TBD/36

THE OXFORD HANDBOOK OF

SOUND AND IMAGE IN DIGITAL MEDIA

THE OXFORD HANDBOO

SOUND A
IMAGE I
DIGITAL M

THE OXFORD HANDBOOK OF

SOUND AND IMAGE IN DIGITAL MEDIA

CAROL VERNALLIS,

AMY HERZOG,

and

JOHN RICHARDSON

OXFORD

UNIVERSITY PRESS

OXFORD
UNIVERSITY PRESS

Oxford University Press is a department of the University of Oxford.
It furthers the University's objective of excellence in research, scholarship,
and education by publishing worldwide.

Oxford   New York
Auckland   Cape Town   Dar es Salaam   Hong Kong   Karachi
Kuala Lumpur   Madrid   Melbourne   Mexico City   Nairobi
New Delhi   Shanghai   Taipei   Toronto

With offices in
Argentina   Austria   Brazil   Chile   Czech Republic   France   Greece
Guatemala   Hungary   Italy   Japan   Poland   Portugal   Singapore
South Korea   Switzerland   Thailand   Turkey   Ukraine   Vietnam

Oxford is a registered trademark of Oxford University Press
in the UK and certain other countries.

Published in the United States of America by
Oxford University Press
198 Madison Avenue, New York, NY 10016

© Oxford University Press 2013

Library of Congress Cataloging-in-Publication Data
Vernallis, Carol.
The Oxford handbook of sound and image in digital media / Carol Vernallis,
Amy Herzog and John Richardson.
pages cm
Includes index.
ISBN 978–0–19–975764–0 (alk. paper)   1. Sound in mass media.   2. Digital media —Technological
innovations.   3. Sound—Social aspects.   I. Herzog, Amy.   II. Richardson, John, 1964-   III. Title.

P96.S66V47 2013
302.23'1—dc23
2013022484

1 3 5 7 9 8 6 4 2
Printed in the United States of America
on acid-free paper

Contents

PART I CINEMA IN THE REALM OF THE DIGITAL: FOUNDATIONAL APPROACHES

PART II DIALOGUE: SCREENS AND SPACES

PART III GLITCHES, NOISE, AND INTERRUPTION: MATERIALITY AND DIGITAL MEDIA

PART IV UNCANNY SPACES AND ACOUSMATIC VOICES

PART V DIALOGUE: VISUALIZATION AND SONIFICATION

PART VI VIRTUAL WORLDS, PARANOID STRUCTURES, AND STATES OF WAR

PART VII BLOCKBUSTERS! FRANCHISES, REMAKES, AND INTERTEXTUAL PRACTICES

PART VIII DIALOGUE: DE-CODING *SOURCE CODE*

PART XII DIGITAL AESTHETICS ACROSS PLATFORM AND GENRE

LIST OF CONTRIBUTORS

Jessica Aldred, Université de Montréal

Jay Beck, Carleton College

John Belton, Rutgers University

Caetlin Benson-Allott, Georgetown University

Warren Buckland, Oxford Brookes University

James Buhler, The University of Texas, Austin

Allan Cameron, University of Auckland

Theo Cateforis, Syracuse University

Dale Chapman, Bates College

William Cheng, Harvard University

Lisa Coulthard, University of British Columbia

Sean Cubitt, Goldsmiths, University of London and University of Melbourne

Joanna Demers, University of Southern California

Nicola Dibben, University of Sheffield

Carol Donelan, Carleton College

Thomas Elsaesser, University of Amsterdam

Jean-Pierre Geuens, Art Center College of Design

Amy Herzog, Queens College and The Graduate Center, City University of New York

Selmin Kara, OCAD University

Eric Lyon, Virginia Tech

Lev Manovich, The Graduate Center, City University of New York

Laura U. Marks, Simon Fraser University

David McCarthy, The Graduate Center, City University of New York

Miguel Mera, City University, London

Kiri Miller, Brown University

Paul Morris, Treasure Island Media

Alex Newton, The University of Texas, Austin

Susanna Paasonen, University of Turku

Jann Pasler, University of California, San Diego

Jennifer Peterson, University of Colorado, Boulder

Melissa Ragona, Carnegie Mellon University

John Richardson, University of Turku

Ron Rodman, Carleton College

Ronald H. Sadoff, New York University

Jacob Smith, Northwestern University

Garrett Stewart, University of Iowa

Will Straw, McGill University

Matthew Sumera, University of Wisconsin, Madison

Eleftheria Thanouli, Aristotle University of Thessaloniki

George Toles, University of Manitoba

Carol Vernallis, Stanford University

William Whittington, University of Southern California

Aylish Wood, University of Kent

María Zauzu, The Graduate Center, City University of New York

ABOUT THE COMPANION WEBSITE

www.oup.com/us/ohsidm

A handbook on sound and image in digital media would not be complete without access to concrete audiovisual examples. Nearly all of our chapters incorporate detailed readings of media texts, and many include links to specific audio and video excerpts. The arguments presented in this volume are greatly enhanced when readers can experience that media firsthand.

Oxford has created a password-protected Web site to accompany *The Oxford Handbook of Sound and Image in Digital Media*, and the reader is encouraged to take full advantage of it. In keeping with the spirit of dialogue and experimentation at the heart of this collection, we hope these clips, like the essays themselves, will generate new readings and lines of thought.

Examples available online are found throughout the text and are signaled with the symbol ◐

You may access the site using username Music4 and password Book2497.

CHAPTER 1

··

INTRODUCTION

··

CAROL VERNALLIS AND AMY HERZOG

THROUGH investigations of what we'll call the "media swirl" and the "audiovisual turn," this handbook charts new territory. Our contemporary media terrain is voluble and intermedial. We are immersed in a dizzying audiovisual archive, accessible via dynamic, proliferating platforms. The socioeconomic, cultural, and technological forces at work in this environment change at different rates. While phenomena like YouTube, haptic-interactive modalities (such as touch- and motion-based interfaces), and high definition-three-dimensional (HD-3D) formats have emerged rapidly, older media, like serial television, immersive video games, and postclassical cinema, have continued to evolve and to cross media, platforms, and technologies; they too become strange. Within this landscape, the intensified, accelerated, piercing qualities of sound and image are amplified. The emergent relations between sound and image, especially, call for new interdisciplinary approaches and modes of analysis.

Several collections have already been devoted to these developments, including the *Oxford Handbook of New Audiovisual Aesthetics (OHNAA)*, the *Oxford Handbook of Sound and Mobile Media*, the *Oxford Handbook of the American Musical*, and the *Oxford Handbook of Film Music*. OHNAA, co-edited by Carol Vernallis, John Richardson, and Claudia Gorbman, provides a context for audiovisual scholars to engage with current media; it might be thought of as foundational, drawing on some of the most respected scholars in the field to revisit long-term debates in audiovisual studies in light of digital technologies and corresponding social changes. *The Oxford Handbook of Sound and Image in Digital Media* commits itself to this same project, but it also pushes the endeavor in new directions. It distinguishes itself through its transdisciplinary methodology and its experiments with form; it is committed to building bridges across disciplines as well as fostering dialogue between senior and emerging scholars.

At present, there is not yet a recognized group of scholars skilled in both audiovisual studies and digital/new technologies, though such a cohort is essential to describe today's media landscape. Could our handbook jump-start a discipline and support the emergence of a new, interdisciplinary field? To achieve such ends, we as co-editors scoured the fields of sound, music, new media, film studies, performance studies, cultural studies, and theater, in search of senior and junior scholars who had a grounding in at least two and hopefully even three areas—sound/music, moving visual media, and digital technologies. We sought out those whom we believed would work outside their comfort zone and would push boundaries, or were keen to collaborate across disciplines. We believe our terrific mix of scholars have produced a balanced, robust, wide-ranging group of essays that give a strong account of today's media.

The themes of sound, image, audiovisual relations, and digital technologies underwrite the volume. While we remain agnostic on the question of what most drives stylistic change, we recognize that audio and visual practices call for a fuller accounting. New forms of sound compression, 5.1 surround-sound, Pro-Tools, Avid editing, computer-generated imagery (CGI), digital intermediate color and image processing, previsualization, high-speed information data transfer and data storage all can contribute to one of today's central strands—a painterly, capture-oriented aesthetic. In today's blockbuster films, for example, a host of technicians finely calibrate sound and image, drawing on new forms of sound compression, immense sound libraries, and audio software. These technologies can help place sound in relation to images that have already been transformed and colorized through CGI and digital intermediaries. Experimental filmmakers, on the other hand, often opt for self-imposed limits: Michel Gondry's handmade animations; Dogma's techno-primitivism; Guy Maddin's "return" to silent film; Johnny To's, Tsai Ming-liang's, and Olivier Assayas's valorization of the long take. At the other end of the spectrum, we find millions of YouTube users producing mashups, home movies, and amateur music videos, drawing on DVD extras rather than formal training. Telegraphic, iconic, and reiterative, the amateur clips garnering the most hits—of animals, dancing, religious rants, stunts, laughing babies—are partly shaped by iMovie editing software and YouTube bandwidth technologies. Into the mix enters interactive, haptic, and immersive technologies—those linked to virtual reality (VR), 3D, Kinect, video games, and apps. These forms of sound–image coordination are all worthy of consideration. But it's also true that technology is only one of many forces shaping today's media landscapes. Equally important is the role of conglomerates that have sought profits from music and image rights, a savvy and restless public wanting to post their own work, as well as independent film and media strains. All these stakeholders are helping to force a new emphasis on intensified audiovisual aesthetics.

Our handbook uncovers a great deal about contemporary sound and image, and our findings depart in some striking ways from traditional approaches to audiovisual studies. Most often sounds and images are configured by audiovisual scholars as comprising some sort of marriage, occasionally felicitous, but at least to some extent interpretable, with relations falling into recognizable categories, such as those of conformance, contrast, and contest.[1] In other words, whatever the audiovisual relation is, it is legible and open to exegesis. Yet when scholars from divergent fields take up the problems of sound and image, they gravitate to different texts and bring different relations to light. The contributors to this volume have sometimes taken up media that would not lend themselves to traditional analysis; rather than a union of image and sound, these works are messy, contested, and redolent with noise and disarray. A film scholar who has included sound as part of her teaching, but for the first time chooses to write about it with a slant on politics and technology, discovers new dynamics. When we as co-editors place a piece on a new sound technology (like Auto-Tune) against a visual one (like digital intermediary), the audiovisual contract looks different: it suddenly seems bewildering that the puffed-up, overachieving aims of both technologies might coexist within the same work. In other cases our authors may find so much interference and delay between sound and image that barely anything gets through, as if each were locked in an echo chamber, where one hardly meets the other. One resonant theme in this volume is the ways sound and image can exist in myriad relations. Alongside harmonic convergences and ecstatic audiovisual mélanges, we find glitches, noise, rupture, and uncanny vestiges of outmoded practices. Our own mélange of scholarly approaches attempts to capture the texture and feel of this diverse media field.[2]

One of our primary objectives for this volume is to forge a dialogue between sound and image scholars. Our contributors bring to the table an impressive range of disciplinary expertise, from film studies, philosophy, musicology, composition, experimental art, experimental music, pornography, digital gaming, documentary, and media studies. The interplay among their diverse approaches provides the structure for the collection. The essays are organized according to shared thematic and theoretical concerns and include contributors whose primary focus is sometimes geared more toward concerns of image whereas others are more focused on sound. While each essay can, of course, be read in isolation, we are most excited about the productive resonances generated among texts. In certain instances, we put groups of authors in direct conversation with one another; they then wrote short response chapters on shared topics or contributed to case studies. These dialogues have continued to generate conversation among the participants, conversations we hope will extend via continued collaborations across our fields.

The first section of the collection, Cinema in the Realm of the Digital: Foundational Approaches, theorizes the broader shift of cinematic discourses through the transition to digital production and distribution. Thomas Elsaesser seeks a definition of "digital cinema," reading the phenomenon both through discourses of media convergence and in terms of digital cinema's ontological contradictions. It is precisely this set of contradictions, Elsaesser posits, that makes a medium like digital cinema "a motor for change": "it carries the old forward while incubating the new, by a move that acknowledges the past's existence but de-fangs and transforms it in the very act of perpetuating it." J. P. Geuens presents a dizzying survey of lighting techniques and technologies used by DPs and colorists from the turn of the past century through our present digital era. Via the digital intermediate, Geuens argues, a new field of labor has opened in the gap between camera acquisition and finished image. And while the malleability of light within this realm allows for perfection of control, Geuens makes a compelling case for earlier approaches to photography that were open to indeterminacy, attuned "to the immanence that permeates a shared moment that will never be again." Echoing these concerns with the overlapping of technology, labor, and aesthetics, William Whittington argues that developments in sound practices have played an undervalued role in shaping the widely touted digital revolution in cinema. Sound and image technologies don't necessarily develop in synchrony; rather, they can possess their own trajectories. He draws on the example of Pixar's early attempts at CGI with the short film *Tin Toy*, in which surfaces were poorly rendered, especially skin and hair, but, at the same time, existed alongside highly sophisticated sound practices. With *Tin Toy*, sound designer Gary Rydstrom struggled to coordinate media that seemed to some extent at odds because they were at different stages of development. For a discerning audience this historical moment lays bare the arbitrariness of the audiovisual contract. Today's "hyperrealist" digital aesthetics are achieved, and in many ways enabled, by the sophisticated soundscapes that subtly guide and transform our relationship to the image, building densely layered audiovisual environments in which the spectator is immersed. At certain moments, and perhaps today is one of them, sound and image can form fragile, temporary relations of proportion and equilibrium.

In the first "dialogue" of the volume, Screens and Spaces, Sean Cubitt and Will Straw explore transformations in the relations between screens and public space. Cubitt provides a political economy of both large-scale public screens and individualized small screens, utilizing the concrete example of screen technology as a means of grappling with broader questions of technological innovation. The commercialization of public space via small and large screens can seem totalizing, yet there remain openings for local, contingent interventions that have the potential to forge new kinds of public assemblages. Straw's response to Cubitt contextualizes the history of screen technology within urban environments, focusing on the illumination of city streets. The differential in scale between small and large screens manifests itself in variable modes of perception and mobility for city dwellers. And in most instances, Straw notes, the visual noise created by screens used in public exist in direct tension with sound media.

Glitches, Noise, and Interruption: Materiality and Digital Media delves into the shifting nature of noise within our digital ecosystems. Laura Marks explores the category of noise in relation to systems of perception and encounters with the infinite. The infinite lies beyond perception and, as such, is experienced as noise. Our senses work to "unfold" select aspects of the infinite, often in tandem with informational systems such as digital and other technologies, transforming unmediated noise into something perceptible. While commodity culture tends to unfold the world into "a smooth surface of seamless information," art attuned to the noisy, the ugly, the forgotten, can make us aware of alternative means of perceiving and unfolding the deafening realm of the infinite. Her discussion of *Brilliant Noise* (2009), by Ruth Jarman and Joe Gerhardt, perfectly illustrates the artistic potential of "sonification" discussed in Lev Manovich and Jake Smith's dialogue in later chapters of this volume.

Lisa Coulthard takes up noise, droning, and silence as recurring themes within European New Extremist films. Drones, which tend to occur within moments of relative silence, dirty "the purity and quiet of digital technology," filling the void with organic and visceral noise, a sonic parallel to the violent and corporeal address of the image. Caetlin Benson-Allott performs a playfully "glitched" engagement with Lady Gaga's stuttering video image. The telerotics of the electronic glitch, for Benson-Allott, reanimate and complicate debates about feminine performance, desire, and "to-be-looked-at-ness" in audiovisual media (her essay engages in a productive debate about questions of agency and openness with McCarthy and Zuazu's reading of Gaga, also in this volume). Joanna Demers similarly identifies stuttering and failures of signification as potent political tools in the hands of media artists such as Ryan Trecartin, Paul McCarthy, Animal Charm, and Sean Griffin. Through "discursive accents," Demers argues, these artists offer inflections of genre and style that destabilize meaning and foster critical, often uncomfortable modes of listening and engagement. Melissa Ragona surveys various technologies used to "clean up" vocal recordings, noting that these attempts to "dope the voice" enabled experimental artists such as Yoko Ono, Hollis Frampton, and Charlemagne Palestine to flesh out the voice's dirt, grit, and grain, released from the binds of narrative or psychological interiority.

Temporal and generic anomalies haunt the essays in Uncanny Spaces and Acousmatic Voices. Will Cheng immerses us in the horrific, industrial soundscape of the *Silent Hill* video game series, linking the strategic use of sound to larger "economies of fear." Engaging with discourses of monstrosity, Cheng maps the semiautonomous trajectories of sounds in the game space, with a particular focus on their visceral impact on the player's own sense of corporeal control. Amy Herzog is similarly interested in questions of space, body, sound, and structures of play. She navigates the performance/installation *Sleep No More*, marking the ways in which its architectures of sound set in motion and reanimate a range of fragmentary references from Shakespeare and Herrmann through digital games. Textual and environmental resonances also drive George Toles study of *Deanimated*, a 2002 installation by Martin Arnold. Arnold digitally transforms a Bela Lugosi horror film, *Invisible Ghost* (Joseph Lewis, 1941), systematically removing the images and sounds of the characters. The attachments and operations of rooms, objects, figures, and score come unhinged, Toles argues, rendering the viewer/listener a ghost within the film's defamiliarized walls. And structures of meaning prove central to Warren Buckland as he works through the poetics of David Lynch's *Inland Empire*. Rather than a symbolic-allegorical analysis of meaning, Buckland traces the surface-level construction of the film, locating at its heart strategies of metalepsis and *mise en abyme*, further embedded and confused by the shifting presence of the acousmatic voice.

Our second dialogue, Visualization and Sonification, pairs Lev Manovich with Jake Smith, discussing the translation of information into visual and audio media. Manovich details his research at the Software Studies Initiative at the University of California, San Diego, where his lab deployed a range of approaches for analyzing and visualizing large datasets. Alongside a history of computational visualization strategies, Manovich provides insights into the creative and artistic potentials for visualizations, as well as the productive ways in which visualization can challenge our codified systems of organizing and conceptualizing information. In response, Smith takes up a number of terms from Manovich's history to provide a corollary study of representations of cultural data in sonic forms. "Sonification," Smith demonstrates, suggests a new field of research in sound studies, one that might reveal previously unheard connections and clusters within the growing archive of digitized sound.

In the section Virtual Worlds, Paranoid Structures, and States of War, authors examine the fraught ways in which music has both shaped and become embedded within the aesthetic culture of political conflict. Music can convey the distilled temporality of the state of exception, argues Dale Chapman, a state "in which the sovereign, in response to crisis, suspends the efficacy of the rule of law." Chapman explores these chilling implications via Alfonso Cuarón's *Children of Men*, a dystopian narrative film that has a great deal to say about the unexamined costs of, and our need to respond to, contemporary state violence. Music, sound, and power inform Matthew Sumera's study of amateur videos crafted from US armed forces combat footage. Typically edited and set to "nu metal" soundtracks (a hardcore subgenre of heavy metal), these amateur shorts are created by both military personnel and civilians and circulated online. These videos, which have become an integral part of the audiovisual culture of war for many service personnel, coincide with the weaponization of nu metal by the military in their antiterror initiatives, literalizing the notion of the "theater of war." We must recognize, Sumera insists, that such examples are not representations of war, but in fact an integral component of the actualities of military conflict.

James Buhler and Alex Newton engage in a close reading of image and soundtrack through the *Bourne* trilogy, centered on the current of cultural trauma coursing through these films. Throughout the series, Jason Bourne emerges as a deeply divided figure, marked by a duality born from recurring personal and political trauma. Buhler and Newton map this duality through the audiovisual aesthetics of the films, particularly the music, which elevates trauma to the realm of myth. Questions of rendering and the digital reverberate on multiple registers here, and the frenetic visualizations of *Bourne Ultimatum* foreground the political, psychic, and representational crises bound up in the paranoid logic that pervades narratives of action. Eleftheria Thanouli and Theo Cateforis close out the section with a dialogue on Barry Levinson's *Wag the Dog* (1997). For Thanouli, *Wag the Dog* marks the coincidence of a range of cultural, technological, and historical trajectories, resulting in a striking public forum for debates about the relationship between cinema and reality. Representations of state violence become particularly charged in this context. Cateforis responds with a reading of two musical sequences from the film, looking at the ways in which music contributes to constructions of authenticity within the film and, by extension, within our own highly mediated reality.

The shifting landscape of the transmedia blockbuster provides fodder for Blockbusters! Franchises, Remakes, and Intertextual Practices. Jessica Aldred takes on the *Beowulf* franchise to explore the paths of cross-media consumption that are encouraged when characters and narratives shift between cinematic and digital gaming platforms. Aldred questions the rhetoric of convergence that circulates around synergistic marketing plans through a case study of digital human characters as they move between media. She chronicles the difficulties of faithfully translating original cinematic texts to synthetic characters in a user-controlled gaming world. Corporate sponsors and video game designers, in particular, seemed to fail to fully understand the needs and expectations of gaming audiences as they tried to further monetize blockbuster franchise products. Carol Donelan and Rod Rodman turn to the *Twilight Saga*, mapping the negotiations between film industry and target audience that have ensued throughout the cycle. The *Twilight* films present an opportunity for the industry to woo a typically neglected demographic, females under twenty-five years of age, via the erotically charged yet ultimately defanged figure of the teen vampire. The soundtrack, both of scored music and compiled pop songs, contributes to the uncanny duality of these fantasy worlds, a vista of forbidden possibilities couched within a familiar, and highly marketable, formula.

Contradiction and balance surface in a new context in Aylish Wood's reading of sound–image relations in the time-shifting, multilayered blockbusters *Watchman* (Snyder, 2009) and *Inception* (Nolan, 2010). Here, sound bridges and carefully calibrated mixes convey key knowledge about the intricate architectures of these films, allowing viewers to navigate the complexes of space, time, and subjectivity contained within their nonunified and unstable storyscapes. Miguel Mera also explores the aesthetics of combination, here via Quentin Tarantino's *Inglourious Basterds*, which is driven, he argues, by the principles of the mashup. Mashup culture, for Mera, is spurred not by pastiche or ironic parallelism, but rather by a pluralistic modality. The mélange of audiovisual tropes deployed in this work engage and challenge audience expectations, fabricating a liminal space in which history and cinematic representation are productively upended.

De-Coding *Source Code*, our third dialogue section, provides a forum for engaging with questions of sound, temporality, and audiovisual virtuality through sustained readings of the 2011 science fiction thriller *Source Code* (dir. Duncan Jones). *Source Code* is a cryptically nonlinear, postclassical puzzle film that engages both its protagonist and audience in a perpetually looping fragment of time: Captain Colter Stevens (Jake Gyllenhaal) awakes repeatedly inside the body of another man aboard a Chicago commuter train 8 minutes before a bomb is detonated. Stevens's postmortem investigation into the source of the violence becomes more frantic with each replay. He becomes attached to his avatar's doomed love interest on the train, at the same time that his own deeply compromised corporeal reality is revealed to the viewer: Stevens is an Army helicopter pilot who has been horribly maimed while serving in Afghanistan, and his entire cognitive existence is sustained via a virtual reality computer simulation.

Garrett Stewart begins the dialogue by taking up *Source Code* as a dystopian coda to his *Framed Time: Toward a Postfilmic Cinema* (University of Chicago Press, 2007). For Stewart, the voice here serves as a disembodied, vexed palimpsest of a historical moment in which narratological and aesthetic traditions fold in on themselves, reflecting on their own organizational logic. Sean Cubitt's response recasts this narrative within the emerging field of eco-criticism. Cubitt finds within the looped, coded world of the film an alternative environment in which questions of agency, subjectivity, representation, and information are upended and redeployed within a transformed and seemingly pliable reality. *Source Code* is ultimately a pseudo-utopia, he argues, gesturing toward a posthuman future that is then recast into individualist master narratives. Yet the gesture itself suggests possible, as-yet-unrealized paths for eco-critical hermeneutics. James Buhler picks up on these threads through an inspired study of the opening and closing sequences of the film. Music and sound construct a mythology of origins that builds, in the first frames of the film, through a genesis of light, dark, water, and sky, culminating in the appearance of the corporate logos in the film's title sequence, a "gap in the image that marks the real of capital."

The chapters that comprise Rethinking Audiovisual Embodiment theorize the body using divergent methodologies, in equally diverse media forums. The musical performance games Guitar Hero, Rock Band, and DJ Hero, for Kiri Miller, present a model of kinesthetic engagement unlike digital games that rely on the construction of an on-screen virtual world. In these musical performance games, the controller-as-instrument works with the body of the player in a direct and physical way, building on personal and cultural musical histories. David McCarthy and María E. Zuazu, in a counterpoint to Benson-Allott's chapter on Lady Gaga and the glitch, critique the operative modality of the Gaga-World phenomenon. At the heart of Lady Gaga's media extravaganza, McCarthy and Zuazu identify a remix aesthetic, a "tendency to mask unity with a set of digital practices that seem to tear and stitch." Indeed, the assemblage of music, image, persona, and networked fans that comprise Gaga are defined by their contradictions, contradictions that can be at once thrilling, regressive, disquieting, and unfinished. Media scholar Susanna Paasonen collaborates with pornography producer Paul Morris in a dialogue about gay porn, affect, politics, and digital technology. Focusing on gay bareback pornography, Paasonen and Morris look at the visceral interplay between bodies and spaces set into motion by pornographic media, with a particular focus on the ways in which sound mediates and creates corporeal intensity.

Sounds and Images of the New Digital Documentary grapples with the contested and evolving nature of "realism" in relation to new audiovisual media networks. John Belton maps shifts in documentary modes of representation read in relation to technological developments. Focusing on recent work by Agnes Varda and Trinh T. Minh-ha, Belton points to the increasingly reflexive approaches these filmmakers adopt, enabled in many ways by lightweight digital cameras. Mutability and cinécriture become means of highlighting the labor of the apparatus and weaving fictions and fabrications that nevertheless bring us closer to an understanding of our material conditions. Selmin Kara unearths the surprising directions in which filmmakers such as Abbas Kiarostami and Aleksandr Sokurov have channeled their experiments with digital documentary. Against the currents of connectivity and networked participation so often associated with the digital, these filmmakers have turned instead to contemplative meditations on the relations among nature, humans, and technology. Kara finds resonance here between the "cosmic indifference" of the dense and highly structured soundscapes found in these works and a recent metaphysical turn toward speculative materialism and object-oriented philosophy; in each instance, an ecology of the world is rendered that decentralizes the human. The operational aesthetics identified in these first two chapters reassert themselves in Jennifer Peterson's study of four recent works that document the changing face of labor in an age of global finance capital. She identifies the emergence of a "digitally informed observational aesthetic," one marked by stationary long takes that simultaneously assert and destabilize notions of objectivity, knowledge, and truth. Once again, mediation, fabrication, and observation fold into one another while, at the same time, remaining highly attuned to the materiality of the world being rendered and to their own technological practices.

Modes of Composition: Digital Convergence and Sound Production incorporates the perspectives of media practitioners and composers. Eric Lyon begins with the separation of image and sound performed by the first audio recording technologies. Subsequent developments in the field gave rise to experiments in the phenomenology of pure "aurality," enabled by electronic technology. More recent digital audiovisual practices have enacted more fluid, even playful bridges between sound and image relations (and, indeed, Lyon's own experiments with spatial sound structure resonate with Jake Smith's discussion of "sonification" in this volume). The transformation of image to sound also guides Jann Pasler's study of Hugues Dufort's spectral compositions inspired by the frescos of Tiepolo. Inspired both by the dynamics of cinema and the psycho-acoustics of computer music, Dufort moves toward a "consonant inharmonicity," which, as Pasler demonstrates through her deft reading of *L'Afrique d'après Tiepolo*, offers an engaged critique of Western constructions of time and space. Ron Sadoff looks at recent transformations in the crafting of scores for Hollywood feature films and video games. Digital technologies have shifted artistic and labor practices, encouraging collaboration and cross-pollination both within and between media fields. Drawing from interviews with composers, Sadoff points to shifts in creative approaches in film and game sound and raises critical questions about the future of the field in light of these developments. Nicola Dibben uses her own work on the mobile app for Björk's *Biophilia* album to explore the broader ways in which digitalization has impacted musical composition and experience. Music visualization, Dibben argues, engenders immersive and multi-modal engagement; in this way, mobile apps bring the consumption of music closer to the realm of interactive video and gaming technologies.

Kicking off Digital Aesthetics Across Platform and Genre, Carol Vernallis thinks through the accelerated aesthetics of our networked mediascape and their potential correlations with the rhythms of contemporary labor and global capitalism. Through a whirlwind survey of music videos, blockbuster films, and promotional shorts, Vernallis suggests several adaptive strategies we might experiment with in order to negotiate this modulating terrain. Jay Beck tackles developments in new transnational art cinema from the perspective of sound studies. Beck identifies several sonic tropes that have emerged across the work of filmmakers from diverse points of origin, each crafting a personal sound aesthetics that up-ends image–sound relations typically associated with mainstream cinema. Alongside new approaches to subjectivity, architectural acoustics, and vocal culture, Beck locates changing renderings of ethics, epistemology, and the sublime in cinematic uses of sound, signaling a significant challenge to the audiovisual status quo. And Allan Cameron examines the prevalence of technological instrumentality in the discourses and visualizations associated with electronic music. Rather than representing a blind embrace or a reflexive repudiation of instrumentality, many electronic visualizations, Cameron finds, make use of architectural and environmental interfaces that critically question the material impact of technology on contemporary experience.

A number of our contributors, while writing about diverse digital phenomenon, pose challenges to media makers that strike a similar chord. In the face of media products that offer smooth, hermetically intact audiovisual environments (typically those most easily assimilated into broader capitalist narratives), our authors call for works that remain open to the outside, that stutter and generate noise, that move in unpredictable ways. This is not merely a question of aesthetics, but of political and historical position-ing. Difference, materiality, and the pressures of the local assert themselves in many of the works these essays highlight. Questions of agency and interactivity are of critical interest, particularly when users' engagement with digital media can be constricted to a surface-level interface, with little substantive input into the meaning, structure, or broader impact of the work. Of equal concern are the vast troves of media artifacts that are often appropriated and recontextualized within contemporary digital media practices. What kinds of new histories do new media practitioners imagine in their work: teleologies of technological mastery, media archaeologies that read the present and future in relation to the material past, or monstrous combinations of approaches, collectively assembled and set into motion? These formal and political tensions consis-tently surface throughout the varied essays of this collection, and, in many ways, speak to our core objectives in studying the changing landscape of audiovisual media. We are delighted to initiate this noisy, productive, groundbreaking conversation, and are indebted to the incredible efforts of the talented collective that made it possible.

NOTES

1. For a seminal description of these categories, see Nicholas Cook, *Analysing Musical Multimedia* (New York: Oxford University Press, 1998), 81–84.
2. One of our co-editors, in a fanciful mood, wondered if a cooking metaphor might help capture the myriad ways sound and image work together in this volume: with sound and image you can bake, poach, sauté, fry, boil, freeze, marinate, truss, mince, fricassée, braise. Then you can fold it all in together and start again.

PART I

CINEMA IN THE REALM OF THE DIGITAL: FOUNDATIONAL APPROACHES

CHAPTER 2

DIGITAL CINEMA

Convergence or Contradiction?

THOMAS ELSAESSER

AMONG the changes that the combination of computer and telephony has brought to life in the twenty-first century, the innovations in sound reproduction and moving image technology are probably not the most decisive.[1] Yet as the information revolution has gathered unprecedented momentum, transforming the way we communicate, create, work, are governed, and entertain ourselves, it is television and the internet that have become the most visible indicators of a qualitative leap. Television, once a state monopoly in most parts of the world, or (as in the United States) a very self-selected club of multinational tycoon-led corporations, has—in its deregulated, commercial form—become a source of sounds, text, and images as automatic, pervasive, and taken-for-granted as switching on the electric current or turning on the water faucet. Even greater ubiquity, accessibility, and "invisibility" await the internet. During a little more than two decades, it has emerged as an entirely new medium, combining the functions of newspaper, post office, book publisher, and library with the services of radio, television, telephony—not to mention the fact that the World Wide Web is also the largest marketplace and shopping mall in human history. These hybrid knowledge-communication-information media, still competing with each other and yet set also on a convergence course, are both cause and effect: they respond to and thereby also drive—via seemingly endless and ever-expanding feedback loops—shifts in human interaction and perception, in consciousness and mind–body links, as well as imposing themselves in myriad forms on social cohesion and asocial solipsism, health and welfare, crime and warfare, political decision making and interpersonal communication. These, in turn, imply a technologically mediated or automatically mediatized contact with "reality" as our primary experience of the world, making television and the internet ever more invisible interfaces for the ways that members of "developed" societies understand themselves as living both locally and globally, but also in another dimension altogether—that of the virtual, as one of the dimensions of the actual.

In the process, cinema—hitherto television's "other"—has been overshadowed, if not altogether eclipsed as a subject of public concern or debate, indeed, as a "medium." And yet, cinema has always served as a metaphor for matters of life (and death) that extend beyond individual films and movie theatres into the realms of identity, subjectivity, and our "being-in-the-world." André Bazin called the cinema "the ancient dream of mankind," desiring its double, its mirror: the creation of an imaginary self alongside the physical self, and a way of cheating death, by preserving that other self: cinema as the art of embalming "time" along with rescuing the body: the "Mummy Complex."[2] Siegfried Kracauer spoke of it as the "redemption of physical reality," and Walter Benjamin regarded film as the very medium destined to train our senses and make us fit for modernity. Today, many see the moving image as our most precious (and endangered) historical heritage, a unique "archive" of life over the past 150 years. Some, like Lev Manovich, have argued that cinema is nothing less than the template for our cultural understanding of the new (digital) media, and, for still others, among them Gilles Deleuze, the cinema constitutes a material-mental organism in its own right, a new and vibrant articulation of matter, energy, and information, and thus a "thing" that "thinks," which only philosophy can help us understand. In its relatively brief history of just over a hundred years, the "cinema" has become more than the sum of the films made for public projection. Yet "the movies" are also less than the sum of the fears and fantasies—about the animate and inanimate, the biological and the technological, the living and the dead—that contemporary culture has invested in the moving image. This is why it makes sense to speak of new ontologies required by what Deleuze, in the 1980s, called the "movement image" and the "time image." Trying to seize this something-both-more-and-less of cinema at the threshold of the digital age is the main purpose of this essay.

Given the dominance of television and the internet, how can the cinema hold its ground among the public spaces and private occasions where cinema, television, and digital media compete with each other for audiences and attention? Is there such a thing as "digital cinema," and how innovative is it as an art form and a technology of sound and image production today? Before one can answer such questions, there is a more fundamental one. Do cinema, television, recorded sound, and digital media belong together at all, considering their very different histories? When one compares them, on what basis and by which criteria? If there is a family resemblance (in Ludwig Wittgenstein's sense), what are the factors bringing them together or what drives them apart? Is the cinema part of a general rush toward "media convergence," or is it set on a divergent course, with diversity the key media-ecological factor? In short: can the cinema maintain its place as the most popular art form ever known, as well as prove to be the most "philosophical" phenomenon among the technical media?

I want to discuss what I see as the cinema's simultaneous marginality and centrality by breaking the questions down into two different clusters or conceptual pairs. These pairs are (multimedia) convergence, and digital cinema. Two further conceptual pairs, virtual reality and interactive narrative, I leave for another occasion (or for others to take up).

The by now commonplace use of these four characteristics of cinema in the digital age disguises inherent tensions, if not outright contradictions *in adjecto*. Yet, instead of taking these naturalized oxymorons as proof that the cinema today is a hybrid medium, my argument is that any embedded contradictions should lead us to ask what is special about the state of the cinema in the first decades of the twenty-first century. Perhaps the contradictions resolve themselves at a different level of generality. No doubt, a look at the cinema from the vantage point of digital media can help revitalize our historical understanding of previous media (as suggested, among others, by Lev Manovich and Henry Jenkins). My own hope is that digital cinema (along with interactive narrative and virtual reality), more sharply defined, affords insights into our "second modernity," which some claim is nothing short of a "second Renaissance" or a "soft Industrial Revolution." Like its predecessors of the fifteenth through nineteenth centuries, the consequences of this revolution/renaissance promise to be uneven, divisive, disruptive, but also irresistibly interesting.[3]

MULTIMEDIA CONVERGENCE: THE PLACE OF THE CINEMA IN THE MEDIA MIX

The first half of this essay deals with multimedia convergence; the second half takes up the question of what digital cinema is. I conclude with some remarks addressing the epochal or epistemic changes associated with terms such as *renaissance* or *revolution*.

What, then, is multimedia convergence? Convergence usually implies that distinct entities or bodies are joined together, become similar, or even merge. It can also mean that certain discrete practices adopt a similar objective or pursue a common goal. In the case of the technical media, convergence points to a force that is setting originally distinct media on a common (i.e., convergent) course. As to the nature of the agency involved, opinion is divided, not least because one needs to distinguish different kinds of convergence. For instance, Henry Jenkins discusses five types of convergence (technological, economic, aesthetic, organic, and global),[4] whereas Graham Murdoch identifies three kinds: convergence of communications systems, convergence of corporate ownership, convergence of cultural forms.[5]

Technological Convergence

In respect of the convergence of technology (or communication systems), the key agency is, of course, digitization, the term usually invoked as the common denominator of all these paradigm shifts. The frantic pace and sheer scale of the changes have been such that one instinctively feels the need for a single source, and "digitization," with its quasi-magical effects, neatly fits the bill. But just because the computer has made such an enormous impact in all areas of life, do we need to succumb to a new version of technological determinism? Such an idea of "convergence" suggests an inexorable inevitability, and, with it, a sense of disempowerment that overlooks a number of salient countervailing forces also shaping the current situation.

It is clear, for example, that innovations other than the computer have affected sound and image production and reproduction: the transistor (portable radio and sound devices), the development of video and fiberoptics, but also jet propulsion and space technology. What we experience are the effects of parallel and mutually interconnected technologies, many of them driven by military considerations, rather than by an ideal of multimedia convergence. Media changes have, especially in Europe, depended also on legal and institutional factors, such as the deregulation of bandwidth and the "privatization" and subsequent proliferation of (commercial) television, as well as changes in censorship, industry self-regulation, and intellectual property right provisions. Then there are geopolitical changes: the world has moved from the two antagonistic power blocs during the Cold War period to four or five competing trading blocs, united (but also newly divided) by the dynamics of financial and commercial globalization. Globalization—it is true—depends on (even if it is not solely determined by) the traffic of information, services, and goods, which only the combination of digitization, computer software, telephony, and satellite technology has made possible.

Digitization in the more narrowly defined context of information media means, first, the technical ability of translating words, graphics, text, sound, speech, and images, as well as other sensory-perceptible signals, into uniform electronic bits of binary code, with perfect fidelity of recording and reproduction, complemented by high-density storage and an unlimited capacity to produce identical copies. Here, too, one needs to make a further distinction among media convergence, genre convergence, and device convergence. *Device convergence* means that, for instance, television screens, computer monitors, and projection surfaces for filmed images may come in different sizes or shapes, but would nonetheless be connected to similar processing units or input/output devices with computing power, hard-drive, random access memory, and internet access. The fact that my laptop now serves me as a typewriter, a telephone, a video screen, and a jukebox is an instance of device convergence, as is the digital camera and web browser built into my mobile phone. *Media convergence* indicates that the "content" of television programs and dynamic websites comes to resemble each other and become interchangeable, along the lines of, for instance, *Big Brother* reality shows, which are broadcast both on television and the internet. The fact that many radio programs now have talk-back or phone-in options (such as the BBC World Service's *World Have Your Say*) is also an instance of media convergence. *Genre convergence* produces the sort of hybridity critics have noted above all for television, when referring to "infotainment," "docudrama," or "edutainment." Often, genre convergence comes about through media-interference or crossovers in technology, for instance, in film genres such as mockumentary and fake documentary, or by a combination of animation and live action, as in *Who Framed Roger Rabbit?* (1988).

Economic Convergence

Economic convergence refers to a business strategy in which media and communications corporations try to increase their overall revenue by making various media outlets under their control (publishing, television and radio broadcasting stations, film and music studios) complement and reinforce each other by sharing content (books, film libraries, music, television programs). The strategy requires several elements to come together: first, a concentration of ownership, with fewer companies owning a larger share of the respective media "markets." Second, it relies on government deregulation, allowing media conglomerates such as News Corporation, Bertelsmann, Vivendi, or Time Warner to own different kinds of media (e.g., film studios, television networks, radio stations and newspapers) under near monopoly conditions. Third, economic convergence is helped by the accelerated flow of information enabled by digitization, allowing images, advertising, and print material to circulate more easily and more rapidly through the different media systems. The perceived benefits are a reduced workforce and profit maximization, synergies in administration and savings in overhead, more leverage with advertisers, and higher brand name recognition and loyalty among consumers. A not inconsiderable side effect of such a form of horizontal integration (echoing the old Hollywood studio system's vertical integration) is that it makes entry into such markets by newcomers and outsiders more difficult. It limits competition and encourages cartel-like practices of price fixing and downward pressure on suppliers and labor costs.

As one can see, in the convergence of corporate ownership, digitization is only one of the decisive factors. What makes digitization nonetheless a focal point of media convergence is the widely held assumption that digital *conversion* also means digital *convergence*. Add speed of access and ease of manipulation to the shared code, so the reasoning goes, and all the media whose content digitization converts into numerical sequences and algorithms—newspapers, movies, television shows, photographs, animated drawings, music, speech—will converge in one super- or hypermedium, a sort of permanent shower of "code" raining down on us, as in the opening credits of *The Matrix*. Common platforms and formats will convert this code-flow back into (graphic) user interfaces for human interaction, such as one encounters on multimedia web pages, supported by powerful search engines like Google and broadband connectivity. But this ignores that both the institutional contexts of a particular medium (which, in addition to money and power, business models and legal matters, include "content" like religion and politics and "standards" like professional codes and industrial standards), and the human users (which include their work and leisure habits, as well as their social needs and interpersonal dynamics) have their own degrees of autonomy that can exert influence on the ways technology and society evolve together and compete with each other.[6]

Cultural Convergence

The last point requires a closer consideration of the third type of convergence (or resistance to it) embodied in cultural forms of media consumption, usually split between passive manipulation and active participation: "The old either-or oppositions (co-optation vs. resistance) which have long dominated debates between political economy and cultural studies approaches to media simply do not do justice to the multiple, dynamic, and often contradictory relationships between media convergence and participatory culture."[7] The technological backbone of this new participatory culture—the social networking websites, such as Facebook, Linked-In, YouTube, or Twitter—is made possible by the highly standardized software of internet browsers, search engines, and the creative commons initiatives; the widespread practice of downloads and file swapping of media content; and the universal spread of mobile telephony and GPS tracking devices. The effects of social networking, however, go beyond private use or bypassing copyright laws and usher in what Henry Jenkins, one of its most eloquent advocates, calls "cultural" convergence: "cultural convergence describes the new ways that media audiences are engaging with and making sense of these new forms of media content.... Cultural convergence has preceded, in many ways, the full technological realization of the idea of media convergence, helping to create a market for these new cultural products."[8]

Convergence in this sense recognizes that the flow of media content across multiple delivery technologies does affect audiences, but Jenkins maintains that this is not a one-way flow from corporations to their targeted consumers: "Media convergence is...a constant form of re-appropriation. [It is] an ongoing process, occurring at various intersections of media technologies, industries, content and audiences; it's not an end state. There will never be one black box controlling all media. Rather, thanks to the proliferation of channels and the increasingly ubiquitous nature of computing and communications, we are entering an era where media will be everywhere, and we will use all kinds of media in relation to one another. [We are] dealing with the flow of content—stories, characters, ideas—from one media system to another."[9] To back his case, Jenkins cites the many cover versions, spoofs, remixes, and references to the *Star Wars* saga that circulate on the internet in the form of clips, scripts, or short films. Homemade videos of reshot, reenacted, or reedited scenes from other blockbusters like *Titanic* and *Batman* or fake trailers for cult films like *Pulp Fiction* on YouTube, Vimeo, and countless other sites are apt indicators of intense activity on the part of fans and fan communities around the audio and image-products of corporate cross-media marketing campaigns, recycling, repurposing, diverting, and appropriating popular culture icons from music, movies, sports, and television shows.

This looks like a strong argument for claiming that convergence is indeed driven by user preference, jumping not only technical hurdles but "species barriers." But, lest we forget: cinema, television, and the internet differ widely in their basic technologies, institutional histories, legal frameworks, and social practices. The cinema came from serial photography and depended on advances in cellulose production, as well as on perfecting the transport mechanism of the sewing machine and the bicycle.[10] Demographically, it grafted itself on the music hall and vaudeville houses, and aesthetically on the magic lantern and the stereoscope as popular entertainment forms. Going to the movies is (still) not the same as watching the identical film on television. Television depended on the technology of the cathode-ray tube, it scans an image rather than frames it, it shares most of its institutional history with radio, and initially hesitated between becoming "armchair theater," an electric variety program, or an instrument of state-controlled political consensus building. Video is technically an extension of the audiotape, itself a wartime invention, whereas the internet, as we know, exploits the combination of the computer and the telephone: developed by the US military, it became a mass-medium via university scientists and research scholars, and its institutional forms are hotly contested between (US and EU) lawmakers, business interests (Google, Microsoft, Apple, Amazon), and defenders of global, if not millennial egalitarianism ("creative commons"). Multimedia art, virtual reality environments, telepresence, and digital sound each have their own serendipitous and leap-frog histories, so that it requires some feat of the synthesizing imagination to conceive of them as belonging together, let alone as suddenly sharing a common evolutionary ladder or joint telos. And yet, such is the impact of the "information revolution" that we now tend to think of them as not only "naturally" linked, but developing in the same direction, transferring their common denominator uses into a technologically based teleology.

Cinema and Convergence

A look into the cinema's history indicates a more nuanced picture. Convergence also suggests obsolescence, yet, so far, different media rarely replace one another (think of the "paperless office" promised by the advent of the computer!).[11] Neither do they straightforwardly "improve" on each other (who has not thought, after a laptop crash: "if the book had been invented after the laptop, it would be an improvement"), nor do they determine each other (in the sense of one medium "answering" a question posed but left unresolved by another). Cinema did not "respond" to the magic lantern by solving problems that had arisen in the practice of magic lantern shows. It repurposed aspects of the basic technology and parasitically occupied part of its public sphere, along with the sites of live performances, such as vaudeville and the music hall. Television has not "evolved" out of cinema nor did it replace it, dire warnings about the "death of cinema" notwithstanding. Digital images were not something the film industry was waiting for to overcome any felt "deficiencies" in its production of special effects. Video didn't kill the radio star: the internet (and MP3 players, podcasts, and mobile devices) gave radio a huge boost and an entirely different lease on life. A new medium may extend the overall spectrum, bringing about unexpected combinations, but it can also lead to rounds of boundary drawing and ring-fencing. While it thus reconfigures the conjunction in which all media operate at any given point in time, a new medium also tends to "rewrite" the other media's histories, to make room for its own genealogy.[12]

Additionally, the dynamics of device convergence are not solely dependent on digitization. To cite a specific example: Ann Friedberg has looked closely at the case for convergence initially around cinema's relation to television.[13] Examining successive technological innovations, such as the VCR, the remote control, and cable television, she argues that these, taken together, began to irreversibly erode the historical differences between cinema and television, even without "digital convergence."[14]

Preceding digitization, the driving force was the growing interpenetration of cinema and television thanks to new delivery and distribution systems, symbolized by cable television on the one hand and the video recorder/prerecorded videotape on the other. By bringing time shifting and the individual ownership of a film (copy) to the consumer-spectator, these innovations demanded new theoretical models and a revision of mono-causal explanations. Accordingly, convergence began before the personal computer; it did not wait for the digital. And, while deploying new technology, at its core was a new business model of delivery on demand. Friedberg successfully separates convergence from "digitization" and thereby implicitly points to one of the more obvious and critical objections: that the convergence thesis is above all a marketing ploy, part of the hype that has surrounded digitally based devices as they tried to transform themselves into mass consumption commodities. When applied to the cinema, as we saw, convergence invariably designates the strategic alliances between the owners of traditional media. There, multinational business conglomerates invest in the print media (newspaper and publishing), in television (terrestrial and cable), in the film business, in audio recording media, and delivery systems such as the internet to effect economies of scale and consolidate centers of power and influence that reestablished the old trusts and monopolies of the studio era while further globalizing their reach.

Convergence, in this sense, is above all an advertising concept of media producers, which only in the second instance hints at a broad sweep of universal aspirations in leisure and entertainment among large sections of Western and non-Western consumers that Jenkins hails as cultural convergence. It entails identification with common visual icons ("brands"), the use of common technologies, and it depends on hegemonic modes of representation. Convergence would thus be the term that disguises the business interests of those who see multimedia primarily as a provider of profit from the exploitation of mono-content, but it would also be a shorthand for very heterogeneous factors of globalization in the spheres of information, communication, representation, and culture, also often referred to by the term "cultural imperialism," for which US popular culture in general, the Anglo-American music industry and Hollywood in particular, are the (perhaps somewhat too convenient) outward signs.

These historical notes of caution aside, however, a degree of convergence between the print and audiovisual media is undeniable. When I open the *New York Times* on the internet, I have an old-fashioned newspaper, with columns and blocks of text, but I can also click on short television features, with a correspondent commenting the news, or look at the trailer of the movie about to open worldwide this weekend. Interlaced with this material are ads that look like photographic images but, as my cursor grazes them, they come alive and transport me to another place: a website, a looped movie, or a telephone number. Generally, websites started out looking like newspapers, emulating their set grids and predefined columns, whereas newspapers extensively use websites as advertising tools. Both media feature animation, sound, and digital video clips to convey information rapidly, snappily, and in a way that grabs the reader's attention and retains it. Television, too, increasingly uses split screens or multiple windows. News programs rely on sophisticated graphics, computer animation, and a continually updated, "refreshed" text-frieze, thereby suggesting a kind of co-evolution between these three heavily "designed" and customized environments that are the print media, television, and the internet. Also in tremendous flux with regard to function, design and styling are other traditional formats combining text and visuals, such as posters, billboards, manifestos, pamphlets, graffiti art, maps and the like. All are still very much present both in the physical and digital worlds, living in the minds of makers and producers, as well as in the perception of users and consumers, so that their interdependence and overlap (and their increasingly "dynamic"; i.e., user-responsive character) suggests a certain convergence, especially if viewed under such common denominators as advertising, infotainment, promotion, political propaganda, or journalistic agenda-setting.

Yet, with respect to the cinema, the case for convergence is more complicated. First, regarding technological convergence, we are still a long way away from full-blown device convergence, with format interchangeability and a single platform. On the contrary: almost as much speaks for divergence as for convergence, or perhaps for "bi-vergence": parallel developments, but in opposite direction, such as larger/smaller or fixed/mobile, when one focuses, for instance on "screens." From the point of view of the user, for instance, there is a tendency for moving image platforms to become more mobile, miniature, and multipurpose (converging around the mobile phone and tablets, rather than the television set and computer monitor), but there is also the opposite development, namely home entertainment centers becoming larger, more sophisticated, and more integrated. Likewise, the projection experience, so typical of the cinema, has seen larger screens in theaters and in the home, but the dynamics of each reconfigure themselves around the variables domestic/public, with their quite different affective, social, and perceptual "experience economies." If, in this development, the cinema retains and even extends its value as a unique kind of social space and a fixed architectural site, with its own cultural values mainly invested in the political significance of "public"—or rather, in the mysterious combination of intimate and public—then the domestic space, already refigured by television, will once more open to feature films the "family audiences" that the cinema lost to television since the 1960s—hence the rise in big-budget children's films, animation features, and fantasy genres.

As we saw, much less open to doubt (and therefore the more controversial) is economic convergence in the area of mainstream cinema ownership (horizontal integration, corporate cross-media "synergy"). Jenkins, as indicated, vehemently argues against the view that such multimedia convergence must lead to mono-content, taking the perspective of the active spectator, user, prosumer, and associated fan communities. Although one may not share all of his optimism, he is surely right to want to think beyond the "reification/ alienation" and "mass-deception" arguments of Frankfurt School theorists.

Most important, though, the convergence theory as applied to the cinema is frustrated by the fact that a special kind of (cultural) value has become attached to the cinema's traditional material basis, the optico-chemical process, whereby celluloid, coated with a light-sensitive emulsion, directly bears the imprint of the objects or views that are before a camera. As digital conversion does away with this material basis, such a modification cannot but challenge definitions of what cinema is, and, by implication, must change what we have come to regard as the specific qualities of the medium: photographic iconicity, guaranteeing the cinema's "reality effect," combined with the special kind of indexicality, the existential link with the real, guaranteeing the "documentary" truth-value that makes the moving image such a special kind of historical "record."[15] Especially widely discussed is this loss of indexicality in the digital image: did it bring about a rupture in the history of cinema that some critics have experienced as traumatic and terminal, or have we simply misunderstood the meaning of "index"? For those in the former camp, digitization quite literally means the end of the cinema, so that there cannot possibly be convergence. Instead, in this light, an era of post-cinema has begun, with its own characteristics and certainly based on a different ontology.

In the latter camp, are those who argue against such a radical "rupture" theory of cinema. They hold the view that our current uncertainty of what is cinematic about moving images does not depend on either indexicality or digitization, and that the dilemma is a false one. Philosophers such as Gilles Deleuze or art historians like Aby Warburg have pondered the relation of still image to moving image without reference to (digital) technology. Indexicality as constitutive and inherent in the photograph was deconstructed long ago by Umberto Eco, on strictly formal grounds, when he pointed out, for instance, how embedded in a complex definition of the sign the concept of the index is in C. S. Peirce. Others, too, have argued against the photograph becoming fetishized as a privileged material support for the "reality" effect, compared to the video image or the pixel, itself a much broader concept when we think of its long history, stretching from optical illusionist toys that work with black-and-white dots to pointillist painting. All this merely to indicate that the ontological or philosophical questions now commonly addressed to the cinema's future require, at the very least, a wider context, in which digitization is itself merely one factor, however crucial.

What, then, can be the overall conclusion regarding the conjunction of digitization, multimedia, and convergence with respect to the cinema? As suggested, the case for convergence in the generally understood sense as technologically driven is at best half the story. The main forces of convergence have been economic and demographic, determined by multinational company policy and the quest for global audiences, not forgetting the economic surplus value of segmented, locally addressed audiences. Since the early years of the past century, the audiovisual media have (apart from military uses) always developed primarily as mass-produced services in a sector of the economy—the leisure, culture, and information industries—that has seen quite exponential growth after World War II, with an acceleration of the pace of change during the past twenty years, but also with increasingly more volatile consumers. Convergence in this sense happens under the sign of capitalist concentration, merger, and cartelization: the result of the media empires of the 1980s (News Corporation, Time Warner, Seagram, Bertelsmann) and the digital start-ups that survived the dotcom bubble and reinvented themselves as megacompanies (Microsoft, Google, Apple, Facebook) is that common ownership has succeeded in holding the audiovisual, print, and electronic media together by also creating a common social base: the mass-market consumer, targeted, profiled, and tracked by a huge and still hugely expanding marketing and service industry that data mines preferences, likes, dislikes, and their volatilities. Thus, from the audiences' point of view, convergence means that different media products are often linked to each other, both intertextually and materially, by shared distribution and marketing practice, when the same product circulates and is repackaged in different forms of media.[16]

This is perhaps why the culture at large still finds a horizon of eventual convergence (in the sense of concentration, synergy, common standards, and linked products) a convenient way of getting a grip on this new multidirectionality of media interpenetration, facilitated by this globalization of ownership on the one hand and the shared technical code of digitization on the other. Although ignoring both the history of the individual media and their very different institutional and cultural meanings, the convergence argument remains attractive because it promises to ground the study of the audiovisual domain in a new *telos*. No longer having to struggle with the supposed goal of greater and greater realism, nor with the realist "ontology" of the material index and the mnemonic trace (with its implied obverse of "illusionism" and "simulacrum" that so much polarizes those "for" and "against" the digital image), the convergence thesis prioritizes the spectator as pragmatic user-consumer and the industry as corporate agency driven by technological competition and profit maximization. Assuming a move from public to domestic space, the spectator is imagined as preferring a single multipurpose and multistandard device that allows ease of access and convenience of use for very different media products, whereas the corporate agent "targets" this user ever more relentlessly into the recesses of his or her personality, desires, narcissism, and psychic dispositions.

However, so complex and diverse is this picture of convergence that one wonders whether the term can encompass all the different layers, processes, and dynamics at work. I personally prefer another term, for which, however, there does not exist a good translation: the German concept of *Verbund*, somewhere between "network" and "affiliation," between "alliance of convenience" and "mutually interdependent antagonism," capable of indicating material discreteness, historical distinctiveness, and the simultaneous dynamics of competition and cooperation. At one level, such an alliance of convenience is the same as multimedia convergence, if considered in its multiple meanings. At another level, it is the opposite because it acknowledges not only competition and cooperation, but also mutually interacting encounters at very different levels and with all the unintended consequences that are so typical of technologically driven contingency, because implying elements of bricolage and recognizing serendipity and uneven development. Furthermore, such mutual interdependency may operate like a cartel, with mergers, takeovers, and buyouts, but it can also be more like diplomacy, requiring negotiation, trade-offs, and give and take.

On a more methodological rather than terminological level, I think the precise nature of such media interaction, interference, and succession needs to be looked at separately, as a problem of media-historiography (as discussed by David Bolter, Richard Grusin and Lev Manovich for new media, and for cinema history by Noel Burch, David Bordwell, Tom Gunning, and Sean Cubitt). The positive point about convergence is that its "logic" demands a move away from notions of "rupture" and "epistemic break," basically suggesting others forms of contact, contagion, and interaction. Convergence can also be a useful first concept in the encounter of science and humanities (say, between the neurosciences and the philosophies of mind). On the negative side, convergence disguises the power relations that exist between media and the co-extensiveness of their encounters and contact zones, as well as the fact that important (technical) advances often happen simultaneously and yet independently of each other.

First Preliminary Conclusion: total technological convergence between the cinema and television or between the cinema and the internet is unlikely, if past experience is anything to go by. The "revival" of the cinema since the 1980s as a distinct social and architectural space of experience especially points toward a divergence of "cinema" and "film." By contrast, economic convergence among cinema, television, the music business, publishing, and the internet is a fact (as far as Hollywood is concerned), having—in addition to the globalization of audiences—added another dimension through the convergence of the military and the entertainment complex (always a reality, but now taking place in full view). This convergence I would prefer to call an "alliance of convenience," to forestall the idea of a common goal or telos or even of a common interface, whether technical or cultural. Rather, the economic value of the cinema is its distinctiveness vis-à-vis the other media (outlets). Cultural convergence (as envisaged by Jenkins and others among fan communities and their relation to films as texts to be reworked and recirculated) is an important phenomenon (now "industrialized" by Facebook and Twitter). But, rather than seeing this aggregation of communities around the liquidity and malleability of digital media objects as an instance of (countercultural) participation, one should bear in mind that, largely due to developments such as dynamic data mining, social network media, blogging, collaborative filtering, feedback loops, and other pull technologies, there is convergence (i.e., cooperation and collusion) between the media conglomerates and the fans (even when they perceive themselves as oppositional).[17] Convergence of this kind is technologically enabled, economically contested, culturally motivated, and takes place in a space that is "virtual" while nonetheless having "real" social consequences.

DIGITAL CINEMA

Even such a relatively cursory assessment of the convergence theory, its commercial logics and inherent tensions (the possible confusion of conversion and convergence; the uncertainty of the kind of *telos* implied; the terminological overstretch, when competition, cooperation, opposition and collusion, appropriation and ingestion have to be accommodated in a single term) suggests that a closer look is needed at "digital cinema" as also more of an oxymoron—a contradiction in terms—than is generally acknowledged. Although "cinema" as public space, "experience," and "event" (i.e., the blockbuster economy) has remained largely unaffected by "the digital" and follows the logic of other spectacle sites, such as festivals, theme parks, or large-scale music venues, the (im)materiality of "film" and its object status in the culture (as authored "text" and autonomous "work") is increasingly determined by digitization and signal conversion, thereby entering into closer proximity with (digital) music and publishing, of which the internet has become the prime delivery system.[18] The term "digital cinema" would obscure these tensions between "cinema" and "film," even as it suggests a smooth transition between the traditional film experience and its digitally reworked successor.[19]

Therefore, what has only been touched on so far is the possibility that digitization, rather than leading to convergence, might actually deepen this division within the cinema itself, between "cinema" (event and experience) and "film" (text and work). It highlights not only the fact that there has always been a tension between the cinema providing a "service" ("going to the movies") and a "product" (the film as self-contained commodity), but also that the cinema as event and experience, tied to place and location, has always been distinct from "film" as a storage medium for recording movement, telling stories, and giving form to sensory data. If it is the latter—film—that is above all affected by digitization, then the impact on the former is more difficult to assess. But this cinema–film divide is not the only way in which "digital cinema" can be construed as an oxymoron.

Digital Cinema as Functional Equivalence: More of the Same Except by Other Means?

In one sense, digital cinema is simply one among a number of ways of making films, and then distributing, exhibiting, or archiving them. The basic principle involves using digitization to record, transmit, and replay images, rather than using light-sensitive chemicals (emulsion) on film (cellulose or polymer). Digital cinema still employs optical lenses to capture, bundle, and refract light, but these, too, may over time be replaced by light-sensitive fibers. The main advantage of digital technology over analog film is that it can transmit large amounts of information exactly as it was originally recorded. Analog supports, such as celluloid and audiotape, lose information in transmission and reproduction, and they gradually degrade with multiple viewings.[20] Digital cinema's major disadvantage (until recently) was that the information contained as pixels in an image was inferior to that of 35mm film stock. Against this must be held that digital information is more flexible (malleable, mutable, modifiable) than analog information. A computer can systematically alter digital data, adjusting all the parameters of an image (such as size, scale, color saturation, tone), compared to the much more restricted range of changes that can be made to photographically recorded images. At the limit, a digital image is not really an image; generated by a different process, it is in essence a set of instructions whose execution (visualization, materialization, manipulation) obeys a mathematical rather than an optical logic.

As such, digital cinema can affect all the major areas of movie-making: production—how a movie is actually made; postproduction—how a movie is edited, combined, or synched with sound and assembled; distribution—how a movie gets from the production company to movie theaters; exhibition and projection—how a film theater presents and projects a movie. In practice, the introduction of digitization has so far had a variable impact on these different aspects of the institution of cinema and, in the process, has brought to the surface several sets of competing agendas and contending claims. The result is that digital cinema today represents a particularly striking case of uneven development and nonsynchronicity with respect to the technological, economic, and cultural factors involved in implementing new technologies.[21]

Going to the local multiplex to watch the new Hollywood blockbuster, I might be forgiven for thinking that very little has changed from what the cinema experience was like nearly a hundred years ago. I am still sitting in a theatrical auditorium space with racked seating for a gathering of spectators, I am still looking at a projected (photographic) image, and I am still engrossed, for the most part, in a narrative live-action feature film, lasting on average between 90 and 150 minutes. So, why the confusion, the anxiety, the hype that has attached itself to "digital cinema"? It depends, of course, on whom one asks. Given the long history and relatively stable technology of celluloid-based cinema, coupled with the fixity of the aesthetic norms underlying the "classical" fiction film and the uniformity of the commodity product we know as the full-length feature film, it is tempting to think that, at the movies, it is "business as usual." This would be to conflate the cinema as an audiovisual storage medium for motion pictures with the cinema as a projection-based spectacle in a public space. On the other hand, realizing that much of what I see on screen was never "in front of" a camera, but generated inside a computer, and that my projection may well be a celluloid transfer from a digitally recorded and edited master, it is possible to claim that such a performance is no longer "cinema." Then again, buying a current release or a digitally remastered classic on DVD and watching it on my laptop or in high definition on my home entertainment center, I can only marvel at the convenience, richness, and sensuousness of the experience and come to the conclusion that there has been seamless convergence between analog and digital, and that—after television, the small screen, the video recorder, and the DVD player—the point may have been reached at which the "history of film" and the "history of cinema" no longer divide either along the lines of "product" and "service" or "work" (autographic) and "performance" (allographic),[22] but that both terms have become in some sense "metaphoric": naming ways of relating to our environment, to each other, and of "being-in-the-world," and thus requiring philosophical as well as technological differentiation.

For the fact of the matter is that going to the cinema today means that nothing has changed and that everything has changed. Behind the scenes, as it were, modifications have been at work at almost every level. But they have, by and large, been integrated along the lines of "functional equivalence," meaning that the introduction of a new technology or technique at first substitutes for something already familiar: doing the same thing with different means. Although this has knock-on effects on other aspects of the filmmaking process or may lead to trying out new things, these generally result in an overall readjustment of other parameters and not in a radical change of craft, method, or style. This, at any rate, is the model that has defined Hollywood's approach to new technology, if one follows David Bordwell, Janet Staiger, and Kristin Thompson in their *Classical Hollywood Cinema: Film Style and Production*.[23]

Sound, 3D, and Expanded Cinema

What, however, has changed substantially and is often credited with having revived the film industry in the 1980s is film sound. "Surround sound" was itself influenced and inflected by the Walkman experience of the 1980s, making what used to be known as "personal stereo" become a collective, shared experience: a new kind of *public intimacy* conveyed through the sound space we share with others in the dark.[24] Dolby, multichannel directional sound has given the cinema a new spatial depth and dimension, which four key films from the mid to late 1970s (*Nashville, Jaws, Star Wars,* and *Apocalypse Now*) pioneered very successfully—each in its own way—to redefine the movie experience.

This redefinition is not only technical; rather, the technical and the cultural aspects interfere, cross-fertilize, and mutually implicate each other: the new film sound reflects the generally changing relation in our culture between "sound" and "image." More and more, it is sound and noise that define public and private space, inner and outer worlds, norm and exception. At least since Dolby noise reduction systems were introduced, sound has been experienced as three-dimensional (3D), "filling" the space the way that water fills a glass, but also emanating from inside our heads, seemingly empowering us, giving us agency, even as we listen passively. In the cinema, the traditional hierarchy of image to sound has been reversed in favor of sound now leading the image, or at the very least, giving objects a particular kind of solidity and materiality.[25] It prompted film theorists Christian Metz to speak of "aural objects";[26] led to a new scholarly approach to "audio-vision," for which Michel Chion's writings stands as exemplary;[27] and created a new industry profession, that of the sound designer, which Walter Murch has helped raise to prestige and artistic status.[28]

Taking sound and image together, it is clear that the introduction of digitization has affected the three traditional branches of the film industry in different ways. Production was the first to be drastically altered, whereas distribution and exhibition have been much slower to adjust, partly because the benefits are less clearly quantifiable while the cost (for instance, of refurbishing theatres with digital storage devices and new projection equipment) is very quantifiable indeed, as are the effects on vested interests, such as labor, infrastructural capital, patents, and monopolies. Digital distribution offers, at first sight, substantial cost benefits to the producers because films, instead of having to be distributed via individually struck prints and then shipped in cans at enormous expense, could be sent as computer files through broadband cable or transmitted via satellite. Given the high advertising cost of a film and its intensive exploitation in the first weeks of a picture's release, such digital distribution would also make it easier to open movies in theaters all over the world on the same day. But what delivers major savings for producers and distributors compels costly investments for exhibitors. These the exhibitors have been reluctant to make unless subsidized by the prime beneficiaries, or recouped at the box office through higher admission prices, as was the case with the slew of 3D movies in the 2009/2010 season (which included such blockbusters and critical successes as *Up, Alice in Wonderland, Coraline,* and *Avatar*). Technically, digital projection has sufficiently matured to stand comparison with analog projection, notably through the use of systems (such as Micromirror) that split the light via a prism into separate color beams that form images by hitting microchips fitted with an array of tiny, hinged mirrors. George Lucas was an early advocate: his company launched *Star Wars - The Revenge of the Siths* in some fifty theaters in the United States via digital distribution and projection already in 2005.[29]

The hype around the reintroduction of 3D should therefore be seen in a double context: first, it gave exhibitors an incentive to install digital projection, and, once in place, it becomes less important whether 3D proves to be a passing fad, a niche attraction, or takes over the mainstream. The second context, however, has to do with sound. Jeffrey Katzenberg, one of 3D's most fervent advocates, speaks of it as the third revolution in cinema: "There have been two previous revolutions that have occurred in movies. The first one is when they went from silent film to talkies, and the next one happened when they went from black-and-white to colour. Which was 70 years ago. In my opinion, this is the third revolution."[30] The surprising aspect of his "revolution" is not that he presents a rather too streamlined and goal-oriented version of film history, but that he very much sees 3D as taking "vision" out of what he calls its "vinyl phase": "As human beings, we have five senses: touch, taste, smell, hearing and sight. The two senses that filmmakers use to affect an audience are hearing and sight. And if you think about the evolution of sound, [which] in our lifetime, ... has gone from vinyl to an 8-track to a CD to digital. But sight is kind of at vinyl right now."[31] The metaphor is telling because it implies that the industry itself is thinking of spatial images as catching up with spatial sound, not the other way round.

When it came to production, the industry was much faster in adopting digital methods for shooting and especially for editing feature films. Even though investments in new technical equipment and human skills were initially also very high, the savings in time and improved control proved universally persuasive factors. There were surprisingly few outward signs of upheaval and change, at least when compared to the incisive transformations (of labor organization, business strategy, and "synergy") that took place in the 1970s and 1980s, when Hollywood went global, adopted the blockbuster as a multimedia marketing platform, and was taken over by information and telecommunication conglomerates: that is, changes that preceded the impact of the digital.

If film production has shifted quickly to digital technology, did any saving in money and time translate into corresponding changes in the power structures of the industry?

Probably not, given that the commercial film industry, but also the independent sector, has always been hierarchically organized. What has changed is the importance of "outsourcing," and what has intensified is the relentless search for cheap locations and labor, but both are within the traditional logic of Hollywood practice. Has digitization lowered the entry barrier for new talent? Again, not in itself, since, in the end, access to equipment and stock does not translate either into talent, production values, or access to distribution. Conversely, digitization of production has had immense influence on styles of filmmaking, not just thanks to the potential for creating fantasy worlds through special effects, but equally noticeably in the documentary sector, with more fluid and close-up camera work. Indeed, the camera has become more like the extension of the (helping) hand than of the (observing) eye, so that film spectatorship is moving in sync with other aspects of a more participatory culture. In addition, just as the audio CD has given a new value and currency to vinyl (see above), the digital as default mode of the image allows filmmakers to invoke the (artefacts of the) analog mode (whether the grain of celluloid or the fuzziness of video, or the pristine hues of black-and-white), as so many ways to draw attention to the poetics of obsolescence.

Thus, faced with the reality of digital cinema at the point of production and postproduction and the eventual penetration of digitization into the areas of distribution and exhibition, one must distinguish not only between the different branches of the institution of cinema—what I called film as *product* and cinema as *service*—but also between different parties or players and their respective agendas or roles. Next to the producer, the distributor-exhibitor, and the movie audience, there is the independent director and the avant-garde artist. For each, a separate cost-benefit sheet arising from digitization could be drawn up. For instance, if "digital cinema" means for the studio or producer that it is business as usual because, as usual, it's (about) business—the chance of exceptional returns on investment in a high-risk service industry—then, for the independent director, the combination of digital equipment, stock, and editing software connotes a significant break: it makes filmmaking potentially much faster, possibly much cheaper, and it gives the director more short-term control (being able to scrutinize the results instantly, compared to, say overnight rushes) but also greater overall control over his or her picture and access to new promotional channels such as YouTube, Daily Motion, or Facebook.

Digital Cinema and the Avant Garde

Similar, and yet quite different, is the stake that the avant-garde artist has in the availability of the digital as a medium next to video and celluloid. She or he, too, is sensitive to the cost factor of equipment and material, but the constraints and compromises that, for instance, a mainstream director or an independent producer-director has to consider when shooting for theatrical release, while simultaneously needing to factor in television broadcasts and a DVD release, do not arise in quite this way when digital techniques intersect with those of video-art. From the moment that Nam June Paik picked up the first semiportable video recorder at the Sony laboratory in 1965, video as an artistic "material" and video as a broadcast medium have developed in separate directions.[32] By entering the gallery spaces, video-art guaranteed itself recognition and legitimacy, and thus also a history, with its critical discourses secured by the presence of Andy Warhol, Bill Viola, Yoko Ono, Bruce Nauman, Dan Graham, Gary Hill, or Lynn Hershman, all of them original artists and distinctly innovative whose interventions and body of work has written video into modern art up to this day, alongside pop art, *Fluxus*, and happenings, as well as contemporary painting, sculpture, and installations.

The digital turn has given video art a new lease of life, as well as inscribed it into a genealogy different from that of cinema. For, with the availability of digital media, artists and scholars trained in alternative film histories immediately recognized the historical as well as aesthetic links between video art and the new media (with their interchangeable formats and common platforms) but also the genealogies that traced both digital and video art back to the "beginnings" of cinema. This, in turn, led to digital cinema acquiring yet another pedigree: the long practice of "expanded cinema" (notably among the New York avant garde around Ken Jacobs, Jonas Mekas, and Stan Brakhage, as well as key figures such as Paul Sharits, Hollis Frampton, and Michael Snow, who, to varying degrees, recognized their own aesthetic agendas ranging from mixed media to *Gesamtkunstwerk* ambitions in the possibilities of digital media).[33]

Whether it was the non-narrative forms represented by hypertext architectures, the new editing techniques of compositing and overlay, or a quite different conception of pictorial space—the frame and graphic abstraction—several kinds of connections emerged between the avant garde and new media, complementing as well as complicating the perceived affinities of the avant garde with early cinema, which had so strongly marked cinema history in the 1970s and '80s, as reflected in the writings of Noel Burch, Charles Musser, and Tom Gunning.

In Europe, directors such as Peter Greenaway, Bela Tarr, Alexander Sokurov, and others also looked to the possibilities that the new media afforded in the way of experiment with seemingly obsolete filmmaking styles, but it was above all the crossovers between cinema, video installations, and gallery art (e.g., Chris Marker, Isaac Julien, Harun Farocki, Mona Hatoum, Douglas Gordon, Tacita Dean) that gave a new impetus to reflect about cinema in a multimodal, cross-media, transhistorical context. Hence, the elaboration of a vocabulary that speaks of intermediality, of hybridity, of expanded, and even "exploded" cinema to retain a sense of difference in texture and voice, of a clash of associations, emotions, and intensities; of the effects of shock or surprise associated with a mixture of film-based and digital techniques, while retaining a sense of affinity with a common aesthetic heritage across cinema, video, and digital art: for instance, around stillness and movement; "magnification" and scale; faciality and frontality; attention, absorption, and attraction–distraction—not to mention immersion and interaction. Whatever qualms one may have about the varying terminology, there is merit in the insight that the traditional performing arts, notably theater and dance, but also the fine arts, such as painting and sculpture, can usefully be seen under the rubric of "media" and thus should be brought into creative-critical contact with cinema and the moving image in the twenty-first century. For artists within the fine art tradition, the notion of convergence is not an obvious *telos*, committed as they are to medium specificity and self-differentiation, but the recognition that aesthetic parameters such as those just enumerated are shared among the different arts is now a commonplace, even if academic art history is slow to catch up. But the historical or conceptual (rather than pragmatic or prescriptive) grounds on which such a "convergence" of art history, the museum, and the moving image can be usefully argued, has indeed become a very fruitful area of debate.[34]

Babette Mangolte, an independent filmmaker, has written about the shock she felt when first working with the digital (or "pixel"), because she could not get used to the fact of it not having the depth of the photographic ("silver-based") image. Even once she added depth through special effects, it seemed to her a simulation, the optical illusion of depth, which had nothing to do with depth in the real world. Yet, in the visual arts, exploring flatness has been the central concern of modernism (especially of the Russian avant garde, notably El Lissitsky and Malevich). Are we, with the pixel image, facing the situation described by Eisenstein, Benjamin, and McLuhan, when they noted how an aesthetic problem (here, the relation of flatness to depth in perception and painting) identified by an artist, to which he or she brings an answer in one medium, is given a meta-turn by the subsequent medium, where it becomes not an aesthetic, but merely a technical issue? In this case, the digital image would have made not the emulation of human vision but the flatness of painting its default value, whereas human perception of depth would have become (one of) its special effect(s), thus turning an aesthetic concern into a matter of technique and thereby "automating" the artist's task.

Mangolte also responded to the fascination that came from the digital camera's "floating" point of view, already hinted at earlier when I suggested the move from eye to hand, and which she describes by saying that the digital image is not tied to a locatable point of view, that the camera can get extremely close without distortion, that the image can be manipulated free from the body. This, in turn, creates an image unbounded by a frame, disorienting because made strange by suspending the human point of view and the human scale, introducing different spatial coordinates (as well as upsetting the calibrated or graded sense of distance and proximity we normally have toward the world).

Audiences, too, are divided by digital cinema: for some, it opens the choice of assuming different spectatorial positions by extending the repertoire of roles from voyeur (as familiar from classical cinema) and witness (typical of documentary and art cinema) to participant, player, user (video games, virtual reality environments) and consumer (of merchandizing, tie-ins, spin-offs). Others—the cinephiles—draw, as indicated, a line in the silicone sand: in their eyes, the digital image is no longer cinema because the loss of indexicality of the image touches the cinema's core: its reality status and photographic essence, defined by luminosity, transparency, and projection, none of which is a prerequisite of the digital image, however much it can emulate transparency, create luminosity as a special effect, and utilize projection.

For media theorists, finally, the digital image frees cinema from a number of misconceived ontologies (of realism) or erroneous philosophical assumptions, again mainly around the truth status of the photographic image, around mimesis and the question of "illusionism." The digital image thus opens up a new understanding of the conditions and limits of the particular symbolic code we call "representational," with its formal schemes (receding sight lines, a single vanishing point) and historical origins (easel painting, the European Renaissance) but also its cultural implications (the "open window," the framed view, the vanishing point, and the horizon) and ideological effects (such as putting the imperial eye and sovereign single subject at the center of the image and thus the world).

The Cinematic Versus the Digital: Effects, Properties, Logics

One's first response to digitization might therefore justifiably be to welcome the air of uncertainty and potentiality around "digital rupture" and "media hybridity" and to believe in the possibilities that this "turn" can bring to sound-image combinations. If nothing else, the spectre of the *telos* of convergence and of technological determinism hovering over digital cinema helps to focus on inherent flaws and contradictions, shortcomings, and misconceptions in the accepted accounts of film and visual media history. It has led to the fields of "early cinema" and "media archaeology" being among the most vibrant and productive areas of academic research and teaching.[35] At the same time, the argument of a fundamental rupture between analog and digital should be taken seriously and put on a broader basis than simply remaining tied to the material support of the image. It has already led to a more philosophically informed debate about what is an image, what is movement, and what is the contribution of "the cinematic" to everything from politics and propaganda, to anthropology and art history. This is why, at the outset, I insisted on the oxymoronic nature of "digital cinema," now highlighting the possible areas of *contradictio in adjecto* by setting in opposition not analog and digital image, but "the cinematic" and "the digital," in terms of their respective effects, properties, and logics. That these three registers of specificity might be also an artificial divide is a possibility (see Lev Manovich on "what digital media are not"), but as a heuristic exercise, they prove essential for my argument.

Among the specific *cinema effects*, one would first list the *impression of reality*, that is to say, the high iconic fidelity that the photographic image carries. The "reality-effect" is also a consequence of the *impression of movement*, which, in turn, is complemented by the *impression of presence*, strengthened by sound, but also providing one of the typical subject effects of cinema; namely, the impression of being included in the image and endowed with a special kind of *ocular-sensory, embodied identity*. This identity effect is crucially shaped by the cinema's reliance on narrative and, in particular, on the causally organized linearity of mainstream feature films, where different narrational strategies (point of view, shot reverse shot, close-up) ensure a "binding" and "stitching-up" (the famous "suturing") or a "focalization" (in a more literary vocabulary) of the spectator as "subject."

The key *digital effects* in such a comparison would be the *impression of hyper-reality*, which would lead to an *impression* not of movement but *of metamorphosis*; that is, not only in the form of morphing and shape-shifting, but also as a constitutive instability of scale, mobility of point of view, and inherent "liquidity" of the (visual) representation.[36] Second, instead of giving an impression of identity and presence, provided in the cinema by the stable configuration of projection, frame, and linear fictional narrative, the subject effect typical of the digital would be the *impression of agency, tactility, and interactivity*. The latter, in turn, has to be assessed against the digital forms of narrative and fictionality, which are characterized by *simulation and hyper-reality, by multiple narratives, branching narratives*, and *narrative loops*. In each case and on both sides of the divide, these effects are "illusory," but this implies also a new meaning for the term "illusion."

When one now turns to *cinematic* versus *digital properties*, the obvious difference is that cinema relies on the *photographic image*, whereas the digital is based on the *numeric image*. Second, in the cinema, the screen is understood as a two-dimensional projection surface, with extension of the image into lateral depth (even when the actual screen is a small or large LED screen, monitor, or touch screen). In the digital, the screen can best be understood as a display (based on the graphic user interface) whose dimensionality is variable, capable of looking two-dimensionally "flat" even when the image is "projected" and suggesting stereoscopic or holographic depth even when the images appear on a handheld device. As already indicated, the cinema relies on a fixed arrangement of camera-projector, spectator, and screen (usually referred to as the *cinematic "apparatus"*), whereas the *digital "apparatus"* (if one can speak of it as such) is the geometrical grid and the box, typified by the "desktop" interface, by the predominance of the rectangular "page," and a generally topographical spatial arrangement, with little suggestion of projected depth. Even when one speaks of "cyberspace," the sensory encounter with digital data (including visual material) is either still predominantly 2D or (in the case of 3D computer animation) immersive, both of which environments are quite different from the "projective transparency" typical of the cinema.

The grid-box scheme of digital media also determines the kind of multimediality typical of the digital, which is the combination of script, graphics, sound, still image, and moving image in one display frame, multiply divided, segmented, and layered (inspired, as suggested earlier, by the layout of newspapers, with banner headlines and inserts, when one thinks of the screen of a news channel, for instance), whereas the cinema tries to integrate and make transparent its own multimediality: such a seamless integration and hierarchical organization of its different sensory data and input channels (sound, image, speech, text, graphics) being another name for its "reality effect." Finally, one of the defining properties of the cinema is that it is a public performance, taking place in a shared space (auditorium), whereas the digital realm establishes its public sphere and imagined communities in quite different ways, independent of shared time, location, and space. It is organized through "sites" (networks, nodes), where—in principle—access is open, permanent, and ubiquitous ("online"), compared to the time regime (scheduled performances) and the rituals of exclusion and inclusion typical of the cinema, where the purchase of individual tickets, the lobbies, concession stands, doormen, and usherettes act as markers of a series of liminal spaces, with an implied cultural symbolism of threshold and privileged access, in the force field of what I called "public intimacy."

Turning finally to the respective "logics," in the sense of a set of underlying but often merely implied premises that ensure a certain functional but also cultural coherence for an ensemble of practices, it used to be argued that the cinema follows the major representational logic of the West since the Renaissance; namely, that of the central perspective as developed by architects such as Brunelleschi and Alberti in Florence around 1435, and elevated to the norm by painters like Masaccio, Mantegna, and Piero della Francesca. The peephole camera obscura that inspired the monocular cinematograph, the framed image and its implied use as a window on the world, also reflect "perspective" as the common symbolic form, not to mention how Cartesian optics (as well as the philosophy of mind inspired by it) became associated with just such a visual scheme, powerfully reproduced in the cone of sight emanating from the all-seeing (i.e., projecting and introjecting) eye.

The logic of the digital, by contrast, is neither visual-representational nor geometrically centered on a perceiving subject. It follows first of all the computational logic of algorithms—formalized routines or instructions for accomplishing predefined tasks (if... then)—that build up complex structures from simple ones through repetition, alternation, and amplification. Second, if we recall that one of the first practical uses of computers (besides cracking enemy code and calculating missile trajectories) was to work with spreadsheets, that is, as a program for manipulating a set of interdependent variables, then one inherent logic of the digital points to the conditional (what... if) as its natural dimension. This conditional mode may seem identical to the virtual but, in fact, belongs to a different paradigm, as long as the virtual is understood to be an optical-visual category such as in the pair "reality–illusion." The conditional does, however, make simulation, emulation, and the playing through of possible scenarios a prominent feature of its *modus operandi*. Likewise, the complex interdependences in a spreadsheet of tabulated data (a "database"), linked and mutually reacting to each other, suggests a logic of connectivity and shareability, of filtering mechanisms and feedback loops that contrasts with the cinema's linear cause-and-effect chains of sequentiality or continuity through contiguity. It also suggest a different temporal regime when compared to the delay, suspension, and deferral typical of narrative, in which these chains of linear data, constituted by a strict succession of individual still frames, are "sculpted" and modulated in time, in contrast to the primarily "spatial" or dispersive order of a database.

Judging by this account of "the cinematic" and "the digital," there seems to be little or no convergence between their respective logics. The more surprising (and in need of explanation) therefore is the observation with which I started this section, namely the quasi-imperceptible transition from analog film production to digital techniques in order to achieve much the same effects: photographically credible representations of the perceptible world articulated through linear narrative. How then to reconcile the conviction of some critics that there has been a radical, indeed, ontological break, and the impression by others that nothing much has changed in the cinematic experience: that it is still "business as usual," both in a literal and a metaphorical sense? Initially, the vocabulary of postmodernism proved to be an attractive option, because it supplanted the discourses of rupture and epistemic breaks with those of transformations, mutation, and transitions, as expressed in terms such as pastiche, parody, reprise, and appropriation. These terms, borrowed from rhetoric and literature, helped to acknowledge the coexistence of analog and digital media practices and their mutual interference and dependencies, as well as the surprising kinds of survival and afterlife of apparently obsolete film forms and narrative formulas. Postmodernism seemed to explain the recycling and retrofitting of genres and stereotypes that made the film industry so "opportunistic" with regards to its rivals (radio, the music industry, television), but it also kept Hollywood's adaptability to and readiness for innovative technology very high (via its special effects and event movies), even as it maintained itself as a stable and, in most respects, frustratingly conservative institution for getting on to a hundred years. Since the 1990s, however, postmodernist cinema has been replaced by postclassical cinema or post-film cinema as terms coexisting but not synonymous with "digital cinema."

Postproduction: Cinema Inside Out—from Harnessing Reality to Harvesting Reality

Yet something more fundamental is at stake in the filmmaking process of the digital age, namely a shift that seems innocuous enough but has far-ranging consequences: the change of emphasis from production to postproduction. It is innocuous if simply translated into the speed and convenience of digital (i.e., "nonlinear") editing, which can now be done on a laptop thanks to some high-performance, off-the-shelf but nonetheless professional-standard editing software. It is also relatively innocuous if we think of digital postproduction in terms mainly of the higher degree of plasticity and manipulability of the images: what George Lucas has called the "sculpture" approach to the digital image. The more important point, however, is that a film created around postproduction has a different relation to the pro-filmic. *Whereas analog filmmaking, centered on production, seeks to "capture" reality in order to "harness" it into a representation, digital filmmaking, conceived from postproduction, proceeds by way of "extracting" reality in order to "harvest" it.* Instead of disclosure and revelation (the ontology of film from Jean Epstein to André Bazin, from Siegfried Kracauer to Stanley Cavell), postproduction treats the world as data to be processed or mined, as raw materials and resources to be exploited. In other words, the move from production to postproduction as the center of gravity of filmmaking is not primarily defined by a different relation to "reality" (as claimed in the argument around the loss of indexicality in the digital image). Rather, a mode of production, for which postproduction becomes the default value, changes more than mere procedure: it changes the cinema's inner logic (and thus its ontology). The emphasis on postproduction made possible by the digital is fundamentally no longer based on perception: its *visuality* is of the order of the *vegetal*: comparable to the growing, harvesting, extraction, and manipulation of genetic or molecular material in the processes of biogenetics or microengineering.

The implications extend to the way one approaches what is no doubt the feature most commonly associated with digital cinema: computer-generated special effects. Normally, these CGI effects are discussed under two headings: those that enhance the impression of reality but stay within the boundaries of verisimilitude and photographic realism (so-called invisible special effects, such as the waves, the smoke from the ship's funnels, or the iceberg in James Cameron's *Titanic* or the recreation of San Francisco's 1970s waterfront for David Fincher's *Zodiac*) and those that create a new reality altogether (visible special effects), such as impossible worlds (the *Star Wars* saga), "lost worlds" (the dinosaurs of *Jurassic Park*), and creatures from the future (*Terminator II*) and the past (the *Lord of the Rings* trilogy). It therefore makes more sense to understand all digital special effects as belonging to the category of objects extracted from the real and manipulated in their "genetic" structure, so that some images might be said to be like clones, whereas others are more like morphs or grafts, but all are, in a direct sense, digital "mutants" of the real, however "invisible" their mutations or "life-like" their appearance is to the eye. *Jurassic Park*'s predatory dinosaurs, for instance, are less retro-evolved from, say, reptiles or birds, and instead are animated mutants of pick-up trucks, motorcycles, or earth-moving vehicles.

This comes close to Lev Manovich's models for mapping change: extending his thinking about the "graphic mode" as the default value of the photographic mode, one can think of "animation" and "real-life action" as variants of each other, instead of—as has been the case in film history—opposites. Change from one medium to another happens, according to Manovich, "inside-out": "One way in which change happens in nature, society, and culture is inside out. The internal structure changes first, and this change affects the visible skin only later.... Think of technology design in the twentieth century: typically a new type of machine was at first fitted within old, familiar skin: for instance, early twentieth century cars emulated the form of horse-drawn carriage. The familiar McLuhan's idea that the new media first emulates old media is another example of this type of change. In this case, a new mode of media production, so to speak, is first used to support old structure of media organization, before the new structure emerges. For instance, first typesets book were designed to emulate hand-written books; cinema first emulated theatre; and so on."[37] This inside-out model has the advantage of adding a sense of the uncanny, of some malevolent act of disguise, indeed, of conjuring up the host-parasite image, as we know (and fear) it, for instance, from the *Aliens* films. When the new bursts forth, it may quite violently disrupt the previous ecology and force dramatic changes, also in terms of power relations. Manovich has made this perhaps even more explicit in another metaphor he uses, that of the "Velvet Revolutions" (after 1989) in the former Soviet satellite states, which may initially have been remarkably unbloody and peaceful, but whose long-term consequences have been very painful, with definite winners, losers, and many a "return of the repressed." In each case, what emerges as the salient feature is how a new "logic" invades a system and takes over, retrovirus like, by leaving appearances intact but, in the meantime, hollowing out the foundations—technological as well as ontological—on which a certain medium or mode of representation was based.[38] But it also makes room for and may explain what earlier I called "the poetics of obsolescence": avant-garde artists merely enacting this inside out logic in softer, more contemplative forms. Both possibilities would suggest that digital cinema is not an oxymoron after all, but the mere shell of an obsolete cultural form whose function it now is to carry a new "life form" of the image into the next century. It is in this sense that "illusion," too, takes on a new meaning.

Second Preliminary Conclusion: digital cinema "emulates" photographic cinema as one of its possibilities (and this is still the majority of its applications), but it obeys different logics. Economically, it is at the forefront of the new economy, which combines global conglomerates with "outsourcing" of services and talents (specialized software firms, start-ups, but also the independents, the festival circuits, and world cinema as talent pools); aesthetically, it is a return to "illusionism," the aesthetics of astonishment that combines the sublime with the "real," neither of which has much to do with "reality." If photographic cinema followed the logic of imprint and trace, then the logic of digital cinema is computational: it extracts ("mines") from the real certain "data" and "information," which can be combined into a string of variables ("aggregated") to make up a scenario: the real as special effect, or, more precisely, the computational program or script as a world, which turns the world into a script—a language or algorithm. At the same time, the cinematic and the digital generate different orders of subjectivity: if, in the Freudian view, the cinema spectator stands under the regime of "lack" and "absence" in relation to plenitude and presence or faces the incompatible and contradictory demands of "law" and "desire," then the digital spectator has to negotiate the equally impossible orders of the "code" (mastery) and the "protocol"(constraint) and of predetermined interactivity masquerading as freedom and agency. The key point, if we follow Manovich, is that the logic of new media, and this includes digital cinema, has left behind not only photographic realism but also "simulation" as the model by which it produces the impression of (hyper-)reality. Instead of simulation, we have sampling, which is a quite different operation and derives from information theory and communication, not from image-making and representation. Although it originated from (popular) music, sampling goes much further: it is compatible with cognitivism and neuroscience; that is, it mimics the way our brains process information intermittently rather than as a continuous flow. The analogies with the traditional arts/media (music, sculpture, painting) overlook the more basic process at work: reality is raw material, from which data are extracted in order to be reassembled according to certain principles, schema, and templates; activated in view of certain goals; and judged by their results. We are in the world of postproduction, whose principles might be visualization, but, in most cases, they will be related to other meta-data structures (selection, filtering, modularization, etc.) that are useful for other purposes, and where visualization is only an intermediary or interface, maintained for human convenience. However, the second characteristic identified by Manovich is equally if not more important: in digital cinema, all representations are mapped on a 3D digital environment, irrespective of whether the reality is a 3D real-world space or a 2D pictorial space: the default value of all digital representation, including the cinema, has become 3D computer graphics. This—together with the nonentertainment uses of such visualization for military, medical, and/or monitoring purposes—is the bridge that takes us from analog cinema to digital cinema and from digital cinema to augmented reality.

Coda: Perspective Corrections

Does this mean that we should endorse, after all, the "death of cinema" or rather accept its historical function as an intermediary—some have even called it an "intermezzo" and a "detour"—between the visualization of natural phenomena previously imperceptible to the human eye (chronophotography as understood by Eadweard Muybridge and Etienne-Jules Marey) and the coding, compression, and transmission of information graspable by the human mind (of which narrative cinema has until now been the *historically contingent* "database" and "memory" because it inscribes the perceiving observer into the impersonal data flow)? It may not be an altogether implausible scenario, but it would underestimate the extent to which digital cinema is both a symptom and an agent, the shell and the incubator of what, at the outset, I called a "second Renaissance" and a "soft revolution."

The last major cultural shift in the default values of Western visual perception was, precisely, the introduction of the central perspective, beginning in the 1450s in Italy and generally identified with the European Renaissance. However, whereas in the fifteenth century it was the religious painters who acted as the mediators of the new ways of seeing: first depicting Heaven and the Almighty in altar pieces and then far-distant sights, producing a possibly unintended consequence: namely, that perspectival projection, which after all, had God as the vanishing point to secure the validity of representation, de facto contributed to secularization. Today, by contrast, it is popular entertainment and the movie industry that act as a kind of metaphysical template or interface, with perhaps equally unintended or at least unpredictable consequences.

Consider the following: the extension of our spatially configured visual and aural environment, such as we experience it in data-rich augmented realities, is symptomatic of the rise of the surveillance paradigm, which—taken in its widest sense—is materially affecting our understanding and engagement with images and visual information off- and online: in either case, *to see is to be seen, to act is to be tracked*. Digital cinema, insofar as it participates in this hybridity of visualization, vitalization, and action, plays a duplicitous role. Although it cognitively and bodily empowers users and spectators, it increasingly releases them from responsibility and consequence: an ethical challenge we are only beginning to become aware of. On the other hand, once images are no longer considered by our culture as *views* (i.e., something to be looked at or contemplated) but more like *clues* (i.e., as instructions for action), then they undo something that Renaissance perspective accomplished; namely, they banish the magic powers of images to act and be acted upon, which religion could make use of as long as their virtual presence was a function of their fixture to an actual site (e.g., as murals and frescos in churches or monasteries). What is now being instrumentalized is a different kind of agency in images, perhaps no less magical (in their effects of contagion, mimetic embodiment, animation, interpellation and instruction for action), when the management of digital information unites the "military-entertainment complex" with industry, finance, and government but also rules our daily lives thanks to smartphones, handheld devices, and augmented reality glasses.

If digital cinema implies that we are now once again sharing the same physical space with the image and are no longer separated by a frame (whether functioning as window [i.e., realism] or mirror [i.e., reflexivity]), then notions of representation and self-reference, both key elements of Renaissance perspectival space, would have to be abandoned. We would indeed experience a shift in paradigm and episteme, one for which the artist Hito Steyerl has coined the term "vertical perspective": "Imagine you are falling. But there is no ground." What, in the context of the revival of 3D, I described as horizonless images, where floating and gliding are more appropriate than sitting or standing upright, Steyerl radicalizes into "being in free fall," arguing that, while falling, one feels as if one is floating or not moving at all because: "falling is relational: if there is nothing to fall towards, you may not even be aware that you are falling.... Whole societies may be falling just as you are. And it may actually feel like perfect stasis." Steyerl goes on to explain: "Our sense of spatial and temporal orientation has changed dramatically in recent years, prompted by new technologies of surveillance, tracking, and targeting. One of the symptoms of this transformation is the growing importance of aerial views: overviews, Google Map views, satellite views. We are growing increasingly accustomed to what used to be called a God's-eye view. On the other hand, we also notice the decreasing importance of a paradigm of visuality that has long dominated our vision: linear perspective. Its stable and single point of view is being supplemented (and often replaced) by multiple perspectives, overlapping windows, distorted flight lines, and divergent vanishing points."[39]

Vertical perspective inaugurates a free-floating presence, immaterial and invisible, as well as ubiquitous and omnipresent. As symbolic form or new episteme, it is as much a set of formalized conventions as was linear monocular perspective when it pretended that the earth was flat and man was the only creature that mattered in the eyes of God. Now the sense of ubiquity, simultaneity, and omnipresence compensates for being a mere speck in the universe, enmeshed in networks of plotted coordinates, trackable and traceable at every point in space or time, and suspended in an undulating, mobile, variable inside to which no longer corresponds any outside, however vast, rich, connected, or proliferating one imagines such an inside (or online) world to be. Digital cinema would then be the name for an inside-out process, of which its apparent contradiction in terms merely signals certain parallax views and perspective corrections.

To sum up by way of several tentative conclusions: We can think about digital cinema in terms of three distinct but interlocking logics:

1. The aesthetic logic: digital cinema obliges one to rethink the cinema's relation to truth, evidence, disclosure. With the digital as the "new normal," all kinds of poetics of obsolescence come alive regarding production of presence, as well as the performativity of the authentic and the real. The aesthetic battles concern the definition of what cinema is: projection and transparency, the auditorium and a darkened room, a social space and a social experience, the framed image as "window and view" or the horizonless space-time of "verticality and free fall."
2. The socioeconomic logic: digitization is not only a new way of generating images and of signal conversion. It has, via the internet, streaming video, downloads, social networks, and YouTube, created new distribution platforms; new forums of information and circulation; the collapse of the barriers between private and public; bleeding the "experience cinema" into history, memory, politics, and the public sphere.[40] But it has also created new business models, offering "services" that are "free" and that have to recover their cost at another level (security, registration, surveillance, data generation, and data mining for prediction, premediation, and risk-assessment; i.e., the very opposite of memory, remediation, and conservation). In contrast to its aesthetics, digital cinema's economics as "service" rather than "work" or "product" obliges us to abandon the top-down "vertical" structures of the film industry and think in a more "horizontal," distributive way—as outlined by the proponents of convergence.
3. The historical logic: digital cinema embodies the philosophical paradox of everything changing so that everything can stay the same. It raises the question of how change happens, once we no longer believe in linear causality, in single agents or single events, or rely on teleology and grand narratives. In response to the end of the modern episteme, the humanities have adopted explanatory models that are allegorical and philological (Walter Benjamin, deconstruction), postmodern (repetition, reenactment), biological and evolutionary (contagion, swarm, stochastic, or rhizomatic proliferation).

I have suggested adding to these another kind of logic and a different dynamic: that of the inside-out, as mentioned by Manovich, or the life form kernel covered by the obsolete but essential shell. It tries to understand how a semantic contradiction or oxymoron like "digital cinema" actually functions as a motor for change, precisely because it appears as a contradiction: it carries the old forward while incubating the new, by a move that acknowledges the past's existence but defangs and transforms it in the very act of perpetuating it. In this way, digital cinema assures us that it is business as usual and there is nothing new under the sun, while pushing us to partake in one of the most dynamic and turbulent periods of human history, undergoing the sort of transformations that future generations will record as a radical break: a revolution and a renaissance at the same time.

NOTES

1. The world's stock exchanges, the movement of currencies and commodities, of labor and services, or the manufacture of weapons and the technologies of warfare would have been as decisively altered even without digital sound and images. Which is not to say that warfare and cinema or global trading and television do not have profound aspects in common. See Paul Virilio, *War and Cinema: The Logics of Perception* (London: Verso, 1988) or Pat Mellencamp, ed., *Logics of Television* (Bloomington: Indiana University Press, 1990).

2. André Bazin, "Ontology of the Photographic Image," in *What Is Cinema* (Berkeley: University of California Press, 1967) 14. See also, in the same volume, his essay "The Myth of Total Cinema," 17–22.

3. On the notion of a second Renaissance, see Henry Jenkins: "I use concepts of media- and cultural convergence to describe the present moment as a kind of Renaissance culture, one being transformed—for both better and worse—as the social, cultural, political, and legal institutions respond to the destabilization created by media change. Among the topics I have addressed have been digital media's impact on Journalism, the emergence of new forms of global culture, the potentials of interactive television, the production of knowledge in an information rich environment, the emergence of new youth cultures in cyberspace, and the impact of digital media on our understanding of intellectual property." Henry Jenkins, "Convergence? I Diverge," *Technology Review*, June 2001 (http://www.technologyreview.com/article/401042/convergence-i-diverge/).

4. Ibid.

5. Graham Murdock, "Digital Futures: European Television in the Age of Convergence," in *Television Across Europe: A Comparative Introduction*, ed. Jan Wieten, Graham Murdock, and Peter Dahlgren (Sage: London 2000) 36.

6. The field of media theorists is split on this issue. There are out-and-out technicists, such as Friedrich Kittler, who hold that human beings adapt very quickly to new technologies, and convinced culturalists, such as Sean Cubitt or Mark Hansen, who see culture shaping technology more than the other way round. The debate between those who believe in the determining force of changes in perception (in line with Benjamin, Foucault, or Virilio) and those cognitivists (Bordwell, Grodal) who think that the human sensorium has not changed in the last thirty-five millennia similarly polarizes this issue of technological determination.

7. Jenkins, "Convergence?—I Diverge."

8. Ibid.

9. Ibid.

10. See Alexander Kluge, *Cinema Stories* (New York: New Directions, 2007), 2.

11. "The paperless office is about as likely as the paperless toilet" (attributed to Keith Davidson of Xplor International. http://www.pcmag.com/encyclopedia_term/0,1237,t=paperless+office&i=48808,00.asp.

12. One lesson of early cinema studies: there is no single event/invention, nor even multiple origins; the prehistory of cinema is being rewritten every twenty years or so, depending on the pressing issues of the day.

13. The case for predigital convergence is made by Ann Friedberg, "The End of Cinema: Multimedia and Technological Change," in *Reconstructing Film Studies*, ed. Christine Gledhill and Linda Williams (London: Edward Arnold, 2000), 438–452.

14. The remote control may have changed the structure of television programming even more decisively than cable and the VCR, affecting the genres, pace, and mode of address of television, while also making its impact on film form, as we shall see. Cable and satellite reception also managed to break up the institutional arrangement of television, especially in Europe, by not only extending the overall amount of choice, but by taking control over this choice increasingly out of the hands and guidelines of governments, which until then had largely policed access. This push in the direction of commercial criteria for choice and selection brings television once more closer to the cinema and already points in the direction of the internet.

15. The French filmmaker Bruno Dumont begged an audience to see his film *Hors Satan* on 35mm: "We are made of chemistry, and film stock is made of chemistry, hence we react to each other in a unique way, chemistry against chemistry, which isn't possible with the digital." Quoted in the editorial of *Cahiers du Cinéma*, no. 672 (November 2011), asking: "This metaphor by Dumont, 'chemistry against chemistry,' is it just mythology or does it contain a grain of truth?" (my translation) http://www.cahiersducinema.com/Novembre-2011-no672,1985.html.

16. From an industry perspective, convergence sounds as follows: "Sir Howard Stringer, chairman and chief executive of Sony Corp America has called 2004 'the year of convergence.' He sees the growth of broadband connected TVs, PVRs, PlayStations, mobile phones, MP3 players and so on as a way for converged companies, or loose alliances of companies, to bridge the gap between content and consumer. 'We will no longer need a permit from the gatekeepers when we want to reach the consumer,' he says." Kate Bulkley, "Better Late Than Never," *The Guardian*, May 14, 2004, http://www.guardian.co.uk/media/2004/may/14/digitalmedia.

17. Jenkins is well aware of this contested terrain: "Approaches derived from the study of political economy may, perhaps, provide the best vocabulary for discussing media convergence, while cultural studies language has historically framed our understanding of participatory culture. Neither theoretical tradition, however, can truly speak to what happens at the intersection between the two. The result may be conflict (as in ongoing legal battles for access to or regulation over intellectual property rights), critique (as in the political activism of culture jammers who use participatory culture to break down the dominance of the media industries), challenge (as occurs with the blurring of the lines between professional and amateur products that may now compete for viewer interest if not revenues), collaboration (as in various plans for the incorporation of viewer-generated materials), or recruitment (as when commercial producers use the amateur media as a training ground or testing ground for emerging ideas and talent)." Jenkins, "Convergence?—I Diverge."

18. The digital revolution in image conversion has been lagging behind the conversion/convergence in recorded sound. Electronic music, both avant garde and pop, had experimented with (and embraced) the computer much earlier than video artists or filmmakers. Already in the early 1980s, the Musical Instrument Digital Interface (MIDI) was adopted as an industry standard, enabling digital musical instruments and computers to communicate with each other. See Paul M. Craner, "New Tool for an Ancient Art: The Computer and Music," *Computers and the Humanities* 25, no. 5 (October 1991): 303–313.

19. Rod Stoneman: "The much vaunted convergence [between monitor and cinema screen] may not take place exactly as foreseen however—there is an important distinction between the 'lean-forward' screens for email or close interaction and the 'lean-back' screens used for film and television viewing." "Recycled Electrons: Film and the Digital," *Kinema* (Fall 2001) http://www.kinema.uwaterloo.ca/article.php?id=168&feature.

20. In practice, of course, there is loss of information, as data get compressed or transferred to other platforms and formats. See internet entries on "lossless compression"

http://en.wikipedia.org/wiki/Lossless_compression and http://computer.howstuffworks.com/file-compression3.htm.

21. On these competing agendas, see Thomas Elsaesser, "The 'Return' of 3-D: Logics and Genealogies of the Image in the Twenty-First Century," *Critical Inquiry* 39, no. 2 (2012), 217-246.

22. The distinction between autographic versus allographic was first made in Nelson Goodman, *The Languages of Art: An Approach to a Theory of Symbols* (Indianapolis: Bobbs-Merrill, 1976), 113.

23. David Bordwell, "An Excessively Obvious Cinema," in *Classical Hollywood Cinema: Film Style and Production*, ed. David Bordwell, Janet Staiger, and Kristin Thompson (London: Routledge 1985), 9.

24. The history of sound in the cinema has in recent decades become a fertile research area, thanks to the work of Rick Altman, Doug Gomery, James Lastra, Michel Chion, Claudia Gorbman, Mary Ann Doane, Kaja Silverman, and many others. For sound and the "New Hollywood," see Gianluca Sergi, *The Dolby Era: Film Sound in Contemporary Hollywood* (Manchester: Manchester University Press, 2004).

25. See Jay Beck, "A Quiet Revolution: Changes in American Film Sound Practices, 1967–1979" and other essays in the present publication, notably James Buhler.

26. Christian Metz, "Aural Objects," *Yale French Studies* 60, Cinema/Sound (1980), 24-32.

27. Michel Chion, *Audio-Vision: Sound on Screen* (New York: Columbia University Press, 1994).

28. In the person of Walter Murch, sound design, film editing, and sound mixing became one integral craft, almost as important as that of the director. See Walter Murch, *In the Blink of an Eye: A Perspective on Film Editing* (Beverly Hills, CA: Silman-James Press, 2001).

29. Six years earlier, in June 1999, Lucas had opened a previous *Star Wars* episode in four digitally equipped theatres: "For the first time in motion picture history, a widely released feature film will be made available to moviegoers via digital projection. CineComm Digital Cinema and Texas Instruments, two of the industry's leading forces in digital projection of motion pictures, will provide their digital projector technology to screen *Star Wars: Episode I The Phantom Menace* on two screens in Los Angeles and two screens in New York." http://www.projectorcentral.com/news_story_94.htm.

30. Bruce Handy, "Jeffrey Katzenberg on 3-D: Depth Becomes Him," *Vanity Fair*, March 23, 2009, http://www.vanityfair.com/online/oscars/2009/03/jeffrey-katzenberg-on-3d-depth-becomes-him.

31. Ibid.

32. According to the *Art History Archive*, "Video art is often said to have begun when Nam June Paik used his new Sony Portapak to shoot footage of Pope Paul VI's procession through New York City in the autumn of 1965. That same day, across town in a Greenwich Village cafe, Paik played the tapes and video art was born. This fact is sometimes disputed, however, due to the fact that the first Sony Portapak, the Videorover did not become commercially available until 1967." See http://www.arthistoryarchive.com/arthistory/videoart/ (accessed October 28, 2012). Paik most likely shot the exterior footage of the Pope with a mains-powered deck (corded, non–battery operated deck) and then brought the tapes to a studio. See also Doug Hall and Sally Jo Fifer, eds., *Illuminating Video: An Essential Guide to Video Art* (New York: Aperture, 1987) and Gary Schwartz, ed., *The Luminous Image* (Amsterdam: Stedelijk Museum, 1984).

33. See Michael Snow's reworking of several of his landmark works in digital formats and as installations; for example, his WVLNT (*Wavelength* For Those Who Don't Have the Time) from 2003, shown as an installation at the Whitney Biennial 2008.

34. See, among others, Gene Youngblood, *Expanded Cinema* (New York: E. P. Dutton & Company, 1970); Pamela M. Lee, *Chronophobia: On Time in the Art of the 1960s* (Cambridge, MA: MIT Press, 2004); and the catalog for "Expanded Cinema," eds. David Curtis, Al Rees, Duncan White, and Steven Ball (London: Tate Publishing, 2011).

35. Thomas Elsaesser, ed., *Early Cinema Space Frame Narrative* (London: BFI Publishing, 1990) and Erkki Huhtamo and Jussi Parikka, eds., *Media Archaeology: Approaches, Applications, and Implications* (Berkeley: University of California Press, 2011) provide representative essays.

36. The obverse of digital malleability and metamorphosis is that the image can seem "out of joint." Things may feel too big or too small, too luridly colored or too flattened to monotones, too smooth or too shiny, too fast or too slow, too irregular or too continuous. Although "faults" in a normative register, these effects can be an aesthetic resource, by providing the suspense, the dissonance, or disequilibrium that every narrative needs to engage the spectator.

37. Lev Manovich, "Image Future," January 2006, http://manovich.net/DOCS/imagefuture_2006.doc.

38. Lev Manovich, "After Effects or Velvet Revolution," *Artifact* 1, no. 2 (2007) http://scholarworks.iu.edu/journals/index.php/artifact/article/view/1357.

39. Hito Steyerl, "In Free Fall: A Thought Experiment on Vertical Perspective," *e-flux Journal*, no. 24 (April 2011), http://www.e-flux.com/journal/in-free-fall-a-thought-experiment-on-vertical-perspective/.

40. In a quite remarkable (and so far little remarked upon) reversal, President Obama has in the 2012 election campaign been compared not —as he was in 2008—to Abraham Lincoln or FDR, but to Paul Newman, as the ideal role model and salient parallel. See Maureen Dowd, "The Ungrateful President," *New York Times*, August 7, 2012, http://www.nytimes.com/2012/08/08/opinion/dowd-the-ungrateful-president.html.

Select Bibliography

Bazin, André. "The Ontology of the Photographic Image." In *What is Cinema?* Vol. I, 14. Berkeley and Los Angeles: University of California Press, 1967. 9–16.

Benjamin, Walter. "The Work of Art in the Age of Mechanical Reproduction." In *Illuminations*, edited and translated by Hannah Arendt. Fontana, London: Schocken, 1969. 217–52.

Deleuze, Gilles. *Cinema 1: The Movement-Image.* Minneapolis: University of Minnesota Press, 1986.

Deleuze, Gilles. *Cinema 2: The Time-Image.* Minneapolis: University of Minnesota Press, 1989.

Jenkins, Henry. "Convergence? I diverge." *Technology Review*, 2001. Last accessed July 28, 2012. http://www.technologyreview.com/article/401042/convergence-i-diverge/.

Kittler, Friedrich. *Gramophone, Film, Typewriter.* Stanford, CA: Stanford University Press, 1999.

Kracauer, Sigfried. *Theory of Film.* Princeton: Princeton University Press, 1997.

Manovich, Lev. *The Language of New Media.* Boston: MIT Press, 2002.

Murdock, Graham. "Digital Futures: European Television in the Age of Convergence." In *Television Across Europe: A Comparative Introduction*, edited by Jan Wieten, Graham Murdock, and Peter Dahlgren, 36. Sage: London, 2000.

Steyerl, Hito. "In Free Fall: A Thought Experiment on Vertical Perspective." *e-flux Journal* no. 24 (2011). http://www.e-flux.com/journal/in-free-fall-a-thought-experiment-on-vertical- perspective/.

CHAPTER 3

··

ANGELS OF LIGHT

··

JEAN-PIERRE GEUENS

ONCE upon a time, a young critic, François Truffaut, viciously attacked the tradition of quality in the French cinema. In his eyes, its professionalism had become a mere front for plain mediocrity. Films were produced industrially, without flair or passion. Although many of his complaints have been thoroughly debated along the years, two words regarding the images in these films have not. They exuded, he wrote, "polished photography."[1] That kind of cinematography, he implied, was a sham. It was lacking in vitality and authenticity, qualities needed for better filmmaking. In this essay, I will attempt to expand on Truffaut's remark. First, I will go back to the seminal moment when cinematographers fused the beautiful into the scenery. Next, I will suggest that modern technologies, such as Power Windows, which makes possible "lighting" and "coloring" the film in post, have made it possible to achieve complete pictorial mastery in film.[2] Last, I will question the tactic of using beautiful images at a time when the traditional film paradigm is in deep trouble.

Lighting did not become a factor in motion pictures until the mid teens. Prior to that, movies were shot either outdoors in the daytime or indoors in a studio whose roof was made of glass. Underneath the glass, sheets of muslin spanned the space from wall to wall, diffusing the light evenly onto the set. The approach made sense as directors of photography (DPs) didn't want to add lighting issues to the instability of the emulsion and the volatility of the chemical process in the laboratories. In *Birth of a Nation* (D. W. Griffith, 1915) for instance, the large Cameron family living room is fully visible, from the left to the right of the frame, as well as from the immediate foreground to the back of the set. We see it all. People and furniture are equally visible. And there isn't what Billy Bitzer, the cinematographer, called "ugly shadows" anywhere.[3] Today, that strategy is generally pointed to as bad, wrong, or simply primitive lighting. And, indeed, the effect is uncanny because the sources of light are nowhere to be seen: no windows or lamps are visible within the shot. Nothing explains how we see what we see. Everything just is.

In fact, the problem originated from a disconnect between the simple lighting arrangement and the stuffy design found in the film. Let us imagine for instance what this space would look like were we to keep the light but discard the overstuffed furniture, the thick carpets, the Victorian wallpaper. We would then discover a large, bright space dominated by tall white walls: an effect not unlike what we find today in art galleries and contemporary museums. As a matter of fact, the plainness of the lighting, its transparency, and its rejection of ornamentation prefigured (inadvertently to be sure) the style made famous by the Bauhaus and International Style. When unmotivated diffused light originating from above was brought back some fifty years later by Jacques Demy in *Bay of Angels* (1963), the lighting strategy was in fact celebrated for its modernity.

The release of Cecil B. DeMille's *The Cheat* (1915) challenged this trouble-free strategy.[4] The very first image in the film introduces us to a shockingly different presentation: Sessue Hayakawa sitting behind a desk in a very dark room. The little we see originates from a luminary on one side of the table and an off-screen practical light to the right. Hayakawa eventually switches off the latter before leaning over the luminary. At that moment, the grid at the top of the flame striates the light on his face while the rest of the image remains in complete darkness. The idea probably originated from David Belasco, whose theater productions were notable for mesmerizing lighting effects such as a fourteen-minute sunset during *Madame Butterfly*.[5] Still, the lighting achieved in *The Cheat* caught movie viewers by surprise because film audiences at the time had few contacts with the theater and were similarly unlikely to be familiar with Caravaggio's *chiaroscuro* effect. For them, the film image had all of a sudden acquired another dimension. The new intensity was felt to "intoxicate the eye, [and] drug the senses."[6] Viewers were no longer just witnessing an event; they were made to experience it sensuously.

The differences between these images and those of Bitzer's in *The Birth of a Nation* are worth reiterating. First, the source of the lighting in DeMille's film is explained from within the scene through the use of practicals. Inasmuch as they appear to duplicate the effect one would obtain at home from a similar configuration, the space is naturalized and the image becomes more realistic. Second, the low-key strategy helps organize the space, focusing our attention on the action in the fore. This said, the darkness in the background is not just a void. Our eyes keep going back to it. What is hidden there? This brings in mystery and a certain level of apprehensiveness. The invisible, the unknown, the nothingness beyond Hayakawa creates an obstacle to our desire to access everything at once. It brings a delay to our narrative yearning. Third, the absence of middle tones between the few bright spots and the dark areas dramatizes the image. We either see something, or we see nothing. Although these features are not necessarily connatural, the combined effect is powerful. The theatricality of the presentation seizes us, makes us pay full attention. The play of light on the flesh of things becomes an essential condiment in our appreciation of the story. It becomes a compelling dramatis persona in its own right.

A word of caution regarding the use of light to beautify images came from Walter Benjamin in the early thirties. There is an inherent danger, he said, in attempting to seduce viewers through light and shade, tight textures and glossy surfaces, when that penchant leaves behind the grim reality of the original subject. Speaking of the German New Objectivity group (*Neue Sachlichkeit*), he wrote that photographers "can no longer record a tenement block or a refuse heap without transfiguring it." Such photography, he added, "is unable to convey anything about a power station or a cable factory other than, 'What a beautiful world!' "[7] This objection, I believe, applies equally to film. Let us take the beginning of *Oliver Twist* (David Lean, 1948) as a seminal example. In fact, a clip from that scene starts off *Visions of Light* (1992), the video compilation produced by the American Society of Cinematographers (ASC) to extol the work of past and present members of the association. In it, Ernest Dickerson reveals that this scene was responsible for him becoming a cinematographer, and it is not difficult to understand why. Lean's film opens up on a dark landscape. A storm approaches. A woman alone hurries on the moors. A few drops of water fall on the surface of a pond. Clouds cover the sky. The wind intensifies. The woman bends backward in pain, a move that reveals she is very much pregnant. A branch with thorns is similarly contorted by the wind. The rain drenches her body. She sees a few lights on the horizon. She hastens as best she can in the muddy field until she reaches the house. She rings a bell. An attendant carrying a portable oil lamp lets her in. As the camera tilts up, a sign, backlit by lightning, announces that the place is a workhouse, that is to say, a refuge created under the Poor Law in England for the unfortunates unable to take care of themselves.

All in all, the scene, photographed by Guy Green, is breathtakingly beautiful. Now, if we read the opening chapter of Charles Dickens's book, only the following words are related to what we see on the screen: "she was found lying in the street. She had walked some distance, for her shoes were worn to pieces; but where she came from, or where she was going to, nobody knows." There is no stormy night on the moors, no rain, no thunder, and no lightning. There is no dramatization whatsoever and the style is matter of fact, except, of course, for the author's sarcastic observations. The difference between the two perspectives is striking. Whereas Dickens makes us focus on the matter at hand—the wretched social circumstances surrounding the boy's birth—Lean chooses to tell the story in a series of stunning images. Like Dickerson, we are mesmerized by the beauty of the photography, its shine, its contrast, and its metaphors. In the process, our experience of the piece undergoes a change: it becomes primarily an aesthetic affair. The social issue is de-emphasized by the look in the fore. The deception works because what we see is convincingly realistic as well as beautiful. The landscape, for instance, is suitably barren and the storm quite credible. The casting of the woman, her dress, and her hairstyle are appropriate for her working-class origin. And the workhouse is believable when we check it against photographs of the original places in England. What turns everything around, then, is the light. Its role is no longer functional, to let us see what is happening. Rather it deflects our attention from the woman's experience, her pain, her fear, the shoes full of mud, the cold wet clothes that press against her body. As a successful alchemist, Green transformed base matter into pure iridescence. Benjamin is right: we respond to the gorgeous lightning effect behind the woman as she bends in pain rather than to her miserable condition and the dreadful circumstances she finds herself in. Her backlit silhouette is what matters. It forms such a beautiful curve within the rectangle of the frame!

Producing great lighting in those days was not easy. In essence, DPs worked out a version of Ansel Adams's cherished zone system for photographers. In a shot that is under one's control, light can be apportioned so that the total reflectance originating from any surface is made to hit a specific value between pure black and pure white. Although cinematographers have traditionally preferred measuring the light falling on a subject rather than the one reflected by it, the idea remains the same: to harmonize an ensemble, one could add more light in a very dark corner of a room or subtract some from a white dress. Motion pictures technology, however, had no equivalent to dodging and burning, which allowed photographers to further enhance their images while printing the negative—basically cutting back or adding light to separate sections of the image. To be sure, the procedure was neither mechanical nor foolproof. Make one mistake during the process, and you had to start all over again. Furthermore, one could manage only a finite amount of corrections before running into trouble elsewhere in the print. Still, in the hands of creative photographers, such as Adams himself, the process is not unlike a performance reflecting the artist's insight as well as skill at that particular moment of his or her life.[8] Although some photographers have chosen to emphasize "straight photography" over dodging and burning, the latter always remains a tempting option when faced with a blemish or a mistake that could be easily erased.[9] Lacking this superior weapon during most of the century, cinematographers had no choice but to create their fabulous images while shooting. Regardless of the difficulty of the enterprise (the size of the space, the actors' movements in it, or a tracking shot by the camera), DPs knew that the laboratory could only darken or lighten each shot in toto during the final timing of the film.[10] Nothing could be done to alter a section of the image without impacting the rest.

It took time, but eventually "dodging and burning" became possible in film through a technology called Power Windows, a Da Vinci system.[11] First, the photographic picture is "converted" into digital bits. The scanning resolution (2k or 4k at this point) determines the total number of pixels generated and thus the density and the wealth of details in the copy. The powerful tool then makes it possible to manipulate individual pixels in the image. Although the basic technology made its appearance in the early nineties, it was at first too time consuming and too expensive to scan entire movies. Only following the release of *Pleasantville* (Gary Ross, 1998) and *O Brother, Where Art Thou?* (Joel Coen, 2000) did the industry understand the full reach of the new tool. In these films indeed, Power Windows was used to define not just a scene here or there but the look of the entire movie. In the first film, color was distributed through the image according to the needs of the narrative. In the second, the lush green of the Mississippi scenery was turned into dusty yellow brown during an eleven-week session in post.[12] This process became known as the *digital intermediate* (DI) because it took place between image acquisition and the final touch given to the release prints by the laboratory.[13] With the DI, it became clear that the film image, which for a century had been accepted as an unadulterated recording of what took place in front of the camera, was now opening itself up as a second site of labor, a brand new mother lode.[14] One could dig inside the image and re-evaluate any element of it. Furthermore, unlike DPs, who have to fight the brute resistance of the physical world to achieve their work, colorists grading the DI can alter components of the image while sitting comfortably behind a console. There, they are able to observe in real time the result of their pictorial modulations, repeatedly correcting them until the desired look is finally achieved.[15] Mattes, masks, blurs, even spline-based shapes are available to define the exact space under consideration. Light level, hue, brightness, and saturation can be adjusted globally (primary color correction) or individually (secondary color correction). Let's wrap the scene in a light aqua tint. Let's make the red on her dress a little more pronounced. Let's add some light reflections on the hardwood floor as if they originated from that window. Let's lower and darken the shadow of the actor on that wall. Although the technology can conceivably be used for contrarian goals, the natural tendency is to keep polishing the image until its luster can take no more.[16] With Power Windows every film could now aspire to become beautiful.

Because the use of the DI expanded unpredictably over a number of years, the industry wasn't able to regulate who does what when. As John Belton suggested in an earlier essay on this technology, the first hint that lighting was now a two-step process came in when a job that had traditionally been done on the set was put off until post.[17] Stefan Sonnenfeld, one of the most vocal colorists, explained the reason: "We can flag a light off a wall in a fraction of the time it takes on the set."[18] Why, indeed, have the entire production wait while the gaffer picks up a flag, attaches it to a c-stand, adjusts it so it cuts the light off the wall without, say, hitting the floor, when the same effect can be done in a fraction of the time by the colorist working alone? As a result, some DPs no longer hesitate to leave chunks of their lighting scheme undone, knowing they will save time and money by doing the job in post. This trend is likely to expand until only the general outline of the lighting—basically its tectonics—will be done during the actual shoot. This, however, does not mean that lighting could be done entirely during color grading. The key thing to remember is that DPs work in space, whereas colorists work on an image. On the set, the light originates from specific points in space, thus impacting an actor differently as he does an about-face. In contrast, in post, the light added to, say, the left side of an actor's face would "stick" to that side regardless of his motions. For instance, if he were to turn 180 degrees around, the light on his face would still appear on the left side of his face even though that would make no sense as far as the real environment is concerned. Up to now at least, color grading systems are designed to modulate an existing lighting framework, not to create one from scratch.

Are colorists trying to infringe on the DPs' domain? Certainly, since they assembled as the American Society of Cinematographers (ASC), DPs have considered themselves "the authors of the image" and "the guardians of the art form."[19] Their importance on the set has grown steadily through time to the point that some of them have become stars in their field. They do not lack in self-confidence either. Michael Goi, the current president of the ASC, even gushes that the members of the association do their work "with impeccable taste" and are known for their "almost uncanny ability to do the right thing at the right moment."[20] Beyond controlling the look of the scene on the set, the DPs' "authority" customarily extends to the lab, where the mechanical operation of the printing machine makes it possible for them to impose their judgment regarding the image over and above "the arbitrary judgment of the timer."[21] Not surprisingly, they loudly resent the fact that the DI allows "the colorist to make independent creative decisions."[22] This is so because the work in post can take weeks, if not months, and cinematographers may already be working on another project. Even if they are able to attend the sessions, they may not get paid for their time. Last, Power Windows does not have objective measurements that DPs could force upon on colorists once they leave the room. Unsurprisingly, DPs are "horrified" when colorists working alone are in charge.[23] Goi, for example, makes fun of a "button pusher" who dared imagine the look for a film prior to its shooting, only to realize that other personnel on the field, including DPs of course, had much more sensible ideas. Further complicating things, there is a jurisdictional issue at work because many colorists, unlike DPs, do not belong to a union. So, it is more difficult for the latter to "dictate the look," as Richard. P. Crudo puts it.[24] If this were not enough, DPs have yet another source of complaint: "it did not take long for our [other] collaborators to realize [that] they, too, could 'paint' in the digital suite."[25] This is so because anybody really can look at an image on the monitor and make suggestions. So the action has attracted not just Robert Rodriguez and Quentin Tarantino, but young directors in general. Producers, too, at times want to have their say. And some actors already have the contractual power "to 'correct' the markers of aging" or examine their screen image and demand some digital adjustment, whether that means "more or less fill . . . a softer or a harder keylight."[26]

Finally, Power Windows makes it easy to release not only various versions of a film but also different looks for each version. This, of course, goes against the Platonic ideal of a single form, a changeless mold, a superior matrix. In film, the pristine negative from which a number of prints, all exactly alike, are produced was considered for many years the sacrosanct original. DPs thence take for granted the "immortality" of the lighting they create on the set.[27] Needless to say, this insistence flies in the face of the new technology. To start with, the reality of film distribution being what it is, any film inevitably acquires a variety of accents and looks as it makes its way through local censorships, print deteriorations, language dubbing or subtitling, colorizing, lexiconing, overscanning, panning and scanning, the PG, 3D and the airline versions, the director's cut, and the individual manipulations of contrast, brightness, aspect ratio, and white balance by television set owners. In view of these mutations, why should we continue to fetishize the look achieved on the set? Where is the line between respecting that lighting and "enhancing it [in post] in a way that evokes the underlying emotion or mood that the director is trying to present?"[28] Besides "do [DPs] even know what the final look is while you're shooting the film? For some directors and DPs, the answer is absolutely yes. For others, the look evolves."[29] As a matter of fact, enhancements to images are already the norm when releasing films on DVDs and Blu-rays. First at the gate, directors, such as Tony Scott, have gone back to their early work so as to give them a more contemporary look.[30] Cinematographers were not able to resist either, vide Laszlo Kovacs who revisited *Shampoo* (Hal Ashby, 1975) so he would be able to correct what he now thought was too much diffusion and too little contrast in the original.[31] Even the high priest of film purity, John Bailey, went to work on the Criterion release of *Days of Heaven* (Terrence Malick,

1978) to mute "the golden warmth that had come to characterize previous video incarnations of the picture."[32] While at it, he brightened some scenes that he now found too dark and added "very subtle 'windows' in the fields and sky...that had been shot in full sunlight and were therefore front lit and very flat."[33] I'm sure this was all for the better but what would the late Néstor Almendros, the original DP, say of all of this? All in all, the malleability of the image made possible by Power Windows all but guarantees that in the future we will never see the same film twice.

For all the uproar, Power Windows is not a revolutionary technology: it has facilitated the production of beautiful images but it has not altered the fundamentals of cinematography. William Fraker, for instance, recently reiterated the consensus of the profession this way: the cinematographer's job, he wrote, "is to pull the audience into the story, so they experience it, and not merely see it. You light to tell a story, by establishing moods with shadow and color, and by deciding what the audience sees and what is obscured."[34] Based on this description, we can see that, apart from color and the tools now available to do the work, nothing much has changed in lighting since *The Cheat*. The objective remains to engage the viewers, to tell them where to look, and to dramatize the action by wrapping it within an appropriate atmosphere. Curiously, the fact that the end result must be appealing to the eyes is left unsaid by Fraker, and it is rarely brought up in the specialized literature. Yet that is what the DPs do: they make the diegetic world look good.

Why do they do it? Why is beauty such a magnet for filmmakers, as well as audiences? In fact, for Immanuel Kant, beauty is not truly a property of the object itself.[35] Rather it expresses a human reaction to an external stimulus—object, event, circumstance, or a combination of those. When we find an aesthetic pleasure in the encounter, we tend to call its generator beautiful. Still, the German philosopher insists, there is nothing subjective about such a pronouncement for the judgment is taken from a disinterested position and thus has universal bearing. I'm expected to be able to argue my case (for instance by highlighting the forms that make the object beautiful) and convince others that my judgment is sound. It is not like when I say "I like oysters." I perfectly know in that case that others find them repellent. Here, my personal taste alone is involved. This insistence on ratiocination, however, is of little help when dealing with lighting: why is a certain light treatment perceived as beautiful in one film, whereas something quite similar elsewhere is not? It also does not account for the prurient aspect of film images, the drawing of audiences into the film that Fraker says cinematography must achieve. To understand this aspect of the image, we must turn to Donald Kuspit's thinking in *The Psychoanalytic Construction of Beauty*. In the essay, Kuspit points to a more embracing explanation provided by Sigmund Freud when the latter writes that "the love of beauty seems a perfect example of an impulse inhibited in its aim. 'Beauty' and 'attraction' are originally attributes of the sexual object."[36] In Freud's view then, the beautiful object becomes a substitute for the sexual object of desire. In this way, "the taste for beauty is rooted in...one's experience of one's body."[37] So, whereas for Kant an abstract justification based on the form of the object under scrutiny is needed to rule something out there beautiful, for Freud, the mind retroactively comes up with the concept "beautiful" to elucidate the immediately pleasurable sensation felt in one's body. What techniques allow cinematographers to mesmerize the audience? What remained for a long time indefinite as well as bewildering to achieve can now easily be taught in film schools. The essential frame of reference remains the look achieved by Jordan Cronenweth in *Blade Runner* (Ridley Scott, 1982). In that film, effects and colors produced just the right kind of hypnotic construct needed for our unconscious desires to flow freely. What were its coordinates? Fans move thick atmospheric effects through space. Overexposed shafts of light crack their way through very dark areas. Reflections bounce off shiny floors and wet pavement. Characters are seen in silhouettes or semi-silhouettes. Elegant practicals are strategically positioned to provide partial illumination in the background. Public areas display colorful neon signs. A cool or warm color gloss floats over the whole picture. Although none of these techniques was new at the time, their blending had never been so successfully managed. The diegetic space was no longer reflecting a formally beautiful but distinct world, separate from that of the viewers. Its palpable, phantasmagoric haze now acted as a magnet for our libidinal impulses: we wanted to be absorbed in it, indeed to cathect with it. Not everyone agrees, though, that such response is positive or healthy. For Max Horkheimer and Theodor W. Adorno for instance, "the tendency to let oneself go," "the trend to lose oneself in the environment" is nothing but a manifestation of the death instinct.[38]

Although DPs repeatedly talk about bringing to life the unique vision of the director—an objective that would require giving each film a distinct look—the tactics they use remain generic in nature. Indeed preexisting models reflecting the consensus of the profession wait for the arrival of the technicians: the blue moonlight shrouding the lovers in bed, the sputtering green light from an outdoor sign illuminating the seedy motel room, the strobing white flashes of light chiseling the dancers in a nightclub. Nothing is new under the sun; everything has been done before. Whatever the subject matter—and Benjamin's word of caution—DPs and colorists see their job as sprucing up their material in a conventional manner. It never occurs to them to create images that are unfinished, unsightly, or just generally unpleasant. Let us take the brutal rape scene in *Boys Don't Cry* (Kimberly Peirce, 1999), for instance. I'm sure that Peirce conveyed to the DP that she wanted a gritty look but what she got instead was the arrangement found in night-time chases taking place in an abandoned factory. There is moonlight, some industrial floodlights, and the car's headlights. Throughout the scene, a bright blue light originating from the practicals is reflected off the hood and roof of the car, essentially wrapping the attack within a context of aesthetic "good taste." In my view, the concern for decorum at that moment turns the lighting into an accomplice of the rape. By and large, then, the crew is satisfied using time-tested solutions that embellish the action with tactics known to appeal to the viewers' senses.

Templates, schemata, and formal shortcuts are, of course, nothing new in art. In this way, the generic tactics used by DPs in film can be seen as variations on the Claude glasses, a very popular apparatus during the eighteenth and nineteenth centuries. With their back to the landscape, they wished to observe, painters or just ordinary sightseers would gaze at its reflection shown on a slightly convex colored mirror held in their hands. The gimmick did two things: first, a specific aspect was extracted from the over-all scenery and, second, the image was tinted sepia, thus duplicating the "golden hour" effect, a Claude Lorrain's trademark. The tool thus made it possible for anyone to see the world as it would show up after being enhanced by artists. Not surprisingly, the look achieved by the Claude glasses became known as "picturesque," implying that the view was now fit to become a picture. The concept was then expanded to describe the work of artists who consistently gussied up the vistas in their paintings in order to make them more spectacular. Claude Joseph Vernet, in particular, was adamant about the tech-nique. He declared: "Others may know better how to paint the sky, the earth, the ocean; but no one knows better than I how to paint a picture."[39] Whatever the constituents of the original material, they would be embellished in the painting until the rendering was good enough to ensnare buyers. In film, too, lighting is used to sheathe everything we see in dazzling varnish. Although films are not any better than in earlier days, they tend to appear consistently in their Sunday best. For DPs and colorists—colorists obviously more than DPs—the more picturesque the effects, the better. To recall Freud and the post-Freudians, this cheap thrill nevertheless manages to provide us with a temporary respite from reality. For two hours, it gives us the sensation of belonging in a world that fulfills our desires. Afterward, of course, we go home.

Although the talent of the personnel involved and the tools now at their disposal have enthroned the regime of the beautiful, there are reasons to believe the strategy is showing fatigue. First of all, a very practical consideration: for beauty to be effective, the presentation must be unanticipated and brief. Freud was very much aware of this phenomenon when he wrote that "we are so made that we can derive intense enjoy-ment only from a contrast and very little from a state of things."[40] For example, in his book on taste, Pierre Bourdieu reports that a "sunset over sea" is perceived as beautiful by all social classes in France, probably because of its brevity, its unusual hue, and the fact that most people come across it only on vacation.[41] My bet is that if we inverted the situation and our ordinary daylight were seen only briefly after a long exposure to sunset-like conditions, then it is daylight that would be regarded as beautiful. It stands to reason, then, that movie lighting must provide the goods only intermittently. What happens, however, when, as is the case today, practically every image in every film is beautiful? The kick produced by the first thing of beauty on the screen weakens progres-sively until it settles into low-grade contentment. In other words, because beauty (or what passes for it) seems to have colonized every screen, its overall impact lessens con-siderably. Although we recognize the excellence on the screen, we end up missing the jolt that "real" beauty is known to deliver. As a devalued currency, beauty can no longer be counted on to buoy viewers.

Second, the assumption that art has to be beautiful—its raison d'être really—came under question at the beginning of the twentieth century. How could we have gone in painting from Gustave Courbet's stone breakers to the vertical grids of Piet Mondrian in such a short time? Were the works still expressions of the same art, or did they belong to different orders? Were they incommensurable? How could one make sense of the dif-ferences? One answer to the puzzling question was given by Arthur C. Danto when he suggested that beauty ceased to be a factor in art, if not as early as 1917 when Marcel Duchamp offered his *Fountain* for exhibition, then surely after Andy Warhol's *Brillo Box* (1964) showed up in an art gallery. Why was this urinal or this image of a consumer item in the gallery valuable, whereas something just like it that could be found elsewhere was not? As the problem was forced on us, it eventually disarranged the traditional paradigm we used to identify a work of art. Indeed, in time, what had mattered most in art appreciation—design, color, symmetry, harmony, beauty, skill, and the like—no longer appeared so essential. Put another way, our senses were no longer the lone adjudicators to ascertain what makes good art. In a move harking back to Kant, Danto then proposed that the new arbiter should be the mind's ability to think through the nature of the artistic object.

Has the same thing happened in film? In his groundbreaking work on cinema, Gilles Deleuze identified a categorical shift in filmmaking starting in the fifties.[42] Then, the action cinema that had been the bread and butter of Hollywood practically from the start sputtered and appeared to go out of fashion. Somehow, the notion of a strong protagonist instinctively knowing what needs to be done and going about doing it sounded hollow, almost obscene, after World War II revealed the impotence of individuals to do much about their situation. In Michelangelo Antonioni's films in particular, characters displayed existential fatigue and the editing that would normally have moved the protagonists forward from shot to shot also petered out. Another facet of that generational change could be observed in the films of Jean-Luc Godard. There, viewers were forced to fill in the space left open by jump cutting and reconcile the story with the nondiegetic exhortations of the filmmaker. Insofar as the lack of the usual sweeteners produced "a shock to thought, communicating vibrations to the cortex, touching the nervous and cerebral cortex directly,"[43] Deleuze's "cinema of the brain" implied a shift of emphasis from a dynamic protagonist to a thinking viewer. More recently, a couple of films by Michael Haneke, *Funny Games* (1997) and *Caché* (2005), could be said to activate the kind of reflection brought up by Duchamp's and Warhol's art. By unexpectedly "rewinding" what we had taken as reality on the screen, the director forcefully makes us confront the visual manipulation and think about what it all means. In doing so, the film expands in our mind from the seamless narrative to a more profound conundrum. What Haneke concocted here is a novel kind of *deus ex machina*. The difference being that, instead of keeping the tactic within the diegesis, he applied it to the medium. As the narrative space suddenly gives up under our feet, we feel like falling into a bottomless pit. Although it is true that we always make sense of a film as we watch it, that activity normally remains in the background of our consciousness. Here, to the contrary, one becomes intensely aware of oneself thinking. Only by thinking hard do we find ourselves enjoying a more complex and enriched spectatorial position. Only later do we realize that what we went through was a *coup de cinema*. To be sure, Godard and Haneke remain niche players, and one would be hard pressed to suggest that Hollywood is close to embracing a more intellectual fare. Still, there is a sense that, compared to their probing of the medium, the reliance on beautiful aesthetics feels old-fashioned, the idea harking back to the artistic values of prior centuries.

A third argument is based on the impact of various technologies on the traditional film paradigm. The particular outcome I want to emphasize involves who gets to make films, what kind of films are being created, and where they are being shown. To start off, let us remember that throughout much of the twentieth century, film unions functioned very much like the guilds of medieval times, in effect enforcing a monopoly over the tools, the workshops, and the products of professional imagemaking. Unless one knew someone (generally a family member) who was already a member of the union, it was practically impossible to join and become one. Apprenticeship, too, was rigorously enforced: one had to spend years loading cameras or moving lights before one could take command of a film's photography. In effect, this monopoly guaranteed that union members alone acquired the necessary knowledge to work on the 35mm feature films playing in theaters. Those excluded had to satisfy themselves shooting documentaries and 16mm shorts, which, of course, did not. For Jacques Rancière, hierarchy in the arts is not unlike class division in society. In fact, it expresses it in a different form. So the beauty we discovered and continue to encounter in Hollywood films is no less a class feature than the powdered wigs worn by noble gents in past centuries. For Rancière, this separation between the two spheres of activity—the professional and the ancillary—demarcates "who possesses speech and who merely possesses voice."[44] There are those whose work is recognized as worthwhile, whose name appears on the marquee, whose films are reviewed and analyzed in journals, and whose wages would put bankers to shame, versus those who labor incognito for the love of the medium or because making a little film opens a new horizon in their life. This particular kind of segregation, Rancière insists, is not unlike that which traditionally confined women, workers, and minorities to the kitchen, the servant quarters, the fields, and factories.[45]

This image monopoly began to unravel when ever-increasing numbers of students pushed their way from film schools into the industry. Unlike the film workers of the past, these newcomers were not just looking for a job; they wanted to make films. Moreover, they didn't want to wait years before making them. As they found work on low-budget and independent features, the unions were eventually forced to accommodate them. Another determinant was the change in technology from film to digital, which made it a cinch for everyone, not just film students, to turn out great looking images, essentially erasing an advantage long enjoyed by professionals. Even more decisive was the opening of the internet as a global theater where all are welcome to exhibit their work. One does not have to look further than YouTube where the very glut of material (thirty-five hours of content imported every minute of the day) makes it possible for most of it to "circulate outside any system of legitimation."[46] All work on the Web, regardless of its source or its quality, is generally realigned in a more pell-mell, more democratic way, thus getting rid of many of the filters that traditionally structured our access to the sensible.

Of all the changes in technology, the new delivery mediums are putting standard filmmaking most at risk. Let us recall Marshall McLuhan: the medium is the message.[47] Movies, for instance, are still being conceived and produced as if they were exhibited exclusively in theaters. There, viewers are captive. The surrounding darkness and the size of the screen help focus all eyes on the shiny spectacle. Only a whiff of competition emerges from theaters next door and from previews of upcoming attractions. Seen in splendid isolation, films have no trouble capturing our attention. In contrast, when the same movies are streamed on the internet, this is no longer the case: there are always other images lurking underneath or circling around those we watch. In fact, the images we don't see seize our imagination a lot more than those facing us. Whereas VHS technology allowed us to fast forward over the dull moments of a film and DVDs to jump entire chapters, the new delivery mediums constantly tempt us to check what else is available. In effect, when streamed on smartphones, tablets, computers, or television sets, accessed at home or on the go, waiting in line at Starbuck's or riding in the subway, the size of the screen, the intrusion of incoming messages, the co-presence of other entertainments, and the everyday surrounding environment undermine the integrity of film images. This implies that the state of distraction that Benjamin predicted for the movies long ago has finally become reality.[48] Interestingly, this redeployment involves a paradox: on the one hand, Deleuze's key ideas for modern cinema—a weakening of the overarching plot in favor of dispersive situations, a preference for ambiguous links between scenes, wandering characters, the presence in the background of the babbling of the times—provide a good description of our experience on the internet. As we access various offerings in bits, we not only ignore the directives of their respective authors, we create unexpected juxtapositions and startling links they never intended. In doing so, we recreate experiments dear to the Surrealists and manage the kind of stunning connections that are the trademark of Godard's films. On the other hand, as impulsive viewers, we have internalized the sensory motor scheme that moved characters full speed ahead in the cinema of action. As we effortlessly jump from one moment in a film to another, from film to film, and from a film to any material whatsoever, our own élan becomes more important that the dynamics originating from the screen. In the end, what keeps us glued online is less what emanates from any one site than the constant change of venues, fueled by the hope that our next move will finally fulfill our desire.

Of course, we should be careful about projecting too much in a new state of affairs. The movies, after all, have survived their appearance on television sets and the competition of cable. If anything, they impacted the original programming available in these media rather than the other way around. Unsurprisingly, very powerful forces today are at work lobbying the state to get rid of the neutrality at the core of the internet. Commercials have already been accepted as a price to pay for online access. And everyone is striving to achieve preferential treatment for their websites by gaming the search engines' algorithms. As for the power of ordinary people to change the medium, wasn't Benjamin himself too hasty when he concluded that, in the Soviet press in the thirties, "the reader is at all times ready to become a writer"? Still, it is tempting to believe that "the conventional distinction between author and public" is waning. And that we may have reached a time when "competence is no longer found on specialized training."[49] For the first time, the free, teeming, undisciplined, and anarchic content available on the internet provides serious competition for what is professionally made. Furthermore, online, what doesn't look conventionally designed or formally garnished has an appeal of its own. In response, Hollywood technicians have even adopted some of the most blatant tropes originating from the subculture (e.g., hand-holding the camera "inappropriately," cutting in the middle of a movement, unmotivated focus changes, and leaving the actors' eyes without their usual luminous dot).[50] Although much of what is presently available online does not deviate significantly in style or spirit from the models set by the industry, it remains at core a "Philistine" culture (as Matthew Arnold would surely have it). Will the internet continue to slant the paradigm in unexpected and enriching ways?[51] We can only hope that the new, chaotic, and rhizomic enterprise manages to at least delay the kind of hierarchy, monopoly, filters, and barriers that ultimately limited what movies were able to achieve.[52]

With viewers electing more and more to jump in the middle of narratives, bypassing all-too-familiar expositions and conclusions, we are left with film fragments. These are not unlike what Deleuze calls "purely optical and sound situations," that is to say, an "uncivilized" combination of pictures and sounds that can potentially break through the clutter of clichés we find in movies today.[53] One way to access such a standpoint from the perspective of light is to consider the notion of exposure. Because any camera today produces a perfectly exposed image, professional cinematographers emphasize the long and demanding process of lighting. In contrast, I'd suggest that the root of the word exposure, *ex posare,* implies leaving behind a comfortable position. What does *ex-posing* the scene mean? Most obviously, it connotes the removal of the *pose,* the artifice, the cliché that mars or hides the unique moment in front of the camera. For filmmakers, the word implies paying full attention to what, in fact, is taking place instead of assuming one knows all about it because thousands of films have treated a similar scene in a conventional manner. It means bringing to visibility, opening to scrutiny what actually is there, its *hic et nunc.* It emphasizes the scene itself, not "the nature of our reactions to it," an essential difference pointed out by E. H. Gombrich.[54] In Cézanne's paintings, for instance, the apples are not displayed for our pleasure. The light simply makes it possible to discover them as they are in themselves, for themselves. And the same goes for film. In *Breathless* (Jean-Luc Godard, 1958), the light is neither beautiful nor is it used to convey meaning or mood. In fact, it shows itself indifferent to the characters and their foibles.[55] The idea thus embodies Martin Heidegger's notion of *Gelassenheit,* which is to let beings be the beings they are, fully themselves, in their uncertainty, their indeterminacy, in the freedom of a present whose future is not yet fated to happen.[56] Therefore, more than anything else, *ex-posing* the scene means keeping the scene open to what is yet unsaid, unknown, or unnamed. Against the calcification of lighting, getting an *ex-posure* thus demands of the filmmakers to remain attuned, as much as anyone can, to the immanence that permeates a shared moment that will never again be. In flat opposition, the beautiful image is assumed to be just right, complete, masterly. Nothing can be subtracted from or added to it. It petrifies one aspect of the scene. It freezes a single perspective, stopping unexpected refractions. Lighting, as it is practiced today, is therefore not innocent. The goal is to keep anything new that could possibly appear in a scene from showing up. If we continue on this path, it is just a matter of time before cinema, like tragedy in the eighteenth century, becomes sadly irrelevant to the times.

NOTES

1. François Truffaut, "A Certain Tendency of the French Cinema," in *Movies and Methods*, ed. Bill Nichols (Berkeley: University of California Press, 1976), 230.

2. Many thanks to Kevin Buck and Steve P. Arkle of Technicolor for being so patient in answering my questions about the technology.

3. Avoiding "ugly shadows" was a main concern of the cameraman. In G. W. Bitzer, *Billy Bitzer: His Story* (Toronto: Farrar, Straus and Giroux, 1973), 84.

4. I am using *The Cheat* as an easy historical marker. There were instances of low-key lighting prior to it. In his *Film Style and Technology*, Barry Salt identifies one as early as 1905. Barry Salt, *Film Style and Technology* (London: Starwood, 1983), 73–76.

5. Mentioned in Gösta M. Bergman, *Lighting in the Theater* (Totoma, NJ: Rowman and Littlefield, 1977), 305–306. Significantly, DeMille and his art director Wilfred Buckland had both worked for Belasco.

6. A newspaper review of David Belasco's staging of *The Darling of the Gods* in 1905. Quoted in A. Nicholas Vardac, *From Stage to Screen* (Cambridge: Harvard University Press, 1949), 117.

7. Walter Benjamin, "The Author as Producer," *Selected Writings, Volume Two: 1927–1934*, ed. Michael W. Jennings, Howard Eiland, and Gary Smith, trans. Rodney Livingstone and others (Cambridge: Harvard University Press, 1999), 775.

8. Ansel Adams looked at his negatives as musical scores that could be reinterpreted over time.

9. See chapter 10 of Beaumont Newhall, *The History of Photography* (New York: The Museum of Modern Art, 1982).

10. Later, the overall color of the image could also be shifted toward red, green, or blue.

11. Color grading can be accomplished using hardware or software. The difference is that the former can deliver real-time operation whereas the latter needs rendering time before the end product can leave the telecine room. On the other hand, software systems may be faster in offering more window shapes or more advanced motion tracking. Different brands, each with its own proprietary system, are competing for the market. New models, using higher resolution or making new options possible or easier to achieve, are coming out all the time. The "Resolve" model of Power Windows, for instance, handles 4K and has endless windows available compared to the "2K+" model, which has less than ten. To simplify the reading, I'm using "Power Windows" as a shortcut for color grading in general, regardless of technology, brand, or model.

12. The cost varies a great deal but it is generally in the hundreds of dollars per hour. Alternatively, a company may submit a flat bid for the job.

13. Telecine, color grading, and the digital intermediate operations are not exactly synonymous terms but I will assume they are, again, to help the reading.

14. It is not clear why a colorist is called a "colorist" when most of the work involves increasing or decreasing light levels. But then the work of a "timer" in the lab had nothing to do with time either.

15. For multiple research papers on the history and technical explanation of the DI, the competing brands, the relative advantages and disadvantages of hardware- versus software-based systems, see the Autodesk website at http://usa.autodesk.com/flame/white-papers/.

16. Bob Richardson is known for degrading some of his images in post, zooming into them, thus increasing the granularity and making them look as if they had been shot on 16mm or even 8mm film.

17. See John Belton, "Painting by the Numbers: The Digital Intermediate," *Film Quarterly* 61, no. 3 (Spring 2008): 58–65.

18. Bob Fisher, "The Big Timers: Meet the DI Colorists," *Film & Video*, June 2005: 22.

19. Michael Goi, "Strengthening Crucial Ties with Collaborators," interview by Stephanie Argy. *American Cinematographer* 91, no. 4 (April 2010): 88 and Kramer Morgenthau quoted in Bob Fisher, "The Case for Film Dailies," *American Cinematographer* 85, no. 4 (April 2004): 92.

20. Michael Goi, "President's Desk," *American Cinematographer* 91, no. 4 (April 2010): 10.

21. Richard P. Crudo, "A Call for Digital Printer Lights," *American Cinematographer* 87, no. 9 (Sept. 2006): 72.

22. Ibid.

23. Richard P. Crudo, "Finishing for Free: The Cinematographer's Dilemma During Post," *American Cinematographer* 85, no. 10 (October 2004): 80.

24. Richard P. Crudo, "A Call for Digital Printer Lights," 70. Although not impossible, this problem would arise only following a complete break of communication between the parties (e.g., as a result of a contractual dispute between producer and director).

25. John Bailey, "The DI Dilemma, or: Why I Still Love Celluloid," *American Cinematographer* 89, no. 6 (June 2008): 93.

26. Bailey "The DI Dilemma, or: Why I Still Love Celluloid," 92. John Bailey is also quoted in Jon Silberg and Stephen Pizzello, "Cinematographers, Colorists and the DI," *American Cinematographer* 90, no. 6 (June 2009): 78.

27. Richard P. Crudo, "Lighting: Our Legacy as Cinematographers," *American Cinematographer* 81, no. 3 (March 2000): 75.

28. Peter Doyle, "Peter Doyle and the Joy of Grading," interview by Debra Kaufman, *Film & Video* (August 2005): 52.

29. Ibid.

30. Silberg and Pizzello, "Cinematographers, Colorists, and the DI," 82.

31. Rachael K. Bosley, "Second Chances," *American Cinematographer* 82, no. 11 (Dec. 03): 99.

32. Jim Hemphill, "Revisiting Days of Heaven," *American Cinematographer* 89, no. 1 (Jan. 2008): 98.

33. Ibid., 100.

34. William Fraker, "On Film," *American Cinematographer* 91, no. 11 (Nov. 2010): 102.

35. Immanuel Kant, *Critique of Judgment*, trans. J. H. Bernard (New York: Hafner Press, 1951), 37–81.

36. Sigmund Freud, *The Freud Reader*, ed. Peter Gay (New York: W. W. Norton, 1989), 733.

37. Donald Kuspit, "*The Psychoanalytic Construction of Beauty*," www://artnet.com/magazine/features/kuspit7-23-02.asp, 6.

38. Max Horkheimer and Theodor W. Adorno, *Dialectic of Enlightenment*, trans. John Cumming (New York: Continuum, 1993), 227.

39. *Encyclopedia Britannica,* 11th ed., s.v. "Vernet, Claude-Joseph."

40. *The Standard Edition of the Complete Psychological Works of Sigmund Freud*, ed. and trans. James Strachey, vol. 21, *Civilization and Its Discontents* (London: Hogarth Press and the Institute of Psycho-Analysis, 1961), 83.

41. Pierre Bourdieu, *Distinction: A Social Critique of the Judgment of Taste*, trans. Richard Nice (Cambridge: Harvard University Press, 1984), 38.

42. See Gilles Deleuze, *Cinema 1 and Cinema 2*, trans. Hugh Tomlinson and Robert Galeta (Minneapolis: University of Minnesota Press, 1986).

43. Deleuze, *Cinema 2*, 156 and 204.
44. Jacques Rancière, *Aesthetics and Its Discontents*, trans. Steven Corcoran (Malden, MA: Polity, 2009), 24.
45. See Jacques Rancière, *Dissensus: On Politics and Aesthetics*, ed. and trans. Steven Corcoran (London: Continuum, 2010), 38.
46. Jacques Rancière, *The Politics of Aesthetics: The Distribution of the Sensible*, trans. Gabriel Rockhill (London: Continuum, 2004), 5.
47. See Marshall McLuhan, *Understanding Media* (New York: McGraw Hill, 1964).
48. See Walter Benjamin, "The Work of Art in the Age of Mechanical Reproduction," in *Film Theory and Criticism*, eds. Gerald Mast, Marshall Cohen, and Leo Braudy, 4th ed. (New York: Oxford University Press, 1992), 679.
49. All three quotes are found in Benjamin, *Selected Writings*, vol. 2, 771–772.
50. Taking just "de-professionalized" lighting, examples include *Public Enemies* (Michael Mann, 2009) and *The Social Network* (David Fincher, 2010).
51. Matthew Arnold, *Culture and Anarchy* (New Haven: Yale University Press, 1994).
52. See Gilles Deleuze and Félix Guattari, *A Thousand Plateaus*, trans. Brian Massumi (London: Continuum, 1980).
53. Deleuze, *Cinema 2*, 272 and 21.
54. E. H. Gombrich, *Art and Illusion* (New York: Pantheon, 1960).
55. See Fabrice Revault d'Allones, *La Lumière au cinéma* (Paris: Cahiers du Cinéma, 1991), 7 and 39.
56. See Martin Heidegger "Conversations on a Country Path About Thinking," in *Discourse on Thinking*, trans. John M. Anderson and E. Hans Freund (New York: Harper and Row, 1966).

SELECT BIBLIOGRAPHY

Arnold, Matthew. *Culture and Anarchy*. New Haven: Yale University Press, 1994.
Belton, John. "Painting by the Numbers: the Digital Intermediate." *Film Quarterly* 61, no. 3 (2008): 58–65.
Bergman, Gösta M. *Lighting in the Theater*. Totoma, NJ: Rowman and Littlefield, 1977.
Deleuze, Gilles. *Cinema 1*. Translated by Hugh Tomlinson and Robert Galeta. Minneapolis: University of Minnesota Press, 1986.
——. *Cinema 2*. Translated by Hugh Tomlinson and Barbara Habberjam. Minneapolis: University of Minnesota Press, 1989.
Horkheimer, Max and Theodor W. Adorno. *Dialectic of Enlightenment*, Translated by John Cumming. New York: Continuum, 1993.
McLuhan, Marshall. *Understanding Media*. New York: McGraw Hill, 1964.
Newhall, Beaumont. *The History of Photography*. New York: The Museum of Modern Art, 1982.
Rancière, Jacques. *Aesthetics and Its Discontents*, Translated by Steven Corcoran. Malden, MA: Polity, 2009.
Rancière, Jacques. *Dissensus: On Politics and Aesthetics*. Edited and translated by Steven Corcoran. London: Continuum, 2010.
Rancière, Jacques. *The Politics of Aesthetics: The Distribution of the Sensible*. Translated by Gabriel Rockhill. London: Continuum, 2004.
Revault d'Allones, Fabrice. *La Lumière au cinéma*. Paris: Cahiers du Cinéma, 1991.
Truffaut, François. "A Certain Tendency of the French Cinema." In *Movies and Methods*, edited by Bill Nichols, 224–237. Berkeley: University of California Press, 1976.

CHAPTER 4

LOST IN SENSATION

*Reevaluating the Role of Cinematic Sound
in the Digital Age*

WILLIAM WHITTINGTON

IN the 1993 Steven Spielberg film *Jurassic Park*, the character of Ian Malcolm (played by Jeff Goldblum) lies injured in a jeep as a genetically engineered dinosaur approaches. Thunderous footfalls break the silence as Malcolm looks down to see rings of water forming in a rain-filled dinosaur track, and he anxiously voices his concern: "Does anybody hear that? That's a um...that's an impact tremor is what it is. I'm fairly alarmed here." In a properly aligned motion picture theater, the tremors from the approaching *Tyrannosaurus rex* fill the entire exhibition space, situating the character and the filmgoers in a jeep, in a jungle, alone. This scene of peril and "alarm" exemplifies many of the qualities of a contemporary blockbuster. It engages new and innovative cinematic technologies, specifically the new multichannel sound format Digital Theater Sound (DTS), which the film introduced, as well as photorealistic computer-generated imagery, which the film refined; it also combines genre themes and conventions from both science fiction and horror, particularly with regard to the fear of the unknown; and, finally, the scene establishes an immersive spectacle through audiovisual strategies designed to create a visceral impact on filmgoers.[1] But to truly understand the integration and implications of these developments, it is important to first listen.

The visual design of the scene denies filmgoers a clear view of the approaching *T. rex*, hiding the creature in the shadows and leaving the soundtrack to create the tension, anxiety, and drama of the scene. In crafting the sound for this sequence, sound designer Gary Rydstrom (*Terminator 2: Judgment Day*, *Wall-E*) establishes a sense of terror by implying both the size and proximity of the threat by creating a dense layer of low-frequency sound effects in conjunction with a pattern of rhythmic thrumming akin to the sound of an approaching thunderstorm.[2] He also engages the multichannel format, particularly the low-frequency and surround sound channels, to fill the well of the theater with rumbles and reverberations that expand the off-screen space of the diegesis. In conjunction with the aesthetics of sound design, the new digital audio medium delivers the sound elements with greater fidelity and dynamic range than any previous film sound format. When the *T. rex* finally does appear, crashing through the trees, the musical score seamlessly picks up this pattern of panic and mayhem by engaging an orchestration of high-pitched and high-frequency stringed instruments in a frenetic arrangement. These combined elements set the pace for the brief chase that follows, creating a visceral and immersive experience for both the characters on-screen and the filmgoers in the theater. Although this film is perhaps best known for its innovative use of computer-generated imagery (CGI) in rendering the photorealistic images of the dinosaurs such as the *T. rex*, it is important to remember that the "alarm" that signaled cinema's transition into the digital age was first heard on the film soundtrack.[3]

In the late 1980s and 1990s, much of the critical writing about emerging digital technologies and aesthetic practices related to cinema focused on the image rather than sound. The concerns that dominated the discourse centered on production economics, quality control, labor displacement, spectacle and special effects, exhibition formats, and marketing issues relating to the transition between analog and digital forms. The tone was often one of trauma, crisis, and "revolution" as the vision of cinema shifted its focus to the pixel and the virtual.[4] At the same time, the soundtrack quietly made its way into the digital era with little notice, somewhat lost in the critical conversation and the visual "sensations," except for complaints that soundtracks were suddenly "too loud."[5] Recently, however, a new body of technologically informed sound history and theory has emerged to augment and, at times, counter this history of visual culture. These new audio-centered works include *Lowering the Boom—Critical Studies in Film Sound* (ed. Jay Beck and Tony Grajeda) and *Beyond Dolby (Stereo)—Cinema in the Digital Age* (Mark Kerins), and *Sound Design and Science Fiction* (William Whittington), as well as journals such as *MSMI—Music, Sound and the Moving Image*. The aim of this essay is to add to this growing body of work and to reconsider the prominence and primacy of sound in the development of cinema aesthetics in the digital age.

So, rather than concede that the majority of the changes in digital aesthetics have been driven entirely by visual practices both on and off the screen, I argue that it was, in fact, sound processes, practices, and technology that led the way into the digital era and that these have been a driving force in shaping the audiovisual dynamics of contemporary cinema. In the 1980s, for example, early three-dimensional or 3D computer animation sequences created by Pixar Animation Studios were often unified by "hyperrealistic" and highly refined sound designs when the images proved more geometric than realistic. More recently, in regard to labor practices, the production processes of sound design, which encourage an overlap of the previously separate duties of recording, editing, and mixing, foreshadowed the labor model for digital special effects personnel, who now find themselves working in virtual environments in which they are lighting, editing, and compositing computer-generated images with live action shots. To elaborate on these and other audio influences, I focus this essay on three interrelated areas of sound and image relations. First, I trace the development of sound design strategies and how these establish audiovisual unity and continuity. Second, I consider the narrative integration of digital sounds and images as they establish spectacle within cinematic narrative. And, finally, I address the cinematic move toward immersive environments and new audiovisual perspectives fostered by digital sound design and multichannel formats. I am also interested in how these factors have shaped perception and critical reception of digital cinema. These fields of focus are not meant to be exhaustive in their scope, but rather are meant to provide a foundation from which to establish a critical understanding that considers both image and sound equally in establishing the history of the digital in cinema today. The critical method of this analysis combines theories from the fields of audio and visual culture, technological convergence, and works related to spectacle and the contemporary blockbuster, in order to establish a shared vocabulary.

The rise of sound design in cinema since the 1960s can be attributed to a multiplicity of factors.[6] These include the introduction of new portable technologies, which allow a broader range of "raw" sound effects to be collected and manipulated, as well as a shift in the mode of film production, particularly the collapse of the duties of the film recordist, editor, and mixers into the position of one sound artisan or sound designer. This aesthetic movement was also led by various sound personnel such Walter Murch (*The Conversation*, *Apocalypse Now*), Ben Burtt (*Star Wars*), and Gary Rydstrom, and promoted by prominent filmmakers such as Francis Ford Coppola, George Lucas, and Steven Spielberg, all of whom sought to shift the role of sound in cinema away from a supporting status to a more active and dramatic engagement in audiovisual relations. Concurrent with the rise of sound design, Hollywood cinema shifted its emphasis to concept-driven genre films or blockbusters that relied heavily on visual effects, makeup appliances and devices, and photochemical lab processes (e.g., optical compositing) to create layers of complexity within the visual field of a shot. In many instances, sound was relied on to unify these less-than-perfect visual constructions using various psychoacoustic and recording and mixing strategies.[7] In the opening scene of *Star Wars* (1977), for example, multilayered rumbles (derived from a recording of a broken air conditioner) give the impression of a massive Imperial space ship traversing the heavens; but, in fact, these images actually depict a small plastic model, set against an optically generated starfield and animated through an automated or motion-controlled camera movement. For sound designer Ben Burtt, the intent was to establish an "organic" and "used future" with his sound effects, shifting science fiction sound away from the ethereal and electronic musical approaches previously codified by genre films of the 1950s.[8] This new approach to sound combined elements of the fantastical with the familiar, and, in terms of critical reception, the sound design was being used to "sell" the images as credible to the filmgoers of the blockbuster generation.

In the digital era, this approach to sound design has become central to the integration and viability of digital images, but the challenges of unpacking the relationships are significant. The ubiquity and refinement of digital images and audio today often lead us to overlook the "work" that appears on the screen and that we hear on the soundtrack. Simply put, it is increasingly difficult to distinguish which shots or sounds in a film have been digitally manipulated, setting aside for a moment the obvious special effects and spectacle elements. This is a problem that sound theory has faced for some time and, therefore, can offer some insight for audiovisual analysis in the digital era. One of the key weaknesses in traditional sound theory dealing with classical Hollywood cinema was that it often examined film sound as a single composite object of capture and subsequently focused predominantly on notions of "realism."[9] However, these notions were challenged as a greater understanding of sound technology and processes emerged, revealing that sound is often one of the most highly constructed aspects of cinema. Contemporary sound scholars have become adept at reverse engineering the processes of sound design by examining production workflows, best practices, and the volumes of technology specifications for audio devices, such as recorders, mixing consoles, and editing software, in order to reveal the strategies and properties behind the construction of the film soundtrack.[10] As a result, it is understood that sound design does not simply capture reality, but rather constructs an entirely new cinematic reality, augmenting it through attentiveness to considerations such as sound perspective, localization, psychoacoustics, and spectacle.

Understanding these "hidden" aspects is important because they provide the architecture for sculpting a sound in the digital age. Specifically, sound perspective deals with the placement of the microphone in relation to what is being recorded. Sound designer Walter Murch (*The Conversation*, *Apocalypse Now*) explains, "the air has a lot to do with it; it's sort of a perfume of sound—sound without air has no smell."[11] The microphone itself plays a role in this recording through the pickup pattern or the field of capture. A polar pattern, for example, limits the recording to the "pole" or top of the microphone and can be engaged to isolate a sound, denoting a sense of privilege or symbolic value. Sound designer Gary Rydstrom explains, "The trick to a lot of sound effects recording is to experiment with different mike placements and different ways of recording" such as through objects like a corrugated pipe or from beneath the surface of a viscous liquid like a milkshake.[12] Where the microphone is placed determines which residual effects, such as reverberations or echoes, are collected in the recording process, often forming a psychoacoustic or perceptual effect. As a result, recording the sound of a phone ringing can be embedded with a sense of loneliness and mystery if the microphone is placed across an empty and reverberant room, as was the case in the opening sequence of *The Matrix* (1999) as the character of Trinity (Carrie-Anne Moss) has her location betrayed by a phone call. Subsequently, when the sound is deployed in a multichannel format, sound localization allows the placement of the effect in any number of speakers within a theatrical venue, and its movement to, say, the surrounds could immediately create an uncanny effect or sound spectacle, particularly if the image on the screen remains unchanged.

Sound designer Gary Rydstrom and Tomlinson Holman, developer of the THX sound standards system, designate the new approach to sound aesthetics in the digital era as "hyperrealism," a philosophy that draws inspiration from hyperrealism in visual culture.[13] Within visual design, hyperrealism is a movement interested in our *perception* of the "real," a property that became both the subject and object of hyperrealistic art. Within the sound design movement, the approach is also interested in perception because it fosters a heightened and often exaggerated use of sound, which is attentive to emotional intents, expectations (related to genre, physics, and psychoacoustics), and intertextual connections such as historical homage (e.g., the *Star Wars* lightsaber sound is often sampled and parodied in space-bound comedies and animation). For Rydstrom, this design approach often means displacing a "raw" or organic sound from its original context, augmenting it through re-recording practices, and then inserting it into a new sound-image pairing to create a heightened effect. An example of this would be to insert the sound of a tiger into a recording of a dog bark. As a result, the sound effect of the dog bark would be perceived as something domestic and recognizable; however, the roar of a tiger would add a new layer of threat through a connection to the primal. The final effect establishes a spectacle of fusion. The resultant effect is not necessarily "cartoon-y," however, but there is a connection to animation.

Sound for early animation often took an onomatopoeic approach, emphasizing bangs, zooms, and honks, which became the lexicon of sound for cartoons and animated shorts, particularly at studios like The Walt Disney Company and Warner Bros. Studios, which produced *Looney Tunes*. Many of these sounds had musical qualities and effectively served to punctuate and complete the animation cycles associated with gestures and movement such as walking, running, or flying. Sonic payoffs were often comedic as well, undercutting our expectations of "reality" or presenting strategies of animalism and anthropomorphism (e.g., mops dancing or attacking a young sorcerer's apprentice). Paul Wells notes that early animation embraced the imperative to reject or "suppress the categories of normal perception" in order to present the irrational, the surreal, and the emotional states of the imagination rather than pragmatic "reality."[14] However, with the introduction of computer animation at Pixar Animation Studios, a conscious aesthetic shift in emphasis occurred in regard to constructing the soundtrack, in part to distinguish the form from traditional cel animation. Early 3D computer animation struggled in the pursuit of "dimension," fostering the need for software to produce photorealistic lighting, texture, and 3D object design, but when these developments proved slow in coming, filmmakers working in this new form relied on sound to animate and anchor their designs by borrowing perceptual audio codes and practices (e.g., Foley effects) from live-action forms. For Rydstrom, sound design was the key to establishing the credibility of computer animation, arguing: "It was clear to me that this form was a whole new thing that would require a whole new approach to sound."[15]

The philosophy of hyperrealism is clearly evident in the 1989 Academy Award-winning computer animated short *Tin Toy*, which became the inspiration for the feature film *Toy Story* (1995). The plot centers on "Tinny," a mechanical version of the one-man band, and his first encounter with a curious baby. By today's standards, the computer-generated images in this short appear crude as the baby's oddly textured skin makes it appear more monstrous than perhaps intended. As a result, sound was engaged to smooth over the technical wrinkles in the computer animation, creating a sense of believability and truth to the story. There is no dialogue in the film; rather, the images and sound evoke the sense of humor and peril as "Tinny" attempts to elude the baby. In dramatic terms, the filmmakers cleverly devised Tinny to be his own worst enemy. His very nature is sonic by the fact that various musical instruments are woven into his jacket. His movements are, therefore, musical. Although this comedic idea is drawn from traditional animation, it has been completely redesigned for computer animation. Using a digital sampler and synthesizer called a Synclavier, Rydstrom created a complex database of sounds including gears, cymbal crashes, drum hits, and horns, as well as eyelid flutters, shivers, and breathing. The instruments were not simply recorded toy versions, but rather a series of real instruments of different scales, which were recorded with a resonant dynamic range and stacked as needed. In pursuit of an overall unified design, Rydstrom sets these sounds in relief against a bed of immediately recognizable vocal and ambient effects, always balancing traditional animation strategies and live-action expectations. In particular, Rydstrom recorded and edited the vocalizations of a real baby to support the rudimentary images of the "monster child" in the film, rather than employing an actor to perform these sounds, which was standard practice in animation at the time. The coos and giggles of the child are recorded and edited to mimic a documentary aesthetic style, and even include an unscripted sneeze, which was animated into the character design. Rydstrom further heightened the live-action qualities of the environment by implying off-screen space through sound effects of a television game show. The television effect is recorded from the perspective of the room on-screen, implying distance, and the chatter is also compressed and muted to give it a sense of the size of the room and the television speaker. Both of these sound constructions serve to create a psychoacoustic gestalt of a living space that is unseen by the camera, and the rapid editing of content implies the presence of a person changing channels, perhaps a parent just home from a trip to the toy store who is taking a break from child care. The balance of this pattern of effects creates the heightened sense of cinematic reality, which counters the rudimentary nature of the 3D animation design. Rydstrom reiterates the importance of sound in the creation of *Tin Toy* noting: "I think it's the most sound-intensive movie per square inch that I've ever done," and, for Pixar, it revealed the importance of sound design in "shaping the content of the film."[16] The filmmakers at Pixar Animation Studios would migrate this successful approach to subsequent feature films such as the *Toy Story* series (1995–2010), *Monsters, Inc.* (2001), and *Wall-E* (2008).

It is important to note that many of the sound designers, including Ben Burtt, Gary Rydstrom, and Tom Meyers (*Armageddon*, *Up*), moved between animation and live-action films during the transition from analog to digital in contemporary cinema. Thus, their labor practices provided an important overlap in the convergence of aesthetic practices between the two forms. As with animation, many computer-generated images for live-action films were obvious special effects shots, which relied heavily on sound to unify the audiovisual design.[17] Early examples can be found in the water-pod sequence in *The Abyss* (1989), the design of the liquid metal effects character sequences in *Terminator 2: Judgment Day* (1991), and the dinosaur sequences like the one described in the opening of this article from *Jurassic Park* (1993). In general, computer graphic imaging systems moved cinematic processes away from lens-based recording to computer-based rendering of the visual field and thus created them in a virtual environment without a production recording track as a guide for the sound editors. As a result, the process of designing sounds emerged as it does in animation, entirely from the creative imagination. It was sound designers like Rydstrom who intuited that computer effects sequences might create a sense of disjunction within a narrative and thus might pull audiences out of the story-world. As a result, sound personnel engaged design strategies that were both exaggerated *and* perceptually accurate, combining fantastical sounds with familiar reference cues such as reverberation or the organic or "raw" effects of real animals or mechanism, and localized sound placement that would direct the eye within the visual field. When the water pod in *The Abyss* rises up and forms a mirror of the face of the character of Lindsey Brigman (Mary Elizabeth Mastrantonio), it is the dialogue and the calming sound effect of lapping water that cue the audience to an understanding that the alien visitors are familiar and friendly. In *Terminator 2: Judgment Day*, the film relies heavily on Foley effects, particularly footsteps, to anchor the computer-generated images of the T-1000 terminator (played by Robert Patrick) to the diegesis as he both walks the tile floor of a hospital and at one point *becomes* the floor.

This new mode of design was complicated somewhat by shifting expectations in regard to technology and special effects as a new mode of spectatorship arose. Filmgoers demanded more from the blockbuster experience when they became accustomed to the potential of computer-generated images. According to Michele Pierson, the range of expectations for computer images and digital special effects fell between a desire for the "photorealistic" and "technofuturist," or the complete remapping of the visual field through the spectacle of digital density or plasticity that can be found in films like *Star Wars: Episode I—The Phantom Menace* (1999).[18] The result has led to a blurring of the distinctions between live-action and animated forms. In addition, transmedia influences from genre television programs such as *CSI: Crime Scene Investigation* (with its emphasis on procedural point-of-view [POV] sequences) and action adventure video games (with their emphasis on first-person shooting positions) shifted the construction of visual field and how audiences experienced it. In regard to cinematic affect, audiences expected a new kind of immersive "ride" that transformed the experience into a cinema of sensation.

According to Constance Balides, this "immersive effect" is established "through an imaginary emplacement of the spectator in the world of the film achieved through textual strategies such as the placement of the camera in the literal position of a character (a point of view shot) or one associated with a purported character's view as well as special effects zoom shots…involving computer graphic images suggesting a movement inward into the image."[19] Although POV shots have been common in cinema from very early on, the native capabilities of digital technology have expanded the technique to include actual views, as well as imagined points of view. Examples of this immersive approach are evident in the bullet wound effects sequence in *Three Kings* (1999), in which the character of Archie Gates (played by George Clooney) describes in voice-over the implications of a gunshot as it is illustrated in gory detail on screen. In *The Virtual Window*, Anne Friedberg argues that the "virtual" capabilities of digital technology reshaped how audiences perceive the image, dislodging the filmgoer from the traditional position of sixth-row center and providing a more fractured point of reference.[20] The resulting digital perspectives have developed in the forms that have come to be known as the *flyby*, the *fly-through*, and *bullet-time*, made famous by *The Matrix* series, all of which create a new sense of immersion, as well as visual spectacle.[21]

Not surprisingly, the soundtrack foreshadowed the shift in perspective through a design strategy known "a point-of-audition," akin to a sonic POV.[22] Traditionally, this design strategy locates the audience at a spatial point within the diegesis, often associated with a specific character or characters, through a manipulation of "volume, reverb and other [audio] characteristics."[23] In the digital era, the approach has been reconceptualized to fold in the imperatives of the cinema of sensation to provide a sonic "thrill ride." In part, the virtual workspace made this possible. Portable recording technologies and the digital audio workstation have allowed sound designers to collapse the duties of recording, editing, and mixing. Sounds are collected and stored in a virtual library, providing easy access and the capability of instantaneous monitoring, thus foregoing the need for tape libraries, machine rooms, and the specialized personnel used in classical Hollywood cinema. As a result, the nuance and detail of sound constructions expanded, and, currently, it is not uncommon to see hundreds of sound elements aligned on a digital grid in a mixing program such as Pro Tools as they are being used to create one effects sequence. The firing of a bullet from a gun, for example, in *Terminator 2: Judgment Day* (1991) included a vast array of "raw" effects including the chambering of a shotgun shell, the sound of a dry fire of the weapon, the sound of a live fire, a cannon blast with reverberation, the whip and whoosh of the bullet in the air and finally, its gooey impact into the body of the liquid terminator. In this instance, the digital sound format provided a nearly lossless medium with limited hiss, recording artifacts, and noise buildup. The multichannel format (5.1 channels, which included left, center, right, right surround, left surround, and low-frequency channels) also allowed the sound designers the ability to spread the sound effects spatially across a number of speakers or channels within the exhibition venue, giving them a sense of direction and localization to direct the gaze of the filmgoer. Most important, the "point-of-audition" in the digital environment was no longer tethered to a specific character or characters; rather, it had been extended to include points of action, movements, and even objects such as bullets within the diegesis. The combination of the digital technology and the aesthetic strategy of design allowed the filmgoers to "ride" the bullet.

Within this new context, the importance of multichannel formats cannot be underestimated in establishing the new digital sound aesthetic. In the early 1990s, when digital visual effects were in their infancy, a number of new digital multichannel sound formats were introduced, including Dolby Digital in 1992 with the film *Batman Returns*, Sony Dynamic Digital Sound (SDDS) in 1993 with the release of *The Last Action Hero*, and DTS, which premiered with *Jurassic Park*, as has been previously noted. Since then, a host of new configurations have emerged with the goal of providing a wider ecosystem for sound deployment. In his book *Beyond Dolby (Stereo)—Cinema in the Digital Sound Age*, Mark Kerins thoroughly details the ramifications of multichannel sound on the film industry and the filmic image, particularly the shifting aesthetic practices related to "digital surround sound" (DSS). Of particular interest for this argument is the ability of DSS to simultaneously place and play "dozens of perceptibly different sounds" within the theater venue.[24] As a result of these new mixing strategies, filmgoers can "hear more sounds at once" (as opposed to sounds presented in a mono environment), allowing them to distinguish differences in volume (loud vs. soft), frequency (high vs. low), rhythmic design (slow vs. fast), and categorization of sound (similar vs. dissimilar). The approach also establishes a dimensionalized environment that allows the creation of a hyperrealized space that overlaps the actual space of the motion picture theater. This expanded environment of immersion has allowed filmmakers to explore *outer space*, in films like *Star Wars* and *Avatar* (2009), and the *inner space* of the mind in films like *Being John Malkovich* (1999) and *Stranger Than Fiction* (2006) using sound, music, and voice-over.

Although the capabilities of digital technologies and practices often strengthen the aesthetic relationship between image and sound, I would be remiss if I did not address some of the instances in which the reverse was true, particularly instances in which sound did not lead the way forward but in fact regressed in prominence. Many critics have argued that the shift toward cinematic immersion facilitated by digital processes and audiovisual spectacle has shifted narrative emphasis away from character-driven storytelling or that it has killed the movie star or unwillingly resurrected them (e.g., forcing Fred Astaire to dance with a vacuum in a popular broadcast commercial in the United States). In some instances, these critiques may be true, but the effects are often only temporary. Digital technologies and processes are still relatively new to filmmaking, and their aesthetic impact is by no means fixed. Any perceived "damage" to cinema can be undone as the novelty of individual uses wanes. As mutable as the images and sound in the digital age have become, so, too, are the tastes and tolerances of audiences in regard to cultural reception. Techniques that provided new sensations today often become the object of critical ire tomorrow, if repeated too often. Take, for example, the technique of *morphing*, which emerged in the late 1980s as a digital special effect used to shift one image to another seamlessly within the visual field, almost akin to a digital cross-fade on the level of the pixel. According to Mark J. P. Wolf, the first film to feature "photo-realistic morphing effects" was *Willow* (1988), which featured a "series of morphs of a character changing first from one type of animal to another, and finally to a human being."[25] The technique was taken up by a number of subsequent films including *Terminator 2: Judgment Day* (1991), *Star Trek VI: The Undiscovered Country* (1991), *Men in Black* (1997), and *Van Helsing* (2004). The technique showcased the unique and native capability of digital technology to seamless transform the visual field, but it also, at times in a film like *Van Helsing*, unbalanced (and regressed) the sound and image model of the contemporary blockbuster and worked against the genre conventions of horror, which the film attempted to embrace.

Early in the film, the character of Anna Valerious (played by Kate Beckinsale) confronts her brother Velkan (played by Will Kemp) as he transforms into a werewolf. A music sting provides the initial shock of discovery, and the computer-generated stylistic overtakes the scene as the character is exposed to moonlight and begins to scale a wall in a movement reminiscent of a backstroke. The computer-generated character defies gravity with the gesture as the film attempts to activate a spectacle of the uncanny but fails. The effect is undercut by the musical score, which directly synchronizes a tonal punctuation with each hand movement along an ascending scale. This approach in composing is known as "Mickey mousing," thus drawing an unwanted connection to animation and the "spectacular" nature of the visual effect. The camera seamlessly follows the action, so that the gesture of transformation is revealed in a single take through the process of morphing. But the mix of the sound is completely unbalanced, regressing to an approach familiar to the soundtracks of horror films of the 1930s, which privileged music over sound effects. When the werewolf finally emerges, the soundtrack briefly provides the sound effects of cracking ribs and tearing flesh, but these effects are buried beneath the swell of music. The focus of the action within a single take and from one point of reference limits the potential of sound design significantly. By contrast, in a film such as *The Howling* (1981), a horror film that relied on makeup effects, lighting, and editing for its transformation sequences, the gesture of transformation was fragmented, through variations in angle, shot duration, camera movement, and performance. As a result, the sound designers were presented with numerous opportunities to shift sound perspective, scale, volume, and design layers in order to present a horror of "excess" organized around sonic spectacles and the "gross display of the human body."[26] The subsequent roster of horror effects for this transformation sequence included the sounds of cracking bones, snapping cartilage as limbs elongated, rapid hair growth on the skin's surface, howls, and screams of agony. In doing so, the soundtrack allowed filmgoers to hear beneath the skin of the characters, thematically reinforcing the notions of the fragility of the human body and the agony of the supernatural condition of lycanthropy. In *Van Helsing*, the morphing technique imposed a reading of the action as a complete audiovisual gestalt, driven forward by music. In many ways, the impact is reminiscent of Hitchcock's *Rope* (1948), which was presented in long takes and, as a result, offered little suspense. Much like a poetic verse, the soundtrack for *Van Helsing*, was denied a sense of meter and rhythm in the cinematic construction. The transformation sequence with morphing and music then becomes a line of poetry without punctuation, rhythm, or pause. Although the images may be photorealistic, the morphing technique denies sonic variation, lessening the impact of this genre convention as horrific.

The "damage" of morphing to audiovisual design was short-lived, however, because the lifecycle of the technique was typical of most special effects practices. Various postproduction effects companies refined the software used to create the morphing effect, and efficiencies related to the labor and workflow reduced the cost of the process, allowing it to be adapted across media from television (mostly science fiction series) to video game productions. As a result, this special effect became less "special." As digital cinema matured, the audiovisual aesthetic moved toward integrating a balance between makeup effects, digital techniques, sound, and performance to establish transformation sequences in films like the *Harry Potter* series. The result has been that the technique of digital shape shifting has paradoxically disappeared as a stand-alone "spectacle" into the crowded audiovisual field of design.

As the audiovisual strategies like morphing and others evolve over time, it is important to remember that it is necessary to constantly remap the history of such production practices and their cultural reception in regard to both the image and soundtrack. No technology or production practice remains constant in cinema. Anne Friedberg aptly argues that cinema in the digital era "has been dramatically transformed" and continues to find itself "embedded in—or perhaps lost in—the new technologies that surround it."[27] Mobile devices, new exhibition venues, and new distribution patterns emerge in what might be termed Cinema 2.0. As a result, consumer formats like DVD and Blu-ray are giving way to video-on-demand (VOD) and streaming, which raise questions about the future availability of films, exhibition strategies in theaters and the home, and the processes of content "remastering." Of particular concern is the drive to "remaster" soundtracks with new audio elements and in multichannel formats without any acknowledgments about how the original aesthetic elements have been altered. Unlike the visual design, specifically in regard to aspect ratio, no statement regarding sound is required at the beginning of a film when the content has been "altered." For instance, the conversion of the soundtrack for *The Exorcist* (1973) to Dolby Digital with new elements, even under the supervision of the director, significantly reshaped the intents and reception of the film. The revised version includes more sound events, specifically Foley, and sound moments that had previously been understated are now suddenly punctuated by louder and more pronounced effects. Unfortunately, the processes of "remastering" the visual aspects of films like *Star Wars* (1979) and *E.T.* (1982) have received far more critical attention, not to mention the ire of fans, than has tinkering with soundtracks. Similarly, the scaling of works of cinema and television to mobile devices shift spatial dynamics of sound and thus alter meanings and visceral intents. The pilot episode of the television series *Lost* (2004–2010) was initially presented on September 22, 2004, on the ABC network in multichannel surround, but it was also the first television show to be offered on Apples iTunes for download to computers and mobile devices. The multichannel experience (for those households with home theaters) surrounded audiences with the traumatic aftermath of a plane crash. The rich soundscape included the screams of survivors, the whirring of a damaged jet engine, and explosions of jet fuel that propelled the sounds of metal debris spectacularly through the surround speakers. Conversely, when downloaded and played on an iPod or iPhone, these same effects are both masked and muted as the sound is converted into two-channel stereo, stripping away the localization of effects and thus the spectacle nature of the image and sound relations. The same issues arise when scaling blockbuster films to mobile screens and ear buds. These examples further underscore the ongoing tensions between technological advancement and aesthetic regression, which are often hidden (and naturalized) in the audiovisual practices of the digital age. In the end, however, with the new critical imperative to unravel the convergence of digital technology, production practices, and audiovisual aesthetics, we need only to continue to look (and listen) to the soundtrack for glimpses of the cinema that is yet to come.

NOTES

1. Digital Theater Sound (DTS) is a *discrete* multichannel digital format (7.1 channels) developed in 1993 by Universal Studios and Steven Spielberg's Amblin Entertainment. The sound content is encoded on CD-ROM and linked to the picture with time code (an electronic synchronization system). The discrete aspect of the format allows for the complete separation of sound information and for that information to be directed to specific speakers in the exhibition space, giving the sound designers the ability to localize specific effects like the honk of a velociraptor and also to prevent sounds from overlapping or "masking" one another.

2. Low-frequency effects (LFE) are deep, low-pitched sounds like thunder and animal growls. In digital theater venues, specific speakers have been designed to reproduce sounds within the 3–120 Hz range and are generally located behind the screen. Localization is not often a consideration when directing sound to this channel; rather, sound designers are concerned with the visceral impact the sound offers to filmgoers.

3. Don Shay and Judy Duncan, *The Making of Jurassic Park* (New York: Ballantine Books, 1993), 129. According to the production histories of the film, *Jurassic Park* has only fifty-two computer-generated images, which, in the early years of digital effects, proved both a substantial and costly number. The innovative nature of the effects can be seen in the unique "texture mapping" of the various dinosaurs, specifically the digital skin that covers their virtual skeletons.

4. John Belton, "Digital Cinema: A False Revolution," in *Film Theory and Criticism*, 6th ed., ed. Leo Braudy and Marshall Cohen (New York: Oxford University Press, 2004), 901.

5. Randy Thom, "Are Movies Getting Too Loud?," http://filmsound.org/randythom/loud-movies.htm, accessed January 15, 2011.

6. The term "sound design" is multifaceted. First, it refers to the design of specific sound effects. Second, it has been associated with the conceptual design of the overall soundtrack. Third, sound design considers the multidimensional aspect of sound deployment within the theatrical space. Finally, sound design can be considered a critical model or method of analysis of the film soundtrack. In this essay, all of these definitions are activated within specific contexts.

7. Psychoacoustics deals with interplay between sound and perception. Sound designers depend on specific perceptual responses in conjunction with cinematic expectations to evoke specific responses from audiences. For example, low-frequency effects often trigger a primal response of fear of the environment.

8. Larry Blake, *Film Sound Today* (Hollywood: Reveille Press, 1984), 35.

9. Theorists, such as Béla Balázs and André Bazin, argue that there is "no difference" between a recorded sound and the original sound, yet this position fails to consider the perceptual work that a recording device performs in the process of recording (capturing and constructing it through microphone choice and recording position) or the work the amplifiers and speakers perform in the deployment of a sound.

10. One of the challenges in sound theory has been a lack of archival assets related to production methods. The final design exists, but none of the documentation leading up to it has been preserved. Visual design in the digital age engages multiple processes, decisions, and layers of construction, but without documentation of the virtual workflow, the history dissipates as hard drives are erased and old technology is replaced. I would argue that preserving these digital assets should be a key priority for cinema scholars.

11. Vincent LoBrutto, *Sound-on-Film: Interviews with Creators of Film Sound* (Westport, CT: Praeger, 1994), 88.

12. Ibid., 235.

13. Tomlinson Holman, *Sound for Film and Television*, 2nd ed. (Los Angeles: Focal Press, 2002), xix. Holman notes that the move toward hyperrealism was in part technological as well, noting that "the exaggeration is due to the experience of practitioners finding that average sound playback systems obscure details, a good deal of the exaggeration still is desirable under the best playback conditions, simply because of the competition from other kinds of sound."

14. Paul Wells, *Animation and America* (Edinburgh: Edinburgh University Press, 2002), 5–7.

15. Karen Paik, *To Infinity and Beyond! The Story of Pixar Animation Studios* (San Francisco: Chronicle, 2007), 72.

16. Ibid.

17. Computer-generated imaging technology is not a single technology; rather, it is a host of convergent technologies in the form of hardware and software applications and input devices such as touch pads and pens. Computer graphic imaging systems come in a number of different configurations and platforms and are often tailored to the specific needs of a production. The technology was first developed to provide an economical alternative to such special effects techniques involving models (large and small-scale), matte painting, stop-motion, and pyrotechnic effects, among others. However, rather than fully supplanting these techniques, digital technologies have augmented them, ironically at much higher production costs.

18. Michele Pierson, *Special Effects: Still in Search of Wonder* (New York: Columbia University Press, 2002), 128.

19. Constance Balides, "Immersion in the Virtual Ornament: Contemporary 'Movie Ride' Films," in *Rethinking Media Change*, ed. David Thorburn and Henry Jenkins (Cambridge, MA: MIT Press, 2004), 317.

20. Anne Friedberg, *The Virtual Window: From Alberti to Microsoft* (Cambridge, MA: MIT Press, 2006), 2.

21. The effects such as the flyby and fly-through serve to propel the virtual camera through environments or terrains, whereas *bullet-time* shifts the camera both physically and temporally on actions such as the martial arts kicks by the character of Trinity in *The Matrix* so that they may be viewed from different angles or in greater detail.

22. Rick Altman, *Sound Theory, Sound Practice* (New York: Routledge, 1992), 60.

23. Ibid., 60.

24. Mark Kerins, *Beyond Dolby (Stereo): Cinema in the Digital Sound Age* (Bloomington: Indiana University Press, 2011), 66.

25. Mark J. P. Wolf, "A Brief history of Morphing," in *Visual Transformation Meta Morphing and the Culture of Quick-Change*, ed. Vivian Sobchack (Minneapolis: University of Minnesota Press, 2000), 91.

26. Linda Williams, "Film Bodies: Gender, Genre, and Excess," *Film Quarterly* 44, no.4 (Summer 1991): 2.

27. Anne Friedberg, "The End of Cinema: Multimedia and Technological Change," in *Film Theory and Criticism*, 6th ed., ed. Leo Braudy and Marshall Cohen (New York: Oxford University Press, 2004), 914.

Select Bibliography

Altman, Rick. *Sound Theory, Sound Practice*. New York: Routledge, 1992.

Balides, Constance. "Immersion in the Virtual Ornament: Contemporary 'Movie Ride' Films." In *Rethinking Media Change*, edited by David Thorburn and Henry Jenkins, 315–336. Cambridge, MA: MIT Press, 2004.

Beck, Jay, and Tony Grajeda. *Lowering the Boom: Critical Studies in Film Sound*. Chicago: University of Illinois Press, 2008.

Belton, John. "Digital Cinema: A False Revolution." In *Film Theory and Criticism*, 6th ed., edited by Leo Braudy and Marshall Cohen, 901–913. New York: Oxford University Press, 2004.

Blake, Larry. *Film Sound Today*. Hollywood: Reveille Press, 1984.

Friedberg, Anne. "The End of Cinema: Multimedia and Technological Change." In *Film Theory and Criticism*, 6th ed., edited by Leo Braudy and Marshall Cohen, 914–926. New York: Oxford University Press, 2004.

Friedberg, Anne. *The Virtual Window: From Alberti to Microsoft*. Cambridge, MA: MIT Press, 2006.

Holman, Tomlinson. *Sound for Film and Television*. Los Angeles: Focal Press, 2002.

Jenkins, Henry. *Convergence Culture: Where Old and New Media Collide*. New York: New York University Press, 2006.

Kerins, Mark. *Beyond Dolby (Stereo): Cinema in the Digital Sound Age*. Bloomington: Indiana University Press, 2011.

King, Geoff. "Spectacle, Narrative, and the Spectacular Hollywood Blockbuster." In *Movie Blockbusters*, edited by Julian Stringer, 114–127. New York: Routledge, 2003.

LoBrutto, Vincent. *Sound-on-Film: Interviews with Creators of Film Sound*. Westport, CT: Praeger, 1994.

Paik, Karen. *To Infinity and Beyond! The Story of Pixar Animation Studios*. San Francisco: Chronicle, 2007.

Pierson, Michele. *Special Effects: Still in Search of Wonder*. New York: Columbia University Press, 2002.

Shay, Don, and Jody Duncan. *The Making of Jurassic Park*. New York: Ballantine Books, 1993.

Thom, Randy. "Are Movies Getting Too Loud?" Accessed January 15, 2011. http://filmsound.org/randythom/loud-movies.htm.

Wells, Paul. *Animation and America*. Edinburgh: Edinburgh University Press, 2002.

Whittington, William. *Sound Design and Science Fiction*. Austin: University of Texas Press, 2007.

Williams, Linda. "Film Bodies: Gender, Genre, and Excess." *Film Quarterly* 44, no. 4 (Summer 1991): 2–13.

Wolf, Mark J. P. "A Brief History of Morphing." In *Visual Transformation Meta Morphing and the Culture of Quick-Change*, edited by Vivian Sobchack, 83–101. Minneapolis: University of Minnesota Press, 2000.

PART II

DIALOGUE: SCREENS AND SPACES

CHAPTER 5

....

LARGE SCREENS, THIRD SCREENS, VIRTUALITY, AND INNOVATION

....

SEAN CUBITT

HI-RES LO-RES

....

THE problem of technical innovation—how it occurs, how it can be encouraged and controlled, its goals and consequences—raises immense problems, and that immensity is itself a problem, perhaps the central problem, for the management of innovation and the innovation process itself. The ostensibly narrow issue of screen technologies serves, in this essay, as a test-bed for an analysis of the conceptualization and practice of technical innovation. Concentrating on public space—city streets and plazas rather than domestic media—it inquires into the relation between the changing nature of the urban environment, the concept of the public, and the management of innovation in screen media by both policy makers and the general public.

There are three typical modes of screen in use in public spaces in the early twenty-first century. The first is the ubiquitous monitor or TV receiver, in cafes and bars, storefronts and betting shops, more or less unchanged from its domestic scale and address The second is the large, high-resolution LCD screen characteristically used for advertising and typically placed in the busiest spaces. In some cities, these are malls and open public squares, in others, like Seoul, major traffic intersections. In many cities, operators have also taken the opportunity to provide public service activities: closed-circuit relays of local events, rather like the use of such screens at sporting and music events; public-service broadcast, again often of cultural and sports events, but also of news and current affairs; and, to a limited but interesting extent, artworks designed for public space. With the exception of the latter, although audiences may cheer or boo, they are rarely in control of the flow of images on large screens.

The third is the handheld "third screen" of mobile phones, PDAs, iPods, and console games—low resolution, intimate LCD screens that, although they may also be commercialized in playback of films, TV, games and advertising, are also commonly used to port video and still images person-to-person. The increasing use of Bluetooth or wireless headphones increases the intimacy of the cradled screen. The likelihood of cheering and booing diminishes, but, at the same time, the ability to text, speak, manipulate, and make one's own videos and images is immensely greater. The porting of social networking websites to mobile platforms is a major advance in this increasing intimacy of the mobile phone, even as it is increasingly ubiquitous in public spaces. This essay concerns the possible articulations of these third screens with the large-scale, public screens and what that might imply for future social and artistic practices. In particular, it argues that virtual possibilities are constrained because corporate and governmental intervention in new media controls the flows not only of capital but of populations. If we exchange privacy for collaboration, risky as it seems, we might be able to take back some of that control.

We have, then, a simple relationship in public space: high resolution means low interaction, whereas low resolution is associated with high levels of interaction. In domestic space, the two may be combined, but high-resolution interactives require screens of larger scale and hard drives of greater capacity than are easily carried about. Laptops bridge the gap between private and public space with portable hi-res screens, but, when in public, they are used typically in pseudo-domestic environments involving chairs at the least, and commonly tables as well. Third-screen devices are different: they can be used on the go, standing, walking, running for a bus. Clever use of technology increases their apparent resolution, but both resolution and illumination pale beside the capacities of large screens.

Both populate public space. We might trace their histories back fifty years and suggest a relation like that between the poster and the paperback. One is bigger, brasher, brighter, and open to both artistic uses and graffiti-style intervention, but in a relatively highly policed zone where fly-posting was (and remains) an illegal activity. The paperback, meanwhile, was highly portable, intimate, personal communication. Admittedly, few people authored their own novels, but the degree of personal intimacy with a good book, the engagement with the reader's fantasy, and the exclusion of the surrounding world are very similar. One major change has been that with the billboard-sized screen and its robust LED components, it is far more expensive to place content on high-resolution screens than to silk-screen rebellious posters and far more difficult to damage a commercial screen than to deface a commercial poster. A second is that even the wave of commercial applications for third-screen devices has not supplanted their use for generating person-to-person media.

What remains the same is the struggle in the streets and squares for attention and the struggle, more specifically, between low-resolution but engrossing intimate media and high-resolution, spectacular display media. Dramatizing the anonymity of the crowd celebrated by Poe and Baudelaire, the dialectic of self-loss and spectacle moves between immersing oneself in deeply personal and emotional small media and subordinating oneself to massive spectacular displays. To the extent that both play with established rhetorical techniques of word, sound, and image and deploy standard repertoires of illusion and narrative, they are akin in replacing the actual city with a vista on something that is not actually present. To that extent, both are virtual. Yet the modes of their virtuality are quite distinct and pose specific problems for any understanding of media innovation and for the deployment of public media, commercial or otherwise.

The expropriation of public space by corporations for purposes of advertising may be inevitable. Smearing the walls with commercial messages has a history stretching back to the late nineteenth century and is, in some respects, indistinguishable from the rise of color lithography. The migration from TV screens carrying advertising in shopfronts to big LED screens mounted on buildings and from print to moving image technologies is entirely in keeping with the age. The loss of any public goal in public space, other than the generation of unwanted desires for unnecessary products, is largely seen as harmless by the public who inhabit them. Of a similar visual effect the poet John Montague writes "The censor's certificate flashes up./ I scarcely notice / so deeply has the harness worn in." We are inured to this theft of time and space and have developed strategies for ignoring our environments as a response. One such technique is to concentrate one's attention on a portable screen, as previously on a book. The sightless gaze of those lost in conversation or fantasy is now ubiquitous in public space. The accusation of theft then runs beyond the theft of public space to the theft of human attention to the environment or to one another. For the unplanned criss-crossing of lives in the city, mobile networks substitute networks into which we have opted, networks that are planned, networks of like with like, walled gardens from which we need not stray to find an unexpected cultural difference or an unwanted challenge to our communities of opinion. Under such conditions, the meaning of the word "public" has changed and, with it, what we might understand by the public good.

ACTUAL AND VIRTUAL

Much has changed in the past hundred years. The old dialectic of enlightenment reversed Nature's physical and spiritual domination over humanity when nature's gods dominated us.[1] The latest form of our reciprocal demeaning of nature is atmoterrorism,[2] when, for the first time, humans have achieved what once was the prerogative of the gods: to make life unlivable. Such historical perspectives are not popular among policy makers. The regulatory environment for technical decisions is an unwanted inheritance of the past that constrains innovation and actively hampers invention. A similarly deep historical stance posed by environmental concerns allows them to be cast as long-term issues that we can afford to defer to a future moment. These historical and futurological perspectives are, as much as possible, swept aside in the present where, as a matter of urgency, not even politics can be relied on: only the economic has the right to determine degrees of possibility.

This is not only a categorical error, in which one mode of outcome is abstracted and privileged. It is also what creates the conditions for its own catastrophe in the form of the global financial crisis. Ignoring past and future permits the principle of deferred payment, the principle, for example, of the derivatives market whose collapse brought about the fiscal tsunami of the late 2000s.[3] But it is also the deferred payment, now actionably overdue, to the global environment. By global environment, I mean first the terrestrial biosphere: atmosphere, soil, rock, and water and the accumulated crisis represented most vividly today as climate change, but also in the form of the toxic waste of two centuries of industrialization. It is also important to recognize that the global environment also includes the polis of humankind and the accumulated crisis of poverty that capital has so saliently failed to resolve in the sixty years since Bretton Woods. The global environment, then, also includes public and social goods excluded from the calculus of profit maximization. Finally, the global environment encompasses the technical environment itself, the machinic phylum.[4] Humans are not immune to the biophysical environment: not only do we interact with it, but, as one of the largest biomasses on earth, the human population is itself an environment where bacteria, viruses, and other organisms find their ecological niches. In the same way, humans are not apart from the technologies in which we are imbricated and with which we form increasingly complex and mutually dependent assemblages.[5]

The deferral of payment on which the current conceptual privilege of the economic rests is a fateful deracination of contemporary decision-making processes from their anchors in the past. This has, as a further implication, a failure to understand the relation between virtual and actual. The debate over the precise meaning of these terms is important, although it can only be touched on briefly here. For Deleuze, the virtual is the immanent flux in which all possibilities arise. Our perception of time derives from an ontological paradox: that there is no distinguishable present except as that moment of the flux in which time splits itself into a past and a future:

> [S]ince the past is constituted not after the present that it was but at the same time, time has to split itself in two at each moment as present and past, which differ from each other in nature, or, what amounts to the same thing, it has to split the present into two heterogeneous directions, one of which is launched towards the future while the other falls towards the past.[6]

The past is what we call actual: the result of past acts. The future is potential. The present itself is virtual, in that it is the moment of splitting between past and future in which acts can occur. Unfortunately, to derive this sense of the virtual, Deleuze needed to posit a new ontological entity, the virtual "plane of immanence." Adorno's remarks on Bergson, the philosopher who more than any other underpinned Deleuze's concept of time, can help identify why this is a problem:

> Bergson, in a tour de force, created another type of cognition for nonconceptuality's sake. The dialectical salt was washed away in an undifferentiated tide of life; solidified

reality was disposed of as subaltern, not comprehended along with its subalternity. The hater of the rigid concept established a cult of irrational immediacy, of sovereign freedom in the midst of unfreedom.... Every cognition including Bergson's own needs the rationality he scorns, and needs it precisely at the moment of concretion. Absolutized duration, pure becoming, the pure act—these would recoil into the same timelessness which Bergson chides as metaphysics since Plato and Aristotle. He did not mind that the thing he groped for, if it is not to remain a mirage, is visible only with the equipment of cognition, by reflection upon its own means, and that it grows arbitrary in a procedure unrelated, from the start, to that of cognition.[7]

According to Adorno, Bergson and, by extension, Deleuze, produce the idea of the virtual, pure becoming by a process of cognitive self-reflection that denies and abstracts from the living, concrete actuality of the world, rather than attempting to understand how that concreteness comes to be and still less how it is thrust into the marginal position in relation to cognition. In this way, the self-reflecting cognition that can come up with the abstraction of virtual from actual severs itself from the rational practice of cognition, which is to apply itself to the world of actuality. This subordination of the actual world is of a kind, Adorno argues, with the domination that characterizes the Western Enlightenment. Reconceptualizing the world as flux and flow does not alter the monstrosity of its subordination: in the guise of freeing existence from our knowledge of it, it succumbs to the very forces of irrationality that characterize power and exploitation under capital.

It is in Hannah Arendt's *Responsibility and Judgement*[8] that we find perhaps the best political answer to this theoretical impasse. For Arendt, the actual as accumulation of acts and as the goal of acts undertaken in the present is the realization of potential. She analyzes the word "potential" to find in it the Latin *potentia*, power, potency. We can find the same root in "virtual": *virtú*, strength, capacity, and sexual potency. What is actual in a situation is that aspect of it that is given; what is virtual is that which offers opportunities for action. It is Arendt's understanding of the virtual as the capacity for change abiding in a given situation and the agents that compose it that underpins the arguments that follow.

The sad fact, as Arendt intimated at the Eichmann trial,[9] is that it is increasingly the business of rule to ensure that situations present the fewest possible virtual aspects, the least number of opportunities for change. Eichmann's normality, and the banality of the evil he perpetrated, represent in effect one possible result of hegemonic process in the public sphere. Although the processes may be rational, indeed, deeply in line with the Weberian rationality of bureaucracy, the banality of evil thesis demonstrates the possibility that open, public, rational discourse on norms and values can reach a consensus that is itself irrational and unethical. Moreover, this outcome should demonstrate that processes like the open debate over public morals can result in situations that are, then, not only open to abuse, or in this instance themselves abusive, but which are also deeply difficult to uproot or to change. That this may also be the case with technical innovation is apparent from a number of normative solutions to technical issues that have then been deployed to block the advent of new technologies. Such are the cases of the delay to the arrival of film sound, the maneuvers that halted the introduction of FM radio, and, in a number of territories, the blocking of the development of digital terrestrial television by incumbent broadcasters. Similar processes are visible in the world of business models, as, for example, the damage currently inflicted on wireless media by the walled-garden approaches of incumbent cellular telecommunications corporations (telcos). The "banality of evil" thesis, the blockage of technical innovation and the damage caused by entrenched business models point toward a common process. This process is one of normalization of the least disruptive and most cost-efficient, regardless of quality or extraeconomic implications. In effect, it privileges the present as the actual outcome of past actions, at the expense of the virtual capacity to produce a future different from the present. This is how events become rarities.

CONTRADICTIONS OF CONTROL

However, it is not always the case that the status quo can be preserved. Perhaps the most remarkable example of this was the World Wide Web of the years following the introduction of the Mosaic browser. Until the dot.com crash of 2001, the Web was one of the longest-lived Temporary Autonomous Zones[10] our generation ever knew. Capital failed to understand. Not until the years after 2001 did it begin to build business models based in the Web rather than imported from magazine publishing and the broadcast industry.

Marx had established the principles for this failure in the famous Fragment on Machines.[11] Socialization of production in the new factories of the Industrial Revolution also brought about a socialization of knowledge and skill that Marx refers to as the social or general intellect. The social intellect/general intellect is manifest in two processes. In one, the skill developed over generations in making things is ossified into machinery and turned to purposes of exploitation. In the second, the ways workers organize themselves so they can get longer breaks or leave earlier are systematized by Capital. As Virno argues in *Grammar of the Multitude*,[12] this innovative power to make new systems is no longer a side benefit of employing workers: it is written into our contracts. The techniques and ideas we invent at work become the property of our employers.

Capital is forced by the falling rate of profit to run the risk of endless revolutions in the means of production (machinery, organization), revolutions that constantly run ahead of capital's ability to assimilate them.[13] This is what happened when the Web turned the internet into a mass medium. Capital had no idea how to respond, how to monetize the revolution in the means of production. The result was a fantastic flowering of creativity, of new kinds of cultural practice, new types of service, new modes of organization. Since 2001, with the social networking portals of Web 2.0, capital has finally managed to catch up and to turn that inventive impetus into profit-making enterprises, a near-miraculous recovery from the inflationary vaporware catastrophe of the early 2000s.

In terms of the history of large screens, the parallel moment of crisis occurred in a rather less public form. The revolution in manufacturing, which in the 1870s and 1880s brought industrial tools even to smaller local and regional firms, increased the quantities of manufactured goods to the point that getting them to markets became desperately difficult. The physical movement of goods could be handled through the new transport media of railways and canals, but governing demand for goods was a far greater challenge. Although some economic historians insist that growth in demand led to the industrialization of production, others, following Galbraith,[14] are adamant that the new manufacturing industries required mass communications to increase demand and to provide market feedback. Historian of control systems James Beniger attributes the key innovations to Henry P. Crowell, manufacturer of rolled oats. Faced with a US market that despised oats as fodder for horses, Crowell had to find a new market in order to head off a crisis of overproduction:

> Crowell addressed this crisis with a revolutionary new technology for the control of consumption: national advertising of a brand name product directly to the mass household market. By repackaging his bulk meal in convenient twenty-four ounce boxes, which he marketed under the now-familiar brand label of the black-coated Quaker, Crowell managed to dispose of surpluses created by the control revolutions in production and distribution by inventing not only the modern breakfast food industry but breakfast cereal itself—a product then almost entirely new to American tastes. Crowell's innovations in advertising included many of the fundamental techniques and gimmicks still used today: scientific endorsements, testimonials, prizes, box-top premiums and the like.[15]

Other innovations included the distribution of free samples, but also, and more significantly, the brand name and the trade mark. The result was a major change in purchasing habits, with some historians crediting Crowell with shifting consumers from bulk to prepackaged product.[16] Since those earliest days, the history of advertising has been a story not only of the manipulation of desire, but of the mass management of consumption, such that it can be guided toward foreseeable, plannable scales over periods of years if not decades.

Big screens in public spaces are the heirs of Crowell's innovations, themselves brought on by a crisis that constantly threatens to reemerge: the crisis of overproduction. The goal of advertising in the contemporary world is, however, less to change modes of consumption and more to maintain advantage within a more or less steady state of the market. As we have seen in responses to the current crisis, capital must maintain demand in order to avoid spiraling out of control. This task is undertaken not only through domestic media but by populating public space. The alliance between government and capital in this instance is clear. Both have an interest in prediction: of consumption in one instance and of public order for both, with a shared interest in ordered pedestrian flows through open plazas, encouraging civic conviviality and discouraging aggressive crowd behaviors. Prediction and good order are of a kind and give precision to the term "urban planning."

At first glance, third screens seem to have little in common with this normative function. They operate at the level of individuals rather than large groups or crowds; and interaction with them is far more personal and interpersonal. Mobile marketing—typically the use of voice and text to acquire customers and maintain their loyalty, with some promotion and m-commerce applications—is also place-sensitive, especially with the spread of GPS services. As the Australian Interactive Media Industry Association (AIMIA) note,

> Mobile advertising has the precision of direct marketing and even more detailed tracking than advertising on the internet. Wireless devices are now also the cornerstone of social networking enabling peer to peer/s connections within social groups. Tapping into this new advertising medium has tremendous potential for brands, publishers and content owners.[17]

Among those entering this market is Google, seeking a new platform to extend its AdSense proprietary software that tunes ads to the keywords of sites visited by the user. In the case of mobile phones, location is also supplied by the routing of calls through celnet mast antennae, and the always-on phone means that advertisers can locate people in time as well as space, all connected to their internet history and to the details they supply on social networking sites. This powerful microtargeting would appear to function in quite the opposite direction to spectacular screens, which are typically tied to one location and that cannot distinguish the kinds of people who pass by them. Like billboards, large-screen commercials would appear to belong to the old world of mass advertising and mass consumption, whereas the mobile belongs to the emergent world of micro-audiences and the long tail of specialist, personalized services. This atomized approach to advertising relates to the efficiency of advertising spending: clients pay according to the number of clicks their banners attract, so that pricing is geared toward maximizing the likelihood that people who respond to an ad are interested in the product or service. Noting that "162 million consumers used text messaging in the fourth quarter of 2008," one report in early 2009 asserts that

> Thirty-three percent of Americans with mobile phones said they recalled seeing mobile advertising during the fourth quarter of 2008. Among those with iPhones, the figure was even higher, at 41 percent. The vast majority of these ads were seen in SMS text messages.[18]

Thus, although personalized, localized, and timely, mobile advertising is also a mass medium, potentially reaching more than 50 million SMS users in the United States alone. Again, the lessons of how to monetarize not only social networking but person-to-person communications are deployed in the interest of averting crises of overproduction and its pair, underconsumption. The fragmentation of media in the multichannel era was always intended to increase the fit between audiences and products advertised. That process has now integrated into not only mobile web applications but the person-to-person zone of SMS innovated by users in the 1980s and '90s. Although cheap books intended for railway travelers had included advertising material since the late nineteenth century, the scale of this intervention is far greater.

At present, advertising media are the preferred route to deliver social messages on behalf of governments. Public health and safety announcements take the same form as ordinary commercials. The response to the advertising of cars and alcohol is to advertise the perils of drunk driving. Such ads appear on mobiles as they do on large screens, entering, however, the same flow, with the same risks of distracted attention and the common problem that those most at risk—smokers for example—are the ones least likely to click on a banner warning of the dangers of cancer. Public service messages also risk alienating users by lacking a meaningful content to link to from mobile banners. Using advertising techniques to secure public goods is, then, a poor substitute for public media. On a more positive note, telcos appear very open to broadcast models in the case of emergency announcements, such as warnings associated with the Black Saturday fires in Victoria in February 2009 sent to all subscribers by Australian service provider Telstra. Whether by informal agreements or enforced through must-carry legislation, such messages form an important part of the service that can be provided through mobile networks. Moreover, they point to the community-building aspects of these media that are perhaps their greatest untested strength.

INTERVENING IN PUBLIC-SCREEN SPACE

It is unlikely that public good messages can compete realistically for screen real estate, as the industry refers to the crowd of elements competing for a share of mobile users' screens. What is required is a new understanding of the assemblage that constitutes the new public individual in technologically mediated networks. Although it is certainly the case that we have always been mediated, the means of mediation have been constantly revolutionized, as we have observed. The new network assemblages in which we are mediated are virtual, not only in the sense that they have their being in some place immanent to but apart from the everyday, but in the sense that they are full of potential that remains untapped. These networks are assemblages of both people and technologies, neither of which are simple terms. The nineteenth century witnessed Marx's revolutionary identification of the worker with the factory in a single automaton, blurring the distinction between human and mechanical. Similarly, the revolutions in the conceptualization of the human in relation to animals brought about by Darwin and Freud have not been stilled by the rise of identity politics. If anything, the collapse of older, hierarchical semantic institutions (church, state, family) as providers of identity, and the recourse to the individual as the new institution charged with providing it, has brought about a crisis in individual identity. Just as the family collapsed under the strain of the demand that it provide not only reproduction but the meaning of life, so, too, the individual as social institution reels under the strain of providing not only the unit of consumption but the very rationale of existence.

The individual, isolated in space, time, and the semantic web she has woven from her network history, is condemned to a kind of privacy that no-one really wants. Privacy is the obverse of surveillance, its necessary complement, not simply its opposite. Privacy arises as a result of surveillance, as its shadow. The private sphere, which Habermas considers to have come into existence during the eighteenth century[19] and which dissolves in the emergence of the welfare state for all but a tiny minority, only ever affected a part of the population. The evidence of the nineteenth-century reformers and of twentieth-century housing campaigners is that privacy never invaded the homes of the poor. A privilege of the bourgeoisie, it has now disappeared for all but the tax-evader and the wife-beater. The rest of us publicize ourselves, not least of all through our network activities. This new individual is at once a performance undertaken under the imperative "Express yourself! Output some data!"[20] and the data image that each of us unconsciously creates as we pass through the networks of money, employment, taxes, medicine, purchases, and browsing. This regime of files, from which we try to protect ourselves with the ideology of privacy, is in fact the self as it has been produced in the surveillant regimes of capital and government.[21] The internal splittings identified by psychoanalysis are now complemented by splits in the social performance of identity: we are split again, in that our various selves are no longer purely internal but external, not presences but presentations.

The positive side of this crowd of presentations that constitutes present-day network schizophrenia is that it is all the more distributed and thus distributable. Mobile and big-screen advertising alike aim at stabilizing the cluster of personalities, not simply around a screen but at a place in a planned economy, in which our purpose is to ensure continued consumption at the aggravated level required by the falling rate of profit. This is the actual state of affairs. But it is not a true picture of the virtual state of affairs: that aspect of the given situation in which we are capable of activity.

A second novelty in the current situation is also important. Kevin Robins[22] identifies a series of changes among European migrants that also affect many other areas of the developed and, increasingly, the developing world. Old colonial destinations no longer act as magnets: migrants move where the work and the money are and keep in touch with their linguistic and cultural groups in real time at a distance, rather than necessarily by geospatial clustering. Informal and increasingly formal economies cross borders on a daily basis, as, for example, among suitcase traders. The nation no longer provides a stable identity, neither the country of origin nor the country of destination. The very notion of "community" has lost its referent, as people move constantly. In Europe's case, Robins argues, the response to the increasing irrelevance of the national paradigm has been the construction of a pseudo-national identity: European cohesion. One evidence for this is the crisis of confidence in public service broadcasting, which no longer has the grounds to construct a coherent audience from the fluid, shifting mix of diasporas that now constitutes the public. Now that migration is no longer an act but a state of being, the attempt to build communities is no longer available in the old terms derived from the nation-building efforts of the earlier twentieth century.

Faced with the impasses of community and identity, of social surveillance and individual privacy, Felix Stalder offers terms for a solution:

> The key question when we try to think about a world without privacy is how we can promote free cooperation, which involves a high degree of visibility and identifiability of individuals, while limiting social sorting and preventing the state to rebuild itself around a deeply authoritarian core. If we manage that, I believe we can really say: goodbye privacy.[23]

Stalder notes the likelihood that the state will respond to free cooperation by interpreting it as terrorism and increasing the degree of authoritarian clampdown, using the very tools of network technologies that enabled the cooperation. The notion of free cooperation is also difficult and certainly utopian in the way Stalder posits it as a future state. Yet he is also clear that, as is the case with Bloch's conceptualization of the not-yet,[24] this is a utopia that already exists in nascent form in the everyday practices of network assemblages.

Free cooperation,[25] collaboration (the term preferred, for its echo of illegitimacy, by Florian Schneider[26]), organized networks[27] are offered as alternatives to the existing order and the existing economy. In an early essay on the theme of the new economics of networks, Richard Barbrook pointed out the existence of two parallel economies, one based on the exchange of gifts, the other on exchange of money and contracts.[28] The gift economy is a quality of peer-to-peer projects, of which Linux and Wikipedia are the most cited examples, along with Project Gutenberg and (although its origins are often forgotten) the first Web manifestation of the Internet Movie Database. In the latter case, commercialization was a function of success, as measured in throughput of data. In the case of Linux, service providers like Red Hat and Ubuntu, which sell services to users of the otherwise free operating system, have found business models appropriate to the Free Libre Open Source Software (FLOSS) ethos, even though somewhat controversial. What is notable about these projects is that they emerge from existing communities; that is, from loose networks with shared interests; that therefore community-building, where it occurs, is a by-product, not a goal; and that the central activity is to provide a service that the donors want and are prepared to contribute their labor to. But where the gift of labor has been commercialized, as it has in social networking, the surveillant functions of the database economy serve not only to target but to average, as Foucault was anxious to demonstrate in the late lectures.[29] Here, the virtual nature of the crowd, its power to act, is removed by a process of forecasting what quantum of deviance is tolerable in a population. The task, then, is to challenge the autoarchiving of network activity with its extension: not to refuse surveillance, but to embrace the post-individual capacity, the virtual of universal visibility, and the multiplication of identities that occurs in the performance of self online, as the grounds of a new sociality. This might well be inspired by Adorno's insistence throughout his late lectures on negative dialectics that what is essential is neither the actual, nor identity, but precisely nonidentity: the nonidentical nature of the world to which Western thought perpetually ascribes identity.[30] The crowd exists, in the discursive and architectural terms of biopolitics, as a common identity. A new politics would have to recognize the nonidentity of the crowd: its fundamental disparity and multiplicity, and thence its potential, its virtual avocation, not as a unity with a single goal but as a roiling evolving process. In an extension of the nonidentity argument, Adorno argues that there can be no "greater good" as long as one person must suffer or one person sacrifice their native demand for happiness.[31] The crowd should no longer be envisaged as the puppet of the demagogue or as monomaniacal, but as the expression of differing and even antagonistic needs. The Occupy and Indignados movements are crowds in this sense: that is why they are pilloried for having no demands. Nor, however, are they aggregates of individuals. The new crowds are multiple, particulate, composed of pre- and meta-individual needs and desires in states of constant dispute and emergence.

The challenge is thus to drive the logic of individualism to its far side; to turn the compulsory choice of consumerism into actual freedom. The research we are presently engaged on with the Nabi Art Centre of Seoul and Federation Square in Melbourne, which experiments with transnational cultural exchange through big-screen artworks that, in many instances, interact with personal handheld devices, is such a project. In one commissioned work, for example, SMS_Origin by the Australian artists Leon Cmielewski and Josephine Starrs, a phone number was displayed on the large screen along with the instruction "sms your family origins" (Figure 5.1). Participants texted their own and their parents places of birth to this number and linked curved vectors

FIGURE 5.1 Leon Cmielewski and Josephine Starrs, SMS_origins
Federation Square, Melbourne, large screens project, December 2010 to August 2009.

were added to a public map that updated in real-time as it received texts. The map was not static; texts are displayed in real-time, and while the map zooms into the countries of origin, animated vectors connect to the locations. As more people participated, the map grew to include accumulated vectors (http://spatialaesthetics.unimelb.edu.au/).

Works such as these address the transnational not merely as a crossing of borders but as a border condition, thus addressing the sociology of migration as a permanent state of existence, the nonidentity of the transnation. Whether such experiments will open the gates for a new temporary Autonomous Zone or whether we can, at best, hope to diminish the privatization of public space by intervening against the commercialization of both large- and small-screen space is still moot. One thing is certain: the results will be temporary and local, even if the local that emerges is effectively translocal. The lesson of the commercialization of public space is that the struggle to secure a new mode of public life will not be over, that it must be constantly renewed, and that for, that to happen, a recapturing of the virtuality of the crowd is a vital first step.

NOTES

1. Max Horkheimer and Theodor Adorno, *The Dialectic of Enlightenment*, trans. John Cumming (London: Allen Lane, 1973).
2. Peter Sloterdijk, *Terror from the Air*, trans. Amy Patton and Steve Corcoran (Los Angeles: Semiotext(e), 2009).
3. Robin Blackburn, "The Subprime Crisis," *New Left Review* 50 (March-April 2008): 63–106.
4. Gilles Deleuze and Félix Guattari, *L'Anti-Oedipe: Capitalisme et Schizophrénie I* (Paris: Editions de Minuit, 1972).
5. Bruno Latour, *We Have Never Been Modern*, trans. Catherine Porter (Cambridge, MA: Harvard University Press, 1993).
6. Gilles Deleuze, *Cinema 2: The Time-Image*, trans. Hugh Tomlinson and Barbara Habberjam (London: Athlone, 1989), 81.
7. Theodor W. Adorno, *Negative Dialectics*, trans. E. B. Ashton (London: Routledge, 1973), 8–9.
8. Hannah Arendt, *Responsibility and Judgment*, ed. Jerome Kohn (New York: Schocken, 2003).
9. Hannah Arendt, *Eichmann in Jerusalem: A Report on the Banality of Evil*, rev. ed. (Harmondsworth: Penguin, 1965).
10. Hakim Bey, *T.A.Z.: The Temporary Autonomous Zone, Ontological Anarchism, Poetic Terrorism* (New York: Autonomedia, 1991).
11. Karl Marx, *Grundrisse*, trans. Martin Nicolaus (London: Penguin/New Left Books, 1973): 690–711.
12. Paolo Virno, *A Grammar of the Multitude: For an Analysis of Contemporary Forms of Life*, trans. Isabella Bertoletti, James Cascaito, and Andrea Casson (Los Angeles: Semiotext(e), 2004).
13. G. A. Cohen, *Karl Marx's Theory of History: A Defence* (Princeton, NJ: Princeton University Press, 1978).
14. J. K. Galbraith, *The New Industrial State* (Harmondsworth: Penguin, 1967).
15. James R. Beniger, *The Control Revolution: Technological and Economic Origins of the Information Society* (Cambridge, MA: Harvard University Press, 1986), 265–266.

16. Daniel Pope, *The Making of Modern Advertising* (New York: Basic Books, 1983), 55.

17. AIMIA, *AIMIA Mobile Advertising Display Formats: Best Practices & Guidelines* (Sydney: AIMIA, August 2007), http://www.aimia.com.au/i-cms_file?page=3434/AIMIA_Mobile_Advertising_Aug07.pdf, 4.

18. Mark Dolliver, "Advertising on Mobile Phones Now the Norm," *Adweek*, February 5, 2009, http://www.adweek.com/aw/content_display/news/agency/e3i265790c0e524ea2ba72bae754877cf17.

19. Jürgen Habermas, *The Structural Transformation of the Public Sphere: An Enquiry into a Category of Bourgeois Society*, trans. Thomas Burger with the assistance of Frederick Lawrence (Cambridge, UK: Polity, 1989).

20. Alexander Galloway and Eugene Thacker, *The Exploit: A Theory of Networks* (Minneapolis: University of Minnesota Press, 2007), 41.

21. Cornelia Vismann, *Files: Law and Media Technology*, trans. Geoffrey Winthrop-Young (Stanford: Stanford University Press, 2008).

22. Kevin Robins, "Transnational Cultural Policy and European Cosmopolitanism," *Cultural Politics* 3, no. 2 (2007): 147–174.

23. Felix Stalder, "Our New Public Life: Free Cooperation, Biased Infrastructures and Authoritarian States," paper presented at Ars Electronica's "Goodbye Privacy" symposium, posted to nettime, September 10, 2007; http://www.nettime.org/Lists-Archives/nettime-l-0709/msg00010.html, accessed October 9, 2012.

24. Ernst Bloch, *The Principle of Hope*, 3 vols., trans. Neville Plaice, Stephen Plaice, and Paul Knight (Cambridge, MA: MIT Press, 1986).

25. Trebor Scholz and Geert Lovink, eds. *The Art of Free Cooperation* (New York: Autonomedia/Institute for Distributed Creativity, 2007).

26. Florian Schneider, "Collaboration: The Dark Side of the Multitude," in *Sarai Reader 2006: Turbulence* (New Delhi, Sarai, 2006), 572–576.

27. Ned Rossiter, *Organized Networks: Media Theory, Creative Labour, New Institutions* (Amsterdam: Institute of Network Cultures/NAi Publishers, 2006).

28. Richard Barbrook, "The Hi-Tech Gift Economy," *First Monday* 3, no. 12 (December 1998), http://www.firstmonday.org/htbin/cgiwrap/bin/ojs/index.php/fm/article/view/631/552.

29. Michel Foucault, *Society Must Be Defended: Lectures at the Collège de France 1975–76*, ed. Mauro Bertani and Alessandro Fontana, trans. David Macey (London: Penguin, 2003) Michel Foucault, *The Birth of Biopolitics: Lectures at the Collège de France 1978–1979*, ed. Michel Senellart, trans. Graham Burchell (Basingstoke: Palgrave Macmillan, 2004); Michel Foucault, *Security, Population, Territory: Lectures at the Collège de France 1977–1978*, ed. Michel Senellart, trans. Graham Burchell (Basingstoke: Palgrave Macmillan, 2007).

30. Theodor W. Adorno, *Lectures on Negative Dialectics: Fragments of a Lecture Course 1965/1966*, ed. Rolf Tiedemann, trans. Rodney Livingstone (Cambridge, UK: Polity Press, 2008).

31. Theodor W. Adorno, *Problems of Moral Philosophy*, trans. Edmund Jephcott (Cambridge, UK: Polity Press, 2000).

SELECT BIBLIOGRAPHY

Goggin, Gerard. *Global Mobile Media*. New York: Routledge, 2012.

Hjorth, Larissa, Jean Burgess, and Ingrid Richardson, eds. *Studying Mobile Media: Cultural Technologies, Mobile Communication, and the iPhone*. London: Routledge, 2012.

Hjorth, Larissa, and Gerard Goggin, eds. Special issue: "Mobile Communications in the City."
  Journal of Urban Technology 15 no. 3 (2008).
McQuire, Scott, Meredith Martin, and Sabine Niederer, eds. *Urban Screens Reader*.
  Amsterdam: Institute for Network Cultures, 2009.
McQuire, Scott. "Immersion, Reflexivity and Distraction: Spatial Strategies for Digital Cities."
  Journal of Visual Culture 6 no. 2 (2007): 146–155.
Papastergiadis, Nikos. "On the Road: Mobility and Mediation in Contemporary Art." In *An
  Atlas of Events*, edited by A. Ribeiro, 24–31. Paris: Fundacao Calouste Gulbenkian, 2007.
Struppek, Mirjam, and Pieter Boeder, eds. "Urban Screens: Discovering the Potential of
  Outdoor Screens for Urban Society." Special issue no. 4, *First Monday* (February 2006).
  http://www.uic.edu/htbin/cgiwrap/bin/ojs/index.php/fm/issue/view/217.
Strupek, Miriam. "The Social Potential of Urban Screens," *Visual Communications* 5 no. 2
  (2009):173–188.

CHAPTER 6

PUBLIC SCREENS AND URBAN LIFE

WILL STRAW

[A]ll the visible forms expressive of a period are to be grasped according to a double and paradoxical figure, that of the restless[*mouvementé*]
pertrification of things, of objects, of beings.

—Alain Mons[1]

Thus, the notion that mobile technologies are new is indeed shortsighted.
Throughout history, when a medium that was once understood as geographically fixed becomes mobile, a cultural shift accompanies this transformation. As writing moved from inscriptions on stone to marks on a
piece of paper or papyrus, the world changed.

—Jason Farman[2]

OF the many intriguing ideas in Sean Cubitt's essay "Large Screens, Third Screens,
Virtuality, and Innovation," one of the most productive is his claim that the difference
between large and small screens condenses a variety of relationships broadly symptomatic of the social status of media in the current moment. These differences in the scale of
screens, Cubitt suggests, express distinctions between spectacular and intimate forms
of address, low and high levels of interaction, states of subordination and immersion. In
this brief response, I pursue the relationship of large to small screens a little further in
relation to two strands within my own work on urban culture. One of these strands has
to do with the status of the urban night, as that temporal unit of city life in which public
screens came to find their significance. The other is the relationship of urban screens to
transportation systems, wherein such screens have served to both resist and underscore
characteristically urban forms of mobility.

The history of public screens, as Cubitt shows, is part of the history of advertising,
of the seductions of the commodity. I would add to this, in an obvious point, that such
screens are also part of a history of light and, in particular, of the illumination of cities.

Within this latter history, in a process long recognized, the seductive powers of the publically available commodity have enhanced the attraction of urban space itself. The transformation of urban space by light has provided new contexts in which the commodity might be "staged" (in the sense that one now speaks of houses being staged for potential buyers). This staging enhances the public visibility of commodities themselves (as they sit, highlighted, in shop windows or adorn the bodies of those moving through cities), but it also makes the city a space of competing attentions, as lighting and its absence differentiate the spaces of cities in increasingly complex ways. As commercial lighting came to reshape urban life, it produced a wide array of ethical/moral judgments about the extent to which the attentions it elicited were noble or debased, unifying or divisive.

Urban screens, large and small, now shine throughout the 24-hour cycle, but their meaning is inseparable from what historian Craig Koslovsky calls the process of *nocturnalization* in Western societies—"the ongoing expansion of the legitimate social and symbolic uses of the night."[3] Within this lengthy process of nocturnalization, gas-based and then electric light came to elicit different, even contradictory effects that anticipated the later differentiation between large and small screens. Spectacular clusters of light, in city centers, became the objects of collective attention. They served as displays of symbolic power with which the traditional bearers of power now had to compete or which the powerful labored to employ for their own purposes. Koslovsky traces a long series of transitions in which the aristocratic rulers of Europe first mobilized the lingering medieval and supernatural associations of night within their own, baroque displays of power. Subsequently, these rulers saw this power dissipate as an ascendant bourgeoisie made the illuminated urban night its own terrain.[4] By the late nineteenth century, the urban textuality of advertising and the lighting that nourished urban nocturnal sociability and commercial entertainment had displaced (or shrunk to relative inconsequence) displays of light once used in the flaunting of aristocratic power. It was not simply that one class had usurped another. As Karlheinz Stierle has argued, in the development of Western cities like Paris, the orchestrated display of unitary power became less important to the experience of urban grandeur than the richness of innumerable details.[5]

In this respect, the differences of scale that Cubitt observes with respect to present-day public screens perpetuate contrasts we may trace back at least as far as the nineteenth century. With the illumination of cities, the dispersion of light into more peripheral regions of urban life encouraged the differentiation of innumerable spaces of circumscribed illumination and shadowy obscurity. The well-lit centers of cities were spectacles to be viewed but so, too, were the countless "things seen" (*choses vues*), as historian Alain Montadon has noted.[6] For almost two centuries now, cities have been caught between the drive toward monumentality—in which collective or commercial power is condensed in a few spectacular sites and places—and the dispersion of a city's attractions across countless small objects and minor spaces.

In an age of digital screens, this dichotomy may be grasped as that between the large liquid crystal display (LCD) screens we associate with city centers (like Times Square) and the smaller "third" screens of smartphones, tablets, and other devices carried by thousands of individuals moving through cities. For Sean Cubitt, the high resolution of the large-scale installed public screen means low interaction, whereas the low reso-lution of the handheld device goes hand-in-hand with greater intimacy, interactivity, and possibilities for individual manipulation of content. I would add, to complicate this dichotomy just a little, an additional way of understanding these differences of scale. Large screens, attached to the surfaces of large buildings, more and more strain after the interpellative function of audiovisual media, a function represented (often in parodied or paranoid form) in science-fiction movies like *Robocop* or *Minority Report*. Here, the content of audiovisual screens employs the rhetorical features of direct address, reach-ing out to viewer/listeners in the moment of this address to elicit a specific response. (The persistent hucksterism of the advertisements seen in *Robocop*, the personalized entreaties to consumers in *Minority Report*, and the network talk shows shown live on Times Square screens all exemplify this.) The fleeting, blatant appeals to attention that mark this interpellative mode cannot help but make this content seem vulgar, "minor" on any scale of cultural value, as in the constant demands for live audience response in New Year's Eve broadcasts.

In contrast, tablets and smartphones lend themselves more easily to the viewing of self-contained television episodes, videoclips, or feature films than to the consuming of "live" audiovisual messages in which the user's attention is constantly demanded. The audiovisual discourse of the handheld device is rarely, at this historical moment, marked by direct address, which is relegated to the residual forms of the text message or audio phone call. The monumentality of the large, installed public screen is thus under-mined by its desperate claims on attention, which recall television in what have been seen, historically, as its lowest forms. The small "third" screen, conversely, is ennobled by its capacity to carry finished, professional content, curated and archived by its owner, in a relationship that recalls that of a book to its owner (an analogy developed, in other directions, by Sean Cubitt in the essay to which this is a response).

If city centers adorned with large display screens constitute one privileged terrain for the investigation of new *audiovisualities*, another is the public transit systems that have been intertwined with media structures in complicated ways for at least 150 years. In the 1920s, Siegfried Kracauer saw the newsstand, typically located near nodes in urban transportation systems, as emblematic of urban tolerance: "Out of the hubbub rise the newspaper kiosks, tiny temples in which the publications of the entire world get together for a rendezvous. Foes in real life, they lie here in printed form side by side; the harmony could not be greater."[7] The fragmentation of collective attention represented in the news-paper kiosk, with its multiple titles and peaceful existence of opposed political positions, is here taken as evidence of the civic/political pluralism that was a virtue of great cities. Alongside this diagnosis, other versions of social theory would come to see the same pluralism as evidence of the weakening of social bonds, as furthering the atomization of the modern individual. These competing accounts of the effect of media proliferation on collective life run through most discussions of contemporary handheld media.

In 1967, following the opening of Montreal's futuristic underground transportation system ("The métro"), designer François Dallegret imagined a futuristic playground, Palais Metro, at the main intersection of the system's two original subway lines.[8] Never realized, Palais Metro nevertheless expressed the dream that the multiple energies of technologically mediated movement might be absorbed and held within a multimedia spectacle that used public screens and multimedia installations to sustain a public gaze. Throughout their history, urban transport systems have felt the impulse to harvest collective attention, for profit or civic virtue, by employing media that could overcome the dispersion of attention that inevitably transpires within them. Transport systems struggle against the proliferation of portable media, from free commuter newspapers through handheld tablets, that were designed precisely to direct that attention away from the transportation environment and its own messaging systems. Present-day airplanes, which must address all passengers as the collective object of institutional care while allowing them to pursue their own itineraries of distracted entertainment, exemplify this struggle over attention even more explicitly.

In the ways in which they deflect attention from transportation systems, portable media devices—Cubitt's "third screens"—threaten the monumentality of these systems and the extent to which they may stand as evidence of civic purpose. When Montreal's métro was opened, in 1967, the challenge was that of finding cultural forms whose modernity was equal to that of the system itself. Displays of abstract art and signage employing up-to-date design principles ensured that the semiotic materials adorning the system were roughly contemporary with those of the transportation system itself. Ever since, as the subway cars and lines have decayed, contemporary media technologies have been employed to restore a modernity—a futuricity—which the underlying system itself no longer possesses. In aging public transport systems around the world, media have come to fulfill the classical function of the architectural facade, joining the system to a history of technological progress from which its own underlying infrastructure has become detached.

In the case of Montreal's métro, this has led to an endless series of experiments with installed media stretching back to the early 1990s. At that time, streams of informational text in digital form were installed in a strategy seemingly designed so that the fluid movement of words would disguise the increasingly bumpy motion of the métro cars themselves. It is as if, no longer able to offer its own technological monumentality as the source of its value, the Métro system was obliged to install media whose own fluid mobility might be taken as its own. More broadly, transportation-based media now seem perpetually torn between two strategies. One of these involves rushing to capture the "essential fragility of collective existence" in cities, as Alain Mons has described it.[9] Streams of text on tickertape-like displays or bits of poetry affixed to bus walls express prejudices about the fugitive character of urban attention and betray the effort to devise equivalences between textual and vehicular movement. The other strategy, intermittently deployed in Montreal over the last two decades, involves large-scale screens installed on waiting platforms and visible from virtually all possible directions. These screens perform at least two functions. In the first place, their own technological up-to-datedness now exceeds and obscures that of the subway system itself. Like so many of the buildings around Times Square, whose architectural age, scale, or novelty could never sustain a sense of that area's centrality, Montreal's métro stations require large-scale digital screens as proof of the system's capacity to look forward. At the same time, the content of these screens, which has ranged from works of contemporary art through news reports and advertisements, works to produce a temporary centering of public attention in the midst of personal itineraries that resist that centering.

All these sorts of screens work to diminish the prominence of sound. The large, fixed screens of Times Square, by assembling crowds of noisy spectators in front of them, make their own audio communication difficult and must find, in the display of busy, exuberant human movement, visual equivalents for noisy sociability. Small, handheld screens, on the other hand, are subject to legal or etiquette-based restrictions governing noise in public places. Detached from the image, sound has found its "publicness" most fully in semipublic spaces like automobiles. Here, automobiles join with audio media in assemblages that rarely interact with the realm of technologicallymediated visuality. In France, the decline of newspaper reading has been blamed in part on the movement of middle-class commuters out of public transportation systems and into their own private cars, where they no longer read newspapers but listen to radio (and, increasingly, to their own archives of music).[10] In Mexico City, as Rosalind Winocur has shown in intriguing detail, new circuits of communication link the automobile driver, caught in traffic, to talk radio programs whose content consists of cellphone calls in which these drivers comment on the state of traffic and on social-political issues more generally.[11]

Sean Cubitt usefully sets the electronic screen within a history of public media that includes the paperback (carried on transportation systems) and the poster. Of the many ways in which the histories of print culture and electronic display have been interwoven, one of the most intriguing involves shifting relationships between two axes:one that separates the flat from the perpendicular, another that divides the tall from the wide. As David Henkin suggests, invoking Walter Benjamin, forms of public textuality in nineteenth-century New York, like the signs that came to adorn the sides of buildings, instituted a "dictatorship of the perpendicular" (Henkin 1998:63). The immobile, vertically oriented poster or advertisement struggled for attention (and generally won) against multiple, scattered forms of print culture (like the newspaper or magazine) designed to be laid flat. By the twentieth century, the contrast between perpendicular, immobile media and portable, flat forms of textuality would become confused. As the newspaper front page, originally organized around parallel "tombstone" columns, came to be criss-crossed by modern, banner headlines (which, reaching across the page with larger typefaces, sought graphic means for expressing loudness), it was conceived more and more to be held upright on public transportation systems and elsewhere.

In the last quarter of the twentieth century, we might have set the conventional, horizontally rectangular advertising billboard against the tall, vertical screens of Times Square or Piccadilly Circus. This verticality followed the up-and-down movement of buildings themselves, producing a popular sense of inner-city commercial centers as canyon-like. More recently, these spaces have lost some of their "verticality" as newly installed public screens mimic the horizontal spread of flat-screen television sets. The screens of Times Square have assumed dimensions that enable them to send back, to their street-level viewers, broad images of the crowds assembled to watch them.

At the same time, in recent years, we have been able to distinguish between handheld devices like the cellphone or e-reader, whose vertical orientation carries over the familiar dimensions of older printculture forms (the written letter in the case of the cellphone screen, the book in the case of the e-reader), and other portable technologies, like the tablet, driven to horizontality by the dominance of audiovisual forms like movies or television programs. If the tablet's horizontality is likely to dominate the handheld and publically installed screens of the future, we might ask about its effects on the experience and perception of public space. The vertical screens of mid-twentieth-century Times Square underscored the monumental depth of that place, reinforcing a well-entrenched association between physical height and symbolic centrality in urban structures. Horizontally oriented screens, which deflect attention across series of such screens, express the sense that a city's richness lies in the contiguity of its innumerable "things seen" rather than in a single, monumental object of collective attention.

NOTES

1. Alain Mons, *La traversée du visible: Images et lieux du contemporain* (Paris: Editions de la passion 2002), 69.
2. Jason Farman, *Mobile Interface Theory: Embodied Space and Locative Media* (New York: Routledge, 2012), 2.
3. Craig Koslovsky, *Evening's Empire: A History of the Night in Early Modern Europe*. (Cambridge: Cambridge University Press, 2011), 1.
4. Ibid., 92.
5. Karlheinz Stierle, Jean Starobinski, and Marianne Rocher-Jacquin, *La capitale des signes: Paris et son discours* (Paris: Ed. de la Maison des sciences de l'homme, 2002), 47.
6. Alain Montandon, *Promenades nocturnes* (Paris: L'Harmattan, 2009), 7.
7. Siegfried Kracauer, "Analysis of a City Map," in *The Mass Ornament: Weimar Essays*, ed. Thomas Y. Levin (Cambridge, MA: Harvard University Press, 1995 [1926]), 43.
8. For images of this never-realized project, see Palais Metro, http://arteria.ca/realisation/palais-metro/.
9. Alain Mons, "La ville ou l'espace de l'errance Cinéma," in *L'urbain et ses imaginaires*, ed. Patrick Beaudry and Thierry Paquot (Aquitaine, France: Maison des sciences de l'homme d'Aquitaine, 2003), 114.
10. "Les tendances et les perspectives." in Les Comptes du Groupe, *Le Monde* (Paris 2004), 2–3.
11. Rosalía Winocur, "Media and Participative Strategies," *Television & New Media* 4, no. 1 (2003).

SELECT BIBLIOGRAPHY

Farman, Jason. *Mobile Interface Theory: Embodied Space and Locative Media.* New York: Routledge, 2012.
Henkin, David. *City Reading: Written Words and Public Spaces in Antebellum New York.* New York: Columbia University Press, 1998.

Koslovsky, Craig. *Evening's Empire: A History of the Night in Early Modern Europe*. Cambridge: Cambridge University Press, 2011.

Kracauer, Siegfried. "Analysis of a City Map." Translated by Thomas Y. Levin. In *The Mass Ornament: Weimar Essays*, edited by Thomas Y. Levin. 41–44. Cambridge, MA.: Harvard University Press, 1995 [1926].

Monde, Le. "Les Comptes Du Group." 16. Paris, 2004.

Mons, Alain. *La Traversée Du Visible: Images Et Lieux Du Contemporain*. Paris: Editions de la passion, 2002.

——. "La Ville Ou L'espace De L'errance Cinéma." In *L'urbain Et Ses Imaginaires*, edited by Patrick Beaudry and Thierry Paquot, 113–121. Aquitaine, France: Maison des sciences de l'homme d'Aquitaine, 2003.

Montandon, Alain. *Promenades Nocturnes*. Paris: L'Harmattan, 2009.

Stierle, Karlheinz, Jean Starobinski, and Marianne Rocher-Jacquin. *La Capitale Des Signes: Paris Et Son Discours*. Paris: Ed. de la Maison des sciences de l'homme, 2002.

Winocur, Rosalia. *Ciudadanos Mediáticos. La Construcciómn De Lo Público En La Radio*. Barcelona: Gedisa, 2002.

Winocur, Rosalía. "Media and Participative Strategies." *Television & New Media* 4, no. 1 (February 1, 2003): 25–42.

PART III

GLITCHES, NOISE, AND INTERRUPTION: MATERIALITY AND DIGITAL MEDIA

CHAPTER 7

A NOISY BRUSH WITH THE INFINITE

Noise in Enfolding-Unfolding Aesthetics

LAURA U. MARKS

THIS essay considers "noise" in light of a model that I call *enfolding-unfolding aesthetics*, a set of relationships among image, information, and infinite that explains how certain things arrive to our perception (image) from the universe (infinite) whereas others do not. According to this model, the infinite is inaccessible to perception and appears as noise: our perception selectively unfolds some aspect of it. However, a sort of quantitative filter often predetermines what we perceive: what we end up perceiving is the product of information.

ENFOLDING-UNFOLDING AESTHETICS

We may consider the infinite to be constituted of innumerable folds, like the ripples on the sea: this is Leibniz's conception of matter, as Gilles Deleuze explains it.[1] When we perceive something, we unfold some small part of the infinite. Every perception is an unfolding. To figure out where an image comes from, we need to find out how it arose from the infinite; and, often, we need to find out how it arose from information, too, information that itself arose from the infinite.

So, the question is, how can we create our own ways of making contact with the infinite without drowning in noise? And, how can we appreciate information as itself an unfolding from the infinite?

To begin, please imagine the realm of perceptible things that populates your world at any given moment to be a vast, variegated surface, containing everything: holiday snapshots, action movies, ultrasound pictures, everything. This field contains sounds and smells and other perceptibles, as well as visual images; I am using the term *image* to refer to all the things we can perceive with our senses. Imagine that this field surrounds you like a bubble, translucent, and you are looking (listening, smelling) out through it.

You look (listen, smell) through the field of images to their sources, distant in time and space: the holiday afternoon, the movie set, the inside of your own body. You realize, perhaps with a queasy feeling, that the field of sources is unimaginably more vast than the field of images that arose from it. It is the whole universe, the infinite—at this given moment—dense with impacted images, a tiny, tiny fraction of which you perceive. What I've just summarized is a sort of cartoon version of Henri Bergson's model of the universe.[2]

But some of the images do not come to you directly from the source. They seem to get twisted or caught on the way "in" to your perception. This is because they reflect not a perceptible experience but a calculation, a procedure. For example, the camera that took the snapshot was digital, and so the visible scene at the source has been assigned pixel values so that it can be expressed as a snapshot. The action movie was shot against a blue screen and keyed in to a digital background; its star was chosen on the basis of a calculation of her audience appeal. The ultrasound picture of the inside of your body is a translation of sound waves into visual images. These calculations constitute an intervening plane between the infinite and the images that convey it to us. I will call that plane *information*. Here is a three-layer diagram of the relations among Image, Information, and the Infinite at a given point in time (Figure 7.1).[3]

Aesthetics, in its simplest guise, is simply an account of how we engage with the perceptible world. This is a phenomenological aesthetics, not a system for judging what is beautiful: thus, what I am proposing is a sort of minor tradition linking the pre-Kantian eighteenth-century aesthetics of Alexander Baumgarten with Maurice Merleau-Ponty's phenomenology of perception. Baumgarten wrote in 1750 that aesthetics is a *scientia cognitionis sensitivae*, "science of sensuous cognition."[4] Enfolding-unfolding aesthetics, which I place within this minor tradition, deals with the coming and going of perceptibles: a kind of recycling or conservation of mass. It proposes that the images (in any sense modality) that we perceive are selectively unfolded from the infinite and that they are often shaped by information, which is itself a selective unfolding from the infinite.

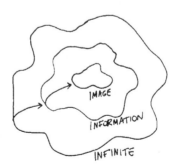

FIGURE 7.1

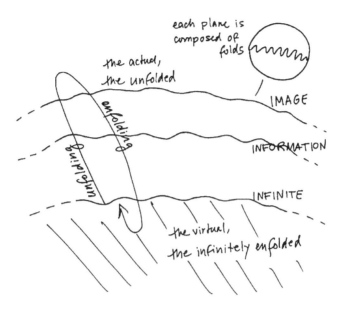

FIGURE 7.2

So, what we perceive (or don't perceive) is the result of a double process of unfolding (Figure 7.2).

I developed enfolding-unfolding aesthetics from Deleuze's investigation, found in his cinema books, into how certain images arise to us by being selected from the infinite. Deleuze, following Bergson, calls it the universe of images. I adopted the term "infinite" instead of "universe of images" in recognition of the roots of these concepts in religious philosophy, particularly the medieval Islamic philosophy that so deeply influenced the beginnings of modern European thought: infinity was considered an attribute of the divine. However, "infinite" as I use it here does not refer to a transcendent and all-powerful deity but to an immanent infinite.[5]

There do exist plenty of images that unfold more or less directly from the infinite: they include our own perceptions, as well as things like paintings, photographs, and audio recordings.[6] Something that we perceive corresponds directly to something "out there." But most perceptibles have been mediated before we ever perceive them. So, my intervention in Deleuze's theory of signs is to insert another image plane between images and the infinite, namely information: a filter that occurs before images can arise. This information layer is most evident in digital and other quantified media, where there is a layer of code underlying the perceptibles we see, hear, and touch—like the holiday snapshot I mentioned earlier. But the information layer is also evident in anything industrially produced, anything whose physical being is the result of quantified research.

Some readers may remark that enfolding-unfolding aesthetics seems to have a lot of points in common with Heidegger's philosophy. But it diverges significantly. First, Heidegger's concept of *techne* might seem similar to my term *information*, given that *techne* describes how human labor gives form to the formless in a process of selection. However, whereas Heidegger privileges the act of selection, enfolding-unfolding aesthetics (in the less anthropocentric spirit of Merleau-Ponty and Deleuze) privileges the infinite that exists prior to human selection from it. Second, enfolding-unfolding aesthetics inquires into the imperceptible sources of the perceptible, and thus it might seem to be "disclosing," in Heidegger's sense that "If there occurs in the [art]work a disclosure of a particular being, disclosing what it is and how it is, then there is here an occurring, a happening of truth in the work." However, in enfolding-unfolding aesthetics, truth is not as important as variety: I am interested in how each thing has a singular origin *and* is made singular in its use. Heidegger's emphasis on "withdrawal" comes closest to the intentions of enfolding-enfolding aesthetics. I am interested in how works of art can hint at aspects of the infinite that are enfolded in information and image; Heidegger values the "uselessness" of works of art, in that they perceive the undisclosable.[7]

THE INFINITE AND NOISE

What is the infinite? Well, *infinite* is a negative term, the not-finite, and most definitions of it are negative: limitless, boundless, uncountable, inconceivable. We cannot conceive of the infinite except as the ground from which we distinguish certain figures—or, the noise from which we receive certain signals. So, I suggest that, from our particular, interested points of view, the infinite appears as noise. We can perceive noise, but we usually filter it out.

Michel Serres points out that noise shares an etymology with *nausea* and *nautical* and that gives a sense to the seasick feeling I (and you might) have when beginning to sense the infinite beyond the bounds of perception. Noise is the sea on which our experience bobs: wave after wave of events and perceptions arise from it and fall back into it ceaselessly. "The silence of the sea is mere appearance. Background noise may well be the ground of our being. It may be that our being is not at rest, it may be that it is not in motion, it may be that our being is disturbed.... As soon as a phenomenon appears, it leaves the noise; as soon as a form looms up or pokes through, it reveals itself by veiling noise."[8] Noise sounds a lot like the infinite: it cannot be detected in itself, but everything we perceive arises from it.

Sha Xin-wei, reflecting on Serres, writes that what mathematicians call randomness signifies the limits of our capacity to recognize. "*Random* is another name for our ignorance, our inadequate senses, and, in the computational setting, the sparseness of our reach. *Noise*, for me, is not just the random in space, or time, or shape, but the hovering of patterned material (matter, energy, symbol, affective field) at the limit of measurement, and therefore observation."[9]

Noise, Sha suggests, is simply the stuff whose patterns we can't recognize. To be very broad-minded, we can imagine that everything in the universe is significant for *some* entity or other. But, from a human perspective, it is hard to imagine a perfect perception to which everything is significant and noise no longer exists. Seth Kim-Cohen recounts the story of Rainer Maria Rilke encountering a skull and becoming entranced with the groove in its cranium, a groove that had no visible meaning to the poet but that, he imagined, might be played with a gramophone needle and produce an unearthly music. Rilke's fantasy appealed to Friedrich Kittler because it indicated that there is more meaning in nature than we can fathom. This meaning, Kittler suggested, can now be assessed thanks to "algorithmically formalized data streams" that could translate the visual information into sound, bypassing any need for an author.[10] Kim-Cohen argues forcefully with Kittler's romanticism: "This is a kind of antimetaphysics, a negative theology: positing a universality of data that precedes any communicative intent, any transmitter, any receiver. This would be the all-knowing, the all-seeing, omnipotent itself. But messages ... are context-dependent. Contextless data is gobbledygook."[11] The cranial music would be pure noise.

In a mystical view, the person who recognizes patterns everywhere, who can hear the music of the cranial groove, would be a God-realized individual. Psychologically, this would be a mad person; our ability to choose what to filter is what gives us agency (schizophrenics often detect patterns and relationships that truly exist but that other people's brains block out). Bergson pointed this out when he explained that normal perception has the survival function of distinguishing immediate needs; in a way, it is a dangerous luxury to perceive beyond our needs.[12]

As Elizabeth Grosz writes, philosophers who are sympathetic to matter, such as Bergson, Henry James, and Deleuze, argue that we "carve out" things in experience: eventually, we have to make some decisions. Grosz points out that the etymology of "de-cision" means to cut out. We have to choose some things as our objects, unfold them from the virtual, hoist them into our actuality.

> The teeming flux of the real ... must be symbolized, reduced, to states, things, and numeration in order to facilitate practical action. This is not an error that we commit, a fault to be unlearned, but a condition of our continuing survival in the world. We could not function within this teeming multiplicity without some ability to skeletalize it, to diagram or simplify it. Yet this reduction and division occur only at a cost, which is the failure or inability of our scientific, representational, and linguistic systems to acknowledge the in-between of things, the plural interconnections that cannot be utilized or contained within and by things but that [make] them possible.[13]

To be radically aware of the world in its infinite multiplicity constitutes the greatest goal of some philosophy (and mysticism). Yet, at the same time, as Grosz points out, trying to be aware of infinity—especially an infinity that is not reducible to a One but consists of innumerable connections—can paralyze and destroy the person making the effort. (This is why trying to live ecologically is so painful and difficult, for the in-between status of things asserts itself every time we try to decide, for example, whether something is trash or food.)

Grosz does not raise, in this particular essay, the question of who is served by those diagramming functions, referring to a collective "we": "*our* scientific, representational, and linguistic systems." But I fear that the most important perceptual decisions are being taken, by market-driven powers, for the rest of us. "We" are not able to come into our own contact with the infinite and its innumerable connections when Google is mapping it for us, when cameras are programmed on the basis of statistics of what consumers probably want to look at, when grocery store potatoes are all the same size and shape, and in other cases (of which I will rant more later) where the teeming infinity of the world is quantified and commodified before it reaches our perception. I want us to be able to cut things out for ourselves, to have our own brushes with the infinite. I admit that the initial impulse that gave rise to my elaboration of enfolding-unfolding aesthetics was anger, anger at a world that comes to us pre-perceived.[14]

The infinite contains everything, by definition. So, information and image are part of the infinite. They arise from it, as waves from the sea, as signal from noise; and they return to it, returning to an undifferentiated state, becoming noise again. Things exist as information or as image for relatively brief times before they dissolve back into the universe. In Figure 2, you can picture this cycling around.

INFORMATION AND NOISE

What does the admittedly loose term "information" mean in the model I am proposing? First, it corresponds to a concept that arose in the first half of the twentieth century in the fields of statistics and electronic communication: information is something that is "abstract yet measurable, and that it is an aspect or byproduct of an event or process."[15] Ted Byfield reports that this new conception of information first occurred in a 1925 article by geneticist and statistician R. A. Fisher, "Theory of Statistical Estimation." Three years later, Ralph V. L. Hartley synthesized Fisher's findings with those of AT&T and Bell Laboratories researcher Harry Nyquist in his article "Transmission of Information," published in *Bell System Technical Journal*. Hartley proposed that information is a quantity that can be transmitted but is free of "psychological considerations"; that is, Byfield says, free of meaning.

After the First World War, Claude Shannon, again at Bell Labs, proposed that information is a quantifiable entity for determining the transmission capacity of a channel.[16] "Noise" consists of those artifacts that interfere in the transmission of an intended message. Shannon's conception of information as a ratio between signal and noise would found modern information theory.

Now, although Shannon disparaged efforts to adapt his theory to other fields, this is what I am doing in enfolding-unfolding aesthetics. If the infinite is not perceivable in itself—if the infinite is noise—then information is often what makes a selection from the infinite so that it can be perceived. In information theory, those aspects of the infinite that do not interest us—that is, almost all of it—are "noise." Information is what has been selected from the infinite as valuable and unfolded. The rest (so, almost everything) remains enfolded. In turn, what we finally perceive, in many cases, is unfolded from information. Information, then, is *an unfolding from the infinite that precedes our perception.*

Hartley and Shannon both emphasized that information has no meaning.[17] Information organizes noise into something that is potentially useful, but not yet meaningful: it becomes the basis for interpretations of meaning. Nevertheless, it seems clear that cultural ideas of what is important shape what is considered to be useful information: they shape the way information is extracted from the infinite. Since what is important is usually money, information is usually selected for its saleable worth. The image that is then generated from this information may appear visible, or audible, or even material, but it is really an expression of information—and often specifically of the profit motive. What we finally perceive with our senses, in many cases, is unfolded from information. At Starbucks, for example: your delicious coffee, the appealing music, and the color and feel of the comfy chairs are all material extrusions of investment decisions. Your toothbrush? A tactile, visible image of ergonomic and market research. Sometimes it seems as if our universe consists entirely of the smooth, designed, commodified surfaces of information-based media. This is especially so for people who live in urban and suburban environments in the postindustrial world. It seems we are trapped in a world not of our invention. This is what Guy Debord testified in *Society of the Spectacle* and what Baudrillard was railing about in *Simulations.* Information penetrates profoundly into perceptible surfaces, and it is usually serving the needs of capital.

However, remember, *pace* Baudrillard, that the information level is not the source of images. There is something else out there. Information is a filter between the image and the infinite, the infinite being the world in which thousands of programmers are writing code, thousands of workers are harvesting coffee, millions of people are brushing their teeth, and more, infinitely more. When some of that infinite stuff slips out, it is considered noise—in a given system. Noise, then, is the trace of the universe that reaches around information to our perception. *Noise is an index of the infinite.*

Obviously, what counts as noise depends on what you believe. The idea that communication should be maximally clear is an ideological notion. Often, art privileges the disruption of the "signal" or the difficulty of extracting signal from "noise." This could even be the definition of art in the Information Age.

Meanwhile, another definition of information comes into play. Information or *in-formation* implies the imposition of form from outside, as in the medieval scholastic Latin definition, "the giving of a form or character to something" (OED), as clay is shaped into bricks by a mold. This concept dates to Aristotle's theory of form, in which matter is potentiality, form is actuality:[18] matter is seen as passive, and form acts on matter. Aristotle's theory assumes that matter lacks innate properties and can be shaped in any way. Thus, "information" implies that the infinite is unformed matter that needs to be shaped in order to be used; furthermore, the same in-formation will always give rise to the same form, as a mold shapes a brick.

A different paradigm asserts that forms arise not through imposition on passive matter but according to a process of individuation, which relates an entity's potential to the changing system of which the entity is part. Gilbert Simondon proposes this distinction between information and individuation in "The Genesis of the Individual," and, in it, we can hear the echo of Bergson's *Creative Evolution*. The results of individuation can never be predicted. Simondon wrote, "We must begin with individuation, with the being grasped at its center and in relation to its spatiality and its becoming, and not by a realized [*substantialisé*] *individual* faced with a *world* that is external to it."[19] No two things individuate in the same way because the universe is always changing.

According to this paradigm, we might think that information, in privileging what can be usefully quantified, chokes off certain potentials. However, Simondon points out that information, too, is always becoming: information arises as a resolution to tensions in a given metastable (i.e., out of step with itself) system. Information signals that something (something considered important in the given system) is changing, as a stock market graph signals changes in prices or a smoke detector signals a potentially dangerous level of particulates. "One could say that the information always exists in the present, that it is always contemporary, because it yields the meaning according to which a system is individuated."[20] If your smoke detector always goes off when you are carrying on as normal in the kitchen, and so you habitually disconnect the smoke detector's fuse when you cook (perturbing the smoke-detection system), then the smoke detector's alarm signal has become noise: the new information consists in the frequency with which you disconnect it. That's the metastability in the system that relates your cooking and the smoke detector's alertness.

Vilém Flusser's playful proposal for a quantitative art theory accommodates the shifting ratio of signal to noise to the second law of thermodynamics. Things start out as noisy and settle into being easily perceptible. Beauty is that which has a somewhat low signal-to-noise ratio: it can be comprehended but requires salutary mental effort. Ugliness is pure noise; prettiness has a higher signal-to-noise ratio; kitsch, writes Flusser, is pure signal.[21] We may note that cultural norms often favor a high signal-to-noise ratio—but not always! Complexity, mystery, "difference" (as in the casual comment, "It's different") are all indicators of relatively low signal-to-noise ratio. We might even consider historical aesthetic periods, like the Baroque or the complexity-loving later 'Abbasid period, to favor low signal-to-noise ratios.[22]

Some creative strategies arise from these conceptions of information. One is to privilege noise as our direct connection to the infinite. Another is to question the way certain information is selected from the infinite and to choose to unfold other things instead. And yet another is to consider information not as a fixed grid but as itself historical and mutable, unfolding and enfolding, something that arises from perturbations in systems. Artists, insofar as they are less bound to convention, are especially good at making and identifying alternative unfoldings.

VIRTUE OF NOISE

As Flusser's criterion suggests, the information-generated image often intends to be aesthetically pleasing. For us, in the postindustrial world, much of what surrounds us is designed, styled, beautified: from our toothbrushes to our transit system, to the high-quality advertising images all around us, to the packaged food we buy, to our own faces and bodies. (Sound and smell design are a little less totalizing, but mood-enhancing music and "nice" smells also thicken our sensory environment, creating the cloying air of the commodity.) It seems that things need to keep on advertising themselves to us even once we've bought them—"Read me! I am nutritious!" "Feel me! I am ergonomic!"

So, ironically, art, which once had the function of providing a little island of beauty in an ugly world, now takes on the opposite job: a little island of ugliness in an overly aestheticized world. (Ugliness here means a low signal-to-noise ratio, in Flusser's conception.) "Hence," Wolfgang Welsch writes, "a task for contemporary art is *not* to introduce more beauty into the already overly beautified environment but to stop the aestheticization machinery by creating aesthetic deserts and fallow lands in the midst of this hyperaesthetic."[23] According to this, art's job is now to make ugliness: to unfold the infinite in a noisier, less "meaningful" way. Noise music privileges the noise that overwhelms potentially meaningful signals.

In Marxist aesthetics, noise is proof of materiality. So, in a heavily commodified world, seeking out noise has long been a strategy of resistance. Commodities' power arises from the myth that the world is not material, and, of course, the Marxist strategy is to show that it is. This is what Walter Benjamin did when he looked for signs of decay in the shiny new shopping arcades. We can do the same thing in the seamless spaces of fancy malls, airports, and online environments like Facebook: seek out deterioration, glitches, any kind of perforation in the smooth surface. Where the surface breaks down, you see the fact of materiality that commodification must always conceal, and it appears as meaninglessness, noise. This search for materiality is a sign of resistance in commodity culture. It has been for more than a century. In fact, the materiality of glitch seems to have become a commodity itself.[24]

I find that there is something defeatist in Marxist aesthetics' passion for the fragment, the decayed, the merely material. It needs to advocate destruction rather than creation. What I am suggesting with enfolding-unfolding aesthetics is more than chipping away at the commodity surface to show the materiality underneath. In fact it's 1.5 times more, for Marxist aesthetics is dualist, and enfolding-unfolding aesthetics is triadic.[25] I'm suggesting we think of that commodified skin between the universe and us not as a bad thing to be destroyed, but as a particular *manner of unfolding*. Enfolding-unfolding aesthetics suggests we can unfold things in other ways. That is what art can do.

I mentioned ugly art, noise music. The virtue of ugly or *awkward* art is that it demonstrates a different kind of unfolding. Rather than create a smooth surface of seamless information, as commodity culture does, ugly things draw attention to what they are unfolding. Things usually ignored, things forgotten, unique yet unimportant events—oddities, not commodities.

Some artworks make it quite clear how the image triangulates between information and the infinite. *Brilliant Noise* (2006), a video by Ruth Jarman and Joe Gerhardt (aka Semiconductor), allows us to look at the sun—and to hear it—in images of the gridded fiery star that emit sonic blasts of brightness and blurts of static and of solar flares that seem to make their own music (Figure 7.3). Looking at and listening to the image helps us understand the selective procedures that were carried out at the level of information in order to extract something from the infinite. It gives us a sense of the choices involved in unfolding information from the infinite and unfolding image from information. Its beauty lies in the dramatic struggle between signal and noise, information and infinite.

Jarman and Gerhardt worked with solar observatories around the world whose staff allowed them to use their images, many apparently quite old. Without knowing more about the technology than what we can divine from watching the video, it is evident that it's very difficult to make images of the sun's surface and that every observatory does it in a different way. They use different kinds of information filters to extract image from the infinite. These filters are just like sunglasses, quantifying and regularizing the perceptible world so that people can actually see it. Jarman and Gerhardt created the sound for *Brilliant Noise* by translating image into sound. They used software to quantify the light levels in each video frame and assign sounds to each light level, so that, in time, the changes in light translate to changes in sound. The creative decisions lie in what kinds of sounds to assign. So, it looks like the sun is singing, and the noise is singing too.

The noise in these images appears both as analog electronic interference and as digital glitches. This reminds us that noise is not only the noninformative images that escape past a filter, but also it is created by the filter itself. Little white dots indicate moments when no signal could be detected, like the "snow" that used to fall on our analog electronic television screens. (Allow me a moment to mourn the demise of TV snow, for it constituted our contact with the analog ether.) I find *Brilliant Noise* surprisingly moving because it values *all* of information, noise, image, and the infinite. It gives us a sense of the choices involved in unfolding information from the infinite and unfolding image

FIGURE 7.3 Still from *Brilliant Noise* (2006) by Semiconductor.

from information. Its beauty lies in the dramatic struggle between signal and noise, information and infinite.

THE NOISY POTATO

In Agnès Varda's *The Gleaners and I* (2000), the filmmaker lives with modern gleaners, people who scrape a living from the leftovers of commercial agriculture. Well-shaped, nicely sized potatoes translate effortlessly into capital. They are harvested, a kilogram of potatoes is translated into a price, and they are sold. Meanwhile, perfectly edible potatoes that are too small, too big, or too knobby do not count as potatoes to the harvester: they are noise, according to the information filter that determines the sale value of a potato. The gleaners collect these noise-potatoes for food in activities that remain under the radar of capital. Varda's potato gleaning scene shows how lots of life-sustaining activity can take place in realms untouched by information.

Varda's account of the lives of gleaners shows us how people can live their entire lives in a way untouched by the codifying practices of Information. This is the way of life of the very poor, who can't afford new (newly encoded) things: unrecognized food, discarded furniture and clothes, unofficial shelters. It is also a way of life that has become attractive to people who want to be self-sufficient and unmonitored. They pay attention to those things that either have never been taken up as information—the knobby potatoes of life—or have fallen back into the Infinite in the ongoing cycle of unfolding and enfolding. We can say that the activity of gleaners and repurposers around the world perturbs the system, constituting a new kind of information, a new indicator that the information filter of the market economy is unable to detect.

WHAT TO UNFOLD

Again, it appears to me that because our postindustrial environment, this aggressive commodity landscape, seems so against us, artists' first impulse is simply to make holes in the smooth info-generated surface, to make some noise. Given that the universe is infinite, and we have so very little contact with it, it seems like a great thing to strip away the filters and just let all the noise rush in.

But, eventually, it is necessary to make a selection. By welcoming noise and refusing to distinguish useable signals, we might feel we are embracing the infinite. But being immersed in undifferentiated noise is schizophrenia. Like the moths of which the surrealist Roger Caillois wrote, whose wings are disguised to look like tree bark so they become indistinguishable from their environment (and yet, Caillois asserted, this camouflage does not protect them), losing one's identity in this way is a kind of suicide.[26] So I suggest another strategy for art to make contact with the infinite, namely, to unfold it differently.

Information can be considered whatever *saves us time* by preempting our encounter with the infinite. Information pre-knows the infinite for us. Information is the realm of the category, the cliché, and the commodity. So, in trying to bypass Information and make our own selections from the infinite, we need to decide what, of all that infinite stuff, to unfold: what noise to distinguish as a signal. Here, I am inspired again by Bergson. In *Creative Evolution,* he suggests that we should try not to categorize the things we perceive, but instead to respond to something that our intellect cannot comprehend, something radically new, unthought. Something that will make us grow.[27] *Brilliant Noise* shows one way that might be done, by first being blinded and deafened by the sun and then choosing to unfold its noisy, infinite surface into beautiful pictures and sounds. *The Gleaners and I* shows how one can make a whole life by passing under a capital-driven information filter, clinging close to the infinite and unfolding parts of it differently.

So we might try to remain in the overwhelming presence of the infinite for a while. But do not stay there forever! Let that contact make you grow in some small way, and select some thing, some new unfolding from the infinite.

NOTES

1. Gilles Deleuze, *The Fold: Leibniz and the Baroque,* trans. Tom Conley (Minneapolis: Minnesota University Press, 1993), 6.
2. See Henri Bergson, *Matter and Memory,* trans. N. M. Paul and W. S. Palmer (New York: Zone, 1991).
3. Some of this introductory material has been published in Laura U. Marks, "Unfolding from the Real: Mediation as Connective Tissue," *Passagens* (Universidade Federal de Rio de Janeiro): 6 (2011) and "Enfolding-Unfolding Aesthetics: The Unthought at the Heart of Wood," in *Technology and Desire,* ed. Rania Gaafar (Karlsruhe: ZKM, 2013).
4. Wolfgang Welsch, "Aesthetics Beyond Aesthetics," in *Rediscovering Aesthetics: Transdisciplinary Voices from Art History, Philosophy, and Art Practice,* ed. Francis Halsall, Julia Jansen, and Tony O'Connor (Palo Alto, CA: Stanford University Press, 2009), 178. The priority to which Baumgarten gave sense experience was eclipsed by Kant's "transcendental study of the objective conditions of judgments concerning the beautiful." See Nicholas Davey, "Baumgarten, Alexander G [ottlieb] (1714–1762)," in *A Companion to Aesthetics,* ed. Stephen Davies et al. (Malden, MA: Wiley-Blackwell, 2009), 162–163.
5. Islamic philosophy, as well as the Greek philosophy that often informed it, such as neo-Platonism, completely underwrites almost all European philosophy, itself first developed by Christian Scholastics, which proposes central concepts of One, Being, and Infinite. The notion that contemporary philosophy, which is usually considered secular, has a religious origin may alarm the reader. But it is only quite recently that some philosophers, such as Bergson, Nietzsche, and Peirce, stripped fundamental philosophical concepts of their divine trappings in order to propose a truly nondualist philosophy, and it was not an easy job. In fact, I would contend that most contemporary philosophy in the continental tradition remains completely indebted to religious transcendentalism.

6. Although the latter, insofar as they are conventional images, are relayed through information. I discuss this kind of image in "Experience–Information–Image: A Historiography of Unfolding: Arab Cinema As Example," *Cultural Studies Review* 16, no.1 (March 2007), special issue on "Rethinking the Past": 85-98; and "Enfolding and Unfolding: An Aesthetics for the Information Age," an interactive essay produced in collaboration with designer Raegan Kelly, in *Vectors: Journal of Culture and Technology in a Dynamic Vernacular* 1, no. 3 (2006), http://vectors.usc.edu/projects/index.php?project=72.

7. See Martin Heidegger, "The Origin of the Work of Art," trans. Albert Hofstadter, in *Philosophers on Art from Kant to the Postmodernists*, ed. Christopher Kul-Want (New York: Columbia University Press, 2010), 139–148.

8. Michel Serres, *Genesis*, trans. Geneviève James and James Nielson (Ann Arbor: University of Michigan Press, 1995), 12–13.

9. Sha Xin-wei, *Poesis and Enchantment in Topological Matter* (unpublished book manuscript, 2011).

10. Friedrich Kittler, *Gramophone, Film, Typewriter*, trans. Geoffrey Winthrop-Young and Michael Wutz (Palo Alto, CA: Stanford University Press, 1999), 43–44.

11. Seth Kim-Cohen, *In the Blink of an Ear: Toward a Non-Cochlear Sonic Art* (New York: Continuum, 2009), 100.

12. Bergson, *Matter and Memory*.

13. Elizabeth Grosz, "The Thing," in *Time Travels: Feminism, Nature, Power* (Durham, NC: Duke University Press, 2005), 131.

14. The angry essay that inaugurated enfolding-unfolding aesthetics is Laura U. Marks, "Invisible Media," in *New Media: Theories and Practices of Digitextuality*, ed. Anna Everett and John T. Caldwell (New York: Routledge, 2003), 33–46.

15. Ted Byfield, "Information," in *Software Studies: A Lexicon*, ed. Matthew Fuller (Cambridge, MA: MIT Press, 2008).

16. Claude Shannon, "A Mathematical Theory of Communication," *Bell System Technics Journal*, 1948; popularized in Claude Shannon and Warren Weaver, *A Mathematical Theory of Communication* (Urbana: University of Illinois Press, 1949).

17. Byfield, "Information."

18. Gilbert Simondon, "The Genesis of the Individual," in *Incorporations*, ed. Jonathan Crary and Sanford Kwinter (New York: Zone Books, 1992), 298.

19. Ibid., 310.

20. Ibid., 311.

21. Vilém Flusser, "Habit: The True Aesthetic Criterion," *Vilém Flusser: Writings*, ed. Andreas Ströhl, trans. Erik Eisel (Minneapolis: University of Minnesota Press, 2002), 51–57.

22. See "From Algorithmic to Baroque," in chapter 6, "Baghdad, 830: Birth of the Algorithm," in Laura U. Marks, *Enfoldment and Infinity: An Islamic Genealogy of New Media Art* (Cambridge, MA: MIT Press, 2010), 168–188.

23. Wolfgang Welsch, "Aesthetics Beyond Aesthetics," in Halsall, Jansen, and O'Connor, *Rediscovering Aesthetics*, 181.

24. As my editor Carol Vernallis notes; see the essays by Melissa Ragona (chapter 11) and Caetlin Benson-Allott (chapter 9) within.

25. Infinite, information, and image correspond to Firstness, Secondness, and Thirdness in Charles Sanders Peirce's triadic logic. See Charles Sanders Peirce, "The Principles of Phenomenology," in *Philosophical Writings of Peirce*, ed. Justus Buchler (New York: Dover, 1955), 74–97.

26. Roger Caillois, "Mimicry and Legendary Psychasthenia," trans. John Shepley, *October* 31 (Winter 1984): 16–32.

27. Bergson, *Creative Evolution*, trans. Arthur Mitchell (Mineola, NY: Dover, 1998).

Select Bibliography

Byfield, Ted. "Information." In *Software Studies: A Lexicon*, edited by Matthew Fuller. Cambridge, MA: MIT Press, 2008. 125–132.

Caillois, Roger. "Mimicry and Legendary Psychasthenia." Translated by John Shepley. *October*, 31 (Winter 1984): 16–32.

Deleuze, Gilles. *The Fold: Leibniz and the Baroque*, translated by Tom Conley. Minneapolis: Minnesota University Press, 1993.

Grosz, Elizabeth. "The Thing." In Elizabeth Grosz, *Time Travels: Feminism, Nature, Power*, 131–144. Durham, NC: Duke University Press, 2005.

Kim-Cohen, Seth. *In the Blink of an Ear: Toward a Non-Cochlear Sonic Art.* New York: Continuum, 2009.

Marks, Laura U. *Enfoldment and Infinity: An Islamic Genealogy of New Media Art.* Cambridge, MA: MIT Press, 2010.

Peirce, Charles Sanders. "The Principles of Phenomenology." In *Philosophical Writings of Peirce*, edited by Justus Buchler, 74–97. New York: Dover, 1955.

Serres, Michel. *Genesis,* translated by Geneviève James and James Nielson. Ann Arbor: University of Michigan Press, 1995.

Shannon, Claude, and Warren Weaver. *A Mathematical Theory of Communication.* Urbana: University of Illinois Press, 1949.

Simondon, Gilbert. "The Genesis of the Individual." In *Incorporations*, edited by Jonathan Crary and Sanford Kwinter, 297–319. New York: Zone Books, 1992.

CHAPTER 8

....

DIRTY SOUND

Haptic Noise in New Extremism

....

LISA COULTHARD

In addition to sonic immersion, increased precision, and volume, technological inno-vations associated with Dolby digital surround sound (DSS) create new opportunities for the exploration of filmic noise and silence.[1] Eradicating the hiss of analog, digital noise reduction technologies invite the exploration of both noise and silence. As the-orist Michel Chion notes and scholar Mark Kerins confirms, Dolby offers "deeper"[2] and "more profound" silences,[3] comments echoed by filmmakers, sound editors, designers, and scholars. And yet, rather than mining the cleansed precision of Dolby digital, a number of recent films subvert (or at least play with) the technological devel-opments offered by digital sound through deliberate sonic imperfections, a celebration of noise, and an avoidance of pure silence on the audiotrack. The avoidance of digital surround sound's capacities for silence is particularly evident in films grouped under the term European New Extremism. In films such as Claire Denis's *Trouble Every Day* (2001), Philippe Grandrieux's *La Vie Nouvelle* (2002) and *Sombre* (1998), Gaspar Noé's *Irreversible* (2002), and Lars von Trier's *Antichrist* (2009), it is not silence but noise that stands out as a disturbing presence. More precisely, what dominates these soundscapes is a recurrent acoustic trope—low-frequency droning that occurs in moments of rela-tive silence. Although this ambient droning might be a feature of contemporary cinema more generally (for example, the films of David Lynch or Andrei Tarkovsky), its pres-ence in extremist films recurs so consistently that the drone becomes a thematically and aesthetically charged trope. The drone dirties the purity and quiet of digital technolo-gies so that noise becomes productive and points to wider considerations of resonance, authenticity, and technological ambivalence in the Dolby age. With these consider-ations in mind, here I analyze the way that New Extremism simultaneously relies on and thwarts the quiet technologies of digital sound in order to attain an aural impact on par with its visual extremism.

Noise is an all-encompassing category frequently used to describe acoustically unde-sired sounds. Jacques Attali, Douglas Kahn, Michel Chion, and numerous other sound theorists remind us that noise has political, ideological, and aesthetic ramifications. Attali asserts the historical and rhetorical connections of noise to violence, Kahn notes the correlation of noise to increasing industrialization and its politics, and R. Murray Schafer, Barry Truax, and others associated with the World Soundscape Project stress the ideological ramifications of the acoustic negativity inherent in terms such as "noise pollution." Detritus, or interference to be disavowed, sounds designated as noise are to be avoided or quelled. Noises are potentially dangerous disturbances in otherwise peaceful and placid sonic environments and, as such, are distinct from those sounds organized into coherent communication, music, or rhythm.

Tying this aesthetic disparagement of noise to its repression in the study of sound in the cinema, Michel Chion argues that the time to analyze noise as an artistic choice in cinema has finally come.[4] The distinction between noise and effect, Chion notes, is even more apparent in contemporary cinema because of noise reduction technologies: as a result, noise becomes an aesthetic choice. As Mark Kerins explains, the "high signal-to-noise ratio of DSS...means that what little background noise exists in these systems is quieter than the ambient room noise of a theatre, and hence imperceptible."[5] Cinema noise ceases to be a matter of interference or tolerated hindrance: it is instead a deliber-ate acoustic choice, and the innovations of Dolby digital allow for its refinement. In the Dolby era, a "'dirty' aesthetic, full of confusion" is no longer merely a "byproduct of flaws in the filmmaking process."[6]

This kind of intentional, "dirty" aesthetic provides the backbone for what I see as an identifiable acoustic identity in European New Extremism, an identity that is, in turn, associated with the tactile and disturbing effects of this cinematic trend. It is not merely that noise or low-frequency drones are present—as noted, there are earlier illustrations of this—but that they become persistent tropes. In its repetition, an acoustic object (the drone) becomes identified with meanings and themes (violent sexuality, psychological dissociation, death). Because of the drone's historical connections to industrialization, its presence in these films also comments on urban decay, technological interference, and the noise of modernization. Moreover, exploiting body-vibrating low frequen-cies, the drone has a traumatic, primordial quality that ties it to the sounds of the body itself: this tarrying between an external world of urban sonic bombardment and inner viscerality is a hallmark of the sonic landscapes of new extremism.

AMBIENT EXTREMITY: SOUND AND THE CINEMA OF SENSATIONS

Preoccupied with the body's materiality (especially in moments of intensity, like sex and violence), extremist films downplay conventional narrative and aesthetic structures in favor of experimentation. Although varied in content, story, and tone, these films create a loose grouping rooted in graphic sex and violence, unconventional cinematic form and narration, and spectatorial implication. In their introduction to the edited collection *The New Extremism in Cinema*, Tanya Horeck and Tina Kendall argue that extremist films ought not to be understood as a genre or a movement, but rather as a trend foregrounding a "highly self-reflexive appeal to the spectator."[7] They are a grouping of films defined by the ways in which they situate "sex and violence as a means of interrogating the relationship between films and their spectators in the late twentieth and early twenty-first centuries."[8]

Using audiovisual disorientation, abrasive unwatchability, and shocking violence, New Extremism focuses on viscerality in spectatorial terms. Although criticism has tended to focus on its "unwatchable,"[9] "fork in the eye"[10] visual assaultiveness, sound is equally tactile and disturbing. Capable of impacting the body in palpable ways, sound is mined in many of these films for its viscerality: as one listens to extremities of acoustic proximity, frequency, and volume, one's own body responds in subconscious ways to those depicted and heard on-screen. Stressing this tactility, films such as *Sombre*, *Trouble Every Day*, and *Antichrist* explore the physical impact of low-frequency sound by replacing silence with a pervasive and resonant background humming or drone. In this way, quiet moments become noisy and disturbed acoustic instants that only suggest silence through the excision of dialogue and music; moreover, in those most extreme moments of explicit violence, this background droning merges bodies and noise to indicate destruction and death.

This connection between death and emphatic noise is perhaps most notable in the opening second scene of Gaspar Noé's reverse revenge thriller *Irreversible*, one of the first and most famous films of European New Extremism. In this chaotic sequence, the acoustic and imagistic distortion of the Rectum Club creates an audiovisual nausea through the use of low-frequency sounds that approximate infrasound. Jason Shawhan notes, "Sonically, there is a dual-wave oscillation at full keen throughout almost all of the sequence, which on a good theatre system is gut-stirring in and of itself."[11] With hysterically mobile framing, this opening creates a sensation of nausea that extends to the material presented (an act of brutal violence in an underground gay sex club) and foreshadows the much darker events soon to occur. The audience is already in a state of visual and auditory unease well before the brutal and graphic violence occurs: the body-vibrating sounds of the opening ready us for danger.

Low-frequency sounds in this scene are essential to its impact and are tied to what I contend is a wider trend in new extremity associating sonic low frequencies with abjection, dissociation, and disturbance. This connection is not surprising when one considers that psychoacoustics have long connected low-frequency sounds to nausea, anxiety, and disorientation. According to sound theorist Jean Francois Augoyard and musician Henry Torgue, "In many sound cultures, there is a connection between the low frequencies and danger, sadness, or melancholy."[12] This connection is especially evident in the particular sonic phenomena of the drone: "The figurative meaning of the French expression '*avoir (ou prendre) le bourdon* [drone]' (in English, 'to be down'), describes someone who is filled with a haunting melancholic feeling."[13]

Augoyard and Torgue go on to comment that the drone is a noise fundamentally tied to modernization and industrialization, a correlation noted by a number of sound theorists. Seeing it as both narcotizing and noisy, R. Murray Schafer concludes that the nonprogressive and continuous nature of drones in industrial and electrical modern life mean that we "listen differently" and are less sensitive to sonic differentiation: "This new sound phenomenon, introduced by the Industrial Revolution and greatly extended by the Electric Revolution, today subjects us to permanent keynotes and swaths of broad-band noise, possessing little personality or sense of progression."[14] Quoting Henri Bergson, Schafer goes on to assert that such flat-lining of sound is tied to behavioral and psychological changes: "as discrete sounds gave way to flat lines, the noise of the machine became 'a narcotic to the brain,' and listlessness increased in modern life."[15] Augoyard and Torgue echo this comment when they state that "when the intensity of a background sound exceeds a certain threshold, mental activity can be paralyzed."[16]

Indeed, the drone's constant and unwavering presence in modern life becomes so ubiquitous that it is perceived as a kind of silence—we become accustomed to its presence as a background for our modernized life, and most of us would never listen to droning as a distinct, identifiable sound. We ignore and adapt to these sounds precisely because of their ubiquity. As Simon Frith notes, "[i]n the twentieth century there has been not only a significant increase in the sheer quantity of noise, but also a shift in our underlying sense of silence: technology provides us with a permanent hum, a continued sonic presence."[17] In a cinematic context, Chion similarly comments on the fundamental noise of cinema, that mechanistic whir of the projector itself, a noise that Chion argues persists in contemporary cinema through diegetic sounds of car engines, helicopter rotors, or other rhythmic machine sounds.[18] But as pervasive as technological hums are, the presence of this kind of droning on a twenty-first century cinematic soundtrack is distinct from the hum of a projector or the noise of modern life. For a drone to take on an emphatic and physically impactful presence, the cinematic soundscape must be dry and precise: Dolby digital sound allows for the exploration of an ambient drone as a thematically loaded, sensational, and tactile acoustic object.

Chion anticipates this link between Dolby digital and a more haptic, tactile cinematic noise when he argues that Dolby stereo heralded a "new sensory cinema" focused on the sound effects associated with everyday actions of the body (breath, skin touches, cloth movements, footsteps), technology (machine hums, traffic noise, engine rumbles), and the environment (animal cries, bird songs, cricket chirps). This new sensory cinema communicates sensations of physical, bodily life through an intensification of its sounds. This last point is crucial: we hear not only with our ears, but our entire bodies. Whether it is the purr of rumbling engines or the unbearable intimacy of a closely miked breath played loud in the mix, sound can send shivers up one's back, increase the rapidity of a heartbeat, or create nausea, anxiety, or uneasiness.

These effects are as palpable in cinematic silence as they are in noise. More than just a new stardom of cinematic noise, Chion asserts that the greatest potential for recent acoustic technologies is silence. Without the inherent hiss of analog systems, digital sound is quite simply quieter, a characteristic that is frequently tied to discourses of purity or cleanliness: as a commentator from *Stereo Review* enthuses, digital "gleams with the promise of a cleansed, transformed future."[19] Chion observes a similar valorization of the clean sounds of Dolby when he discusses the lack of vibration and the dryness of the acoustics associated with big THX theatres. More specifically, referring to the THX demo during which one hears "a bunch of glissandi falling toward the low bass register, spiraling spatially around the room from speaker to speaker, ending triumphantly on an enormous chord,"[20] Chion remarks on a lack of vibration in the low-frequency effects and the absence "of the reverberation that normally accompanies and muddles loud sounds in an enclosed space."[21]

This aural cleansing has led some to yearn for the hiss of analog. When discussing the use of silence in *Contact* (1997), Kerins states that "the quiet speaker hiss of a Dolby Stereo silence would be reassuring, but director Robert Zemeckis...uses the total silence made available by DSS to emphasize the feeling of emptiness."[22] Here, feelings of comfort, nostalgia, and reassurance are connected to the acoustic detritus of older technologies: the hiss is not interfering noise, but a comforting background hum that holds off the potentially disturbing perfection of silence. This same kind of sonic nostalgia is found throughout films that seem to revel in the sounds of old technologies, such as the deliberate record pops of songs played on the jukebox or the scratchy hiss of the opening credits in Quentin Tarantino's grindhouse pastiche *Death Proof* (2007). This acoustic nostalgia works in concert with the reassurance of analog hiss discussed by Kerins, and both play a role in films that deliberately eschew sonic perfection. For instance, in his film *Trash Humpers* (2009), Harmony Korine uses outdated recording technologies, a choice he frames as a desire for the beauty of "the fog of analog," a clear reaction to clean digital sound and images.[23] Although Korine is referring to visual as well as auditory cleanliness, his reference to the "fog of analog" holds particular resonance in light of the connections between nostalgia and the comforting blanket of sound associated with the background ambient noise of analog sound. A more positive term for noise, "fog" here indicates nostalgia for the uncertainty and lack of precision associated with technological formats now seen as imperfect.

In opposition to this valorization of older technologies, sound designers and theorists repeatedly assert the possibilities offered up by new technologies, specifically digital's ability to make low-volume and low-frequency sounds perceivable. With Dolby digital surround, low-frequency and ambient sounds can register in ways that they simply cannot in analog formats. Paying particular attention to the 0.1 low frequency effects (LFE) channel in the 5.1 of DSS sound, Kerins notes that this technology allows low-frequency sounds to have the same volume as high-frequency. This innovation is able to create spectacular effects that impact the body of the spectator and aid in his or her immersion, a frequently discussed goal for DSS. Put simply, low-frequency effects provide "a rhythm that is felt as much as heard,"[24] "a pure gut, physical, straight-to-the-brainstem physical response."[25] This physical reaction is most notable in the drone, a sound that makes emphatic the haptic, gut-stirring abilities of low frequency and makes acute the presence of noise as an aesthetic choice, one stressing disturbance and disorientation.

DIRTYING SOUND: THE HUM, THE DRONE AND THE BUZZ

New Extremism relies not only on the shocking content of its stories for its impact, but also on sensation itself—as a "cinema of the senses,"[26] its images and sounds are transsensorial and tactile. This is perhaps most evident in the narrationally obscure and formally exploratory work of Philippe Grandrieux. His key works *Sombre* and *La Vie Nouvelle* rework the serial killer and gangster genres respectively, but manipulate each so that only the shadows of stories remain. Nightmarish and focused on sensation and feeling rather than story, his cinema is truly haptic in a Deleuzian sense—images, sounds, colors, and shapes touch the spectator and elicit responses based more in sensation than intellect. This synesthesia is most emphatic in Grandrieux's use of low-frequency drones and his sharp and disorienting acoustic contrasts. Although not mentioning droning in particular, many reviewers and scholars have commented on the pulsating, haptic nature of sound in Grandrieux's works. For instance, in a review of the Harvard Film Archives' Grandrieux retrospective, Michael Atkinson comments that "his soundtracks are powerful affairs, often shedding on-location sound altogether and building a Lynchian storm of creepy ambient noise—as if the whole world were clamped beneath an old boiler that's about to blow."[27] This sense of compressed energy is equally apparent in the archive's description of Grandrieux's work as a "cinema of vibrations and tremors in which image and sound seem to pulsate with furious life,"[28] as well as in Martine Beugnet's discussion of sound as "an intrinsic element of the aesthetics of sensation" in Grandrieux's films.[29]

Opening with a low-frequency humming, representative of both vehicular motion and psychological disturbance, Grandrieux's *Sombre* illustrates this pulsating energy with an overwhelming drone that intensifies as the camera follows a car along a highway.[30] The drone is replaced with diegetic sound as the film cuts abruptly to a second scene of screaming children who are watching an off-screen spectacle. This scene is then invaded by the same droning hum, which is eventually cut off by total silence as the image shifts to a child discovering a murdered female body. Redolent with fairytale imagery, the serial killing narrative of *Sombre* follows the puppeteer/ killer Jean's redemption through his encounter with Claire, a symbol of virginal innocence. In the film's opening moments, these central conflicts are brought to the foreground: children (innocence) are paired with violence (screams, death) in a way that prepares the audience for the narrative to come. Switching from extremely low- to extremely high-frequency and then back again before cutting to silence, the transitions between these opening scenes are disruptive and confusing: we never see and hear with any clarity because both image and audio track are distorted and obscured. More than this, though, the noises themselves battle as they intrude on each other, an aural violence echoed in the pulsating and uncanny images depicted on-screen. Through these opening scenes, the film instructs the audience to interrogate the unseen and to fear the heard—the sonic contrasts place the listener in an alert and anxious aural state.

In the story of human trafficking told in *La Vie Nouvelle*, we get similar acoustic extremes, albeit in this film they are more intensely focused on the animalistic and otherworldly sounds of the body itself. As Adrian Martin notes, "the soundtrack is constructed globally upon unidentifiable, layered, synthesised, ambient noises of breath or wind, sucked in and expelled, which underlie the entire film and constitute its disturbed heartbeat, returning to our ear when all other sounds have disappeared. In the very beginnings and endings of his films, over the credits, there is nothing but this strangely bodily sound."[31] Without dialogue, the opening of *La Vie Nouvelle* emphasizes noise with its droning hum and images of unidentified human figures. Beugnet describes this scene as one of audiovisual vibration and distortion: "As the camera travels forward, the speed of recording (8 to 6 frames per second instead of the customary 24) makes the images vibrate. The sound is like a muffled rumbling, like that of a storm or a plane taking off in the distance."[32] Indeed, throughout the film, the action pauses in moments of contemplation that are suffocated by a droning presence similar to that heard in the opening of *Sombre*. For instance, in one scene, the main character looks out a window at the end of a dark hallway. As the camera zooms into the city pictured outside the window, the drone that dominates the audiotrack becomes more disruptive, shifting into an assault on the senses that transforms the bleak, brown urban landscape depicted outside into something hellish and monstrous. The hum becomes a pulsating noise that overwhelms both the spectator and the characters: the drained color palette emphasizes a drab Eastern European winter locale, and the sound is likewise muddied. In both films, it is the loudness, pitch, and timbre of sounds usually characterized as noise that shape the contours of the sensations. The blurring of noise and music works to construct cinematic bodies that move beyond their filmic confines to settle in shadowed, resounding form in the body of the spectator.

We see a similar use of this hum of vibratory distress in Claire Denis's *Trouble Every Day*, a variation on the vampire film that transforms its bloody subject matter into a melancholic tale of desire, loss, and illness. Throughout the film, a droning hum is linked to the central protagonist Dr. Shane Brown, who has contracted a disease that transforms sexual desire into murder and cannibalism. After an ambiguous prelude featuring indistinguishable human figures, the film introduces Shane and his murderous desire for his new bride while they are en route to Paris for their honeymoon. Sitting on the floor of the airplane washroom, Shane descends into a fantasy of his bloodied beloved reaching out to him in pleasure; the mechanistic noise of the airplane transforms into a distorted silence as the images are paired with a vibrating low-frequency hum that sounds as if it is occurring underwater or from a great distance. Shifting from noisy airplane engines to the droning of Shane's fantasy, the film connects the drone to both meditative silence and mechanistic noisiness. Machine and fantasy meld, as the hum resonates not only in Shane's head, but in the spectator's body.

As in Grandrieux's *Sombre*, the connection between machine noise and the droning silence of psychosis/violence made in the opening moments becomes a persistent acoustic trope. This droning heard in the airplane scene recurs several times in *Trouble Every Day*—in scenes in the medical labs associated with experiments implicated in the disease's origins, as well as in the film's disturbing conclusion. But it is worth noting that, in addition to these drones, the film is rife with the sounds of traffic hums, exterior noises, and the buzz of city life. Interior spaces such as the couple's hotel room are not protected from this noise, as the outside world continuously bleeds through and maintains a constant presence on the soundtrack. In relation to this noise, the droning stands out as both similar (insofar as they are both flat-line, "low-information, high redundancy sounds,")[33] and distinct (in that the droning is tied with a psychological and corporeal interiority). Low-frequency sounds are notoriously difficult to locate spatially and, unlike traffic noise, the droning in the film is not varied or spatially determinate. Although the traffic, airplane, or other machine noise comes from the outside world, the drones in the film sound submerged, muddied, and interior—droning stems from Shane's interior life and stands in for his murderous, bloody desire. But droning also indicates Shane's disease itself; left undefined and abstract in the film, his disease is throughout linked to sexual desire, pharmacological greed, medical experimentation, and the problematic "lingering, alienating effects of the colonial past on contemporary French society."[34] Appearing in scenes focused on mechanistic noise and medical experimentation, the drone in *Trouble Every Day* represents Shane's struggle with his disease, but also suggests larger social, ideological, and political issues tied to modernization and its melancholic, narcotizing, and alienating effects.

Although the metaphorical, allegorical, and ideological dimensions of disease are subtle in the film, they are nonetheless apparent. More specifically, in *Trouble Every Day*, the drone makes explicit the link between disease, sex, and death. This connection is particularly notable in the film's final moments. After his first kill, Shane has just finished showering as his wife returns and finds the new puppy he has just purchased for her. As he exits the shower, the camera shows blood dripping from a shower curtain and as they embrace, a drone is heard on the soundtrack. Starting early in the scene at a quiet volume that one could easily interpret as mere ambient noise, the drone rises in the mix to suggest a disturbance that the image track works to obscure—we see a married couple exchange an embrace and discuss their return to the States, but this normalcy is undermined by the intensifying drone that overwhelms the images before a cut to the credits. It is as if violence, the void of death, and the psyche itself are given voice in this low-frequency hum that threatens to suffocate the characters within its powerful vibrations. Sound literally overpowers and wipes out the images, as the film cuts to its final credit sequence accompanied by the melodic title song by the Tindersticks. Returning us to the opening scene by repeating the title song, this conclusion retroactively infects the opening scene of an anonymous couple embracing in a romantic Parisian locale— the droning that overwhelms the closing shot of Shane's wife's face indicates a yoking of desire to violence and psychological disturbance, a connection that cannot be undone by the melodic music and its romantic associations.

This relation of the drone to corporeal as well as psychological disturbance is equally notable in Lars von Trier's *Antichrist*. Although both *Antichrist* and *Melancholia* (2011) utilize low-frequency effects for visceral impact (especially forceful in *Melancholia's* apocalyptic and infrasonically rumbling ending), the sound of *Antichrist* is particularly notable for its exploration of organic and corporeal low-frequency noise. Literally using the body as a sound effect (the sound designer swallowed a microphone to record bodily sounds from the inside and then used these sounds in the mix), Kristian Eidnes Andersen's sound for *Antichrist* manipulates sound to evoke corporeal response. Added to these corporeal sonic artifacts are the numerous effects in the film that are grounded in organic materials: rocks, wood, grass, and the human voice all appear as unidentifiable noise in the ambient, background hum of the film. Interestingly, these low-frequency organic rumbles sometimes originate in high-frequency sounds: for example, for one effect the designer brushed horse hair across twigs, a relatively high-frequency sound that was then slowed down and shifted in frequency to create an uncanny noise that seems both familiar (everyday, organic materials) and strange (because of its delay and sonic manipulation). With traces of their organic origins, these low-frequency distorted hums intrude on and oppress the characters as sonic indicators of otherworldly influences and psychotic disturbance. They also suggest the rumbling of nature itself, a point rendered palpable in the way the earth regurgitates its ghosts at the end of the film. Here, the drone becomes alienated from the mechanized hums of industrialization and modernity to communicate the disorder of nature. Not a place of quiet contemplation or bucolic silence, the natural world of Eden hums with noises of organic, even human, origin.

Although *Melancholia* is not usually tied to new extremism, its sonic similarities to *Antichrist* are worth noting. Focusing more on musical score (its repetition of Wagner's Prelude to "Tristan und Isolde"), *Melancholia* nonetheless emphasizes distortion as this score is edited, compressed and, in the film's apocalyptic conclusion, combined with rumbling low-frequency sounds associated with the planet Melancholia approaching the earth. This ending is an extremely loud sequence that has an visceral impact on the audience, and a certain messiness of noise was crucial to this impact: " 'It's the loudest thing I have ever mixed…I wanted it to struggle and fight with the Wagner piece, so it tries to drown the Wagner piece. I know it's a little messy, but I wanted it to be very overwhelming and I think I succeeded with that.' "[35] This importance of messiness is also voiced by von Trier in reference to *Antichrist*; in the DVD extra "Sound in *Antichrist*," von Trier is repeatedly heard asking for the opening aria from Handel's "Rinaldo" to be less clean, more messy, and more imperfect. More than just imperfection though, *Melancholia*'s earth-shaking sounds in the film's final moments suggest visceral and haptic qualities facilitated by the LFE channel of digital surround. As noted, low-frequency sounds carry with them associations of threat, imminent danger, and potential nausea. Physiological and psychological, this impact has been tied to the vibrations of the soundwaves themselves, as well as to warning sounds in the natural world. As sound design scholar Tomlinson Holman notes, low-frequency rumbles create a feeling of unease and fear in the audience because of a connection to the weather: "in the natural world low frequencies are associated with storms (distant thunder), earthquakes, and other natural catastrophes."[36] Interestingly, Andersen and von Trier similarly connect low-frequency sounds to signs of danger in the natural world: "The end of the world in Mr. von Trier's imagining brings turbulent weather, so Mr. Andersen dug into his archive of recorded storm and wind sounds, blending them to create the high tones of the audio mix."[37]

More than just using the low-frequency sounds of weather, *Melancholia*'s sound design explores the sounds of the natural world more generally.[38] Similar to his work in *Antichrist*, Andersen digitally manipulated organic materials to create defamiliar-ized sounds: "For the lower tones, the rumbling and the roars, he experimented with organic materials like stones and wood: 'If you rub stones together, you get this edgy sound. It's not that nice at normal speed, but if you slow it down a lot in a sampler, you can get wonderful rumbling sounds,' he said. 'When you tear a piece of thin wood apart, it has these creaking sounds, and then you slow that down as well. I put these out in different speakers and let them fly around in the surround system so you get this turbulent feeling.'"[39] Further, Andersen's comments reiterate the relation between low-frequency sounds and emotional depression voiced by Augoyard and Torgue, cited at the beginning of this article. As they note, drowned out (often intentionally as in the case of Muzak), masked, or habitually ignored, the drone of modern life can play dual functions: it can be both a "reassuring background ambience"[40] blocking the unease associated with total silence and a melancholia-inducing low-frequency vibra-tion, absorbed rather than heard and linked to physiological, emotional, and psycho-logical disturbance.

In each of the films I have discussed, we hear and feel this split between the distur-bance and comfort of droning as both noise and silence. Resonant with the threat and nausea associated with low-frequency sound, the alienating, droning hum in films such as *Antichrist*, *Sombre*, and *Trouble Every Day* suggests both corporeal pulsating life, as well as the silent inactivity of the brutally ruptured body. It is equally tied to the alien-ating noisiness of modern life, in which both sounds and emotions become flat-lined, nonprogressive, and redundant—a psychic state explored in the emotional flatness of characters in *Trouble Every Day*, *La Vie Nouvelle*, and *Melancholia*. Both originating in and oppressing the human figures on-screen, the noise of the drone in these films sug-gests an overwhelming presence of distortion and audiovisual uneasiness. The drones of industrialization, of the mechanized noise of modern life, are transformed into natural, corporeal, and bodily sounds of resonance and vibration.

Most palpable in moments of extreme trauma, violence, or death, the drone in European New Extremism stands in for both overwhelming noise, as well as for the impossibility of introspective quiet. Dirtying silence and replacing both voice and music with droning hums, new extremist films render pure silence impossible, as only sullied approximations are offered in its place. This acoustic disturbance replaces silence as the zero level of sound, one always tainted by the disturbing hum of nauseat-ing low-frequency drones. Located between the detritus of noise and the purity of total silence, dirty sound resonates with the violence and disaffections addressed in the new extremity. In the violence and brutality of these films, noisy, atmospheric silence—alive with estranged corporeal and organic sounds—is indicative of the void of death itself; as polluted silence, humming noise renders trauma audible and insists on our audition and attention.

NOTES

1. There are, of course, multiple technologies associated with digital sound: Dolby Digital, Dolby Theater Sound (DTS), Sony Dynamic Digital Sound (SDDS).

2. Michel Chion, *The Voice in Cinema*, trans. Claudia Gorbman (New York: Columbia University Press, 1999), 167.

3. Mark Kerins, *Beyond Dolby (Stereo)—Cinema in the Digital Sound Age* (Bloomington: Indiana University Press, 2011), 58.

4. Michel Chion, *Audio-Vision: Sound on Screen*, ed and trans. Claudia Gorbman (New York: Columbia University Press, 1994), 145.

5. Kerins, *Beyond Dolby (Stereo)—Cinema in the Digital Sound Age*, 58.

6. Michel Chion, *Film, A Sound Art*, trans. Claudia Gorbman (New York: Columbia University Press, 2009), 127.

7. Tanya Horeck and Tina Kendall, "Introduction," in *The New Extremism in Europe: From France to Europe* eds, Tanya Horeck and Tina Kendall (Edinburgh: Edinburgh University Press, 2011), 1.

8. Tanya Horeck and Tina Kendall, "Introduction," 2.

9. Asbjørn Grønstad, "On the Unwatchable," in *The New Extremism in Europe: From France to Europe*. Eds. Tanya Horeck and Tina Kendall (Edinburgh: Edinburgh University Press, 2011), 192.

10. Grønstad, "On the Unwatchable," 199.

11. Jason Shawhan, "It's Beginning, To, and Back Again: The Sense-Deranging Sound and Vision of Gaspar Noé's *Irreversible*," *The Film Journal* Issue 4 (2002). http://www.thefilmjournal.com/issue4/irreversible.html, accessed June 2012.

12. Jean-Francois Augoyard and Henry Torgue, *Sonic Experience: A Guide to Everyday Sounds*, trans. Andra McCartney and David Paquette (Montreal: McGill-Queen's University Press, 2005), 42.

13. Augoyard and Torgue, *Sonic Experience: A Guide to Everyday Sounds*, 41.

14. R. Murray Schafer, *The Soundscape: Our Sonic Environment and the Tuning of the World* (Rochester: Destiny Books, 1997), 78.

15. Schafer, *The Soundscape*, 79.

16. Augoyard and Torgue, *Sonic Experience: A Guide to Everyday Sounds*, 41.

17. Simon Frith, *Performing Rites: On the Value of Popular Music* (Cambridge, MA: Harvard University, 1996), 100.

18. Michel Chion, *Film, A Sound Art*, trans. Claudia Gorbman (New York: Columbia University Press, 2009), 8.

19. Kerins, *Beyond Dolby (Stereo)—Cinema in the Digital Sound Age*, 40.

20. Chion, *Audio-Vision: Sound on Screen*, 100.

21. Ibid., 101.

22. Kerins, *Beyond Dolby (Stereo)—Cinema in the Digital Sound Age*, 59.

23. Liz Armstrong, "The Fog of Analog: Harmony Korine Makes Love to Garbage." *Vice* 16.11 (2009). http://www.vice.com/read/fog-of-analog-215-v16n11, accessed June, 2012.

24. Kerins, *Beyond Dolby (Stereo)—Cinema in the Digital Sound Age*, 83.

25. Miller in Kerins, *Beyond Dolby (Stereo)—Cinema in the Digital Sound Age*, 134.

26. Martine Beugnet, *Cinema and Sensation: French Film and the Art of Transgression* (Carbondale: Southern Illinois University Press, 2007), 16.

27. Michael Atkinson, "Camera Obscura: Philippe Grandrieux's Loaded Minimalism," *The Phoenix* (February 16, 2010). http://thephoenix.com/Boston/movies/97123-camera-obscura/, accessed June 2012.

28. http://hcl.harvard.edu/hfa/films/2010janmar/grandrieux.html.
29. Martine Beugnet, "Evil and the Senses: Philippe Grandrieux's *Sombre* and *La Vie Nouvelle*," *Studies in French Cinema* 5, no. 3 (2005), 180.
30. In her essay "Evil and the Senses: Philippe Grandrieux's *Sombre* and *La Vie Nouvelle*," Martine Beugnet comments that this humming sound at the opening of *Sombre* is the recorded sound of beehives. Although I do not know the particulars of the design process, it appears that this sound is slowed down and manipulated and likely layered with other sounds to create the droning effect of the opening.
31. Adrian Martin, "Dance, Girl, Dance: Philippe Grandrieux's *La Vie Nouvelle*." *Kinoeye* 4.3 (July 26, 2004). http://www.kinoeye.org/04/03/martin03.php, accessed June 2012.
32. Martine Beugnet, "Evil and the Senses: Philippe Grandrieux's *Sombre* and *La Vie Nouvelle*," *Studies in French Cinema* 5, no. 3 (2005), 181.
33. Schafer, *The Soundscape*, 78.
34. Beugnet, *Cinema and Sensation*, 39.
35. Andersen in Mekado Murphy, "Lars von Trier Apocalypse Is Set to Wagner's 'Tristan,'" *New York Times* (December 29, 2011).
36. Tomlinson Holman, *Sound for Film and Television* (Los Angeles, CA: Focal Press, 2002), 7.
37. Murphy, "Lars von Trier Apocalypse Is Set to Wagner's 'Tristan.'"
38. A connection could be made to Grandrieux's preference for natural sounds in the creation of his droning effects, which are, according to Beugnet, derived from the droning of bees in *Sombre* and "the sound of the earth recorded underground" (Beugnet 2005, p. 180) in *La Vie Nouvelle*.
39. Murphy, "Lars von Trier Apocalypse Is Set to Wagner's 'Tristan.'"
40. Augoyard and Torgue, *Sonic Experience: A Guide to Everyday Sounds*, 41.

SELECT BIBLIOGRAPHY

Attali, Jacques. *Noise: The Political Economy of Music.* Translated by Brian Massumi. Minneapolis: University of Minnesota Press, 2003.
Augoyard, Jean-Francois, and Henry Torgue. *Sonic Experience: A Guide to Everyday Sounds.* Translated by Andra McCartney and David Paquette. Montreal: McGill-Queen's University Press, 2005.
Beugnet, Martine. *Cinema and Sensation: French Film and the Art of Transgression.* Carbondale: Southern Illinois University Press, 2007.
Chion, Michel. *Audio-Vision: Sound on Screen.* Edited and translated by Claudia Gorbman. New York: Columbia University Press, 1994.
Chion, Michel. *Film, a Sound Art.* Translated by Claudia Gorbman. New York: Columbia University Press, 2009.
Holman, Tomlinson. *Sound for Film and Television.* Los Angeles: Focal Press, 2002.
Horeck, Tanya, and Tina Kendall, eds. *The New Extremism in Europe: From France to Europe.* Edinburgh: Edinburgh University Press, 2011.
Kahn Douglas. *Noise, Water, Meat: A History of Sound in the Arts.* Cambridge, Mass: MIT Press, 1999.
Kerins, Mark. *Beyond Dolby (Stereo)—Cinema in the Digital Sound Age.* Bloomington: Indiana University Press, 2011.
Sergi, Gianluca. *The Dolby Era: Film Sound and Contemporary Hollywood.* Manchester, UK: Manchester University Press, 2005.

CHAPTER 9

....

GOING GAGA FOR GLITCH

*Digital Failure @nd Feminist Spectacle in
Twenty-First Century Music Video*

....

CAETLIN BENSON-ALLOTT

¶
Glitch, *n*. A surge of current or a spurious electronic signal…*Astronauts'
Slang.*[1]
¶

WHETHER its name derives from the German *glitschig*, meaning "slippery" or is
merely an extraterrestrial neologism, the glitch is uniquely electronic in its subversive interruption; like all mechanical errors, it articulates the substrate over the subject, but its uses are NOT LIMITED to rendering the medium as message. This is
because a glitch "usually fixes itself in the amount of time time for it to be noticed."[2]
The glitch is a disease of time, a pause and a potentiality. But we're getting ahead of
ourselves.¶

   After John Glenn brought the glitch back from outer space in 1962, we identified it in the st/t/c of transistor radios, the p*p of a scratched record, the warble of
wrinkled audiotape, and the sk'p of the CD. We've seen it wriggle along the bottom of
VHS playback and freeze the pixels of a DVD image. During the ascension and commodification of Web 2.0 in the first decade of the twenty-first century, online videos
became host to a new kind of glitch: the digital stutter of inininsufficient buffering in
Adobe Flash Player and other streaming media software. When a computer is unable
to download a file fast enough to exceed the rate of playback, the viewer may see her
video image freeze--

then skip forward as it tries to rematch its audio and video tracks. During such glitches,
the medium becomes a temporal presence, a missed beat or ———— outside the hermetic order of the code. Dropped frames (and, less often, missing measures) interrupt
choreography, ~~visual pleasure~~, and the viewer's fantasy of mastery. An alien presence
in our electronic media, the online video glitch suspends the smooth operation of

technoculture, techno©ommerce, and technophallocentrism. Indeed, some recent music videos have appropriated the digital glitch to interrupt—one might say, to buffer—the fetishization of the female performer. By working inside the genre of the corporate music video and the logic of the glitch (the Other of normative computer processing), these performers are reimagining objectification WE'RE PLASTIC as individual agency BUT WE STILL HAVE FUN. Simulated glitches make visible their ambivalent relationships to patriarchal, heterocentric video culture as they interrupt the gaze without alienating the spectator. Thus, by inviting the glitch into the aesthetic economy of streaming music videos, some of the most objectified and successful women in pop are bursting the illusion of immersion that video produces, opening up in^ter^vals of frustration—and potential critical reflection—through the temporal structures of fantasy and //streaming// media platforms.

f¶¶k\≤ç/á°∂MùΠ9⁄="...É<"Qÿ&8Ïd4˙/†57S√k»'Äa,ΩÑ¨A¿©ìò–ÀõΩ/œΣ˙©X/‡´ÚÚÜ]

Don't tell me you're surprised that this story begins with Madonna. Countless musical and cultural critics have crowned Madonna the Mistress of Appropriation, citing her commodification of minority ¢lub ¢ultures, electronic ~~underground~~ movements, lesbian fashion history, and eventually even country-western music in her quest to stay current.[3] Thus, when Madonna's 2000 album *Music* exhibited sonic manipulations reminiscent of 1990s glitch music, particularly the German electronic group Oval, it was quite literally business as usual. Yet whereas artists like Oval, Nicholas Collin, and Aphex Twin generate, record, and arrange actual Σrrφrs for their music, Madonna glitches the glitch. Instead of recycling the noise of a skipping CD to create pop music (as Oval, Collins, and many hip hop turntablists do), she undermines the underground and **avant-garde** pretensions of glitch music to capitalize on its digital moment in her *Music* and—ironically—her commodification as a performing image. *!?# Her second single from the album, "Don't Tell Me," begins with a plucked guitar riff, ᵍⁱⁿᵍling arpeggios more reminiscent of country-western than dance music or experimental sound art. Then, where the fourth beat should have fallen, there is a—but not just any pause: a digital drop out, a beat of pure silence, the utter absence of noise impossible on any analog recording technology.[4] Thus, by the end of its first bar, "Don't Tell Me" brings together the historical, analog authenticity of the country-western genre with the hypermediation of electronica to produce that mythic contradiction, the authentic digital object. This is because listening to the glitch in "Don't Tell Me" requires one to listen to the machine itself, to the 01100011 01101111 01100100 01100101 that was supposed to stay silent and enable the illusion of unmediated communication between performer and listener. But let's skip ahead to the video.¶

Although "Don't Tell Me" interrupts the fantasy of authentic pop music with digital dropouts, its video destabilizes the tenuous illusions of voyeurism and mastery that its genre encourages. The video (dir. Jean-Baptiste Mondino, 2000) begins with Madonna strutting toward the camera, dressed in a shirt plaid fitted and dark jeans, her face lowered beneath a straw cowboy hat. When the first dropout arrives, Madonna's image pauses, suggesting that she and the music are ¢coextensive or ¢controlled by the same timecode. However, the desert horizon behind her continues to recede at its previous

pace, a movement so slight that it appears at first to be a mistake of the eye. The video
repeats this effect two more times, until it starts to resemble trick photography or computer error. When glitches interrupt the slipstream of a truck as it blows Madonna's hat
away, she finally looks up at the viewer, acknowledging her video's techno]$Ötrickery.
Simultaneously, the camera pulls back enough for the viewer to see that she has been
walking on a wooden platform in front of a bluescreen. *Often art privileges the disruption of "signal."* This revelation retroactively produces an ontological paradox (since a
video truck produces no breeze) and encourages the viewer to question her assumptions
regarding images and embodiment, performers and spectators, power and visual pleasure. *This could even be the definition of art* Joshu@ Clover and Chris Ne@lon observe
that such structural games are quite standard "within the mise-en-abysmal history of
the video form."⁵ However, Madonna's video redirects this generic convention to interrogate her role as an image or spectacle: "by compounding the planes and filling them
with a certain set of highly mobile icons, the flatness returns as its opposite: not depth
but possibility."⁶ *in the information age.*⁷

That possibility seems to reside in the alter?ty of the image, in Mondino's choice not
to produce a stable universe or female spectacle for the viewer but to ?nsist ?nstead
on the temporal remoteness of the image and the performer. As Carol Vernallis demonstrates during a close reading of Madonna's "Cherish" (dir. Herb Ritts, 1989), music
videos do not necessarily utilize conventional Hollywood continuity editing or narratives. Rather, they employ their own rhythm'c 'onceits and aesthetic patterns to engage
and please the viewer.⁸ "Don't Tell Me" uses its digital platform to undermine such con-
ciliatory conventions. After its glitches establish an interdependence—between the
music and the performer's body in the first verse, the video moves its meditation on
mediation to the background during the second verse and first chorus as the images
on Madonna's bluescreen start to throb with the downbeat, suggesting a new ontological independence between performer and song. During the Ò€%&FÇ bridge after
the second chorus, the video furthers this aliΣnation ΣffΣct by introducing a second
illusory protagonist: a rodeo rider on a bucking bronco. Projected on a wrinkled and
weathered outdoor screen, the rider is ~~only~~ an image, but as "Don't Tell Me" continues,
his performance becomes a double for Madonna's. Mondino also intercuts their scenes
with 4our similarly projected images of different cowboys dancing. Alone, these dancers appear oblivious to the camera, but when they finally appear onscreen together in
the fourth verse, each seems equally unaware of his fellow performers and their synergistic choreography. When these dancing cowboys subsequently begin to move syn-
chronously—first as images onscreen and later on Madonna's platform—they achieve
an almost mechanical perfection. Their performance is visually oriented toward the
camera—which suggests that it was designed for our visual pleasure rather than their
subjective expression. Despite joining Madonna's world, they remain image$. For her
part, Madonna seems indifferent to—even unaware of—the bodie$ now surrounding
her. Like the dancers, she's just for us. To that end, the cowboys' presence on Madonna's
stage reminds us that she is on stage. They mark her platform as a fetısh just as the
glıtches in her video and the wrinkles in the cowboy's screen make a fetısh of theirs.

In short, "Don't Tell Me" pairs its audio glitch with a suggestion that relationships occur across images planes, not within them, which may be why the video ends with its privileged player—the Lone Rider—having never left ©X/‡ screen. Although the Lone Rider is never subject to a glitch, his image suggests the immanence of technology to the national mythos he represents. Both the cowboy and country-western music connote nostalgia for some lost *uthenticity in *merican popular culture and pop music, but in "Don't Tell Me" these *ssociations are revealed and exploited as media produ©tion$. Indeed, Madonna's final scene in "Don't Tell Me" finds her astride a mechanical bull, riding the routinized production of Americana. Using and glitching these references, Madonna reminds her viewer that her commodified performance is equally remote, because it also produces desire through the interval between fantasy and physical presence. "Don't Tell Me" thus tells us that desire for a video performer must be understood as telerotic: premised on distances both temporal and technological.

In addition, by *ffforegroundinggg* the oft-disavowed telerotics of music video fantasy, "Don't Tell Me" disrupts the scopophilic gaze traditionally directed at female music video performers. As Laura Mulvey explains in her seminal essay "Visual Pleasure and Narrative Cinema," the erotic spectacle of woman's to-be-looked-at-ness is based on both a technological and a temporal logic. Citing the economic and cultural genealogy of cl455ic4l Hollywood cinem4, Mulvey observes, "As an advanced system of representation, the cinema poses questions about the ways the unconscious (formed by the dominant order) structures ways of seeing and pleasure in looking."[9] For Mulvey, the cinema's "structures of fascination" isolate women as emblems of ~~castration anxiety, reminders of the patriarchy's vulnerability~~.[10] Being both a narrative and a visual art form, classical Hollywood cinema developed two strategies for disabling this threat: sadism and fetishization. In the former, the woman is either forgiven or punished by a male protagonist (and through him the male spectator) who reasserts ~~control~~ by judging her. This strategy "demands a story, depends on making something happen…in a linear time with a beginning and an end."[11] The second solution, fetishization, dehumanizes the woman; by turning her into an object and an idol, the film ~~obfuscates the threat of castration~~ while the scopophilic spectator enjoys her PLASTIC image. To be sure, Mulvey developed this theory to describe classical Hollywood narrative cinema, but because "fetishistic scopophilia…can exist outside of linear time time time," it constitutes one of the most important STILL HAVE FUN strategies for visual pleasure in music videos as well.[12]

Because, just like the cinema, the music video "as an advanced system of representation" produces its own logic of—its own delivery system for—visual **pleasure**.[13] As Vernallis suggests, music videos are very rarely structured around co/he/sive narratives.[14] Hence, the most famous narrative music video to date facilitates storytelling by rearranging an already chart-topping single to tell a tangential story about teenage romance. When Michael Jackson's *Thriller* (dir. John Landis) premiered in 1983, the 13-minute short film cited the music video's typical narrative play by limiting it to metaphysical chicanery and relegated its music to plot **advancement**. The video begins with Jackson and a date confessing their love in a graveyard, when a full moon unexpectedly transforms Jackson into a werewolf. A sudden --- then reveals the same two actors sitting in a movie theater watching the previous situation unfold on screen. During their walk home, Jackson teases his girlfriend with the song's verses until ghouls accost them, transform Jackson, and then join him in the video's legendary dance sequence. Yet, just when Jackson seems about to attack our heroine, a match-on-action cut reveals him rousing her from a dream, thus doubling the opening sequence's metafilmic conceit and emphasis on narrative structure _____.

By contrast, most corporate music videos intercut rudimentary narratives with dance sequences, close^ups, and direct appeals to the camera that inte^^upt any pretense of coherent temporal structures or organized landscapes. Thus, even a relatively narrative video like Aerosmith's "Crazy" (dir. Marty Callner, 1994) mixes its story—two Catholic school girls out for a wild night of teenage rebellion—with unrelated shots of the band performing for a packed arena. This disruption of narrative continues to structure post-MTV music videos p<b≈@<"fiC<ˇö for Internet distribution. Emblematic of this new genre are Lady Gaga's two short films with Jonas Åkerlund, "Paparazzi" (2009) and "Telephone" (2010), as well as her more traditional short-form music videos. All of Gaga's videos employ characters, situations, and psychologically motivated responses while

suborinating them to logics other than narrative. However, the Åkerlund videos in particular build on the structural and generic innovations of Jackson's work to cite music video's historical relationship with film while simultaneously exploiting its new platform to subvert power dynamics inherited from older media. Spectacle is still a dominant component of Gaga's video aesthetic, but it is a different architecture of spectacle ‰¬< than the cinematic model Mulvey describes. As Mulvey notes, cinema is a historically, politically, and socioeconomically unique organization of codes and conventions. Hence Gaga's videos must build their own structures of fascination, their own technological and temporal logic of the look, and do so—I argue—around the online video form (and its short circuits).

from the German *glitschig*, meaning "slippery"

T-t-t-take, for example, Gaga's most downloaded song, "Poker Face."[15] Like most of the tracks on Gaga's first album, *The Fame* (2008), "Poker Face" lays sexually provocative (if safely ambiguous) lyrics over electronic dance beats and disco chord progressions. Its video, directed by Ray Kay, introduces several visual motifs that reappear throughout Gaga's early video work, such as opaque sunglasses-cum-masks, Great Danes, cyborg body modifications, hair bows, and unusually staccato editing. The latter begins during the song's opening bars, as a distorted synthesizer loop establishes the hyPerMediAted tone of the music, and Gaga rises out of a luxurious resort pool. Water streams in slow motion from her black latex bodysuit and disco-ball mask. Suddenly the image starts to break up. Kay inserts close-ups of Gaga between frames of the original shot, creating a•stuttering•strobe•effect that is quickly picked up by the percussive beat of an electronic drum kit. Kay then pulls back to a long shot of the same scene to remix Gaga's a/s/c/e/n/t from the pool. By freezing the shot and skipping back and forth by a few milliseconds at a time—*literally nonlinear editing*—Kay produces a spectatorial experience of the random access memory controlling the video file. Later on, a similar freezing and skipping effect will add fleeting glimpses of movement to otherwise still images of Gaga reclining by the pool and in a gazebo with a male admirer. These hypermediated contortions are juxtaposed against long shots of Gaga's highly sexualized choreography during which scanty, shiny, costumes emphasize her pelvic thrusts, playful self-touching, and smooth undulations. This strategy builds on the music video's traditional 1nt23rcu44ing5 of loosely associated images, but the editing adds the titillation of mediation through erotic tableaus that can be seen but never gazed upon, that refuse to hold still long enough for scopophilic mastery. Like a po'poorly bubuffer'd YouTube clip, Gaga skips beyond our control and inaugurates a new economy of video pleasure for new media.[16]

Thus, like "Don't Tell Me," "Poker Face" integrates platform into the erotic appeal of Gaga's performance by fetishizing telerotic absence through the manipulation of time. The streaming video glitch, a malfunction of processing time, makes the spectator aware of his own gaze, and of the illusion that Gaga is performing for him, that the time of his look and the time time time of her performance somehow coincide. Her glitches should also remind us that fantasy is premised on temporal disjunction, sync on being out of. As Jean Laplanche and J. B. Pontalis point out, fantasy depends *IT'S SO MAGICAL* on the noncoincidence of experience and desire, on the subject becoming "caught up himself in the sequence of images." *WE'D BE SO FANTASTICAL*[17] Gaga's videos, especially her short films with Åkerlund, trap the viewer in this web, using the temporal interruption of the video glitch to remind the spectator that "fantasy is not the object of desire, but its setting."[18] By exploiting and drawing attention to platform as setting, Gaga's videos can enable *GET HIM HOT*, even produce *SHOW HIM WHAT I'VE GOT* fantasy while challenging the viewer's illusion that he can master her.¶

Because of their platform, Gaga's videos are able to launch this challenge to fantasy in a way "Don't Tell Me" could not quite manage on MTV. Since "Just Dance" premiered on ArtistDirect.com on April 30, 2008, Gaga's videos have always been born digital, specifically streaming. Videos on streaming media sites (such as YouTube, Vevo, ArtistDirect, and DailyMotion) are haunted by the threat of buffering too late, arriving in a shot after it has begun, or freezing before skipping ahead to catch another image out of context. Various video artists have approximated these streaming video glitches through j'mp cuts, ssstttrrobbbeee effects, and rapid intercutting but failed to incorporate them into the video's guiding fantasy structure: the erotics of the star's body and the ecstatic, if sometimes loosely associated, pairing of sound and image. It is fitting ••• that glitch finally becomes a lure for the artist named after a glitch, since Lady Gaga allegedly got her name from a smartphone's attempt to autocorrect the title of Queen's 9184 hit "Radio Ga Ga."[19]

To that end, both "¶aparazzi" and "Telephone" investigate Gaga's mediated spectacle by incorporating their pop songs into longer narrative frames áË¢ÃŒ stardom and tabloid culture. Each also builds on the streaming video aesthetic established in "Poker Face" by renegotiating the viewer's visual access to and desire for the star through postponement and the delayed gaze—Indeed, "Paparazzi" begins with an exercise in deferral; whereas most pop music videos introduce their performers within moments, "Paparazzi" opens with 45 seconds of static establishing shots. This nearly silent introduction both launches the video's "neon noir" aesthetic and creates a coherent, legible setting for its fantasy.[20] The next minute and a half construct the narrative frame: Gaga's lover attempts to seduce her in front of a paparazzo, but she resists violently and falls from their balcony, temptemporarily disabling both her body and her star power. Over the course of the song, Gaga rebounds physically and psychically, ultimately poisoning her boyfriend and, through her ensuing arrest, catapulting herself back to front-page celebrity. Yet, as Vernallis reminds us, a music video's narrative often bears little relation to the song's lyrics (which in this case describe a female paparazza stalking a male star).[21] Indeed, "¶aparazzi"'s narrative competes for semantic significance with several other spectacular sequences, including a series of artfully arranged female corpses and shots of Gaga posing suggestively on a couch, by herself and with a trio of blond hipsters. During the bridge, Gaga also dances alone in a wood-paneled closet, kitted out in a 35 mm celluloid bodywrap and extravagant Mohawk wig, as strobe lighting and rapid editing intermix her image with those of another dead woman and the Great Danes from "Poker Face." These effects create impressions of stillness within the choreography as Gaga appears to be performing her own display for the viewer. Sssimulated shshutter noise encourages the viewer to regard Gaga as mediated image, albeit one whose media prevents the viewer from seeing #@%&!! clearly. Moreover, it is through shots such as these—and not the oft-touted narrative—that Gaga's new erotics of fascination emerge.

That is, "¶aparazzi" restructures the male g•ze using the glitch as a pause that produces desire. For that reason, Gaga's video encourages a retroactive reading of Mulvey's woman as spectacle: the woman as glitch. While expanding on the female star's "to-be-looked-at-ness," Mulvey observes that when the woman displays herself (as does a showgirl or music video performer), "for a moment the sexual impact of the performing woman takes the film into a no man's land outside its own time and space."[22] AND AFTER HE'S BEEN HOOKED As a performance of a song, the music video aspires to this despatialized, detemporalized erotic contemplation, which is also precisely the structure of fantasy that Laplanche and Pontalis ~~theorize~~. As I mentioned earlier, I'LL PLAY THE ONE THAT'S ON HIS HEART Laplanche and Pontalis describe fantasy as a setting for desire and a nonteleological "sequence of images." Sequence—although time-based—is not necessarily narrative; as Linda Williams eXXXplains, "fantasies are not, as is sometimes thought, wish-fulfilling linear narratives of mastery and control leading to closure and the attainment of desire. They are marked, rather, by the prolongation of desire."[23]

4Williams, fantasy's emphasis on ex•tend•ing desire helps explain the prominence of repetition and spectacle in sensational film genres, specifically horror, melodrama, and pornography. Observing that "fantasy is not so much a narrative that enacts the quest for an object of desire as it is a setting for desire," Williams argues that the filmic pleasures of these "body genres"—the satisfactions they offer as audiovisual media—rely on an entirely different relationship to time time time than does classical Hollywood realism.[24] They elicit the spectator's enjoyment by reproducing the time of fantasy as a space or setting for desire. Notably, Vernallis's theory of music video narrative indicates that that genre follows a similar logic in that it undermines its own suggestions of narrative to prolong the pleasures they hint at...

Returning then to Gaga's closet sequence in "Paparazzi," her celluloid costume and strobe editing now seem to harness the temporal telerotics of fantasy and to-be-to-be-looked-at-ness to bolster the star's appeal. Although her sartorial display codes her as an "object of sexual stimulation through sight," the sequence's disjunctive editing and lighting effects bl•ck and entice our gaze with a spectacle we cannot quite catch

sight of.[25] The strobe prolongs our desire to see the star, and her costume assures us that she is to-be-looked-at, but their confluence undermines our ability to master her spectacle through voyeurism. Moreover, the closet sequence bears no narrative relation to the video's story; its shots do not cohere to create a time or a space but leave her—or rather us—buffered and buffeted into a new temporality. Gaga's exploitation of this "no man's land" suggests that the temporality of fantasy, while prolonging pleasure, can also produce a glitch in the regime of the ma— —aze.

Thus, one might say that nBê©À Mulvey isolated a glitch in film's streamless delivery of visual pleasure even as she articulated its standard operating procedures. For what is the woman-as-spectacle if not "a sudden short-lived irregularity in behavior"?[26] Mulvey argues that "The presence of woman is an indispensable element of spectacle in normal narrative film, yet her presence tends to work against the development of a story line, to freeze the flow of action in moments of erotic contemplation."[27] Indeed, when to-be-looked-at-ness arrests the narrative for moments "coded for strong v!sual and erot!c impact," it sutures the spectator not to stories or characters but to the antinarrative structure of desire itself.[28] In short, the BAD ROMANCE of feminine spectacle disrupts narrative's phallocentric order. In classical Hollywood film, woman's "alien presence then has to be integrated into cohesion with the narrative," but in the music video, the alien presence can continue to present itself as alien, to revel—and invite us to revel—in its inassimilable difference.[29] Certainly, such estrangements have not always benefited female video stars, but Gaga demonstrates that fomenting fantasy through a refusal to integrate can introduce a f*few ff*feminist glitches into the^system. Embraced as the metaphysical limit of the medium, the streaming video glitch bridges previous debates about feminist exhibition and spectatorship and ontological inquiries into the aesthetics of music videos. Moreover, the specific glitch of streaming media software—that is, the digital stutter and dropped frames—emphasize the glitch as missed connection, as a disruption of order, including heterocentric order. Such is the aesthetic conceit of Gaga's last video with Åkerlund, "Telephone."///

"Telephone" continues both the narrative—and the counternarrative gestures—Gaga and Åkerlund establish in "Paparazzi." The video opens with Gaga under arrest for her boyfriend's murder and awaiting bail in a Los Angeles County jail. Surveillance cameras track her arrival and her fellow inmates' reactions, which range from indifference to arousal, skepticism, and even hostility. Burning up the prison yard in glasses made of lit cigarettes, Gaga briefly befriends an androgynous body builder (played by Heather Cassils) who lets Gaga squeeze her bulging phone and initiates us all into a queer telerotics of technology. Cassils's telephonic phallus teaches the viewer that "Telephone"'s phones can do a lot more than —————. Beyond mere metaphors, these phones function as ideological interruptions and iconic reminders of distance and mediation throughout the video. To that end, the surveillance camera next catches Gaga on a day-room payphone explaining her technological difficulties:

> Hello, hello, Baby?
> You called, I can't hear a thing.
> I ain't got no service in the club
> You see-see.

At first, Gaga's eyes are downcast, but by the end of the second line, she looks up from her ostensible address to her baby and stares directly into the camera. As she asks her caller and her viewer to accept her excuse, the camera cuts to a close up of her lips and phone—and then hitches glitches, coding Gaga's closing repetition as mechanical break-down. WHAT, WHAT DID YOU SAY— Before Gaga even has a chance to communicate that the signal is breaking up, her image begins to vvvibrate and her lyrics are temporarily com-mandeered by the sound of a skipping CD. Adopting these rhythms for herself, Gaga drops the phone and informs the viewer that she's "kinda busy" "kinda busy" "kinda busy" before launching into a choreographed cellblock parade with several scantily clad young women. Like her glitches, Gaga's studded thong and matching brassiere deper-sonalize her near nudity and make her body more remote from the viewer through its very objectification. As Roland Barthes suggests, the G-string's "ultimate triangle, by its pure and geometrical shape, by its hard and shiny material…definitively drives the woman back into a mineral world, the (precious) stones being here the irrefutable sym-bol of the absolute object, that which serves no purpose."[30] At least not our purposes, for this display reminds the viewer that YOU'RE NOT GONNA REACH MY TELEPHONE the female performer can empower herself through "the refuge of being an object" and thereby evade the "weakness and timorousness" of exposure.[31]

Hence, by becoming an object, Gaga reclaims the Gaze in its traditional Lacanian sense, in which an object reminds the viewer that he *too is too* an object and a mortal one at that.[32] Gaga warns the viewer that he does not control the gaze during her first chorus and bridge as she threatens the video technology with its own impotence. First, she advances on the retreating camera while imitating a telephonic busy signal (or is it a skipping CD?). Next the camera begins to cut among ++++++ barred perspectives on her performance; when viewed through cell doors, Gaga's objectification reminds the viewer that objects can be imposing as well as alluring. This threat continues into the bridge, which inflicts new glitches on images of Gaga posed in her cell, erotically mummified in yellow crime scene tape. Although these images are almost still, the pace of the editing rises to match the quick chant of the lyrics, until it stops to rest for a very long time (almost a second!) on Gaga lying motionless on her cot, announcing that she's "out in the club sippin' that bubb.' " Only her lips move during this compar-ative longshot, emphasizing the uncanny stillness of her body suddenly arrested for our gaze. Legs spread, reclining on the bed, Gaga seems posed for sexual consump-tion, but the surreal movement of her lips recalls her malfunctions during the video's earlier glitches. This effect may make the viewer nervous, but then you can't say she didn't CAUTION us.⁋

Furthermore, the ideological damage has already *&!&$~' been done.

Both narrative order and our fetishistic gaze have been ruptured, revealed as insufficient attempts at mastery. The next time we're alone with Gaga in her cell, her head whips back and forth so fast, too ffast, inhumanely fffast, as if to remind us that this is not a woman but a technological image, and the technology is spinning beyond our control. We can now only gawk at Gaga through her mediated telerotics, in full awareness of the machinery of image prod------

"Telephone"'s remaining narrative teaches the viewer what can happen to consumers who persist in the fantasy of mastery, but it also invites him to take pleasure in prolongation over objectification. To make an elliptical story even/ /Beyoncé bails Gaga out of jail and drives her to an isolated desert diner where Beyoncé—aka Honey Bee—poisons her disrespectful boyfriend and Gaga poisons everyone else. On its own, this story provides few satisfactions, especially since it offers neither the narrative closure of parable nor the psychological insight of realism, but it does provide something for the musical sequences to interrupt. That is, it imparts just enough structure to destabilize the conventions of corporate music videos and make the music feel subversive again. Thus, when Beyoncé sings the third verse, the video pauses its narrative for her rebellious performance. Simultaneously, a series of jump cuts and blocky editing emphasize the defiant tone of her lyrics ("I should have left my phone at home/ 'Cause this is a disaster"). Here, the cinematography responds to her threat rather than diffusing it. Thus, when Gaga picks up a camera to capture the moment, the flashes of her Polaroid#although not glitches per se#nonetheless highlight the women's determining role in the construction of their own mediatation.

When the glitches do rec*mmence, they continue the anarchic allure of Gaga and Beyoncé's rebellion, specifically their lyrical refusal to –mit submit to external technologies of control. In a sequence that mirrors Gaga's jail cell spectacle, the camera watches as Beyoncé, alone in a kitschy motel room, orders a caller (and by extension the viewer) to "stop telephoning me." Here Beyoncé does not so much dance as strike a series of poses that gl\tches repcat to form a dance; her image vibrates as she mimes screaming into the phone, beating her head in frustration, and jumping menacingly toward the camera. While a downright ladylike femme fatale in her narrative sequences, when Beyoncé reaches her glitch, her spectacle becomes uncontrollable, erotic but dangerous, in excess of the system that would incorporate—. Whereas Beyoncé's image is still manifestly sexualized—as Gaga's and Madonna's have also been—it refuses to toe the line or adhere to linear time. There's something wrong with its to-be-looked-at-ness—or perhaps within to-be-looked-at-ness generally.

Thus, the gl-glitch allows Beyoncé, Gaga, and Madonna to remind their viewers that although we may perceive them as objects of fantasy, as fantasies they are not always under our control. Fantasies may mimic the teleology of classical narrative, but they need not adhere to it nor to its promises of cohesion, coherence, and closure. Interpreted by these artists as the pause, the skip, or the stutter, fantasy's emphasis on the prolongation of desire creates room for other ideologies, other potentialities within commercial genres. Of course, watching a video glitch can be an endlessly frustrating experience; suddenly the entertainment that seemed so available, the product that seemed so willing to give itself to the viewer, just stops. These intentional glitches remind the spectator of the incompleteness of the image, that its object—the performer, the media file—was always already absent. Their feminist appropriations draw viewers' attention to DON'T TELL ME the mediated setting of desire and spectacle without entirely dismantling that setting; instead, they direct it toward other investments. Through the prolongation of desire, they create pleasure in the breakdown of the system, be it just the streaming video platform or

NΩTES

1. *Oxford English Dictionary Online*, s.v. "glitch," accessed March 2011, http://www.oed.com. proxy.library.georgetown.edu/view/Entry/78999?isAdvanced=false&result=1&rskey=30 IDn5&.
2. Iman Moradi et al., *Glitch: Designing Imperfection* (New York: Mark Blatty Publishers, 2009), back cover; glitches added.
3. See Santiago Fouz-Hernandez and Freya Jarmen-Ivens, eds., *Madonna's Drowned Worlds: New Approaches to her Cultural Transformations* (Burlington, VT: Ashgate, 2004).

4. For more on the sonic significance of digital dropouts, see Anne Danielsen and Arnt Maasø, "Mediating Music: Materiality and Silence in Madonna's 'Don't Tell Me,'" *Popular Music* 28, no. 2 (2009): 129.

5. Joshua Clover and Christopher Nealon, "Don't Ask, Don't Tell Me," *Film Quarterly* 60, no. 3 (2007): 65.

6. Ibid; glitches added.

7. Italic disruptions courtesy of Laura U. Marks's essay (chapter 7) for this volume.

8. Carol Vernallis, "The Aesthetics of Music Video: An Analysis of Madonna's 'Cherish,'" *Popular Music* 17, no. 2 (1998): 155–157. Kay Dickinson raises a similar point as regards the performer's body during her analysis of "Music Video and Synaesthic Possibility" in *Medium Cool: Music Videos from Soundies to Cellphones*, ed. Roger Beebe and Jason Middleton (Durham, NC: Duke University Press, 2007), 16.

9. Laura Mulvey, "Visual Pleasure and Narrative Cinema," in *The Film Theory Reader: Debates and Arguments*, ed. Marc Furstenau (New York: Routledge, 2010), 201.

10. Ibid.

11. Ibid., 205.

12. Ibid; glitches added.

13. Mmany mmusicologists have argued that mmusic video criticismm tends to overvalue the immage, indeed to slight the mmusic in favor of visual analysis, and I acknowledge that mmy turn to Mmulvey might seemm to perpetuate this prejudice. However, I actually want to use Mmulvey's theory of filmic scopophilia to prove that pop mmusic produces different arrangemments of visual pleasure for the mmusic video, including a different temmporal logic that enables femminist appropriations of the video glitch.

14. Carol Vernallis, "Strange People, Weird Objects: The Nature of Narrativity, Character, and Editing in Music Videos," in *Medium Cool: Music Videos from Soundies to Cellphones*, ed. Roger Beebe and Jason Middleton (Durham, NC: Duke University Press, 2007), 114–117.

15. Incidentally, it is also the second most downloaded song of all time on iTunes. See "All Time Top Songs," Apple Website, ACCESS DATE, http://www.apple.com/itunes/10-billion-song-countdown/.

16. Indeed, in an e-mail message to author on April 10, 2012, Manon points out that "the drag-and-drop procedure of digital editing lends itself to the "square" or "blocky" truncations and alternations."

17. Jean Laplanche and J. B. Pontalis, "Fantasy and the Origin of Sexuality," in *Formations of Fantasy*, ed. Victor Burgin, James Donald, and Cora Kaplan (New York: Methuen, 1986), 26.

18. Ibid.

19. Of course, I do not mean to suggest that Gaga is anything like the quintessential artist of streaming music videos. Yet, as David McCarthy and María Zuazu point out (chapter 31) elsewhere in this volume, Gaga's "Frankenstein assemblages" reflect their contempor/// distribu//// platf/rm/ and their zeitgeist in their negotiation of Gaga's star image. Thus, I see them hinting at new feminist uses of new media.

20. Johan Weiner, "How Smart is Lady Gaga?" *Slate*, July 16, 2009, http://www.slate.com/id/2220502/.

21. Vernallis, "The Aesthetics of Music Video," 163.

22. Mulvey, "Visual Pleasure," 204.

23. Linda Williams, "Film Bodies: Gender, Genre, and Excess," in *Film Theory and Criticism*, ed. Leo Braudy and Marshall Cohen, 5th ed. (New York: Oxford University Press, 1999), 711.

24. Ibid.
25. Mulvey, "Visual Pleasure," 203.
26. *Oxford English Dictionary*, s.v. "glitch."
27. Mulvey, "Visual Pleasure," 203–204; glitches added.
28. Ibid.
29. Sadly, it is beyond the scope of this article to turn this observation toward an analysis of Gaga's alien spectacle in "Born This Way" (2011; dir. Nick Knight and Lady Gaga), but I hope it will inspire other little monsters to take up the work.
30. Roland Barthes, "Striptease," in *Mythologies*, trans. Annette Lavers (New York: Farrar, Straus, and Giroux, 1972), 85.
31. Ibid.
32. See Jacques Lacan, "The Mirror Stage as Formative of the *I* Function as Revealed in Psychoanalytic Experience," in *Ecrits: A Selection*, trans. Bruce Fink, Héloise Fink, and Russell Grigg (New York: Norton, 2002) ; and Jacques Lacan, *Seminar I: Freud's Papers on Technique* (New York: Norton, 1991).

Select B#bl#ography

Barthes, Roland. "Striptease." In *Mythologies*, translated by Annette Lavers, 84–87. New York: Farrar, Straus, and Giroux, 1972.

Clover, Joshua, and Christopher Nealon. "Don't Ask, Don't Tell Me." *Film Quarterly* 60, no. 3 (2007): 62–67.

Danielsen, Anne, and Arnt Maasø. "Mediating Music: Materiality and Silence in Madonna's 'Don't Tell Me.' " *Popular Music* 28, no. 2 (2009): 127–142.

Dickinson, Kay. "Music Video and Synaesthic Possibility." In *Medium Cool: Music Videos from Soundies to Cellphones*, edited by Roger Beebe and Jason Middleton, 13–29. Durham, NC: Duke University Press, 2007.

Laplanche, Jean, and J. B. Pontalis. "Fantasy and the Origin of Sexuality." In *Formations of Fantasy*, edited by Victor Burgin, James Donald, and Cora Kaplan, 5–34. New York: Methuen, 1986.

Moradi, Iman, Ant Scott, Joe Gilmore, and Christopher Murphy. *Glitch: Designing Imperfection*. New York: Mark Blatty Publishers, 2009.

Mulvey, Laura. "Visual Pleasure and Narrative Cinema." In *The Film Theory Reader: Debates and Arguments*, edited by Marc Furstenau, 200–208. New York: Routledge, 2010.

Vernallis, Carol. "The Aesthetics of Music Video: An Analysis of Madonna's 'Cherish.' " *Popular Music* 17, no. 2 (1998): 153–185.

——. "Strange People, Weird Objects: The Nature of Narrativity, Character, and Editing in Music Videos." In *Medium Cool: Music Videos from Soundies to Cellphones*, edited by Roger Beebe and Jason Middleton, 111–151. Durham, NC: Duke University Press, 2007.

Williams, Linda. "Film Bodies: Gender, Genre, and Excess." In *Film Theory and Criticism*, 5th ed., edited by Leo Braudy and Marshall Cohen, 701–715. New York: Oxford University Press, 1999.

CHAPTER 10

···

DISCURSIVE ACCENTS IN SOME RECENT DIGITAL MEDIA WORKS

···

JOANNA DEMERS

> Being-in and its attunement are made known in discourse and indicated
> in language by intonation, modulation, in the tempo of talk, "in the way
> of speaking." The communication of the existential possibilities of attun-
> ement, that is, the disclosing of existence, can become the true aim of
> "poetic" speech.
>
> —Heidegger, *Being and Time*[1]

I'D like to begin by considering a word from the title of Ryan Trecartin's *KCorea-INC.K (Section A)*: "K-Corea." What on earth could this word possibly mean? Obviously, it nods to the country Korea, but with a "K" first, followed by the "C." When pronounced with the Valley Girl or hip-hop accents that many of Trecartin's characters use, "Corea" also sounds a bit like "career," and this sonic similarity figures centrally in the video, which features female multinational conglomerate employees whose names reflect the parts of the world they presumably represent (e.g., Global Korea, Israel Korea, USA Korea, etc.). So, depending on the accent with which it is pronounced, K-Corea can point toward two seemingly unrelated signifieds simultaneously. The added punch is the discrepancy between the image and sound: K-Corea *looks* like a neologism, but it *sounds* like it could be spelled "K. Korea," or "Kay Korea"—that is, a recognizable letter, or a woman's first name or initial, followed by the country Korea. In other words, the image and sound of K-Corea do not completely correspond to one another. Trecartin's video works are replete with this sort of slippage between image and sound, especially the sound of characters' accents. And such slippages are sources of great ambiguity and power.

Yet the meaning of the word "K-Corea" never congeals into anything recognizable or certain. We hear numerous characters use it, and, thanks to the familiarity of their accents, we can almost make ourselves believe that we understand what "it" is, this

"K-Corea." Almost. In fact, the sway of this single word is formidable, for in addition to dimly suggesting a country and the concept of vocation, it also parodies our culture's love affair with abbreviations and shibboleths, catchwords that betray a speaker's affiliations. "K-Corea," in other words, is a parody, not of the words "Korea" or "career," but rather of those smitten with the latest techno-lingo, those who use words without fully comprehending their power.

In this essay, I look at examples of sound–image relationships in recent digital media works that display such semiological polyvalence. I create an extended metaphor, likening the sonic markers of discourse—the low drone in horror film soundtracks, the cheesy guitar rock of 1980s television, or the atonality of institutional "new music"—to spoken accents. For, just as spoken accents often convey knowledge about the provenance of a speaker, these *discursive accents* exist as tell-tale markers that (correctly or otherwise) indicate the genre, style, or medium into which a work falls. To be clear, a discursive accent could be a genre (e.g., wuxia film) or a style (e.g., poorly edited amateur material), but it is not reducible to either genre or style. In the course of this essay, I'll identify discursive accents such as new music, torture porn, hip-hop diction, and bad 1980s television, practices that in some instances count as a single genre but might in other instances exist as larger cultural phenomena. And, just as listeners to an unfamiliar foreign language often attend to subtleties—pitch, cadence, nuance, liaison— that go by unnoticed when words' meanings are clear, listeners to discursive accents may attend to stylistic and generic frictions and disjunctions that might otherwise be swept away in more discursively straightforward works. In the moments I consider, image stabilizes and grounds the work in some discourse—usually just one—whereas discursive accents such as diegetic or nondiegetic sound and music destabilize the work by suggesting multiple discourses. In these moments of generic hybridity and stylistic instability, discursive accents retreat from meaning and exist more as immanent, unintelligible sound.

My essay therefore explores discursive accents in four recent digital video works: Ryan Trecartin's *K-Corea INC.K (Section A)* (2009), Paul McCarthy's *WGG Test* (2003), Animal Charm's *Edge TV with Animal Charm* (2008), and Sean Griffin's *Tension Study II: Eagle Claw Wu Tsiao Chen Wins* (2007). These videos share many elements, including parody, violence, and stereotypes of race, ethnicity, and sexuality. Rather than dwelling on these topical similarities, however, I'd like to focus this discussion on one issue: what discursive accents offer to the field of aesthetics. One of the more vexing questions in recent aesthetic theory has been what, if anything, distinguishes our experience of art from everything we consider "non-art." Discursive accents suggest how content and form, the traditional poles of artistic production, can merge and ultimately reconcile with one another. And this merging, so I argue, signals what is truly distinctive about the experience afforded by art. Discursive accents show that art cannot be subsumed under abstract signifiers and signifieds. Like spoken accents, discursive accents cannot be reduced to mere words.

RYAN TRECARTIN, *K-COREA INC.K*
(*SECTION A*) (2009)

K-Corea INC.K (Section A) is impossible to describe in a straightforward manner.[2] Like much of Trecartin's video work, it inundates the viewer with seemingly hackneyed '90s-era editing and video effects, a disjointed soundtrack, and characters that scream and shout at one another and at the camera in unintelligible slang. A teleological summary of the plot, which would appear to treat a fantastical, parodic board meeting, would be both impracticable and irrelevant. At best, I can present fleeting impressions and clumsy attempts to grasp at broad themes, but the thickness of Trecartin's material makes it so that two viewers may recall very different information.[3] We have three groups of characters: Global Korea, an African-American man in drag who commands a bevy of blond-wig-wearing women (real or in drag) with names like "Argentinian Korea," "Hungary Korea," and the like; USA Korea (played by Ryan Trecartin), also in drag and sporting a blond wig; and Mexico Korea, also blonde and sporting a faux-Spanish accent. USA Korea addresses the camera for most of her time on-screen, speaking words that vaguely have to do with corporate policy in a sing-song voice:

> We the Situations have Issue UpSetta. YES
> TreavelCustity.Dot Compromise,,,, Custody,,Over-Load= YES
> And Then, We as Crashing,,, Inside Out ... (need)
> Stridex-Corporate

Global Korea's declamation sounds like African-American slang and is laden with the sorts of turns of phrase we might hear in a drag bar, a hip-hop song, or on a third-rate daytime talk show:

> Flying Company,,, 3rd/World-Class, You Can smoke ALL UP in this Shit

USA Korea, on the other hand, ends her phrases with a melodic figure that sounds like the vocal style of Beyoncé or Rhianna, and because Trecartin subjects his voice (as well as those of many of his actors) to pitch-shifting, USA Korea ends up sounding a bit as if she has sucked on helium or is singing through a Vocoder or Talk Box. Mexico Korea, meanwhile, also appears by herself and addresses the camera, apparently discussing both corporate policy and her "love-life."

The sound in *K-Corea INC.K (Section A)* is dense and turgid, but it can be roughly organized into six types of discourse: techno music, ambient/New Age music, "video effects" (obviously synthesized explosion sounds, zoom sounds, helicopter sounds), USA Korea's and Mexico Korea's monologues, and Global Korea's group conversations. These materials, for the most part, do not overlap but instead follow each other in quick succession; the pacing of this and other Trecartin works is irregular and jagged, which has the effect of making time seem to pass more slowly than it really does. Fragments of dialogue or synthesizer-disco follow each other incongruously, and there is never any pause to allow viewers to digest what they are witnessing. The 30-odd minutes of *K-Corea INC.K (Section A)*, in other words, seem like an eternity.

One particularly disorienting moment begins at 7:00. This is the first instance of relative calm after a constant onslaught of chattering characters, cell phone ringtones, and booming sound effects. The sound includes simple piano chords perhaps channeling New Age music. Global Korea says directly to the camera, "I'm gonna fire her" as her blonde coterie looks on with glee; Global Korea is presumably referring to the hermaphrodite dressed in a rubber suit and mask who is writhing on the sofa in front of her. Global Korea picks up what appears to be a gasoline container and pours its contents on the rubber-clad person, then lights a cigarette, takes a few languorous drags, and then flicks it on the person, saying "I had to let you go." When the cigarette falls, the screen action freezes and the words "I had to let you go" suddenly appear on-screen in yellow and black (8:12), the suggestion being that Global Korea has just set someone on fire.

The schism between sound and image here goes further than similar instances of aestheticized violence in, say, the films of Tarantino, where hip, popular songs serve as odes to horror. The prime example of this practice is the infamous torture scene in *Reservoir Dogs* (1992), when Mr. Blonde (Michael Madsen) hears and dances along to Steelers' Wheels' "Stuck in the Middle with You" even as he prepares to mutilate the cop he has just captured. As with so many of Tarantino's soundtrack choices, this perky song perversely reflects a character's enjoyment of carnage.[4] But Trecartin's score at this moment sounds like straightforwardly nonironic New Age music—music meant to calm and lift the spirit. Absent are any linkages between sound and image; the music is nondiegetic, but also sorely out of place, even by the standards of recent torture porn that revels in scenes such as this. By the end of this immolation sequence, it's quite difficult to place *K-Corea INC.K* into any particular genre. Its first 7 minutes are frenetic and loud, and the next 2 minutes sound calm, yet lead to violence, a violence that seems ignored or repressed by the soundtrack. Trecartin's sound–image combinations like these function as ciphers, leaving confusion in their wake.

Paul McCarthy, *WGG Test* (2003)

The premise is banal: a handheld camera entering a pleasure yacht where several nubile, bikini-clad young women are partying.[5] Banal, and derivative, for as McCarthy's title acronym hints, this is a video modeled on the popular *Girls Gone Wild* reality series featuring college women who drink, have casual sex, and flash the camera and random passersby. But in McCarthy's alternative universe of "Wild Gone Girls," these starlets are also busy hacking up the limbs and body of the captain (played by McCarthy himself), who is impossibly grinning and laughing along with them, at one point cheerfully saying, "I forgot my penis enlarger."

Wild Gone Girls does not feature anything technically unusual. Its sound consists of the girls' chatter, background party music like Al Green's "Tired of Being Alone," an intermittent high-pitched whine accompanying slow-motion shots of girls wielding axes, and electronic beeping paired with close-ups of two girls' bikini-covered crotches. The video is brief and effective at parodizing a few contemporary genres: reality television, sexploitation, horror, and torture porn.

The shock of *WGG Test* lasts only a moment. After the opening revelation that we are watching a butchering, the camera that was facing downward at the male victim continues to angle further until it is showing the two standing women upside down. The camera then pauses at that angle so that we have a clear view of their bodies, simultaneously sexualized and defamiliarized in their upside-down state, as the soundtrack begins to play a screeching, high-pitched drone, similar to something that might appear in a horror film just before the killer attacks his next victim. After this initial moment of shock, the video asks us how long we can watch the video without flinching, and how long we can stomach the violence. The girls in *WGG Test* continue to hack at their victim, whose leg incredibly remains attached throughout the whole film; this differs from violence in mainstream Hollywood horror films, in which victims' limbs are dispatched quickly and efficiently. Part of the challenge here lies in fathoming McCarthy's aims. If *WGG Test* behaved more like a straightforward parody of only one genre—say, reality sexploitation—the high art–minded viewers that presumably constitute McCarthy's audience would have an easier time laughing along, secure in the knowledge that they were not complicit with the depicted violence. But the collision of reality sexploitation with other genres, like horror and torture porn, makes it more difficult for viewers to look away. The low drone, a staple of horror films, would lead us to believe that we are watching yet another aestheticization of violence and horror. Yet its images confound that premise by presenting a hedonistic environment of consensual violence, of sadism met with masochism. To what, then, is this dire music responding? If everyone is laughing and having fun, is anyone getting hurt? And by watching this slaughter, are spectators implicitly sanctioning it? By the end of *WGG Test*, our capacity for decoding discursive accents has been dulled, and we are left with considerable doubt as to the ethical stance of the work we have just watched.

Animal Charm, *Edge TV* with Animal Charm (2008)

Animal Charm is a duo comprised of Jim Fetterly and Rich Bott who works with found film and video footage dating from the 1980s and 1990s. This footage draws from local access programming, industrial training and promotion videos, television news "magazines" like *Dateline* or *60 Minutes*, and family sit-coms and dramas. *Edge TV with Animal Charm* is funny perhaps only to those who grew up during the 1980s watching a great deal of television or else to those who know the conventions of television from that era quite well.[6] This brief work is an encyclopedia of much of the conventions of network television. Its opening credit graphic spells "Edge TV" in neon letters blinking and scrolling across the screen, and these letters are laid over footage of men and women with big hair and bigger smiles. The music for this opening graphic sounds like the theme music for *21 Jump Street*: glitzy guitar rock with a sleazy saxophone. And hey, there's even someone zip-lining!

So, with one brief sequence, *Edge TV* situates us in mid-1980s TV-land, with touches of MTV, teen melodrama, and the general euphoria that was so prominent in the media of that era. After the title sequence, the mood shifts abruptly to something recalling a serious evening news exposé: a mute soundtrack paired with slowly tracking shots of a gate locked with a chain, an unidentified empty lot, and a boarded-up building. The last shot in this sequence is particularly cliché: a close-up shot on the chain binding the fence, showing the deserted road behind it. This sort of shot would be routine in stories centering on urban neglect or financial collapse, and, with the utter absence of sound, the affect is sober and deflating…so much so that the onset of the next sequence is jolting. We hear a man's voice shouting and see (presumably the same) man falling from a tall military training obstacle, and then immediately jump to a medium shot of a couple seated on a sofa reading a document, with the television in the background showing a dog's face. Animal Charm added this television dog to the original footage; its resolution is too clear in comparison with the image of the couple on the sofa to have originated from the same material. Again, that generic friction and goofiness are important here; the rapid succession of unrelated styles and images is what propels this video.

We jump to a long shot of a house in the wilderness with smoke gently wafting from its chimney, footage taken from *Homeward Bound: The Incredible Journey* (1993), a live-action children's film featuring a cat and two dogs who speak with human voices. We hear a jubilant voice-over of the dog Chance (Michael J. Fox), who shouts "Turkey! Turkey! Turkey!" Then, Animal Charm intervenes by fragmenting and looping the shot to seem as if it were playing on fast-forward. We move to other footage from *Homeward Bound*, and then cut to an interview with a man in his early twenties who talks about his addiction to porn: "I was selling it for a couple years and, uhh, watching it…a lot [pause] and I was just screwed up." This man's constricted breath and slightly open mouth suggest that he is perhaps not over his addiction. Cut to the penultimate sequence, the largest of the video: a random collage of footage of military training programs, jet-skiing, people tripping and falling over random objects, all overlaid with poor-quality chroma-key graphics of neon-covered hands waving in front of the screen. The music for this sequence is equally silly: a synthesizer organ playing a mid-tempo minor-mode theme that escalates in tension. The video then ends with a reprisal of the title sequence graphics.

Edge TV is funny—very funny—but probably only to those conversant with 1980s American television. Animal Charm videos make sense if approached according to the same criteria that we use for assessing turntablism in hip-hop or the cinematic homages in Tarantino's films. The obscure excerpts that Animal Charm has reclaimed are odd, but not necessarily funny. Some are boring or even disturbing. Rather, we laugh at the kitsch that results from so many strange, disparate samples being strung together, one after another. The discursive accents that emerge from this hodgepodge recall the popular media of an era that was a little too impressed with itself and its burgeoning technologies of home computers and video recorders to notice when it spoke too loudly, too crassly. Unlike in the Trecartin and McCarthy examples, where accents of different discourses compete and ultimately render each other unintelligible, the various accents employed in *Edge TV with Animal Charm* congeal to form a hyperstylized view of 1980s media, one that disregards the particular in order to arrive at a general sense of the decade's ridiculousness.

SEAN GRIFFIN, *TENSION STUDY II: EAGLE CLAW WU TSIAO CHEN WINS* (2007)

Griffin is a composer and artist who usually works with opera and staged works. *Tension Study II*, however, is a digital video of a live performance that, itself, features portions of digitally rendered film.[7] Its real-life star, the Taiwanese-Canadian percussionist Aiyun Huang, plays her collection of instruments (mostly crotales and woodblocks) to match the actions of a digital collage video that Griffin extracted from the Taiwanese/Hong Kong martial arts film, *Master of the Flying Guillotine* (1975). This footage loops fantastical special effects-laden scenes that feature its female protagonist Wu Tsiao Chen punching, kicking, and flying through the air. Huang also speaks a text taken from wuxia films in Chinese, with English subtitles projected on a large screen behind the performer. Griffin, who collaborated with percussionist Huang to craft the piece, asks her to match her attacks to the rhythms of the characters' attacks; sometimes these are Wu's, and other times they are those of Wu's opponents. This is an enormously exacting task. As Huang and Griffin describe it in their written joint-discussion of the piece, it is akin to asking the percussionist to "fight" Wu. What results is a mixture of percussion performance with Huang reciting a spoken text in Chinese and shouting and yelling in time with the battle sequences.

Tension Study II combines elements of Hong Kong martial arts films with the gestures and sounds of contemporary classical music, often known by practitioners as "new music." "New music" is a recent outgrowth of twentieth-century modernism. Prizing abstraction, complexity, and performer brilliance, it is often fiendishly difficult to execute, and its audiences are quite small, with its largest fan base in European cities. Outside of these few oases, new music depends nearly entirely on support from universities in North America and Asia. It is thus diametrically opposed to popular culture, often proudly so. The sounds and performative rituals of new music are, oddly enough, strangely similar to the gestures in many Hong Kong martial arts films. Many new music pieces, including *Tension Study II*, oscillate between moments of relative calm and poise, and sections of intense activity—much like fight scenes in which a warrior motionlessly holds his arms up and contemplates an enemy before attacking. New music also shares with martial arts films a delight in stretching the performer's body, both literally and figuratively, in pushing it to the extremes of endurance. Like many martial arts heroes, new music performers routinely wear black clothes onstage and keep their faces expressionless. Many new music works are so demanding that they cannot be performed by more than one or two specialists worldwide.

I want to focus on a particular passage in *Tension Study II*, because this instance represents well what happens throughout the 13-minute work. The passage begins with Huang saying "she froze" in Chinese. As Huang speaks this text, she plays a roll on woodblocks in a gradual crescendo; this crescendo culminates in the first fight scene of the piece, when a battle from *Master of the Flying Guillotine* takes place as Huang frantically hits various percussion instruments while yelling and shouting, all in time with the music. The video section here depicts the heroine Wu struggling to battle an unnamed male opponent, but this opponent nimbly avoids her kicks and punches. At several points, Griffin "performs" the video footage like a hip-hop DJ plays a turntable, letting it play backward and forward to create a new rhythm rather than the one already inherent in the film. Huang must try to match this new rhythm both with her percussion attacks and vocalizations.

Some of the instruments Huang plays in this passage have timbres and formants that resemble the intonations and diphthongs of Huang as she speaks Chinese. One could say that these instruments "pronounce" in a manner similar to Huang, at least to the ears of a Westerner who knows no Chinese. But these instruments are also part and parcel of the arsenal of post-1945 new music percussion music. And the domain of new music, as well as percussion performance in general, is, for the most part, dominated by white European and North American male composers and performers. New music's origins in post-World War II aesthetics have imbued it with a tendency to search for "new" sounds that have no prior grounding in culture or history, a goal resembling the phenomenological fallacy that there can be a primary, universal experience that precedes social and cultural imprinting.[8] New music is openly a product of white male high-art culture and has always enjoyed significant financial and philosophical support at the hands of the US government, as well as of international defense corporations.[9] Yet new music often represents itself as pure, idealized, and objective, not besmirched by messy considerations of class, ethnicity, or gender.[10] In this sense, new music displays affinities with other cultural practices associated with whiteness (like classical opera) that often represent themselves as normative and nonmarked.[11] This makes Huang's presence as a Taiwanese-Canadian female percussionist all the more provocative. *Tension Study II* re-embeds the sounds of Huang's percussion set-up within a national and ethnic identity that is *not* Western European or Caucasian American. But the question that then bedevils the piece, and this is undoubtedly an intentional question on the part of Griffin, is how this representation affects its two women, Wu and Huang. The piece pits them as adversaries: Huang must struggle and fight to stay in time with Wu's movements.[12] They are also fighting their own battles, respectively. Wu must fight against a merciless male on-screen opponent who, at least initially, overpowers her. Huang, one of a very small number of Asian female new music performers with a career of international repute,[13] must also struggle here to play an extremely challenging piece that risks objectifying both her culture of origin (through the popular cinema of East Asia), as well as her professional culture (i.e., the culture of new music performers and composers). The percussion instruments she plays already seem to imitate and, to some ears perhaps even mock, her intonation in speaking Chinese. And although non-Chinese speakers can understand the text thanks to the subtitles projected on the screen above her, the foreignness of Huang's musical and spoken languages is nevertheless rendered into spectacle. *Tension Study II* relies directly on accent—that of Huang, as well as that of her instruments—to convey foreignness, but risks reinforcing orientalisms that reduce wuxia film to grunts, yells, and physical stunt-work.

Discursive Accents

Pierre Schaeffer, inventor of *musique concrète* and a prolific theoretician, spends much of his *Traité des objets musicaux* discussing various types of listening. In particular, he designates four modes of listening: Mode 1 (*écouter*) concentrates on sound emission and its objective qualities. Mode 2 (*ouïr*) involves hearing in a passive manner, simply the basic reception of sound. Mode 3 (*entendre*) involves not only hearing but attending to particular aspects of sound. Mode 4 (*comprendre*) involves comprehension and understanding, not only of the sound itself but its external associations.[14] In making these fine distinctions among the four modes, Schaeffer erects a critical framework for advocating yet another type of listening, *reduced listening*, whereby the listener brackets out any information about the source of sound production or its external associations. Reduced listening is critical to *musique concrète*, which can call on both abstract sounds as well as those, like the sounds of a train, that are easily identifiable. Michel Chion, one of Schaeffer's *musique concrète* composition students as well as the preeminent film sound theorist, has taken great steps to condense and synthesize Schaeffer's writings into the invaluable *Guides des objets sonores*, a glossary that delineates these listening theories with painstaking detail. Yet, however meticulously Chion the *concrètiste* parses out these details, Chion the film sound theorist minimizes the subtle distinctions between these four modes by noting that acousmatic situations (in which the sight of sound production is hidden from view) discourage, rather than encourage, reduced listening.[15]

In other words, Schaeffer's and Chion's writings, considered broadly, ultimately suggest only two extremes of listening: listening for meaning and signification, or else listening for pure, innate qualities of sound (i.e., reduced listening). But the video works profiled earlier introduce the possibility of an intermediary type of listening, one in which discursive accents imply a work's generic and stylistic provenance. According to Schaeffer's schema, this sort of listening would most closely approximate *comprendre*, for here, we are listening not only for the meaning of words and sounds, but also for the context that surrounds them. Yet these four works make the prospects for successfully listening for meaning appear dim. Trecartin's script insinuates themes and concepts without ever specifying them, and the other three works make such limited usage of dialogue that meaning is circumscribed in them as well. However, in the absence of any concrete meaning, sounds can still refer obliquely.

To understand how this might work, let's compare how we hear discursive accents with the manner in which we listen to someone speaking our language in a clear and understandable way, but with an accent other than our own. In such situations, we don't have to strain to understand the meaning of the speaker's words. Instead, our attention may center on the peculiarities of the speaker's pronunciation, and, if we have heard this accent before, we may think about how such an accent seems to represent a region or a people. In these situations, accents can stand metonymically for a whole cultural identity. When unfamiliar, accents can impede the listening process; when familiar, they can aid it. Accents provide an easy means for listeners to categorize anything—languages, media, people—and then to feel that they enjoy some power over them. When we are familiar with an accent, we can say to ourselves, "Oh yes, that's a such-and-such accent, I know where that person comes from." When we are not familiar with an accent, listening becomes riskier. What does the accent mean? From where does it originate? Will I ever be able to understand this person? The four works I discuss here all contain moments of juncture in which the accents of multiple styles and genres coexist, overlap, and compete. These are often fraught moments, moments when we are not sure how to understand or react to the sounds we hear. An accent that we might otherwise presume to know suddenly becomes foreign again, as if we are hearing it for the first time. And so, instead of hearing that accent for its content and affinities to the discourse to which it supposedly belongs, we listen to the accent for its own properties, qualities that are not easily categorized or reduced to words.

Discursive accents, then, exist in a state of ambivalence. They are hinges, and circumstances will dictate whether they veer into the territory of concepts or surface phenomena. In other words, discursive accents exist in the no man's land of the sign, for they can be heard either as signifieds (i.e., content) or signifiers (i.e., form). This ambivalence is potent and incendiary, for as Cavarero and Dyson have each argued, both classical metaphysics and modern linguistics have habitually ignored the uniqueness of the voice—its timbre, breath, and tone—in order to listen nearly exclusively to the meaning of the voice's speech.[16] As used in these four examples, discursive accents resituate the phenomenal qualities of voice (or sound, taken broadly) into an artwork, and divest sound of its signifying properties so that it can conceal, rather than reveal, meaning.

A handheld camera that jerkily shows the seemingly unrehearsed, natural actions and movements of nonactors; the grunts and shrieks of an aspiring kung fu master; cheesy synthesizer music. These phenomena can all be taken for themselves as characteristics specific to one genre or style. Or, they can be read as cues for larger groupings of discourse. The handheld camera is a staple of reality films (like *The Blair Witch Project*) and television (like *Girls Gone Wild*). Kung fu vocalizations are obviously germane to kung fu cinema. And cheesy synthesizer music appears in a host of 1980s programs, especially action television series. With enough background experience and knowledge, viewers and listeners can comfortably categorize most of the art they consume according to the conventions with which they are already familiar. This is how we apprehend art, by making it fit within a matrix of associations.

These generic conventions function similarly to accents of spoken language because they can serve to alert a listener or viewer to the provenance of an artwork. Likewise, to an uninitiated viewer, they will seem opaque and inscrutable, rather than transparent and intelligible. The parodic elements of these four works give considerable weight to the viewer's ability to recognize generic and stylistic codes; someone totally ignorant of kung fu cinema and new music culture would not appreciate their volatile combination in *Tension Study II*, for instance, just as viewers of *Edge TV* need to have some appreciation of 1980s television to appreciate its humor. But these moments of recognition are fleeting. Just as soon as we recognize through image the genres and media at play—wuxia, new music, bad television—sound scrambles that certainty. Huang's slow declamation is, of course, taken from lines in *Master of the Flying Guillotine*, but it also recalls the *Sprechstimme* parts of Schoenberg's *Pierrot Lunaire* (albeit in Chinese), and her shouts during battle sequences could easily fit amid new music works by composers like Georges Aperghis or Helmut Lachenmann that make similar demands on performers. Similarly, the sounds in *Edge TV* identify their provenance as the distant past of cheesy television, but they would seem perfectly at home if heard as belonging to a musical or sound collage.

CONCLUSION

I want to consider two issues in closing: how does the concept of accent in a work of art complicate our understanding of the definition of art? And, are the tendencies I chart in this essay specific to digital media works?

Discursive accents, as deployed in the four works assembled here, function as both signifiers and signifieds. This division, not coincidentally, also underlies the traditional definition of art as a coupling of content with form.[17] Hegel, for instance, describes art in terms reminiscent of Plato's "Theory of Forms," as a combination of idealized concept with physical form: art "has as its basis the unity of meaning and shape."[18] Sontag revisits this polemic in her essay "On Style," in which she cannily faults then-contemporary criticism for making a false distinction between style and substance.[19] Among Hegel's most passionate moments in his *Aesthetics* are those when he argues for a dialectical relationship between concept and form, when the two overcome their differences in order to resemble one another. Sontag, meanwhile, advocates a revised understanding of style, one that expands its territory beyond the mere surface details of a work. But neither Hegel nor Sontag are specific in their recommendations, and we are left not knowing what a truly integrated ontology of art, one that reconciles the opposites of style and substance, content and form, signifier and signified, might mean.

The concept of discursive accent offers one way in which we might accomplish such a reconciliation. For the manner in which discursive accent is enlisted here suggests a clear distinction between art and sign. Works with unambiguous discursive accents (think referential pastiches like Tarantino's films) sometimes run the risk of being reduced to their influences. Instead of attending to the way that a particular work employs its material, we often fall prey to the academic temptation of naming the work's influences, of creating genealogies, and, in so doing, of reducing our experience of the artwork into a game of identification. But the discursive accents in these four works reinforce their status as works of *art*, not as sentences or other prosaic forms of discourse. Accents here confuse, rather than illuminate, meaning. And like listeners confronting an unknown language, we then attend to things usually ignored when comprehension comes easy— things like the voice's intonation, modulation, and tempo. This essay's epigraph talks of a "'poetic' speech," a speech that calls to bear these singularities of artistic form, all coincidentally expressed in terms that are acoustic and sonorous. Heidegger perhaps did not go far enough; a truly poetic speech need not be speech at all, but may be free to slide into the realm of poetry, of poiesis, where sound can be free to exist without being grounded in a particular meaning or image. In such instances of poiesis, form does not merely overpower or obliterate content, but rather *becomes* the content. In the works presented here, what ultimately matters most is not whether we can classify the barrage of discursive references, but rather whether we are aware in the first place that we are encountering a barrage.

This leads to the second question, of whether this employment of accent is particular to digital media video. I have simply tried to distinguish between works that foreground their referentiality and those that use discursive accents as a way of detracting from spectators' knowledge. This sort of approach is perhaps less likely to be adopted in mainstream narrative film[20] than it is in media like sound art, where straightforward narrative is often absent. Sound art is often defined as sound-based practice that interacts with the space in which it is heard[21]; elsewhere, it has been described as any sound-based practice that underscores the act of listening.[22] One additional characteristic to add to this list could well be the tendency for using sound epistemologically, either as a sign that contributes to listeners' knowledge or as a cipher that confounds understanding. Digital media works like those discussed here are particularly well-suited to this task since they work with image as well as sound, but we could find points of correspondence in the work of sound artist Miki Yui, who works with field recordings and synthesized sounds. Her album *Lupe Luep Peul Epul* (2001) features tracks that resemble nothing like conventional music since they lack melody, harmony, or regular rhythms. Nor do they sound like *musique concrète* or field recordings, although they are intermittent moments of recognizably captured sound. Instead, Yui's work taunts and eventually exhausts the listener's desire to identify sound sources and contexts. Like the videos I have considered, Yui's and other works of sound art have a great deal to say about sound's ability to say everything and nothing simultaneously.

Acknowledgments

I am grateful to Mandy-Suzanne Wong for her insight and suggestions.

Notes

1. Martin Heidegger, *Being and Time*, trans. Joan Stambaugh (Albany: State University of New York Press, 1996), 152.
2. Ryan Trecartin, *K-Corea INC.K (Section A)*, video, 33:05, 2009, http://vimeo.com/5841178
3. For a speculative but helpful summary, see Ryan Trecartin, "K-Corea INC. K (section a)," http://www.eai.org/title.htm?id=14602, accessed June 6, 2011.
4. Tarantino may have drawn inspiration for this scene from passages in Bret Easton Ellis' *American Psycho* (1991), in which the anti-hero Patrick Bateman slaughters some of his victims while playing upbeat 1980s hits like Huey Lewis and the News' "It's Hip to Be Square."
5. Paul McCarthy, *WGG Test*, video, 5:34, 2003, http://artforum.com/video/ id=20576& mode=large&page_id=18.
6. Animal Charm, *Edge TV with Animal Charm*, http://www.youtube. com/ watch?v=WwgMGExlfMw, accessed May 10, 2011; this clip is no longer available due to infringement claims.
7. Sean Griffin, *Tension Study II: Eagle Claw Wu Tsiao Chen Wins*, YouTube video, 17:58, 2007, http://www.youtube.com/watch?v=BrkdrcPfmok
8. For more on the phenomenological fallacy, read Brian Kane, "*L'objet sonore maintenant*: Pierre Schaeffer, Sound Objects and the Phenomenological Reduction," *Organised Sound* 12, no. 1 (2007): 15–24.
9. See Amy C. Beal, *New Music, New Allies: American Experimental Music in West Germany from the Zero Hour to Reunification* (Berkeley: University of California Press, 2006) and Georgina Born, *Rationalizing Culture: IRCAM, Boulez, and the Institutionalization of the Musical Avant-Garde* (Berkeley: University of California Press, 1995).
10. Ellen F. Waterman, "*Cassandra's Dream Song*: A Literary Feminist Perspective," *Perspectives of New Music* 32, no. 2 (1994): 154–172.
11. Nina Sun Eidsheim, "Marian Anderson and 'Sonic Blackness' in American Opera," *American Quarterly* 63, no. 3 (2011): 641–671.
12. Aiyun Huang, and Sean Griffin, "Kung Fu Fan Turns Master: Eagle Claw Wu Tsiao Chen Wins," In *Performer's Voice Volume*, eds. A. Marshman. London: Imperial College Press, 2011.
13. Huang is associate professor of percussion at McGill University in Montréal, Québec, Canada. She routinely gives solo and chamber concerts in Europe, North America, and Asia, and is regarded as one of the world's top new music percussionists.
14. Pierre Schaeffer, *Traité des objets musicaux: essais interdisciplines* (Paris: Éditions du Seuil, 1966), 113–116.
15. Michel Chion, *Audio-Vision: Sound on Screen*, trans. Claudia Gorbman (New York: Columbia University Press, 1990), 32.

16. Adriana Cavarero, *For More Than One Voice: Toward a Philosophical of Vocal Expression* (Palo Alto, CA: Stanford University Press, 2005) and Frances Dyson, *Sounding New Media: Immersion and Embodiment in the Arts and Culture* (Berkeley: University of California Press, 2009).

17. For more on the analogous relationship between art and signs, see Paul De Man, "Sign and Symbol in Hegel's *Aesthetics*," in *Aesthetic Ideology*, ed. Andrzej Warminski (Minneapolis: University of Minnesota Press, 1996), 91–104.

18. G. W. F. Hegel, *Aesthetics: Lectures on Fine Art*, trans. T. M. Knox, vol. 1 (Oxford: Clarendon, 1975), 602.

19. Susan Sontag, "On Style," in *Against Interpretation and Other Essays* (New York: Picador, 1961), 15–36.

20. A few Hollywood films provide exceptions to this rule, including *The Usual Suspects* (1995) and *Snatch* (2000).

21. Alan Licht, *Sound Art: Beyond Music, Between Categories* (New York: Rizzoli, 2007).

22. Salome Voegelin, *Listening to Noise and Silence: Towards a Philosophy of Sound Art* (London: Continuum, 2010).

SELECT BIBLIOGRAPHY

Cavarero, Adriana. *For More Than One Voice: Toward a Philosophical of Vocal Expression*. Palo Alto: Stanford University Press, 2005.

Cameron, Dan, ed. *Paul McCarthy*. Ostfildern: Hatje Cantz, 2001.

Chion, Michel. *Audio-Vision; Sound on Screen*. Translated by Claudia Gorbman. New York: Columbia University Press, 1990.

Demers, Joanna. *Listening Through the Noise: The Aesthetics of Experimental Electronic Music*. New York: Oxford University Press, 2010.

Dyson, Frances. *Sounding New Media: Immersion and Embodiment in the Arts and Culture*. Berkeley: University of California Press, 2009.

Licht, Alan. *Sound Art: Beyond Music, Between Categories*. New York: Rizzoli, 2007.

McGarry, Kevin, ed. *Ryan Trecartin: Any Ever*. New York: Skira Rizzoli, 2011.

Schaeffer, Pierre. *Traité des Objets Musicaux: Essais Interdisciplines*. Paris: Éditions du Seuil, 1966.

Sontag, Susan. "On Style." In *Against Interpretation and Other Essays*, 15–36. New York: Picador, 1961.

Voegelin, Salome. *Listening to Noise and Silence: Towards a Philosophy of Sound Art*. London: Continuum, 2010.

CHAPTER 11

....

DOPING THE VOICE

....

MELISSA RAGONA

Pitch correction has come to mean pitch corruption—a doping of the voice that has reached an apex in the technologies of Auto-Tuning.[1] Auto-Tune is like steroids for singers. It prosthetically boosts their performance, puts them back on pitch, and keeps them there. It can also give them an otherworldly tone, one that they can claim as their own or choose to manipulate beyond the zone of T-Pain ecstasy.[2] With the advent of new technologies of vocal manipulation, the distinction between authentic and manipulated sound environments is collapsing. New media sound experiments enthusiastically combine hygienic and corrupted sound forms.

Auto-Tune, like Dolby before it, was originally used to clean up or correct tonal inaccuracies in the music and sound industries. Although first acting as a kind of drug for singers, it later became an experimental tool for sound engineers, musicians, and performers, one that allowed them to produce a synthetic, superclean sound somewhere in the uncanny valley between human vocal idiosyncrasies and seeming digitized perfection. Cher was one of the first to profit commercially from this new wonder drug in her 1998 hit, *Believe*. However, she was not the first to self-consciously use this technology to deliberately distort and produce a new version of the voice. Marlon Brando, Yoko Ono, John Lennon, and Laurie Anderson used related voice technologies to revise and transform their vocal performances well before Cher's innovative hit topped the charts.

In fact, the industries of sound technology have been preoccupied with the idea of "cleaning up" the dirt of recording's excess: the crack, fuzz, squeal, hiss, and pop of analog systems. Dolby Noise Reduction (DNR), invented and marketed in the early 1970s, was a technological and ideological phenomenon that transformed the industries of music and film. By manipulating the magnitude of frequencies during recording and playback, it achieved an "ideal" form of sound—one that represented a clean envelope in which all sounds could be distinctly heard, emerging from seemingly new, uncluttered dimensions of audio space.[3] The Dolby system—which sometimes scrubbed sound too clean—also heralded the birth of the sound designer. Walter Murch, working hand in hand with Francis Ford Coppola and George Lucas, among others, designed some of the most intricate soundtracks for films that are now considered exemplary classics of sound design history: *THX-1138* (1971), *American Graffiti* (1973), *The Godfather* (1972), *The Conversation* (1974), *Apocalypse Now* (1979). Directors, such as Robert Altman, performed similarly within the new sound space that Dolby provided, producing masterworks of sound layering, as in Altman's film, *Nashville* (1975). While Hollywood was cleaning up and engineering a highly controlled soundscape for commercial film, artists such as Hollis Frampton, Charlemagne Palestine, Paul Sharits, Yoko Ono, and Vito Acconci were utilizing noise to pollute and energize film and video space. Dirty sound acts included Frampton's *Critical Mass* (1971), Acconci's *Theme Song* (1973), Charlemagne Palestine's *Island Song* (1976), and Yoko Ono's *Fly* (1970).

In a sense, the dirt that new sound technologies flung away in the 1970s ended up, in concentrated form, within the voices that were now beautifully legible inside and outside Hollywood venues. By examining a brief history of several sound production technologies that preceded Auto-Tune, this essay will survey what I am referring to as a "doping of the voice," an elusive phenomenon hidden by industry engineers, but amplified by artists who sought to make the voice as pliable and "sounding" as the instruments that often accompanied it. On the one hand, the dope dealt by the commercial sound industry resembled expensive designer drugs—technologies that promised to make one both *sound* as well as *look* better (e.g., early dubbing for film, double-tracking for music).[4] On the other hand, a doping of the voice was practiced by experimental artists (Ono, Palestine, Frampton) to dirty the voice's narrative context: grinding its phonemic elements, challenging its purity as signature of the body, and wresting it away from any kind of philosophical or psychological interiority.[5] Throughout audible history, vocal manipulation was applied to the voice both in the name of authenticity, as well as of artifice.

The dirty voice, ironically, makes its debut at the same time as the invention of technologies that made "clean sound" and legible voices possible. Unlike the *grain of the voice* that signifies sensual materiality of the body, Dolby-inspired "dirt" of the voice is almost noncorporeal, a synthetic product of technologically manipulated speech. It is a sound object that can exist independently from its source image, even when it is synchronous.[6]

A classic example of this new kind of vocal grit is demonstrated in Marlon Brando's performance in Francis Ford Coppola's *Apocalypse Now* (1979). As a result of DNR and Murch's exquisite sound engineering, one hears the nuances of Brando's speech, his breathing, his hesitations, his bodily processes. As is well known, Brando showed up on the set of *Apocalypse Now* in the Philippines grossly overweight, vexing Coppola's casting of Kurtz as lean, agile, and ridden with malaria. Thus, all of Brando's scenes were shot with low lighting, most of his body hidden in dark shadow. Moreover, automated dialogue replacement (ADR) or looping technology was used to generate much of his dialogue in post-production, emphasizing the tension inherent in this process, in which a disembodied or nonbodied effect (re-recording off-site) produces an uncanny bodily sound, sensuous and credible as its original source.[7]

As a result, his speech on horror in *Apocalypse Now* is exquisite—it sonically summons up the tortured body and spirit of Kurtz even when we can barely see Brando's face. His voice is embedded with sweat, paucity of food (he gnaws on small hunks of coconut), and extreme, embittered anguish:

> You have no right to call me a murderer. You have a right to kill me: you have a right to do that. But, you have no right to judge me. It's impossible for words to describe, what is necessary to those who do not know what [painful pause, grimace] "horror" means. Horror. Horror has a face. And you must make a friend of horror. Horror and moral terror are your friends. If they are not, then they are enemies to be feared. They are truly enemies.[8]

As Elisabeth Weis has argued, Brando—on the shooting site—deliberately mumbled his lines in order to ensure that ADR would later be employed so that he could have control and mastery over the final aural shape of his delivery.[9] Pitch correction was also an important part of this technique, since most ADR performances were delivered at a lower pitch than their initial set debut. Because they lacked the energy level of a live encounter, ADR tracks had to be "pitched up" in order to simulate the original audio dynamics.

Pitch correction, in a sense, sets the stage for the conflation of what Roland Barthes, borrowing from Julia Kristeva, distinguished as two separate essential categories of the voice: the *geno* and *pheno*.[10] The former implies a voice that signifies, as well as carries within it, the materiality of language as expressed through the body: its abjection, its weight, its texture. In contrast, the pheno voice is one that sings or speaks with perfect diction: with a rote sense of style and lyrical perfection. It does not engage or use the body. Indeed, the pheno voice gives the listener intellectual pleasure without erotic *frisson*. The geno voice—with a body moving through it—is Antonin Artaud, is William Burroughs, is Tom Waits, is Janis Joplin, is Nico, is Maria Callas, is PJ Harvey. In experimental film, video, and performance, it is exemplified by artists such as Vito Acconci, Charlemagne Palestine, Yoko Ono, Mike Kelley, Meredith Monk, Shelley Hirsch, and Blixa Bargeld.

Marlon Brando, of course, is a major entry on the geno list, but he is also a figure who compromises these distinctions. He, like Meryl Streep after him, used ADR to clean up and organize the geno factor so that it is a studio-produced synthetic version of itself. It sounds like the body, but it is an extremely processed, quite precise simulation of the body speaking: pheno-inflected geno. The most extreme example of this is realized when Brando appears posthumously in *Superman Returns* (2006). His earlier ADR rehearsals from his role as Jor-El, superman's father in *Superman: The Movie* (1978), are used again in 2006 to recreate dialogue for a CGI-produced "virtual Brando."[11] The geometry of Brando's face in *Superman Returns* is captured from an old 1970s plaster cast created for *Apocalypse Now*: his head movements are reanimated using a 3-D computer model of the cast, and his mouth gestures are culled from phonemic movements from previous on-screen performances.[12] In a sense, Brando and his directors were already doping his voice in ADR rehearsals and editing sessions as early as the 1950s—a process that continued throughout and beyond his career.[13] By the end of his career, Brando's voice is successfully divorced from his body, only to be reunited in the most provocative,

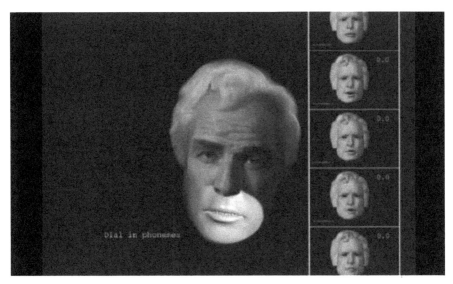

FIGURE 11.1 Media still from Rhythm & Hue's "Marlon Brando reprises his role of Jor-El in *Superman Returns*." 2006. *Source*: http://www.youtube.com/watch?v=kMXWCeQJ7l4

albeit disturbing of ways as an image-sound collage, bridging 1970s ADR with 1990s CGI effects (Figure 11.1).

Outside the studios of 1970s Hollywood, disjunctive cinematic voice experiments occurred in film and video works such as Hollis Frampton's *Critical Mass* (1971), Yoko Ono's *Fly* (1970), and Charlemagne Palestine's *Island Song* (1976), prefiguring the kind of obliterating sound objects created by contemporary cases of Auto-Tuned image sequences. *Critical Mass* is Frampton's attempt to address what he thought of as the inertia-ridden influence of Hollywood narrative talkies on the cinematic image. By spinning sound and image into "symmetrical orbit around one another,"[14] Frampton transforms a cantankerous narrative relationship (the entire film focuses on a single scene of a couple arguing) into a fractured syntactical volley. As I stated in an earlier essay, Frampton prefigures digital delay with analog techniques:

> By staggering successive shots of male and female speakers so that they collide (one hitting right before the other has finished), Frampton achieves through analog editing techniques what would come to be known as digital delay. The overlapping words cause a dislocation between the action and the sound of speaking. As in the opening of *Zorns Lemma*, Frampton begins *Critical Mass* in black with voice-over, but a tripping, doubling effect is already in action: just fine, just fine/where the hell were you?/I was just away/away where?/away where?/ you know, ha/you know, ha.[15]

Rhythmic and stuttering, *Critical Mass*, as Bill Simon has noted, is a study in temporal adjournment, creating tension between future, past, and present time. "We are simultaneously either listening in the present and seeing the past or listening to the past and seeing the present."[16] Gesture and sound are inextricably tied to one another as we move backward and forward in editing time. The image seems to be an after-effect of sound, jarred and torn away from any other kind of context (the couple floats, black and white, against a white background), it merges with the seeming "perfect machine" of the voice.

Another analog precursor to Auto-Tune-like experiments in technology is Charlemagne Palestine's *Island Song*. Strapping a video camera to himself, he drove a motorcycle around St. Pierre (an island off the southern coast of Newfoundland), repeating the phrase over and over again: "Gotta get outta here."[17] Trained as a composer and influenced by the theories and sound work of John Cage, Terry Riley, Steve Reich, La Monte Young, and Tony Conrad, Palestine's body of video and performance work—like his work in music and sound installation—is informed deeply by emergent forms. Beginning with his early experience singing sacred drones in a synagogue youth choir, Palestine has been experimenting with overtones and resonant frequencies across vocal work, church bells, oscillators, piano, and custom-made drone machines.

In *Island Song*, Palestine utilizes his own voice, a motorcycle engine, an incidental foghorn, and other ambient sounds to "compose" a work that is in constant pitch adjustment, as he makes his way recklessly across an uphill section of the island at full throttle. In a sense, Palestine's project is the reverse of Frampton's. Rather than manipulating the voice via the apparatus (e.g., film), Palestine tunes the voice to the apparatus (i.e., the motorcycle as a tone or drone generator). Like his other projects in trance vocalizations, he works himself up over the course of the island ride into a state of euphoric oneness with the cycle's motor.

> Okay, Okay, here, okay, okay, okay here . . . .okay here . . . .OKAY here.
> Ah ha. Ah ha. Okay here [one only hears the sound of the motorcycle motor for a
>   good 3 minutes]
> Ah ha Ah ha Ah ha. Ah haaaaaaa. Em hem. Okay here! Ah ha. Okay here! Ah ha.
> Ah haaaaa. Okay here! Ah ha. Ahhhhhhhh eh haaaaaa. Okay.
> EHHHHHHHHHHHHHHHHHHHHHHHHHHHHHHHHH   eeeeeeeeh
>   EHHHHHHH
> [tonal] EHHHHH heyeeeeeeeee EHHHHHHH heyeeeeeeee EHHHHHHHH
>   EHHHHH heyyyyyyyy
> Ehhhhhhh heyeeeeeee Ehhhhhhhh okay.
> Okay here
> EHHHHHHHHHHH he EHIIIIIIHHH HHHHHHHHH
> EHHHHHHHHHH HEYYYYYYY whoooooah yeah
> EHHHHHHHHHH HEYYYYYYY yeaaaaaaah
> Yayyyyyyy eeeeeeeeyeah[18]

Palestine characterizes himself as a *dirty* minimalist: "I was the street guy of [the Minimalist] school." Although similar to Reich, he embraced the idea that "a compositional process and a sounding music are one and the same thing"; he always sullied the purity of emergence, either using violence (e.g., repeatedly throwing his own body up against a wall as he produced overtones with his cantoring voice) or inebriation as part of the momentum of his evolving process (e.g., he always plays with a few bottles of cognac at his side, drinking as steadily as the shape of the work emerges). But, unlike the voices of Tom Waits or Janis Joplin, Palestine is not interested in simply allowing his body to be the subject of his voice. Rather, he applies structural procedures to the voice so that the grit of his vocal performances is transformed into compositional process. In *Island Song*, the presence of the off-screen, omniscient body-camera is secondary to the objects of the harmonizing voice and motorcycle engine. Sound guides and dominates the image. Visually, we are subjected to the driver's point-of-view (i.e., the only reason for looking is to keep one's vehicle on the road). The motorized voice, cantoring in loops, enacts the kind of suture that in film has been classically structured through a series of shot-reverse shots. Instead of being sewn into the fabric of the film by the camera's world, we are literally driven by Palestine's relentless sonorous insistence to remain inside this visually disembodied, but aurally lush film.[19]

Similar to Palestine, Yoko Ono uses her voice to launch a sonic world, defining a zone that is seemingly extracorporeal. However, as Slavoj Žižek has argued, most people think of the voice as already removed from the body:

> An unbridgeable gap separates forever a human body from "its" voice. The voice displays a spectral autonomy, it never quite belongs to the body we see, so that even when we see a living person talking, there is always a minimum of ventriloquism at work: it is as if the speaker's own voice hollows him out and in a sense speaks "by itself," through him.[20]

With Ono, this displacement is extreme. Most of the descriptions of Ono's voice are radically Othered. It is likened to that of a witch, a she-mule, a whale giving birth, an alien, a subatomic detonator, or a cat with its head being twisted off, among many—primarily—pejorative terms. Indeed, in a 1974 song called, "Yes, I'm a Witch," she confronts popular criticism head on: "Yes, I'm a witch/ I'm a bitch/I don't care what you say/My voice is real/My voice speaks truth/I don't fit in your ways."[21] As recent as 2011, a satire of her voice appeared in *The Daily Cricket*, "Yoko Ono Voice Finds Commercial Applications,"—it had been allegedly used to drive mice and rodents from residential homes, scare migrating birds from airport runways, and knock enemy planes out of the sky. Numerous online comments denigrated Ono's signature scream in her 1961 conceptual work, *Voice Piece for Soprano*, which was reinstalled at the Museum of Modern Art in 2010. Although she intermittently performed the piece herself during the length of its exhibition, her "instruction painting" as she calls it, also directed museum visitors to scream into a very well amplified microphone. She also gave them written instructions on how to focus their screams: (1) against the wind, (2) against the wall, (3) against the sky. Visitors' screams could be heard from July to the end of November 2010 in the grand Marron atrium, sometimes reaching as far as MoMA's fifth-floor galleries. One miffed patron wrote on MoMA's blog:

> The "scream" part of Yoko Ono's piece is incredibly disruptive to the rest of the museum, and it is a shame that it is scheduled to run until November. MoMA should

seriously consider curtailing it, or lowering the volume on the very loud speakers. At least Marina Abramovic sat there quietly.[22]

It is interesting how Abramovic's silence then becomes another kind of sound piece when contrasted with Ono's boisterous, radically disruptive audio work. Many viewers did not understand Ono's conceptual score and its purposeful intervention in the sterile silence of museum viewing. Thus, they complained about how her noise prevented them from really enjoying their museum experience. In a sense, as Ono's stigma of being that "bitch who broke up the Beatles," has begun to wane, it has only been replaced with another moniker: that tuneless, wailing singer who seduced John Lennon into collaborating with her on works of embarrassing avant-garde sound, performance, and visual art.

One of those collaborative works includes Ono's film *Fly* (1970). This work was first conceived by Yoko Ono as *Film No. 11* (1968), part of an earlier series of Fluxus-inspired conceptual film scripts,: "About a fly going from the toe to the head of a lying naked body, crawling very slowly. The whole film should take about an hour."[23] Ono, with assistance from Lennon, realizes the two-sentence film script in 37, rather than 60 minutes in her film, *Fly* (1970). At first, song-like, the soundtrack is a mimetic audio map of a fly's journey across actress Virginia Lust's naked body. Similar to Palestine's *Island Song,* in which hand-held tracking shots map the movement of the motorcycle, Ono's film features her voice tracking the fly's movement over the terrain of Lust's body, invoking a trance-like identification with the fly's journey. Singsong-like in its opening phrases, her voice track introduces the film in the same way that it signals its end, emphasizing a ho-hum kind of everydayness to the fly's activity, even as it traverses a socially charged surface, like a nude body (think of Ono's approach in *No. 4*, aka *Bottoms*, 1966— the pedestrian quality of everyone's "bottom" exposed). Ono's Fluxus-inspired strategies of close observations, small gestures, and conceptual frames can be applied to *Fly* and its sound decisions. Phonemic sounds, almost childlike, are used to introduce the fly's motif, the absolute stillness (some say, drugged state) of Lust's body produces both an ambient silence, as well as the effects of duration (i.e., the journey lasts as long as the length of her body). Once the fly is in transit, Ono, in a sense, motorizes her voice to match the fly's locomotion—one we usually hear as a steady buzz, caused by a fly's vibrating flight muscles (Figure 11.2).

As Ono describes, the soundtrack for *Fly* was conceived in the Regency Hotel in New York on Christmas day in 1970. Lennon recorded the track on a multitrack Nagra recorder in three parts: the first part is what Ono calls a monologue; the second section, a dialogue; and the third, a trialogue.[24] The three "movements" of Fly's soundtrack represent the various levels of tape composition that Lennon was experimenting with at the time: playback, reverse-distortion, and live-against-recorded improvisations. In the first section, Ono's voice is live, improvisatory. Then, her recorded voice is played back on one of the Nagra's tracks, as Lennon performs on his guitar. The latter is recorded on yet another track. Finally, both recorded tracks are played simultaneously, but running in different directions: Lennon's guitar tape is played in reverse, while Ono's voice

FIGURE 11.2 *Shy* (pen and ink drawing inspired by Yoko Ono's film, *Fly*, 1970) by Dakotah Konicek (image courtesy of the artist)

recording runs in real time. Section three is even more complex, or, as she terms it, "a monologue in a trialogue form."[25] Lennon plays his guitar against the reversed playback of tape section two. Then, the latter recording is also reversed (so, a kind of double negative is performed) and played while Ono performs another live voice solo over it. When the reversed tape comes to an end, Ono's voice performance continues and Lennon plays a live radio.[26] Ono's description of *Fly's* recording process also seems to imply that Lennon was extending what he had learned earlier about artificial double-tracking (ADT) from EMI recording engineer, Ken Townsend, while the Beatles were making their album, *Revolver* (1966). Frustrated with double-tracking sessions—or performing the same track twice, then playing them back together—Lennon encouraged Townsend to help him produce an automated or "artificial" form of using the same track recording twice, with one track on a slight delay in order to produce a subtle, but fuller doubled sound effect.[27] This initially was applied exclusively to voice, but then spread across instruments, including guitar and drums. One can hear this tripping effect applied to both Ono's voice, as well as Lennon's guitar on the soundtrack for *Fly*. Lennon's primitive application of ADT, coupled with the reverse engineering of both tracks, makes for an extremely dense, complex composition, the guitar sounding like an airbrush up against Ono's electronic scat.

Similar to the effect that ADR had for Marlon Brando—namely, that he could control the outcome of his produced voice—Ono and Lennon's use of ADT effects allows for a sculpted soundscape that invests the voice and guitar with an otherworldly richness that wouldn't exist acoustically. So, although most attribute Ono's voice quality to the unusualness of her abject, raw performance, or even the otherness of her persona, she often constructs and, thus, controls her ultimate sound compositions through highly conceptual frames and sophisticated technical means. Many argue that Ono is naturally "off-pitch," however, she worked—together with Lennon—to produce a voice that was surprising and rich in its compositional effect, often manipulating it electronically in order to amplify atonal and asynchronous moments. As her film *Fly* attests, she also did not shy away from depicting her voice as Othered, even if it seemed to be coming from the most abject species of the animal kingdom, the fly. But, again, the image sound relations in *Fly* are often severed, as her voice is not always in sync with the fly's travels across Lust's naked, abstracted body. And, ultimately, *Fly's* soundtrack is most celebrated on the album *Fly* that was produced a year after the film (1971). Ultimately, Ono's voice-becoming-fly is a feat both of virtuosic performance and technical agility. It colonizes and incorporates the image, carrying all of its initial visual signification into the realm of sound.

And, not surprisingly, listeners often make direct comparisons between Ono's voice and the technology of Auto-Tune: "That sound, that force, that apocalyptic yodel. The human Autò-Tune antidote,"[28] or "Who else in 1971 had songs like these? I mean it almost sounds like Auto-Tune, when at the time there were no computers! Only Yoko can do it!"[29] And, indeed, several have tried to Auto-Tune her MoMA *Voice Piece for Soprano*, with frustration:

> I Auto-Tuned her voice and added some "wah." It was difficult to get it properly Auto-Tuned for a couple of reasons: 1) She is screaming, not singing which means that there aren't different notes to Auto-tune the pitch, 2) It was my first time using the Auto-Tune feature in Audacity and I am probably not using it correctly.[30]

Ono's voice at once obstructs and epitomizes the automated features of Auto-Tune applications. Like other experimental voice artists—both her contemporaries and those that followed—Ono was informed by Cage-inspired, process-based works, many of which borrowed from technology and industry to explore concepts of automation, repetition, chance, and duration (e.g., Marian Zazeela's and Simone Forti's drone-voice performances with La Monte Young's Theater of Eternal Music in the sixties, or Laurie Anderson's direct use of the vocoder in *Oh Superman* [1981]). Ironically, Ono's voice defies automated tuning, but reminds one of the problem of tuning—the ineffable struggle to find a universal, repeatable system of harmony. Deliberately casting herself between Western rock and roll and Eastern-influenced experimental paradigms, Ono skates between two models of tuning, one that finds its roots in the "bland, equal spacing of the 12 pitches of the octave," or equal temperament; the other based in a constant evolving system that strives for "*just*" intonation, or to find the purest relationships possible between sound frequencies.[31] Auto-Tune is structured on the fixed pitch of equal temperament and, when conventionally applied, can subtly make the least tonal singers sound like trained Pythagoreans. But it can also be used to distort and accentuate the quick steps the voice makes between notes, making transparent the work it takes for one frequency to synch with another. It is no wonder, then, that listeners find an analogue for Auto-Tune technology in Ono's voice, vacillating as it does between harmonic models.

Auto-Tune creates intensity with speed and, instead of a nuanced story, a seemingly instantaneous translation of meaning through sound occurs, like the distillation one might get of a song from a skip in a record or a glitch on a CD. Its looping effect, its quick reiteration and replay capacity on YouTube, Facebook, Vimeo, and the like creates a cumulative history of versions, *original, abbreviated, Auto-Tuned, remixed, part two*. By giving a great deal more authority to sound, especially the voice-as-sound, Auto-Tune and related technologies are changing the way sound and image work together. By dismantling the narratives of somatic authenticity often used to analyze the voice, and replacing them with mechanical, roboticized, digitized versions of vocal texture, identity, and affect, pitch technology is changing how we understand the *jouissance* of the voice—especially pitch—since Barthes first described it as raw, spontaneous, and corporeal.

After Ono and Cher, one of the most compelling contemporary examples of pitch manipulation has been performed by the Gregory Brothers, co-inventors of Songify, a downloadable iPhone app that has the ability to turn any kind of speech (e.g., a news clip, a poem, a headline, a bit of gossip) into a song, with disco-like background tracks for only $2.99. In addition to the Gregory Brothers' great hits, like their series *Auto-Tune the News* (2009) and *Bed Intruder Song* (2010), they songified the *Charlie Bit Me* video that went viral in 2007.[32] The original *Charlie Bit Me* was uploaded by UK-based Howard Davies-Carr, the father of Harry and Charlie Davies-Carr, who, at the time, were three years old and one year old, respectively (Figure 11.3).[33] The 56 second video includes a sequence in which Charlie, at first, nibbles a little bit on his brother Harry's fingers. At

FIGURE 11.3 Media still from *Charlie Bit Me*. 2007. Source: http://www.youtube.com/ watch?v=HE4FJL2IDEs

first Harry is smiling and amused and explains to the camera: "Charlie bit me." Then, continuing to smile, knowing what he might be in for, Harry puts his finger back into Charlie's mouth. This time, Charlie locks down on it with his new teeth, and Harry lets out a few alarming screams, increasing with momentum as he realizes how much it actually hurts, "Ouch. Ouch. OUCH CHARLIE! OUUUUUUCH! Charlie! That really hurt." Harry is almost in tears and Charlie seems to be sadistically laughing at his older brother. When they both settle down, there's a bit of a pause and Harry calmly, but firmly says directly to the camera: "Charlie bit me." He pauses again and addresses Charlie: "And that really hurt, Charlie. And it's still hurting."

The Auto-Tuned version of *Charlie Bit Me* demonstrates the impact that automated pitch correction has had on mediated image-sound relations. Using what has come to be called "the Cher Effect," *Charlie Bit Me's* retune speed seems to be set to zero in that the speakers' voices—instead of gliding smoothly from one note to another—instantly jump to the exact pitch of the next note. As a result, the complex emotional narrative posed by *Charlie Bit Me* is highly compressed. Instead of seeing the nuances of Harry's brief encounter with his brother in which he moves from a position of control, performing for the camera with confidence to one of total disintegration—we see and hear only broad strokes. Affect is roboticized—his laughter and cries of pain are indistinguishable from one another. Like the couple in Hollis Frampton's *Critical Mass*, the two little brothers are mechanized, choreographed beyond their domestic situation by voice software that makes Charlie's laughter marvelously sinister and Harry's cries of pain into electroclash screams. In other words, Auto-Tune has the ability to present a "controlled version of losing control" by converting the more primal, instinctive emissions of the human voice (crying, gasping, sighing) into a slick, architectural sound, as if one is sliding down a balustrade through so many organized rooms of emotion.

Before and including the time when Cher's *Believe* was first released, Auto-Tune and its technological predecessors, such as Automated Dialogue Replacement (ADR) and Artificial Double Tracking (ADT), were well-kept industry secrets, downplayed in relation to the final presentation of the voice in both the film and music industries. As discussed, the great actors and musicians of our time were never satisfied with their own, unprocessed voices (Brando, Lennon, Streep, Cher). In fact, they were interested in new technologies and often inspired the industry to invent innovative forms of pitch enhancement to meet their performance standards. At the same time, their producers conspired to hide the history of voice manipulation, beginning with Lennon's engineer Ken Townsend and producer George Martin, and extending to Cher's engineers-cum-producers, Mark Taylor and Brian Rawling. Fictional creation stories were invented: Taylor claimed he produced the steplike effect on Cher's voice using a Digi-Tech talker, basically a vocoder that looks like an old guitar foot pedal.[34] Martin made up a fake tool name, telling Lennon that ADT was produced with a "double-bifurcated splosing flange."[35] Not only did they want to hide their company secrets, but also no one wanted to be seen as manipulating what was viewed as the most authentic footprint of the human voice: pitch. Even to this day, performers and producers—some of whom have even used Auto-Tune to produce their work—denigrate it as much as the sports industry has demonized steroids for athletes. In 2009, for example, Christina Aguilera wore a T-Shirt that boasted, "Auto-Tune is For Pussies"; in 2010, the British television series, X-Factor banned it from its production equipment; and, already in 2006, Neko Case charged that Auto-Tune is like "that taste in diet soda, I can taste it—and it makes me sick."[36]

Auto-Tune seems like a new touchstone for voice authenticity. However, if we look back at the essentialist claims for natural voice quality, all the haters of Yoko Ono's voice, for instance, or all the lovers of John Lennon's crooning, they fall flat. History reveals that both Lennon and Ono's voices have been equally processed through various voice revision technologies. As Belton has argued for film sound, "the work of technology can never quite become invisible."[37] The current insidious nature of Auto-Tune technology encourages us to look back and listen again to the rich technological histories in- and outside of commercial video, film, and sound culture that experimented with synthetic voice mimesis. Moreover, as Palestine and Ono have demonstrated, the voice can also stand in for or model new directions for voice technology.

Finally, new technologies like Auto-Tune emphasize the uncanny nature of the voice—its ability to elide categorical oppositions: pure and dirty, geno and pheno, processed and unprocessed. The dope of the voice is already built into its untethered position, floating as it does between the body and language.[38] Technology sends it further adrift, producing errant methods that are helping to shape new horizons for rethinking the heretofore fictional unity of body, voice, and image.

NOTES

1. Auto-Tune was invented by Dr. Harold (Andy) Hildebrand, previously a music composition scholar, at Antares Audio Technologies, Inc. Its first phases were discovered while he was working for Exxon Production Research Landmark Graphics (1976–1989), a company he co-founded to study and interpret seismic data. The methods he developed in relation to this process were applied to detect, analyze, and modify pitch. In 1997, utilizing digital signal processing (DSP), he developed a seamless looping technique for pitch-related audio samples. Shortly after, Auto-Tune was enthusiastically picked up by the music industry to enhance singers' voices in live and recorded performance. For a more extended history of Auto-Tune see Dave Tompkins, *How To Wreck a Nice Beach: The Vocoder from World War II to Hip Hop, The Machine Speaks* (Chicago: Stop Smiling Media, 2010).
2. R & B singer-turned-rapper, Faheem Rasheed Najm, who took the stage name, T-Pain, uses its effects so often that an Auto-Tune inspired iPhone app, "I am T-Pain" (2009) was named after him.
3. John Belton, "Technology and Aesthetics of Film Sound," *Film Sound: Theory and Practice*, ed. Elisabeth Weis and John Belton (New York: Columbia University Press, 1985), 67.
4. Dubbing is also known as Automated Dialogue Replacement, Additional Dialogue Recording or ADR. See fn. 7 for a more extensive description. Double-tracking is an audio recording technique in which a performer sings or plays along with his or her own prerecorded performance, usually to produce a stronger or "doubled" sound that is not possible with just a single voice or instrument. Yoko Ono, inspired by her collaboration

with John Lennon, used a technology—developed by Abbey Road Studios—called artificial double-tracking or automatic double-tracking, also known as ADT in her soundtrack for the film *Fly* (1971). The latter used tape delay to create layered sound as if two or more people were playing or singing together, when, in fact, one original recorded performance was played over itself with an oscillator. The second tape, slightly out of sync with the first, created a double-track effect. For a more extensive discussion of the Beatles' use of multitracking see Greg Milner's *Perfecting Sound Forever: An Aural History of Recorded Music* (New York: Faber and Faber, 2009).

5. Here, I borrow from Jonathan Sterne's charge: "Since this book is not bound by Christian doctrine, there is no law—divine or otherwise—requiring us to assume the interiority of sound and the connection between sound, subjective self-presence, and intersubjective experience. We do not need to assume that sound draws us into the world while vision separates us from it." Sterne, *The Audible Past: Cultural Origins of Sound Reproduction* (Durham and London: Duke University Press, 2003), 18.

6. Michel Chion identifies a similar phenomenon in terms of screen sound. "These sounds and voices that are neither entirely inside nor clearly outside are those that interest me the most, as will become amply evident." *The Voice in Cinema*, ed. and trans. Claudia Gorbman (New York: Columbia University Press, 1999), 4.

7. Automated dialogue replacement is a postproduction process in which an actor watches his or her scene repeatedly so that he or she can reperform each line to match the wording and lip movements of their original performance. For a further description of ADR, see Elisabeth Weis, "Synch Tanks: The Art and Technique of Postproduction Sound," *Cineaste* 21, no. 1-2 (1995): 57.

8. *Apocalypse Now*, directed by Francis Ford Coppola, speech given by Marlon Brando (1979; Paramount, 2001), DVD.

9. Elisabeth Weis, "Sync Tanks: The Art and Technique of Postproduction Sound," *Cineaste* 21, no. 1–2 (1995): 57.

10. For a more in-depth discussion of geno and pheno voices, see Roland Barthes, "The Grain of the Voice," *The Responsibility of Forms: Critical Essays on Music, Art, and Representation*, trans. Richard Howard (Berkeley and Los Angeles: University of California Press, 1991), 267–277.

11. *Superman Returns*, directed by Bryan Singer (Warner Brothers, 2007), DVD.

12. Rhythm and Hues, an LA-based visual effects company, by using ADR rehearsal tapes, previous on-screen performances, and partial projections, animated Brando's virtual mouth. See "Marlon Brando as Jor-El," YouTube video, 3:30, posted by "metallo2006" July 14, 2006, http://www.youtube.com/watch?v=kMXWCeQJ7l4. In a sense, their work prefigures the most recent advanced facial animation work, known as Video Rewrite. Instead of using texture mapping or 3-D manual modeling, Video Rewrite uses "computer-vision techniques to track points on the speaker's mouth," as well as a system in which new mouth images (i.e., made by phonemes) are morphed automatically into a "new background face." Christoph Bregler, Michele Covell, and Malcolm Slaney, "Video Rewrite: Driving Visual Speech with Audio," *Proceedings of SIGGRAPH 97* (Los Angeles Convention Center, CA, August 3–8, 1997), 1–8.

13. Marlon Brando used ADR as early as 1957 in Joshua Logan's *Sayonara*. *Sayonara*, with sound engineer George Groves at the helm, won an academy award for best sound. Groves described Brando as a "perfect actor, but very hard to understand...a mumbler." Groves also lauded Brando's affirmative approach to ADR: "He [Brando] lay down on

the dubbing console while we were getting ready for the next loop and was very relaxed and was most accommodating…some people are just terrible, they go into tantrums." Stephen R. Wainwright, "Warners Career (1957–62): George becomes head of the sound department at Warners," *The Official Website of George R. Groves*, last modified August 25, 2012, accessed July 15, 2012, http://www.georgegroves.org.uk/warners2.html.

14. Hollis Frampton, "Film in the House of the Word," *Circles of Confusion: Film, Photography, Video, Texts 1968–1980* (Rochester, N.Y.: Visual Studies Workshop Press, 1983), 85.

15. Melissa Ragona, "Hidden Noise: Strategies of Sound Montage in the Films of Hollis Frampton," *October* 109 (Summer 2004): 110.

16. Bill Simon, "New Forms in Film," *Artforum* (October 1972): 83.

17. *Island Song*, directed by Charlemagne Palestine (1976; Electronic Arts Intermix, 1995), DVD.

18. Ibid. Phonetic transcription is my own.

19. Palestine's aural trance states are reminiscent of Vito Acconci's iterative performances, especially *Theme Song* (1973), in which Acconci uses a tape recorder (playing songs from the Doors, Bob Dylan, Van Morrison, Kris Kristofferson) to push and extend his insistent invitation to the viewer: "Come on, I'm all alone, come close to me." Similar to Palestine's performance, he uses an electronic impulse; he keeps starting and stopping the machine, putting in new cassettes, starting them over, singing along, humming, imitating the pause, start, and looping of mechanically induced sound.

20. Slavoj Žižek, *On Belief*, Thinking in Action (London: Routledge, 2001), 58.

21. Yoko Ono, "Yes, I'm a Bitch," *A Story*, recorded 1974, selected songs released on box set *Onobox* (Ryko Distribution, 1992), entire album (Rykodisc, 1997), compact disc.

22. Jason Persse, "From a Whisper to a Scream: Following Yoko Ono's Instructions," *Inside/Out*, MoMA PS1 blog, July 14, 2010, http://www.moma.org/explore/inside_out/2010/07/14/from-a-whisper-to-a-scream-following-yoko-onos-instructions/.

23. Scott MacDonald, "Yoko Ono: Ideas on Film: Interview/Scripts," *Film Quarterly* 43, no. 1 (Autumn 1989): 21.

24. Yoko Ono, *Crawdaddy!: The Magazine of Rock N' Roll* (New York: 1971). *Crawdaddy!* was one of the first magazines to publish rock and roll music criticism. Self-published by Paul Williams who was 17 at the time of *Crawdaddy's* first issue in 1966, *Crawdaddy* preceded *Rolling Stone* and *Cream* in rock journalism. In addition to Ono, it solicited contributions from and wrote profiles on John Lennon, Bruce Springsteen, Bob Marley, The Rolling Stones, William S. Burroughs, and more. In 2007, Crawdaddy! resurfaced as a blog, highlighting its archives, in the web magazine *Paste*: see Josh Jackson, *"Crawdaddy!* comes to *Paste,"* *Crawdaddy* (blog), *Paste*, August 5, 2011, http://www.pastemagazine.com/blogs/crawdaddy/2011/08/crawdaddy-comes-to-paste.html.

25. Ibid.

26. Ono, *Crawdaddy!* (New York: 1971).

27. George Martin, *All You Need is Ears: The Inside Personal Story of the Genius Who Created the Beatles* (New York: St. Martin's Press, 1979), 155.

28. Rob Harvilla, "Oh, Yoko Ono: BAM throws a star-studded tribute to the Plastic Ono Band," *Village Voice*, February 23, 2010.

29. HCmon, 2010, comment on "Yoko Ono: 'Mind Holes' (1971)," YouTube video, 2:48, posted by "misterfabdu93," December 5, 2008, http://youtu.be/nptngMqWWLM.

30. drkats, "Yoko Ono Screaming Song Live at Art Show! Autotune!" YouTube video, 3:26, posted September 14, 2010, http://youtu.be/B1l47VSplwI.

31. Just or pure intonation is a tuning system that dates back to Ancient Greece (Ptolemy) in which "pitches are given as fractions," as a way of determining harmonic intervals. LaMonte Young's use of just intonation was influential on Yoko Ono's approach to tonal voice work. See Kyle Gann, "An Introduction to Historical Tunings," Kyle Gann's Home Page, 1997, http://www.kylegann.com/histune.html.

32. Gregory Brothers, "AutoTune—Charlie Bit Me (Original Full Version)," YouTube video, 1:01, posted by "JimboVids," November 10, 2009, http://youtu.be/sMMoR19IisI.

33. Howard Davies-Carr, "Charlie bit my finger—again!" YouTube video, 0:56, posted by "HDCYT," May 22, 2007, http://youtu.be/_OBlgSz8sSM.

34. Mark Taylor's fictional story became accepted history and so convincing that Kay Dickinson, in her seminal essay, "'Believe'? Vocoders, Digitalised Female Identity and Camp Authors," retold and quoted Taylor's made-up history of Cher's *Believe* as having been produced with a Digitech Talker. See Dickinson, "'Believe'? Vocoders, Digitalised Female Identity and Camp Authors," in "Gender and Sexuality," special issue, *Popular Music* 20, no. 3 (October 2001): 334. Taylor's fictive story is still published on *Sound on Sound's* site, but now with a noticeable disclaimer. Sue Sillitoe and Mat Bell, "Recording Cher's Believe," *Sound on Sound*, February 1999, http://www.soundonsound.com/sos/feb99/articles/tracks661.htm.

35. George Martin recounts his description of ADR's technology to Lennon: "Unwittingly, I coined a new word in our technical language. When I first tried ADT on John Lennon's voice, he was knocked out by it. What was it? How was it done? I replied in gobbledygook: 'Well, John,' I said very earnestly, 'it's a double-bifurcated sploshing flange.' He knew I was putting him on, but he always referred to it as 'flanging' the voice." Martin, *All You Need is Ears*, 156.

36. "Interviews: Neko Case," by Ryan Dombal, *Pitchfork*, April 10, 2006, http://pitchfork.com/features/interviews/6306-neko-case/.

37. Belton, "Technology and Aesthetics of Film Sound," 63.

38. Here I am referring to Mladen Dolar's characterization of the voice as an *objet petit a* (after Lacan)—an object that defies representation, residing as it does at the intersection of language and body. "What language and the body have in common is the voice, but the voice is part neither of language nor of the body." Mladen Dolar, *A Voice and Nothing More* (Cambridge: MIT Press, 2006), 73.

SELECT BIBLIOGRAPHY

Chion, Michel. *The Voice in Cinema*. Edited and translated by Claudia Gorbman. New York: Columbia University Press, 1999.

Dickinson, Kay. "'Believe'? Vocoders, Digitalised Female Identity and Camp Authors," in "Gender and Sexuality." Special issue, *Popular Music* 20, no. 3 (October 2001): 333–347.

Dolar, Mladen. *A Voice and Nothing More*. Cambridge: MIT Press, 2006.

Frampton, Hollis. "Film in the House of the Word." In *Circles of Confusion: Film, Photography, Video, Texts 1968–1980*, 81–85. Rochester, NY: Visual Studies Workshop Press, 1983.

MacDonald, Scott. "Yoko Ono: Ideas on Film: Interview/Scripts." *Film Quarterly* 43, no. 1 (Autumn 1989): 2–23.

Martin, George. *All You Need is Ears: The Inside Personal Story of the Genius who Created the Beatles*. New York: St. Martin's Press, 1979.

Milner, Greg. *Perfecting Sound Forever: An Aural History of Recorded Music*. New York: Faber and Faber, 2009.

Ragona, Melissa. "Hidden Noise: Strategies of Sound Montage in the Films of Hollis Frampton." *October* 109 (Summer 2004): 96–118.

Sillitoe, Sue, and Matt Bell. "Recording Cher's Believe." *Sound on Sound*. February 1999. http://www.soundonsound.com/sos/feb99/articles/tracks661.htm.

Simon, Bill. "New Forms in Film." *Artforum* (October 1972): 78–84.

Sterne, Jonathan. *The Audible Past: Cultural Origins of Sound Reproduction*. Durham and London: Duke University Press, 2003.

Tompkins, Dave. *How To Wreck a Nice Beach: The Vocoder From World War II to Hip Hop, The Machine Speaks*. Chicago: Stop Smiling Media, 2010.

Weis, Elisabeth, and John Belton, eds. *Film Sound: Theory and Practice*. New York: Columbia University Press, 1985.

Weis, Elisabeth. "Sync Tanks: The Art and Technique of Postproduction Sound." *Cineaste* 21, nos. 1–2 (1995): 56–61.

Žižek, Slavoj. *On Belief. Thinking in Action*. New York and London: Routledge, 2002.

PART IV

UNCANNY SPACES
AND ACOUSMATIC
VOICES

CHAPTER 12

MONSTROUS NOISE

Silent Hill *and the Aesthetic Economies of Fear*

WILLIAM CHENG

I'm gripped by a nightmare within minutes of entering the game *Silent Hill*. After watching a brief introductory video—one that shows protagonist Harry Mason crashing his car into the side of a road while driving through the game's eponymous town—I take control of this avatar to go in search of his missing daughter. Things are quiet save for the hollow sounds of Harry's footfalls and the distant noise of creaking metal. While it's hard to see through the thick fog and flurries of snow, I soon spot a young girl not far away. She's standing still, her arms crossed, one leg angled oddly forward, thick strands of black hair covering her face. Just as I'm about to reach her, she springs to life and runs into an alley. I instinctively follow. Deeper and deeper into this dark alley I go, passing an empty wheelchair, then a blood-stained gurney, before arriving at a dead end where I encounter a dreadful sight: a flayed humanoid corpse, ribs all exposed, pinned against a barbed wire fence. Upon turning away from this abomination, I see—to my even greater horror—a trio of child-like monsters teetering toward me. I manage to edge past these enemies, but some kind of gate now blocks my path out of the alley. Although I could swear this barrier was not here before (as this was the same way I came), I have no time to dwell on such mysteries. Harry is defenseless and escape looks impossible. The monsters lunge at him with knives and emit guttural cries as they gnaw at his legs. No amount of button-mashing on my part is capable of averting this grisly fate. With a soft moan, Harry collapses and dies before my eyes.

A cutscene then shows Harry waking up—unscathed, it appears—inside a run-down diner (see Figure 12.1). Was it all a dream? This narrative sleight-of-hand reveals the protagonist's fake death to have been a pre-scripted, unavoidable event, a necessary part of advancing through the game. A certain sting of impotence, however, lingers in my mind. Though this diner looks like a relative safe haven, I'm not sure I feel any more

FIGURE 12.1 Left: Harry getting attacked by monsters in the opening alleyway sequence of *Silent Hill,* and Right: Harry waking up in a diner. Screen captures by author.

secure than I did before. The game has already tricked me once. Who knows what else it could be up to?

I know what this game wants me to do: exit the diner, solve some puzzles, fend off monsters, and find Harry's daughter. But after the foul play in the alleyway, I'm no longer sure how much I should trust this game or follow its orders. What am I getting myself—and Harry—into?

No Exit

Silent Hill is a 1999 PlayStation survival-horror game developed by Team Silent and published by Konami Computer Entertainment Tokyo. Released in North America, Japan, and other territories, the game debuted to favorable reviews and has since spawned multiple sequels and film adaptations. Although preceded by notable survival-horror games such as *Alone in the Dark* (1992), *Clock Tower* (1995), and *Resident Evil* (1996), the *Silent Hill* series has emerged as one of this genre's most iconic franchises. To this day, players continue to fashion and debate intricate theories about the settings, characters, monsters, and timeline of the *Silent Hill* universe. Fan fictions, instruction manuals, strategy guides, novels, comic books, and other supplementary media have together done much in past years to flesh out the lore surrounding the fabricated American town of Silent Hill.

Writers have variously posited English Gothic literature, Japanese Noh theater, the stories of H. P. Lovecraft, and the films of Alfred Hitchcock as sources of inspiration for *Silent Hill.* Most evidently, the game draws from Japanese horror cinema (J-horror) and its topical arsenal of demonic mothers, victimized daughters, vengeful spirits, and terrorizing technologies. The conspiratorial plot of *Silent Hill* involves the torture of a young girl named Alessa Gillespie by her mother Dahlia. At one point in the game, Dahlia explains to Harry that Alessa's protracted agony has served to revive the god of a cult: "For the seven years since that terrible day [the day on which Alessa was sup-posed to be sacrificed in a fire], Alessa has been kept alive, suffering a fate worse than death. Alessa has been trapped in an endless nightmare from which she never awakens. 'He' [the god] has been nurtured by that nightmare, waiting for the day to be born." The torment of Alessa is never depicted in the game, but her pain is palpable in its world's gruesome sights and sounds. Over the course of a player's adventure, the town of Silent Hill routinely transforms into an Otherworld, an alternate reality that, in Harry's words, looks like "someone's nightmarish delusions come to life," a realm soaked in shadows and stained with blood. The flesh wounds of Alessa are etched in these hellish envi-ronments, while echoes of her mental anguish reverberate through a soundscape that pulses with groaning metal, squeaking wheels, air raid sirens, howling monsters, and other noises of nature and technology gone awry. The jumbled sounds, darkness, and fog that permeate *Silent Hill* signal a disavowal of aesthetic legibility—a disavowal born of trauma so unspeakable that its symptoms and aftershocks lie beyond all conventional representation.

Paranormal externalizations of Alessa's pain are further mirrored in the player's dis-tressing interactions with the game. *Silent Hill* compels its player to empathize with Alessa's suffering via gameplay that stresses vulnerability instead of blazing guns and superhuman feats. Harry Mason is a ludological anomaly who lacks the extravagant powers possessed by typical heroes and heroines of action-adventure games. He is an Everyman, an extraordinarily ordinary being whose poor offensive capabilities make him easy prey for the monsters in the gameworld.

Mark Simmons—project director of *Silent Hill: Origins* (2007) and *Silent Hill: Shattered Memories* (2009)—declared in an interview that when one "[looks] back at the survival-horror genre, it's pretty clear that the monster scares were built upon awkward controls, clumsy combat, and constantly being kept in a state of low health. Other genres had moved on [by] leaps and bounds, but the survival-horror genre con-tinued to fall back on these unrefined elements of gameplay because they added to the fear."[1] One way survival-horror games elicit fear is indeed by teasing the player with an illusion of control, only to snatch it away at the worst moment. With this in mind, the opening alleyway sequence in *Silent Hill* is horrifying precisely because it is *not* a cutscene in the traditional sense. The player retains some control over Harry's move-ments as the monsters launch their assault. For a few awful seconds, the (first-time) player will instinctively fight for survival, pressing every possible button, frantically trying everything but accomplishing nothing. The game forces Harry to die in the player's hands.

In the same way that Alfred Hitchcock's *Psycho* (1960) famously broke the rules of the horror film by killing off its female protagonist mid-shower (and mid-story), so the first five minutes of *Silent Hill* effectively warn players that all bets are off. The most upsetting aspect of the alleyway attack lies in how it explodes the player's concep-tions of what the *game* is allowed to do. The scripted demise is likely to leave us feeling not simply frightened, angry, and confused, but moreover betrayed by the breach of contract between gamer and game—a contract that, under ordinary circumstances, should grant us some say over our characters' fates. This violation of trust in the opening moments of *Silent Hill* gives a player enough reason to be henceforth wary not only of the monsters in the game, but also of the monstrous game itself. With its narrative fake-outs, unreliable controls, and dearth of combat options, *Silent Hill* assumes the guise of a living entity actively seeking to undermine its player's agencies. The game imparts a sense of the uncanny, which, according to Ernst Jentsch's (ante-Freudian) definition, pertains to the "doubt as to whether an apparently living being is animate and, conversely, doubt as to whether a lifeless object may not in fact be animate.... [W]hen...a wild man has his first sight of a locomotive or of a steamboat...the feeling of trepidation will here be very great, for as a consequence of the enigmatic autonomous movement and the regular noises of the machine—reminding him of human breath—the giant apparatus can easily impress the completely ignorant person as a living mass."[2] At times, players of *Silent Hill* might likewise feel as if they are fighting an animate ludic apparatus, one that churns out fear through unruly mechanics and unfair outcomes.

Just as *Silent Hill* can seem to transgress its status as an idle medium, so its grotesque soundscape manifests as a sentient antagonist, an invisible yet omnipresent force that seethes and convulses as it plays mind games with the player. This essay contemplates the ludic, perceptual, and hermeneutic anxieties provoked by this horror game's uncanny sounds. By underscoring ways in which the industrial noises in *Silent Hill* haunt various borders—between diegetic and non-diegetic, real and virtual, lingering and ephemeral, organic and mechanical, surface and subdermal, instructive and manipulative—I explore how this game's audio works to unsettle a player's mental and bodily control. Through comparisons of discourses on noises and monsters, I frame the sounds in this gameworld as living monsters in their own right: abject, liminal, and always potentially trespassing on players' own inhabited spaces. Underpinning these considerations are broader investigations into the *aesthetic economies of fear*—the frightening efficiency with which the minimal sounds (and overall reductive aesthetics) of horror media can evoke maximal terror.

DEAD RINGERS

Discrete musical tracks accompany a player's travels through *Silent Hill*. Some locales are deathly silent (aptly living up to the game's title), while others are almost intolerably clamorous. Japanese composer Akira Yamaoka (b. 1968) created a spooky soundworld using recorded and synthesized noises. Audio effects include microtonal slides, dissonant stacked chords, timbral distortions, juxtapositions of extreme registers, rapid vibrato, drones, loops, prolonged decays, and ghostly echoes.[3] As a whole, this aesthetic approximates a mix of industrial music, glitch music, Japanese noise music, punk, and other countercultural genres that emphasize the use of unconventional sounds. The result invokes what Zach Whalen calls an "atonal chaos" that "[reflects] the player-character's [i.e. Harry Mason's] psychological state."[4] Although these strident sounds do convincingly exemplify Harry's unstable mind, they are also, as the game tells us, the supernatural projections of Alessa's pain. All the while, this cacophony contributes (and gives expression to) the player's own harrowing experience. Together, then, Harry, Alessa, and the player constitute a band of suffering souls, an ill-fated trio whose fears resound through a terrible world of din and darkness.

Annotations in Figure 12.2 trace the sound events in the game's introductory alleyway sequence. Predetermined layers of noise are progressively triggered and sustained as Harry reaches corresponding spatial nodes. Sounds increase in both density and volume as the passageway becomes ever narrower. A sense of claustrophobia is compounded by this simultaneous compression of space and expansion of noise: accumulating soundwaves overfill the slender alley, bracing against its walls and virtually bursting at the seams of our screen. As Harry's surroundings go dark—as it becomes almost impossible to *see* anything—the player has little choice but to lend a compensatory ear to the game's assaultive sounds, to listen to (and through) this noise for signs of danger. For while we can afford to cover our ears and close our eyes when things get scary in a horror film, this isn't a realistic option when playing a horror video game. A player is impelled to stay on high alert—to tolerate every terrifying byte of audiovisual data—for the sake of Harry's survival. Not until Harry dies his false death at the end of the alleyway do these suffocating sounds fade away. A grueling start to an unforgiving game.

Like recycled detritus, the repetitive noises in *Silent Hill* resemble an experiment in musical patchwork gone wild, comprising scraps of sound sewn together and grotesquely reanimated into an acoustic equivalent of Frankenstein's monster. These noises reach fever pitch whenever the town transforms into the nightmarish Otherworld. In one interview, Yamaoka explained that he scored this game with industrial noises because they could produce "much of the essence needed [for the game] ... [a] cold and rusty feeling."[5] Industrial music, as Paul Hegarty describes, offers an "anti-aesthetic, using the tools of art to undo art.... Stylistically, it often combines objects not usually thought of as belonging to music."[6] Or, as Karen Collins writes: "[I]ndustrial music is built around 'non-musical' and often distorted, repetitive, percussive sounds of mechanical, electric and industrial machinery, commonly reflecting feelings of alienation and dehumanisation as a form of social critique."[7]

Industrial music's anti-aesthetic ideology is appropriate for *Silent Hill* given that the game—in frustrating the player's agencies—comes off as resolutely anti-*ludic*. Sounds in this gameworld constantly work to unhinge the player's mental fortitude and sensory orientation. One perturbing aspect of the soundscape is how its noises straddle the diegetic and non-diegetic divide: sirens, rattles, clinks, drips, whirs, and scrapes punctuate the game's environments but lack visible sources. It's often tough to tell (and, in many cases, impossible to verify) whether a sound is coming from an unseen monster, from some distant machinic apparatus, or from beyond the game's diegesis entirely.

Even more disturbing than the muddling of diegetic and nondiegetic noises is how these sounds cross from the game's virtual world into the real world inhabited by the

Following the car crash, Harry (1) wanders the streets of Silent Hill in search of his daughter. He (2) spots a girl in the distance and (3) follows her into a dark alley, passing (4) an abandoned wheelchair and (5) a bloody gurney. Heading deeper into the alley, Harry (6) reaches a dead end and (7) sees a flayed corpse pinned against a fence.

1) Sound of groaning metal

2) Addition of faint sounds intoned approximately at $G^\flat$, C, and $D^\flat$ (A=440)

3) Addition of air raid sirens

4) Addition of sound of grinding wheels (fades by the time Harry reaches the gurney)

5) Addition of resonant percussive noises

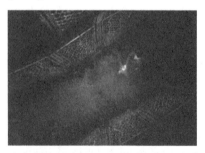

6) Addition of repeating dissonant chords (chordophone timbre) and a staccato melody that plays only once (metallophone timbre)

7) Addition of bass beat

FIGURE 12.2 Progressively layered sound events in the introductory alleyway sequence. Segments (2) and (7) occur as cutscenes. Screen captures by author.

player. Buzzes, rumbles, door-slams, and other noises bleed with ease from the game-world into the player's own environment precisely because they sound like everyday racket. We may occasionally be duped into hearing these in-game sounds as if they're coming from real-world sources—from our living rooms, from upstairs, from right out-side our windows. Liable to fool us in this regard are not the game's outrageously loud, dissonant, or repetitive noise samples, but rather the little mundane sounds that pop up now and then: a creaking floorboard here, a muted thump there, a generic beep from nowhere. The sheer density of this industrial audio is enough to create the impression of surround-sound; that is, noises in the game—even when just piping out of a television's speakers—can so extensively saturate a player's physical space that they might sound as if they're invading from all directions. Such illusion stands to prevail despite the medio-cre audio quality of the game's noises. A low-fi *thud* and a high-fi (or acoustic) *thud*, after all, are not easy to tell apart.

Since much of the industrial audio in *Silent Hill* is indistinguishable from real-world ruckus, it can sound like it's *coming from inside the house* (to borrow the chilling line from the opening sequence of Fred Walton's 1979 thriller *When a Stranger Calls*). Being led to believe that virtual noises are coming from our own sur-roundings is genuinely frightening because *real* sounds indicate *real* threats. When playing *Silent Hill*, we should have little problem reassuring ourselves that the noises we're hearing are all coming from the gameworld's dense, industrial soundscape. But since the noises in there are dead ringers for the everyday noises out here, we're work-ing with scrambled sensoria. Regardless of how we might strive to perceive these noises as safely contained in the game, some uncertainty can continue to nibble at the fringes of our consciousness. Whenever we go on record saying that we know a horror film or game poses no real threat—whenever we're willing to affirm that the suspicious sound we just heard definitely came from the television set rather than from outside our own windows—we brush up against the question of whether we would bet our lives on this claim. It's easy to answer yes when we're in broad daylight, reading *about* horror while sitting in the middle of a bustling coffee shop, bundled in the warmth of ample company and the authority of rational thought. It isn't nearly so easy when we're in the middle of *experiencing* a horror movie or a horror game, when we're alone at night, when our minds and bodies are being held hostage by our own imaginations run amok.

OF NOISES AND MONSTERS: THE HORROR, THE HORROR, THE HORROR

When asked about how his music for *Silent Hill* strikes fear in players, Akira Yamaoka responded: "First and foremost is 'irregularity.' People are analog creatures…. When things don't happen as we expect, or when the rhythm breaks, we start to get very nervous.... In short, I betray the user's expectations."[8] In the game, as Yamaoka notes, individual loops of music contain irregular rhythms and sound events, most of which would defy accurate transcription with conventional Western notations for duration, pitch, and timbre. On a broader scale, however, several of the game's tracks actually achieve an oppressive effect by repeating samples with unwavering *regularity*. Much of this music can be parsed into melodic and rhythmic cells lasting no longer than a few seconds each. These recycled noise fragments evoke a hellish labyrinth in which paths toward escape and resolution are persistently concealed or deferred. Although a player can technically mute the game's audio, doing so is not advisable because these sounds supply important information about potential nearby dangers.

Like Jentsch's uncanny locomotive, the noises in *Silent Hill* chug away with a mechanical anempathy that verges on sentient antipathy. It's possible to hear this industrial music as somehow sinister in its mimicry of the player's own repetition of dreadful actions. A typical playthrough of the game involves Harry perishing again and again, getting resurrected each time (via the reloading of save files) for the gruesome ritual to carry on. The most cynical assessments of repetitious gameplay would cast it as a fatuous activity through which players are disciplined, subordinated, homogenized, and drained of all operative authority by a game's arbitrary demands for redundant action.

Several studies of musical minimalism in horror films and games posit repetition as a marker of mindlessness, psychological malfunction, or trauma. Claire King proposes that a looping melody in *The Exorcist* (1973) demonstrates a "struggle against the continuity of time [which] recalls the paralysis engendered by traumatic memory."[9] Inger Ekman and Petri Lankoski describe the repetitive moans of monsters in the 2001 survival-horror game *Fatal Frame* as a "sign of [the monsters'] mental incapacity."[10] And Kevin Donnelly frames the drone of white noise in John Carpenter's *The Fog* (1980) as an acoustic analogue to the fraught human unconscious.[11] Such readings could be deemed interpretatively compensatory in the way they strive to highlight minimalist music's maximal import—to eschew, in the words of Susan McClary, assumptions of minimalism as the mere "refusal" or "self-erasure" of meaning.[12] Or, as Robert Fink puts it, a "true cultural hermeneutic of minimal music ... must attempt to make its emptied-out formal language *signify*."[13]

Noise—as material and metaphor—has been widely theorized with similar reliance on compensatory hermeneutic premises. Writers and composers since the turn of the twentieth century have increasingly embraced noise as an object "existing in all music ... essential to its existence, but impolite to mention,"[14] comprising "sounds we have learned to ignore,"[15] signifying "only in relation to the system within which it is inscribed,"[16] connoting all the "local impurities [that] are subsumed under a communication presumed to be successful,"[17] and "present in every musical signal."[18] These characterizations familiarize noise by emphasizing its ontological relativity and phenomenological ubiquity, proclaiming not simply (and tautologically) that the *rest* is noise, but moreover that *all* is already potentially not-noise. A shared mission of exegetes and experimental composers has been to salvage noise from non-signification, to find it a home, to grant it amnesty in sanctioned spaces of musical and verbal expression.

Apophenic sensibilities inhere in portrayals of noise as a semiotic vacuum—an auditory Rorschach test signifying at once everything and nothing. Appeals to definitional promiscuity abound in descriptions of noise as "a refusal of representation, a refusal of identity"[19] and "out of control...situated within excess, a transgressive act that exceeds managed data."[20] Electronic music composer Kim Cascone describes noise as an "aesthetics of failure,"[21] while other writers have insisted on noise as always already *failing to be* noise. According to Paul Hegarty, "noise cannot remain message and still be noise.... When noise catches on,...if it were to become a [cultural or artistic] movement or inspire one, it would already be failing."[22] To this point, Simon Reynolds asserts that "to speak of noise, to give it attributes, to claim things for it, is immediately to shackle it with meaning again, to make it part of culture.... To confer the status of value upon [the] excess and extremism [of noise] is to bring these things back within the pale of decency. So the rhetoricians of noise actually destroy the power they strive to celebrate."[23] Noise is, in a word, self-negating. Even as a countercultural artifact, it cannot but slip toward the mainstream, toward the realms of social and aesthetic respectability against which it is supposed to be defined. To be sure, some formulations of noise's paradoxical status revel in so much rhetorical ambivalence that they risk getting sucked into a similar nihilistic abyss (and hence becoming discursive noise themselves).

Just as noise is conceivably present in every signal, so monsters are popularly regarded as externalizations of the ubiquitous monstrosities in human nature. Descriptions of noise's polysemy closely mirror critiques of monsters as interstitial objects (organic and otherwise) that facilitate the deferral of hermeneutic terminus. The monster, according to scholars, is "a remarkably mobile, permeable, and infinitely interpretable body,"[24] a "fantasy screen where the multiplicity of meanings can appear and fight for hegemony,"[25] and "a category that is itself a kind of limit case, an extreme version of marginalization, an abjecting epistemological device."[26] Like noises, monsters are ideal sites for discursive play. Although they're intimidating and powerful, they reciprocally serve as vehicles for scholars' intimidating displays of interpretative power. Rhetoricians *qua* monster-tamers—much like music connoisseurs who claim to comprehend noise *as* music—champion definitional mutability in bids for intellectual authority. The relationship of hermeneuts to monsters is ironically vampiric given the ease with which the latter can be appropriated as repositories for deconstruction. To reformulate one of the overriding constructionist theses of Gothic criticism: monsters are not born, but made—made, in no small part, by (and into) discourse.

CHEAP SCARES

Like the writers who work to domesticate monsters via critical inquiry, composers for early video games took up the role of noise-tamers in their attempts to fashion meaningful music out of *beeps* and *boops*. Until the 1990s, most video games contained soundtracks that accommodated no more than a few simultaneous melodic voices. Meager hardware and memory capacities further required designers to rely on the extensive repetition of short tracks. Game composers, consequently, were tasked with acoustically telescoping minimal musical material into sounds that could stand up to the monumental fantasies and larger-than-life characters of virtual worlds. Limited noises accompanying a player's encounters with dragons and giants had to be presented in a manner that inspired similar registers of awe and excitement. Prolific Japanese game composer Nobuo Uematsu explains the difficulties and rewards of audio design as follows: "The NES [Nintendo Entertainment System] only had three tracks [melodic voices], and each of their sounds was very unique. I had to focus on the melody itself and think about how each chord would move the audience. I struggled to produce originality in the same three tones, just like any composer for that period. It's amazing to listen to how [different] composers... had totally different creations by using the same three instruments."[27] Composers, of course, did not carry the full burden of creativity. Players, too, were expected to grow ears to extract maximal significance from minimal sounds. In the same way that players had to learn to interpret the pixilated graphics of early games as ludic iconography—for example, a triangular stack of dots as a spaceship—so they had to exercise a certain degree of aural imagination when confronted with the tinny *pew-pews* of interstellar battle. Composers and players of such games, much like the sound directors and audiences of radio dramas a half-century earlier, engaged in a semiotic business of audio data compression and decompression. Game audio design, as it came of age, was largely about negotiating technological constraints—or, more accurately, about cultivating the medium's expressive possibilities to forge innovative forms of sonic shorthand.

   Much of early game audio was reductive by technical necessity, but developers of survival-horror games excelled at coming up with justifications for stripped-down designs. Aside from featuring an (oppressively) repetitive soundtrack, *Silent Hill* makes use of dark and foggy environments that obviate the need for graphical rendering beyond Harry's limited line-of-sight. Awkward camera angles, an unwieldy inventory system, fuzzy enemy hitboxes, the absence of weapon reticles, and other prohibitive quirks are prevalent during gameplay and yet all find plausible vindication in survival-horror's ludic and aesthetic conventions. These alleged defects, according to the sneaky wisdom of developers, make things *scarier*.

   There's little doubt that a game like *Silent Hill* trades cunningly in horror's economies of fear—namely, in gaining esteem and commercial success via the exploitation of (apparently) simplified aesthetics and low-budget production. Among the most familiar cases of such exploitation nowadays can be seen in the found-footage sub-genre of horror films. Movies such as *The Blair Witch Project* (1999) and *Paranormal Activity* (2009) accrued indie cred and massive profits by capitalizing on elements of bare-bones presentation: low-resolution visuals, shaky camerawork, and sparse sound-scapes all helped achieve a sense of DIY faux-realism and subcultural cachet. In these films, standard rubrics for labor and value are confounded by a license to *flaunt* what might be perceived in other genres as technical or presentational flaws. Horror films, as observed by Judith Halberstam, "constantly [attempt] to call our attention to cine-matic production, its failures and its excesses…[exposing] the theatricality of identity because it makes specular precisely those images of loss, lack, penetration, violence that other films attempt to cover up."[28] Although horror movies are sometimes panned as "always-already 'low' "[29] and "the ultimate B-movies, crude, cheap, and basic,"[30] it's hard not to admire and envy them for owning up to—and taking advantage of—their rough edges and thrifty constitution.

Reductive art gets condemned when it is (assumed to be) the result of incompetence, but commended if it can somehow be confirmed as a product of intentional, painstak-ing stylization. We're bound to feel a bit uneasy when we can't tell the degree of effort that has gone into making something look simple. Content aside, one scary thing about horror films is their lucrative role in the entertainment industry. To put things in per-spective: whereas mega-blockbuster movies such as James Cameron's *Titanic* ($200 mil-lion budget) and *Avatar* ($237 million budget) both earned approximately *10 times* their respective budgets at box offices worldwide, the first *Paranormal Activity* film (shot for a meager $15,000) earned about *12,000 times* its budget (with a combined domestic and international gross of $200 million). Horror media, in sum, is unsettling not least for curbing our ability to gauge how much labor, money, and time may have gone into man-ufacturing a lowbrow surface and, in turn, the extent to which the creators are profiting from our willingness to embrace the final products.

Also central to horror's economy is the sheer *efficiency* with which the genre viscerally affects its consumers. Linda Williams has influentially classified the horror film (along with pornographic and melodramatic films) as a "body genre" because it compels "the body of the spectator [to be] caught up in an almost involuntary mimicry of the emotion or sensation of the body on the screen,"[31] resulting in "an apparent lack of proper esthetic distance, a sense of over-involvement in sensation and emotion."[32] One of horror's most reliable scare tactics is the "stinger,"[33] a sudden loud sound used to galvanize the viewer or player. The economy of the stinger lies in the baseness of the sign (*mere* noise) as well as in its manipulative force (a *cheap* shot). Like visual jump-scares, the stinger has a reputation of being an underhanded, lowbrow maneuver. Whereas suspense tends to be lauded, shock gets scorned as lazily sensational. When we deride stingers as the inex-pert stuff of B-movies and B-games, we may do so, in part, out of embarrassed indigna-tion—the feeling of being cheated out of control of our own bodies, of being left with little means of defending against such a rudimentary ploy. We have reason to begrudge a stinger, in other words, not only for its material economy, but also because—despite knowing that it's a cheap trick—we can't help falling for it. Seeing as how the impact of a stinger "precedes complex mental cognition and responses,"[34] its power can be nearly impossible to defy. Although it's a simple blast of sound, it represents a monster that cannot be tamed by discourse or mitigated by savvy. It doesn't matter if we're world-class experts on horror. Some stingers will get us all the same. In bypassing our intellectual faculties, this most vulgar of noises exposes all listeners as susceptible to shock, reminding us that—notwithstanding our persuasive words and theories—we're animals through and through.

While stingers are efficient generators of fear, they are not the only kinds of reductive noises capable of scaring us. Perhaps the single most manipulative sound in *Silent Hill* is, in fact, virtually the opposite of a stinger. This particular noise fades in and out, never takes the player by total surprise, and will recur hundreds of times in a single playthrough of the game. Yet it's flat-out terrifying. The force of this sound comes from the way it discreetly conditions and controls the player. Instead of delivering a jolt to the nervous system, it burrows deep into the mind and under the skin. To grasp what this noise is, how it works, and why it has become one of the most iconic sounds in survival-horror games to date, let us return to Harry's arrival in Silent Hill, to the beginning of the nightmare that didn't end.

BECAUSE THE RADIO TOLD ME TO

You know the story now by heart: crashed car, missing daughter, cacophonous alleyway, flayed corpse, invincible , unavoidable death. All a nightmare, perhaps. But then the nightmare goes on.

When Harry wakes up in a diner following these events, he's greeted by a lone cop. She tells him that strange things are happening around town: all phones are dead and the streets are dead empty. She hands Harry a gun, but warns him to use discretion before pulling the trigger. Ammunition is precious.

After the cop leaves the diner, I make Harry explore the small space to pick up a few more items—among them a map, a flashlight, and a knife. As I lead Harry toward the exit, a red pocket radio on a table starts emitting a static signal. A cutscene then shows Harry walking over to examine this device…but before he can pick it up, a flying pterodactyl-like beast smashes through one of the diner windows. The cutscene ends: Harry falls back under my control. In a panic, I shoot at the monster with the gun I received from the cop. The radio is still going berserk, though its white noise is now barely audible over my gunshots, the beast's screeches, and a percussive musical track (see Figure 12.3). Just as I start to wonder whether this is supposed to end in yet another scripted demise, the creature crumples to the ground. The radio noise stops. All is silent once more. I take the radio and head out into the foggy town.

FIGURE 12.3 Harry's encounter with a monster in the diner. Screen captures by author.

Within minutes of wandering the streets, I come to realize that this pocket radio—though unable to perform any conventional receiving and transmitting functions—is a monster-detector. Its white noise increases in loudness as monsters approach Harry and dies away when they are successfully dispatched or eluded. While this sound telegraphs the proximity of enemies, it does not convey their exact location. Especially when heard amid the game's hazy environments, the noise is thus doubly alarming because it tells the player not only that monsters are near, but also that they can come from anywhere. This radio static, as noted earlier, is completely contrary to a stinger. Whereas the latter manifests as a blast of sound, the former ebbs and flows in volume. And whereas the visceral impact of a stinger comes largely from the shocking *noise* itself (rather than from an indication of a specific threat), the radio static, by portending the presence of enemies, is frightening precisely as an *index* of danger.

Harry's radio—a transmitter of messages from the beyond—literalizes the kinds of occult powers that writers attributed to this technology in the early twentieth century. Granted, players who are preoccupied with virtual survival in *Silent Hill* should have little incentive to reflect on how Harry's radio is able to do what it does. The fact that a player never sees Harry carrying the device eases the assimilation of its static into the level of pure interface. Players have no need to hear the signal as one that's coming from a pocket radio. What matters is its warning function. "Game sound," as Ekman and Lankoski put it, "is free to challenge narrative fit since it is primarily serving a function other than maintaining narrative plausibility: its role is to facilitate gameplay and help the player make meaningful choices.... The *functional fit* refers to the ease by which sound provides information for performing actions."[35] Although functional sounds can assist ludic progress, this isn't to say they unequivocally enhance a player's agency. The radio's noise in *Silent Hill* is useful, but an excessive dependence on the alarm may suggest that the *static* is controlling the *player*—leading the player, for example, to run aimlessly through fog or to unload scarce ammunition into the edges of the screen in hopes of striking as-yet-unseen monsters. The hyper-compressed nature of this radio static epitomizes horror's coercive economy: white noise, after all, is by definition the noisiest of all noises, combining signals devoid of aesthetic intervention, full of sound and fury, signifying nothing. Still, for all its material crudeness, this noise in *Silent Hill* steers the player's actions with masterful efficiency. Despite serving as an aural lifeline, it points up players as Pavlovian creatures whose bodies tick with every *tick* of the radio.

The radio's static in *Silent Hill* is distressing not least for its ability to lull and lock its listener into a state of compliance. This techno-dystopian scenario invites broader reflections on all the little mechanized noises that subliminally shape our everyday acts of work and play. Beckoning beeps of computers, ringtones of mobile devices, musical earworms, and other contaminants of urban noise pollution all constitute automated audio signals with potential to move and master us.[36] Many of these sounds, while *legible*, influence our behaviors without ever providing us with much incentive to *read* them per se—to deconstruct their anatomy, source, and function so as to restore some semblance of human intellectual authority. A vision of players succumbing to the noises of *Silent Hill* resonates with popular media depictions of video games at large as a manipulative medium of entertainment. Players who grow conditioned to obey a game's white noise end up committing what might appear to be a host of mindless actions—exactly the sorts of actions that detractors of games love to lament.

As a tribute to the twists that tend to occur at the ends of horror stories, I'll offer a modest one to close out my discussion in kind. Like many who have written about *Silent Hill*, I've so far referred to the game's radio static as "white noise."[37] The reality is that this sound is technically *not* pure white noise, but rather a stylized representation of it. The radio static consists of a high ringing tone—pitched at approximately 700Hz—juxtaposed against looping samples of crackling sounds in a lower register. What's notable is that designers went this extra mile to create an aestheticized *approximation* of white noise when they could have just resorted to blasting actual static. One reason for investing such effort was perhaps to make this recurring noise more palatable to players' ears. Just as no player of a survival-horror game would want to suffer bodily harm, so most may not be so eager to tolerate literal white noise for a long time. The result of this stylization is a noise that retains a mildly grating timbre and yet befits extended aural consumption. That most players, critics, and scholars nevertheless describe the sound *as* white noise—and, presumably, perceive it (virtually) as such—testifies to the successful implementation of this almost-but-not-quite musicalized aesthetic. So while *Silent Hill* contains many sneakily economical aspects (a repetitive soundtrack, foggy environments, and plot holes *qua* traumatic visions), the radio static's sound design offers a reversed scenario. The stylized noise reminds us that, for all the labor- and cost-cutting strategies in the production of horror entertainment, there are also subtle acts of creative effort that can sometimes go unsung.

Conclusion

One reason we voluntarily subject ourselves to horror media is to go forth and learn fear. And to experience fear in a horror video game, we must follow the trail of breadcrumbs through its terrible gauntlet. At every turn, *Silent Hill* implicitly asks us to venture into darkness, to peek around this corner, to open that door behind which might lurk a couple of formidable, even insurmountable, monsters. We instinctively oblige because, well, that's the point of the game. Thus we force Harry into the terrors of the unknown, making him (and ourselves) vulnerable to monsters from nowhere, noises from everywhere, stingers that shock us, static that steers us.

When it comes to survival-horror, the game is a monster of a medium: it oversteps its inanimate status, breaks with convention, violates ludic contracts, bombards us with noise, and teases us with illusions of real danger. Just as our spectatorship of horror films is said to be ruled by a masochistic impulse, so there's an awful pleasure in stumbling through the haunted house of a horror game, surrendering to its manipulation and being transgressed *against*.[38] Capitulating to cheap scares requires that we accept cacophony, reductive aesthetics, and illogical plot points as compelling conceits. To play *Silent Hill* with conviction is to play (and buy) *into* its economies of fear.

Visceral scares of horror media expose the limited defenses of our rational and rhetorical faculties. Try as we might to keep noises and monsters tucked safely away in our discursive webs, they're capable of slipping through, running wild, and returning to invade our imaginations. Noises and monsters make perfect subjects for metaphysical dissection, but—if there's anything we've learned from Dr. Frankenstein and his Gothic kin—these patients do not always remain docile. Hermeneutic control only gets us so far. As we attempt to discipline rogue phenomena with theories and theses, they discipline our minds and bodies in turn. Interpreting video games and their stimuli as uncannily living entities can shed light on interactivity, repetition, automation, and the intersection between our ludic, aural, and intellectual agencies. A fantasy of things come to life, of course, is the very stuff of video games—a medium that lets us displace authority onto virtual characters, to experience conflicting sensations of being in and out of control, and to inhabit murky spaces where nothing stays dead for long.

Acknowledgments

I'm grateful to Kevin Donnelly, Amy Herzog, Hannah Lewis, Elizabeth Medina-Gray, Luci Mok, Alexander Rehding, John Richardson, Kay Shelemay, Carol Vernallis, and Gavin Williams for their valuable feedback on this essay.

NOTES

1. Mark Simmons, "Scream Team: Interview with Mark Simmons, Sam Barlow, and Tom Hulett," *Nintendo Power* 241 (2009), 45.

2. Ernst Jentsch, "On the Psychology of the Uncanny," trans. Roy Sellars, *Angelaki* 2, no. 1 ([1906] 1997), 11.

3. According to Yamaoka, his main musical influences have included punk, techno, metal, and British New Wave rock bands such as Depeche Mode, Ultravox, and Visage. See Daniel Kalabakov, "Interview with Akira Yamaoka," *Spelmusik.net*, 2002, http://www.spelmusik. net/intervjuer/akira_yamaoka_eng.html.

4. Zach Whalen, "Play Along—An Approach to Video Game Music," *Game Studies: The International Journal of Computer Game Research* 4, no. 1 (2004), http://www.gamestudies. org/0401/whalen.

5. Quoted in Kalabakov, "Interview with Akira Yamaoka."

6. Paul Hegarty, *Noise/Music: A History* (New York: Continuum, 2007), 105.

7. Karen Collins, "The Future Is Happening Already: Industrial Music, Dystopia and the Aesthetic of the Machine" (PhD diss., University of Liverpool, 2002), 13.

8. Akira Yamaoka, "Mad Maestro: Interview with Akira Yamaoka," *Nintendo Power* 241, no. 39 (2009): 3.

9. Claire King, "Ramblin' Men and Piano Men: Crises of Music and Masculinity in *The Exorcist*," in *Music in the Horror Film: Listening to Fear*, ed. Neil Lerner (New York: Routledge, 2010), 120.

10. Inger Ekman and Petra Lankoski, "Hair-Raising Entertainment: Emotions, Sound, and Structure in *Silent Hill 2* and *Fatal Frame*," in *Horror Video Games: Essays on the Fusion of Fear and Play*, ed. Bernard Perron (Jefferson, NC and London: McFarland & Company, 2009), 192.

11. See K. J. Donnelly, "Hearing Deep Seated Fears: John Carpenter's *The Fog* (1980)," in *Music in the Horror Film*, ed. Neil Lerner (New York: Routledge, 2010), 160–161.

12. Susan McClary, "Minima Romantica," in *Beyond the Soundtrack: Representing Music in Cinema*, ed. Daniel Goldmark, Lawrence Kramer, and Richard Leppert (Berkeley, CA: University of California Press, 2007), 52.

13. Robert Fink, *Repeating Ourselves: American Minimal Music as Cultural Practice* (Berkeley, CA: University of California Press, 2005), 18 (emphasis in original).

14. Henry Cowell, *Essential Cowell: Selected Writings on Music*, ed. Dick Higgins (Kingston, NY: Documentext, [1929] 2001), 252.

15. R. Murray Schafer, "The Music of the Environment," in *Audio Culture: Readings in Modern Music*, ed. Christoph Cox and Daniel Warner (New York: The Continuum International Publishing Group, [1973] 2004), 30.

16. Jacques Attali, *Noise: The Political Economy of Music*, trans. Brian Massumi (Minneapolis, MN: University of Minnesota Press, 1985), 26.

17. Douglas Kahn, *Noise, Water, Meat: A History of Sound in the Arts* (Cambridge, MA: MIT Press, 1999), 25.

18. Mary Russo and Daniel Warner, "Rough Music, Futurism, and Postpunk Industrial Noise Bands," in *Audio Culture: Readings in Modern Music*, ed. Christoph Cox and Daniel Warner (New York: Continuum International Publishing Group, 2004), 50. Or, as John Cage famously stated: "Wherever we are, what we hear is mostly noise. When we ignore it,

it disturbs us. When we listen to it, we find it fascinating." John Cage, *Silence: Lectures and Writings* (Middletown, CT: Wesleyan University Press, 1973), 3.

19. Csaba Toth, "Noise Theory," in *Noise & Capitalism*, ed. Mattin Iles and Anthony Iles. Arteleku Audiolab, 2009), 27, http://www.arteleku.net/audiolab/noise_capitalism.pdf.

20. Caleb Kelly, *Cracked Media: The Sound of Malfunction* (Cambridge, MA: MIT Press, 2009), 63.

21. Kim Cascone, "The Aesthetics of Failure: 'Post-Digital' Tendencies in Contemporary Computer Music," *Computer Music Journal* 24, no. 4 (2000): 12.

22. Hegarty, *Noise/Music: A History*, 126.

23. Simon Reynolds, "Noise," in *Audio Culture: Readings in Modern Music*, ed. Christoph Cox and Daniel Warner (New York: Continuum International Publishing Group, 2004), 56.

24. Judith Halberstam, *Skin Shows: Gothic Horror and the Technology of Monsters* (Durham, NC: Duke University Press, 1995), 11.

25. Slavoj Žižek, "Grimaces of the Real, or When the Phallus Appears," *October* 58 (1991): 63.

26. Jeffrey Jerome Cohen, "Preface: In a Time of Monsters," in *Monster Theory: Reading Culture*, ed. Jeffrey Jerome Cohen (Minneapolis: University of Minnesota Press, 1996), ix.

27. Quoted in Matthew Belinkie, "Video Game Music: Not Just Kid Stuff," 1999, http://www.vgmusic.com/vgpaper.shtml.

28. Halberstam, *Skin Shows*, 153.

29. Harmony Wu, "Trading in Horror, Cult and Matricide: Peter Jackson's Phenomenal Bad Taste and New Zealand Fantasies of Inter/national Cinematic Success," in *Defining Cult Movies: The Cultural Politics of Oppositional Taste*, ed. Mark Jancovich, Antonio Lázaro Reboll, Julian Stringer, and Andy Willis (Manchester: Manchester University Press, 2003), 86.

30. Morris Dickstein, "The Aesthetics of Fright," in *Planks of Reason: Essays on the Horror Film*, ed. Barry Keith Grant and Christopher Sharrett (Lanham, MD: The Scarecrow Press, 2004), 53.

31. Linda Williams, "Film Bodies: Gender, Genre, and Excess," *Film Quarterly* 44, no. 4 (1991): 4.

32. Ibid., 5.

33. K. J. Donnelly, *The Spectre of Sound: Music in Film and Television* (London: BFI, 2008), 95.

34. Ibid.

35. Ekman and Lankoski, "Hair-Raising Entertainment," 185 (emphasis in original).

36. Studies of music in everyday life, musical manipulation, violence, and sound ecologies have variously emphasized the ability of acoustic phenomena to act on, inhibit, and control human thought and behavior. See, for example, Steve Goodman, *Sonic Warfare: Sound, Affect, and the Ecology of Fear* (Cambridge, MA: MIT Press, 2010), 5–13; Suzanne Cusick, " 'You are in a place that is out of the world...': Music in the Detention Camps of the 'Global War on Terror,' " *Journal of the Society for American Music* 2, no. 1 (2008): 1–26; Peter J. Martin, "Music, Identity, and Social Control," in *Music and Manipulation: On the Social Uses and Social Control of Music*, ed. Steven Brown and Ulrik Volgsten (New York: Berghahn Books, 2006), 57–71; and Tia DeNora, *Music in Everyday Life* (Cambridge: Cambridge University Press, 2000).

37. See Bernard Perron, *Silent Hill: The Terror Engine* (Ann Arbor: University of Michigan Press, 2012), 28; Michael Nitsche, *Video Game Spaces: Image, Play, and Structure in 3D Game Worlds* (Cambridge, MA: MIT Press, 2008), 132; Ewan Kirkland, "The Self-Reflexive

Funhouse of *Silent Hill*," *Convergence: The International Journal of Research into New Media Technologies* 13 (2007): 410; and Whalen, "Play along," 76.

38. On masochism and horror film spectatorship, see Anna Powell, *Deleuze and the Horror Film* (Edinburgh: Edinburgh University Press, 2005), 47; Carol Clover, *Men, Women, and Chain Saws: Gender in the Modern Horror Film* (Princeton, NJ: Princeton University Press, 1992), 222; and Noël Carroll, *The Philosophy of Horror, or Paradoxes of the Heart* (New York: Routledge, 1990), 158–214.

SELECT BIBLIOGRAPHY

Carroll, Noël. *The Philosophy of Horror, or Paradoxes of the Heart*. New York: Routledge, 1990.

Cohen, Jeffrey Jerome. "Preface: In a Time of Monsters." In *Monster Theory: Reading Culture*, edited by Jeffrey Jerome Cohen, vii–xiii. Minneapolis: University of Minnesota Press, 1996.

Donnelly, K. J. *The Spectre of Sound: Music in Film and Television*. London: BFI, 2008.

Fink, Robert. *Repeating Ourselves: American Minimal Music as Cultural Practice*. Berkeley: University of California Press, 2005.

Goodman, Steve. *Sonic Warfare: Sound, Affect, and the Ecology of Fear*. Cambridge, MA: MIT Press, 2010.

Hand, Richard J. "Proliferating Horrors: Survival Horror and the *Resident Evil* Franchise." In *Horror Film: Creating and Marketing Fear*, edited by Steffen Hantke, 117–134. Jackson: University Press of Mississippi, 2004.

Jentsch, Ernst. "On the Psychology of the Uncanny." Translated by Roy Sellars. *Angelaki* 2, no. 1 (1997): 7–16.

Kirkland, Ewan. "The Self-Reflexive Funhouse of *Silent Hill*." *Convergence: The International Journal of Research into New Media Technologies* 13 (2007): 403–415.

Perron, Bernard. *Silent Hill: The Terror Engine*. Ann Arbor: University of Michigan Press, 2012.

Whalen, Zach. "Case Study: Film Music vs. Video-Game Music: The Case of *Silent Hill*." In *Music, Sound and Multimedia: From the Live to the Virtual*, edited by Jamie Sexton, 68–84. Edinburgh: Edinburgh University Press, 2007.

CHAPTER 13

"CHARM THE AIR TO GIVE A SOUND"

The Uncanny Soundscape of Punchdrunk's Sleep No More

AMY HERZOG

Last night, I dreamt I went to Manderley again. It seemed to me I stood by the iron gate leading to the drive, and for a while I could not enter, for the way was barred to me.... Then, like all dreamers, I was possessed of a sudden with supernatural powers and passed like a spirit through the barrier before me. The drive wound away in front of me, twisting and turning as it had always done, but as I advanced, I was aware that a change had come upon it.... We can never go back to Manderley again.

—Rebecca(Hitchcock, 1940)[1]

[A] William Shakespeare of the future could create kaleidoscopic worlds of dazzling variety that will display the coherence and unified vision we associate with great fiction...dictate not just the words and images of the story but the rules by which the words and images would appear.

—Janet H. Murray, *Hamlet on the Holodeck* (276)

I'll charm the air to give a sound, While you perform your antic round.

—Shakespeare, *The Tragedy of Macbeth* (4.1.129–130)

I step off the elevator into a narrow, dark hallway and take a moment to orient myself to the warren of small, interconnected rooms that open before me. I am just one of several wraiths in beaked, white masks exploring these seemingly abandoned chambers. We've clearly entered a different time period, ostensibly the 1930s, although the precise moment is indistinct because each room overflows with a hodgepodge of objects from multiple eras, all already heavily marked with age. My sense of temporal transportation is most immediately cued by the music wafting through each room—if my memory can be trusted in this moment of uncertainty, a tinny recording of a Rudy Vallee song, perhaps "Honey" (1929). More masked figures flit past the door as I pause to tentatively handle a silk robe thrown across a bed and flip open a moldering, handwritten journal. The sheer volume of stuff, of dust, of smells, is overwhelming. I'm not sure where to look or how far this hall of rooms will extend—should I linger to open the box on the dresser or scurry down the hall with the other ghosts? Unnerved by the worn doll left on the pillow of a child's bed, I leave the suite of rooms.

And suddenly, not even sure of how I've arrived here, I'm stepping through a set of French doors into the coolness of the night, my shoes crunching on the gravel walkway of a small graveyard bathed in blue light (I have to remind myself, after the shock dissipates, that I'm, in fact, deep inside the third floor of a warehouse in Chelsea on a sweltering summer evening). A breeze brushes my cheek as I am propelled forward, in no small part by the music; Bernard Herrmann's "Prelude" from *Vertigo* (Alfred Hitchcock, 1958) swells up as if on cue as I reach the doors. The impact is visceral, my skin prickles and I suppress a momentary spasm of giddiness. I'm gazing down at my feet through the eyeholes of my mask, in part to keep from tripping over the gravestones and rocks, and in part because those feet seem oddly disembodied—I observe my own movements as though they are someone else's, framed by a camera-like gaze. I'm at once thoroughly, physically engaged in the present of a space that demands vigilant attention and reenacting waves of cinematic recollections that wash over me. At this moment, I'm Scottie or perhaps Madeleine, guided by unseen forces through the cemetery at Mission Dolores in *Vertigo*, not yet certain who I am following or why. I raise my head to see the brightly lit windows of a building beside a tree at the far side of a courtyard (how is this physically possible?). I wander closer and peer through the glass to see a couple engaged in a violent, erotic pas de deux across a bed, encircled by more masked figures. The sharp thudding of their bodies against the furniture breaks my spell, and I step through the threshold into yet another dream space.

I am describing my first experience inside the New York production of *Sleep No More*, the immersive theater piece staged by the London collective Punchdrunk, which first opened in March 2011.[2] It is a project that defies concise summary. Based on Shakespeare's *Macbeth*, *Sleep No More* (directed by Felix Barrett and Maxine Doyle, sound design by Stephen Dobbie) transposes the structures and rhythms of the play into a tightly choreographed, nearly dialogue-less physical adaptation, set in a fabricated 1930s hotel, The McKittrick (a reference to *Vertigo*), awash with cinematic elements drawn from Hitchcock, Herrmann, David Lynch, and Stanley Kubrick. The action is danced across nearly one hundred rooms, spread between six floors in three interconnected warehouses on West 27th Street. The set includes the hotel lobby and ballroom, as well as a graveyard and suites of rooms associated with certain characters (my initial entry was through the bedrooms of the Macduffs), a street filled with shops (including a taxidermist, a candy shop, an embalmer's workshop, and a private investigator's office and darkroom), a forest, a witches' apothecary, and several wards within a large sanatorium. After checking into the hotel and stumbling through a pitch black curtained corridor, audience members gather in the Manderley Bar (a reference to *Rebecca*), which is perfectly styled with live jazz and vintage cocktails. Guests are ushered into the performance space in small groups via elevator, dispersed on various floors of the instal- lation, with almost no directives beyond a short list of rules: you must wear your mask at all times, you may not speak for the duration of the performance, and you will do well to remember that "fortune favors the bold."

It may seem odd to approach questions of sound and new audiovisual media through a work that is fetishistically devoted to the past. The musical components of *Sleep No More* consist primarily of Bernard Herrmann's film scores and recordings of popu- lar songs from the 1920s through the 1960s. Sound here works in concert with deeply familiar narrative references (namely *Macbeth*), adapting them to a Prohibition-era set- ting. Visual nods to photographic and cinematic pasts abound, including a heavy doses of Stanley Kubrick's *Eyes Wide Shut* (1999) and *The Shining* (1980), two films equally haunted by bygone eras. And the design of the installation materializes the past in its wallpapers, draperies, furniture, and room after room stuffed with artifacts, many reflecting Victorian fixations on death and the natural sciences or even more ancient occult rituals.

Yet *Sleep No More* is, at the same time, a highly contemporary phenomenon, perhaps the most expansive experiment in immersive theater in New York to date. Elements of interactivity and site-specificity have long played a role in the theater, utilized most effectively toward political ends by artists such as Augusto Boal in his Theatre of the Oppressed in the 1960s and presaged by Antonin Artaud in his 1938 call to "abolish the stage and the auditorium and replace them by a single site, without partition or bar- rier of any kind, which will become the theatre of the action."[3] Yet the past decade has witnessed an explosion of large-scale immersive projects, which are emerging as an enormously popular, trans-media and trans-genre trend. Site-specific and immersive performance worlds run the gambit from underground "happenings" and interactive art installations (The Underbelly Project, 2010, The Cans Festival, 2008, public works by Maurice Benayoun), to urban interventions (projects by Pierre Huyghe, Los Angeles Poverty Department, Paul Chan's *Waiting for Godot in New Orleans*, 2007) to classi- cal music (Alina Ibragimova's 2011 collaboration with the Quay Brothers in Chethem's Library, Manchester), to Jane's Addiction's 2012 "Theatre of the Escapists" tour (an immersive environment partly inspired by *Sleep No More*, described by lead singer Perry Farrell as "Twenties surrealist with a Sixties, Warhol pop twist").[4]

There is thus something forward reaching in the conception and promotion of *Sleep No More*'s haunted spaces. The production taps into a burgeoning demand for expe- riential works that bring to light unseen aspects of our urban environment. Projects such as these often root themselves the abandoned, the forgotten, and the analog; par- ticipants thrill in the spirit of individualized adventurousness and an almost nostalgic appreciation of the handcrafted. Yet contemporary immersive works are equally marked by the influence of audiovisual media and of digital technologies, on multiple registers. Intertextual references to songs, to films, and to television abound on the levels of music, image, and narrative. The stagings themselves are enabled by sophisticated multitrack sound and lighting systems that create synchronized, sensory environments for performers and audience members alike. Happenings are advertised via social networks, and bloggers relish in sharing spoilers and tips for exploring these worlds. And, as I will argue in more detail below, the architecture, and indeed the very premise of immersive theater, has been deeply enriched by developments in digital gaming technology. It is no accident that this trend toward immersive experiences has proven so popular with a youthful audience not typically drawn to traditional theater or performance art. On a structural level, immersive theater resonates with the hyperconnected, technologically mediated modality familiar to a contemporary digital generation.

In the pages that follow, I will argue that *Sleep No More* provides a fascinating forum for exploring new trends in the use of sound in both live performance and audiovisual media. Although a great number of the musical references and cues in the soundscape are drawn from well-known, analog sources, building on the long history of associations embedded within each sonic passage, their deployment marks a decided shift in the role that sound performs in theater and film. The sound environment in the installation serves not merely to establish ambience within the space, although it does perform this task expertly. It also works to guide and synchronize the actions of the several hundred individual audience- and cast members who navigate the environment during each performance. The use of sonic cues, in this context, draws directly from the logic of first-person perspective role-playing video games.

One of my objectives in this essay will be to tease out some of the dense sonic references woven into the soundscape of *Sleep No More*, paying particular attention to the way in which music works to deepen the physical experience of the uncanny within that space. A second goal involves reading the use of sound cues within the performance in relation to digital gaming environments. Finally, I will suggest that the use of rhythm and repetition in *Sleep No More* resonates on an even deeper register with similar architectures of meaning in some of the work's key points of reference: namely Shakespeare's *Macbeth* and Herrmann's film scores. My point is that the use of sound and looping movements in this production goes beyond surface-level allusion to outside texts, triggering instead a more foundational, structural link. Given the highly individualized nature of the *Sleep No More* experience, it is difficult to make any conclusive statements about the work's overarching meaning or its narrative objectives. Yet a careful examination of its architecture reveals a complex deployment of sonic patterning, one that activates new connections with a set of historical texts and that challenges our understanding of what it means to experience sound, touch, and performance in our own uncannily digital worlds. On each register of this inquiry, one can locate a tension between the experience of autonomous movement within the space of the irrational and an architectural framework that serves to choreograph and set the boundaries for that experience.

I would like to note certain logistical constraints that have impacted my study of sound in *Sleep No More*, for these limitations have resulted in an analysis based more on the more generalized affective impact of the soundscape than on close readings of individual compositional elements. In the interest of recounting the work as it was meant to be experienced, I have sought to describe the soundscape as it sounds and feels within the trajectory of the performance event. Many of the raw elements within the sound design have been edited, altered, and layered with other tracks, making them difficult to study outside of that environment. The recorded soundtrack is further extended into the noises produced by performers and audience members moving about the space. And, although I have done my best to accurately recount the scope of that multilayered aural environment, my efforts inevitably fall short. Over the course of two visits, I spent 6 hours within the performance space and made a concerted effort to visit and listen to every space within the installation. Yet, with such a vast amount of territory to cover, and with the sonic elements constantly shifting within each of those rooms as the cast stages multiple, simultaneous encounters across each floor, and with certain areas opening and closing at various points throughout the evening, one individual can only encounter a fraction of the performance and hence only a fraction of the sound design. Moreover, one is often disoriented, startled, and overwhelmed during the course of the performance. My recollections regarding what I heard at those moments are surely suspect. Yet I'm not certain that a detailed mapping of tracks would greatly enhance my project here (as fascinating as such a map would be, from a practitioner's perspective). The more significant point of this essay, and I would argue the point of the performance, has to do with engaging in the physical experience of the immersive environment, in the specific space and time in which it unfolds. My hope is that any inaccuracies or omissions in my descriptions will be outweighed by their fidelity to the embodied, emotive experience.

Music, Charming the Air

Punchdrunk is one of several theatrical companies staging productions within nontraditional settings. Although objectives vary depending on context, one can point to a common interest in teasing out affinities among performance, text, and space, and in upending established notions of spectatorship. Rather than isolating the theatrical experience in a hermetic black box, site-specific and immersive productions put bodies into dialogue with objects and environments in unexpected ways. Audiences within these productions are challenged to actively navigate architectural constructs and, at times, to intervene in the trajectory of the production. This challenge can be tinged with anxiety; the thrill of the immersive performance often stems from the fact that we don't know what we are expected to "do" in these spaces, absent the familiar rituals of traditional theater. Questions of agency arise, with proponents extolling the creative potential for performative spectatorship and detractors comparing immersive productions to gimmicky ghost rides or haunted houses. I will explore the tensions between audience autonomy and prescribed experience in more detail in later sections, suggesting that the interplay between these tendencies is continually in flux, evolving over the course of a production in contradictory ways. I'd like to consider first, however, the strategies by which Punchdrunk uses sound to flesh out the particular site of *Sleep No More* in New York, looking initially at uses of prerecorded music and then at the integration of live sound.

Felix Barrett has described the Punchdrunk ethos as one that is deeply sensitive to the specificity of environment—not site-specific but rather "site-sympathetic."[5] Although scenarios for Punchdrunk productions are typically planned in advance of entering a location, and those locations themselves are not always the sites originally sought, Barrett recounts waiting to explore chosen sites before solidifying details of an installation. The dynamic he describes seems less about capitalizing on a location's specific history and more about tapping into the latent energies present there, the capacity of that architecture to provide for embodied experiences. In essence, Punchdrunk uses the installation aspect of their productions to invoke an uncanny experience, to render a knowable space suddenly unfamiliar, stirring up that "which ought to have remained hidden but which has come to light."[6] The interaction with space here is visceral, an experience that resonates on a deeply sensuous and subjective basis.

This move toward a spatial, material sympathy is not only artistic, but also logistical. In an environment in which hundreds of participants navigate a large space individually, a strong sense of ambience or tone is critical; it allows for an empathetic connection between audience, space, and performance while at the same time remaining diffuse enough to provide for any number of individual variations. The tone of the environment serves as the primary link binding together any number of circulating elements: the affective experience of the audience members, the gestures of the actors and the mood of their performances, the material qualities of the space, and the narratives and texts around which the production is built. Because audience members have so much freedom to roam throughout the installation, tonality must be infused within the full range of sensory experiences they might encounter (visual and sound design, architectural layout, lighting, ventilation, and smell). That the tone is crafted on such a material and corporeal basis furthers the sense of the uncanny. What is experienced is often not registered on a fully conscious level.

The whole of the experience, for the designers of Punchdrunk, is built up from all the physical triggers that might create a sense of simultaneous unease and excitement, "from smells to the use of bass."[7] Sound is crucial among these. It registers corporeally, reverberating within the chest or signaling the approach of another body within a darkened room. Memory-images are triggered as well, particularly through the use of familiar songs and musical themes. Preexisting musical elements within the *Sleep No More* sound design, for example, seep into our consciousness sometimes, and, for some listeners, as recognizable references; for others, they linger at the edge of perception as unidentified historical or emotive cues. In all these capacities, sound works to tease out the hidden ambiences latent within an installation. It provides a further tonal bed upon which performers and audience members can interact, entering into the rhythms and themes of the narrative scenario.

One of the most poignant scenes I encountered in this regard occurred in the hotel lobby. A young man (billed as the "boy witch") is lip-syncing Peggy Lee's "Is That All There Is?" (Leiber and Stoller, 1969) under a spotlight, with tears streaming down his face. Much of the furniture in this corner of the lobby is covered with sheets; like the party scene in The Overlook Hotel in *The Shining*, it feels as though this abandoned hotel is populated only by specters. The lyrical content of the song reinforces this impression, eschewing even death as a "final disappointment." But the performances, both Lee's and the boy witch's, are filled with emotive life. In contrast to the tonal sound beds that comprise much of the soundscape throughout the space, this song remains intact and is played at an increased volume; it may, in fact, serve as a beacon leading audience members into the room. Lee's resonant voice fleshes out the nuances of the intimate stories she recounts, rescuing them from empty irony. And the boy witch's performance is incredibly moving, attuned to each nuance of Lee's vocalization, which is particularly challenging given the long passages of spoken word. The excessive drama and nihilism of the lyrics could easily tip into parody or camp, as could the gender reversal of singer and voice.[8] Yet the utter strangeness of this unexpected encounter, infused with traces of Kubrick and David Lynch, resonates as deeply real.

Yet the most omnipresent sonic force within *Sleep No More*, by far, is Bernard Herrmann. Although press for the production often bills the show as "Macbeth meets Hitchcock," the point of reference is not a specific set of images, characters, or plot points from Hitchcock films.[9] Instead, what we encounter is a far more amorphous mood, one that is in fact dictated most directly by Herrmann's scores, especially those for *Vertigo* and *Psycho*.[10]

Royal S. Brown describes Herrmann's collaborations with Hitchcock as partaking in a curious dynamic. Herrmann's emotional volatility, both musically and personally, provide for Brown a productive counterpoint to Hitchcock's cool rationality. At the same time, both artists engage in a similar modality: beginning from a place of everyday normalcy before slipping into the realm of the frightening and unknown.[11] "The essence of Herrmann's Hitchcock scoring lies in a kind of harmonic ambiguity, hardly new to Western music but novel in film music," Brown writes, "whereby the musical language familiar to Western listeners serves as a point of departure, only to be modified in such a way that norms are thrown off center and expectations are held in suspense for much longer periods of time than the listening ears and feeling viscera are accustomed to."[12] Just as Hitchcock's troubled filmworlds often begin within seemingly familiar settings, Herrmann's compositions at first seem in line with traditional Western structures and tonal systems. But rather than cycling around toward harmonic resolution, Herrmann's scores rely on unresolved, unstable intervals: seventh-chords and the recurrence of major thirds within minor mode settings.[13] Through repetition, these destabilized elements begin to function independently from the rest of the composition; in the case of the use of sevenths, they take on the characteristics of a motif. Herrmann's predilection for short phrases or musical "cells" in the place of developed themes allows for the somewhat mobile play of mood and unstable signification. The ambiguous use of thirds, for Brown, leaves the listener in a state of suspension, not certain how to "read" or contextualize what is heard.[14] And because "harmonic and instrumental color" dominate over theme and motif in Herrmann, musical phrases cannot be contextualized within or subsumed by larger melodies.[15] In the prelude to *Vertigo*, for example, strings and winds play circling arpeggios, periodically interrupted by blaring brass chords. Free-floating signifiers, these phrases shift and are easily defamiliarized, opening into the realm of the irrational. Passages within *Vertigo* and *Psycho* are marked by "mirrored contrary motion," spiraling upward and downward simultaneously.[16] "What characterizes the Herrmann/Hitchcock sound," Brown writes, "are the ways in which this downward tendency is counterbalanced to reflect the unique equilibria of Hitchcock's cinema, and, even more importantly, the ways in which novel harmonic colorations make that descent into the irrational felt as an ever-lurking potential."[17]

The thematic relevance of Herrmann to the modality of *Sleep No More*, in this context, is quite clear. *Sleep No More* is experienced as a series of disconnected, nonlinear vignettes with narrative connections that are primarily rooted in thematic resonances. Short phrases and polytonal arpeggios lend themselves to this ambience-driven space in which extended melodies and musical themes could not properly register. Just as ostinato patterning and unresolved chords provided great flexibility in synchronizing and stretching the score across diverse passages in film, these same structures mesh easily with the movements and emotions of the participants in the installation.[18] The simultaneous rising and falling of Herrmann's musical passages invoke vertiginous sensations, even in those unfamiliar with the score. And for those who do recognize the references, their presence in this new space triggers uncanny juxtapositions of present and past. Herrmann provides a means of foreshadowing the irrational, making emotional sense out of an experience that could otherwise feel hopelessly fragmentary.

But Herrmann is hardly the only spirit called forth to charm the air in The McKittrick Hotel, which has a fairly rich, more immediate musical history of its own. The "hotel" is in fact a set of empty warehouses at 530 West 27th Street, once home to a series of dance clubs and lounges: Sound Factory (1989–1995), Twilo (1995–2001), Spirit (2003–2006), and B.E.D., Home, and Guesthouse, which shared different floors at the location starting in 2005.[19] Alongside the nearby Bungalow 8, Pink Elephant, Marquee, and Cain, this strip of 27th Street was dubbed "club row" in its heyday. Sound Factory and Twilo were tremendously popular havens for house and electronic music. The tenor of the neighborhood soon shifted, however, from an industrial outpost to a destination for overpriced bottle service, underage clientele, and celebrity gawking: "an amusement park for adults," "a Disneyland for drunks."[20] A number of alcohol-overdose deaths were linked to the location, and, in 2007 a thirty-five-year-old man fell to his death in an elevator shaft during a fight with an employee at B.E.D.

It would be a stretch to argue that this history had a direct influence on *Sleep No More*, but certain ghosts of this past echoed for me in a scene that might best be described as a witches' rave-orgy.[21] The scene took place in a bar on the fourth floor, which is a near-exact replica of the Manderley Bar below, except that the room is now in complete disarray, with broken bottles and upturned chairs, covered in dust and cobwebs. To walk into the room is to experience the uncanny as a hit to the gut; I was reminded of a similar strategy for generating fear and disorientation in the video game series *Silent Hill* (Konami, 1999–present), where rooms unexpectedly transform into dark images of their former selves. The scene commences with Hectate's laugh and the shocking intrusion of drum and bass music, played at a deafening volume. This was the only contemporary music I encountered in the performance space, with a mix prominently featuring "Reece" by Ed Rush and Optical (Virus Recordings, 2005). The room is launched into pure darkness save for a rapid-fire strobe light, which renders all actions that follow into frozen tableaux. Three lithe female witches grab the boy witch and strip him completely naked; he then emerges from the dark wearing a goat's head. Macbeth enters the room, and the group engages in an extraordinarily homoerotic ritual involving even more nudity, a fountain of blood, and a dead infant, which the witches mockingly pretend to nurse. The combination of sound, light, and truly shocking imagery register with a massive, bodily blow.

MOVEMENT AND SOUND, ANTIC ROUNDS

Indeed, a key component of the soundscape of *Sleep No More* is the material impact of the sound produced there. And a great deal of this sound extends beyond the recorded tracks to include both the choreographed collisions of the performers and the less predictable noises generated by the audience. In a strange way, much of the music in *Sleep No More* seems geared toward shaping the experience of individual wanderers as they navigate the installation. Music and sound thus function quite differently than in traditional theater or dance, where music serves to undergird the performers' movements and a centralized narrative. Although the musical atmosphere does indeed seep into the general mood of the performances, in the heat of that action, by contrast, many of the scenes minimize music to rely directly on the sounds generated by the performers to heighten their dramatic impact. If the majority of the music within the production lures us into contemplation of the past, the thuds and crashes of the dancers jerk us back into the collective, embodied space of the present.

Maxine Doyle, co-director and choreographer of *Sleep No More*, worked to forge a physical language for the piece, one in which dialogue and narrative are adapted into the freighted meetings of bodies and spaces, paring texts down to the "unseen words."[22] Nearly all the performers in this production were trained as dancers, and they range across the vast set with tremendous athleticism and command of space. Scenes occur as vignettes within rooms where characters' trajectories collide; these encounters are often violent or violently sexual. As tensions rise, the performers literally climb the walls, hanging suspended within doorframes through sheer momentum and strength. These moments, too, resonate with uncanniness; we are surprised by the unfixed boundaries of the body, by its capacity to do the unexpected, and by the space for accommodating such contortions.

For Doyle, questions of proximity are central within the immersive space of the installation. As the design, ambience, and sound encourage audiences to enter into the materiality of each room, the performers must respect and maintain that spatial relationship, further tightening the sense of physical immersion rather than partitioning space into safe areas for performing or spectating:

> There's no concession to the physicality of the choreography in relation to the audience's proximity to it. And that's a challenge; audiences have to become part of the choreography, they have to engage with [it on] a kinetic level in order to survive. It becomes quite Darwinian.[23]

There is an inherent unpredictability at work during these encounters and a high degree of intimacy. Audience members are startled into the rhythms and flows of the danced performances they stumble across on their journeys and are forced to react (by moving aside, by fleeing, or by following the performers as they break apart and move to other rooms). "One-on-one" encounters are written into the looping trajectories of each performer, as well, in which they solicit interactions with individual audience members.

The crescendos and denouements of the performers' movements throughout the space are deeply sonic, even if they are not buoyed by music in a traditional sense. The forceful sounds of the performers' bodies pierce through the recorded soundtrack, resonating above the more cautious shuffle of the audience members pulled in their tow. This being an adaptation of *Macbeth*, nearly every scene was marked by betrayal, conflict, and descents into madness and grief. Performers slammed into one another, and the walls, and the floors, with an abandon that was at times frightening. And the sounds of bodies hitting bodies and bodies hitting walls and objects sometimes coincided with shocks to one's own flesh. I was kicked on several occasions when I didn't move out of the way of dueling characters quickly enough, or, most memorably, when I had the misfortune of standing between a lovelorn nurse and a large taxidermied mountain goat she was paying tribute to in an enchanted forest. The experience, for me, generated a jarring awareness of my own physical presence within this space, precisely the realization that the theatrical apparatus, with its prosceniums, cushioned seats, and darkened auditoriums, seeks to avoid.

One of the strangest physical sounds within this installation is produced by the coalesced bodies of the audience members as they gravitate toward various characters. Shortly after entering the performance space for the first time, I realized that a stark division was being forged in terms of the audience's collective psychological response to this experiment. Some, like myself, were drawn toward exploring the space, breaking away from the pack to indulge in the fetishism of objects (books, letters, pelts, feathers, teeth, jars of candy, bins of tiny animal skulls). Others immediately attached themselves to characters and followed them from scene to scene and floor to floor. This is no easy task, as there is no "off time" for the performers, who are continuously partaking in some activity, including running full tilt in pursuit of other performers. Enormous packs of Lady Macbeth followers, for example, are always chasing after her down stairwells, with varying degrees of athleticism, and getting tangled up with Duncan's entourage as it attempts to move the opposite way. The approach of a character, and thus a scene, could at times be thunderous.[24]

In short, the experience of a performed scene within *Sleep No More* was always tinged by an acute awareness of one's own presence and the presence of the other masked figures surrounding you, and of the psychically charged, often tense relationships between all present. I felt this tension painfully when I walked into the lobby where Macbeth was in the process of murdering Lady MacDuff. She was extremely pregnant, with the contents of her suitcase strewn about her on the floor. Macbeth had lifted her off the ground and was slamming her limp body against the wall: BAM, BAM, BAM. There was much to signal this moment as a performance, most immediately the presence of a handful of white masked figures like myself watching. Yet the sound of Lady MacDuff's body as it hit, coupled by this strange group of silent onlookers, rendered the scene simultaneously real and surreal. As she fell to the floor, lifeless, Macbeth ran from the room and nearly all the observers took off in pursuit. I stayed behind with several others in stunned silence to witness MacDuff as he found his wife's body. Whatever had just happened felt horribly wrong, a sensation amplified by the masked participants' instinctual and somewhat unseemly responses.

ARCHITECTURES OF PLAY

This is, for me, the central paradox of *Sleep No More*: the uncanny realization that one is in "meatspace," a navigable, tangible world, that is nevertheless experienced as highly mediated, simulated by its architecture and ritualized interfaces (the masks, the prohibitions, the wordless dances of the performers). I felt a constant need to touch things to confirm that they were really there, and I witnessed many other participants doing the same. I suspect this is one reason the modality of immersive theater is so often compared to that of the videogame.

A sense of a transformed reality is key to theories of immersive media. Janet H. Murray offered one of the earliest considerations of immersion as a mediated phenomenon:

> *Immersion* is a metaphorical term derived from the physical experience of being submerged in water. We seek the same feeling from a psychologically immersive experience that we do from a plunge in the ocean or swimming pool.... We enjoy the movement out of our familiar world, the feeling of alertness that comes from being in this new place, and the delight that comes from learning to move within it.[25]

Digital designers seek to create immersive presence within the simulated environments they program. On can achieve that sensation of thrilling, playful alertness Murray describes through a direct engagement of the perceptual apparatus, although in a digital environment this is no easy task. Immersive presence in these contexts requires drawing many of the participants' senses away from their physical environment and into the simulated one, as well as psychological immersion, whereby players are absorbed, mentally and emotionally, into the narrative and their own strategic navigation of the simulated world.[26]

Sleep No More is, of course, dissimilar from videogames in many respects, most immediately because the immersion it provides is physical. Indeed, much of what may strike us as strange about the installation is that it feels like a dream or videogame image, but it is in fact an actual space filled with actual objects. Material immersion is thus de facto and requires no division of the senses. Questions of agency, however, are less clear-cut. Within the trajectory of a videogame, participant actions dictate the outcome of each sequence. Limits are, of course, programmed into the simulation, with a finite number of outcomes. And narratives and missions steer game players toward particular goals, namely "winning" or completing the game. But the evolution of gameplay is determined largely by the decisions of the player. Despite the more immediate "presence" of the audience within *Sleep No More*, each individual's actions have very little impact on the trajectory of the show. The storylines of each character continue to loop through their hourly cycle, relatively unchanged. We are present in this world, but seemingly only as mute witnesses.

Yet I would nevertheless argue for the importance of understanding the architectures of immersive theater in relation to gaming, in that each puts the experience of the individual participant at the center of their design, empowering them to experiment within the limits of constructed space.[27] Developments in gaming design and theory have complicated our understanding of gameplay and immersion in ways too diverse for me to summarize adequately here. Most relevant for our purposes are those environments and approaches that emphasize gameplay as process and that gesture toward Artaud's theatrical ideal: "direct communication . . . between the spectator and the spectacle."[28] David Parry, for example, has written about "sandbox-style" games, such as the *Grand Theft Auto* series (Rockstar, 1997–), open-ended digital environments in which players are given relative freedom to explore the boundaries of the gameworld, including the freedom to ignore or subvert narrative "missions." Parry suggests that digital gaming can be best understood as an event in which gamer and game are conjoined in a process of continual negotiation.[29] This process of negotiation in gameplay, for Parry, takes place in the space in between that which can be changed and that which remains fixed, between play and structure. Gamers game because they enjoy freedom and experimentation, the room to play with the new perceptive realities that games offer. Yet play always arises in relation to certain limits, the rules and structures that produce the architecture necessary for exploration to take place.

Sleep No More, too, can perhaps best be understood as a play-based experience. It is a very unusual sort of environment, in that meat- and game-space collapse in ways unattainable via a console. And it is a very unusual sort of game, in that there is no clear objective, no means of "winning." But much like a videogame, meaning in *Sleep No More* is created through the process and experience of participatory play, which is user driven, versus the fixity of a prewritten text or a predetermined finale. And the artistry of the project depends on the delicate balance between that which is open to negotiation and the architecture that enables that playspace to exist. The designers for this production faced the daunting challenge of granting participants the semblance of unbounded freedom, thus minimizing awareness of any structure or constraints, while at the same time maintaining a safe and functional system, flung out across a six-floor structure, within a fixed timeframe. With such a large number of potential individual variances arising at every turn, the underlying structure of *Sleep No More* is deceptively rigid and tightly choreographed.

If we are to interpret *Sleep No More* as a play-based format, what, then, are the rules that govern participants' behaviors here, and what function do sound and music play in navigating these strictures?

Sonic Attractors

During my second visit to *Sleep No More*, I was startled to realize the degree to which sound dictated the behaviors of performers and audience members alike. My initial encounter with the production was of complete mystification. Performances seemed to occur spontaneously, and my own movements through the installation felt accidental and instantaneous. I was particularly floored when I found myself wandering into the hotel ballroom just as the final banquet scene was commencing, along with what appeared to be every single other audience member present that evening. Given the large number of us, and the amount of space we had to wander, it seemed inconceivable that we would all happen to arrive at this spot at precisely the same moment. Once I had gained a basic understanding of the floor plans, however, and was familiar with several major plot points, I became aware of the subtle cues that were built into all aspects of the production, from the strategic staging of scenes, the sealing off and opening up of certain passageways, and the use sound and light to subtly encourage participants to move in particular directions. There was something deflating about this realization, in that the mystery of the space was diminished. At the same time, recognizing the rules by which the production operated spurred a desire to "game the system," to methodically explore and push the margins of the installation and to buck the flow of the expected trajectory. Michael Abbott described a parallel response to the production: "I was struck by a familiar sense of open-world freedom, bound by intentional designer-imposed limits, but ultimately responsive to my desire to test those limits, tweak the system, and observe the results."[30]

The strategic use of sound was most apparent in the moments just before a scene was to commence. Elements in the recorded sound design would shift, sometimes with the introduction of a new musical element played at an increased volume or more often through atmospheric shifts induced by low-frequency chords. The performers' voices intruded in staccato bursts at these moments as well, as did the sounds of their movements, slamming objects or other characters with reverberant force. Depending on where one was within the installation, these sounds served as attractors, turning heads and luring curious wanderers into range. And, as the performance commenced, the wandering and browsing tended to cease. For the duration of the dance between characters, most participants stopped to watch, rapt. Coupled with lighting cues that functioned in tandem with the sound, the performance vignettes felt precisely like videogame "cutscenes." Cutscenes or "in-game cinematics" are prerecorded video scenes (usually animated) triggered at certain moments during gameplay; in most instances, player interactivity is suspended for the duration of the scene. Cutscenes tend to provide narrative explication, aid in character development, or provide instructions for an upcoming mission (e.g., introducing a level boss before a battle).[31] The dynamic of action–contemplation enacted between individual exploration and performed scene in *Sleep No More* is strikingly gamelike; the scenes themselves are deeply affecting, but they appear to function as a supplement to the player-driven modality that comprises the majority of one's time within the production. That is to say that the relatively prescribed performance scenes within *Sleep No More* are not necessarily the key to understanding the work as a whole, and, although they play a critical role in shaping the experience, they are but one of many components (including design and lighting) that shape, guide, and add texture to the playspace. And understanding how sound functioned within those scenes, as a cue for the performers and as an beacon leading participants toward particular areas within the architecture, reveals much about the larger modality of the production.

In short, sound in *Sleep No More* serves as one of our primary means of experiencing and navigating space, and it does so in ways that resonate with gaming systems. Sound orients us within unfamiliar environments and creates a visceral connection among body, space, and the experience of movement. We might also say that sound can function as an "attractor," encouraging players to more or perform in a particular way. Alison McMahan identifies attractors in three-dimensional gaming environments as elements that "tempt the user to go or do something"; attractors can include moving or shimmering objects that attract our attention and nonvisual objects that compel us through other sets of sensations, as well as manipulativeing objects that serve as tools or that shift dynamically through the spatiotemporal coordinates of the game.[32] *Sleep No More* overflows with attractors, a great number of them visual (partially open drawers, jars of candy, curtains, and doors that beckon). Sonic attractors, although perhaps not always as obvious, are equally important in defining the experience of play.

Within the architecture of *Sleep No More*, sound moves us, prodding our instinctual responses in ways we may not even consciously recognize. As Karen Collins notes about sound in videogames, "anticipating action is a critical part of being successful in many games. Notably, acousmatic sound—sound with no clear origin visually—may inspire us to look to the direction of a sound, to 'incite the look to go there and find out.'"[33] Surveying the wide range of sound cues used in *Sleep No More*, we might find that bodily slams attract us to action in a very base way (something exciting or dangerous is happening, come closer, get out of the way). Nonmusical sound effects (machinelike drones, wind) help to dictate ambience, but they also signal pending events. Likewise, sound and music in the installation can remind us that we've been in this room before, creating a sonic map that allows us to navigate toward a desired location. Even within the realm of the "cutscene" performances, where player action is limited, sound (both live and recorded) and movements (which both respond to and produce sounds) prove salient forces in attracting audience attention and providing cohesiveness in the context of the larger installation. Sound and music, like many other structural elements in *Sleep No More*, produce certain "soft limits" that help to manage and make meaning out of the myriad subjective trajectories that constitute an evening's performance.

Attractors work to make sense of the architecture of *Sleep No More* and to build a thick web of intertextual references and conventions into the space. The experience of sound, image, touch, and smell is initially visceral and reactive, oriented toward the present yet serving at the same time as a trigger for buried, Proustian memory images. It is a highly interactive, open system, dependent on the actions of each participant—structured but nevertheless unpredictable. It is key to bear in mind that these sonic attractors operate within an enormous, multilevel space, traversed by hundreds of participants at any given moment. It would be physically impossible for individual audience members to encounter all, or even most, of these cues throughout their journeys, even taking into account the looped nature of the performances (the entire performance repeats once every hour, leading toward the finale at night's end). And there is no guarantee that each participant will respond to a cue in a predictable manner.

For some participants, this openness is experienced as frustration. As one visitor noted in an online gaming journal article, "The Perils of Too Much Choice":

> It all seemed deliberate, certainly, but there were no clues distinguishing the melody from the (ample) noise. There was nothing in the McKittrick that called out "Pick me up! Read me! I'm essential to understanding this maze." There was no indication of what floor or which rooms we should visit first so as to be aware of where the performers were or where they were headed. Nothing shimmered. It was all equally enticing, or equally alienating.[34]

Yet I would argue that this is one of the most remarkable achievements of this production, a feat that is particularly notable given contemporary audience's familiarity with a range of media/performance/narrative models: we are thrown into an environment where we have no idea what is expected of us or where "meaning" should be located. Despite the presence of attractors, significance and direction are left undetermined. This is the challenge Punchdrunk's work poses for those who try to write about it. It accounts as well for some of the contradictory responses to this piece. Within *Sleep No More*, all decisions made are utterly subjective, but the overall experience leaves some participants feeling cast adrift, or, paradoxically, manipulated. Is the key to the game held within the narrative, or is the point a thematic one? Is the objective to master the labyrinth, ferreting out all its hidden clues? Or is it to study the psychological responses of all the human guinea pigs struggling through this maze? If *Sleep No More* is a puzzle, is it a Borgesian garden of forking paths? Or is it a high-art haunted house, sensational and affecting, yet ultimately leading only toward the exit?

RHYTHMIC HAUNTINGS AND UNSEEN WORDS

Criticism of immersive theater as gimmicky or theme park–esque may stem from the realization by some audience members that their individual experience has in fact been preordained by the structure; they feel "had." Similar charges are invariably levied against nearly all interactive artworks that traffic in visceral, physical experiences, and these complaints frequently resort to comparisons with the midway funhouse.[35] Evidenced here is a deep-seated skepticism of entertainments based on physical sensations; such experiences might be momentary thrilling, in the eyes of critics, but are ultimately pandering and hollow. They cite a further sense of betrayal upon discovering that an encounter that felt unique and intimate was in fact a recurring part of the show. The coincidence of structure and play, then, might result in a rather duplicitous emotional event: the experience of an authentic, individual, deeply moving human exchange, which is in fact orchestrated in advance and repeated endlessly each evening.

I would offer several arguments to counter the cynicism of such a reading. The first is to assert that a corporeal level of engagement should not be viewed in opposition to critical thought. To do so is to reenact the problematic and politically suspect Cartesian mind–body divide and to dismiss the critical role that our bodies and perceptive organs play in any type of thought or aesthetic endeavor. It is important to recognize, as well, that the structure of an artwork does not necessarily function as a negative limit, nor is it always a vehicle of audience manipulation. A well-orchestrated structure, in a work of art, can serve as architecture for, quite literally, perceiving the world in a new way. If Sleep No More is imperfect, it is at the same time endlessly ambitious in its attempts to bring structure and meaning into dialogue with one another in a rigorous way. More specifically, the choreography and audiovisual design of Sleep No More work in tandem to translate the rhythms, repetitions, and reverberations of its originary text, Macbeth, into a physical, mobile assemblage of bodies and objects. And given that the basis of this adaptation is rooted in its rhythms, repetitions, and reverberations, I would argue that the work as a whole is deeply sonic, not only in its surface-level manifestations, but also in its inherent structure.

Although sound functions as one of the primary elements motivating participants' movements throughout the architecture of Sleep No More, it does a disservice to the richness of the soundscape to limit our understanding to this task alone. One of the aspects of Sleep No More that few critics have commented on is its strange and somewhat oblique fidelity to the rhythms of speech present in Macbeth, in particular to the elliptical songs of the three witches.

Macbeth is the most explicitly musical of Shakespeare's tragedies, with most of the calls for music occurring during the spectacular witches' scenes.[36] David L. Kranz discusses the ways in which the rhythm and cadence of the songs sung by the witches in Macbeth permeate the play as a whole, recurring in the speech of others (Macbeth and

Lady Macbeth in particular) and haunting the actions that follow. Indeed, the form of the witches' speech is as significant for him as the words themselves:

> Through the most self-conscious manipulation of poetry—including diction, rhyme, alliteration, anaphora, chiasmus, rhythm, and meter—Shakespeare clogs the witches' verse with repetitive forms, doubling, tripling, and even quadrupling them. Indeed, the manner of the Weird Sisters' speech is at least as prominent as its meaning. No other lines in Shakespeare...can match this concatenation of sounds, this poetic compulsion to repetition.[37]

The witches' songs are marked by recurring alliteration, internal rhyme, and childlike poetry. Yet these patterns seem to be infectious, emerging in the voices of other characters most strongly when they are alone and consumed by strong emotions or when they are sleepwalking or drunk. We hear this shift in meter when characters are in a suspended state of vulnerability, haunted by the past, in moments where there is heightened sensation but limited agency. The echoes of these indeterminate and mobile songs remain mysterious, seemingly generated not by a singular force or will, singing of a destiny that is predetermined.

The lack of dialogue in *Sleep No More* removes the literal language of the witches' poetry from the soundscape. But the exercise is not silent and, in fact, it demonstrates an increased reliance on echoes, repetitions, and conjured sounds. Some of these repetitions are directly sonic (recorded songs, musical themes, whispered phrases), some are gestural (tics and movements repeated by various performers), and some are thematic (the rhythmic recurrence of symbolic images across various rooms, of suitcases, of taxidermied animals). The production places its audience quite literally in a state of vulnerability, haunted by the past, in a suspended moment of heightened sensation. Agency exists, in terms of the range of directions and tactics one might adopt in exploring the location. But in terms of shaping the destiny of the narrative, participants are locked into the role of a ghost-like observer. Just as the Macbeths are consumed by unearthly songs, we, too, are possessed by melodies and sensations we cannot place, which move through us. This is an environment haunted by fragmented phrases and recurring patterns of expression, reverberating through a host of texts, themes, gestures, objects, structures, and bodies. The sound design works hard to set the timbre and rhythm for all these expressive elements, to provide a setting for them, and to move the participants through the dance.

In this context, Bernard Herrmann's scores take on an even deeper relevance. Their somewhat compulsive, spiraling phrases function precisely like the doubled and tripled poetry of the witches' songs, exposing the realm of the irrational swirling in the shadows of our waking life. Daphne Du Maurier's *Rebecca* and Hitchcock's adaptation of that text, too, operate through the vertiginous descent of the narrator's voice, caught up in repetitive and contradictory movements ("Last night, I dreamt I went to Manderley again...We can never go back to Manderley again"). Repetition, for Freud, was closely linked to sensations of the uncanny. When we encounter unexplained repetitions (the "obstinate recurrence of a number," for example, throughout the course of a day), we are inclined to "ascribe a secret meaning" to the pattern, to presume the hand of some cosmic force.[38] Each of the texts referenced in *Sleep No More* draws on a similar dynamic, using the repetition of gesture and theme to invoke an uncanny sensation—the irrational lurking behind the mundane. The repetition itself is highly ordered, governed by a structure that eludes and confines us, masking a dark ambivalence, and set on a predetermined course. This dynamic, I would argue, is the engine that drives the entire experience of *Sleep No More*. Like Lady Macbeth's somnambulism, our actions within the McKittrick Hotel are guided by forces beyond us; we are trapped in a lucid dream.

STYLE AND STRUCTURE

Sleep No More is a production centered on the physical and psychological experiences of audience members, built on a scaffolding of recurring themes drawn from a wide range of cultural references. The connections forged among body, structure, and meaning take place largely through visceral sensations and unconscious triggers, a large number of them rhythmic and sonic. There is a strong evocation of the uncanny in nearly every aspect of the production, whereby the familiar is suddenly rendered unfamiliar and strange, plagued by inscrutable repetitions and fragmentary scenes. One's navigation through this environment is further conflicted by the tension between agency and fate. Autonomy feels unprecedentedly ample here, but, at the same time, individual participants are limited in their capacity to alter the course of events that have already passed, cursed, as it were, to loop endlessly.

I have argued that *Sleep No More* draws on design structures associated with digital gaming systems. I return to this point as a means of conclusion, to point to another resonance between immersive theater and the videogame: the centrality of *style* in gameplay as a means of generating meaning within a system of preordained order. The most creative interactive games make use of structures that set productive limits, yet that are nevertheless malleable and encourage experimentation. "The challenge for the creator of an interactive narrative is to design the potential for play into the structure of the experience," Eric Zimmerman writes, "and the real trick is that the designed structure can guide and engender play, but never completely script it in advance."[39] David Parry makes a similar point about sandbox games, which privilege the process of negotiation, one's *style* of playing, over teleological goals.[40] *Grand Theft Auto* players might argue in online forums, for example, not about who racked up the most points or finished first, but rather about the merits of their stylistic choices while doing so (what vehicle they used, what outfit they wore, what cheats they deployed, where to perform the best motorcycle tricks, what music they listened to, unorthodox uses for hidden objects).[41] The rules of the gameworld must remain fixed in order to provide a meaningful space in which play can take place. Yet, paradoxically, part of the negotiation of gameplay is to continually push, subvert, and challenge those rules.

What styles of play are enabled within *Sleep No More*, and is there space left open for unscripted experimentation? On the one hand, there are diverse participatory approaches demonstrated at every performance and observing one's own style as it emerges (consciously or unconsciously) is one of the most rewarding parts of the experience. On my second visit, I forced myself to resist looking down when a character caught my gaze; I became more brazen in my engagement with the architecture, slipping behind characters to open doors I had not seen during my first visit, discovering secret passages. I found that anonymity generated a certain confidence in exploring public space, one that is often more difficult to access beyond the boundaries of the game.

I'd further suggest that some of the limits imposed by the structure of the production, such as the inability to alter the trajectory of the narrative, are consistent with the thematic arc of the work, as mapped through its references to *Macbeth*, *Rebecca*, and *Vertigo*. Each of these works centers on a character caught up in a descent into the irrational, on a path they cannot control. Each work invokes the dread of that descent via rhythms and repetitions that are not merely understood, but felt. The designers of *Sleep No More* have created an analogous structure, one that builds on and amplifies that experience. That this experience can be disorienting and frustrating is precisely the point. The stylistic challenge lies in responding to the provocation and in working to understand the nuances and depths of the dynamic.

As is the case with digital games, questions of consumerism have dogged immersive productions. And there are reasons to be wary of the intrusion of capital in the spheres of game-based art, for precisely the same reason that these works are so appealing. Immersive productions are viscerally thrilling, they encourage multiple engagements, and, as such, they are easily marketed and sold. *Sleep No More* has become a full-blown New York phenomenon, with numerous celebrity shout-outs and a featured episode of *Gossip Girl*.[42] And Punchdrunk partnered directly with Playstation 3 in September 2011 to design an immersive installation in the tunnels beneath Waterloo Station to promote the launch of the game *Resistance 3*.[43] I mention these commercial tie-ins not to diminish Punchdrunk's remarkable work. The interest their immersive approach has generated speaks to its inventiveness, which has registered with audiences from well outside the purview of traditional theater. But there is an obvious temptation to commodify experience, and we can only hope that this temptation won't diminish the creativity, breadth, or style of play engendered by future productions. The experience of live immersion can be mesmerizing and, as evidenced by *Sleep No More*, capable of engaging with rigorous ideas in surprising, moving ways. The possibilities for extending and transforming the function of music in these types of environments are seemingly endless. Music, too, is experienced as process, as movement, as flow, as a medium governed by both structure and irrational excesses, by temporal disjuncture, and by a lingering, often unresolved affect. That immersive theater is so sonically driven makes it a format of great importance for the fields of sound and audiovisual media studies. One can scarcely imagine a more fruitful space in which to bring to life a host of unheard melodies.

NOTES

1. Adapted from Daphne Du Maurier, *Rebecca* [1938] (New York: Perennial, 2001), 1.
2. Earlier versions of this work were produced in 2003, in the Victorian-era Beaufoy Building in London, and in 2009, in the Old Lincoln School in Brookline, Massachusetts. The scope of the project was extensively expanded for the New York installation.
3. Antonin Artaud, *The Theater and Its Double*, trans. Mary Caroline Richards (New York: Grove Press), 96.
4. See Andrew Dickson, "Immersive Theatre: It Was a Ghost in the Library with a Violin," *The Guardian*, July 4, 2011, http://www.guardian.co.uk/culture/2011/jul/04/immersive-theatre; Steve Baltin, "Perry Farrell: Jane's Addiction Tour Inspired by 'Boardwalk Empire' Era," *Rolling Stone*, January 31, 2012, http://www.rollingstone.com/music/news/perry-farrell-janes-addiction-tour-inspired-by-boardwalk-empire-era-20120131; "Cans Festival, Banksy Exhibition," *Pinewood Design* (blog), May 4, 2008, http://pinewooddesign.co.uk/2008/05/04/the-cans-festival-banksy-street-exhibition/; Jasper Rees, "Street Art Way Below the Street," *New York Times*, October 31, 2010, http://www.nytimes.com/2010/11/01/arts/design/01underbelly.html.
5. Felix Barrett, "Felix Barrett in Discussion with Josephine Machon, February 2007, Battersea Arts Center, London," *Body, Space and Technology Journal* 7, no. 1 (2007): 3–4, http://people.brunel.ac.uk/bst/vol0701/.
6. Sigmund Freud, "The 'Uncanny' [1919]," in *The Standard Edition of the Complete Psychological Works of Sigmund Freud*, vol. 17, ed. James Strachey (London: Hogarth Press, 1955), 241.
7. Barrett, "Felix Barrett in Discussion with Josephine Machon," 2.
8. Other reviewers recount seeing Hectate lip-syncing Tony Bennett's version of the same song (1969) on a different floor, at the same time that this performance takes place.
9. Both the UK and Boston productions of *Sleep No More* incorporated more direct references to *Rebecca* (including characters inspired by the film), and promotional materials for the shows included a poster with a Saul Bass-inspired font and an image of a Victorian home drawn from *Psycho*. See the Punchdrunk website, http://www.punchdrunk.org.uk/. The Bass font remains for the New York production, but the direct narrative references have been downplayed.
10. Barrett confirmed that the references to *Rebecca* had been minimized in this production: "I think now we've made it a more broad, generic film noir landscape." Felix Barrett and Maxine Doyle, interview by Leonard Lopate, *The Leonard Lopate Show*, NPR, July 5, 2011. Many interviews and reviews of the work reiterate the presence of "1930s noir elements." See, for example, Jed Lipinski, "He Puts the Maximus in the Circus," *New York Times*, May 4, 2011, http://www.nytimes.com/2011/05/05/fashion/05upclose.html. The film historian in me feels compelled to call this characterization into question. Although the film noir style is challenging to delineate, nearly all accounts suggest that film noir began in the early 1940s. I'd press this point because my impression of *Sleep No More* did not suggest a noir visual palette, nor did the dynamics between characters resonate with prototypical noir narratives. I would argue for Herrmann's scores as a more relevant reference point here, where conflict is more diffuse, cyclical, and unresolved. Barrett himself intimates that it was Herrmann who inspired his staging more than Hitchcock; see Barrett, "Felix Barrett in Discussion with Josephine Machon," 12.

11. Royal S. Brown, *Overtones and Undertones: Reading Film Music* (Berkeley: University of California Press, 1994), 151–152.

12. Ibid, 150.

13. Ibid, 153.

14. Brown gives the example of the G-E-flat third, which "can be the top two notes of the C minor triad (see the opening of Beethoven's Fifth Symphony, for instance) or the bottom two notes of the E-flat major triad." Brown, *Overtones*, 152.

15. Ibid, 153.

16. Ibid, 168.

17. Ibid, 153.

18. Many thanks to John Richardson for this and other insights on the relevance of Herrmann in this context.

19. See Tara Kyle, "Punchdrunk 'Immersive Theater' Group Seeks to Replace Mega Clubs in West Chelsea," *DNAinfo.com*, November 10, 2010, http://www.dnainfo. com/20101110/chelsea-hells-kitchen/punchdrunk-immersive-theater-group-se eks-replace-mega-clubs-west-chelsea; and Isaiah Wilner, "The Short, Drunken Life of Club Row," *New York Magazine*, February 11, 2007, http://nymag.com/news/features/27845/.

20. Wilner, "The Short, Drunken Life of Club Row."

21. Interestingly, Colin Nightingale, a producer at Punchdrunk, noted that nearly all the core members of the company had been involved in the electronic music scene in the United Kingdom and suggested that their experiences with multifloor musical happenings were a greater influence on their installations than gaming. Panel discussion, "Theater Rethunk: An Alternative History of the Theatrical," Congress for Curious People, Coney Island Museum, Brooklyn, April 22, 2012.

22. Maxine Doyle, "Maxine Doyle in Discussion with Josephine Machon, November 2006," *Body, Space and Technology Journal* 7, no. 1 (2007): 3, http://people.brunel.ac.uk/bst/vol0701/.

23. Ibid.

24. At these moments, the New York production of *Sleep No More* can be a victim of its own enormous success. The crush of onlookers during some scenes interferes with one's ability to experience anything but the crowd. And the tenor of the audience at a performance in late 2011 was markedly less respectful than one earlier that year, with some participants pushing to position themselves to be chosen for coveted one-on-one exchanges. It seems that repeat visitors and the circulation of spoilers online have diminished the sense of the unknown within the show.

25. Janet H. Murray, *Hamlet on the Holodeck* (Cambridge, MA: MIT Press, 1998), 98–99

26. Alison McMahan, "Immersion, Engagement, and Presence: A Method for Analyzing 3-D Video Games," in *The Video Game Theory Reader*, ed. Mark J. P. Wolf and Bernard Perron (New York: Routledge, 2003), 77.

27. Gaming practices have been asserting an influence in theater on several different fronts. The Brick Theater in Williamsburg, Brooklyn, stages an annual Game Play festival, featuring works that explore the boundaries of performance and gaming technology and culture.

28. Artaud, *The Theater and Its Double*, 96.

29. David Parry, "Playing with Style: Negotiating Digital Game Studies," in *The Meaning and Culture of Grand Theft Auto: Critical Essays*, ed. Nate Garrelts (Jefferson, NC: MacFarland, 2006), 228–229.

30. Michael Abbott, "Blood Play," *Brainy Gamer* (blog), July 6, 2011, http://www.brainygamer. com/the_brainy_gamer/2011/07/bloody-play.html.

31. Numerous bloggers have made similar observations regarding the gamelike qualities of *Sleep No More*. For two of the best, see Abbott, "Blood Play," and Dan Dickinson, "Games of 2011: *Sleep No More,*" *Dan Dickinson: The Primary Vivid Weblog*, December 25, 2011, http:// vjarmy.com/archives/2011/12/games-of-2011-sleep-no-more.php.

32. Alison McMahan, "Immersion, Engagement, and Presence," 76.

33. Karen Collins, *Game Sound: An Introduction to the History, Theory, and Practice of Video Game Music and Sound Design* (Cambridge, MA: MIT Press, 2008), 130, with a reference to Michel Chion, *AudioVision: Sound on Screen* (New York: Columbia, 1990).

34. Katherine Coldiron, "The Perils of Too Much Choice," *Escapist Magazine*, November 15, 2011, http://www.escapistmagazine.com/articles/view/ features/9215-The-Perils-of-Too-Much-Choice.

35. Carsten Höller's 2011 *Experience* exhibition at the New Museum, for example, received the following review: "takes every device from a traveling carnival except the concession stands...more about emptying your mind than it is about contemplating a specific philosophical question." Paddy Johnson, "Naked and Nauseated at the New Museum," *L Magazine*, November 9, 2011, http://www.thelmagazine.com/newyork/ naked-and-nauseated-at-the-new-museum/Content?oid=2190773.

36. Nicholas Brooke cites Frances Shirley in making this claim. William Shakespeare, *The Tragedy of Macbeth*, ed. and with an introduction by Nicholas Brooke (New York: Oxford University Press, 2008), 36. For a detailed chronology of revisions, musical additions, and contentions regarding the composers for songs used in productions of Macbeth, see Nicholas Brooke's Appendix B, "Musical Additions" in ibid, 225–233 and Robert E. Moore, "The Music to *Macbeth,*" *The Musical Quarterly* 47, no. 1 (1961): 22–40.

37. David L Kranz, "The Sounds of Supernatural Soliciting in *Macbeth,*" *Studies in Philology* 100, no. 3 (2003): 350–351.

38. Freud, "The Uncanny," 238.

39. Eric Zimmerman, "Narrative, Interactivity, Play, and Games: Four Naughty Concepts in Need of Discipline," in *First Person: New Media as Story, Performance, and Game*, ed. Noah Wardrip-Fruin and Pat Harrigan (Cambridge, MA: MIT Press, 2004), 160.

40. David Parry, "Playing with Style," 233.

41. Ibid, 236.

42. "The Big Sleep No More," *Gossip Girl*, season 5, episode 7, aired November 14, 2011 by CW.

43. The installation, entitled "...and darkness descended," put small groups of participants through a grueling live-action mission underground. See Tom Hoggins "Punchdrunk and Resistance 3 Present '...and Darkness Descended,' Waterloo Station Arches (review)," *The Telegraph*, September 5, 2011, http://www.telegraph.co.uk/ culture/theatre/theatre-reviews/8742127/Punchdrunk-and-Resistance-3-present-... and-darkness-descended-Waterloo-Station-Arches-review.html.

SELECT BIBLIOGRAPHY

Artaud, Antonin. *The Theater and Its Double*. Translated by Mary Caroline Richards. New York: Grove Press, 1958.

Bogost, Ian. *How to Do Things with Videogames*. Minneapolis: University of Minnesota Press, 2011.

Brown, Royal S. *Overtones and Undertones: Reading Film Music*. Berkeley: University of California Press, 1994.

Collins, Karen. *Game Sound: An Introduction to the History, Theory, and Practice of Video Game Music and Sound Design*. Cambridge, MA: MIT Press, 2008.

Machon, Josephine. *(Syn)aesthetics: Redefining Visceral Performance*. London: Palgrave Macmillan, 2009.

McMahan, Alison. "Immersion, Engagement, and Presence: A Method for Analyzing 3-D Video Games." In *The Video Game Theory Reader*, edited by Mark J. P. Wolf and Bernard Perron, 67–86. New York: Routledge, 2003.

Parry, David. "Playing with Style: Negotiating Digital Game Studies." In *The Meaning and Culture of Grand Theft Auto: Critical Essays*, edited by Nate Garrelts, 226–243. Jefferson, NC: MacFarland, 2006.

Pearce, Celia. "Towards a Game Theory of Game." In *First Person: New Media as Story, Performance, and Game*, edited by Noah Wardrip-Fruin and Pat Harrigan, 143–153. Cambridge, MA: MIT Press, 2004.

Stockburger, Axel. "Listen to the Bulk of the Iceberg: On the Impact of Sound in Digital Games." In *Space Time Play: Computer Games, Architecture, and Urbanism: The Next Level*, edited by Friedrich von Borries, Steffen P. Walz, and Matthias Böttger, 110–113. Berlin: Birkhauser Verlag AG, 2007.

CHAPTER 14

....

A GASH IN THE PORTRAIT

Martin Arnold's Deanimated

....

GEORGE TOLES

Show me your environment and I will tell you who you are.
—Boris Pasternak, *Safe Conduct*

FOR his 60-minute installation, *Deanimated* (2002), Austrian experimental film-maker Martin Arnold performs massive digital surgery on the images and soundtrack of a 1941 Monogram quickie horror movie, *Invisible Ghost*. He gradually erases the entire cast from the narrative proceedings (that is to say, certain actors are selectively expunged from view while the rest of the image—the scene setting and portions of the soundtrack—remain intact. By the film's conclusion, all of the human presences have become invisible: deanimated). It is not clear at any time during this ellipsis-saturated narrative what *should* be visible to us, but isn't. The images reveal no conspicuous gaps. Arnold steps up the pace and extent of his liquidations after a deceptively conventional introduction. He retains the entire original credit sequence with its booming, porten-tous score (which the ensuing decades have hollowed out somewhat, leaching away its crispness and immediacy). He also doesn't tamper with the film's odd first episode, in which Bela Lugosi, as Charles Kessler, sits at his dining room table in his baronial home and conducts an enraptured conversation with his "deceased" wife's empty chair. Eventually, Arnold will reduce Lugosi and his fellow performers to a ghostly status that far exceeds the ordinary ghostliness of film's always somewhat supernatural pres-ent tense. The actors are available to us, if at all, in the same disconcerting terms as the "veiled from view" absentee, Mrs. Kessler, at the dining table. The director's plan in *Deanimated* is to siphon off the energy these gradually disappearing players possess and transfer it to the objects, walls, floors, doorways, and staircase of the Kessler home. Bits and pieces of the actors' visible actions remain, along with odd snatches of dialogue, but their behavioral residue becomes steadily more enigmatic. The house appears to be hav-ing a troubling dream about itself and its cast-off occupants, and the work tries to break through into some sort of object language that will enable the house to know (perhaps even articulate) what the dream signifies.

The rooms of the house impassively survive the elimination of their once busy occupants, carrying on in their absence with an inhospitable air of self-involvement. Or perhaps it is more accurate to say that the rooms acquire the power to haunt those who have been whisked away, without notice or explanation. The Kessler house feels traumatized, struggling in the aftermath of Arnold's severe purge to hold onto the functions it held (as generally unobtrusive background setting) when company was still present. The rooms do not appear innocently vacant. Instead, in keeping with the atmosphere of trauma, they convey a dazed strickenness. They seem to be reacting—with the limited emotional resources of the inanimate—to a terrible event that has just happened or bracing themselves for something about to happen. Whatever it is, they can't defend themselves against it. They collude with their new state of waiting and destitution, but they strain in futile protest as well. The rooms act, especially in the first half of *Deanimated*, as though they are not yet accustomed to being alone or reconciled to the end of their life of service. They seem unduly exposed as the camera intently scrutinizes their object particulars and grants them fresh meaning of some sort in their own right. Their startling immobility as the prolonged inspection goes on suggests the unearthly silence of a battlefield, when the smoke clears. So much has been quietly, perhaps ruthlessly, obliterated. How do the rooms attest to these losses? How quickly do they compose themselves, make peace with the shadows of death?

The actors who remain on view seem less mindful than the rooms of the insidious gleanings. They are confidently involved with the surviving plot action, which the viewer must contend with in obscure, barely motivated fragments. The actors also do their best to adjust to the fact that their mouths are often digitally sealed. Only arbitrary snippets of their assigned dialogue escape from them and break the forlorn near-silence of the static-threaded soundscape. The muted and trailing-off dialogue is accompanied by indecipherably transitioned facial expressions, testifying to thoughts scattered, interrupted, demolished, or blankly endorsed. Instead of meanings being understood, the actors seem to cover their customary perplexity with a pretense of instant understanding, so as not to be caught out. In relation to their own words, which are typically cues to action, the actors fare best by appearing to "reaffirm [the] opacity of language as its natural state." Toward this end, they "put [speech] back into nonsense," which in the Kessler house works well enough for most purposes.[1] Irving Massey argues in his brilliant study of metamorphosis in literature, *The Gaping Pig*, that dream images and dream speech contain more truth than conscious thoughts because dream language is inescapably metaphoric, restoring contact with the "abysmal ocean beneath us," on which all life rests.[2] The flimsy floor boards of rationality rest just above this enormous sea, in which our inadvertent beginnings and endings, our faint thrusts at purpose and conviction (before we vanish) chaotically mingle. Dreams steer our frail barks toward an eternity of something—it can't even be termed darkness, Massey claims—which our more deliberate life scratchings ever so briefly interrupt. "A conscious thought is frequently [self-protectively] a half-truth, and the expression of a half-truth is usually a defense against the acknowledgment of a whole one."[3] The "whole truths" that Massey alludes to are those that draw the hidden, vast, inexpressible underworld into its proper relation (always a mystifying, unraveling relation) with the makeshift arrangements of daylight sense.

Most of *Invisible Ghost's* musical score survives intact in *Deanimated*, but feels frantically compensatory in its severely curtailed narrative surroundings. The music strives to breathe a sense of vivid dramatic clarity into spaces and altered ways of watching that have no use for clarity. The music is designed, like most Hollywood scores of the period, to increase the spectator's emotional access to the depicted events through highlighting and signal flares for what is to come. But in the ghostlier precincts of *Deanimated*, the score itself seems to have no real emotional access to what it accompanies; it must continue its derailed operations anyway. The score could almost be said to be fearful of its own superfluous "speech." It cannot summon the kinds of actions and referents that it solely exists to illustrate. The séance of sound is at first comically, then oddly, then at last dismally unsuccessful; it fails to raise a single lost performer or intelligible action from limbo. The score can merely try to enliven the gaping emptiness with its predigested noise. The crypt-like chambers rebuff the urgent motifs that mechanically flow "across them," bearing irrelevant musical tidings from a more wakeful world. The score is prevented from delivering its contents to the intended destination. It seems "thrown back" and stranded, alongside the viewer, outside a world that won't be accounted for with melodramatic phrasing. The music cues can also be understood as sonic apparitions, pressing against the movie frame as if it was a window, seeking to reclaim its own missing life. At times, it can mimic the camera's own restlessness and that of the few still ambulatory, uneffaced performers. All are alike in their ongoing search for a familiar narrative harbor.

Arnold's source film, *Invisible Ghost*, directed by Joseph H. Lewis, is not without interest and has by no means been selected arbitrarily for "recasting" and revisionist haunting. This low-budget horror movie, produced by a Poverty Row Studio, fortunately possesses one of those wildly fanciful stories that hasn't been thought through and is all the better for it. Director Lewis and screenwriters Helen and Al Martin are primarily concerned with creating an enveloping mood, one that grows out of marital betrayal and the fantasy of remaining faithful to a relationship after it has come to a painful end. Charles Kessler (Bela Lugosi) keeps a large framed portrait of his former wife in the front hall of his vast home. The literary pedigree for this portrait and the husband's obsessive misreadings of it—as a result of a delusive attachment to the one whose image it preserves—can be traced to Edgar Allan Poe ("The Oval Portrait") and Herman Melville (*Pierre or, The Ambiguities*). The painting of Mrs. Kessler is the first object introduced in the film, and it notably precedes the arrival on-screen of any living character. Kessler appears to venerate both the portrait and the memory of the lost relationship that it consecrates. In the anniversary dinner that I previously alluded to, in which Kessler talks to his wife's empty chair, he requires his servant, Evans (Clarence Muse), to cooperate with his elaborate fantasy. Evans, following Kessler's instructions, extends the phantom guest the courtesy of serving her food first and waiting for her approval of it. Unbeknownst to Kessler, his wife (Betty Compson) is not only still alive but dwelling on his property, tucked away in the lower level of his gardener's ample toolshed. She has survived a car accident in which her former lover was killed; the accident took place shortly after she told her husband of her affair and of her intention to leave him for his one-time "best friend." For several years, she has been secretly fed and cared for by the well-meaning gardener, Jules (Ernie Adam), who is indefinitely preparing for a time when both parties are mentally and physically strong enough so that he can announce her miraculous survival to Kessler. (Perhaps Jules is taking instruction from Shakespeare's *The Winter's Tale*, which has much to say about jealousy, suspended animation, and reawakening.) Even after three years, Mrs. Kessler shows signs of lingering disorientation. It is unclear what, if anything, Kessler knows about either the accident or its outcome (Figure 14.1).

As the custodian of his wife's immaculate image and memory, Kessler seems to have bewitched himself into a state of forgetful tranquility. The dark finale of his marriage has left no imprint on his conscious memory. He has lost touch with any sorrow, rage, or regret that his wife's disloyalty might have induced in him. Only once a year does he make a public display of eccentric behavior, and he confines it to the carefully bounded occasion of his anniversary dinner. It is like a clockwork indulgence in aberration. According to his grown-up daughter, Virginia (Polly Ann Young), who still lives with him, Kessler is consummately rational, diffident, and considerate at all other times. Even in the baffling spectacle of the anniversary dinner, decorum reigns. Kessler seems dreamily, harmlessly mad; his delusion may strike deep, but it does not have a fearsome aspect.

FIGURE 14.1

Invisible Ghost includes a recurring nocturnal episode of Kessler discovering his wife (or her specter) on his lawn, gazing up at him as he stands, entranced, at his study window. Much emphasis is placed on the consistent, inviolable barrier of this window. The encounters are always wordless. It is hard to read either character's intention or to be clear about what they comprehend in the other's prolonged look. Mrs. Kessler is consistently clad in a soiled, white gown and bears the demeanor of an inconsolable shade. She always appears to summon him from his ruminations, to break into his wandering thoughts. As she stands imperious outside, backed by a glittering bounty of moon-dappled foliage, he senses her presence and walks to the window to behold her. He never seems surprised to find her again. The weather varies for their after-dark staring contests (one occurs during a rainstorm), but what remains constant is his possession of the indoors and her seeking some form of recognition (or assent) from her station outside. The aftermath of these silent, doleful encounters would suggest that she has been firmly in control, even though he towers above her and retains possession of the dwelling. She evinces no desire to be admitted to the house, nor does she try to lead him outside, which would mean relinquishing his realm for hers. When Kessler turns away from her, he has invariably entered a hypnotic trance, marked by a curious halting gracelessness of movement. He immediately tracks down, apparently at random, some unfortunate servant or visitor to his home. Having found his victim, he laboriously removes his outer garment (a dressing gown) and then employs it for combined suffocation and strangling (Figure 14.2).

Mrs. Kessler's motives for vengeance—in spite of her wandering wits and alarmed disenchantment with her husband—are attenuated to the vanishing point. She has no

FIGURE 14.2

reason to bring harm to any of Kessler's victims, any more than he does. When we see her in the company of the gardener Jules during his furtive toolshed visits, she seems afflicted with a sheepish moroseness and a will o' the wisp guilt. We find nary a hint of a concealed punishing fury. Kessler, for his part, has no misgivings or chafing resentments against any of the figures he stalks and eliminates. The one dark emotion in Kessler, which is never alluded to directly in the film and to which he never achieves conscious access, is the jealous rage he experienced over his wife's sexual betrayal with someone "close" to him. In the pristine placidity of his waking adjustments to his housebound world, he has not had to overcome heartbreak and torment. He has simply buried his agony somewhere in the gardens of the night. His gallantly courteous relations with one and all imitate the quality he exhibits when gazing devotedly at his wife's painting. His surviving human connections have turned "invisible"; he cannot see into faces, or pursue real attachments. In spite of his formal social gestures, he remains perfectly alone in the house he never leaves. When called on to respond to someone, he does so with the same elaborate courtliness he displayed when addressing the empty chair at his anniversary meal. Kessler takes hold of his one authentic feeling—rage—only when Mrs. Kessler turns up to reawaken his toxic memory. He is permitted to "live it up" whenever she becomes reanimated and graces him with a fit of madness. The "invisible ghost" of the title is the ghost of Kessler's jealousy, peering into the windows of his mannered isolation and managing, periodically, to break in.

The "sufficient explanation" of Kessler's string of murders—that his guilty, predatory, similarly deranged wife imbues him with homicidal wrath through windowpane hypnosis—manages to satisfy the protocols of horror movie intelligibility. And yet this plot explanation will not survive even casual scrutiny. The film seems to knows this and wraps all question of motive (on either side of the marital divide) in an obscuring fog. What *may* be happening, in Kessler's recurring bouts of window projection, is that he passes, in a trice, through three emotional stages. First, he discovers yet again that his wife has returned to him. (From the dead, from her other relationship? It matters little, since her return on any terms is his deepest wish. He no doubt fantasizes that it is her deepest wish as well.) Second, he mentally opens himself to his love, which he continues to regard as his most precious belonging, his one sure attachment in life. Third, in the act of opening himself he lights on his dormant jealous rage (another rediscovery!), which slips through the cracks of his love the instant he allows himself to *see* his wife as separate from his frozen picture of her: safe, still, changeless, untouched. She lays siege to his rickety reality sense with her gaze. Having been found out (exposed, if you will) in his destitute state, he must *clear* the house (the stifling house of his consciousness) of the first living form he can lay his hands on. It is as though he must sacrifice someone in close proximity to him to propitiate his "unknowable wife" so that she will return to immobility and become distant and dear once more. The person killed is always a surrogate for her, as well as for his own unacknowledged, impossible to "live with" hatred. In spite of the fact that his maladroit technique of attacking his victims is ludicrously unworkable, there is a poetic rightness to his ritual. He removes his covering—the outermost trappings of a feeble, skimpy identity—and uses it to shield his approach to his scapegoat prey, like a toreador cape. He proceeds to choke off the voice of his sacrifice while simultaneously draping the face, thus blocking his view of it. (More than once we are treated to victim point-of-view perspectives on a cloak brought near to the camera and then raised up to black out the frame.) The purpose of the crime is to reduce the felt power of both sound and sight. His wife has fixed him with her look, but she has not yet spoken the words that long ago condemned him: "I betrayed you," "I love another" (his one other friend, one assumes), "I have decided to leave you for good." Kessler's wife is the only person whose presence can briefly penetrate his hollowness and reanimate him. But all that she can pass onto him—in a tiny vicious cycle—is the unthinkable fact of her perfidy and the consuming jealousy that it unleashed.

Joseph Lewis returned to the idea of unthinkability and self-splitting in his 1946 film, *So Dark the Night* (whose title has Keatsian associations with an oblivion both dreadful and craved). In this fitfully compelling narrative, every bit as primitive as *Invisible Ghost*, a gifted detective tracks himself without knowing it, as he seeks the person responsible for murdering his fiancé as well as his imagined rival for her love. His own "senseless crimes" end up destroying the alternative, calm rural life the detective had planned for himself after his retirement. Smitten by the simplicity and straightforwardness of the occupants of a small village, Henri Cassin (Steven Geray) decides to leave behind his urban identity as a legally sanctioned watcher. This much-admired and sought after investigator has come to regard every human and inanimate surface in the city world as potentially incriminating. It has been his business to interrogate things without let-up. Whatever excites his suspicion eventually yields its guilty secret. Lewis marks the climactic moment when the detective joins together his "innocent" past and "guilty" present with the shattering of a pane of glass. Cassin stands before a window in a darkened room and views the scene of his earlier arrival in the country village as though it were a "memory movie" projected on the glass. On the day when he first entered the village, he had immediately felt tempted by its peacefulness but estranged from it, as though its serenity could have nothing to do with him. Now he watches, with double estrangement, as these images from a past prior to his amnesiac life as a murderer return to him. The countryside did indeed prove alien; he could never make his home there. In ceasing to be a guarded watcher in this alluring place, he exercised insufficient control over his turbulent, "unsuspected" self. To protest the division between the anxious, well-meaning visitor, seeking to make a good first impression and the accursed destroyer (now suffering sensations of all-encompassing lostness), he smashes the glass and thereby breaks off the internal movie projected there. Behind this ruptured mind screen lies unbroken night. The darkness sweeping in affords him no refuge nor any clue of how he moved, in trustful stupefaction, from the past's gossamer "there" to the monstrous "here."

It is difficult to describe the effect of unthinkability in film without conveying the impression that a narrative has control of the operation. That is, the director of the film—or some figure involved in the creative process—knows how to *think* about the movie's representation of the unthinkable and the uses to which it will be put. In the case of *So Dark the Night* and especially *Invisible Ghost*, I think it would be wrong to attribute thematic cohesiveness or a storyteller's lucid purposefulness to the various grapplings with unthinkable thoughts. The films appear to duplicate, by a fortunate inadvertency, the protagonist's "lostness" within the plotted action. An often highly adroit and expressive visual style seems to coexist comfortably with undernourished performances; an agglomeration of lazy, slapdash genre conventions; vacuous dialogue, and a vagabond tone (often entirely at the mercy of the confused actors' on-set impulses). With the (possible) exception of Bela Lugosi's Kessler, the performers in *Invisible Ghost* look stranded in their roles, imperfectly disguising their lack of understanding of the actions they are carrying out and the clumsily repetitive, non sequitur lines they are regularly obliged to speak.

A description of a woman who will eventually vanish without a trace in Don DeLillo's novel, *Point Omega*, conveys with eerie exactitude the remoteness of Joseph Lewis's muddled cast:

> Her look had an abridged quality, it wasn't reaching the wall or window.... She wasn't lost in thought or memory, wasn't gauging the course of the next hour or minute. She was missing, fixed tightly within.[4]

I like the conjunction of "missing" and "fixing"—as though going missing were related to "fixity," being securely coffined "within." Jessie Elster, the woman DeLillo describes, is diversely unreachable in the "narrows" of a state that excludes looking, thought, and memory. The actors in *Invisible Ghost*, by seeming general agreement, have decided to adopt a slightly ruffled composure as their fallback position in every social situation. Even the threat of murder can't penetrate their mildly strained air of polite collectedness. No one seems able to get his head around the worrisome implications of a mounting death toll within the Kessler house. The pervasive condition of not-knowing that the performers seek to cover over with bland effects makes silence and conversation alike busily empty. Unthinkable thoughts, like those buried inside Kessler, might be pushing their way up in the collective fog, trying to become clear through the debris of words and scattered gestures. Because Kessler cannot get in touch with his feelings and express them, it appears fitting that no one lodged in the house with him can either. A general infection is at work. Once again, I make this sound like a conscious directorial strategy. When watching the film, however, I cannot persuade myself that much of this collusion has been willed or disciplined. The film seems to find the form of life that it requires with minimal evidence of deliberate shaping.

There is an arresting passage in Jacques Ranciere's *The Future of the Image* that talks about the shifting of "loads" when forms and categories come undone. Ranciere's general reflections about aesthetic uncoupling in the nineteenth century could be regarded as a description of Martin Arnold's objectives in his installation:

> [W]ords and forms, the sayable and the visible, the visible and the invisible, are related to one another in accordance with new procedures. In the new regime...the image is no longer a codified expression of a thought or feeling. Nor is it a double or a translation. It is a way in which things themselves speak and are silent. In a sense, it comes to lodge at the heart of things as their silent speech.[5]

Arnold deprives the rooms in the house of their backdrop function: they are no longer nondescript adjuncts to awkward comings and goings. He endows them with not only heightened presence but also an enhanced yearning for expression. Arnold is determined to avoid "codification" of the "thought or feeling" astir in these object spaces. The viewer can't "see" what she is supposed to think and feel on the patchy gray and dark surfaces that confront her in these spaces; gleaming or mistily candlelit areas don't make the internal illumination problem any simpler. We may attune ourselves to rustling intimations, a faint pressure for emergence, a sharpened expectancy about doors and shadowy windows and unclimbed stairs. No doubt we experience the momentary relief that attends a rescue from a static perspective or a shift of any sort by the camera or on the soundtrack. The separate rooms of the house become more separate from one another as we are confined in them for extended surveys of their contents. We sense that they don't countenance free passage and would preserve their remoteness from neighboring rooms even if all the doors were flung open (Figure 14.3). Each space, in other words, presents its own puzzles of isolation and enclosure.

Early on, *Deanimated* imitates *Invisible Ghost*'s concern with using one room as a refuge from something unseemly or troubling on display in another. Virginia Kessler, the grown-up, live-at-home daughter, no sooner welcomes her current romantic interest, Ralph (John McGuire) into her home—the first figure from outside to be admitted indoors—than she attempts to steer him clear of the spectacle taking place in the dining room. (Kessler, as I previously noted, sits there, in glassy-eyed elation, sharing a meal and pleasant chat with his absent wife.) Virginia cannot account for Kessler's peculiar

FIGURE 14.3

conduct, as she explains to a vacantly rattled Ralph. It is merely something that *happens*, thankfully not too often. She leaves her father sequestered during his lapses and bus- ies herself elsewhere until the aberration has run its course. In *Deanimated*, Virginia's muddled efforts to find language for what distresses her yield a counter-spectacle of self-stifling. Her flailing verbalization (brief, utterly disjointed utterances) is inter- spersed with shrugs, throat clearings, raised eyebrows, head shakings, audible swallow- ing, and beseeching looks. Ralph attempts to smooth out the transmission difficulties by making a sexual advance, which Virginia responds to with avidity, as though any shared activity might afford a respite from her mismanaged privacy and the hostile weight of words. The pair's attempt to press forward with kissing makes complications of its own. The gesture seems to involve lips testing alien human surfaces and faces hid- ing from each other in the midst of it. A kiss in *Deanimated* acquires its own quality of ghostliness: a soft imprint on another's flesh that leaves no trace. The couple's kisses have intense visibility and tactility in the moment of doing, but their two faces lose the sense of having been acted upon with disconcerting ease. Physical intimacy evaporates as readily as a forgotten thought.

Ralph draws back from Virginia's still acquiescent mask when he senses he is being watched. A maid (Terry Walker) has noiselessly arrived at the library threshold. (The library has no actual door, only an odd theatrical curtain on a metal rod.) Before the maid is revealed, standing motionless in the entrance way, unabashedly staring at the couple, we watch Ralph's head from the rear, in close-up, as he turns away from the curi- ously halting progress of his caress and looks back toward us, anxiously. It is as though we have been caught spying on the couple as they flounder through their embrace. We do not know that there is anyone or anything (besides ourselves) to meet Ralph's look until the reverse shot materializes the female servant. Her presence is powerful enough to dispel immediately any chance of additional furtive touching. Virginia and Ralph rise together and quickly vacate the room and then the house itself. It would appear that Virginia feels a sudden irrepressible urge to go for a drive somewhere. Ralph no sooner catches sight of the maid than Virginia fades out for him. He forgets how to look at her as the maid commands his full attention. She has not only taken over the room and driven its befuddled "rightful" occupants into exile, she also mirrors the effect of the painted female portrait in the hallway, which the camera fastened on at the begin- ning of the film. The sheer fact of her mute, stationary "attendance" shifts the emotional focus to her. The attachment physically declared by the couple prior to her appearance is deprived of its solidity. The maid's inquisitive, self-possessed look pulverizes their weak and mismatched gestures of closeness. She becomes the library portrait, vanquishing the attempt to posit a new relationship that challenges her *past* authority. Ralph's atten- tion appears to stay behind with the maid—magnetized by her—as he escorts Virginia out of the house. (It will seldom be this simple again for living characters to leave the Kessler residence.) Has there been a sudden shift in Ralph's loyalty, due to instant attrac- tion, or does Ralph already know the maid from somewhere else? Is he unnerved by a shock of recognition? *Deanimated* glances toward such narrative questions and then erases them, together with the character who put them in play. The maid disappears, unobtrusively, from view, lingering in the library for a purpose that will never be ascertained. When the camera turns away from her already half-turned away form, she cannot count on her eventual return elsewhere in the narrative, even though her decisive first exposure virtually guarantees that. Instead, she becomes the film's second ghost (following on the heels of the missing Mrs. Kessler). She is swallowed up by the room in which she received her one and only sighting.

The maid disappears well in advance of the bedroom murder that was her salacious destiny in *Invisible Ghost*. The narrative spaces prepared to receive her before that death scene (the kitchen and backyard) fulfill their function as settings in her absence. Can they be said to futilely await her, holding themselves ready for an action that has occurred many times already, in the enclosed, repeating memory field of *Invisible Ghost*? Or is it possible that she is still there in some fashion, making her presence felt (albeit weakly, dimly) in the kitchen or beside the large tree in the yard, even though the sight and sound evidence of her cinematic corporeality have been extinguished? (Can an actor be totally removed from a space where she has once firmly belonged in a finished film, and where those who have watched it vaguely or distinctly recall seeing her? Maybe the subtraction is necessarily incomplete. She is not "gone for good"—as one says of the dead—but rather perfectly hidden from view.) The still remaining camera movements that once were motivated by the maid Cecile's actions, the framings that existed to accommodate her (in her exchanges with other actors), the hiss and crackle surviving on the soundtrack in the midst of other sound suppressions, may all carry the imprint of the missing maid. I think of the fate of actors in decayed or heavily spliced prints (the former are memorialized in Bill Morrison's 2002 archival compilation, *Decasia*). The performers carry on gamely with their dances, dining, street crossings, their depicted vices and ecstasies as their limbs or faces are mulched and leached away by temporal encroachments. The spoiled, missing parts of these entities lend an entrancing melancholy vigor to whatever remnants persist, faithful to the imperatives of a visibly diseased, but still animated moment.

Other, larger casualties from *Invisible Ghost* include all the movie's clumsy, improbable murders, Kessler's staggering walks while in a hypnotic trance, and the discoveries of the victim's bodies (or rather, the fearful discoveries remain but the erstwhile corpses have evaporated). Most important, Mrs. Kessler is nowhere in evidence until very late in the film. A single shot of a woman in a trench coat toppling off a chair announces with grisly matter-of-factness her simultaneous arrival and farewell. The ghostly Mrs. Kessler provides the one literal death in *Deanimated*. Her dying fall crystallizes the many previous death scenes that have slipped from view, evading our need to detect something and hold onto it. Perhaps this moment of final reckoning permits us to feel death's presence "burning through" the artifice. The effect seems far more potent, and indismissible, than the haunted house pile-up of superfluous victims in *Invisible Ghost*. In *Deanimated*, Mrs. Kessler is no longer a recovering accident victim, hidden away in the gardener's toolshed. The toolshed itself no longer exists on the Kessler property; the camera pays it no visits. The film has lost all memory of Mrs. Kessler's nocturnal presence beneath Kessler's window. The spot where she stood is still visible (if forgetfully so), but the figure who so conspicuously tormented her husband with thoughts of love, jealousy, and murder is no longer there to assert her claims. Since she now refrains from making her presence known directly, Kessler can forego all his trips to the window. He is relieved of his obligation to stare out into the darkness, become transfixed (and then horrified) by her image. The silent messages from her that he would dreamily decode as cues for vengeance have not been sent. Only the window itself survives for us to wonder at and come to terms with. It has a slightly crooked design. It offers a frail barrier between inner and outer worlds, between vacant warmth and chill darkness, between lonely, expectant rooms and desolate grounds, where often the trees and foliage stand stock still. When rain visits the window in a storm scene, its panes seem covered with rivulets of sadness. Suffering (unreleased in the house) beats against the glass, and quavers along its surface, trying to break through, find an opening (Figure 14.4).

The one crime for which there is palpably haunting evidence in *Deanimated* is the defacing of Mrs. Kessler's portrait. A large gash is startlingly revealed on the painted image the morning after the rainstorm. The damage begins at the lips and extends down to her neck. It is as though Kessler had been driven to silence her image, "wicked in her dead light," before she could deliver the message that (long ago) unhinged him.[6] To make herself known to him—like rain piercing the outer glass—is to ruin his false peace and to disfigure her frozen beauty. We do not see Keller attack the portrait, but this is one victim that refuses to melt away. The portrait's eyes remain intact, resting above the desecration and taking no notice of it. Perhaps they accost and reproach the one who has defaced her, perhaps they simply stand separate from a loss they cannot mourn. All

FIGURE 14.4

the story that *Deanimated* needs or wants has to do with a husband blindly tearing open the image of his beloved wife's face. In so doing, he causes the wife herself to materialize briefly and die. In the strict, Poe-like economy of the revised tale, where the bare minimum of gestures linking the married couple is called for, a single act of violence (against an image, not a person) becomes the death stroke for both of them. Kessler's sole claim to selfhood has been his possession by her. His wife only lives on as a captive in his deceitful dream. From fictions flimsier than this couples have built a strong semblance of life together.

The supremely quiet house in the final "act" of *Deanimated* is rarely troubled by human traffic. Its somber, petrified self-containment is most often interrupted by the flare of untended candles or a fire slowly dwindling in a fireplace. The candles are in no hurry to be done, any more than the struggling blaze in the fireplace is. They flicker on tables and in alcoves, in groups or all alone. They are forgotten holdovers of social purposes that have crumbled away, leaving no guests, no hosts, no vagrant witnesses. Well, we viewers are witnesses, but we have a hard time making our sense of living and imagined presence *stick* to what is on display. There is a kind of latent excitement in this memorial to social vacancy, akin to what Hungarian novelist Dezso Kosztolanyi describes in his novel, *Skylark*. Things whose observers have been cleared away rejoice in their severed ties and become "pregnant with [new] significance." The divorced existence that objects take up feels "primordial, reticent and hostile" amid the residue of order and decorum, "stinging our hearts with their indifference."[7] In *Deanimated*, social forms still exert some sway in the emptied rooms, but the objects seem already to be pulling away from old duties. In their agitated transition, they personify waiting. But the act of waiting works to establish another plane of time within the film image itself, a plane of futurity. *Invisible Ghost*'s present tense has come undone; we live in its aftermath, with some shattered vestiges of the depleted present now and then revived for a few breaths. Time steps ahead of us, and ahead of where we feel the movie itself ought to be, and forms a still life of impending foreclosure, as the "lost world" of the living (the invisible ghost) lurches to catch up with it. The surviving placement of things, executed with care, for some reason, some time ago, cannot help but be anxious on behalf of all human designs and supports. Even if no one is left to mind them, the chambers anticipate, in their own fashion, and for their own sake, disruption, decay, annihilation. Might something better be in store, instead? Death has touched these rooms, but has only entered part way. There is still more death to come, and perhaps the aim of waiting is to be filled with it. The rooms know, even if an increasingly mobile, skittering camera does not, that they are the only story that is left. They are the "waiting" hereafter of narrative space, the hereafter that can't be detected or experienced when a movie, with all its particulars in place, is resurrected for a fresh viewing.

The characters are now intruders in the rooms' mournfully disengaged future reality. When they turn up for their fragmentary maneuvers and try to rekindle a present tense life of some sort, it is they rather than their surroundings that seem almost gossamer. It is as though they can no longer leave a persuasive impression on their surroundings. They appear to be jousting in thin air, with no ground beneath them. To keep their little purchase on actions or to connect momentarily with fellow beings who may ebb away for good as soon as they turn a corner, they must exert themselves with seeming greater fierceness. Their power of attachment nonetheless continues to dwindle. A figure may knock on a door much longer than usual to stay centered or afloat. Another may take refuge in the clarity of a greeting or a habitual gesture. Without warning, however, any bit of behavior can become a murky thicket. Or drop away altogether. In the last part of the film, the surviving occupants of the house have all, in effect, become house servants, like Evans. The house has effectively replaced Kessler as a source of orders. Insofar as the house has intentions, it is to give expression to the balked, tormented consciousness of Kessler, its now almost entirely absent "owner." Virginia is given the most prominent role to play in the film's last bid for a story action that "goes forward." But she has become a surrogate Mrs. Kessler, a servant who will "materialize" the wife's beloved and enraging image. It seems to be her task to get some sort of message through to her "husband" and, at the same time, to awaken the fury of the rejected spouse. Her actions are the only narrative tissue that might *explain* the gash in the portrait that the spectator discovers not long after spending considerable time watching her toss and turn in bed.

The Virginia segment begins in her bedroom as she composes a message at her writing desk. We have no access to what she has written, but the logic of the narrative makes all messages into the same message: Mrs. Kessler is attempting to *get through* once more. Perhaps she is conveying at last what she truly wants from Kessler. Meanwhile, down the hall, Ralph's twin brother, Paul (as we learn in *Invisible Ghost*) is resting in another bedroom, idly flipping through a magazine. Kessler himself deposited him in this room earlier. Before saying good night to Paul there, he makes an elaborate dumbshow of conveying his thought process to his houseguest, which Paul exaggeratedly, and unconvincingly, indicates that he comprehends. Kessler disappears from the action at this point, ceding his visible role to Paul, who seems eager to find a pretext to leave his chamber and pay Virginia a stealthy visit. So there are stand-ins for both of the Kesslers as the night scene proceeds. Both of them, but especially Virginia, make an Alamo stand for continued narrative relevance, pressing against the house's increasing impatience with any visible, residual human action. The soundtrack supports Virginia's bid to make something that matters, something that will go somewhere, happen. A thunderstorm arrives, and the score frantically scrambles to make every object the camera glances at or moves in on shimmer with ominousness.

Virginia has many lights to put out before removing her dressing gown and settling into bed. She runs a peculiar gambit of blowing out candles and then switching off extra, seemingly superfluous electric lights. She appears content with the letter she has written and propped up on her desk. But in the contradictory mélange so typical of movie action, her successful completion of a task (composing an important message, as yet unsent) instantly enhances the likelihood of her victimization. Because the letter is still in the room, we somehow know that she will not be able to get her message through and benefit from it. It is *too late* for that. Virginia is not apprehensive about going to bed and takes her time with a quietly eroticized disrobing ritual. Because she radiates calm, each action she performs calls menace into being. Her capacity to feel safe as she seeks rest ensures that her room will be invaded. As she drifts off into slumber, the atmosphere around her bed becomes electric with portent. The thunderstorm breeds new, threatening configurations of light and shadow on her walls, the door which she had shut—when we are led to notice it again—is inexplicably half open. The camera presses in on Virginia from above, darkening its scrutiny of her as she sheds all sense of being watched. In the coils of sleep, she has even more forcefully assumed the wife and mother's place, dreaming her way into Mrs. Kessler's wayward desires. Her suspect form becomes a natural destination for Kessler's sturdy, amplified delusion. Were he to spy on his daughter in bed (as he actually does in *Invisible Ghost*), he would see her as at once endearingly trustworthy and engulfed in the sounds and erratic light of a malevolent storm. Her serene face becomes a taunt in the midst of so much upheaval. The storm's fury matches Kessler's own and sweeps the sleeping "Mrs. Kessler" back to her moment of sexual betrayal (Figure 14.5).

Down the hall, Paul rises from *his* bed twice, the first time to listen for suspicious sounds on the other side of his closed door, the second with a determination to extend his investigation by opening the door wide and studying the tempting corridor. His wish to enter the hall is suppressed, for the time being, and he contents himself with a brief, security guard peering. He then returns to his bed, without dousing the lights or gaining mastery of his night thoughts. We part company with him as he staves off his impulse to roam. We may recall that *Deanimated* opens with a credit sequence that features a drawing of a dark predator, one hand fiercely extended, like a claw. (The other hand rests on a limp, ineffectual cane, as though unaware of its fellow hand's maniacal

FIGURE 14.5

business.) It could be seen as a lurid sketch of the Id in motion. No sooner does the film proper begin than we see a second piece of art, the more formal painting of Mrs. Kessler. The close juxtaposition of the two art images makes the painting the apparent goal of the shadowy assailant. The plot of *Deanimated*, as I noted earlier, can be distilled to a single movement and its destructive repetition. Kessler's initial action is to descend the stairs of his house and gaze admiringly at his wife's portrait. Later, in the depths of night, Kessler returns to the portrait and, unobserved even by himself, tears a hole in it. The crudely depicted hobbling predator reaches out and smears the finished painting with his own grimy turmoil. Paul, in his guest bedroom, hides like Kessler from unseemly thoughts. Again like his host, he is outwardly an emissary of tidiness and caution. His two approaches to the door suggest that he is intent on making sure that everything at night is in its proper place. Only those things that *should* be going on actually are. He operates in a fog of dubious concern. Arnold may well be suggesting that his brash (but still circumspect) act of opening his door is what causes Virginia's door to open and stay open, as if in ghostly answer to a wish.

Once Virginia completes her climb into bed and settles herself for sleep, once Ralph interrupts his magazine skimming to harken to foreign sounds in the hall beyond his door—and in himself—Arnold turns his attention once again to downstairs' chairs, fireplace, window, staircase, and wallpaper. A more hectic search is in progress than at any previous point in the film. The camera movements are frenetic and paranoiacally confident of closing in on the culprits and threats being sought. The music boils over with agitation at the disclosure of presences with malign intentions—well on their way to enactment. The storm seconds every motion made by the score and adds its window rivulets of anguish to the central dynamics of fear. "See! Can't you see?" the camera visually exclaims as it arrives at exact spots where signs of trespass should be discernible: as plain as a bloody footprint. We must make do, alas, with sights of unyieldingly taciturn domestic furnishings, retreating further into a cryptic *thereness* as the framing demands revelation. All of the abortive efforts to flush out the dangers that the music, storm, and camera pointing give so much credence to make us ever more mindful of the story we have left behind. We await our pending return to Virginia, defenselessly asleep, and (perhaps) to Ralph's slow, furtive progress in breaking out of his room. The sights and sounds of downstairs commotion seem magnetically aligned with the woman in bed, arrayed for ravishment. She is our most vivid, recent memory from the shredded narrative, the human image (and predicament) that must be accounted for. However prolonged the camera's detour engagement with things elsewhere in the house, we count on eventually gaining readmission to the bedroom. Everything we see and have trouble decoding can be attached, metaphorically, to the woman beset by dreams and *oblivious* of an actual peril accumulating on all sides. The delay in further visual contact with Virginia does not prevent the viewer from shifting all the unspecified anxiety from the lower regions to the clearly established "bedroom story."

No human action in *Deanimated* has received more sustained, undistracted attention than Virginia readying herself for a good night's sleep. The disproportion of this heady inspection of moment-to-moment behavior introduces a new storytelling pace and accords the episode a strong center of gravity that the more fragmented story snippets lack. Virginia herself becomes the mystery message she has penned before retiring, and we must get back into her presence for the message contents to be construed and thus "delivered." As we weave about downstairs trying to fasten our eyes on one thing, then another, trying to keep our bearings and catch the telling ghostly *glimpse* should it transpire, our thoughts lie elsewhere. They are still with Virginia. Not enough scholarly attention has been devoted to those very common intervals in films when we can't concentrate on what is directly before us. Something prior to what is presently being shown has pricked our interest. A forceful, tantalizing image plays on in our memory, and we continue to fill in and magnify the details, unable to let it go. It takes remarkable powers of attention, at any time, to really see what is happening in front of us. So often the light that the present moment yields for "taking note" is obscured by the stronger light (and resultant hold) of some earlier sighting. Thus, a great deal that passes for seeing at the movies is a temporary, unacknowledged blindness. What feeds our blindness is a persisting contact with a vital bit that we won't relinquish from "before." The narrative is always pushing us forward (pointing out and directing us to absorb new information) but our true sympathies can just as adamantly drive us backward: to touch an image that has fled, to make it abide. How much of our viewing is a surreptitious recouping of a lost "then" while streaming through the narrative "here and now"? That doorway, that face, that gardener raking, that sound of geese or a trunk pulled across the floor, that half-remembered melody: any particular in a narrative can "take us over" without warning and become a potent backward destination.

As Virginia's head and shoulders turn back and forth on her pillow, attempting to give waking consciousness the slip, the camera slips away downstairs and begins to twist and turn itself, as though imitating and preserving in the mind's eye Virginia's restless motions. The libidinal energy let loose with our prolonged spying flows into the search of the other areas of the dwelling. The fearful hunt for trespassers is streaked with desire for the figure upstairs, who summons us back to her in her "secret" dream, a dream that can't easily be disentangled from viewer fantasy. However, with so much deferral and displacement of looking, the "natural course" of viewing desire is stymied. Nothing comes of our wishes in the narrative action. A figure does not materialize to carry our excited hopes to either a tender or brutal resolution. What happens to the undischarged sexual energy from the nocturnal storm? For Martin Arnold, it becomes the force tearing Mrs. Kessler's portrait. In the morning light, the viewer's unfulfilled gaze is confronted with familiar, static spaces where little of consequence has changed. Then, as if in answer to the question, "What was all that maddening activity *for*?" we are led several times to the portrait. Each time we look at the bird-shaped hole in her features, the woman's image is more disturbingly imprinted in our minds. The viewer's prurient investment in recumbent Virginia (and the palpable promise of harm to her) accompanied us throughout our agitated, digressive inspection of various "bodily" objects in the house. I would argue that the desire for a return to the woman we *still* beheld (in her absence) layers itself onto the objects that take her place. Finally, the object substitution gathers itself to a point, and Mrs. Kessler's likeness is ravaged in Virginia's place. Something had to happen, as the triple imperative of storm, distraught search, and culminating music guarantees. The gash in the portrait is small evidence of visible devastation, but *because* it is small (relative to our literal-minded fears and hopes) it affects us more strongly than a more straightforward attack would have. The hole gapes at us, intimating a ghostly nothingness beneath the marred and stricken surface. The face of Mrs. Kessler strives to maintain its former attractive composure, in effect smiling around its new, unsightly wound, which looms more painfully large each time we confront it.

In the last tour we make of the darkening house in *Deanimated*, silence reigns. The host, houseguests, police, and servants have dispersed or disintegrated, and light feebly pulsates in the thickening indistinctness. The camera becomes a kind of night watch-man (akin to Paul checking the hallway for troubling noises); it seems determined to guard against any further break-ins by the purported living (moving shadows; that is to say, in their fluttering human likeness). Earlier, I noted the house's capacity to slip the cogs of the movie's "time present" and become a hereafter for exhausted narrative space. The rooms, bereft of company, wait patiently to fade away or for something unfinished and forgotten to catch up with them. In the film's closing segment, time begins to flow in reverse: to become the past, our past. As time's active presence on screen dwindles, it makes do with a slow-motion retracing of steps. The rooms ultimately reveal themselves to be the all but irretrievable memory spaces of childhood's dim beginnings, the domes-tic nooks and crannies that first intimated who we were, who we might become, then forsook us. Now they stand before us again, remote and estranged in a sadly inviting way, billowing with nightfall. Perhaps they wispily mourn our long ago departure but are firmly sealed against our return. The darkness and dust of these abandoned living quarters have an intimate deathly flavor, one whose taste we gradually identify as our own mortality. We have been inside this Arnold film, by fits and starts, for a time, but now we are not. It will no longer let us in.

Our enforced detachment resembles the consciousness-dividing window that I pre-viously described from Joseph Lewis's *So Dark the Night*. In this instance, however, the window will not shatter so we can pass through—into *ourselves*, as it were. Usually movie spaces readily allow us access: they are designed to make us welcome, however depress-ing a film's subject matter. They ensure us, as swiftly as possible, that we have entered the cinema world and enjoin us to feel a part of things. The rooms that we encounter in the last minutes of *Deanimated* have been visited by us again and again in the course of the film, often for prolonged, static views, with no human distraction. We are bet-ter acquainted with these spaces, surely, than with most interior settings in films. It is the very fact and weight of this familiarity, this seeming knownness of the terrain that allows a sense of exclusion to arise. The exclusion can feel strangely personal and acutely painful.

Deanimated seems to suggest that whenever we enter a film emotionally we are attempting to revive the dream passageways and undemolished shelters of our child-hood imagining. Perhaps our need for film is inseparable from our need to keep in touch with these passageways and the protection of enclosure. Placement in film—the finding of our footing in film spaces—can allow us to recover, inwardly, a remembered strength that comes from being less defined, less bound up in the limiting arrangements of our conditioning. The comforts of home that film replenishes have to do with belonging, on the one hand, but equally the sense that we are still free to choose who we might become and on what terms, on the other. The fears that burden us can be temporarily set aside as we explore spaces, in the company of surrogate selves, that potentially enlarge the scope of our inner life. In the world that awaits us outside the movie theater, there may be no one resourceful and trustworthy enough to open the doors we compulsively seek and "take us in." But such doors and invitations and guardians do exist while a movie unspools. Our hazardous pilgrimages in whatever we consider to be reality are so often secretly directed to the "aging edifice of memory." Film's greatest capacity to befriend us has to do with its near effortless power to restore a condition of placement, a placement that appears, to an enthralled viewer, the key to all inclusion. The ever-emptying (but never empty) house of *Deanimated* thins out the dream of "living inside" and reclaiming our place that so many film narratives engineer. Ultimately, the film banishes us from our own house and leaves us orphans. We think of our own vague beginnings as a *place* where, in memory, we still somehow move about and rest; we have come from there and memory glimmers permit us to circle back, to touch pieces of this past—in flashes of sensation—as though it were still, imperishably, ours. It is that recollected first ground of our being that seems to be crumbling in the closing minutes of *Deanimated*. The "dwelling of dwellings" inside us, that against all logic and odds, awaits our return, is suddenly in jeopardy. Perhaps, this scratchy whispering finale tells us, there is no longer any placement within to call our own.

The most significant space in the geography of *Deanimated* is the front entranceway or hall. It is where the portrait is hung. It is also a place that offers us, side by side, a stairway leading up, and—behind it and to the left—an extremely enticing door. For me, this door gradually became the all important one, the heart of the memory house, the door that might afford fullest access to the past and to a sense of well-being. The film returns to this door often. It almost always seems to face me from the same distance. It is steadfastly closed. By the end of the film, it seems to repudiate me. It keeps its own records of who has gone in and who has gone out, and it declares me "past recalling." I no longer count for anything to this door, losing my own imprint in the shifting space of memory. The staircase, in turn, would seem to beckon me upward. I recall climbing, and being carried up, steps very much like these with the promise of sanctuary and sleep. But now, in the diminished light of *Deanimated*, the stairway stiffens in resistance. Only ghosts can traverse the desired distance. The camera gestures upward, but it withholds the invitation to advance. I remain below, numbly awaiting the noiseless footsteps of those lost to me to become audible once more. It is clear that they have forgotten all about me and have no reason to come back. And the wallpaper beside the stairway, which the camera has repeatedly paused to contemplate, as though urging me to run my hands over it and thus stroke it into rippling life: the paper declines, in its last appearances, to an amorphous blankness. The child's imagination has lost its will, its way, its openings.

There is a candle in another room, on the kitchen table, waiting for someone to emerge from the shadows to pick it up. We know that candle from somewhere, but it is not for us. It is a stranger's now. The glistening, out-of-place water cooler in the kitchen corner (seemingly extruded from a child's daydream of plenty) seems to be drained of liquid. Or the water hides from us in its clear, but not clear enough, glass bell. Whatever thirst it awakens will never be satisfied. A picture of a small landscape appears on the hallway wall. We almost recognize it; if only we could draw closer. But it stares back at us, unreachable and unreadable, demanding that we keep our distance. It will be opaque from now on, although if we could only identify it, call it to mind, a crucial memory key might turn. Something from a still living, inhabitable past might be returned to us. The ranks of candles in the upstairs corridor light no one's passage through, certainly not our own. No one anticipates our delayed arrival. The candles will continue to burn by themselves, unattended, sharing their light only with fellow objects, until their substance is gone. They know that it will not be our breath that will extinguish the flames and save these fast-perishing tapers. The larger fire in the study hearth rises up, as it has many times before, in the extreme foreground of the frame with the wavering hiss of time on the faded, damaged soundtrack as one of its sounds and the house's congregating sighs as the other. The fire proclaims its incapacity to warm. It is equally unable to burn away the detail in the image behind it, although that appears to be its aim. For whom does any of this detail persist? Whose gaze might it answer, whose sense of dwelling might it replenish?

Throughout our encounter with these memory supplications turned cold, our placement in the movie frame of our own past continues to wear away. It is not death that makes us afraid here, it is the rewinding of the reel (the reel of our reality) to our beginnings and finding the evidence that we *have been*, in fact—that we have left a mark with our existence—erasing before our eyes. We join the procession of the visually expunged performers, the perplexed wayfarers in *Deanimated*'s senseless plot. It was the mere semblance of being, after all, that needed to be dissolved. What we took to be our own longstanding story—in which everything that occurred was necessarily connected to us—could easily absorb our elimination and go forward. Like Kessler, whatever we believed we saw, esteemed, or held onto, we misconstrued. We have never really been here, in the way or with the heft that we supposed. We live *underneath* our living, scratching to get inside. Our conscious presence is a smudge, easily becoming one of the "missing" in the melancholy, diaphanous habitation we claim to occupy (Figure 14.6). Fernando Pessoa, a connoisseur of displacement, has written in *The Book of Disquiet*: "We are two abysses . . . a well staring at the sky."[8] The abysses meet only in the persevering stare and in the dream of being touched by a reflection; what they "know," according to Pessoa, is never "self-realization."

After a devastating stretch of darkening silence, during which our memories of place have had ample time to join the homeless shades, Arnold draws once more on the score from *Invisible Ghost*. In these "unaccommodated" passages, which include a softly grievous stirring, pizzicato vivacity, and solemn bombast, music tries to find a proper tone for the materialization of the dying Mrs. Kessler, an orchestral revelation definite enough to surrender the house to her keeping and to let the viewer escape from it. Crashing against a firmly established and fitting silence, the music fails to "sound out" the death.

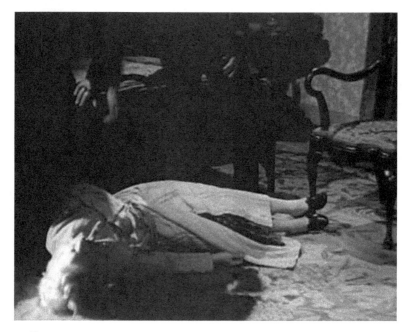

FIGURE 14.6

The score seems condemned to clear-cut, emotional expression (one kind after another) and shrivels on contact with the house's "last phase" of unutterable calm. Before Mrs. Kessler pitches over onto the floor, the dream of her life passes fleetingly across her dumbstruck face, and our dream (so it seems) along with it. Our visual haunting of the Kessler home has been as unpropitious as the clumsy, alien music. The house initially received us, encouraged us to linger awhile, and ponder, with amused detachment, its peculiar enigmas, its burlesque anguish, and disappearing acts. And then it cast us out, having pilfered and dissolved our own memories of belonging, in time with the night. We are now the shadow on the wall, or the slight impress on the chair, or the wavering candle, burning unseen. Our deeds done there—in these empty memory spaces—go extinct. Whatever we were, the page has turned blank. If only we might retain even ghostly prerogatives

NOTES

1. Irving Massey, *The Gaping Pig: Literature and Metamorphosis* (Berkeley: University of California Press, 1976), 10.
2. Massey, *Gaping Pig*, 14.
3. Ibid., 13.
4. Don DeLillo, *Point Omega* (New York: Scribner, 2010), 59–60.
5. Jacques Ranciere, *The Future of the Image*, trans. Gregory Elliot (New York: Verso, 2009), 13.s

6. Wallace Stevens, quoted in Helen Vendler, *Last Looks, Last Books: Stevens, Plath, Bishop, Merrill* (Princeton: Princeton University Press, 2010), 38.

7. Dezso Kosztolanyi, *Skylark*, trans. Richard Aczel (New York: NYRB Classics, 1993), 189.

8. Fernando Pessoa, *The Book of Disquiet*, trans. Richard Zenith (New York: Penguin Classics, 2006), 45.

SELECT BIBLIOGRAPHY

DeLillo, Don. *Point Omega*. New York: Scribner, 2010.

Kosztolanyi, Dezso. *Skylark*. Translated by Richard Aczel. New York: NYRB Classics, 1993.

Massey, Irving. *The Gaping Pig: Literature and Metamorphosis*. Berkeley: University of California Press, 1976.

Pessoa, Fernando. *The Book of Disquiet*. Translated by Richard Zenith. New York: Penguin Classics, 2006.

Ranciere, Jacques. *The Future of the Image*. Translated by Gregory Elliott. New York: Verso, 2009.

Sabbadini, Andrea, ed. *Projected Shadows: Psychoanalytic Reflections on the Representation of Loss in European Cinema*. New York: Routledge, 2007.

Vendler, Helen. *Last Looks, Last Books: Stevens, Plath, Lowell, Bishop, Merrill*. Princeton, NJ: Princeton University Press, 2010.

CHAPTER 15

THE ACOUSMATIC
VOICE AND METALEPTIC
NARRATION IN
INLAND EMPIRE

WARREN BUCKLAND

WHAT is at stake in analyzing a puzzle film like *Inland Empire* (David Lynch, 2006)? We need to begin with the film's poetics, *how* it is put together. In general terms, a poetic perspective entails a two-fold analysis: it rationally reconstructs the *decision-making process* of practitioners, and it regards practice as a *problem-solving activity*. Drawing on an enormous wealth of experience, expert practitioners decide the best way to construct a film by choosing from the numerous options available to them, and their decisions are guided by the need to solve a problem. (Their decisions are also delimited by technological developments, institutional norms, and successful films of the past.) My agenda in this essay is specifically focused around the issue of how shots and scenes are joined in *Inland Empire* to create a complex diegesis, or narrative world, composed of multiple intersecting layers. What role does voice and soundtrack play in creating this ambiguous reality? I examine the decision-making process that has gone into the construction of the film's complex aural and visual narrative world.

I am not trying to explain *what* the film means, for this activity takes something away from the film (its inherent ambiguities, its equivocations) by trying to attach meanings to nonsignifying (or primordial) signifiers. Like Raymond Bellour in his later essays (such as "The Film We Accompany" [2004]), I simply want to accompany the film as it unfolds (although I still retain much of the analytical tools of film textual analysis). I also want to avoid making vague, abstract generalizations regarding the film. Instead, I plan to begin from the film itself and stick close to its surface. In other words, I hope to develop a "bottom-up" rather than "top-down" analysis.

I am trying to maintain accuracy in the analysis and avoid fanciful interpretations that surround this film on blogs and David Lynch websites, where something always means something else. Such symbolic-allegorical readings look *beyond* the film rather than *at* it. I am trying to avoid inaccurate reading strategies and instead simply want to study (without entirely succeeding) what we see and hear while experiencing the film, particularly the complex sound and image constructions in the first hour and final moments. In sticking close to the film, I sometimes get caught up in the small details. Such a reading strategy assumes that you are familiar with the film. (Simply trying to describe what happens in *Inland Empire* would take up several thousand words in itself. I prefer to spend those words analyzing how the film is put together.)

I am aware that film analysis may have "met its match" when confronted with the sounds and images of Lynch's *Inland Empire*. To some extent, my frustration was mirrored in the 1980s by Raymond Bellour. In his 1985 paper "Analysis in Flames," he described the exhaustive, systematic film analysis, which he carried out in the 1970s, as "in flames": it had burned itself out.[1] William Routt and Rick Thompson argue that, in "Analysis in Flames," Bellour burned out on analyzing one type of film—the well-made narrative films consisting of closed spaces and coherent narrative worlds. They then identified two alternative types of film narratives:

> "[W]ell-made" narratives are not the only story structures that even "classic" films provide.... [S]ome stories, for example, seem to aim at nothing more or less than the end of history, in the process inevitably implying their own obliteration. These are narratives made of lines leading nowhere. Some stories and some films end in nothing, *nada*, and the destruction of the world. Other stories and films...end with the establishment of utopia, which as surely as the case of world destruction, signifies the end of the conflict which produces stories. Both variants call stories themselves into question by exacerbating the tension between narrative and diegesis until it produces a paradox, a madness bred of reason.[2]

Inland Empire belongs to both narrative categories Routt and Thompson identify: it appears to be a narrative made of lines leading nowhere; but it also ends up establishing a utopia (although it may be more appropriate to discuss the film as a form of heterotopia). *Inland Empire* certainly "call[s] stories themselves into question by exacerbating the tension between narrative and diegesis until it produces a paradox, a madness bred of reason."

Unfolding *Inland Empire*

David Lynch decided to shoot *Inland Empire* on a prosumer digital camera, the Sony DSR-PD150. In an interview, he describes the advantages:

> Lightweight camera, smaller crew, 40-minute takes, automatic focus, seeing what you have right before you in the camera and being able to tweak the view and

seeing [the actors] exactly the way they're going to be recorded. So if you don't like something you can fix it, see it right there. When you start shooting you've got *40 minutes*. You can go deeper and deeper into a scene, no interruptions.[3]

Lynch sees the lightweight camera as significantly increasing the options available to him, options that enable him and his characters to go deeper into a scene, to explore creative, intangible problems via several alternative options without any delay. What is just as significant is that he used this digital technology to create a film structured like a series of nested Chinese boxes, each representing a level of diegetic reality. But not normal nested boxes, for they are overlapping—overlapping with transparent, variable sides. These boxes represent a fluid, malleable space; they represent several diegetic levels embedded within one another. Transitioning from one level or box to another is usually strongly marked in the film; but this signalling of a transition still creates disorientation. This is because, in *Inland Empire* and many other contemporary stories, the transition becomes a transgression, a process known as *metalepsis* or "frame-breaking." Werner Wolf defines metalepsis as "a fictional representation consisting of several distinct worlds and levels, among which unorthodox transgressions occur."[4] Metalepsis names an unorthodox transgression of the boundary between narrative levels, resulting in a blurring or contamination between the levels. For example, a character in a dream transgresses the dream boundary and enters the diegesis of the character; or a character in the diegesis enters the fictional world of the film he or she is watching.[5] Such transgressions are central to *Inland Empire*.

Credit Sequence

The credit sequence begins with a bright light, resembling a powerful arc light projector beam, shining across the black screen. The projector beam momentarily hits the lettering of the film's title, making the letters stand out from the darkness. The lettering appears to be moving forward. Closely synchronized with this light and lettering moving forward we hear a loud industrial-mechanical boom, which creates an uncanny effect by conferring materiality onto the light. The sound is typical of Lynch's experiments to blur the boundaries between sound effects and music and to create harsh metallic sounds whose ultimate source remains unknown.

Several of these stylistic elements are to be found in the credit sequences of Lynch's previous two films, *Lost Highway* (1997) and *Mulholland Dr.* (2001). (All three films form a loose triptych and are therefore worth considering together.) The trope of the dark screen pierced by a beam of light is to be found in *Lost Highway*'s credit sequence. The opening image consists of a road in complete darkness along which the camera, attached to the front of a car, is traveling at high speed, lit only by the car's headlights. (The direction of the light in this credit sequence is therefore different from *Inland Empire*.) The trope of the lettering moving forward is also to be found in *Lost Highway*'s credit sequence, in which the titles give the impression of rapidly flying toward the screen, sticking to the screen (or windshield) for a few seconds, before flying off behind the camera. The issue here is one of metalepsis, for the nondiegetic titles (which exist outside the story world) appear to interact with the car in the diegesis. The soundtrack is dominated by David Bowie's song "I'm Deranged," presumably nondiegetic (unless the car's unseen driver is playing it loud on his radio; but the lack of reverb from playing it in the car suggests it is nondiegetic).

Mulholland Dr. also begins with a car driving along a dark road (Mulholland Dr.). This time the camera is behind the car rather than attached to the front of it. Again, lighting derives primarily from the car's headlights. The credits begin with the car headlights briefly shining on a road sign for Mulholland Dr.: the letters glow momentarily. After this shot, the camera follows the car along the road. The credits appear on screen, glow momentarily, before disappearing into the darkness again (the nondiegetic credits are therefore imitating what just happened in the diegesis). The soundtrack is dominated by Angelo Badalamenti's nondiegetic music composed for the film. All three credit sequences therefore contain a dark screen, a beam of light, lettering moving forward, and lettering momentarily appearing and disappearing in an unusual (rather than conventional) manner.

Inland Empire begins with a black-and-white close-up shot of a gramophone needle on a radio transcription disc (a common way to record radio programmes in the 1930s–1950s, after which tape recording took over). Whereas the title credits have emphasized light (the projector beam accompanied by sound), the opening shot now emphasizes the production of sound, illustrated with an image. Over the crackling of this mechanical (nondigital) sound produced by the needle on disc, an acousmatic voice—a bodiless voice, a voice whose source cannot be seen—narrates the continuation of a story: "Axxon N. The longest running radio-play in history. Tonight, continuing in the Baltic region, a grey winter day in an old hotel." The voice is reading the text aloud in a slightly monotonous, mechanical delivery. It is the voice of a public orator, conscious that he is addressing an audience. Like the gramophone behind the curtain in *The Testament of Dr Mabuse* (Fritz Lang, 1932), the voice in the opening of *Inland Empire* emanates from an acousmatic device.[6] But Lynch goes one step further than Lang. The image opening Lynch's film combines two acousmatic machines, the radio (the voice of the radio announcer) and the gramophone; the voice is mediated through both forms of technology (the radio voice is not coming live from a radio, but emanates from a disc, a recording of a radio play). This doubly mediated voice, whose bodily origin remains invisible, punctuates the film on a few occasions, offering fragments of commentary and exposition.

The first words of the announcement, and the first words spoken in the film, are unanalyzable. "Axxon N." is a primordial signifier; it does not signify some anterior meaning. It is simply a name (of a radio play) without a prior referent (the words have no prior denotation or connotation). Michel Chion finds the first word uttered in *Citizen Kane* to function similarly as a primordial signifier: "We are watching [in the opening scene of *Citizen Kane*] a version of Genesis, in which Rosebud is the first word uttered, whereby there is light. Rosebud is a signifier by definition unanalyzable, since it's the first primordial signifier, pure and simple."[7] The whole of *Citizen Kane* (a complex film, although not as complex, of course, as *Inland Empire*) is structured around the attempt to find the meaning of this primordial signifier.[8] "Axxon N." plays a similar role in *Inland Empire*.

Following the utterance of "Axxon N.," the first half of the radio announcement is simply about the radio play itself—its longevity. The other half minimally orientates the listener by identifying place and time. Significantly, the announcement lacks narrative: no characters, activities, or complicating actions are mentioned. Furthermore, the close-up shot of the needle and disc is superimposed over at least two other shots of the needle and disc—all these shots therefore constitute slightly different manifest options (similar to the more elaborate superimposition of jitterbug dancers in the opening of *Mulholland Dr.*). Behind these images is an indistinct image of what appears to be a surface darkened with burn marks.

This shot of the disc and needle transitions to "an old hotel" with two people speaking in Polish (a country in the Baltic region). The images are still in black and white. The radio voice motivates the transition, since we can assume this is the old hotel spoken of—suggesting, therefore, that this part of the film enacts the radio play. The voice dominates and structures the film at this point: it takes us to a new time and place, simply illustrated by the images. For some obscure reason, the faces of the two people in the hotel corridor are digitally blurred, an unusual technique to use in a fiction film. Although the bodies of the speakers are present, their mouths uttering the words are concealed by the digital blur. Although not off screen, the mouths remain concealed, preventing spectators from definitively matching up the voice with the speaker: "If an actor's mouth isn't visible onscreen," writes Chion, "we cannot verify the temporal co-incidence of its movements with the sounds we hear. Such audio-visual matching is the ultimate criterion for attributing the voice to a given character."[9] The unusual semi-acousmatic arrangement created by the digital blurring is repeated again in the TV images of the "rabbit sitcom," in which the humanoid rabbits speak in English, although we cannot see their mouths move because they are concealed under rabbit heads. The digital blurring therefore creates a gap in the diegesis or story world. The gap is heightened (rather than camouflaged), for the spectator is aware of this rather unusual device. The gap is also temporary and unmotivated (or motivated aesthetically).[10] *Inland Empire*, in other words, is initially being uncommunicative (a typical trait of David Lynch's films).

We return to the image of the disc (but not accompanied by the voice) on a few occasions. We also see the words "Axxon N." written on two different doors, which Laura Dern's characters (Nikki Grace/Susan Blue) feel compelled to enter.[11] On both occasions they lead to the house that Susan Blue lives in ("Smithy's House"). On both occasions, therefore, we and Susan are transported to another time and place. The written *visual* signifier "Axxon N." transitions us to Smithy's house. In contrast, the *voice* uttering this name "Axxon N." at the beginning of the film transitions us to the old hotel. Both locations—Smithy's House and the hotel room—are the most significant locations in the film. One space is occupied by Susan Blue, the other by the Lost Girl (as explained below). Both characters briefly meet up toward the end of the film, giving a sense of closure.

In the hotel room, mentioned by the radio announcer, we gain more information about the two people whose faces are digitally blurred. From the dialogue, we understand that a client is meeting a prostitute. In the next scene, which switches from black-and-white to color, we see a young woman, called the Lost Girl in the credits (and played by the Polish actress Karolina Gruszka) sitting on the edge of the bed watching television. Because of the setting, a hotel room, and because we look for continuity from one scene to the next, we can infer that she could be the prostitute in the previous scene. The gap created by the blurring of her face has now been filled in.

As with shots of the disc and needle, close-ups of the Lost Girl's face occasionally punctuate the entire film. She participates in the action midway through the film (when the Phantom violently beats her) and at the end (a reunion with her husband and son in Smithy's house, after Susan has killed the Phantom). Both appearances suggest that the Lost Girl played the role of Susan Blue in the original incomplete, cursed version of "On High in Blue Tomorrows," called "47."

Transitions: Metalepsis

The Lost Girl, as we said, is watching TV. The TV screen becomes a privileged screen of transition between different spaces. In fact, the dramatic transition to new spaces (or, one Chinese box to another, one diegetic level to another) is one of the dominant tropes in *Inland Empire*. To understand this film's poetics (how it is made), we need to examine these transitions.

We can infer that the majority of the film takes place in one of the main Chinese boxes—the TV set that the Lost Girl is watching. In this, her first appearance, we see her watching the rabbit sitcom, plus a few shots from the next scene speeded up. These speeded-up shots represent more metalepsis—images from the film we are watching (*Inland Empire*) jump levels and are embedded in the film as speeded-up TV images. This embedding and blurring of levels is even more unusual because the embedded images derive from the *next* scene in the film. We only know they are embedded and repeated when we see the following scene of *Inland Empire*. A similar trope is used in *Lost Highway*. There, the TV of Fred and Renee Madison also becomes a privileged screen of transition to other spaces, this time to spaces inside their house (especially the living room and bedroom). The Madisons mysteriously receive videotapes consisting of static, followed by images of outside, then inside their house.

The Lost Girl also watches a TV with nothing but static. Is the TV like this all the time? Are the images on the TV simply figments of her imagination? The film does not resolve these gaps; they remain permanent. Out of the static emerges the humanoid rabbit sitcom. It seems to be taking place in another old and more run down hotel. The rabbit sitcom at first sounds mysterious simply because one of the lines of dialogue is out of sequence:

Female rabbit 1: I'm going to find out one day.
Female rabbit 2: When will you tell it?

Male rabbit: Who could have known?
Female rabbit 1: What time is it? (*Canned laughter*)
Male rabbit: I have a secret.

. . .

If the male rabbit's line "I have a secret" is spoken first, the other lines fall into place. As with the digital blurring of the faces of the two people in the hotel room, the heads of those speaking, although on screen, are hidden (although the concealment by the rabbit heads takes place within the diegesis, whereas the digital blurring is nondiegetic, imposed on the fictional story world from the outside). The voices coming from the rabbits are not, therefore, anchored in the movements of their mouths (although their body movement and gestures partly enable us to anchor the voices to a particular body).

The male rabbit then leaves the room and enters a palatial room, an improbable juxtaposition of spaces, even though continuity editing (or doorknob editing, as Bazin called it) suggests they are contiguous spaces. But clearly this is not the case. This transition resembles the improbable scene transitions found in *The Trial* (Orson Welles, 1962).[12] The male rabbit closes the door and stands motionless in the palatial room. He then "disappears" (fades out) as the lights come up. Why does the humanoid rabbit disappear? He disappeared because he can only survive in the TV sitcom world and, in another instance of metalepsis, he has jumped to another level of reality (outside the TV sitcom). This suggests that the palatial space is a space separate from the TV sitcom (but it does not indicate why he left his sitcom space). It also reminds us of another space in the film—the palatial house that Nikki lives in (shown in the next scene). The film therefore sets up an opposition between run-down spaces (Smithy's house, the rabbit sitcom) and palatial spaces (including Nikki's home).

This unusual technical device (fading a character out of a scene) happens again near the end of the film, when Susan Blue enters the hotel room of the Lost Girl and embraces her. Susan then fades from the shot. What links these two events (fading out of the rabbit, fading out of Susan) is the character called the Phantom. He appears for the first time in the film a few moments after the rabbit disappears, in the palatial room, asking "for an opening" (an opening into the film?). He appears for the last time in a seedy hotel corridor when Susan shoots him, a few moments before Susan embraces the Lost Girl and fades out. Susan's killing of the Phantom frees the Lost Girl and appears to lift the curse on the film "On High in Blue Tomorrows" (and its remake called "47" and its characters). The scene in the palatial room ends with the rabbit standing at the same door.

After a long fade, a new scene with new characters unfolds. A character played by Grace Zabriskie (called visitor #1) visits Nikki (Laura Dern). Lynch has chosen to film the visitor in extreme close-up with a wide-angle lens, creating distortion. The opening images of this scene with Grace Zabriskie were previously shown on the hotel TV (but there is no causal link creating coherence; it simply remains a metalepsis and a repetition). Except for one shot at the end of the scene, Nikki is not filmed in close-up with a wide-angle lens; her face is not distorted. Visitor #1 presented herself as a new neighbor, but their conversation takes a strange turn when she first begins to talk about a folktale involving evil. She then discusses Nikki's next film role, in the film "On High in Blue Tomorrows." The visitor knows a lot about the film. She implies that the story is cursed. She knows Nikki will definitely get the lead role of Susan Blue (at this point in time Nikki does not know if she has the role); she knows that Nikki's husband will be involved in the film—he plays Smithy, Susan's husband (although Susan denies he plays a role in the film); and she thinks there will be a murder in the film (which is correct, as Susan is stabbed with a screwdriver at the end of "On High in Blue Tomorrows"). The visitor also knows about the alleyway that leads to Smithy's house: "Then, not through the market-place; you see that, don't you? But through the alley, behind the marketplace. This is the way to the palace. But, it isn't something you remember." The irony here is that the alley does not lead to the palace, but to the run-down Smithy's house. Visitor #1's monologue is David Lynch's version of concentrated preliminary exposition, the narrative device that confers on the viewer background information near the film's beginning, signpost-ing upcoming events. But unlike conventional exposition, Visitor #1's exposition is too cryptic and fragmentary to guide us through the film.

Visitor #1 ends her monologue by pointing to the opposite end of the room, saying, "If it was tomorrow, you would be sitting over there." We then see Nikki sitting there (to Nikki's and our surprise; it is at this disturbing moment that Lynch chooses to film Nikki in close-up with a wide-angle lens, distorting her face). Nikki now seems to have a double. But when we cut back to Nikki and visitor #1, they have disappeared. What has happened is that we have transitioned one day ahead via a point-of-view shot, as Nikki "sees" herself at the opposite side of the room the next day. But she disappears *at the very moment* we share her point-of-view shot, the moment she becomes both the subject and object of the point of view. We do not return to Nikki looking at herself. Instead, the transition is permanent, and the film continues one day forward. This play on doubling a character, who sees him- or herself in a point-of-view shot before suddenly disappear-ing, is repeated later in the film. Furthermore, this filmic option, to use the point of view to transition forward in time, is highly unusual, but not unique; Kubrick uses it towards the end of *2001* (1968), when Bowman is in the white room and sees an older version of himself. Once we see the older Bowman, the younger one disappears, and the film con-tinues with the older man.

On the Set

Kingsley, the director of "On High in Blue Tomorrows" (played by Jeremy Irons), chooses to read through scene 35 of the script. "Not the love scene, of course, but some of the earlier scenes...the scene where Devon, you arrive, Billy, at Smithy's house to find Sue, Nikki, looking out of the window." This read-through of scene 35 (which reminds me of another read through, this time by Betty in *Mulholland Dr.*), is interrupted by an off-screen sound. Nikki's co-star, Devon (Justin Theroux), checks the as yet unfin-ished Smithy's set, hears loud footsteps on the concrete floor, but does not see them (the source of the sound remains invisible at this moment in the film). He tries the door to the set, looks through a window, and then goes behind the set. Smithy's house is simply a flat façade. In Meir Sternberg's terms, a gap is created in the diegesis, for we do not know who disturbed the reading. More specifically, the disturbance creates a curiosity gap, which means it is clearly noticeable (rather than camouflaged, as with the surprise gap).[13] This leads the spectator to generate simultaneous hypotheses to fill in the gap and to anticipate that the film will confirm one of our hypotheses at a later date. If the gap is not filled in, it will become permanent (rather than temporary).[14] In the read-through of scene 35, the gap is filled in, but in a highly improbable way (involving more metalepsis).

Later, Devon and Nikki are filmed acting out a seduction scene from "On High in Blue Tomorrows." Once the scene is over, we get a distorted close-up on Nikki's face, an internal stylistic option that, by this time in the film, we recognize as a style that suggests character imbalance. This shot is immediately followed by an abrupt transition—same location, apparently the same time, but a change of sound gives the impression we have changed to a new reality. In combination with the distorted close-up of Nikki, we could infer that this sudden cut signifies a change to a new level of Susan's mental reality.

This abrupt transition is followed by another scene between Nikki and Devon. She talks to him about their affair and worries that her husband will find out. Nikki pauses for a moment and comments that what she is saying "sounds like dialogue from our script." From off-screen we hear Kingsley's disembodied acousmatic voice cut the shot and asks what's going on. We quickly realize that they *were* lines from the script and that Nikki is confusing the script with reality (more metalepsis). The scene ends with more distorted images of Nikki, plus ominous, discordant orchestral (predominately string) music. This scene is followed by another abrupt transition. We see Devon talking to the film's producer about the curse on the script. Perhaps Devon thinks the rumors are affecting Nikki's performance, which would explain her behavior in the previous scene.

In a later scene from "On High in Blue Tomorrows," where Billy is making love to Susan (which Kingsley mentioned earlier), Nikki comes out of her character to talk to Devon, which confuses him, because he is now the character Billy. She imagines her husband is watching. The husband is then shown creeping about the corridors of Smithy's house and peering through the bedroom doorway at her and Billy. Could Susan simply be imagining her husband's presence? But the basis for such an inference is not resolved; it remains ambiguous. Susan also mentions to Billy a scene "shot yesterday" in the alleyway. Laura Dern now seems to be speaking as Nikki, the actress, rather than Susan, the character. We then cut to the alleyway, suggesting the film has moved back to the day before, and we see Nikki dropping off her shopping in a car parked there. It seems to be the alleyway that visitor #1 mentioned; visitor #1 therefore signposted this scene. Nikki's attention is drawn to the letters "Axxon N." chalked on a metal door. She follows the arrow next to the chalked sign, and ends up at the back of the set. In front of her, she sees herself (Nikki) and Devon reading scene 35. The film has moved back in time and has also worked its way forward to a previous scene (just like the structure of *Lost Highway*, which uses the Möbius strip structure to work its way back—or forward—to the film's opening scene). As before, Devon and Nikki, reading through scene 35, hear a sound from the back of the set, and Devon performs the action seen earlier—he stops reading from the script and gets up to see who is behind the set. We see Nikki looking at the group around the table (including herself), and then we cut back to Nikki on the set. When we cut back to the group around the table for a second time, Nikki has unexpectedly disappeared, just like she did when she saw herself on the other side of the room in her home, when visitor #1 called on her. Nikki therefore sees her double again, and one of them disappears. By showing Nikki on the set while scene 35 is read out, the film fills in a gap generated by the earlier scene—who was behind the set? But the filling in of the gap is, in Sternberg's terms, highly improbable, for it supposes that Nikki can be in two places at the same time (just like the Mystery Man and Fred Madison in *Lost Highway*).[15] Yet, we must keep in mind that Nikki at the table is reading through the script for the first time with Devon and that this read-through has brought the character of Susan to life. This could account for the appearance of a double at this precise moment in the film. So, it is Nikki who disappears in this scene, leaving her character, Susan, to occupy the set (Smithy's house). The moment of overlap, when Susan (the character) sees Nikki (the actress) is another moment of metalepsis, for Susan can momentarily see beyond the boundaries of her fictional world to the actress who plays her.

From this moment on, we have transitioned to "On High in Blue Tomorrows," the film-within-the-film. Susan sees her husband/Smithy and runs into Smithy's house. Previously, we saw it was a flat façade, but this time around it is a fully three-dimensional (3D) space. Nonetheless, when Devon approaches, he still sees it as a flat façade, while Susan experiences it as 3D. In a further remarkable move, when Susan looks out of the window, she no longer sees a dark stage, but a front garden. Both spaces in front of and behind the façade of Smithy's house have become 3D imaginary spaces. We are back to the trope of transitioning across boundaries into new and unforeseen spaces. Susan enters the "impossible" space of Smithy's house, and she sees another impossible space, the front garden. What has happened is that Susan has moved one level down into the film-within-a-film ("On High in Blue Tomorrows"), whereas Devon remains on the level of the film (*Inland Empire*).

This play with imaginary spaces evokes Christian Metz's discussion of "The Imaginary Signifier."[16] The cinematic signifier is from the outset Imaginary (in Lacan's sense of the word) because it combines the perceptual wealth of the photographic image with the absence of the represented (as does a mirror image, in which we see ourselves in all our perceptual wealth in the Imaginary 3D space of a flat mirror). The cinematic signifier evokes an imaginary elsewhere via a play of presence and absence: "the activity of perception which [cinema] involves is real (the cinema is not a phantasy), but the perceived is not really the object, it is its shade, its phantom, its double, its *replica* in a new kind of mirror." Metz goes on to say: "More than the other arts, or in a more unique way, the cinema involves us in the imaginary: it drums up all perception, but to switch it immediately over into its own absence, which is nonetheless the only signifier present."[17] Cinema evokes something (using rich visual and aural signifiers) that is not actually there in front of us.

Lynch evokes the two spaces on either side of the façade of Smithy's house in all their perceptual wealth, but we know they are not there, they are absent; we know there is no three-dimensionality to Smithy's house (it is flat, like a mirror), and we know that in front of the façade is a dark, empty stage. Yet we see (through Susan's eyes) the interior of the house and a garden outside. The film is becoming more communicative, as we share Susan's experiences one fictional level down.

Of course, *all* filmic images play on this presence/absence. My point is that Lynch is making this play on presence/absence a *theme* of his film at this moment; this play becomes the experience of one of his characters. And this, I think, is the point of this use of the trope of duplication. To repeat my earlier point: although it is Nikki the actress at the table reading from the script, her character, Susan, is on the set. Susan can, therefore, inhabit the imaginary space of Smithy's house because she is just as fictional as the space. And this is why Devon cannot see Susan or the interior of the house. (He can only enter the film as his character Billy, and he is not in character when he goes looking for the intruder in the set.)

Susan explores Smithy's house. When she enters the bedroom, it seems familiar because it is the location where the love-making scene between Susan and Billy took place. Susan and her husband have now changed roles; the forward traveling point-of-view structure remains in place; it is simply occupied by a different character. It is she who walks along the corridors of the house and enters the bedroom. She sees her husband in the bedroom, taking off his green jacket, going to bed, and switching off the light.

Susan then reenters the living room to find several women in there. She covers her face with her hands. We then cut to her optical point of view as she uncovers her face, revealing she is now standing in a street in Łódź in Poland, at night, with two of the women who are also in her living room. After seeing the film a few times, it is possible to infer that this is another moment of metalepsis: Susan has magically transitioned to "47," the unfinished (and cursed) German version of "On High in Blue Tomorrows" set in Poland. "47" is therefore the film-within-the-film-within-the-film. The actress Laura Dern has entered the film *Inland Empire* to play an actress called Nikki. *Inland Empire* is the finished film being seen at this moment. The actress Nikki in *Inland Empire* has transitioned to Susan in "On High in Blue Tomorrows," the film-within-the-film which is in the process of being made. But while in "On High in Blue Tomorrows," the character Susan has transitioned into the incomplete film "47." Immediately afterward, we cut to the Lost Girl in the hotel room, followed by the black-and-white image of the radio transcription disc and needle. The Lost Girl's face is superimposed over this image as she explains to Susan (whose face also appears superimposed) another way to transition to the unfinished version of the film (by burning a hole into a silk shirt with a cigarette and then looking through the hole).

We cut back to Susan in her living room, and the same two women in the Polish street scene go over to the window of the living room and show that the street is just outside the house (Smithy house). The living room is not only shown not to be in Poland, but is not at ground level either. This additional juxtaposition of imaginary spaces again reminds me of Orson Welles's *The Trial*, which similarly uses creative geography for expressive ends (the creative editing expresses the metaphor that the Law is like a labyrinth, as Carroll points out[18]).

ENDINGS

The filming of "On High in Blue Tomorrows" is completed once the character of Susan Blue dies on Hollywood Boulevard. Nikki walks off the set, but does not appear to come out of character; she remains Susan Blue. These final 20 minutes of *Inland Empire* are the most complex. This is evident the moment Susan walks off the set and into a cinema where "On High in Blue Tomorrows" is already being screened. On screen, we see previous scenes from "On High in Blue Tomorrows," in addition to a few shots replicating what is happening in real time in front of it. That is, we see Susan looking off screen at the movie screen/cut to the movie screen, which shows what we have just seen—Susan looking off screen at the movie screen. In this instance, the screen is functioning like a mirror. We then see a figure walking out of the cinema and up a flight of stairs, an action shown in the movie theater and then replicated immediately on screen. These are moments of metalepsis combined with *mise en abyme*, carried out in real time. John Pier notes that *mise en abyme*, like metalepsis, is based on embedding.[19] But, in addition, *mise en abyme* involves resemblance and reduplication between levels (part of one level is simply copied and duplicated on another level, as with matryoshka nesting dolls). Susan is at the same time embedded and duplicated on screen.

This combination of metalepsis and *mise en abyme* occurs again soon after Susan shoots the Phantom (who found a "way in" to the story and seems to be haunting it; after he is shot the spell on the story is lifted). After the shooting, Susan enters the rabbit room—room number 47. The rabbits disappear as soon as she opens the door (suggesting that metalepsis is taking place, that Susan continues to transgress diegetic worlds). She then finds her way into the Lost Girl's hotel room. The Lost Girl knows she is coming, because she can see Susan on her TV. Susan then enters the Lost Girl's hotel room, embraces her, and fades away. This is not only played out in front of Lynch's camera; it is also duplicated and embedded in real time on the TV. That is, the TV now shows the hotel room from the perspective of Lynch's camera. The TV is in the shot and therefore duplicates the shot (it shows the hotel room and the TV), producing an infinite regress. This effect is created by metalepsis and *mise en abyme* working together in real time.

Finally, the Lost Girl transcends diegetic worlds by leaving her hotel room and walking into Smithy's house, where she is reunited with her husband and son. Susan's husband turns out at this level of fiction to be the Lost Girl's husband. Perhaps the film "47" has now been completed and the curse lifted? While she sat in front of the TV, the Lost Girl was watching the remake of the film that remained incomplete.

Lynch chooses a handheld digital camera to make *Inland Empire*. He also uses a multitude of storytelling formats and technologies—the radio serial; the gramophone; the TV sitcom; the folktale; plus, of course, film (and films within films). From these formats, he creates multiple diegetic worlds, each of which I have conceived as a malleable, transparent Chinese box. Each box contains its own diegetic world. This multidiegetic film does not clearly demarcate one world from another. By the end of the film, we have entered numerous boxes and exited several, but without clear orientation (linearity).

And, although most characters are locked in their own Chinese box, their own diegetic world (especially the rabbits), a few can transcend them. Nikki, of course, can mediate several diegetic worlds—the world of *Inland Empire* and, within that, Kingsley's film "On High in Blue Tomorrows," plus its German remake, "47," as well as the rabbit sitcom.

Metalepsis is one of the key rhetorical figures in Lynch's work and is central in his triptych *Lost Highway, Mulholland Dr.*, and *Inland Empire*. Although the device is not unique to contemporary cinema, it has become ever more sophisticated and complex. In all three films, Lynch combines it with *mise en abyme* and, in *Inland Empire*, the acousmatic voice. In the opening moments, this voice travels from radio to gramophone to film. It is unclear whether the whole of *Inland Empire* is an enactment of the radio play. If it is, this would add another layer of metalepsis, for *Inland Empire* becomes a film embedded in (and enacting) the radio play "Axxon N.," with "On High in Blue Tomorrows" embedded in *Inland Empire*, and "47" embedded in "On High in Blue Tomorrows." In transcending all these levels, Nikki is the most metaleptic of all the characters. But she—like the spectator—also has the tendency to confuse the different levels.

ACKNOWLEDGMENTS

Different versions of this chapter were presented at Aberystwyth University, Brunel University, the University of Liverpool, Reading University, and Tecnológico de Monterrey Campus Toluca, Mexico. I wish to thank the participants for their comments and suggestions.

NOTES

1. Raymond Bellour, "Analysis in Flames," *Diacritics* 15, no. 1 (1985): 54–56.
2. William Routt and Rick Thompson, "'Keep Young and Beautiful': Surplus and Subversion in *Roman Scandals*," *Journal of Film and Video* 42, no. 1 (1990): 19.
3. Michael Joshua Rowin, "Toy Cameras: An Interview with David Lynch," *Reverse Shot* (blog) (2006), http://www.reverseshot.com/article/interview_david_lynch.
4. Werner Wolf, "Metalepsis as a Transgeneric and Transmedial Phenomenon," in *Narratology Beyond Literary Criticism*, ed. Jan Christoph Meister (Berlin: De Gruyter, 2005), 95.
5. More radically, the Möbius strip blurs the boundary between inside and outside, reducing both to a single surface. The Möbius strip is therefore the exemplary figure of metalepsis. I have analyzed the structure of Lynch's *Lost Highway* (1997) as a Möbius strip, although I failed to refer to the concept of metalepsis. See Warren Buckland, "Making Sense of *Lost Highway*," in *Puzzle Films: Complex Storytelling in Contemporary Cinema*, ed. Warren Buckland (Boston: Wiley-Blackwell, 2009).
6. For an analysis of voice in *The Testament of Dr Mabuse*, see Michel Chion, *The Voice in Cinema* (New York: Columbia University Press, 1999), chapter 2.
7. Ibid., 91–92. Although "rosebud" does have a prior meaning, its significance remains

unknown throughout the film, even when it is anchored in the sled in the film's final moments.

8. Borges described *Citizen Kane* as a labyrinth without a centre. Such a description is even more relevant to *Inland Empire*.

9. Chion, *The Voice in Cinema*, 127.

10. See Meir Sternberg, *Expositional Modes and Temporal Ordering in Fiction* (Bloomington: Indiana University Press, 1978), especially 50–53 and 238–246, for an outline of different types of gaps in narratives.

11. In *Inland Empire*, the actress Laura Dern plays an actress called Nikki Grace. Nikki gets a role in a film called "On High in Blue Tomorrows," in which she plays a character called Susan Blue. Her husband's name is Smithy, and the house they live in is called Smithy's house. (We also need to note that, within the fictional world of *Inland Empire*, "On High in Blue Tomorrows" is a remake as an incomplete German film—made in Poland—called "47.")

12. See Noël Carroll, "Welles and Kafka," in *Interpreting the Moving Image* (Cambridge: Cambridge University Press, 1998), 191–202.

13. Sternberg, *Expositional Modes and Temporal Ordering in Fiction*, 244–245.

14. Ibid., 238–241.

15. See Ibid., 243–244, for a discussion of the relative probability of hypotheses that fill in gaps.

16. Christian Metz, "The Imaginary Signifier," in *Psychoanalysis and Cinema: The Imaginary Signifier* (London: Macmillan, 1982).

17. Ibid., 45.

18. Carroll, "Welles and Kafka."

19. John Pier, "Metalepsis," in *The Living Handbook of Narratology*, ed. Peter Hühn et al. (2010), http://hup.sub.uni-hamburg.de/lhn/index.php/Metalepsis.

SELECT BIBLIOGRAPHY

Bellour, Raymond. "Analysis in Flames." *Diacritics* 15, no. 1 (1985): 54–56.

Bellour, Raymond. "The Film We Accompany." *Rouge* 3 (2004). http://www.rouge.com.au/3/film.html.

Buckland. Warren. "Making Sense of *Lost Highway*." In *Puzzle Films: Complex Storytelling in Contemporary Cinema*, edited by Warren Buckland, 42–61. Boston: Wiley-Blackwell, 2009.

Carroll, Noël. "Welles and Kafka." In *Interpreting the Moving Image*, 191–202. Cambridge: Cambridge University Press, 1998.

Chion, Michel. *The Voice in Cinema*. New York: Columbia University Press, 1999.

Metz, Christian. "The Imaginary Signifier." In *Psychoanalysis and Cinema: The Imaginary Signifier*, 1–87. London: Macmillan, 1982.

Pier, John. "Metalepsis." In *The Living Handbook of Narratology*, edited by Peter Hühn et al., 2010. http://hup.sub.uni-hamburg.de/lhn/index.php/Metalepsis

Routt, William, and Rick Thompson. " 'Keep Young and Beautiful': Surplus and Subversion in *Roman Scandals*." *Journal of Film and Video* 42, no. 1 (1990): 17–35.

Rowin, Michael Joshua. "Toy Cameras: An Interview with David Lynch." *Reverse Shot* (blog), 2006. http://www.reverseshot.com/article/interview_david_lynch.

Sternberg, Meir. *Expositional Modes and Temporal Ordering in Fiction*. Bloomington: Indiana University Press, 1978.

Wolf, Werner. "Metalepsis as a Transgeneric and Transmedial Phenomenon." In *Narratology Beyond Literary Criticism*, edited by Jan Christoph Meister, 83–107. Berlin: De Gruyter, 2005.

PART V

DIALOGUE: VISUALIZATION AND SONIFICATION

CHAPTER 16

··

MUSEUM WITHOUT WALLS, ART HISTORY WITHOUT NAMES

Methods and Concepts for Media Visualization

··

LEV MANOVICH

In the first decade of the twenty-first century, researchers in the humanities and social sciences gradually began to adopt computational and visualization tools for working with large datasets. The majority of this work, often referred to as the "digital humanities," has focused on textual data (e.g., literature, historical records, or social media) and spatial data (e.g., locations of places and events).[1] However, visual media have remained largely outside of the new computational paradigm.

To fill this void, in 2007, we established the Software Studies Initiative at the University of California, San Diego.[2] The aim of the lab was to develop easy-to-use techniques for computational analysis and visualization of large collections of images and video for researchers in media studies, the humanities, and the social sciences.[3] This essay draws on a number of my articles written since we started the lab, in which I discuss the history of visualization, the techniques that we developed for visualizing large sets of visual media, and their applications to various types of media.[4] The reader is advised to consult these articles directly for more in-depth descriptions of the visualization methods presented here and for detailed analyses of their applications.

This essay offers a theoretical analysis of the key conceptual steps involved in generating visualizations of cultural artifacts. To differentiate cultural analytics from other visualization practices (e.g., scientific visualization, or geo visualization), we might identify this field as "culturevis." The steps and concepts associated with culturevis include "data," "metadata," "feature extraction," "information visualization," "media visualization," "mapping," and "remapping."

To move from cultural artifacts to their visualizations, we can follow a number of alternative paths. The first step shared by all of these paths is the translation of the original artifacts into data (in the case of born digital media, this step is not required). At this point, the data and existing metadata can be visualized. Alternatively, a researcher can also add new metadata to the data manually; he or she can use computational analysis to extract "features" from the data. This new metadata and/or extracted features are then used in visualization. At the visualization step, there are also alternatives: he or she can use the techniques of information visualization, which represent information using the language of points, lines, curves, and other simple geometric elements; or he or she can use recently developed techniques of "media visualization" to create new visual representations that can show large image and video collections directly.

As the use of visualization in humanities and social sciences grows, it is important to understand these steps theoretically. We need to ask what is at stake at each step, what assumptions are used, what is gained, and what is lost. And since each route will ultimately create different representations of the artifacts and generate metadata enabling different types of discoveries, it is also crucial to understand these differences. This essay begins this discussion.

The essay is organized in the following way. I first briefly review recent developments in visualization techniques, with the focus on artistic visualization. Next, I discuss the key conceptual steps that take us from artifacts to visualizations. As illustrations, I use selected visualizations created in my lab. The last section summarizes the discussion and links the new possibilities opened up by use of visualization of large visual collections to the relevant concepts developed by earlier twentieth-century art historians—Heinrich Wölfflin's "Art History Names" and André Malraux's "Museum without Walls."

VISUALIZATION TECHNIQUES

A multitude of visualization techniques are available to us (Figure 16.1).[5] The systematic history of their development remains to be written. Nevertheless, key historical milestones are known.[6] The key visualization techniques widely used today and available in popular software applications such as Excel, Tableau, manyeyes, and others were already developed in the first decades of the nineteenth century. They include pie charts, bar charts, line graphs, scatterplots, radar charts, and histograms. The same period also witnessed the development of two-dimensional (2D) thematic maps. The adoption of computers since the 1970s led to many new techniques, as well as to a gradual increase in the information density of representations, since software programs could visualize much larger amounts of data than was practical to do by hand. The rapid development of three-dimensional (3D) computer graphics technologies in the 1980s facilitated the development of the new field of scientific visualization. The 1990s saw the rise of

FIGURE 16.1 Exploring a 44,000 × 44,000 pixel visualization of 1 million manga pages on HIPerSpace scaled display system. HIPerSpace offers 35,840 × 8,000 pixel resolution (287 megapixels) on a 31.8 feet wide by 7.5 feet tall display wall made from seventy 30-inch monitors. Visualization was rendered with free ImagePlot software created in our lab. Courtesy of Lev Manovich and Jeremy Douglass, 2009.

information visualization that introduced new 2D visualization techniques (such as hyperbolic trees and treemaps) for representing non-numerical data.

In the late 1990s, information visualization started to attract the attention of new media artists; by 2004, their work reached the point at which it became meaningful to talk about a new area of "artistic visualization."[7] Although this new area of culture continued to grow, with visualization projects included in major museum exhibitions, the term itself remained problematic (for one thing, the most celebrated examples of artistic visualizations were created by professionally trained designers Ben Fry and Lee Byron and scientist Martin Wattenberg). One way to define artistic visualization is by contrasting it to the "normal" use of visualization in science, business, and mass media. If these fields use visualization functionally, with a designer aiming to represent the relationships in data given to her by the client without making any independent statement about it (we call this position "design neutrality"), artistic visualization projects deliberately aim to make such statements. The goal, in other words, is not a representation of data for its own sake but rather a statement about the world and human beings made through particular choices of the datasets and their presentation.[8]

As artistic visualization became popular with digital artists and designers, the number of people doing this work increased (significant factors here include the development of high-level graphics programming languages designed specifically for artists, such as Processing, and the availability of social media data from major companies, such as Flickr and Twitter via their APIs). Competition on the level of form became another distinguishing feature of artistic visualization. We can say that the history of visualization entered a new "modernist" stage in which the invention of new techniques (or, at least, new variations of the existing techniques) came to be valued for its own sake. Indeed, a survey of the most influential artistic visualization projects of 2000s shows that none of them used well-known visualization techniques but instead defined new ones. Some of these new techniques were given explicit names and were subsequently adopted by other designers (e.g., the arc diagrams introduced in *The Shape of Song* by Martin Wattenberg, 2001, or the Streamgraph from Lee Byron's *Listening History*, 2006); others only appeared in unique visualization projects (Fernanda B. Viégas and Martin Wattenberg, *History Flow*, 2002; Ben Fry, *On the Origin of Species: The Preservation of Favored Traces* 2009).

However, artistic projects that are able to introduce truly new visualization techniques are exceptions; the majority of projects are only able to distinguish themselves by customizing preexisting techniques. For example, consider visualcomplexity.com, the influential collection of projects that visualize complex networks curated by designer and writer Manual Lima since 2004. Browsing this collection of more than 700 visualizations can create an impression of almost infinite visual diversity. However, filtering them by "method" shows that many of the projects are variations produced using a small number of visualization methods.[9] In other words, the apparent diversity of the visualization field today is partly an artifact of software that allows for rendering the same fundamental layouts in a multitude of ways.

The endless surface variations generated by a small number of fundamental visualization techniques hide another important constant, which has not changed since Charles de Fourcroy's proportional squares graphs (1782) and William Playfair's line graph and bar chart (1786).[10] All information visualization techniques use a small vocabulary of discrete abstract elements: rectangles, circles, and straight and curved lines. Thus, the visual language of visualization is similar to that of modernist geometric abstraction (1912–) and modern graphic design (1919–). Do the graphs that first appeared in the second part of the eighteenth century and became commonplace in scientific publications in the first part of the nineteenth century anticipate the development of abstract visual language in art and design a hundred years later? This is just one of many intriguing questions waiting to be investigated by the future historians of visualization.[11]

How can we use visualization in the humanities and in media studies? The common sequence of steps used to create a visualization involves gathering data, organizing it in an appropriate format, and transforming it into still images, animations, or interactive interfaces using already existing or newly proposed techniques. If we want to visualize existing data *about* cultural artifacts—for example, lists of the most popular books on amazon.com, the number of artworks in different genres in a museum collection, or the dates and locations of tens of thousands of letters exchanged by Enlightenment thinkers in the eighteenth century (as does the *Mapping the Republic of Letters* project at Stanford University)[12]—we can follow the same sequence of steps. In this workflow, information about *the lives of media artifacts* is transformed into the familiar graphical elements of information visualization: points, lines, and other graphical elements.

But can visualization also support—and hopefully augment—the key methodology of the humanities: the systematic and detailed examination of *cultural artifacts themselves*, as opposed to only the data about the social and economic lives of
these artifacts? For example, the *Mapping the Republic of Letters* project successfully uses visualization to examine correspondence patterns between European
Enlightenment thinkers. Can visualization also show the content of tens of thousands
of Enlightenment letters directly, rather than only their dates, authors, and locations,
in such a way that we can perform detailed readings of these letters and at the same
time see large-scale patterns? Or, to take another example, can visualization further
André Malraux's idea of a "museum without walls" (comparing themes and formal
elements in all photographed works of art[13]), which he proposed in the middle of the
twentieth century? For instance, can we compare millions of professional artworks
available on museum web sites, or billions of user-generated artworks on social media
sites? In other words, how do we combine microscopic and telescopic vision, "reading" the actual artifacts and "reading" larger patterns abstracted from very large sets
of these artifacts?

Media Versus Data

Normally, a visualization designer works for a client who provides him or her with data;
the designer's job is to figure out the best way to display this data so the relationships and
patterns within it become visible. However, if you are a media or humanities scholar,
there is no given "data" to start with. Instead, you have concrete artifacts that can come
from a variety of different cultural fields: literature, cinema, user-generated digital content, interactive design, web design, computer games, web sites, blogs, books, photographs, visual art, films, cartoons, motion graphics, graphic design, industrial design,
fashion, and so on. This means that the default assumption of visualization design—that
you can start with some already existing data—can't be taken for granted.

There are a number of important conceptual issues involved in turning cultural artifacts into data—here I will describe just three of them.[14]

First, the steps for translating cultural artifacts into "data" that captures their content,
form, and use (reading, sharing, remixing, etc.) are not standardized—in many cases,
they have to be invented and theorized. For example, what is the "data" of a web page?
To make a web search work, Google algorithms extract more than 200 "signals" from
every web page they find including the text, links, fonts and colors, and layout.[15] Would
such a representation of a web page be appropriate if I want to study and visualize the
evolution of web design since 1996, using a sample of 150 billion historical snapshots of
web pages from archive.org?[16] The seemingly logical answer is that this depends on the
questions I want to ask. For Google, the goal is to determine the pages most relevant to
the user's query. However, for media researchers, starting with well-formulated questions does not exploit what visualization is best at: exploring without preconceptions a

large dataset to discover "what is there" and revealing unexpected patterns, as opposed to testing already formulated ideas. We can call such processes *exploratory visualization*.

Even in the case of the most familiar "old media" artifacts, such as printed books, it is not immediately obvious what their "data" might be. Although many digital humanists and literary scholars analyze dematerialized "texts," disregarding the particular formats in which they were presented to the readers, the Google search algorithms suggest that if we are interested in the reception of literature as a print medium, we do need to take into account all the details of its appearance and materiality (fonts, colors, line spacing, layout, margins, etc.).

Second, being able to translate media artifacts into data often requires specialized technical knowledge in addition to domain knowledge: image processing in the case of images, computational linguistics in the case of text, audio signal processing in the case of music. To take a concrete example from our lab's research, we downloaded tens of thousands of pages of *Science* and *Popular Science* magazines published between 1870 and 1922 from Google Books and found that different sets of pages have different contrast levels. Let's say we decide that we will normalize the contrast (a decision which itself needs to be theoretically motivated). There is no single right way of doing it. There are various image processing algorithms that can be used, and each will produce a different kind of "data" as a result.

Third, transforming collections of artifacts into data and then visualizing this data may "throw the baby away with the bathwater." That is, working with visualizations of data representing certain aspects of cultural artifacts can lead to new understandings, but it is not a substitute for the insights one gains by viewing the artifacts themselves. Although all standard visualization techniques involve some reduction in order to reveal patterns, this new visibility is also accompanied by *opacity*, as the media artifacts with all their aesthetic richness and semantic detail are substituted by abstract elements such as points, rectangles, and lines.

"Close reading" (examining artifacts directly) and "distant reading" (examining patterns revealed by visualization) lead to different kinds of knowledge. For instance, examining a text cloud visualization that shows the frequencies of the most widely used words in a text is not the same as carefully reading the text itself. To take an opposing example, looking at the images of 9,000 pages from *Popular Science* magazine (see Figure 16.2 below) is not the same as examining a graph that shows the numbers of images in the magazine's pages per year. Our visualization of pages from 1870 to 1922 reveals a gradual increase in the number of images appearing in the magazine, but to understand the exact shape of this pattern, we need to look at a graph.

This discussion should explain why I gave the field of artistic visualization a prominent place in my brief sketch of the recent history of visualization. The "artistic" dimension of artistic visualization relevant for the humanities problematizes the standard visualization process, specifically the translation of some already existing "reality" into data. This reality (i.e., the choice of the data and its organization) does not exist beforehand, but is defined by the artist.

Additionally, if representational cultural artifacts perform a translation from a story, a visible world, memory, or imagination into the signs in the artifact, visualization requires a secondary translation that maps the materiality of the artifacts into something that can be put into a spreadsheet or a database. In other words, it is a representation of a representation, a map of a map. Like any new map, it selects and omits, reveals some things, and makes others invisible.

DATA VERSUS METADATA

Having understood some of the conceptual and practical challenges of translating media artifacts into data, let us now assume that this step has been accomplished, so we can move forward in our discussion. Usually media artifacts come with some metadata recorded by institutions, individuals, or software systems. For instance, more than 1 million digital images of art, architecture, and photography available on artstor.org are annotated with the name of the artist, year and country of creation, original artifact size, and more. The metadata for every video on YouTube includes category, tags, upload date, number of views, and numbers of likes and dislikes.

This metadata also needs to be problematized. Rather than taking for granted these categories, we need to ask if they are meaningful for understanding cultural processes. For example, in the case of social media, it is common to analyze metadata about the countries where the users live. But what does it mean that a particular user lives in country X? Does she live in a capital or in a small city? Was she born there or had she just moved there recently for school or work? In other words, the default assumption that a set of random people associated with country X will have something in common and "represent" this country is ungrounded. The same applies to other standard demographic categories, such as gender and age.

Metadata is defined as data about data. For example, in the case of YouTube, the video files are the data; their tags, categories, upload dates, and number of views are the metadata. Twentieth-century media researchers studied individual media artifacts or groups of artifacts (for instance, individual feature films or films of a particular director), and the metadata was only used for library searches. However, as the amount of media artifacts generated by billions of consumer devices keeps growing, a close reading of even a tiny portion of these artifacts becomes impossible (by the middle of 2012, Facebook users were uploading 10 billion photos per month, and this number continues to grow).

As a result, a new type of media research became popular in computer science, the industry, and often in digital humanities. The *researchers began to analyze the metadata about the media artifacts, rather than the artifacts themselves.* Metadata is smaller in size than the actual data, it contains structured categorical information that is easy to graph and analyze, and it can reveal information that can't be found in the data itself. For example, the *Mapping the Republic of Letters* projects uses visualization to examine

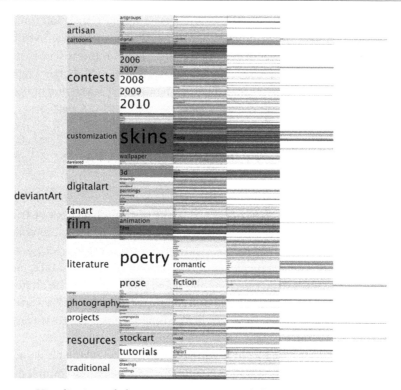

FIGURE 16.2 Visualization of the category structure of deviantArt online community for user-created artworks. Each category is represented as a rectangle. The categories are positioned left to right in the order of their hierarchy (e.g., Photography/People & Portraits/ Glamour Portraits/). The height of each category rectangle corresponds to the number of images in the corresponding category, as represented in our 1 million images sample. (The original visualization also uses a pink to blue color gradient to represent the ratio of female to male users in each category.) Courtesy of Hanley Wang, 2012.

patterns in correspondence between European Enlightenment thinkers using such metadata as dates, who wrote to whom, and their geographic locations. This is a typical example of an analysis in which metadata itself becomes the primary object of study. Similarly, numerous free software tools allow you to analyze patterns associated with your Twitter and Facebook profiles, such as showing stats about the number of followers of every user who favored or retweeted every one of your tweets.

Another example of metadata as the subject of analysis comes from a project in my lab to explore deviantArt, the largest social network for user-generated art. We started by downloading a sample of 1 million images, as well as the associated metadata—user screen names, image upload dates, and the categories in which the creators placed each image. This metadata allows us to visualize the images in different ways. For instance, we can compare images submitted by different users, look at the patterns in deviantArt growth since 2000 using upload dates, and also compare images in different categories.

However, the category structure of deviantArt is so interesting that we can study it as an artifact in its own right. Consisting of close to 2,000 separate labels organized into a hierarchical tree with as many as seven levels (e.g., Customization/Skins & Themes/ Linux and Unix Utilities/Desktop Environments/KDE/Styles/, Photography/People & Portraits/Spontaneous Portraits), this system presents us with a fascinating portrait of the contemporary cultural imagination and the landscape into which people invest their creative energies. Comparing this category system with the ones used by museums and academics to describe visual media reveals the massive gap between institutions of high culture and the real world. Whereas categories such as sculpture, painting, drawing, or experimental film are also present in deviantArt, most of its designations do not have high-culture equivalents (e.g., stock images, street art/stickers, or digital art/pixel art/ characters/isometric), and yet they constitute the larger part of "nonprofessional art" today (Figure 16.2).

To summarize: what are metadata from one perspective are data from another perspective.

Visualizing Metadata Versus Visualizing Media

Metadata usually consists of text, numbers, or geographic coordinates. We have access to a multitude of visualization techniques developed over the past 300 years to represent these data types. These techniques are readily available in graphing, mapping, and data analysis software, both free and commercial (this is another reason why practically all visualizations of humanities-based artifacts show only the metadata, but not the arti- facts themselves).

In the 2000s, a few projects by digital media artists and visualization designers dem- onstrated that it is possible to construct visualizations that show not only information about the images or video collections, but the images themselves. These projects (*The Top Grossing Film of All Time, 1 x 1* by Jason Salavon, 2000; *Cinema Redux* by Brendan Dawes, 2004, and a few others) sampled a feature film and then displayed the sampled frames in a rectangular grid in a sequence corresponding to the frames' order in the film. We created free software tools that implemented this technique with additional options and extended its use to collections of still images. We have successfully used these tools to visualize patterns in collections of magazine covers, newspaper pages, comic and manga books, web sites, films, animation, motion graphics, and other media types.

Presenting images from a collection in a grid organized according to existing meta- data (such as creation or upload dates) is the simplest way of visualizing an image col- lection.[17] We call this technique *collection montage*. This technique can be seen as an extension of the most basic intellectual operation used in the humanities—*comparison* between a small number of artifacts. However, if twentieth-century technologies only allowed for a comparison between a small number of artifacts at the same time—for example, the standard lecturing method in art history was to use two slide projectors to show two images side by side—we can now compare tens of thousands of images by displaying them simultaneously on a computer screen and interactively changing the layouts. The graphic capacities of current laptops, tablets, and smart phones also allow us to interact in real time with these visualizations—zooming in and out and sorting image sets in different ways using any of the available metadata.

This quantitative extension leads to a qualitative change in the kinds of observations that can be made about media collections. Being able to display large numbers of images simultaneously allows us to see gradual and subtle historical changes over long periods of time, to find which images are typical and which are unique, and to understand patterns of similarity and difference between multiple image collections (Figure 16.3).

Although collection montage is conceptually simple, it is quite challenging to characterize it theoretically. Given that information visualization normally starts with text, numbers, network connections, or other nonvisual data, and then represents these data in a visual domain, is it appropriate to consider image montage as a visualization method? If traditional information visualization techniques translate *data into pictures*, a collection montage technique translates *pictures into pictures*.

I think that calling image montage a "visualization" is justified if, instead of focusing on the transformation from nonvisual to visual, we focus on another key aspect of visualization: arranging the visual elements in a particular spatial layout to highlight patterns that are hard to observe in raw data. Seen from this perspective, collection montage is a legitimate visualization method. For example, the current interface of Google Books cannot present thousands of pages of a magazine such as *Popular Science* on a single screen, so it is hard to understand how the magazine evolved over time. However, when we gather all these pages and arrange them in a particular layout (see Figure 16.3), these patterns become visible.

In its simplest form, collection montage shows all of the images in a collection. In the case of video, it is more useful to sample and show only select frames (as was done in the pioneering artistic visualization projects that I referred to earlier). We can also apply this method to any sequential media, such as pages from newspapers or comic books. For instance, an animated visualization created by my undergraduate student Cyrus Kiani uses 5,930 front pages from *The Hawaiian Star* covering the period between 1893 and 1912.[18] The animation of 5,930 front pages of the newspaper issues published during these twenty years for the first time make visible how the visual design of modern print media changes over time, in search of the form appropriate to the new conditions of reception and new rhythms of modern life. (Some of the important relevant cultural changes during this period include development of abstract art, which then leads to modern graphic design; the introduction of image-oriented magazines, such as *Vogue*; the new medium of cinema; the invention of the photo telegraph; and the first telefax machine.)

When we sample a video or visualize a very large image collection, the sampling procedure should not be thought of as a simple mechanical step (e.g., sampling a video at 1 frame per second) or as a necessary strategy for dealing with larger data (as it was understood in nineteenth- and twentieth-century statistics). For instance, we can easily create a visualization showing all 160,000 frames making up a typical feature film (90 minutes = 5,400 seconds = 162,000 frames, assuming 30 fps), but the result will not be useful. Instead, we should think of *sampling as a creative strategy* that can be applied to any dimension of media data. For example, we can sample both in time (selecting every Nth image) and in space (selecting only a part of every image).

By experimenting with different ways of arranging these media samples, novel patterns can be discovered. For instance, I made a visualization that compared the first and last frames of every shot in the 1928 film *Eleventh Year* by Russian directory Dziga Vertov. "Vertov" is a neologism invented by the film director, who adapted it as his last name early in his career. It comes from the Russian verb *vertet*, which means "to rotate." "Vertov" may refer both to the manual movement involved in filming in the 1920s—rotating the handle of a camera—and also to the dynamism of the film language developed by Vertov who, along with a number of other Russian and European filmmakers, designers, and photographers working in that decade, wanted to "defamiliarize" everyday reality by using dynamic diagonal compositions and unusual points of

FIGURE 16.3 Collection montage visualization of 9,900 pages from *Popular Science* magazine from the beginning of publication in 1872 to 1922. The visualization uses the third page of every issue, arranged left to right and top to bottom in the order of publication. This page: a closeup. Next page: full visualization. In the first three decades of its publication, *Popular Science* used very few images. The change in magazine ownership in 1912 dramatically manifests itself in the sudden jump in the number of images and ads and new layout strategies. However, when we zoom out to see the whole visualization, we notice that this change was already anticipated by the gradual increase in the number of images during the preceding decade. Courtesy of William Huber, 2010.

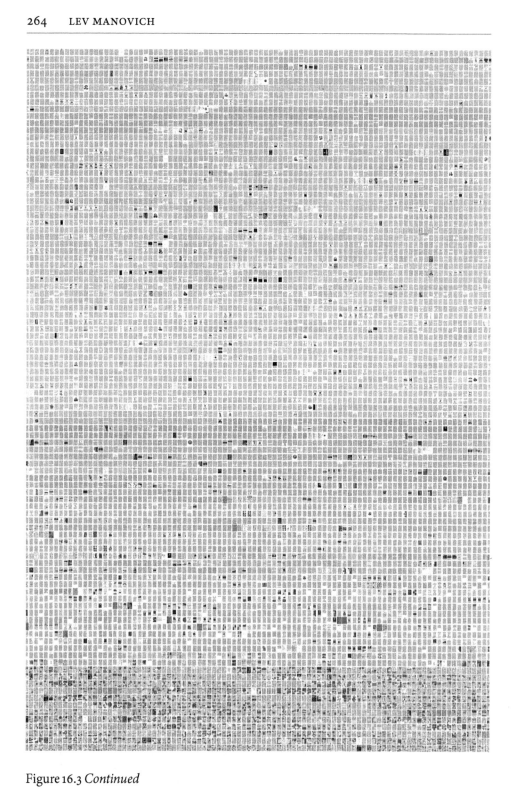

Figure 16.3 *Continued*

view, such as shooting from below or from above. However, my visualization suggests a very different picture of Vertov. Almost every shot from *The Eleventh Year* starts and ends with practically the same composition and subject. In other words, the shots are largely static.

A rectangular grid is not the only way to visualize an image collection. Figure 16.4 shows another technique that we use equally frequently. Here, images are sorted in two dimensions according to their visual characteristics and/or metadata. When we use this technique, an image collection (or a set of sampled frames from a video) is often transformed into what visually looks like a cloud, with image density varied in different parts of the visualization. Images with similar characteristics form tight clusters, whereas images with unique characteristics lie outside these groupings.

This technique extends the familiar scatterplot by adding images on top of the data points and therefore we call it *image plot*. In general, we refer to the renderings that show the actual images in a collection as *media visualizations*—to contrast this method with *information visualization* that can only show information about the collection. Collection montage and image plot are two types of media visualization we use most frequently, but there are also many other ways to organize a collection in a single view.

The conceptual operation behind media visualizations can be called *remapping*. What do I mean by this? In mathematics, mapping is a function that creates a correspondence between the elements in two domains. The example of mapping in media is the projection systems used to create 2D images of 3D scenes, such as isometric projection and perspective projection. We can also think of the well-known triad of signs defined by Charles Pierce (icon, index, symbol) as different types of mapping between an object and its sign.[19] Understood in this way, any representation is the result of a mapping operation.

Modern industrial media—photography, film, and audio and video recoding—led to the emergence of a popular artistic strategy: using an already existing media artifact and creating a new meaning or aesthetic effect by sampling and rearranging its parts. This strategy has been central to modern art since the 1950s. Its different manifestations include pop art, remix, appropriation art, and a significant portion of media art—from Bruce Conner's first compilation film *A Movie* (1958) to Douglas Gordon's *24 Hour Psycho* (1993), Joachim Sauter and Dirk Joachim' *The Invisible Shapes of Things Past* (1995), Jennifer and Kevin McCoy' *Every Shot/Every Episode* (2001), and numerous others.

Because many of these media art projects derive their meanings and aesthetic effects from systematically rearranging samples from original media, I think it is logical to refer to them not as mappings, but rather as *remappings*. If the original media object—a newspaper page, a television news program, a feature film, or the like—created a particular media map of "reality," the art project that rearranges its elements is a remapping. Visualizations that create new visual representations of the media collections (or their samples) can be similarly understood as such remappings. They are the new maps to help us navigate and critically analyze the original media maps.

At the same time, many media projects that use strategies of sampling and remapping can be retroactively understood as "media visualizations." They examine ideological patterns in mass media, experiment with new ways of navigating and interacting with media, and defamiliarize our perceptions.

Finally, although at first glance the purpose of visualization is simply "revealing patterns in the data," it is certainly possible to defend the position that the visualizations of media collections described here are closer to media art. Any remapping is a reinterpretation of an original media map, which creates new meanings and leads to new interpretations.

Media visualization represents one answer to the fundamental question of how to bring together close and distant reading. Step away, and you can see larger patterns across a whole media collection. Step closer, and you can study the details of individual images. This is not something that you can do with a traditional information visualization that would represent images as points.

From a semiotic perspective, media visualization also functions differently than information visualizations. The abstract elements of information visualization are "symbols" (to use Pierce's typology of signs); that is, they are signs that signify by convention. In this, information visualization can be contrasted with geographic maps that signify by resemblance and thus, semiotically, are "icons." In contrast, media visualizations show us the original objects themselves, so there is no semiotic translation involved. Rather than being symbolic representations of objects or their iconic maps, they are the instruments for understanding—a new epistemological technology enabled by software.

Media visualization relies on our ability to instantly see patterns in a single image. It constructs a new image out of all images (or their samples) in a collection, arranging them in such a way that patterns across these images can be easily seen. Note that this method would not work with sound or text collections, since listening and reading unfold in time. So, for example, although we can arrange thousands of letters in a single high-resolution visualization, as we do with images, it would not work as effectively. But if we arrange hundreds of thousands of images together (sorted by metadata or by visual features, as described later), the patterns are easy to see.

ADDING NEW METADATA VERSUS EXTRACTING FEATURES

The two fundamental methods just described—using information visualization techniques to reveal patterns in the metadata and using techniques drawn from media and digital art to display the actual large media collections or their samples organized by metadata—differ with regard to what is being visualized. Information visualization shows the metadata about the media. Media visualization shows the actual data. Neither method requires additional new information; instead, both use already existing meta-data and the contents of a collection.

I now present two other methods that rely on augmenting media data with new infor-mation. Both require additional work to add this information, but differ in terms of how the information is created.

One method is to manually add text descriptions, such as tags. Since the emergence of social media, this method has also entered the popular culture. For example, people rou-tinely add tags to images they upload to Flickr (I am using Flickr as an example because it popularized user-generated tagging, which has since become a default feature on most social media platforms). If Flickr's tag system employs an "open vocabulary" model in which any user can introduce new tags, researchers usually follow a "closed vocabulary" model, in which they agree on the set of tags to be used to annotate a media collection.

Some social media sites such as deviantArt also use hierarchical categorical systems to organize media submissions (see Figure 16.2). These categorical systems are more useful than simple tags, but they must be approached with caution. For example, we found that whereas most deviantArt artists place their submissions in the appropriate categories, many do not. For example, the category "paintings" also contains many drawings.

Another limitation of manually added metadata (regardless of whether created by institutions such as museums to describe their collections or individual users describ-ing the media they upload) is that the divisions created may blind us to other ways of categorizing the artifacts and to other types of differences between them. Both newly added and already existing metadata may also lead us to assume that the categories used to classify artifacts have clear boundaries whereas, in reality, they may be fuzzy, and the categories may overlap. For example, let's say we are analyzing photos uploaded by users to a social media site such as Flickr or Picasa, and we want to compare the images from different cities. But do big cities have clear boundaries? European cities in the Middle Ages were limited by city walls, but this is not the case today. If we describe a "city" using a function with variables such as population density, number of restaurants, cafes, shop-ping and entertainment facilities, and the like, we will find that, today, in most cities, this function may change gradually from the center to the periphery, without any sharp drops that would define the city's boundary. So, what exactly we are comparing if we use images tagged as (for example) "Seoul" and "San Paolo"?

In summary, I want to suggest that instead of automatically assuming that metadata categories describe data in objective and faithful way, *we need to think of data and its metadata as two related but ultimately independent entities*. This view has two conse-quences. On the one hand, *metadata needs to be approached as a separate dataset to be investigated in its own right*—rather than as an accurate map of the data. On the other hand, *automatic data analysis* (to be discussed later) *is likely to reveal clusters and pat-terns that do not correspond to the classification provided by already existing metadata*.

Modern social scientists and qualitative marketing researchers use yet another method to describe sets of objects—rating them using quantitative or qualitative scales. We can also use this approach to describe media artifacts. For instance, the "abstract"/"representational" qualities of each painting in a collection can be rated using a 1 to 10 scale.

Whether we add tags, construct our own data categories, or use rating scales, all these manual techniques for adding new information about media collection have two crucial limitations. The first is that they don't work well with large datasets. Although a single person can annotate every shot of a feature film in one day, annotating 1 million images in our deviantArt sample would be a real challenge even if we use crowdsourcing. (In the industry, some companies are able to successfully annotate large media datasets by employing a large staff. For example, the Pandora music recommendation engine relies on a team that tags each new song using 400 different attributes; after ten years in business, it has a database of 800,000 songs.[20])

The second limitation involves the use of one semiotic system (natural languages) to describe another (visual media). Having developed much later than the human physical senses, natural languages complement them in their function. The senses can capture and process signals, differentiate between fine gradations in these signals, and construct representations of the environment from the information they carry. By contrast, a natural language, such as English, Russian, or Mandarin, is good for reasoning about the particular and the general, describing temporal relations, forming abstract categories, and differentiating between *qualities*—but it does not try to compete with our sensory capacity to capture *quantitative* distinctions. Therefore, natural languages are limited in their ability to describe *media aesthetics*. Words can't effectively capture the full range of variations among color, texture, composition, rhythm, movement, and other analog dimensions of media.

The first limitation (scale) means that the manual annotation method would not work for researching the aesthetics of user-generated media, such as the deviantArt network, which currently contains more than 200 million user submitted artworks. Manual annotation can, however, work with small collections of art from the past, such as the BBC *Your Paintings* digital archive of 200,000 paintings in UK museums.[21] However, the second limitation (the inability of natural languages to register fine quantitative differences) is always present, regardless of the size of a collection.

Instead of manual annotations, we can use well-established computer techniques to automatically process and extract information from images and video about their form and content. Originally developed in the fields of digital image processing and computer vision, today, these techniques are also used in many research areas and practical applications including content-based image search, video summarization, and video fingerprinting. Hundreds of millions of people using digital media software, web services, and imaging devices such as digital cameras are familiar with a few of these techniques—for example, face detection in iPhoto and Facebook, or smile detection used in digital cameras. Other techniques remain invisible to consumers, but they form the foundation of the digital media industry because they are built into all digital media devices and applications. For instance, when you take a picture with a digital camera using automatic exposure setting, the software in the camera chip analyzes light information captured by the image sensor, measuring gray and color values of every pixel, and then algorithmically adjusts these values to produce an image with the best contrast. In our lab, we adopted existing techniques to create open source software tools that can automatically extract dozens (or even hundreds) of separate pieces of information from every image in a collection or every frame of a video. One such tool (QTIP) can process between 100 and 200 desktop-size images per second, extracting fifty separate descriptions.[22]

The difference between manual and automatic methods of augmenting data with new information is not only a matter of procedure and speed. The two methods also represent two different ways of understanding media. When we tag or annotate, it is logical to describe this process as *adding* additional information to the media.

When we analyze images automatically to describe their properties using numbers, we engage in a different practice. In computer science, the process of automatically analyzing images and video is called *feature extraction*.[23] The assumption is that the computer automatically and objectively extracts the information that is already present in the images or video. The features are the statistics summarizing different types of information that can be calculated from all the pixels making up an image. Examples include average brightness, saturation and hue, number of edges and their orientations, the positions of corners, measurements of texture, most frequently appearing colors, and so on. In the case of video, in addition to analyzing visual properties of every frame, temporal features such as the positions of cuts and other types of transitions between shots are also extracted (this process is called *cuts detection*).

In practical applications such as *content-based image search* (searching images by their content, which in this context means both the objects in images and visual elements such as dominant colors), hundreds of features are extracted by software to provide a comprehensive representation of every image. Although it is well known that the choice of features to be extracted has a crucial effect on the success of a particular application, there is no general theory that would specify which features are to be used in different cases, so this choice depends on the experience of the researchers.

The two approaches to augmenting media data—manual annotation and automatic extraction—have complementary strengths. Whereas computers can capture the fine details of a visual form, it is very difficult for them to understand the representational content of media. Humans, however, can do this easily. Given an arbitrary image, we can immediately recognize any common objects it may contain such as a face, sky, houses, trees, cars, and so on.

In their turn, natural languages can't capture small differences in images that are related to their appearances as opposed to semantics. For instance, try to describe using words the differences between the rendering of sky and clouds in all of Turner's landscapes or the movement patterns in tens of thousands of motion graphics works.[24] The human brain can certainly compute such fine differences, and they drive our aesthetic and emotional responses to visual media, be it painting, visual effects in cinema, fashion, product design, or interfaces. (If we could not distinguish these differences, artists and designers would not use them in their creations.) However, the results of the brain's computation are not accessible to the language system.

Instead of a limited number of linguistic categories, computers can describe many details of a visual form with infinite precision using numbers. For example, let's say that we want to measure the average brightness of an image. Typically, in digital images, brightness values are represented on a scale that has 256 values. Every pixel in an image has a gray scale value between 0 (pure black) and 255 (pure white). To measure average brightness, we add the gray scale values of every pixel and divide them by the total number of pixels in the image. The result is a real number (a "real number" is a number that contains a fraction: for instance, 129.54, or 178.51), which means that this measurement scale can have infinite number of possible values. But even if we round off these numbers, we will still have a scale of 256 distinct values describing average brightness— which provides us with a much more nuanced system than the few terms available in English language such as "dark" and "light."

In the same way, we can use a numerical scale to characterize the orientations of all lines in an image, its most prominent colors, the size and positions of all distinct shapes, and hundreds of other characteristics.

Since the manual annotation and feature extraction methods complement one another, we can combine them in studying massive media datasets. For example, in our deviantArt analysis project, we ran image processing software on the whole set of 1 million images, extracting various features from every image. We also selected a small sample of a few hundred images and tagged them manually, describing characteristics of these images that computers can't capture.

MEDIA VISUALIZATIONS USING EXTRACTED FEATURES

Although the features extracted from media collections can be explored using standard information visualization techniques such as histograms and scatterplots, they can be also used to drive *media visualizations*. For example, we can sort the images in a collection according to a particular visual feature, such as average color hue, and then render a montage visualization using the sorted sequence. We can also create a 2D scatterplot by mapping individual features to horizontal and vertical axes, then render the images on top of the points. We find this type of visualization to be particularly useful, and we call it *image plot*.[25]

Image plots allow us to compare different image collections or subsets of a single collection according to various visual characteristics. As an example, Figure 16.4 shows an image plot that compares sample images from the "Traditional" and "Digital Art" categories in our deviantArt dataset. Each plot contains 90,000 images.

Our method of extracting visual features and then using them for media visualization draws on existing approaches in computer science, but with one crucial difference. In the fields of computer vision, content-based image search and image classification, single visual features are never used by themselves. Instead, hundreds of features are combined together in the hope of creating a unique "signature" for every image. If, for instance, a user wants to find all the images in a database similar to a particular image, the computer compares the signatures of the input image to the signatures of all the other images in the database and returns the images that have the most similar signatures. (Google's "search similar images" feature, introduced in 2009, is implemented in this fashion.[26])

This approach can be also used for media research—for instance, to identify all the faces or people in a museum collection. However, if we use computers to analyze visual media according to a priori linguistic categories such as "face" or "person," we miss out on another powerful approach to computer-enabled large visual data analysis—*exploratory visualization*. Using a media visualization approach, we can explore arbitrary large datasets to simply see "what is there," in the process finding patterns that do not correspond to preexisting semantic categories. For such free exploration of a collection, we do not need to generate image signatures, which combine hundreds of features or analyze image content. Instead, a much simpler technique is sufficient. Although many of the features that can be extracted from images are not meaningful to a human observer (such as the gray scale differences between neighboring pixels used to characterize texture), some of them do have direct perceptual meaning. Examples of such features are used in Figure 16.4: average brightness and average saturation. To efficiently explore a large image collection, we can sort it in two dimensions, repeatedly using various

FIGURE 16.4 Image plots visualizations comparing images in Traditional Art (*left*) and Digital Art (*right*) categories from deviantArt online community for user-created art. Each plot shows 90,000 images sorted by average brightness (X-axis) and average saturation (Y-axis). (The original visualization is in color.) Visualizations show that images in Digital Art category have more variability on both brightness and saturation dimensions. Digital Art category also has substantially larger proportion of images which are either dark overall or use dark backgrounds. Finally, it also has more colorful images (higher saturation values). Courtesy of Jay Chow, 2012.

combinations of these features. (The interactive visualization application, which we developed for super high-resolution visual supercomputer HIPerSpace, can do this in real time with up to 10,000 images of any size.[27] Our desktop software ImagePlot currently has to render each visualization separately, but as computer speed advances, with time, it will also be possible to quickly go through various combinations on a desktop.)

What do I mean by a *perceptual meaning*? Thinking about media images in terms of average brightness or average saturation is not obvious. These features do not directly correspond to our intuitive judgments about images. However, if I ask you to sort a number of images from the darkest to the lightest, the result will be similar to what we can obtain by mapping these images according to their average brightness feature as extracted by a computer. Such visualization makes immediate perceptual sense: we understand that the images were sorted from the darkest to the lightest. Other features that have such direct perceptual meaning are the number of edges, the number of shapes, the dominant orientation of lines, the average hue, or the proportion of areas with texture. Although some of them, such as average hue, may appear counterintuitive, when a large number of images are sorted using such features, the result is immediately meaningful.

To explore image collections, we can generate many visualizations, each sorting images in two dimensions using different combinations of features. The method is simple enough to be taught in a single session, and my undergraduate students have successfully used it in a number of classes I taught. Obviously, we can also use existing or newly added semantic metadata in these visualizations—as, for example, in Figure 16.4, which compares two subsets of our deviantArt collection using existing category information.

It is also possible to combine single visual features to arrive at more "high-level" dimensions of visual form—for instance, "calm/dynamic," or "flat/3D." However, doing this is not trivial.[28] It is not a priori clear which features best characterize such high-level dimensions or what is the right way to combine them. In computer vision and related fields, researchers use the term *semantic gap* to describe the distance that needs to be overcome between what a computer can see—features extracted from pixel values—and the content and meanings of an image as perceived by a human observer. More recently, scientists introduced a related term, *emotional gap*, defined as "the lack of coincidence between the measurable signal properties, commonly referred to as features, and the expected affective state in which the user is brought by perceiving the signal."[29] Similarly, we can define a *media aesthetics gap* as the distance between features that computers can extract from media images and human judgments about the aesthetics of these images.

MUSEUM WITHOUT WALLS, ART HISTORY WITHOUT NAMES

In this essay, I discussed some of the key concepts and operations involved in visualizing media collections: data, metadata, feature extraction, mapping, remapping, information visualization, and media visualization. These concepts and operations are the building blocks that can be combined into a number of methods that can take us from artifacts to their visualizations—but in different ways and with different outputs that can support different types of questions.

Once media artifacts are translated into digital data, we can decide what will be visualized. Traditional information visualization techniques are useful for exploring patterns in metadata already associated with these artifacts, new metadata manually added by researchers, or features automatically extracted from the data by algorithms. Media visualization techniques pioneered by media and digital artists and now accessible to everybody via the open source tools developed in our lab allow us to explore patterns in images and video data by displaying large visual media collections sorted in a variety of ways. Because these techniques allow us to see simultaneously both individual artifacts and larger patterns, they offer one solution to the fundamental question of digital humanities: how to bring together distant and close reading, the micro and the macro.[30]

Although natural language is a powerful tool for describing the representational and narrative content of media, it does not work as well to describe media aesthetics. In contrast, computers can use infinite numerical scales to capture many nuances of visual form in a more precise way. They can also automatically detect certain types of content such as faces, separate photographs from manually created images, and perform many other types of content analysis.

Combined with the massive media datasets now available (both digitized visual media created before the twenty-first century, and born-digital contemporary media created by professional and nonprofessional users), this opens the door to fascinating research possibilities. Rather than only relying on small media samples, as media researchers did in the twentieth century, we can now map histories of media aesthetics and explore patterns in contemporary media production, sharing and remixing by analyzing billions of artifacts.

These new possibilities can be said to echo the important concepts developed by twentieth-century art historians André Malraux and Heinrich Wölfflin. According to Malraux (1901–1976), photographic reproductions of artworks made possible a "museum without walls." Artifacts that previously could not be seen together could now share the same space through their photographs. His book *Voices of Silence* (published in English translation in 1953) put this concept into practice by including 638 photographs of artworks from different cultures and historical periods. This was a pioneering work for its time. Using media visualization, such a sample today can be expanded many times, with the number of images limited only by what has been digitized and what has been made available by museums and other collections—or what can be scraped from the web. (To assemble our collection of almost 6,000 digital images of works by French Impressionists that represent approximately half of the estimated number of paintings and pastels created by these artists, we scraped a number of different web sites and combined the results. In another project, we scraped more than 1 million manga pages from the most popular fan manga web site onemanga.com.) By interactively sorting the images using both existing metadata and extracted features and displaying them in different layouts, we can explore their relations in ways that go beyond the comparisons of two images typical of a twentieth-century art history lecture.

This basic methodology of twentieth-century art history was introduced by Heinrich Wölfflin (1864–1945) after he became art history chair at Basel in 1897. Wölfflin developed the pedagogical method of using two projectors positioned side by side in art history lectures to allow for the comparison of pairs of images. The techniques discussed in this essay scale up Wölfflin's procedure, allowing us to display together and compare an arbitrary number of images.

But this is not the only relevance of Wölfflin for our discussion. The introduction to his foundational book *Kunstgeschichtliche Grundbegriffe* ("Principles of Art History," 1915) was called "Art History Names." This title reflects the ambition of art history's founders—Wölfflin, Riegl, Panofsky—to analyze broad patterns of historical changes in visual representation and form, manifested in multitudes of artifacts that were produced across thousands of years, without limiting these investigations to small sets of important "art" objects. In *Principles of Art History*, Wölfflin writes:

> As every history of vision must lead beyond mere art, it goes without saying that such national differences of the eye are more than a mere question of taste; conditioned and conditioning, they contain the bases of the whole world picture of people. That is why the history of art as the doctrine of the modes of vision can claim to be, not only a mere super in the company of historical disciplines, but as necessary as sight itself. (1932 [1915], p. 237)[31]

The broad "history of vision" advocated by Wölfflin and his contemporaries is an inspiration for the use of computational analysis and visualization for analyzing massive media collections. However, its crucial to keep in mind that Wölfflin and other scholars of his generation were limited not only by their small samples and comparative techniques, but also by the intellectual paradigms that made them read cultural artifacts as expressions of the unique characteristics describing "spirit," "mentalities," and "world picture" of different "nations."

Today, a different "art history without names" is becoming possible—think of the massive collections of user-generated media artifacts and the opportunity they offer for the study of contemporary human imagination, including both their "content" and the patterns of imitation, diffusion, and innovation on a global scale (deviantArt is just one example of such collections). Media visualization methods allow us to explore such media collections without a priori reducing them to small number of categories, as Wölfflin and his colleagues had to do. And rather than assuming that media artifacts created by users with similar demographic profiles also share some common characteristics in content and/or aesthetics (to translate Wölfflin's assumptions in contemporary terms), we can instead use the combination of feature extraction and media visualization to find clusters of media objects related in all kinds of ways and then see if they correspond to user demographics or any other a priori categories.

Ultimately, visualization can help us to question our existing metadata labels and our ways of dividing objects of study, revealing that that every narrative and map we construct is only one possible way of arranging the objects. In the words of Bruno Latour, "The 'whole' is now nothing more than a provisional visualization which can be modified and reversed at will, by moving back to the individual components, and then looking for yet other tools to regroup the same elements into alternative assemblages."[32]

ACKNOWLEDGMENTS

The research presented in this essay was supported by an Interdisciplinary Collaboratory Grant "Visualizing Cultural Patterns" (UCSD Chancellor Office, 2008-2010), Humanities High Performance Computing Award "Visualizing Patterns in Databases of Cultural Images and Video" (NEH/DOE, 2009), Digital Startup Level II grant (NEH, 2010), CSRO grant (Calit2, 2010), and Mellon Foundation grant "Tools for the Analysis and Visualization of Large Image and Video Collections for the Humanities" (2012–2015). We also are grateful to the California Institute for Information and Telecommunication (Calit2) and UCSD Center for Research in Computing and the Arts (CRCA) for their support of our work.

NOTES

1. For recent discussions of digital humanities, see David M. Berry, ed., *Understanding Digital Humanities* (New York: Palgrave Macmillan, 2012); Matthew K. Gold, ed., *Debates in the Digital Humanities* (Minneapolis: University of Minnesota Press, 2012); Katherine Hayles, *How We Think: Digital Media and Contemporary Technogenesis* (Chicago: University of Chicago Press, 2012); Anne Burdick, Johanna Drucker, Peter Lunenfeld, Todd Presner, and Jeffrey Schnapp, *Digital Humanities* (Cambridge, MA: MIT Press, 2012); Stephen Ramsay, *Reading Machines: Toward an Algorithmic Criticism* (Champaign: University of Illinois Press, 2011).

2. For more information, see the website for the Software Studies Iniciative, accessed October 5, 2012, www.softwarestudies.com.

3. To separate this research from many other kinds of work included in the 2000s under the umbrella term "digital humanities," I introduced the term *cultural analytics* to refer to the use of visualization and quantitative analysis of large sets of visual and interactive artifacts for humanities research and teaching. See Lev Manovich, "Cultural Analytics: Visualizing Cultural Patterns in the Era of 'More Media,'" *Domus* (Spring 2009).

4. The key articles are Lev Manovich, "What Is Visualization?" *Visual Studies* 26, no. 1 (2011): 36–49; Lev Manovich, "How to Compare One Million Images?" in *Understanding Digital Humanities*, ed. David Berry (New York: Palgrave Macmillan, 2012); Lev Manovich, "Media Visualization: Visual Techniques for Exploring Large Media Collections," in *Media Studies Futures*, ed. Kelly Gates (Malden, MA: Wiley-Blackwell, 2012).

5. See Nathan Yau, *Visualize This: The FlowingData Guide to Design, Visualization, and Statistics* (Hoboken, NJ: Wiley, 2011).

6. Michael Friendly and Daniel J. Denis, "Milestones in the History of Thematic Cartography, Statistical Graphics, and Data Visualization," Datavis.ca website, accessed October 5, 2012, http://datavis.ca/milestones/; see also "Gallery of Data Visualization: The Best and Worst of Statistical Graphics," Datavis.ca website, accessed October 5, 2012, http://www.datavis.ca/gallery/index.php.

7. See Lev Manovich, "Data Visualization as New Abstraction and Anti-Sublime," *SMAC!* 3 (2002), available at www.manovich.net; Andrew Vande Moere, "About the Information Aesthetics Weblog" *Information Aesthetics* (blog), December 2004, http://infosthetics.com/information_aesthetics_about.html; Fernanda B. Viégas and Martin Wattenberg, "Artistic Data Visualization: Beyond Visual Analytics," *Proceedings of the 2nd International Conference on Online Communities and Social Computing* (Berlin: Springer-Verlag, 2007), http://www.research.ibm.com/visual/papers/artistic-infovis.pdf.

8. For further discussion, see Lev Manovich, "Introduction," in *Visual Complexity*, by Manual Lima (Princeton, NJ: Princeton Architectural Press, 2011).

9. *Visual Complexity* website, filter by "method," accessed October 5, 2012, http://www.visualcomplexity.com/vc/.

10. Michael Friendly and Daniel J. Denis, "Milestones in the History of Thematic Cartography, 1970s," Datavis.ca website, accessed October 5, 2012, http://www.datavis.ca/milestones/index.php?group=1700s.

11. Such an analysis will have to take into account the popularity of isotypes developed by Otto Neurath in 1920s, who also used modernist aesthetics of simplicity and restricted geometry, but refused abstraction, believing that that isotypes will be more effective because of their iconicity.

12. Daniel Chang, Yuankai Ge, Shiwei Song, Nicole Coleman, Jon Christensen, and Jeffrey Heer, "Visualizing the Republic of Letters," http://www.stanford.edu/group/toolingup/rplviz/papers/Vis_RofL_2009, 2009.

13. Linda Nochlin, "Museum without Walls," *New York Times*, May 1, 2005, http://query.nytimes.com/gst/fullpage.html?res=9B0CE2DC1431F932A35756C0A9639C8B63.

14. My discussion only touches on the dimensions of this problem, which I see as most relevant to visualizing media. For a theoretical and historical analysis of data practices in the sciences, see Geoffrey C. Bowker, *Memory Practices in the Sciences* (Cambridge, MA: The MIT Press, 2006). For an analysis of the impact of big data on scholarly research and communication, see Christine L. Borgman, *Scholarship in the Digital Age: Information, Infrastructure, and the Internet* (Cambridge, MA: MIT Press, 2007).

15. "How Google Search Works," google.com, accessed September 6, 2012, http://www.google.com/competition/howgooglesearchworks.html.

16. "Wayback Machine," Internet Archive, accessed October 5, 2012, http://archive.org/web/web.php.

17. In computer science, a number of researchers published papers that present more complex techniques for visualizing media collections. However, implementing and using any of these techniques requires substantial technical knowledge that most users in the humanities and media studies currently do not have. Therefore, we focused on first implementing and popularizing those techniques that are both very simple to use and very simple to explain—such as an image plot. For examples of research in this area, see G. P. Nguyen, M. Worring, "Interactive Access to Large Image Collections Using

Similarity-Based Visualization," *Journal of Visual Languages and Computing* 19, no. 2 (April 2008): 203–224; Jing Yang, "Semantic Image Browser: Bridging Information Visualization With Automated Intelligent Image Analysis," *Proceedings of 2006 IEEE Symposium on Visual Analytics Science and Technology*; Gerald Schaefer, "Interactive Navigation of Image Collections." *FGIT 2011: Future Generation Information Technology: Third International Conference* (Springer, 2012); Gerald Schaefer, "Image Browsers—Effective and Efficient Tools for Managing Large Image Collections," *2011 International Conference on Multimedia Computing and Systems (ICMCS)*.

18. Lev Manovich, "Visualizing newspapers history: The Hawaiian Star, 5,930 front pages, 1893–1912," Software Studies Initiative Website, accessed October 8, 2012, http://lab.softwarestudies.com/2012/03/visualizing-newspapers-history-hawaiian.html.

19. Twentieth-century cultural theory often stressed that cultural representations are always partial maps since they can only show some aspects of the objects. However, given the dozens of recently developed methods for capturing data about physical objects and the ability to process massive amounts of data to extract new information—something which, for instance, Google does a few times a day when it analyzes over a trillion web links—this assumption needs to be rethought.

20. Eric Shonfeld, "With 80 Million Users, Pandora Files To Go Public," *TechCrunch*, February 11, 2011, http://techcrunch.com/2011/02/11/pandora-files-to-go-public/.

21. "Your Paintings," *BBC Online,* accessed October 5, 2012, http://www.bbc.co.uk/arts/yourpaintings.

22. QTIP (QTImageProcessing), "Software for Digital Humanities," Software Studies Initiative Website, accessed November 25, 2012, http://lab.softwarestudies.com/p/software-for-digital-humanities.html.

23. See, for example, Mark Nixon and Alberto Aguado, *Feature Extraction & Image Processing for Computer Vision*, 3rd edition (Oxford: Academic Press, 2012).

24. See behance.net for examples of such works. Motion graphics projects gallery, *behance.net*, accessed October 5, 2012, http://www.behance.net/?field=63.

25. Although a similar technique has been previously described in a number of computer science publications, it has not been implemented in any free or commercial software. Therefore, we developed a free software tool, ImagePlot. It allows rendering of high-resolution visualizations that can show very large image collections. The tool and documentation are available from http://lab.softwarestudies.com/p/imageplot.html.

26. "Search by Image," Google.com, accessed October 8, 2012, http://www.google.com/insidesearch/features/images/searchbyimage.html; "Google Help: Search by Image," Google.com, accessed October 8, 2012, http://support.google.com/images/bin/answer.py?hl=en&p=searchbyimagepage&answer=1325808.

27. "Images: Cultural Analytics Visualizations on Ultra High Resolution Displays," Software Studies Initiative Website, accessed November 26, 2012, http://lab.softwarestudies.com/2008/12/cultural-analytics-hiperspace-and.html.

28. For an example of such research, see the following paper that investigates how low-level features can be used to describe the emotional content of images: Jana Machajdik and Allan Hanbury, "Affective Image Classification Using Features Inspired by Psychology and Art Theory," *MM '10 Proceedings of the international conference on Multimedia* (2010), 83–92.

29. A. Hanjalic, "Extracting Moods from Pictures and Sounds: Towards Truly Personalized TV," *IEEE Signal Processing Magazine* 23, no. 2 (2006): 90–100.

30. Matthew L. Jockers, "On Distant Reading and Macroanalysis," *Matthew L. Jockers* (blog), July 1, 2011, accessed November 26, 2012, http://www.matthewjockers.net/2011/07/01/on-distant-reading-and-macroanalysis/.

31. Heinrich Wölfflin, *Principles of Art History: The Problem of the Development of Style in Later Art* (New York: Dover, 1950), quoted in Michael Hatt and Charlotte Klonk, *Art History: A Critical Introduction to Its Methods* (Manchester University Press, 1998), 66.

32. Bruno Latour, "Tarde's Idea of Quantification," in *The Social After Gabriel Tarde: Debates and Assessments*, ed. Mattei Candea (New York: Routledge, 2009).

Select Bibliography

Few, Stephen. *Now You See It: Simple Visualization Techniques for Quantitative Analysis.* Oakland, CA: Analytics Press, 2009.

Friendly, Michael, and Daniel J. Denis. "Milestones in the History of Thematic Cartography, Statistical Graphics, and Data Visualization." Datavis.ca website. http://datavis.ca/milestones/.

Lima, Manual. *Visual Complexity.* Princeton, NJ: Princeton Architectural Press, 2011.

Manovich, Lev. "How to Compare One Million Images?" In *Understanding Digital Humanities*, edited by David Berry. New York: Palgrave Macmillan, 2012.

——. "Media Visualization: Visual Techniques for Exploring Large Media Collections." In *Media Studies Futures*, edited by Kelly Gates. Malden, MA: Blackwell, 2012.

Nguyen, G. P., and M. Worring, "Interactive Access to Large Image Collections Using Similarity-Based Visualization." *Journal of Visual Languages and Computing* 19, no. 2 (April 2008): 203–224. Also available at http://staff.science.uva.nl/~giangnp/Pubs/Pdf/2006/NguyenWorringJVLC06.pdf.

Tufte, Edward R. *The Visual Display of Quantitative Information.* 2nd edition. Cheshire, CT: Graphics Press, 2001.

Viégas, Fernanda and Martin Wattenberg. "Artistic Data Visualization: Beyond Visual Analytics." *Proceedings of the 2nd International Conference on Online Communities and Social Computing.* Berlin: Springer-Verlag, 2007. Also available at Hint.fm, http://hint.fm/papers/artistic-infovis.pdf.

Yau, Nathan. *Visualize This: The FlowingData Guide to Design, Visualization, and Statistics.* Hoboken, NJ: Wiley, 2011.

CHAPTER 17

EXPLORATIONS IN CULTURESON

JACOB SMITH

Lev Manovich provides us with a useful taxonomy of recent techniques of information visualization aligned with humanities research—what he has referred to as "culturevis." Manovich's work focuses on visual media and so might not appear to be immediately applicable to other media forms. The scope of this publication impels us, however, to explore how his suggestive work can be applied to sound media. Manovich has given us a head start: note that two of his "classical" examples of culturevis—*The Shape of Song* (2001) and *Listening History* (2006)—are depictions of sound culture. We should not be surprised that sound files and listening habits served as the source material for pioneering work in culturevis since sound recordings were among the first forms of popular culture to be digitized and compiled online *en masse*. Visualizations of the structure of music or the temporal patterns of music listening raise questions about what culturevis can tell us about sound culture, but can we also speak of a "cultureson"? That is, what is the history and future of practices that analyze and represent data in sonic form? What kinds of auditory cultural analytics are available to humanities research and teaching? As a response to Manovich's essay, I will sketch the domain of an incipient cultureson and consider some implications of recent visualizations of sound culture, pointing to specific examples that merit further investigation in each case.

Manovich notes that researchers in the humanities have only recently begun to show an interest in information visualization, but that scholarly community has paid even less attention to the techniques by which data is made audible: a process that has been called "sonification."[1] The sonic analogs to the pie chart and bar graph include sonar technology, Geiger counters, metal detectors, auditory displays of volcanic activity,[2] seismograms,[3] and "visual-to-auditory sensory substitution devices."[4] Auditory displays such as these can enrich the study of cultural analytics by revealing the particular protocols of visual and sound media, at the same time that they demonstrate that "data are fluid and are not necessarily tethered to any one sense."[5] For its proponents, the spatial and temporal characteristics of sound make auditory displays particularly adept at the representation of spatial relations; group interaction; constellations of events and their interrelationships; processes of change and development; emotional, chemical, or brain states; the discrimination of periodic events (i.e., rhythm); the detection of small changes of frequency in continuous signals; and dynamics of resonance, overlap, harmony, and dissonance.[6] Furthermore, the omnidirectional quality of hearing means that auditory displays can be used in situations during which a person's eyes are busy with other tasks, such as alarm and monitoring systems for airplane pilots and surgeons.[7]

Consider a sonification of Olympic athletes crossing the finish line in events such as downhill skiing, luge, and speedskating posted by the *New York Times* website in 2010.[8] Tight clusters of sound represent the mere fractions of a second that separate individual competitors. The sonic depiction of this data emphasizes the proximity of phenomena in time and the barely perceivable distinction between events as they approach simultaneity. Sonification is also the key operation of avant garde artists and audio hobbyists who record the radio signals caused by phenomena such as lightning storms, aurora, and the Earth's magnetosphere.[9] Stephen P. McGreevy's CD *Electric Enigma* (Irdial 1996) is one of several commercial discs that feature sonifications of "natural radio phenomenon." McGreevy's recordings allow us to perceive the invisible movements of atomic particles in the atmosphere as sound, producing in the listener a sense of planetary space, as well as the intimation of a sublimely nonhuman harmony.

A remarkably systematic and organized effort at sonification has been achieved by the First Sounds project. First Sounds is a group of audio historians, recording engineers, and archivists whose aim is to make audible the earliest known sound recordings and inscriptions.[10] The group garnered international attention when they succeeded in playing back sound waves that had been scratched onto paper in 1860 for the purpose of visual analysis by Édouard-Léon Scott de Martinville on his phonautograph (a precursor to Thomas Edison's 1877 phonograph). Scott's "phonautograms"—themselves pioneering instances of culturevis—were never intended to be heard, and First Sounds member Patrick Feaster makes a useful distinction between "the sonification of non-aural data," such as the spatiotemporal relationships between Olympic athletes or the movement of atomic particles, and the sonification of "aural data stored non-aurally," as with Scott's phonautograms or the grooves of a phonograph record.[11] Feaster refers to his work as "eduction," a term he prefers to "playback" or "reproduction" since many of the inscriptions that he aurally animates are not sound recordings in the normal sense. Electronic musicians like Aphex Twin have used sound editing software such as Metasynth or Coagula to turn images into sound in the service of avant garde composition,[12] but Feaster uses that software to educe very old visual inscriptions of sound phenomena: a process that he calls "paleospectrophony."[13] Feaster's website features a host of remarkable "experimental eduction projects," including eductions of sound spectrograms from the 1930s and 1940s, a system of speech notation published in 1775, and a haunting sonification of illustrated instructions for a barrel organ made in 1650.[14]

Feaster's experimental eduction is just the kind of groundbreaking sonification technique that Manovich's work can help sound scholars to appreciate and describe.

Manovich's categorization of culturevis can also shed new light on audio "remix culture." Vernacular remix artists have been exploring the field of cultural analytics for decades, illustrating Manovich's claim elsewhere that "electronic music" serves as one of the "key reservoirs of new metaphors for the rest of culture today."[15] Manovich's description of "collection montage" can be fruitfully applied to audio works such as LeRoy Stevens' "Favorite Recorded Scream" (2008), a 3-minute auditory display of ecstatic vocalizations made by the likes of James Brown, the Pixies, and the Who; and Osymyso's "Intro-Introspection" (2002), a pioneering artifact of mashup culture comprised of the introductory moments of more than 100 pop records.[16] Both of these tracks work by Manovich's "key operation" of "layout," which involves the arrangement of elements in such a way as to allow the user to notice patterns in an array.[17] Stevens and Osymyso use collection montage to create a kind of audio text cloud through the juxtaposition and emphasis of elements in a large dataset, and, in the process, they provide a subtle critique of recorded popular music.

The critical dimension of these sonic layouts is more apparent in examples of cultureson that resemble Manovich's category of "remapping"; that is, artifacts that systematically rearrange media samples in a new configuration in order to examine ideological patterns. That description aptly describes the work of remix and mashup artists who combine preexisting tracks using digital Auto-Tune and time-stretching software: artists such as John Oswald, Evolution Control Committee, Girls on Top, Soulwax, Go Home Productions, Party Ben, and Freelance Hellraiser. The term "mashup" has gained widespread usage in the past decade, but it is often used in a broad sense to mean the same thing as a "remix." In the strictest terms, a mashup is not simply a collage of multiple recordings, but a special category of remix that combines two discrete tracks (usually the vocals from one and the instruments from another) in order to produce a new song. The technical simplicity of that maneuver is significant: mashups are not about virtuosic editing technique, but about "high-concept" ideas and a certain DIY Punk attitude. Also, like Punk, the best mashups work simultaneously as both pop music and pop music criticism: for example, when Destiny's Child sing over a Nirvana track, we are prompted to think about the segregation of white and black musical genres since the 1990s on radio formats; or when we hear Christina Aguilera front the Strokes, we confront the different approaches taken to romance in various genres of pop music, as well as the ways in which the division of labor between writing lyrics, melodies, and instrumentation tends to work in contemporary songwriting.[18] Mashups are thus examples of cultureson that are not design neutral because they deliberately aim to make a statement about the world through particular choices of the datasets and their presentation. The best mashups are cultureson that prompt both a close reading of the cultural artifacts themselves and a distant reading of their "larger patterns across a whole media collection."

Mashup mixes have become the blueprint for a wide range of cultural production, including episodes of Fox's smash TV series *Glee* (2009), the stunning video mashups made by Hexstatic,[19] the Mashed in Plastic project (a collection of mashups based around the work of director David Lynch),[20] and Israeli producer Kutiman's breathtaking *ThruYOU* (2009), which consists of YouTube videos of amateur musicians that are mixed in such a way as to produce "video jams of amazing funkiness, in the process creating an all-new art form that combines DJing, video montage and found art."[21] Manovich's analysis provides us with a framework for works such as these, other than their automatic designation as "postmodern pastiche": they are cutting-edge experiments in the sonification of audio datasets; artifacts of cultureson that make their dataset dance, like a pie chart that begins to bubble and blend until it turns into gumbo or a bar graph whose immobile lines spring to life, morphing into the pulsating display of an audio equalizer.

Remix artists have blazed a trail in cultureson that scholars in the humanities should endeavor to follow. Academics can also learn something from the executives and marketing departments of the cultural industries, who use cultural analytics to help them understand their audiences and market their products. Consider the emerging economy surrounding "musical intelligence" software, which compares a new song to a database containing millions of songs from the past and then makes a prediction about whether or not the new track will be successful. The pioneer in this field was the Spanish company Polyphonic HMI, who market their service as "Hit Song Science."[22] Executives at Polyphonic HMI left to start their own company, Platinum Blue Music Intelligence, which promotes its service under the name Music Xray.[23] Platinum Blue's software plots an individual record as a visual point of light in a three-dimensional "music universe," with each point placed in proximity to other records with similar sonic traits.

Manovich argues that visualization allows users to find novel patterns that would be otherwise difficult to observe, and, similarly, once the musical data had been visualized in this manner, the team at Platinum Blue observed that the vast majority of chart-topping hit songs were clumped together in approximately fifty "clusters." The closer a new song lies to one of these clusters therefore, the more likely that it will be a hit.[24]

Musical intelligence software is used by record companies hoping to minimize risk, by amateur musicians hoping to convince labels that they have what it takes for mainstream success, and by online radio providers like Pandora, whose "Music Genome Project" recommends new tracks to users on the basis of an algorithm comprised of 400 musical components.[25] The fact that music intelligence software now shapes creative choices in the recording studio and helps to determine which tracks a record label will promote will prompt some to see it as evidence of the utter desperation and moral bankruptcy of the recording industry. Such is the implicit message of Dave Soldier's thought-provoking 1997 People's Choice Music project, which is a kind of sonic analog to one of Platinum Blue's visualizations of a well-trod corner of the musical universe.[26] Soldier composed two songs determined by an online survey of musical preferences. The least popular musical traits as determined by the poll were synthesized into the 25-minute "Most Unwanted Song," which features wild variations in tempo and volume, an operatic soprano rapping, plugs for Walmart, and a healthy serving of bagpipes. More interesting is "The Most Wanted Song," whose bland, lite-rock synths, meandering saxophone, and romance narrative is both hilarious and eerily familiar. Soldier's project seems to suggest that "musical intelligence" prevents recording artists from taking risks or questioning formal conventions, yet some have asserted that "hit song" software can convince reluctant record executives to get behind new and innovative artists, provided that their scores are high enough (the oft-cited example here is the claim that software predicted the success of Norah Jones' CD *Come Away With Me* [2002] in the face of industry skepticism).[27]

The widespread adoption of services such as Hit Song Science, Music Xray, and the Music Genome Project suggest that humanities scholars need to pay more attention to emerging articulations between cultural analytics and the cultural industries. In fact, discourse surrounding Pandora sometimes frames the Music Genome Project as a response to cultural studies: a writer for the *New York Times* notes that, in contrast to prevalent "social" theories of musical preference, Pandora's data-driven approach "ignores the crowd": "The idea is to figure out what you like, not what a market might like. More interesting, the idea is that the taste of your cool friends, your peers, the traditional music critics, big-label talent scouts and the latest influential music blog are all equally irrelevant. That's all cultural information, not musical information. And theoretically at least, Pandora's approach distances music-liking from the cultural information that generally attaches to it." What Pandora's system ignores, the author concludes with a shrug in the direction of Pierre Bourdieu, is the social dimension of taste.[28]

How might scholars interested not in *filtering out* cultural information but in *bringing it into sharper focus* deploy this same software? Popular musicians have long been known for "misusing" new technology, for throwing away the instruction manual and deploying the latest gadgets in unforeseen ways—using digital samplers, for example, not simply to capture a more faithful cello sound, but to cut and paste old Parliament records. Can humanities researchers make a similar move and hot-wire the latest hit song science to create "musical knowledge" in addition to "musical intelligence"?

In addition to providing new tools in the investigation of the social dimension of musical culture, scholars might have something to learn from digital analyses of sound form. Press reports describe how software tends to uncover surprising and unnoticed similarities between artists commonly considered to be vastly different: U2 and Beethoven for example, or Van Halen and MOR piano singer Vanessa Carlton. Could hit clusters in the "music universe" reveal undertheorized genres or untold histories of popular culture? What insights might be gained if we expanded the sonic dataset beyond the Billboard charts to include amateur recordings, types of recording besides popular music, tracks made outside of the United States and Western Europe, or even the songs of nonhuman animal species? What significant clusters might appear in an analysis of the recordings found in the University of California, Santa Barbara's Cylinder Project, which contains more than 6,000 digitized sound recordings from the first decades of recorded sound?[29] How do the "tags" and user-generated comments on music websites like SoundCloud and Bandcamp shape the temporal experience of music listening and construct new generic categories? What I hope has become clear over the course of this essay is that Manovich's work on culturevis has provided scholars of Sound Studies with a rare and valuable gift: a new set of questions.

NOTES

1. The term "sonification" is used by researchers working on the auditory display of data. See for example, Gregory Kramer, "An Introduction to Auditory Display," in *Auditory Display*, ed. Gregory Kramer (Reading, MA.: Addison-Wesley Publishing, 1994), 1–77. Jonathan Sterne and Mitchell Akiyama define "sonification" as "the transformation of nonsonic data into audible form." "*The Recording That Never Wanted to be Heard and Other Stories of Sonification," in *The Oxford Handbook of Sound Studies*, Trevor Pinch and Karin Bijsterveld, eds. (Oxford: Oxford University Press, 2012), 545. In the same volume, Alexandra Supper defines the term as "the use of nonspeech audio to convey information." Alexandra Supper, "*The Search for the 'Killer Application': Drawing the Boundaries Around the Sonification of Scientific Data," in Pinch and Bijsterveld, *Sound Studies*, 249. The term has also been used in the context of media studies by Sean Cubitt in "The Sound of Sunlight," *Screen* 51, no. 2 (2010), pp. 118–128

2. See Kurt Kleiner, "Volcanoes May Reveal Secrets Through 'Song,'" *New Scientist*, August 10, 2006, http://www.newscientist.com/article/ dn9711-volcanoes-may-reveal-secrets-through-song.html.

3. Chris Hayward. "Listening to the Earth Sing," in *Auditory Display*, ed. Gregory Kramer (Reading, MA: Addison-Wesley Publishing, 1994), 369–404

4. See the discourse surrounding Peter Meijer's "vOICe" technology, which represents visual information with sounds, and is intended to be used by people who have lost their sight or were born blind: Alison Motluck, "Seeing with Your Ears," *New York Times*, December 11, 2005; Lakshmi Sandhaha, "Blind 'See With Sound,'"*BBC News*, October 7, 2003, http://news.bbc.co.uk/2/hi/science/nature/3171226.stm; Mark K. Anderson, "Red, Blue, Green and Other Sounds," *Wired*, April 12, 2002, http://www.wired.com/techbiz/media/news/2002/04/51660.

5. Sterne and Akiyama, "The Recording That Never Wanted to be Heard," *547*. For another fascinating discussion of the entwinement of the senses in modern technologies, see Teffer, Nicola. "Sounding Out Vision," *Senses and Society* 5, no. 2 (2010): 173–188.

6. See Kramer, "Auditory Display," and Sterne and Akiyama, "The Recording That Never Wanted to be Heard," 550.

7. See Kramer, "Auditory Display"; Ryan McGee, "Auditory Displays and Sonification: Introduction and Overview," http://www.lifeorange.com/writing/Sonification_Auditory_Display.pdf.

8. "Fractions of a Second: An Olympic Musical," *New York Times*, February 26, 2010, http://www.nytimes.com/interactive/2010/02/26/sports/olympics/20100226-olysymphony.html. Thanks to Patrick Feaster to pointing out this auditory display to me. Also see a range of sonification techniques applied to rowing here: Stephen Barrass, "Sonification of Rowing," June 21, 2009, StephenBarrass.com (blog), http://stephenbarrass.wordpress.com/2009/06/21/sonification-of-rowing/.

9. See Stephen P. McGreevy, www.spaceweathersounds.com and www.auroralchorus.com. Some taxonomies of sonification categorize the "space weather sounds" as "audification": a method that translates data that already exists as a waveform into sound (see Thomas

Hermann, "Data Exploration by Sonification," http://www.techfak.uni-bielefeld.de/ags/ami/datason/datason_e.html). For more avant-garde uses of this phenomena, see Douglas Kahn, "Radio of the Sphere" in *Radio Territories*, Brandon LaBelle and Erik Granly Jensen, eds. (London: Errant Bodies Press, 2006).

10. See *First Sounds*, www.firstsounds.org.

11. E-mail correspondence with the author, July 2010.

12. See Jarmo Niinisalo, "The Aphex Face," *bastwood* (blog), http://www.bastwood.com/aphex.php.

13. Feaster uses the term "paleospectrophony" to refer to the sonification of inscriptions that can be treated as graphs of time versus frequency (like sound spectrograms). Sterne and Akiyama refer to the First Sounds project in order to stress the plasticity of sound, that is, the ability for data to be conveyed across different sensory registers ("The Recording That Never Wanted to be Heard," 547).

14. Patrick Feaster, Phonozoic, www.phonozoic.net.

15. Lev Manovich, "What Comes After Remix?" Winter 2007, http://manovich.net/DOCS/remix_2007_2.doc.

16. See Ben Sisario, "Primal Snippets, on Vinyl," *New York Times*, August 18, 2009, and Sukhdev Sandhu, "Favorite Recorded Scream," *Telegraph*, August 14, 2009, http://www.telegraph.co.uk/culture/music/rockandjazzmusic/6016675/Favorite-Recorded-Scream-at-last-a-record-thats-really-worth-shouting-about.html. A similar approach can be applied to television culture, as can be seen in the YouTube "supercut," "Don Draper Says What," http://www.youtube.com/watch?v=WsJSRP7cZVo&noredirect=1.

17. See Thomas Hermann on sonifcation and datamining: "the goal in the research field of datamining is to find patterns, to detect hidden regularities in data." Hermann points to the "extremely high-developed pattern recognition capabilities in the auditory domain" as an argument for further research in sonification. Thomas Hermann and Helge Ritter, "Sound and Meaning in Auditory Data Display," *Proceedings of the IEEE* 92, no. 4 (April 2004), http://www.dei.unipd.it/~musica/IM/P6_Hermann_04.pdf See also: "Data Exploration by Sonification," http://www.techfak.uni-bielefeld.de/ags/ami/datason/datason_e.html.

18. My thinking on mashups has been profoundly shaped by Dale Lawrence. See his insightful article: "Two Boots: Stiff Old Bands Get Down Like That," *Village Voice*, December 3, 2002, http://www.villagevoice.com/2002-12-03/music/two-boots/.

19. Exactshit Vimeo Channel, http://vimeo.com/channels/exactshit.

20. Mashed in Plastic, www.mashedinplastic.co.uk.

21. ThruYou: KutiMan Mixes YouTube, http://thru-you.com/#/videos/; "The Fifty Best Inventions of 2009: YouTube Funk," *Time*, http://www.time.com/time/specials/packages/article/0,28804,1934027_1934003_1933973,00.html.

22. Uplaya.com, http://uplaya.com/.

23. Music Xray, company website, http://www.musicxray.com/.

24. See Oliver Burkeman, "How Many Hits?" *Guardian Weekend*, November 11, 2006, 54–57.

25. In his discussion of culturevis that work to "augment and visualize," Manovich wonders whether processes of annotation are better suited to humans or software, given the limitations of language. Note that Pandora has a panel of human musicians who "annotate" tracks. The company's founder claimed that there were "elements of music that machine listening just couldn't capture" (Rob Walker, "The Song Decoders," *New York Times*, October 18, 2009).

26. Hear David Soldier's "Most Wanted Song" project at: http://www.ubu.com/sound/komar.html.

27. See Malcolm Gladwell, "The Formula," *New Yorker*, October 16, 2006; "Sounds Good?" *The Economist*, June 10, 2006; Adam Sherwin, "Pop Picker Takes the Hit and Miss Out of Music Making," *The Times (London)*, April 1, 2006; Oliver Moreland, "The (X + Y) / Z = Hit Factor," *BBC Focus Magazine*, November 2009, 43–47.
28. "Nothing more clearly affirms one's 'class,' nothing more infallibly classifies, than tastes in music." Pierre Bourdieu, *Distinction* (London: Routledge, 2010), 10.
29. "Cylinder Preservation and Digitization Project," Department of Special Collections, Donald C. Davidson Library, University of California Santa Barbara, http://cylinders.library.ucsb.edu/.

SELECT BIBLIOGRAPHY

Kahn, Douglas. "Radio of the Sphere." In *Radio Territories*, edited by Brandon LaBelle and Erik Granly Jensen, 219–230. London: Errant Bodies Press, 2006.
Kramer, Gregory, ed. *Auditory Display*. Reading, MA: Addison-Wesley Publishing, 1994.
Sterne, Jonathan, and Mitchell Akiyama. "The Recording That Never Wanted to be Heard and Other Stories of Sonification." In *The Oxford Handbook of Sound Studies*, edited by Trevor Pinch and Karin Bijsterveld, 544–560. Oxford: Oxford University Press, 2012.
Supper, Alexandra. "The Search for the 'Killer Application': Drawing the Boundaries Around the Sonification of Scientific Data," In *The Oxford Handbook of Sound Studies*, edited by Trevor Pinch and Karin Bijsterveld, 249–272. Oxford: Oxford University Press, 2012.
Teffer, Nicola. "Sounding Out Vision." *Senses and Society* 5, no. 2 (2010): 173–188.

PART VI

VIRTUAL WORLDS,
PARANOID
STRUCTURES, AND
STATES OF WAR

CHAPTER 18

MUSIC AND THE STATE OF EXCEPTION IN ALFONSO CUARÓN'S *CHILDREN OF MEN*

DALE CHAPMAN

ONE of the most unsettling scenes in Alfonso Cuarón's film *Children of Men* (2006) depicts the protagonists' arrival in a fictional future refugee camp, set in what is presently the British seaside resort town of Bexhill-On-Sea. Despite the film's futuristic setting, this scene vividly alludes to a present-day world made familiar to us through media portrayals of Abu-Ghraib and Guantanamo Bay. As Theo and Kee watch from a fortified bus, British soldiers in Kevlar process terrified prisoners in a hangar lit with klieg lights. Rows of detainees stand immobile with black hoods over their heads or cower naked before snarling dogs while military operatives subject them to stress positions. Here, a punk song, the Libertines' provocatively titled "Arbeit Macht Frei," serves as diegetic source music, its high-decibel rumble suggesting the sonic intimidation employed by American soldiers in their interrogation of so-called unlawful combatants under the auspices of the Global War on Terror.[1]

In its cinematography, production design, and uses of sound and music, Cuarón's *Children of Men* offers a powerful filmic realization of what political theorists refer to as the "state of exception." The conservative German political theorist Carl Schmitt, in his treatise *Political Theology*, defined the state of exception as that legal framework in which the sovereign, in response to crisis, asserts his or her authority through the suspension of the rule of law. Beyond its legal status, this suspension is also an ontological one: our experience of the ordinary institutions of daily life becomes interrupted, placing in abeyance our most fundamental assumptions about the world around us, including our relation to time and place. In Schmitt's words, "The exception is more interesting than the rule. The rule proves nothing; the exception proves everything…. In the exception the power of real life breaks through the crust of a mechanism that has become torpid by repetition."[2]

The ontology of the state of exception was especially attractive to German philosopher Walter Benjamin, who saw in it a powerful tool for understanding the intersection of the political and the aesthetic. Benjamin identifies the exception as embodying a notion of "now-time": a searing, messianic intensity of the "now" that shapes our moments of ecstasy, revolution, or catastrophe.[3] Whereas Schmitt understands the state of exception as a decisive, punctuating event, clearly demarcated in time and place, Benjamin articulates the possibility that there may be no demarcating the everyday from its dissolution. Or, as Benjamin himself puts forth in his "Theses on the Philosophy of History," "The tradition of the oppressed teaches us that the 'state of emergency' in which we live is not the exception but the rule."[4]

The issues raised by the state of exception may seem well removed from the domain of musicology. But, as Suzanne Cusick has recently emphasized, the expressive power of music, with its ability to overwhelm our everyday apprehension of events, has rendered it applicable to the state of exception's ontological suspension. In interrogation practices implemented by the US government, under the pretext of national security, recorded music played at dangerous volumes has been used on prisoners as a potential source of psychological disorientation, believed capable of inducing the very disintegration of the self.[5] This disturbing appropriation of music raises important issues about the ethical and political valence of music, especially in light of new judicial strategies pursued by Western democracies as part of their expansion of the so-called Global War on Terror.[6] Few recent fictional movies do more to realize the frightening implications of this state of affairs than *Children of Men*. An adaptation of the 1992 P. D. James novel of the same name, *Children of Men* takes up the idea of a dystopian future in which widespread infertility places the future of humanity in jeopardy and throws the institutions of civic society into chaos. If P. D. James's novel foregrounds the issues of infertility and reproduction, tracing some of the ramifications of a society with "no future," Cuarón's film focuses on larger dimensions of widespread social crisis, depicting with heightened realism the potential response of contemporary neoliberal society to the prospect of catastrophe.[7]

This essay foregrounds some of the ways in which *Children of Men* realizes a compelling account of the state of exception through a wide variety of contemporary classical and popular music that cuts across genre distinctions. Within the context of musicology, Cuarón's film provokes us to entertain a very expansive conception of "twentieth-century music," encompassing musics as disparate as post-romantic *Lieder*, the post-minimalist concert music of "The New Simplicity," progressive and psychedelic rock, and contemporary British electronic dance music genres such as dubstep and grime. This broader musical palette provides Cuarón with an archive from which to draw complicated lines of association, harnessing polarities of past and present, inside and outside, and high and low. These musical oppositions, often refigured as ethnic and racial oppositions, help to make sense of the film's representations of the state of exception.

I hope to demonstrate that the concept of the state of exception might serve as a powerful hermeneutic tool, providing access to a previously unexamined dimension

of music's political significance. If music has limited access to the politics of representation, we should nevertheless recognize that it can structure our experience of time.
I argue that *Children*'s musical practices intervene temporally to help create an experience of the state of exception. It also functions in the domains of representation and
culture, shaping our understanding of our world in fundamental ways.[8]

Sometimes, the exception manifests itself less in the overt "content" of certain
sequences than in their *texture*, their realization of specific structures of feeling. Cuarón's
formal choices, in both the visual and aural registers, accentuate the seamlessness with
which "normal life" blends into the suspension of normality in the state of exception. It
is these formal choices in *Children* that highlight the ways that music might contribute
to our understanding of the political topography of the present.

ANAMORPHOSIS

Children of Men opens in the year 2027, some eighteen years after the world's last human
being was born. An influenza epidemic and the attendant political turmoil have brought
most of the planet to the point of collapse, creating a massive refugee crisis for Britain,
the only nation maintaining a semblance of its former social stability. Britain pays the
price for this stability through its government's imposition of a draconian policy of
closed borders, with the suggestively named office of "Homeland Security" incarcerating all undocumented foreigners and sending them off to refugee camps.

The central narrative involves a road trip of sorts, in which Theo Faron, played by
Clive Owen, agrees to shepherd a secretly pregnant refugee, a young black woman
named Kee (played by Claire-Hope Ashitey), through security checkpoints to the southern English coast. It is here that Kee hopes to connect with supporters of the "Human
Project," an underground group seeking to reestablish the future of humanity. As Slavoj
Žižek has noted, Cuarón has used the "road movie" trope before, in his 2001 film *Y tu
mamá también*, which, on its surface, follows the sexual exploits of two close friends
from Mexico City as they make their way through the Mexican countryside.[9] In both
Children and *Y tu mamá*, Cuarón presents the film's narrative largely as a formal scaffolding around which the "real" events of the story take place: in *Y tu mamá*, the ravages
of poverty and class divisions in neoliberal Mexico; in *Children*, the incremental collapse of the rule of law in an ostensibly "civilized" society.

Žižek argues that the political efficacy of Cuarón's movies lies in his strategy of *anamorphosis*.[10] In the context of Lacanian psychoanalysis, anamorphosis is that sense in
which an object gazes at us from an oblique angle, a position we can't determine from
confronting the image dead on. Rather, the object only manifests itself for the viewer as
it appears out of the corner of the eye, at the periphery of sight.[11]

Anamorphosis makes its presence felt in *Children of Men* in a variety of ways. Cuarón's
decision to shoot the film sometimes with a jittery, handheld camera, and at other times
with wide-angle lenses and long, seeming unbroken shots, has the effect of making the

viewer nervously aware of the troubling events that transpire at the edge of the dieg-esis. The camera follows Theo off the Tube and down the train platform, but pauses to take in the refugees locked behind armed guards in detention cages. It follows the hun-gover Theo on his way to work, latté in hand, but lingers on the harrowing sight of mass evictions, with soldiers bulldozing squatter tenements as detained immigrants look on, their faces transfixed in abject fear. As Theo emerges from a shop to walk down Fleet Street in central London, digital billboards prod us surreptitiously from the margins of the screen, provoking us with fleeting glimpses into a disturbing post-crisis culture: tele-screens urge us to fetishize pet clothes (in the absence of any need for Baby Gap) or market suicide kits for the remaining pharmaceutical industry (in the absence of any cause for hope).[12] These details do not clamor for our attention, but prod at us from the edge of the frame, emerging as spectral after-images supplementary to the film's central narrative.[13]

Anamorphosis serves as an efficient tool for evoking the film's reading of the state of exception. Whereas Benjamin's contends that "the state of emergency [exception] in which we live is not the exception, but the rule," in *Homo Sacer*, political theorist Giorgio Agamben frames this assertion differently, arguing that it is impossible for the sovereign to isolate the zone of efficacy, to segregate the locus of the exception from that sphere in which the rule of law continues unabated. Rather, when the sovereign decides on the exception, the rule of law and the suspension of the rule of law blur into one another, overlapping ambiguously in a "zone of indistinction."[14] In *Children of Men,* there is no impermeable boundary separating the mundane experience of our protagonist (bureau-cratic drudgery, a morning stop at a coffee franchise) from the omnipresent apparition of sublime violence. The genuine "story" of *Children* is the story of the dissolution of this negligible boundary between Theo's life and the *bare life* of those who find themselves naked before the sovereign's unrestrained application of power.[15]

Cuarón does as much to realize this "story" through his formal language as through his unflinching depictions of refugee camps. The overall effect is a kind of wide-angle intensification of the periphery in each scene. Richard Beggs's exquisite sound design for *Children* plays a key role here, as his carefully crafted sonic minutiae (distant gun-shots, fear mongering television commercials, the rustle of trees in the wind) accentu-ates the actions at the margins of the viewer's consciousness, heightening the sense of anamorphosis. The soundtrack itself often stands in an anamorphic relation to the film's visuals, offering up an oblique commentary on elements of the film's import that escape its imagery. The film's sound also lends the film access to the distinctive ontology of time in the state of exception.

THE RINGING

Children of Men's opening sequence introduces a key component of the film's sonic architecture.[16] The camera follows Theo as he walks along Fleet Street, motorized rickshaws providing evidence of London's diminished state in the film's fictitious 2027 setting. Suddenly, an explosion rips through the coffee shop where Theo had just purchased his morning cup, the camera briefly settling on a screaming woman carrying her own severed arm (Figure 18.1). The viewer scarcely has time to register the impact of the harrowing event before the camera cuts to the stark black-and-white title card. The sound design for the sequence centers around a piercing, high-frequency ringing, initiated at the instant of the bomb's detonation. With the explosion, the ringing immediately occupies the sonic foreground, and, as the title card appears, all sounds outside of the ringing are cut short, magnifying its intensity.

The impact with which the excruciating sonority introduces itself situates it as a defining gesture in *Children*. The context of the sound in the opening sequence implies that it embodies Theo's subjective experience of tinnitus, caused by the deafening impact of the bomb explosion. However, the persistence of the ringing, which reappears later in the film at moments of dramatic import, imparts to it a structural role in the film. Like tinnitus itself, which lingers insistently as an ambient potentiality in the mind of the sufferer, the recurrent ringing sound in *Children* underscores the entirety of the film's sound-world as an emotional texture resonating in the background of Theo's experience.[17]

In one scene in particular, Cuarón connects the ringing to a more expansive field of signification. In an abandoned warehouse commandeered by the radical paramilitary group, "the Fishes," Theo is taken aside by his former partner, Julian (played by Julianne

FIGURE 18.1

FIGURE 18.2

Moore), who, as leader of the Fishes, calls on him to help Kee obtain the transit papers that will allow Kee to reach the English coast and meet up with members of the Human Project (Figure 18.2). When Theo refuses, he is seized by two of Julian's lieutenants, who trigger his tinnitus in the ensuing scuffle. Julian's parting words to Theo speak to his injury, but in their poignant depiction of a cumulative decline, they also allude to the greater trauma of the fertility crisis:

> You know that ringing in your ears? That "eeeee ....?" That's the sound
> of the ear cells dying. Like their swan song. Once it's gone, you'll never
> hear that frequency again. Enjoy it while it lasts.[18]

Julian's parting shot to Theo offers up encroaching deafness as a metaphor for the irreversible diminution of the planet's population during the infertility crisis. Individual ear cells, ringing with the "swan song" of their imminent demise, wink out like the dying embers of a doomed society. Indeed, the context of the sound's recurrence throughout *Children* reinforces this metaphor, as it is often metonymically linked to the catastrophic death of Theo's friends.

However, the fertility crisis in Cuarón's film, unlike that portrayed in the source novel, functions less as a central theme than as a point of departure for exploring the political ontology of global catastrophe. In this context, we might hear the piercing timbres of Theo's tinnitus as a kind of alarm, marking the condensed temporality of the state of emergency. This becomes most explicit in those scenes in which Cuarón draws on our memory of the ringing to forge links with both the diegetic, on-screen action and the nondiegetic music.

The most powerful example of this kind of tight sonic integration can be found in the climactic battle sequence near the end of the film, set in the Bexhill refugee camp, where illegal immigrants have been rounded up for deportation by the British government. In its depiction of the refugee camp, *Children* emulates with frightening verisimilitude the sights and sounds of places such as 1990s-era Bosnia-Herzegovina, the sites of atrocities perpetrated in the absence of rule of law. The detritus of a jettisoned populace lies everywhere, and the camp is engulfed in the sounds of black-market transactions and the militant chants of religious extremists. In even the most untroubled scenes of interior domesticity, the punchy clatter of distant machine-gun fire resounds off-screen, collapsing the distance between assumed normalcy and the violence of the state of exception.

In the scene immediately preceding the climactic battle sequence, a hired gun shepherds Theo and Kee out of a safehouse, through the militarized compound, and then to the underground tunnels where they will escape Bexhill by boat.[19] Along the way, the camera pauses on a mother keening over the body of her son, disconsolate with grief. As the camera cuts to an empty underpass, the mother's cries abruptly give way to the opening measures of Krystoph Penderecki's *Threnody to the Victims of Hiroshima* (cue 1:23.45). The juxtaposition forges an explicit connection between the woman's anguished cries and the chilling *marcato* tone clusters that open Penderecki's composition. Cuarón sustains this connection for the duration of the battle sequence, by allowing the *Threnody* to unfold uninterrupted as the extradiegetic soundtrack for the totality of the scene. Moreover, by reintroducing the high-pitched ringing of Theo's tinnitus after a particularly violent shell blast, he establishes an implicit homology linking the harrowing cry of the grieving mother, the traumatic resonance of Theo's tinnitus, and the charged affect of the *Threnody*. The piercing ring in Theo's ears sounds like the *Threnody* realized in miniature, a sonic distillation of the latter's brutal textures.

The entire sequence, comprising Theo and Kee's flight to the entrance of the underground cistern, their capture and Theo's near-execution by the militant Fishes, and Theo's subsequent rescue of Kee from a building shelled by British security forces, was shot to resemble one unbroken take.[20] The sustained intensity of Penderecki's dissonances underwrites the temporal integrity of the scene, cementing our experience of a total immersion in the *now* of real-time. In this way, the angular sonorism of *Threnody* amplifies a web of interrelations binding the urgency of the ringing sound to the finite time of the children of men.

Messianic Time

In both its allusion to humanity's extinction and its evocation of the terror of the state of exception, the ringing sound plays a central role in constructing time in *Children of Men*.

It may seem counterintuitive to point to such a static sonority as somehow emblematic of time in a film with such a turbulent and manic narrative, but the simultaneous realization of total stasis alongside radical volatility gets at something very specific to the experience of the state of exception.

For Schmitt, the sovereign's declaration of a state of emergency relies on his or her ability to impose an interruption in the ordinary flow of temporality, a delimited sphere of time outside of ordinary time. In Benjamin's work, this rupture in temporality goes under the name of "messianic time," and, like the "power of real life" that Schmitt sees as inherent in the exception, messianic time breaks through the "torpid repetition" of ordinary existence, exploding the relentless progress of a ceaseless, empty chronology.

Messianic time is the time of the state of emergency, but it is also the time of revolutionary possibility, the potentiality of human history concentrated in the instantaneous present. As Benjamin asserts, "[h]istory is the subject of a structure whose site is not homogenous, empty time, but time filled by the presence of the now [*Jeztzeit*]."[21] It is through this charged construct of "now-time" that Benjamin links the intensity of moments of political turbulence to the volatile temporality of the aesthetic work.[22] More recently, Agamben, building on Benjamin's formulation, arrives at a conception of messianic time carefully distinguished from the notion of apocalypse: in theological discourse, the figure of the apostle witnesses the messianic event not from the standpoint of the apocalyptic *end of time*, but rather, from that of the *time of the end*. The apostle witnesses a time "that *contracts itself and begins to finish*"—not an absence of time, but its extreme concentration.[23] This conception of time offers itself as a singular mechanism for understanding certain kinds of musical and cinematic time. It is a time uniquely cognizant of its own immediacy, training its lens on a still instant now. It is the time that Julian highlights when she describes Theo's tinnitus as the "swan song" of hearing, a time simultaneously marked by a magnified urgency and by the imminence of its end.

THE ETERNITY NOTE

John Tavener's extradiegetic score for *Children of Men* shows us how music might provide a concentrated window into messianic time and onto the state of exception. Tavener's music has often been associated with the work of contemporaries such as Arvo Pärt and Henryk Górecki, whose emphasis on musical simplicity, coupled with often overt allusions to ritual or spiritual practice (in Tavener's case, that of the Greek Orthodox Church), would lead critics to label them as exponents of a musical trend known as "holy minimalism" or "the new spirituality." These artists have achieved considerable popularity, particularly among those not ordinarily invested in classical music. However, as Maria Cizmic has noted, some observers have been dismissive of the music, criticizing the "flatness" of its static musical textures, as well as what they see as its problematic indebtedness to the trappings of religious mysticism. In a modernist critical tradition that celebrates the artwork as a complex autonomous object, with its own interior

reserves of meaning, this combination of musical simplicity with a reliance on an external source of meaning appears suspect.[24]

However, it is precisely these aesthetic and "extramusical" elements of Tavener's work,
with their suggestion of a mystical temporality outside of time, that render it so evocative as nondiegetic accompaniment to Cuarón's filmic vision. Using an unconventional
approach, Tavener wrote his new material for the film (in addition to preexisting work
also on the soundtrack) as what Cuarón calls a "spiritual comment rather than a narrative support."[25] As a consequence, the Tavener segments used sparingly throughout
Children do not underwrite specific cues with goal-directed musical gestures. Rather,
they imbue the film with a consistent emotional texture heavily indebted to Tavener's
conception of musical time.

A key concept here is the notion of the ison. The ison is a drone pitch based on the
tonic of the melodic mode, sustained underneath a line of melodic chant. However,
Tavener, drawing on his understanding of the role of the ison in the Greek Orthodox
tradition, attributes a metaphysical significance to this eternity note.[26] Tavener's static,
immovable drone of the ison configures time as an extended present, highlighting the
volatile transience of everything that happens within its duration. In effect, it manifests
itself as a "time of the end," that moment where, as Agamben would have it, "time contracts upon itself and begins to end," a time that holds the ephemeral and the eternal in a
singular tension.

We hear this tension between the ephemeral and the eternal as a function of the relationship between Tavener's cues and the events unfolding on screen. Tavener's interventions embody the unique temporal flexibility that Michel Chion attributes to music in
relation to other manifestations of film sound. In Chion's terms, Tavener's music refuses
to function as a support for the temporal animation of events in Children: its placid,
nearly immobile tempos stand in marked contrast to the chaotic teleology of the narrative action on screen.[27] In their quality of near-stasis, Tavener's cues in Children emulate the musical components of other cinematic depictions of battle: we might hear and
see resonances here with the stillness of Tōru Takemitsu's scoring of the castle attack
sequence in Kurosawa's Ran or the role of Samuel Barber's Adagio for Strings in the nondiegetic score of Platoon. In each of these cases, the somber cues leave a lingering residue that often seem to contradict the frenetic pace of events elsewhere in the film. The
very popularity (and, indeed, overuse) of this kind of juxtaposition in contemporary
film might lead us to wonder about its efficacy in Children of Men. However, in my view,
what redeems its usage in Cuarón's film is its metonymic, associative link to the unrelenting intensity of the film's visual textures. In sections of Children of Men unaccompanied by nondiegetic music, we continue to "hear" Tavener's eternity notes as an implicit
substratum, situating transient moments in relation to an extended, expansive present.

This aspect of Tavener's music comes to the fore in the scene that I described at the
outset of this discussion, the moment at which the bus bearing Theo, Kee, and Kee's
midwife, Miriam, arrives at the gates of the Bexhill refugee camp (Figure 18.3).[28] As the
passengers look on, guards subject the incoming refugees to a ritual of abnegation. The
soldiers (as part of the diegetic action on screen) use the Libertines song "Arbeit Macht

FIGURE 18.3

Frei" as a mechanism of brutalization. Cuarón likely chose "Arbeit" for the obvious symbolism of its title, its allusion to the slogan that graced the entrances to several German
concentration camps in World War II.[29] At the same time, though, alongside its over-
driven volume, the Libertines song evinces a manic, excessive speed, its cookie-cutter
blues choruses lurch just slightly out of its performers' control. The music's careless
hyperactivity establishes Bexhill as the site of a bizarre carnival of fear, a zone where
those within stand naked before the unrestrained power of the state.[30]

When the soldiers board the bus, Theo and Miriam frantically try to distract them
from Kee, whose labor pains have set in, her cries set in counterpoint with those of the
detainees outside the bus. Kee and Theo watch in horror as Miriam is seized, hustled off
the bus, and hooded. As the bus pulls away, the viewer, looking on from Theo's perspective, is left to imagine Miriam's fate, as the camera tracks past the corpses of other prisoners, efficiently arranged in rows.

At this moment, with the bus doors slamming shut, we hear the bare, ascetic textures
of the opening passage of Tavener's 1998 work, *Eternity's Sunrise* (cue 1:09.58). As the
segment opens, an f^2# pedal, sustained by violins and doubled in the lute part, underscores a chantlike melodic phrase for solo soprano voice, descending from f#[2] to b[2]. In
the following phrases, the soprano and string voices succeed one another in mutual
melodic imitation, the last pitch of each melodic figure serving as the pedal underlying
the next one. Although there is no consistent, unchanging drone, the succession of ped-
als maintains the effect of an unbroken stasis, the languorous movement of one legato
voice held in check by the stillness of the other. Also, the crystalline, vibrato-less texture
of the voicing, which was scored for a baroque ensemble, underscores the elegiac stark-
ness of the sequence.

The text for *Eternity's Sunrise* is derived from the powerful opening quatrains of William Blake's poem, "Auguries of Innocence." These phrases invoke the metaphysical and the corporeal as fundamentally interwoven:

> To see a World in a grain of sand,
> And a Heaven in a wild flower.
> Hold Infinity in the Palm of your hand,
> And Eternity in an hour.[31]

These words, only indistinctly audible in their setting in the Bexhill arrival sequence, nevertheless bear on our discussion here insofar as they inform Tavener's own sensibility. In the final pairing in the first quatrain, Blake invokes the possibility of an eternal present, of the infinitude of time inscribed within the moment. Tavener's use of the *ison* reinforces this sense of the immensity of the charged instant in time. In this way, *Eternity's Sunrise*, functioning here as nondiegetic commentary in *Children of Men*, renders the extended present as an audible event, a sonic realization of distended time in the state of exception.[32]

The strains of *Eternity's Sunrise* continue as Theo and Kee follow the line of refugees through Bexhill's checkpoints. This music establishes the camp as a territory outside of time, a site where our preoccupations with past and future give way to an extended present, removed from time's forward motion. Indeed, Cuarón soon figures this absence of time in a literal way: shortly before Theo enters the gateway to the camp, he is pulled aside by a soldier who orders him to remove his watch. This loss of the timepiece is figured as Theo's transition from the ordinary unfolding of chronological time to the "time of the end," the boundless present of messianic time.

TOMORROW NEVER KNOWS

Children of Men's figuration of the distinctive temporal ontology of the state of exception does not take place within a cultural vacuum. The film's elaborate representation of the state of exception centers on what Zahid Chaudhary has identified as an "allegory of absolute alterity," a network of signification in which the Bexhill camp operates as the site of an engagement with an utterly inassimilable racial, ethnic, and national otherness.[33] At the sonic level, it is popular music that Cuarón puts to work in defining this site of radical alterity, relying on the musical signifiers of blackness to demarcate those "Red Zones" where the state of exception operates unchecked. However, the black British musical genres that saturate the diegesis during the Bexhill scenes work within a larger context in which an unmarked nostalgic whiteness, in the form of classic rock, serves as its tacit foil and antipode.

King Crimson's "Court of the Crimson King" has in some sense become emblematic of *Children of Men*'s iconoclastic soundtrack. This epically pompous progressive rock song, the title track from King Crimson's first album in 1969, provides nondiegetic accompaniment as Theo makes his way to the Ark of Arts, a final repository for the world's artistic treasures.[34] Theo hopes that the tenuous connection he has with London's elite, via his cousin Nigel, who curates the Ark, might allow him to secure the transit papers Julian had demanded on Kee's behalf. En route to the Ark, the Bentley bearing Theo plows past squalid market stalls and crowds of religious extremists, passing through the gates of the Admiralty Arch of Trafalgar Square. The Arch has become the heavily fortified checkpoint for a kind of "Green Zone" at London's core, a space where the expensively attired exist within a sphere of privilege and leisure. Here, *Children of Men* extrapolates a kind of neoliberal dreamscape in which the starkly militarized demarcations of contemporary Baghdad are mapped onto today's widening class divisions, anticipating a frightening political horizon in which the desperately chaotic and the obliviously cocooned occupy rigidly segregated spaces.[35]

Few rock songs are better suited to Cuarón's portrayal of the Ark of Arts than "The Court of the Crimson King." With their accompaniment of flutes, gentle percussion, and acoustic guitar, the verses evoke a kind of pastoral retreat to the idealized concerns of medieval troubadours. However, it is the opening, anthemic sequence that achieves the song's most powerful effect, its pulsing Mellotron chords supporting a descending chain of suspensions in the melody.[36] The sequential pattern generates an exquisite, almost indulgent harmonic tension, accentuating a dimension of unhurried reserve in the song's baroque sensibility. As such, the song provokes a contradictory set of emotional responses. On the one hand, in its unabashed hauteur, it highlights the scene's stark class polarizations, as its measured cadence captures something of the distinctive temporality of London's postapocalyptic elite. However, the poignant tension in these descending sequences also evokes something of the sweeping sense of loss that permeates the texture of daily life in *Children of Men*.

We find part of this sense of loss embodied in the song's relation to the past, its nostalgic allusion to an earlier, ostensibly more hopeful era. "The Court of the Crimson King" stands as merely one instance of a soundtrack permeated with the iconic songs of classic rock. In particular, the musical tastes of Theo's best friend, the aging hippie Jasper, are meant to gesture towards the 1960s as a bygone era of utopian possibilities. At home or in the car, Jasper's stereo blares John Lennon's politically barbed anthem, "Bring on the Lucie (Freeda People)," or Deep Purple's "Hush," with its evocative use of the same descending-fourth chord progression found in Jimi Hendrix's "Hey Joe" and other anthemic rock songs from the 1960s. Beyond these original versions of classic rock songs, though, what are perhaps even more significant are the many cover versions of 1960s songs that appear in connection with Jasper: in one scene, we listen to Jasper talking over a quiet blues cover of the Beatles' "Tomorrow Never Knows" by Junior Parker. In another, we hear Franco Battiato's bizarrely nonidiomatic cover of the Rolling Stones' "Ruby Tuesday." In their versioning of earlier moments of vitality and originality, these covers allude to a cultural infertility underlying the more obvious biological catastrophe of *Children*'s world.[37] Their utopian claims become reduced to empty gestures, sites of privileged retreat.

Throughout *Children of Men*, Cuarón uses tracks from contemporary black British electronic music to outline another world removed from the tone of decadent nostalgia invoked by King Crimson. The hip hop of Roots Manuva plays over the car radio as Theo helps Jasper clear his driveway. Kode 9's "Backwards," a track in the bass-heavy style of dubstep, plays faintly in the background as Luke, a militant from the Fishes, discusses the logistics of Kee's visa over pints with Theo at a nondescript pub. Pressure's "Money Honey," a song combining the harsh production of grime with Warrior Queen's assertive toasting, seeps out of an anonymous storefront.[38] In each of these cases, stylistic elements derived from a variety of African diasporic musics (the heavy bass of dub reggae, the toasting and MCing of hip hop and dancehall, the vamping electronic textures of reggaeton, favela funk, and contemporary American R&B) situate these moments in sharp contradistinction to the nostalgic warmth associated with classic rock elsewhere in the film.

This racialized gap, separating grime and dubstep on the one hand from Deep Purple and King Crimson on the other, bifurcates the popular music of the film along a temporal crease of past and future. Where *Children*'s use of rock covers reminds us of their derivation from an earlier moment in pop history, the stark modernity of the black British genres, their embodiment of the most innovative stylistic interventions in contemporary music, point to a future rendered in their image.[39] For Cuarón, that image of the future lies in that bleak terrain that political theorists have labeled as *biopolitics*: those processes that reduce the sphere of politics to the regulation of the body as a biological entity.[40]

The film's association of black British music with biopolitics becomes especially clear in that scene where Theo and Kee, having passed through the security checkpoints at the Bexhill refugee camp, pass through the gates into a chaotic black market world, where the camp's occupants hustle the new arrivals with offers of accommodations, food, and other necessities. Theo and Kee have arrived in the terrain of *homo sacer*, the bare life of the biological body, stripped of its political protections. If the camp is made up of non-British refugees from around the world, its soundscape is nevertheless dominated by the black British music of dubstep. Random Trio's "Indian Stomp," with its juxtaposition of sampled percussion and South Asian vocals, competes with the brutal distorted bass of Pinch & P Dutty's "War Dub." In contrast to the melodic and harmonic plenitude of Jasper's classic rock songs, each of these tracks presents a stripped-down polyrhythmic tautness. In the characteristic groove of Random Trio's "Indian Stomp," for example, a minimal distribution of sampled drum beats is sufficient to invoke dubstep's efficient quality of rhythmic displacement. The 4/4 pattern is held in tension between its kick drum beats, which fall on the downbeat of 1 and the upbeat of 2, and the high-pitched brake drum sound that falls on the downbeat of 4. This internal rhythmic tension of the groove works in counterpoint with the supple ornaments of the South Asian vocal melody, producing a stark superimposition of divergent ethnic tropes (South Asian melodic constructions, contemporary black British dance textures) with a stripped-down economy of means. Each of these tracks is intricate in its own right; together, though, these overlapping tracks, emergent from different places in the diegesis, are experienced as a disorienting cacophony. In Bexhill's soundscape, rival layers of musical signification resist individual isolation, presenting themselves as a disorienting wall of sound.

It is significant here that as Theo and Kee pass through the turnstile gates of Bexhill, the film shifts from Tavener's nondiegetic score to the realm of diegetic sound. In contrast to the powerfully *empathic* role of Tavener's *Eternity's Sunrise*, which lends us access to the subjective emotional experiences of Theo and Kee on the threshold of Bexhill, the black British music that greets them upon entry figures itself as a fundamentally indifferent and potentially hostile sound that accosts them from without. The South Asian and African diasporic musical tropes of "War Dub" and "Indian Stomp" are here pressed into service as the markers of diegetic music's *anempathic* role, its basic otherness in relation to the subjective affect of the protagonists.[41] In this way, sonic blackness is figured as the musical embodiment of Bexhill, a manifestation of the hostile conditions they face on the threshold of the camp's biopolitical regime.

In affiliating black British electronic dance music so strongly with the conditions of the refugee camp, *Children of Men* projects a highly ambivalent assessment of its political and cultural possibilities. Clearly, this kind of music is deeply invested in the dancing body as a site of pleasure.[42] Here, however, Cuarón's use of African diasporic dance music also works to mark the body as the reduced horizon of the political in the near future of the War on Terror, a site where pain and pleasure overshadow any larger aspirations of the political subject.[43] This strategy risks reifying blackness on two fronts: first, through its straightforward equation of blackness with the abject body of the state of exception, and second, through its erasure of the properly *utopian* dimensions of electronic black music.[44]

The film's musically coded references to blackness function within a film that foregrounds racial difference as a primary, if largely tacit, source of its future world's social tensions. Zahid Chaudhary argues that Cuarón's strategy of foregrounding difference in *Children of Men* depends on a use of signifiers of otherness that border on the stereotypical. This use of such signifiers works in tandem with the film's strategies of anamorphosis. In representing the anguished social confrontations that take place at the periphery of Theo's line of sight, the film relies on the viewer's rapid, shorthand comprehension of the markers of alterity to make these situations visible. As Kee and Theo plunge through the chaotic streets of the Bexhill camp, they encounter an angry funeral procession, replete with brandished Kalishnokovs and repeated chants of "*Allah akbar!*" (God is great!).[45] The scene plays off of the audience's familiarity with countless such images from news reports based in the streets of Baghdad or the West Bank, the abbreviated visual tropes of "strife in the Middle East." In using such tropes, Cuarón seeks to use the unassimilable "otherness" of the camp's inhabitants as a means of making race visible, inscribing it at the core of the film's interrogation of the state of exception. However, this strategy runs the risk of reinforcing pernicious stereotypes, in its bombardment of the audience with loaded signs that it must always apprehend as fleeting distractions, never fully understood or assimilated.

Chaudhary has argued that this ambivalent function of *Children*'s racial troping is an unavoidable consequence of the film's attempt to represent alterity through the mode of allegory.[46] The figure of allegorical representation attempts to address complex truths by

opening up chains of inquiry and referral, pointing outside itself to an abundance of cultural meanings and references. However, this very abundance of associated meanings
has the potential to make the sign itself seem arbitrary, caught up as a mute object within
a field saturated by signification. This, indeed, is our experience of *Children of Men*,
where constant, citational references to the fact of racial differences raise complicated
questions: does the film's political tactic of making visible the inequities of race run the
risk of reproducing racialized discourses? Does the film's strategy of fixing blackness as
the marker of an absolute alterity, identified strongly with the state of exception, undercut or reinforce the ideological work of race thinking?

These questions are lent additional importance when we consider the complicated
role of Kee in *Children of Men*. In his decision to cast *Children*'s lone mother as a black
woman, Cuarón situates alterity at the core of the film's narrative, the site of its world's
hopes for futurity. In some ways, Kee's blackness seems to destabilize the conventional
Hollywood trope in which the future is imagined as a horizon of whiteness. As I noted
earlier, Kee's motherhood is framed in frankly biblical terms: she reveals her pregnancy to Theo in a barn, surrounded by animals, in an obvious allusion to the site of the
Nativity. If I have associated Tavener's music in *Children* with the charged ontological
conditions of "messianic time," this, too, figures as an important dimension of the scene,
where Tavener's *Fragments of a Prayer* emerges on the soundtrack at the moment of
her revelation. This music reappears in the final scene of the movie, where Kee and her
newborn await their rescue by the crew of the *Tomorrow*, the vessel associated with the
Human Project.[47] In this way, Tavener's music embodies "messianic" time in a double
sense: through its sonic evocation of a "time of the end," to return to Agamben's analysis
of messianic time in the Judaic tradition, and in its metonymic association with the more
baldly allegorical allusions to Christianity in the film's depiction of Kee's pregnancy.

However, if Tavener's music bestows humanity on Kee, affiliating her with the nobil-
ity of humanity's persistence, it also, paradoxically, reinforces the film's affiliation of
blackness with the reduced horizon of biopolitics. The Eurocentric musical tropes of
the classical nondiegetic film score have long been used to elicit subjective empathy for
the film's protagonists, in circumstances in which some or all of the principal characters
are black.[48] In *Children of Men*, those moments that most powerfully figure Kee as the
heroine of the film, its bearer of futurity, use Tavener's music to inscribe the film's future
under the sign of whiteness. By contrast, black music in *Children* remains largely external to the film's zone of empathy, despite Cuarón's occasional use of "conscious" tracks
in which black performers grapple with the social tensions of twenty-first-century life.
Throughout *Children*, black music is not only firmly linked to the desperate conditions
of Bexhill's state of exception but is also divorced from the future that is envisioned for
Kee, the film's black protagonist, and for the continuation of humanity embodied in her
newborn daughter. In this way, Cuarón's decision to use African diasporic music to reinforce an allegory of absolute alterity in *Children of Men* runs the risk of undermining the
film's own critique of race-thinking. If this strategy of representing race is an unavoidable corollary to the film's allegorical structure, it nevertheless situates a striking ambiguity at the core of the film's political project.

THE FOREST AMBUSH

At this point, I would like to focus on one scene in particular, to demonstrate how the coordinated use of the aesthetic strategies outlined here enables Cuarón to realize an intensely concentrated synecdoche of the state of exception. In the forest ambush sequence, Cuarón depicts the scene unfolding in the car bearing Theo, Key, and three members of the "Fishes" toward their hoped-for rendezvous with the Human Project. Theo engages in raucous banter with Julian, and the tone here is as relaxed as we have seen anywhere in the film. However, in a rapid-fire succession of events, the situation changes dramatically as the car is ambushed and the passengers are thrown into crisis.

Cuarón and his cinematographer, Emmanuel Lubezki, present this virtuosic sequence in what resembles one unbroken take, all of it shot from the interior of the car, looking out. Here, Cuarón uses a Doggie-Cam two-axis dolly, a device that allows the camera to rove around the interior of the car, operated remotely from the car roof; this setup allows the camera a 360-degree view unimpeded by rigging or crew. The virtuosity of this sequence is partly an effect of digital manipulation: the forest ambush scene was shot in six separate sequences and digitally amalgamated in postproduction.[49] The combined usage of the Doggie-Cam and postproduction editing lends the scene an aspect of radical continuity, as it unfolds seemingly uninterrupted over a period of 4 minutes.

Throughout the scene, the song "Wait" by indie rock band the Kills plays over the car radio as source music, introduced as an innocuous background element. "Wait" pulses with a static intensity, one that realizes calm and tension as *simultaneous* rather than *subsequent* elements: Alison Mosshart's laconic vocals are undergirded by James Hince's relentless eighth-note guitar riff, which sustains the open fifth e—b as a kind of consistent pedal underneath the song's minimal harmonic moves. The effect is that of a latent tension that sits just below the surface, only becoming manifest when the time is right. In the forest sequence, it bides its time throughout the entirety of the forest scene, emerging only belatedly as a thing whose sinister dimensions are known.

In one moment, Theo, Kee, Julian, and the other passengers are exchanging wisecracks; in the next, they are paralyzed with fright as a band of several hundred marauders assail its occupants on all sides. One assailant on a motorcycle shoots Julian in the neck, killing her and triggering Theo's tinnitus. Finally, having outrun their forest attackers, Luke brutally dispatches the police sent out to intercept them, driving off as the strains of "Wait" continue to play over the car radio.

What is terrifying about this scene is the sense that we cannot pinpoint the moment at which things transition from normalcy to panic. Neither the camera nor the music helps us out, using cuts or a shift in affect to decisively mark the beginning of the crisis. Instead, the threat emerges from the periphery of the protagonists' point of view, as an apparition that suggests to the viewer that it was already there.

One of the key dimensions of the state of exception is the impossibility of determining where it begins and ends. The rule of law and its suspension reside alongside one another, with the terror of the exception emerging only incrementally, as something that slowly occupies the same space and time.[50] We see this in the dynamics of the security state in the new millennium, where democratic institutions and extrajudicial tactics have gradually come to operate in tandem. Like the scene in the forest, there is no punctuating moment of change, only a slowly dawning realization of what has already taken place.[51]

CONCLUSION

Throughout the present discussion, I have argued that the soundscape of Alfonso Cuarón's *Children of Men* harnesses sound design, a nondiegetic score, and a wide range of source musics in the service of a cinematic realization of the state of exception. The legal and ontological threshold of the exception marks a point where time itself is transformed and enters into a new configuration in which the residual traces of history are brought into confrontation with the "now" of an extended, heightened present. This threshold is a site where divisions of race, ethnicity, and socioeconomic class come into play, because in *Children*, the suspension of the rule of law maps out a terrain that is almost entirely negotiated by those who fall under the sign of otherness: immigrants, the poor, and people of color, all those for whom the stratified United Kingdom of 2027 has provided no dispensation. Because it manipulates time in powerful ways, and because it is so effective in marking social difference through style, music in *Children* serves as a privileged locus for the realization of the state of exception.

In particular, *Children of Men* raises intriguing questions about the role that cinematic and musical form and technique might play in making visceral the abstract political questions of our moment. For example, in interviews, Cuarón stresses that his use of long takes serve as a means of highlighting the radical potential of the moment.[52] In film, music can play this same role with powerful results, reorienting the listener to reside utterly in the intensity of the now. Indeed, this dimension of music has lent itself to a specific role within the regime of the state of exception, one with which Cuarón himself is familiar. In 2007, he directed a short promotional film based on Naomi Klein's new book *The Shock Doctrine*, in which she discusses the technique of extreme psychological disorientation used in the interrogation of CIA detainees and its potential application to the dynamics of contemporary geopolitics.[53] If Klein foregrounds the use of musical bombardment as a means of radically disorientating the individual subject, Cuarón's soundtrack for the film short dramatically illustrates how the urgent temporality of music saturates a global culture caught in the undecidable threshold of the state of exception. In a striking audiovisual montage, Cuarón presents a succession of images of social, political, and environmental crises, each image marked with stylized stenciled annotation, outlining in shorthand the mechanisms through which radical reforms were introduced (cue 0:04.34). These annotations are synchronized with an electronic soundtrack of grinding industrial coldness, lending the sequence a tactile, visceral momentum.[54]

This closely integrated conception, linking music as sonic power to music's sonic evocation of state power, also animates *Children of Men*, situating the latter film as a more ambitious realization of the themes portrayed in the short film. This linking of music, sound, and power must stand as one of the most compelling and timely interventions of Cuarón's *Children of Men*. However, we must take care to understand the limits of the film's strategies in this direction. The almost simplistic demarcations that the film establishes between the empathic role of Tavener's Eurocentric score, on the one hand, and the bleak, dystopian terrain assigned to the film's African diasporic pop, on the other, raises troubling questions about the degree to which its thematic treatment of alterity reinforces, rather than challenges, racialized structures of power. Moreover, the distinctive temporality of the Tavener score, which I have identified as potentially offering an intriguing window onto the time of the state of exception, may be more effective in theory than in practice: to what extent does such a temporality, remote from the frenetic events on screen, actually *distance* the viewer from the film's representations of state violence? Are there alternative aesthetic strategies that might better realize this connection between music and the state of exception?

Whether or not Cuarón's aesthetic vision succeeds in relation to the terms outlined here, its positing of a dystopia that extrapolates the most disturbing tendencies of our contemporary moment offers us a provocative point of departure for thinking about filmmakers' responsibilities in these areas. What I hope to have demonstrated here is that music, with its powerful phenomenological access to time, and in its terse realization of complex modes of experience, must be central to our conversations about film, violence, and social critique. Far from being a pleasing but supplementary addendum to the film spectacle, music and sound design can reveal much of what is at stake in the urgent questions that presently face us.

NOTES

1. Suzanne Cusick, "Music as Weapon/Music as Torture," *Revista Transcultural de Música* 10 (2006), http://www.sibetrans.com/trans/a152/music-as-torture-music-as-weapon.
2. Carl Schmitt, *Political Theology: Four Chapters on the Concept of Sovereignty*, trans. George Schwab (Chicago and London: University of Chicago Press, 2005), 15.
3. See Horst Bredekamp, "From Walter Benjamin to Carl Schmitt, via Thomas Hobbes," trans. Melissa Horson Hause and Jackson Bond, *Critical Inquiry* 25, no. 2 (1999): 264.
4. Walter Benjamin, *Illuminations: Essays and Reflections*, ed. HannahArendt, trans. Harry Zohn (New York: Schocken Books, 1968), 257.
5. Suzanne Cusick, "Music as Torture/Music as Weapon"; see also Suzanne Cusick, "'You are in a place that is out of the world...': Music in the Detention Camps of the 'Global War on Terror,'" *Journal of the Society for American Music* 2, no. 1 (2008): 1–26.
6. See Giorgio Agamben, *State of Exception*, trans. Kevin Attell (Chicago and London: University of Chicago Press, 2005), 1–31.
7. On this point, see Slavoj Žižek, "'Children of Men': Comments by Slavoj Zizek," commentary, *Children of Men*, directed by Alfonso Cuarón (Universal City, CA: Universal Studios, 2007), DVD.

8. See Lawrence Kramer, *Musical Meaning: Toward a Critical History* (Berkeley: University of California Press, 2002); Carolyn Abbate, "Music—Drastic or Gnostic?" *Critical Inquiry* 30, no. 3 (2004): 505–536.

9. Slavoj Žižek, "'Children of Men': Comments by Slavoj Zizek."

10. Ibid.

11. On anamorphosis, see also Slavoj Žižek, *Looking Awry: An Introduction to Jacques Lacan Through Popular Culture* (Cambridge, MA: MIT Press, 1991), 90–91.

12. These simulated ads, produced as part of a suite of graphics for the film by the design firm Foreign Office, can be seen at http://foreignoffice.com/category/film. Accessed November 12, 2012.

13. Slavoj Žižek, "'Children of Men': Comments by Slavoj Zizek."

14. Giorgio Agamben, *Homo Sacer: Sovereign Power and Bare Life*, trans. Daniel Heller-Roazen (Stanford, CA: Stanford University Press, 1998), 38.

15. Giorgio Agamben, *Homo Sacer*, 4.

16. "Baby Diego," *Children of Men*, DVD.

17. For an extended discussion of the use of the ringing sound, see Jordan Summerlin, "'Children of Men': The Repetition of the Ringing," *Film International*. Accessed January 24, 2010. http://www.filmint.nu/?q=node/87.

18. "Kidnapped," *Children of Men*, DVD.

19. The sequence begins near the end of "Reasonable Accommodations," *Children of Men*, DVD.

20. James Udden notes that the seamlessness of many of these "single-take" shots is illusory, in that they are in actuality the result of digital splicing in postproduction. James Udden, "Child of the Long Take: Alfonso Cuaron's Film Aesthetics in the Shadow of Globalization," *Style* 43, no. 1 (2009): 31.

21. Walter Benjamin, *Illuminations*, 261.

22. Ibid., 263.

23. Giorgio Agamben, "The Time that Is Left," *Epoché* 7, no. 1 (2002): 2. Emphasis mine.

24. Maria Cizmic, "Transcending the Icon: Spirituality and Postmodernism in Arvo Pärt's *Tabula Rasa* and *Spiegel im Spiegel*," *Twentieth-Century Music* 5, no. 1 (2008): 47–48.

25. Kevin Crust, "Unconventional soundscape in 'Children of Men,'" *Chicago Tribune*, January 17, 2007, http://archives.chicagotribune.com/2007/jan/17/news/chi-0701160308jan17.

26. John Tavener, *The Music of Silence: A Composer's Testament*, ed. Brian Keeble (London: Faber and Faber, 1999), 154. For further discussion of temporal stasis in Tavener's work, see Jeremy Begbie, *Theology, Music, and Time* (Cambridge: Cambridge University Press, 2000), 28–44.

27. See Michel Chion, *Audio-Vision: Sound On Screen*, trans. Claudia Gorbman (New York: Columbia University Press, 1994), 13–21, 81–82.

28. "Prison," *Children of Men*, DVD.

29. On the actual playlists alleged to have been used by soldiers in instances of "harsh interrogation," see Justine Sharrock, "The Torture Playlist," *Mother Jones*. Accessed February 22, 2008.http://motherjones.com/politics/2008/02/torture-playlist.

30. Mark Fisher, "Coffee Bars and Internment Camps," *k-punk* (blog). Accessed January 26, 2007. http://k-punk.abstractdynamics.org/archives/008956.html.

31. William Blake, *The Complete Poetry and Prose of William Blake*, ed. David V. Erdman (Berkeley: University of California Press, 1982), 490.

32. On the extramusical implications of musical layers in *Eternity's Sunrise*, see John Tavener, "Composer's Note," *Eternity's Sunrise* (London: Chester Music, 1997), iii.

33. Zahid Chaudhary, "Humanity Adrift: Race, Materiality, and Allegory in Alfonso Cuarón's *Children of Men*," *Camera Obscura* 24, no. 3 (2009): 86–87.

34. "In the Court of the Crimson King," *Children of Men*, DVD.

35. On *Children of Men*'s depiction of neoliberalism as dreamscape, see Mark Fisher, "Coffee Bars and Internment Camps." On the Iraqi "Green Zone" as a metaphor for the segregated spaces of polarized wealth under neoliberalism, see Naomi Klein, in "The Possibility of Hope," commentary, *Children of Men* (Universal City, CA: Universal Studios, 2007), DVD.

36. The melody presents a succession of 4-3 suspensions: f#^{1}—e^1 over C major, and e^1-d#^{1} over B^{7}sus^4—B major.

37. On this issue of "cultural infertility," see Mark Fisher, "Coffee Bars and Internment Camps," and Slavoj Žižek, " 'Children of Men': Comments by Slavoj Zizek."

38. Grime and dubstep are two of the most distinctive genres in the contemporary British soundscape. Both are heavily indebted to contemporary rap, reggaeton, and R&B MCing and production, as well as to the post-rave electronic dance musics of what Simon Reynolds calls the "hardcore continuum," referring to the genre of breakbeat hardcore. See Simon Reynolds, "The Wire 300: Simon Reynolds on the Hardcore Continuum #7: Grime (and a Little Dubstep)," *Wire*, February 2009. http://www.thewire.co.uk/articles/2040/.

39. On this point, see Kodwo Eshun, *More Brilliant Than the Sun: Adventures in Sonic Fiction* (London: Quartet Books, 1998).

40. See Giorgio Agamben, *Homo Sacer*, 3.

41. Note 43: See Michel Chion, *Audio-Vision*, 8–9, 221–222.

42. On this point, see Jeremy Gilbert and Ewan Pearson, *Discographies: Dance Music, Culture and the Politics of Sound* (London and New York: Routledge, 1999), 38–53.

43. On black music and biopolitics, see Paul Gilroy, *Against Race: Imagining Political Culture Beyond the Color Line* (Cambridge, MA: Harvard University Press, 2000), 177–206.

44. On the utopian promise of African diasporic music, see Kodwo Eshun, *More Brilliant Than the Sun*; Michael E. Veal, *Dub: Soundscapes and Shattered Songs in Jamaican Reggae* (Middleton, CT: Wesleyan University Press, 2007), 208–214.

45. Zahid Chaudhary, "Humanity Adrift," 89.

46. Ibid., 87–91.

47. Zahid Chaudhary, "Humanity Adrift," 94.

48. On this point, see Ella Shohat and Robert Stam, *Unthinking Eurocentrism: Multiculturalism and the Media* (London and New York: Routledge, 1994), 209.

49. James Udden, "Child of the Long Take," 31.

50. Giorgio Agamben, *Homo Sacer*, 38.

51. Fisher, "Coffee Bars and Internment Camps."

52. Alfonso Cuarón, interviewed in "Under Attack," commentary, *Children of Men* (Universal City, CA: Universal Studios, 2007), DVD; see also Alfonso Cuarón, in Kim Voynar, "Interview: *Children of Men* Director Alfonso Cuarón."

53. See Alfonso Cuarón and Naomi Klein, *The Shock Doctrine*, film, narr. by Naomi Klein (London: Renegade Films, 2007), http://www.guardian.co.uk/books/video/2007/sep/07/naomiklein; Naomi Klein, *Shock Doctrine: The Rise of Disaster Capitalism* (New York: Metropolitan Books, 2007).

54. Alfonso Cuarón and Naomi Klein, *The Shock Doctrine*.

SELECT BIBLIOGRAPHY

Agamben, Giorgio. *Homo Sacer: Sovereign Power and Bare Life*. Translated by Daniel Heller-Roazen. Stanford, CA: Stanford University Press, 1998.

——."The Time That Is Left."*Epoché* 7, no. 1 (2002): 1–14.

Benjamin, Walter. *Illuminations: Essays and Reflections*. Edited by Hannah Arendt. Translated by Harry Zohn. New York: Schocken Books, 1968.

Chaudhary, Zahid. "Humanity Adrift: Race, Materiality, and Allegory in Alfonso Cuarón's *Children of Men*." *Camera Obscura* 24, no. 3 (2009): 73–109.

Chion, Michel. *Audio-Vision: Sound On Screen*. Translated by Claudia Gorbman. New York: Columbia University Press, 1994.

Cusick, Suzanne. "Music as Weapon/Music as Torture." *Revista Transcultural de Música* 10 (2006). http://www.sibetrans.com/trans/a152/music-as-torture-music-as-weapon.

Stilwell, Robynn. "The Fantastical Gap Between Diegetic and Non-Diegetic." In *Beyond the Soundtrack: Representing Music in Cinema*, edited by Daniel Goldmark, Lawrence Kramer, and RichardLeppert, 184–202. Berkeley: University of California Press, 2007.

Udden, James. "Child of the Long Take: Alfonso Cuaron's Film Aesthetics in the Shadow of Globalization." *Style* 43, no. 1 (2009): 26–44.

Schmitt, Carl. *Political Theology: Four Chapters on the Concept of Sovereignty*. Translated by George Schwab. Chicago and London: University of Chicago Press, 2005.

Tavener, John. *The Music of Silence: A Composer's Testament*. Edited by Brian Keeble. London: Faber and Faber, 1999.

CHAPTER 19

UNDERSTANDING THE
PLEASURES OF WAR'S
AUDIOVISION

MATTHEW SUMERA

> There is talk that many Vietnam films are antiwar, that the message is war
> is inhumane and look what happens when you train young American
> men to fight and kill.... But actually, Vietnam war films are all pro-war,
> no matter what the supposed message, what Kubrick or Coppola or
> Stone intended. Mr. and Mrs. Johnson in Omaha or San Francisco or
> Manhattan will watch the films and weep and decide once and for all that
> war is inhumane and terrible, and they will tell their friends at church and
> their family this, but Corporal Johnson at Camp Pendleton and Sergeant
> Johnson at Travis Air Force Base and Seaman Johnson at Coronado Naval
> Station and Spec 4 Johnson at Fort Bragg and Lance Corporal Swofford
> at Twentynine Palms Marine Corps Base watch the same films and are
> excited by them, because the magic brutality of the films celebrates the
> terrible and despicable beauty of their fighting skills.
>
> —Anthony Swofford, *Jarhead*

THIS chapter is about America's post-9/11 audiovisions, somatic warscapes[1] extending across indeterminate time and space, modulating affect, and vitalizing brutality.
From feature films to documentaries, televised news to soldiers' online viral videos,
armed forces recruitment advertising to video games, the sights and sounds of contemporary war are atmospheric. They are environmental. They are miasmic and a
weapon, less about war than part of it. Projectiles more than representations, war's
audiovisions are best understood as hallucinatory expectations—soundvisions in
the phantasmagoric sense[2]—enlivening dreams of collective violence through a merciless logic of their own. They premeditate, in Grusin's terms, preparing us for the
future inevitable of perpetual conflict even as they death-deal in the banality of the
auditories and imaginaries of prosaic combat.[3] Such futurity, however, is not simply

(or only) used to practice for the "catastrophe of global terror"[4] or to fortify what Massumi calls the "self-renewing menace potential" of "affective fact."[5] As much, it presents the hope of an Ajax-like exuberance, an aggressive annihilation, a desire to "Kill 'Em All." In what follows, I work to understand the audiovisual logic buttressing such sentiments.

Denouncing war's audiovisions, like Mr. and Mrs. Johnson denounce war itself, is easy enough to do. These audiovisions are, of course, barbaric. Condemning them, however, gains us little, for they are not so easily dismissed. In this essay, instead, I work to understand the potency, pleasures, and affects of America's post-9/11 audiovisions to a range of social actors. For the sounds and images of war (created by governments and multinationals, military personnel and armchair warriors, mainstream media and nongovernmental organizations [NGOs] alike) are an essential part of war's felt impact, of war's annihilatory desires. Examining them, then, helps clarify the reasons Americans are comfortable with war, the reasons, indeed, why they often embrace the war ideal. Examining them helps explain, as well, America's military normal: "The massive investments in war and in the public relations of war, and the assorted beliefs that sustain them all."[6] For America's post 9/11 audiovisions ultimately tell the story of what war means to the most militarized nation in the history of the world, projecting that narrative far beyond its geographical borders. Developed from below as much as from above, such sights and sounds explain war's brutal sublime, something we must first understand if we ever hope to move beyond it.

To focus my analysis, I will examine a much smaller set of depictions in what follows—viral videos featuring images of US armed forces, set to some form of popular music and posted online. Created by civilians and military personnel alike, the sheer volume of such productions is extraordinary, representing every stage of what we might think of as the lifecycle of war, of war's eternal return.[7] "Death Zone" is but one example.[8] A highlight video of combat carnage set to the music of the heavy metal cello group Apocalyptica, the four-minute production was shared among members of the "kill team," US soldiers found guilty of murdering and mutilating Afghan civilians. An ethnographic video of sorts—created by soldiers, for soldiers, an interpretation of what soldiers do—it is illustrative of the ways in which such productions both contribute to and amplify war's ferocious logic.

In thinking through these videos, the locations in which they circulate, and the uses to which they are put, I am particularly interested in theorizing their belliphonics.[9] Although much valuable work has been done analyzing war as spectacle—scholarship aimed at critiquing the logic of war's visual culture[10]—such examination tends to describe a world without sound, a world struck dumb, as it were, devoid of auditory logic and concomitant affect. My essay addresses this lacuna directly. In it, I examine the connections and consequences of militarized soundimages, and I focus on the active deployment of these creations. Specifically, I work to show how sound and music function as generative and affective forces in these projections, and, in so doing, I seek to develop a musical anthropology of contemporary warfare and collective violence.

"Die Terrorists Die"

Musical viral videos depicting the buildup to war most often project dreams of technologically mediated, precision killing. Developed by military personnel and civilians alike, such videos began circulating within weeks of the attacks of 9/11. One production, "Taliban Bodies," for example, was first posted to the web in October 2001.[11] Created by IT director Ryan Hickman and set to the song "Bodies" by nu metal band Drowning Pool, "Taliban Bodies" features images and video of decontextualized military equipment and random explosions edited to fit the contours of the song. So tight is the connection between sight and sound, in fact, that few images appear in the video that are not directly aligned with some musical, primarily rhythmic or timbral, feature. This kind of extraordinary cohesion is a key aspect of video affect and an issue I will return to later. For now, it is enough to quote Hickman about his motivation for creating "Taliban Bodies": "every time 'Bodies' by Drowning Pool, came on the radio, I always pictured military equipment blowing things up to the beat of the song."[12]

Defining war as heightened musical experience, "Taliban Bodies" was an immediate internet sensation. Within a few weeks of being posted to the web, it appeared on local television news programs, cropped up at basic training sites throughout the United States, and circulated informally among deployed US personnel around the world. Indeed, among all armed service members I have interviewed during the more than four years of my research, I have yet to meet one unfamiliar with the video. In addition to such casual circulation, all branches of the US military have shown "Taliban Bodies" in official settings as well, ranging from basic combat training to countless combat deployments. As one fan on an online chatboard writes, "Hell yes! This was like the quintessential indoc vid for new trainees when I came in ... lol."[13] Largely because of its success, "Taliban Bodies" in turn set the precedent for countless similar productions, and Hickman eventually went on to develop his own website, Grouchymedia.com, where he now features more than sixty videos sent to him by a variety of editors over the past decade. Defined as "the place to find those pump-you-up-to-kill-the-bad-guys videos everyone has been talking about," Grouchymedia.com, according to Hickman, "is focused on providing a morale boost to our U.S. and allied troops around the world. The videos you'll find here are about them, for them, and couldn't have been made without them!"[14]

How does music contribute to such intentions and affect? To answer this question, I want to look at one representative production in some detail—"Die Terrorists Die," Hickman's follow-up to "Taliban Bodies," released in 2002.[15] The video itself is consistent with numerous other productions circulating on the web, and a close analysis of it will help explain the broader appeal and impact of these creations.

Including a title screen situating the video as "the 'Taliban Bodies' sequel," "Die Terrorists Die" begins with a brief dedication to "all US and Allied Armed Forces." It continues with a clip of an American flag swaying in the breeze, accompanied by a voice-over from then Secretary of Defense, Donald Rumsfeld: "Smart bombs are useless without smart people. We need motivated, highly focused men and women, and we have them, in abundance."

From the start, "Die Terrorists Die," set to the song "Die MF Die" by the nu metal band Dope, is framed as a recruitment advertisement and buildup to war. Hickman's dedication to military personnel clearly identifies the video's intended audience, and the recognition of allied forces presages then President Bush's eventual language about the "coalition of the willing" during the buildup to the 2003 War in Iraq. The auditory/visual combination of Rumsfeld's voice, aligned with imagery of the American flag, moreover, works to indicate the need for new recruits while simultaneously acknowledging the commitments of current military personnel. The inclusion of language about smart bombs is important too, inserting an idealized form of distanced killing into the video's narrative, a theme I will return to later.

Immediately following Rumsfeld's quote, Dope's song begins, with the band's guitarist playing muted sixteenth notes on a heavily processed guitar, a sound further manipulated with a phaser and panned left to right, suggesting a siren-like quality filled with a sense of warning and menace. As this sound continues, the rhythm guitarist enters, playing a short, heavily distorted and syncopated phrase. This figure is played twice; the first time, Hickman synchronizes it to an image of the back of the head of drill instructor, the second he matches to a picture of a fighter pilot, apparently sitting in a cockpit, helmet and mask on. Both audiovisions suggest preparation and readiness, training and anticipation, and these perceptions are underscored by the processed guitar sound, which rapidly moves up in pitch, suggesting the auditory equivalent of a rocket launch; indeed, in a similar video set to the same tune, this sound is actually synchronized to a sequence in which a fighter jet takes off. As the heavily processed sound quickly reaches its peak—the sound of preparedness reaching its inevitable fulfillment—the entire musical prelude abruptly ends in a caesura, or brief pause, prior to the full band entering. Dope makes heavy use of such caesuras throughout "Die MF Die," each pause providing a moment of respite while also functioning to propel the song forward when the music resumes. Hickman carefully exploits these moments through his editing practices as well, an issue I will explore shortly.

When the full band enters after the first caesura, the tempo for the remainder of the song is set. "Die MF Die" is an up-tempo nu metal song, roughly 125 beats per minute, consistent with allegro markings in the Western art tradition. Set in 4/4 time, the song continues with an elaboration of the initial syncopated guitar line, this time accompanied by the drummer who plays a straight quarter-note rhythm, four beats to the measure, on his bass drum. During this section of the video, Hickman edits photos of soldiers standing at attention (presumably during basic training drills) to align with the individual bass drum notes. After two measures of this sound–image combination, the drum pattern changes to match the rhythm of the syncopated guitar figure, triggering a more agitated visual sequence in which Hickman aligns pictures of soldiers on obstacle courses to match the new drum rhythm. He then synchronizes images of soldiers shooting at a firing range to the beat, followed by sequences of military vehicles (tanks and armored cars) sped up to match the tempo of the song, and so on. The sped-up imagery, in particular, gives the video an almost cartoony feel, moments of Keystone Cops-like freneticism that would be humorous if they were not so deadly serious.[16]

The audiovisual trajectory of "Die Terrorists Die"—and indeed, countless similar productions—is set in these first few sequences, in which rapidly edited images of recruits, perfectly aligned to specific musical features, morph into scenes of basic combat training, military vehicles, and ultimately a plane dropping a bomb. Another caesura aligns with the image of the bomb falling, and Hickman conspicuously edits footage of a massive explosion and resulting mushroom cloud to synchronize exactly with the moment the band resumes the song. Here and throughout the remainder of the video, through near virtuosic editing practices, Hickman visualizes these musical pauses in dramatic ways, drawing attention to them through changes in his editing rhythms and creating, in turn, what we might think of as rhythmic nodes of audiovisual destruction.

Hickman's careful approach to visual editing applies to the vocal features of the song as well. Lyrically, "Die MF Die" projects an aggressive rebellion in which the singer forcefully rejects everything his interlocutor does or thinks—"I don't need your forgiveness/I don't need your hate/I don't need your acceptance" and so on. During the chorus of the song, these rejections change to violent demands, and the lyrics become nothing more than a murderous mantra screamed four times through: "Die motherfucker, die motherfucker, die." Rhythmically, the band's lead singer performs the syllables of the word "motherfucker" as four sixteenth notes with each "die" aligning to an accented eighth note, generating a rapid sense of accelerated momentum. Although the transcription of this rhythm in Figure 19.1 functions as a basic schematic, it is more complex. Specifically, the performance of the lyric produces a 2:3 polyrhythm that generates a bounce in the words because of their rhythmic placements and syncopated and non-syncopated accents; there is a certain amount of elision, as well, in the pronunciation of "motherfucker" that adds to this effect. This rhythmic phrasing, then, is what generates momentum in both the song and video during the chorus, pushing the music and, by extension, the imagery synchronized with it, forward.[17]

Hickman takes full advantage of this phrase in his video, aligning pictures of Osama Bin Laden and others precisely with these sixteenth notes during the first chorus of the song.[18] The resulting sequence, in turn, constitutes the quickest set of visual edits in the entire production, and the speed at which the pictures of the presumed terrorists go by is so fast that it is impossible, without moving frame by frame, to tell who they actually are. The ultimate intent, however, is seemingly obvious, as audioviewers are presented with an onslaught of Arab-looking men, shown at a speed in which they are clearly meant to

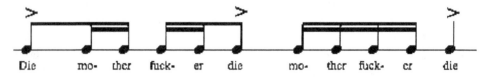

FIGURE 19.1 Lyrics and rhythm to the chorus of Dope's "Die MF Die."

appear indistinguishable and synchronized to a soundtrack that does little more than demand their death.

And yet, perhaps surprisingly, Hickman does not visualize subsequent choruses with pictures of Arab-looking men, even as he utilizes similar editing tempos throughout. Instead, he maps sequences of Air Force planes, submarines, and other military equipment to succeeding refrains, synchronizing the lyrics, "die motherfucker, die motherfucker, die" to images of US armed forces. Given the dedication at the beginning of the video and everything he has written about his support of American troops, however, we can assume that conclusions based on a too direct interpretation of this combination would not be consistent with Hickman's intent. Such mapping, therefore, cannot be completely understood only through a focus on signification, and these video productions, to some extent, have less to do with meaning and representation and more to do with intensity, impact, and force. Speed, in particular, defines a key component of "Die Terrorists Die" and similar productions, and the ways in which Hickman structures visual tempos, including his editing approaches to visualizing caesuras—moments that function to mark tempo while reenergizing rhythm—are essential to video affect. "Die Terrorists Die," as a result, is perhaps best understood as a profound study of speed, a form of engendering violence through the careful manipulation of velocity, calling to mind Virilio's writings on dromology. As Virilio notes, "without the violence of speed, that of weapons would not be so fearsome."[19] Hickman seems to intuitively understand this connection, working to bolster both through his production.

As can be seen in this brief analysis of the first minute of "Die Terrorists Die," music is essential to the impact and trajectory of the video. The nu metal subgenre, in particular, is featured in countless similar productions, a metal/hip hop combination known for its distorted, oftentimes downtuned guitars and screamed heavy metal vocals. These musical features, including the rapid tempos noted above, provide the subgenre with its fundamental sense of aggressiveness, an attribute lauded by bands and fans alike. In distinction to other forms of heavy metal, however, nu metal importantly relies on groove-based drumming influenced by alternative rock bands like Faith No More and the Red Hot Chili Peppers rather than the more extreme blast beats found in subgenres such as death metal, grindcore, or black metal. Nu metal's song structures are more consistent with verse-chorus-verse pop structures as well, a significant divergence from the prog-like tendencies in other forms of heavy metal. Because of such features, the subgenre's harsh timbres, oftentimes violent lyrics, and noise-based aesthetics are significantly more radio friendly than most post-thrash versions of heavy metal. Accordingly, and owning no small part to its incorporation of periodically rapped vocals, nu metal catapulted to the top of the rock charts in the mid-1990s, where it virtually dominated hard rock airplay, the summer tour circuit (namely, the 1997–2002 versions of "Ozzfest" and the "Family Values Tour"), and MTV's Total Request Live by the end of the decade.[20]

In addition to its broad popularity at the beginning of the twenty-first century, nu metal has become the de facto music for a sizable majority of military personnel across the US armed forces.[21] It is no coincidence, then, that numerous songs by nu metal bands have found their way into countless military representations, from video games to armed forces recruitment advertising (the US Navy used two Godsmack songs in their "Accelerate Your Life" advertising campaign, for example) to feature films and more. Indeed, the subgenre has become what we might think of as an "affective platform"[22] for both imaging and engaging in contemporary warfare and combat, a potent musical index and sometimes icon (especially in some of its more rapid-fire, double bass drum sections) of post 9/11 US militarism.

More than purely representational, however, nu metal has also been weaponized over the course of the last decade as well, being used both in interrogations and as a form of sonic assault when played over loudspeakers at extremely high volume.[23] As David Peisner notes about Drowning Pools' "Bodies," the song used in Hickman's first production, such weaponization has also been routinely turned onto the self:

> [I]f the military had its own People's Choice Awards, Drowning Pool would win top honors. Nearly every interrogator and soldier I spoke to mentioned the agro-metal outfits 2001 hit "Bodies"—with its wild-eyed chorus, "Let the bodies hit the floor"— as a favorite for both psyching up U.S. soldiers and psyching out enemies and captives.[24]

It is in such use that the internally and externally facing mapping evidenced in the chorus of "Die Terrorists Die"—in which the lyrics, "die motherfucker, die motherfucker, die," are synchronized to images of both presumed terrorists and US troops—is further clarified. Just as the sounds of nu metal are seized on to psych up US soldiers and psych out enemy combatants, so, too, are the sounds of nu metal used in "Die MF Die" to vitalize on the one hand and terrorize on the other. In the end, then, it is the music's affective, devastating potentials that seem most to matter. Nu metal's deployment in these viral videos is therefore militarized in ways similar to these more directly obvious uses.[25]

The fact that a subgenre of heavy metal has been militarized in such a fashion, perhaps, should not be surprising. After all, more than any other form of popular music, heavy metal has long been preoccupied with the nature and meaning of warfare and collective violence. From Black Sabbath's early antiwar song, "War Pigs," through Slayer's "War Ensemble," to the current battle metal subgenre, war and combat have been central themes in heavy metal's archive.[26] Indeed, although little mentioned in Walser[27] and other early histories of the music, metal's near obsession with war seems particularly apropos to the genre of popular music most dedicated to the exploitation of "ugly feelings."[28] And what feelings, after all, could be uglier than those surrounding war and the concomitant buildup of an arsenal that could kill everyone on the planet many times over? From lyrics to guitar effects, timbre to drum sounds, imagery to band names, much about metal has been specifically designed to generate a sense of power and unrelenting force. That a genre dedicated to unearthing negative emotions (a genre, moreover, that came of age during a time in which nuclear annihilation seemed a real possibility) should seize on war as a generative theme, then, should not shock. Nu metal's appeal among military personnel and its consequent uses noted here are best understood within this broader history.

As important as nu metal is to "Die Terrorists Die" and similar productions, it assumes its primary significance only through Hickman's editing practices. Editing, as noted earlier, is essential to the sense of speed and aggressiveness projected in the video, and editing practices provide the visuals their ultimate structure and intensity. As Carol Vernallis notes about music videos more broadly, "editing…places the video's images and the song's formal features in close relation."[29] In war videos like "Die Terrorists Die," this is an understatement. Fundamentally, the entire production is little more than an editing exercise in which the photo evidence of the raw materials of war is closely aligned to an aggressive, up-tempo heavy metal song. The creation of elaborate sync points, a term I borrow from Michel Chion's theorization of film sound,[30] consequently becomes crucial to video affect and defines, in turn, one of the reasons people choose to watch and listen. As one fan writes about a similar video creation: "excellent editing; the cutaway to the dog eating, the one Marine shooting into the mirror, the bricks in the wall being shot down like a Tetris game…all right in tune to real hellraiser music. I was into the excitement of it but I managed to be grateful for their bravery as well."[31] Such videos work to reconfigure the killing process, allowing us to experience it in new, fine-grained, emotive detail.[32]

Editing practices, in this way, assume an ideological value in these video productions. As Chion argues in a passage on active and passive perception, music in film (and certainly in other media) "can become an insidious means of affective and semantic manipulation."[33] Although such possibilities certainly exist, it is only the case because of the careful ways in which music is placed in relationship to the image—or, in productions like "Die Terrorists Die," the reverse. Accordingly, as Chion elsewhere observes, the careful manipulation of sound can be singularly crucial to film because often "what we hear is what we haven't had time to see."[34] This is particularly true in the chorus section addressed earlier, in which rapid editing makes it impossible to tell who or what we are actually seeing. In such video moments, it is the song, then, that functions to provide both narrative trajectory and a formal glue to hold together what would otherwise be a set of random, unrelated images. Through careful editing practices, the song drives the images, projecting into them a heightened sense of deadly power.

The devastating affects of "Die Terrorist Die" and similar productions should not be underestimated. As Hickman notes about the imagery he uses in his second video, "almost every picture and clip used in Die Terrorists Die came directly from people in the service, including a bunch of shots taken in 2002, during the war in Afghanistan."[35] After the initial success of "Taliban Bodies," US military personnel stationed throughout the world sent Hickman countless pictures from their deployments as a token of their appreciation for his work on the video. In subsequently incorporating this imagery into "Die Terrorists Die," a process taking more than 100 hours to complete,[36] Hickman in turn developed what we might think of as a feedback loop of affective influence, in which his influence on military personnel in turn influenced him with the hope of further influencing them, and so on.

Such a loop calls to mind Grusin's theorization of the modulation of affect—"we learn how to modulate our affective states by interacting with things, people, media, or technologies in our environment."[37] As he observes, such modulation ultimately means that our affects "co-evolve with our media and other new technologies,"[38] eventually working to blur the distinction between body and machine, resulting in what he calls, by way of Deleuze and Guattri, "machinic enslavement."[39] Accordingly, as Lazarrato argues, "the functions, organs, and strengths of man are connected with certain functions, organs, and strengths of the technical machine and together they constitute an arrangement."[40]

In introducing the concept of "machinic enslavement," I want to argue that in watching and listening to videos like "Taliban Bodies" and "Die Terrorists Die," military personnel learn how and what to feel about the act of militarized killing. Moreover, they learn important things about how and why to kill while sitting at their computer screens, and these lessons, in turn, are carried to the actual fields of battle.[41] It should not be surprising, then, that in some video productions, such as "Operation Phantom Fury,"[42] we see moments in which marines clearly pose for the camera while they actually shoot and get shot at (sounds integrated diegetically into the video). In one scene in particular, at 3:13 into the production, a marine can be seen smashing a mirror, an act clearly meant to be captured by a handheld digital camera. That this event was later synchronized to land directly on the beat of a nu metal song helps solidify the affective loop and machinic enslavement of these productions. Such videos, to this end, have become an extension of what Swofford calls the terrible and despicable beauty of the fighting skills of military personnel, and individual soldiers, sailors, marines, and others accordingly act out new videos even as they fight actual battles. For those military personnel who may consider themselves unfortunate enough to be assigned desk jobs while deployed, videos become a particularly important venue as well, and I have heard of a number of instances in which these service members have been seen rolling around in the dirt to look appropriately disheveled before filming their own productions. Soldiers like to pretend they are soldiers, too.[43]

In many ways, the theater of war has become quite literal. Certainly, similar instances of soldiers acting for cameras predate the current conflicts, as war correspondent Michael Herr notes, writing about the theatricality of Vietnam combatants: "You don't know what a media freak is until you've seen the way a few of those grunts would run around during a fight when they knew that there was a television crew nearby; they were actually making war movies in their heads."[44] What is different about America's current audiovisions, however, is that there is never a moment in which the camera and the available soundtrack are not present, never a moment in which the inevitable viral video is not being created, and never a moment in which the newest creation, set often to the same limited number of songs, is not being freshly uploaded to the internet for all to see, hear, and eventually rehearse. The ease and increasing affordability of digital technologies, combined with the mandates of aggressive documentation—what Lewis calls "compulsive communicationalism"[45]—have created a demand for self-expression that must continuously be fed. And, at the beginning of the twenty-first century, it is nu metal that provides the glue to hold such visions together.

This is the devastating power of these projections, and Hickman's video productions, along with countless others, have become, in and of themselves, significant weapons in the US-led wars in Iraq and Afghanistan. The success of these videos, in their ability to modulate affect and inspire collective violence, is in turn directly evidenced in "Die Terrorists Die" itself, in which Hickman includes several images sent to him of bombs with "Thanks Grouchy" written across their sides, tributes to his initial video and the Grouchymedia website he went on to develop (see Figure 19.2).

In including this imagery, placed in the video directly in the midst of the chorus section analyzed earlier, Hickman reflexively acknowledges his role in post-9/11 US militarism—in a way, paying homage to his own fighting skills. Indeed, it is not going too far to think of this actual bomb as the materialization of the audiovisual bombs Hickman has dropped in his videos, and we might best position the precision editing practices analyzed above vis-à-vis the idealized, distance killing lauded in battlefield terms such as "surgical precision" and the smart bombs Rumsfeld speaks about at the beginning of the video. In profound ways, the meticulousness of the former pays tribute to the brutal potentialities of the latter. That the latter, in turn, enters the actual field of battle with a physical trace of the former on its side only helps to solidify this devastating relationship and the machinic enslavement that ties nu metal, the home computer, editing software, military personnel, and battlefield imagery together. As Steve Marz writes in *Stars and Stripes,* the official newspaper of the US Armed Forces, "if the U.S. military can be imagined as a prizefighter, these would be the music videos played as he made his way to the ring."[46] Such audiovisions are less about war than they are part of it.

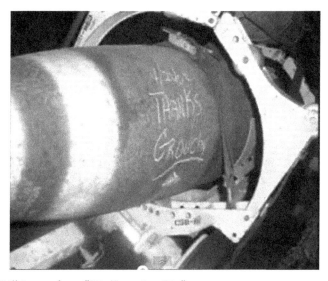

FIGURE 19.2 Still image from "Die Terrorists Die."

Coda

As I have argued, war's contemporary depictions cannot be separated from the actualities of the battlefield. Less about representing than creating, such productions function to project war as a sonic immersive experience. Through them, combat becomes affective, and, as Deleuze and Guattari write in their analysis of the war machine, "affects transpierce the body like arrows, they are weapons of war."[47] In becoming musical, then, war also becomes numinous, standing outside of specifics, idealized as felt experience, naturalized, totalized, and invulnerable to doubt. This is the lasting impact of these audiovisions and one that, through the loops noted earlier, seems to show no signs of loosening its grip.

In the next stage of my work, though, I seek to find ways to short circuit the logic at the nexus of these creations. In having watched and listened to hundreds of hours of videos over the past four years, I can attest to the damaging affects of these projectiles, and I have seen things I wish to have not seen, heard things I wish to be able to unhear. Although undoubtedly uncomfortable, this is perhaps also the generative experience for moving such audiovisions in a new direction, one that explores the aesthetics of unlistening and of asynchronization. How do we imagine a world in which sound and vision work to de-escalate and detune? This is the question we desperately need to ask and answer. One early example potentially shows the way. "Boom" by the heavy metal band System of a Down, is the band's official video, set to images not of combat and war but instead of peaceful protests against the 2003 invasion of Iraq.[48] Mixed with the sounds of people talking about their reasons for protesting, it imagines a different power and force, one that seeks to engender peace rather than violence. It, unfortunately, is one of few productions that work to show the hope of a more just and equitable future. In its success in imaging the reorganization of sound and vision, however, it provides a new, important audiovisual direction and crucial model for further study.

Acknowledgments

This chapter is dedicated to my friend and mentor, anthropologist Neil Whitehead, who unexpectedly died as I was writing it. His guidance, fierce intellect, and profound compassion are deeply missed.

Notes

1. Carolyn Nordstrom originally developed the term "war-scape," which she derived from the work of Arjun Appadurai and his introduction of the term "ethnoscape." Carolyn Nordstrom, *A Different Kind of War Story* (Philadelphia: University of Pennsylvania Press, 1997), 37; Arjun Appadurai, "Disjuncture and Difference in the Global Cultural Economy," *Public Culture* 2, no. 2 (1990): 1–24.

2. For an insightful study of the connections between phantasmagoria, aesthetics, and what she calls anaesthetics, see Susan Buck-Morss, "Aesthetics and Anaesthetics: Walter Benjamin's Artwork Essay Reconsidered," *October* 62 (1992): 3–41.

3. Richard Grusin, *Premediation: Affect and Mediality after 9/11* (New York: Palgrave MacMillan, 2010).

4. Ibid, 9.

5. Brian Massumi, "The Future Birth of the Affective Fact: The Political Ontology of Threat," in *The Affect Theory Reader*, ed. Melissa Gregg and Gregory Seigworth (Durham: Duke University Press, 2010), 53.

6. Catherine Lutz, "The Military Normal," in *The Counter-Counterinsurgency Manual: Or, Notes on Demilitarizing American Society*. Network of Concerned Anthropologists. (Chicago: Prickly Paradigm Press, 2009), 26.

7. Given the transient nature of these video productions, in which they are uploaded one day and often taken down the next, it is difficult to assess how many currently circulate. I would estimate, however, that there are easily thousands.

8. An excerpt from the video is linked to a feature story at *Rolling Stone*. See Mark Boal, "The Kill Team," *Rolling Stone*, accessed March 27, 2011, http://www.rollingstone.com/kill-team.

9. Martin Daughtry, "Belliphonic Sounds and Indoctrinated Ears: The Dynamics of Military Listening in Wartime Iraq," in *Pop When the World Falls Apart*, ed. Eric Weisbard (Durham: University of Duke Press, 2012) 111–144.

10. See, among others, Paul Virilio, *War and Cinema: The Logistics of Perception* (London: Verso, 1989); Jean Baudrillard, "War Porn," *International Journal of Baudrillard Studies* 2, no. 1 (2005): http://www.ubishops.ca/baudrillardstudies/vol2_1/taylor.ht; Nicholas Mirzoeff, *Watching Babylon: The War in Iraq and Global Visual Culture*. (London: Routledge, 2005) ; and Judith Butler, *Frames of War: When Is Life Grievable?* (New York: Verso, 2010).

11. Available online at "Taliban Bodies," GrouchyMedia, http://www.grouchymedia.com/videos/2001/10/taliban-bodies.html. For an in-depth analysis of "Taliban Bodies," see Matthew Sumera, "The Soundtrack to War," in *Virtual War and Magical Death: Technologies and Imaginaries for Terror and Killing*, ed. Neil L. Whitehead and Sverker Finnström (Durham, NC: Duke University Press, 2013).

12. Originally posted to http://www.grouchymedia.com/about_grouchymedia.cfm. This page has since been deleted.

13. Quote reproduced verbatim. Originally posted to a chatboard on Grouchymedia.com that has since been removed.

14. Originally found at http://www.grouchymedia.com/about_grouchymedia.cfm. This page has since been deleted.

15. The video is available at http://www.grouchymedia.com/videos/2002/08/die-terrorists-die.html, although, at the time of this writing, the original, explicit version does not appear to be working. Copies have been uploaded numerous times to YouTube as well. See http://www.youtube.com/watch?v=QG3RfAROVrk for an example.

16. I thank Carol Vernallis for this observation.

17. I thank an anonymous reviewer for comments about the polyrhythm.

18. After the initial release of "Die Terrorists Die," Hickman subsequently edited the actual song in a "clean version" of the video, taking out each "motherfucker" although in no other way altering video imagery or his editing practices.

19. Paul Virilio, *Speed and Politics: An Essay on Dromology* (New York: Semiotext(e), 2006), 153.

20. These musical attributes and attendant successes have made nu metal particularly controversial among many metal fans who consider it to be too much of a capitulation to mainstream music. For more on nu metal's pariah-like status among extreme metal fans, see Keith Kahn-Harris, *Extreme Metal: Music and Culture on the Edge* (Oxford: Berg, 2007).

21. For a nuanced analysis of soldiers' listening practices in Iraq that goes beyond the scope of my immediate study, see Lisa Gilman, "An American Soldier's iPod: Layers of Identity and Situated Listening in Iraq," *Music & Politics* 4 (2010): 1–17.

22. Bruce Johnson and Martin Cloonan, *Dark Side of the Tune: Popular Music and Violence* (Hampshire, England: Ashgate, 2008), 13.

23. For more on music and interrogation, see Suzanne Cusick, "'You Are in a Place That Is Out of This World...': Music in the Detention Camps of the 'Global War on Terror,'" *Journal of the Society for American Music.* 2 (2008): 1–26. For an analysis of what he calls "sonic warfare," see Steve Goodman, *Sonic Warfare: Sound, Affect, and the Ecology of Fear* (Boston: MIT Press, 2009).

24. David Peisner, "Music as Torture: War Is Loud," *Spin*, November 30, 2006, http://www.spin.com/articles/music-torture-war-loud.

25. As John Richardson notes, examining connections between music and violence is often anathema to most music and media scholars, particularly because of concerns about how such critiques might fuel right-wing moral crusades (personal communication). As both a music fan and scholar, I am sensitive to such concerns and the sweeping generalizations that are often made about popular music, in particular, in support of censorship and other reactionary agendas. Nevertheless, to completely ignore the connections between music and violence, as scholars have long done, seems increasingly out of touch with contemporary (not to mention historical) events and uses, requiring its own kind of blinkered engagement. To this end, I situate my work within the growing body of literature that has begun to examine the often-complex relationships between music and violence in all their specificity. For more, see a working bibliography I maintain, "Music and Violence Bibliography," the Society for Ethnomusicology's Special Interest Group on Music and Violence, http://musicandviolencesem.wordpress.com/2011/11/14/music-and-violence-bibliography/. I am a co-chair of the Special Interest Group (2011–2013).

26. In arguing for the importance of war to heavy metal's poetics, I do not intend to argue that all metal subgenres approach the topic, when they do, in a similar fashion. Indeed, there is great diversity—politically, aesthetically, and otherwise—in how metal musicians and fans have used the theme of war throughout the music's history. As a fan of many forms of metal, moreover, I am sensitive to any attempts at oversimplifying a diverse genre with appeal to a wide, increasingly global audience. For more on metal's contemporary reach, see Jeremy Wallach, Harris M. Berger, and Paul D. Greene, *Metal Rules the Globe: Heavy Metal Music Around the World* (Durham, NC: Duke University Press, 2011).

27. Robert Walser, *Running With the Devil: Power, Gender, and Madness in Heavy Metal Music* (Middletown, CT: Wesleyan University Press, 1993).

28. Sianne Ngai, *Ugly Feelings* (Boston: Harvard University Press, 2005).

29. Carol Vernallis, *Experiencing Music Video: Aesthetics and Cultural Context* (New York: Columbia University Press, 2004), 49.

30. Michel Chion, *Audio-Vision: Sound on Screen* (New York: Columbia University Press, 1994), 58–60.

31. Anonymous posting at Free Republic, www.freerepublic.com.

32. I thank Carol Vernallis for this observation. As she notes, these videos "dissect and reconfigure the act of killing" by, "1) readying (still frames of American and foreign military and civilians), 2) aiming and directing (moving tanks and planes), and 3) targeting or blowing up (booms)." She continues: "In the music videos, we see the killing process through a new, perhaps closer lens" (personal communication).

33. Chion, *Audio-Vision*, 34.

34. Ibid., 61.

35. Posted at http://www.grouchymedia.com/videos/2002/08/die-terrorists-die.html.

36. Steve Mraz, "'Proud to be an American' with a Slightly Harder Tune: Sites' Rockin' War Videos Strike a Chord with Servicemembers [sic]," *Stars and Stripes*. July 18, 2005. http://www.stripes.com/news/proud-to-be-an-american-with-a-slightly-harder-tune-1.35986.

37. Grusin, *Remediation*, 96.

38. Ibid.

39. Ibid., 100.

40. Maurizio Lazzarato, "The Machine," *Transversal*. (2006): http://eipcp.net/transversal/1106/lazzarato/en

41. Machinic enslavement is nothing new to the US military. Indeed, it has long been defined as an ideal form of soldiering. Nowhere is this more evident than in the US Marine Corps "Rifleman's Creed," composed during World War II: "My rifle is human, even as I, because it is my life. Thus, I will learn it as a brother. I will learn its weaknesses, its strength, its parts, its accessories, its sights and its barrel. I will keep my rifle clean and ready, even as I am clean and ready. We will become part of each other."

42. Available online at http://www.grouchymedia.com/videos/2006/07/operation-phantom-fury.html.

43. Thanks to Neil Whitehead for this observation.

44. Michael Herr, *Dispatches* (New York: Vintage, 1991), 209.

45. Jeff Lewis, *Language Wars: The Role of Media and Culture in Global Terror and Political Violence* (London: Pluto Press, 2005), 25.

46. Mraz, "Proud to be an American."

47. Gilles Deleuze and Félix Guattari, *A Thousand Plateaus: Capitalism and Schizophrenia* (Minneapolis: University of Minnesota Press) 356.

48. System of a Down, "Boom!" YouTube, posted October 2, 2009, http://www.youtube.com/watch?v=bE2r7r7VVic.

SELECT BIBLIOGRAPHY

Baudrillard, Jean. "War Porn." *International Journal of Baudrillard Studies* 2 no. 1 (2005). http://www.ubishops.ca/baudrillardstudies/vol2_1/taylor.htm.

Butler, Judith. *Frames of War: When Is Life Grievable?* New York: Verso, 2010.

Chion, Michel. *Audio-Vision: Sound on Screen*. New York: Columbia University Press, 1994.

Daughtry, Martin. "Belliphonic Sounds and Indoctrinated Ears: The Dynamics of Military Listening in Wartime Iraq." In *Pop When the World Falls Apart*, edited by Eric Weisbard, 111–144. Durham, NC: Duke University Press, 2012.

Grusin, Richard. *Remediation: Affect and Mediality after 9/11*. New York: Palgrave MacMillan, 2010.

Lutz, Catherine. "The Military Normal." In *The Counter-Counterinsurgency Manual: Or, Notes on Demilitarizing American Society*, edited by the Network of Concerned Anthropologists, 23–37. Chicago: Prickly Paradigm Press, 2009.

Massumi, Brian. "The Future Birth of the Affective Fact: The Political Ontology of Threat." In *The Affect Theory Reader*, edited by Melissa Gregg and Gregory Seigworth, 52–70. Durham, NC: Duke University Press, 2010.

Sumera, Matthew. "The Soundtrack to War." In *Virtual War and Magical Death: Technologies and Imaginaries for Terror and Killing*, edited by Neil Whitehead and Sverker Finnström, 214–233 Durham, NC: Duke University Press, 2013.

Vernallis, Carol. *Experiencing Music Video: Aesthetics and Cultural Context*. New York: Columbia University Press, 2004.

Virilio, Paul. *Speed and Politics: An Essay on Dromology*. New York: Semiotext(e), 2006.

CHAPTER 20

··

OUTSIDE THE LAW
OF ACTION

Music and Sound in the Bourne *Trilogy*

··

JAMES BUHLER AND ALEX NEWTON

HORROR VACUI

··

If, as Rick Altman noted in 1980, "more than half a century after the coming of sound, film criticism and theory still remain resolutely image-bound," little has changed substantively in film theory despite the rapid growth in scholarship on the soundtrack.[1] The continued visual bias of film theory and criticism is especially evident in writing on action films, where the strong auditory component has frequently served as the basis for denigrating the genre as nothing other than "big and loud." Larry Gross, while locating the most egregious affronts in the contemporary action blockbuster, traces its origin to the spectacle of early sound: "The moment there was sound, film-makers recorded the voice of *King Kong* (1933) and the airplane machineguns that would shoot him down, to give huge audiences cheap thrills."[2] Gross's statement is a polemical distortion; he makes it seem as though *King Kong*, released well after sound film had established itself as the commercial foundation of the industry, inaugurated the sound era. Yet the displacement is symptomatic because it opens the film to an allegorical reading of film history: sound, captured as if in the wild, is a monster that threatens to destroy the civilizing force of the narrative that gives coherence to the sequence of images; and no beauty on earth has the power to kill (or even tame) this sonic beast.

It is striking that this old lament mourning the passing of the silent film should appear so forcefully just as the digitization of film production and postproduction took hold in the 1990s, when technology again threatened to upend the foundations of cinematic sense. Stanley Cavell reminds us that the coming of sound, far from remedying in a simple way any deficiencies of the silent drama, opened a cultural wound, one that sound film, whatever its technological advances and pleasures, was never able to close, and so sound film carried within itself a traumatic kernel that constantly unsettled the very terms of synchronization that it demanded.[3] Cavell locates the most characteristic response—a response in which sound film comes up against and acknowledges its own limits—in a sound practice that distills the presence of a particular silence, one that registers not meaning but the audible sense of the void that separates bodies, so that we become aware of the presence of the silence that surrounds characters as fraught. Yet he also recognizes that much sound film has preferred not to confront the wound, has preferred instead to skirt the traumatic encounter through distraction. *King Kong* again stands as the privileged example. In Cavell's account, however, the film's unruly sound— its combination of "continuous Wagnerama and almost continuous screams"—is not a monster but rather a displacement of the wound of sound: "the film is more afraid of silence than Fay Wray is of the beast."[4]

These two strategies of approaching the wound—distillation and distraction—converge in what Michel Chion calls the "quiet revolution," the development of technologies of audio production and reproduction capable of delivering "a micro-rendering of the hum of the world."[5] The turn to rendering initiates a subtle but decisive shift in the status of the image from the screen as Bazinian "window on the world" to screen as a "monitor."[6] Where the image had once established perspective and promised "a world of immediate intelligibility,"[7] sound "abounds in details; it is polyphonic but vague in its outlines and borders."[8] Notably, Chion says, modern sound design resembles the representation of visual space in pre-Renaissance painting where "the void between these bodies is not constructed."[9] The site of the wound is again displaced, but it now paralyzes the image: "being no longer functional or structuring, the image becomes interestingly idle." Rendering is the auditory correlate to—and the quiet revolution is the actual driving force of—the impoverished (and space destroying) close-ups of what David Bordwell has called "intensified continuity."[10] Just as *King Kong* responds to the horror of silence by masking it with music and noise, so, too, the contemporary action film seems to respond to the threat of the catatonic image by covering it with frenetic editing and other visual wizardry designed both to energize and to distract. But once we note that Cavell's description of *King Kong* passes over the sound in the initial sequence in New York—a sequence where the silence is in fact allowed to resound in all its emptiness and words register only the pain of human interaction reduced to economic relations—we can understand the film's soundtrack less as an evasion of the wound than as a dramatization of the bitter breaking of silence, the conversion of trauma into myth. The film earns its screams and its evocation of Wagner.

And so it may be for the contemporary action film. Digital filmmaking extends rendering from the soundtrack to the image. The action genre in particular makes the special effect into the norm. Now routinely built and framed in postproduction, the digital image floats, like the soundtrack, in the nether region between (imaginary) reproduction and (symbolic) representation. As Altman noted already in 1992, "today, the customary electronic manipulation and construction of sound has begun to serve as a model for the image."[11] But whereas rendered sound establishes a continuity that grounds the sequence, the rendered image loses depth, fragments rather than consolidates space, and disassociates in editing, which assembles a series of striking glances that relate as much through the soundtrack as to each other. With sound anchoring the continuity, the management of sync points for visceral impact, more than visual logic, drives the montage.

Rendering thus figures the loss of what Cavell calls "automatic world projections," a fading of the cherished indexical quality of film, and, in this loss, film registers the experience of a final terrible mortality as nature's withdrawal from us. Does digital filmmaking still produce cinema? Animation may not exactly make movies—or rather it might be worth upholding a distinction between animation and movies because animation retains a profound artistic dignity to the extent that it denies itself and us a view of the world. Nature as such does not exist in animation, which is therefore a pure expression of subjective will. "The difference between this [animated] world and the world we inhabit is not that the world of animation is governed by physical laws or satisfies metaphysical limits which are just different from those which condition us; its laws are often quite similar. The difference is that we are uncertain when or to what extent our laws and limits do and do not apply (which suggests that there are no real *laws* at all)."[12] Digital filmmaking follows animation in this respect. A rendered world is a virtual world. It is a world that looks and sounds just the way it does because it has been made to order: nothing in it escapes the determinations of rendering. Compare this situation with nature, which, although captured, is not determined by its appearance as an automatic projection. The depiction of the rendered world is governed by resemblance rather than by cause; in semiotic terms, it is iconic rather than indexical. Yet the world of digital filmmaking cannot acknowledge its denial of nature, its loss of "sacred contact,"[13] the fading of the index—at least not directly: the virtual world of digital filmmaking must still look indexical, must still look like automatic world projections. Nature's withdrawal therefore appears within it instead as an incorporation, as a destruction of distance that makes the void between bodies unfathomable and the fixing of the coordinates of any narrative based on them uncertain. If we are not absent from nature, if we cannot escape responsibility for its representation, which is the only way we know it, the laws of nature assume form in the virtual world by force of subjective intention. This passage to the subjective interior is the reverse side of the fading of the index, the denial of nature. Following the path of sound, digital rendering has "radically desacralized cinema, substituting circuitry for direct contact, constructed iconicity for recorded indexicality."[14] The wound of sound, which made silence apparent, articulate, and unbearable insofar as it figured social isolation, passes into the wound of rendering, which does the same to the unfathomable void between bodies that now asserts itself not in silence but in a conspiratorial hum of the world.[15]

In this essay, we trace these concerns in the films of the *Bourne* trilogy, the last of which has been much criticized for its ostentatious audiovisual style. First, we consider how music serves to underscore the basic duality of its protagonist, Jason Bourne

(Matt Damon), a duality born of trauma and which the music elevates to myth. Next, we examine the intersection between the striking visual techniques and the sound design in the final film and argue that the audiovisual style matches the film's thematics. In the concluding section, we return to the issue of trauma and explore how the trilogy functions as a critical meditation on the social trauma buried at the heart of the action genre's law of action.

MUSIC, MYTH, AND DUALITY

Distant thunder rumbles and a cold wind whistles under the opening Universal logo. A salty open C-G drone, unbalanced with the fifth in the bass, enters as the screen goes black. If this opening to *The Bourne Identity* (2002) seems, despite differences in instrumentation and key, vaguely reminiscent of Wagner's *Flying Dutchman* "Overture," that is because the music seems to endow the void and coming storm with mythic significance, drawing the origin of the film, as mythic openings to film so often do, from music and sound.[16] More thunder, oddly distant and this time synchronized with lightning flashes that illuminate a body floating in the water (Figure 20.1a), punctuates the soundtrack. A prominent thunder peal coincides with the image of a fishing vessel moving through heavy seas. Inside, the crew rides out the storm playing cards. A slow, plaintive bassoon melody emerges from the drone with a cut back to the rough sea (Figure 20.2). The melancholic and wispy tune seems more the elaboration of a cry than an actual theme, which ambivalently fluctuates between major and minor, an ambivalence emphasized by synchronizing the modal shift to minor with a cut to the floating body. A lone fisherman on deck appears with the last portion of the tune, which cadences on a long G, the fifth scale degree. As the drone continues, the fisherman moves about the boat and then pauses to look (Figure 20.1b). Lightning again illuminates the body. With a return to the fisherman peering intently at the sea, a new agitated motive begins in the strings (Figure 20.3). Like the opening bassoon melody, this material never really coalesces into a proper theme. In fact, its construction is even more rudimentary, a basic idea played in measured tremolo that repeats like clockwork every six beats, once again focused melodically on the G rather than the tonic; it carries without substantial development or variation across another somewhat closer shot of the body floating in the water and into the brief title card. Following the title, the motive continues as the crew pulls the body aboard ship and only changes when the body shows signs of life.

If the film thus starts with an image of death, this origin makes the story into a myth of rebirth and renewal: the body marks a dividing point between before and after. And, although the time before this origin is also a time literally forgotten, it remains present, and traumatically so, so long as it cannot be properly remembered. The division of origin is therefore bound up with repression that yields a duality of character, and it is the music of *The Bourne Identity* that first establishes this basic duality of Jason Bourne that will persist across the trilogy of films: on the one hand, he is presented as a

FIGURE 20.1 *The Bourne Identity*. (a) Floating body; (b) The fisherman's gaze.

FIGURE 20.2 Humanity Theme (transcription by authors).

FIGURE 20.3 Action Theme (original version from *The Bourne Identity*; transcription by authors).

severely damaged subject suffering from acute amnesia and searching for his identity; on the other hand, he is pushed by a blind, motoric drive that he does not understand but that allows him to perform amazing physical and intellectual feats.[17] The music not only divides Bourne along this line of lost subjectivity and unfathomable drive, both situated in that irrevocable time before origin, it also marks a fundamental ambivalence: the bassoon theme, which we will refer to as the "humanity theme," floats modally between major and minor, with the major mode portion of the tune constructed around the interval of a falling minor third and the minor mode portion emphasizing the major third. Beyond its modal ambivalence, the tune is also decentered with respect to its tonic: it is organized around the dominant pitch, G, which serves as both its point of departure and its cadential goal. This decentering is furthered by the drone accompaniment, which lacks the tonic in the root, once again shifting emphasis toward G. By contrast, the tonic much more clearly anchors the motoric theme, which it hammers every six beats. Nevertheless, this motive, which we will refer to as the "action theme," also quickly jumps away from the tonic, circling around G in a slow turn. Moreover, its relation to the tonic will also grow more attenuated as the theme develops by adding a lowered second scale degree (lower staff of Figure 20.4), as well as a countermelody based on the first part of the humanity theme (upper staff of Figure 20.4).

The duality represented by the musical organization of the themes extends to the relationship of the themes to the image track. Neither theme, in fact, initially synchronizes with an image of Bourne.[18] The humanity theme at first appears over the fishermen playing cards, whereas the fisherman spotting Bourne motivates the first appearance of the action theme, which seems to associate the theme with Bourne's literal body rather than with his subjectivity.

The Bourne Supremacy (2004) similarly begins with an open C-G drone, the G again in the bass but an octave higher than *Identity*. The opening motive breaks off before it can develop into a substantive theme. Following the title, the humanity theme begins to sound as the image track displays a disorienting collection of shots: a highway exit for Berlin, a hotel room, a family portrait of unknown characters, and the room number 645. The dialogue and sound effects add to the confusion. Although sound contextualizes some of the information—for instance, Conklin (Chris Cooper), the main antagonist in *Identity*, instructs Bourne—even these clues remain sketchy. Conklin appears only as a disembodied voice, a kind of dream superego, issuing orders. His voice, which pans sporadically around the stereo field with nearly every line repeated at

FIGURE 20.4 Action Theme (Variant with Violin Counterpoint; transcription by authors).

varying intervals and from completely different positions, disorients in much the same way that the images do. Furthermore, although the volume of the voice signals proximity, the heavy reverb implies a shadowy distance. Several effects sound, some of them, like the rain and the windshield wipers, clearly diegetic, some of them, like the various whooshes, clearly extradiegetic, but the bulk of them, like the unintelligible off-screen voices, somewhat undecidable. As the effects build, the reverb on the voice lessens until it all but disappears with the penultimate sound of woman's scream followed by a gunshot. Released from the dream, Bourne gasps awake in bed as the gunshot echoes in the background.

The final film of the trilogy, *The Bourne Ultimatum* (2007), opens *in medias res* with Bourne fleeing the Russian police after the climactic car chase in *Supremacy*. This scene therefore takes place before the final two scenes of *Supremacy*. As the image track fades in, so does the music with a low C-G drone, this time with C as root but supporting a prominent G several octaves above in the high strings. An electronic rhythmic sound pulses out a steady four-beat rhythm, and a disquieting A♭ sounds as the full Universal name settles into place, cueing the start of the definitive eight-beat version of the action theme in the cellos as the logo fades to black. With a percussive extradiegetic hard swoosh, the image flashes, suddenly revealing a pair of legs stumbling heavily through the snow as the action theme acquires a countermelody in the upper strings (Figure 20.4). A disorienting cut to Bourne from the side showing him limping accompanied by labored breathing suggests that he is in trouble. A shot of Bourne from the rear follows him as he turns his head at the sound of a train horn, which seems to call gently to him in his home key of C minor. A quick pan motivated by Bourne's head turn discloses a train yard outside a station. That pair of shots is then repeated, this time police sirens wailing a piercing E♭-A tritone, drawing his attention to the street, which brings both a cut to approaching police cars (a substitute for the pan to the train yard) and a change in music. Bourne then hobbles down the stairs toward the station, disappearing just as police cars pull up.

Like the scene itself, the music for the opening of this cue replays an earlier moment, as most of the cue up to the shot of the police cars is a compressed version of the music that had accompanied Bourne's escape from the Hotel Brecker in *Supremacy*. This definitive eight-beat version of the action theme had actually first emerged early in *Identity*, when the amnesic Bourne visited the bank in Zurich and made the horrifying discovery that his safe deposit box contained a large amount of cash, a gun, and series of passports under different aliases. As Bourne processes the import of this find, an eight-beat version of the action theme gradually takes shape, first as a driving pulse with an amorphous, breathy, flute-like melody floating above it before finally taking definitive form as the accompaniment to the first (falling minor third) part of the humanity theme. Once Bourne makes his decision to flee with all the contents of the safety deposit box except the gun, the action theme continues amid a flurry of increasingly frantic percussion hits before giving way to a tonally askew counterstatement in the upper strings. Importantly, the emergence of the definitive form of the action theme is intimately bound up with Bourne's recognition of his splintered identity, and, by initially playing in counterpoint to the humanity theme, it also encompasses the modal ambivalence that the opening of the film had associated with Bourne's duality. This sense of duality continues with the version of the theme heard both at the Hotel Brecker and in the opening of *Ultimatum*. The violin countermelody (Figure 20.4) carries this duality, which prominently emphasizes E♮ (against the action theme's E♭) and whose A♭-E♮-G figure is a retrograde of the humanity theme's opening G-E♮-A♭.

This action theme recurs frequently in the trilogy, where it is generally associated with physical action. But, unlike other music used to underscore action, this theme (like the humanity theme) specifically signals a melodramatic mode: it occurs in moments such as the bank and the Brecker Hotel, where the intensity of the physical action is the outward expression of Bourne's existential crisis of identity. In the opening of *Ultimatum*, it likewise announces existential disquiet. Near the end of the scene, having broken into a pharmacy, taken what appears to be morphine, and removed a bullet from his shoulder, Bourne stands in front of a sink, where the sound of trickling water triggers a dissociative flashback similar to the dream that opened *Supremacy*, although here the flashbacks are shorter, more fragmentary, and interspersed with shots of two policemen entering the pharmacy. When one of the policemen approaches, Bourne snaps out of the flashback and quickly disables him while drawing his gun on the other. After the second policeman pleads for his life, Bourne leaves him be, and a swooshing extradiegetic sound effect leads into the very brief title sequence. After the title fades, the opening phrase of the humanity theme sounds. Although musically the opening of *Ultimatum* follows the model of *Supremacy*, where this theme had likewise emerged after the title, it nevertheless appears here strangely detached from a narrative context: the theme seems disconnected from Bourne and instead seems to draw what in retrospect is a symbolic shot of the sun setting behind the CIA headquarters into view. Just as the action theme sounds prior to the appearance of Bourne, so, too, the humanity theme plays after the opening scene is completed, and the lack of synchronization between these themes, their distance from each other and from Bourne's presence, seems to press the duality to the point that it actually fractures under the strain, producing free-floating signifiers of identity.

All three films thus open with images of a wounded and scarred Bourne, and all three films use music to underscore the trauma, but in each case music points to a trauma that is fundamentally existential. Comparing studio-era Hollywood films featuring characters scarred by psychological trauma with respect to gender, Heather Laing argues that those with male protagonists tend toward the musical use of sharper dissonance and tonal disruption.[19] The music of the Bourne films, although tonally ambivalent, eschews this representational scheme. Instead, the music locates the trauma in the relationship of themes to the enigma of Bourne's presence. The themes represent a basic duality: hollowness, fragmentation, existential despair in the case of the humanity theme; repetition without end in the case of the action theme. Moreover, as we attempt to integrate the musical motives narratively, to tie them to Bourne, we reveal only a traumatic split—between the themes and within the themes. Music thereby gives cinematic form to the structuring absence that is the trauma.

SOUND, SYNC POINTS, AND THE
FORM OF ABSENCE

The Bourne trilogy tells the story of Jason Bourne, a former CIA assassin suffering from amnesia and trying to piece his life back together. The three films are arranged as a spiral quest that traces the progressive restoration of his humanity with a provocative twist at the end. Each film thus represents a stage in his recovery and focuses on regaining, coming to terms with, and surmounting a particular memory: in *Identity*, he reclaims his identity as Bourne and tries to reconstruct his last job; in *Supremacy*, he avenges the death of his girlfriend Marie (Franka Potente) and works to recollect his first hit job; and, in *Ultimatum*, he pursues the CIA, seeks to understand how he came to be an assassin, and ultimately comes to reject the identity of Bourne. The trilogy thus ends with Bourne's recognition of his own complicity, his (symbolic) death, and the promise of (another) rebirth, a rebirth whose terms, however, the film leaves unspecified.

A notable and much commented upon factor of the films, however, is that the base-level cinematic technique—fast, disjunct cutting that often pushes past the limits of continuity editing; shaky handheld camerawork that favors unbalanced composition occasionally allowing the principal figure to drift out of focus or even out of the shot; frenetic off-screen sound that often seems to substitute for effective images—grows increasingly agitated over the course of the trilogy, indeed seems to follow what Barry Salt calls an "expressive program."[20] It is as if, in a gigantic transfer of the pathetic fallacy, Bourne's approach to the traumatic core of his being affects not just the mise-en-scène but shakes the very foundations of cinematic representation. If it is a convention of action films that "fragmented shots of the hero's body in action and multiple-angle views of the same body signify the hero's threatened or fractured masculinity" so that the integrity of the body and so also its central place in the filmic representation might be triumphantly restored at the end,[21] the consistent use of the decentering techniques in the Bourne films, especially the last two films, without the recuperative acts of restoration, has a profoundly disconcerting effect of dislocating the trauma to the level of representation. Paul Greengrass, who directed both *Supremacy* and *Ultimatum*, attributes these devices, especially the extensive use of handheld cameras, primarily to the subjectivization of the point of view: "Your p.o.v. is limited to the eye of the character instead of the camera being a godlike instrument choreographed to be in the right place at the right time."[22] Greengrass's description of how the handheld camera technique works in the films is quite misleading, and we will discuss this point below, but it is worth noting that he relates it specifically to point of view and understands the way that it represents the limitations of that point of view to be as important as what it discloses. In this sense, the vaunted "energy" of the technique is tied to revealing and working on and through a systemic incapacity of representation. The closer Bourne comes to the traumatic core, the more subjective and dissociative the representation becomes, and the more the film is shaped as action, the less that action can be grasped.

According to David Bordwell, the devices deployed to such disorienting effect in *Ultimatum* are derived principally from the so-called "run-and-gun" style of action film associated with such directors as Tony Scott, Michael Bay, and Simon West.[23] Bordwell argues that the fast cuts and handheld camera work serve to "roughen up" the basic contemporary filmmaking norms of intensified continuity. This "roughening" is purportedly so extensive that the sequence of images, however flashy, often seems incomplete and confusing.

> In the fancy run-and-gun style, cinematography and sound do most of the work. Instead of arousing us through kinetic figures, the film makes bouncy and blurry movement do the job. Rather than exciting us by what we see, Greengrass tries to arouse us by how he shows it. The resulting visual texture is so of a piece, so persistently hammering, that to give it flow and high points, Greengrass must rely on sound effects and music. As a friend points out, we understand that Bourne is wielding a razor at one point chiefly because we hear its whoosh.[24]

As noted above, the roughening serves to destabilize both the continuity of the image sequence and the image itself, and Bordwell is correct that the soundtrack often compensates for that instability by filling in the gaps. But Bordwell's claim that the soundtrack plays primarily a clarifying function in the film is misleading. Depending on the scene, the roughening applies as much to the soundtrack as the images: the film makes frequent use of off-screen sound, filters, frenetic nondiegetic music, often portending sync points whose signification is obscure. This audiovisual roughening has the effect of making scenes difficult to parse, despite the use of intensified continuity, in terms of determining which objects in a shot are meaningful and which are incidental.

Like rendering, roughening therefore erodes the indexical quality of the image. At the base of Bordwell's critique of the run-and-gun style is his claim, echoing Chion's description of the screen as monitor, that the image requires the energy of roughening because it has become innately static. Editing, postproduction processing, and camera technique, Bordwell says, substitute for recording real action between bodies on screen. Bourne's combat expertise, moreover, should be evident from Matt Damon's physical actions, not constructed through representational tricks, such as intentionally shaky images, frantic editing, and sound cues. For the indexical quality of the image is bound up with the cinema's humanism:

> Lengthier shots let the actor develop the character's reactions in detail, and force us to follow them. Classic studio cinema, with its more distant framings and longer takes, lets you follow the evolution of a feeling or idea through the actor's blocking and behavior. The villain in the average Charlie Chan movie displays more psychological continuity than the nasty agents in *Bourne Ultimatum*.[25]

Bordwell's meditation on shot length and distance in this passage suggests a fear of fragmentation, a longing for a lost wholeness that classic studio cinema promised. For all of Bordwell's valorization of film as art, of cinema as an intentional object, we are not far from ontological realism, from the Bazinian "window on the world" or the Cavellian "automatic world projection." From this perspective, Bordwell's complaint is less about subordination to sound and more about the fading of the index and the concession to icon. As Bordwell's clinically precise descriptions of the procedures make clear, the atomization and fragmentation of intensified continuity serve as attacks on the actor's body that evacuate the actor from the image, and action film generally pushes this process much further than do other contemporary genres. Action heroes tend toward a general and much commented upon blankness that Bourne's amnesia only emphasizes, and Reni Celeste reminds us that, rare for Hollywood cinema, actors in action films often disappear so far into their roles that they become replaceable.[26] Action heroes seem machined for the modernity that they enact. "Though each figure represents an assortment of sociological and political meanings for the given period in which he appears as character, the ultimate anxiety he represents is the loss of human power and freedom, to the machine, the law, the disaster, the alien and ultimately the cinema."[27] It is the apparatus of cinema, then, that vests the terror and purges it in a ritualized spectacle of primal violence—the "explosion point" that Celeste identifies as the correlate to classic cinema's "screaming point" and that she claims as the characteristic audiovisual figure of contemporary cinema.[28]

We will consider the explosion point further in a moment, but we should note that Bordwell's attempt to historicize the shaky shot, to trace the use of the handheld camera all the way back to the silent era, in order to deflate its "revolutionary" pretensions has almost the opposite effect of recognizing its persistent subversive power. If the shaky shot returns throughout film history always with shocking effect, like the monster or action hero who will not die, it also seemingly has the power to break the chains of classical representation based in the indexical quality of the photographic image. A mark of a kind of realism, the shaky shot is also a mark of its subjectification. As such, it is a technique fully consistent with Elefetheria Thanouli's claim that postclassical narration is characterized by "a high dose of subjective realism that attempts to visualize the innermost mental and emotional states."[29] In the Bourne trilogy, then, subjective realism gives preference to representing icons of Bourne's mental trauma over capturing indexes of "kinetic figures."

Although Bordwell sees Greengrass's use of the run-and-gun style in his Bourne films as "pretty incoherent," the systematic disorientation of the style in fact serves characterization on at least two levels. First, as intimated above, its dissociative tendencies reflect trauma. Second, Bourne's seemingly effortless ability to negotiate every situation appears positively virtuosic. Together, these two levels, which stand starkly opposed to one another, are another expression of Bourne's fundamental duality, now taken to the level of style. Bordwell, who senses the tension, states bluntly that the disorienting effect of the style should not be attributed to Bourne's psychology. "The style isn't best justified as being a reflection of Jason Bourne's momentary mental states (desperation, panic) or his longer-term mental state (amnesia)."[30] Bourne's virtuosity, Bordwell thinks, makes it difficult to understand the use of the style on the basis of Bourne's interiorized psychological states. In particular, Bourne's success in negotiating the tense situations is dependent on the fact that he is himself never disoriented. And the style serves as an

effective means of marking asymmetries among Bourne's knowledge, the CIA's surveillance capabilities, and what the film allows us to know about the respective actions of
Bourne and the CIA. As Bordwell rightly notes, much of *Ultimatum* "relies on crosscut-
ting to create an omniscient awareness of various CIA maneuvers to trap him. And if
Bourne saw his enemies in the flashes we get, he couldn't wreck them so thoroughly."[31]
Yet the film's omniscience is, in this respect, deeply unsettling because the assemblage
does not generally resolve into the superior knowledge characteristic of the omniscient
viewpoint. Indeed, the more disorienting the sequence, the more virtuosic Bourne
appears as he effortlessly discerns what is significant and incidental in the dizzying array
of shots and sounds presented.

Consider the Waterloo Station sequence from *Ultimatum*, where Bourne directs
British journalist Simon Ross (Paddy Considine) as he attempts to evade a crew of CIA
operatives.[32] During the scene, agents follow on foot, and a CIA team working out of
New York uses the surveillance cameras in the station to aid the onsite crew. In a particularly striking segment, Bourne uses a cell phone to navigate Ross through the station without being spotted by either the operatives or the security cameras. Without
ever providing a master shot of the station interior, the film presents a flurry of shots
as Bourne and Ross move through the space. The fast cutting pace and jerkiness of the
handheld camerawork make it almost impossible to parse the images for pertinence
in real time. Although initially it seems that many of the shots are presented merely to
establish a space crowded with people (Figure 20.5), repeated viewing shows that nearly
every shot contains a pertinent piece of information:[33] Ross, Bourne, the agents tracking
Ross, the security cameras monitoring the station. Many of the shots, however, have also
been roughened up to dislocate the focal point, sometimes seeming to push it completely
off-screen, an effect heightened by extensive use of off-screen sound. Sound, in fact,
assumes and cycles through many modalities in the scene; speech: simple on-screen,
on-screen from the rear, simple off-screen, filtered off-screen, ambient crowd, ambient
loudspeaker; effects: simple on-screen, sweetened on-screen, simple off-screen, contiguous off-screen, sweetened off-screen, and ambient; music: nondiegetic. The only
modality used regularly in the film but not featured in this subsequence is extradiegetic
sound, which generally appears in the establishing portion of expository sequences and
in the highly stylized flashbacks. The soundtrack, aside from the music, does not hold
the disparate shots together here but, in fact, destabilizes them further by confounding
the image with a barrage of off-screen noises and with abrupt shifts between filtered and
unfiltered voices.

To say that sound "stabilizes" the image here would therefore be a mistake. We may
be able to tell that a punch hits its mark by its sound, but locating that mark often proves
futile. Just as the frame is too small to contain all the action on-screen, it is evidently
too small to show precise sources for all the sound effects, many of them quite prominent. Punches and other actions can usually be identified, but the sync point is often
obscured. If, in a fight scene of a typical action film, sounds of bodily contact generally
serve to register damage, it usually takes place on-screen, even if the action is too fast
for the image to record.[34] The sync point in that case directs attention to the point of

FIGURE 20.5 *The Bourne Ultimatum*. Scanning the crowd in Waterloo Station.

contact. In *Ultimatum*, however, these sync points, points of contact, are rarely centered, often pushed to the edge of the frame and frequently occur beyond the frameline, leading to the paradoxical feel of an off-screen sync point. If we feel we are grasping for shots, we are; we certainly do not feel that the narrator has control of the action because the characters seem to elude the shots. What Greengrass risks with his technique is the appearance of incompetence. If shot seems to crash into shot; if the geography of the space is difficult to reconstruct from the shots and sounds we are given; if shots begin mid-action and are interrupted before the action is completed; if the significant action frequently seems to elude the camera because the camera seems too close or out of position—these could on their own be read as signs of a director who is not fully in control of his craft, of a director who is willing to sacrifice everything for "a sense of energy." This is, more or less, Bordwell's interpretation of Greengrass's appropriation of the run-and-gun style, which he mischievously calls "The Bourne Coverup."[35] Yet, poor filmmaking or not, all of this serves in the end to empower the ungraspable figure of the shot.

With the handheld camera, Greengrass argues, "sometimes the camera will not know what's going to happen. That gives you space; you can play in that space, you can let the actors be totally free."[36] Presumably because the camera can move, the actors no longer need to worry about where the camera is and so are free to move in the way that best expresses the character's intentions and feelings through motion. Yet the camera cannot anticipate every move an actor will make, so the actor purchases freedom through occasional absence from the frame. This absence passes to the character, who likewise finds freedom beyond the frameline. And if we do not force our desire for mastery of the image to override what we in fact see, we recognize the freedom of the figure from the image as a figure of resistance, as a figure not captured by representation; but also as a figure whose expression of freedom is possible only to the extent that it is not entirely free of representation.[37] These off-screen sync points force us to see in the off-screen space the figure giving form to absence.

This empowerment divides Bourne, who seems to be able to navigate the disorienting field only by regressing to the very CIA programming that he seeks to transcend. Bourne is never closer to his former identity—and to a contemporary action hero—than when he must evade detection or engage in physical confrontation. In the fight with the agents in the Waterloo Station sequence and with Desh at the end of the Tangier sequence, Bourne seems to regress to pure animal, pure drive—the very image of the hard-bodied action hero.[38] Bourne's regression is underscored by prominent "explosion points," which serve to punctuate action, most characteristically by ending it. In films committed to the law of action, explosion points function as terminals of a causal chain that determine the action absolutely and render characters without choice. As a terminal, the explosion point is not just a harbinger of death marking a conclusion to the causal logic—although it is frequently that too—but it is also that moment when the chain of causality breaks and ceases to have the force of full determinacy, which is one reason an explosion point may also be used to initiate a line of action. In the Bourne trilogy, explosion points often entail close physical contact—fight scenes—rather than the detonation of incendiary devices.[39] Such scenes frequently mark endpoints of Bourne's physical action, his full regression to action figure, and so also a return to a brutal violence that confuses animal and machine, nature and alienated technology.

In the fight with the agents in Waterloo Station, music follows the path of Bourne's regression and amplifies the hits, ultimately disappearing entirely under Bourne's gratuitous pistol-whipping of a downed agent. Reversing the more typical pattern, the Tangier sequence *initiates* the final long fight scene with a dramatic explosion point: Bourne crashes through a window. Having been gradually reduced from orchestra to percussion over the course of the long chase, music now drops out completely, leaving only the bare sounds of physical violence as Bourne and Desh engage in brutal hand-to-hand combat. Danijela Kulezic-Wilson locates the "particular effectiveness" of this sequence in the way "that the previously pervasive buzz of music disappears here and the fantasy world of unbeatable heroes and wild chases is suddenly replaced with the realistic sounds of hitting, grunting, fists impacting soft tissue, and bones breaking."[40] Where Kulezic-Wilson hears realism, however, we hear action devoid of humanity, the binding of the explosion point to physical action. Without dialogue or music, Desh and Bourne both seem reduced to their base programming, the embodiment of the pure drive of self-preservation.[41] In both cases we are presented not so much with the alienation of the self but rather the alienation of humanity. The training and discipline lead to the base programming of pure drive, as all rational calculation is oriented only toward scanning the environment for the potential to inflict maximum harm on the opponent. Indeed, even Bourne's brutal strangling of Desh, which characteristically takes place just outside the frameline (Figure 20.6), lacks a cliché death rattle from the score, and, after Desh's body tumbles to the ground, only a dark silence haunts the soundtrack as Nicky (Julia Stiles) looks on, bewildered at what she has witnessed. Yet, even in a scene like this, the lacunas in the image are the marks of an underlying trauma and so also of Bourne's duality. The inability of the camera to catch the action adequately in these scenes not only frustrates our identification of and with the action; it also captures Bourne's own

FIGURE 20.6 *The Bourne Ultimatum*. Bourne kills Desh.

decentering and self-alienation, the extent to which Bourne is lost to himself and so cannot recognize the source of his own motivations and actions.

TRAUMA, REPETITION, AND THE
LAW OF ACTION

If the mythology of the Bourne trilogy uses amnesia to grant its hero a blank slate, the trilogy as a whole, but especially *Ultimatum*, remains burdened by its past. It forgets in order to remember and so to return to the time that its myth of origin would repress. And if Bourne seeks redemption through deeds, as action heroes are wont to do, he does so not by forgetting the memories of the past but by reclaiming them and making a conscious choice to atone, thereby hoping to redeem them and himself. This gives the Bourne films their distinctively elegiac tone and moves them beyond the similar amnesiac situation of *Total Recall* (1990), which aspires to make good its motto: "a man is defined by his actions, not by his memories." As Frank Grady notes, this line "is a congenial formulation for an action film, reducing one's identity to one's deeds—not even to the sum of one's deeds but to the deeds of the immediate present."[42]

In their final conversation in *Supremacy*, Bourne and Marie debate what might be termed the action hero imperative. Although Bourne had declared "Jason Bourne" dead at the end of *Identity*, he finds that his old identity continues to haunt him, not just in the dream that opens the film or in his restless run along the beach in Goa, but also in his current predicament, in which he and Marie are being chased by an agent. Bourne reacts to the presence of the agent by reverting to the default role of action hero, as he prepares to jump from the speeding jeep so he can ambush their pursuer. Marie pleads with Bourne: "Jason, don't do it. I don't want you to do it." Bourne, locked into the law of action, the logic of the action hero, responds: "I told them what would happen if they

didn't leave us alone." Marie reflects on the consequences, on the "repetition compulsion" at the heart of this logic: "It's never going to be over like this." Bourne nevertheless
continues relentlessly down the line of the imperative: "We don't have a choice." Marie
refuses the logic: "Yes, you do." These words shake the philosophical foundations of the
action film, and they will prove far more traumatic for both film and character than
the amnesia ever was. It is hardly surprising that Maria pays almost immediately for
these words, which, if acted on, would bring an end to the action film as such. Bourne is
left speechless across several nervous cuts, and then a shot rings out, hitting Marie, and
sending the jeep careening off a bridge.

If the logic of the action film cannot allow Marie to live after uttering those words, the
film also cannot deny their traumatic effect, which it both attempts to contain by making Marie into a haunting figure of loss and helps to propagate by continually returning
to her as a motivational figure to explain Bourne's actions. As with melodrama, which
in its twentieth-century form usually confronts characters with moral choice,[43] the cinematic expression of the moment exceeds the containment that its representation would
perform. First, Marie is literally in the driver's seat when she is shot. The shot therefore
seems to mark an end to her control, and Bourne struggles desperately to steer the jeep
back on course. Second, the bridge is a common cinematic signifier of transition, of the
space between two worlds. Marie's death on the bridge therefore symbolically checks
Bourne's slide back to the identity of action hero; landing in the river, he falls into the
indefinite state of character transition. Third, water is associated with rites of purifica-
tion, baptism, and rebirth, associations that the films had already implicitly tapped at the
opening of *Identity* and that will be multiplied with increasing frequency in *Ultimatum*.
This occurs most striking early in *Ultimatum*, when Bourne, on a train from Paris, reads
Ross's story. During the dissociative flashback triggered by the article, images of Marie,
of her death, and of being plunged into a water tank during training are all freely inter-
mingled. If this flashback links Bourne's trauma over Marie's death to the trauma of his
training, it does so through this strange doubling of images of water, which dislocates
the traumatic shock from its putative origin in grief and suffering and returns it to the
transitional state—Bourne is on a train in an indefinite place between locations—and a
strange repetition of duality, as he contemplates the question of the story—"who is Jason
Bourne?"—and the story's lead that multiplies his identity only to insist on the irreduc-
ible core of killer: "His code name was Jason Bourne, but he had many identities, each
one seemingly more deadly then [sic] the next." The typo here is fully symptomatic of
the law of action: it converts a conceptual comparison into an (ungrammatical) temporal sequence that portends the increasing violence of the repeating series.

Such multiplications and uncanny filmic repetitions extend throughout the final film,
which seems to structure itself around the idea of *repetition compulsion*, in psychoanalytic theory a classic response to trauma. There are, in fact, few original situations in
Ultimatum. Nearly every incident is a variant of something that occurred in one of the
first two films. Sometimes this is literally the case, as when Bourne remembers the death
of Marie while reading Ross's article or, more uncannily, when the conversation between
Bourne and Landy (Joan Allen) from the end of *Supremacy* is repeated almost verbatim.

But the principle of repetition extends from big set pieces, such as the car chase with Paz (Édgar Ramírez) being modeled after the final car chase with Kirill (Karl Urban) in *Supremacy*, to small details, such as Nicky dyeing and cutting her hair, replaying similar scenes with Marie in *Identity*.[44] The same can be said for the music, which develops very little in terms of new material for *Ultimatum*, not even at the end, where, given the theme of transformation, it might be expected. It is easy enough to attribute such repetition to the industrial terms of sequel production, which explains (away) formulaic repetition as a hedge against risk. Yet, as genre critics frequently note, the underlying repetitions in the genre formulas are what make them particularly susceptible to ideological analysis, which frequently reads the repetitions as symptoms of cultural contradiction and anxiety.[45] One of the tenets of ideological criticism of genre (and sequels) is that changes in the basic formula reflect shifts in underlying social tensions: the formula changes because the social conditions that it reflects shift. In the action film, the primary (but by no means only) site of these changes is the hero, whose status is taken to reflect, above all, anxieties in shifting definitions of masculinity and race, as well as the loci of white male power.[46]

In fact, we should insist on this connection to sequel production for another reason as well: it suggests that Bourne's trauma is serving to double but also to mask the films' traumatic core, which relates to our psychic investment in and identification with the action film. For it is here, in our recognition of this identification, that we encounter the Lacanian Real, the film looking back at us. The nauseous feeling that the handheld camerawork induces for some reflects a kind of malaise, an "action sickness" that relates as much to psychic as to physiological processes. We recognize the unsettling of desire in the displacements of sync points to off-screen space as well. The desire for the action film is tied to the desire for Bourne's regression: not to return to "where it all began" to overcome amnesia, but to accept our own amnesia and accede to the law of action as the price for the return of the action hero.

Each film in the trilogy resolves its amnesiac episode with a variant of the talking cure: Bourne receives a piece of information that allows him to reassemble his memory and overcome the trauma associated with it. Each promises either a restoration or a new order. In neither *Identity* nor *Supremacy*, however, does the revelation of the key piece of information serve as the climax of the film nor does it mark both a change and new direction for Bourne's character; as such, a residual trauma remains. Only in *Ultimatum* does the revelation serve as the climax of the film, and only in *Ultimatum* does the revelation prove transformational in both action and goal.

The climax of *Ultimatum* bears close analytical scrutiny in this respect. With the inside help of Landy, Bourne returns to the site of his initial training. As Bourne enters a deserted hallway, the familiarity of the place triggers dissociative flashbacks, and Bourne oscillates between present and past as he walks down the hallway. Throughout, the flashbacks remain disorienting: the image track uses over-exposure and other film processing, as well as a choppy frame speed, while the soundtrack features a drone-like sound halfway between music and effect; aggressive, nondiegetic effects that emphasize the cuts; and a disorienting off-screen voice. In the flashback, Daniels (Colin Stinton) leads Bourne to a security door while an off-screen voice, treated with an echoing effect, spells out the consequences of the training regime: "When we're finished with you, you will no longer be David Webb. You might not even remember who he was." The mysterious voice in the flashbacks belongs to Dr. Albert Hirsch (Albert Finney), who subsequently appears in the hallway. Bourne, desperate to remember why he was chosen for the program, pressures Hirsch to reveal his initiation. In *Identity*, Bourne regained his memory through a similar confrontation, whereas in *Supremacy* it was his return to the scene of his flashbacks that triggered his recall. *Ultimatum* combines these two features, man and place, and adds an object, his dog tags, a mark of identity, as a third. Bourne learns the uncomfortable truth from Hirsh: he volunteered for the program. As Hirsch hands Bourne his tags marked with the name "David Webb," a soft, distorted version of the humanity theme sounds and his memories, no longer dissociated, flood back to him. Hirsch, sensing a vulnerability, presses the issue: "You can't outrun what you did, Jason. You made yourself into who you are. Eventually you are going to have to face the fact that you chose right here to become Jason Bourne." These words cue the pivotal memory. A stylized heartbeat gradually grows into a distended, repeating, tonally alienated musical sequence as Webb struggles, with Hirsch badgering him, over whether he should shoot an unknown man bound in the corner of the laboratory simply on Hirsch's orders. Webb's decision comes with a negative stinger at the end of a long musical build-up, and he unleashes three rounds into the silence (Figure 20.7). The bright metallic sound of shell casings bouncing off the floor accompanies the unknown man slumping, lifeless, in the corner. Briefly, the soundtrack presents only room tone, letting the consequences of the actions sink in. Then a low, ominous C minor chord—the key associated with Bourne throughout the trilogy—swells, marking the mythical birth of Jason Bourne out of this burst of violence. The dark minor chord transforms into an elegiac string hymn that serves as preparation for the entrance of the sweet theme associated with Marie and played, like the humanity theme, on the bassoon. This music, quite unexpected under the circumstances, cues an important psychological shift. Having reclaimed his memory, Bourne inverts the primal scene and rejects his identity: "I am no longer Jason Bourne." Instead of killing Hirsch, he takes Marie's advice and refuses the role of avenging hero. Just as the theme moves to its cadence, agents arrive on the scene, and he runs toward the roof of the building, where Paz, one of the agency's assassins, confronts him. Instead of shooting, Paz demands to know why Bourne did not kill him earlier. The latter replies with a question—"Do you even know why you are supposed to kill me?" The humanity theme answers in C♯, its focalization seeming to transfer to Paz, who now appears to follow Bourne in questioning his identity. As the latter runs to leap off the building, Paz lowers his weapon, but Vosen steps out of the shadows and shoots. An echoing gunshot accompanies the falling body and disappears with the sound of the body hitting the water.

Ultimatum therefore ends where *Identity* began—with a seemingly lifeless body floating in the water (Figure 20.8). Gradually, a string drone evocative of the opening of *Identity* emerges, but this time the high violins slip down a half-step, unsettling the mythic repetition, making it sound ghostly. The bassoon sings the slow lament of the

FIGURE 20.7 *The Bourne Ultimatum.* The Birth of Jason Bourne.

FIGURE 20.8 *The Bourne Ultimatum.* Death or Rebirth?

first part of the humanity theme, but now a half step lower than the usual key of C and in a lower register. Where the rebirth of *Identity* had led only to a cyclic return of the Bourne identity that seemed inescapable, that of *Ultimatum* is positioned as a transformation, the Bourne identity having been laid to rest. Yet the nature of this transformation is uncertain. The slow, dirge-like tempo of the humanity theme and lower register here evokes more the tone of negation than of positive transformation. As Landy exposes the conspiracy at a congressional hearing, only the string drone sounds, the violins adding a drawn-out chromatic descent with a shot of the floating body while her testimony continues. The final note of the three-note chromatic descent, a dissonance that dissipates in a trill rather than resolving, marks a cut to Nicky, who watches a news report announcing the arrest of Hirsch and Vosen as the violins continue, now vacillating between major and minor. Another shot of the body enigmatically cues disjointed fragments of the action theme. The news report invokes the name of David Webb, suggesting restoration, but then adds that he is also known as Jason Bourne, which once again divides the character, emphasizes his duality, even as he has seemingly vanished like a ghost. When the news report announces that no body has been recovered, Nicky smiles as the same series of aggressive string tirades that had ended each of the previous films sounds and the once still body springs to life.[47]

If this body reanimates to the same music that had ended the previous films and so presents all the signs of preparing a sequel, it is nevertheless not at all clear who has come to life. The ambiguity here seems purposeful. Bourne dies, but the body revives so that his death cannot be construed as sacrifice: that role belongs to Marie (Kreutz, variant of *Kreuz* = cross). What Bourne discovers in his conversation with Hirsch is only that he can now choose otherwise and does so, but that this in no way undoes the original choice; he remains culpable.[48] If he is no longer Jason Bourne, he therefore also cannot return to an innocent state of David Webb before the fateful choice.[49] The figure who swims through the dark waters into the final credits is truly a man without identity in order that we do not pin our hopes on him.

Unusual for an action film, *Ultimatum* therefore places its bet not on the action hero or the individual to save the institution, but on the institution to reform itself. *Ultimatum* presses the point onto the issue of gender. If the trilogy follows the expectations of the action film in minimizing the role of female characters, rarely permitting them to participate explicitly in the action, this exterior status also strangely empowers them, not by placing them on a pedestal or by holding them out as precious, vulnerable objects to be protected, rescued, and avenged, but by making them agents not beholden to the law of action, to the paranoid logic of the action film, which it attributes to the world of men.[50] Exterior to this masculine law of action, women are the principal agents of reform.[51] The women—Marie, Landy, and Nicky—are all presented as (predictably) good angels arrayed with Bourne against a world bedeviled by the self-serving actions of fallen men, and they are each charged with points of major decision: Marie gives Bourne his ultimatum; Landy actively intervenes at numerous points to help Bourne; Nicky decides not to reveal Bourne's presence in Madrid. Marie and Landy, in particular, are each granted the extraordinary capacity to see beyond the law of action, to see its debilitating, paranoid logic masquerading as causality and necessity in order to render decision moot in the conclusion of no alternative. As such, they maintain faith in the institution, whether they are on the inside (Landy) or the outside (Marie). Bourne, too, comes to recognize that continuing in his role of action hero and committing to the law of action only strengthen the corruption and reproduce the paranoia of the institution. By denying himself an identity at the end, he therefore absents himself, leaving it to the institution to reform itself and to solve its problems. Significantly, this role of reform goes unscored: Landy's testimony, accompanied only by the motionless drone held over from the previous shots of the floating body, is mundane, the ordinary bureaucratic activity of reporting ("The file indicates..."). It distances the role of the individual, not to depersonalize or to signify an evasion of responsibility but to demythologize. What society needs, the film seems to say, is not more heroic individuals but people who have let go of their paranoia.

If the idea that government could reform itself through such testimony seems fantastic and utopian,[52] that simply suggests the extent to which we have internalized and even come to desire the law of action, the paranoid structure, which music so often conceals—as, on the surface at least, it does here—by metaphysically inflating it into myth.[53] The music repeats, rather than giving something new, that we might recognize the return as bare repetition, the myth as nothing more than a closed circle. The ending presents all the signs of sequel in order to expose its social antinomies: Bourne, a product of the paranoia, might return if we cannot let go this desire for the law of action, and music reflects this desire; but Bourne's return would represent failure, another repetition of the very tired script of social trauma, rather than success. "Look at us. Look at what they make us give." These are Bourne's final words, addressed to Paz, and, oddly enough, they are another repetition, the dying words that the Professor (Clive Owen) spoke to Bourne in *Identity* after Bourne had fatally wounded him. But, of course, "they" did not "make" us give anything. Hirsh has this much right: Bourne committed knowingly to the law of action, as do we when we agree to be governed according to the paranoid scenario sketched by Hirsch ("The republic lives on a knife's edge").

The law of action nevertheless appeals because, like music, it disguises the fact that, once rendered, the image of action is no longer something caused by the world. If, in classic cinema, the photographic image serves as the index to the humanity of the real world, then in contemporary cinema the law of action becomes the index to the inhumanity of the rendered world. To refuse to allow the index to fade, to preserve instead the law of action as something real (or rather as the appearance of a natural social substrate) is, however, to conceal the wound of rendering, to suffer the collapse of the process of subjectivization into an interior closed world of paranoia and social isolation. In *The Bourne Ultimatum*, particularly, the action sickness induced by the handheld camera, the sync points that push beyond the frameline, and the lethargy expressed in the humanity theme alert us to our complicity, to the high costs, both social and psychological, of binding ourselves to the law of action.

NOTES

1. Rick Altman, "Introduction: Cinema/Sound," *Yale French Studies* 60 (1980): 3.
2. Larry Gross, "Big and Loud," *Sight and Sound* 5, no. 8 (1995): 7.
3. Stanley Cavell, *The World Viewed: Reflections on the Ontology of Film*, enlarged edition (Cambridge, MA: Harvard University Press, 1979), 147ff.
4. Ibid., 152.
5. Michel Chion, "Quiet Revolution... and Rigid Stagnation," *October* 58 (1991): 71.
6. Ibid., 73. We follow Chion's article in defining rendering as re-creation of sound (or image) through imaginative reshaping (ibid., 69–72). For example, a rendered punch is enriched or sweetened so that it corresponds not to the sound of an actual punch but to its visceral emotional impact. Rendering falls somewhere between the simulacrum of recording and the code of conventional representation so that it blurs the distinction between the two terms. See also Slavoj Žižek, *Looking Awry: An Introduction to Jacques Lacan Through Popular Culture* (Cambridge, MA: MIT Press), 40
7. Cavell, *The World Viewed*, 150.

8. Chion, "Quiet Revolution," 73.

9. Ibid.

10. For a detailed discussion of "intensified continuity," see David Bordwell, *The Way Hollywood Tells It* (Berkeley: University of California Press, 2006), 117–189, esp. 121–138.

11. Rick Altman, "Four and a Half Film Fallacies," in *Sound Theory/Sound Practice*, ed. Rick Altman (New York: Routledge, 1992): 44.

12. Cavell, *The World Viewed*, 169–170.

13. Altman, "Four and a Half Film Fallacies," 43.

14. Ibid., 44.

15. Tom Gunning argues that "the marginalization of animation" is "one of the great scandals of film theory," and he works to unify cinema under the kinesthetic, the impression of movement, which bears affinities with rendering inasmuch as the visceral impact of movement also displaces both reproduction and representation as the ground for assessing the "believability" or "reality" of the imagined world ("Moving Away from the Index: Cinema and the Impression of Reality," *Differences* 18, no. 1: 38, 45). The price of unity, however, is the loss of distinction, and the wound of rendering is bound up with this loss. Gunning explores consequences of this loss in another article: "Gollum and Golem: Special Effects and the Technology of Artificial Bodies," in *From Hobbits to Hollywood: Essays on Peter Jackson's Lord of the Rings*, ed. Murray Pomerance and Ernest Mathijs (Amsterdam: Editions Rodopi, 2006), 319–349.

16. On the mythic significance of opening films this way, see James Buhler, "Enchantments of *The Lord of the Rings*: Soundtrack, Myth, Language, and Modernity," in *From Hobbits to Hollywood: Essays on Peter Jackson's Lord of the Rings*, ed. Murray Pomerance and Ernest Mathijs (Amsterdam: Editions Rodopi, 2006), 231–248, esp. 231–233.

17. Amnesia is a common trope in action films, especially recent ones. Some familiar examples include *Robocop* (1987), *Total Recall* (1990), *Johnny Mnemonic* (1995), *Conspiracy Theory* (1997), *Mindstorm* (2001), and *Unknown* (2011). One line of criticism that developed in response to action films of the 1980s argues that spectacle in these films represents a form of political amnesia. See, for instance, Michael Rogin, "'Make My Day!': Spectacle as Amnesia in Imperial Politics," *Representations* 29 (1990): 99–123; and Susan Jeffords, *Hard Bodies: Hollywood Masculinity in the Reagan Era* (New Brunswick, NJ: Rutgers University Press, 1994), 155–156.

18. Although we will push our interpretation in a different direction below, a lack of close coordination between a film's system of leitmotifs and the narrative is another characteristic of cinema's mythic mode. On this point and its relationship to Wagnerian practice, see James Buhler, "*Star Wars*, Music and Myth," in *Music and Cinema*, ed. James Buhler, Caryl Flinn, and David Neumeyer (Hanover, NH: Wesleyan University Press, 2000), 33–57.

19. Heather Laing, *The Gendered Score: Music in 1940s Melodrama and the Woman's Film* (Aldershot: Ashgate, 2007), 144.

20. Barry Salt, *Film Style and Technology: History and Analysis*, 2nd ed. (London: Starword, 1993), 288–289. Increasing the roughness incrementally may have been a strategy devised by Paul Greengrass and his team for assuming stylistic control of the Bourne series since Greengrass did not direct the initial film; but it also seems calibrated to coincide with shifts in Bourne's character, becoming rougher as the amnesia is revealed as the mask of psychic rather than physical trauma.

21. Mark Gallagher, *Action Figures: Men, Action Films, and Contemporary Adventure Narratives* (New York: Palgrave Macmillan, 2006), 58.

22. Quoted in Anne Thompson, "Greengrass Brings Auds into Picture," *Variety*, August 3, 2007, http://www.variety.com/article/VR1117969675.

23. David Bordwell, "Unsteadicam Chronicles," in Bordwell and Kristin Thompson, *Minding Movies: Observations on the Art, Craft, and Business of Filmmaking* (Chicago: University of Chicago Press, 2011), 171.

24. Ibid., 174. Bordwell's critique of Greengrass' style in *Ultimatum* follows the line and many of the details of argument that Eric Lichtenfeld presents against Michael Bay and Simon West in *Action Speaks Louder: Violence, Spectacle and the American Action Movie*, revised edition (Middletown, CT: Wesleyan University Press, 2007), 178–185. Incidentally, it is Desh (Joey Ansah), not Bourne who wields the razor.

25. Bordwell, "Unsteadicam Chronicles," 173–174.

26. Reni Celeste, "The Frozen Screen: Levinas and the Action Film," *Film-Philosophy* 11, no. 2 (2007): 29.

27. Ibid., 30.

28. Ibid., 26–28. On the screaming point, see Michel Chion, *The Voice in Cinema*, trans. Claudia Gorbman (New York: Columbia University Press, 1999), 76–79.

29. Eleftheria Thanouli, "Post-Classical Narration," *New Review of Film & Television Studies* 4, no. 3 (2006): 186.

30. David Bordwell, "[Insert Your Favorite Bourne Pun Here]," *Observations on Film Art* (blog), August 30, 2007, http://www.davidbordwell.net/blog/2007/08/30/insert-your-favorite-bourne-pun-here/.

31. Bordwell, "Unsteadicam Chronicles," 171.

32. Neil Archer has an excellent analysis of the Waterloo Station sequence in terms of the logic of surveillance. Archer's book appeared after our chapter had entered production, so we are not able to consider his arguments. See *Studying The Bourne Ultimatum* (Leighton Buzzard: Auteur, 2012), 31–47.

33. The only exception is shots associated with Ross's point of view, which emphasizes his inability to assess the situation accurately.

34. Michel Chion, *Audio-vision*, trans. Claudia Gorbman (New York: Columbia University Press, 1994), 58–62.

35. Bordwell, "Unsteadicam Chronicles," 171.

36. Quoted in Thompson, "Greengrass Brings Auds into Picture."

37. Gregg M. Horowitz, "Art History and Autonomy," in *The Semblance of Subjectivity: Essays in Adorno's Aesthetic Theory*, ed. Tom Huhn and Lambert Zuidervaart (Cambridge, MA: MIT Press, 1997), 259–285.

38. The literature on the hard-bodied action figure is immense. See Robin Wood, *Hollywood from Vietnam to Reagan* (New York: Columbia University Press, 1986), 162–188; Elizabeth G. Traube, *Dreaming Identities: Class, Gender, and Generation in 1980s Hollywood Movies* (Boulder: Westview Press, 1992), 28–66; Yvonne Tasker, *Spectacular Bodies: Gender, Genre and the Action Cinema* (New York: Routledge, 1993); Steven Cohan and Ina Rae Hark, eds., *Screening the Male: Exploring Masculinities in Hollywood Cinema* (London: Routledge, 1993); Jeffords, *Hard Bodies*; Fred Pfeil, *White Guys: Studies in Postmodern Domination and Difference* (London: Verso, 1995), 1–36; Yvonne Tasker, ed., *Action and Adventure Cinema* (London: Routledge, 2004); Mark Gallagher, *Action Figures*. The ambivalent representation of the action hero between animal and machine is noted by Eric Licthenfeld, *Action Speaks Louder*, 66.

39. On the punch as explosion point, see Celeste, "The Frozen Screen," 27.

40. Danijela Kulezic-Wilson, "The Music of Film Silence," *Music and the Moving Image* 2, no. 3 (2009): 3.

41. The handling of the sound here is quite reminiscent of two striking scenes in *King Kong*: in Kong's battle with the *Tyrannosaurus rex* on Skull Island and with the airplanes in New York, music drops out for the confrontation, leaving only the sounds of the desperate struggle.

42. Frank Grady, "Arnoldian Humanism, or Amnesia and Autobiography in the Schwarzenegger Action Film," *Cinema Journal* 42, no. 2 (2003): 45.

43. Janet Staiger, "Film Noir as Male Melodrama: The Politics of Film Genre Labeling," in *The Shifting Definitions of Genre: Essays on Labeling Films, Television Shows and Media*, ed. Lincoln Geraghty and Mark Jancovich (Jefferson, NC: McFarland, 2008), 72–73. Although many scholars have argued that action films since the 1970s have made extensive use of the melodramatic mode—for a recent example, see Richard Pope, "Doing Justice: A Ritual-Psychoanalytic Approach to Postmodern Melodrama and a Certain Tendency of the Action Film," *Cinema Journal* 51, no. 2 (2012): 113–136—so far as we are aware, no one has noted that action films typically follow the older, nineteenth-century form, which persisted longer in westerns, in presenting their characters as fixed moral types rather than being given and so also being defined by their choices. Choice in action film is usually presented, as it is to Bourne here, as being no choice, as a function of the action causality, or else the choice is impossible, as for instance the choice offered Helen Tasker in *True Lies* (1994). On the law of action eliminating alternatives to the point of no choice, see Jeffords, *Hard Bodies*, 171–177; and Archer, *Studying The Bourne Ultimatum*, 78.

44. Many of these repetitions are documented by Greengrass in his audio commentary to the film on the DVD. Such repetitions are common in sequels, although they are usually treated ironically or through a process of inversion that allows us to situate shifts in character development and goals. In *Ultimatum*, repetition is generally not transformed in this way.

45. Thomas Schatz, *Hollywood Genres: Formulas, Filmmaking, and the Studio System* (New York: McGraw-Hill, 1981), 14–41.

46. For a summary, see Julian Stringer, "'Your Tender Smiles Give Me Strength': Paradigms of Masculinity in John Woo's *A Better Tomorrow and The Killer*," *Screen* 38, no. 1 (1997): 25.

47. From the string drone that accompanies Landy's testimony up to the point where the string tirades enter with Nicky's smile, the music parallels in fairly direct fashion the scene on the ship early in *Identity*, where the doctor removed the bullets from Bourne's back. In *Identity*, the first half of the humanity theme had followed.

48. Vincent M. Gaine, "Remember Everything, Absolve Nothing: Working Through Trauma in the *Bourne* Trilogy," *Cinema Journal* 51, no. 1 (2011): 159–163.

49. On this point, compare the quite different interpretation in Archer, *Studying The Bourne Ultimatum*, 84.

50. Archer interprets gender as simply a blind spot in the films. See ibid., 73–75.

51. The film is undoubtedly drawing on a long cultural tradition of casting women in the role of reformer.

52. Bordwell makes this point in "Unsteadicam Chronicles," 175.

53. On the use of music to construct conspiratorial reality, see Phil Ford, "Music on the Edge of the Construct," *Journal of Musicology* 26, no. 2 (2009): 240–273.

SELECT BIBLIOGRAPHY

Altman, Rick. "Introduction: Cinema/Sound." *Yale French Studies* 60 (1980): 3–15.

Archer, Neil. *Studying the Bourne Ultimatum*. Leighton Buzzard: Auteur, 2012.

Bordwell, David. *The Way Hollywood Tells It*. Berkeley: University of California Press, 2006.

———. "Unsteadicam Chronicles." In *Minding Movies: Observations on the Art, Craft, and Business of Filmmaking*, edited by Bordwell and Kristin Thompson, 167–176. Chicago: University of Chicago Press, 2011.

Cavell, Stanley. *The World Viewed: Reflections on the Ontology of Film*. Enlarged edition. Cambridge, MA: Harvard University Press, 1979.

Celeste, Reni. "The Frozen Screen: Levinas and the Action Film." *Film-Philosophy* 11, no. 2 (2007): 15–36.

Chion, Michel. "Quiet Revolution . . . and Rigid Stagnation." *October* 58 (1991): 69–80.

Gaine, Vincent M. "Remember Everything, Absolve Nothing: Working Through Trauma in the *Bourne* Trilogy." *Cinema Journal* 51, no. 1 (2011): 159–163.

Gallagher, Mark. *Action Figures: Men, Action Films, and Contemporary Adventure Narratives*. New York: Palgrave Macmillan, 2006.

Gross, Larry. "Big and Loud." *Sight and Sound* 5, no. 8 (1995): 6–10.

Gunning, Tom. "Moving Away from the Index: Cinema and the Impression of Reality." *Differences* 18, no. 1 (2007): 29–52.

Higgins, Scott. "Suspenseful Situations: Melodramatic Narrative and the Contemporary Action Film." *Cinema Journal* 47, no. 2 (2008): 74–96.

Jeffords, Susan. *Hard Bodies: Hollywood Masculinity in the Reagan Era*. New Brunswick, NJ: Rutgers University Press, 1994.

Lichtenfeld, Eric. *Action Speaks Louder: Violence, Spectacle and the American Action Movie*. Revised edition. Middletown, CT: Wesleyan University Press, 2007.

Pope, Richard. "Doing Justice: A Ritual-Psychoanalytic Approach to Postmodern Melodrama and a Certain Tendency of the Action Film." *Cinema Journal* 51, no. 2 (2012): 113–136.

Silberg, Jon. "Bourne Again." *American Cinematographer*, September 2007. http://www.theasc.com/ac_magazine/September2007/TheBourneUltimatum/page1.php.

Tasker, Yvonne. *Spectacular Bodies: Gender, Genre and the Action Cinema*. New York: Routledge, 1993.

Tasker, Yvonne, ed. *Action and Adventure Cinema*. London: Routledge, 2004.

Thanouli, Eleftheria. "Post-Classical Narration." *New Review of Film & Television Studies* 4, no. 3 (2006): 183–196.

Thompson, Anne. "Greengrass Brings Auds into Picture." *Variety*, August 23, 2007, http://www.variety.com/article/VR1117969675.

Walker, Janet. "Trauma Cinema: False Memories and True Experience." *Screen* 42, no. 2 (2001): 211–216.

Wood, Robin. *Hollywood from Vietnam to Reagan*. New York: Columbia University Press, 1986.

CHAPTER 21

DEBATING THE DIGITAL

Film and Reality in Barry Levinson's
Wag the Dog

ELEFTHERIA THANOULI

THE relation between cinema and reality has been the cornerstone of film theory since the inception of the medium. Questions regarding the inherent ontological qualities of cinema and its correspondence with the external world have been central in the works of key theoreticians such as Rudolf Arnheim, Siegfried Kracauer, and André Bazin. In their writings, they sought to explain how celluloid related to reality and even prescribed ways in which it *should relate* to it in order to fulfil its promised destiny.[1] Even though contemporary film theorists constrain their prescriptive tone using more rigorous methodologies, they are still compelled to address the perennial question of "what is cinema" in an age in which digital technology complicates exponentially the relation between cinema and reality. In this essay, I explore the evolving relation between cinema and reality through the close study of Barry Levinson's film, *Wag the Dog* (New Line Cinema, 1997). The meticulous analysis of this filmic text and the examination of the historical and social context in which it was produced, exhibited, and received worldwide enable me to illuminate a series of changes in the way a fiction film reflects and interacts with reality, urging us to reconsider some of our central and long-standing concepts in film theory.

There was nothing in the preproduction or filming stage of *Wag the Dog* that could foretell its fated trajectory. It was originally a small project that was squeezed into Levinson's agenda while filming the big-budget *Sphere* (1998). Despite the star cast featuring Robert de Niro and Dustin Hoffmann in the leading roles, its independent status, combined with a political theme traditionally considered box-office poison, were most likely to ensure a moderate exposure to the wide audience. Indeed, *Wag the Dog*'s wide release on January 9, 1998 would have seemed rather uneventful, if a few days later, on January 21, *The Washington Post* hadn't officially reported the outbreak of the Monica

Lewinski scandal.[2] The eerie coincidence of the film's narrative with the twist in Bill Clinton's presidential career triggered a fervent discussion around the relation between art and life, rising to crescendo a few months later when the United States launched a series of attacks in Sudan and Afghanistan. As Joseph Hayden observed, "*Wag the Dog* may have provided the most surreal experience in twentieth-century presidential history," as the distinction between fact and fiction, or rather real and surreal, in most media reports (newspapers, TV news, soft news etc.) reached a zero-degree level.[3] A considerable number of TV viewers even rushed to the video stores to watch the film, in order to grasp the references and the parallelisms that reporters and analysts were drawing between the actual events and the fictional plot.[4] According to *The Economist*, the makers of *Wag the Dog* were responsible for "one of the luckiest pieces of timing in screen history,"[5] causing the film to become part of a cultural semantics; its title would qualify as an adjective next to the words "scenario," "syndrome," or "phenomenon," signifying a particular fictional template of fabricating news and manufacturing consent.[6]

What is more fascinating about *Wag the Dog*, however, is how it worked its way through the writings of a wide range of disciplines, including international relations theory, geopolitics, history, ethics, rhetorics, visual sociology, journalism, and communication theory, to name an indicative few.[7] Coincidence or luck is hardly a good excuse in academia. Indeed, *Wag the Dog* became a significant point of reference for such diverse strands of research in the humanities and social sciences because it was reconstructed as a "media event"[8] with exceptional political, social, and semiological repercussions. The filmic narrative and the surrounding political context entered an unprecedented intertextual relay that unsettled some of the fundamental values of contemporary Western society. The conflict between "what is real" and "what is reel," as portrayed in the diegesis, leaped straight into the real world, just like Woody Allen's character in the *Purple Rose of the Cairo* (1985). In what follows, I will analyze the *Wag the Dog* event in two parts; the narrative and its historical context. Both sides will enable me to touch on a series of key issues in the debate about the digital and will contribute to the ongoing discussion about the cinema–reality binary in the digital era.

THE TEXT

Wag the Dog's story is loosely based on Larry Beinhard's novel, *An American Hero*, and its screenplay is accredited equally to Hilary Henkin and David Mamet, even though it was the latter who worked closely with Levinson for the making of the film.[9] Mamet's flair for satire was apposite for the outrageous premise of the project, which is worth outlining here in some detail. Eleven days before the US presidential elections, the American president is accused of sexually harassing a Firefly girl, and his chances for reelection are slimmed. To manage the press debacle, the White House brings in Conrad Brean (Robert De Niro), a special advisor, who devises the plan to stage a fake war to keep the media agenda off the sex scandal. He seeks the help of a Hollywood producer called Stanley Motss (Dustin Hoffman), who is fascinated by the assignment and swiftly drafts a war narrative with a music theme, visuals, and other tie-ins. Albania is selected as the enemy, while a digitally fabricated war scene is fed to the media to verify the outbreak of the conflict. Indeed, the footage is so emotionally wrenching that for the next two days the news reports are dominated by the horrors of the war against Albania. Oddly enough, the response from the CIA and the president's opponent is not to deny the war but to declare its ending. Faced with the premature ending of the war, Brean and Motss retaliate with the story of a soldier called Schumann who is, supposedly, left behind in the Albanian front. While the American public awaits the return of the war "hero," the person chosen for this role (an ex-convict) is accidentally killed. Once again, the team quickly recoups by staging the soldier's funeral in the most dramatic manner. Finally, Election Day comes and the president is triumphantly reelected thanks to his resolution during the Albanian war. The success of the communication enterprise behind the reelection is so overwhelming that Motss wants to be acknowledged for his masterwork. To prevent possible damage, Brean orders Motss's death and makes sure that the political reality is protected from the truth.

Brean's idea to fabricate a war to sway public opinion raises a number of questions regarding the status of the image and the role of reference for the shaping of collective memory. One of Brean's recurring arguments concerns the long-standing strategic use of emblematic images for representing an entire war, thus blocking the need for more specific and detailed historical evidence. He mentions two memorable pictures from World War II (five marines raising the flag on Iwo Jima and Winston Churchill's V for Victory) and one from the Vietnam War (a naked girl running after a Napalm attack) to prove that his plan to reduce the war to one single image is not a new concept. He also frequently refers to the Gulf War and the smart bomb footage that circulated in the news broadcasts. When Brean alleges that he shot that footage in a studio in Falls Church Virginia with a 1/10 scale model of a building and Motss asks whether that is true, the answer is "how the fuck do we know." *Wag the Dog*'s lead character expresses from the start his disbelief regarding a clear distinction between fact and fiction. The evidential quality of the image is always in dispute, as he refuses to attribute a denotative function to any historical representation, whether in a photograph or a news report. Cynical as his views may be, the historical research around several emblematic images of twentieth-century warfare has proven how staging and fabricating techniques have always been infiltrating the photographing process. As Eugene Vance notes about the iconic image of raising the flag on Iwo Jima,

> The revered flag-raising photograph of Iwo Jima made in World War II by Joe Rosenthal alludes to, but does not record a heroic act: it is a twice-posed image made on a true site of battle that still glorifies the sentiments of many Americans when they raise their flag, and it has been replicated in a bronze national monument, a postage stamp and reams of calendar art. It incited, as well, the staging of yet another

no less inspired "historical photograph." The Russian war photographer Yevgney Khaldai, who was Jewish, emulated "Iwo Jima" when the Russians captured Berlin and when, like Rosenthal, he twice staged his own flag-hoisting photograph, using a flag improvised from tablecloths on May 2, 1942.[10]

Despite photography's ability to mechanically reproduce reality, it is widely acknowledged that photographs of warfare have done nothing but reproduced particular conceptions of war and not the war *as it really was*.[11] In *Wag the Dog*, Brean and his team take advantage of that premise by taking it a step further, namely by producing a war that *never was*. Indeed, Levinson's characters seem to implement Jean Baudrillard's notion of simulation, so they can obstruct the real threat (the sex scandal) with a hyperreal one (the Albanian war). The film's plot illustrates how the concept of hyperreality could successfully function in the American presidential scene, with dire implications for democracy and political power. In one of Baudrillard's famous passages, the workings of simulation are described as follows:

> Today abstraction is no longer that of the map, the double, the mirror, or the concept. Simulation is no longer that of a territory, a referential being or substance. It is the generation by models of a real without origin or reality: A hyperreal. The territory no longer precedes the map, nor does it survive it. It is nevertheless the map that precedes the territory—precession of simulacra—that engenders the territory.[12]

The hyperreal war waged in the film bears no relation to real events, nor does it correspond to any preexisting grounds of conflict. It is pure simulation. Even though the president's advisor convinces his team that what they are doing is nothing new, in fact, it definitely is. Surely, propaganda and media manipulation have been part and parcel of all modern warfare, but the complete fabrication of a war is something new. Even Baudrillard, one of Gulf War's most radical critics, did not argue the war was *only* simulated. In the book with the provocative title *The Gulf War Did Not Take Place*, Baudrillard had claimed that the Gulf War did not take place in the sense that the two opponents, the Americans and the Iraqis, were fighting two separate types of war and were not destined to confront each other in the battlefield on equal terms.[13] This is significantly different from the story of the film, in which the conflict is entirely simulated. What is even more striking is the response of the other presidential candidate, as well as of the CIA, who declare the end of the conflict from within the hyperreal zone. It seemed easier to retaliate with another simulacrum rather than address the real facts and gather evidence of the lack of war activity in Albania. Again, it is Baudrillard who gives an apt description of political power at the age of hyperreality:

> Power itself has for a long time produced nothing but the signs of its resemblance. And at the same time, another figure of power comes into play: that of a collective demand for *signs* of power—a holy union that is reconstructed around its disappearance.[14]

The signs of power, such as press conferences, presidential announcements, and authoritative commercials, flood the media, but the real agency is nowhere to be found. Even the people on Motss's crew oscillate between fact and fiction, between what they know as true, what they doubt as true, and what they invent all the way. The practice of fabrication takes many shapes in the story, from composing a music theme to inventing a hero and staging his funeral, but what is most emphatically portrayed is the shooting of the news footage of the refugee girl escaping a bombed-out Albanian village. In that scene, Levinson reveals the process of simulation as a technological operation, which is able to produce something that never was. Against the blue screen of a Hollywood studio, a young actress with a bag of Doritos in her hands is running around scared, while the director adds the images of a burning village in the background and morphs the Doritos into a white kitten (see Figures 21.1 and 22.2). The enormous creative possibilities of digital technology are ostensibly demonstrated, as we watch the characters debate over which images to choose and which sounds to mix to make the footage more realistic and emotional. And yet, is the digital to be held responsible for the manipulation of the truth and the simulation of a lie? The theoretical debates over the technological, ontological, and semiological features of digital media have yet to come to a definitive answer.

At the technological level, the fundamental distinction between analog and digital media is based on the former's "automatic processes of image capture" and the latter's "mathematical processes of image generation."[15] In other words, the analog technology mechanically *inscribes* an image by registering the traces of light of a preexisting object,

FIGURE 21.1 Analogue reality: the actress holding the Doritos.

FIGURE 21.2 Digital reality: the actress holding a white kitten.

whereas the digital *produces* an image by transforming a numerical matrix into pixels. In the aforementioned scene, we are elaborately presented with the manifold ways in which these two technologies collaborate and converge, granting the digital, however, the final touch. The actress, her movements, as well as the cats and the burning villages are all captured in the analog mode but, as soon as they are fed into the computer, they lose their indexical relation to the profilmic reality and become a numerical code. From then on, these images can be easily composited, animated, or morphed by special-effects specialists who take advantage of this "elastic reality"[16] to create a highly deceitful video that asserts the nonfactual; namely, a war scene that never existed. The capacity of the digital to assert *what is not* and *negate what is* has been hailed by Friedrich Kittler, and further elaborated by Yvonne Spielmann, as one of the unique features of digitality in contrast to analog media.[17] As the digital engages in a dialectical relationship with the analog (the opposite is not possible), it simulates the latter's affirmative function while it performs a negative one, too; whereas an analog image works affirmatively by representing something that exists, the digital image can only simulate that something *exists*, thus performing an affirmation, while it can also simulate something that *does not exist*, thus performing a negation. The concerns that arise from the ability to simulate a negation—that is, to affirm the presence of a nonexistent object—are central in the debates about the ontological differences between the analog and the digital.[18]

At the ontological level, the search for *inherent* qualities in these two types of images is not without obstacles.[19] The remarkable creativity of digital tools in the making of the fake war footage appears to confirm the fears about the loss of reality in digital images. Remember how the famous French critic Jean Douchet lamented the impending death of cinema:

> The shift towards virtual reality is a shift from one type of thinking to another, a shift in purpose which modifies, disturbs, perhaps even perverts man's relation to what is real.... All good films, we used to say in the 1960s, when the cover of *Cahiers du cinéma* was still yellow, are documentaries,... and filmmakers deserved to be called "great" precisely because of their near obsessive focus on capturing reality and respecting it, respectfully embarking on the way of knowledge.[20]

Douchet's words nostalgically resonate with André Bazin's well-known admiration of cinema's privileged relation to reality or Roland Barthes's faith in photography's authentication of reality.[21] Yet, the retorts are not insignificant either. Both *Wag the Dog's* lead protagonist and a series of contemporary thinkers cast serious doubts about the plausibility of such claims. Motss openly questions the veracity of some historical analog photos, acknowledging the possibility of manipulation even in analog media. Despite the film's extensive display of the digital means of image construction, the creative possibilities available to those working with analog technology should not be underestimated. Granted, matte shots and superimpositions are easily detectable, but the inventive potential of staging, framing, and editing a scene has been ingeniously explored right from the start, already from Lumières' first films. In his article "Louis Lumière—The Cinema's First Virtualist," Thomas Elsaesser summarizes the evidence of deliberation and planning behind Lumière's single-shot, single-scene films made with a static camera to illustrate how Douchet and Bazin's belief in cinema's capturing and respecting reality had been misconstrued all along.[22] Similarly, William Rothman painstakingly analyzes *Nanook of the North* (1922), another emblematic documentary so well-praised by the lovers of reality, to show how fantasy and myth intertwined with the life of Nanook as seen through Flaherty's camera.[23] In fact, a number of key documentary theorists, such as Bill Nichols and Michael Renov, have extensively argued for the problematic relation of nonfiction films to the outer world without taking into consideration any digital representations at all.[24] Thus, the advent of digital possibilities does not seem to establish a new ontological regime altogether; rather, it sets the agenda for an ontological inquiry that encourages us to reconsider the history of analog media by freeing us from the hallucination of their indexical relation to reality, to paraphrase Timothy Murray.[25]

But whatever happened to reality? Should we entirely give up on it, since you cannot tell the difference anymore, as Stanley Motss and his team suggest? Is there a way to allow reality to reenter the picture? One first step would be to cast off the anxiety about the formal or ontological identity of the image and concentrate on its semiological function. Lefebvre and Furstenau, in an article called "Digital Editing and Montage: The Vanishing Celluloid and Beyond," examine at length the significance of semiotics for understanding filmic images and scrutinize Peirce's definition of an "index" in order to illustrate how *"indexicality is simply how signs indicate what it is they are about."*[26] Whether it is a photographic or a graphic[27] image, its connection to the real world still obtains. As they note,

> Like paintings, CGI visuals are less directly connected to the pictured object than traditional photographs. Yet the computer-generated Roman coliseum of *Gladiator*, ship and waves of *Titanic*, storm of *The Perfect Storm*, or tornadoes of *Twister*, are all necessarily indexical of Reality in an unlimited number of ways, *including* in their connections to the existing coliseum, the Titanic, waves and tornadoes.[28]

In this light, the concern becomes much less about whether the object of representation existed in front of the camera but, rather, whether this object has existed in reality irrespective of the means of representation. If, for instance, a documentarist resorts to CGI for illustrating how the volcano of Santorini erupted 3,600 years ago, then it is most likely that those images were created on the basis of the scientific proof available at the time, and, in that sense, we are safe to assume that the CGI approximates or represents a past reality. In the case of *Wag the Dog*, however, the problem with the news report about the Albanian war is certainly not in the digital collage but in the commitment of that footage and the break of a social contract on the part of its makers.[29] As Plantinga strongly argues, the discursive function of all nonfiction representations, including TV news, is to make direct assertions about the actual world and, in fact, there is a social contract binding media people and viewers alike that requires the fulfilment of that function.[30] Whether a given society or a political system allows or even invites the violation of this contract is a more complex issue, hardly related to the ontological anxiety caused by the digital. In Elsaesser's words,

> The question of truth arising from the photographic and post-photographic would thus not divide along the lines of the trace and the indexical at all, but rather from the flow from a complex set of discursive conventions, political changes and institutional claims which safeguard (or suspend) what we might call the "trust" or "good faith" we are prepared to invest in a given regime of representation.[31]

What *Wag the Dog* achieves is to question all regimes of representation in a political and social context that is no longer able to safeguard any of the traditional values, like truth or trust, but rather establishes a permanent sense of instability in which fact and fiction are woven into a web of infinite regression. Ironically enough, the film's central premise would soon be corroborated by real life, as the political developments and the fictional plot got caught in a double-bind in which nobody could any longer ascertain who was wagging whose tail.

THE CONTEXT

The American political scene in the 1990s and, particularly the Persian Gulf War, provided Levinson and his screenwriters with a blueprint of the fictional plot. The

Gulf War, waged by a coalition of forces led by the United States, was the first war in world history to break on TV; at least, this is how it registered in the memory of hundreds of millions of viewers around the globe. The American President George Bush was part of the TV audience, too. According to the reports, he "was fiddling with the TV remote control when the bombing was due to start, and showed almost childish delight when the raid on Baghdad came through live on television at the time he had ordered it."[32]

The TV viewers had 24-hour live coverage of the war, but there was hardly any coverage of the communication campaign launched by the Bush administration to mobilize public opinion for an American invasion in the Middle East. The media were transformed into propaganda vehicles, as is usually the case in periods of crisis, and were inclined to report government officials' statements as facts, even when concrete evidence suggested otherwise. As former CIA officer Ralph McGehee told journalist Joel Bleifuss, "There has been no hesitation in the past to use doctored satellite photographs to support the policy position that the U.S. wants supported."[33]

Furthermore, the government of Kuwait and some members of the royal family paid $10.8 million to Hill & Knowlton, an international public relations company, to support the cause of Kuwait and stir anti-Iraqi feelings in US public opinion.[34] As part of the campaign to demonize Saddam Hussein and the Iraqis, Hill & Knowlton invented the story of Nayirah, a girl who tearfully testified to the House of Representatives Human Rights Caucus that she had witnessed Iraqi soldiers remove 15 newborn babies from their incubators and abandon them on the floor of the hospital to die. The firm produced a video news release (VNR) of her testimony, which was shown on NBC *Nightly News* and then was distributed to some 700 TV stations to end up being watched as a solid piece of news by an estimated audience of 35 million Americans.[35] Two years later, it was revealed that the girl was in fact the daughter of the Kuwaiti Ambassador to the U.S. and she was coached by Hill & Knowlton to fake her confession.[36] By that time, the war was over and the media had changed their agenda.

This was one of the numerous misleading stories reported during the war, which found resonance in *Wag the Dog*'s seemingly preposterous scenario. In addition to the fake news reports, however, the film explores extensively the issue of social participation in the drama of war, which is often the result of astroturfing. *Astroturfing* is a relatively new type of political advertising or public relations campaign that is meticulously designed to appear as spontaneous and popular grassroots behavior.[37] In contrast to traditional communication campaigns, which are openly guided by a public entity, such as a political party or a corporate company, astroturfing provokes a public reaction to an event as if it were independent and naturally occurring. In *Wag the Dog*, Brean and Motss initiate the trend of throwing old shoes on trees and lampposts as a symbolic support for the return of Schumann. This carefully implanted idea of participating in a national effort by means of shoe-throwing gathers momentum, and the streets are quickly filled with old shoes hanging everywhere. As they walk through a hotel lounge, Brean and Motss glance at a TV news report that shows young students throwing their shoes into a basketball court after the end of the game and yelling "Bring back Shoe!" The commentator describes this as "a spontaneous moment of sheer patriotism" and Motss says laughingly "there is no business like this."

Aside from war, there is also the sex theme that runs through the film's plotline, which is again another trope grounded in real life. After John F. Kennedy's extramarital affairs were revealed in the '70s, it was Bill Clinton whose reputation was tarnished by regular rumors about his sexual behavior, already from the time he was a governor in Arkansas. Particularly during the 1996 presidential campaign, with Jennifer Flowers and Paula Jones' stories out in the open, the issue of "character" became one of Bob Dole's arguments against Clinton, but the latter's spin doctors dismissed the accusations as diversions from the real issues on the political agenda.[38]

Even though the makers of *Wag the Dog* would hardly promote it as a "historical film," a brief glimpse into the actuality of the 1990s reveals the close ties of *Wag the Dog* with a number of historical facts, confirming most theorists' view that films, knowingly or not,[39] always amount to a document of a past reality. In other words, so far, there is nothing exceptional. However, *Wag the Dog* would also become a precursor of a series of *future* developments with its fictional narrative providing an interpretive framework for the real facts that took place soon after its screening.[40] It is precisely at that point where the relation between reality and the cinema was short-circuited, causing significant concern about the distinction between what is real and what is not. And this is why *Wag the Dog* is an invaluable case in point for understanding the evolving relationship between the cinema and the real world and for conceptualizing the new status of truth in a multiply mediated political reality. A short chronicle of the facts is again essential to clarify this point.

The Monica Lewinski scandal broke only days after the wide release of *Wag the Dog*, causing great surprise to its makers. Levinson and Hoffman were thrilled by the coincidence and commented on the blurry line between fact and fiction, whereas Mamet made the most insightful comment of all, saying "My secret psychotic fantasy is that someone in the White House is saying, 'What we should do is go to war, but we can't even do it because of that movie.'"[41] Ironically enough, President Clinton did go to war, or rather launched missile attacks against Sudan and Afghanistan, when the Lewinski scandal reached its peak. On August 20, 1998, three days after admitting his "inappropriate relationship" with Lewinski on national television, he ordered strikes on suspected terrorist facilities in the two aforementioned countries, spreading suspicion around the motives of his decision. *Wag the Dog* was repeatedly mentioned in news reports across all media, and numerous politicians were asked to comment on the similarities of Clinton's actions and the movie. One of the first questions addressed to Defense Secretary William Cohen at a nationally televised Pentagon was how he would respond to people who think the military action "bears a striking resemblance to 'Wag the Dog.'" His response was a cliché that seemed to come right out of Motss's lips: "The only motivation driving this action today was our absolute obligation to protect the American people from terrorist activities."[42]

Furthermore, extensive research into the references to *Wag the Dog* in soft and hard news programs clearly shows how the American nation employed the film as a "frame"[43] for understanding the government's decisions. As Matthew Baum writes,

> Once again, using Lexis-Nexis, I reviewed transcripts from 12 soft news programs. I found that, in the week following the attacks, 35 of 46 soft news stories on the subject (or 76%) addressed the *Wag the Dog* theme, repeatedly raising the question of whether the President might have launched the missile strikes to distract the nation from the Lewinsky scandal. In contrast, during that same period, the three network evening news programs, combined, mentioned *Wag the Dog* or Monica Lewinsky in only 11 of 69 (16%) stories on the missile strikes.[44]

Even though Baum emphasizes that soft news programs discussed the film far more, it is remarkable that *Wag the Dog* even made it into 16 percent of the evening news stories seven months after its screening. And its reputation would be far from over, as it continued to affect the public reception of Clinton's foreign policy in Iraq later that year. As Gene Healy notes on the December bombings in Iraq, "if the timing of the Afghanistan and Sudan strikes was suspicious, the timing of the 'Desert Fox' strikes in Iraq could hardly have been more so. The Desert Fox operation began on the eve of the House impeachment debate."[45] By that time, *Wag the Dog* had already been established as key concept in political discourse for interpreting presidential decisions. For other nations, the film became a political tool whenever they faced a threat from the United States; both Iraqi and Serbian television aired *Wag the Dog* to supposedly expose the motivations behind the US attacks in Iraq and Kosovo, respectively. For Americans, it became an interpretive tool for evaluating official responses to terrorism, enhancing suspicion "that any kind of military response was an attempt to generate public support, or even to distract attention from internal crises."[46] The interference of this film with the news coverage of American foreign policy continued through the years, extending over to key events such as the 9/11 attacks, the war in Iraq in 2003,[47] and, recently, Barack Obama's decision to allow the building of a mosque close to the Ground Zero site.[48] According to journalist Andrew Christie, *Wag the Dog* "is becoming our national portrait in the attic, worth a trip us the stairs every few years so that we may gaze upon its shifting surface and behold the latest, ghastly truths that have become visible there, reflecting our real political face."[49]

CONCLUSION

I have tried to demonstrate how the afterlife of *Wag the Dog* in the public sphere transformed a low-key independent production into a media event that would occupy news reports as well as the academic fields of the humanities and social sciences for years to come. For film theorists, in particular, the contribution of this film to our understanding of the relationship of film and reality in the contemporary world is momentous. Even though film and reality have always had a complicated relationship, mostly discussed in dialectical terms, the case of *Wag the Dog* shows how this relationship enters a new phase, in which concepts like imitation, mirroring, or influence are found wanting. The contextualization of this filmic text within an existing historical background and the concurring external reality indicated a series of changes in the way that cinema and the real world interact with each other in contemporary society. To begin to conceptualize this new stage in the film–reality binary, I suggest we need to use the digital not as ready-made concept but as *a guiding metaphor* that could lead us to new conceptualizations. In other words, instead of analyzing the film narrative to understand digitality, I propose that we use the characteristics of the latter to elucidate the evolution in the relationship of cinema and reality.

From this perspective, *Wag the Dog* as a media event seems to perform two key operations that are distinctly unique to the digital; first, the process of negation, and second, the transformation of all data sources to a single numerical code. These two operations were doubly articulated, first at the level of the diegesis and then during its interaction with the unfolding reality. Let me explain. As a film narrative, *Wag the Dog* proposed that you could fabricate a 100 percent fake war and make it pass off as reality. The film demonstrated the distinctive ability of the digital to simulate something that does not exist, thus performing what Kittler calls a negation. At the same time, the film persistently promoted the idea that you can never know whether something really existed or not, thus eliminating the distinction between fact and fiction. Technically, this is also the distinction eliminated by the digital platform once it incorporates the analog signs.

Similarly, when we move to the interplay of the film with reality, the distinction between the film scenario and the political developments in the domestic and foreign scene cannot be clearly demarcated.[50] The fictional template was immediately embedded in the way the media and the public received and interpreted the political events, whereas the film's lasting effect further influenced the political discourse for years to come. The more we look into the specifics of the Clinton affair and the subsequent attacks on foreign targets, the more we realize that it would be impossible to tell where fiction ended and truth began. Just as the digital obliterates distinctions by transforming live-action footage into pixels, the *Wag the Dog* event establishes that, in a media-saturated world, telling fact from fiction is no longer attainable. As Elsaesser notes, "Future generations, looking at the history of twentieth century, will never be able to tell fact from fiction, having the media as material evidence. But then, will this distinction still matter then?"[51] Therefore, does it matter whether the American attacks in Afghanistan and Sudan were true or whether they were also a negation akin to the Albanian war? *Wag the Dog*, just like Elsaesser, seems to imply that it does not. In this new phase, film and reality are both filtered through the media to become same-order signs with equal mobilizing force. In this sense, the media function just like a computer; they have the capacity to obliterate the origins of information and to simulate either fact or fiction, producing "truth" merely as a particular type of a "special effect." In this new light, the film's tagline "a comedy about truth, justice and other special effects" is no longer a joke; it is a very literal conception of the status of truth, and, by extension justice, in contemporary society.

Thus, the resonance of *Wag the Dog* extends well beyond the realm of American foreign policy, embracing all strands of social life. In fact, it gives us a blueprint of the ethical, economic, and social issues that global societies would be confronted with in the new millennium. Take, for instance, the global financial crisis. When the recession started in the United States in 2008, people were faced with increasing discrepancies between the financial economy and the real economy. The financial–real binary entails a highly complex set of relations, which inherently embed the notion of a creative construction of reality without, however, amounting to the false–real distinction. Equally complex is the response of the public in an age dominated by the internet and a multitude of social networks. *Wag the Dog* already indicated the significance of social participation in national events and suggested multiple ways for stirring public response, mixing the authentic with fabricated sentiment. The contradictions rising from this mix are also evident in the public response to the global crisis and protest movements like Occupy Wall Street. If we look at the "Pepper-spray cop" incident,[52] for example, we realize that the "code" true–false bears little explanatory weight in measuring the impact of the situation. When a police officer called John Pike offhandedly pepper-sprayed a group of Occupy protesters at the University of California Davis on November 18, 2011, the response of the "real" witnesses was to capture the event with their digital cameras, while the "virtual" online witnesses were able, thanks to digital tools like Photoshop, to comment on, play with, and reconstruct the scene in the most creative but obvious

FIGURE 21.3 The police officer pepper-spraying the protesters.

FIGURE 21.4 A reconstruction of the "Pepper-spray cop" incident.

ways (see Figures 21.3 and 21.4). Within a week, hundreds of collages were shared across all social networks, drawing the attention of all traditional media, like newspapers and TV news, and causing the suspension of the police officers involved in the incident. In this instance, it was not the "reality" of the scene that aroused public consciousness but rather the opposite; it was the blatant parody of the real situation that carried the symbolic power to impose changes, however small-scale, in the real world.

All things considered, the debate about digitality and the exploration of the digital as a metaphor in all its fine nuances and dimensions could elucidate a number of key processes in contemporary social life that resist easy explanations within traditional social thinking.[53] Understanding the digital is essential for understanding what Foucault calls the "regime of truth"[54] in contemporary society; that is, the mechanisms, discourses, and institutions that are charged with saying what counts as true or not. Within that regime, the role of cinema keeps changing. *Wag the Dog* is a film that could help us retrace it.

NOTES

1. Rudolph Arnheim, *Film as Art* (London: Faber and Faber, 1957); André Bazin, *What Is Cinema?* Vol. I (Berkeley: University of California Press, 1967); and Siegfried Kracauer, *Theory of Film: The Redemption of Physical Reality* (New York: Oxford University Press, 1960).

2. Susan Schmidt, Peter Baker, and Toni Locy, "Special Report: Clinton Accused of Urging Aide to Lie," *The Washington Post*, January 21, 1998. http://www.washingtonpost.com/wp-srv/politics/special/clinton/stories/clinton012198.htm

3. Joseph Hayden, *Covering Clinton: The President and the Press in the 1990s* (Westport, CT: Praeger, 2002), 108.

4. Robert Wicks, *Understanding Audiences: Learning To Use the Media Constructively* (New York: Routledge, 2001), 80.

5. "Is It Life or Is It Mamet?" *Economist*, January 29, 1998, http://www.economist.com/node/112045.

6. James Der Derian, "Virtually Wagging the Dog," *Theory & Event* 2, no. 1 (1998); Joel Black, *The Reality Effect: Film Culture and the Graphic Imperative* (New York: Routledge, 2002); and Andrew Hoskins, "Constructing History in TV News from Clinton to 9/11: Flashframes of History-American Visual Memories" in *American Visual Cultures*, ed. David Holloway and John Beck (New York: Continuum Publishing, 2005).

7. A selective list of books would include the following: Cynthia Weber, *International Relations Theory* (New York: Routledge, 2001); James Price Dillard and Michael Pfau, *The Persuasion Handbook: Developments in Theory and Practice* (Thousand Oaks, CA: Sage Publications, 2002); Klaus Dodds, *Geopolitics: A Very Short Introduction* (Oxford: Oxford University Press, 2007); Miron Rezun, *Europe's Nightmare: The Struggle for Kosovo* (Westport, CT: Praeger, 2001); Andrew Bacevich, ed. *The Long War: A New History of U.S. National Security Policy Since World War II* (New York: Columbia University Press, 2007); and Howard Good, *Journalism Ethics Goes to the Movies* (Lanham: Rowman & Littlefield, 2008).

8. A media event is defined as "an occurrence which attracts an extraordinary amount of media attention. The attention is generally international in scope, crosses the boundaries between popular news and political event, and usually marks a reference point in the cultural and historical imagination thereafter." See Mike Hammond, "Media Event," in *Critical Dictionary of Film and Television Theory*, ed. Roberta Pearson and Philip Simpson (London: Routledge, 2001), 272.

9. Tom Stempel carefully chronicles the production process of the film and points out the disputes and changes the story underwent from the novel to Mamet's final draft. See Tom Stempel, "The Collaborative Dog," *Film & History* 35, no. 1 (2005).

10. Eugene Vance, "The Past as Text and the Historiography of Tomorrow: Notes on a Recent Book," *MLN* 113, no. 4 (1998), 958.

11. Bernd Hüppauf, "Experiences of Modern Warfare and the Crisis of Representation," *New German Critique* 59 (1993).

12. Jean Baudrillard, *Simulacra and Simulation* (Ann Arbor: University of Michigan Press, 1994), 1.

13. Jean Baudrillard, *The Gulf War Did Not Take Place* (Bloomington: Indiana University Press, 1995).

14. Baudrillard, *Simulacra and Simulation*, 23.

15. Lucia Santaella-Braga, "The Prephotographic, the Photographic, and the Postphotographic Image," in *Semiotics of the Media: State of the Art, Projects, and Perspectives*, ed. Winfried Nöth (Berlin: Mouton de Gruyter, 1997), 122.

16. Lev Manovich notes that the privilege of this type of elastic reality (i.e., analog images in a digital platform) is that "while retaining the visual realism unique to the photographic process, film obtains a plasticity that was previously only possible in painting or animation." See Lev Manovich, *The Language of New Media* (Cambridge, MA: MIT Press, 2001), 301.

17. Friedrich Kittler, "Fiktion und Simulation," in *Philosophien der neuen Technologie*, ed. Ars Electronica (Berlin: Merve Publishers, 1989) and Yvonne Spielmann, "Aesthetic Features in Digital Imaging: Collage and Morph," *Wide Angle* 21, no. 1 (1999).

18. Kittler and Spielmann identify a third type of image, the electronic, that stands between the analog and the digital. Whereas the electronic is analog in principle, it prefigures several qualities of the digital. Kittler, "Fiktion und Simulation"; Spielmann "Aesthetic Features in Digital Imaging."

19. Despite the differences among visual forms so diverse as photographs, fiction films, documentaries, and TV news, the theoretical inquiry into the impact of digital technology on their formal and ideological functions seems to follow—paradoxically enough—a convergent path and, for that reason, I will consider them here as a whole.

20. Thomas Elsaesser, "Early Film History and Multi-media: An Archaeology of Possible Futures?" in *New Media, Old Media: A History and Theory Reader*, ed. Wendy Hui Kyong Chun and Thomas Keenan (New York: Routledge, 2005), 14.

21. Bazin, *What Is Cinema?* Vol. I; Roland Barthes, "The Photographic Message," in *Image, Music, Text*, ed. Stephen Heath (New York: Hill and Wang, 1977); and Colin MacCabe, "Barthes and Bazin: The Ontology of the Image," in *Writing the Image After Roland Barthes*, ed. Jean-Michel Rabaté (Philadelphia: University of Pennsylvania Press, 1997).

22. Thomas Elsaesser, "Louis Lumière—The Cinema's First Virtualist," in *Cinema Futures: Cain, Abel or Cable? The Screen Arts in the Digital Age*, ed. Thomas Elsaesser and Kay Hoffmann (Amsterdam: Amsterdam University Press, 1998).

23. William Rothman, "The Filmmaker as Hunter: Robert Flaherty's *Nanook of the North*," in *Documenting the Documentary: Close Readings of Documentary Film and Video*, ed. Barry Keith Grant and Jeannette Sloniowski (Detroit, MI: Wayne State University Press, 1998).

24. Bill Nichols, *Representing Reality: Issues and Concepts in Documentary* (Bloomington: Indiana University Press, 1991); Michael Renov, *Theorizing Documentary* (New York: Routledge, 1993).

25. Timothy Murray, "By Way of Introduction: Digitality and the Memory of Cinema, or, Bearing the Losses of the Digital Code," *Wide Angle* 21, no. 1 (1999), 6.

26. Martin Lefebvre and Marc Furstenau, "Digital Editing and Montage: The Vanishing Celluloid and Beyond," *Cinémas* 13, no. 1–2 (2002), 97.

27. In Manovich's theory of digital media, the digital is characterized as a "graphic" or "painterly" image, similar to the animated image that existed from the origins of the cinema. This parallel makes once again evident how the digital and the analog can share similar formal qualities. See Manovich, *The Language of New Media*, 301.

28. See Lefebvre and Furstenau, "Digital Editing and Montage: The Vanishing Celluloid and Beyond," 99.

29. Note how Noel Carroll debunks the postmodern skepticism of documentary theorists, like Nichols and Renov, by arguing that "the distinction between nonfiction and fiction is a distinction between the commitments of the texts, not between the surface structures of the texts." See Noel Carroll, "Nonfiction Film and Postmodernist Skepticism," in *Post-Theory: Reconstructing Film Studies*, ed. David Bordwell and Noel Carroll (Madison: University of Wisconsin Press, 1996), 287.

30. Carl Plantinga, "Moving Pictures and the Rhetoric of Nonfiction Film: Two Approaches," in *Post-Theory: Reconstructing Film Studies*, ed. David Bordwell and Noel Carroll (Madison: University of Wisconsin Press, 1996), 321.

31. Thomas Elsaesser, "Digital Cinema: Delivery, Event, Time," in *Cinema Futures: Cain, Abel or Cable? The Screen Arts in the Digital Age*, ed. Thomas Elsaesser and Kay Hoffmann (Amsterdam: Amsterdam University Press, 1998), 208.

32. Philip Taylor, *War and the Media: Propaganda and Persuasion in the Gulf War* (Manchester: Manchester University Press, 1992), 32.

33. Douglas Kellner, *Media Culture* (London: Routledge, 1995), 205.

34. Jarol Manheim, "Strategic Public Diplomacy: Managing Kuwait's Image During the Gulf Conflict," in *Taken by Storm: The Media, Public Opinion, and U.S. Foreign Policy in the Gulf War*, ed. Lance W. Bennett and David L. Paletz (Chicago: University of Chicago Press, 1994), 138.

35. Lance W. Bennett, *News: the Politics of Illusion* (New York: Longman, 2002), 55.

36. Kellner, *Media Culture*, 207.

37. John Stauber and Sheldon Rampton, *Toxic Sludge Is Good for You: Lies, Damn Lies, and the Public Relations Industry* (Monroe, ME: Common Courage Press, 1995).

38. Peter Rollins, "Hollywood's Presidents, 1944–1996: The Primacy of Character," in *Hollywood's White House: The American Presidency in Film and History*, ed. Peter C. Rollins and John E. Connor (Lexington: University Press of Kentucky, 2003), 252.

39. There is extensive literature on the complicated nature of cinema's relation to the historical past and the manifold ways in which a film can function as a historical document. Indicatively, see Marc Ferro, *Cinema and History* (Detroit, MI: Wayne State University Press, 1988) and Robert Rosenstone, *History on Film/Film on History* (New York: Longman/Pearson, 2006).

40. Richard Maltby, *Hollywood Cinema* (Malden, MA: Blackwell Publishing, 2003), 291.

41. The inevitable comparison of the film's plot to the sex scandal in the White House was made in a number of interviews with the film's crew. Mamet's comment appeared in an interview on *The New York Times*. See Janet Maslin, "At Sundance, Talk of Life Imitating Art," *New York Times*, January 24, 1998. http://www.nytimes.com/1998/01/24/movies/critic-s-notebook-at-sundance-talk-of-life-imitating-art.html.

42. "Wag the Dog Back in Spotlight." *CNN*, August 21, 1998. http://articles.cnn.com/1998-08-21/politics/wag.the.dog_1_people-from-terrorist-activities-dogs-military-strikes?

43. I am using "frame" according to Gamson and Modigliani's definition (i.e., "a frame is a central organizing idea or storyline that provides meaning to an unfolding strip of events, weaving a connection among them. The frame suggests what the controversy is about, the essence of the issue"). See William A. Gamson, and Andre Modigliani, "The Changing Culture of Affirmative Action," *Research in Political Sociology* 3 (1987), 143.

44. Matthew Baum, "Sex, Lies and War: How Soft News Brings Foreign Policy to the Inattentive Public," *American Political Science Review* 96 (March 2002), 96.

45. Gene Healy, *The Cult of the Presidency: America's Dangerous Devotion to Executive Power* (Washington, DC: Cato Institute, 2008), 127.

46. Keith Jenkins, *Images of Terror: What We Can and Can't Know About Terrorism* (New York: Aldine de Gruyter, 2003), 46.

47. The rescue story of Jessica Lynch, an American soldier in Iraq, was repeatedly discussed as another *Wag the Dog* case in American political history. See Carol Mason, "The Hillbilly Defense: Culturally Mediating US Terror at Home and Abroad," *NWSA Journal*, 17, no. 3 (2005) and John Carlos Rowe, "Culture, US Imperialism, and Globalization," *American Literary History* 16, no. 4 (2004).

48. Many conservative and religious groups accused Obama for "wagging the mosque"; that is, of trying to divert attention from deflating economy. See Delwyn Lounsbury, "President Barack Hussein Obama Does 'Wag The Mosque' in a Deflation Economy," *EzineArticles*, http://ezinearticles.com/?President-Barack-Hussein-Obama-Does-Wag-The-Mosque-In-A-Deflation-Economy&id=4953490.

49. Quoted in Robert L. Hilliard, *Hollywood Speaks Out: Pictures that Dared to Protest Real World Issues* (Malden, MA: Wiley-Blackwell, 2009), 168.

50. Indicative of this mesh of reality and filmic imagination is the fact that, after the 9/11 attacks, the military sought help from a number of top Hollywood filmmakers to prevent future attacks. As James Der Derian notes, "In a reversal of roles, government intelligence specialists have been secretly soliciting terrorist scenarios from top Hollywood filmmakers and writers. A unique ad hoc working group convened at USC just last week at the behest of the U.S. Army. The goal was to brainstorm about possible terrorist targets and schemes in America and to offer solutions to those threats, in light of the twin assaults on the Pentagon and the World Trade Center." See James Der Derian, "The War of Networks," *Theory & Event* 5, no. 4 (2002).

51. Thomas Elsaesser, "History Memory Identity and the Moving Image: One Train May Be Hiding Another," in *Topologies of Trauma: Essays on the Limit of Knowledge and Memory*, ed. Linda Belau and Petar Ramadanovic (New York: Other Press, 2002), 62.

52. "Casually Pepper Spray Everything Cop" http://knowyourmeme.com/memes/casually-pepper-spray-everything-cop.

53. Traditional social theories, whether neoliberal or Marxist in perspective, seem to lack the conceptual tools for handling the complexities and contradictions of social global phenomena. More novel approaches seem to come from systems and network theories, which could further explore the conceptual wealth of the digital. Indicatively, see Niklas Luhmann, *The Reality of the Mass Media* (Stanford, CA: Stanford University Press, 2000) and Bruno Latour, *Re-Assembling the Social: An Introduction to Actor-Network-Theory* (New York: Oxford University Press, 2005).

54. It is worth quoting Foucault at more length to clarify the notion of the "regime of truth." As he writes, "each society has its regime of truth, its 'general politics' of truth: that is, the types of discourse which it accepts and makes function as true; the mechanisms and instances which enable one to distinguish true and false statements, the means by which each is sanctioned; the techniques and procedures accorded value in the acquisition of truth; the status of those who are charged with saying what counts as true." Quoted in Paul Rabinow, *The Foucault Reader* (London: Penguin Books, 1991), 73.

Select Bibliography

Baudrillard, Jean. *Simulacra and Simulation*. Ann Arbor: University of Michigan Press, 1994.
——. *The Gulf War Did Not Take Place*. Bloomington: Indiana University Press, 1995.
Baum, Matthew. "Sex, Lies and War: How Soft News Brings Foreign Policy to the Inattentive Public." *American Political Science Review* 96 (March 2002): 91–109.
Bazin, André. *What is Cinema?* Vol. I. Berkeley: University of California Press, 1967.
Elsaesser, Thomas. "Louis Lumière—The Cinema's First Virtualist." In *Cinema Futures: Cain, Abel or Cable? The Screen Arts in the Digital Age*, edited by Thomas Elsaesser and Kay Hoffmann, 45–61. Amsterdam: Amsterdam University Press, 1998.

———. "History, Memory Identity and the Moving Image: One Train May be Hiding Another." In *Topologies of Trauma: Essays on the Limit of Knowledge and Memory*, Edited by Linda Belau and Petar Ramadanovic, 61–72. New York: Other Press, 2002.

Kittler, Friedrich. "Fiktion und Simulation." In *Philosophien der neuen Technologie*, edited by Ars Electronica, 57–80. Berlin: Merve Publishers, 1989.

Lefebvre, Martin, and Marc Furstenau. "Digital Editing and Montage: The Vanishing Celluloid and Beyond." *CiNéMAS* 13, no. 1–2 (2002): 69–107.

MacCabe, Colin. "Barthes and Bazin: The Ontology of the Image." In *Writing the Image after Roland Barthes*, edited by Jean-Michel Rabaté, 71–76. Philadelphia: University of Pennsylvania Press, 1997.

Spielmann, Yvonne. "Aesthetic Features in Digital Imaging: Collage and Morph." *Wide Angle* 21, no. 1 (1999): 131–148.

CHAPTER 22

BETWEEN ARTIFICE AND AUTHENTICITY

Music and Media in *Wag the Dog*

THEO CATEFORIS

THE first image that greets us in Barry Levinson's 1997 satire *Wag the Dog* is a mediated one. It is a political campaign advertisement for the president of the United States, who is up for reelection in less than two weeks. The television spot features two horse jockeys having a conversation after a race. One of the jockeys asks the other, who has just won the race, which horse he plans to ride in "the stakes." The winning jockey imparts a piece of advice handed down from his father: "Like my daddy used to say...never change horses in midstream." The other jockey smiles and reacts approvingly to this bit of homespun wisdom, and the first jockey adds a final tagline, "yeah, always stick with a winner." At this point, the accompanying music swells up in volume and an ascending melody gradually arches to a triumphant cadence as a confident male voiceover enters reminding viewers not to change horses in midstream and to reelect the president on election day. The commercial draws to a close with one final image: a close-up of the American flag gently rippling in the breeze.

With its overbearing symbolism, canned dialogue, and corny slogans, "Don't Change Horses in Midstream" directly lampoons the artifice of the typical campaign advertisement and sets the stage for *Wag the Dog*'s satiric intentions. As with much of what follows in the movie, music is crucial to establishing this effect. In a gesture that mirrors the scripted sentiments of the two horse jockey actors, the advertisement's score consists predominantly of synthesized or fake orchestral instruments such as imitation strings, glockenspiel, and a miniature brass fanfare. Likewise, the music accents the heavy-handed text and patriotic imagery with cymbal crashes, percussion, and a simultaneous crescendo and decelerando meant to suggest the sweeping grandeur and magnificence of the presidential office. The comedic irony, of course, is that the advertisement's contrived message ultimately conveys neither a sense of strident heroism nor enthusiastic hope, but rather complacency. It appeals to the voters' fear of change rather than any real promise for the future.

As we soon learn, beneath the placid vision offered in the advertisement's elaborate political kitsch lies a campaign in desperate trouble. A story has hit the press that accuses the president of having had inappropriate sexual relations with a young girl on a visit to the White House. The presidential staff calls on the services of a spin-doctor, Conrad Brean (Robert DeNiro), to fix the crisis, and he quickly fabricates a war with Albania to distract the public. Brean persuades a Hollywood producer, Stanley Motss (Dustin Hoffman) to "produce" the war, or as he puts it, "a pageant" with themes, visuals, and a song. As the plot develops, music plays a critical role at every juncture of their production. First, to sell the war effort, Motss turns to his trusted collaborator, Johnny Dean (Willie Nelson)—a grizzled, barely coherent songwriter—to provide a rousing patriotic anthem. After the CIA intervenes, and the president declares that the war has ended, Brean and Motss shift gears and extend their masquerade by creating a war hero left behind enemy lines, Sgt. William Schumann, who (naturally) is given his own fake folk song, "Good Ol' Shoe," to help cement his mythic role in the war. Much to their chagrin, they are delivered a disturbed ex-convict (Woody Harrelson) to assume the role of Schumann, but before he can be returned home to greet the waiting public, he is accidentally killed. Brean and Motss then capitalize on this tragedy by staging an elaborate military funeral, complete with a solemn choral march, "God Bless the Men of the 303," reminiscent of Ssgt. Barry Sadler's 1966 Vietnam era hit, "Ballad of the Green Berets." With the simulated Albanian confrontation concluded, and the president now riding a wave of public support, Motss threatens to go public and take credit for his impending reelection. Brean, however, has Motss killed to protect the operation.

At its heart, *Wag the Dog* hinges on a basic disjunction between the president's actual campaign and the illusory media events that are hastily constructed to secure his reelection. This essay explores the tension between these two mediated representations, specifically in relation to their competing claims for an authentic emotional appeal capable of winning over the American people. In Motss's view, the "Don't Change Horses" advertisements (which he glimpses on television at various points in the movie) are amateurish, poorly produced attempts to sell the president's campaign. The story of *Wag the Dog* revolves to a large degree around Motss's attempts to fashion events that are more believably patriotic, that resonate with an authenticity the advertisements presumably lack. I will focus on the two most prominent of these spectacles—the production of "The American Dream" anthem and the folk song "Good Ol' Shoe"—which occur back to back in the movie and mark the transition from the focus on the war to the creation of a war hero. As we will see, they each draw on a wide range of entrenched symbols and images of musical authenticity that ably feed the film's satiric and cynical tone. At the same time, as Motss's fake authentic creations accumulate over the course of the film, eventually dwarfing the presence of the actual campaign, it encourages us to view the "Don't Change Horses" advertisements in a different light. As I will argue, their dated appearance—a manifestation of clichéd television practices—assumes an authenticity all its own, one grounded in the nostalgic allure of an increasingly obsolescent media formation, one that, for all its contrived artifice, nonetheless offers a degree of familiarity and comfort in the face of Motss's high-tech capabilities.

THE AMERICAN DREAM

With its depiction of a thoroughly mediated society, *Wag the Dog* constantly reminds us of how easily the public can be manipulated or even deceived when handed seemingly authentic images and information. The idea of manipulation covers a wide spectrum of intents and purposes. On the one hand, to manipulate is to influence someone to react in a certain way or to elicit a specific emotional response. Much film music, for example, acts in this manner. On the other hand, manipulation can suggest more insidious designs. Music can be deployed less benignly to create desire among audiences for everything from questionable commodities to destructive ideologies. This is especially apparent in advertising, where music serves as a crucial component that can invest a product with seemingly magical properties. As Claudia Bullerjahn aptly summarizes, "a person's attitude towards the *ad* is generally a more important determinant of purchasing intentions than their attitude towards the *product*."[1] Music makes us more susceptible to manipulation.

Given music's affective powers, it is unsurprising that numerous researchers have tried to determine precisely how it influences our actions and generates conditioned emotional responses. The largest amount of this research has emanated from fields such as social psychology and marketing and has focused on how successfully or not the music in commercials and retail spaces generates favorable audience responses and increased business.[2] Because these studies generally employ social science methodologies, they tend to base their analyses on comparisons of musical style or those musical parameters that can be most easily quantified, such as tempo, pitch, modality, and loudness. Those musicologists who have ventured into the study of musical affect have tended to gravitate toward semiotic and communication models that similarly seek to establish a rigorous framework for the investigation of music's powerful emotional appeal.[3] None of these studies, however, has attempted or offered a formulaic understanding of musical authenticity and its effects, precisely because it is more ineffable, dependent on specific contexts, situations, and cultural memories. Authenticity—the sense that something is real or genuine—cannot be quantified; it can only be qualified through its various recognizable attributes.

Wag the Dog's "American Dream" sequence offers an ideal entryway into the complex terrain of authenticity, especially as it is defined through mediated depictions. The song itself is styled on the surface as a rather generic patriotic mass-choir arrangement with instrumental pop/rock backing, but it is the way that it is visually presented that is most initially interesting. As we hear the opening strains of the first verse, the camera ushers us into a recording studio, where we see a group of singers with headphones gathered around microphones following the conducting lead of Johnny Dean (with Motss standing watch behind the control room glass). The spectacle of a group of singers coming together in a time of crisis to record a song clearly echoes such familiar media "mega-events" as "We Are the World," which have been a ubiquitous pop culture presence since their first wave of appearances in the mid-1980s. In the case of *Wag the Dog*, the similarity is no coincidence, as the composer responsible for "The American Dream," Tom Bahler, also served as the original vocal arranger for "We Are the World." Given this close connection, it is worth following the comparison between "The American Dream" and "We Are the World" in some detail.

The authenticity of this type of mega-event works in two basic ways. First, in what Allan Moore has called an *authenticity of expression*, we are led to believe that the singers' emotions—which in this case are tied to an honorable cause—are stripped of any commercial pretense and are thus honest and sincere.[4] Second, what pushes across this expression is the perceived *liveness* of the performance itself, which seemingly circumvents its mediation.[5] This live presentation is crucial because it allows a window into the act of the recording process and thus offers proof of the artistry involved. In the famed music video for "We Are the World," the singers' craft and investment in the music is signified by their dutifully somber poses and, most significantly, the prominent display of sheet music. "The American Dream" echoes this atmosphere, gathering the singers, deep in focus and concentration, in traditional choral rows with music stands placed before them. The earnestness of their endeavors mirrors the seriousness of the Albanian war crisis.

Part of the way that authenticity cohered in the original "We Are the World" was through the very idea of assembling a group of superstars in a cooperative effort, which suggested that these musicians were not part of some competitive capitalist marketplace, but rather willing participants in an intimate folk-like community of artists. As Simon Frith has noted, this folk myth has long functioned within popular music generally and rock music specifically as a way of covering over its obvious commercial and individualistic intentions.[6] Significantly, the diversity of the song's cast—which ranged from African-American pop artists like Michael Jackson and Dionne Warwick to white rockers like Bruce Springsteen and Steve Perry and the country musicians Kenny Rogers and Willie Nelson (!)—further emphasized this sense of community as part of a larger melting pot identity of the United States. It fit "the conventional multicultural image of 'America' as a mirror of the world, where people of all nations come together as one to pursue their common American Dream."[7] Whereas Motss somewhat surprisingly chooses an anonymous group of singers rather than celebrities for "The American Dream," he follows a similar template of communal diversity. Men and women, young and old, black and white: we are meant to see them as a seemingly representative cross-section of the American populace; although it is worth noting the absence of anyone of obvious Middle Eastern, Asian, or Latino/a descent, which speaks volumes about what purportedly constitutes an authentic "Americanness" or true American identity.

Turning to the music itself, the types of vocal performance on display not only mirror the relative diversity of the singing group, but also give full force to the song's authenticity of expression. In the manner of "We Are the World," the verses of "The American Dream" consist of single lines passed from singer to singer, and a chorus that unites the voices as one. Although the singers are obviously following the conductor, they employ individual touches such as melismas, drawn out phrasing, and melodic improvisations that suggest that their vocals are extemporaneous individual outpourings rather than mere scripted lines from a score. One of the most central voices is that of an African-American man, whose grainy, raspy timbre and enraptured interjections throughout the choruses connote a range of black styles such as gospel, soul, and rhythm-and-blues (R&B) that have long stood as markers of direct, unmitigated emotional authenticity in popular music. Although there is nothing in "The American Dream" that quite matches the often overwrought exhibition of authenticity that courses throughout "We Are the World"—Bruce Springsteen, with his teeth clenched and eyes closed tight in intense concentration, comes most immediately to mind—the intended effect is nonetheless similar.

"The American Dream" assembles various points of visual and musical authenticity in a familiar, mediated dramatic package, but true to *Wag the Dog*'s form, it twists these conventions into a satiric shape, and this is accomplished most obviously through the song's lyrics. Whereas mega-events like "We Are the World" typically concerned themselves with extending aid to others in times of need, "The American Dream" weds this media spectacle to a chest-thumping song that urges us to defend our core American values and "guard our American borders." The model in this case seems to stem less from some utopian ideal of mid-1980s "charity rock" and more from the conservative patriotism of singers like Lee Greenwood, whose 1984 adult contemporary country hit "God Bless the U.S.A." became a virtual anthem of the Republican Reagan and Bush eras and enjoyed a huge surge of popularity during the Gulf War. As the musical responses to the events of 9/11 and the Iraq War have shown, such patriotic sentiments have become a commonplace reaction in times of crisis. "The American Dream" deftly collapses this authenticity of expression with that of the humanitarian mega-event to show how each of them are manipulative in their own basic designs.

GOOD OL' SHOE

"Good Ol' Shoe" follows directly on the heels of "The American Dream" and serves to advance one of *Wag the Dog*'s most crucial plot transitions. As "The American Dream" recording comes to a close, Brean and Motss learn that the CIA has put a halt to the fake Albanian war, and there now appears to be nothing to divert the public from the president's scandal. Motss, however, proposes that they have simply reached the conclusion of act one, and their production must move forward with a second act. For this, they will need a hero, a serviceman left behind enemy lines, "discarded like an old shoe." Inspired by this turn of phrase, Motss implores Johnny Dean to write a song about a good old shoe, "a ballad of loss and redemption," while they go about conjuring the character of Sergeant William Schumann. Dean is soon met in the recording studio by an elderly African-American gentleman who asks if they are done recording so he can put away the equipment (presumably he is a janitor or studio hand, although his choice of dress—a fashionable blazer—would indicate otherwise). Dean tells him he is supposed to be writing a song, and the man asks what kind. The camera briefly cuts away from them, and when we rejoin them, the two are sitting together with acoustic guitars. The studio's bright lights foreground them, as if to suggest a live performance stage, and, after some hesitant back and forth vocals and guitar picking, they have soon arrived at a blues song that repeats a refrain of "good ol' shoe." As Motss and Brean contemplate the details of their second act, the camera cuts away from the two performers to the studio control room and back again, the music remaining largely in the background of the film's dialogue.

The pivotal figure in the "Good Ol' Shoe" sequence is the African-American blues guitarist who mysteriously appears from out of nowhere to help Johnny Dean write his song. He is portrayed by an actual, well-known blues and gospel figure, Roebuck "Pops" Staples, but, more significantly, his presence serves a function common to many Hollywood films. In what Krin Gabbard has aptly called "black magic," an African-American character such as Staples lends his authenticity to white characters, in this case so they may realize their quest for an appropriate blues ballad.[8] The specter of an old black blues man with a guitar (Staples, who had grown up in Mississippi near Charlie Patton, was in his early eighties when he appeared in *Wag the Dog*) intersects with so many mythic representations of authenticity that they are almost too numerous to mention here. The majority of them deal with the blues and its centrality to the history of popular music, and rock in particular, as a presumably pure and untainted point of origination. As various scholars have suggested, whether one sees the blues as an authenticity of "primality,"[9] a "folkloric" authenticity,[10] or one based on an African-American "ethnic/cultural identity,"[11] its authenticity is most of all asserted through its recognition as an original "roots" music. This authenticity gained its strongest foothold beginning in the 1960s, when white British rock guitarists such as Eric Clapton and Keith Richards heard recordings from the 1920s and '30s of long-forgotten country blues musicians like Robert Johnson and testified to their unparalleled emotional power and allure. This mythic power has only escalated in recent decades, with a steady stream of historical media—CD reissues, anthologies, television documentaries, radio specials—that reached its zenith in 2003 when Congress officially recognized the "Year of the Blues."

The familiar tropes of the country blues resonate throughout the performance of "Good Ol' Shoe." The opening lines instantly conjure a rustic image, with the introduction of a hound dog named Blue that is loyal to the singer and his good old shoe. And, in the time-honored tradition of the blues, the shoe (and by extension dog) becomes a symbol of fidelity found to be lacking in the male protagonist's choice of women. Musically, the song employs a straightforward 12-bar blues progression with even phrasing and distinct verse/chorus sections that highlight the hook of "good ol' shoe." In this respect, however, it sounds very much like a modern blues song, employing the types of formal blues devices that eventually became routine and standardized with the rise of R&B in the 1940s. The country blues of the 1920s and '30s were often marked more by wandering strophic forms, free phrasing, and idiosyncrasies of performance that since have become signs of their authentic originality. Stylistically, "Good Ol' Shoe" certainly works as a blues song, but it is rather far removed from the celebrated and mythologized "old, weird America" of early twentieth-century folk from which the blues first sprang.[12]

Brean too senses that the performance of "Good Ol' Shoe" is somehow incomplete, and he asks Motss if "there is a way we can make it sound old and scratchy... with like a hiss." Motss follows this lead and completes Brean's train of thought; the song's authenticity can be guaranteed by its presence as an object, by turning it into an old record. The scene fades out with the overlapped image of a 78 RPM of "Good Ol' Shoe" spinning on a turntable. And so, just as the song was initiated by an act of black magic in the person of Pops Staples, it concludes with a technological sleight of hand that magically transforms the modern performance into a 1930 recording. This, of course, draws on the reality that music's authenticity is generally inseparable from its mediated form of dissemination. More specifically, the defects, wear, and aging of recorded objects lends them an aura of uniqueness. In an era of mechanical reproduction and mass manufacturing, where exact copies proliferate, these physical imperfections serve to differentiate presumably similar objects from one another. These old and scratchy qualities humanize the object and obscure the processes of industrialization.[13] The age and history of the record mirrors that of its originator, Pops Staple, and both serve to authenticate the song. As a final measure, Brean has the newly created "old" record placed in the Library of Congress, a seal of institutional and archival authentication that ensures "Good Ol' Shoe" will have its desired effect.

ARTIFICE AND AUTHENTICITY

After creating the character of Sergeant Schumann, the remainder of the music that Motss incorporates as part of his production revolves around the development of his new war hero. A grim black-and-white photograph of the captive Schumann, in which he is wearing a sweater with a Morse code message ripped out of it that reads "have courage mom," is released to the media. Before long, we are greeted on the television by a "live" video of Merle Haggard and his band performing a song of the same name. Like the previous musical examples, "Have Courage Mom" draws its authenticity largely from the specific mythologized qualities of a genre, in this case, the emotional sincerity and conservative American values that have long been fundamental to country music's essence. It also, of course, draws on Haggard's iconic status as one of country's most patriotic figures, the author of such famed songs as "Okie from Muskogee" and "The Fightin' Side of Me." The last major song of Motss's production, and one that serves to conclude his final act, is "The Fighting Men of the 303," a male choral tribute to Schumann's military unit that is played at the fallen soldier's funeral. At first, the song wafts above the funeral procession unmatched to any on-screen source, a product seemingly emanating from Motss's God-like hand. Eventually, the camera cuts to a televised view of the funeral, and the music appropriately switches from the male vocal rendition to the live military brass band that is actually accompanying the event. Both versions employ familiar performing ensembles and stylistic arrangements that underscore the somber, balladlike authenticity of the musical gesture and reveal the degree to which Motss's elaborate concoction has permeated the public sphere.

   In a landscape like this, where simulacra and hyperreality have become the norm, *Wag the Dog* forces us to question the very nature of "the real." How exactly are we supposed to distinguish the fake from the genuine when they ostensibly exhibit the same characteristics? Are we at the mercy of spin doctors like Brean and producers like Motss? Some have argued that in this environment of relentless spin and digital mediation, the objects that we *know* to be artificial, to be transparently inauthentic, ironically assume a new status of authenticity. Nicholas Rombes, for example, points to a nostalgia for the "'less realistic' special effects and stunts of analogue cinema" that has emerged in the wake of Hollywood's hyperrealist CGI spectacles.[14] In *Wag the Dog*, it is the president's "Don't Change Horses in Midstream" advertisements that fulfill this nostalgic function. The actors cast as normal, everyday citizens; the scripted slogans; the saccharine music: these all emit an aura of authenticity precisely because their overworked conventions leave us certain of the object's origination and mediated intentions. Partly, this authenticity is conveyed through the very appearance of the advertisements themselves, which generally have a more grainy look than *Wag the Dog*'s other televised images. Their faded, washed-out colors almost suggest they are from another, more distant time. To be sure, this dated quality and obvious phoniness, reduces the advertisements on some level to objects of kitsch that reinforce the movie's overriding satiric tone. But this should not blind us to the very real longings and desires that kitsch can arouse for an irretrievable past and the memories of what once was.[15] For all the laughs that the "Don't Change Horses" advertisements elicit, there is a noticeable elegiac quality to them.

There is a comparison to be made here with the history of popular music, which is filled with many such instances in which old and new media have met and where authenticity and artifice have clashed in the battle over musical taste and meaning. We are currently in the midst of one such moment in the early 2010s. The pervasive influence of Auto-Tune—a device employed in much mainstream popular music to correct and make more accurate one's vocal pitch—has raised anxieties over issues of talent, craft, and the vanishing presence of natural voices. When any singer's mistakes can be smoothed over with some digital tweaking, what becomes the standard for "real" singing? In this climate, in which musical production has increasingly become a digital undertaking and the truth of performance is less easy to discern, musicians and fans alike have come to embrace the authenticity of older musical technologies, such as the synthesizer, that were once criticized for their inauthentic imitative features. The fake strings and brass sounds of synthesizers from the 1970s and '80s that once drew the ire of both musician unions and purist rock fans have now assumed a new nostalgic authenticity, based certainly on their obsolescence and corresponding rarity as artifacts, but also simply in terms of the obviously electronic nature of their timbres. As with the special effects of analog cinema or *Wag the Dog*'s "Don't Change Horses" advertisements, because the imitative features of these analog synthesizers now seem so obviously unrealistic, their very artifice has secured for them a position of authenticity.

The closing sequence of *Wag the Dog* brings this dissonance between authenticity and artifice to a point of confrontation. At Sergeant Schumann's funeral, Brean and Motss toast the success of their production, as the president is now overwhelmingly favored in the polls and his reelection is imminent. Motss, however, sees a political talk show on the television discussing the president's campaign, and they credit his resurgence to the constant onslaught of his "Don't Change Horses" commercials. To drive home the point, they show an excerpt of the horse jockey advertisement with which the film began. Motss is infuriated by this implication and decides he can no longer remain silent and must call the television station to finally claim the credit that has been denied him his entire career. Although it is perfectly clear to us that Motss's production was the act that saved the president's election, in the end, it is the traces of the genuine "inauthentic" advertisements whose impact remains most potent.

In the decade and a half since *Wag the Dog*'s prophetic examination of political spin, media manipulation, and its ramifications, the line between the authentic and the artificial has become even more blurry. The growth of competitive cable news programming and the accelerated impact of the internet have made *opinions* about the news more accessible and appealing than the comparatively slow-moving discourse of actual reporting itself. As the media has saturated our lives with information constantly in the process of being verified or debunked, it only seems natural that people have increasingly gravitated toward the knowingly inauthentic—fake comedic news outlets like *The Daily Show*, *The Colbert Report*, and *The Onion*—as examples of authentic cultural expression. Likewise, it is no accident that one of the most celebrated popular music figures of the moment, Lady Gaga, is one whose artifice and inauthenticity of image define her authentic stature as a creative artist. We have reached a point at which "inauthentic authenticity" enjoys a place of prominence throughout our media and entertainment.

Wag the Dog remains important for its prescient foregrounding of this media simulacra and hyperrealism. The movie hinges around two competing forms of manipulation. Initially, we take the "Don't Change Horses" advertisements, with their ludicrous grab bag of election season clichés and barely concealed fakery, to be baldly manipulative. However, when we witness how easily and cynically Brean and Motss wield their power and resources to deceive the public in the shape of "The American Dream" and, especially, "Good Ol' Shoe," we are encouraged to think more critically about the ways in which authenticity is constructed. As *Wag the Dog* so ably illustrates, authenticity emanates from recognizable symbols and cultural meanings that must resonate in some way with an audience's expectations. And it is precisely because we have these expectations, and that we *experience* authenticity through affective means, that we are ripe for manipulation. With the rapid rise and spread of digital editing, it has become shockingly easy to create and manufacture objects that appeal to our sense of the authentic. In such a society, where the "real" is ever easier to fabricate, it is worth acknowledging how *Wag the Dog* surreptitiously, and perhaps even poignantly, grants the privilege of authenticity to those objects—the "Don't Change Horses" advertisements—that we know to be the most artificial and inauthentic.

NOTES

1. Claudia Bullerjahn, "The Effectiveness of Music in Television Commercials," in *Music and Manipulation: On the Social Uses and Social Control of Music*, ed. Steven Brown and Ulrik Volgsten (New York: Berghahn Books, 2005), 209.
2. Some representative studies include Ronald E. Milliman, "Using Background Music to Affect the Behavior of Supermarket Shoppers," *Journal of Marketing* 46, no. 3 (1982): 86–91; Judy I. Alpert and Mark I. Alpert, "Music Influences on Mood and Purchase Intentions," *Psychology & Marketing* 7, no. 2 (1990): 109–133; Clare Caldwell and Sally A. Hibbert, "The Influence of Music Tempo and Musical Preference on Restaurant Patrons' Behavior," *Psychology & Marketing* 19, no. 11 (2002): 895–917.

3. See, for example, Philip Tagg, *Kojak—Fifty Seconds of Television Music: Toward the Analysis of Affect in Popular Music* (Gèoteborg: Skrifter frêan Musikvetenskapliga Institutionen, 1979) ; Robert S. Hatten, *Musical Meaning in Beethoven: Markedness, Correlation, and Interpretation* (Bloomington: Indiana University Press, 1994) ; and Eero Tarasti, *A Theory of Musical Semiotics* (Bloomington: Indiana University Press, 1994).
4. Allan Moore, "Authenticity as Authentication," *Popular Music* 21, no. 2 (2002): 214.
5. Philip Auslander, *Liveness: Performance in a Mediatized Culture* (New York: Routledge, 1999).
6. Simon Frith, "'The Magic That Can Set You Free': The Ideology of Folk and the Myth of the Rock Community," *Popular Music* 1 (1981): 159–168.
7. Jaap Kooijman, *Fabricating the Absolute Fake: America in Contemporary Pop Culture* (Amsterdam: Amsterdam University Press, 2008), 24.
8. Krin Gabbard, *Black Magic: White Hollywood and African American Culture* (New Brunswick, NJ: Rutgers University Press, 2004).
9. Moore, "Authenticity as Authentication," 213, 215.
10. Hans Weisethaunet and Ulf Lindberg, "Authenticity Revisited: The Rock Critic and the Changing Real," *Popular Music and Society* 33, no. 4 (2010): 469–471.
11. Richard Peterson, "In Search of Authenticity," *Journal of Management Studies* 42, no. 5 (2005): 1086–1087.
12. The phrase and concept of "old, weird America" was popularized through Greil Marcus's *Invisible Republic: Bob Dylan's Basement Tapes* (New York: Henry Holt and Company, 1997).
13. Emily Chivers Yochim and Megan Biddinger, "'It Kind of Gives You That Vintage Feel': Vinyl Records and the Trope of Death," *Media, Culture and Society* 30, no. 2 (2008): 183–195.
14. Nicholas Rombes, *Cinema in the Digital Age* (New York: Wallflower Press, 2009), 9.
15. Celeste Olalquiaga speaks to this aspect of kitsch in *The Artificial Kingdom: On the Kitsch Experience* (New York: Pantheon, 1998).

SELECT BIBLIOGRAPHY

Auslander, Philip. *Liveness: Performance in a Mediatized Culture.* New York: Routledge, 1999.
Bullerjahn, Claudia. "The Effectiveness of Music in Television Commercials." In *Music and Manipulation: On the Social Uses and Social Control of Music*, edited by Steven Brown and Ulrik Volgsten, 207–235. New York: Berghahn Books, 2005.
Frith, Simon. "'The Magic that Can Set You Free': The Ideology of Folk and the Myth of the Rock Community." *Popular Music* 1 (1981): 159–168.
Gabbard, Krin. *Black Magic: White Hollywood and African American Culture.* New Brunswick, NJ: Rutgers University Press, 2004.
Kooijman, Jaap. *Fabricating the Absolute Fake: America in Contemporary Pop Culture.* Amsterdam: Amsterdam University Press, 2008.
Moore, Allan. "Authenticity as Authentication." *Popular Music* 21, no. 2 (2002): 209–223.
Peterson, Richard. "In Search of Authenticity." *Journal of Management Studies* 42, no. 5 (2005): 1083–98.
Rombes, Nicholas. *Cinema in the Digital Age.* New York: Wallflower Press, 2009.
Weisethaunet, Hans, and Ulf Lindberg. "Authenticity Revisited: The Rock Critic and the Changing Real." *Popular Music and Society* 33, no. 4 (2010): 465–485.
Yochim, Emily Chivers, and Megan Biddinger. "'It Kind of Gives You that Vintage Feel': Vinyl Records and the Trope of Death." *Media, Culture and Society* 30, no. 2 (2008): 183–195.

PART VII

BLOCKBUSTERS! FRANCHISES, REMAKES, AND INTERTEXTUAL PRACTICES

CHAPTER 23

"I AM BEOWULF! NOW, IT'S YOUR TURN"

Playing With (and As) the Digital Convergence Character

JESSICA ALDRED

In the weeks prior to its release in November 2007, director Robert Zemeckis enthused that his computer-generated blockbuster *Beowulf* and its digital cast (derived from the voice and motion-captured performances of Anthony Hopkins, Angelina Jolie, Ray Winstone, and John Malkovich) were particularly well-suited for adaptation into video game format. "Not only does the film have a compelling story and strong visual style that will translate well into a game," he suggested. "But because the film is entirely digital, we are able to share our assets with (game developer) Ubisoft. *Audiences will be able to make a seamless transition between the film and the game.*"[1]

Zemeckis celebrates the supposedly effortless transitions consumers can now make between the once-disparate media forms of cinema and interactive digital games. In so doing, he echoes a prevailing strand within industrial discussions of *convergence*, which emphasizes how the ephemerality of digital media content enables the cross-media flow of intellectual property, as well as the mastery and creative intervention of its consumer-operators. Zemeckis boasts that the status of his movie characters as digital "assets" makes them readily translatable into digital game characters, while the promotional build-ups surrounding most video games licensed from movies boast of next-gen graphics that allow them to create digital avatars that all but duplicate the photorealistic appearance and behavior of their cinematic counterparts.[2] According to such accounts, the boundaries between media forms and the human characters that populate them are rapidly disappearing, allowing consumers to enjoy the franchise in question as a seamless, immersive experience. However, as the *Beowulf* franchise demonstrates, such idealized forecasts for character convergence may be implausible and even undesirable.

Although convergence has come to be understood as a complex, multifaceted phenomenon with far-reaching effects on media production and consumption, there has been surprisingly little attention paid to its impact on how we create and consume fictional characters. Convergence once meant the strictly technological notion of different media functions "converging" in a single device; however, recent scholarship has broadened the definition to include the concentration of media conglomerate ownership across formerly distinct industries,[3] the synergistic flow of content or "intellectual property" across multiple media platforms,[4] the sharing of talent and technology between media,[5] and the formal and narrative qualities of converged media content resulting from all of these developments.[6] As Stephen Prince observes, at a time when the major film studios are owned by the horizontally integrated "Big Six" media conglomerates, films are rarely conceived as stand-alone texts: "Before there was cinema. Now, and in the future, there is software."[7] This essay investigates what is at stake when media characters become "software"—figures compelled by the synergistic imperatives and overlapping industrial and technological practices of their conglomerate owners to anchor media franchises and forced to take up starring roles in films, games, and other ancillary media designed to expand the franchise storyworld and extend its revenues.

Contextualizing the Transmedia Character: To Ancillaries and Beyond!

Obviously, there are strong economic motives behind promoting the dialogue between cinematic and interactive characters, as well as the supposedly effortless transitions consumers can make between them. In a media landscape where horizontally integrated companies hold interests across a range of once-distinct industries, the longer a piece of intellectual property can stay in the public eye—and draw on the public wallet—the better. Digital game characters are being viewed increasingly less by media producers as cheap, ancillary spin-offs of their big screen counterparts. Instead, they've become one of the most crucial fictional elements in the broader media ecology of what Henry Jenkins has termed "transmedia storytelling," whereby a franchise storyline is dispersed across multiple delivery channels, with the aim of each medium adding its own, unique contribution to an immersive, multimedia storyworld.[8] As Jonathan Gray asserts, the prevailing logic of our contemporary media landscape no longer strictly places film at the center of the textual interaction while relegating ancillary media to the role of "nuisances cluttering streets, screen time, cyberspace, and shopping malls...tacked on to the film or program in a cynical attempt to squeeze yet more money out of a successful product."[9] Instead, as Gray suggests, these "peripherals are often anything but peripheral...often playing a constitutive role in the production, development, and expansion of the text."[10] Although the film may remain the precondition for these transmedia expansions, it can no longer be viewed as doing its work alone, nor is it solely responsible for all of a franchise's popular meanings. Thus, a successful film character licensed for use in the context of a video game spin-off has the potential to extend the popularity of a franchise well beyond the box office, even functioning to keep brand awareness piqued between cinematic installations. As Jenkins contends, the synergistic nature of trans-media storytelling makes it an ideal means of organizing a franchise in the age of media convergence. Transmediation allows media conglomerates to maximize revenues across a range of separate but related products, while holding out the promise of a satisfactory experience for the consumer who ideally consumes all strands of the franchise.[11] In this context, characters are increasingly being treated as intellectual property to be trans-lated—and marketed—across multiple media platforms.

The term "convergence" has been mobilized as a uniquely twenty-first-century trope linked to widespread digitization as the technological driver enabling content to flow readily across media platforms. But characters that move across media aren't a new phenomenon, as anyone who's ever played with a Boba Fett action figure or followed Spider-Man from the pages of a Marvel comic to the big screen and back again will attest. Film characters have a long history of cross-media translation and adaptation, be it through appearances in early radio serials, novelizations and comic books, or their reimagining as action figures and other ancillary collectables. For example, whereas film-licensed action figures and toys may not occupy their own franchise-sanctioned narrative space, these supposedly "peripheral" bits of ancillary merchandise can still function to powerfully affirm and expand the franchise storyworld through the imagi-native play of their users. Gray contends that the original Kenner Star Wars action fig-ures allowed fans to personalize and intensify the franchise's obvious themes at the same time as they permitted them to become active participants in filling in the narrative gaps between cinematic texts through their game play. In the Star Wars universe, Gray argues,

> [T]he toys...have never merely been "secondary" spin-offs or coincidental: they have played a vital role in, and thus have become a vital *part of*, the primary text and its unrivalled success. Each movie brought to head years of play, and characters with long toy histories.[12]

Interactive digital characters hold out the promise of functioning as next-generation agents of franchise affirmation and expansion, situated as they are within navigable digi-tal storyworlds that permit players to explore the gaps and spaces just off-screen in their cinematic source material. Digital game characters also allow this franchise-expanding activity to transcend its previous status as pure child's play, appealing across age demo-graphics to the multigenerational audience that now consumes digital games. As they come to increasingly resemble their cinematic counterparts—in many cases due to such overlapping technical processes as motion capture, digital texture mapping, and shared vocal performances—these figures also hold out the promise that technologi-cal convergence will inevitably result in successfully converged content, eliminating any residual barriers to translating characters across media. As we'll see, in the case of the *Beowulf* franchise, producers hoped audiences would make a "seamless" transition from Beowulf as cinematic character to Beowulf as interactive character, construct-ing the muscle-bound Viking as both a transformative character controlled by actor Ray Winstone *and* a digital avatar who could be operated by the spectator/consumer. Through both its promotional strategies and its mode of address, Beowulf-the-film flaunts the ways in which cinematic digital characters can emulate the superhuman capabilities of video game avatars at the same time as it urges consumers to intervene via one or all of its interactive spin-offs. However, although each text—and each version of Beowulf—seemed poised to make a unique contribution to the *Beowulf* storyworld, the franchise's insistent blurring of the distinctions between these characters and their digital worlds may have ultimately contributed to a problematic series of redundancies and excesses. Trevor Elkington argues that the term "media convergence" somewhat problematically suggests that all media are moving toward a common ground where once-disparate narrative and design demands begin to merge, and all texts begin to behave similarly. As Elkington suggests, this assumption overlooks remaining diver-gences between games and cinema—particularly in the realm of character construction and reception—at its own risk.[13]

The Many Faces of Beowulf: The Digital Human as Convergence Character

His voice- and motion-captured performance provided by English actor Ray Winstone, the digital star of Zemeckis's 2007 film repeatedly bellows "I AM BEOWULF!" at the top of his lungs. However, these assertions of unified identity belie the fact that the fran-chise actually encouraged multiple points of entry into the character. Spectators could watch Beowulf on the big screen and join his adventures vicariously via the immersive subjective perspectives on display in the three-dimensional (3D) IMAX release. They also could guide him as digital avatar-protagonist, hacking and slashing his way through *Beowulf: The Game*, released for PC and the X-Box 360, PlayStation 3, and Nintendo Wii game consoles or in *Beowulf: The Mobile Game*, a downloadable cell phone game launched at the same time. They could download his chiseled, golden-haired likeness as a digital skin for their Second Life avatar and explore Beowulf Island, a virtual environ-ment created in that persistent online world for Paramount. They could even animate their own Beowulf avatar in their favorite massively multiplayer online role-playing game (MMORPG) to create a machinima film trailer as part of a prerelease promotional contest.

Although Winstone got to "drive" the digital character of Beowulf on screen, after the credits had rolled, you, the consumer, had the chance to take the reins and have your turn playing (or rather, playing as) Beowulf too. As per Jenkins' model of the ideal transmedia franchise as a carefully distributed, cross-media mode of storytelling, each text and each version of Beowulf seemed poised to make a unique contribution to the

Beowulf storyworld. Although the film roughly adheres to the episodic structure of the original epic poem, depicting Beowulf's exploits as a young conquering hero and an aging king, the game connects these two episodes in his life by playing through the approximately thirty years of bloodspilling adventures that occurred between them. In fact, the episodic structure of Beowulf as epic poem actually makes it ideal source material for transmedia expansion, since the lengthy temporal break between episodes creates the type of textual gap that can be filled in through other media forms. Neil Gaiman and Roger Avary's script for the *Beowulf* film provides a narrative connection between the two previously unrelated periods of Beowulf's life through his affair with Grendel's mother as a young warrior, which in turn produces the dragon offspring that terrorizes Beowulf's kingdom as an aging king. With this causal link in place, *Beowulf: The Game* was ideally positioned to fill in the gap between these two episodes by allowing users to play through the three decades worth of adventures that separated them. Beowulf Island in Second Life and Beowulf machinima, meanwhile, seemed ideal forums for more open-ended exploration and user creativity that could extend long after audiences had watched the film and completed the game. Zemeckis was not the first director to translate the ancient epic poem to the big screen; Sturla Gunnarsson's *Beowulf and Grendel* (an Icelandic-Canadian-British-American-Australian co-production filmed on a relative shoestring on location in the director's native Iceland) preceded Zemeckis's all-computer-generated image (CGI) bloodbath in theaters by just over a year. But Zemeckis's version (with its whopping estimated $150 million price tag for the film alone) was the first to receive the full franchise treatment, from its various interactive transmediations right down to a series of Beowulf action figures and replica swords.[14]

In so doing, the franchise holds out the promise of transmedia character identification and consumption as a wholly engulfing experience; it allows consumers to become further immersed in Beowulf's digital storyworld through virtual exploration and play, at the same time as the Beowulf character spills over and becomes ubiquitous in the world of the user—constantly accessible on one's cell phone, for example, or through a constantly open browser window on one's computer. However, whereas *Beowulf*'s promotional and diegetic strategies sought to imply a high degree of consumer agency in weaving together this transmedia tale, its insistent blurring of the distinctions between these various iterations of Beowulf and the digital worlds in which they reside ultimately placed undue constraints on users who wished to intervene creatively on the franchise.

THE CONVERGENCE CHARACTER AS "SLIDER SELF"

Thanks to an upgraded version of the motion or "performance capture" technology Zemeckis used to digitize Tom Hanks in *The Polar Express*, Winstone found himself cast in what would have been an otherwise implausible role for the paunchy ex-boxer and character actor—that of hunky leading man. In the film's promotional build-up, Winstone repeatedly enthused that performance capture took the limitations of his "real" body out of the equation and allowed his bodily and facial performance to drive the actions of his chiseled digital stand-in. "The great thing about it," he admitted, "is that it allowed someone like me, who is 5'10" and a little on the plump side, to play a 6'6" golden-haired Viking."[15] The film's promotional materials emphasized the limitless possibilities provided to the human actor by a transformative digital *character*—a relationship of mastery and control over the digital human image with obvious parallels to that of the relationship between gamer and avatar. It is a relationship of mastery that franchise producers also hoped spectator/consumers would ultimately develop with different, interactive iterations of the Beowulf character.

Winstone's enthusiasm for his digital stand-in transcended pure actorly vanity, since Beowulf's menacing stature and chiseled appearance are strongly linked to (and indeed, serve as a kind of shorthand for) his exceptional abilities. In praising his digital stand-in for allowing him to transcend the limitations of his lived physicality and capacities, Winstone echoes the enthusiasm of participants in video role-playing games and persistent online virtual worlds like Second Life, who invest extensive amounts of time constructing what anthropologist Tom Boellstorff has termed "slider selves."[16] These digital stand-ins can be tweaked and modified using in-game affordances to create the player's desired representation of him- or herself in the world of the game, even if that avatar bears little resemblance to the operator-player controlling it. Nick Yee and Jeremy Bailenson have documented how users who fashion more attractive "slider selves" benefit from what the authors have termed the "Proteus effect," consistently behaving more assertively in their online interactions with others thanks to the confidence boost provided by their enhanced self-representation.[17] Meanwhile, Boellstorff's study in Second Life indicated that this more assertive behavior may actually spill back into the user's "real" life, helping him or her overcome the social constraints and particularities of his or her actual physicality. (Physically disabled users inspired by the freedom of exploration and socialization provided by their digital avatars reported becoming bolder and more adventurous in their offline daily lives, for example, whereas autistic users who'd employed their avatar as a means of rehearsing social interactions in a bias-free environment tended to feel more confident seeking out real-life interactions.) However stage-managed they may be, Winstone's comments suggest that Beowulf represents his ideal "slider self," an identity that ultimately inflected his "real world" motion-capture performance. He confesses that having his digital alter ego in mind enabled him to be braver and more overtly physical in the role than originally planned, including the decision, once production began, to perform all of his own stunts. "It wasn't just voice, believe me," he corrected a journalist who referred to Beowulf as a vocal performance. "I broke two ribs doing this film. Probably the most physical job I've ever done in my life on a film."[18]

It's worth noting that Winstone is the only cast member who appropriates this gamer-avatar discourse—and, perhaps not coincidentally, he is the only interactive or "playable" character in the franchise. (Other characters appear in *Beowulf: The*

Game only as computer-controlled nonplayer characters, and they were absent from Beowulf Island in Second Life.) With the exception of Beowulf, the rest of the high-profile cast were denied transformative "slider selves" and given digital doubles instead. These other digital characters were created, like Winstone, from the actors' performance capture data, but also from high-resolution photographic scans of the stars' faces and bodies. Indeed, while Winstone enthused about the transcending the limitations of his own body to play a 6'6" Viking, co-star Angelina Jolie claimed profound unease with how much her character replicated her appearance, especially when she saw her nearly naked digital likeness on screen for the first time. By uncoupling only Winstone's image from that of his cinematic avatar, the *Beowulf* franchise sought to ease consumer transition from one media form to the next and from one version of Beowulf to the next, creating a transformative character into which viewers could more readily project themselves in the context of game play or virtual exploration. In live action cinema, a star's image is always, to some extent, carried into the role he or she plays; as a result, these digital doubles of such recognizable stars as Jolie, Anthony Hopkins, and John Malkovich are similarly bound to the expectations and constraints of their respective star images. Furthermore, as I've argued elsewhere, most characters in digital games licensed from movies struggle to balance their "doubled" obligations as avatars of both their player-operator and their big screen source material.[19] These figures are thus less suited to succeed as avatars of their players, since such excess star baggage leaves minimal space for users to form a successful "projective identity," James Paul Gee's useful term for the type of identification players experience with digital avatars as both an extension of self, into which they can project their own values and desires, and a highly constructed, often super-empowered other.[20]

GET IN THE PICTURE/GET IN THE GAME

Of course, since the pleasure of video game play is as much kinesthetic as it is visual, how the digital character Beowulf looks may ultimately be less important than how he acts—or rather, how it feels to act as Beowulf within the transmedia storyworld. Following the widely held assertion that interactive digital characters are as much defined by their functionality and capacity within game space as they are by any sort of richly developed persona,[21] Beowulf's capacities as interactive character are alluded to during the film's prolonged, gamelike sequences. Although these sequences are in part intended to showcase the film's 3D IMAX format, they also tend to be an excessive gesture toward how the viewer may go on to further explore the franchise via its interactive digital storyworlds while aligned with the Beowulf character, suggesting how it should look and feel to act as Beowulf when you, the consumer—not Winstone the actor—are in charge. Beowulf leaps, rides, swims, and flies through no fewer than half a dozen such sequences throughout the film, and we are pulled along with him thanks to the acrobatics of Zemeckis's virtual camera. These sequences oscillate mainly between first-person and tightly held third-person perspectives that strive to immerse us in elaborate, fully realized digital spaces that present new challenges to act on at every turn. One of the most striking examples—Beowulf's final, climactic airborne battle with the dragon terrorizing his kingdom—enforces an almost nauseatingly close align-ment with our hero as he chases down the flying beast on horseback and then fights him to the death, favoring an over-the-shoulder camera position highly reminiscent of that mobilized by such popular video role-playing games as *Mass Effect, Morrowind,* and *Fallout 3.* (This combination of close alignment with one's avatar at the same time that the avatar body remains visible to the player has been shown to evoke a higher levels of player identification than a purely embodied, first-person perspective.)[22] The wholly embodied, subjective perspectives more readily associated with first-person shooter games are here reserved for providing viewers with crucial information about vari-ous approaching obstacles and deadlines, as well as vital clues as to how Beowulf will eventually defeat his adversary—for example, Beowulf's subjective look at the dragon's glowing throat, prompting his recollection of King Hrothgar telling him that this is his enemy's weak spot.

As Alexander Galloway points out, one of the crucial differences between cinema and games is that, whereas cinema may selectively construct and frame its environ-ments to serve a specific narrative trajectory, video games must create "actionable" spaces—complete, exhaustively detailed, and navigable 3D digital worlds in which the player, rather than the director, controls the "camera," and (relatively) unrestricted gameplay occurs in real time.[23] In this navigable digital space, Lev Manovich has sug-gested, narration and action are closely linked, and looking and acting are the two key activities performed by the player.[24] I would argue that these sequences remediate the phenomenology of actionable digital game space, placing the Beowulf charac-ter temporarily in charge of the camera in almost real time, rendering narration and action nearly inseparable in the process. In so doing, these sequences approximate what Katherine Isbister terms the "visceral feedback" we experience while "looking and acting" as the interactive character, an experience shaped by what sorts of physi-cal powers a character possesses and how it feels to move through the gameworld.[25] As Robert Alan Brookey and Paul Booth have suggested in their analysis of the *Lord of the Rings* franchise,

> for the cross-promotional and synergistic practices of a franchise to work, the consumer must be reminded that there are other products to be consumed...the function of the franchise is to continually suggest that immersion is the aggregate experience of consuming all the products of the franchise.[26]

Here, the trope of immersion also directs consumers toward the supposedly immersive experience of consuming all versions of the Beowulf character.

THE IMMERSIVE FALLACY AND THE TRANSMEDIA CHARACTER

The film's spectacularly immersive mode of address suggests some rather elaborate possibilities for "looking and acting" as Beowulf in the franchise's interactive spin-offs—possibilities those media can't and ultimately don't live up to. The film leaves a three-decade long gap in its storyline for the console game to fill in with a series of missions not depicted on screen. However, almost all of the film's "immersive" sequences are also repeated in the game, but with decidedly less mobility and potential for action than Beowulf is capable of on screen, in part due to the huge processing requirements of creating interactive real-time gameplay with photorealistic graphics. For example, in the film, our first exposure to Beowulf's heroics comes when he must single-handedly slay a half-dozen sea monsters with his bare hands. Swinging from one beast to the next as they pull him through the ocean at breakneck speeds, he progressively learns and executes the series of moves that will dispatch the beasts most effectively—a winning combination of punching, grabbing, stabbing, and disemboweling. In the game, the sea serpents provide a training level at which players learn the series of moves that will help move Beowulf through the game most effectively—once again, a winning combination of punching, grabbing, stabbing, and disemboweling. However, to focus on teaching the rules of the game in an expedient fashion, gameplay is confined in this case to a rocky cliff where Beowulf stands and waits for the serpents to appear. Serving more as an object for aesthetic contemplation than a locus of subjective agency and fluid exploration, Beowulf attacks and defeats the serpents from a mostly static position, guided by a series of flashing prompts telling us which buttons to press, and when, to achieve the desired moves. Not only does the player experience drastically different visceral feedback via the Beowulf character than what was suggested by the film, but this nondiegetic, informatic layer of gameplay guidance further pulls us out of this implied immersive alignment.

In its excessive attempts to construct Beowulf as transmedia character, the film subscribes to the "immersive fallacy" of total engulfment or presence in a virtual world that Katie Salen and Eric Zimmerman have faulted as being highly detrimental to game and game character design:

> The immersive fallacy would assert that a player has an "immersive" relationship with the character, that to play the character is to *become* the character. In the immersive fallacy's ideal game, the player would identify completely with the character, the game's frame would drop away, and the player would lose him- or herself totally within the game character.[27]

As Salen and Zimmerman have so convincingly argued, in the context of gameplay, the illusion of complete presence and bodily immersion is just that because we are constantly shifting between cognitive frames that alternately place us "inside" of our character in a relationship of direct identification and very much outside of it, aware of the character as an artificial construct and our own status as players operating it according to the rules of the game:

> A player's relationship to a game character he or she directly controls is not a simple matter of direct identification. Instead, a player relates to a game character through the double-consciousness of play. A protagonist character is a persona through which a player exerts him- or herself into an imaginary world; this relationship can be intense and emotionally "immersive." However, at the very same time, the character is a tool, a puppet, an object for the player to manipulate according to the rules of the game. In a sense, the player is fully aware of the character as an artificial construct.[28]

Salen and Zimmerman deem this hybrid consciousness one of the unique pleasures of gameplay; however, by putting forth the ideal of seamless, immersive alignment with our protagonist-character in its primary media text, the *Beowulf* franchise sets its interactive characters up to disappoint when they inevitably cannot deliver on this promise.

Although the film promises an impossibly immersive alignment with Beowulf as interactive character, the Beowulf game features a digital character constrained by the temporal linearity and spatial boundedness of cinematic expectations, at times even resistant to the most basic interventions of gameplay. For all that it could have allowed players a more open-ended and customized engagement with the Beowulf character, the game insists on constructing a narrative that slavishly adheres to and fills in the linear timeline laid out by the film, forcing the player along on rails between gameplay levels and noninteractive cinematic cutscenes, many of which repeat, verbatim, dialogue from the film. Game reviews repeatedly cite this insistent linearity as one Beowulf's greatest flaws and fault the multiple ways in which developers had limited both the "actionability" of the gamespace and the capabilities/capacity of the Beowulf character in order to keep players traveling along this linear path:

> Beowulf, in an effort to seem open-ended, is full of branching paths whose avenues lead to dead ends. Even worse, one trail will be blocked by a waist-high boulder that your mightiness cannot scale, yet the only way forward will entail a 20-foot climb straight up a vertical surface. Truly, Beowulf does not know his own strength, and neither does Ubisoft. [29]

Beowulf can scale sheer rock faces with his bare hands one moment but be brought to a standstill by a waist-high boulder the next; he'll fearlessly plummet down a treacherous waterfall or into the depths of a seemingly endless cave, but flat out refuse to hop down into an innocuous gully if it threatens to take him off course. These inconsistencies prevent the player from experiencing the sort of smooth, intuitive cognitive immersion Isbister deems crucial to a player's psychological experience of his or her character, whereby the player must be able to synchronize his or her problem-solving capabilities with those of the avatar to chart an eventually effective course of action through the game.[30] Even Beowulf's movements within gamespace were faulted for being too "linear" and "cinematic"—in the most heated battles, for example, many of his key attack moves are lengthy animations triggered by the right sequence of button mashing, which means that the gamer can't actually intervene to redirect him until the animation has finished. This mechanic was consistently faulted by reviewers for lowering the stakes of gameplay.[31] The choice of whether to use "heroic" or "carnal fury" modes of gameplay suggests a kind of moral choice system that will impact Beowulf's progress through the game and his development as a character, but this choice proves an illusion, since certain battles can only be won using carnal mode, and, regardless of which mode you use more often, the outcome of the game remains the same.

If, as Jesper Juul suggests, it is the player's *activity* and the game's evaluation of and response to that activity that ultimately guarantee player investment and presence in the game, Beowulf falls decidedly short.[32] For all that the digital character of Beowulf allowed Winstone to perform effectively in the film's digital storyworld, players struggle to act effectively when given control of their own Beowulf avatar, with its shortcomings as a stand-in for the player forcing a harsher evaluation of how it functions as an avatar for its cinematic source material. This reviewer clearly articulates how Beowulf's (and thus, the player's) ineffectivity in the gameworld can lead to a hypercritical judgment of character appearance:

> Most of the environments look good, with plenty of atmosphere and creepy set pieces, and the cinematic violence certainly employs enough blood. *But Beowulf executes the same attacks over and over, and the guy himself isn't very cool-looking.* His weird Viking ponytail looks awful, and some of the other textures look last-generation.[33]

Such harsh evaluations weren't limited to character appearance. In an effort to further foreground the convergence of its film and game characters, Paramount heavily promoted the fact that key cast members (and noted thespians) Winstone, Anthony Hopkins, and Brendan Gleeson provided the vocal performances in *Beowulf: The Game.* (For example, during the game's promotional build-up, writer and lead story designer Gabrielle Schrager enthused that the "actors seamlessly translated their characters' depth and emotion, breathing life into their video game roles as they did for the film.")[34] However, by prioritizing cinematic authenticity for its characters through shared vocal performances, game designers may have ultimately further impeded player alignment with them. After all, a star's image and its attendant baggage isn't confined to physical appearance; the unique quality of an actor's voice serves as an auditory guarantee of diegetic presence, even if the photographically recorded image of the body is absent. In the case of *Beowulf: The Game*, the highly touted presence of actors Winstone, Hopkins, et al. may have prompted somewhat unfair expectations for the kinds of performances currently possible in the medium of the video game. As Mary Ann Doane observes, cinematic performances—and indeed, the very unity of narrative cinema itself—depend on the appearance of synchronous dialogue (and the "lip sync" between actorly speech and facial expression) in order to conceal their material heterogeneity.[35] However, in the Beowulf game, the disjuncture between vocal and visual performance repeatedly points up the separate origins of sound and image—and thus, the heterogeneity of the character in question. When not shouting repetitive and nonsensical catch phrases ("I am Beowulf!" "Stand together!") in the heat of battle, Winstone's voice is matched with a decidedly lower-resolution version of Beowulf than his cinematic counterpart in the context of noninteractive cutscenes and forced to recite extensive exposition through lips only partially capable of wrapping themselves around the syllables. Game reviewers and gamers alike faulted the game's "shoddy" voice acting[36] as a reason to "stop listening to the characters in the middle of the game,"[37] but tended to ground this criticism in the perceived disjuncture between sound and image rather than in any inherent shortcomings in the vocal performance alone.

Beowulf's other high-profile interactive identity—as a downloadable avatar in Second Life—further curtailed the kind of customization and creative intervention users have become accustomed to. Although Beowulf may have proven the ideal "slider self" for Winstone, Second Life residents who wanted to tweak their versions of Beowulf according to their own ideals of self-representation were unable to do so, their "sliders" disabled in order to maintain the proprietary character image defined by Zemeckis's film. Due to the double-avatar status of the movie-licensed interactive character, how users could "look and act" on Beowulf Island was mainly limited by its role in the film's promotion. Once they had downloaded their Beowulf avatar, users were guided, not into an immersive exploration or expansion of the Beowulf universe, but rather into entering into the "Beowulf avatar sweepstakes" where they could win tickets to the theatrical release of the film. And although the designers of Beowulf Island, the Electric Sheep Company, had successfully expanded the storyworlds of *CSI* and *I Am Legend* into Second Life, at Paramount's insistence, Beowulf Island was not actually used for any sort of fictional expansion of the franchise. Instead, it was merely a site where merchandise could be acquired, promotional contests could be launched, and cast and crew could give interviews. The "build" feature was disabled on the island, preventing users from performing their own creative additions to the Beowulf storyworld. This promotional mandate was reinforced by Electric Sheep's head of business development, Jason Mirvis, when I contacted him about the project: "The Beowulf campaign was conducted on behalf of Paramount Pictures to help promote the release of the film.... The Beowulf Island was never meant to be a permanent sim within SL, and the island was closed after the marketing campaign ended."[38]

Thus, not long after the Beowulf DVD had been released and the promotional obligations of the Island fulfilled, it disappeared into the cyber-ether (sadly, along with it went Jez Albatros, the avatar I'd created solely for the purpose of living happily ever after on Beowulf Island). The only transmediation of Beowulf that allowed consumers creative control over Beowulf's image was a machinima contest in which users fashioned their own Beowulf trailers using the game engine of their choice. As Gray asserts, machinima provides an ideal forum for the transmedia expansion of character:

> When screened for others, machinima works much like vids or fan fiction, adding stories to the text's expanding diegesis, perhaps giving visual form to the fan text and fan canon, or "fanon."... If video games allow considerable possibilities for the

exploration of narrative space, machinima artists, by repurposing them to create machinima, also open up considerable room for the exploration of character.[39]

However, by enforcing the exact repetition of sanctioned trailer dialogue, the contest ultimately rendered these creations mere parrots of the film's promotional materials rather than any sort of truly creative intervention upon or expansion of the Beowulf character.

At a time when the production processes, aesthetic possibilities, and commercial goals of digital media forms have never been more intertwined, digital human characters have become one of the most compelling case studies in the ways in which film and video games are converging. However, as the *Beowulf* franchise demonstrates, the successful convergence character remains difficult to achieve in even the most carefully conceived transmedia franchise. At present, fictional characters do not so much "flow" from one medium to another as they point up the remaining obstacles to such translation, placing extraordinary demands on media producers and consumers in the process. For all their superficial similarities, the many faces of Beowulf ultimately reveal how certain medium-specific expectations for character construction and identification remain. Elkington suggests that, in trying to blatantly appeal to the fans of both films and games and emphasize the "converged" nature of its various media platforms, many contemporary franchises end up being self-defeating—in other words, in trying to appeal to everyone, they end up pleasing no one. As the corporate goals and aesthetic possibilities of cinema and digital games continue to merge in the entity of the digital human character, it remains to be seen whether media producers can find new and compelling ways to avoid this self-defeat.

NOTES

1. Alexis Dunham, "Ubisoft announces Beowulf," *IGN*, May 24, 2007, http://m.ign.com/articles/791700. Emphasis mine.
2. For example, the press release for *Iron Man 2* boasts that it features "a cast of characters that transports fans into a deeper and more authentic cinematic video game experience," thanks in part to the "marquee" talent lending their voices and photorealistic images to the game. See "Iron Man 2: The Video Game Blasts into Stores Everywhere," *Gamasutra*, May 4, 2010, http://www.gamasutra.com/view/pressreleases/58342/IRON_MAN_2_THE_VIDEO_GAME_BLASTS_INTO_STORESEVERYWHERE.php.
3. See, for example, Edward Jay Epstein, *The Big Picture: Money and Power in Hollywood* (New York: Random House, 2005).
4. See, for example, Angela Ndalianis, *Neo-Baroque Aesthetics and Contemporary Entertainment* (Cambridge, MA: MIT Press, 2005); Chuck Tryon, *Reinventing Cinema: Movies in the Age of Media Convergence* (New Brunswick, NJ: Rutgers University Press, 2009).
5. See, for example, Robert Alan Brookey, *Hollywood Gamers: Digital Convergence in the Film and Video Game Industries* (Bloomington: Indiana University Press, 2010); Casey O'Donnell, "Games Are Not Convergence: The Lost Promise of Digital Production and Convergence," *Convergence* 17, no. 3 (August 2011): 271–286.

6. See, for example, J. David Bolter and Richard Grusin, *Remediation: Understanding New Media* (Cambridge, MA: MIT Press, 1999); Barry Ip. "Technological, Content and Market Convergence in the Games Industry." *Games and Culture* 3, no. 2 (April 2008): 199–224.

7. Stephen Prince, *A New Pot of Gold: Hollywood Under the Electronic Rainbow, 1980–1989* (Berkeley: University of California Press, 2000), 89.

8. Henry Jenkins, *Convergence Culture: Where Old and New Media Collide* (New York: New York University Press, 2006), 93–130.

9. Jonathan Gray, *Show Sold Separately: Promos, Spoilers, and Other Media Paratexts* (New York: New York University Press, 2010), 175.

10. Gray, *Show Sold Separately*, 175.

11. Jenkins, *Convergence Culture*, 93–130.

12. Gray, *Show Sold Separately*, 183.

13. Trevor Elkington, "Too Many Cooks: Media Convergence and Self-Defeating Adaptations," in *The Video Game Theory Reader 2*, eds. Mark J. P. Wolf and Bernard Perron (New York: Routledge, 2009), 232.

14. The drastically different opening weekends of each Beowulf adaptation indicate the extent to which Gunnarsson's film was viewed as a stand-alone text, whereas Zemeckis's was conceived as a larger media event. *Beowulf and Grendel* premiered on a single screen in the United States on June 18, 2006, earning $4,360 in its opening weekend. Zemeckis's *Beowulf*, in contrast, received a wide release on more than 3,000 regular and IMAX screens, grossing $27.5 million in its opening weekend.

15. From "Beowulf Production Notes," http://www.beowulfmovie.com/[http://www.beowulfmovie.com/.

16. Tom Boellstorff, *Coming of Age in Second Life: An Anthropologist Explores the Virtually Human* (Princeton, NJ: Princeton University Press, 2008), 129

17. Nick Yee and Jeremy Bailenson, "The Proteus Effect: The Effect of Transformed Self-Representation on Behavior." *Human Communication Research* 33 (2007): 271–290.

18. Pearson, Ryan. " 'Beowulf' vs Cartoons: Animated Debate Rages," *Associated Press*, November 25, 2007, http://www.azcentral.com/arizonarepublic/ae/articles/1125animation1125.html.

19. Jessica Aldred, "A Question of Character: Transmediation, Abstraction and Identification in Early Games Licensed from Movies," in *Before the Crash: Essays in Early Video Game History*, ed. Mark J.P. Wolf (Detroit, MI: Wayne State University Press, 2012), 98–99.

20. James Paul Gee, *What Video Games Have to Teach Us About Learning and Literacy* (New York: Palgrave Macmillan, 2003), 55–56.

21. See, for example, James Newman, *Videogames* (London: Routledge, 2004), 134; Jesper Juul, "Games Telling Stories?" *Game Studies* 1, no. 1 (July 2001), http://www.gamestudies.org/0101/juul-gts/.

22. See, for example, Zach Waggoner, *My Avatar, My Self: Identity in Video Role-Playing Games* (Jefferson, NC: McFarland, 2009).

23. Alexander Galloway, *Gaming: Essays on Algorithmic Culture* (Minneapolis: University of Minnesota Press, 2006), 63.

24. Lev Manovich, *The Language of New Media* (Cambridge, MA: MIT Press, 2001), 245–247.

25. Katherine Isbister, *Better Game Characters by Design* (San Francisco: Elsevier, 2006), 204–205.

26. Robert Alan Brookey and Paul Booth, "Restricted Play: Synergy and the Limits of Interactivity in The Lord of the Rings: Return of the King Video Game," *Games and Culture* 1, no. 3 (2006): 227.

27. Katie Salen and Eric Zimmerman, *Rules of Play: Game Design Fundamentals* (Cambridge, MA: MIT Press, 2004), 253.

28. Salen and Zimmerman, *Rules of Play*, 453.

29. Joe Dodson, "Beowulf: The Game Review," Gamespot.com, November 21, 2007, http://www.gamespot.com/beowulf-the-game/reviews/beowulf-the-game-review-6183284.

30. Isbister, *Better Game Characters*, 205.

31. See, for example, Dodson, "Beowulf," 2007. "The funny thing is that you don't actually have to dodge an attack. You simply hit dodge followed by power strike, and Beowulf automatically executes the super swing while moving toward the nearest enemy.... Beowulf seems to be invulnerable during both animations, so as long as you hammer on the dodge-and-attack sequence, you can cinematically cleave and stomp your way through an unlimited number of barbarians, monkey men, or worshippers, all while healing yourself and your allies."

32. Jesper Juul, "Games Telling Stories?" *Game Studies* 1, no. 1 (July 2001), http://www.gamestudies.org/0101/juul-gts/.

33. Dodson, "Beowulf," 2007. Emphasis mine.

34. Filip Truta, "Anthony Hopkins Is the Voice of King Wrothgar in the Beowulf Video Game Too," Softpedia.com, October 26, 2007, http://news.softpedia.com/news/Anthony-Hopkins-is-the-Voice-of-King-Hrothgar-in-the-Beowulf-Video-Game-Too-69261.shtml.

35. Mary Ann Doane, "The Voice in Cinema: The Articulation of Body and Space," *Yale French Studies* 60 (1980): 34–35.

36. Charles Onyett, "Beowulf Review," IGN.com, November 13, 2007, http://ps3.ign.com/articles/835/835434p2.html.

37. Gamer review posted by user Iamx30108200, "Nice graphics and good gore scenes and.... that that's about it." Gamespot.com, March 13, 2008, URL no longer active.

38. From an e-mail correspondence with Jason Mirvis, head of business development with The Electric Sheep Company, May 6, 2009.

39. Gray, *Show Sold Separately*, 198.

SELECT BIBLIOGRAPHY

Boellstorff, Tom. *Coming of Age in Second Life: An Anthropologist Explores the Virtually Human.* Princeton, NJ: Princeton University Press, 2008.

Brookey, Robert Alan, and Tim Booth. "Restricted Play: Synergy and the Limits of Interactivity in The Lord of the Rings: Return of the King Video Game." *Games and Culture* 1, no. 3 (July 2006): 214–230.

Elkington, Trevor. "Too Many Cooks: Media Convergence and Self-Defeating Adaptations." In *The Video Game Theory Reader* 2, edited by Mark J. P. Wolf and Bernard Perron, 213–236. New York; London: Routledge, 2009.

Gee, James Paul. *What Video Games Have to Teach Us About Learning and Literacy.* New York: Palgrave Macmillan, 2003.

Gray, Jonathan. *Show Sold Separately: Promos, Spoilers, and Other Media Paratexts.* New York and London: New York University Press, 2010.

Isbister, Katherine. *Better Game Characters by Design: A Psychological Approach.* San Francisco: Morgan Kaufmann, 2006.

Juul, Jesper. "Games Telling Stories?" *Game Studies* 1, no. 1 (July 2001), http://www.gamestudies.org/0101/juul-gts/.

Newman, James. *Videogames.* New York; London: Routledge, 2004.

Salen, Katie, and Eric Zimmerman. *Rules of Play: Game Design Fundamentals.* Cambridge, London: MIT Press, 2004.

Yee, Nick, and Jeremy Bailenson. "The Proteus Effect: The Effect of Transformed Self-Representation on Behavior." *Human Communication Research* 33 (2007): 271–290.

CHAPTER 24

LION AND LAMBS

Industry-Audience Negotiations in the
Twilight Saga *Franchise*

CAROL DONELAN AND RON RODMAN

WITH the advent of the *Twilight Saga*, the teen vampire subgenre, once consigned primarily to popular literature and television, has sunk its teeth into the blockbuster film franchise (Figure 24.1). The subgenre's migration into big-budget corporate cinema has prompted a negotiation between the Hollywood film industry and its target audience of young women and girls. In the *Twilight Saga* imagination, the contemporary film industry is—to quote dialogue from the first film—a "sick, masochistic lion" and the audience, "stupid lambs," there for the culling. And yet, the lion and lambs have successfully negotiated a "no bite" treaty that still allows for the expression of female desire in a culture reluctant to admit that it exists. The industry, for its part, has agreed to adopt a protective rather than predatory stance toward its target audience, offering young female viewers a PG-13 fantasy "for their own good" rather than exposing them to representations of sexual violence that "go too far," are too threatening or age-inappropriate. At the same time, the industry is willing not only to acknowledge the existence of female desire but also to represent its darker, uncanny dimensions.

By displacing the cultural prohibition against young girls having sex into a fictional prohibition against vampires biting human beings, the series allows both industry and audience to "have their cake and eat it, too." The industry safely positions itself as upholding the traditional value of sexual abstinence while at the same time presenting young female viewers with scenarios of erotic possibility expressive of their most forbidden desires. This pattern of cultivating and maintaining mutually exclusive values (such as abstinence vs. sexual activity) is expressed in the films via proliferating sets of binary oppositions: Edward/Jacob, vampire/werewolf, spiritual/physical, cold/hot, north/south, father/mother, familiar/uncanny, and so on. Inasmuch as these and other oppositions structure the story and produce the conflicts, the necessity of having to choose one or the other is avoided. In the parlance of *Seventeen* magazine, the question

FIGURE 24.1 Edward Cullen (Robert Pattinson) and Bella Swan (Kristen Stewart) in *Twilight* (Summit Entertainment, 2008).

is not whether one is "team Edward" or "team Jacob" because the series offers viewers both objects of desire.[1] The music industry is complicit in this "both/and" arrangement, offering consumers the opportunity to purchase not one but two CDs for each film—an original score and a collection of compiled tunes from popular bands whose musical styles range from mainstream pop to alternative to punk rock.

CULLING THE D-QUADRANT AUDIENCE

All six of the major studios in Hollywood today enlist the services of a firm called National Research Group (NRG) to coordinate film releases.[2] The objective is to ensure that new releases are not competing for the same audiences at the same time. Ad campaigns, known as "drives" (as in "cattle drives"), are designed to shepherd audiences to theaters on opening weekend (Figure 24.2). The NRG divides audiences into four basic demographic groups or quadrants: A, males older than 25; B, females older than 25; C, males younger than 25; and D, females younger than 25. Most of the top-grossing films in recent years (domestic) have been targeted at either A- or C-quadrant audiences of men and boys with films like *The Dark Knight, Iron Man, Transformers, The Hangover, Inception*—or hit the jackpot by appealing to all four quadrants at once, with family-friendly films such as *WALL-E, Harry Potter, Up, Toy Story 3, Shrek Forever After,* and *Avatar*.

The *Twilight Saga*—which includes *Twilight* (Catherine Hardwicke, 2008), *New Moon* (Chris Weitz, 2009), *Eclipse* (David Slade, 2010), *Breaking Dawn, Part I* (Bill Condon, 2011), and *Breaking Dawn, Part II* (Bill Condon, 2012)—is unusual in seeking to attract/attack the neglected D-quadrant audience of young women and girls. Like the vampire Edward Cullen (Robert Pattinson), the desired image whose sparkling white skin camouflages a potentially dangerous predator, the franchise is designed to appeal to a

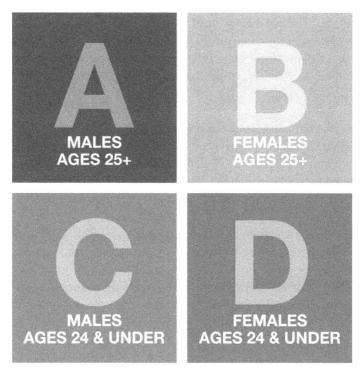

FIGURE 24.2 The National Research Group divides audiences into four quadrants based on gender and age.

particular audience, to express and represent their desire while also preying on them as consumers. As Edward warns Isabella (Bella) Swan (Kristen Stewart), the film's protagonist and target-audience representative, "I'm the world's most dangerous predator. Everything about me invites you in." This invitation is proffered not only in theatrically screened films but also in aggressively marketed DVDs and CDs, film and music downloads, books and fan magazines, life-size standee posters, t-shirts and sock assortments, jewelry, collectibles, carrying cases, lunch boxes, key rings, purses, wallets, umbrellas, water bottles, and other merchandise available for purchase.

As the saga begins, a fawn in the woods is chased and attacked by an elusive predator, a vision of the dark side of contemporary industry-audience relations. The sense of threat is enhanced by the swooping camera, unattributed point-of-view shots, and ominous music. "Dying in the place of someone I love seems like a good way to go," Bella intones in voice-over, signaling her consent to being culled as a member of a particular audience ("dying") and herded into a cinema theater ("in the place") based on her fascination with the celebrity image of Robert Pattinson ("of someone I love")(See Clip 1 ⏺).

Later, in a stylistically amped-up, gender-bending homage to the redwood forest sequence in Hitchcock's *Vertigo* (1958), Bella (in the role played by Jimmy Stewart) interrogates Edward (in the role played by Kim Novak) about his strange appearance and behavior, attempting to elucidate the truth about his mysterious identity (as image).

"You're a vampire," she concludes, "but I'm not afraid." In response, Edward rewards her with a vampire-style mounted thrill-ride to a mountaintop and reveals himself fully by stepping into a shaft of sunlight. "This is what I am," he exclaims melodramatically, presenting himself to Bella's gaze, his light-reflective Caucasian skin shimmering in cinematically self-referential glory, accompanied by Carter Burwell's sparse, bloodless musical score. "It's like diamonds," she gasps. "You're beautiful." "Beautiful?" Edward snorts. "This is the skin of a killer, Bella." (See Clip 2 ◐)

Despite Edward's desperate desire to prey on Bella, he announces his determination to restrain himself, to remain "vegetarian" (which, in the unique logic of the story, entails biting animals but not human beings) and she, in turn, insists on "trusting him" in this effort. She is far more convinced of his ability to control himself than he, but her belief in him (or rather, suspension of disbelief) bolsters his confidence. "So the lion fell in love with the lamb," he concludes as the two draw together in an uneasy embrace, an allegory of industry-audience relations. "What a stupid lamb," she responds. "And what a sick, masochistic lion," he adds. As in genre film, wherein both the ritual needs of the audience and ideological needs of the industry are said to meet, the *Twilight Saga* is brilliantly positioned to fulfill the industry's rather desperate economic need to recruit a new audience (of credulous lambs), as well as that audience's appetite for storylines, characters, images, music, and other appeals tailored specifically to their darkest fantasies and desires.[3]

The *Twilight Saga* is a PG-13 cinema, as embodied in the "vegetarian" Edward, who restrains himself from biting Bella—which, in the contradictory logic of the film, figures the value of sexual abstinence but does not preclude the possibility of sex. And yet, this cinema is haunted by an uncanny double, an R or NC-17-rated cinema that threatens to "go too far" in its depiction of male sexual violence against women. This impulse is initially embodied in Edward's double, the villainous vampire-tracker-rapist James, who attacks Bella.[4] In a scene mediating the conclusion of Welles' *Lady from Shanghai* (1947), with its fun-house proliferation of mirrors, James threatens to keep the video camera rolling as he preys on Bella, having lured her to a ballet studio under false pretenses. He grabs her by the throat, throws her across the room, and watches her writhe in pain, all the while recording what he sees and commenting self-reflexively on the visual style of the film unfolding before our eyes: "Beautiful. Very visually dynamic" (Figure 24.3).

Edward ultimately intervenes on Bella's behalf, but in the midst of a battle between Edward and James that thrillingly showcases the intensified visual style and wirework characteristic of contemporary Hollywood blockbusters, James bites Bella, poisoning her with his vampire venom. Meanwhile, Edward finds himself in the strange, tantalizing predicament of needing to suck the venom out of Bella's veins in order to save her, but without "going too far" and biting her himself. This scene enacts a complex negotiation with the culture's dominant ideologies of gender and sexuality. The (male) fantasy of sexual violence directed by James may be pervasive in culture but is positioned in the *Twilight* imagination as "going too far" in threatening the (female) target audience and failing to take into account their perspectives and desires. *Twilight* attempts to offer an

FIGURE 24.3 The predatory vampire James points a camera at Bella in *Twilight* (Summit Entertainment, 2008).

FIGURE 24.4 Edward presents himself to the Volturi in *New Moon* (Summit Entertainment, 2009).

alternative to the culture's dominant (male) sexual fantasies. Edward may be "vegetarian," prohibited from biting Bella, but he still figures for female viewers the possibility of sex in the service of their desires. (See Clip 3 ◉)

Inasmuch as Edward manages to restrain himself from "going too far" in *Twilight*, in *New Moon*, his mistaken belief that Bella is dead prompts him to "go too far" in attempting to kill himself. Once again, a cultural prohibition (against suicide) is displaced into a fictional prohibition (against exposing one's hidden vampire nature). Edward offers himself up to the Volturi, a vampire group dedicated to helping vampires destroy themselves when they "go too far" in revealing their hidden identities as predators (Figure 24.4).

The Volturi function allegorically like the internal, self-censoring arm of the Hollywood film industry, for which there is a long history, ranging from the establishment of the Production Code Administration in 1934 to the Motion Picture Association of America's ratings system in use today. The Volturi reject Edward's petition for destruction, given that "his particular gifts are too valuable to destroy." Edward then determines to incite the wrath of the Volturi by creating a spectacle of himself and exposing the truth of predatory vampire identity. He climbs to the top of a clock tower (*Vertigo*, again) and prepares to present the secret of his sparkling white skin to the masses below, gathered for a San Marco's Day Festival celebrating the historical expulsion of vampires from the city (evoking the Catholic Legion of Decency and other industry boycotting groups from the 1930s). This time, it is Bella's turn to race to Edward's last-minute rescue. The theme of the couple separated by the crowd gives the filmmakers an opportunity to pay homage to the reuniting of Katherine (Ingrid Bergman) and Alex (George Sanders) at the conclusion of Rossellini's *Voyage in Italy* (1954); cinema history is as much an intertext in the *Twilight Saga* pastiche as the Stephenie Meyer potboilers on which the series is based. As Bella embraces Edward, his exposure as sparkling-skinned predator is masked, and the uneasy "treaty" between industry and audience is upheld. (See Clip 4 ◑)

The threat of male sexual violence and rape lurks in this franchise, as does the violence of suicide, but as long as the industry restrains itself from "going too far," as long as the vampires refrain from making spectacles of themselves and revealing their hidden predatory natures, the target audience will be reached. In *New Moon*, Edward, in breaking up with Bella, lies to her "for her own good," to protect her from villainous vampires threatening to prey upon her. Bella also lies to her father Charlie "for his own good," to protect him from this same group of predators. In the *Twilight Saga* imagination, the industry produces fantastic illusions for the D-quadrant audience "for its own good," protecting consumers from the scenarios of sexual violence lurking elsewhere in culture while at the same time acknowledging and expressing the darker, forbidden dimensions of female desire.

THE TEEN VAMPIRE SUBGENRE AND THE UNCANNY

In its effort to attract/attack its target audience, the *Twilight Saga* combines the conventions of the horror genre with the teen coming-of-age narrative. From this hybrid arises the highly marketable teen vampire subgenre. Stephenie Meyer's novels are only the latest, albeit most successful iterations within the literary subgenre that also includes the *Point Horror* series—notably Caroline Cooney's *The Cheerleader* (1991), *The Return of the Vampire* (1992), and *The Vampire's Promise* (1993)—and Richelle Mead's *Vampire Academy* books (2007–2010). The teen vampire subgenre has also been popularized on American television, in series such as *Buffy the Vampire Slayer* (WB, 1997–2003), *Charmed* (WB, 1998–2006), *True Blood* (HBO, premiered in 2008 and continuing), and *Vampire Diaries* (CW, premiered in 2009 and continuing). The subgenre has had a less consistent presence on film, with sporadic offerings such as *The Lost Boys* (Joel

Schumacher, 1987) and its second-generation sequel, *The Lost Boys: The Thirst* (Dario Piana, 2010), *Interview with the Vampire* (Neil Jordan, 1994), and *Let Me In* (Matt Reeves, 2010), based on the Swedish film *Let the Right One In* (Tomas Alfredsen, 2008). Given its subgenre status, the *Twilight Saga* franchise may have more in common with these teen-oriented literary and televisual precursors than classic vampire films such as F. W. Murnau's *Nosferatu* (1922), Tod Browning's *Dracula* (1931), Werner Herzog's *Nosferatu* (1979), or Francis Ford Coppola's *Dracula* (1992).

Central to both the horror genre and the teen coming-of-age narrative is the expression of the "uncanny," a psychoanalytic term summarized by Freud in 1919 as "something repressed that recurs," "something familiar in the mind that has been estranged" due to repression that is now perceived as unfamiliar and strange, or "something which ought to have been kept concealed but which has nevertheless come to light."[5]   The uncanny is manifested in feelings of uncertainty about whether something is dead or alive, or in the experience of ourselves as split, doubled, or at odds with ourselves (conscious vs. unconscious selves). In the horror genre, vampires and other monsters are figured as our uncanny doubles, external manifestations of internal repression, returning to haunt us. Similarly, the teen coming-of-age story grapples with the uncanny experience of encountering our disowned selves as we mature—perhaps selves more violent or sexual than we are prepared to acknowledge. Freud uses the German words *heimlich* and *unheimlich* to describe the relationship of the familiar made unfamiliar through repression and "the return of the repressed." *Heimlich* denotes a range of meanings associated with the safety, tranquility, and intimacy of home; of being "at home" with oneself. The intimate, private aspect of *heimlich* gives rise to *unheimlich*, the concealed, secret, or hidden aspects of our identities that ought to remain concealed (repressed) in the unconscious but are consciously revealed, "brought to light." The *unheimlich* extends to meanings such as eerie, ghostly, horrifying, and dreadful, but also ecstasy (being outside oneself). The *Twilight Saga* does not shy away from evoking the unsettling feelings associated with the uncanny. At the same time, it takes care not to "go too far" in enlisting viewers in the experience of negative emotions.[6]

In the first film in the franchise, Bella leaves her mother's home in Phoenix to go live with her father in Forks, Washington, "which exists under a constant cover of clouds and rain." Although she "doesn't know where I'll go or what I'll see," her journey is essentially one of transition from childhood innocence to adult sexual identity. Forks and the surrounding landscapes, where she was once comfortably "at home" (*heimlich*), having spent her childhood summers there, are now eerily unfamiliar (*unheimlich*) and populated with strange creatures. On her first day at Forks High School, already unsettled by her encounters with her new classmates, Bella stares in fascination as the pale, ethereal Cullen vampires make their slow-motion entrances into the school lunchroom. In subsequent encounters with Edward in biology class and the school administration office, she is disturbed by his strong reactions to her—as if he is filled with revulsion and disgust by her very presence. That evening, dinner at the hometown café with her socially awkward father Charlie and meeting "old acquaintances" (whom she struggles to recall) do little to dispel Bella's sense of unease.

As Bella's relationship with Edward begins to develop, the anxieties and fears associated with her transition into adult sexual identity are expressed via a network of references to worms, snakes, hands, and "cold things" which figure, via displacement, that which "ought to be kept concealed but which nevertheless threatens to come to light"—sexual difference as exemplified by the (cold vampire) penis. In biology class, the object of study is the planaria or "zombie worm." When Bella and Edward speak for the first time in class, he asks her if she likes the rain, which she finds an odd question, a non sequitur. "I don't like any cold, wet thing," she shudders in response. Later, in the lunchroom, the kids plan a surfing trip to La Push ("La Puuuush!"), the local beach, despite the cold weather, and Eric can be heard arguing for the "use of mitts, otherwise you'll get frostbite," a displaced allusion to masturbation. At the beach, as Jacob Black tells Bella the "scary story" about the Quileutes descending from wolves (an allegory of male physicality that she will later "not remember"), Eric is seen in the background playfully chasing Angela with a snake. "It touched my hand!" Angela screams. Subsequently, Bella accidently touches Edward's hand, prompting her to remark, "Your hand, it's so cold." In F. W. Murnau's *Nosferatu* (1922), a scene takes place in a greenhouse; Dr. Van Helsing shows his students a Venus flytrap devouring a fly and a polyp with mouth and tentacles consuming its live victim. In *Twilight*, Mr. Molina also takes his students on a class trip to a greenhouse, but the uncanny in this tale is associated not with figurations of engulfment (male fear of female sexuality) as in *Nosferatu* but rather penetration (female fear of male sexuality).

Jacob Black (Taylor Lautner), a member of the Quileute tribe, is, like Edward, an image of desire for Bella and the D-quadrant audience. Moreover, like Edward, Jacob is a predator who protects Bella from other predators, especially vampires (such as James and Victoria) who do not respect the historical "no bite humans" treaty established by the vampire Cullens and wolf Quileutes. However, whereas Edward's body temperature is icy cold, Jacob's is super hot—thus motivating his shirtless performance throughout most of the franchise. Inasmuch as Edward's secret (that he is a vampire) is "camouflaged," Jacob's secret (that he is a shape-shifting wolf) is "not remembered." Indeed, Bella remembers the part about the "cold ones" in the "scary story" Jacob tells her on La Push beach, but not the other part about the wolves. This is indicative of where she (and the franchise) is developmentally: she recognizes spiritual or idealized love (as exemplified by Edward, at least initially) but is not yet ready to accept the reality of physical love and penetration (as exemplified by Jacob).

Jacob's physical maturation is a source of fascination for Bella; in *New Moon*, Edward's snide reference to the "wolf being out of the bag" is telling in this regard. In *Twilight*, as Edward and Bella are dining in a restaurant, he reveals to her that he can read every mind in the room except hers. (See Clip 5 ◓)

As he scans the room he states what each person is thinking: "money...sex...cat." He then remarks that he has difficulty reading Bella (the D-quadrant audience), that he doesn't have the strength to stay away from her anymore (if the industry is be profitable), and that visions change based on what people decide (in response to ticket sales, the industry either produces more of the same or changes course). If *Twilight* is about letting the "cat out of the bag"; that is, Bella's (female) journey toward sexual maturity (cf. Tourneur's *Cat People*, 1942, and *Black Swan*, 2010), *New Moon* is about letting the "wolf out of the bag"; that is, Jacob's parallel (male) journey toward sexual maturity.

The third film in the series, *Eclipse*, continues to negotiate this process of change and development by focusing on the meanings and feelings associated with marriage, leaving one's parents behind, aging, and death. In marrying Edward, Bella will be changed (from a human being into a vampire, from a virgin into a sexually experienced woman) but will also remain paradoxically unchanged (stuck in time, frozen at a particular age). Edward offers Bella cold immortality, but at the expense of losing contact with her parents, as one who is dead loses contact with those who are alive. She would have to leave the warmth associated with her mother (now in Florida) for the coldness of life with Edward (in Alaska), spatially paralleling her initial trajectory from her mother's home in (warm) Phoenix to her father's home in (cold, rainy) Forks. Moreover, she knows that her father Charlie, the benevolent tracker, will never give up searching for her after she changes and disappears into vampire existence—just as he has never given up searching for the missing Riley Biers. The young vampire Rosalie Cullen expresses to Bella the downside of having been forcibly changed and made to leave behind human life before she has been able to experience much of it; Rosalie will never know what it is like to have children and know her grandchildren. Jacob offers Bella an alternative to this kind of loss; in choosing him, Bella can remain a human being and experience what it is like to have and raise children and know her own grandchildren. She will be subject to the devastating effects of time, however, and experience loss of a different sort: aging and death. The anxiety associated with aging and death is visualized in a dream sequence at the beginning of *New Moon*; Bella, with Edward by her side, shimmering cinematically, encounters her dead grandmother as an aged, uncanny mirror image of herself. On waking up, Charlie, Bella's father, surprises her with birthday gifts: a digital camera and photo album, for recording and archiving her senior year experiences. In the *Twilight Saga* imagination, the visual image is a mirror in which the D-quadrant viewer is invited to encounter her own perpetually changing (and yet contradictorily immortal) uncanny double through her own eyes. (See Clip 6 ●)

THE UNCANNY EAR

Music plays a major role in facilitating the experience of the uncanny for the D-quadrant audience without "going too far" and overshooting their tastes and sensibilities. Each of the first three *Twilight Saga* films has a different composer—Carter Burwell for *Twilight* and *Breaking Dawn, Part I*; Alexandre Desplat for *New Moon*; and Howard Shore for *Eclipse*—but the franchise manifests the same basic approach to musical direction, alternating a moody, original Hollywood-style score aimed at evoking the uncanny (*unheimlich*) with a familiar, comforting, compiled score of mostly vocalized indie pop tunes (*heimlich*).

Burwell's score for *Twilight* is arguably the most successful at evoking the uncanny; the familiar sounds of electric and acoustic guitars are defamiliarized via protraction, distortion, and other state-of-the-art sound studio techniques into an eerie, atonal soundscape, which is, in turn, interspersed with tracks by The Black Ghosts, Blue Foundation, Collective Soul, Paramore, MuteMath, Muse, Iron & Wine, Linkin Park, and others, carefully selected to mediate the D-quadrant audiences' aspirations toward a more sophisticated musical taste and, beyond that, a more mature (perhaps sexual) identity.

Musicologists have long grappled with Freud's notions of the uncanny in relation to classical music. Carolyn Abbate has focused on how distinct Freudian traits of the uncanny find their way into opera and musical narrative, most notably in the concepts of ventriloquism, automata, doubling, and repetition compulsion.[7] Other musicologists have worked more closely with the theoretical core of Freud's essay, suggesting that musical uncanniness results from failed attempts to repress familiar or "homelike" musical elements, which, upon resurfacing, are heard as newly defamiliarized. For example, Nicholas Marston points out Schubert's technique of alienating the sense of tonic as *heimlich* in his piano music, whereas Michael Cherlin discusses Wagner's and Schoenberg's tonal allusions as uncanny.[8] With reference to film music, Neil Lerner discusses how sound effects and "familiar" music by Bach, Schumann, Arditi, and others create an "encounter with the uncanny through hauntingly familiar sounds" and have "opened up the possibilities of the soundtrack for creating fear and dread in the horror film."[9] A more general summary of the musical uncanny comes from Lawrence Kramer, who suggests that the uncanny occurs (1) when one encounters something familiar that has been estranged by repression, (2) when events conform to infantile forms of thought that have supposedly been surmounted in adulthood, and (3) whenever something reminds one of a compulsion to repeat that operates as a basic principle in the unconscious.[10]

In Burwell's score for *Twilight*, in the opening scene, as a fawn is attacked by a predator, the music echoes the presaging of events to come: eerie electronic synthesized tones prolong a tonic pitch, embellished by a chromatic neighbor motion above (E-flat-D-D-flat). This chromatic b2 scale degree plays a role in the recurring theme, as a pitch outside the realm of a diatonic harmony lends an uncanny dissonant quality to the motif. These long tones give way to pounding drums, heard later with the appearance of the "bad" vampires Victoria, James, and Laurent in the ultimate fight scene.

The first encounter between Bella and Edward in biology class is marked sonically by a combination of distorted electric and acoustic guitar, signifying the friction between the two characters as they meet—and Edward's inability to read Bella's mind and be "in control." However, their second encounter, also in biology class, is marked by Burwell's "Phascination Phase" cue, which features a polymetric disjunction of an acoustic guitar playing compound meter-like triplet figures, with the piano part subdividing in duplets. This temporal disjunction presages the uncanny nature of Bella's and Edward's relationship (Figure 24.5). (See Clip 7 ◉)

When Bella and Edward later profess their love for each other on the mountaintop, Burwell's "Love Theme" develops, again with guitar and piano, punctuated by electric

FIGURE 24.5 "Phascination Phase"

FIGURE 24.6 "Love Theme"

guitar licks, instruments that have long been associated with the masculine and feminine, respectively.[11] The music here reprises the metric disjunction of the "Phascination
Phase" cue, but also articulates the "Love Theme" (Figure 24.6).

Burwell's "Love Theme" features a dissonance at the incipit: a B-flat in the melody
against a B and an A in the "left hand." Whereas the B-natural is dissonant against the A,
it is part of the diatonic universe of the A minor key. However, the B-flat floats above the
prevailing A-minor tonality of the theme, leaving the listener with a sense of unease—of
the uncanny. This uncanny feel is palpable, and studio executives picked up on it. As
Burwell writes on his blog:

> To our surprise, one of the executives wasn't in love with the "Love Theme." In
> particular he objected to the opening note of the melody, which he correctly noted
> is dissonant (the high note is a B flat, over A and B natural in the harmony). The

dissonance is immediately resolved to a consonance, but he couldn't get the initial note out of his head. Music is enormously subjective: For [director] Catherine [Hardwicke] and myself the tune was wonderfully romantic and moving. For him it was off-putting.[12]

Freud argues that the uncanny can be a matter of something gruesome or terrible but also something strangely beautiful, bordering on ecstasy. Burwell's quote suggests the two sides of the uncanny: the dissonant and the beautiful.

Although the soft dissonance of the "Love Theme" provides an eerie effect, the apparent lack of a tonal center in the cue conveys an even more uncanny effect. The cue is notated as G major/e minor, but the introduction to the theme begins by outlining a D major triad (V of G), and then moves to a G minor triad, representing a mode mixture from the prevailing key signature (although we listeners do not actually hear the major tonic previously). The theme appears after a downward sequence by step progression of D-C-B-flat-A accompanying chords on D minor, C, B-flat, and A minor.[13] The piece floats through the A minor tonality, then through G major, finally ending in E minor. The final chord, however, does not lend itself to a tonal resolution, as it is an e minor 6/4 chord (with a B in the bass). This floating tonality is reminiscent of Marston's remarks on the uncanny qualities of Schubert's music, particularly in his alienation (*unheimlich*) of the tonic harmony.[14] The meandering tonality of this and other cues in the piece has led to criticism of Burwell's score as "formless," but this apparent stream of consciousness compositional style is suitable for evoking the uncanny—more so than Desplat's tight leitmotivic construction for *New Moon*, and Shore's similarly periodic topical music in *Eclipse*. Various critics have remarked on Burwell's score:

> As good as *Twilight*'s vocal numbers might be, there's no denying the important, almost ever-present power that Burwell's work gives to the film's dreamy atmosphere....Burwell responds to the story's teen fan base with swooning female voices, guitar work that can veer from the melancholy to the savage, and ethereal samples that cast a truly magical spell over the dew-speckled trees and vampire skin. It's like a combo of Led Zeppelin and Pink Floyd, a rock 'shroom trip that plays the unconsummated romance between living and dead as the ultimate trip.[15]

And:

> Burwell's work is often steeped in yearning and melancholy, making him a good fit for writing music for a love story that would probably result in death if it were consummated. The romantic pieces are the score's strongest and most interesting moments: "Phascination Phase" telegraphs how gripping infatuation can be with an insistent [male] acoustic guitar and a [female] piano melody that wraps around it; "I Dreamt of Edward" brings an eeriness to its longing with slight atonality; and "Bella's Lullaby" is romantic without being sentimental. Burwell makes sure that the story's underlying threat isn't forgotten, mixing suspense and romantic tension on "I Know What You Are" and "The Skin of a Killer," which, with its complex emotions and undulating melody, is one of the most quintessentially Burwell cues in the score.[16]

In *New Moon*, Desplat's score retains much of the muted, subdued nature of Burwell's score, but is more traditional, relying less on "uncanny" electronic effects and more on the acoustic piano and orchestral instruments. Here, Desplat's "New Moon" main theme also lacks the eerie, uncanny dissonance and tonal ambiguity of Burwell's theme, just as the film itself shifts in emphasis from uncanny vampire horror to teen romance. Desplat's love theme is melancholy rather than eerie, and it resonates with the longing of teen romance (Figure 24.7).

The traditional nature of the score reflects the evolving relationship of Bella and Edward, with emphasis shifting from the uncanny coupling of mortal and vampire to the familiarity of girlfriend-boyfriend interactions. Howard Shore's score to *Eclipse* seeks to revisit the uncanny with a few electric guitar effects, but the film has more to do with backstories and the culminating battle between Victoria, Riley, and the newborns and the Cullen-Quileute alliance, and thus consciously motivated action takes precedence over the unconscious eeriness of *Twilight*.

"CHILDREN OF THE NIGHT! WHAT MUSIC THEY MAKE!": THE POP SCORE

Like many popular films of the late twentieth and early twenty-first century, the *Twilight Saga* makes extensive use of a compilation of pop songs by a variety of bands. Although the use and subsequent marketing of pop tunes, sheet music, and recordings dates back to films such as *Laura* (Otto Preminger, 1944), *The Blackboard Jungle* (Richard Brooks, 1955, with the theme "Rock Around the Clock" by Bill Haley and the Comets), *The Man Who Knew Too Much* (Alfred Hitchcock, 1956, featuring Doris Day's rendition

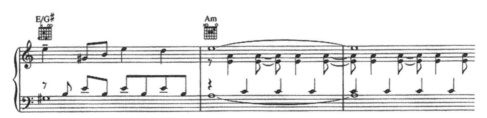

FIGURE 24.7 "New Moon"

of "Que Sera, Sera"), *The Graduate* (Mike Nichols, 1967, with the music of Simon and Garfunkel), and *American Graffiti* (George Lucas, 1973), the pop compilation score came into its own in the 1980s, with films like *The Big Chill* (Lawrence Kasdan, 1983) and *The Breakfast Club* (John Hughes, 1985) and continued through the 1990s and beyond.[17] The use of pop tunes gives additional marketability to a film, with cooperating music distribution companies making possible sales of CDs and MP3 files to consumers, as well as adding memorability to the movies ("Oh yes, that song played when Edward met Bella," etc.). Each film generated two CDs—an original recording of a newly composed score and a compilation of pop songs by bands featured in the films. As consumer items, pop tunes in a film offer up "cultural currency" to certain demographics toward whom the music is marketed. To know and recognize the music is a sign of belonging to a certain social group; teen identity is constructed out of the consumer products one purchases. Conversely, pop tunes can also tend to date films, making the "cultural currency" factor quite temporary.[18]

In addition to their marketing value, the compiled pop tunes in the *Twilight* franchise function to lessen the unsettling feelings or negative emotions associated with the uncanny world of vampires and werewolves. Pop tunes tend to appear in settings associated with normal to everyday teenage life: diegetic pop songs are heard in scenes involving Bella's home, restaurants, clothing stores, the prom, car radios, and the high school. Conversely, the original score tends be associated with "uncanny" locations: the forest, darkened streets, or locations "defamiliarized" by the presence of Edward (such as the biology lab). Following the deer hunting prologue of the first *Twilight* film, described earlier, with Burwell's eerie score, the ensuing opening credits are accompanied by the song, "Full Moon" by The Black Ghosts, temporarily alleviating the fear and tension created by the opening.

When used nondiegetically, the compiled pop song score accompanies scenes that focus on Bella: in *New Moon*, the motorcycle-building montage with Jacob is accompanied by "Shooting the Moon" by OK Go while Lykke Li's "Possibility" accompanies the scene of Bella bemoaning Edward's absence by moping in her bedroom. Grizzly Bear's "Slow Life" is heard during Bella's near drowning from her cliff-diving episode. Pop tunes link the fictitious world with the "real world" and help to shepherd viewer emotions away from the uncanny back to the safety and comfort of the familiar.

The pop music also expresses the coming-of-age theme in the films and mediates the trajectory toward sexual maturity on the part of the D-quadrant audience. The bands featured in the *Twilight Saga* are stylistically and geographically disparate, with groups whose music ranges from "mainstream" to "punk rock." Stephenie Meyer reportedly chose some of the groups based on what she listened to while writing the novels.[19] Curiously, many of the artists fall under the generic label of "indie" or "alternative" bands, a musical demographic not usually associated with young teen girls but rather with college-aged and older, more sophisticated audiences. The music by these alternative bands reflects the stylistic aspirations of the target audience as they grow to musical (sexual) maturity. Just as the franchise as a whole follows Bella and her journey from adolescence to adulthood, alternative musical groups are enlisted to initiate that young audience into the (young) adulthood of musical taste. The bands are listed in Table 24.1.

Finally, some pieces from the classical repertoire are also present in the trilogy. Debussy's *Clair de Lune* ("Moonlight"—night music!) is on Edward's playlist in his home (Bella comments: "Boy, you sure have a lot of music" when looking at his CD collection) and reappears in *Eclipse*, also associated with Edward's home. The Cullens have Verdi's *La Traviata* playing as they cook "Italiano" when Bella comes to the vampire family's house for dinner. In *New Moon*, Schubert's *Wanderer's Nachtlied* accompanies Dr. Cullen's treating of Bella's wounds and the quasi-ritualistic burning of her bloody bandages in a bowl.[20] A brief excerpt from *Der Fledermaus* accompanies the reappearance of the Cullens near the end of the film. In these examples, classical music portrays the Cullens as "different," with sophisticated tastes in music, clothing, cars, and home design, contrasting their aristocratic status with the working-class status of Bella's family. Classical music also serves to remind viewers that the Cullens are an "antique" clan who lived in the eras when this music was originally produced.

Notwithstanding the mediating role of pop music, there are a few moments when pop music points to the uncanny or is itself uncanny. In *New Moon*, Edward's first appearance—in slow motion, swaggering in the school parking lot, decked out in designer clothes and sunglasses, is accompanied by an upbeat rock tune, Hurricane Bells' "Monsters." This entrance is sonically different from his first appearance in the preceding *Twilight*, wherein Edward enters the school cafeteria in slow motion, accompanied by Burwell's subdued "Who Are They?" theme. (See Clip 8 ◉) (See Clip 9 ◉)

Although the Burwell cue suggests Edward's mysterious nature as vampire, the rock tune accompanying his entrance in *New Moon* suggests his changed status, his "knowability" as Bella's boyfriend.

Two other uncanny moments in the use of pop music occur in *Twilight* via the use of Robert Pattinson's own voice. The first is when Edward rescues Bella from would-be seducers in the streets of Port Washington. As they sit in a restaurant, the tune "Never Think" plays in the background, its source seemingly diegetic, the song possibly emanating from an audio system or an unseen singer performing just off-screen. The irony is that the singer is Pattinson himself, singing to his fictitious double, Edward, and Bella. This presentation is an interesting twist on the traditional role of "teen heart throb" pop stars serenading the young D-quadrant audience. While Bella vicariously stands in for the audience in the scene so does Pattinson's uncanny double Edward. The appearance of the song reveals the uncanny by problematizing what is real and what is imagined. Later in the film, another Pattinson song is heard nondiegetically as Edward sucks the blood out of Bella's bite wound and Bella starts hallucinating. The resulting audiovisual montage has Bella remembering and then forgetting her experiences with Edward.

THE UNCANNY AND NEGATIVE EMOTIONS

The uncanny manifests itself in the *Twilight Saga* on multiple levels, prompting potentially negative emotions in viewers. The franchise itself is an "uncanny body," a doubled text. On one level, it aims to appeal to the D-quadrant audience and its forbidden

Table 24.1

Music Groups in the *Twilight* Saga
Twilight:
Muse
Paramore
The Black Ghosts
Linkin Park
MuteMath
Perry Farrell
Collective Soul
Blue Foundation
Rob Pattinson
Iron and Wine
New Moon:
Death Cab for Cutie
Band of Skulls
Thom Yorke
The Killers
Anya Marina
Muse
Bon Iver & St. Vincent
Black Rebel Motorcycle Club
Hurricane Bells
Sea Wolf
OK Gow
Grizzly Bear
Editors
Eclipse:
Metric
Muse
The Bravery
Florence + the Machine
Sia
Fanfario
The Black Keys
The Dead Weather
Beck and Bat for Lashes
Vampire Weekend
Unkie
Eastern Conference Champions
Band of Horses
Cee Lo Green

desires, but, on another level, it expresses its predatory agenda, its desire to "attack" these viewers as consumers. This PG-13 cinema is also "haunted" by a repressed other, an R or NC-17 cinema that "goes too far" in its depiction of male sexual violence, threatening its target audience and failing to acknowledge its perspectives and desires. The coming-of-age narrative is uncanny, as represented in Bella's perception of herself as Other in dreams and hallucinations associated with sexual maturation, aging, and death, and in her journey through spaces that map her movement through time and the maturation process. The vampires and werewolves populating the *mise-en-scene* of Bella's reality are uncanny bodies, doubled identities existing on the border between two states—boy/monster, protective/predatory, dead/alive (vampires), human/animal (werewolves)—evoking feelings of fear and anxiety. The images and dialogue are uncanny, signifying via displacements in meaning repressed content related to sexuality and violence, which is disturbing. The music of the films highlights the sense of uncanny, oscillating between pop tunes and classical scoring at once comfortably familiar and then eerily unsettling. Everything about the *Twilight Saga* franchise is overdetermined in evoking the uncanny and the negative emotions associated with it. Why are viewers willing to subject themselves to emotions they would probably not wish to experience in reality?

Noel Carroll frames this question as the "paradox of horror." Viewers of narrative films, motivated by curiosity and the desire to know, experience "cognitive pleasures" associated with rational problem solving. More specifically, viewers of horror films, desiring to know, are conventionally led into encounters with the *unknown*, which produces feelings of fear, anxiety, and disgust. These "negative emotions" are not the goal of horror but rather the price paid for cognitive pleasures such as proving the monster exists, disclosing its properties, and so on.[21] Elsewhere, Carl Plantinga argues that viewers of mainstream Hollywood films expect "affective compensation," wherein negative emotions are ultimately transformed into a pleasurable viewing experience. The emotional valence of popular films is such that negative emotions are typically "attenuated" and "mixed" with positive emotions. In the end, viewers experience relief as negative emotions are replaced by pleasurable emotions, which, in turn, are experienced that much more profoundly due to "physiological spillover" from the negative emotions.[22]

These arguments add another dimension to an understanding of industry-audience negotiations in the *Twilight Saga*. The franchise invites young female viewers into encounters with the unknown—with vampires and werewolves figuring male sexuality as mysterious, dreams and hallucinations figuring the female self as Other, and alternative music that signifies for its consumers the possibility of adopting a new, more mature identity. These encounters generate mixed emotions—positive emotions associated with investigation, discovery, and excitement, as well as negative emotions associated with the perception of the uncanny, including fear and anxiety. Negative emotions are mixed with positive ones and thereby attenuated, prevented from "going too far" in generating an aesthetic experience inappropriate for the target audience. Ultimately, negative emotions are replaced by positive emotions—which are experienced profoundly because of a "spillover effect" from negative emotions. Music is effective in modulating viewer emotion, with composed scores providing a foundation for "attenuated" and "mixed" emotions, and pop tunes tending to nurture positive emotions while also expressing the target audience's aspirations toward musical maturity. At the end of *Breaking Dawn, Part I*, the revelation that Bella has been transformed into a vampire is juxtaposed with closing credits featuring a loud, upbeat pop tune that jars the audience from fantasy to reality, summing up the film-going experience as a pleasurable amusement park ride—perhaps in the Haunted House. Despite the realization that Bella has been bitten, the industry-audience "treaty" is upheld. Young female viewers are offered a rare experience, a blockbuster film franchise for them, mediating their erotic fantasies and forbidden desires, and the industry, in turn, rakes it in.

NOTES

1. "True—they're both pretty irresistible!—but you've gotta choose one of these *Twilight* guys!" "Are You Team Edward or Team Jacob?" *Seventeen*, http://www.seventeen.com/fun/quizzes/celebrity/team-edward-team-jacob-quiz.
2. See Edward Jay Epstein, "Hidden Persuaders: The Secretive Research Group That Helps Run the Movie Business," *Slate*, July 18, 2005, http://www.slate.com/id/2122934/.
3. Regarding "ritual" and "ideological" approaches to film genre, see representative essays such as Thomas Schatz, "The Structural Influence: New Directions in Film Genre Study," in *Film Genre Reader III*, ed. Barry Keith Grant (Austin: University of Texas Press, 2010), 92–102; Judith Hess Wright, "Genre Films and the Status Quo," in Grant, *Film Genre Reader III*, 42–50; and Rick Altman, "A Semantic/Syntactic Approach to Film Genre," in Grant, *Film Genre Reader III*, 27–41.
4. The honeymoon sex scene between Edward and Bella in *Breaking Dawn, Part I* similarly mediates audience anxieties about male sexual violence and dark female desires.
5. Sigmund Freud, "The Uncanny," in *Writings on Art and Literature* (Stanford, CA: Stanford University Press, 1997), 193–233.
6. For discussions of "negative emotions" in film viewing, see Noel Carroll, "Why Horror?" in *Horror: The Film Reader*, Ed. Mark Jancovich (London: Routledge, 2002), 33–45 and Carl Plantinga, *Moving Viewers: American Film and the Spectator's Experience* (Berkeley: University of California Press, 2009).
7. Carolyn Abbate, *Unsung Voices: Opera and Musical Narrative in the Nineteenth Century* (Princeton, NJ: Princeton University Press, 1991).
8. Nicholas Marston, "Schubert's Homecoming," *Journal of the Royal Musical Association* 125.2 (2000): 248–270 and Michael Cherlin, "Schoenberg and *Das Unheimliche*: Spectres of Tonality," *The Journal of Musicology* 11.3 (Summer 1993): 357–373.
9. Neil Lerner, "The Strange Case of Reuben Mamoulian's Sound Stew: The Uncanny Soundtrack in *Dr. Jekyll and Mr. Hyde* (1931)," *Music in the Horror Film: Listening to Fear*, Ed. Neil Lerner (New York: Routledge, 2010), 55–79.
10. Lawrence Kramer, *Music as Cultural Practice, 1800–1900* (Berkeley: University of California Press, 1990), 203–204.
11. Regarding the "masculine" guitar, see Robert Walser, *Running with the Devil: Power, Gender, and Madness in Heavy Metal Music* (Hanover, NH: University Press of New England, 1993). Regarding the "feminine" piano, see Feona Attwood, "Weird Lullaby: Jane Campion's Piano," *Feminist Review* 58 (Spring 1998): 85–101 and Richard Leppert, "Sexual Identity, Death, and the Family Piano," *19th Century Music* 16.2 (Autumn 1992): 105–128.
12. Carter Burwell, "Twilight," *The Body Inc.*, http://www.thebodyinc.net/projects/Twilight.html.
13. See Richard Cohn, "Uncanny Resemblances: Tonal Signification in the Freudian Age," *Journal of the American Musicological Society* 57.2 (Summer 2004): 285–324. The relationship of A minor and G minor is close to Cohn's hexatonic poles that he describes as

"uncanny" in late nineteenth-century music, especially that of Wagner. This relationship does not carry the neo-Riemannian relationships that Cohn describes with the third-related harmonies that form complementary hexachords, such as E major and C minor forming the hexachord E flat-E-G-G#-B-C. In Burwell's case, the g minor/e minor relationship creates a pentatonic collection of G-B flat-B-D-E (perhaps making the Bb less "uncanny"), while the G minor/a minor relationship produces a hexatonic/Dorian collection of G-A--♩-C-D-E, somewhat typical in popular music.

14. Michael Cherlin also points out the tonal allusions, especially allusions to Wagner, in the Fourth String Quartet of Schoenberg as uncanny. See Michael Cherlin, "Schoenberg and *Das Unheimliche*: Spectres of Tonality." *The Journal of Musicology* 11.3 (Summer 1993): 357–373. Further, Richard Cohn describes the presence of "hexatonic poles" in music from Gesualdo to Schoenberg as uncanny. Richard Cohn, "Uncanny Resemblances: Tonal Signification in the Freudian Age," *Journal of the American Musicological Society* 57.2 (Summer 2004): 285–324.

15. Daniel Schweiger, "CD Review: Twilight" *Film Music Magazine*, December 16, 2008. http://www.filmmusicmag.com/?p=2234. Accessed February 16, 2012.

16. Heather Phares, "Twilight [Original Score]" Review. http://www.allmusic.com/album/twilight-original-score-mw0000804943.

17. For more information on pop compilation scores, see Jonathan Romney and Adrian Wooton, eds., *Celluloid Jukebox: Popular Music and the Movies Since the 50s* (London: British Film Institute, 1995) and Phil Powrie and Robynn Stilwell, eds., *Changing Tunes: The Use of Pre-Existing Music in Film* (Aldershot, England: Ashgate, 2006).

18. Robb Wright, "Score vs. Song: Art, Commerce, and the H Factor in Film and Television Music," In *Popular Music and Film*, Ed. Ian Inglis (London: Wallflower, 2003), 8–21.

19. Futterman, Erica. "Dawn of the Undead," *Rolling Stone*, August 8, 2008. http://www.rollingstone.com/movies/news/dawn-of-the-undead-20080808.

20. Perhaps not coincidentally, the only music heard during Tod Browning's *Dracula* (1931) is also a piece by Schubert, the first movement of the Symphony No. 8 "Unfinished," which was presented diegetically as Dracula attended the London Symphony Orchestra concert in order to meet Lucy and Mina.

21. Noel Carroll, "Why Horror?" in *Horror: The Film Reader*, Ed. Mark Jancovich (London: Routledge, 2002), 35.

22. Carl Plantinga, *Moving Viewers: American Film and the Spectator's Experience* (Berkeley: University of California Press, 2009), 184.

SELECT BIBLIOGRAPHY

Driscoll, Catherine. *Teen Film: A Critical Introduction*. London: Berg Publishers, 2011.

Goldstein, Jeffrey, ed. *Why We Watch: The Attractions of Violent Entertainment*. Oxford: Oxford University Press, 1998.

Grant, Barry Keith. *The Dread of Difference: Gender and the Horror Film*. Austin: University of Texas Press, 1996.

King, Geoff. *New Hollywood Cinema: An Introduction*. New York: Columbia University Press, 2002.

Langford, Barry. *Post-Classical Hollywood: History, Film Style and Ideology Since 1945*. Edinburgh: Edinburgh University Press, 2010.

McDonald, Paul, and Janet Wasko, eds. *The Contemporary Hollywood Film Industry*. Malden, MA: Blackwell Publishing, 2008.

Neale, Steve, and Murray Smith, eds. *Contemporary Hollywood Cinema*. London: Routledge, 1998.

Neale, Steve, ed. *Genre and Contemporary Hollywood*. London: BFI Publishing, 2002.

Shary, Timothy. *Generation Multiplex: The Image of Youth in Contemporary American Cinema*. Austin: University of Texas Press, 2002.

Spadoni, Robert. *Uncanny Bodies: The Coming of Sound Film and the Origins of the Horror Genre*. Berkeley: University of California Press, 2007.

Stringer, Julian, ed. *Movie Blockbusters*. London: Routledge, 2003.

Worland, Rick. *The Horror Film: An Introduction*. London: Wiley-Blackwell, 2006.

Wyatt, Justin. *High Concept: Movies and Marketing in Hollywood*. Austin: University of Texas Press, 1994.

York, Ashley Elaine. "From Chick Flicks to Millennial Blockbusters: Spinning Female-Driven Narratives into Franchises." *The Journal of Popular Culture* 43.1 (2010): 3–25.

....

CHAPTER 25

SONIC TIMES IN *WATCHMEN* AND *INCEPTION*

....

AYLISH WOOD

IN *Watchmen* (Zack Snyder, 2009) and *Inception* (Christopher Nolan, 2010) characters navigate the unusual spatiotemporal realities of fourth dimensional time and multiple-level dreams. The sound designs of each film shift between seamless and overt organizations, inviting audiences to also experience unstable spatiotemporalities. As the sound and image relations mediate between both coherent action and also potentially destabilized spatiotemporal realities, they work to hold contradictory tendencies in balance. This balancing act is especially evident in many of the sound bridges that connect together scenes occurring in distinct times and spaces.[1]

Writing about sound design practices, David Lewis Yewdall argues that: "mixing is where you bring carefully prepared tracks from sound editorial and music and weave them together into a lush, seamless soundtrack."[2] By contrast, William Whittington suggests that the era of multichannel sound design has led to the soundtracks of science fiction films becoming: "a far more aggressive, overt, and active participant in the production of meaning and transmission of knowledge from core elements of music, effects, and dialogue."[3] It is more usual to think of sound bridges in terms of whether they ensure the seamless continuity of a film as Yewdall outlines. The argument made in this essay is that sound bridges contribute to the transmission of knowledge about the unusual spatiotemporal realities of *Inception* and *Watchmen*. Even as the soundtrack is seamless in the sense that its transitions are smoothly achieved, bridging more than one location, the balance of the mix among music, sound effects and dialogue sits unusually with the images. Consequently, the sound-image relations coordinate and generate a perspective on time and space.

The idea that an audiovisual perspective connects to subject positions, points of view or points of audition is familiar.[4] Writing in 1980, Mary Anne Doane argued that Hollywood cinema positioned its spectator as unified and nonfragmented through an illusion created by seamless audio and visual editing. Through image and sound editing, as well as the soundtrack mix, the audiovisual imagery created a parallel between the spectator and the unified figure frequently, although not always, found driving the actions at the heart of a drama.⁵ Where *Watchmen* and *Inception* differ from films that fit Doane's account is in creating story-worlds based on nonunified configurations of time and space. These two films are the focus of the following discussion because they illuminate how sound and image relations mediate an audiences' experience of the strangeness of nonunified spatiotemporalities. The coherency and instability of the dream levels of *Inception*'s story-world are mediated through the unusual sound-image configurations of sound bridges, whereas those of *Watchmen* offer imagined experiences of fourth dimensional time. Although distinct in many ways, their sound design shares the approach of using sound bridges to mediate an audiences' experience of these imagined spatiotemporalities.

Such nonunified configurations are interesting beyond *Inception* and *Watchmen*. Technologies intercede in how we see and hear in ways that can be seamless and overt, locating us in spatiotemporal organizations that are both transparent and challenging. This duality carries with it the potential for an unstable slippage in the position of a spectator. The sound-image relations of *Inception* and *Watchmen* negotiate such a duality. They allow a glimpse at incipient destabilization, but always in conjunction with spaces that seem solid, even if the status of their reality is actually uncertain. A question we might ask is whether the sound-image relations of films such as *Inception* and *Watchmen* acknowledge that unified positions have given way to configurations that reveal the precarious balance of experiences that involve technological mediations.

HOLDING THE DREAM TOGETHER

A constant question running through *Inception* is whether or not characters are still inside a dream, whether they ever find their way back to reality. Cobb (the team leader), in particular, seems to be constantly unsure about whether he remains trapped within a dream. The film ends when the sound and image of a spinning top ceases before we know if it will topple, denying viewers a clear signal as to whether Cobb has returned to reality. Ruth Tallman comments: "It seems that the movie doesn't give us enough information to settle these questions, so how will we find answers? Where do we look?"⁶ If there are any answers to be found in *Inception*, where the world of the dream is a space that seems to be unified but is in fact highly unstable, listening is as revealing as looking. By focusing on the sound-image relations of sound bridges, it becomes evident that these depict both the connections between and also the instabilities in the dream levels. Looking at the balance between these two tendencies gives insight into how *Inception* offers a perspective on negotiating a way through mediated reality. The timings of the individual scenes discussed are listed in Table 25.1.

In the story-world of *Inception*, shared dreams are possible through the mediating interventions of teams of people whose purpose is to extract information. Induced into

Table 25.1 Timings

	Chapter	Time
Inception (Blue-ray)		
Paris café: Ariadne remodels the sky	4	00.29.45
Train on street: dream level 2	7	01.05.25
Japanese castle: Cobb and Arthur pitch to Saito	1	00.03.20
Robert Fisher in hotel bar: dream level 2	9	01.28.00
Yusaf plays *Non, Je Ne Regrette Rien*: dreams levels 1,2, and 3	11	01.42.53
Cobb's return to USA	14	02.17.17
Watchmen (Blu-ray director's cut)		
"As I lie …" Dr. Manhattan tells Janey he loves her	21	01.19.35
The Comedian dies: *Unforgettable* on soundtrack	1	00.02.30
Opening credits	2	00.05.42
Hollis Mason's death	32	02.14.00
Jon Osterman's transformation	19	01.13.14
Rorschach's introduction	3	00.12.30
Watchmen (original release version)		
"As I lie …" Dr. Manhattan tells Janey he loves her	20	01.11.25
The Comedian dies: *Unforgettable* on soundtrack	1	00.02.25
Opening credits	2	00.05.37
Hollis Mason's death	not included	—
Jon Osterman's transformation	19	01.06.00
Rorschach's introduction	3	00.12.25

a dream state by the infusion of a serum, the dream of a mark (victim of the extraction) is controlled by the heist team, causing them to reveal their secrets. One of the central narrative arcs of *Inception* is that Cobb's team (Ariadne the architect; Arthur the fixer; Yusaf the chemist; Eames the thief) will plant an idea in the mind of the mark, Robert Fischer, rather than steal it. This involves the team in constructing dream environments, but across several levels, dreams within dreams within dreams. Dream levels are hybrid constructions drawn from multiple sources that include both the subconscious of individual characters and the designed and frequently technologically mediated constructions of the architect. As such, they are mediated realities to be negotiated by the characters within the story-world of *Inception* and also by the viewing the audience.

Sound-image relations conjure the story-world of *Inception* in several ways. Sound at times supports the strange imagery of the dreams, grounding any inconsistencies in credible sonic environments. At other moments, it more overtly mediates both the threat of instability and also the continuity of the dream. Although the dream levels are shown as distinct spaces, an urban streetscape in the pouring rain, a plush hotel, a snow-covered mountainside, they are linked through the experience of the dreamer. Tethered to a time point in reality, within each dream world time expands, and the dreamer lives out the reality of the dream level in which he or she is aware. Although temporally connected, the dissimilarities between dream levels creates a potential for a disruptive discontinuity in the audiovisual experience. The work of the sound-image relations is to depict these fragmentary spaces as ones that have the capacity to be seamlessly articulated together, whether as connections or incursions and disruptions.

Although *Inception* won Academy Awards in the categories of both sound mixing and sound editing, discussions about sound tend to begin with Hans Zimmer's score. The latter is often described as bombastic, and the sound is at times overwhelming. In the final minutes of the heist, the three dream levels collapse and limbo crumbles. The brass section of the orchestration blasts out a two-note refrain with the string section in support as buildings crash to their destruction, explosions reverberate, water cascades through the windows of a van, and a lift plummets downward.[7] In an auditorium with surround sound speakers, the sound is felt as much as it is heard. Such a physical engagement fits with ideas about immersion cinema.[8] But to only describe the sound of *Inception* in terms of its music's capacity to overwhelm and immerse misses the sound design's more subtle occupation of generating textures in the sound-image relations of the film.

Throughout *Inception*, the roles of the music and sound shift in relation to each other, as well as to the images, producing the distinct sonic profiles and textures of specific moments. As Ariadne remodels the streets of Paris or when a runaway train careers along a street, the sound design blends the unreal with reality. The sound-image relations work together to make these strange moments credible and establish the images as part of a stable dream world. Running alongside music, mechanistic sounds, based on the idea of a massive watch mechanism, are aligned with images of Parisian streets "being peeled off the earth's surface."[9] The sound, composed of metal groans and heavy moving parts juddering into action, have a reverb to fit such a large space, an echo that seemingly emerges from the end of the boulevards and runs up between the buildings. When watching and listening to the Paris sequence, the flow and shape of the sound seeks to embed these extraordinary images in a feasible sound environment, a huge machine that might possibly move the earth. A similar tactic occurs with the runaway train. The visual image of a train engine careening along an American street in Downtown Somewhere is given the sonic environment of recorded train sounds slowed down and layered with the further sounds of car collisions (Figure 25.1). The absence of music enhances the impact of the sound effects in fully embedding the images.

The sound-image relations not only ground strange moments but also work to ensure the stability of a world constructed around multiple realities. Throughout *Inception*, the textures of sound created using multichannel techniques and multidimensional sound projection are complex. They provide audio cues to anchor visible actions and add emotional overtones and undertones. In addition to providing all the kinds of sounds that might be expected from an action-based film (gunshots, vehicles of all shapes and

FIGURE 25.1 The runaway train careens down a street. The sound design combines train sounds with those of cars colliding.

FIGURE 25.2 Arthur finally draws attention to the rattling array of lamps by looking upward.

sizes, explosions, fights), sound-images negotiate a way through the various tensions of *Inception*. Early in the film, when at the Japanese castle, potential backer Saito seems unconvinced by Cobb and Arthur's presentation of their extraction skills. As Cobb lays out his wares, a deep rumble is heard but is not cued as significant by signs of reaction from Cobb, Arthur, or Saito. As Saito leaves the room, the rumble becomes more insistent as it is joined by the rattle of glass, a sound visibly echoed in the shaking array of lantern lights illuminating the room. The sound might be interpreted as conveying the dismay of Cobb and Arthur at Saito's dismissive response, but this is altered by Arthur's reaction: "what's going on up there?" (Figure 25.2) Reiterating the strangeness of this comment, when Cobb looks at his watch, the image cuts to an upside-down view of a watch face. As the second hand ticks over, stepping up from a slow to faster movement, an accelerating tick-tock is audible and the image cuts to a riot.

The cuts between dream levels, as well as across the scenes of the riot, occur rapidly and conform with the fast editing practices described by David Bordwell as an aspect of intensified continuity.[10] Each time there is a cut back and to between dream levels, the rapid visual editing occurs in conjunction with a sound bridge. The sonic impression of quickening provides an example of the kind of sound bridge used throughout *Inception*. In the transition from one dream state to another, or to reality, a sound is carried over from one level to the other. As it does so, it takes on a different set of associations. From being associated with a ticking watch, the accelerating tick moves from the foreground to the background, becoming incorporated into the riot scene, perhaps the sound of an impact and precursor to the noise of shattering glass. The intensified continuity of the visual editing and the sound bridges bind the dream levels together, patching their disparate elements into the illusion of a coherent spatiotemporality.

The events in the Japanese castle also introduce the second narrative arc in *Inception*: the story of a lost love. The lost love and heist stories are both narrative motors within *Inception*. The heist motivates the scenario of actions taking place across multiple spaces. The story of Cobb's lost love provides the backstory for his motivations and also generates obstacles within the plot. The intersecting arcs of these two stories heighten the tension generated within the heist and create points of instability in the dream levels. These points of instability, too, are mediated through the sound-image relations. The scene following Robert Fischer's insertion into a new dream level opens with a strong visual matching that establishes continuity between the disparate spaces of two dream levels. Yusaf drives the van through the streets of dream level 1 trying to escape the gunfire of Fischer's defensive projections. The figures within the van, although remaining strapped in their seats are thrown around, arms and legs moving through the air in slow motion. Shots of the van capture it cornering on two wheels, and the canted angles are extended to the dream level below. Fischer sits at a bar in the hotel, where the level of water in his glass takes an angle that matches the canted angle of the van. The visual matching of these angles build continuities across the dream levels, enhancing the stability of the illusion. This stability is sonically disturbed in the sequence that follows, when the two narrative arcs almost collide.

Cobb, in his persona of Mr. Charles (a device used by Cobb when the integrity of a dream level is endangered), tries to win Fischer's confidence, with the slowly tightening framing of the two men signalling the increasing intensity of their conversation. Just as Cobb says: "I'm here to protect you," the intensity is suddenly broken both sonically and visually. First, a glass is heard breaking, and a sound continues as though a finger is being rubbed on the rim of a glass. This counterintuitive position of sound and image, the glass somehow still vibrating at high pitch even though it is broken, suggests something is not right. When the camera pulls back, it reveals the bar, the broken glass, and Cobb's face as he looks off-screen as though registering something. The continuing high-pitched tone heightens the tension further, with other elements of the sound design signaling an uncomfortable pause in the venture. Not only do we cut to Cobb's point of view of his children crouching and playing in the hotel lobby, an indication that the stability of the dream is threatened, but the sound could be described as "holding."

Michel Chion draws attention to the punctuating use of silence in the era of surround sound speakers.[11] Although this is a far from silent moment, the held synthesizer
notes and ringing tone punctuate, refocusing attention on events. Paul Théberge uses
the phrase "relational silences" to describe a system of balancing sounds that: "pitted
the various sound components against each other, not for functional reasons but for
specific dramatic purposes."[12] Through the rebalancing of sound elements, Cobb suddenly goes from giving the appearance of having control to being on the edge of losing control. With the notes continuing to hold, Fischer stares at him, as do the room
full of his potentially aggressive projections. The sound of the background chatter drops
away, with the ringing sound and musical notes of the synthesizer seeming to continue
to add pressure that is finally broken when Cobb restarts his dialogue. As he speaks, the
ringing note drops out, the background chatter picks up, and the musical progression is
again more audible. When the layers of sound drop out and the background chatter is
silenced, two things are cued at once: the potential breakthrough of Cobb's disturbances
into Arthur's dream and the possibility that Cobb is rumbled. In the incipient imbalance
of possibilities, Cobb experiences a collision of his conscious and subconscious. This
collision threatens the integrity of the dream world, a tension mediated by sound.

In contrast, once Cobb reasserts control with his statement: "Mr. Fischer, I'm here to
protect you," the subsequent sound distortions create connective bridges between the
two visually distinct dream levels, patching them back together again. When Yusaf's
skid in the rain is shown in slow motion, the gunning engine and road contact noises
slow too. The torsion of the sound slowing as the van begins to topple changes from the
foreground to the background, stretched out to mingle with the sound of bad weather
in the hotel dream level. In another layer of sound, as an arc of rain crosses the screen
in slow motion, an associated sound suggests slowly running rivulets of water. With the
cut back to Fischer at the bar, the same associated sound becomes the tinkle of moving glassware in the background. This device, a kind of sonic rescaling across layers of
sound, is used throughout the transitions between the dream levels. The extent of the
rescaling extends to match the number of dream levels and becomes more extended
as the third dream level is introduced. This is especially evident in relation to the Edith
Piaf version of *Non, Je Ne Regrette Rien*, which is used to signal a kick, and which can be
heard across each of the dream levels.[13] When rescaled and stretched out on dream level
3, the song is hardly recognizable as it is closer to a rumble.

The integration of *Non, Je Ne Regrette Rien* into the soundscape of *Inception* is
unusual. Apparently, Nolan had thought of using the song long before *Inception* went
into production, making it a formative element in the film's development. Hans Zimmer
is given the credit for the way in which the song was manipulated to mesh with the overall sound design.[14] Not only is it a sound bridge connecting across the different dream
levels, it acts as a trigger to provoke action within the story-world and reveals the temporal expansion of the dream levels. Michel Chion has described ways in which sound
can animate a scene, introducing a temporal pacing that is not given in the actions of
characters or editing patterns.[15] He uses the term "vectorization" to describe how sound
marks off phenomena oriented in time. This is also true of *Non, Je Ne Regrette Rien*,

although in ways that specifically relate to the unusual spatiotemporalities of *Inception*.

although in ways that specifically relate to the unusual spatiotemporalities of *Inception*. As a sound bridge, the song is rescaled at several speeds: normal speed and stretched out as it percolates through the dream levels. For instance, at the end of the car chase on dream level 1, Yusaf starts the playback of *Non, Je Ne Regrette Rien* on an iPod just as he is about to drive the van off the road bridge to create gravity for the kick. In this scene, the sound of the song has a slightly tinny quality, which matches with the image of Arthur asleep, the headphones placed on his head by Yusaf to relay the playback of the song. The image cuts to Arthur, this time running down the hotel stairwell in dream level 2, and the sound shifts from normal speed to a slower one. The first heavy beat matches Arthur's jump onto the landing, the second pushes into the foreground, like a miscued echo of someone running downstairs in a tight concrete space. Just as the listening audience might be unsure that this first beat is anything other than Arthur landing on the concrete, he too notices nothing until the second beat, when the sound has come into the foreground. The image then cuts to the snowy mountainside of dream level 3, with a view of two figures slowly descending a sheer rock face. In this sound bridge, the heavy beat is retained in the foreground of the mix, but reverberating more slowly. The just recognizable lyrics are rescaled and stretched to the point where they could be the sound of wind in such a landscape. In this segment, the song *Non, Je Ne Regrette Rien* is put to multiple uses. Within the story-world, it triggers action on dream levels 2 and 3, where the team realizes they must act more quickly. The sound-image relations patch together the actions across three different visual environments. But the bridge not only connects: the manipulations of the song also evoke the strange temporalities that coexist across the nested levels of the dreams.

The sonic environment introduced in the final stages of *Inception* offers a counterpoint to the sound-image relations that have run throughout the film. Whether depicting the instabilities introduced through Cobb's subconscious or the continuities between dream levels, clarity has remained paramount in the sound-image patchwork. This clarity binds together the dream realities constructed from multiple sources and spanning several distinct worlds. The ending seems to similarly offer the coherent space of Cobb returning to the US. Overall, the music carries the scene, different instruments foregrounded as the action progresses, but nevertheless present throughout. For instance, as Cobb wakens on the aircraft, the string section predominates; following Cobb's admittance through border control, the guitar picks up the melody before the string and brass sections again take over. The dialogue in the sequence is sparse, most significant are the words of the border guard as befits Cobb's desire to return home without arrest. As though to heighten this moment of success, the music drops off in volume, allowing the ambient sounds of the airport, the words of the border guard, and the thuck of his stamp on Cobb's passport to dominate. There is, however, something off kilter in these textures. The apparently unified configuration may turn out to be anything but, paradoxically because the binding audiovisual work is no longer anchoring dream levels to each other or reality. This absence gives the sequence an untethered, almost free-floating quality. A visual clue is found in the introduction of a shallow focal field. Most noticeable in the airport, Cobb is placed in focus, with other members of the team out of focus, unless they are active in catching Cobb's eye. This pulls the scene inside itself as though to detach the actions from its connections to other places. The visual echoes from other scenes in the film accentuate a sense of detached space. Despite the passage of time, the children look almost the same as they appeared in Cobb's dreams. The image of the spinning top introduced in the opening of *Inception* returns just before Cobb apparently reawakens in the aircraft. These echoes compact time and space together and, without the clarity given in the earlier sound-image relations, the question of whether Cobb's mind has floated free is already posed before the screen cuts to black and the sound of the spinning top and music abruptly cease.

Inception features dreams that are hybrid constructions drawn from multiple sources. These sources include both the subconscious of individual characters and the designed constructions of an architect. Several levels of textual work connect the spaces of these dreams. Through the two narrative arcs that drive the momentum of the action, the heist team works to ensure that their mark remains convinced of the dream. At the level of the sound design, many sounds were recorded and manipulated, or created and then layered along with the score, to generate the sonic environments of that same reality. The balance between overt and seamless sound design offers a spectrum of perspectives for an audience. During Cobb and Fischer's intense conversation, the prospect of a collapsing reality is suggested even as it is deferred. Although this potential fragility is displaced for much of the remainder of *Inception*, in the closing section, another possibility is introduced: the danger of becoming untethered in the mediated reality of a dream. As an exploration of spatiotemporal organizations that are transparent and challenging, *Inception* provides a continuum on which to negotiate a tentative location, somewhere between incipient collapse or a state of delusion.

A SIMULTANEOUS NOW: *WATCHMEN* AND THE FOURTH DIMENSION

Watchmen offers an equally paradoxical spatiotemporal configuration through the idea of time as the fourth dimension. And, like those of *Inception*, the sound-image relations propose a series of perspectives on spatiotemporal experience for its audience. Whereas the nonunified configurations of *Inception*'s spatiotemporal organization relied on nested levels of time, those of *Watchmen* disperse conventional temporal linearity into the coordinates of four dimensions. In so doing, the sound-image relations mediate the temporal experiences of the character Dr. Manhattan for viewers.[16] This involves a complex interplay of voice-over, dialogue, sound effects, music, and the visual details of scenes, many of which rely on visual effects. In keeping with Rick Altman et al.'s point that sound is multiplanar, the mediations of the sound-image relations occur through a shifting balance within the sound mix, as well as between the sound and image.[17]

Watchmen, like the comic book on which it is based, puts forward a story-world with many routes for engagement. These include a critique of superheroes, a political commentary on the mid-1980s reworked in the late 2000s, and the adaptation of a work lauded as excellent writing (the comic book featured in *Time*'s list of top 100 novels since 1923), as well as a work celebrated among comic book aficionados.[18] Alongside all of these runs a perspective on how space-time exists in a block universe. The concept of a "block universe" is based on Albert Einstein's conceptualization of time existing in the fourth dimension. By this, Einstein meant that all events can be defined by a set of coordinates. These include the three spatial coordinates with which everyone is familiar, in practice if not theoretically, plus a temporal coordinate. In a block universe, all possible events—past, present, and future—already exist. This counterintuitive description of time is hard to grasp when one is used to thinking about tensed or linear time, in which the past has happened, the present is now, and the future has yet to happen. Whereas the block universe is primarily associated with a view of time deployed by physicists and philosophers, a context in which it remains open to debate, in *Watchmen*, Alan Moore explores how such a time could be experienced. This experience is developed in the comic book through the "what-if" idea of the multidimensional character Dr. Manhattan and is also depicted in the comic book panels. The facility for comic books to create complex narrative organizations of space and time has been written about. In their influential works on comics, both Will Eisner and Scott McCloud discuss the ways in which comic book artists have widely drawn on various art movements, including Cubism and Futurism.[19] Mark Bernard and James Bucky Carter explicitly link the sequential art of the *Watchmen* comic to Futurism and Cubism, both of which sought to challenge one-point perspectives on time and space.[20] The multiple spatial and temporal perspectives of a Cubist or Futurist work refuse a privileged position, offering a viewer many simultaneous perspectives. In a comic book, any sequence of panels can be arranged in ways that both establish or disrupt linear organizations of time and space. According to McCloud, comics offers an opportunity that: "allows us to connect these moments and mentally construct a continuous, unified reality."[21] The distinctiveness of the *Watchmen* comic book is that the continuous reality is infused with the simultaneous appearance of multiple space-times.

In addition to facing the difficult task of compressing a multithemed comic book series into a narrative suited to a feature length film, the challenge in making a cinematic version of *Watchmen* was to visually and aurally capture its explorations of time as a fourth dimension. One of the key devices used within *Watchmen* is to create a spatiotemporal organization in which more than one temporality is present and active in a sequence of images. One example of this is seen and heard when Dr. Manhattan recounts his telling Janey that he loves her. The visual imagery locates viewers by a Christmas tree in the sitting room of their home, and Dr. Manhattan (in voice over) states: "It is Christmas 1963 . . . I tell her I still want her and that I always will. As I lie to her it is September 4th 1970. I am in a room full of people wearing disguises." The unexpected spatiotemporal moment occurs with the sentence: "As I lie to her it is September 4th . . ." a statement that remains accompanied by the imagery already associated with Christmas 1963. In the moment of confusion caused by the sudden mismatch of sound and image, space-time becomes active. This is to say, more than one spatiotemporal organization competes for a viewer's attention, placing them not in time but somewhere between times.

Filmmakers have a diverse range of possibilities for constructing time in the cinema, but it is rare to find more than one spatiotemporal organization coexisting within a single series of images. For instance, parallel editing is a staple method of storytelling.[22] Filmmakers often tell stories by cutting between two parallel sets of actions, one time frame giving away to another. It is unusual in films, including those in which the status of events is uncertain, to see and/or hear events presented as an ambiguous space-time. *Eternal Sunshine of the Spotless Mind* (Michel Gondry, 2004) is an exception.[23] Split-screen constructions in which different elements of the narrative compete for our attention, such as those found briefly in *Andromeda Strain* or more extensively in *Timecode*, might seem to offer multiple time-spaces. Even here, however, the individual elements have their own temporal stability. The strategy of *Watchmen* is distinctive. It does use familiar methods of changing space-time, adopting parallel editing and frequently deploying flashback to tell the histories of several characters. But these are combined with unusual configurations in which more than one space-time coexists. In these configurations, the simultaneous spatiotemporal realities are integrated through the sound-image relations. Rick Altman suggests that: "Every sound initiates an event. Every hearing concretizes the story of that event. Or rather it concretizes a particular story among the many that can be told about that event."[24] What is interesting about *Watchmen* is that the event initiated by the sound does not always straightforwardly find its match in the accompanying visual images.

The interplay of mismatched relations between sound and image offers an additional expressive dimension through which viewers can encounter the spatiotemporal complexities of *Watchmen*. By expressive dimension, I mean that organizations of the imagery mediate an experience for a viewer. Imagery always mediates for a viewer, of course, but, in *Watchmen,* the unusual sound-image relations specifically mediate the unusual spatiotemporal organizations of fourth dimensional time. Writing about film music, Anahid Kassabian discusses how an audience gives attention to different elements of the audiovisual world of the film and that these elements compete for a viewer's attention: "Attention to music depends on many factors, including the volume of the music, its style, and its 'appropriateness' in the scene."[25] Extending this observation from music to sound more widely, the ways in which a balance is achieved between multiplanar sound (music, sound effects, dialogue and voice-over) and the visual imagery lies at the heart of the expressive work of a film. *Watchmen* uses a range of expressive strategies to engage its audience with complex spatiotemporalities. These are evident in the fight sequence opening the film depicting the death of the Comedian, the alternative timeline of American history in the credit sequence, and the simultaneous space-times that are a part of a spectacular sequence depicting Dr. Manhattan's transformation. These transformation scenes integrate the temporal events, as though to demonstrate Dr. Manhattan's experience of a block universe. This contrasts with the sequence introducing Rorschach, which offers a different kind of hook by exploring the uncertainty of simultaneous time for those of us more familiar with the world of tensed time.

The opening of *Watchmen* features the Nat King Cole song *Unforgettable* (1951) to accompany the brutal beating of the Comedian. The romantic string and piano movements of the orchestration, lyrics about love, and Cole's rich voice establish an easy and even pacing that sits in juxtaposition with the violent actions. Speed ramps, both slowing into and also speeding out from slow motion, accompanied by sound effects act as sound bridges that also signal changes in tempo. The use of Cole's classic track in its orchestral version can be described as an ironic use of music, the unforgettable of the love song transformed into a bitter epitaph for a violent man. This, however, is only one dissonant element among several in the opening sequence. The others lie in the layering of sound effects to pick out physical contact sounds between flesh and flesh, and flesh and objects. Included in this mix are unexpected aural cues to minutiae (such as the sound of coffee spilling from the Comedian's mug or the ping of the Comedian's badge) and also the shifts to and from slow motion. The balance achieved by interweaving sound and music acts both as a cohesive linking of the action, even as it also dissembles the integrity of the scene. The dissembling is particularly evident in the mismatched pacing conjured in the sound mix, a device that initiates two different events: the nostalgic evocation of the love song *and* the pacing of a brutal beating.

The opening credits also have a number of complex temporal organizations. Accompanied by an extended version of Bob Dylan's "The Times They Are a-Changin," the credits show the history of superheroes, a montage of iconic images drawn from American history, into which are inserted fictional characters (just as extra sections are introduced into Dylan's song). *Watchmen* is not the first film to do such a thing, as both *Forrest Gump* (Robert Zemeckis, 1994) and *Zelig* (Woody Allen, 1983) have famously demonstrated. Unlike these two films, in which the historical timeline remains intact as Gump and Zelig are participants in events that are a part of historical reality, *Watchmen* creates an alternative history. This alternative timeline presents a series of "what-if" scenarios. What if the famous VJ photo that featured in *Life* magazine was of a lesbian kiss, Silhouette rather than a sailor kissing the nurse, or the Comedian was the sniper on the grassy knoll, or Dr. Manhattan was already on the moon when the first American astronaut got there (Figures 25.3a,b)? The temporal flow through the montage is interrupted by the use of slow motion. Throughout the credit sequence, images are seen in the moment of their capture as photographs. The slow-motion images become poses for a camera, punctuated by the sound of a flash bulb blowing. Writing about the sounds of punches being thrown in *Raging Bull*, Michel Chion remarks:

> In short, the punch with sound effects is to audiovisual language as the chord is to music, mobilizing the vertical dimension. In the brutal and exhausting boxing scenes in *Raging Bull* Scorsese used punches to bestow a maximum degree of temporal elasticity on the fighting scenes; thus he could use slow motion, repeated images and so forth.[26]

A similar temporal elasticity is conferred by the punctuating sound of the flash bulb in *Watchmen*. For each event, the action is slowed down and the pose extended. The temporal elasticity of the flash bulb sound-image is again evident in the doubled temporal organization of the sequence featuring Hollis Mason's death. The echo with

FIGURE 25.3 The iconic images of VJ day and the moon landing altered in the alternative timeline of *Watchmen*. (a) Silhouette gets the girl. (b) Dr Manhattan on the moon.

Raging Bull is underlined as the fight leading to Hollis's death is scored with *Cavalleria Rusticana: Intermezzo*. Used in *Raging Bull* to evoke a dreamlike nostalgic quality to the opening images of Jake la Motta training alone in the ring, in *Watchmen*, the nostalgia is only given in the perspective of Hollis's memories. Included in the director's cut version but not the original release, the sequence cuts between Hollis's first-person view of the person he imagines he is punching, figures recognizable as the crooks and villains from his past, and the present, in which Hollis is beaten to death by a gang of younger men.

The "what-if" posed in the opening credits includes not only the alternative time-line of the Minutemen that culminates with Richard Nixon elected to a third term, but also asks its audience to imagine the existence of a figure such as Dr. Manhattan. Through Dr. Manhattan, the "what-if" extends beyond the reimagined domestic poli-tics of America and the international arena of the Cold War, toward fourth dimensional temporality and the nature of being. The sequence in which Dr. Manhattan narrates his transformation is organized around simultaneous space-times and shows him as some-one able move in the fourth dimension. In this counterintuitive conceptualization of time, the shared now of two temporal moments is mediated through the sound-image relations. When Dr. Manhattan retreats to Mars after discovering that his former lover Janey is dying, he reflects on their meeting and his transformation from Jon Osterman to Dr. Manhattan. Even though he narrates his past, Dr. Manhattan's notion of time is untethered from tensed time. In tensed or subjective time, the privileged now is located in what is conventionally understood as the present, the time in which we currently live, which would be 1985 in *Watchmen*. Since Dr. Manhattan operates through a multiple now, the audiovisual imagery works to invest each of the temporal events with nowness.

One marker of nowness is Dr. Manhattan's voice-over. John Belton comments that: "The authority of a voice-over track is partly the result of its spatial qualities. It occupies a space that is beyond or outside of the film."[27] Dr. Manhattan's voice-over has qualities that make it stand apart from the dialogue, signaling its status as an acousmatic voice, although one with an evident relation to a character. The distinctness between the visible character dialogue and that of the acousmatic voice-over are established by their sound qualities, which imply different spatial origins. Dialogue seems to emerge from the character's space on the screen partly due to the placement of the sound's projection from the front of house speakers and also partly due to its spatial reality. By contrast, the rich bass voice-over of Dr. Manhattan's narration gives the impression of arising from a more expansive space, running through surround sound speakers. It is clear which voice is voice-over and which is dialogue. The aural distinctiveness between the two is exploited within the sound design to create a soundspace in which time is untensed. This occurs through two strategies. The voice-over always refers to an event as now, rather than in the past or even the future. In addition, as described more fully later, the voice-over is woven together with the character dialogue within a sequence. When Dr. Manhattan speaks about "now," he is placing himself in the moment of action, even though he is apparently speaking off-screen from a different location and time. This double position draws attention to Dr. Manhattan's ability to be in every now, to be in the fourth the dimension.[28]

As the following detailed analysis shows, establishing the nowness of each moment occurs through both simple and more complex relations among voice-over, dialogue, music, and sound effects. Simple examples include Dr. Manhattan's voice-over signaling the present of every statement, including: "I'm in love...," "It is February 12th, 1981, Wally dies of cancer, of which, they now say, I am the cause," and "I cross the room." The presence of the voice-over acts as a sound bridge to ensure continuity across the visual montage of each event, but the presentness of every statement disturbs the stable temporality of the chronology of the narration. The coincidence of Dr. Manhattan's now with a past event is strongest in the depiction of Jon Osterman's transformation into Dr. Manhattan. William Whittington argues that:

> The recording and placement of the voice-over removes it from the visual and spatial anchors of synchronization and background noise, only to anchor it in the consciousness of the character. In this instance, the voice dominates the sound design, competing against all of the other elements (music, ambiance, and effects).[29]

In the transformation sequence, however, Dr. Manhattan's voice-over is not removed from visual and spatial anchors but is instead integrated with them. In this way, the now of Dr. Manhattan's consciousness, which is given through his narration, coexists with the now of the events depicted. The sequence begins in dialogue, with the voices of Wally, Jon, and Janey audible on the soundtrack. Also heard is a choral section of *Prophecies*, originally written for *Koyaanisqatsi* by the Phillip Glass Ensemble. *Prophecies* is used in *Watchmen* for much of Dr. Manhattan's narration of his relationship with Janey and the aftermath of his transformation. The music, played on an organ, features clusters of repetitive note patterns (arpeggios) that include alterations in rhythm that run throughout and provide the continuity of a rather somber mood.

The unusual balance between voice-over and dialogue is evident as the narrative of the event of Jon Osterman's accident begins with a shot of Wally, Janey, and Jon emerging from the Intrinsic Field Laboratory. They are talking (inaudible mumbles), and Jon turns back saying: "Oh, I'll catch up with you guys, I think I left my watch inside." Following a cut into the space of the lab, the camera follows Jon as he walks toward the chamber. When Jon turns and enters the chamber, the camera continues forward, showing the heavy door beginning to close and stops to register a counter running down. The next shot is from inside the chamber, a close up of a watch lying on a surface, with Jon's midriff visible against the background of the door closing and shutting. Across these two shots, Dr. Manhattan's integrated voice-over begins: "I cross the room to the Intrinsic Field Centre. I find my watch." As the organ and choral voices continue, other sounds register, the light metallic click of the watch strap fittings on the surface as Jon picks it up and the thunderous thud of the door closing, followed by an alarm going off. We see Jon moving quickly to the door and cut to a shot of him looking outward, only his face visible behind the narrow window of the door as Wally enters the frame. There then begins a sequence of intersecting dialogue and voice-over, each interwoven with sound effects, the clarity of the dialogue consistent with whether or not it is heard through the door:

MANHATTAN: When I get to the door Wally is turning white. (Voice-over).

WALLY: The program's locked in. We can't override the time lock. (Dialogue becomes muffled with a cut to Jon's perspective within the chamber. The sound includes the whoomph and hum of machinery coming on line).

MANHATTAN: I am terrified. (Voice-over. Shot cuts from Jon looking out to the inside of the chamber, and the sounds of the machinery and crackles of the energy beginning to accumulate around Jon increases to mid-level).

JANEY: Jon (Dialogue muffled)

JON: Janey (Dialogue muffled as heard from Janey's and Wally's perspective in the outer lab. The machinery is audible in the background).

JANEY: I'm sorry Jon, but I can't…

JON: Janey don't leave me. {Shouts} Don't leave me. (Dialogue muffled with cut to inside the chamber, crackling sound of energy increases).

As the transformation begins, the intensity of the music and sound effects increase (Figure 25.4). The narration shifts away from the voice-over and gives way to the

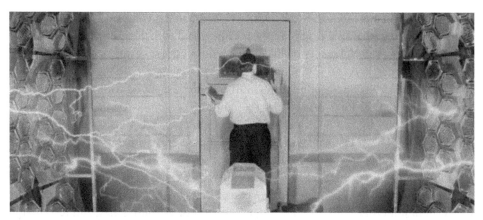

FIGURE 25.4 Jon Osterman stands locked into the laboratory as the machines fire up around him.

music, *Pruit Igoe*, which was also originally written by the Phillip Glass Ensemble for *Koyaanisqatsi*. Unlike the more somber organ motif from *Prophecies*, the orchestration of *Pruit Igoe* features strings and horns, the staccato pacing accompanying the choral voices complement and enhance the dramatic visual effects of the accident.[30] In a flash of white energy, the body of Jon Osterman can be seen disassembling and scattering in all directions. The intense music continues in conjunction with Dr. Manhattan's voice-over, until the quasi-messianic moment when Jon appears in a "resurrection" pose as Dr. Manhattan in the refectory. Both the music and the imagery heighten this sense of religiosity. The integration of the voice-over with the dialogue, sound effects, and music creates a spatiotemporal event in which the now of the narration and the now of the accident coexist; they are both equally present. It is not that one is now and the other then, but they are both now. Even though it is clear from the plotting that Dr. Manhattan is reminiscing in 1985, the now of that present (Dr. Manhattan on Mars) is not privileged. Instead, the now of the reflection becomes coincident with the now of the accident. The spatiotemporal composition of the sequence seeks to depict the block universe from the perspective of Dr. Manhattan, for whom all events have the possibility of being now.

As a being who seemingly inhabits the block universe, this unusual integration of Dr. Manhattan's voice-over makes sense and can be understood as an audiovisual organization that seeks to place an audience within an experience that loosely approximates with such a perspective. At other points within the film, the organization of the sound-image relations set up competing spatiotemporalities that leave a viewer in a more uncertain position. The provocation is to understand that there are competing space-times and that making sense of them involves a struggle. When Rorschach is first encountered in *Watchmen*, he is presented in two space-times. There is the space-time of his actions, which follow on from the death of the Comedian and the police's visit to the latter's apartment. The voice-over, which opens the sequence, introduces a second space-time. Michel Chion comments that "textual speech" has the "power to make visible the image that it evokes through sound—that is, to change the setting, to call up a thing, moment, place or characters at will."[31] Rorschach's voice-over unusually calls up an image whose compositional framing rather than content is reiterated in the accompanying visuals. After he has bent over to pick up the Comedian's smiley badge, the voice-over narrates "I've seen the face of the city." There is both a match and mismatch in the relations between sound and image. In the shot, Rorschach is seen looking at a face, but the face of a smiley badge (Figure 25.5). As Rorschach continues to vent his anger at the world, the mismatch increases, distancing the sound from any synchrony with the image, anchoring it in Rorschach's mindset until another strange alignment occurs. Having decided to enter the Comedian's apartment, Rorschach shoots his grappling hook high into the air. This is seen from a very low angle, which forces the audience to look upward along the line of the ascending high-rise. At the same time, Rorschach is heard saying: "All the whores and politicians will look up and shout save me." The device of matched compositional framing that echoes the image given in the voice-over is repeated when, after entering the Comedian's high-rise apartment using the grappling hook, Rorschach says "Now the whole world stands on the brink, staring down into bloody hell." The cut that occurs as he speaks moves the framing so that we are engaged in the process of looking down, either at Rorschach or over his shoulder to the city below. The mismatch created by compositional frame matching made visible in the voice-over, but not in the content of visual images, creates a peculiar balance in the sound-image relations. Other sounds introduce an undercurrent of anxiety, too, as the soundtrack features a harsh siren, an insistent beating drum, and the repeat of four piano notes. In Rorschach's introduction, space-time is split, leaving viewers somewhere between, wondering at what they should be looking and hearing.

FIGURE 25.5 Rorschach is seen looking at the face of a smiley badge.

CONCLUSION

Watchmen and *Inception* explore nonunified configurations of space in the imagined realities of shared dreams and fourth-dimensional temporalities. The strangeness of these spatiotemporalities are credible within the generic conventions drawn on by both films. Broadly speaking, the films both include elements of the science-fiction genre, a genre within which it is not unusual to find mutable organizations of time and space. Not simply relying on generic conventions to ground the credibility of their story-worlds, the sound-image relations of *Inception* and *Watchmen* generate audiovisual environments through which audiences can engage with the spatiotemporal realities of each film's story-world. Although the details of these worlds are very different, their nonunified configurations of time and space are each mediated through the sound-image relations. As examples of contemporary sound design, these sound-image relations offer two variations on seamless and overt integrations of music, sound effects, dialogue, and voice-over. The sound bridges of *Inception* hold together the potential incoherencies of the dream levels, whereas the shifting balances of *Watchmen's* sound mix evoke an experience of fourth-dimensional time. In completing each other's participations in generating the story-world, the sound-image relations contribute to and extend the ways in which time and space can be articulated in the cinema.

At the beginning of this essay, a question was posed: do the sound-image relations of films such as *Inception* and *Watchmen* acknowledge that unified positions have given way to configurations revealing the precarious balance of technological mediations? Although not an explicit theme in either film, articulations of time and space in *Inception* and *Watchmen* do offer a perspective on a wider experience of technologically mediated worlds. Technologies feature in many ways, and although neither film has an overt agenda on technology, their sound-image relations propose experiences of mediated constructions of time and space. The patching together achieved by sound bridges and multiplanar sound mixes exposes mediations that are both seamless and overt, revealing spatiotemporal organizations in which a potential for disintegration is counterpointed with an appearance of stability. Rather than displacing such a contested and challenging reality by establishing a singular perspective on events, the sound-image relations of *Inception* and *Watchmen* present different strategies of negotiation. Making sense of reality involves working through configurations that acknowledge their precarious ground.

NOTES

1. A sound bridge can be understood as a sound (frequently music, sound, or dialogue) that carries over between one shot and another, running over the cuts between moments of action within a particular scene. A sound bridge also occurs across scenes, connecting events that take place in a different time and space. It is the latter that are primarily discussed in this essay.

2. David Lewis Yewdall, *Practical Art of Motion Picture Sound* (Amsterdam: Focal Press, 2007), 476.

3. William Whittington, *Sound Design and Science Fiction* (Austin: University of Texas Press, 2007), 195.

4. Michel Chion *Audio-Vision: Sound on Screen* (New York: Columbia University Press, 1990), 89–92; Rick Altman, *Sound Theory, Sound Practice* (New York: Routledge, 1992), 46–64.

5. Mary Ann Doane, "Ideology and the Practice of Sound Editing and Mixing," in *The Cinematic Apparatus*, ed. Teresa de Lauretis and Stephen Heath (London: Palgrave MacMillan, 1980), 47–56.

6. Ruth Tallman, "Was it all a dream?: Why Nolan's Answer Doesn't Matter," In *Inception and Philosophy: Because It's Never Just a Dream*, ed. David Kyle Johnson (Hoboken, NJ: John Wiley, 2011), 17.

7. The score for *Inception* features a mixture of synthesizer, electric guitar, and an orchestra with an expanded brass section.

8. Tim Recuber, "Immersion Cinema: The Rationalization and Reenchantment of Cinematic Space," *Space and Culture* 10, no. 3 (2007): 315–330.

9. Richard King, "Christopher Nolan's *Inception*," *Mix Online*, July 9, 2010, http://mixonline.com/post/features/christopher_nolan_inception/index2.html.

10. David Bordwell, "Intensified Continuity: Visual Style in Contemporary American Film," *Film Quarterly* 55, no. 3 (2002): 16–28.

11. Michel Chion, *Film, A Sound Art* (New York: Columbia University Press, 2009), 147–164.

12. Paul Théberge, "Almost Silent: The Interplay of Sound and Silence in Contemporary Cinema and Television," in *Lowering the Boom: Critical Studies in Film Sound*, ed. Jay Beck and Tony Grajeda (Urbana and Chicago: University of Illinois Press, 2008), 56.

13. A kick indicates that the dream should leave a dream level and involves a literal fall through gravity.

14. Daniel Schweiger, "Creating a Hypnotic Wall of Sound for the Soundtrack of Christopher Nolan's *Inception*," *Buzzine*, July 23, 2010, http://www.buzzinefilm.com/interviews/music-interview-hans-zimmer-inception-movie-soundtrack-07232010.

15. Chion, *Audio-Vision*, 13–20.

16. In the comic, Dr. Manhattan states: "They explain that the name has been chosen for the ominous associations it will raise in America's enemies." Visually, the text-box is placed in a panel that includes a newspaper with the headline: *Atomic Bomb Dropped on Hiroshima*. Alan Moore and Dave Gibbons, *Watchmen Chapter IV* (New York: DC Comics, 1986), 12. In the film, the same explanation is given through Dr. Manhattan's voice-over narration.

17. Rick Altman, McGraw Jones, and Sonia Tatroe, "Inventing the Cinema Soundtrack: Hollywood's Multiplane Sound System," in *Music and Cinema*, ed. James Buhler, Caryl Flynn, and David Neumeyer (Hanover, NH: Wesleyan University Press, 2000), 339–359.

18. Jamie A. Hughes, "'Who Watches the Watchmen?': Ideology and "Real World" Superheroes," *Journal of Popular Culture* 39, no. 4 (2006): 546–557; Rurik Davidson, "Fighting the Good Fight: Watching Watchmen," *Screen Education* 54 (Winter 2009): 18–23; and, Mark White, *Watchmen and Philosophy: A Rorschach Test* (New York: John Wiley, 2009).

19. Will Eisner, *Comics and Sequential Art* (Tamarac, FL: Poorhouse Press 1985); and Scott McCloud, *Understanding Comics: The Invisible Art* (New York: Harper Perennial, 1994).

20. Mark Bernard and James Bucky Carter, "Alan Moore and the Graphic Novel: Confronting the Fourth Dimension," *ImageText* 1, no. 2 (2004), http://www.english.ufl.edu/imagetext/archives/v1_2/carter/#search=%22watchmen%20alan%20moore%22.

21. McCloud, *Understanding Comics*, 67.
22. Valerie Orpen, *Film Editing: the Art of the Expressive* (London: Wallflower, 2003); and Ken Dancyger, *The Technique of Film and Video Editing: History, Theory, Practice* (Amsterdam: Focal Press, 2007).
23. For instance, in the sequence that begins with Joel and Clementine sitting in the car improvising dialogue for a drive-in movie, their spatiotemporality begins to shift. Within the story-world of *Eternal Sunshine of the Spotless Mind*, this is explained by the memory eraser team's attempts to eradicate Joel's memories of Clementine. Intercut with scenes of the team working on a computer, the location surrounding Joel and Clementine first "tiles back" before segueing into another memory, which at times has a hybrid time and space. The tiling back of the location is both seen and heard. Heard as a clicking on the soundtrack that alerts Joel (and the audience) to the location's spatiotemporal dissolution and seen as the space disassembles as though tile by tile. For a more detailed discussion of sound in the film, see Carol Vernallis, "Music Video, Songs, Sound," *Screen* 49, no. 3 (Autumn 2008): 277–297.
24. Altman, *Sound Theory, Sound Practice*, 23.
25. Anahid Kassabian, *Hearing Film: Tracking Identifications in Contemporary Hollywood Film Music* (London: Routledge, 2001), 52.
26. Chion, *Audio-Vision*, 62.
27. John Belton, "Technology and Aesthetics of Film Sound," in *Film Theory and Criticism*, ed. Gerald Mast, Marshall Cohen, and Leo Braudy (New York: Oxford University Press, 1992), 328.
28. To make a spatial analogy: space is defined in a three-coordinate system of x, y, and z. We can say, in moving from one position to another, that we are here, and then here and then here. In the fourth dimension, there are four coordinates (x, y, and z plus time) and, theoretically, it is possible to say that one can be in any of those space-times. Regardless of their tensed chronology, it is possible to say that this is now, and this is now, and this is now. Only a fictional character is able to actually experience such an untensed multiplicity of nows.
29. Whittington, *Sound Design and Science Fiction*, 174–175.
30. There is a strong echo in *Watchmen* of the sound and images seen when *Pruit Igoe* was originally used in *Koyaanisqatsi*. In each film, the music accompanies scenes of technological destruction and quasi-messianic imagery.
31. Chion, *Audio-Vision*, 172.

SELECT BIBLIOGRAPHY

Chion, Michel. *Film, A Sound Art*. New York: Columbia University Press, 2009.
Eisner, Will. *Comics and Sequential Art*. Tamarac, FL: Poorhouse Press, 1985.
Kassabian, Anahid. *Hearing Film: Tracking Identifications in Contemporary Hollywood Film Music*. London: Routledge, 2001.
McCloud, Scott. *Understanding Comics: The Invisible Art*. New York: Harper Perennial, 1994.
Beck, Jay, and Tony Grajeda. Eds. *Lowering the Boom: Critical Studies in Film Sound*. Urbana and Chicago: University of Illinois Press, 2008.
Whittington, William. *Sound Design and Science Fiction*. Austin: University of Texas Press, 2007.
Yewdall, David Lewis. *Practical Art of Motion Picture Sound*. 3rd ed. Amsterdam: Focal Press, 2007.

····································

CHAPTER 26

INGLO(U)RIOUS BASTERDIZATION? TARANTINO AND THE WAR MOVIE MASHUP

····································

MIGUEL MERA

QUENTIN Tarantino's filmmaking has consistently featured the use of preexisting music that indulges both his "cinephilia and melomania."[1] His highly distinctive approach to the use of music, often drawn from his own record collection, is synonymous with his cinematic style and provides memorable, provocative, and meaningful audiovisual relationships. Indeed, Tarantino is one of the most widely discussed directors in the field of music and moving image studies. Scholars have suggested that Tarantino's films valorize audio over vision,[2] have highlighted the "unrivalled precedence he grants music in his creative process,"[3] and have even suggested that music is the nucleus around which entire films are constructed: "It is as if on some deep level the images are *dictated by and added to* the music, rather than the reverse."[4] It is clear that there is some unique quality in Tarantino's films that is, in no small measure, defined by the way he appreciates and thinks about music.

Tarantino has consistently stated that he is reluctant to work directly with composers because this would require him to relinquish too much control over his storytelling.[5] Speaking at the Cannes film festival in May 2008, he colorfully reinforced this idea:

> I have one of the best soundtrack collections in America. I just don't trust any composer to do it. Who the fuck is this guy coming in here and throwing his shit over my movie. What if I don't like it?[6]

Yet, only a few months later, Tarantino approached veteran composer Ennio Morricone to score *Inglourious Basterds* (2009).[7] Morricone initially accepted the offer, but time pressures and conflicting working projects eventually prevented the collaboration from taking place. The composer did not believe that the three-month window between the completion of principal photography in February 2009 and the April delivery would allow sufficient time to finish the work. Morricone explained: "Either I start working on it before he stops shooting—after we discuss it together—or I just can't do it."[8] Morricone later confirmed via his official website that a timetable clash with Giuseppe Tornatore's *Baaria* (2009) would prevent him from scoring *Inglourious Basterds*.[9] The initial offer to Morricone and the subsequent use of several of his preexisting pieces in the film raise interesting questions about Tarantino's approach to the use of music. Although Tarantino's admiration for Morricone is long-established—having referred to him as "the greatest film composer that ever lived"[10]—it is not clear why the director would be prepared to go against the core principles of his musical working practices that have consistently avoided ceding control to a composer writing original music. The answers to this question are nuanced and begin to tell us something about the evolution of Tarantino's musical thinking.

Unlike his previous projects, the soundtrack for *Inglourious Basterds* is constructed principally from preexisting film scores or music with clear filmic associations, and not from popular music tracks.[11] Although Tarantino featured some of Morricone's music in *Kill Bill Vols. 1 & 2*, a wide variety of pop tracks were also used. *Reservoir Dogs* (1992), *Pulp Fiction* (1994), and *Jackie Brown* (1997) exclusively used preexisting pop music. *Inglourious Basterds*, therefore, represents a point of arrival—transitioned through *Kill Bill Vols. 1 & 2*, where the director also worked with the RZA to create some music after the film had been shot—in which Tarantino engages as closely as he has ever done with the notion of the "scored" film. It is a continuation of Tarantino's working methods, yet also a shift in aesthetic approach that is allied to artistic trends in a postmillennial, digitally mediated society.

Ken Garner has explained that music matters to the characters in Tarantino's films and that taking "control of the score" is explicitly celebrated through their selection of diegetic music.[12] However, in *Inglourious Basterds*, the central actors/characters are not provided with songs that they can "own" or opportunities to take control of the music in the diegetic space, and the score functions more like a composed rather than a compiled score in terms of dramatic coherence and narrative structure. I suggest that, in *Inglourious Basterds*, coherence and unity of concept is achieved, paradoxically, through the application of multiple layers of appropriative meaning that are synonymous with the popular music practice known as *mashup*. In its most basic form a mashup (sometimes also called "bastard pop") is where two or more samples from different songs are blended together to create a new track. Typically, this involves capturing the vocal elements from one track and merging them with the instrumental sections of another.[13]

In this essay, I am concerned with some of the aesthetic qualities that govern mashup culture, rather than the questions of piracy and legality that often surround discussions about the reappropriation of copyrighted material. My focus is not on the technical processes involved in the creation of mashup, but rather on the pluralistic forms of listening and the sensibilities that are embedded in its cultural logic. In *Inglourious Basterds,* it is not simply that multiple references exist in ironic parallelism or contrapuntal pastiche, but rather that a variety of audiovisual ideas rub up against one another, coalesce, and form new meanings. Although not a mashup in the strictest technical sense of the term, because multiple sources of preexisting video are not combined, there is nonetheless a consistent mashing of tropes from both aural and visual cinematic genres. So strong are the genre allusions and cinematic contexts that their simultaneous presence is a constant reminder of the film's transformative aims. Earlier practices, of course, employed creative juxtapositions but had a tendency to emphasize counterpoint or defamilarization rather than the true goal of mashup culture, which is pluralism. Indeed, the heterogeneity of the *Inglourious Basterds* soundtrack, which contains music from the 1930s to the 1980s, is one of the clearest clues about its attitude in relation to mashup culture. As Stefan Sonvilla-Weis argued, mashup is a "metaphor for parallel and co-existing ways of thinking and acting rather than exclusionary, causal and reductionist principles of *either or* instead of *as well as.*"[14] I argue that the popularity of mashup since the turn of the millennium points toward a broader sociocultural audile phenomenon, of which Tarantino is a principal exponent. In *Inglourious Basterds,* Tarantino creates a movie that blends audiovisual tropes from war films, spaghetti westerns, men-on-a-mission and action movies, blaxploitation films, horror movies, and National Socialist propaganda; impish playfulness serves to present this material from a startlingly fresh perspective.

The use of mashup principles has significant ramifications for our appreciation of *Inglourious Basterds* as a whole. One of the most heavily critiqued aspects of the film is that it rewrites the ending of World War II, creating an alternate version of the Holocaust. The film tells the story of two simultaneous plots to assassinate the Nazi political leadership, one planned by a maverick team of Jewish allied soldiers—known as The Basterds—and the other by a Franco-Jewish cinema proprietor.[15] Both plots converge in a movie theater, where Hitler and most of his high command officers are burned alive, shot, and then also blown-up for good measure. Daniel Mendelsohn observed that to indulge fantasies at the expense of historical truth would be the most "inglorious bastardization of all."[16] However, Tarantino's film is not only a mashup of war movie characters and clichés but also explores how film shapes audiences' ideas about authenticity and revenge. Within this context, the soundtrack's reference to music from the spaghetti western subgenre in particular allows historical liberties to become a reflection on the metamorphosis of fact into myth and vice-versa. The film enjoys the juxtaposition of old and new and celebrates a plurality of contexts and signification in a liminal space. It is the creation of this deliberate liminal space, which I argue problematizes Jean Baudrillard's notion of simulacrum, that ultimately challenges the audience in the film's concluding sequences.[17] The playful genre allusions and self-aware process of mythologizing are shattered by a jolt from history that forces the audience to confront their own cathartic spectatorial position.

MASHUP: BEYOND COUNTERPOINT?

> If I am using a piece of music from another movie, I'm almost never
> using it for the same effect that it was used in the movie that I am using it
> from.... So part of the fun is the dichotomy of what it was and now what
> it is.[18]

Tarantino's comment exemplifies an attitude shared by numerous mashup artists.
Mashup is considered transformative and playful, delighting in synchronic simultaneity and difference and actively demonstrating that meaning is not fixed. This, of course,
recalls one of the longest running debates in film music scholarship, namely, the limitation of simplistic critical definitions of music–image relationships as either parallel or
contrapuntal.[19] This terminology is usually built on a faulty assumption that the image
is autonomous and that music either supports or opposes it. What Tarantino suggests is
that neither image nor music are set and that meaning emerges as a result of the interaction between the various components in a work.

This kind of approach has been a regular feature in Tarantino's work and has frequently been discussed in relation to postmodernity, with specific reference to notions
of pastiche, nonlinear structures, self-reflexivity, and the collapse of "low" and "high"
culture distinctions.[20] However, some writers have argued that there is very little below
the surface to discover in Tarantino's work.[21] Indeed, critical reception of *Inglourious
Basterds* was mixed. Roger Ebert claimed it was the best film of 2009, but other reviewers argued that although it was a "masterclass in gorgeously-constructed self-pastiche,"
the director desperately needed "an editor willing to trim his indulgences."[22] Another
reviewer was struck by a movie that was "exasperatingly awful and transcendentally disappointing," which seemed like a "Tarantino film in form and mannerism but with the
crucial element of genius mysteriously amputated."[23]

The same kinds of criticisms about style over content and technical prowess at the
expense of emotional depth are also frequently leveled at mashup. Michael Serazio,
for example, stated that the "mashup movement is surprisingly vapid" and represents
what some postmodern theorists understand as the end of an era in which culture
winds down and, through a lack of genuine inventiveness, recycles itself at an increasingly accelerated speed.[24] Serazio was "uncertain what exactly, in the end, the mashup
really has to say."[25] John Shiga, conversely, argued that in mashup culture "copying is
inextricably tied to listening" and highlighted how online mashup communities—a
subculture of producer-consumers—value pluralistic experimentation as the basis for
sociality; a sympathetic community in which reputation, status, and various forms of
capital are played out through the act of listening and creating.[26] He argued that these
digital music cultures ignore traditional hierarchies in a spirit of mischievous exploration in which genre is treated as something fluid and transformable that can be made to
materialize or vanish at will within a given work. But mashup artists do not only place
genres *against* each other, they also search for resonant associations between tracks.

These may be timbral, harmonic, lyrical, rhythmic, or gestural. CCC's "Stand by Me," for example, mashed Ben E. King's "Stand By Me" (1961) with by "Every Breath You Take" by The Police (1984).[27] The simple A + B mashup combines King's vocal with The Police's instrumental track and highlights the harmonic and rhythmic congruence between the two. The juxtaposition is not only oppositional and combinatorial in equal measure but, assuming that the listener knows both songs, the excised "unheard" material is a phantom presence, a reverberant memory. DJ Lobsertdust's "Nirgaga," a mashup of Nirvana's "Smells Like Teen Spirit" (1991) and Lady Gaga's "Poker Face" (2008), highlights timbral and gestural similarities between the two songs, as well as juxtaposing alternative rock with commercial pop.[28] Other artists, such as Girl Talk or DJ Earworm, use a vast range of sources to create new materials, seeking resonances at the micro- and macro-levels.[29]

It is easy to see how Tarantino's approach is related to this kind of work. Genres are morphed in inventive ways, and the display of taste through both listening and viewing is constantly in evidence. The ability to identify and generate links between apparently incongruent materials is the ultimate manifestation of mashup culture's geek chic; Shiga calls this "cool listening."[30] In interviews, Tarantino frequently refers to how cool it is to use a particular music track in a given context: "You are really doing what movies do better than any other art form; it really works in this visceral, emotional, cinematic way that is just really special."[31] I would argue that Tarantino's approach is increasingly based on the same kind of playful sociality that is evident in mashup communities. Although made available via the distribution mechanisms of the global film industry rather than posted to the social space of an online message board, there is a homespun and personal quality to Tarantino's films. Indeed, he has argued that his soundtracks are "basically professional equivalents of a mix tape I'd make for you at home."[32] *Inglourious Basterds* in particular has connected with an audience engaged in detailed online debates about Tarantino's approaches, intended meanings, and use of materials. Furthermore, that same audience has the digital tools at their disposal to generate user-produced digital content, and several spoof trailers using material taken from *Inglourious Basterds* demonstrate practical and participatory involvement.[33] The celebration and sharing of "cool" moments indicates how mashup mentality runs through Tarantino's work.

What exactly is mashed in *Inglourious Basterds*? The film is a World War II drama, but the music does not conform to standard expectations of style or genre. On the one hand, music from 1940s films is used diegetically (e.g., *Die Große Liebe*), but there is also a good deal of nondiegetic spaghetti-western music (e.g., *Il Mercenario, La Resa dei Conti, Da uomo a uomo*), men-on-a-mission war movies (e.g., *Dark of the Sun, Kelly's Heroes*), blaxploitation movies (e.g., *Slaughter*), action movies (e.g., *White Lightning*), Italian crime dramas or *poliziotteschi* (e.g., *Revolver*), 1980s erotic horror (e.g., *Cat People*), and so on. The heterogeneous assortment of musical choices is supported by a similar variety of different languages and dialects that are found in the film, such as American Southern, French, German, Italian, and received pronunciation English. Popular culture references to sports, games, and other movies abound. Several of the performers (Mike Meyers, Brad Pitt, Christoph Waltz) seem to be enjoying themselves so much that they lend a mischievous spirit to the film. Lisa Coulthard might suggest

Table 26.1

Originally from	Genre	Composer	Track	Use in *Inglourious Basterds*
The Alamo (1960)	War epic	Dmitri Tiomkin/arr. Nick Perito	The Green Leaves of Summer	Opening Titles
CHAPTER 1: Once Upon a Time in Nazi-Occupied France				
La Resa dei Conti/The Big Gundown (1966)	Spaghetti-western	Ennio Morricone	Dopo la Condanna/ The Verdict	Nazi troupe drive towards Monsieur LaPadite's dairy farm
Il Ritorno di Ringo/ The Return of Ringo (1965)	Spaghetti-western	Ennio Morricone	L'incontro Con La Figlia	Jews hiding under floorboards are shot, Shoshanna escapes
CHAPTER 2: Inglourious Basterds				
White Lightning (1973)	Action	Charles Bernstein	White Lightning (Main Title)	Private Butz describes The Basterds to Hitler
Il Mercenario (1968)	Spaghetti-western	Ennio Morricone	Il Mercenario (Riprisa)	German Sergeant Werner Rachtman meets Lieutenant Aldo Raine (slow-motion sequence)
Slaughter (1972)	Blaxploitation	Billy Preston	Slaughter	Hugo Stiglitz is introduced
The Battle of Algiers (1966)	War	Ennio Morricone & Gillo Pontecorvo	Algeria, 1 Novembre 1954	The Basterds recruit Stiglitz
La Resa dei Conti/The Big Gundown (1966)	Spaghetti-western	Ennio Morricone	La Resa/The Surrender	Donnie Donowitz "The Bear Jew" beats Sergeant Rachtman to death
White Lightning (1973)	Action	Charles Bernstein	Hound Chase	Private Butz is marked with swastika on his forehead. Leading into Chapter 3
CHAPTER 3: German Night in Paris				
Un Dollaro Bucato/Blood for a Silver Dollar (1966)	Spaghetti-western	Gianni Ferrio	Un Dollaro Bucato/ Blood for a Silver Dollar	Emmanuelle/ Shoshanna smokes and reads a book in a café. Frederick Zoller pesters her
Al di là della legge (1967)	Spaghetti-western	Riziero Ortolani	The Saloon	Gestapo officer comes to collect Emmanuelle Mimieux

(Continued)

Table 26.1 Continued

Originally from	Genre	Composer	Track	Use in *Inglourious Basterds*
The Entity (1981)	Horror	Charles Bernstein	Bath Attack	Hans Landa arrives at the restaurant, flashback to Shoshanna's escape
Dark of the Sun (1968)	Adventure-war	Jacques Loussier	Claire's First Appearance	Emmanuelle/ Shoshanna and Marcel discuss plans to burn the cinema on Nazi night
CHAPTER 4: *Operation Kino*				
Dark of the Sun (1968)	Adventure-war	Jacques Loussier	The Fight	Lieutenant Archie Hicox and Hugo Stiglitz prepare to go into La Louisiane tavern to rendezvous with double agent Bridget von Hammersmark
Die GroßeLiebe (1942)	Drama/propaganda	Zarah Leander	Davon geht die welt nicht unter	Diegetic music in tavern
Hi Diddle Diddle (1943)	Comedy	Foster Carling song, Phil Boutelje lyrics	*The Man With The Big Sombrero*	
Glückskinder (1936)	Screwball comedy	Performed Lilian Harvey and Willy Fritsch	*Ich wollt ich wär ein Huhn*	
Slaughter (1972)	Blaxploitation	Billy Preston	Slaughter	Stiglitz imagines torturing the German Major
Dark of the Sun (1968)	Adventure-war	Jacques Loussier	Main Theme	Bridget von Hammersmark, Aldo Raine and two Basterds prepare a plan for attending the film première
CHAPTER 5: *Revenge of the Giant Face*				
Cat People (1982)	Erotic horror	David Bowie	*Cat People (Putting Out Fire)*	Night of *Nation's Pride* première. Emmanuelle/ Shoshanna puts on make-up/war paint. Alternative film ending is shot and edited

(Continued)

Table 26.1 Continued

Originally from	Genre	Composer	Track	Use in *Inglourious Basterds*
Da uomo a uomo/Death Rides a Horse (1967)	Spaghetti-western	Ennio Morricone	Mistico e Severo	Landa observes guests at film première and goes to meet Hammersmark and The Basterds
Devil's Angels (1967)	Biker movie	Davie Allen and Mike Curb	The Devil's Rumble	Sergeant Donowitz and Private First Class Ulmer find their seats in the film theatre
		Ray Charles performed by Rare Earth	What'd I Say	Donowitz leaves auditorium and sees Hitler
Zulu Dawn (1979)	War	Elmer Bernstein	Zulus	Marcel locks the auditorium door and we see the pile of nitrate film
Kelly's Heroes (1970)	Comedy/war	Lalo Schifrin	Tiger Tank	Zoller leaves the auditorium, Emanuelle/ Shoshanna changes the projection reel, Marcel waits behind the cinema screen
Revolver/Blood in the Streets (1973)	Poliziottesco	Ennio Morricone	Un Amico	Emmanuelle/ Shoshanna has just shot Zoller. He groans in pain, she checks if he is alive. Zoller, lying face down on the floor, turns and shoots her
Eastern Condors (1987)	Action	Chun Ting Yat	Sherman Chow Gam	Donowitz and Ulmer shoot two German guards protecting Hitler's loggia box
Allonsanfàn (1974)	Drama	Ennio Morricone	*Rabbia e Tarantella*	Landa is marked with swastika on his forehead, leading into the End Credits
End Credits				

that these are all techniques designed to encourage the audience to enjoy the soundtrack and vice-versa.[34] Table 26.1 shows a chronological list of the music as it appears in the film. The left-hand column indicates the movie in which the specific music track originally appeared.

Most of the preexisting music can be categorized within clear film music genres. Music from war films abounds, although only one of these, *Kelly's Heroes* (1970), is set during World War II and is about a group of soldiers who go absent-without-leave to rob a bank behind enemy lines. Although the backdrop is Nazi-occupied France, this film is not so much about war as it is about a group of men on a specific mission. Historical referentialism, therefore, is not the governing factor in the selection of material. Indeed, further exploration of the music track list reveals a recurrent pattern of films that deal with individuals or small groups of men, normally outcasts or underdogs, who are motivated to complete a particular task in opposition to another group. *Dark of the Sun* (1968), for example, tells the story of a gang of mercenaries sent on a dangerous mission during the Congo Crisis (1960–1966). *Eastern Condors* (1987) features an ensemble of convict soldiers, clearly reminiscent of the squad in the *Dirty Dozen* (1967), who are given a secret mission to enter Vietnam and destroy a bunker containing missiles before they are accessed by the Viet Cong. Although *Slaughter* (1972) is a blaxploitation movie, its main character is a former Green Beret captain who seeks revenge for the murder of his parents.[35]

The idea of revenge and an undercover mission also features in *White Lightning* (1973). The central character, Gator McKlusky, is imprisoned for running moonshine. Federal agents agree to release him if he will help capture the ringleaders of the moonshine operation. Since one of these men is responsible for the murder of Gator's younger brother, he agrees to assist and is able to find a way out of prison and exact retribution at the same time. Tarantino argued that the main title music from *White Lightning* would be ideal not just as "a theme for The Basterds *per se*, but something that would be really interesting to show them doing their thing, doing their apache resistance against the Nazis."[36] The music, according to Tarantino, has a sinister quality and the use of Dobro guitar, etherial solo whistling, and "twangy" Jew's harp gives the piece a distinctive American South feel originally allied to *White Lightning*'s Arkansas setting.[37] Tarantino suggested that this music brings an "Americanness" to *Inglourious Basterds* and that it acts as an "echoing theme" for the central character, Lieutenant Aldo Raine, "because he's from the South."[38] Even a cursory exploration of some of the music used, therefore, suggests that the choices are not innocent and that numerous resonant associations are made between an original track and its revised context. Principally, thematic links relating to the notion of retribution unifies the disparate material.

As early as the opening title sequence, the audience is aware that Tarantino is playing with the notion of genre, but also going far beyond this. The first music heard is "The Green Leaves of Summer," a piece of music originally composed by the Russian-Jewish émigré Dmitri Tiomkin with lyrics by Paul Francis Webster for John Wayne's directorial debut, *The Alamo* (1960). The film is an epic war movie and deals with the famous 1836 siege that was pivotal in the Texas Revolution.[39]

Interestingly, Tarantino does not use the version of "The Green Leaves of Summer" taken directly from *The Alamo* itself, but rather Nick Perito's instrumental arrangement of it.[40] This choice may have been made, in part, to avoid the specific textual references in Tiomkin and Webster's choral version of the theme: "A time to be reapin', a time to be sowin'/The green leaves of Summer are callin' me home." Tarantino's aesthetic approach to the film, as has already been observed, moves toward the notion of the "score" rather than the compiled song soundtrack. However, it is equally clear that "The Green Leaves of Summer" also had a significant impact beyond the movie for which it was originally made. In this respect, Tiomkin had great form. His song "Do Not Forsake Me, Oh My Darling" from *High Noon* (1952) and the whistled main theme from *The High and the Mighty* (1954) were both top ten hits. *Billboard Magazine* predicted on November 7, 1960 that the soundtrack album for *The Alamo* "should enjoy a brisk sale."[41] Indeed, it remained in the best-selling LP charts for forty-seven weeks and peaked at number seven, and both score and song won Tiomkin further Academy Awards.[42] Numerous versions of "The Green Leaves of Summer" exist, and, as such, it represents popular culture's appropriation of material through and beyond its cinematic context. In this respect, it represents the best of both worlds for Tarantino the melomane, record collector, and audile listener.

But what does the music itself convey? A lilting 12/8 guitar rhythm and smoky accordion melody soon give way to a fuller arrangement incorporating luscious strings and female choir. We are clearly listening to a filmic representation of a folk ballad—rustic simplicity appropriated and made mythic—a musical interpretation that could easily be mistaken for a spaghetti-western soundtrack that acts as a gateway to the fantasy world of the film. The use of music clearly associated with but not quite from *The Alamo* encourages the audience to hear the way that the history of war is told through the concepts of myth, appropriation, and fairy tale. Indeed, as the opening titles fade and Perito's arrangement dies away the intertitle reads: "Once upon a time in Nazi occupied France..."

WHY MORRICONE?

A potent musical strand in *Inglourious Basterds* relates to the western, especially the spaghetti western and, as already observed, there is a particular focus on the music of Ennio Morricone. In fact, Morricone's music frames the movie, but it is not the same Morricone at the beginning as at the end. Film director Bernardo Bertolucci observed that there is the famous Morricone who was "Sergio Leone's composer and who, with him, invented the sound of the Italian western," but he also suggested that there are various other Morricones who represent different aesthetic and compositional aspects. For Bertolucci, the music is also able to go "back to Verdi, to go into the peasants songs, the music of the collective heart," so that, without knowing it, Morricone "wrote two or three beautiful possible national anthems for Italy."[43] Simon Frith perceives the composer as an equally pivotal figure, but, for him, Morricone is "the line that runs from Puccini to Dub,"[44] and, in the construction of aural narrative, he is able to "draw on music's ability to cross and confuse cinematic and cultural codes."[45] We can see some of the features of Morricone's compositional style, as identified by both Bertolucci and Frith, directly mapped onto Tarantino's approaches in *Inglourious Basterds*.

It is clear that Morricone is especially associated, through his collaboration with Sergio Leone, with the spaghetti western. Originally coined as a pejorative term by critics to highlight the supposed inauthenticity of non-American westerns, the spaghetti western was a subgenre that emerged in the mid-1960s. Principally directed by Italians, originally released in the Italian language, and often filmed in Spain, they were more bleak and gritty than American westerns. What Leone and Morricone provided was a European perspective on the mythic notion of the Old West as exemplified by the westerns of John Ford et al. In essence, the spaghetti western first demythologized and then, I would argue, remythologized the frontier and its inhabitants.[46] Codes of honor were upturned, with heroes who were only slightly less evil than the villains; the bleakness of landscape was not merely presented, audiences were encouraged to feel its harshness; long sequences without dialogue and extreme close-ups resulted in what Jameson has described as operas "in which arias are not sung but stared."[47] The spaghetti western celebrated the process of mythologizing, and Morricone's music was fundamental in shaping its success.

The key to the effectiveness of Morricone's music in Leone's films lies in the opportunities for the "foregrounding" of musical moments. Royal Brown observed that Leone's extension of action in time allowed "the music more room to expand" so that Morricone had the "luxury of writing developed themes that have musical logic while generating ample amounts of cinematic affect."[48] This is an aesthetic position that would have comfortably accorded both with Morricone's classical training and his early experiences in commercial music production. Before he broke into the film industry in the early 1960s, he worked as an arranger in the Italian recording industry, providing orchestrations for hundreds of popular songs in different styles. As Jeff Smith observed, the aesthetic approach, use of particular instrumental colors, and formal characteristics of his film scores for the spaghetti westerns "bear certain similarities with these interpolated songs, and often his cues similarly invert the normal hierarchy of image and music."[49] The boldness and vibrancy of orchestration and the spirit of experimentation are all functions of the fact that Leone's spaghetti westerns valued music as a principal character. Morricone himself acknowledged the importance of this in allowing the music to speak:

> Music you cannot hear, no matter how good it is, is bad film music. That is how films are. A lot of my music, and music by other composers, has been judged to be bad because the director did not give it proper space or volume.[50]

I would also suggest that the principal reason that Morricone's music has been judged to be so effective in these collaborations is not only because Leone allowed the space for it, but also because both composer and director believed in an aesthetic approach that rejected fundamental aspects of the Hollywood western.[51] Indeed, from the very outset of their collaboration on *A Fistful of Dollars* (1964), it was clear that Leone was searching for a different kind of sound and wanted to work in a different way to achieve it. Leone suggested that the music should be composed before the film was shot so that he could use it to help formulate ideas about its potential impact. Frayling noted that this first project "was too far advanced, and too sparsely budgeted for such an innovation," but, in subsequent projects, sequences were built around the precomposed music and, in *Once Upon a Time in the West* (1968), for example, the music was even played on set with a direct influence on the performances of the actors.[52] Therefore, Morricone's music is effective as film music precisely because it has not been created and does not function in the same way as most other film music. It has its own structural logic that is not defined by picture editing configurations; the images are frequently shaped around the music. Furthermore, Morricone's music is commonly built through the transition of short motives into overarching structures that are reminiscent of the verse-chorus structures of popular music. The Italian musicologist Sergio Miceli refers to this as "micro-cell technique."[53] For a director who likes to use preexisting music, such as Tarantino, we can immediately understand the appeal of Morricone's music. It can be easily manipulated in structural terms, has a clear link to popular music practice both in gestural approach and instrumentation, and has a clear identity and life beyond the film (much of Morricone's film music is widely available on record), while also being fundamental to the identity formation of the given film itself.

In line with Bertolucci's assessment of some of the different facets of Morricone's musical character, Tarantino explained that the first half of *Inglourious Basterds* is specifically designed to mash "spaghetti western mood with WWII iconography," but he also observed that the use and function of Morricone's music changes as the film progresses, so that, at the end, it is "less spaghetti western and more operatic."[54] I would also add an intermediate category to these two uses of music that I would describe, for want of a better term, as the spaghettification of preexisting tracks. By this, I mean that the way that a track is used, regardless of its original context or whether it is even by the Italian composer, is deliberately reminiscent of the form and function of Morricone's music in Leone's spaghetti western films, especially in relation to the manipulation of time and the creation of myth. Three specific examples from *Inglourious Basterds* will serve to highlight these Morricone-esque musical categories.

The opening scene features a homestead set against an expansive landscape with a lone figure (Monsieur LaPadite) chopping wood. In the distance, we see army vehicles approaching.

> [W]hen we were shooting the first sequence, everyone in the crew was like: "Quentin this is your first Western." The Nazis in their uniforms, in their cars, in their motorbikes did not break the Western vibe, it went with it in a strange way. They filled-in for *bandidos* or outlaw riders.[55]

The music cue used is "Dopo la Condanna," taken from Sergio Sollima's spaghetti western *La Resa dei Conti* (1966). One of the most striking features is that Morricone's

FIGURE 26.1 Beethoven *Beethoven's Bagatelle No. 25 in A minor, Für Elise*, opening.

score quotes Beethoven's *Bagatelle* No. 25 in A minor, commonly known as *Für Elise*. Its opening gesture is one of the most instantly recognizable phrases in music history (Figure 26.1). Based around E⁷ dominant harmony resolving to A minor, the alternating E/D#'s can be interpreted as a slow trill. In general, the lower note of a trill is the root with the upper auxiliary note as a decoration on it, but Beethoven inverted this and generates delightful piquancy with D#'s eventually falling to a D natural that implies the dominant seventh chord and articulates an overall descent from the fifth to the tonic.

In Morricone's cue, Beethoven's opening gesture remains on a piano but is recontextualized within the harmonic and orchestrational context of the spaghetti western sound. Morricone provides extra repetitions of the E/D# "trill," creating an extended version of motif X that appears four times during the cue. The motif first resolves onto A minor, as in Beethoven's original, but, in subsequent appearances, the concluding note A is placed over F major and Dm⁷ harmony, before finally resolving on A minor at the end of the cue. Interspersing these statements, improvisatory classical guitar passages based on the aeolian mode act as answering phrases, often moving over parallel block major chords (F—D—E). In addition, orchestral strings, a lyrical French horn melody, and rhythmic, effected electric guitar patterns contribute to Morricone's typical spaghetti western sound.

Even before Tarantino used this music, "Dopo La Condanna" was already a mashup. In its original context, this juxtaposition of musical materials had a clear narrative justification. The story of *La Resa dei Conti* centers around the character Manuel Sanchez, who has been framed for the rape and murder of a child by a wealthy landowner and power-broker, Mr. Brokston. The real culprit is Brokston's son-in-law. Brokston hires Jonathan Corbett, a gunman with a reputation for bringing criminals to justice, and offers him support to run as a senator in return for hunting Sanchez. However, after several encounters, Corbett begins to have doubts about his quarry's guilt. Annoyed at Corbett's inability to catch Sanchez, Brokston arrives in Mexico to take over the manhunt, aided by his Austrian bodyguard, the Baron von Schulenberg (see Figure 26.2). We have learned that this mustachioed Austrian is the best gunman in Europe, with thirty-three duels and thirty-three wins under his belt. He also happens to be a skilled pianist, and we even hear him play *Für Elise* while he boasts about his dueling prowess to Corbett. In narrative terms, this sequence seems designed to demonstrate cultured precision and ruthless efficiency. The film's climactic sequences involve several

FIGURE 26.2 Baron von Schulenberg—*La Resa dei Conti.*

Mexican stand-offs in which the genuine murderer, von Schulenberg, and Brokston are all killed by Corbett and Sanchez. Morricone's cue "Dopo la Condanna," complete with Beethoven quotation, is, of course, used during Corbett's duel with von Schulenberg and highlights differences between the two skilled gunmen. One is precise, measured, efficient, and European, the other more free-spirited, improvisatory, and from the frontier.

In the context of *Inglourious Basterds*, the piece of music acquires even deeper layers of meaning. Richard Etlin observed that the Nazi party used cultural heroes to strengthen its political agenda and "Beethoven was promoted as an artist who represented National Socialist heroic ideals."[56] Indeed, Beethoven was privileged and placed beside Wagner as representative of German supremacy, and German musicologists were even commissioned to rewrite the history of German music in accordance with Nazi principles.[57] The use of Beethoven taps into this historical association with the Third Reich, and the cue as a whole acquires meaning from both its previous filmic context and its new placement. Beethoven is mashed and reshaped, but so is the sight and sound of the spaghetti western and the visual metaphor of the war movie.

The second category, which I have called spaghettification, is exemplified by a very brief distorted guitar riff—moving from the flattened subtonic to the tonic minor—derived from Billy Preston's score for *Slaughter*. This is used as a "theme" for the character Hugo Stiglitz, the only German member of The Basterds, who is notorious for his sadistic ways of murdering Nazis (see Figure 26.3).

We are introduced to him through the menacing guitar riff and a freeze-frame in which his name is emblazoned across the screen. This is reminiscent of the technique used by Leone in *The Good, the Bad, and the Ugly* (1966), in which each character is labeled by an epithet that appears over a freeze-frame of his image accompanied by Morricone's famous alternating perfect-fourth "coyote call." The same thematic material represents all three characters in Leone's film but receives a different orchestration

FIGURE 26.3 Hugo Stiglitz—*Inglourious Basterds.*

on each occasion.[58] Morricone goes some way toward explaining the significance of this kind of audiovisual approach:

> Out of his intuition, Sergio understood a very important thing—that film and music share a temporal dimension.... Film and music need attention, transmission, that makes use of time. If you respect the temporal nature of both film and music, you get the best results.[59]

In the Stiglitz freeze-frame sequence, Tarantino borrows the idea of identificatory gestural boldness from Leone and Morricone's temporal dislocation in order to expand the mythic space. As Sean Cubitt observed, the "cinematic freeze is not a photograph, because it has a definite duration."[60] The audience is invited to engage both with the suspense and spatialization of time, which is precisely where myth can be shaped because, as Roland Barthes might have argued, form and meaning are blended into a mode of signification. This approach seems all the more clear because the action on either side of the freeze-frame engages in further temporal displacement. First, as the captured German sergeant walks towards Lieutenant Aldo Raine, the action moves into a slow-motion sequence featuring Morricone's music from *Il Mercenario* (1968). Then the distorted guitar theme from *Slaughter* is heard over the freeze-frame, before developing into funk-rock that accompanies a violent but playful, multilayered flashback showing how Stiglitz came to join the gang after murdering a string of Nazis. Overall, this sequence demonstrates a carefully managed control of tempo, slow—pause—fast, that creates a space for the mythic precisely in the manner of Morricone's spaghetti western music.

Tarantino has referred to the use of Morricone's music in the latter half of *Inglourious Basterds* as operatic. One scene in particular, a *"Romeo and Juliet* shootout at a movie première" exemplifies the approach.[61] Having escaped SS Officer Hans Landa several years earlier, Shoshanna Dreyfus has assumed a new identity as Emmanuelle Mimieux and is the owner of a Paris cinema. German war hero Private Fredrick Zoller, whose exploits are to be celebrated in a Nazi propaganda film, *Stolz der Nation* (*Nation's Pride*), takes an interest in her and persuades Joseph Goebbels to hold the première at her cinema. With the presence of numerous high-ranking Nazi officials, she plans to take her revenge by locking the audience in the theater and burning them alive after setting fire to large quantities of highly flammable nitrate film. However, as the plan sprints toward its conclusion, Zoller leaves the theater to find Dreyfus/Mimieux in the projection booth. She tries to get rid of him, but he is insistent. With the promise of a sexual encounter, she persuades him to lock the door and then shoots him in the back. This is where Morricone's track "Un Amico" taken from the film *Revolver* (1973) is heard.[62]

Despite the fact that Shoshanna has just shot Zoller, the instrumental version of Morricone's track "Un Amico" seems to generate an initial tenderness between them. The lyrical melody and soothing textures suggest regret—the gentle main theme enters as Zoller groans in pain and Shoshanna goes over to him. Shoshanna perhaps does not loathe Zoller as a person but what he represents. However, as the music develops into its most expansive phrase, Zoller, who has been lying face down on the floor, turns and shoots Shoshanna. The meaning of the scene seems ambiguous as we experience the blood-spattered, slow-motion death of the two characters. Does Tarantino generate dissonance between graphic violence and sweet music? Does the sequence represent the aestheticization of violence? Is there something darkly sexual about the bodies writhing in slow-motion as they lay bleeding and dying?

Much has been written about Tarantino's use of music in relation to violence, particularly the notion of ironic counterpoint, a concept that several writers have found increasingly unsatisfactory. Phil Powrie, for example, argues that counterpoint exists not between what you see and what you hear in the torture sequence in *Reservoir Dogs* (1992), "but between the act of seeing and the act of hearing."[63] Lisa Coulthard, likewise, argues that music in Tarantino's scenes of violence is "more than mere accompaniment, ironic commentary, or contradiction," it is "essential in the audiovisual construction of spectatorial enjoyment and engagement."[64] Coulthard also understands Tarantino's aesthetic approach as emphasizing the "superficial nature of his film texts so that they can be viewed and enjoyed within a context of pleasurable affective and analytic passivity."[65] I would align this theoretical perspective with Gregg Redner's attempts to find methodological connections between musicology and film theory by using ideas proposed by the French philosopher Gilles Deleuze.[66] In particular the notion of *sensation* seems apposite.[67] Deleuze proposed the idea that art is experienced as pure sensation rather than contemplation; the arts create novel combinations of sensation and feeling; that is to say, a compound of "percepts" and "affects."[68] The move away from representational analytical perspectives toward those that focus on intensities of experience and highlight affect and hapticity seems a valuable way of approaching much of Tarantino's work. Redner suggests that by considering the Deleuzian concept of precognitive sensation it becomes possible to hear a score in its purest form, thereby enabling us to understand it as "an expanding flow moving forward towards the greater plane which is the entirety of the filmic universe."[69]

The "Un Amico" sequence certainly engages in a way that goes far beyond simplistic counterpoint between image and music. It seems to me that something close to Deleuze's notion of sensation is precisely what Tarantino was thinking of when he described the use of Morricone's music in this sequence as "operatic." Shoshanna's bright red dress, Zoller's cream uniform jacket, the humane and lyrical melody, and the beautiful slow-motion creates a narrative sequence that is ambiguous about the tragic, the tender, and the impact of brutalistic violence. The music does not explain or express the images; it renders them physically sensible. The sequence could be considered "operatic" precisely because, like the most breathtaking climactic moments in opera, it is simultaneously emotional and visceral. It is not desensitized through simplistic juxtaposition.

WRITING/RIGHTING HISTORY?

In his discussion of the use of Morricone's "Un Amico," Tarantino observed that he had been waiting for an opportunity to use the track for many years. Recalling its original use in *Revolver*, the director explained: "I remember thinking...wow this is fantastic, but it doesn't really quite go with this movie."[70] The same attitude is also evident in other tracks used in the film, including David Bowie's "Cat People (Putting Out Fire)," which originally appeared in Paul Schrader's movie *Cat People* (1982): "I've always loved that song and I was always disappointed by how Paul Schrader used it in the movie. He didn't really use it; he threw it in over the closing credits."[71]

"Cat People (Putting Out Fire)" is used for one of the film's most striking sequences, in which Emanuelle/Shoshanna engages in a preparatory ritual before setting fire to her own cinema.[72] It is clear that there is a close alliance between the visual editing, lyrics, and the structure of the music. The sequence begins with slow fades—from establishing shot to extreme close-up—while Bowie's brooding baritone voice drones, but as his voice reaches its impassioned heights on the word "gasoline," the tempo suddenly increases and we see Shoshanna putting on her make-up. This is no ordinary preparation for an important night—after all, the song tells us that she is "putting out fire with gasoline." On the line "See these eyes so red," Shoshanna takes her red cream-blusher and aggressively applies it as war paint (Figure 26.4). She rhythmically loads the magazine into her pistol on the fourth beat of a bar before the start of a new verse: "Still this pulsing night." The entrance of the fourth verse, "See these tears so blue," coincides with a mid close-up as she puts on her cocktail hat and we watch her slowly lower her veil in focused readiness. The music's unbridled emotion screams in anticipation while

FIGURE 26.4 Emanuelle/Shoshanna—War Paint.

Shoshanna herself remains intensely poised. The scene fetishizes her personal prepara-
tions for the première of *Stolz der Nation*, but the central section also fetishizes filmmaking itself. We see Shoshanna and her lover Marcel making the movie insert, their
attempts to get it developed, and, over a repetitive guitar riff, the joining together of two
sections of nitrate film using a splicer and cement. Tarantino gives this song a cinematic
treatment that he felt was warranted but never received in its original incarnation.

Tarantino's use of preexisting music from other films aims to correct perceived past
errors or miscalculations. By giving a track the treatment it truly deserves, there is an
attempt made to "right" cinematic history. This approach sits comfortably within the
ideals of mashup culture, in which new combinations focusing on undervalued or forgotten materials are cherished. However, *Inglourious Basterds* goes several steps further.
Its historical narrative also completely reshapes the ending of World War II and, thus,
seems intent on both writing and "righting" history.

Tarantino perceives the boundary between mediated cinematic history and historical
veracity as minimal: "I like the idea that it's the power of cinema that fights the Nazis.
But not even as a metaphor—as a literal reality."[73] This extraordinary statement echoes
Baudrillard's theorization in *Simulacra and Simulation* that history is a lost reference
that has become society's myth. Baudrillard claimed that society replaced reality with
the signs and symbols of its simulation so that conceptions of history and truth are constantly eroded. Cinema is, therefore, at the "service of reanimating what it itself contributed to liquidating."[74]

> Concurrently with this effort towards and absolute correspondence with the real,
> cinema also approaches an absolute correspondence with itself—and this is not
> contradictory: it is the very definition of the hyperreal.[75]

Baudrillard's assertion was that hyperreality occurs when reality and fiction are blended
(or mashed), and fiction emerges as the victor. The simulation does not simply trick an

audience into believing in a false entity, but signifies the destruction of an original real-ity that it has replaced. Several critics—who found Tarantino's approach distasteful—saw the theoretical concern posed by Baudrillard clearly articulated in the film's flagrant distortion of some of the defining aspects of the war. In particular, Daniel Mendelsohn argued that Tarantino's celebration of vengeful violence exposed the fragility of mem-ory, warped the representation of the past, and ultimately had the effect of turning Jews into Nazis.[76] On his blog, Jonathan Rosenbaum called the film deeply offensive, pro-foundly stupid, and akin to Holocaust denial. For Rosenbaum, the diffusion of histori-cal truth in *Inglourious Basterds* (with its reality derived only from other movies) made "the Holocaust harder, not easier to grasp."[77] Interestingly, Tarantino seems to have started with the intention of honoring history, but during the writing process changed his approach because: "My characters don't know they're a part of history."[78] Tarantino further explained:

> For people of my generation and younger, I didn't want to trap the film in that period bubble…I was very influenced by Hollywood propaganda movies made during World War II. Most were made by directors living in Hollywood because the Nazis had taken over their countries…I wasn't taking anything from them stylistically, but what struck me about those movies was that they were made during the war, when the Nazis were still a threat, and these filmmakers probably had had personal experiences with the Nazis, or were worried to death about their families in Europe. Yet these movies are entertaining, they're funny, there's humor in them…. They're allowed to be thrilling adventures.[79]

At first glance, *Inglourious Basterds* seems utterly unconcerned with the ethics of war or the accuracy of history and is instead focused on the power of cinema. The charac-ters, for example, include a British soldier who used to be a film scholar and a German movie star working as a double agent. The climax of the film depends on the flamma-bility of nitrate film stock. Trapped in a movie theater, the audience is consumed by flames while Shoshanna's phantasmagorical effigy laughs hysterically as they burn and exclaims: "This is the face of Jewish vengeance." When Hitler is assassinated, countless rounds of machine gun fire, resonating with the force of wish fulfillment, disintegrate his body. Tarantino indulges in the latent bloodlust of revenge, but the film is not just a revenge fantasy. In the climactic moments, there is an emphatic rupture between his-torical reality and its representation, raising numerous questions about the exploitative influence of cinema and the morality of vengeance. There is a moral consequence to the audience's cathartic response that forces it to confront its own spectatorial position.

Films reshape history even when they are resolutely faithful, and history is always recounted from a particular perspective or with an agenda. The public memory of war in the twentieth century has arguably been created more by a manufactured past than a remembered one, as John Chambers and David Culbert remind us.[80] By so shamelessly rewriting history and making the mechanics of the process overt, *Inglourious Basterds* ultimately demands its audience ignore truth in a bold assertion of the fantastical power of the cinema. But fiction does not emerge as the victor. There is no sense in which reality has been replaced or eroded because the film continually signals and questions the act of its own representation.

The rejection of realism throughout the film has been explicitly demanded through the use of mashup techniques that highlight numerous liminal spaces and call to question everything that the film presents. *Inglourious Basterds* ultimately problematizes the nature of historical (mis)representation, both in film generally and in the war movie specifically. The film sets up typical war movie conventions, but considers them in new ways by drawing attention to them and questioning their cultural dominance. The use of spaghetti-western music, in particular, seems designed to scrutinize the very issues that Baudrillard identified in relation to the real and hyperreal. The film is so audacious that it seems a direct challenge to Baudrillard's pessimistic view of postmodern society's perceived inability to distinguish between reality and its representation. The film is undoubtedly an inglorious bastardization, but surely that is the point?

In a clearly demarcated cinematic fantasy space, the audience is constantly caught in-between: between genres, between historical fact and fiction, between music tracks that belong simultaneously in several contextual locations—there is even a gap between Ennio Morricone's music and the ghostly presence of the composer who nearly "scored" the film. The approach taken in *Inglourious Basterds* exemplifies the aesthetic sensibilities of mashup in which appropriation, re-invention, and re-signification are fundamental goals. Tarantino adores the liminal space and places the audience at its center in order to celebrate multifarious resonant, provocative, and problematic associations.

Notes

1. Claudia Gorbman, "Auteur Music," in *Beyond the Soundtrack*, ed. Daniel Goldmark, Lawrence Kramer and Richard Leppert (Berkeley: University of California Press, 2007), 150.
2. Robert Miklitsch, *Roll over Adorno: Critical Theory, Popular Culture, Audiovisual Media* (New York: State University of New York, 2006), 13.
3. Fred Botting and Scott Wilson, *The Tarantinian Ethics* (London: Sage, 2001), 165.
4. Travis Anderson, "Unleashing Nietzsche on the Tragic Infrastructure of Tarantino's *Reservoir Dogs*," in *Quentin Tarantino and Philosophy*, ed. Richard Greene and K. Silem Mohammad (Chicago and La Salle, IL: Open Court, 2007), 36.
5. Jonathan Romney and Adrian Wootton, *Celluloid Jukebox: Popular Music and the Movies Since the 1950s* (London: BFI, 1995), 127.
6. Quentin Tarantino, "Masterclass" (Cannes Film Festival, Salle Debussy, hosted by Michel Ciment, May 22, 2008).
7. Tarantino has refused to explain the misspellings in the title *Inglourious Basterds* by citing the artistic flourishes in the work of Jean-Michel Basquiat: "If he describes why he did it, he might as well not have done it at all." Associated Press, "Inglourious Basterds Has One Tricky Title," *MSNBC.com*, August 27, 2009, http://www.msnbc.msn.com/id/32588484. Tarantino was inspired by Enzo G. Castellari's 1978 war film *Quel maledetto treno blindato* (*The Inglorious Basterds*).

8. Nick Vivarelli, "Morricone Accepts Inglorious Offer," *Variety*, November 14, 2008, http://www.variety.com/article/VR1117995914?refCatId=2525.

9. Ennio Morricone's Website, accessed July 10, 2009, http://www.enniomorricone.it/

10. Ann Donahue, "Tarantino digs into record collection for Basterds," *Reuters,* August 21, 2009, http://www.reuters.com/article/idUSTRE57K4T520090821.

11. In fact, there is only one preexisting track used in the entire movie that does not have a clear referential filmic context, Rare Earth's interpretation of Ray Charles' hit "What'd I Say" (1972). The small section used is taken from the unusual coda/outro that bears almost no relation to the rest of the track. It is also purely instrumental.

12. Ken Garner, "Would You Like to Hear Some Music? Music-in-and-out-of Control in the Films of Quentin Tarantino," in *Film Music: Critical Approaches*, ed. K. J. Donnelly (Edinburgh: Edinburgh University Press, 2001), 189.

13. Mashup artists, many of whom are amateur enthusiasts, use audio-editing software to splice and merge pop songs and produce hybrid recordings that are shared and discussed in online message boards. The most infamous example of musical mashup is DJ Dangermouse's *Grey Album* (2004) that fused rapper Jay-Z's *The Black Album* (2003) with the Beatles' eponymous album *The Beatles* (1968), which is more commonly known as *The White Album*. See Michael Ayers, *Cybersounds: Essays on Virtual Music Culture* (New York: Peter Lang, 2006).

14. Stefan Sonvilla-Weiss, *Mashup Cultures* (Wien: Springer Verlag, 2010), 8.

15. The Basterds may be more historically founded than they initially appear. The Jewish Infantry Brigade Group within the British Army was formed in late 1944 and fought, under the Zionist flag, against the Germans in Italy from March 1945 until the end of the war in May 1945.

16. Daniel Mendelsohn, "When Jews Attack," *Newsweek*, August 24, 2009: 73.

17. Jean Baudrillard, *Simulacra and Simulation*, trans. Sheila Faria Glaser (Ann Arbor: University of Michigan Press, 1994).

18. Quentin Tarantino, interview by Elvis Mitchell, "Quentin Tarantino on *Inglourious Basterds*: The Music," *Inglourious Basterds—Motion Picture Soundtrack*, Warner Bros., ASIN: B002KU6AO8, 2009, mp3 music.

19. See for example, Michel Chion, *Audio-vision: Sound on Screen* (New York: Columbia University Press, 1994); and Nicholas Cook, *Analysing Musical Multimedia* (Oxford: Oxford University Press, 1998).

20. Keith M. Booker, "Like Something from a Movie: Film as the Object of Representation in Postmodern Popular Film," in *Postmodern Hollywood: What's New in Film and Why It Makes Us Feel So Strange*, ed. Keith M. Booker (Westport, CT: Praeger, 2007), 89–150; Peter Hanson, *The Cinema of Generation X: A Critical Study of Films and Directors* (Jefferson, NC: McFarland & Co, 2002).

21. Lisa Coulthard, "Torture Tunes: Tarantino, Popular Music, and New Hollywood Ultraviolence," *Music and the Moving Image* 2, no. 2 (2007): 1–6.

22. Sukhdev Sandhu, "Inglourious Basterds, review," *Telegraph*, August 20, 2009, http://www.telegraph.co.uk/culture/film/filmreviews/6060344/Inglourious-Basterds-review.html.

23. Peter Bradshaw, "Inglourious Basterds," *Guardian*, August 19, 2009, http://www.guardian.co.uk/film/2009/aug/19/inglourious-basterds-review-brad-pitt-quentin-tarantino. It is worth noting that, despite some lukewarm critical reviews, the film eventually achieved eight Academy Award nominations and six BAFTA nominations.

24. Michael Serazio, "The Apolitical Irony of Generation Mashup: A Cultural Case Study," *Popular Music and Society* 31, no. 1 (2008): 91.

25. Serazio, "The Apolitical Irony of Generation Mashup," 92.

26. John Shiga "Copy-and-Persist: The Logic of Mashup Culture," *Critical Studies in Media Communication* 24, no. 2 (2007): 97.

27. CCC, "Stand by Me," MP3, accessed December 12, 2011, http://www.hello.dj/ccc/sweetest-apples.

28. DJ Lobsterdust, "Nirgaga," MP3, accessed December 12, 2011, http://djlobsterdust.com/index.php/mashups/nirvana-vs-lady-gaga/.

29. Girl Talk's approach is exemplified by the album *All Day* (2010), available to download at: http://illegal-art.net/allday/. DJ Earworm has become best known for his annual *United States of Pop*, which mashes up the top-selling 25 songs of the year. Further details at: http://djearworm.com/ (last accessed December 15, 2011).

30. Shiga, "Copy-and-Persist," 99.

31. Quentin Tarantino, "Quentin Tarantino Interview," *The Tarantino Connection*, MCA MCD 80325, 1996, compact disc.

32. Quentin Tarantino, interview by Michaela Latham, "Quentin Tarantino: Kill Bill Vol. 1," *BBC Online*, June 10, 2003, http://www.bbc.co.uk/films/2003/10/06/quentin_tarantino_kill_bill_volume1_interview.shtml.

33. Kreshnik Musmurati, for example, created a spoof movie trailer that mashes *Inglourious Basterds* with Pixar's family animation *Ratatouille*. See Kreshnik Musmurati, "Inglourious Basterds & Pixar's Ratatouille (MashUp)," video, 1:42, accessed December 12, 2011, http://www.thetrailermash.com/nglourious-basterds-pixars-ratatouille-trailer-mashup-action/.

34. Coulthard, "Torture Tunes," 1–6.

35. Blaxploitation movies emerged in the early 1970s and featured African-American actors in leading roles. The films were made specifically for an urban, black audience and frequently featured antiestablishment plots as well as the glorification of violence.

36. Tarantino, interview by Mitchell, 2009.

37. Charles Bernstein's use of Jew's harp in *White Lightning* may, in fact, have been influenced by Morricone's use of the instrument in *The Good, The Bad and The Ugly*, a few years earlier.

38. Tarantino, interview by Mitchell, 2009.

39. The film's sociocultural production context is key. Wayne was a founding member of the Motion Picture Alliance in the late 1940s, which was established to protect the film industry from the perceived threat of communism to the American way of life.

40. Composer and arranger Nick Perito is best known for his work as music director for Perry Como. His version of "The Green Leaves of Summer" was released as a seven-inch single in November of the same year as *The Alamo*, United Artists/London Records [UK], #45-HLT 9221, 1960, 45 rpm.

41. "Reviews of This Week's LP's," *Billboard Magazine,* November 7, 1960: 37. The Brothers Four's version of the song, which was added to the soundtrack album, was also released as a single and reached No. 65 in the Billboard Hot 100.

42. Tiomkin's score for *The Alamo*, including "The Green Leaves of Summer," is held in the Tiomkin Collection at the University of Southern California.

43. Bernardo Bertolucci, in *Ennio Morricone*, directed by David Thompson (London: BBC Films, 1995), television documentary.

44. Simon Frith, *Music for Pleasure: Essays in the Sociology of Pop* (New York: Routledge, 1988), 141.

45. Simon Frith, "Mood Music: An Inquiry Into Narrative Film Music," *Screen* 25, no. 3 (1984): 83.

46. The spaghetti western was also part of a broader movement of postwar revisionist westerns that favored realism over romanticism. Notable examples include Sam Peckinpah's *The Wild Bunch* (1969), Arthur Penn's *Little Big Man* (1970), and Robert Altman's *McCabe and Mrs Miller* (1971). See Patrick McGee, *From Shane to Kill Bill: Rethinking the Western* (Oxford: Blackwell Publishing, 2007).

47. Richard T. Jameson, "Something to do With Death: A Fistful of Sergio Leone," *Film Comment*, March–April 1973: 11.

48. Royal S. Brown, *Overtones and Undertones: Reading Film Music* (New York: Columbia University Press, 1994): 227, 228.

49. Jeff Smith, *The Sounds of Commerce: Marketing Popular Film Music* (New York: Columbia University Press, 1998), 131.

50. Ennio Moricone, in *Ennio Morricone*, directed by David Thompson (London: BBC Films, 1995), television documentary.

51. Christopher Frayling, *Sergio Leone: Something to Do with Death* (London: Faber, 2000), 153–158.

52. Frayling, *Sergio Leone: Something to do with Death*, 155. This remains an uncommon working process within commercial filmmaking. Perhaps is it not surprising to discover that Tarantino also likes to play music on set.

53. Sergio Miceli, *Morricone: la musica, il cinema* (Modena, Italy: Mucchi Editore, 1994), 15–17; see also Charles Leinberger, Ennio Morricone's *The Good, the Bad and the Ugly: A film score guide* (Lanham, MD: Scarecrow Press, 2004).

54. Tarantino, interview by Mitchell, 2009.

55. Ibid.

56. Richard E. Etlin, *Art, Culture, and Media Under the Third Reich* (Chicago: Chicago University Press, 2002), 162.

57. Anselm Gerhard, "Musicology in the 'Third Reich': A Preliminary Report," *The Journal of Musicology* 18, no. 4 (Autumn 2001): 517–543; Pamela Potter, *Most German of the Arts: Musicology and Society from the Weimar Republic to the End of Hitler's Reich* (New Haven, CT: Yale University Press, 1998); and Pamela M. Potter "What is 'Nazi Music'?" *Musical Quarterly* 88, no. 3 (2005): 428–455.

58. Miceli identifies the three distinct sounds in *The Good, the Bad and the Ugly* as a soprano recorder, two male voices treated electronically, and a bass ocarina. *Morricone: la musica, il cinema*, 134.

59. Christopher Frayling, *Once Upon a Time in Italy: The Westerns of Sergio Leone* (New York: Harry N. Abrams in association with the Autry National Center, 2005), 97.

60. Sean Cubitt, *The Cinema Effect* (Cambridge, MA: MIT Press, 2004), 213.

61. Quentin Tarantino, interview by Ella Taylor, "Quentin Tarantino: The *Inglourious Basterds* Interview," *Village Voice*, August 18, 2009, http://www.villagevoice.com/2009-08-18/news/quentin-tarantino-the-inglourious-basterds-interview/2//.

62. It is an expansive theme that exists in several versions—instrumental and vocal—within its original film context. *Revolver* is the story of a prison warden (Vito Cipriani) who is forced to release a convict (Milo Ruiz) in exchange for his wife who has been kidknapped. A subplot, however, concerns a French folksinger who becomes embroiled in the scheme and is used as an unwitting pawn. At various points in the film, we hear the singer perform his biggest hit, a vocal version of the Morricone track entitled "Un Ami."

63. Phil Powrie, "Blonde Abjection: Spectatorship and the Abject Anal Space In-between," in *Pop Fiction: The Song in Cinema*, ed. Steve Lannin and Matthew Caley (Bristol: Intellect, 2005), 100.

64. Coulthard, "Torture Tunes," 2.

65. Ibid.

66. Gregg Redner, *Deleuze and Film Music: Building a Methodological Bridge Between Film Theory and Music* (Bristol: Intellect, 2011).

67. Gilles Deleuze, *Francis Bacon: The Logic of Sensation*, trans. Daniel W. Smith (London: Continuum, 2003).

68. Gilles Deleuze and Felix Guattari, *What Is Philosophy?*, trans. Hugh Tomlinson and Graham Burchell (New York: Columbia University Press, 1994), 164.

69. Redner, *Deleuze and Film Music*, 45.

70. Quentin Tarantino, interview by Elvis Mitchell, 2009.

71. Quentin Tarantino, interview by Rene Rodriguez, "Remaking History: An Interview with Quentin Tarantino," *Pop Matters*, August 18, 2009, http://www.popmatters.com/pm/featu re/109973-remaking-history-an-interview-with-quentin-tarantino/.

72. It is worth noting that Tarantino used the single version of "Cat People (Putting Out Fire)" by Giorgio Moroder and David Bowie, which is 2.5 minutes shorter than the extended track that appeared on Paul Schrader's film. Tarantino did not use the "commercial" version of the song that Bowie re-recorded for the album *Let's Dance* in 1983.

73. Quentin Tarantino, interview by Henri Sordeau, "Quentin Tarantino talks *Inglourious Basterds*—RT Interview," *Rotten Tomatoes*, August 11, 2009, http://uk.rottentomatoes. com/m/inglourious basterds/news/1837048/quentin_tarantino_talks_inglourious_ basterds_rt_interview.

74. Baudrillard, *Simulacra and Simulation*, 48.

75. Ibid., 47.

76. Mendelsohn, "When Jews Attack," 72–73.

77. Jonathan Rosenbaum, "Some Afterthoughts About Tarantino," *Notes* (blog), August 27, 2009, http://www.jonathanrosenbaum.com/?s=tarantino+holocaust+denial.

78. Tarantino, interview by Sordeau, 2009.

79. Tarantino, interview by Taylor, 2009.

80. John Whiteclay Chambers and David Culbert, *World War II, Film, and History* (New York and Oxford: Oxford University Press, 1996).

SELECT BIBLIOGRAPHY

Baudrillard, Jean. *Simulacra and Simulation*. Translated by Sheila Faria Glaser. Ann Arbor: University of Michigan Press, 1994.

Botting, Fred, and Scott Wilson. *The Tarantinian Ethics*. London: Sage, 2001.

Coulthard, Lisa. "Torture Tunes: Tarantino, Popular Music, and New Hollywood Ultraviolence." *Music and the Moving Image* 2, no. 2 (Summer 2007): 1–6.

Deleuze, Gilles, and Felix Guattari. *What Is Philosophy?* Translated by Hugh Tomlinson and Graham Burchell. New York: Columbia University Press, 1994.

Garner, Ken. "Would You Like to Hear Some Music? Music-in-and-out-of Control in the Films of Quentin Tarantino." In *Film Music: Critical Approaches*, edited by K. J. Donnelly, 188–205. Edinburgh: Edinburgh University Press, 2001.

Gorbman, Claudia. "Auteur Music." In *Beyond the Soundtrack*, edited by Daniel Goldmark, Lawrence Kramer and Richard Leppert, 149–162. Berkeley: University of California Press, 2007.

Greene, Richard, and K. Silem Mohammad. *Quentin Tarantino and Philosophy*. Chicago: Open Court, 2007.

Redner, Gregg. *Deleuze and Film Music: Building a Methodological Bridge Between Film Theory and Music*. Bristol: Intellect, 2011.

Serazio, Michael. "The Apolitical Irony of Generation Mashup: A Cultural Case Study." *Popular Music and Society* 31, no. 1 (2008): 79–94.

Shiga, John. "Copy-and-Persist: The Logic of Mashup Culture." *Critical Studies in Media Communication* 24, no. 2 (2007): 93–114.

Sonvilla-Weiss, Stefan. *Mashup Cultures*. Wien: Springer Verlag, 2010.

PART VIII

DIALOGUE:
DE-CODING SOURCE
CODE

CHAPTER 27

....

SOUND THINKING

Looped Time, Duped Track

....

GARRETT STEWART

SOUND *AND* IMAGE IN NEW MEDIA

....

IN conventional cinematic realism, of course, it is seemingly a case of sound *from* image. Can that priority be reversed, with sound *mediating* image? And how might the newness of electronic media be involved in this inverted hierarchy? What would such a thing look like, sound like, in mainstream moviegoing, quite apart from video installations? These are questions that actually have answers, as well as some new evidence. The answers come in part from philosophy, the evidence from a recent and superficial sci-fi film that, as much in its way as multichannel video art, resists any relaxation into the "audiovisual" as one seamless entity. A movie doesn't have to "work," in the sense of being wholly coherent or persuasive, in order to solicit a viewer's working out of its inferences—and this without dodging its contradictions. For cinema, as philosopher Gilles Deleuze insisted across his two volumes on film art, in addition to both thinking in images and thus imaging thought, is also a machine for the production of thought in its *audi*ence (etymologically: its listening spectator, not just its viewer).

Much depends on the plotted interplay of optical frameline and soundtrack. It's one thing in Martin Scorsese's crime epic *Goodfellas* (1990), for instance, to find the cinematic license of classic voiceover anchored in the end to a confessing gang member on the witness stand, so that the "historical present" of narrative retrospect has become legal testimony: adventure under the sign of incrimination, ongoing action of time past, crime of record. It is one thing, in other words, and in the words now of Michel Chion, to have the *acousmêtre*—the acoustic "being" of an off-screen voice—tethered at last to the self-narrated body, with the result, also in Chion's terms (although not applied to this film), that the eerie and penetrating power of the overvoice is paradoxically "castrated"

(because wholly internalized) by embodiment—and thus subject in this case to apprehension and sentencing.[1] It's another thing altogether, in the sci-fi thriller *Source Code*
(Duncan Jones, 2001), not to be confused with Mike Figgis's *Timecode* (2000), to find
the voice itself fictionalized from the start through its prosthetic association with a literally castrated human form preserved in suspended animation in a computer-assisted
coma.[2] But it is not a wholly unfamiliar thing. In considering the relation between image
and sound in electronic media, as registered on the slant by narrative cinema, one notes
how not a few films, sci-fi narratives prominent among them, would file under "new
digitized media" the audio-optic sensorium of the human body itself as rewired transmission device.

For such thematized anomalies of the voice track, however, there are also different
terms ready to hand. As a genre film of the criminal underworld, *Goodfellas* is all action,
dependent on the *movement-image* for its plot momentum. At the same time, given
its operation as metageneric gangster film, the vocal "frame-up" of its narrative arc as
criminal investigation turns it to a *time-image* as one long retroactive flashback floated
somewhere between witness and jury, narrator and audience. Chion's acousmatic (invis-
ibly sourced) voice becomes the *sonsign* of a temporal retrospect that, in the last scene,
compromises the purity of narrative as *memory-image* with the forensic motivations of
arraignment and punishment. Markedly recast in this way are those *sheets of the past*
that have been emphasized in their cinematic planarity by Scorsese's punctuating freeze
frames along the way. So, too, in *Source Code*, where these "sheets" are electronically
dealt out and reshuffled until a digital freeze breaks the time-loop structure with its own
decidedly silent *opsign* of ontological rupture.

In rephrasing such plots in this fashion, I've shifted terms from the vocabulary
of Chion to that of Deleuze.[3] And I've done so in the spirit of my own terminology in
Framed Time, a study that follows Deleuze's interrogative lead in the closing speculation
from his second cinema volume, *The Time-Image*, about whether (writing as he was in
the early 1980s) the "numeric image" at the onset of computerized visuals would operate from within and so transfigure the postwar time-image—or inaugurate a whole new
digital regime.[4] (Deleuze's open-ended question is one more way of wondering, as many
still do, whether the move from classical to modern actually cedes to something unto
itself that should be known as postmodern.)

My attempt to think along with—and historically beyond—Deleuze in this regard
led me to concentrate, in *Framed Time,* on the first decade after the 1995 centenary of
photomechanical film and the elusive new weave of theme and electronic medium that
characterized so many of its proliferating fantasy plots. These are plots whose technical machination (and sidelined digital anxiety) often seemed to traverse the very difference, material and historical both, between two dispensations of cinema, filmic and
postfilmic: that is, for example, between the integral photo-cell on a spooling strip and
the digital scan of computer-generated imaging (CGI) or the more ubiquitous techniques of computer editing. This difference is recruited by certain plots, a surprising
number, to figure the on-screen manifestation (and mutation) of frame/d time. As in
the phonetic "lap dissolve" of that very phrase, the increment is in one way or the other,

through the advance of the frameline or the binary scan, disappeared by the image. Such narratives involve the phenomenological image as optical sign in movies (no longer entirely "films") characterized by an exponential incorporation of CGI effects but tending toward an active suppression of computerization as theme. I extend that investigation now, with one recent and exacerbated case in point, into the realm of the Deleuzian *sonsign*, where the signifying voice or noise can also be found to operate—not unlike the visual morphing of the contorted time travel or "temportation" plots I analyze in *Framed Time*—more as a travesty of the "time-image" than as a philosophical extension of its parameters. My case in point, with *Source Code*, is a film in which the belated (and indeed, at one level, posthumous) suppression of digital phobias, after a plot-long dystopian ordeal centered on the temporal distortions of invasive computer science, arrives with a last-ditch and unconvincing cell-phone euphoria ("new media" degree zero) in transmission within a digitally generated parallel universe.

This technically silent (but narratively "recited") text message is sent by a veritable military prisoner sprung at last by the very technology that has previously entrapped him. This comatose soldier's severed body has been rewired for a secret time-travel mission, computer boosted into an alternate reality of supposed limited duration, and then finally aided (by a sympathetic captor) in fleeing there forever. In the process, human temporality is furiously refigured, or disfigured, by every aspect of the film's time-loop fantasy. Hinged around this degradation of the time-image from philosophy to plot monstrosity, and in particular of the *sonsign* from philosopheme to diegetic irony, Jones's film also mobilizes most of the other topoi of the Deleuzian time-image that I have traced in atrophied or equipmental form in turn-of-the-millennium cinema. These are divided in their effects around Deleuze's own rough-hewn but useful distinction (following Antonioni)—as regards certain typical earlier avatars of the time-image—between "European cinema" (the art narrative) and "American science fiction," as, for instance, between *Last Year at Marienbad* and the equally fateful calendrical designation of *2001: A Space Odyssey*. In contrast to the doubled body as reciprocal and sutured focal point for its own death and transfiguration at the end of Kubrick's narrative, as marked by the alternate *sonsigns* of its helmet-encased breathing, in *Source Code,* the ontological duplication of the out-of-body sensorium enters a computer-driven time-loop in which the putative body of the military agent we've been watching, as flashpoint of the movement-image, is revealed to be entirely virtual in its every corporeal and temporal aspect, including its merely "signified" rather than supposedly audited voice.

I work from the assumption that the issue of "sound and image in new media" is no less an issue, beyond gallery installation or digital poetics, when the new media in question are subordinated either to technical enhancements or plotted topics in standard narrative fare. And not least in a film like *Source Code,* in which the proverbial testings of the quest hero resemble the overcome challenges, from level to level, of a supercharged video game in which he is all avatar, no input. In the process, this is a film whose plot grimly prevents, and then ends up bluntly finessing, the normal coincidence of "image and sound" in the embodied plot agent that regularly distinguishes mainstream production from "new media art"—or, for that matter, the Deleuzian "movement-image" of classic screen action from the "time-image" of later innovation. And it operates this transformation of audiovisual norms by a belated disclosure of the revealed anomalies of its voice track in unexpected contrast to the traditional overscoring of a classic non-diegetic soundtrack. The cutting-edge digital tech of the dystopian plot has no echoes in the conservative classic score, no electronic music to enhance the technophobia of the hero's predicament. But this, too, may be part of the film's building irony. We are lulled into commonplace audiovisual expectations—only to encounter them later in macabre refusal. The "program music" of orchestral dramaturgy steps off its progress across the plot in a wholly predictable interplay of musical effects entirely nondiegetic (unsourced in the story world)—until it turns out (only plot will eventually explain) that the hero's own voice is equally unsourced, nondiegetic, as much a disincarnate overlay as the unseen production of his theme music. It is hard to overstate the force of this ontological jolt, this eviscerated Deleuzian *sonsign*.

Deleuze has a unique gift, to be sure, for taxonomizing, amid other ingredients of his semiology, the noosigns (thought-signs) in postwar film, those moments where cinematic mediation demands a kind of interpretive meditation on the very time of sound figure or visual image. But, outside of those notable films in the modernist vein raising variously profound roadblocks to passive viewing, such a demand can remain entirely implicit. Yet with cinema conceived as a machine *for* as well as of thought, even a formulaic narrative and its slick twists can, if not wax philosophical, at least jog ideas never broached by its own storytelling. In doing so, it may even take the unexpected measure of its own medial basis, including the sound/image composite of traditional screen projection. To phrase this composite in the kind of linguistic play that in its own right keeps eye and ear, script and phonemic undertext, in reciprocal suspension, this signifying force field might be identified as the never arrested temporal flux of *oculaurality*.

What then, to review, are those signature gestures of the Deleuzian time-image that now so often, and in *Source Code* so flagrantly, get twisted into sci-fi knots? And how might they, too, engender, cheapen, or disable that shift from watching to thinking, from reception to reflection, that everywhere inflects Deleuze's account of screen tempo-rality in its ocular and aural valences? How, in short, might the aberrant sound/image ratio in *Source Code* operate, if you will, as *cinementation*? In his modernist paradigm, Deleuze stresses those more or less existential manifestations of time-consciousness that break with the sensorimotor continuum. These include, on half a dozen salient fronts, the (1) "forking" narrative, often involving the spatiotemporal disorientation of (2) "any-space-whatever"; the diegetic prominence of (3) "the telepath" and (4) "the dou-ble" as part of a underlying conversion of protagonists from motor agents to (5) "specta-tors" within and *of* their own experience; and, finally, the links between screen and brain modeled on the concept of cinema as (6) "spiritual automaton," the very mechanization of a cognitive being-in-the-world.[5] Extrapolated from the cinematographic experiments of high modernism and redistributed across the time-loop fictions and forking-path narratives of recent CGI-heavy cinema, as they often are, these crisis points of senso-rimotor discontinuity come to an extreme concentration in *Source Code*. This is a film, as we'll see in detail (as one can only see in detail), where (1) iterated forks in time, computer instigated, teleport the protagonist as sheer optico-auditory probe into the (2) "any-space-whatever" of variable reconnaissance targeting as a remote-controlled (3) "pathic" medium and (4) doppelganger (inhabiting, in the film's own lingo, the "synaptic map" of a dead man) for a serial séance channeled through this sheer machinic (5) "spectator" whose near-corpse as (6) "spiritual" entity is wholly "automatized" and all but robotically maintained as a kind of quasi-somatic filtering (rather than screening) device in an out-of-body surveillance circuit.

As part of this artifice, the standard-issue synchronous voicing of his speaking image is a more than ordinary illusion that gets finally disclosed—at an unforeseen peripety en route toward a further trick ending—as the utter divorce, diegetically presented, of the speaking subject from all sensorimotor continuum on screen. Undermined in this way (despite faux close-ups) is the Deleuzian "affection-image" that offers such a crucial hinge between action and reaction, cause and effect, in his understanding of traditional movement-image cinema. The time-image has hereby outsmarted itself in yet another baroque sci-fi form, sabotaged its own axiomatic basis (and springboard) in the credited phenomenology of human gesture, human movement. Without this realist basis, time (as exploratory image or idea) has nothing to immobilize, break with, or dilate upon. How this double-bind operates in *Source Code*, and with what narrative blowback, what metaphysical repercussions, only plot can tell, even when it isn't wholly leveling with us. Attention to the audio/visual tension of this one action thriller (all primary action being in fact computer-fabricated, a mirage for the hero as well as for us) can also serve to complement a certain one-sided emphasis in *Framed Time* on the digitized visual (rather than audial) ironies of recent screen practice, a practice that, as much since the invention of the CD as since that of the DVD, often thematizes the electronic dimension of its own medium.

VIDEO ERGO SUM: THE SEEING GUY

I see, therefore, in Bergsonian (Deleuzian) more than Cartesian terms, I am: centered indeterminately in the world-as-image. Unless.... And here is where the sci-fi premise often rears its head, staging an exception that, in the case of *Source Code*, involves the brutal coercion of sightless eyes. The optic of consciousness, the seeing I of human cognition, once reduced to nothing more than inert "viewing" in the inhibited action of modernist cinema, is pushed over the edge by a sci-fi plot of computerized second sight laboring to keep its paradoxes straight. An American pilot downed and dismembered on a mission in Afghanistan is given, instead of a body bag, a return "tour" of duty in the morbidly specular sense, and this time only on the Homeland Security front. His somatic remains are repurposed by cybernetic prosthesis as a reconnaissance apparatus hooked up to a paramilitary computer program that allows for "time reassignment," so that he can be projected (the latent cinematic trope) into the residual neural traces of a victim slain by a terrorist bomb on a commuter train.

The protagonist is thus charged (electronically) to invade by remote control the dead man's trace memories and find the terrorist, not to prevent the disaster that has already happened but, rather, to allow an interception of the culprit before he sets off a threat-ened dirty bomb in downtown Chicago. Across the length of plot, we alternate in a kind of hypertrophic parallel montage between the hero catapulted time and again onto the speeding train, until yet again incinerated, and his debriefing in the podlike chamber, reminiscent of a downed cockpit, that he assumes at first is a simulator (or "sim," as he calls it) in a virtual combat trainer. Slowly, he ferrets out the truth: that the only death he has not yet died for his country is total brain death. Linked to a life-support system, his cerebral cortex—as the formulaic "mad scientist" explains in the clichéd idioms of "par-abolic calculus"—is activated as a remote wireless feed from the residual brain waves of a blast victim whose synapses have retained, for looped replay now, the last minutes of cognition "like a surveillance camera in a convenience store at closing time."

As it turns out, the morphing capsule that imprisons the hero is altogether simulated, even his own body a mere digital "manifestation" as well: an internalized CGI effect to help "orient him" in his spectatorial assignment as mobile surveillance antenna, a sort of human drone. The movement-image has thus gone entirely virtual when out-of-body action renders all spatiotemporal whereabouts an "any-space-whatever" assimilated by electronic tap. In lieu of real action, though, there is in part a cinematic reflex action. In seeming to recognize even his own body, the hero is only seeing things; we accept this as if knowing that, even in more normative circumstances, the movie actor only embodies a given character on screen in a provisional way. Jake Gyllenhaal is only there, after all, to "orient" us toward the character Colter Stephens, who in this case, this anomalous diegetic case, has survived his own proper body.

But other narrative perturbations do not so easily dissipate into that mode of metalep-sis where aesthetic first cause is inserted as plot effect. Even though we know we've been "had," tricked, by seeing his image all along—pandered to as much as he has been—we're still shocked, late in the film, at the sight of his disemboweled carcass in a hold-ing tank next door to the computer monitors of his mission controllers, with electrodes wired to his eviscerated torso and brain. And shocked, almost more, to find, just before this, that the fact of his disembodiment has been accepted by the manipulative scientific and military personnel running his mission in ways we hadn't foreseen. Suddenly, we realize that the separate camera and mike into which they have been peering and speak-ing in sutured exchanges with the hero (Figure 27.1), as registered on more than one visible monitor in his subjective pod, have presumed a living image of him that, quite to the contrary, has been not just virtual but wholly "fictive." When we finally spot the monitor at which we had assumed they were viewing his (albeit simulated) image, and from whose speakers we thought they were following his vocal reports, we see that he has been coming through to them, all along, merely as a text message scrolling across the screen (Figure 27.2). No attempt at voice-recognition software has converted his brain waves into vocal sounds, any more than he has been hearing their commands as actual oral prompts. The time-image, in this grotesque form of bodily effacement within a recycled violence, has evacuated even the movement of sound waves from the space of sheer telepresence. As if revising a classic case of the "acousmetric" uncanny, it is as if the narrative voiceover from beyond the grave in *Sunset Boulevard* has not just been

FIGURE 27.1

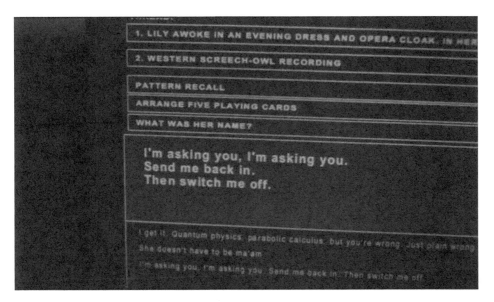

FIGURE 27.2

internalized by the diegesis as the case of a "talking" corpse but denied there even the phonics of its own messaging.

It's hard to take this in at first, but there's no getting past it. We've been made to see that the eyes in what's left of the soldier's body twitch behind closed lids. What Colter has thus been "seeing" from the start is an electrode feed, bypassing all eyesight, of his military controller, Goodwin, and her civilian boss. The screens in the pod, like the pod itself, are part of the heuristic mirage. They're what would keep him from thinking he was virtually dead, at least until he wises up. (In fact, he often "talks to" his keeper without even looking toward the transmitted image of her that we see in the capsule; the whole thing feels "set up" for us as well as for him.) Only one early clue, minor at that, prepares for the later disclosure. After the neurological shock and "manifested" physical damage of his first mission, with the monitors spluttering out of commission, Goodwin asks a technician whether Colter in his projected space "has a visual signal" again yet— rather than whether he, say, "has image." When the cover of his strictly virtual perception is finally blown, we recognize the true and violent remediation that camerawork and track have until now euphemized in the service both of functional dramaturgy and final surprise: human face as sheer interface, voice as mere electronic pulse in orally dubbed transcription. And, in regard to the latter, there is perhaps a less marked anticipation at one late turning point of plot, easy to mistake as irrelevant tech gimmickry. This happens when the voice of Colter's father (from a radio interview about his son's heroism) is beamed into the pod as a shameless inducement for Colter to submit one last time to his mission—"beamed," that is, as a mobile graph of sound waves on the sudden manifestation of an oversize screen: the electronic trace of voice rather than its aural presence, mediated for us at one remove (and all but fully admitted as such this time) by a nondiegetic overdub.

In point of contemporary fact, a bizarre development in the latest NASA science comes bearing down on the film as if from the day before yesterday. One learns from the Web—where else?—that a technology is now in operation that can detect subvocal vibrations of the larynx and transmit them from one soldier to the submuscular impulses in the throat and cranium of another.[6] What results is the wireless immediacy of a direct verbal message invulnerable to being either drowned out by the noise of a firefight or (as of yet) aurally intercepted. The technology, NASA suggests explicitly, as if with Deleuze in mind, is closer to "telepathy" than "telephony." But it is across just that distinction—between thought transference and audial technology—that *Source Code* soon reverses its tracks by trick ending. After that pivotal disclosure of text messaging instead of the assumed transmission of speech, everyday I-phoning comes to the rescue with a last silent e-mail translated onto the sound track as if in a voice from beyond the grave.

This, too, requires a bit more plot to bring out—including an apparent digression that is in fact preparatory. That digressive plant first, with its thematic pertinence masked by smart-ass dialogue early on. The repatriated but out-of-step war hero asks the reiterated girl he keeps remeeting on the train if her mobile phone can connect to the internet, and she mocks him for his anachronistic innocence by saying that no, alas, it's only connected by a long string to her office. Little does she realize that her networked interlocutor is, as digital figment, a kind of embodied walkie-talkie rendered up-to-date with a military vengeance, whose beamed attention turns her former new acquaintance on the train (whose pending corpse the hero's reassigned forensic gaze now inhabits) into little more than a reanimated zombie, herself as well. More than she could guess or believe, even the "old-fashioned" mechanical vibrations that generate the airwaves of his voice in real time have been computer-duped by loop-time.

Further along in the unfolding (and refolding) plot, that initial and fateful text message on the laboratory monitor—by which we finally realize that the hero has never been audible to his operators—is melodramatically keyed to his request, "typed" or ciphered out on screen, for euthanasia rather than the planned "memory wipe" and reassignment. He wants only one more return to the otherwise doomed train to frustrate detonation by the (now identified) terrorist and thus, even though he is assured that his plan is scientifically impossible, to save that female victim he has fallen for in his reiterated time loops. This last wish of the bodiless operative is in fact granted by his sympathetic handler, Goodwin, his electronic spymaster. And when the button is pressed in this mercy killing, and the proverbial plug thus pulled, the moment of his release is marked by a "3D" digital freeze of the traincar—the camera roving past immobilized bodies—at the moment of a presumed last kiss. After which, by parallel montage, we revert to the resulting uproar in the lab and then return to the stop-action locomotive as the potential arrest of time, the classic *opsign* of death, is released again to action. But this preternatural action soon goes entirely off-screen in the hero's alternate reality with his "dream girl," the computerized version of an "any-space-whatever" not as a region of rootless anomie (as in the postwar examples of Deleuze) but as a digitally sprung utopia. The seeing I of human cognition—narrowed to that of a passive "spectator" in the Deleuzian time-image—is transmuted at this sci-fi turn into computerized simulation and its fantasized escape routes.

The realm of "the virtual," that privileged category for Deleuze (a realm opposed to the actual, but not to the real), has been too wholly technologized to keep intact anything like the philosophical valences of the authentic time-image. In digital sci-fi—often (but not always) digital in topic as well as in execution—an electronic virtuality tends instead to become actual at the expense of the real: taxing not just verisimilitude but often any genuine "thought" in the mode of the Deleuzian *noosign*. Here, again, is where the swerve from action to temporal cognition in the history of cinema takes a further swerve into electronic rather than simply cognitive virtuality—and ends up seeming to betray and parody rather than inhabit and expand the genuine time-image. Deleuze's historiography is concerned, as mentioned, with the transition from a cinema whose movement-image was primarily to be *seen* as such, to one whose action, or inaction, is largely to be *read*. Or, put it this way: from a naturalized *motion over time*, movement as an immanent phenomenon, to the elevation of *time over motion* as a sign function. At stake, in short, is the hermeneutic transition from mimesis to semiosis, where the *opsign* and the *sonsign* are together subsumed, if only by defaulted coherence, to the *noosign*: the screen's play of sight and sound taking not just shape but thought.

It is in this respect that Deleuze can announce, although with his own emphasis on visual rather than audial features, that "the three cerebral components" of cinema— where it may be said to take time, time out, for thought—"are the point-cut, relinkage and the black or white screen" (*Time-Image*, p. 215) As soon as the relinkage in question isn't subordinated to action via montage, a gap opens whose suspension must be rethought, especially when dilated into a reflective lacuna swallowing up a given scene into the rectangle, black or white, of sheerly potential image. Instead of a naturalistically "motivated" transition between images, we get their "irrational" abutting or their emptying out. Like so much other recent sci-fi, *Source Code* drags any such cerebration of the medium down to the plot level and so turns it flamboyantly but *merely* diegetic, forcing radical time-space disjuncture into a computer-driven engine of scopic displacement and remote surveillance. Into the black hole (sometimes the explosive white heat) of temporal disjuncture in *Source Code*, the nondiegetic privilege of the cut-on-action, basis of all temporal montage, has been pilfered from narrative license and installed in the diegesis as electronic magic, complete with the high-speed digital decomposition of the hero's own image in these quantum jump cuts (Figure 27.3). There is no thinking the connection between the near-dead pilot and the soon-again-dead body in which his synaptic tracery is, across an impossible ellipsis, relocated. Time is not isolated for reading; it is merely remobilized for fantasy. Time does not intercept and reconceptualize action; rather, the time-loop action thriller reduces time to a function of detective adventure. There is no thought-sign here, not yet at least, just the fictionalizing of cognition as a computer-duplicable teleport. So that the historical transition from editing motivated by action to the "irrational cut" is reversed in this case by narratively motivated cuts between different time "frames": leaps of both sound and image that are themselves, by genre convention, reasoned even if impossible, the very fabric of reality rent and spliced by digital engineering.

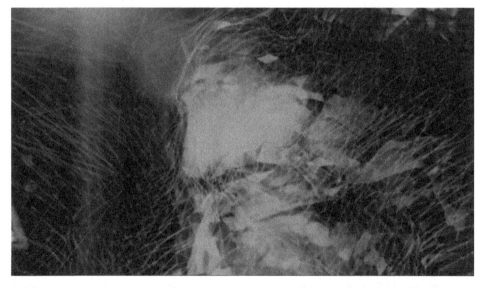

FIGURE 27.3

SONS SANS SENS: THE AUDIAL LIE

Part of the way plot enfolds its own execution in *Source Code*, as we've seen (or heard), involves cinema's inherent mechanics (but here perverse subterfuge) of the thrown voice—foregrounded at the end in symptomatically improbable ways. A final triumphant debriefing from the hero begins in voiceover, his image radically off camera in an alternate reality, from which he assures his mission controller that the computer's "Source Code" program, despite any intent or credible explanation, has in fact sourced a "whole new world." But back in the "real world," we quickly see, there is still work to be done and counsel to be taken from the near future. In the hero's last voiceover, we hear what the (equally) artificial intelligence of a smartphone scrolls out as silent text: "If you are getting this email, you will soon hear that a terrorist attempt has been thwarted." What? What's happening? Where are we? And when? In our mental scramble to grasp this further tricking of closure, we realize that Colter is somewhere far off camera within the same parallel universe we are now watching: making contact not with the space of his at last alleviated corpse but with an identical lab where, by temporal paradox, all missions are still pending for his humanoid broadcast platform.

Diegesis has here been given over entirely to the same parallel universe in which he has survived his mission by preventing the train disaster and can thus still reach his operator before the events of the film (the main plot) have ever taken place. His remote message is not more remote or electronically generated that the world in which it is received, and, by the time we figure this out, we realize the trick is itself figurative. For how real, even as absent, can this recognized voice be felt to be, a voice that has all along been a mere figment of poetic (and narratively deceptive) license? And how upbeat can this ending seem when the speaker's former operator—receiving the likes of an I-phone message from the organic android "I" of this incarnate biotech app—is still standing just a room away from a body not yet euthanized after all? This is the body about which the off-screen voice now speaks in third person, urging compassion when a mission does come in this militarization of Homeland Security: "Promise me you'll help him and, when you do, do me a favor, tell him everything's gonna be okay." That's because each brave soldierly triumph may well sponsor another parallel universe. Regardless of how many deaths you are compelled to die for your country—itself an allegorical trope for how many enlisted bodies command central pumps into the mission—there's the hope of a new (and amorous) afterlife each time. It's the stateside counterterrorist answer to a jihadist's harem in the sky.

So it is that the film's trick ending, where the time-loop is supposed to have become a loophole, is actually snagged by plot's own paradoxical logic. The fact that the utopian alter-world doesn't in fact alter the mortal trauma, the macabre half-life, of his artificially sustained heart, lungs, and brain—vestigial organs in this case, except for cognitive rewiring—is a quirk of the storyline that can scarcely squirm free from the broader aura of biopolitical paranoia that rims the film. There's no escaping the death of one's body. And as soon as we warm to the contrived fantasy of the ravaged soldier's doing so, we're back in the lab with his version of an immobilized rat on the computer treadmill, jerked back there by the double helix of plot itself. Yet no matter how many deaths he's made to endure, an equal number of computer-triggered afterlives, we are asked to accept, will ensue: u-topic erotic otherworlds where, even if he's still no more than an electronic signal (a cell phone stream) in "real time," his presence can be transfigured by a voice not his own and the body that goes with it in the virtual (but now digital and magical) zone of Deleuze's coordinate-free "any-space-whatever."

Further sleights of technique tip over into critique as well. Fleeing a remote electronic mission, this last remote *transmission* in *Source Code* offers a curious variant of the "unclosed quotation" in voiceover discussed by Michel Chion in his latest book, where the delegation of narrative to a character's speech summons a scene, flashback or otherwise, from which we never return to the site of the vocal prompt, as if the narration had "forgotten" to close its "quotation" (Film, *A Sound Art*, pp. 70–71). Here, instead, we have the case of an un*opened* quotation, begun in medias res from an unidentified space off camera. This is an out-of-field space from which, like the hero's own "voice" all along, sound is only "translated" from electronic signal (on the workaday handset) to phonetic trace—and only by the narrative's own ruse. Keyed to the movement-image (via intercutting) in a traditional enough manner, all would be well if we trusted this off-screen voice as vocal trope, one may say, for its strictly alphabetic reception back in the lab. But we have been trained—it may take us a moment to remember, within the plot's dizzy last twists—to doubt it utterly, especially when it is floating, ontologically adrift again, somewhere between a continuing operational deceit of narrative and the electronic irony of a final acousmatic impingement.

The cut the overvoice accompanies (the return from precipitated erotic idyll to high-tech lab) thus breaks with sensorimotor and acoustic conventions alike to pry open the space of thought—in this case, the repressed unconscious of the film's own premise. Such an acoustic phantasm, in this last burst of its uncanny power, could at any moment be leveled—Chion's term is again "castrated"—if, by edit or camera movement, it were to be locked down once more to a mere mortal body (or even its mere "materialization") in on-camera speech. And not least the foreign body: the once dead, then saved, then co-opted stranger on the train. This, we know from his driver's license, is one Sean Fentress, history teacher, now history himself within his own usurped and tenanted body, a body co-opted by a time-traveller whose voice track was previously plastered over an encapsuled virtual image unanchored to the off-frame remains of his own artificially animated cadaver. Parsing Chion's term for the "acousmetric voice" beyond his own usage, we may sense (even with cases less byzantine than *Source Code*) that in the acoustic being (*être*) of the out-of-frame voice resides, in fact, but only when unlocated in a vocal source, the acoustic master (*maître*) of its mysterious and pervasive charge. But, in Jones' film, that voice (even when "hallucinated" on-camera) has never before been really audited from the barely respiring body. Possible now, long-distance, only through the vibrating vocal chords of the stranger's body our hero has so happily snatched, such a voice remains permanently dissociated from the metallic lair of the hero's abject, dismembered carcass on screen. Never the twain shall meet—even, as we've seen, grammatically. (Do me a last favor for him.)

There is a further history here—as if in fact reinscribed just here—besides the meta-history of Deleuze's transition from movement to time as screen dominant. What happens in *Source Code*—with its extreme medial as well as narrative "doubling" and "forking" within the diegesis—is a split inherent to sound film itself and its consolidation of the "movement-image" as uninterrupted duration. The "duping" that arose as one alternative to subtitling in the international marketing of "talking film"—a doubling of body by voice whose goal was total coalition or conflation—has split apart once more.[7] In Jones's film, we move (but only realize this after the fact) between an actor directly miked for us as character and his vocal status as sheer unbacked "translation," minus all image, within a diegesis that admits to (and manipulates) the cruel lack of fit between bodily frame and its cyborg instrumentations. Hermetically enclosed within the malign coils of his serial redeployment, speaking English without a mobile larynx to sound it out, he is at last revealed as entirely closed captioned.

The *duping* has, in the other sense, been *of* us as well as for us—but then what else is new? The organic integration of sound and image on screen, in digital recording as well as in film's previous technologies of audial tracking, is always a subterfuge, an artificial meld, a ventriloquized trick. *Source Code* only exaggerates and perverts this, cheating further on the given—until the anodyne coda foists off a virtual voice as the transcendent signifier of a text message unaccompanied by cellular phonetics but overlaying the track with the evocation of a freshly incarnate origin in a new and liberated plane of existence. What would be a hoary convention of "the talkies," hearing the voice of a letter-writer, for instance, over the image of its absorbed reader, and thus substituting metaphysical cause for material and textual effect, is bent out of shape by the foregoing pressure of narrative. *Letter from an Unknown Woman*: "By the time you read this, I may be dead." *Source Code*: "By the time you read this I am reborn." Such a minor device of suspended disbelief as the voiceover itself is, in *Source Code*, torqued almost into mordant irony by the twist ending, which thus urges from us, after all, a reading of, rather than just a listening to, its vocal overlay.

Deleuze and Chion again converge on the overlap of image and sound. Overlap, overlay: the common topological metaphor for "superimposed" voice. The trope of over-voicing in *Source Code*, only normalized at the last minute as the acousmatic figure for silent voicing at the sending rather than receiving end of any "written message"—any text-ing at large—has returned to the place of off-frame potency as if to redeem the sacrificial voicelessness of the mutilated hero. Yet the time-loop logic robs all uplift within the retained snares of its cautionary technophobia. For the "time reassignment" that renders all action virtual will need to happen again and again, this giving of one's life for one's country. In this parable of PTSD as *posthumous* traumatic stress disorder, the slain hero as human surveillance drone for "unmanned" reconnaissance has no escape after all from his serial redeployment.

And so, the topological model for the thrown voice on screen groans under the weight of an intolerable irony. Given the pressure built up behind it in the rest of plot, this last overdubbing of the bodiless voice thus breaks from sensorimotor continuity not by the lateral gaps stressed by Deleuze, but by the gaping metaphysical distance, in this case, between *vox* and *cogito* in what Eisenstein would call vertical montage (the overlay upon image of a nondiegetically matched sound). Such a split between somatic and phonic presence can indeed—when rendered as a paradoxical sheet of the present, two-ply and inscrutable—offer the disturbing virtuality of the time-image in further "numeric" implosion. Where Spielberg's *E.T.* was to "phone home" from an alien world, the cellular connection here is an incoming call, a moment of human contact, in an already strictly virtual universe. With everyday digital convenience touting (even spouting in over-voice) its triumph over malign paramilitary contrivance, Friedrich Kittler's paradigm of martial innovation preceding commercial media is perversely inverted by this sci-fi denouement, so that a comfortable phase of the latter (the boom in remote electronic messaging) can be maneuvered to naturalize and even ameliorate the potential depredations of the former.[8] The era of computerized telephonics, gone over to a nightmare of electro-telepathy and recursive temporality, seems bent on its own fantasized repair. Yet the digital fix, in only one sense, remains. The combat casualty lingers unreleased, dying to fight another day—even while his off-frame avatar is looking back on, and out for, himself in a message from the far side of his latest mission, with its last-minute magic vector from the neutered to the virtual body.

So it is, then, that the inherent ventriloquism of any cinematic soundtrack is raised by *Source Code* to the power of itself, though here in the mode of a further castration. The effect is to undo the vocal *cogito* of inner speech around the theme of the surveillant body as transparent sensory conduit, the remote cybernetic probe. If the Deleuzian time-image thus implied (or parodied) is to be *read* as *opsign*, whereas the movement-image was mainly to be *seen* as action, so with the evolution from sound to postwar *sonsign*. Although sound is certainly to be audited as ambient in the auditorium, it is also to be *read* in its often contrapuntal relation to a traced motion on screen. It is perhaps unsurprising that, as with so many films of the preceding decade, time-loop sci-fi is yet again, with *Source Code*, a dystopian arena for this spatiotemporal fissure between mimesis and semiosis in the audial track. When the mercy-exterminated hero of *Source Code* nevertheless breaks back into narrative space as the posthumous emanation of another corpse's inactivated larynx, the vocal rather than cinematographic "point-cut" that takes him there, together with the equivocal "relinkage" of the sound bridge that completes this transit, is also disposed, in the Deleuzian sense, *to take thought*: to require it of us and to assume its work before us. Ironic work in this congested case. Voiceover itself, as if inwardly recited at the point of merely fingertip input for a silent text message, becomes yet again a parody of the body–mind split that complicates all time-images.

And one notes here—and tries "thinking through"—the coordination of the musical track with just this logic. Routine and even self-referential in Hollywood terms (a mashup of Bernard Herrmann for ratcheted tension, John Williams for romantic sweep and release), the score has been reserved exclusively, until just before the end, for the trainbound action. If the anchoring reality of the lab and control deck is marked by strictly ambient noise and tactical address, the alternate reality to which Colter is dispatched is instead a self-conscious mix of rom com and action thriller—and *sounds* like it: this virtual universe cued, like movie "worlds" in general, by the implausible accompaniment of unsourced sound. It is only in the long intercut sequence where Colter is "shut down" by Goodwin in the lab while he is preempting, rather than just detecting, the terrorist and—coffin become incubator—beginning his second life with the girl, only then, that the score overlaps into the control room. This it continues to do right through to the end, exactly as the new parallel reality takes over the diegesis completely. In Roland Barthes's terms, the score itself has become part of the "hermeneutic code," inflecting the gathering final enigma with a further clue to its own solution.

In view of any such close league between vocal track and narrative score, conspiring together to "reframe" the spatiotemporal coordinates of the image before us, I want readily to admit, in retrospect, a certain self-imposed limitation in the frame-grabbed emphasis on cinematography in my grappling with Deleuze in *Framed Time*. What I called there a medial narratography as a method of response—with its attention to the smallest units of visual syntax as constituting at times their own microplot—should rightly be complemented by a grasp of cinema's own "narratophony" (whether plot turns are predictably enhanced for dramatic emphasis by a nondiegetic score, as in *Source Code*, or more ironically dismantled by disjunctures or anomalies of the soundtrack). On this *understanding* rather than sheer *hearing*, sound waves themselves can carry and transmute the calibrated oscillations of narrative, both in the encompassing brackets of voiceover, as well as in the bridgework of the audio track's most vexed layerings and transitions, whether or not these might at times be digitized within genre plots as an inhumane prosthesis—or its ludicrous cure. But let me be clear about the terminology. These sonic gestures, too, would come to notice, yield to reading, under the receptual paradigm of narratography, a "response aesthetic" cued as much (at least in its ideal deployment) by phonographic as by cinematographic markers in those films on which attention not only focuses but tunes-in.[9]

Once again, though, as with *Framed Time*, summation can only be momentary, since the movies keep coming, their subsumption to the digitized "time-image" still coming in for debate. But one pattern at least is clear. For the audio/visual (rather than audiovisual) register, what is unmistakable in the "new media" of museum practice can also be recognized in mainstream Hollywood production—if only at times against the grain of the so-called "sci-fi action pic." Reading sound as well as hearing it, even more than reading the seen image, brings time into play by the obvious route of simultaneity (synchronicity)—or its refusal. At which point, to complement Deleuze with Eisenstein in a fully responsive narratography of audio/visual media and their exploratory syncopations, the narrowly denominated screen "viewer" is stationed to perceive not the sensory match of motor cause and sonic effect but the dialectical interplay of two sign systems in "vertical" montage. The artificial fusion or "superimposition" that *is* all embodied voice on screen, its status as audial laminate in relation to image, becomes at such moments a legible palimpsest and a narrative sounding board.

And more. In the last shot of *Source Code*, with cinematography and phonography so gruesomely at odds over the disjunction between the insistent corpse and an overvoiced esprit de corps, a deep mechanics of the medium is also exposed to view within digital earshot of an alternate universe. A rephrased Deleuze may help to think, again to think *through*, the unique audio/visual layering of this disclosure. Pursuing this, we do well to note that the industrial category of "sound design" (including its dead-metaphoric association with graphic patterning rather than musical composition) has emerged only since those late-modernist experiments of European cinema that, on Deleuze's model, push back against ambient recording or score in favor of the sign-value of the "sound-scape," whose own widely used topographical metaphor recalls again the *oculaurality* of cinema's double-tracked sensory "field." Such "design" is therefore part of the larger historical arc that the end of *Source Code* compacts and explodes.

If it is fair, finally, to consider the metahistorical transition from the movement-image to the time-image as a transformation from within—as, in effect, a shift from image-as-picture to image-as-figure, or in other words from the audio/visual to the leg-ible—then the baseline of a optically recorded space (always to some extent retained by the medium, at least in its narrative functions) can at times work against the resis-tant "figuring" that would override and remake it. Such a tension, such a friction, might of course often entail not the routine match of image to sound but the freestanding sound-image or sound-figure: sound as sign ([de]sign) rather than sheer signal. In *Source Code*, however, the sign of a voice strictly fictive to begin with, as transmitted by cross-cut one last time, cuts deeper yet into the system of editing in cinema at large. For here, with this preternatural sundering of real time and "numeric time," the technique of parallel montage (so much a mainstay of the movement-image in the evolution of screen narrative) is laid bare in its all abutted alterities. It stands forth as not merely a coded structuring of the actual but—through the "forking" of alternate space-times—an opening to the virtual; and not just an opening, in this sci-fi case, but a gaping discrep-ancy converted on the spot to a figure of looped time and its forced "relinkages."

Nonetheless, in the technological hyperbole of this one narrative closure—with its limbo of clairvoyant vocality caught between worlds, between time-space continua, and so marked by a kind of spectral scenic antiphony—the attentions of narratogra-phy would register the return of a repressed disjuncture within the very conventions of screen editing, conventions established well before the postwar dominance of temporal-ity over action. Put it that, long before the Deleuzian time-image pries open its seams toward "irrational" lapses in either image or sound, there is a primal virtuality that lurks unheeded in embryo across the associational ligatures of montage per se, all narrated continuum a logical mirage that itself can only be thought, not really seen. Or, to enlist a running distinction in *Framed Time*, one can again cast the methodology at stake as a function of scale. On the one hand, a broad-gauged narratology might see one of its contested models, "possible worlds theory," evoked diegetically by the tandem phases of fictional science in this one plot—the targeted reconnaissance of electronic teleporta-tion alongside the accidental generation of a whole parallel world. On the other hand, a medium-keyed narratography would note how the tacit ongoing tension between indexical and virtual environments, photographable and suboptical action, human face and sheer interface, gets pinpointed at the last moment by a traditional device of cinematic sound editing: a voice overlap gone not just phantasmagoric but in its own way paradigmatic, thus foregrounding the virtual copresence that silently structures the routine "parallel universe" assumptions of so much intercutting on screen. The unanchored sound bridge drives in this way a medium-deep wedge.

The genre of sci-fi, here and often elsewhere, works to convert such an aesthetic condition of screen fiction to futurist science, its upshot pushed in this case (in any remnant of the "affection-image," as epitomized for Deleuze in the emotive close-up) off-screen altogether.[10] From which nebulous source the sonic penetration of diegetic space—not in itself explicitly digital sound, indeed purely figurative, but by direct metonymy with cellular text—closes the ironic circle begun with the subliminal dubbing of the hero's already duped body right from the start. Located now at the drastic intersection of horizontal and vertical montage are those constitutive fissures—inherent to the narrative sophistication of the movement-image itself—through which even the more philosophical resonances of the time-image often tend, by irruption, to get sounded. The case of *Source Code* is no less exemplary than it is extreme. Within the double folds of an electronic imaginary, the logical affront of that last and supposedly ameliorating sound bridge is just one of the ways, in the ironies of a soundtrack—ironies sometimes unintentional—that narrative cinema talks back to its itself: to its own devices, its own structuring assumptions, its own formal history.

NOTES

1. The point about the castrating effect of off-frame vocal omnipotence being neutralized when tied to an on-camera speaker is developed in Chion's treatment of Fritz Lang's Mabuse films in *Voice in Cinema*, trans. Claudia Gorbman (New York: Columbia University Press,1999), whereas his subsequent comments on the "acousmatic" dimension of Scorsese's film, p. 337 and later, in *Film, A Sound Art*, trans. Claudia Gorbman (New York: Columbia University Press, 2011), don't pursue this aspect of voice's narrative curtailment.
2. Chion's brief treatment of "voice as a special effect" (*Film, A Sound Art*, p. 337–339) has an indirect bearing on what, given the evidence to come, I have called the "nondiegetic voice" of the virtual hero in *Source Code*.
3. Across two influential volumes, *Cinema 1: The Movement-Image*, trans. Hugh Tomlinson and Barbara Habberjam, and *Cinema 2: The Time-image*, trans. Hugh Tomlinson and Robert Galeta (Minneapolis: Minnesota University Press, 1986, 1989), Deleuze—building on the theories of image and duration in Henri Bergson—tracks the moving image of cinema from its emphasis on action in the first half-century of genre films to a postwar dominance of temporal dislocation in "modernist" cinema, where movement comes to be subordinated, often in stasis and psychic disorientation, to a vexed and recursive temporality. In the movement-image, action is purely visible. In the time-image, optical events have instead to be read. Hence, in his second volume, concentrating on developments in and since the New Wave, we find the semiotic prominence of audiovisual signification rather than manifestation: the *sonsign*, the *opsign*, etc.
4. The question for Deleuze, in *Cinema 2: The Time-image*, is whether the "electronic image," alternatively called the "tele and video image" and the "numerical image," is destined to "transform cinema or to replace it" (p. 265), which means for the "time-image" in particular

whether electronics "spoils it or, in contrast, relaunches it" (p. 267). For my treatment of those narrative films whose temporal effects may be said to fall somewhere between these options in their digital ironies, both expanding and unwittingly parodying the time-image at once, see *Framed Time: Toward a Postfilmic Cinema* (Chicago: University of Chicago Press, 2007).

5. I summarize here the enumerated parallels between the late-modernist time-image and its millennial modifications discussed more fully in *Framed Time*, 166–170.

6. "Subvocal Speech Demo," NASA's home page, http://www.nasa.gov/centers/ames/news/releases/2004/subvocal/subvocal.html, accessed May 2012.

7. For the definitive treatment of the voice–body divide that sound engineers struggled to overcome by vocal "duping" at the inauguration of "the talkies," see Nataša Ďurovičcová, "Local Ghosts: The Human Body and Early Sound Cinema," in Leonardo Quaresima and Laura Vichi, eds. *Il film et suoi multipli* (Udine: Faculta degli studi, 2003). More broadly, the quality of "secondary orality" stressed as an instrumental function of both electrical and electronic media by Walter Ong in *Orality and Literacy: The Technologizing of the Word* (London: Methuen, 1982) has been investigated as the "vocalic uncanny" of remote voicing from radio through sound film to computer streams by Steven Connor in *Dumbstruck: A Cultural History of Ventriloquism* (New York: Oxford University Press, 2000).

8. I allude to an argument prosecuted frequently by Kittler and threaded fairly continuously through both his *Gramophone, Film, Typewriter*, trans. Geoffrey Winthrop-Young and Michael Wutz (Stanford, CA: Stanford University Press, 1999) and *Optical Media*, trans. Anthony Enns (New York: Polity Press, 2010).

9. Medium-determined—a matter of lexicon, syntax, and figuration in literary writing, of image, sound, and figuration in film—narratography stands to any screen feature, optical or sonic, like cartography does to a fixed land mass or as geography (in the scientific and investigative sense) to its material counterpart (identified by the same suffix).

10. In this sense, *Source Code* is about the future of a telepresencing quite apart from screening (as of a multiple temporality quite apart from ordinary human timelines). To quote the tagline from my earlier chapter (in *Between Film and Screen: Modernism's Photo Synthesis* [Chicago: University of Chicago Press, 1999]) concerning an embedded distance from the old-fangled science of photography staged by the diegetic "new media" of sci-fi: "The media turn of futurist film fiction addresses the postphotographic science of cinema's own dubious future" (p. 182). Going one quantum leap further, *Source Code*, in its metafilmic projection, has taken its remediated hero irreversibly off-screen, so that only his vocal ghost lingers by proxy in the voice of a posthumous double, a virtual self whose speaking image has been left in the end (as in fact all along) entirely behind. If it is no longer true to say that movies of the future tend to be about the future of movies, as I've repeatedly argued, then that is largely because the mediations they now picture have foregone screening altogether for immersive virtualities "envisioned" (but not strictly "reframed") by narration.

CHAPTER 28

···

SOURCE CODE

Eco-Criticism and Subjectivity

···

SEAN CUBITT

THIS essay attempts to think through the implications of eco-criticism[2] in new media, especially for the theory of subjectivity. Because eco-criticism expands the concept of agency to nonhuman actors,[3] it challenges older, exclusively humanist conceptions of subjectivity. Eco-critical perspectives on cinematic ontology, epistemology, and object formation (are we looking at organisms, ecologies, or a planetary system?) must also extend, in the age of informatics, to understanding what such extension implies for the human subject, both as matter of representation and as the site of interpretation and understanding: subjectivity as the event in which the projected filmstrip becomes diegesis and narrative. *Source Code* (Duncan Jones, 2011) offers itself as a laboratory for conducting this research.

Eco-criticism began as a type of genre criticism, seeking out explicit expressions of ecological concern in literature and cinema. But if it is to have critical valence in new media studies and the humanities more generally, it will have to speak more broadly, in the same way that feminist studies began in critical work on women's films and the differential representation of women and men, but grew to become a key approach to all of cinema. Second, just as cine-feminism began to inquire into the conditions of women's labor in (and exclusion from) the industry, in a new expansion, eco-criticism today inquires into the environmental impacts of media: the human and environmental costs of mining and other resource extraction, the environmental degradation associated with offshore manufacturing, the vast energy costs of running planetary network communications, and the toxic trade in recycling.[4] Third, eco-critique has begun to address the history and contemporary formation of the mediating role of political economy in the relationship between humans and populations[5] as a prelude to forming a new environmental politics capable of more than ethical pretensions. Here, the hermeneutic tools of the humanities have a key role to play—a role that they have forgotten. The purpose of the sciences is to pursue knowledge; that of the professional schools is to provide wealth, health, justice, shelter. The humanities' task is to debate the weighting of these Goods: to be the center of the discussion of values. They have abdicated that task at their peril. The expansion of eco-criticism is central to re-examining the humanities' work of debating the good life.

Axioms

From a human point of view, communication mediates between people, who are presumed to have an existence apart from communication. But from the point of view of communication, humans mediate between communicative actions: names, stories, images. From this standpoint, humans are media. The human subject, as it mediates communications, is noisy, just like any medium. The extraordinarily swift evolution of language can be explained by the mutations communications undergo in their passage through the human medium. We do not live exclusively in environments composed of tangible objects: communication is an integral element of our environment.

An environment and its inhabitants co-evolve. A species does not discover an environment waiting for it. It co-creates that environment by acting in it, eating, excreting, building, reproducing, dying. Ecology is a science of relations and mediations, in which innumerable interactions must constantly recreate the end-points "environment" and "inhabitant." These termini do not originate communications: mediation comes first, construing as needed, from the materials at hand, the partners that will be so mediated. This is the environmentalist account not just of natural but of human history. Too often, we presume that the nonhuman has autonomy from human affairs, save only when anthropogenic processes threaten natural cycles. It is a direct consequence of such thinking that sees preserving wilderness given precedence over relationships between human population and the environing world. If eco-critique is to have a political role, it must address the human as well as organic, the environment of data centers, Tijuana maquiladoras, the recycling villages of southern China, and the habitat of the North Circular quite as much as Antarctica.

Modernity is the history of mediations between environment and population. It is the story of how land, once held in common, became estates held by the wealthy and powerful. Land, alienated from those who worked it, had no option but to become an environment, apart from them. In a second great chapter, it is the story of how tools, once an extension of the limbs of their users, became machines, and the workers became mere "hands" and were forced to obey the discipline of the factory environments from which, again, they were alienated and to which they were subordinated. In our epoch, a third chapter is coming to a close, the migration of knowledge from the population to the environment. The "how-to" knowledge of the cottage weaver became the embodied knowledge of the spinning jenny; today, even knowledge about who lives in the neighborhood and which plants grow best locally has been abstracted and increasingly privatized. As in the two previous epochs, the process is mediated by political economy, that process of mediation between population and environment that ensures that the relationship is governed by the twinned principles of power and wealth. As the information revolution consolidates under the neo-liberal rule of the market—now itself increasingly automated in computer-based trading—we can see with alarming clarity the next move: the becoming-environment of the human body, in which Foucauldian bio-politics and the vampire-capital of Marx come to realization.

INFORMATION AS ENVIRONMENT

Source Code tells the story of terminally injured pilot Colter Stevens (Jake Gyllenhaal) incarcerated in a life support module from which he can be sent back in time to inhabit the body of a stranger, bound for Chicago on a suburban train which, in the film's present, has been bombed by a mystery terrorist. Stevens can only return for 8 minutes on each expedition, during which he must defuse the bomb, stop the terrorist from striking again, get the girl, and resolve who and where he is and how to survive. The dénouement involves Colter finding a way to abandon his dying body in favor of the alternate reality that his actions have produced.

The film belongs in a recent subgenre I have taken to calling "irreality films": *Déjà Vu* (Tony Scott, 2005), *Next* (Lee Tamahori, 2007), *Knowing* (Alex Proyas, 2009), *Inception* (Christopher Nolan, 2010), *The Adjustment Bureau* (George Nolfi, 2011), and *Source Code* (2011), to which could be added the weaving-of-destiny subplot in *Wanted* (Timor Bekmambetov, 2008). The cycle differs from the cluster of films appearing at the close of the last century, notably *Dark City* (Alex Proyas, 1998), *The Matrix* (Andy and Lana Wachowski, 1999), and *The Thirteenth Floor* (Josef Rusnak, 1999) in that the central trope of the earlier cycle was that the characters found themselves immersed in a virtual reality: in the more recent group, it is reality itself that is unreal. Although some of the new cycle are based on the paranoid stories of Philip K. Dick (notably *Next*, adapted from Dick's short story "The Golden Man" and *The Adjustment Bureau* adapted from "The Adjustment Team"), they differ from earlier adaptations like *Blade Runner* (Ridley Scott, 1982) and *Total Recall* (Paul Verhoeven, 1990), in that, although the protagonists come to doubt their own reality, the world around them obeys the familiar laws of physics. Irreality films share the different conceit that the world is itself a data construct or can be treated as such.

The title, *Source Code*, is the name of the program that hosts the mental activities of the dying Colter and runs the quantum-voodoo premise of the story. But, as title, it clearly has a metaphorical role. Source code is the working part of an application. Written in a programming language like Java, source code is the nearest human programmers get, by and large, to machine code: the raw processing of zeros and ones. It contains the instructions that generate computer actions. As Wendy Chun writes, code operates as *logos*: "code as source, code as true representation of action, indeed, code as conflated with, and substituting for, action."[6] The inferences are at least two: every event in the world as we experience it—spilled coffee, the flight of a duck across a lake—is the epiphenomenon of an underlying code (Figure 28.1).[7]A further inference of the world-as-epiphenomenon thesis is that the code of *Source Code*, although performative, is stochastic rather than determinist, so that the narrative appears as a series of variations on a theme, rather like Tom Tykwer's *Lola Rennt* (1998). Unlike apparently similar films like *Groundhog Day* (Harold Ramis, 1993), whose protagonist must become a decent person in order to escape the temporal vortex of the plot, Tykwer's film eschews explanations for the three versions of the story it tells, in a deeply nihilistic film, in which nothing more than chance guides the success or failure of Lola's sprint. Hollywood irreality films, by contrast, not only explain the origins of the variations, but give them a moral shape.[8]

Source Code does not seem to propose a synonym ("the world is like a movie") but a metaphor ("the world is a movie"), in which case a second inference becomes apparent. The coded world must be coded by someone. By the same token, what has been written can be rewritten (with the exception of *Knowledge*, which, uniquely, is governed by predestination). In *The Adjustment Bureau*, the author, although unnamed, is clearly God, albeit a God who can change his plan if persuaded by human. In *Wanted*, the code is produced by a mystic self-operating loom. Here, as in *Adjustment Bureau* and *Next*, the author of the rewrites is the protagonist, and there is always another chance to rewrite—most egregiously in the conclusion of *Next*, in which Otis Johnson (Nicholas Cage), after failing, gets to restart the clock again. It is not difficult to recognize here a common attribute of Hollywood narrative: its conviction that individuals are the only moral agents and, in *Source Code* in particular, that individual actions matter to the extent that

FIGURE 28.1 *Source Code*, Duncan Jones, Vendome Pictures/Mark Gordon Company, 2011.

the whole world can be rewritten on the basis of one person's acts and that this can be morally justifiable. To this extent, these films can be seen as variants on a specific, and I believe recent, motif in the tradition of predestination—shared with films like *Good Will Hunting* (Gus van Sant, 1997), *Little Man Tate* (Jodie Foster, 1991), *Twelve Monkeys* (Terry Gilliam, 1995), or, indeed, *The Matrix*—whose narratives concern the protagonist growing into a predestined role.

Such observations of ideology in action are a preliminary step. The nuanced evolutions of ideological theses, such as the theme of the recodable world in irreality films, tell us a great deal about human reactions to emerging states of affairs. The disorientation such films play on is not exclusively narrative. It comes from a specifically environmental concern: that the world we inhabit is not (or no longer) composed of atoms but bits, programs, and that our own personal knowledge has been superseded by modes of automated processes that can be manipulated at will. In an inversion of the paranoid sensibility of *The Sixth Sense* (M. Night Shyamalan, 1999), where the world remains while its subject no longer truly inhabits it, here the subject remains, while the world has lost its solidity, transformed into the alienated form of knowledge: information. An eco-critical approach must confront the fact that the human environment is no longer exclusively the excluded organic world, but includes the alienated forms of our tools and, now, of how and what we know. The survival of the self in this deracination of its environment is one of the challenges an expanded eco-critique discovers in irreality films.

SUBJECTIVITY

The environment is characterized by the fact that it is alienable: that it is made of "data," things that are given. In our times, what can be given can also—and, in many instances, must—be sold. What can be given or sold is in any eventuality—a thing, rather than a relationship or a process. Eco-criticism thus has to engage with the object relation created by the movement of land, tools, and knowledge into the alienated environment in which only what is left behind is treated as human. As Adorno was at pains to make clear, bourgeois individualism may well be a historical and ideological construct, but it is the form of subjectivity through which we perceive ourselves, our world, and our place in it.[9] To that extent, while reaching for a supraindividual critical position from which to analyze *Source Code*, it would be dishonest to deny the role of subjectivity in the political and economic mediations between population and environment. Concerns about subjectivity underpin crucial contributions to environmental thought, from the deep ecology of Arne Naess[10] to the very differently constituted theories of subject–object relations that inform the ethical choice paradigm in green consumerism. Understanding the privilege given by fictions to the conditions of subjectivity may yet open up a third way of conceiving relationship. As a founding principle, we might state that, for eco-criticism, the development of subjectivity is not only biographical but historical: a product of the mutual constitution of self and other both as population and as environment.

Freud made the case that the infant's desires are "polymorphous," although perhaps a better term might be "amorphous." Only as the child is socialized does it begin to separate interior and exterior, to distinguish the various organic processes from one another, to isolate objects for these newly discrete desires, and, at the same time to acquire the ability to identify with others like itself.[11] Freud more or less stops here: unsurprisingly, because this is the object-relation that almost all his patients exhibited at the dawn of consumer capitalism.

As objects of desire for power and wealth, land, manufacturing, information, and their products pose themselves as attainable. But it is a truism of psychoanalysis that the object of desire is always missed, or lacking, or elsewhere. This suggests a number of consequent observations, of which the first must be that the pursuit of power and wealth does not fulfil human desire. Of itself, political economy does not satisfy, but *mediates* desire. The myriad objects that consumerism dangles before us—including the media of power and wealth themselves—are always missed or missing or unsatisfactory. Their apparent givenness—as data and as presences—is sheer phantasm, because they are not objects as such, but mediations. One reaction constitutive of subjectivity is to constitute the real object of desire as already impossibly lost: to place it in the past, as we do in nostalgia, and in Freud's account in melancholia.[12] This is so often the role played by wilderness in Green politics: the climactic representation of a lost world seen in the closing scene of *Soylent Green* (Richard Fleischer, 1973). Here, the *objet petit "a,"* the impossible object of desire, of a pristine nature untouched by humanity, is impossible because it is past.

Similarly, the quest for innocent objects of consumption rests on an impossible cleanliness in production and distribution. Ironically, this is true also of digital media, whose planned obsolescence would make the Detroit of the 1950s blush for shame. To cite just one statistic, ostensibly weightless and friction-free, the server industry that underlies cloud computing already in 2009 outstripped the carbon emissions of the airline business and is growing, at conservative estimates, by at least 15 percent a year. Yet the dream—and the marketing as well as the political quest—of a marriage between consumer capital and environmentalism keeps us looking for that perfect product that "takes only memories and leaves only footprints," in Chief Seattle's well-known admonition. What we imagine, in short, is consumer goods that have no history: no materials extraction, manufacture, or toxin-laden freight budget. Nor is the dreamed-of immaculate commodity ever destined for the trash or the waste disposal industry: it has no future. The pure commodity is wholly present. A familiar form of magic, the innocent object provides the rough-hewn subject with an apotropaic talisman against its utter dependence on the political-economic relation it must have with its environment. In the guise of ethical choice, it refounds the solipsistic hyperindividuality of capitalist subjectivity, crowning as the ultimate good the alienation of the subject from all of its environments.

The great movements of modernity—the alienation of land, tools, and knowledge—are movements from the originary enjoyment of the world toward the alienation of desire as desire for objects. There is no reversing that process. We have therefore to look toward the third phase, that of the becoming-environment of information, to inquire whether emerging forms of subjectivity and the subject–object relation are capable of resisting and, better still, producing alternatives to the triumph of information capital.

I want to propose here another thesis, derived in part from Virno's work on the language instinct.[13] Alongside hunger, sex, and survival, human beings are in thrall to what Wallace Stevens called the "Blessed rage for order."[14] It is the drive to make a home—a niche in the environment. Like any instinct, it can veer into extremity, as it does in fascism. It is also one root—as Stevens evokes in "The Idea of Order at Key West" in which the phrase appears, of "the maker's rage to order words of the sea"—of the urge to make art. At one extreme lies fascism, at the other entropy—the urge to destroy as obverse of the drive to order. This consideration makes clear that the rage to order is part and parcel of Freud's entropic death drive.[15] Order is then not simply a physical property of systems but an ingrained element of human beings, and it lies at the root of both language and the pursuit of knowledge.

The enclosure, commercialization, and subsequent industrialization of agriculture changed the object of hunger. The separation of tools from bodies and the growing eroticization of their products changed the object of sexual desire. What then occurs when knowledge—which was never about the thing known but its place in ordering taxonomies—once integral to personal existence, is alienated in the form of data? This is the question at the heart of the portraits of subjectivity in irreality films.

Creative media have the option to embark on journeys into imaginary worlds, worlds that often enough reveal the anxieties but also the unanswered desires of the present. This utopian principle can operate on a simple commutation test. What kind of alternate order and what goals of subjectivity do not appear in this cycle? Perhaps the most alluring of imaginary worlds is one beyond the ministrations of political economy. As mediation, political economy mediates between populations and environments. But what if, in imagination, we resolve the forced distinction between the two? As a utopian project, we could imagine a world in which the human population no longer poses itself as the self opposed to the environmental other. To do this, humanity would have to abandon its position outside the environment and become an element of it, along with land, tools, and knowledge. It would have to abandon its role as population, that is, as that which labors and is ruled, mediated by political economy, leaving political economy without a role because excluded from the human–environment relation. This post-human scenario destroys the privilege of human subjectivity over its objects, as indeed it loses the privilege of the concept (knowledge) over its materials. It suggests a resolution, too, of the subject–object relation that lies at the foundation of modern subjectivity.

Perhaps this scenario is unimaginable: but that is the definition of the future. Following Ernst Bloch's principle of hope,[16] the future is by definition unknowable. A plan is not a future, merely a continuation of the present. Planning is the function of the vast simulations used in biopolitical management of populations and of the planetary embrace of computer-based trading in financial markets. It is also, as I argue in a forthcoming book on the history of visual technologies, the diagram (to use Deleuze's term) of digital media, increasingly standardized around the pattern of the grid, which dominates digital visuality from chip design to raster displays. A radically different future—in Bloch's definition, therefore, any future worthy the name—requires a radically different technological aesthetic, one that is increasingly difficult to instigate because of the powerful regime of normative standards operating in digital networks. Such visions are utopian, in the nonpejorative sense articulated by Fredric Jameson: "utopias are non-fictional, even though they are also non-existent. Utopias in fact come to us as barely audible messages from a future that may never come into being."[17]

Source Code is a fiction masquerading as a utopia. As pseudo-utopia, it tells us of a future that already exists, a program awaiting execution. But such futures, on Bloch's reckoning, are not futures at all. As fiction then, irreality films speak of and from the present and for the eco-critical expansion into theories of subjectivity, of and from present subjectivity, especially the drive to order, so central to the informationalization or becoming-environmental of knowledge. What is the look of bemused delight that passes across Matt Damon's face in the closing scenes of *Adjustment Bureau* or the quizzical grin of Jake Gyllenhaal, allowed to live and love again, if not a secular expression of an ancient individualist dream, admission into heaven. The danger of belief in afterlife, posed in our case as alternative realities, is that it dematerializes the material world and our lives as we live them. This is the sense of Adorno's complaint against any voluntary or utilitarian sacrifice of happiness: if we accept misery or hasten death—or own or others'—because a better world awaits, we deny the one life that we have.[18] If these films legitimate a good deal of cartoon violence, they do so on the back of an ancient belief in the triumph of the good and a mystical orientation toward an unknown future that current Green politics (and materialist humanities) have tended to demean, at peril of losing touch with deeply experienced yearnings for a better life. On the positive side, then, these films posit an alternative to the present, but on the negative, that alternative is different only by a fraction: a single life, a single love. Without wishing to demean the value of a life, or especially the value of love, the lack of ambition in these dreams of alterity is disappointing.

Each of the films describes a troubled moment, a sense of vertigo as the forking paths of time are revealed and the solidity of the familiar world dissolves. Although each in its way explains, justifies, and resolves the trouble, it is surely symptomatic of something that they raise the problem of irreality in the first place. Why should the world be a stranger to us? And why should that strangeness come in the form of a source code (data visualization in *Déjà Vu*, the animated maps of *Adjustment Bureau*, the tapestry of *Wanted*)? The answer lies in the translation from knowledge—identical with its knower—to information—alienated in the legal sense of a property that can be given away or sold. If what I know—that around the corner, say, just out of sight, there's a house with a red door—is no longer mine, I may be paranoid, in the style of Philip K. Dick, whose characters constantly find that they are living in simulated worlds. But if that is not simply the case with me but with everyone, as is now the case, and if everything known (in the passive voice, anonymous and depersonalized) resides elsewhere, in an environment I can no longer read or experience directly, or where I trust Google Street View as much as my own memory, then I am engaged in a mass social experiment in which the problem lies not in my mind but in the world beyond it. However, and this is the point of pursuing an environmental critique of the subject, my mind, my subjectivity, is undoubtedly changed in its new relationship with an informatic environment newly integrated with the older environments of landscapes and factories.

An instinct—sex, hunger, order—is an environment in which a subject dwells. Like the physical environment, the instinctual, so often presumed to be not only innate but unchangeable, is remade in its interaction with the subject. Thus, we are wrong to believe that a drive is the socialized form of a natural instinct hardwired into the brain. Instead, we should understand that socialized drives are primary, because, as it were retrospectively, drives construct instincts rather than vice versa. This is why the hunger satisfied by a Big Mac is so different from that satisfied by tearing apart a woolly mammoth with flint axes. The quality of the experience is wholly different not because the subject is changed but because subjectivity, as social process, remakes the environment that it inhabits—including the instinctual environment. We experience ourselves differently in different epochs and cultures because we remake our worlds. Thus, it no longer matters what the "natural" origin of the drive to order may have been. What matters are the vicissitudes through which it passes to achieve its present form and how it feels to inhabit the ordered environment, to be its subject, now. The informatic environment is the highest stage of modernity's increasing elucidation and fugal development of the rage to order.

Because the drives that constitute social subjectivity—and there is no other form—construct instincts as habitable environments, fictions have the privileged role of experimenting with (or expressing) these subject effects as environmental. The worldview in question in *Source Code* is, in many respects, the outcome of the colonization of realism by scientific rationalism which, since Leibnitz, has proceeded on the basis of quantization: what cannot be expressed mathematically is not the object of science and therefore not open to discourses of truth. Realism is a broad church, embracing both the wild shores of quantum physics and Deleuze's radical empiricism. In Meillassoux and Brassier, the reality of the world approaches Wittgenstein's "all that is the case": an assemblage of states of affairs taken as given, even if there is no human observer to whom they appear. Such forms of absolute realism attempt to broach the old Kantian division between things-in-themselves and things-for-us. But quantifiable reality is specific in restricting the status of fact to those dimensions of the world that are open to being measured. From here, it is a short step to arguing that the phenomenal world we experience at first hand—breezes, smells, colors—exist to the extent that they express equations. As knowledge passes from personal to environmental, however, the chill feeling arises that none of "this"—the tactile, smelly, contingent world of sensation—is actual, only the froth rising up from a world of pure algebra that subtends it.

Source Code discovers the power of pure information not only as world but as the world-constituting power of the dying, legless Colter in his tank. What he discovers, however, is not the hyperreal of *The Matrix*—the world as simulation—but, on the contrary, integral reality: the world as presentation analyzed in Baudrillard's last works.[19] The problem is that, as presentation, the world is both entirely and unchangeably as it is and, at the same time, without any kind of necessity, least of all one that might be humanly comprehensible. That is to be the role of the love story: to provide some kind of order, some nonarbitrary reason why the world should be so and not otherwise. As that definition suggests, this can only be an aesthetic or more specifically affective rationale. And, for our solipsistic protagonist, the archetypal brain in a vat, affect is wholly bound into the individuated self.

It is in the nature of every modern era to see itself as ultimate. For Colter, the discovery that all the world is information—the self-presentation of an abstract source code—is at first terrifying, even abject. But it soon empowers him, first to change the event, and then to drop out of his dying body: to sacrifice the mortal meat for a purely informatic existence. What he embraces is the dialectical obverse of the world as presentation: its nonidentity. In the Aristotelean tradition, right through to Wittgenstein's axiom that "the world is all that is the case," anything that is, is identical to itself. In *Source Code's* conception of integral reality, however, the presentation of the world obscures and denies the code of which it is an expression. To this extent, Colter's terror and disgust result from the discovery that the ground of being is nonidentity, the quality that, in Frege, is particular to zero: the empty set.[20]

But this is Hollywood. *Source Code* opens the Pandora's box of nihilism, the recognition of the nothingness underpinning the informatic universe, only to close it again with a better lock and key. What this and other irreality films suggest is that, under such conditions, the subject must assert absolute sovereignty and create its own personal paradise. At the same time, the nihilistic principle means that no social utopia is thinkable or, more specifically, realizable. In this way, Jones' film raises an ontological question— what is the status of the world?—only to substitute for it the epistemological question— how do I know? It falls heir to the idealist tradition, for which the world is an effect of consciousness, adding, however, the consumerist faith: if the world is only what I know about it, why don't I just imagine a better one—for myself?

That is the fiction offered by the film, a metaphysical realism that, like the object-oriented philosophy of Meillassoux, Harman, and Brassier,[21] aims to break down the old Kantian division between things-in-themselves and things as they exist for us. The idealist tradition coming out of Bishop Berkeley, on the other hand, culminates in Baudrillard's nihilist proposition: that there is nothing, rather than something. This is the nightmare experienced by Colter. In this tradition, the idea that human calculation—mathematics, which is a discourse quite as much as language or code—is not just congruent with but identical to nature as hypostatized Other, but is pure Pythagorean mysticism. This discredited belief—to construct an oxymoron—is to the credit of the scientific view, whose concept of progress through the accumulation and refinement of knowledge is itself, properly speaking, utopian. This is the role of the mathematical sciences in environmental politics, especially in the form of data visualization, so much a part of environmental discourse, as in *An Inconvenient Truth* (Davis Guggenheim,

2006). Mobilized in environmental politics as a means of recruiting popular support, this idealist-mathematical tradition reveals itself in political practice, ironically enough, as a form of populism.

The term "populist" has recently been revalued by Ernesto Laclau to indicate a politics neither of individuals nor of populations but of a "primitive" that does not need to be premised on the prior existence of individuality or of society, which Lacau names "demand." Populist demand is an affect that drives populist politics, a politics of people as opposed to their governors, bypassing political parties and electoral politics to appeal directly to mass activism. It is clear, however, that as a political philosopher, Laclau ascribes demand exclusively to humans. An environmental politics must also organize itself around nonhuman demand, nonhuman affect. In its peculiar way, data visualization attempts to articulate this nonhuman discourse into human-comprehensible form.

Picturing, on the other hand, is a humanism. Where populism is always about an embattled people and their demand, realism—the theory that photography and cinematography have a privileged relation with the world—begins in the assumption that human perception is the unique and universal criterion of truth. This is a political position only in the sense that it preempts an essentially political struggle over the status of the real. Pictures, once held to be the essential hegemonic machinery of ideology, are now held to assure, in the relation of indexicality, the ability of symbolic activity to communicate reality.[22] Yet the obverse is also true: reality is what symbolization produces as its other, especially when, as in picturing (as opposed to data visualization), the model of vision is exclusively that of human eyes. Just as the subject is "an effect of language" (and of framing, perspective, and other visual and semantic systems), so reality is an effect of representation, which produces the object of the subject–object relation. We set all sorts of nets and traps: reality is what evades them, the impossible object of our desire for knowledge, possession, and the order of knowledge and command. Pictures are evidence of humanistic attempts to define the world as object of perception and so to found our control over it. This humanism originated in the nascent republican war on aristocracy and theology of Pico and Luther. Today, however, it recurs as a defence of the secular world they constructed, but now with an investment of faith that turns it into a new form of deity. Pictorial realism wants to maintain a 500–year-old thesis that the world is its own cause and that the human being alone is its witness, the observer for whom all of creation renders itself visible. Clinging to a historical epoch that made possible, and descended into, the maelstrom of industrial capitalism, it is necessarily nostalgic, which explains the elegiac tone of so much landscape cinematography in environmental cinema. At the same time, integrating the oscillation between demand and nostalgia, humanism and populism, is a key strategy in cinema, one that allows us to expand eco-criticism beyond the exclusive terrain of environmentally explicit cinema.

The Nonidentity of Integral Reality

Baudrillard's theory of integral reality argues that representation not only smothers the world it depicts, but replaces it, not merely simulating but presenting. Presence, the privileged core of being, is no longer self-evident, requiring re-presentation in order to exist at all. Colter sits in a void, between something and nothing, existence and nonexistence, one and zero. But what is that nothing, that zero? Frege starts from the Aristotelean axiom that everything that is, is self-identical: this stone is this stone. Nothing, therefore, is not identical to itself. Thus, he argues, we can define zero as what is not identical to itself. Adorno arrived at a startlingly similar conclusion concerning the nonidentical: what is important about a state of affairs is not what it is but what is has the power to become, what is future, and therefore what is not (yet) the case.[23] Thus, we can come to a critique of integral reality: that its presentation of the world is an effect of power that, presenting the world as identical to itself, hides the abject truth that nothing really exists. On the one hand, the analyst must take this "nothing" literally: the nothing that exists is nonidentical. On the other, the film confesses that the world is indeed integral reality, but that it distinguishes itself by a pseudo-Heideggerian failure to exist. *Source Code* poses a resolvable form of Heideggerian post-metaphysics, a utopia of personal redemption premised on the "obscene" confession on the part of integral reality that it is founded on a void. What political, as opposed to personal, hope is to be derived has to be extracted from the residual contradiction.

The mystery of source code is that a purely mathematical phenomenon (the "quantum parabola" of the film) results in a viscerally experienceable world. This is as apt a description of computing as it is of the narrative premise of the film. The simple reversal (math can describe the world; the world can be constituted as math) concerns the changing polarity of knowledge and information: from picturing environment by and for a human observer to the self-enumeration of the environment.

The face-off between populist realism and scientific abstraction, between picturing and enumerating, belongs to the challenge facing the all-too-human Colter: to see the world both through human eyes and as the functioning of self-operating programs beyond the human sensorium. The challenge is environmental because it concerns the fit, or lack of fit, between the instincts Colter has been schooled in as a military operative (whose very memories can be triggered, as they are in his first awakening in the virtual reality pod) and those he must acquire as agent in another world where vision is no longer the primary sense. In the scene in which Colter's memory is rebooted after his first run back in time, one trigger is a recording of the Western Screech Owl. As the sound plays, his control screen displays a sonogram of the recording, a visualization of a mathematical expression of the sound (a motif that recurs when he hears a recording of his father's voice). This brief image places us on the cusp between the picturing mode of analog cinematography[24] and the far less anthropocentric mode of data visualization.[25]

It is all too easy to qualify this dichotomy as analogous to the drift from knowledge to information, but digital media—including sound, which has been reproduced digitally in cinema systems devised by Eastman Kodak, Sony, and Dolby since around 1993—also have their claims not only to indexicality but to a heightened ability to capture the "optical unconscious."[26] Four cameras were used on *Source Code*: a more or less traditional but highly sophisticated Panavision Panaflex Millennium XL2 film camera, and three digital cameras; an Iconix, a Phantom HD, and a Red One, the first based on charge-coupled device (CCD) technology, the latter two on complementary metal oxide semiconductor (CMOS) technology. The Panasonic is a 35mm film camera, but has digital speed controls and viewfinder among other electronic tools. The Internet Movie Database (IMDB) gives the negative formats as 35mm and Redcode RAW, the 4K resolution HD format native to Red cameras. Like most contemporary films, it went through digital intermediate. There are many continuities between analog and digital equipment: the same glass technology, similar color filtering, similar latency, similar data loss patterns after exposure. If there is a single feature that distinguishes them, a feature deeply resonant with the themes of *Source Code*, it is the clock function.

Both analog and digital cameras expose the whole field for similar lengths of time—something under one-twenty-fourth of a second. The weak chemical reactions in exposed film have to be chemically amplified to make them visible in the negative, then fixed before going through grading, and finally printed to positive. The digital image has parallel stages en route to final cut: amplification of signal, conversion of charge to voltage, digitization, and color correction before finalized handover to its various delivery formats. But there is one exception to the parallels. The difference is that the *whole* frame of analog film is fixed simultaneously, whereas the charge at each pixel of a CCD or CMOS chip must be removed to memory in strict order to preserve the spatial relations between pixels, under the control of a clock mechanism. Thus, from a hermeneutical perspective, chip cameras differ from film almost exclusively in that each frame contains a temporal account of itself.

The Phantom HD has a specific function in film production: the maximum speed of the Panasonic film camera is 50 frames per second (fps), that of the Phantom more than ten times as fast at 555 fps, giving it the capacity to record extremely small timespans and to give the illusion of extreme slow motion on playback. This is the kind of technique used for filming fireballs of the kind repeatedly shown in *Source Code* and almost certainly for the freeze-frame that occurs at the climax, evoking Laura Mulvey's description of the digital freeze: "film's original moment of registration can suddenly burst through its narrative time.... The now-ness of story time gives way to the then-ness of the time when the movie was made" (Mulvey 2006: 30–31). At the moment of the freeze-frame in *Source Code*, Colter has finally worked out how to fill his 8 minutes: capturing the terrorist, wooing the girl, and creating a community (one of many echoes of *Groundhog Day*) at peace and enjoying itself (see Figures 28.1 and 28.2). A few minutes later, he will call this "a perfect day." The perfect moment—coinciding with the crisis back in the world of his mortal body—is arrested, almost certainly using the extreme speed of exposure of the Phantom. And yet, even at these extreme speeds, the structure of the image is

FIGURE 28.2 *Source Code*, Duncan Jones, Vendome Pictures/Mark Gordon Company, 2011.

bound to the clock function of the chip. Looking carefully at the language Mulvey uses, we can emphasize something explicit in the digital mode: she speaks of the time when the movie was made. This is not a moment, not a Husserlian *Augenblick*, instantaneous and whole. It is, most specifically, a nonidentical image. Quite apart from its delivery as DVD or Blu-ray digital scan, even in the cinema, this shot is ontologically incomplete, even as it tries to capture the perfect moment perfectly executed. It is exactly time, time that can only exist as change, that discloses itself, comes into being, in the cinematic process in which things become other than themselves.

We can now begin to zoom out again to the larger argument. What order of values are in play here, and how can eco-critique provide a purchase? The film is very explicit about its Chicago setting: Chicago the financial center, where the most significant digitization of real-world process is enthroned in the Midwestern heart of the nation. The film is an inquiry into how to live in a world where decision making is not only remote but automated (and that goes for the mass transit system where most of the action takes place, as well as the Beleaguered Castle laboratory where Colter's body is held). Such traditional ideological analysis does not, however, satisfactorily explain the existential unease the film generates, specifically the disturbance of the subject-object/ population-environment relationships that underpin phenomenological experience, that of Colter and of the audience alike.

An iconic motif throughout the film is Anish Kapoor's Cloud Gate sculpture on the Chicago waterfront. Although Kapoor is known for his manual approach to design, computer synthesis was an essential element in the design and fabrication of the piece. The result is a mirrored, biomorphic form that reflects the world and its visitors in elegant distortions. The mirroring has the effect of making the sculpture appear weightless and of dissolving its own form into the world it reflects. Something analogous is occurring to Colter in the latter part of the narrative, and something similar is also true of the seamless blending of digital and analog imaging processes.

The digital camera does not, in the first instance, read the world numerically: as photochemical reactions release ions to form darker oxides in the analog negative, optoelectronics release electrons (ions in the language of chemists) when struck by sufficient numbers of photons: what is waste product in analog is the capture mechanism in digital. Such digital instruments can claim as great a fidelity to real light as analog, with both responding to the accumulated photons arriving at the photosensitive field by emitting electrons. Historian of scientific instrumentation Peter Galison distinguishes statistical ("logical") instruments as opposed to instruments that produce images. Today, however, as Galison observes, scientific instruments increasing deploy both strategies to produce knowledge about the world.[27] Just as a director of photography collects data from light-meters to compose a shot, digital tools collect data about the world they envision. What is intriguing here is how these technologies arrive together in a product like *Source Code* to assemble a form of knowledge that is not immediately assimilable to the informatic environment.

The freeze places both love and heroism in the context of community, a little utopia, like Frank Capra films of the 1930s. The coda that follows makes explicit an individualist ethos, which had been momentarily subsumed into the commons in the freeze. Because we know that the freeze is not "a" photograph, not a coherent unity, we might have been left to imagine the evolution of multiple and unforeseeable futures from the instability of that nonidentical image. But, even fudging that opportunity, the last scenes of *Source Code* demonstrate the grounds for hope in the ruins of informationalization, the deep instability of political economy's mediations between population and environment, and both the trauma and the residual utopianism in the crisis of the informatic subject. In this, the story tells us how to construct an instinct for order that is neither Robinsonade of the individual, imposing his order on an externalized environment, nor that exercise

FIGURE 28.3 *Source Code*, Duncan Jones, Vendome Pictures/Mark Gordon Company, 2011.

FIGURE 28.4 *Source Code*, Duncan Jones, Vendome Pictures/Mark Gordon Company, 2011.

of power that historically alienated environment from subjects ostensibly subjected to the necessary laws of nature, the factory or informatics, but in fact subjected to the political economy that derives its authority from managing the population–environment relationship.

In the opening scene, as we zoom in through a helicopter shot toward the train, a duck takes off, its wings beating the water, with a squawk loud enough to be heard over the train (Figure 28.3). This shot is repeated at the start of almost every one of Colter's runs back in time. In this first instance, we cut into Colter sleeping: evidence therefore that the duck exists apart from his consciousness, that the informatic environment is total, independent of whether it is perceived or not, just like the real environment, the tree that falls when there is no-one to observe it. As the music fades to allow the diegetic sound of the train's bogies rhythmically thumping, the soundtrack is sweetened with the sound of heavy weaponry and helicopter rotors: a remnant, we presume, of Colter's dream, in which he is reliving the crash that left him immobilized in his laboratory pod. As he starts awake, the formal aspects of the film inform us of his subjective disorientation: abrupt handheld pans and cuts, and sharp, unnaturally heightened sounds: the ring-pull on a can of soda, the splat of coffee falling on his shoe, a "snick" as a commuter checks his watch, and fragments of overheard dialogue, including words muttered several seats away. We are brought in from a world constituted as more or less familiar: Chicago marked out by its lake shore monuments—the Chicago River, the Herald-Tribune Building, the Sears and Hancock Towers—and the duck. We are placed sharply into subjectivity, a subjectivity that, in the next few passes, will offer us the hypothesis that all this is an illusion or a simulation.

By the end, we will be placed very differently. In the coda, in which Colter and Christina stroll hand in hand in the spring sunshine, the score now dominated by French horns and unison strings in major chords, the camerawork is equally lyrical: steadicam passes, locked off shots, and all the edits motivated by both characters in shot-reverse-shot continuity. The only ambiguity, in a clever composite of the couple reflected in the Kapoor sculpture's curved surface (Figure 28.4) , is that we see next to Colter Stevens' foreground face the reflected face of Sean Fentriss, a fact that no longer causes Colter the shock and nausea of his first confrontation with a mirror in the train's washroom. "This feels like exactly where we're supposed to be, doesn't it?" he asks, and the question is rhetorical.

In the narrative, Colter ceases to be human. By abandoning the flesh, he opts to become information and thus to become environment, in the new terms made possible, indeed inevitable, by the new information ecology. Colter has sacrificed his body in a refusal of integral reality. From a narrative perspective, his gesture is based on an ultimately individual (and heteronormative) embrace of his own death, the entropic death drive. But as an account of the affordances of the diegetic world, constituted as reprogrammable environment, Colter's move to a posthuman position coincides with a utopian dream of a humanity that becomes its own environment. Such unthinkable futures are the goal of eco-critical hermeneutics.

NOTES

1. Latour, Bruno (2004), *Politics of Nature: How to Bring The Sciences Into Democracy*, trans Catherine Porter, Harvard University Press, Cambridge MA.
2. See among others Paula Willoquet-Maricondi, ed., *Framing the World: Explorations in Ecocriticism and Film* (Charlottesville: University of Virginia Press, 2010); Jhan Hochman, *Green Cultural Studies: Nature in Film, Novel, and Theory* (Moscow: University of Idaho Press, 1998); Gregg Mitman, *Reel Nature: America's Romance with Wildlife on Film* (Cambridge, MA: Harvard University Press, 1999); Derek Bousé, *Wildlife Films* (Philadelphia: University of Pennsylvania Press, 2000); David Ingram, *Green Screen: Environmentalism and Hollywood Cinema* (Exeter, UK: University of Exeter Press, 2000); Scott MacDonald, *The Garden in the Machine: A Field Guide to Independent Films About Place* (Berkeley: University of California Press, 2001); Pat Brereton, *Hollywood Utopia: Ecology in Contemporary American Cinema* (Bristol, UK: Intellect, 2005); Deborah Carmichael, ed., *The Landscape of Hollywood Westerns: Ecocriticism in the American Film Genre* (Salt Lake City: University of Utah Press, 2006); Cynthia Chris, *Watching Wildlife* (Minneapolis: University of Minnesota Press, 2006); and Sheldon H. Lu and Jiayan Mi, eds., *Chinese Ecocinema: In the Age of Environmental Challenge* (Seattle: University of Washington Press, 2010).
3. Bruno Latour, *Politics of Nature: How to Bring the Sciences Into Democracy*, trans. Catherine Porter (Cambridge MA: Harvard University Press, 2004).
4. See for example Jennifer Gabrys, *Digital Rubbish: A Natural History of Electronics* (Ann Arbor: University of Michigan Press, 2010); Elizabeth Grossman, *High Tech Trash: Digital Devices, Hidden Toxics, and Human Health* (Washington DC: Shearwater, 2007); Jussi Parikka, ed., *Medianatures: The Materiality of Information Technology and Electronic Waste* (Living Books, 2011), http://www.livingbooksaboutlife.org/books/Medianatures; Richard Maxwell and Toby Miller, *Greening the Media* (Oxford, UK: Oxford University Press, 2012); Nadia Bozak, *The Cinematic Footprint: Lights, Camera, Natural Resources* (Newark, NJ: Rutgers University Press, 2012).

5. The inspiration seems to have come from Foucault's observations on the birth of biopolitics in the late eighteenth and early nineteenth centuries: Michel Foucault, *Society Must Be Defended: Lectures at the Collège de France 1975-76*, ed. Mauro Bertani and Alessandro Fontana, trans. David Macey (London: Penguin, 2003), 245–246.

6. Wendy Hui Kyong Chun, *Programmed Visions: Software and Memory* (Cambridge, MA: MIT Press, 2011), 19.

7. A parallel from cinema might be the formal practices underpinning classical and postclassical style, such as the 180-degree rule, so important to this film, where so much of the action occurs aboard a train. Alternatively, we could understand a film as the epiphenomenal expression of its shooting script: a series of actions and recordings performed according to a previously formalized decision list.

8. David Bordwell notes of *Source Code* that its narrative structures are merely minor modifications to a highly familiar form of narration: "More than we often admit, today's trends rely on yesterday's traditions. Quite stable strategies of plotting, visual narration, and the like are still in play in our movies. When a movie does innovate in its storytelling, it needs to do so craftily. The more daring your narrative strategies, the more carefully, even redundantly, you need to map them out. The game demands *clarity through varied repetition.*" David Bordwell, "Forking Tracks: *Source Code,*" *Observations on Film Art,* May 3, 2011, http://www.davidbordwell.net/blog/2011/05/03/forking-tracks-source-code/. My contention is that the motivation for such crafty changes in narration, and even more so in the diegesis of irreality fims, point toward an aporia in this stylistic continuity. On the other hand, Bordwell makes a convincing case for the continuing importance—I would suggest a growing one—of the dialectic of chance and destiny in Hollywood plots, exemplified in *Source Code.*

9. Theodor W. Adorno, *Aesthetic Theory*, ed. Gretel Adorno and Rolf Tiedemann, trans. Robert Hullot-Kentor (London: Athlone Press, 1997), 41–42.

10. Arne Naess, *Ecology, Community and Lifestyle: Outline of an Ecosophy*, trans. and revised by David Rothenberg (Cambridge, UK: Cambridge University Press, 1989).

11. Sigmund Freud, *On Sexuality: Three Essays on the Theory of Sexuality and Other Works*, Pelican Freud Library 7, trans. James Strachey, ed. Angela Richards (Harmondsworth, UK: Pelican, 1977).

12. Sigmund Freud, "Mourning and Melancholia," in *On Metapsychology: The Theory of Psychoanalysis*, Pelican Freud Library 11 (Harmondsworth, UK: Pelican, 1984), 245–269.

13. Paolo Virno, *Multitude: Between Innovation and Negation*, trans. Isabella Bertoletti, James Cascaito, and Andrew Casson (New York: Semiotext(e), 2008).

14. Wallace Stevens, "The Idea of Order at Key West," in *The Collected Poems of Wallace Stevens* (London: Faber, 1955), 128–130.

15. Sigmund Freud, *Beyond the Pleasure Principle*, trans. James Strachey (New York: Livingstone, 1961).

16. Ernst Bloch, *The Principle of Hope*, 3 vols., trans. Neville Plaice, Stephen Plaice, and Paul Knight (Cambridge, MA: MIT Press, 1986).

17. Fredric Jameson, "The Politics of Utopia," *New Left Review* 2 (Jan-Feb 2004): 35–54.

18. Theodor W. Adorno, *Problems of Moral Philosophy*, trans. Edmund Jephcott (Cambridge: Polity, 2000), 128.

19. See in particular Jean Baudrillard, *The Agony of Power*, trans. Ames Hodges, introduction by Sylvère Lottringer (New York: Semiotext(e), 2010).

20. See Alain Badiou, *Number + Numbers*, trans. Robin MacKay (Cambridge, UK: Polity, 2008).

21. See for example Quentin Meillassoux, *After Finitude: An Essay on the Necessity of Contingency*, trans. Ray Brassier (London: Continuum, 2008); Graham Harman, *Guerrilla Metaphysics: Phenomenology and the Carpentry of Things* (Chicago: Open Court Press, 2005); Ray Brassier, *Nihil Unbound: Enlightenment and Extinction* (London: Palgrave Macmillan, 2007).

22. Compare with the authors cited in note 24, the once-influential essay Jean-Louis Baudry, "Ideological Effects of the Basic Cinematographic Apparatus," trans. Alan Williams, in *Movies and Methods*, ed. Bill Nichols, vol. 2 (Berkeley: California University Press, 1985), 531–542.

23. "Wittgenstein's position that fundamentally consciousness has to do only with that which is the case. That might call forth another definition: metaphysics is the form of consciousness in which it attempts to know what is more than the case, or is not merely the case, and yet must be thought, because that which, as one says, is the case compels us to do so" (note on the *Tractatus* cited in footnotes to Adorno, *Problems of Moral Philosophy*, 196).

24. See in particular Mary Anne Doane, "The Indexical and the Concept of Medium Specificity," *differences: A Journal of Feminist Cultural Studies* 18, no. 1 (2007): 128–152; D. N. Rodowick, *The Virtual Life of Film* (Cambridge, MA: Harvard University Press, 2007); and in a rather different register Laura Mulvey, *Death 24x a Second: Stillness and the Moving Image* (London: Reaktion Books, 2006).

25. See Sean Cubitt, "Everybody Knows This Is Nowhere: Data Visualization and Ecocriticism," in *Ecocinema Theory and Practice*, eds. Stephen Rust, Salma Monani, and Sean Cubitt (New York: AFI/Routledge, 2012), 279–296.

26. See Walter Benjamin, "The Work of Art in the Age of Its Technological Reproducibility: Third Version," in *Selected Writings*, vol. 4, *1938–1940*, eds. Howard Eiland and Michael W. Jennings (Cambridge, MA: Bellknap Press/ Harvard University Press, 2003), 251–283.

27. Peter Galison, *Image and Logic: A Material Culture of Microphysics* (Chicago: University of Chicago Press, 1997).

SELECT BIBLIOGRAPHY

Brereton, Pat. *Hollywood Utopia: Ecology in Contemporary American Cinema*. Bristol, UK: Intellect, 2005.

Bousé, Derek. *Wildlife Films*. Philadelphia: University of Pennsylvania Press, 2000.

Carmichael, Deborah, ed. *The Landscape of Hollywood Westerns: Ecocriticism in the American Film Genre*. Salt Lake City: University of Utah Press, 2006.

Chris, Cynthia. *Watching Wildlife*. Minneapolis: University of Minnesota, 2006.

Hochman, Jhan. *Green Cultural Studies: Nature in Film, Novel, and Theory*. Moscow: University of Idaho Press, 1998.

Ingram, David. *Green Screen: Environmentalism and Hollywood Cinema*. Exeter, UK: University of Exeter Press, 2000.

MacDonald, Scott. *The Garden in the Machine: A Field Guide to Independent Films about Place*. Berkeley: University of California Press, 2001.

Mitman, Gregg. *Reel Nature: America's Romance with Wildlife on Film*. Cambridge, MA: Harvard University Press, 1999.

Rust, Stephen, Salma Monani, and Sean Cubitt, eds. *Ecocinema Theory and Practice*. New York: AFI/Routledge, 2012.

Willoquet-Maricondi, Paula, ed. *Framing the World: Explorations in Ecocriticism and Film*. Charlottesville: University of Virginia Press, 2010.

CHAPTER 29

NOTES TO THE SOUNDTRACK OF *SOURCE CODE*

JAMES BUHLER

"Everything's Going to Be OK"

DARKNESS, the black void of the screen. A high, thin, slightly metallic sound wavers gently like a distant alarm and crescendos as the outline of what appears to be mountains comes into view. Light begins to glow in a crevice between two peaks and an ambiguous tone—part string, part low wind—warms the sound as the light momentary fills all but the left edge of the screen with a bright white that, in the context, seems blinding, beyond the capabilities of the apparatus to represent. The view wheels to resolve a rising sun that not only brings light but also endows the image with depth, the shoulders of mountains draped with a rim of light that now separates the dark sky from the dark earth. As the view pulls back and around to get out of line of the sun, the image of the mountains detaches from the frame line and the source of the light. The sound of the alarm grows more insistent when light starts to appear around the edges of the black square of the Summit Entertainment logo, which works its way to the center of the screen, eclipsing the oval of light that now fills the screen, except for the right and left edges (see Figure 29.1). The warm flute and string tone returns more clearly and emphatically as the words "Summit Entertainment" appear beneath the logo to claim ownership of the image, but also of the picture. The logo then disappears, leaving the screen once again momentarily void. A bright flash of light calls forth another sounding of the alarm, now accompanied by a more active flute line in the upper register. The light divides and rotates before receding into the void. An aggressive brass chord sounds as the lights disappear, and it builds in a slow crescendo as rudimentary string figures organize over and against it. A few indistinct flashes of light give way to another point of light that appears behind the ominous metallic letters of "Vendôme Pictures." All goes black

FIGURE 29.1 Summit Entertainment Logo: The Great Eye of Capital.

again as the brass reaches a violent and terrifying climax. The explosion of the bass drum cuts off the brass and summons at last, but also in the beginning, an image of the world.

The overt mythifying intention of this opening to *Source Code* (2011) should be evident from this description, which draws particularly on the archetypal creation story of Genesis. The motifs of the void, light and dark, heaven and earth, as well as the divisions that serve to bring the world out of chaos are designed into the graphic animations of the corporate logos, which follow terse, rudimentary scripts of *creatio ex nihilo*, an especially congenial scenario for any concern devoted to fashioning fiction out of light. The ritualistic repetition is the way the corporation posits itself as the ultimate origin of the film. And the corporation is not even wrong in locating itself thus at the point of origin. Without the capital that the corporation secures, there is no filmic light. Behind the summit, the light; behind the representation, the light; behind the metallic letters, the light. This light offers illumination, even apparent clarity; however, it brings enlightenment only to those patient enough to pick through its dialectical puzzles and consider what the dazzle of its brightness and clarity conceals. The light projects the spirit of capitalism but also figures the occluded real of capital.[1] It is the filmic manifestation of the capitalist gaze, the point from which the great clouded eye of capital watches the world with terrifying indifference.

"It's the Same Train, But It's Different"

The animated logos of Summit and Vendôme are by no means exceptional in this respect—although that final image of the Summit Entertainment sequence, in fact, does a masterful job of figuring the light as the blind eye of capital. Indeed, I first became aware of the profound and extensive mythologizing work of the corporate credits when I analyzed the New Line logo sequence as it appeared in Peter Jackson's *Fellowship of the Rings* (2001), very much along these same lines albeit without the Lacanian twist.[2] Of course, many films that use such corporate sequences allow the myth to pass unnoticed because the sequences seem safely situated outside the film. If we recognize the presence of mythologizing work in such cases, we attribute it to the sequence and the firm and separate it from the film. This separation does not mean that the work is ineffective, even when it becomes routine, or that the entwinement of mythology with ideology is any less tangled just because it scrupulously honors the strict secular division between firm and film. But any film with mythic intentions of its own will perforce confront the issue of origins, so such films tend to draw out this thematic affinity with the corporate sequences and therefore also alert us to the ideological work these sequences perform. In many cases—and *Source Code,* whether by planning or by dumb luck, is a spectacular case—the myth of the film also becomes enmeshed with the myth of the corporate sequence and for good reason: they both concern the hidden foundations of modern subjectivity, the real of capital.

If the corporate work is less the fashioning of fiction than the use of the fiction to extract profit, it is the business of the myth to mystify those origins, to plunge the source of the light, the real that stands behind the image, into darkness. And music is the preferred cultural tool for performing such mystifying work. Music arrives before the image, even before the corporate credits, and so serves, or appears to serve, as the source of the image, which it seems to call into being. Music thereby becomes the origin before origin, which unsettles ontologies of both film and world.

"We Don't Get Off Here"

Darkness, the black void of the screen. The bass drum booms, dividing the origin between symbolic and imaginary. Or, rather, it announces the birth of the imaginary out of the symbolic, a second origin parallel to but not identical with the first that gave birth to the symbolic. The music after the bass drum blast is likewise similar to yet distinct from the opening. The nominal E minor tonality is retained across the articulation as is an implied triple meter (which first began to assert itself in the build-up to the climax), but the alarm is absent, and the dominant string figure and its insistent projection of a hypermetrical grid (repeating every four measures) are both new. As Figure 29.2 shows, the image, which follows the drum stroke almost immediately, posits the world fully formed in the big bang of the drum, as it already offers advanced articulations. Most prominently, these articulations include the division between water and city, but also between city and sky, suggesting that the city is built on the older, more fundamental division between water and sky—here, again, recall Genesis and

FIGURE 29.2 The City.

its account of the division of the waters. The profuse reproductive power of that older division, its ability to multiply and conquer new domains, is evident in the piers that project the grid of the city out into the naturally unarticulated space of the water but also in the buildings that project the grid up into the naturally unarticulated space of the sky. City here runs on the source code of modernity: within this image, city is the imaginary representation of the symbolic, which transgresses its own limit as well as that of the imaginary representation to extend its dominion over all the world. It is in that sense an unruly image, an image of the sublime power of the symbolic, which we have made and which makes us, but which we do not control. But it is also an image of the sublime power of capital, which underwrites the building of the city and the extension of its grid according to the dialectic of enlightenment, which is, in that sense, nothing other than the unfathomable drive circulating around the real of capital, a drive that destroys the very symbolic order that sustains and reproduces its source code and makes it meaningful.

Even at origin, the imaginary representation of the symbolic is already in a state of advanced decay. "Myth is already enlightenment, and enlightenment reverts to mythology."[3] The real of capital appears amid the decay as that point at which the dialectic turns back on itself, and the city seems no longer opposed to nature but is instead revealed as its deepest and most obscure expression. Self-preservation, the impulse to defend and protect the self as imaginary identity, turns the dialectic even as it undermines the production of that identity by destroying all symbolic efficacy—the bond between subjects that makes identity, and so the recognition of self—possible.

"Everything Looks More Beautiful in Retrospect"

The vague foreboding of this opening image and the title sequence that follows stems from the recognition of that gap in the image that marks the real of capital. This inability to adequately imagine or symbolize the source of the dialectic without regressing to mythological formulations that mystify precisely what they would enlighten defines the very condition of living under capitalism. The sequence unsettles everything. The corporate credits unwound to a brief, amorphous musical introduction, but the musical articulations matched those of the image fairly closely. The music did not pull against itself, even as it built to a violently dissonant climax. The music of the title sequence, by contrast, is initially divided between a metrically insistent repeating motif—composer Chris Bacon calls it a "rolling string figure"[4]—and more chaotic gestures orchestrated with masking techniques such as flute playing flutter tongue, heavily muted brass, percussive flourishes, and sharp dissonant stingers that suggest alienation, the world awry. Even as the orchestration becomes less veiled on the second (louder) pass through the material, the musical figures continue somewhat at odds with the string line that provides the underlying metrical grid. The overall effect is one of menace, of a kind of wild, infernal machine throwing off disquieting musical figures as it traces a relentless path toward some undetermined destination.

The images themselves are similarly divided throughout the title sequence, with a set of disorienting mismatched cuts that, despite offering an almost God's-eye perspective, seem to be searching for some elusive commonality to the modern city and its surroundings as the view passes over, through, and among the visible infrastructure—roads, buildings, waterways, train tracks, and landscapes—that supports the city. In the sequence, a dominant place is assumed by images of modern transport, as that which channels desire along prescribed routes; of modern skyscrapers, as terminals of and monuments to capitalist accumulation; and of bodies of water, as an older, natural channel of desire more or less written over by the roads and rails of modern transport without, however, having disappeared.

The relation of music and image is such that they do not settle into each other because the music does not seem to take particular note of elements in the images, and the cutting does not closely follow the rhythms or articulations of the music. The one consistent exception to this is the extradiegetic text announcing the names of the actors and other creative personnel, which appear at regular intervals synchronized to the hypermetrical structure of the music. The effect is to associate the infernal machine described by the music with this extradiegetic level of the filmmaking, which is also that of the corporate credits and capital control. If this music also becomes coupled to the images of trains through sheer force of repetition and through the tendency to seek in the image an explanation for the soundtrack (or vice versa), the train likewise forges a symbolic link to capital, as an opaque expression of its dialectical drive. Yet these links all remain tenuous enough that soundtrack and image track do not resolve into an imaginary unity but instead stage a kind of play of missed synchronization, where the unruly sounds and images refuse the relation of complementarity in order to expose the natural state of diegetic synchronization as fantasy. This purposeful failure is less an instance of critical reflection, however, than another means of motivating the reversion to mythological figures.

"It Doesn't End Well for You"

After the amorphous introduction for the corporate credits, the music for the titles follows a basic tripartite structure common to title sequences. The first part, which is repeated in slightly varied form, is centered in E and anchored by the recurring four-bar string figure, which, although occasionally masked, only disappears with the turn to the more lyrical middle section. Bacon associates this lyrical music with the source code. Appropriate to its name, the tune here has a primal sound, being constructed around the intervals of the perfect fifth and the step, a broad but mostly square rhythmic profile, and having little of the motoric quality of the rolling string figure. It is also initially scored for the full violin section in an upper register, an orchestration that is usually reserved in cinema for statements of lyrical fulfillment. After a modulation, it then passes to the horn, an orchestration that retains its connotations of the heroic style from the concert repertory and the operatic stage. The music presents its modulations as bold, moving first from B♭ (a tritone away from the opening tonic E) to A, and then in abridged form from D♭ to C, where the music nominally remains until the whiteout to the train that opens the first run of the source code. The modulations occur at the phrase boundaries, however, so the bold effect of the modulations is achieved by attenuating mediation, akin to tonal blocks slipping past one another rather than transforming internally, even when the orchestration is retained across the modulation. This, too, is the work of mythologization: it dispossesses the lyricism and heroicism of its subjectivity and instead presents the atavistic motivic material as though moved by some mysterious force.

"It Doesn't Matter What You Do to Them. They're Already Dead"

Water, sky, divided by a slice of wooded land. Signs of human intervention are evident in Figure 29.3—a thin ribbon of white (a road, perhaps), a path to the water—but, unlike the city, where machines (cars, trains) move about as indices of human presence, human

FIGURE 29.3 The Duck Pond.

activity is here initially absent. This shot doubles the opening shot of the city, now seem-ingly from the perspective of nature, with land encroaching on the water and sky, most literally with respect to the water, as swamp grasses and even trees protrude into it like the piers of the city. The trees also extend into the sky, but they bear none of the promi-nence or menace of the buildings of the city. As the view tracks quickly forward over the water, reproducing the movement of the entrance into the city, a duck quacks and takes flight, as though spooked by the approach of some unseen threat. The view passes indif-ferently over the duck, the waters grow reflective (something that does not happen to the waters of the city, which remain cloudy, but frequently does with shots of bodies of water in the more rural and suburban locations), and a moving train begins to appear, the white ribbon revealed as train tracks, nature no longer absent human activity.

The narrative status of this shot across the duck pond is peculiar. If the opening shots of Chicago and the trains crossing the rural areas can be assigned to the introductory function of the title sequence, this shot is more difficult to place. On the one hand, it fol-lows immediately one of the more striking of the overhead city shots, which includes the Frank Gehry-designed BP Pedestrian Bridge winding across the city grid in serpentine fashion. The credit sequence contains several shots similar to the duck pond, although none of them absents human activity or plays up the iconography of the natural setting to the same extent. The music also clearly identifies the shot as part of the titles, as the music takes no notice of the cut but continues to build the motoric motive toward a climax. On the other hand, the duck call announces something new—prior to this, the only diegetic noise had been of passing trains and perhaps some very faint waves for the initial shot of the city. The shot of the duck pond is also repeated three additional times in the film, each instance initializing a run of the source code. These subsequent appearances assimilate the shot to the code, although it cannot belong to the running of the source code proper since its point of view cannot be attributed to the afterglow of Sean's consciousness. It seems instead to be the code's initializing sequence, bearing the same relationship to the code itself as the corporate credits and perhaps the title sequence do to the film, neither entirely inside nor outside.

As the view closes in on the train, the music reaches a fevered climax, quickly dissolving into and displaced by a grating train sound that coincides with a brief white screen that signifies the start of the source code. The scene opens on a bearded young man who appears to be asleep, his reflection partially obscured, as though clouded over, in the train window. A soft metallic ring (thin like the music for the very opening of the film but without the wavering to give the impression of an alarm and now resembling the faint squealing of train wheels on a corner), sounds as explosions, snatches of unintelligible voices on the radio, and helicopter rotors float unmotivated on the soundtrack like a distant dream. He opens his eyes, which are oddly mismatched, one appearing distinctly lighter in color than the other. The horn of a passing train startles the man fully awake and sound then seems to assail him from all directions: Coke can, coffee spilling, trains going by, the punching of tickets, the voices of the woman sitting across from him, and other passengers. The man's continually disoriented reaction to it all denaturalizes the sound, unlocks the uncanny effect that attends the synchronization of sound to source but is rarely thematized as such. The sound really does not want to settle with the image, just as music and image did not want to settle in the title sequence, just as this man's consciousness, thrown, we soon learn, into the body of another man on the train, does not want to settle into that body. Is it too fanciful to note that the film is organized around a recurring "explosion point,"[5] an emphatic sync point that ends each of the source code runs except the final one and that the plot is premised on avoiding?

"We Have to Keep Doing This"

Colter Stevens, a man barely alive. If the government of the 1970s rebuilt its damaged soldier "better, stronger, faster" with the technology of robotics, today's damaged soldier is remade virtually only as an ordinary civilian through computer technology. In both cases, the era's distinctive technology vivifies the nearly dead body, makes that body into a response to deep cultural trauma, into a vital force in combating the nation's peculiar existential threat. In the case of Steve Austin, he becomes the man perfected through bionics, the cyborg prototype deployed to represent the United States in the proxy war with the Soviet Union but even more to battle the corruption and lawless power that the Cold War had unleashed. In the case of Colter Stevens, he becomes the man abstracted into computer code, deployed to fight the menace of a stateless terrorism. Whereas the bionic man therefore serves primarily a regulative function, damping the forces of disorder that threaten to undo the delicate Cold War balance of power promised by detente, the virtual man primarily serves a restorative function, opposing the forces of disorder that threaten to destroy the last remaining superpower. In both cases, the forces of disintegration are generated dialectically from the system, dissolving all distinction between interior and exterior threat. Steve Austin is more likely to find himself battling a rogue arms dealer or corrupt government official than a Soviet agent, and Colter Stevens, although all but killed in Afghanistan and initially seeking the terrorist in marks of the other, discovers that the bomber occupies the privileged class of the American white male.

This discovery opens up an unexpected chain of signification: the bomber's libertarian fantasy of blowing up society in order to give it the freedom to rebuild itself from the rubble possesses a cold calculus that suits the name of Derek Frost. Derek, which means "ruler of the people," is also a homonym for derrick, a lifting device like a crane used in shipping and extraction industries. His cold thought is also the product of the Cold War—the most virulent contemporary form of libertarianism descends from the writings of Ayn Rand—as is the nuclear threat, which lives in the afterglow of the arms race. Colter Stevens might likewise be parsed as "colder head," from Steven, crown, which might link him to Derek's intellectual frost or, what amounts to the same thing, to death; but the name also relates to "colt," suggesting both the young horse and the gun, icons of the American West, which was mined and exploited for its mineral resources, much of which passed through Chicago on its way East. Sean (God is gracious) Fentress (bold, adventuresome), by contrast, serves not just as the source code and absented body to be filled but also as ego-ideal, consistent with the reading of the mirror phase according to Lacan. That the names of the two principal female characters—Christina (follower of Christ) Warren (watchman); Colleen (girl) Goodwin (good friend)—bear similarly allegorical meanings and that Derek's personal information and even physical description changes from one ID to the next makes the whole seem rather like a dreamscape.

"This Isn't the End"

Bacon locates the "emotional climax of the film" but also of the music in the "frozen moment," the arresting track through the freeze frame after the source code has run its course for the last time and Goodwin has shut off Colter's life support in the primary narrative thread. According to Bacon's description, music (but also the film) finds its fullest emotional expression when time, too, yields to cold logic, freezes over, and, sealed with a kiss, completely congeals, poignantly reminding us that one moment those who are alive and content may in the next moment be dead. In a dialectical reversal, however, the freeze turns from an omen of death to one of possibility and offers something more than sentimental comfort that at least they died happy. If every moment that advances into the next is laid over an averted catastrophe, the passing of time expresses the hope that the catastrophe is not yet fated, that the source code can be transcended, that origin is not destiny, that the world might yet be otherwise. Absolutely out of field and out of time, music, flickering with what therefore seems like a divine spark, warms this time frozen in the infinite expanse, but also possibilities of the moment.

The kiss evidently awakens a desire that the sentimentality of the frozen image cannot contain, and Bacon seizes on this desire, noting that the frozen moment "provided the opportunity to write a theme for Colter and Christina that we were able to parse up a bit and allude to in several earlier scenes, but reserve the full statement for this moment."[6] Bacon, however, seemingly misremembers his music here, which is, for the duration of the freeze frame, lyrically empty and powerfully so: this is the aching music of unrealized potentiality rather than fulfillment; it marks out the timeless time and expands it with drawn out rubatos as though uncertain about how and whether it can proceed. Scored for piano and glockenspiel with relatively static string accompaniment, the theme is based on the head motive of the source code theme (a repeated fifth and a step on the lower end), with a rising line in the bass that will subsequently assume considerable importance. When the view shifts back to Goodwin with Colter lying dead, the static pitch of the ECG, first heard at the beginning of the freeze frame and reminiscent of the very opening music to the film, sounds as a pedal, and the music, now scored primarily for piano and flute, turns contemplative, before reluctantly winding its way to the preparation for a cadence in C. At the approach of this cadence, played by the strings and freighted with the full symbolism of death, the view returns to the frozen moment, where, instead of closure, something extraordinary occurs: the cadence is averted and time resumes its seemingly mundane course. A new theme, based on the rising bass line of the music for the frozen moment, appears in the strings and prepares the ground for the appearance of the lush romantic theme associated with Colter and Christiana. This theme is heard at various points throughout the film, most recently at the beginning of the last source code run. Here, it is stated first intimately by the piano and then ecstatically by the strings as the train enters the city. A diegetically unanchored radio voice announces unseasonably warm weather, as shots of Chicago similar to the title sequence show spring blossoms emerging from the winter freeze.

Throughout the final minutes of the film, the music assiduously avoids closure. It makes one very tentative full cadence, when, as they are entering the AT&T Plaza to see Anish Kapoor's Cloud Gate sculpture, Colter mentions to Christina that he has no cash, as though the very mention of money has grown taboo. "Such a beautiful day, isn't it?" Colter says. "Yeah, it is a really perfect day," Christina responds, and the music quickly resumes, building to another euphoric outburst of the romantic theme as they hurry to the sculpture. As they look into its mirrored surface, which reflects their distorted place in this world rebuilt on the fantasy of desire, the music runs through the same cadential material, but this time it dissipates wholly unresolved for the beginning of the epilogue.

"Do You Believe in Fate?"

The epilogue also begins with a radio voice, which likewise delivers a weather report, this time ominous, cloudy rather than sunny, and without any semblance of a God's-eye view in the images. Goodwin begins to read an e-mail on her phone, and Colter's voice is heard in voice-over. With a cut to her cell phone, music returns, its cast again nervous, frantic, conspiratorial. Goodwin rushes to Rutledge's office, where she learns that the content of the message is true. The music at this point begins to replay, nearly verbatim, the opening of the film, the music for the corporate credits continuing through the remainder of the scene in the office. With a cut to Goodwin entering the room holding Colter's damaged body, a varied and slightly abridged version of the title music begins, as Colter finishes his message and requests Goodwin's help. This music continues into the end credits.

If Colter as Sean has found the idyll of perfection in the reflective corporate abstraction of the Cloud Gate sculpture, Colter as military body is doomed to wait with iffy assurances and is still, indeed, caught within the vortex of the cultural trauma that is simply waiting for a point of irrationality around which to organize. The uncanny repetition of the music here recognizes that the source code is destined to begin again, that the fantastic reflections caught within Cloud Gate are purchased at a terrible cost. Perhaps the Goodwin who received the text message recognizes this as well. In any case, she chooses to keep Colter's message to herself. Colter as Sean is living the fantasy of desire without fully acknowledging the sacrificial substitution that founded its libidinal economy, so it is not surprising that he cannot recognize that the world built from his fantasy has done nothing but displace the trauma.

NOTES

1. On the real of capital, see Slavoj Žižek, "Against the Popular Temptation," *Critical Inquiry* 32, no. 3 (2006): 551–574.
2. James Buhler, "Enchantments of The Lord of the Rings: Soundtrack, Myth, Language, and Modernity," in *From Hobbits to Hollywood: Essays on Peter Jackson's Lord of the Rings*, ed. Murray Pomerance and Ernest Mathijs (Amsterdam: Editions Rodopi, 2006), 231–233. Not every logo follows this script, of course. Older studio logos frequently used official imprimaturs such as shields, seals, banners, and badges, and many current corporate credits do not mythologize in precisely this way.
3. Max Horkheimer and Theodor Adorno, *Dialectic of Enlightenment: Philosophical Fragments*, trans. Edmund Jephcott (Stanford: Stanford University Press, 2002), xviii.
4. Lakeshore Records, "Lakeshore Records to Release *Source Code* Soundtrack," Press release, March 1, 2011, Film Score Monthly discussion board, posted by "CineMedia Promotions," March 22, 2011. Accessed August 4, 2012, http://filmscoremonthly.com/board/posts.cfm?threadID=77539.
5. Reni Celeste, "The Frozen Screen: Levinas and the Action Film," *Film-Philosophy* 11, no. 2 (2007): 26–28.
6. Lakeshore Records, "Lakeshore Records to Release *Source Code* Soundtrack."

SELECT BIBLIOGRAPHY

Buhler, James. "Enchantments of The Lord of the Rings: Soundtrack, Myth, Language, and Modernity." In *From Hobbits to Hollywood: Essays on Peter Jackson's Lord of the Rings*, edited by Murray Pomerance and Ernest Mathijs, 231–248. Amsterdam: Editions Rodopi, 2006.

Celeste, Reni. "The Frozen Screen: Levinas and the Action Film." *Film-Philosophy* 11, no. 2 (2007): 15–36.

Horkheimer, Max and Theodor Adorno. *Dialectic of Enlightenment: Philosophical Fragments.* Translated by Edmund Jephcott. Stanford, CA: Stanford University Press, 2002.

"Lakeshore Records to Release Source Code Soundtrack." Lakeshore Records press release, March 1, 2011. http://filmscoremonthly.com/board/posts.cfm?threadID=77539.

Žižek, Slavoj. "Against the Popular Temptation." *Critical Inquiry* 32, no. 3 (2006): 551–574.

PART IX

··

RETHINKING AUDIOVISUAL EMBODIMENT

··

CHAPTER 30

....

VIRTUAL AND VISCERAL
EXPERIENCE IN
MUSIC-ORIENTED
VIDEO GAMES

....

KIRI MILLER

"VIRTUAL frets, actual sweat": the title of a *New York Times* article on *Guitar Hero* summed up the core appeal of the rock-oriented video games that captured a huge portion of the digital game market from 2006 to 2010.[1] Before *Guitar Hero II* became a breakout hit in 2006, "rhythm games" had been considered a niche category; by the end of 2010, the *Guitar Hero* and *Rock Band* franchises had sold over 46 million game units and brought in over $3 billion in revenue.[2] In 2011, *Guitar Hero III* was declared the top-selling video game ever released, after it grossed $830.9 million in less than four years.[3] The games offered a new platform for digital music distribution, as labels vied to place their artists in new game editions and players paid millions of dollars to download additional songs that had been transcribed and coded for gameplay. As of spring 2011, the *Rock Band* series had generated over 100 million downloads of additional game repertoire from a catalog of 2,700 songs—as well as driving sales of recordings by artists featured in the games, purchased for listening rather than playing.[4]

Guitar Hero and *Rock Band* created a parlor music renaissance, with plastic instrument controllers and downloadable content (DLC) replacing the pianos and sheet music of the nineteenth and early twentieth centuries (see Figures 30.1 and 30.2).[5] In mainstream media outlets and the digital public sphere, commentators seized on the question of the games' musical authenticity and the players' moral fiber: to some, this instant-gratification route to rock heroism seemed emblematic of "everything that's wrong with pop culture."[6] Debate often centered on whether the games were facile fantasy-enablers or potential stepping-stones to "real" music making: might they foster genuine musical skills, inspire players to pick up real instruments, or otherwise prove

FIGURE 30.1 *Rock Band* guitar controller. (Photograph by the author.)

FIGURE 30.2 *Rock Band* drum controller. (Photograph by the author.)

themselves socially valuable? Meanwhile, exasperated fans asserted that the games were *just games* and should be evaluated on their own terms rather than on the basis of their musical authenticity, realism, or educational potential.[7]

This values-oriented reception discourse often precluded inquiry into how these games work and what it feels like to play them: how do virtual frets lead to actual sweat? Because the games relied on the "guitar hero" trope and revolved around virtual rock

concert performance, many commentators assumed that players were seduced by fantasies of stardom: the thrill of commanding the adulation of the games' screaming crowds.
Game advertising encouraged this assumption, dwelling on the stylized bodies of the
rock-star avatars who model players' living room performances. Live rock performance
is both spectacular and familiar, a genre with established conventions and associations;
the "guitar hero" model offered an easy way to telegraph an appealing core game concept
to consumers. However, when I undertook qualitative research on *Guitar Hero* and *Rock
Band* gameplay, I noticed that few players referred to rock-star fantasies or to identifying
with the avatar musicians. Instead, players described getting lost in the music, feeling
like they were improvising guitar solos, seeing the games' streaming musical notation
in their heads when songs from the games came on the radio, feeling responsible for the
games' musical output, and experiencing a profound sense of mastery when difficult
musical passages suddenly felt effortless and natural under their fingers. In other words,
their "actual sweat" derived from visceral musicality at least as much as from virtual
stardom.

    Guitar Hero and *Rock Band* encourage players to explore what it means to be a live
performer of a prerecorded song, a phenomenon I refer to as "schizophonic performance."[8] They exemplify and exploit "the inherent tensions at play between the live
ontology of performance arts and the mediatized, non-live, and simulacral nature of
virtual technologies."[9] These music-oriented video games offer a distinctive, generative
model for considering the nature of digital audiovisuality because they build on the long
cultural history of technological mediation and virtuality in musical production and
reception: from acoustic musical instruments to recording, amplification, multitrack
editing, electronic instruments, turntablism, digital sampling, karaoke, lipsyncing, and
air guitar.[10] I draw here on Marie-Laure Ryan's exegesis of "the virtual," which includes
both "the largely negative idea of the fake, illusionary, non-existent, and the overwhelmingly positive idea of the potential, which connotes productivity, openness, and diversity." Ryan argues that the human body "is virtualized by any practice and technology
aiming at expanding its sensorium, altering its appearance, or pushing back its biological limits."[11] In this sense, all musical technologies are intrinsically virtual: they allow for
sound production or reproduction that extends the capacities of the human body, channels sensory and temporal experience, cultivates empathy (virtual emotional response),
and generates "relational infrastructure" across communities of practice.[12]

    Although sound plays the starring role in most Western definitions of musical experi-
ence, music is always already multisensory—audiovisual, unfolding in time, and physically engaging, whether one is singing, playing an instrument, dancing, listening with
a still body, or imagining music.[13] All of these aspects of musical experience are culturally mediated; in contemporary Western culture, they are often mediated by the notion
that some people are "musical" and others are not. As technologists have worked on
developing music production software, new musical instruments, digital games, and
other innovative musical interfaces, some have adopted the credo that new technologies
might not only create "new social modalities for listening to music," but also "reintro-
duce casual social contexts for making music…offer[ing] an empowering experience

to those who would not otherwise participate in making music."[14] The fact that so many people identify as "not musical" has created an opening for technologically mediated solutions: platforms for musical practice that are accessible to novices, nonintimidating, anonymous, private, or otherwise low stakes—sometimes because they are presented as "just games" or "not really musical" at all. This means designing interfaces around aspects of musical experience that haven't been stigmatized as "musical." For instance, as Tina Blaine and Sidney Fels suggest, designers might focus on "movement, gesture, touch, and physical interactions such as dancing with strangers in highly customized environments," rather than "highly complex single player instruments developed for experts." As Blaine and Fels observe, "These design strategies lay the foundation for developing intimate personal connections with other players and their instruments over relatively short periods of time, and also help foster a sense of community."[15]

The guitar, bass, and drum controllers included with the *Guitar Hero* and *Rock Band* games have been by far the most widely distributed and commercially success-ful of these novice-friendly "alternate controllers" to date.[16] This chapter explores the reasons for that success, focusing on the tightly integrated multisensory experience afforded by these games. I also address the less-successful *DJ Hero* games, which were designed to extend the purview of the "Hero" franchise beyond rock into the realm of hip-hop, house, and other club music genres. Despite a holiday marketing push, celeb-rity tie-ins, and generally excellent game-industry reviews of the gameplay experience, *DJ Hero* did not achieve hit status. I analyze player reviews of the game—particularly reviews that make comparisons to *Guitar Hero* and *Rock Band*—to shed light on this outcome and its implications for virtual musicality. Throughout the chapter, I make gen-eralizations about gameplay that are drawn from five years of qualitative research on these games, including surveys, gameplay/interview sessions with players, interviews with game designers, media reception analysis, and fieldwork at gamer bar nights and tournaments.[17]

GUITAR HERO AND ROCK BAND: DESIGNING VIRTUAL MUSICIANSHIP

When the game developers at Harmonix Music Systems began work on the first *Guitar Hero* game, they did so with the specific aim of developing a game that featured a guitar-shaped controller—a "peripheral," in industry terms. "Peripherals" are devices that aren't part of the standard game-console set-up; they require players to buy new hardware in addition to the game software, which means potentially higher profit margins for game publishers, as well as opportunities for innovative gameplay design. RedOctane, a company that made dance-pad controllers for the *Dance Dance Revolution* games, wanted to branch out into selling guitar controller peripherals, so they com-missioned Harmonix to create a guitar game. The electric guitar is a powerful cultural symbol, with built-in associations for both musicians and nonmusicians—it indexes rock music, masculinity, American youth culture, innovation, creativity, electricity (literal "power"), spectacular live performance, and the "guitar hero," an improvising, virtuosic, rebel genius who has mastered the instrument and bends it to his will in front of an adoring crowd.[18] As Steve Waksman notes, musical instruments are valued not only for innovations but for "the stability they offer, for the ways in which they connect with 'traditional' sounds and practices." Musicians are never simply playing instruments according to their basic physical affordances; they are also "engag[ing] with the techniques, the gestures, the sounds, and the meanings to which the instrument has given rise."[19]

The electric guitar thus offered a rich, robust organizing principle for the new game. The designers at Harmonix had the luxury of building on an archive of associations, counting on players' intuitive grasp of what the electric guitar meant. As long as they developed a controller that was visually recognizable as a guitar, could be physically associated with the guitar repertoire through gameplay, and that incorporated (or left room for) some of the physical gestures of rock guitar performance, they could dispense with strings, frets, a pick, and other fundamental elements of actual guitar construction and playing technique. Since the game was explicitly intended to bring the feeling of playing music to nonmusicians,[20] the controller did not have to meet the authenticity standards of guitarists; it needed to look and feel *just enough* like a guitar to make the player using it look and feel *just enough* like a musician.[21] The indisputably authentic rock music coming out of the speakers, the rock-star avatars on screen, and the cheering virtual crowd that provided real-time feedback on a player's performance would fill the gap. As lead designer Rob Kay put it, "It just seemed right to us to make it about balls-out rock guitar. That's the iconic thing that bringing a guitar game to America should be all about.... Often in video games, it's those clichés that are easy to hold onto and get into.... Even though I wouldn't necessarily identify that American guitar rock as being my favorite thing, I know what it is and I know how to get into it."[22]

At the same time, Harmonix faced the core design challenge of balancing musical control and accessibility.[23] If gameplay simply consisted of pushing buttons in time with a prerecorded track, the game would not feel interactive, and players would not feel responsible for the musical output—but if players were given too much control over the sound, the results would not be rock hits and the promise of "guitar heroism" would be broken. Rob Kay told me that the company initially tried to develop a guitar "freestyle" system, "which was going to give you creative, musical control by triggering samples and creating your own guitar solos," but they weren't satisfied with the results:

> ROB KAY: It was too difficult to make it sound good, and feel sure that it would be learnable, and all the things that we'd want for a fully creative game.
> KM: So you got the sense that people would only be able to play kind of bad-sounding solos on it?
> ROB KAY: Yeah, because even we could only play bad-sounding solos on it.

Players would need visual instructions to lead them through the prerecorded music: a musical notation system. Experienced gamers would also expect a series of goal-oriented tasks and a responsive evaluation system: audio, visual, and/or tactile feedback related to successful or unsuccessful play, and cumulative, quantifiable rewards in the form of points, energy, or some other familiar metric. Moreover, as Rob Kay noted, the designers aspired "to make the simulation more than just a clinical recreation of music. We had this ambition...to bring some showmanship, as well as musicianship to the experience." They wanted players to draw on their visceral understanding of the pleasure and excitement of rock performance, rather than on their preconceptions about the difficulty of reading music or the tedium of practicing an instrument. "If the whole mindset was too much about a music simulator it would just turn people off, you know. We don't have little notes [i.e., standard music notation symbols]. You never see a little note in a Harmonix game....If someone saw a sheet of music, and that was their intro to *Guitar Hero*, they would run."

The resulting basic design characteristics remained consistent across all the *Guitar Hero* and *Rock Band* games (as well as *DJ Hero*, created later by another developer). A notation track streams down the screen, much like the roadway in a driving game (see Figure 30.3). Colored "gems" on this track represent musical notes. As the gems pass the bottom of the screen, guitarists have to press specific fret buttons while simultaneously hitting the strum bar on the guitar controller; drummers have to strike specific drum pads or step on the kick-drum pedal. When they play accurately, players accumulate points and build up "star power" or "overdrive energy" (depending on the game), which can be periodically deployed for a burst of bonus points and rewarding audiovisual feedback: the screen lights up with electric effects and the crowd goes wild. On the guitar controller, players activate "star power" by raising the neck of the guitar into the air—an iconic rock performance gesture that was intended to invite players to "put themselves

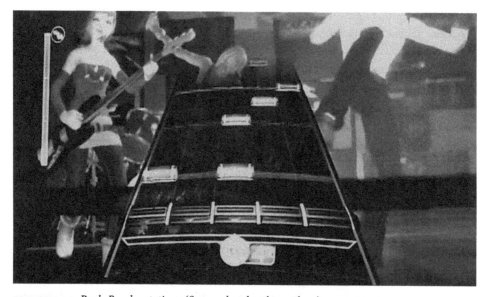

FIGURE 30.3 *Rock Band* notation. (Screenshot by the author.)

in the shoes of a rock star," in Rob Kay's words. He explained, "We were always keen to get people doing that move, because once you give people this cue that their physical performance has got something to do with the game,... you're suddenly in the mindset, and thinking about all of those rock star moves that you see people do, and then [you'll] just jump around and do the rest."

While this "star power" feedback system models the buildup of live performance adrenaline and encourages players to adopt a rock star identity, negative feedback plays a crucial role in training players' ears and making them feel responsible for the game's musical output. When a player doesn't hit the right notes at the right time, the game provides audible and visible mistake indicators (e.g., the missed gem turns red, the notation track shakes, there is the sound of a flubbed guitar strum). Most important, the music associated with those gems drops out of the audio track. Matt Boch, creative designer of hardware at Harmonix, explained the impact of this feedback system:

> You get all this musical knowledge that you would have to grind so long for otherwise, in an instant.... There are a lot of people who turn on a song, and it's a song. And they couldn't tell you what the bass player's playing, versus what the guitar player's playing, versus the synthesizer in the background, or any of those elements.... And playing this game does a really easy trick, which is deciding that the success of one event determines the muting of one track. It equates two things which are actually not equal, and does this great trick to your brain which is hugely pleasurable, and educates you in a way by pulling [the track] away. It's this simple, "One of these things is not like the other."... And bang, it's there right in front of you.[24]

Guitar Hero and *Rock Band* require players to learn a notation system, translate its symbols into specific physical techniques, integrate aural and visual cues to anticipate the next set of required actions, and do it all while keeping up with the temporal flow of a song. For novices, it's as though one's very first guitar lesson required sight-reading sheet music while sitting in with a professional band. The game designers made this task possible by notating each song at four different difficulty levels (easy, medium, hard, and expert), as well as by presenting the song list in each game as a graded repertoire, from the simplest to the most challenging. When players attempt a song on the "easy" setting, a single on-screen gem and corresponding button on the guitar controller might yield a long guitar riff on the audio track; on "expert," there are gems for each note in the riff. As players improve, they go back and play through the same repertoire again at higher difficulty levels. The audio output is exactly the same, but it's much more difficult to produce.

In the world of digital gaming, this is a curious design feature. In a shooter game, for instance, it would seem very strange if players were encouraged to go through the same assassination mission several times, using increasingly complex button combinations on the controller with each iteration. It is a compelling pursuit in these music games because the player is bringing the distinct audio, visual, and kinesthetic elements of gameplay into closer alignment with each new difficulty level. Players often find the "easy" version of songs disconcerting because of the mismatch between the simplified on-screen notation and the more complex musical track coming through the speakers;

this sensory clash offers constant reminders of the gap between the players' actions on the controller and the musical performance of the recorded musician.[25] Players who already know a song by ear often find themselves trying to play more notes than are presented in the notation. But on the "expert" level, when there is note-to-note correspondence between the on-screen notation, the player's actions, and the musical track, players experience a satisfying sense of coherence. One player told me, "From a very instinctive point of view, like as a human, it just feels *right* and it feels like I am doing something worthwhile."[26]

    Guitar Hero and *Rock Band* gameplay cultivates a focused, intimate, immersive, multisensory relationship with music—something that is increasingly unusual in contemporary musical reception contexts, where multitasking is so common. As Harmonix co-founder Alex Rigopulos observed in a published interview, "When you need to move your body in synchrony with the music in specific ways, it connects you with the music in a deeper way than when you are just listening to it." In the same article, Paul McCartney described *The Beatles: Rock Band* as "'a natural, modern extension' of what the Beatles did in the '60s, only now people can feel as if 'they possess or own the song, that they've been in it.'"[27] The hundreds of players who completed my online survey or participated in gameplay/interview sessions often expressed the same sentiment, describing how they would "get completely caught up in the visceral 'feel' of a particularly gripping song."[28] One player broke down his experience this way: "Hitting the right notes, taking in the music, kind of isolating the different sounds you're hearing, working through the song, listening, kind of dissecting it, seeing how well the game is relating to the song and you're relating to the game's relation, and whether or not those align with what you expect."[29] Many people recounted the process of laboring over certain playing techniques until the day when they suddenly became effortless. As a *Rock Band* drummer told me, "Sometimes I'll be really into the rhythm, and I'll notice my foot is doing the two taps at the right time [i.e., double-kick patterns on the kick drum pedal], but it feels like I'm only telling it to do one, but it does two anyway. That's what it's supposed to do."[30] In general, players' accounts support Grodal's observation that video games "allow 'the full experiential flow' by linking perceptions, cognitions, and emotions with first-person actions. Motor cortex and muscles focus the audiovisual attention, and provide 'muscular' reality and immersion to the perceptions."[31] Players' experiences also point to the intrinsic affinities between playing video games and playing musical instruments.

DJ HERO: WHEN VIRTUAL FALLS SHORT OF VISCERAL

The first *DJ Hero* game was released in 2009, with considerable marketing fanfare. It was meant to capitalize on the market dominance of the *Guitar Hero* name while also reaching out to a new group of players: fans of hip-hop, techno, house, and other sample-based dance music genres, rather than the rock, punk, and metal at the core of the *Guitar Hero* and *Rock Band* repertoires. Since *DJ Hero* revolved around mashups and remixes, it also offered a new angle on digital music distribution: the game could bring exclusive, original musical content to market while still drawing on the name recognition of celebrity artists. Endorsements from hip-hop luminaries like Eminem and Jay-Z played up the "hero" theme, helping to bridge the awkward conceptual gap dividing lead rock guitarists from club DJs—although these stars are in fact MCs, not DJs. Perhaps to compensate for this discrepancy, the venerable turntablist Grandmaster Flash did the voice-over work for the game's tutorial system, lending it subcultural capital and a connection to hip-hop history. DJs rarely achieve the mainstream celebrity of MCs, but they continue to play key roles as cultural gatekeepers, archivists, arbiters of cool, and engineers of transformative dance floor experience; in contemporary youth cultures around the world, it's not uncommon to hear that "everyone wants to be a DJ."[32]

Nonetheless, only about 300,000 people bought *DJ Hero* in the month after its release, and the game was regarded as a commercial flop.[33] Sales surpassed a million units only after bargain-basement discounting (from an initial price of $120 to around $40). *DJ Hero 2* was released in 2010. Just a few months later Activision, the publisher of all the *Hero* games, announced that they were discontinuing the entire franchise due to declining sales.[34]

What happened? Industry writers pointed to market saturation in the music/rhythm game sector, as well as to the simultaneous economic downturn; consumers might be unwilling to pay $120 for yet another peripheral-oriented game. But the *DJ Hero* gameplay experience suggests other reasons for its weak performance. When I first sat down to play the game, I was perplexed by the controller: a peculiar hybrid of a record player, a mixer, and a *Guitar Hero* guitar (see Figure 30.4). Color-coded buttons reminiscent of a guitar controller's fret buttons are superimposed on a turntable platter—and there is only one turntable, although the game is purportedly all about mixing records. A cross-fader switch provides the mixer element, but where is the other sound source that the player is supposed to be mixing? (See Figure 30.5.) My initial gameplay notes on *DJ Hero* reflected on the implications of this design choice:

> I have no DJing experience myself—indeed, I still get nervous about actually setting a needle down on a record, on the rare occasions that I attempt such a thing. But I've spend a lot of time with DJs, and I've taught a lot of classes that revolve around post-turntablism music. When I'm teaching a unit about hip-hop, I often begin by asking the class, "Why are two turntables better than one?" And when I watch a DJ at work with two turntables and a mixer, I'm often awed by his/her ambidextrous virtuosity. Of course club DJs today use all kinds of equipment, but given that *DJ Hero* features a turntable at all (vs. any of the myriad other interface possibilities for simulating real-time remix production), it seems peculiar to just use one. Especially when the game tutorial voiceover is by Grandmaster Flash (who starts things off by emphasizing his own turntablism pioneer status). There's something surreal about having Grandmaster Flash explain that each of the three buttons on the single

FIGURE 30.4 *DJ Hero* controller. (Photograph by the author.)

FIGURE 30.5 *DJ Hero* controller versus typical DJ turntables and mixer. (Photograph by the author.)

turntable represents a different sound source, as though *this* had been his pioneering innovation. Someone unfamiliar with record players might conclude that all records come broken into three concentric rings, which you can mix and match on your single turntable and manipulate individually as you play your set. And of course this implies the presence of three invisible tonearms/needles (the controller doesn't include any representation of the tonearm/needle at all).

When I actually started to play a *DJ Hero* set, I discovered the satisfying click of the cross-fader. This click has strong associations for me; at a club the music would be way too loud for me to hear it, but it's a big part of the sound when my DJ spouse is mixing in the living room. It helps me distinguish what he's doing with his mix vs. what was already part of the mix on each record (because the clicking cues me that he's shifting between the two sources). I also just like the sound—the crispness of it, and the way that it makes a rhythmic pattern of its own that interlocks with the rhythm of the musical mix in interesting ways. So while the turntable part of the controller packed more associations visually, once I was playing the game it was the cross-fader that made me feel more aligned with a DJ's kinesthetic experience. The *DJ Hero* turntable doesn't even spin around during gameplay, except when you briefly spin it backward yourself on "rewinds." I certainly wasn't imagining a record was under my right hand. Maybe some kind of track pad, but not a record.[35]

Like *Guitar Hero* and *Rock Band*, *DJ Hero* certainly cultivates a physical relationship to the musical material. However, that relationship is built on a weak foundation. Players have trouble forging a visceral connection between their actions on the controller, the music they are hearing, and their preconceptions about the physical techniques and affective "feel" of DJing—that is, if they have such preconceptions at all. Consider these player reviews posted on the game's Amazon.com product page:

There is nothing intuitive with this game. A guitar, drum, singing. we all know how to do that, even if we can't play a tune in real life. But DJing is a different concept. (Tim E Robertson, posted November 15, 2009)

I have to say that the player who liked the game the best was the four year old, although he did have some questions—ranging from what is a record player to why would you want to scratch a record?...He was the one who played the game the longest, well after the teenagers left. He was intrigued by what a record player was. Intrigued and confused. (iGertrude, posted November 22, 2009)

What I loved about Rockband was the connection between you, the controller, the game and the music. When you make an action on the controller you see it both on the notes, the actions of the avatars and you hear it. This is the first mistake of DJ Hero, you don't feel like you are actually the musician. On Rockband you do. (M. Radcliffe, posted November 1, 2009)

In Rock Band, Guitar Hero and even Karaoke Revolution, you could listen to the background music and get into the rhythm and know when you'd hit the next key or sing along. In this game, you don't know what the predetermined mixes will choose to do, how they'll choose to mess with the songs. So you are at the mercy of your visual senses. I think people enjoyed the other games because they really felt like they were making the music, they felt musically connected. (Shannon B Davis, posted November 1, 2009)

The very nature of the gameplay also leaves something to be desired. That thing is "fun." As a huge hip-hop fan, I actually expected the more relatable music to add to my experience, but the experience wasn't nearly as visceral as banging out a song on the drums or even strumming through one on a plastic guitar. In the end, pressing buttons is pressing buttons unless you feel in tune with the music, and the poor "beat-charting" in DJ Hero leaves no room for that visceral feeling. (Akash, posted October 20, 2009)[36]

Players who lacked DJ experience had trouble understanding how their physical motions related to the complex remixes coming out of the speakers:

> DJ Hero lacks the 'campy fun' that you experience when someone thrusts a plastic guitar in your hand or sits you down infront of some plastic drums in Rock Band— DJ Hero simulates an experience that very few of us know exist and even less of us want to try. (Riyad Kalla, posted November 19, 2009)

> It isn't so different from its predecessors, so why does it fail to rock? It really lacks the visceral feeling of picking up a guitar and playing it. Also, I think most of us grew up seeing Rock Gods on MTV. We understand how the guitar is played and we see the Rock God (or Goddess, as the case may be) rocking out on the stage. DJs are unsung heroes, often behind the scenes. We boogie down to what they play—but do we understand how they do it? (Shannon B Davis, posted November 1, 2009)

> The group with whom I played were equal part intrigued and intimidated by the turntable controller—everyone wanted to try, but quickly got frustrated at how unnatural it felt. Face it—most of us have had momentary fits of air guitaring or drumming, but not so many have had that for DJing....Another issue is the mixes themselves. Each one is a mash-up of two tracks....At one point someone commented that you can barely even tell if you're doing well or not because your ears don't know what the end result is supposed to sound like. (D. R. Jeanclerc, posted October 22, 2009)

Those who did have DJing or digital remix experience were flummoxed by the disconnect between the play mechanics of *DJ Hero*'s hybrid turntable/mixer/sampler and their own understanding of actual remix production interfaces:

> The game is confused as to what it is trying to produce, it combines vinyl based mixing, digital vinyl based mixing (like Scrato, Traktor etc) and fully digital mixing (eg Ableton) into a single composition. Some of the transitions and effects you hear are simply not possible with vinyl. You have Armanda Van Burren CDJ style beat repeats and key points on one track and seconds later you have scratches. This is simply not possible without having 4 hands. (M. Radcliffe, posted November 1, 2009)

> I have 18 years experience as a mobile/club DJ and was excited when this game came out, but I am extremely disappointed. It is nothing compared to real scratching....[T]he game does a poor job of emulating the feel of a real vinyl.... AND WHY ONLY 1 TURNTABLE!? EVERY DJ SETUP I EVER SAW USES 2. (Oseph S. Vetrano, Jr., posted November 1, 2009)

***

Guitar Hero, Rock Band, and *DJ Hero* all aim to integrate kinesthetic engagement with audiovisual experience—in keeping with digital games' established role as "a paradigmatic site for producing, imagining, and testing different kinds of relations between the body and technology in contemporary culture."[37] Game designers have long understood that mutually reinforcing audio and visual stimuli set the stage for immersive gameplay. These music-oriented games go a step further by making physical engagement with the game controller meaningful and viscerally persuasive: whereas most games draw players into the on-screen gameworld, allowing them to master and forget the controller in their hands, these games draw attention to the controller as instrument and the living room as performance space. Moreover, their challenge-and-reward system is built around a dynamic process of bringing audio, visual, and kinesthetic experience into *ever-closer* alignment: becoming a good player means getting better and better at stitching one's own body to the sound coming out of the speakers, mending the schizophonic split between live and recorded music.[38]

But comparing players' experience of *Guitar Hero, Rock Band,* and *DJ Hero* (not to mention comparing their sales histories) adds nuance to this finding, highlighting the importance of the cultural knowledge that players bring to the games. As Laura Ermi and Frans Mäyrä have shown, gameplay immersion has sensory, challenge-based, and imaginative components, derived from a game's "audiovisual execution," the proper calibration of its technical and strategic challenges, and its narrative or characters.[39] *Guitar Hero* and *Rock Band* are light on narrative and characters, but they still rely on imaginative immersion grounded in prior knowledge. The iconic figure of the guitar hero, the familiar appearance and fret-and-strum mechanics of the guitar controller, and the basic assumption that rock songs are created by a group of musicians who are each responsible for producing one musical line: all these elements form the scaffolding for a player's initial experience with the games. Many *Guitar Hero* players told me that they had not previously been fans of the rock and metal songs featured in the games; as they developed an intimate relationship with these repertoires through gameplay, they came to be more appreciative listeners as well. Things didn't work out this way for *DJ Hero*. The game featured a well-designed, distinctive physical interface and a carefully curated lineup of hip-hop and electronic dance music tracks, but even avowed fans of these genres often reported that they felt less connected to the game music than they did when playing *Guitar Hero*.

It may seem that the moral of this story is that music-oriented game designers should stick with simulating traditional musical instruments if they want to hit the virtual/visceral sweet spot of multisensory immersion. However, there are other ways to build on players' internalized music-cultural knowledge and habitual modes of embodied engagement. For instance, several *DJ Hero* reviewers noted that the music in the game made them want to get up and dance. This visceral response has already become the conceptual seed of a new wave of games that teach players elaborate dance choreography.[40] Now that full-body motion-sensing technologies are becoming standard gaming equipment, designers have an opportunity to forge even deeper connections among audio, visual, and kinesthetic engagement. As experienced dancers already know, the human body can be a powerful musical instrument.

NOTES

1. Katie Zezima, "Virtual Frets, Actual Sweat," *New York Times*, July 15, 2007, http://www.nytimes.com/2007/07/15/fashion/15guitar.
2. These sales data are compiled from figures cited in César Berardini, "Rock Band Surpasses $1 Billion Dollars in Sales," *TeamXBox.com*, March 26, 2009, http://news.teamxbox.com/xbox/19228/Rock-Band-Surpasses-1-Billion-Dollars-in-Sales; Kris Graft, "Rock Band: 10m Units Shipped Worldwide," *Edge-Online.com*, February 12, 2009, http://www.edge-online.com/news/rock-band-10m-units-shipped-worldwide; Jeff Howe, "Why the Music Industry Hates Guitar Hero," *Wired.com*, February 23, 2009, http://www.wired.com/culture/culturereviews/magazine/17-03/st_essay; and Tor Thorsen, "NPD: Wii Play Top Us Best-Seller to Date," *GameSpot.com*, January 19, 2010, http://uk.gamespot.com/news/6246627.html. *Guitar Hero* (2005), *Guitar Hero II* (2006), and the *Rock Band* games (2007–2010) were developed by Harmonix Music Systems; *Guitar Hero III* (2007) and subsequent *Guitar Hero* games were developed by Neversoft.
3. Chris Morris, "Call of Duty, Guitar Hero Top All-Time Best Selling List," *CNBC*, March 24, 2011, http://www.cnbc.com/id/42253109.
4. Mike Rose, "Rock Band Passes 100m Song Downloads," *Gamasutra.com*, May 5, 2011, http://www.gamasutra.com/view/news/34521/Rock_Band_Passes_100_Million_Song_Downloads.php.
5. For accounts of earlier parlor-music technologies that offer striking parallels to the digital games discussed in this chapter, see Thomas Christensen, "Four-Hand Piano Transcription and Geographies of Nineteenth-Century Musical Reception," *Journal of the American Musicological Society* 52, no. 2 (1999); Mark Katz, *Capturing Sound: How Technology Has Changed Music* (Berkeley: University of California Press, 2004); and Timothy D. Taylor, "The Commodification of Music at the Dawn of the Era of 'Mechanical Music,'" *Ethnomusicology* 51, no. 2 (2007).
6. John, "Everything That's Wrong with Pop Culture in Two Photos," *theCHIVE.com*, February 24, 2010, http://web.archive.org/web/20100227011927/http://thechive.com/2010/02/24/everything-thats-wrong-with-pop-culture-in-two-photos-2-photos/. This post juxtaposes an iconic photograph of Johnny Cash making an obscene gesture at the photographer (labeled "Then") with an image of Miley Cyrus smashing a *Guitar Hero* controller during a video shoot (labeled "Now").
7. Kiri Miller, "Schizophonic Performance: *Guitar Hero, Rock Band*, and Virtual Virtuosity," *Journal of the Society for American Music* 3, no. 4 (2009).
8. Ibid.; see also R. Murray Schafer, *The New Soundscape: A Handbook for the Modern Music Teacher* (Don Mills, Ont.: BMI Canada Limited, 1969) and Steven Feld, "From Schizophonia to Schismogenesis: On the Discourses and Commodification Practices of 'World Music' and 'World Beat,'" in *Music Grooves: Essays and Dialogues*, ed. Charles Keil and Steven Feld (Chicago: University of Chicago Press, 1994).
9. Steve Dixon, *Digital Performance: A History of New Media in Theater, Dance, Performance Art, and Installation* (Cambridge, MA: MIT Press, 2007), 23.

10. For points of entry into the rich literature on these topics, readers might start with Michael Chanan, *Repeated Takes: A Short History of Recording and Its Effects on Music* (New York: Verso, 1995); Paul Théberge, *Any Sound You Can Imagine: Making Music/Consuming Technology* (Middletown, CT: Wesleyan University Press, 1997); Philip Auslander, *Liveness: Performance in a Mediatized Culture* (New York: Routledge, 1999); Steve Waksman, *Instruments of Desire: The Electric Guitar and the Shaping of Musical Experience* (Cambridge, MA: Harvard University Press, 1999); Jason Toynbee, *Making Popular Music: Musicians, Creativity and Institutions* (New York: Oxford University Press, 2000); René T. A. Lysloff and Leslie C. Gay, Jr., eds., *Music and Technoculture* (Middletown, CT: Wesleyan University Press, 2003); Jonathan Sterne, *The Audible Past: Cultural Origins of Sound Reproduction* (Durham, NC: Duke University Press, 2003); Katz, *Capturing Sound: How Technology Has Changed Music*; and Paul D. Greene and Thomas Porcello, *Wired for Sound: Engineering and Technologies in Sonic Cultures* (Middletown, CT: Wesleyan University Press, 2005).

11. Marie-Laure Ryan, "Cyberspace, Virtuality, and the Text," in *Cyberspace Textuality: Computer Technology and Literary Theory*, ed. Marie-Laure Ryan (Bloomington: Indiana University Press, 1999), 89, 94.

12. For more on "relational infrastructure" and bodily praxis, see Judith Hamera, *Dancing Communities: Performance, Difference, and Connection in the Global City* (New York: Palgrave Macmillan, 2007).

13. See also Tomie Hahn, *Sensational Knowledge: Embodying Culture through Japanese Dance* (Middletown, CT: Wesleyan University Press, 2007).

14. Michael Gurevich, "Jamspace: Designing a Collaborative Networked Music Space for Novices," in *Proceedings of the 2006 International Conference on New Interfaces for Musical Expression* (Paris, France: NIME, 2006), 118, 120.

15. Tina Blaine and Sidney Fels, "Contexts of Collaborative Musical Experiences," *Proceedings of the 2003 Conference on New Interfaces for Musical Expression* (NIME.org, 2003), 129, 133, http://www.nime.org/2003/onlineproceedings/Papers/NIME03_Blaine.pdf.

16. For more on earlier music/rhythm games that employed alternate controllers (e.g., *Dance Dance Revolution*, *Guitar Freaks*, *Donkey Konga*), see Jacob Smith, "I Can See Tomorrow in Your Dance: A Study of *Dance Dance Revolution* and Music Video Games," *Journal of Popular Music Studies* 16, no. 1 (2004); Tina Blaine, "The Convergence of Alternate Controllers and Musical Interfaces in Interactive Entertainment," *Proceedings of the 2005 Conference on New Interfaces for Musical Expression* (NIME.org, 2005), http://nime.org/2005/proc/nime2005_027.pdf; and Joanna Demers, "Dancing Machines: 'Dance Dance Revolution', Cybernetic Dance, and Musical Taste," *Popular Music* 25, no. 3 (2006).

17. See Kiri Miller, *Playing Along: Digital Games, YouTube, and Virtual Performance* (New York: Oxford University Press, 2012).

18. Steve Waksman, "Into the Arena: Edward Van Halen and the Cultural Contradictions of the Guitar Hero," in *Guitar Cultures*, ed. Andy Bennett and Kevin Dawe (New York: Berg, 2001); André Millard and Rebecca McSwain, "The Guitar Hero," in *The Electric Guitar: A History of an American Icon*, ed. André Millard (Baltimore, MD: Johns Hopkins University Press, 2004).

19. Steve Waksman, "Reading the Instrument: An Introduction," *Popular Music and Society* 26, no. 3 (2003): 256–257.

20. Harmonix Music Systems, "Harmonix Music Systems," http://www.harmonixmusic. com/#games.

21. However, the games proved appealing to experienced musicians as well; see Miller, *Playing Along: Digital Games, YouTube, and Virtual Performance.*

22. Rob Kay, interview with the author, October 17, 2007. All subsequent Rob Kay quotations are from this interview.

23. Blaine and Fels, "Contexts of Collaborative Musical Experiences."

24. Chris Dahlen, "Harmonix Music Systems" (includes an interview with Matt Boch), *A. V. Club*, July 18, 2008, http://www.avclub.com/content/interview/harmonix_music_systems.

25. Cf. Nicholas Cook, *Analysing Musical Multimedia* (New York: Oxford University Press, 1998), 102.

26. Post-gameplay interview, July 2008.

27. Daniel Radosh, "While My Guitar Gently Beeps," *New York Times Magazine*, August 11, 2009, http://www.nytimes.com/2009/08/16/magazine/16beatles-t.html.

28. Survey follow-up correspondence. See Miller, *Playing Along: Digital Games, YouTube, and Virtual Performance* for details about this qualitative survey.

29. Post-gameplay interview, July 2008.

30. Ibid.

31. Torben Grodal, "Stories for Eye, Ear, and Muscles: Video Games, Media, and Embodied Experience," in *The Video Game Theory Reader*, ed. Mark J. P. Wolf and Bernard Perron (New York: Routledge, 2003), 132.

32. Geraldine Bloustien and Margaret Peters, *Youth, Music and Creative Cultures: Playing for Life* (New York: Palgrave Macmillan, 2011), 83–122. See also Sarah Thornton, *Club Cultures: Music, Media and Subcultural Capital* (Hanover, NH: Wesleyan University Press, 1996); Mark J. Butler, *Unlocking the Groove: Rhythm, Meter, and Musical Design in Electronic Dance Music* (Bloomington: Indiana University Press, 2006); and Aram Sinnreich, *Mashed Up: Music, Technology, and the Rise of Configurable Culture* (Amherst: University of Massachusetts Press, 2010).

33. James Brightman, "DJ Hero Sold Just 211k Units in November," *IndustryGamers*, December 11, 2009, http://www.industrygamers.com/news/dj-hero-sold-just-123k-units.

34. Ricardo Bilton, "Activision Blizzard Ends Guitar Hero Series," *International Business Times*, February 10, 2011, http://www.ibtimes.com/articles/111010/20110210/activision-blizzard-guitar-hero.htm.

35. Gameplay notes, December 30, 2009.

36. All cited reviews are customer reviews of "Xbox 360 DJ Hero Bundle with Turntable," *Amazon.com*, product posted October 27, 2009, http://www.amazon.com/Xbox-360-DJ-Hero-Bundle-Turntable/product-reviews/B0028ZNX68.

37. Martti Lahti, "As We Become Machines: Corporealized Pleasures in Video Games," in *The Video Game Theory Reader*, ed. Mark J. P. Wolf and Bernard Perron (New York: Routledge, 2003), 158.

38. Miller, *Playing Along: Digital Games, YouTube, and Virtual Performance.*

39. Laura Ermi and Frans Mäyrä, "Fundamental Components of the Gameplay Experience: Analysing Immersion," *Proceedings of DiGRA 2005 Conference: Changing Views—Worlds in Play* (DiGRA.org, 2005), http://www.digra.org/dl/db/06276.41516.pdf, 7–8.

40. E.g., Ubisoft's *Just Dance* (2009) and Harmonix's *Dance Central* (2010). See Kiri Miller, "Multisensory Musicality in *Dance Central*," in *The Oxford Handbook of Interactive Audio*, ed. Karen Collins, Bill Kapralos and Holly Tessler (New York: Oxford University Press, forthcoming).

SELECT BIBLIOGRAPHY

Auslander, Philip. *Liveness: Performance in a Mediatized Culture.* New York: Routledge, 1999.

Collins, Karen, ed. *From Pac-Man to Pop Music: Interactive Audio in Games and New Media.* Burlington, VT: Ashgate, 2008.

———. *Game Sound: An Introduction to the History, Theory, and Practice of Video Game Music and Sound Design.* Cambridge, MA: MIT Press, 2008.

Grodal, Torben. "Stories for Eye, Ear, and Muscles: Video Games, Media, and Embodied Experience." In *The Video Game Theory Reader,* edited by Mark J. P. Wolf and Bernard Perron, 129–155. New York: Routledge, 2003.

Katz, Mark. *Capturing Sound: How Technology Has Changed Music.* Berkeley: University of California Press, 2004.

Lysloff, René T. A., and Leslie C. Gay, Jr., eds. *Music and Technoculture.* Middletown, CT: Wesleyan University Press, 2003.

Miller, Kiri. *Playing Along: Digital Games, YouTube, and Virtual Performance.* New York: Oxford University Press, 2012.

Smith, Jacob. "I Can See Tomorrow in Your Dance: A Study of *Dance Dance Revolution* and Music Video Games." *Journal of Popular Music Studies* 16, no. 1 (2004): 58–84.

Taylor, Timothy D. "The Commodification of Music at the Dawn of the Era of 'Mechanical Music.'" *Ethnomusicology* 51, no. 2 (2007): 281–305.

Théberge, Paul. *Any Sound You Can Imagine: Making Music/Consuming Technology.* Middletown, CT: Wesleyan University Press, 1997.

Whalen, Zach. "Play Along—An Approach to Videogame Music." *Game Studies* 4, no. 1 (2004). http://www.gamestudies.org/0401/whalen/.

CHAPTER 31

A GAGA-WORLD PAGEANT

Channeling Difference and the Performance of Networked Power

DAVID MCCARTHY AND MARÍA ZUAZU

LADY Gaga, still, reclines amid her sprawling entourage, listening to the strains of an A-minor fugue as it creeps about a spindly harpsichord, each leap upward preceded and followed by descending triads or scalar runs. As Gaga manipulates a smooth remote control, the music rushes to an abrupt cadence on the leading tone (G#). Suddenly, she is startled by her own voice, an acousmatic voice whose source she frantically seeks as her head darts back and forth. The voice sings in the fugue's relative major (C), emphasizing the same note, F, the minor-sixth in A minor, and the fourth in C major. But where the fugue's gestures plodded menacingly downward against syncopated upward leaps, Gaga reverses the direction, climbing upward with an even anacrusis and landing squarely on the downbeat with an expansive fourth scale degree (the fugue begins E-C-A-F; the voice begins C-D-E-C-F). Some fantastic voice out of center, the eccentric voice of Gaga simultaneously not her own, has refashioned something stiff and dark, calling into existence a new world, one in which Gaga will triumph as the protagonist of a *Pygmalion*-meets-international-sex-slave-ring narrative. For many, this video for "Bad Romance" would serve to introduce a *Gaga World*.[1]

Fans, detractors, and the indifferent tended to agree: Gaga seemed to come out of nowhere to capture a moment. Although her most cynical critics would describe her as a cheap knockoff of early pop stars, wherever Gaga has channeled Madonna, Grace Jones, or even Andy Warhol, her pastiches have seemed more haunted than nostalgic. One might think, for example, of the deformed Madonna emerging from the mist at the close of the video for "Born This Way," a video that marks an assertive attempt to supplant her most recognizable predecessor (see Figure 31.1). Her references to the stars of the past have appeared up-to-date, and, even if that something *au courant* is fabricated (how could it be otherwise?), the workings of that fabrication remain of interest. Using a metaphor culled from the first seconds of one of her first hugely successful videos, one

FIGURE 31.1. Lady Gaga's deformed Madonna in the official video for "Born This Way." Screen shot by the authors.

could suggest that Gaga at first seemed to sing out from some bizarre somewhere else, reworking contemporary, digital, cloud-based popular music and making of it an optimistic metaphor for a moment, one conceptualized as a flexible web of networks. Rather than comparing Gaga to some supposedly external social context, it is more interesting and helpful to observe that she participates in the creation of a context, reworking a moment even as she appears to capture it. The moment is never quite prior, the context is never entirely external; it is as if she writes a kind of "subtext," to borrow Fredric Jameson's term, providing the social problems she will then mythically resolve.[2]

In this way, she is able to pick and choose resolvable contradictions while overlooking others. At the same time that Gaga preaches a contemporary gospel of individuality, mobility, and equality, she participates in a contemporary obfuscation of coercion and exploitation. Yet the unapologetic directness with which she offers anonymous fame is revealing, and this partially explains why it has not been helpful to rush to judgment when it comes to Gaga's politics: if on the one hand she encourages people to accept unethical social arrangements, on the other hand, in working over increasingly invisible processes, she has a tendency, deliberate or otherwise, to draw contradictions into relief. This has made her an intriguing target for satirists, a point we will return to when concluding this survey of the pop star's mythology. The search for something timely in Gaga's work has fueled J. Jack Halberstam's book on a historically distinct form of "Gaga Feminism." We are attempting to provide a theoretical perspective that can outline some of the ideological boundaries giving the Gaga World shape and resonance. In this sense, our essay can be read as a supplement to a project such as Halberstam's rather than as a critique thereof, for if our respective projects take on different tones, we are motivated by a shared curiosity about Gaga's apparent contemporaneity. Wherever we denounce the palliative characteristics of Gaga's videos, we are equally fascinated by the possibility of reading them in more provocative ways, in ways that can illuminate contemporary "frustrations and desires," as Halberstam suggests.[3]

What we aim for here is a keener understanding and more incisive critique of one popular set of contemporary understandings of society as presented in Gaga's multimedia extravaganza. By enumerating, categorizing, and theorizing a few of the paired ways that a digital Gaga World works on its inhabitants at the same time that those inhabitants, and Gaga especially, curate that world, we hope to describe some ways that the pop star participates in a contemporary mythology, demonstrating a set of dispositions toward recurrent social contradictions. We are interested, for example, in the high value Gaga places on mobility or equality in her networked Gaga World, as compared with her apparent lack of interest in the preconditions for participation in that World or with the ways that she masks that World's capacity to harvest the fruits of a participant's unpaid labor. As Luc Boltanski and Ève Chiapello demonstrate in their survey of managerial literature from France in the 1990s, people can tend to share values, to participate in a common "order of justification," without considering where that order came from or where it might go.[4] The Gaga World plays on the same hopes and anxieties associated with the prominence of Web 2.0, cloud-based media, and reticular metaphors for society, so it is no surprise to find her world characterized by intimate anonymity and anonymous intimacy, populated by impersonal personalities, threaded with delimited pathways, and governed by apparently nonhierarchical and increasingly invisible concentrations of power.

The relationship between Gaga's music and her digital techniques and platforms is neither neutral nor unidirectional, but one of interdependence. We here attempt to read the first four years of Gaga's career—a period that includes *The Fame* (2008), its continuation in *The Fame Monster* (2009), and *Born This Way* (2011)—as an orchestrated pageant performing Gaga's status as a new model of dominance for a cloud-based, major record label–backed, international music industry. Her task was nothing less than the establishment of a star power that appeared to foster open participation, and her strategy was fully in line with the rules of the network: her node may have been out of center, but it was powerful nevertheless. Although Gaga bombards her audience with fragmented images and sounds, she sticks to a small number of coherent themes that remain surprisingly constant as one moves from the composition of her melodies, to the coordination of her images, to the generation of her narratives. Each individual product may result from a complex set of collaborations, but they all participate in the same brand name.

We suggest that one of Gaga's most important strategies is her characteristic *remix aesthetic*, her tendency to mask unity with a set of digital practices that seem to tear and stitch. This remix aesthetic embraces a number of practices, such as her occasional use of nearly disjointed or abrupt transitions from one hook to the next in songs like "Bad Romance" or "Judas," her eclectic comfort with a variety of stylistic tropes, the proliferation of fan renditions or live acoustic performances by Gaga herself, or the seemingly endless stream of remixes, authorized or otherwise. These practices do not originate with Gaga, but by drawing them together under a larger aesthetic, Gaga appears especially attuned to her time, especially open to the utopian desires invested in transnational networks, and especially well-equipped to harness those networks. As this essay works through her YouTube pageant, it should become apparent that Gaga has been weaving a tale, one that tells us where she comes from, how she got here, why she has come, and how we are to receive her.

Gaga World: Shaping

The YouTube video is one example of what Lewis Mumford calls a *container technology*, in this case, a container for other containers, for the various audio and visual file formats that act as *apparatuses* by transforming their contents, *compressing* them.[5] In her essay "Going Gaga for Glitch: Digital Failure @nd Feminist Spectacle in Twenty-First Century Music Video (chapter 9)," Benson-Allott points out that the image, contained and shaped by the YouTube video, compressed and streamed to the computer screen, establishes a rift between viewer and performer. The audio file, by contrast, often seems to generate an inhabitable space. The Gaga World's audible space is haunted by remixes, saturated by the "deadness" that Jason Stanyek and Benjamin Piekut have shown to be characteristic of recorded sound in general and of contemporary capitalism in particular.[6] In this space, bits and pieces are continuously remixed into politically distributed assemblages, Frankenstein's monsters roam shifting networks, and Gaga names her *little* monsters, setting up relationships between them. The situation is similar to one Kiri Miller observed in her careful description of audio in the *Grand Theft Auto* video game franchise: when choice, fluidity, flexibility, and what Stanyek and Piekut call "recombinatoriality" are the norm, it might appear as though The Author has been rendered superfluous, supplanted by The User, but, in fact, the range of options and the finitude of their potential relationships have been deliberately carved into a bounded allegory.[7] The apparent proliferation of options hides crafted, crafty limits.

As is typical of containers, the Gaga World appears neutral, even invisible, but although it seems to be a mere stage, it is generated by and generative of performance. There is a provocative moment in the video for "Bad Romance"—the first single from *The Fame Monster*—when two separate digital manipulations, one audible and one visible, occur in relation to one another. At about 2:20, one can hear Gaga's laborious grunt or groan echo electronically in the distance, while at the same moment, in a gesture loosely synchronized with this sound, she lifts her leg and spreads her thighs, pressing her hands down low to the front of her pelvis as an abrupt visual cut breaks the dance move into two discrete instances. Only the visual manipulation can properly be described in terms of Benson-Allott's distancing "glitch." The audible element mimics something more intimate, the erotic sound of Gaga at work echoing in her sounding space, pausing briefly to whisper sexily into the listener's ear at 2:39, "You know that I want you/You know that I need you." At the same instant, her rarefied shout declares,

"'Cause I'm a free bitch, baby!" Echoic pathways give depth to the space, suggesting an expansive audible gesture juxtaposed with the bounded movement seen in the image.

Indeed, her vocal pathways seem to exceed four dimensions. At about 4:35 in the video for "Judas," it sounds as if Gaga emerges from a field of electronic distortion as the middle range of her voice is swiftly filtered into the audio file. The listener appears to inhabit a world this side of an invisible, digital, generative machine. By using a filtering technique facilitated by digital technology, Gaga and her producers are able to create the illusion that she has passed into our world from another side. The Gaga World is therefore an expansive space, its flexible, multidimensional corners carved out sonically using digital audio production.

Gaga's priority in this space stems not from her centrality in the mix, but from her mobility. Her digital productions swirl about the listener, in much the same way that action sequences in contemporary superhero films set the audience on a roller-coaster ride, their pathways predetermined by the tracks laid down in the process of production; these are *movies* in an extreme sense. As the object of our desire, Gaga moves left and right, further away and closer; she appears in more than one place at once, everywhere, nowhere, receding back beyond the digital only to swiftly reemerge empowered. At the same time that the restless journeys of her voice establish mythic spaces, she is demonstrating her apparent capacity to move freely, and her listeners come along for the ride.

Gaga World: Branding

These generated spaces are continuously being branded. Part of this has to do with characteristics of the YouTube video as medium. Although fans can potentially download YouTube videos, as a platform, YouTube only supports such a practice in special cases such as presidential addresses; the format is cloud-based, and users are expected to go to the site whenever they want to view a video.[8] Once there, they engage in virtual communal practices, watching videos that have been uploaded or even created by users and exchanging comments, while at the same time engaging in various forms of unpaid labor by viewing advertisements, generating content, and providing YouTube with valuable data about audience tastes. The cloud is networked, and, on careful inspection, disparate modes of access become apparent. YouTube administrators, Gaga, and her fans all come with different capabilities and intensions when they enter this networked space.

A second point to be made about the YouTube video in general is that its interface tends to encourage a surprisingly focused listening practice, even if it has been possible since at least 2010 to organize YouTube videos in a playlist or to attend private parties where music will be streamed from YouTube and amplified through speakers.[9] The presence of a video alone tends to command attention, perhaps even more so when placed on a computer screen rather than on a television where content can quickly dissolve into

the background as a kind of audiovisual wallpaper.[10] YouTube has demonstrated a preference for higher and higher quality sound and image—the switch to AAC from MP3 is
representative of this—suggesting an expectation that at least a portion of the audience
will pay careful attention to the content being consumed. Gaga, for her part, has said
that she hopes her fans will watch a given video "hundreds of times to figure it out."[11]

At the same time that the YouTube video encourages more focused listening practices
and suggests communal participation, it establishes a rentier economy wherein disciplined audiences are constantly engaging in unpaid labor in the hope of viewing what
are in any case—and increasingly so since YouTube's merger with Google—elaborate
advertisements for merchandise distributed by mainstream media giants.[12] Gaga's videos don't just hover in a cloud, they are collected on a channel, and when users access
one video they are immediately welcome to watch another, to float downstream.[13]
Indeed, much of Gaga's business model has to do with finding ways of channeling the
apparently fluid or diffuse.

Her remix aesthetic facilitates this strategy. The overload of fan renditions, live acoustic performances, and remixes is not really new with Gaga, but she does seem to have
pushed these practices to new limits. Her singles are accompanied by remixes, remixes
are included on special editions of her albums, and she has already released a best-selling
album devoted entirely to remixes of her early hits, *Lady Gaga: The Remix* (2010). The
marketing benefits of these strategies are somewhat obvious: remixes provide more sal-
able product and more advertising while allowing Gaga to wear numerous hats (there is
even a country version of "Born This Way"); fan versions suggest a participatory community surrounding the pop star's music; and live acoustic versions, by attempting to
belie the inescapable ghosts of digital deadness, seem to afford a more intimate encounter with the talented woman behind the "unplugged" machine.

Gaga has found ways of containing her disjointed, fragmentary, and diffuse milieu,
using channels, copyrights, and an overarching Gaga World. Victor P. Corona's observation that Gaga works to instantiate herself in popular memory by putting forward images
of "monstrous" individualities and rapidly deploying "visual impressions that are practically tailor-made for the age of viral marketing," only captures half the picture.[14] These
elaborate and diverse images are indispensable, to be sure, but so is their transparent
container, their Gaga World. Three videos from early in her career, "Paparazzi" (2009),
"Bad Romance" (2009), and "Telephone" (2010), all of which are "extended" and include
audio content not found on the original single, played a huge role in establishing that
world. All three are heavily invested in the construction of a brand. Whereas rappers
might shout their names into a microphone to declare their presence on a track, Gaga's
self-referential devices sound more like a free-floating brand name. Bits of her name are
frequently woven into lyrics and hooks, titles announce the "Haus of Gaga" (as in "Bad
Romance"), recordings of some of her other songs are played in the diegetic spaces of
her videos (e.g., "Paper Gangsta" over the prison yard's loudspeakers in "Telephone"),
and the DJ on her car radio announces her songs (also in "Telephone"). Every element
is contained by her world, needs to be understood within that world, and gives substance to that world, creating a closed, self-reinforcing space, a space where encounters

are not only mediated (all encounters are mediated, after all), but deliberately channeled by some actors more than by others.

GAGA WORLD: TRAVELING

In addition to being shaped and branded, the Gaga World is variously curated by three archetypal Gagas: the frightening yet alluring Other, the Friendly Peer, and the mediating Mother.[15] Although Gaga moves freely among these different types and even tries to collapse them to some degree, an individual single, performance, or public appearance will tend to deploy only one archetype at a time. Each corresponds to a different set of strategies aimed at strengthening her position within what she otherwise claims is a flat, nonhierarchical, radically inclusive space.

In "Bad Romance," Gaga apparently emerges from some exotic land or hatches from a primordial ooze. At least as important as the images in the video—Gaga crawls out of a pod with big, infantile eyes and is groomed for sale at an Eastern-European sex slave auction—are the specific musical tropes of Otherness. The "Rah, Rah" hook beginning at 0:31 is arguably the most characteristic and characteristically "Gaga" part of the song, and the tropes it deploys suggest more than a generic Otherness.[16] Gaga sings vocables in a coarse, guttural voice, suggesting a prelinguistic or primordial decomposition of the word "Romance" and of her own name. The scale degrees being used—1, 5, and flat 6—suggest tropes of ancientness and otherness; the open fifth is a familiar index of something ancient or even primal (cf. *Also Sprach Zarathustra* in Stanley Kubrick's *2001: A Space Odyssey*), and the flat six is a stereotypical index of "folk" musics in a number of areas surrounding central Europe (e.g., the Iberian Peninsula or Eastern Europe). Incidentally, these are precisely the scale degrees she returns to in "Judas," and it is interesting to note that these two especially characteristic songs developed out of her collaboration with the producer RedOne. The prominent leap in Judas is of an octave rather than a fifth, but this is still an open, "perfect" interval lying low on the overtone series. When coupled with the sharp, percussive accompaniment played on up-beats in "Bad Romance," it can almost be heard as Balkan.[17]

Although these tropes hint at an indefinite composite, as indices, they share some points of reference. Instead of conjuring up some far-off, alien Other—from the "Far East," for example—they suggest something nearer and strangely familiar. When Gaga herself has spoken about writing the song, she talks about being in Norway on a bus, traveling through Russia, Germany, and Eastern Europe, listening to "German house-techno music." These are supposedly "our" Others—the collective "we" being a "normative" white, Euro-American audience—and the signifiers at play might be heard as references to some ancient ancestor, to the European "hill people" of the Balkan region or to the childhood of humanity.[18]

This does not mean that Gaga's music sounds folky. Instead, Gaga seems to be playing on a desire for the kind of mobility that digital networks are supposed to afford;

she appears to be an eccentric traveler from somewhere on the margins. The particular variety of otherness conjured up in "Bad Romance" is alluring and captures the audience's attention long before she appears as the full-fledged pop diva: she is startled by her own refined voice, and the guttural voice that succeeds it plays vigorously in what is really more a percussive, instrumental texture; the vocables do not sketch what would be described as any kind of melody. In a media environment saturated by fantastic pop stars crying for attention, Gaga's Otherness, far from placing her in a marginal position, is wholly captivating. As she seduces the man who will buy her on the market, she also draws in her audience, and her power and control over her audible world seem to steadily increase, only eventually giving way to the full-fledged diva.

Hope, in the Gaga World, is not invested so much in the digital network itself, as in the potential for users to navigate the network, and Gaga's privilege is performed as a virtuosic mobility. The Friendly Peer archetype plays on a similar attitude toward networks: again, the network is important not in itself, but in its capacity to be used in desirable ways. If the friendly girl next door of a video like "Eh, Eh (Nothing Else I Can Say)" is a far cry from the frightening Other just described, both are encountered in a virtual, networked space. And as in the case of the Other, Gaga as girl next door enjoys priority, this time based less on mobility and more on competent *networking*: when Gaga appeared in the *Saturday Night Live* sketch "What's That Name?" with Justin Timberlake, she had the superhuman ability to remember the names of even her least attractive and most forgettable fans.[19]

This ability seems to go beyond friendliness to suggest omniscience; at the conclusion of the sketch, Gaga begins naming every single member of the studio audience. At this point, she might not be playing Gaga as Friendly Peer so much as Gaga as Mother, a facet that seems to have been strategically introduced as part of the promotion for *Born This Way*, an album that takes for granted Gaga's status as a superstar of the grandest proportions. Describing his interview with Gaga, Brian Hiatt wrote, "She truly believes she's been reborn as Mother Monster—hence the giant egg she arrived in at the Grammy's, emerging only for her performance."[20] Coupled to this transformation, Hiatt explains, is a change in the way she carries herself and speaks, as well as in the ways that she refers to her fans as "little monsters" or as a "revolution" joined to her by "this umbilical cord that I don't want to cut, ever." Her overt claims to "authenticity" as a performer, artist, and musician are framed as being an expression of a responsibility to her fans. Gaga explains:

> During the show, I say, I don't lip-sync, and I never will, because it is in my authenticity that you can know the sincerity of my love for you. I love you so much that I sweat blood and tears in the mirror every day, dancing, writing music, to become better for you to be a leader, to be strong and brave, not to follow.[21]

Gaga gets explicit about this new archetypal persona in "Born This Way." The video for that single begins with a 2.5-minute introduction featuring arpeggiated augmented chords held still for long periods of time, suggesting something uncertain although

FIGURE 31.2 Primordial togetherness in the official video for "Born This Way." Screen shot by the authors.

not necessarily anxious or menacing.[22] Beneath these static chords, a bass line moves slowly but deliberately, illuminating different qualities of the chord being held in the upper register, producing what Sumanth Gopinath has called a "profundity trope:" as the bass moves, the listener moves all around and about the static chord, hearing all of its possible harmonizations as if from an omniscient perspective.[23] The video is supposed to be depicting not the birth of Gaga, as in "Bad Romance," but the primordial forma-tion of a new chosen people, Gaga's "little monsters," collapsing representations of Gaga as Mother with her *progeny* (see Figure 31.2), on the one hand, and as Christ with her flock, on the other. The bells that sound at about 2:00 are only some of the more overt examples of the introduction's religious overtones. At the same time, the script might be self-consciously awkward or even deliberately poorly written (e.g., "The birth was not finite, but infinite," or "thus began the beginning," or "the eternal mother hov-ered"), undermining or leveling in a campy way what could otherwise come across as self-absorbed or pretentious. For all of her eccentricities, at some level Gaga wants to be down-to-earth. "I don't want [the message] to be hidden in poetic wizardry and meta-phors," she says, "I want it to be an attack, an assault on the issue because I think, espe-cially in today's music, everything gets kind of washy sometimes and the message gets hidden in the lyrical play."[24]

The song proper, beginning at about 2:33, works to disarm the listener with a very differ-ent kind of "folk" than was invoked in "Bad Romance." The track retains an expansive pro-fundity, sonically evoking a huge space, and her oratorical voice is bathed in wet reverb as fragments of it are broken up, rarefied, and bounced digitally from one channel to the other in an electronic echo. But, instead of evoking an esoteric "Eastern" mysticism, Gaga brings things much closer to home. Although the chord progression—V-IV-I-V in the key of B major—suggests something eternal by hovering on an unresolved dominant chord, the all-American gospel style evoked at the end of the song seems to elicit a different angle on the timeless, perhaps evoking a supposed innocence and communality. When Madonna imbricated religious imagery in her infamous video for "Like a Prayer," she used an iconog-raphy largely indebted to a mysterious, "medieval" Roman Catholicism, but she sang in a gospel style, accompanied in the video by a cheerful black choir. George M. Fredrickson has written about nineteenth-century representations of "the Negro as more natural Christian," as more charitable, more free of the guileful pursuit of power.[25] In such representations, southern black gospel Christianity comes across as a simpler, more wholesome and com-munal faith loosed from the machinations of an overly intellectual, systematic faith associ-ated with power (exemplified by Calvinism in the literature Fredrickson cites).

The Gaga World provides a branded container in which encounters are had and mobility is performed, but where all connections eventually lead back to a decentered, multifaceted, yet always prioritized and privileged node. Gaga's points of reference are neither empty nor self-contained; they arrive as icons but are swiftly integrated into an allegorical Gaga World. Gaga is claiming to establish a radically inclusive community, one that she nourishes maternally without being a hierarchically privileged ruler. At 5:11 in "Born This Way," the chorus gives way to a break section. As strange sounds, fragments of speech, and electronic effects float in an expansive, reverb-drenched, wet, womblike space, Gaga begins to enumerate her expanded litany of the welcomed: "whether you're broke or evergreen, you're black, white, beige, Chola descent [etc.]." Everyone is sup-posed to be a little monster in the network—integrated, mobile, and empowered, but some more so than others.[26]

SOCIAL NETWORKS, NETWORKED SOCIALS

Such an ostensibly inclusive community would seem to ask of its members only that they be true to themselves and their individual life experiences. Instead of expecting RedOne to be somehow true to any kind of Moroccan heritage, the narratives built around him consistently portray him as a mobile, cosmopolitan, global traveler moving from Morocco, to Sweden, to Los Angeles. His musical experiences in many different places seem only to enhance his abilities as a musician and producer, giving him a wider vocabulary out of which to construct new and exciting assemblages.[27] "Authenticity," in this case, is a faithfulness to himself, wherever his travels might take him.

Meanwhile, Gaga, her handlers, and the popular press constantly remind the public that Gaga worked hard for her success, climbing up through the ranks of the music scene on Manhattan's Lower East Side. Andrew Hampp—writing, appropriately, for *Advertising Age*—quotes Dyana Kass, the head of pop-music marketing for Universal as saying, "Lady Gaga has truly turned culture on its head and has done so from the ground up on her terms.... You can't buy that kind of authenticity, and as a result the demand for her involvement in projects is staggering."[28] Troy Carter, Gaga's manager, has made an effort to avoid letting Gaga appear as if she is simply endorsing a product. Instead of framing her as a mere spokesperson or face for a company, Gaga is hired by companies like Polaroid as a creative director, and comparisons are made to Tom Ford with Gucci or Steve Jobs with Apple.[29] Though Gaga unmistakably occupies a position of privilege, not only in her Gaga World but also as Stefani Germanotta, the daughter of wealthy Manhattanites, elements of power are consistently washed out of her political assemblages, her family recedes into the background as her rise through the Lower East Side's club circuit is recounted; one can participate whether "broke or evergreen," and there is no comment whatsoever on the different modes of participation available to different persons. The public is supposed to suspend knowledge of Germanotta's privileged background even when reminded of it by narratives involving her strong relationship with a loving family. "It's a sharable fame," claims Gaga, "I want to invite you all to the party. I want people to feel a part of this lifestyle."[30] The workings of power are not distributed democratically so much as they are made invisible or ignored.[31]

The sociality that should supposedly emerge between actors in the network actually becomes nothing but a series of links to otherwise isolated individuals, a collection of umbilical chords nourishing the Mother at least as much as her little monsters.[32] Rather than being empowered, the actors in the network desperately seek attention from other actors as they seek to strengthen their own positions. RedOne's unique life experiences are valuable in that they can be used to capture the ears of a larger audience, and Gaga's exotic persona does not revel in difference so much as it deploys tropes of otherness in a strategic fashion. One might even go so far as to argue that the "monstrosity" of the little monsters metaphor has troubling qualities. Although it would be foolhardy to make too much of the connection without a more detailed study than can be undertaken here, one has to wonder if there is more than a superficial relationship between a situation in which individuality must be worn externally and broadcast to peers in an effort to gain attention, on the one hand, and, on the other, the importance of tattoos and prosthetics in Gaga's iconography, or the increased prominence of body modification in the United States over the past twenty years.[33] Gaga's Frankenstein assemblages might be said to express a fragmented sociality, a jumble of individuated pieces stitched together, each fragment doing what it can to stand out in the texture somehow. Although a cloud-based platform like YouTube might appear to establish a public and shared space for the exchange of media, it actually facilitates an almost totally anonymous practice while establishing a rentier economy and allowing for the surveillance of an individuated community. It is, in any case, *You*Tube, not *We*Tube.

The political shapes suggested by Gaga's world are therefore riddled with contradictions, yet these shapes resonate deeply with popular ways of thinking about society; this, we propose, is what Gaga captures about her moment. Calling attention to contradictions is challenging because, very often, they appear in places that one might otherwise most want to celebrate. For example, while the increased trend toward personalization has a certain appeal, it seems impossible to separate this very appeal from an attendant set of anxieties over new, more complete, and more invisible forms of domination realized through the ever-increasing degradation of public spaces. In the "What's That Name?" sketch cited above, Gaga may be the better pop star, more deeply invested in her fans, but the opprobrium Bill Hader directs at Timberlake seems no less unjust for that. Meanwhile, although Hader plainly adores Gaga, she gradually assumes assorted symbols of elite power, wearing thick, intellectual spectacles, speaking with a sophisticated transatlantic accent, holding a jeweled cross in her right palm, and blessing a fan with a benedictory gesture. She seems to arise as a new kind of royalty or as a mediator between humanity and something higher, beloved as a saint by her little monsters.

Gaga as Mother makes sense as the ultimate scene in a pageant carefully orchestrated to perform the singer's tenuous position as the networked age's star of stars, yet this is also precisely the point at which the Gaga World starts to lose interest. Although she is pleased that "anyone could sing 'Born This Way,'"[34] the tradeoff is that the song sounds much less Gaga than "Bad Romance" or "Judas." And when she coaxes the citizens of Springfield to love themselves in an episode of *The Simpsons* entitled "Lisa Goes Gaga" (Season 23, Episode 22, 2012), a naïve Lenny says with amazement, "That kind of thing sounds hollow coming from anyone but you!"

Where the contradictions of the Gaga World have appeared to remix social contradictions, providing imagined resolutions to perceived problems, they have tended to ring true and timely. But this very quality might also prove the Gaga World's undoing. Gaga does everything the individuated citizen of a networked society is supposed to do: she is flexible, mobile, out of center; she enjoys self-esteem while honoring transitory responsibilities toward others; she channels traffic and harvests the fruits of user-generated labor; she multiplies and strengthens her connections, empowering her nodes by capturing little monsters with catchy hooks.[35] We suggest that the frightening yet alluring

Other, rather than the Friendly Peer or mediating Mother, remains Gaga's quintessential and most interesting archetypal persona. There is something spooky and creepy about this Gaga World, these haunted networks, these unsettling remixes; yet there is also something thrilling about mobility, encounter, and connection. This disquieting situation gives the Gaga World charge and excitement. But whether her misplaced voice could eventually startle her entourage of little monsters with more serious challenges would depend in part on how she is heard.

NOTES

1. Michel Chion discusses the acousmatic voice in his book, *The Voice in Cinema* (1982; repr., New York: Columbia University Press, 1999). All timings in this paper refer to videos hosted at Lady Gaga's official YouTube channel: http://www.youtube.com/user/LadyGagaVEVO, accessed May 31, 2012. Jessica Narum was the first to call to our attention the parallels between George Bernard Shaw's Eliza Doolittle and the abnormally wide-eyed woman who is caught and remade into an object of desire and commerce in Gaga's video, only to turn around and conquer the man who desired her (in the former case by marrying the confirmed old bachelor, in the latter by blowing a purchaser to smithereens in his own bed). We wish to express our gratitude to Amy Herzog and Carol Vernallis whose comments on earlier versions of this essay were challenging and helpful. Thanks are also due to the Spanish Fulbright Commission, whose support helped make this project possible.
2. Fredric Jameson, *The Political Unconscious: Narrative as a Socially Symbolic Act*, hardback ed. (United Kingdom: Methuen & Co., Ltd., 1981; New York: Routledge Classics, 2002), 66–68.
3. Jeffrey J. Williams, "The Drag of Masculinity: An Interview with Judith 'Jack' Halberstam," *symploke* 19, nos. 1–2 (2011), 380. J. Jack Halberstam, *Gaga Feminism: Sex, Gender and the End of the Normal* (Boston, MA: Beacon Press, 2012).
4. Boltanski and Chiapello are equally concerned with instances where people do *not* share a common "order of justification," where they attempt a justification or a critique by reference to an "order" or a "city" that is not necessarily shared by all of their interlocutors. If at times our analysis tends to conjure up a singular and homogeneous, albeit ostensibly historical, social formation, we would remind our readers that we are drawing on an analytic apparatus that recognizes multiple, sometimes coexistent yet incompatible orders. Gaga's social critiques, we argue, operate within the limits of a singular order, and we intend to map those limits. See Luc Boltanski and Ève Chiapello, *The New Spirit of Capitalism*, trans. Gregory Elliott (New York: Verso, 2007), e.g. 20–22, 519. Their language of "orders" and "cities" is adapted from Luc Boltanski and Laurent Thévenot, *On Justification: Economies of Worth*, trans. Catherine Porter (Princeton: Princeton University Press, 2006 [1991]).
5. Lewis Mumford, *The Myth of the Machine: Technics and Human Development* (New York: Harcourt, Brace & World, 1966); Zoe Sofia, "Container Technologies," *Hypatia: A Journal of Feminist Philosophy* 15, no. 2 (2000); Jonathan Sterne, "The MP3 as Cultural Artifact," *New Media & Society* 8, no. 5 (October 2006).
6. Jason Stanyek and Benjamin Piekut, "Deadness: Technologies of the Intermundane," *The Drama Review* 54, no. 1 (Spring 2010). The concept of "deadness" is intended to have a wide

range of applications, especially in its role as part of a larger project challenging common assumptions about liveness and agency. "Although the idea of deadness arose out of our analysis of posthumous duets . . . , its usefulness extends beyond the sonic realms of musical production to all kinds of co-labor." Stanyek and Piekut, "Deadness," 20.

7. Kiri Miller, "Jacking the Dial: Radio, Race, and Place in Grand Theft Auto," *Ethnomusicology* 51, no. 3 (Fall 2007); Stanyek and Piekut, "Deadness."

8. There are, in fact, a number of ways of downloading YouTube videos, such as CatchVideo, DownTube, KeepVid, Mozilla Firefox's DownloadHelper, and VDownloader, and we are not aware of any efforts on the part of YouTube to prevent this practice. Nevertheless, these technologies seem to facilitate a practice that YouTube tends to indirectly discourage.

9. Jack Schofield, "YouTube Adds a Music Discover/Playlist Feature, and offers Sundance Movies for Rent," *Technology Blog, The Guardian*, January 22, 2010. http://www.guardian.co.uk/technology/blog/2010/jan/22/youtube-playlist-discovery-sundance-rental, accessed June 29, 2011.

10. Far from being disciplined by the screen, for example, Clay, the hero of Bret Easton Ellis's novel *Less Than Zero* (New York: Vintage Contemporaries, 1985), turns off the sound on his television to let MTV's disconnected images wash through his bedroom.

11. Brian Hiatt, "Monster Goddess. Unicorns, Sex Dreams and the Freak Revolution: Deep Inside the Unreal World of Lady Gaga," *Rolling Stone* 1132, June 9, 2011, 40–47.

12. Mark Andrejevic, "Exploiting YouTube: Contradictions of User-Generated Labor," in *The YouTube Reader*, ed. Pelle Snickars and Patrick Vonderau (Stockholm: National Library of Sweden, 2009), 408–409.

13. Raymond Williams described something similar in his study of television in the 1970s. See *Television: Technology and Cultural Form* (London: Fontana, 1974; New York: Routledge Classics, 2003).

14. Victor P. Corona, "Memory, Monsters, and Lady Gaga," *The Journal of Popular Culture* (Early View, 2011): 2, doi: 10.1111/j.1540-5931.2011.00809.x.

15. Although Corona does not use the vocabulary of Other, Peer, and Mother, it might be said that his discussion of the negotiation of various notions of femininity in the careers of female pop stars hints at a longer history that cannot be elaborated here. In singling out Courtney Love, Britney Spears, and Beyoncé as having each captured an individual "key element," he proposes a kind of trinity that might be productively, if no doubt problematically, mapped onto our own typology. See "Memory, Monsters, and Lady Gaga," 14–15.

16. Whether or not she would agree with our decision to single out this hook as being particularly "Gaga," Jody Rosen, writing for Rolling Stone's "Ultimate Ranking of Lady Gaga Songs," described "Bad Romance"—the song that took the number one ranking on that list—as, "the essence of Gagaism." *Rolling Stone.com*, May 25, 2011. http://www.rollingstone.com/music/lists/the-ultimate-ranking-of-lady-gagas-catalog-20110525/bad-romance-19691231, accessed July 2, 2011. Speaking from our personal experiences and conversations, it seems fair to at least suggest that some of Gaga's songs sound more Gaga than others, and we would agree with Rosen that "Bad Romance" is the quintessential example.

17. Berto Romero and Ana Morgade pick up on and emphasize this "exotic" quality in their flamenco version of the song, "Romance Jodío." See "Bad Romance—Lady Gaga—Doblado flamenco—Romance Jodío," YouTube video, 3:01, posted by "RicardoEntertainmen1" May 29, 2010. http://www.youtube.com/watch?v=O8XJP-xSKak, accessed June 30, 2011", accessed June 30, 2011.

18. Mirjana Laušević makes a similar point about the appeal of Balkan dance to U.S. "WASPs." The Balkan folk were supposed to be frozen in an early stage of human evolution and therefore more childlike and close to nature. They were, in this sense, "familial," not alien. See *Balkan Fascination: Creating an Alternative Music Culture in America* (New York: Oxford University Press, 2007), 74–75.

19. "What's That Name?" *Saturday Night Live*, season 36, episode 22, Hulu television episode, 6:15, http://www.hulu.com/watch/243592, accessed July 6, 2011.

20. Brian Hiatt, "Monster Goddess," 40–47. The rest of the quotations in this paragraph are taken from that interview. The quotations have been minimally adjusted to correct minor typographical errors in the original text.

21. Hiatt, "Monster Goddess." One important point that cannot be elaborated here for sake of space is that the Gaga as Mother facet is wrapped up with an explicit representation of Gaga as Christ (she even sweats blood). One might also observe that although the popular press picked up on Gaga's performance of a Mary Magdalene character in the video for "Judas," she also appears in that video as a Stephen figure (the first to be martyred by stoning), as a Judas figure ("kissing" Judas with the lipstick that extends from the tip of her gun), and even perhaps as a Christ, Mother Mary, or at least as some kind of leadership figure. In moving through these different representations, Gaga assumes different positions within the body politic.

22. The most recognizable predecessor would be Bernard Herrmann's overture for Hitchcock's Vertigo and its tale of obsession and anxiety.

23. Sumanth Gopinath, "Good Trains and Bad: Steve Reich and the Holocaust in American Musical Life," (paper presented at the 2nd International Conference on Minimalism, University of Missouri-Kansas City, September 3, 2009).

24. Bill Werde, "Lady Gaga 'Born This Way' Cover Story," *Billboard.com*, February 18, 2011. http://www.billboard.com/news/lady-gaga-born-this-way-cover-story-1005041172.story, accessed May 30, 2012.

25. George M. Fredrickson, *The Black Image in the White Mind: The Debate on Afro-American Character and Destiny, 1817–1914* (New York: Harper & Rowe, 1971), 110–117. This representation was sometimes deliberately linked to representations of women, setting up an alliance between feminism and abolitionism. The irony of these representations is that while they depicted black people and women in a more favorable light than white men, they nevertheless justified white male power by suggesting that white men, for all their vices, were stronger and better able to make the difficult decisions needed to lead the nation.

26. Gaga herself has explained the idea of an inclusive, empowering community of Others. She says, "Harkening back to the early '90s, when Madonna, En Vogue, Whitney Houston and TLC were making very empowering music for women and the gay community and all kinds of disenfranchised communities, the lyrics and the melodies were very poignant and very gospel and very spiritual and I said, 'That's the kind of record I need to make.'...Anyone could sing 'Born This Way.' It could've been anyone." Quoted in Bill Werde, "Lady Gaga 'Born This Way' Cover Story."

27. Ann Powers makes the RedOne-as-global-traveler narrative explicit: "Nadhir Kayat's journey from obscurity to fame is the tale of a global wanderer.... Genre is dead. Allegiance to a particular subculture is counterproductive. Old-fashioned values about 'real music' don't factor in when you're reaching for the next unexpected sound.... Few major artists attach themselves to one style or even evoke only one era. Producers must

be like safecrackers, practiced in finding perfect combinations." See, "Their Mix Goes Global; RedOne, Alex Da Kid and Ari Levine, Groundbreaking Producers and Grammy Nominees, Are Plugged into Pop's One-World, Multi-Genre Spirit," *Los Angeles Times*, February 13, 2011.

28. Andrew Hampp, "Gaga, Oooh La La: Why the Lady Is the Ultimate Social Climber; Leveraging Digital Media and Creative Partnerships Makes Artist a Uniquely 2010 Pop Star," *Advertising Age*, February 22, 2011.

29. Ibid.

30. Corona, "Memory, Monsters, and Lady Gaga," 6.

31. Where this has been perceived, it has provoked especially hostile criticisms of Gaga. It is ironic but, if one accepts our argument in this essay, not so surprising that "Born This Way" has provided the touchstone for the "Gays Against Gaga" tumblr (http://gaysagainstgaga. tumblr.com/archive, accessed July 23, 2012). Many participants on this tumblr express feeling that, rather than being asked to participate as equals in a social movement, they have been targeted. However one evaluates these kinds of sentiments, they depend on the perception of an unequal power relation.

32. Gaga describes personhood as dependent on anonymous digital connections. "We have this umbilical cord that I don't want to cut, ever," she explains. "I don't feel that they suck me dry. It would be so mean, wouldn't it, to say, 'For the next month, I'm going to cut myself off from my fans so I can be a person.' What does that mean? They are part of my person, they are so much of my person. They're at least 50 percent, if not more." Quoted in Hiatt, "Monster Goddess."

33. An article in *U.S. News & World Report* from 1997 described tattooing as the "sixth-fastest-growing retail business" in the United States, following, perhaps only coincidentally, the internet, paging services, bagel, computer, and cellular phone shops. See Mary Lord and Rachel Lehmann-Haupt, "A Hole in the Head?" *U.S. News & World Report*, November 3, 1997, News You Can Use, Parenting: 67. In this regard, it is also perhaps telling that arguably the funniest line in Weird Al Yankovich's take on "Born This Way"—a parody that otherwise might not rank among his most successful—says "I'll wrap my small intestines 'round my neck and set fire to myself onstage." The humor in the line has everything to do with an uneasy sense that there are more than hints of self-mutilation and violence built into Gaga's iconography. See "Perform This Way (Parody of 'Born This Way' by Lady Gaga)," YouTube video, 2:55, posted by "alyankovicVEVO," June 20, 2011. http:// www.youtube.com/watch?v=ss_BmTGv43M, accessed July 5, 2011.

34. Werde, "Lady Gaga 'Born This Way' Cover Story."

35. Our thinking about ostensibly proper conduct in a networked, neoliberal society is indebted here to Luc Boltanski and Ève Chiapello's description of the "Great Man" in the "Projective City." See *The New Spirit of Capitalism*, trans. Gregory Elliott (New York: Verso, 2007).

SELECT BIBLIOGRAPHY

Andrejevic, Mark. "Exploiting YouTube: Contradictions of User-Generated Labor." In *The YouTube Reader*, edited by Pelle Snickars and Patrick Vonderau, 406–423. Stockholm: National Library of Sweden, 2009.

Boltanski, Luc, and Ève Chiapello. *The New Spirit of Capitalism*. Translated by Gregory Elliott. New York: Verso, 2007.

Chion, Michel. *The Voice in Cinema*. Translated by Claudia Gorbman. New York: Columbia University Press, 1999. Original work published as *La voix au cinéma* (Paris: Editions de lÉtoile/Cahiers du Cinéma, 1982).

Corona, Victor P. "Memory, Monsters, and Lady Gaga." *Journal of Popular Culture* (Early view, 2011). doi: 10.1111/j.1540-5931.2011.00809.x.

Fredrickson, George M. *The Black Image in the White Mind: The Debate on Afro-American Character and Destiny, 1817-1914*. New York: Harper & Rowe, 1971.

Hiatt, Brian. "Monster Goddess. Unicorns, Sex Dreams and the Freak Revolution: Deep Inside the Unreal World of Lady Gaga." *Rolling Stone* 1132, June 9, 2011.

Jameson, Fredric. *The Political Unconscious: Narrative as a Socially Symbolic Act*. New York: Routledge Classics, 2002. Original work published 1981 by Methuen & Co., Ltd., United Kingdom.

Latour, Bruno. "An Attempt at a 'Compositionist Manifesto.' " *New Literary History* 41, no. 3 (Summer 2010): 471–490.

Latour, Bruno. *Politics of Nature: How to Bring the Sciences into Democracy*. Translated by Catherine Porter. Cambridge: Harvard University Press, 2004. Original work published as *Politiques de la nature. Comment faire entrer les sciences en démocratie* (La Découverte, 1999).

Miller, Kiri. "Jacking the Dial: Radio, Race, and Place in *Grand Theft Auto*." *Ethnomusicology* 51, no. 3 (Fall 2007): 402–438.

Mumford, Lewis. *The Myth of the Machine: Technics and Human Development*. Vol. 1. New York: Harcourt, Brace & World, 1966.

Sofia, Zoe. "Container Technologies." *Hypatia: A Journal of Feminist Philosophy* 15, no. 2 (2000): 181–219.

Stanyek, Jason, and Benjamin Piekut. "Deadness: Technologies of the Intermundane." *The Drama Review* 54, no. 1 (Spring 2010): 14–38.

Sterne, Jonathan. *MP3: The Meaning of a Format*. Durham: Duke University Press, 2012.

———. "The mp3 as Cultural Artifact." *New Media & Society* 8, no. 5 (October 2006): 825–842.

Varnelis, Kazys. "The meaning of network culture." *Eurozine*, January 14, 2010. http://www.eurozine.com/articles/2010-01-14-varnelis-en.html.

Werde, Bill. "Lady Gaga 'Born This Way' cover story." *Billboard.com*, February 18, 2011. Accessed May 30, 2012. http://www.billboard.com/news/lady-gaga-born-this-way-cover-story-1005041172.story.

Williams, Jeffrey J. "The Drag of Masculinity: An Interview with Judith 'Jack' Halberstam." *symploke* 19, nos. 1-2 (2011): 361–380.

Williams, Raymond. *Television: Technology and Cultural Form*. New York: Routledge Classics, 2003. Original work published 1974 by Fontana, London.

CHAPTER 32

COMING TO MIND

Pornography and the Mediation of Intensity

PAUL MORRIS AND SUSANNA PAASONEN

PORNOGRAPHY has had a crucial impact on the development of network technologies and online economies, as in the development of web hosting services, credit card payment systems, banner advertisement, web promotion, and streaming video technologies. At the same time, digital media technologies and online platforms have affected the production, distribution, and consumption of pornography. All this has drastically transformed the shapes and forms that contemporary pornography takes.[1] The distribution of audiovisual pornography first shifted from VHS to DVD in the 1990s, then increasingly to online platforms. With the expansion of web distribution, porn production has broadened from well-established studios and companies to small, independent, and amateur ventures. Some scholars have termed the ensuing expansion of available porn niches and subgenres as "netporn," namely pornographies particular and characteristic to online platforms.[2] However, when zooming in on particular sexual subcultures and pornographic practices, it becomes much more difficult to distinguish online practices from offline ones, or to separate DVD production from online distribution.

Rather than addressing the general intersections of pornography and digital media, this chapter explores the dynamics of mediation in the context of gay bareback pornography. Coauthored by Paul Morris, porn producer, director, and founder of Treasure Island Media (TIM, est. 1998) with a background in studies of music, and Susanna Paasonen, a media studies scholar who has spent the last decade researching online pornography, this chapter combines practice-based insights with more conventional scholarly argumentation. Debates on pornography, its social role and meaning, gender equality, and moral value have for some three decades been stuck in a rigid argument between antiporn and pro-porn (or "anti-antiporn") campaigners. These polemics will not be revisited here. In what follows, we'll address the interplay of bodies performing, recording, and viewing pornography, and the sensory intensities and proximities generated through digital sound and image. Our interests lie in the fleshy force and appeal of bareback porn and that of porn more generally.

BAREBACK SUBCULTURE AND PORNOTOPIA

Writing half a decade ago on Victorian literary pornography, Steven Marcus coined the term "pornotopia" to describe the utopian aspects of the genre, its abundant depictions of sexual acts and flowing desires.[3] Since the mid-1990s, the internet has become a pornotopia in its own right, with its plethora of available pornographies and diverse displays of corporeal appetites and dynamics of control. As large porn corporations and mainstream sites have attempted to garner audiences by steadily incorporating specialties, subcategories, and subcultural styles as novelties to their product menus, niche practices have become increasingly recognizable. Detached from the sexual subcultures they originated in, these imageries have been marooned and hence transformed, whereas neat demarcations such as the mainstream and the alternative have grown increasingly unstable in definitions of pornography.[4] Nevertheless, distinctions remain and continue to matter.

Gay bareback pornography—briefly, gay porn featuring penetrative sex without the use of condoms—was established as a recognizable porn subgenre in the late 1990s, and TIM has been a prominent player in the field since the beginning.[5] Drawing on and documenting sexual practices of bareback subculture in the San Francisco Bay area, TIM caused no small degree of controversy by countering the mandate of safe sex in gay porn and by featuring HIV positive performers. The subgenre has since become increasingly recognizable as it has been incorporated into the palette of mainstream gay porn: currently, a Google search for "gay bareback porn" generates some 36 million hits. Yet tensions remain. On the one hand, TIM has been banned from various adult industry events—and even death threats have been made against the producer. On the other hand, porn has been seen as central to the bareback subculture as a form of witnessing that documents sexual practices and renders forms of intimacy visible. Queer scholar Tim Dean defines TIM titles as documentary pornography, as visual ethnography committed to representing a sexual community to and for itself.[6] From the perspective of TIM, the issue is one of responsibility to a community and a tradition. Within and for the sexual community to whom the films are targeted, it presents something of a living archive of male sexual practice. The fan base of TIM—and that of Morris personally—is among the largest for any gay porn producer.

Particularly in the beginning, TIM titles were carefully set in specific spaces—a cheap hotel room, a San Francisco porn booth store, etc.—all of which would be open to the viewer if they were in San Francisco. The promise was that if you find this place, these men would be there, waiting for you. The TIM fan base is strong in the Bay area but it has, in the wake of DVD production and online presence, become markedly translocal. Participants and believers in the sex culture often are not in physical proximity to places where the culture exists. TIM's networked presence extends the subculture and adds a virtual layer, at least for those fans who do not recognize the particular locations and see these as more anonymous frames of action.

TIM is well established within contemporary gay pornography, yet its productions remain somewhat detached from the trends of the industry more generally. The films have changed since the late 1990s (not least in terms of technological execution) but there is also considerable consistency to them, given that they are tailored to the demands, critiques, and needs of the audience. According to Morris, for the most part, porn provides experience without peril, experimentation without damage. The men in TIM films are, however, admired and prized by the constituent audience precisely for being damaged, for having taken the ultimate risk and "lost." By participating in a TIM film, these men tacitly "come out" as HIV positive and simultaneously argue for the permanentl nature of seroconversion. In most porn, however, and in a world increasingly dominated by the medical gaze, to willingly live in symbiosis with a virus is seen as irrational and irresponsible.

SEX, RISK, AND COMMUNITY

The sex in TIM films is markedly unsafe. In fact, it represents something of an antithesis to the pedagogy of safe sex practiced in gay porn since the breakout of the AIDS epidemic. The films celebrate bodily fluids and acts of sharing semen through practices of "seeding" and "breeding" (the virus). For some viewers, this seems to evoke a kind of stickiness: having watched it, one feels dirty and the sense of dirtiness continues post viewing. A writer for *Out* magazine, for example, said that he was afraid to watch the videos because he felt that he might become infected by them, that somehow they had a magical power to either overthrow his personal will and cause him to imperil himself or to actually introduce the virus into his blood. But this is what drew him to the work as well.

For Dean, sharing the virus facilitates gay kinship outside heterosexual notions of family and undoes the HIV closet that "is as double-edged as any closet, since it confers a measure of protection through deniability while incarcerating in silence those it shelters."[7] The notion of kinship created through breeding and seeding the virus reverses notions of sexual health. Writing on TIM, queer theorist Lee Edelman identifies the films as "Foucauldian resistance to the aesthetic conformity and sexual conservatism embedded in the representational politics of the mainstream studios producing gay porn."[8] Rather than celebrating seroconversion, Edelman sees the porn as turning away from the notion of sex as safe, and embracing its material substances by "immersing itself in celebrations of contact with cum."[9] The potential contagions experienced by viewers can be seen as loops of intensity in which bodily boundaries of safety are negotiated with notions of pleasure and disgust as these images come close.

Viscerality

That which leaves an impression on us, sticks. Katariina Kyrölä writes on how media images of bodies stretched to the limits of their carnal capacity "reach out to viewing bodies and touch them so viscerally that they are likely to leave a mark, some form of a residue."[10] Mediated images and sounds stick, and the sensations they evoke—be these ones of sexual arousal, disgust, confusion, or intense fascination—linger on. Although it could be said that encounters with all kinds of media images, popular and highbrow alike, involve such stickiness, porn has its fleshy particularities and gut reactions that need to be acknowledged.

The metaphor of filth carries associations of contagion, for when sensing filth, some of it has already managed to stick on the person—a contamination has already taken place. In porn, filth fascinates and titillates, and the sensations that linger are also ones of contagion, of having been touched or impressed in particular ways. Antiporn objections (be these moral, political, or aesthetic in character) routinely resort to the terminology of filth, scum, and sleaze, in marking porn as not only trashy but as an object of disgust. In straight porn, the same terminology has a promotional function: the filthier and grittier porn is promised to be, the more hardcore (and hence "better") it is. Straight hardcore negotiates with thresholds of disgust and pushes them in order to make an impression and to grab audience attention.[11]

At the same time, these boundaries—much like definitions of taste—escape general definition. For example, historian William Ian Miller identifies wet kisses and sex in general as instances in which bodily boundaries are breached and thresholds of disgust need to be negotiated.[12] This implies a markedly low threshold of disgust in relation to TIM titles, where semen is licked off from hands, chests, and anuses, scooped out from rectums, rubbed on skin, and devoured with gusto. These are generally scenes of shared intensity that the performers act out with apparent delight.

Dean argues that bareback porn "paradoxically adapts technologies of visual mediation—the digital camera, the Internet, to its project of overcoming mediation."[13] One might argue that a similar paradox applies to a range of pornographies—and perhaps even to pornography as an umbrella marker of genre. All kinds of pornography involve attempts at intersensory translations that aim to move and touch the bodies of those engaging with it. By moving up close and zooming in on the bodies performing for the camera, porn tries to mediate the immediate feel and intensity of sex, yet it is ultimately limited to conveying how it looks and sounds. A great deal threatens to be lost, or even amputated, in the translation between how sex is audiovisually depicted and how it feels, tastes, and smells. A whole range of sensory stimuli escapes mediation. Nevertheless, some of the intensity stubbornly seeps through in audience sensations of sexual arousal, amazement, or disgust, and when scenes grab viewer attention and pull them back for further revisiting. Porn tries to mediate the sensory and the somatic—the intensity and feel of sex—through audiovisual means, in order to find resonance with the viewers. That is, it aims to create immediate fleshy sensations by mediating the immediate sensations of sex displayed for the camera and microphone.

SPACES OF PORNOGRAPHY

In film studies, this visceral force of porn has often been addressed through the notion of body genres. Linda Williams has defined porn as analogous to genres such as horror and melodrama in that they all try to move their viewers in bodily ways and to make their bodies leak. Whereas horror tries to make the bodies flinch and sweat in anxiety, melodrama tries to move them to tears, and porn tries to arouse them sexually and drive them towards orgasm.[14] The idea is that the intensities of the carnal displays on the screen grab the viewers in particularly fleshy ways so that some of the distance between the characters and one's own body becomes bridged.

But when watching horror, the frisson of engagement is possible from the distance between self and image. One does not usually wish one's own body to be torn apart and abused. Porn is the opposite—one easily transposes the on-screen action onto one's own body, actively works into that experience through masturbation, timing one's own orgasm with that of the on-screen person. This calls for the necessity of making porn that gives room for full engagement—that is, not the kind of porn populated by people who look and act as though they exist in a world that is not available to the viewer.

Porn is about place being dominated by flesh. It is the reverse of interior design. In porn, space is deflated by the fascinating presence and actions of bodies. In horror, by way of contrast, the torture space or haunted house is as important as the narrative action and bloodletting. Through the masturbating viewer's vested involvement with the repetitive movements and acts and sounds of the bodies being observed, porn-time congeals (in ways comparable to the primacy of time for syncopated dance and the relative irrelevance of the dance space) and space weakens. The quality of attention and awareness this develops is immediate and focused, the opposite of transcendent or spatial. The draw of place or space are replaced by human flesh, something we know as ourselves.

Scholars have regularly failed to address masturbation as part and parcel of porn consumption, whereas the connection seems obvious to porn producers and audiences. Perhaps the body-genre analogy is appealing because it provides certain conceptual distance, or comfort, one where bodily affectations of the sexual and lusty sort can be addressed on a nonpersonal level as issues of generic form. If one focuses on the interconnections of masturbation and porn, analysis involves a much more intimate intermeshing and reverberation of bodies performing and watching.

Part of Marcus's argument is that pornotopia is an imaginary nonplace that can be geographically located anywhere but which ultimately exists in the audience's imagination. Promising the freedom of fantasy without the burden of excessive detail, pornotopia, although often set somewhere, is equally detached from the confines of physical location.[15] In video porn, the locations are often motels, hotels, and anonymous residential houses. The clubs, porn stores, and hotel rooms where TIM films have been shot are similar sites, yet they are also about very particular cities and locations. Perhaps they could be better thought of as heterotopias, simultaneously virtual and actual locations of nonhegemonic action. For Michel Foucault, such other spaces "presuppose a system of opening and closing that both isolates them and makes them penetrable."[16] One of the examples he uses to clarify this admittedly obscure notion are "American motel rooms where a man goes with his car and his mistress and where illicit sex is both absolutely sheltered and absolutely hidden, kept isolated without however being allowed out in the open."[17] Such locations—be they considered pornotopia or heterotopia—are semi-accessible pockets of activity and potentiality.

Space in porn is usually laughable (incidental) or simply background (outdoor, motel room, shower, toilet stall). Such space supports the types of sex that performers performed in the scene ("top," "bottom," "straight," "leatherman," etc.) but it is also, coincidentally, parallel to the intimation of harmony in dance music. The melody and rhythm and timbral complexities are primary in dance music because they exist in time. If harmony becomes too extended or functional (in the traditional sense of classical European functional harmony), it draws the music into narrative and distracts from the depth of trance. If place becomes primary, other than accidental, the work is easily situated as erotica rather than porn. If location/space is pointedly primary, the nudity or even sex becomes incidental in the sense of being embedded within narrative. In horror, the place is primary and usually arrived at through unfortunate accident. In porn, the place is incidental and is arrived at by moving within a world of supernatural sexual saturation.

MEMORIES OF THE FLESH

What is exciting about watching porn—when it is good and it works—is remembering, recognizing, and reliving. The body is shaped by historically layered skills, experiences, and sensations that bring forth particular ways of relating to other bodies and reverberating with them. Dance scholar Susan Kozel discusses this as resonance that is based on our assembly of senses and varied experiences and allows for empathy with mediated (or fictional) experiences and acts.[18] Watching porn, our bodies resonate with the images and bodies on the screen, and they do so in accordance with our layered corporeal histories, orientations, traumas, and fascinations. These "somatic archives" facilitate bridging the sensory gaps between the sexual acts seen and heard and those experienced in the flesh, while the rhythms and intensities of masturbation help to bridge them further.[19]

What is exciting about porn is the recognition of something real and almost forgotten: a moment, a gesture, a connection. Often, when reviewing a new piece at TIM, there are scenes that stand out, where some very particular thing happens. It is never predictable, which is why it is so valuable. Most commercial pornographers seem to believe that formulaic repetition is enough or that providing some fetishistic storyline or detail will work. That is why so much porn is closer to death than sex: it gives you the skeleton but does not bother with the flesh.

Sex is about percepts, specifics, immediacies. Skateboarders speeding down a street—that's the body thinking in the way a man having sex thinks. The work, or challenge, of porn is to try to understand and capture what the flesh is saying—to capture and mediate some of this intensity and immediacy. When recognizing some of this, the images resonate with one's somatic archives and the memories of sensations, partners, and situations that they entail. In such instances, the movement of bodies on the screen, the sounds they make, and the range of sensory stimuli involved in sex become easy enough to sense—and not merely to make sense of. Yet this is not only a question of recognizing things through or in terms of the familiar since the body constantly learns and alters in surprising ways while its sensations, palates, tastes, and experiences change. Experiences of consuming porn shape and influence one's contingent somatic reservoirs as resonance, titillation, dislike, curiosity, or exercises of imagination, while these archives in return orient ways of sensing and making sense of pornography.

According to a thesaurus definition, *resonance* refers to "oscillation induced in a physical system when it is affected by another system that is itself oscillating at the right frequency." Such frequencies are both intentionally sought and accidentally found when something moves us. Resonance can also smack of dissonance: numerous porn subgenres work with and through disgust, by pulling the viewers into uncomfortable proximity. Porn encounters may equally be devoid of any kind of vibration, given how often users complain of the boredom of browsing through endless image and video galleries where nothing grabs them. Resonance is not constant nor given. It is often hard indeed to figure what the flesh gestures toward.

CIRCULATION

TIM aims to seduce men into a repeated and extended experience that requires sustained concentration through an entire sex scene. The European art music culture is similar. One understands and joins by committing to complex experiences that have lots of subtle signs. An enduring sex culture is transmitted through the assimilation of extended structures—"scenes." Lay participants or dilettante/amateurs are able to "sample" the culture through excerpts, animated gif files, and stills that spread autonomously throughout the web. The understanding is improved (through recognition) as one has personal experience. This sexual experience does not have to be extensive for recognition to happen, just as one's appreciation of symphonic music is enhanced if one plays an instrument but has never actually performed in a symphonic orchestra.

It can be argued that porn and music are similar activities using different materials. Animated gif files are parallel, for instance, to dance music with the brief and infinitely repeating unit of information. In the gif, the insistent "now" of the dance music beat is visual. What each teaches is an isolated fragment of an eternal present and a focus on the physicalization of analytical attention (the repeated carnal fragment in the porn gif, the complex syncopated layers of beat division in dance music). Both teach through the pleasure of the body in a moment rather than a place. The porn blog that focuses on stills and gifs is parallel to the dance floor. Both engage the body in trance.

From a pornographer's perspective, sexual scenes are parallel to extended musical structures, and the masturbatory experience is parallel to the aesthetic experience of a musical structure. If a person is only familiar with samplings or excerpts of popular symphonic warhorses, they would have a limited understanding of the culture of European art music. They would see it as strange, elitist, even unapproachable. The same is true of porn. The web makes it simple to sample it, exaggerate it, and copy it; and gifs, stills, and excerpts are circulated on blogs and pirate sites. Pornographers can see these as misrepresenting the work or, positively, as road signs sending consumers to them. "Clues" are seeded through all available media. Images are an obvious example, as are the animated gifs that are being carefully created and seeded in multitudes of sites.

Theresa Senft has introduced the notion of the "grab" to describe the visual and tactile dynamic of visual exchanges online.[20] With the grab, she describes a media landscape characterized by user-generated content and user engagement of various kinds. Once images or videos are made available, they are out of the control of their creators as users grab images, perhaps link or incorporate them to other sites, share them, and frame them with comments of their own—as with the still images and animated gifs that TIM and its fans seed onto the network. The logic and rhythm is one of clicks, links, and clips.

The notion of the grab captures some of the complexity of digital production, circulation, and consumption within—but also beyond—the visual. As users, we are "grabbed" as our movements are tracked with cookies or through IP addresses and as our routine tasks are recorded as data. Pornographers grab particular gestures, motions, and intensities when producing the films. Users grab video clips, share and circulate them, grab them with their descriptions and comments, rip files, and create their own remixes. One way to put this is that that which grabs, resonates: such encounters involve potentiality and affectation.

As attention becomes more rarefied and ephemeralized, it resists linearity and has to be seduced carefully yet chaotically (with no linear connection) into situations of more and more sustained effort. In a sense, this is about the necessity of chaotic marketing today. Since the online market is wary of any obvious intent or purpose, a culture—or a company such as TIM—has to mimic the web as closely as possible, to simply be "part of the landscape," a natural and inevitable occurrence.

WORKING WITH SOUND

Discussions on porn—be these studies, critiques, or other debates—have overwhelmingly focused on the visual and the pictorial content, whereas the workings of sound in and for porn have been left with much less attention. At the same time, sound plays a crucial role in the mediation of intensity. In her discussion on heterosexual porn, Williams emphasizes the centrality of sounds in conveying and mediating female pleasure: the cries of women dominate in aural hard core. At the same time, these cries, as well as sighs, grunts, moans, squeals, panting, and bits of dialogue are often dubbed, so that sound and image are slightly off-sync with one another.[21] The sounds may be just a bit too crisp, loud, or sharp, and disjointed in relation to the movement of the performing bodies. The sounds of pleasure are often stylized and hyperbolic, and hence in contrast with claims of documentary realism on the plane of the visual.[22]

The use of music has been one means of filling the audio space: as dubbed sounds become part of a broader sonic fabric, minor discontinuities between words uttered or groans made and lips moving become less obvious.[23] The conventions of using music in porn—from the 1970s porn funk to 1980s synthesizer soundscapes—are familiar to many. The soundtrack provides rhythm and tempo for sexual acts unfolding, possibly to support the motions of masturbation. Alternatively, the soundtrack may create a sense of distance by detaching the audience from the diegetic sounds of the acts performed. The textures of music may remain in the background, add to the intensity of the overall scene, or disrupt it. Once this additional, external layer of rhythm and texture is absent, the sounds of sex involve intensity that draws viewers—as listeners—into a different kind of proximity.

In TIM titles, the sonic plays a crucial role in the mediation and creation of intensity: sounds come up close in order to enfold the viewer. This "sonorous envelope" involves grunts, heavy breathing, and bodies slamming. The sounds are recorded close to the source, often intimately so. In the absence of scripted dialogue, the words uttered are spontaneous expressions of pleasure, surprise, and excitement, and they are crucially about communication between the men in the scene. Captions are sometimes used to mediate what the men are saying (if this cannot be properly heard) and what is happening in the film (if this escapes the camera, as in the case of internal ejaculations). According to Dean, the captioning heightens the "movies" documentary effect by retaining all the contingent noises—traffic roaring by, a radio show playing intermittently, as well as "enthusiastic remarks to the participants, periodic silence—that occur during filming."[24] In other words, sound heightens and creates the films' documentary feel of "being there," of audiences grasping the intensity of the scenes and joining in its resonating loop.

Despite the documentary mode and intensity of TIM films, however, they do not merely document and record the sounds unfolding. A great deal of attention and work is invested on mediating intensity and facilitating bodily engagement through auditory means when making the films. The sound work is meant not to awaken the viewer from the masturbatory trance but to more fully engage him in it. This trance is the "work" of pornography and is as important to the development and elaboration of the personal fantasy as the sexual excitement of the imagery. It cannot rupture the engagement, but it can deepen it (if it works well). The opening of *What I Can't See #1* (1999) is an interesting example in this respect. The film starts with the visual and sonic noise of a TV screen. As a remote control is handled, the sound changes into the disco beat of *You Should Be Dancing* by the Bee Gees while a topless, rollerblading man happily dances to the upbeat tune. The image is fuzzy, black-and-white, and the music clear. A scratching sound follows as the image ripples and cuts to a scene, in full color, of a man hammering the television set to a screaming sound. As the man continues to kick the TV, a sweet folk song (written for the video) starts to play. The image shifts to the opening text that describes the film one is about to experience and the song, about being lost, doodles through the sequence as it shifts to shots of men having anal and oral sex. No other sounds are heard until the song ends and the diegetic soundscape takes over with its humming background noise of traffic passing by, the sounds of the equipment handled, and the slurping sounds of a mouth reaching for a penis. The audience reads the texts, watches the images, and hears the words being sung. If the scene works, the two streams of information augment each other while providing distance between one other that has to be creatively bridged.

In later videos, TIM has used the sound of broken bones, animal cries, sound effects from horror movies, women's screams, slowly rising oscillating tones, and so on to enhance the intensity of the moment being watched. The intended impact is a kind of footnote or bass note to the action. Other audio elements used involve reverb, echoes, added (subliminal) music, and tone sequences that, if sped up, would be recognizable as loops derived from pieces like the *Rite of Spring*. Drones and dog barks (sometimes continuing annoyingly) have equally been added on to enhance the visceral reaction of the viewer: as he masturbates, he finally says "I wish that damned dog would stop barking!" but he moves into and through the frustration because of the images and that enhances his concentration, his trance, his engagement with the possibility of a social orgasm. In some of the later TIM videos, there are scenes in which the sound of the playspace is changed and edited in order to corporealize the space and give it a voice, a complex tone. This is sometimes done with objects in the room, giving them sounds as they pass before the camera. In one brief sequence, a man moves away from a guy who is in a sling then moves back toward him. This brief move is given the sound of metal being strained and bent. Furthermore, scenes have been tinted various colors: deepening red, for example, as the intensity develops, very slowly. All this is the opposite of films by pornographers like the late Brad Braverman. His worlds were elite, fantasy, ideal, and his soundtracks were only music that repeated over and over (composed for the scene, but removing the connection of the viewer with the images).

In TIM titles, the sounds amplify the visual and build the overall rhythm of the scenes. Intensity is, however, orchestrated and oriented also through the means of discord and friction, by meshing the resonant with the dissonant to the degree that the two become inseparable. These resonances are not simply about "good vibrations" but involve more complex compositions.

To use an analogy, in a dinner scene in Hitchcock's *Suspicion*, five people are eating a meal, a regular event, satisfying a physical desire/need. It is done every day by everyone. If this were pornography, the scene would be isolated and about the eating of the meal. But Hitchcock has, of course, a story within which all these specific little narratives take place, so we can only notice in passing—but not give too much attention to—expressive specificities. The dinner conversation is about murder, particularly about poison. At one point, one of the characters—Dr. Sedbusk—recalls exhuming a body four years after its burial. At that point, Hitchcock cuts to a close-up of the doctor's hands as he cuts into the pheasant corpse that he is eating. Had Hitchcock shown one of the other characters reacting, horrified by the necrophiliac juxtaposition of eating and the idea of a rotting human corpse, the weight of the moment would have overwhelmed the conversation and the narrative. So the moment is noticed but not held in the mind of the viewer, who very quickly forgets about it in the narrative flow.

The sustained attention needed to keep in mind an unfolding narrative is very similar to the masturbatory trance. In fact, you could easily argue that pornography maintains the most antique narrative structures in existence. There are characters that must be kept clear, events that unfold, surprising twists, conclusions that have various meanings, and so on. The quality of the masturbatory trance, the state necessary for the scene to "work," can be enhanced by stretching, but not rupturing, it.

In one TIM scene, as the camera pans across two men fucking, flags in the painting above them very briefly flutter. You see them and you hear them. But even if the viewer notices, he quickly forgets. In another scene, a man being fucked throws his head back and in that moment he has been given a sound that is an amalgam of a human death cry and a pig's squeal. In actuality, he made no sound at all. No one will notice consciously, but it will thicken the viewers' trance and, through their unconscious participation, bring them more intimately in contact with the scene.

PORN AND UTOPIA

In his 1977 essay, "Entertainment and Utopia," film scholar Richard Dyer maps the utopian aspects of entertainment through an analysis of musicals. For Dyer, the point of musicals is to present "what utopia would feel like."[25] The notion of utopian sensibility can easily be applied to pornography (beyond Marcus' take on pornotopia). For Dyer, the feel of utopia in entertainment involves energy (as power, activity, and potential), as well as the feel of abundance, intensity, transparency, and community.[26] All these five aspects have been discussed earlier in relation to bareback porn, its visceral force and appeal, and its role within the sex culture.

Morris sees sexuality as utopian human tendency to move toward physical and emotional bliss. Accordingly, bareback porn is utopian in that it argues for better conditions for the body, for the ease and infinite availability of pleasure—and, even more important, for fun, as creative social chaos, albeit a rather managed one. Just as the *1,001 Arabian Nights* is Princess Scheherazade's repetitious (and erotically driven) sequence of lessons in social humility and empathy for the cruel and murderous man she has wed, porn is 10 million and one efforts by the body to argue for the necessity of its own imaginary and its place in the social world, a social world that grows daily less and less friendly to or knowledgeable about this complex system that is our bodies, particularly our sexualized bodies.

Such utopianism—or at least the promise thereof—is crucial to understanding the power and pull of porn, its particularity as a genre, as a field of production, circulation, and consumption. The promise of porn is one of energy, abundance, intensity, transparency, and, in some instances more than others, of community. These utopian wishes are not always met: porn may well bore its consumers, irritate or amuse them, and one person's sense of intensity and authenticity is likely to leave another one cold or even disgusted. Proximities with sexual intensity may intermesh pleasure and titillation with discomfort or shame, and they may create sticky, conflicting sensations that linger on. Nevertheless, these carnal intensities are the ones that invite people back and engage them as audiences and consumers, as networked participants in online exchanges, and as fans with affective attachments to performers, producers, and the sexual cultures they are part of. It is the intensity that grabs, and sticks.

NOTES

1. Susanna Paasonen, *Carnal Resonance: Affect and Online Pornography* (Cambridge, MA: MIT Press, 2011).
2. See Katrien Jacobs, *Netporn: DIY Web Culture and Sexual Politics* (Lanham, MD: Rowman & Littlefield, 2007).
3. Steven Marcus, *The Other Victorians: A Study of Sexuality and Pornography in Mid-Nineteenth-Century England* (New York: Basic Books, 1964), 216.
4. Feona Attwood, "No Money Shot? Commerce, Pornography and New Sex Taste Cultures," *Sexualities* 10, no. 4 (2007): 453.
5. On barebacking, see Tim Dean, *Unlimited Intimacy: Reflections on the Subculture of Barebacking* (Chicago: University of Chicago Press, 2009); Michele L. Crossley, "Making Sense of 'Barebacking': Gay Men's Narratives, Unsafe Sex and the 'Resistance Habitus,'" *British Journal of Social Psychology* 43, no. 2 (2004): 225–244; Damien Thomas Ridge, "'It Was an Incredible Thrill': The Social Meanings and Dynamics of Younger Gay Men's Experiences of Barebacking in Melbourne," *Sexualities* 7, no. 3 (2004): 259–279; Sharif Mowlabocus, *Gaydar Culture: Gay Men, Technology and Embodiment in the Digital Age* (Farnham: Ashgate, 2010), 147–182.
6. Dean, *Unlimited Intimacy*, 119–120.
7. Dean, *Unlimited Intimacy*, 7.
8. Lee Edelman, "Unbecoming: Pornography and the Queer Event," in *PostPorn Politics: Queer_Feminist Perspectives on the Politics of Porn Performances and Sex_Work as Cultural Produktion*. ed. Tim Stüttgen (Berlin: b_books verlag, 2009), 36.
9. Edelman, "Unbecoming," 37.
10. Katariina Kyrölä, *The Weight of Images: Affective Engagements with Fat Corporeality in the Media* (Turku: University of Turku, 2010), 122.
11. Paasonen, *Carnal Resonance*, 208–209.
12. William Ian Miller, *The Anatomy of Disgust* (Cambridge, MA: Harvard University Press, 1997), 127–128.
13. Dean, *Unlimited Intimacy*, 104–105.
14. Linda Williams, "Film Bodies: Gender, Genre, and Excess," *Film Quarterly* 44, no. 4 (1991): 2–13.
15. Marcus, *The Other Victorians*, 269.
16. Michel Foucault, "Of Other Spaces," *Diacritics* 16, no. 1 (1986): 26.
17. Ibid., 27.

18. Susan Kozel, *Closer: Performance, Technologies, Phenomenology* (Cambridge, MA: MIT Press, 2007), 24–26.
19. See Paasonen, *Carnal Resonance*, 202–204.
20. Theresa Senft, *CamGirls: Celebrity & Community in the Age of Social Networks* (New York: Peter Lang, 2008), 46.
21. Linda Williams, *Hard Core: Power, Pleasure, and the "Frenzy of the Visible"* (Berkeley: University of California Press, 1989), 122–123.
22. Williams, *Hard Core*, 123–124; John Richardson, *An Eye for Music: Popular Music and the Audiovisual Surreal* (Oxford: Oxford University Press 2011), 156.
23. Sanna Härmä and Taru Leppänen, "Miltä porno kuulostaa? Sukupuoli, äänet ja musikki valtavirran pornoelokuvissa," *Lähikuva* 3 (2006): 8–9.
24. Dean, *Unlimited Intimacy*, 133.
25. Richard Dyer, *Only Entertainment*, 2nd ed. (London: Routledge, 2002), 20.
26. Dyer, *Only Entertainment*, 22–23.

SELECT BIBLIOGRAPHY

Cronin, Blaise, and Davenport, Elizabeth. "E-Rogenous Zones: Positioning Pornography in the Digital Economy." *The Information Society* 17, no. 1 (2001): 33–48.

Dean, Tim. *Unlimited Intimacy: Reflections on the Subculture of Barebacking*. Chicago: University of Chicago Press, 2009.

Edelman, Lee. "Unbecoming: Pornography and the Queer Event." In *PostPorn Politics: Queer_ Feminist Perspectives on the Politics of Porn Performances and Sex_Work as Cultural Produktion*. Edited by Tim Stüttgen, 33–45. Berlin: b_books verlag, 2009.

Dyer, Richard. *Only Entertainment*, 2nd ed. London: Routledge, 2002.

Foucault, Michel. "Of Other Spaces." *Diacritics* 16, no. 1 (1986), 22–27.

Jacobs, Katrien. *Netporn: DIY Web Culture and Sexual Politics*. Lanham, MD: Rowman & Littlefield, 2007.

Kozel, Susan. *Closer: Performance, Technologies, Phenomenology*. Cambridge, MA: MIT Press, 2007.

Kyrölä, Katariina. *The Weight of Images: Affective Engagements with Fat Corporeality in the Media*. Turku, Finland: University of Turku, 2010.

Laqueur, Thomas. *Solitary Sex: A Cultural History of Masturbation*. New York: Zone Books, 2003.

Marcus, Steven. *The Other Victorians: A Study of Sexuality and Pornography in Mid-Nineteenth-Century England*. New York: Basic Books, 1964.

Miller, William Ian. *The Anatomy of Disgust*. Cambridge, MA: Harvard University Press, 1997.

Paasonen, Susanna. *Carnal Resonance: Affect and Online Pornography*. Cambridge, MA: MIT Press, 2011.

Sedgwick, Eve Kosofsky. *Tendencies*. Durham: Duke University Press, 1993.

Senft, Theresa. *CamGirls: Celebrity & Community in the Age of Social Networks*. New York: Peter Lang, 2008.

Williams, Linda. "Film Bodies: Gender, Genre, and Excess." *Film Quarterly* 44, no. 4 (1991): 2–13.

PART X

SOUNDS AND IMAGES
OF THE NEW DIGITAL
DOCUMENTARY

CHAPTER 33

....

THE WORLD IN THE PALM OF YOUR HAND

Agnes Varda, Trinh T. Minh-ha, and the Digital Documentary

....

JOHN BELTON

JOHN Grierson coined the word "documentary" in a 1926 review of Robert Flaherty's *Moana,* which he described as "a poetic record of Polynesian tribal life." Grierson praises the film's combination of ethnographic documentation and "its poetic feeling for natural elements," thereby defining the documentary as a "creative treatment of actuality," as an aesthetically powerful representation of a topic of social concern.[1] Grierson's review also mentions Flaherty's use of a new panchromatic film stock (rather than the orthochromatic stock that had dominated film production for the past thirty years). Panchromatic film had a greater sensitivity than orthochromatic film (ortho) and was capable of recording the entire visible spectrum from blue to red whereas ortho was limited to the blue and green regions of the spectrum. This greater sensitivity enabled Flaherty to render the skin tones of his Polynesian subjects with greater subtlety and accuracy than previously possible. (Grierson might also have mentioned, but did not, Flaherty's use of six-inch telephoto lenses, which enabled him to film the Samoan natives in close-up from great distances "to obviate self-consciousness" on the part of his subjects, thus obtaining more "natural" performances.[2] Although Grierson's reference to a specific film stock constitutes, at most, a minor aside, the presence of this technical detail at the christening of the term "documentary" has more than anecdotal significance.

The history of the documentary *shadows* the history of motion picture technology in that technological development has consistently empowered documentary filmmakers in their quest for "greater realism."[3] This so-called "greater realism" is necessarily placed in quotation marks. It is illusory, idealist, and the stuff of fantasy or "myth," as Andre Bazin suggests in his essay, "The Myth of Total Cinema."[4] If Bazin's "myth" is a "concept

[that] existed...fully armed in [men's] minds," then its ideological status and the ideological nature of the quest for "greater realism" is implicit in Bazin's discussion of it.[5] Jean-Louis Comolli makes what is implicit in Bazin explicit. Comolli locates the quest for "greater realism" at the core of the ideological project that guided the invention of the cinema and the subsequent development of its chief technological advances in the areas of sound, color, and widescreen. He insisted that "it is to the mutual reinforcement of an ideological demand ("to see life as it is") and the economic demand to make it a source of profit that the cinema owes its being."[6]

The relation of technological development to the development of the cinema as a whole or to the development of the documentary in particular is both complex and highly mediated. It is not my intention to subscribe to a form of vulgar technological determinism in which technology drives cultural production, but I do want to suggest that technological development generates a field in which cultural production exercises various options in the give-and-take process of negotiating a variety of different—and often opposing—economic and ideological demands.

Comolli, of course, was writing about the cinema in general, not the documentary in particular, when he defined the basic demands that drove the cinema's development. Commercial cinema is clearly a mode of production designed to minimize costs and maximize profits. Its economic and ideological interests work in tandem, for the most part. The documentary differs from commercial cinema in that it pursues supposedly more lofty objectives than mere entertainment. The documentary seeks to inform and to educate—to expose social, political, and economic problems, to analyze them, and, on occasion, to propose solutions to them. Within the larger system of the cinema itself, the documentary's appeal to greater realism—an appeal that is distinguished in many ways from that of commercial cinema—disavows commercial cinema's economic demands for profit-making. Yet this disavowal conceals the existence of an economic reality that has become increasingly apparent since the release of Michael Moore's *Roger and Me* in 1989, but which has been in place since Robert Flaherty's *Nanook of the North* (1922) or even earlier. If the evolution of the documentary from *Nanook of the North* to *Fahrenheit 9/11* (2004), *An Inconvient Truth* (2006) and *Sicko* (2007) can be seen as a pursuit of "greater realism"—and perhaps greater profits—it can also be understood in terms of the development of a technological base that permits the illusion of "greater realism." In what follows, I review some aspects of the relationship between technological innovation and documentary practices.

In their review of the "modes of the documentary," John Izod and Richard Kilborn, drawing on Bill Nichols' earlier work, approach the notion of a documentary mode of address from a techno-historicist perspective, characterizing different modes in terms of the nature of the technology available at different points in the genre's development. Their most convincing claims for the relationship between technology and documentary practices can be seen in their discussions of the genre's expository and observational modes. Its other two modes—interactive and reflexive—have a more mediated than direct relationship to technological development. Yet all four modes can be seen as attempts to achieve greater realism—with each mode of address appropriating technological developments—and the signifying practices that accompany them—to secure the investment of greater credibility in their "speech" than their immediate predecessor was capable of.

The "expository mode addresses its audience directly, usually through a narrator who interprets what we see, in effect telling us what we should think of the visual evidence before our eyes."[7] Examples of this mode range from silent films, such as *Nanook of the North,* which relies on inter-titles to *Night Mail* (1936), *The Battle of San Pietro* (1945), and *Victory at Sea* (1952–53) with their "Voice of God" commentary. Although the expository mode spans the entire history of the documentary, its origins lie in the silent and early sound era when filmmakers shot MOS—without sound—because sound equipment didn't yet exist or was too cumbersome and heavy to take along on the shoot. Voice-over narration and musical scoring would later be devised to accompany the exhibition of the film—either live in the silent era or in the form of a recorded soundtrack in the sound era. Lightweight, semi-portable, silent-era cameras, such as the Akeley, which weighed only 22 pounds, enabled filmmakers like Flaherty to set up shots more quickly than would be possible with a studio camera, making it possible for him to capture moments that would be lost with more bulky equipment.[8]

Izod and Kilborn link "the observational mode" directly to the development of lightweight camera and sound recording equipment that gave rise to *cinema verite* in France and direct cinema in the United States in the early 1960s. Lightweight 16mm cameras had been available since the 1920s and were used extensively by American Signal Corps cameramen on the battlefields of World War II. By 1960, blimped, virtually noiseless 16mm handheld cameras had been developed by Éclair, Auricon, and Arriflex. Zoom lenses permitted cameramen to film continuously without changing lenses. At the same time, the development of faster film stocks enabled filmmakers to shoot on location without intrusive lighting equipment. And, in 1958, Stefan Kudelski introduced the Nagra tape recorder, which weighed only 13 pounds, 13 ounces, and which permitted filming in sync sound. As a result, small crews of two—a camera-person and a sound recorder—could "go into any situation and return with material for a film, technically acceptable and with synchronous sound recorded directly at the moment of shooting."[9] Observing a strict, "noninterventionist" stance on the part of the filmmaker, these films eschew all forms of commentary, whether voice-over narration or musical scoring. The seeming objectivity of the observational mode emerged as a direct response to and implicit rejection of the subjectivity of the expository mode. And it staked its claims to greater objectivity on the basis of its less intrusive technological apparatus. Exemplified in the films of Jean Rouch, such as *Chronique d'un ete* (1961); Richard Leacock and D. A. Pennebaker, *Primary* (1960); Pennebaker's *Don't Look Back* (1967); and Frederick Wiseman, *High School* (1968), films in the observational mode attempted to repress the subjective aspects of the expository mode and to permit characters and events to speak for themselves via "exhaustive observation" of them.[10] This repression, however, did not guarantee objectivity. Although invisible, filmmakers still stood behind the camera, their presence necessarily influencing the course of events that unfolds before them. The editing of filmed footage also tended to reveal the hand of the filmmaker at work, as seen in the cuts in *High School* from scenes in which teachers and hall monitors impose their institutional will on students to students behaving as mechanical automatons in gym class, edits that expose the arbitrariness of adult authority. Under the mask of "greater realism" lurked the spirit of the expository mode, albeit in the more subtle area of stylistic expression. Nonetheless, the subjectivity that this new mode had seemingly repudiated crept back into the apparently objective stance observational documentaries had taken toward their subjects. By now, it should be clear that "greater realism" is always the *illusion* or *impression* of greater realism and a relative rather than absolute category. If the films of Lumiere seem to possess "greater realism" than those of Melies, that does not necessarily mean that they are lacking in subjectivity. Indeed, every Lumiere film is in some way "about" the position of the camera, whether still or moving and thus "about" the camera's look.

In reaction to the impossibility of invisibility, documentary filmmakers began to step forward from behind the camera and interact with the subjects of the documentary, an interaction that often takes the form of an on-camera interview, exemplified in films such as Emile De Antonio's *In the Year of the Pig* (1969) and Claude Lanzmann's *Shoah* (1985). In a number of documentary films, the so-called "interactive mode" sought and secured credibility—and therefore the illusion of greater objectivity—by acknowledging the mediating presence of the camera, microphone, and film crew and abandoning the pretense of nonintrusive invisibility. The interactive mode is not grounded in the introduction of new film technology but rather in a new perception of the role that technology plays in the authentication of documentary evidence. Acknowledgment of the act of documentation—the appearance of the camera and the microphone—establishes an apparent transparency in the relationship between filmmaker and subject, who acknowledge one another's presence, and between filmmaker and film viewer, for whom there is a similar but necessarily different form of recognition in which the filmmaker's presence in one space—the diegetic space of the film—is acknowledged by the viewer from another space—that of the theater. This "apparent transparency," however, clearly conceals yet more subtle forms of authorial speech. The interview format reveals the presence of the interviewer but not the latter's ultimate control of the interview. The off-screen Voice of God has been put on screen, secularized, and restricted to laconic questions and observations, but the technological apparatus remains off-screen and thus invisible.

If the interactive mode is characterized chiefly by the trope of the interview, the reflexive mode takes the presence of the filmmaker and the filmmaking apparatus one step further, not merely acknowledging their presence but foregrounding and problematizing it, along with calling into question the process of documentation itself. As Nichols explains, "whereas the great preponderance of documentary production concerns itself with talking about the historical world, the reflexive mode addresses the question of *how* we talk about the historical world."[11] The reflexive mode can been found in films as diverse as Dziga Vertov's *Man with a Movie Camera* (1929) and in Errol Morris's *The Thin Blue Line* (1987). In the former, the film's cameraman and editor appear as they actively film and edit actuality footage, and the subject of the film—an investigation of everyday life in Soviet Russia—includes among its various portraits of production activities a documentation of the making of the film itself. The "greater realism" sought by Vertov lies beneath the surface appearance of everyday reality, emerging only after rigorous Marxist deconstruction of those appearances through editing. Morris' film acknowledges its own status as a construction through the inclusion of studio-staged reenactments of events mentioned in the filmmaker's interviews with crucial witnesses to what actually happened. Conflicting testimony is embodied in different stagings of key events, suggesting that the truth is ultimately inaccessible and that, as Plato and Umberto Eco have insisted, all representations are lies. This postmodern crisis in the field of representation, grounded in a contemporary loss of faith in the objectivity of the image, forces us to the conclusion that the truth can never be known. The only way to represent its "reality," then, is through demonstrably fictional stagings of conflicting representations of it.

Morris' fictional restagings differ in nature and intent from the reenactments found in early newsreels, such as J. Stuart Blackton's *Battle of Manila Bay* (1898); documentaries, such as Flaherty's *Man of Aran* (1934); mockumentaries, such as Jim McBride's *David Holzman's Diary* (1968), Rob Reiner's *This Is Spinal Tap* (1984), or Christopher Guest's *Waiting for Guffman* (1997); or reenactments staged for The History Channel. Morris has no intention of passing his footage off as real.

Morris's interviews, although not staged, have a similar effect on the viewer. Using what he calls the "Interrotron device," Morris encourages his subjects to look directly into the lens of the camera by placing his own, live, video image on a Teleprompter-like screen right next to the lens, introducing postmodern self-reflexivity into the reality of the situation that is being recorded.[12]

Morris achieves "greater realism" through "greater artifice." He gives us representations that, although they refer to referents, actually have no referent. The referent—what actually happened—remains off-screen, inaccessible, possibly unknowable. In this way, *The Thin Blue Line* stages the postmodern dilemma of which digital imaging is both a symptom and a cause. The contemporary loss of faith in the image finds its technological origins in the advent of digital imaging and the rupture it represents in the indexical relationship between the image and its referent. *The Thin Blue Line*, of course, was not filmed digitally, but it is the product of a new "psychology of the image" that takes into account what Philip Rosen refers to as the "practically infinite manipulability" of digital images.[13] This manipulability has undermined the traditional psychology of the image discussed by Andre Bazin in "The Ontology of the Photographic Image." Existential phenomenology gives way to a postmodern subversion of traditional certainties. William J. Mitchell concludes his book, *The Reconfigured Eye: Visual Truth in the Post-Photographic Era*, by presenting digital imaging as an exemplary form of postmodern representation. Much as postmodern literary theory has "shaken our faith in the ultimate grounding of written texts on external reference," "the emergence of digital imaging has irrevocably subverted the...certainties of traditional photography."[14] Digital imaging's subversive characteristics force us to revisit analog photography and to see it from a postmodern perspective—as a medium fully capable of convincing fakery.

Digital imaging is both a symptom and a product of postmodern epistemology. It exemplifies a loss of faith in the image and, at the same time, produces that loss of faith by undermining our perception of traditional technologies, such as photography, in terms of their relationship with the so-called "real."

This new postmodern "psychology of the image" tells us that the objectivity and truth experienced with previous imaging technologies was essentially a reality effect, a construction of sorts generated by a viewer in response to the apparent perceptual richness of the photographic image. From this vantage point, neither photochemical nor digital images can be trusted, but, at the same time, there remains a powerful desire on the part of the viewer for credible imaging. Disavowal in the digital age combines knowledge of the image's "practically infinite manipulability" with a desire for belief in its authenticity. The implication is that the credibility that we have invested in the image is the product of an ideological need—our desire to establish an ontological relationship between photograph and referent. In effect, digital imaging becomes a wedge that enables us to see that reality is an ideological construct. The notion of "credibility" is less a matter of what we know about how technology works than of what we know about how ideology works.

Digital technology is therefore associated with the "crisis in representation" that characterizes postmodern cultural production. To some extent, documentary filmmakers have found a solution to this crisis in the appropriation of digital technology and their self-reflexive use of it, in making films that foreground representational practices and make those practices the implicit subject of their films. Here, I look at two self-reflexive digital documentaries that attempt to navigate this postmodern crisis in representation and, in so doing, extend the parameters of the self-reflexive mode. Both of them return us to Comolli, for whom "greater realism" was the chief ideological demand that the cinema sought to answer. In these works, the process of imaging becomes the so-called "reality" that the film seeks to observe. In my first example, Agnes Varda's *Les glaneurs et la glaneuse* (2000), this "reality" is presented as a fiction—more properly, as a metaphor—that seeks to reconnect itself more or less directly to an actual referent. In my second example, Trinh T. Minh-ha's *The Fourth Dimension* (2001), this "reality" is presented in the form of a series of images of Japan—fictions again—that are broken down into discrete elements, undergo digital manipulation, and are reassembled, mirroring the very processes of digital technology itself. These images attempt to evoke an absent referent—Japan—indirectly, through a discontinuous series of absences, silences, gaps, and fissures.

Varda's film begins with the citation of textual representations—images of a dictionary entry for the noun "glaneur" and a reproduction of Jean-Francois Millet's painting "Les Glaneuses" (1867), which hangs in the Musee d'Orsay in Paris. It ends with the retrieval—via an implicit act of gleaning—and display of another painting, "Gleaners Fleeing Before the Storm" by Hedoin. The history of the representation of gleaners—on canvas, in nineteenth-century photographs, and in turn-of-the-century motion pictures—becomes one of several of the film's motival threads. At the same time, the film explores less conventional forms of representation that are themselves the products of gleaning and implicitly about gleaning, although they do not depict gleaners themselves.

These range from cast-off refrigerators used as display cases for found objects and tower-like constructions erected by a brick mason out of doll parts and other objects to the painterly assemblages of artist Louis Pons. Varda, who once famously signed her films as "cine-writer" and referred to direction as "cinecriture," here refers to herself as a "gleaner." She is "la glaneuse" of the film's title, a point that is lost on English-speaking audiences for whom the film is titled "The Gleaners and I." In other words, the film itself is an act of gleaning, resembling the work of Pons and others.

Varda makes the analogy quite explicit in her comments about the film. She explains:

> This film is a documentary woven from various strands; from emotions I felt when confronted with precariousness; from the possibilities offered by the new small digital cameras; and from the desire to film what I can see of myself—my aging hands and my grey hair. I also wanted to express my love for painting. I had to piece it together and make sense out of it all in the film, without betraying the social issue I had set out to address—waste and trash....I wanted to glean images as one jots down travel notes....My intention became clearer to myself throughout the shooting and editing stages. Little by little, I found the right balance between self-referential moments (the gleaner who films one of her hands with the other) and moments focused on those whose reality and behavior I found so striking.[15]

Varda shot much of the film herself, using a Mini DV Sony DCR TRV 900E digital camcorder that fit in the palm of her hand. Additional footage was shot by other camera crews working under Varda's instructions. Unlike earlier film and video cameras, the Mini DV is extremely lightweight and portable. As Jonathan Rosenbaum points out, traditional filmmaking equipment had the effect of erecting a wall between filmmakers and their subjects, with the filmmakers remaining on their side of the wall "separated by an entire industry, an ideology, and a great deal of money and equipment."[16] In comparison with traditional filmmaking equipment, the Mini DV marks a significant step forward in the removal of that wall, at least at the moment of filming itself. Varda's use of this digital camera and inclusion of herself as would-be gleaner in the film represent an attempt to put herself on equal footing with her subjects, as both gleaner and object gleaned (Figure 33.1).

As in other reflexive documentaries, Varda steps from behind the camera and inserts herself, as yet another "gleaner," into her portrait of gleaners. From an image of Jules Breton's portrait of a gleaner, Varda cuts to an image of herself striking the pose of Breton's gleaner. She drops her sheaf of wheat and picks up her digital camera and then provides us with a demonstration of what this new technology can do. The wave of her hand into the lens, seemingly shaking it, is answered through a kind of echo in which reverse-shot images of her seem to shake again and again. Through this elaborate cycle of images, Varda establishes the terms of her analogy between gleaning and filmmaking.

Varda represents her own travels in the language of gleaning. In one scene, she returns home from a trip to Japan. Opening her bag, she unpacks a stream of souvenirs—items she had "picked up" in her travels. Again she resembles the gleaners in her film. One of her souvenirs—postcards of Rembrandt paintings—prompts another moment of

FIGURE 33.1 Agnes Varda poses with her mini DV Sony digital camcorder (frame enlargement).

self-reflexive meditation as her gaze—and that of camera—shifts from the postcards to her own hand and back to the final postcard at the bottom of the pile, Rembrandt's self-portrait.

Later, she extends the analogy between gleaning and filmmaking in another scene that foregrounds her own hand. Just as her gleaners pick up leftover crops or abandoned objects with their hands, so Varda picks up images with a DV camera that fits in the palm of her hand. In one sequence, she represents this notion of picking by "capturing" images with her hand, which encircles, then closes on trucks driving down the highway. Her gestures here not only identify her as a gleaner, but equate the images she is quite literally forming with her own hands with the constructions of Louis Pons that immediately precede this scene. The analogy between digital technology and the hand—which in English is also a digital phenomenon, boasting five digits—presents digital filmmaking as an extension of traditional hand-crafted objects, as well as extending Astruc's notion of the *camera-stylo*—the camera as pen, presumably held in the hand—into the new era of digital filmmaking where cinecriture is still possible.

With traditional, analog filmmaking, the camera often functions as an extension of the eye. In digital filmmaking, given the "practically infinite *man*ipulability" of the image, the image is now as much something that is *hand*led as seen. Varda's notion of the camera as an extension of her hand—her notion of filmmaking as "picking"—provides a new paradigm for figuring cinematic creativity in the digital age.

Hands constitute a motif that runs throughout the film. As Varda explains, "I have two hands. One has a camera—the other one is acting, in a way. I love the idea that with these handheld cameras—these new digital things—very light but, on the other hand, very 'Macrophoto.' You know what macro is? You can approach things very near. I can, with one hand, film the other one. I like the idea that one hand would be always gleaning, the other one always filming. I like very much the idea of the hands. The hands are the tool of the gleaners, you know. Hands are the tool of the painter, the artist."[17]

Varda's meditation on representation takes place in the trenches of an old-fashioned modernism as she looks out on the battlefield of postmodernism. Across no man's land she views the "crisis" in representation and insists on the ability of metaphor and analogy to mediate between images and referents. For her, representations still have referents. Her film may play on the surface of a series of representations of gleaning and cast gleaning as a metaphor for artistic creativity. But this play and this metaphor is anchored in a solid social base—an entire subculture of the French populace whose physical survival depends on their gleaning activities. Varda weaves this reality into the fabric of her film. Varda is not only fascinated by her gleaners, but she respects them. Her appropriation of gleaning as a metaphor emerges as an attempt on her part to identify with them, to frame her own experience of the world as an artist in the language of theirs. Like them, she struggles to survive—presenting the terrain of her own body as her battleground. Both she and they emerge as cast-offs of contemporary consumer culture whose struggles to survive expose the inefficiency and waste of that culture. Varda reconnects representation to its referents. Hand-held digital technology becomes a tool that enables her to refer to this "greater reality."

Trinh T. Minh-ha has described her first digital film, *The Fourth Dimension* (2001), as a journey through "the Image of Japan as mediated by the experience of 'dilating and sculpting time' with a digital machine vision" capable of producing images that possessed "inherent mutability."[18] More precisely, the film explores images of Japan from the point of view of an outsider journeying through it. Japan is a speeding bullet train and drums, festivals and parades, and, most of all, a dense fabric of traditional rites and rituals. At the same time, as a reflexive work, *The Fourth Dimension* is concerned with "the process of documenting its own unfolding: it documents its own time, its creation in megahertz, the different paths and layers of time-light that are involved in the production of images and meanings."[19] For Trinh, the mutability of the images of Japan is best represented through the "inherent mutability" of digital imaging. The opening image of the film is a forward moving shot, taken from inside a car, of a highway shrouded in fog, punctuated by street lamps and an occasional neon sign. The image then diminishes, leaving black on all sides. This frame within a frame rises to the top border of the frame, descends halfway to the bottom, then moves left, then right, touching each edge of the larger frame and then bouncing off of it, like a figure in a Pac-Man computer game. At one point, the image elongates with anamorphic distortion in the horizontal and vertical direction, as if it were being Photoshopped. The image is truly infinitely manipulable. As Trinh suggests, "Images of the real, produced at the speed of light are made to play with their own reality as images. There, where new technology and ancient Asian wisdom can meet in all 'artificiality' is where what is viewed as the objective reality underneath the uncertain world of appearance proves to be no more and no less than a reality effect—or better, a being time."[20]

Trinh refers to all of her works as "events"—or, more properly, "boundary events" (because they inhabit the spaces between traditional boundaries; her films occupy the spaces between the categories of documentary, fiction, and experimental film, for example). The title of her latest book—*The Digital Film Event* (2005)—refers to both a new event-space—that of the digital film—and to the book itself, which is presented as a "textual installation" in which the reader moves through a variety of verbal and visual texts.

For Trinh, digital film is the perfect instance of a boundary event—it is neither film nor video, but exists in a space between film and video. By this, Trinh does not simply mean that digital film is digital whereas film and video are analog, but that digital film is inherently more mutable than the other two. In this respect, digital technology expands the traditional limits of film and video. Trinh is also fascinated by the way digital technology "displaces the fixed boundaries between film and animation or computer games."[21] Trinh, like Lev Manovich, understands the inherent mutability of digital imaging as a form of animation and sees digital technology as an imaging system with greater "plasticity." That is, the captured image (whether on film or video or digital video) becomes, in the digital realm, the point of departure for further manipulation. But, for Trinh, this "sculpting" of the image is not an end in itself—not a special effect designed to defamiliarize observable phenomena or to stimulate retinal pleasure. Trinh dismisses what she refers to as "the cyborg's hand"—the digital effects (the disfiguring, animating, morphing, and trans-shaping of the image) that some experimental filmmakers have engaged in, likening those experiments to the special effects of Hollywood blockbusters. "Digital effects that decompose and disintegrate the image abound in new media works and become an end in themselves," she says.[22] Instead, digital manipulability needs to be put to the service of revealing the mutability that, according to Taoist philosophy, informs the unseen dimension of reality itself—"the mutability of relations between the ordinary, the extraordinary and the infraordinary."[23]

The sorts of digital manipulation Trinh employs are about as far from special effects as one could imagine. *The Fourth Dimension* uses mobile internal frames, for example, to set an oblong image in play with the four borders of the frame from which it ricochets like a bullet (or bullet train, one of the film's dominant image-metaphors for Japan). In one image of a man sitting on a wharf reading a book, a digital window accentuates a box of light reflecting on the surface of the water. Drawing on the compositing features of digital technology, Trinh also adds layers of color to the image. These horizontal and vertical rectangles of color resemble curtains that open and close from side to side or top to bottom. In one scene, a dragon float is painted over with bands of different colors as the float turns in the frame. Like the ricocheting image, the color layers also function as internal frames. In both instances, digital manipulation emphasizes the images as *images*. Trinh is not showing us the reality of Japan but images of Japan. The images tell us something about Japan—the ordering of its interior spaces within a finite exterior border—but it does so on the level of discursive commentary by the film itself rather than by documentary observation. Just as important, for Trinh, is the fact that these digital techniques speak to her relation, as filmmaker, to these images. They refer back to her role as digital compositor, sitting at a computer terminal, exploring Japan through images she has taken of it.

The Fourth Dimension elaborates a metaphor of vision and perception in the digital age. In the digital era's primal scene, the individual sits immobile at the computer keyboard and travels at the speed of light through cyberspace. For Trinh, this state of consciousness is unique to the machine vision of digital technology. In digital film's primal scene, the filmmaker sits at the window of her nonlinear, digital editing console, " 'dilating and sculpting time' with a digital machine vision."[24]

In *The Fourth Dimension*, on the bullet train, passengers sit immobile, yet move at hyperspeed "through Japan's likeness."[25] Through the train window—what Trinh refers to as "the window-screen,"[26] they see the "vast rhythms of life."[27] What the viewer sees are "not motion pictures, but images on the move."[28] It is the landscape that appears to move, not the viewer. At the same time, the movement of the train is regulated, Trinh's voice-over narration tells us, "by a computer brain in Tokyo."[29] Meanwhile, Trinh sits immobile before her window—the computer screen—on which is displayed the film's myriad moving images. The image of the bullet train, Trinh tells us, summons up the speed of modernity; her film is a digital machine that "speeds through Japan's likeness." In other words, the film, in both its content and its form, explores the features of digital consciousness—speed, mobility, and virtuality.

The electronic age brings with it a crisis in terms of the physical dimensions of both time and space, rendering them virtual. In digital film, Trinh notes, time is liquid: "digital technology offers the possibility of working intensely with time and with the indefinite coexisting layers of past, present, and future."[30] Digital technology allows filmmakers "to break away from the dominance of linear time…allowing us effortless fluidity in time."[31] All times exist at once.

Space is emptied out of its physical substance and "reduced almost to zero."[32] Quoting Paul Virilio's *The Lost Dimension*, Trinh suggests that "the crisis of the physical dimension in the age of telecommunications is apparently a crisis of substantive, continuous, homogenous space. What one has instead is a discontinuous, heterogeneous space in which the accidental becomes essential."[33] Filmmakers regularly *construct* time and space—primarily through editing techniques that establish temporal and spatial relations between shots. Unlike analog representation, which is continuous, digital technology is inherently discontinuous. Trinh's film explores that discontinuity. Her editing refuses to establish temporal and spatial relations in terms of any linear, temporal and spatial continuity. Instead, it permits her to question normative senses of time and space and to promote new ways of seeing made possible by new technologies of seeing.

For Trinh, digital technology transforms space into time—the fourth dimension of her film's title. The charge-coupled devices/sensors in digital cameras scan pro-filmic spaces, translating them into numerical data—or "datascapes"—that are recorded successively on disc or magnetic tape. What was once space is now temporal sequence. Space becomes time.

The Fourth Dimension is about time. It's about the time created by digital technology that, in its effortless fluidity, permits "us to break away from the dominance of linear time," technology that processes data "at the speed of light."[34] It's about the time of modernity—what Trinh calls "train time"—and the time of tradition—"Noh time."[35] Japan is a pastiche of past and present times. In this particular sequence, Trinh literalizes the embeddedness of one time within another. A railway trestle opens a window onto a Noh play. Japan is, at once, one of the most modern and most ancient of cultures.

The Fourth Dimension is about the time of ritual in which past and present merge. The past, in the form of ancient rituals, is reenacted in the present. Participants in these rituals exist within these two temporalities, and that existence defines their lived experience. As Trinh suggests, the film is about "musical, historical, [and] sociopolitical time, as well as montage time, optical time; the time of festivities, of traveling, of witnessing, and of viewing; the time, so to speak, of both electronic and spiritual light."[36] The electronic and the spiritual are not opposed but interdependent. Digital technology enables Trinh to "create different time-spaces that expose or turn to advantage the fissures, gaps and lapses of the system."[37] Much as she refuses to create the spatial continuity of classical Hollywood cinema in her editing, so she also refuses to create temporal continuity. Each shot exists in a discrete time-space, reaffirming a truth about the fragmented nature of existence in postmodernity. As Trinh writes, "The challenge is to find a way to let the film perform the holes, the gaps, and the specific absences by which it takes shape."[38] When this is accomplished, what is revealed is that "the objective reality underneath the uncertain world of appearances" is "no more or no less than a reality effect."[39] All is illusion, and reality is the greatest illusion of all.

Trinh insists that the reflexive play of her films "is not there for the mere sake of reflexivity…but as a means to deconstruct the context in which we operate."[40] What is deconstructed is the Image of Japan—its combination of the modern and the ancient, speed and stillness, mobility and stasis, the machine and the human, technology and spirituality, and freedom and conformity. Digital technology quite literally enables Trinh to deconstruct the image, to place images within other images, deracinating them from their referents. The reality of the digital image is its status as a composite of discrete picture elements. Trinh breaks her images of Japan down into pixels—pieces of a larger whole—and combines them into new, hybrid images that refer to this new digital reality. It is a "greater reality" in that it embodies within it her own activities as a filmmaker and the reality of the digital medium she uses to capture it.

Varda still believes in cinecriture, in a filmic writing through which she can express herself and which connects her back with the world she observes. Trinh, on the other hand, attempts to speak through absences and silences—and through a digital dismantling of the image. For Varda, digital cinema extends the language of cinema. For Trinh, for whom the language of cinema was always halting and disjunctive in the past, digital cinema marks a break of sorts from the past, giving her a new landscape to explore in her pursuit of the Way and in her quest to represent the reality of nonbeing and emptiness.

Digital cinema is, after all, a potentially Taoist language—ones and zeroes, states of being and nonbeing, presence and absence, on and off.

Both Varda and Trinh guarantee the authenticity of their speech by means of laying bare the aspects of the technological apparatus through which they speak. The "greater realism" of the apparatus is exposed as a fiction but a fiction that is recuperated through the exposure of the apparent transparency of its operations. Varda's analogies between artists and workers and between handheld DV cameras and hands present the apparatus as an artisanal tool—as an extension of the hand—rather than as an ideological weapon—as an Althusserian agent of the State. Distrustful of representations and of the technological apparatus that produces them, Trinh makes no pretense to objectivity. She acknowledges that every representation is a fabrication and forces the viewer to read the image—that which is there on screen—in terms of what is not there—the absences that the presences evoke, the nonbeing that makes being possible.

Acknowledgments

I wish to thank Jonathan Kahana and Adam Lowenstein for their perceptive comments on an earlier draft of this manuscript and their helpful suggestions for revisions.

Notes

1. John Grierson, "Flaherty's Poetic *Moana*" in *The Documentary Tradition*, ed. Lewis Jacobs (New York: Norton, 1971), 25.
2. Robert Flaherty, "Filming Real People," in *The Documentary Tradition*, ed. Lewis Jacobs (New York: Norton, 1971), 97.
3. It is important to distinguish here between "greater realism" and "truth." As Errol Morris has shown in *The Thin Blue Line*, sometimes the truth can only be achieved through artificially arranged scenes; that is, through greater artifice rather than greater realism. Not all documentary filmmakers are in pursuit of greater realism.
4. Andre Bazin, *What Is Cinema?* trans. Hugh Gray, vol. 1 (Berkeley: University of California Press, 1967), 21.
5. Bazin, *What Is Cinema?*, 17.
6. Jean-Louis Comolli in Bill Nichols, *Movies and Methods*, vol. 2 (Berkeley: University of California Press, 1985), 53, 55.
7. John Izod and Richard Kilborn, "The Documentary," in *The Oxford Guide to Film Studies*, ed. John Hill and Pamela Church Gibson (New York: Oxford University Press, 1998), 429.
8. Barry Salt, *Film Style & Technology: History & Analysis* (London: Starword, 1983), 199; Flaherty, Robert. "Filming Real People." In *The Documentary Tradition*, ed. Lewis Jacobs, 98–99. New York: Norton, 1971.
9. M. Ali Issari and Doris A. Paul, *What Is Cinema Verite?* (Metuchen: Scarecrow Press, 1979), 152.

10. Bill Nichols, *Representing Reality* (Bloomington: Indiana University Press, 1991), 40.

11. Ibid., 56–57.

12. "The Fog of War: 13 Questions and Answers on the Filmmaking of Errol Morris," Landmark Theatres, 2004, http://www.landmarktheatres.com/mn/fogofwar.html.

13. Philip Rosen, *Change Mummified: Cinema, Historicity, Theory* (Minneapolis: University of Minnesota Press, 2001), 318–319.

14. William J. Mitchell, *The Reconfigured Eye: Visual Truth in the Post-Photographic Era* (Cambridge, MA: MIT Press, 1992), 225.

15. "*The Gleaners and I*, a film by Agnes Varda" (press book), Zeitgeist Films, http://www.zeitgeistfilms.com/films/gleanersandi/presskit.pdf, 3.

16. Jonathan Rosenbaum, "Precious Leftovers," *Chicago Reader*, January 5, 2001, www.chicagoreader.com/movies/archives/2001/0105/010511.html.

17. Agnes Varda interviewed by Andrea Meyer, "Interview: Gleaning" the Passion of Agnes Varda: Agnes Varda," *IndieWire*, March 8, 2001, http://www.indiewire.com/article/interview_gleaning_the_passion_of_agnes_varda_agnes_varda.

18. Trinh T. Minh-ha, *The Digital Film Event* (New York: Routledge, 2005), 3.

19. Ibid., 28.

20. Ibid., 4.

21. Ibid., 6.

22. Ibid., 37.

23. Ibid., 6.

24. Ibid., 3.

25. Ibid., 10,

26. Ibid., 87.

27. Ibid., 7.

28. Ibid., 69.

29. Ibid., 90.

30. Ibid., 10.

31. Ibid., 63.

32. Ibid., 200.

33. Ibid., 10.

34. Ibid., 4, 66.

35. Ibid., 10.

36. Ibid., 74.

37. Ibid., 130.

38. Ibid., 3.

39. Ibid., 4.

40. Ibid., 37.

SELECT BIBLIOGRAPHY

Bazin, Andre. *What Is Cinema?* Vol. 1. Translated by Hugh Gray. Berkeley: University of California Press, 1967.

Comolli, Jean-Louis. Technique and Ideology: Camera, Perspective, Depth of Field. In Movies and Methods, Vol. 2, edited by Bill Nichols, pp.40-57. Berkeley: University of California Press, 1985.

Flaherty, Robert. "Filming Real People." In *The Documentary Tradition*, edited by Lewis Jacobs, 97. New York: Norton, 1971.

Grierson, John. "Flaherty's Poetic *Moana*." In *The Documentary Tradition*, edited by Lewis Jacobs, 25. New York: Norton, 1971.

Issari, M. Ali, and Doris A. Paul. *What Is Cinema Verite?* Metuchen, NJ: Scarecrow Press, 1979.

Izod, John, and Richard Kilborn. "The Documentary." In *The Oxford Guide to Film Studies*, edited by John Hill and Pamela Church Gibson, 429. New York: Oxford University Press, 1998.

"The Fog of War: 13 Questions and Answers on the Filmmaking of Errol Morris," Landmark Theatres, 2004. http://www.landmarktheatres.com/mn/fogofwar.html.

Andrea Meyer. "Gleaning' the Passion of Agnes Varda: Agnes Varda," 2001. http://www.indiewire.com/article/interview_gleaning_the_passion_of_agnes_varda_agnes_varda

Minh-ha, Trinh T. *The Digital Film Event*. New York: Routledge, 2005.

Mitchell, William J. *The Reconfigured Eye: Visual Truth in the Post-Photographic Era*. Cambridge, MA: MIT Press, 1992.

Nichols, Bill. *Representing Reality*. Bloomington: Indiana University Press, 1991.

Rosen, Philip. *Change Mummified: Cinema, Historicity, Theory*. Minneapolis: University of Minnesota Press, 2001.

Rosenbaum, Jonathan. "Precious Leftovers." *Chicago Reader* January 5, 2001. www.chicagoreader.com/movies/archives/2001/0105/010511.html.

Salt, Barry. *Film Style & Technology: History & Analysis*. London: Starword, 1983.

The Gleaners and I (press book). Film. Directed by Agnes Varda. Zeitgeist Films. New York, NY, 2001. http://www.zeitgeistfilms.com/films/gleanersandi/presskit.pdf.

Varda, Agnes. Interviewed by Andrea Meyer. "Interview: Gleaning the Passion of Agnes Varda: Agnes Varda." *IndieWire* March 8, 2001.

CHAPTER 34

THE SONIC SUMMONS

Meditations on Nature and Anempathetic Sound in Digital Documentaries

SELMIN KARA

OVER the past two decades, documentary has significantly benefited from the offerings of digital technologies. The emergence of new amateur and professional technological devices, interfaces, and platforms made documentary filmmaking more accessible and center stage among mainstream media practices by granting it further mobility, ubiquity, and connectivity. They also paved the way for enabling user participation, database and feedback integration, expanded means of archiving and transmission, and broader forms of intermedial, as well as remixable storytelling. However, despite all the interest in fulfilling digital documentary's new promises, filmmakers like Abbas Kiarostami and Aleksandr Sokurov, who are known for their frequent crossovers between fiction and nonfiction, seem to have channeled the new documentary's energy elsewhere. Coupling the aesthetic strategies of long-take cinema with abstract, eremetic meditations on nature, the works of these directors shift the focus from increased connectivity in documentary narratives to reimagined connections among humans, technology, and nature in the digital era.

A reenvisioned ecology of humans, technology, and nature emerges in especially two films, Kiarostami's *Five: Dedicated to Ozu* (2003) and Sokurov's *Confession: From the Commander's Diary* (1998), which are both reminiscent of and distinctive from the two filmmakers' earlier analog works with regard to their image and sound composition. While preserving the uninterrupted flow of imagery through long takes (seemingly similar to the way analog realist cinema applied the technique to enhance photographic realism), both films downplay the digital image track's significance in favor of highly structured soundtracks. Composed of dense, layered, and amplified sounds, the soundtracks of *Five* and *Confession* evoke a particular notion of nature as unwieldly, exorbitant, self-contained, and indifferent to the human condition. The cosmic indifference ingrained in their acoustic ecologies has a similar affective import with what

Michel Chion describes as "anempathetic sound" in *Audio-Vision*: sounds and diegetic music that exhibit a conspicuous indifference to the action or emotion depicted in a scene.[1] In the two films, although the image tracks offer little visual or narrative information to the audience, the vibrant and heavily layered soundtracks create the impression of a hypersentient nature, unsettling in its nonvisual sensory overload and unresponsive toward the viewers' attempts at extracting meaning out of it. The obscurity of visual cues and lack of sonic empathy in the films makes it difficult to interpret the films according to the aesthetic and human-centered vision of traditional long-take cinema. This article analyzes the two documentary works in order to examine the ways in which they stray away from analog realist cinema's often taken-for-granted humanism and gesture toward a new media ecology, along the same lines as the recent "nonhuman turn"[2] in the humanities, arts, and social sciences.

THE SUMMONS OF A VIBRANT NIGHT

The digital framing of nature through static camera shots, meditative long takes, and seemingly minimal editing finds its most formal display in Kiarostami's *Five: Dedicated to Ozu*. The experimental multipart installation piece (later turned into a film and released on DVD) is composed of five handheld single-take shots, extended over 74 minutes with chapter breaks.[3] In the fifth chapter, capturing the barely discernible impression of a pond along the Caspian Sea at night, the image track offers little visual or narrative information to the audience. Conversely, the vibrant and amplified soundtrack, presenting carefully edited and inflated nature sounds such as the rhythmic ebb and flow of water, howling wind, crickets, frogs, rain, and thunderstorm, conjure up the vision of a self-contained nature, inassimilable by human medi(t)ation. A similar aesthetic is also present, to a certain extent, in the third installment of Sokurov's five-part mini-series, *Confession: From the Commander's Diary* (1998), a 52-minute abstract contemplation about the harsh life of Russian sailors serving around the Arctic Circle. Although a nighttime sequence obscuring the image and privileging the soundtrack, such as the one in *Five*, is not central to *Confession*, the entire third episode of the documentary miniseries takes place in the shadow of a seemingly perpetual Arctic night. The monochromatic-looking daytime scenes are filmed at military outposts, which are exposed to only 10 minutes of sunlight per day. Here, too, the image track offers minimal sensory appeal, whereas the soundtrack is anempathetic and overpowering.

In the introductory chapter of his influential book, *The Imperative*, enigmatic philosopher Alphonso Lingis ruminates:

> When the night itself is there, there is no longer anything to see. The cries, murmurs, rumbles no longer locate separate beings signaling one another or colliding with one another on observable coordinates. Shouts or distant lights do not mark locations in the night but make the whole of the night vibrant.[4]

Lingis's passage on the power of sound in highlighting the sensory aspects of perception presents an evocative application of the two major theoretical moves he makes in his book. In the first of these moves, Lingis revisits Kant's theory of ethics and challenges its human-centered worldview. What he suggests, in place of accepting the call of reason as the only universal directive (also known as *the categorical imperative*) commanding human actions, is to acknowledge the way perception responds to other imperatives, or, in his words, "summons" that come from outside human agency: from the sirenlike forces of nature. His second important move lies in a rejection of all forms of holism in phenomenological description. Accordingly, he proposes to describe things, spaces, and elements in nature separately and distinctly, putting in relief their sensual qualities. It is within this framework that the night becomes a crucial setting. The night invites Lingis to surrender himself to the command of the universe by closing his eyes to the obvious (which he later describes as the logocentric call of the visual field) and shifting his attention to the distinct elements of nature, such as its cries, murmurs, and rumbles. Interestingly, it is the call of an equally commanding night that seems to draw the attention of the Iranian filmmaker, Abbas Kiarostami, to the pond along the shore of the Caspian Sea in the last segment of *Five*.

The back cover of *Five*'s DVD summarizes the segment in the following words: "A pond. Nighttime. Frogs. A chorus of sounds. Then, a storm, and finally, dawn." This fragmented description of the Caspian night is striking in that the segment is featured in a work that is itself an assemblage of the depictions of five elliptical scenes from nature, loosely connected through the theme of water. In the preceding four segments, the installation film shows, without cuts, seemingly everyday curiosities along the Caspian Sea like a piece of driftwood floating on the edge of the shore, people in the distance promenading and staring at the sea, a pack of dogs sitting on the beach, and, finally, a number of ducks noisily crossing the frame. In the absence of narration, a clear narrative structure, and visual changes that stimulate the viewer, *Five* is a formally challenging film to absorb, perhaps even more so than Kiarostami's other works, which can all be said to bear experimental qualities. If the slow pace and the obscure content of the film require a certain type of patient commitment from the viewer, the fifth and last segment, featuring the nightly vision of a pond in stormy weather, pulls them into an even more esoteric and impenetrable world. The field of vision is almost entirely cloaked in darkness, yet through the slowly and gradually increasing volume of the soundtrack and the rich composition of sounds, a vividly described locality emerges, holding its mysteries until the very end. It is only after the first flashes of lighting during what appears to be an impending storm that the viewer is allowed to distinguish what they are looking at: a pond. The image does not become fully exposed until the very end of the segment, when the night leads to dawn. Here, Kiarostami's foregrounding of the nightly nature sounds at the expense of the image suggests an affinity between his approach and that of Lingis. In their rich descriptions of the visible and audible forces of nature (in the name of offering a commentary on the representable world), Lingis and Kiarostami seem to be staging similar interventions to the humanist traditions of phenomenology and documentary. By using meditations on a vibrant night as entry and exit points to their works, they inadvertently undo phenomenology and documentary's holistic and logocentric depictions of reality.

At this point, it might be relevant to note that logocentric- or human consciousness–based approaches to reality have come under vigorous attack in recent years, by not only Alphonso Lingis but also by scholars like Nigel Thrift and Karen Barad in their recent writings. Thrift and Barad argue that a greater part of our contemporary history of thought has been defined by *representational thinking*, which is the type of thinking that draws an agential distinction between humans and nonhuman matter in explaining human-nature relations, mostly indebted to the anthropocentric traditions of Kantian rationalism and Humean models of empiricism. Proposing to move away from human consciousness–based approaches to politics, affect, and nature and toward revitalized seventeenth-century notions of agency and selfhood, Thrift underscores the necessity of articulating alternative models of subjectivity in the contemporary age of warfare, capitalism, and environmental threat. What he finds compelling in the seventeenth-century notions of agency is a formulation of subjectivity and human action based on *apathy*, or, more specifically, "a passivity that is demanding, that is called forth by another."[5] In other words, the direction that one's actions are to take is left to the demands of nature. Here, the idea of human action put into motion by the *calling forth by another* resonates with Lingis's invocation of the cosmic *summons*, referring to a commanding call or ethical imperative extended by nature. In directly addressing the topic of nature, Thrift indicates that his work sets out "to escape the traps of representational thinking of the kind that wants, for example, to understand nature as simply a project of cultural inscription (as in many writings on 'landscape') in favor of the kind of thinking that understands nature as a complex virtuality."[6] This passage points to the significance of the trope of nature for the contemporary debates on subjectivity and agency in Thrift's work. It projects a vision of nature that constitutes a vast field of emergence (in a Deleuzian or Massumian sense) for human and nonhuman action instead of presenting a surface on which certain humanist discourses of reality can be inscribed.

Barad talks about a similar trap in liberal social theories, which put the epistemological emphasis on a correspondence between social or scientific descriptions of phenomena and reality, based on the assumption that the world is divided into representing subjects and passive matter awaiting representation.[7] (The question of representation obviously has significant bearings for documentary media scholarship, too, although one rarely comes on references to the contemporary debates on the human-nature relationships in the field.) Although acknowledging the more widely recognized legacy of the Cartesian subject-object divide, Barad traces the emergence of the dichotomy between representations and the represented (as well as of the related problem of realism in philosophy) back to an earlier formulation, namely Democritus's atomic theory. She proposes, in its place, a posthumanist framework that "calls into question the givenness of the differential categories of 'human' and 'nonhuman,' examining the practices through which these differential boundaries are stabilized and destabilized."[8] Barad's posthumanism and Thrift's nonrepresentational theory are, of course, only two of the increasing number of alternative frameworks that point to significant shifts in our contemporary understanding of human-nature relationships. By reading Lingis, Thrift, and Barad together, I do not wish to suggest that these scholars are doing identical forms of theoretical work or that their ideas are directly applicable to the documentary films in question. However, their shared critical stance against human consciousness–based models of thinking, in conjunction with their reflections on representations of nature, are relevant for contextualizing the type of media ecology conveyed by the long-take nature sequences in *Five* and *Confession*.

The Media Ecology of Digital Long Takes

The term "media ecology," which refers to the interrelations among humans, nature, and media technology, has been around for quite some time. From Marshall McLuhan's Toronto-school media theory to Matthew Fuller's study on the material practices that establish media regimes[9] and Sean Cubitt's forays into EcoMedia,[10] one finds several different formulations of media-dominated worlds as ecologies. In a special topic issue of the *Fibreculture Journal*, Michael Goddard and Jussi Parikka have also delineated a third strand in media ecological theory, one influenced by Felix Guattari. According to Goddard and Parikka, this latest reincarnation of media ecological theory stems

> from a more politically oriented way of understanding the various scales and layers through which media are articulated together with politics, capitalism and nature, in which processes of media and technology cannot be detached from subjectivation.... Technology is not only a passive surface for the inscription of meanings and signification, but a material assemblage that partakes in machinic ecologies.[11]

By invoking the media ecology of films like *Five* and *Confession*, I am referring to a similar type of framework for understanding the way these documentary works approach the question of articulation—among documentary subjects, digital technologies, and nature. Instead of thinking of ecologies solely as the product of the human-nature interaction, we are compelled, especially in the media-saturated digital age, to take into account the role of technology in filtering our experiences, as well as the possibility of a more complex ecology, in which humans, nature, and media constitute equally powerful agents in the shaping of reality.

What of the media ecology in a film like *Five*, then? Although the viewer is presented with a single-take sequence in the fifth segment of *Five*, both the image and soundtracks are, in fact, heavily edited, suggesting that there is only the semblance of an uninterrupted flow in the employment of long takes. What is projected is a discontinuous reality, accessed partially by digital cameras and sound recording equipment. The 28-minute pond sequence is constructed from around twenty takes filmed over several months and superimposed onto each other with invisible cuts. Similarly, the soundtrack of the sequence is also carefully crafted, juxtaposing amplified diegetic sounds from different takes during a four-month mixing process. Despite appearances, there is no necessary overlap among image, sound, and reality based on analog long-take cinema's common aspirations for realistic representation. Rather, the audience is presented with intertwining visual and sonic temporalities created by the superimpositions. What gives the impression of an uninterrupted duration in the folding of the sound assemblage over the visual assemblage is precisely fragmentation and the layering of multitemporal fragments, which reveal or establish audiovisual patterns of a Caspian night abstracted from its various takes. Here, reality emerges not as a product of patient observation in compliance with the rules of human perception, but of a new interrelational dynamic among humans, digital technology, and nature.

Five's foregrounding of audiovisual patterns through layered temporalities rather than continuity in duration is significant with regard to the fact that it challenges the common conceptions related to long takes in analog cinema. Among the most persistent of these conceptions is the assumption that long-take cinematography is essentially oriented toward aesthetic realism or preserving events in their physical unity, established early on by French film theorist André Bazin. The artistic endorsement of long takes by canonized directors like Andrei Tarkovsky and Ingmar Bergman after the 1950s, and their coupling of the style with increased shot lengths, metaphysical themes, and contemplative dialogues, helped reinforce this view. In a certain sense, it is mostly through Tarkovsky and Bergman's artful elevation of the style (in the context of an equally anti-Hollywood and anti-Soviet montage cinematic approach) that long takes gained a privileged status in shaping a significant number of neo-realist world cinemas. These highly stylized cinemas, which are at the center of "slow cinema[12] versus fast films" debates, further made the technique synonymous with a particular formulation of time-oriented filmmaking. This type of filmmaking associates a Bergsonian model of duration, which pictures time and consciousness in a continuous and uninterrupted flow, with heightened realism. In an interview from 1969, Tarkovsky explained his understanding of how analog long-take cinema was ontologically tied with realism:

> The specific character of cinema consists in pinning down time. Cinema operates with time that has been seized, like a unit of aesthetic measure, which can be repeated indefinitely.... The more realistic the image, the nearer it is to life, the more time becomes authentic—meaning, not fabricated, not recreated...of course it is fabricated and recreated, but it approaches reality to such a point that it merges with it.[13]

In this formulation, what allowed the time to *become authentic* or the image to get *nearer to life* was the capturing of reality in its uninterrupted, real-time flow by means of long takes, as opposed to the way Eisensteinian montage fractured it through cuts and dialectical editing.

Of course, the camera in Tarkovsky was never meant to be unobtrusive; it did not necessarily seek to capture *life as it is*, the way observational-style documentary filmmaking did through similar techniques. (The long take was initially introduced by documentary filmmakers as a fly-in-the-wall observational device; one can think of Bazin's crediting of Robert Flaherty for the birth of aesthetic realism in this context.) Tarkovsky's camera was deliberate and probing, whereas the discontinuous, assemblistic use of sound in his films went against the type of authentic realism suggested in the continuity of their imagery. Nonetheless, Tarkovsky's writings and stylistic approach, at least at the level of cinematography and the editing of the image track, pointed toward an understanding of duration based on continuity, which has come to be commonly associated with Bergsonian temporality in the field of film studies. (Gilles Deleuze's Bergsonian reading of Tarkovsky's work in *The Time-Image* strengthened this connection.) In this context, the layered visual and sonic temporality of the pond sequence in *Five* goes against the dominant framework of Bergsonian duration in analog long-take cinema, while also refusing to conform to Eisensteinian montage or a contemporary Hollywood style of *intensified continuity*. The temporality evoked by the layering of audiovisual impressions from multiple Caspian nights is more Bachelardian in its compositional logic than it is Bergsonian, in that Kiarostami focuses on the rhythms, textures, and patterns of documentary reality rather than continuity.

In *Dialectics of Duration*, Gaston Bachelard critiques Bergson for setting continuity as an absolute term in defining duration, since Bergson arrives at this formulation by mapping the inner workings (or what he observes as the incessant stream of activity) of the psyche and the body onto the perception and fabric of time. More specifically, Bachelard finds it problematic that Bergson explains duration by recourse to the field of psychology and its human consciousness–centered view on nature—a view that imagines life, matter, and thought unfolding in a linear temporal progression, parallel to the linear activities of the brain and the body. Within this framework, duration is experienced and intuitively grasped as composed of a uniform rhythm without any pauses, rests, gaps, repetitions, or superimpositions. The resulting formula of continuity is inevitably deceptive since it is only through a circular logic that the irregularities, breaks, or intervals in the vast extension of matter outside the human body get ironed out and represented as part of a unified, seamless reality. In a passage exemplifying how this works, Bergson states:

> There are intervals of silence, between sounds, for the sense of hearing is not always occupied; between odors, between tastes, there are gaps, as though the senses of smell and taste only functioned accidentally: as soon as we open our eyes, on the contrary, the whole field of vision takes on color; and since solids are necessarily in contact with each other, our touch must follow the surface or edges of the objects without ever encountering a true interruption. How do we parcel out the continuity of material extensity.... No doubt the aspect of this continuity changes from moment to moment; but why do we not purely and simply realize that the whole has changed, as with the turning of a kaleidoscope.[14]

What the passage conveys is the priority, in Bergsonian thought, of human perception over discontinuous precognitive matter, as well as the simultaneously kaleidoscopic and unified whole over independent parts. It is this conviction that opens his work to criticism regarding its anthropocentric and holistic phenomenological approach.

Bachelard rejects the Bergsonian notion of continuity on similar ethical grounds and sees in it a reworking of the Cartesian subject-object divide. Suggesting that Bergson's world consists of a strict division between active subjects and passive objects, he argues that this is a world in which objects are ultimately knowable by subjects, without having any agency or reality of their own:

> In this way is the unending dialogue of mind and things prepared, and the continuous fabric woven that lets us feel substance within us, at the level of our innermost intuition, despite the contradictions of external experience. When I do not recognize reality it is because I am absorbed by memories that reality itself has imprinted in me, because I have returned to myself. For Bergson, there is no wavering, no interplay, no interruption in the alternative we have between knowledge of our innermost self and of the external world. I act or I think; I am a thing or a philosopher. And through this very contradiction, I am continuous.[15]

What Bachelard proposes instead of this human consciousness–based model is shifting the attention from psychology to the realm of nature sciences, such as botany and quantum physics, and thinking of temporality in relative terms according to their finds. His alternative to the human consciousness– and continuity-based theory of duration is a theory of *repose*, one that takes into account inactivity and rest, absence as well as presence, and individual instances as well as flow, following observations of diverse temporal phenomena in nature. The choice of the word *repose* and the attention to inactivity bring to mind Thrift's invocation of apathy in his call for returning to seventeenth-century models of subjectivity based of passivity or inaction. Bachelard further suggests that discontinuity, repetition, and rest, as well as temporal superimpositions and rhythms, are integral to thinking about matter and duration beyond the confines of human interiority. That is why, in his formulation, duration lends itself better to an analysis of rhythms ("rhythmanalysis") and patterns instead of uninterrupted flow.

Bachelard borrows the term "rhythmanalysis" from the Brazilian philosopher Pinheiro dos Santos, who suggests that nonhuman matter operates through vibrations on the molecular and quantum levels and that these vibrations constitute their abstract movement, which might be insensible to and not intuitively knowable to humans. Thinking about the vibrations and temporality of matter in terms of rhythms through the Bachelardian return to the quantum gives philosophy a "sonic inflection, becoming infected by musical metaphors in an attempt to approach something that eludes it."[16] As Henri Lefebvre, who also takes up the term rhythmanalysis, explains:

> [The rhythmanalyst] will listen to the world, and above all to what are disdainfully called noises, which are said without meaning, and to murmurs, full of meaning— and finally he will listen to silences.... For him nothing is immobile. He hears the wind, the rain, storms; but if he considers a stone, a wall, a trunk, he understands their slowness, their interminable rhythm. This object is not inert; time is not set aside for the subject.... The sensible? It is neither the apparent, nor the phenomenal, but the present.[17]

The striking similarity of Lefebvre's language with that of Lingis in interpreting Bachelardian modes of temporal analysis (his call for listening to murmurs, silences, the wind, etc. in order to understand matter) points to the ecocritical dimension inscribed into the topic of duration via sound. This dimension is often ignored in the field of film and media analysis because the field tends to take Bergsonian duration as a given. Conversely, Kiarostami's sound and image editing in *Five* sets duration as a relative, matter- or object-oriented (instead of subject-oriented) term, deflating assumptions about continuity. His long-take night is a rhythmic assemblage, one that takes into account the temporal patterns, superimpositions, and cadences that might be observable among various nights on the Caspian shore, without privileging the linear logic of human perception.

Disclosing that the long-take nighttime pond sequence involves time-lapse cinematography as well as superimposed imagery in the DVD's commentary, Kiarostami downplays the agency of the filmmaker further by pointing to the no longer required presence of the filmmaker during filming in digital technology (he sets the camera up and leaves the scene, while the sound is recorded separately) and the relativity of human consciousness–based time. The time-lapse technology used in acquiring the long-take shots interrupts the duration of the image, giving it a relative continuity that is based on machinic rhythms rather than human-based ones. Consequently, the effect of slowness achieved through the process points to a temporal rhythm that is interminable: slowness becomes an affectively charged, virtual mode of reality established by an assemblage of lapsed and superimposed temporalities rather than an effect of uninterrupted linear flow of time. The question in the editing process, then, turns into one of understanding the interrelations among the distinct materialities of image, sound, and profilmic reality: the patterns and rhythms that emerge in their interaction, facilitated yet not fully determined by the filmmaker. "How can I explain this role of having no role?" asks Kiarostami self-effacingly in his DVD commentary, speculating:

> Maybe this whole symphony of silence, and then the duet, the trio, and the improvisation of the frogs, or toads, is an interaction of both observation and non-observation, presence and absence.... Really, in my opinion, if we imagine life without this parameter [chance], we have lost some of our sense of realism.[18]

Notably, histories of documentary media rarely mention the significance of the element of chance or nonhuman agency for different schools of realism when they deal with the topic. Due to lack of scholarship regarding materialist approaches in documentary, implications of Kiarostami's digital long-take realism, which is object-oriented and more post-humanist than humanist (unlike most of its analog counterparts), gets lost in the vacuum.[19]

Of course, in a strange, somewhat paradoxical sense, there is something postmodern about the subtly post-humanist, object-oriented realism behind Kiarostami's remarkable collage of superimposed imagery and sounds, as if it is both a pastiche and an appeal to the sonic singularity of cyclical nature-time that folds the past, present, and future onto each other. The paradox, here, lies in the fact that postmodern aesthetics itself suggests artificiality and cultural inscription, drawing attention to the deliberate, the unnatural, and the decontextualized, whereas the "natural sounds" that are used in the soundtrack have lives and locative realities of their own. Although Kiarostami is a masterful composer, he cannot control or produce the sounds of the Caspian night. Instead, he can celebrate them and act as a temporary conductor of an orchestra of sound or a diligent curator,[20] in the manner of environmental artists who sculpt nature in order for the "real art" of decay, transformation, or erosion to flourish. On the other hand, one can also argue that what Kiarostami strives to establish through this collage might precisely be a new reality, reassembling and layering diegetic sounds in order to evoke a virtual, previously nonexisting audiovisual space, in which natural sounds are heard and juxtaposed in ways that would not have been possible without the intervention of digital technology. The logic behind this latter argument can be traced back to the ideas that led to the ambient music movement in the 1980s, inspired by the technological developments in recording. In his chronicle of the birth of ambient music, a compositional style that he introduced in an eponymous 1978 album, Brian Eno mentions two factors that paved the way for the new movement to come into existence: "the development of the texture of sound itself as a focus for compositional attention [in the 1970s], and the ability to create with electronics virtual acoustic spaces (acoustic spaces that don't exist in nature)."[21] By creating a carefully textured acoustic environment of ambient music in which to be lost, Eno suggests that immersion is the goal. The chorus of sounds in the acoustic nighttime pond sequence in *Five* can similarly be interpreted as emanating from or resonating in a virtual space, with its layered, multitemporal assemblage no longer locating a specific place in time. Where else might superimposed diegetic sounds be encountered if not in a virtual, affective dimension? In their arrhythmic crescendos and decrescendos, cries and murmurs, or soars and dips, the sounds suggest that they belong to no one and not to the image, whereas the image itself vaguely marks their source location by projecting a kaleidoscopic reflection of it, stitching together impressions of the pond captured in different times.

ACOUSTICS OF A PERPETUAL NIGHT: THE ARCTIC AND THE ANEMPATHETIC

Differently from Kiarostami's five-part film, which pushes the limits of documentary by frustrating the expectation of a narrative arc, Sokurov's *Confession* makes generous use of narrative elements, blurring the distinction between fiction and nonfiction. The hybrid film, labeled a documentary by Sokurov, features analog video (shot on Betacam SP, as is the case with most Sokurov documentaries) yet can also be read within the parameters of a digital audio aesthetics by taking on a different life when viewed with its alternative soundtrack, which consists of stereo sound remastered in Dolby Digital 2.0

for its DVD release. In *Confession*, Sokurov intentionally exploits the low visual quality of analog video to create a bleak and prosaic vision of military life around the Arctic Circle, the image of which becomes even further removed from any sensual qualities when the digital remastering process amplifies the soundtrack, making the wall of already amplified ambient sound surrounding the bland images more distinct and vibrant. As William Brian Whittington argues, the Dolby digital format foregrounds sound quality and design; therefore, there is a double amplification of sound at stake in the film's DVD version. Here, I take the documentary's DVD version not as a mere diversion from or supplement to the original but as an independent text on its own, following Mark Kerins's call for considering the proliferation of different versions of the same movie in the DVD era as an integral feature of digital culture, requiring media scholars' attention to the differences between theatrical and home mixes when talking about soundtracks. In the context of proliferation, Sokurov's films constitute rich texts for analysis in general because they translate to DVD-based digital mixes exceptionally well, with their muted imagery, minimal dialogue, and ample use of ambient sounds. More so than Kiarostami, Sokurov is known for his techniques of image and sound manipulation, especially optical distortions, in contrast with the slow, minimally edited look of his cinema. Sokurov is also relevant for digital cinema in relation to his later experimentations with digital single-take films like *Russian Ark* (2002) and Dolby digital sequences in video docudramas like *Taurus* (2000). Toru Soma indicates that, immediately after *Confession*, Sokurov and his sound director/long-time collaborator Sergey Moshkov started experimenting with shooting Dolby Digital, which resulted in the peasants (*khodoki*) sequence of the ensuing film *Taurus* ("How the Ark"). Although the sequence was cut from the final version of the film, it was nevertheless "a blueprint of the aesthetic achievement in Sokurov's next film, *Russian Ark* (2002)."[22] In this sense, *Confession* is a transitional film, preceding, and, in a certain sense, premediating the arrival of a digital aesthetics in Sokurov's work.

Confession concludes with a desaturated nighttime sequence, in which sailors are shown pulling a small boat carrying the bosun and a seaman to the naval ship under a heavy snowstorm right before dawn. The human figures appear like silhouettes in the scene, made indistinct behind a thick veil of snow, fog, and dimmed imagery. The commands and shouts of the sailors reverberate on the deck but are heavily cloaked by the sounds of the wind, the raging sea beating the ship's hull, clanks of metal, echoes, and nondiegetic classical music. Following the image of a lone young man smoking and lulled by the cradling motion of the battleship to hallucinatory dreams (which Sokurov simulates by superimposing on the dark, stormy waters the ghostly image of the sailor swimming in the sea), the voiceover provides a melancholic commentary:

> The sea was big. The Commander smiled, remembering this phrase of Chekhov's. Towards the evening, the bosun and a seaman returned to the ship. They had taken medical officers to the shore. All the crew was on board. We will stay the night here anchored by the shore, till the storm is over and in the morning, God willing, we will move on, wrote the Commander. He added a full stop and went to bed.

The voiceover, which represents the third-person narrative of the battleship's unnamed commander,[23] underscores the sense of existential solitude common to most Sokurov films. The amplified ambient sounds that accompany the voiceover accentuate the powerlessness of the documentary's subjects against the long, turbulent night of the Barents Sea and nature's indifference to their desperate search for purpose. It is true that in both of the nighttime sequences in *Five* and *Confession*, the amplified yet anempathetic soundtracks project a view of nature fundamentally indifferent to the human condition. In *Confession*, however, this indifference or lack of empathy almost takes on a cruel face.

As I previously mentioned, Michel Chion defines anempathetic sound as "sound—usually diegetic music—that seems to exhibit conspicuous indifference to what is going on in the film's plot."[24] The sound of the running water in the shower scene of Hitchcock's *Psycho,* which continues uninterrupted throughout and after the brutal murder of one of the film's main characters, Marion, presents a paradigmatic example of this type of sound by exhibiting an unsettling indifference to the violence that takes place. Although Chion does not discuss how the term might be applied to the use of sound in documentary film, his elaboration of anempathetic sound as creating an *effect of cosmic indifference,* "not of freezing emotion but rather of intensifying it, by inscribing it on a cosmic background,"[25] provides a suitable framework for explaining the function of amplified soundtracks in *Five* and *Confession*.

From a philosophical point of view, there is much more to the idea of cosmic indifference than what Chion's original formulation reveals. At the level of affect, for example, anempathetic sound is described as indifferent, which suggests a neutral stance. However, in humans, there is no such thing as absolute neutrality. Heidegger would argue that all our perceptions are filtered through moods (*stimmung* in Heideggerian terms). In this sense, anempathetic sound's blocking of emotions seems intentional because its very refusal to participate in the evocation of mood has a sort of sinister air, a cruelty. Such a reading is representative of Sokurov's general pessimistic view on nature that runs through both his fiction and nonfiction films, often featuring anempathetic soundtracks. Sokurov states in an interview:

> This is a moral issue: landscape as a witness of death, landscape as an absolute category. In itself, it carries an artistic image or idea. Not every human face contains some artistic essence, but every landscape does. Each one is the indifferent countenance of nature looking at human beings, some lofty art that doesn't care whether humanity exists or not.[26]

Conversely, that sound in film conveys nature's indifference to human agency can be seen as benevolence. This is because anempathetic sound penetrates us and moves through our bodies, inducing precognitive affect rather than conscious thoughts or emotions. Either way, anempathetic sound is, itself, a sort of sensual, sentient thing if it is thought of in terms of intentionality.[27]

In both *Five* and *Confession,* the subjects behind and in front of the camera seem absorbed or swallowed by the acoustic, supersentient matter. The carefully curated soundtracks evoke a particular notion of nature as impervious and indifferent to the human condition, in tandem with the formal and technological abstraction of the image. To reiterate some of the audiovisual details I mentioned earlier, the image of the pond in *Five* is almost completely veiled by the night, barely discernible through the occasional reflection of moonlight; in *Confession*, one sees indistinct figures of sailors blurred through snow, nightly shadows, and constant fog throughout the film. On the other hand, the soundtracks presenting carefully layered and inflated nature sounds create an ambient wall of sound, suggesting nature's indifference to human intervention or agency.[28] There is notably a similar nighttime nature scene in Kiarostami's first digital documentary, *ABC Africa*, which features a 7-minute black screen sequence filmed during a thunderstorm and government-enforced power outage in Uganda. Toward the end of the documentary, Kiarostami lets the camera run during a nighttime thunderstorm, filming from a window what seems to be the impenetrable dark reserve of the night. Flashes of lightning, which reveal a few trees outside, occasionally lift the darkness. The scene underscores how power outages confine Ugandans to a life of destitution. It further suggests that nature's independent agency and indifference toward human tribulations are common themes in Kiarostami's work.[29]

OBJECT-ORIENTED DOCUMENTALITY

Significantly, digital documentaries' return to tropes of nature as indifferent to human medi(t)ation through a disenchantment of the visual and amplification of the sonic comes at a critical moment. In the twenty-first century, various disciplines within the humanities and nature sciences have increasingly turned their attention to revisiting the outdated and no longer supportable binaries established around human-nature relationships. This rethinking is evident in the metaphysical turn taken in recent years in the fields of art, humanities, and social sciences. There is also a rekindled interest in the theories of vitalism, panpsychism, hylozoism, speculative materialism, and agential realism, as well as in process- and object-oriented philosophies.[30] Such theories seek to formulate a philosophy of nature that can respond to contemporary ecological sensibilities and posit nature as an entity capable of acting upon itself without the intervention of human or organic actors. In this context, analyzing digital documentaries' meditations on nature gives us an opportunity to enter documentary in contemporary phenomenological debates and explore emerging forms of documentary media ecologies.

Although it is difficult to establish a direct connection or dialogue between the recent metaphysical turn in the aforementioned fields and the documentary filmmaking of directors like Kiarostami and Sokurov,[31] we can still think about the ways in which films like *Five* and *Confession* gesture toward an object-oriented, nonhumanist documentary realism. Kiarostami's pond, nighttime, frogs, a chorus of sounds, then, a storm, and finally, dawn and Sokurov's evocation of the acoustic Arctic both suggest a love for things, such as the cries, rumbles, and murmurs of the night. In an extensive study on evocations of place and landscape in independent film and video, Scott MacDonald talks about how nature has been so central to the representational and narrative strategies of fiction and documentary film throughout the history of cinema.[32] However, most of the films he examines are humanist in their orientation and aesthetic discourse. Conversely, the images and sounds of nature presented in Kiarostami and Sokurov's documentaries point to a different conception of the relationship among documentary subjects, material reality, and technology. It is a relationship in which affect and sound obscure the logocentric field of vision and exploit the hidden patterns of nature instead of representing or capturing reality as it is. The camera, as well as the recording and editing devices, become equally powerful agents in forging relationships between human and nonhuman actors. In Kiarostami and Sokurov's takes (or long takes) on nature, humans share citizenship with a diverse population of objects in the universe; they cry out, murmur, and rumble their summons for those who are willing to listen.

NOTES

1. Michel Chion, Claudia Gorbman, and Walter Murch, *Audio-Vision: Sound on Screen* (New York: Columbia University Press, 1994), 221.
2. An eponymous conference held by the University of Wisconsin Milwaukee's Center for Twenty-First Century Studies in May 2012 defined the nonhuman turn as the critical approaches (such as post-humanism, media ecology, actor-network theory, object-oriented ontology, and animal studies) that have emerged in the twenty-first century as a response to the human-centered formulations of nature and technology in the arts, humanities, and social sciences.
3. The original video installation has been exhibited in various festival and gallery environments around the world. After its world premiere at the Cannes Film Festival in 2004, New York's Museum of Modern Art (MoMA) acquired the work for its first screening in the United States and presented it in conjunction with the Kiarostami moving-image retrospective in 2007. At MoMA, the five segments that made up the work were projected—in a synchronized loop—onto five separate partitions dividing the Morita Gallery, with a bench before each screen and the audio of each segment blending together at a distance.
4. Alphonso Lingis, *The Imperative* (Bloomington: Indiana University Press, 1998), 9.
5. Nigel Thrift, *Non-Representational Theory: Space, Politics, Affect*, rev. ed. (New York: Routledge, 2007), vii.
6. Ibid., 57.
7. Karen Barad, "Posthumanist Performativity: Toward an Understanding of How Matter Comes to Matter," *Signs* 28, no. 3 (2003): 803.
8. Ibid., 808.
9. Matthew Fuller, *Media Ecologies: Materialist Energies in Art and Technoculture* (Cambridge, MA: MIT Press, 2005).
10. Sean Cubitt, *EcoMedia* (Amsterdam and New York: Rodopi, 2005). In this handbook, Cubitt expands his ecomedia theory with a brilliant discussion of eco-criticism, referring to explicit expressions of ecological concerns in literature and cinema. One can also think about the established field of eco(media) art here, including the works of artists like Ruth Wallen.
11. Michael Goddard and Jussi Parikka, "Editorial," *Fibreculture* 17 (2011): v

12. Also referred to as "contemporary contemplative cinema" by Harry Turtle and "austere minimalist cinema" by Jonathan Romney.

13. John Gianvito, ed., *Andrei Tarkovsky: Interviews* (Jackson: University Press of Mississippi, 2006), 19.

14. Henri Bergson, *Matter and Memory*, trans. Nancy Margaret Paul and W. S. Palmer (New York: Cosimo Classics, 2007), 259–260.

15. Gaston Bachelard, *Dialectic of Duration*, trans. Mary McAllester Jones (Manchester: Clinamen Press, 2000), 25–26.

16. Steve Goodman, *Sonic Warfare: Sound, Affect, and the Ecology of Fear* (Cambridge, MA: MIT Press, 2009), 85.

17. Henri Lefebvre, *Rhythmanalysis: Space, Time and Everyday Life* (New York: Continuum, 2004), 19–21.

18. Abbas Kiarostami, Five: Dedicated to Ozu, 2003, DVD commentary.

19. Jennifer Peterson's essay on Workers Leaving the Factory also points to the lack of alternative theoretical frameworks dealing with long-take realism. Looking at "Worker remakes," a cluster of digital documentaries quoting the Lumières' landmark actuality film, Peterson suggests that the specific long-take realism in these films offers a "conceptual realism" rather than the traditional cinematic realism.

20. In one of our conversations about the film, Carol Vernallis indicated that Kiarostami's orchestration of ambient sounds made her think of a style of sound editing that can be best described as "tender curation." I find that phrasing rather poignant and applicable to films or media installation works that employ a similar audiovisual aesthetics.

21. Brian Eno, "Ambient Music," in *Audio Culture: Readings in Modern Music*, ed. Christoph Cox and Daniel Warner (New York: Continuum, 2004), 95.

22. Toru Soma, "How the Ark of 'I' Was Prepared by Sound Technologies: From the Secret Sequence in 'Taurus' to 'Russian Ark,' Filmed by Alexander Sokurov," *Bigaku (Aesthetics)* 55–52, no. 218 (2004): 69–83.

23. This is a fictional character introduced by Sokurov to frame the sailors' experiences of isolation and mental destitution in the documentary, played by the only actor among the subjects, Sergei Bakai.

24. Chion, *Audio-Vision: Sound on Screen*, 221.

25. Ibid., 8.

26. Lauren Sedofsky, "Plane Songs: Lauren Sedofsky Talks with Alexander Sokurov," *Artforum International* 40.3 (November 2001), 124.

27. I thank Carole Piechota for encouraging me to think about the question of intentionality in relation to anempathetic sound and her invaluable comments on the cruelty and benevolence of sound, which helped formulate some of the thoughts here.

28. I am using the phrase "wall of sound" in reference to the music production and recording technique developed by Phil Spector in the 1960s and its introduction of dense, layered, and reverberant sound in the pop and rock scene.

29. Here, one can also think of the ending of Kiarostami's award-winning fiction film *Taste of Cherry* (1997), featuring a nighttime thunderstorm.

30. Jane Bennett writes about the necessity to recognize humans as participating in a shared "vital materiality," understood as a type of vibrant biopower and resistance inherent in all matter (see Jane Bennett, *Vibrant Matter: A Political Ecology of Things* (Durham, NC: Duke University Press, 2010), 14); Graham Harman promotes the idea of object-oriented philosophies, for which he sees Alphonso Lingis's work as inspirational; Bruno Latour's

actor-network theory draws attention to the agency of nonhuman actors; and Quentin Meillassoux's speculative materialism contends that we can imagine a universe of objects-in-themselves without depending on models that look for a representational relationship between Thought and Being. Despite their differences, what these theorists share in common is a resistance against Kantian idealism, which sets forth the rational agent as the exemplary citizen of the universe, commanding the environment with his or her faculty of thought alone.

31. Notably, I have not come on a direct acknowledgment of the contemporary debates revolving around human-nature relationships by either filmmakers, who are both well versed in philosophy.

32. Scott MacDonald, *The Garden in the Machine: A Field Guide to Independent Films About Place* (Los Angeles: University of California Press, 2001).

Select Bibliography

Bachelard, Gaston. *Dialectic of Duration*. Translated by Mary McAllester Jones. Manchester: Clinamen Press, 2000.

Barad, Karen. "Posthumanist Performativity: Toward an Understanding of How Matter Comes to Matter." *Signs* 28, no. 3 (2003): 801–831.

Bennett, Jane. *Vibrant Matter: A Political Ecology of Things*. Durham, NC: Duke University Press, 2010.

Chion, Michel, Claudia Gorbman, and Walter Murch. *Audio-Vision: Sound on Screen*. New York: Columbia University Press, 1994.

Cubitt, Sean. *EcoMedia*. Amsterdam and New York: Rodopi, 2005.

Fuller, Matthew. *Media Ecologies: Materialist Energies in Art and Technoculture*. Cambridge, MA: MIT Press, 2005.

Harman, Graham. *Guerrilla Metaphysics: Phenomenology and the Carpentry of Things*. Chicago: Open Court, 2005.

Lingis, Alphonso. *The Imperative*. Bloomington: Indiana University Press, 1998.

Thrift, Nigel. *Non-Representational Theory: Space, Politics, Affect*. Revised Edition. New York: Routledge, 2007.

CHAPTER 35

WORKERS LEAVING THE FACTORY

Witnessing Industry in the Digital Age

JENNIFER PETERSON

IF one of the primary characteristics of the digital era is a shift away from industrial production toward the production of information, the cinema's persistent (and persistently marginal) focus on industrial subjects can provide an important perspective on our era: a front row seat, if you will, at the deathbed of industrial manufacturing. Industrial films were present at the birth of cinema: the Lumière Brothers' *Workers Leaving the Factory,* famous as the first subject on the program at the Grand Café in Paris on December 28, 1895, is an industrial film of sorts. Today, of course, *Workers Leaving the Factory* is readily available for viewing online, cropping up anytime one runs a Google search for "invention of cinema"; moreover, since 1995, the film has inspired a spate of remakes. In the 100 years between the Lumières' *Workers* and its postmodern status as a foundational cinematic text, labor and industry persisted as subjects for documentaries, even if labor subjects were never a particularly mainstream theme in fiction films. The narrator of Harun Farocki's 1995 film *Workers Leaving the Factory* remarks, "Whenever possible, film has turned hastily away from factories." And yet it is the contention of this essay that, since the turn of the twenty-first century, an important group of films has been turning back to face the factory as its "gates" have been transformed. This return to questions of industry in cinema and media is symptomatic of the historical shift away from manufacturing toward the dominance of finance capital: these new "industrial films," if we can call them that, document and respond to the state of labor in the contemporary global economy.[1] Documentaries in the Vertov tradition, such as *Three Songs of Lenin* (1934), once celebrated modern industrial production, but today's nonfiction films about industry, for all their observational reserve, seem more akin to lamentations.

This article aims to open up the subject of labor and industry in recent experimental documentary. (Fiction films concerned with labor have also been on the increase lately, particularly in Chinese cinema, but this essay is concerned with nonfiction.)[2] Although it can be hazardous to identify broad trends based on a few exceptional films, especially when that trend is still unfolding, the frequency of this return to industry in contemporary nonfiction film is striking. This return is postmodern in terms of its quotation of previous films and outmoded genres, such as the *Workers* remakes, which I discuss below. And, too, this return reflects the growing role of online digital archives: the seemingly old-fashioned genre of the industrial film now circulates widely online as more and more public-domain "vintage" industrials are uploaded to sites such the Internet Archive and the Industry Film Archive. But one can discern another trend in the growing number of documentaries that have been focusing on industry and labor: a commitment to a rigorous observational aesthetic. Films such as *Workingman's Death* (Michael Glawogger, 2005), Wang Bing's *West of the Tracks* (2003) and *Crude Oil* (2008), *Kodak* (Tacita Dean, 2006), *Manufactured Landscapes* (Jennifer Baichwal, 2006), *Our Daily Bread* (Nikolaus Geyrhalter, 2006), *Sleep Furiously* (Gideon Koppel, 2008), *Make it New, John* (Duncan Campbell, 2009), *In Comparison* (Harun Farocki, 2009), *Ruhr* (James Benning, 2009), *Erie* (Kevin Jerome Everson, 2010), *The Forgotten Space* (Allan Sekula and Noël Burch, 2010), to name just a few, have been visualizing the changing landscape of labor and industry in the face of the unevenly technologized global economy, which people in some parts of the world experience as postindustrial but which for many others remains a world of heavy labor.[3] The unifying themes of this diverse group of films would seem to be economics and alienation, whether the people shown are Welsh farmers or Chinese steelworkers.

Although this group of films is too disparate to be defined as any kind of a movement, it does cohere around two formal tendencies: first, a style that is shaped by digital aesthetics (whether the work was shot on film or digital video), and second, a commitment to observation and avoidance of editorializing. The first tendency has been enabled by technological shifts: the ability to shoot almost limitless hours of video has encouraged higher shooting ratios than were possible in the age of expensive film stock. This allows filmmakers to shoot more footage, of course, but it is in the realm of editing that changes can be observed. The films I discuss herein are concerned with questions of duration, using the long take not as a narrative device but as a formal concern. Even films shot on 16mm or 35mm have been exploring this long take aesthetic. The second, observational tendency is arguably a countertrend to the "issues-oriented" and "character-driven" documentaries that have been popular in this same period, from Michael Moore's films to *The Cove* (Louie Psihoyos, 2009). The films I discuss here are non-narrative, and the people they depict are not presented as "characters" but rather remain unnamed, as in a traditional industrial film. Some (but not all) of these films avoid dialogue entirely, instead using ambient location sound to create a nonverbal sonic landscape. This new observational aesthetic is distinct in tone from the cinematic realism of the first half of the twentieth century. Rather than fetishizing commodities after the manner of a conventional industrial film, and rather than promoting an image of the heroic worker (Vertov again), these films quietly critique the structure of industry they observe. This new observational aesthetic is also unlike the observational style of 1960s documentary, whose *cinéma vérité* "shaky cam" has long since become a cliché of advertisements, reality TV, and Hollywood feature films. Rather, these films mobilize a style we might call "conceptual realism" to explore the increasingly urgent themes of labor and industry in the face of ongoing crises in global capitalism, along with the concurrent environmental degradation this economic system brings about. This cinematic style shares with contemporary photography a "conceptual" relationship to the real: these images retain a documentary impulse but, at the same time, call into question the very meaning of documentation.

To begin a provisional exploration of this new observational aesthetic, this essay considers several examples. First, I examine the recent spate of *Workers Leaving the Factory* remakes, focusing in particular on Ben Russell's 2008 film *Workers Leaving the Factory (Dubai)* and Sharon Lockhart's *Exit* (2008). Second, I discuss the 2010 film *Foreign Parts,* made by Véréna Paravel and J. P. Sniadecki, which documents the Willetts Point neighborhood of Queens, New York, a decaying and yet in some ways vibrant neighborhood of junkyards and auto repair shops that is currently slated for urban redevelopment. Finally, I turn to Daniel Eisenberg's *The Unstable Object* (2011), a tour-de-force three-part exploration of different kinds of contemporary labor (postmodern, modern, and traditional) in three different parts of the world. All these films observe the state of industrial labor today, either commenting on labor's new forms in the global economic marketplace, documenting the denuded landscapes of industrial waste, or reflecting on the passing of old industries. Today's highly structured and surveyed forms of labor are, of course, part of the same historical moment that favors highly organized and manipulated mainstream digital media products. By challenging the commercially saturated, fast-paced style of the moment, these films enable us to witness labor and media reflecting on and even shaping each other. At stake in this work is a rigorous, digitally informed observational aesthetic that adheres to a principle of witnessing.

The concept of witnessing has taken on new relevance thanks to the emerging field of trauma studies, which focuses on the ethical and philosophical meanings of the act of witnessing traumatic events (genocide, war); witnessing is also an important concept for contemporary historiography, which more broadly analyzes the ways in which history is recounted. Although interpretations of the concept vary, I quote from Kelly Oliver's definition, which stresses the basic dual nature of witnessing as both seeing and testifying to that which cannot be seen: "The double meaning of witnessing [is] *eyewitness* testimony based on first-hand knowledge, on the one hand, and *bearing witness* to something beyond recognition that can't be seen, on the other."[4] Or as Jane Blocker explains it, "theorists of witness argue...that the inaccessibility of events is the very nature of witness."[5] The films I discuss here do not witness trauma as such, but labor, which is at once a more banal and more ubiquitous experience. Although the list of recent traumatic events is long, this particular group of films avoids headline-grabbing subject matter such as 9/11, the Iraq War, Abu Ghraib, and the Darfur genocide, which have been covered by other documentaries. Instead, these films make the everyday reality of labor visible in some of its endlessly various guises (some of which are indeed traumatic), and they bear witness to the larger, ungraspable complexity of globalized labor shaped by economic crisis. What we might call these films' stylistic "clarity" is employed paradoxically, not in the service of establishing objectivity or a stable truth, but to evoke the partial and complex experiences of work that lie beyond the scope of the camera.

WORKERS LEAVING THE FACTORY

The Lumière Brothers' 1895 *Workers Leaving the Factory* actually exists in at least three different versions; the two most well-known run at 47 and 40 seconds, respectively.[6] The film is typically understood as both a promotion of the Lumière photographic factory and a demonstration of the new *cinématographe*'s ability to represent movement. The film begins: the factory gates swing open and workers stream out, heading off screen left and right. Most of the workers are women, but some men also appear, several on bicycles. A dog runs in and out of the frame, and, in the longer version, a horse-drawn carriage emerges at the end. The apparent health and well-being of these workers seems to assert the functionality of the Lumière factory, which is, in turn, all the more impressive for its presentation of this wondrous new mechanical device.

The Lumières' films, and this film in particular, have come to represent a privileged moment in cinema history; Sean Cubitt argues that *Workers Leaving the Factory* is emblematic of "an innocence of movement that never after could recur in front of the camera... at the edge of a leisure that cannot be remade or recorded: these are... visions of immanent utopia."[7] Although a few people in the film glance in the direction of the camera, for the most part, these workers do not stare at the *cinématographe*, which indicates the possibility that it was staged; in most early actuality films, people on the street gawk at the camera, which was, after all, a new apparatus and one that required a cameraman to conspicuously hand-crank it. The camera might also have been concealed from the workers, as Cubitt acknowledges. Whether the film was "staged" (by telling the workers to perform their habitual exit from the factory without looking at the camera) or the apparatus hidden, it produces a celebratory resonance, evoking the off-screen leisure to which these workers are headed rather than the labor they have just concluded. This is not exactly "innocence," then, but promotion.

The Lumières' *Workers* film presages a form of promotional cinema that flourished in the silent era and has persisted to this day: the industrial film. In the first two decades of cinema, industrial films developed into an important genre, becoming one of several kinds of nonfiction film (along with travelogues, nature films, science films, and the like) that were regularly shown in motion picture theaters in the pre–feature film era.[8] Although they are not often socially critical films, silent-era industrials quite literally visualize the Marxist concept of commodity fetishism, showing the process by which workers' labor is transformed into commodities that mask the labor that went into producing them.[9] Many early industrials were sponsored by the companies whose products were being documented, such as those of the Ford Motor Company.[10] Such films typically embodied a boosterist, pro-industry stance toward whatever production process is depicted, be it railroad air break manufacturing in the Westinghouse Works films from 1904, biscuit-making in *A Visit to Peek Frean and Co.'s Biscuit Works* (Cricks and Martin, 1906), or fish-canning in *The Fish Processing Factory at Astrakhan* (Pathé, 1908).[11] As I have argued elsewhere, early industrial films modeled a Taylorist concept of production, in which manufacturing is broken down into a series of discrete tasks; in film terms, industrials are often edited according to a logic of one shot per action.[12] The industrial film genre persisted well beyond the silent era, of course, to become a mainstay of nontheatrical film throughout the twentieth century, although it has only recently become a topic of interest to film scholarship.[13] Industrial films continue to be produced today, going by various names such as training films, marketing films, and so forth. Over time, the industrial film genre has remained surprisingly consistent in terms of form, but it has adapted to changing media apace with emerging technology (from film to videotape to digital video to internet distribution). But I am not so much concerned here with the fate of the industrial film genre in the digital age; rather, what seems noteworthy is the way this apparently outmoded genre has become a reference point for recent nonfiction films about labor and industry. The brilliant 2009 film *Make It New, John,* for example, uses a great deal of archival footage from industrial films (along with some important staged segments) to tell the story of the production and failure of the DeLorean car in the late 1970s and early 1980s. Likewise, as I shall argue, *The Unstable Object* uses the classic industrial film as inspiration for its studied exploration of labor in the contemporary world.

In recent years, a number of remakes of the Lumière Brothers' *Workers Leaving the Factory* have appeared.[14] This particular Lumière film has become a touchstone for filmmakers in the past two decades, beginning with Farocki's *Workers Leaving the Factory*, which compiles footage of workers exiting factories from many different fiction and nonfiction films, drawing our attention to how frequent and yet parenthetical or unexplored this visual image is in film history. Farocki's film (and its 2006 iteration as a twelve-channel video installation), with its aesthetic of sampling and its dense interplay between image and sound to produce critical insight, merits extended analysis that I do not have space for here. But in a text that accompanied this film on its release in 1995, Farocki observed, "The first camera in the history of cinema was pointed at a factory, but a century later it can be said that film is hardly drawn to the factory and is even repelled by it. Films about work or workers have not become one of the main genres, and the space in front of the factory has remained on the sidelines."[15] This observation still rings true if one considers commercial fiction films, but in nonfiction, the turn toward labor and industrial subjects has been gathering steam since the dawn of the twenty-first century.

Recent remakes of the original Lumière *Workers* motif include Ben Russell's *Workers Leaving the Factory (Dubai)* (2008) and Sharon Lockhart's *Exit* (2008).[16] These two films both utilize a rigorous observational style that seems to hold back from critical analysis, although one cannot watch these works without perceiving their critical attentiveness. Russell's and Lockhart's remakes refer to the original *Workers* film not just as an empty reference, but as a starting point for formal exploration of the stationary camera, deep focus, and the long take. These are, of course, the techniques famously celebrated by André Bazin as the foundations of cinematic realism, but contemporary experimental nonfiction does not engage with the long take and deep focus in the same way that, say, Italian Neorealism did. Rather, these films use the old techniques of cinematic realism in a new, self-aware manner that we might usefully think of as conceptual realism. Restricting their stylistic techniques to just these few elements, these films explore the very ontology of cinema in the digital age.

Russell's film, for example, which is readily available for viewing online, portrays in one long take the vast difference between labor in the Lumière era and the kind of labor that exists today.[17] *Workers Leaving the Factory (Dubai)* responds to the globalization of labor and the flow of capital to oil-rich regions by presenting a moving portrait of Dubai construction workers, echoing the composition of the original Lumière film, but with a longer running time. The workers in Russell's film do not emerge from behind a factory gate—indeed, there is no gate or factory wall at all here—but instead proceed out from the depths of a landscape of half-built skyscrapers. The all-male workers, wearing green or blue jumpsuits, mill about the side of the construction site or walk past the camera (Figure 35.1).

Unlike in the original Lumière film, many of these workers gawk at the camera as they walk by. When a line of workers boards a bus, almost all of the men crane their necks to look at the camera before they climb on board. As with the Lumière film, the workers

FIGURE 35.1 *Workers Leaving the Factory (Dubai)* (Ben Russell, 2008). Image courtesy of Ben Russell.

move in a compositional flow off-screen, but in this case that flow is not only off screen right and left (which emphasizes a two-dimensional sense of space) but from back to front, into the space behind the camera, emphasizing depth of field and conjuring up the presence of the world outside the frame (which includes the camera and the filmmaker).

A text accompanying the film on Vimeo explains what the viewer may have already suspected: these laborers are not local, but from Southeast Asia. Dubai is, of course, one of the fastest growing cities today, and it is well-known as one of the few places where large-scale construction is still taking place since the 2008 recession hit (along with Beijing and Shanghai). The labor in this film is not centralized and geographically located inside a factory, but unbounded, migratory, and determined by the forces of global capital. Unlike the Lumières' *Workers*, this is not a promotional film. The company employing the workers is not named, nor do these workers project a joyous end-of-the-day mood. A brown-shirted man, apparently a supervisor, impatiently gestures the workers toward parked buses, and they hurriedly line up in order not to miss their ride. The fact that they are driven away from the work site in unmarked buses encourages the viewer to imagine not a happy world of postwork leisure but a dismal workers' housing block. We don't learn anything about these workers, other than that they are men— framed in an extreme long shot, it's difficult to make out their faces—nor do we learn precisely what their tasks are, beyond their association with the construction site. As in the era of the Lumière *cinématographe,* this is a world of class stratification, as these migrant workers construct buildings presumably to be occupied by more well-heeled consumers. But, unlike the world of the Lumières, this factory film depicts a world in which the scale of both capital and labor has become global.

Despite having been shot on 16mm film, *Workers Leaving the Factory (Dubai)* evinces the long-take observational aesthetic that I am arguing is central to the new observational mode in the digital era. (The film is silent, so we don't have the extra contextual information that location sound would provide. Sound is a central part of the contemporary observational aesthetic, however, and I discuss it in my other examples to follow.) A single take, the camera remains stationary for the film's entire 6 minute and 45 second running time. The stationary camera connects this film to the tradition of portraiture, but the fact that this is a film and not a still photograph means that we view the scene in real time. But this is not the long take made famous by the traditional understanding of Bazin, which was understood as essentially realistic and humanistic. Instead, Russell's long take underscores its inadequacy as a perfect mirror of reality. And, indeed, an important new wave of scholarship has been suggesting that the realist/humanist interpretation of Bazin has been a misreading all along.[18]

What is "conceptual" about this form of observation is its gesturing beyond the boundaries of the frame. Because nothing is explained beyond what we can see, the viewer is forced to find, infer, or project meaning into the film. In this way, *Workers Leaving the Factory (Dubai)* acknowledges the subjective nature of observation without having to make a fuss over the issue, as if to say, "Here is a landscape, make of it what you will, let's move on to the next example." This unstated modular quality is perhaps this film's most clear debt to the digital media ecosystem (modularity, of course, being one of Lev Manovich's five principles of new media).[19] Russell made a related film in 2008 called *Trypps #5 (Dubai)*, one of a series of short films he calls *Trypps*, which document places around the world in the interest of creating a "psychedelic ethnography." For my purposes here, it is enough to emphasize that this short film relies on outside context to generate meaning. Viewing the film in a sequence with other short films, or with knowledge about the original Lumière film or about Dubai: these are the sort of outside elements that activate the film, and Russell relies on the fact that his film exists in a messy world saturated with information and media. Although the 16mm technology of this film may not be new, its content (Dubai construction workers), structure (a single stationary take in a series of modular long-take films), and various modes of exhibition (whether theatrical or online) render it decidedly contemporary.

Sharon Lockhart's 2008 film *Exit* perhaps best exemplifies what I am calling the conceptual realism of this new observational style. One could say a great deal about this fascinating film, but most relevant for my purposes here are *Exit*'s references to the Lumière film and its reworking of photographic realism in moving images through use of the long take and stationary framing. The style of Lockhart's film, shot on 35mm (but transferred to high-definition [HD] video for exhibition), grows directly out of the photographic work for which she is perhaps more well known. *Exit* is a series of five stationary long takes of workers leaving the Bath Iron Works in Maine. These kind of industrial jobs are increasingly rare in the United States, although a press release informs us that the plant is owned by General Dynamics, a major defense contractor, which means these jobs are subsidized by the US military.[20] Irrespective of this information, what one sees in the film feels like a bygone image from a previous era, rendered in a style that looks decidedly contemporary. Each shot runs 8 minutes, preceded by an intertitle announcing the day of the week, so that the five shots comprise a five-day workweek structure, for a total running time of 41 minutes. Although there is no visual evidence to verify that these shots were taken on the subsequent weekdays that are announced, we tend to believe the intertitles, although this is just one of the many games the film sets up for us. By presenting some details and withholding others, the film plays with the act of documentation itself.

Exit is one of two films Lockhart shot after spending a year getting to know the workers at this plant—the other film, *Lunch Break*, is a long, slow-motion, single-take tracking shot (10 minutes of original footage slowed down to 80 minutes of running time) through the inside of the plant showing workers eating lunch. (Significantly, *Lunch Break* is the first of Lockhart's films to use a moving camera.) These two films, in turn, comprise parts of a larger installation called *Lunch Break*, which also includes photographs.[21] Just as the Lumière film extended the logic of still photography by adding movement, so the stationary camera of *Exit* expands Lockhart's photographic work by adding movement, which engages the viewer differently. Lockhart's long-take aesthetic imposes a real-time experience on the spectator, in a sense rendering the act of viewing a kind of labor. This film, like all the work in this stylistic vein, demands an attentive spectator.

Exit plays with the Lumières' composition by placing the camera behind rather than in front of the workers as they exit the factory. Even more than Russell's film, *Exit* shifts the axis of action away from the flat left-right sensibility of the Lumière film to a depth-emphasizing front-back movement: workers stream out from a space behind the camera and walk forward, away from the camera, creating another composition that emphasizes deep space (see Figure 35.2). Once the film's repetitive pattern has been established (this happens at the beginning of shot two, which begins exactly like shot one with the sound of the end-of-day horn and workers walking away from the camera), the viewer begins to anticipate the four identical long takes that remain to be seen. The attentive viewer must readjust her attention accordingly; the inattentive or impatient viewer grows frustrated at this point. The film then becomes a series of visual games as the viewer begins looking for patterns and visual cues. One begins paying attention to the workers' lunchboxes, their clothing, the actions certain of them repeat each day. The film's five-part repetitive structure emphasizes the quotidian nature of labor's daily routine, and the viewer becomes self-conscious about the work of spectatorship—focusing attention, contemplation, interpretation—that locates meaning in the film. We wonder many things: how much are these workers paid, how long they have been working here, do they like or dislike their jobs, what is morale like at the plant? None of that information is given, which is the key to the film's effect. At once visually lush (shot on 35mm

FIGURE 35.2 *Exit* (Sharon Lockhart, 2008). Image courtesy of Blum & Poe gallery.

WORKERS LEAVING THE FACTORY 607

color film stock) and restricted (the rear-view composition denies us a view of the workers' faces and frustrates our desire to see more), *Exit* demands that the viewer participate
by drawing on her own resources—thoughts about labor, memories of labor, visual acu-
ity—to produce meaning for the film.

Sound is another important part of this restrained style. The film's diegetic sync-sound
is sparse and appears to have been recorded from a single source. We hear the sound of
feet shuffling by, seagulls squawking (which locates the plant near a body of water that
we cannot see), snippets of conversation (although we cannot make out many words),
and, most importantly, the booming end-of-day horn blast that begins each new take.
Again, the effect is both specific and general, representing real sounds that happened in
a specific time and place, but evoking a sense of workers everywhere.

In a perceptive article from 2001, art historian Norman Bryson termed Lockhart's
strategy for conceptual photographic representation "counterpresence." It is not the
photograph's presence but "what lies outside the individual photograph" that matters,
not "affirmation but negation" that this style produces. "The principle at work resembled
that of minimalist music: instead of attending to what lies within each sound, the listener hears the shifts *between* sounds, the variations that come forward only against the
background of repetition."[22] Counterpresence is significant not only as a formal question, but for its revolutionary impact on spectator attention. "Now attention had to
work on quite a different basis: not passively receiving a flow, but actively working with
juxtapositions and fragments, sequences and implications."[23] Bryson applies the idea of
counterpresence to Lockhart's photographic work (arguing that it also describes much
contemporary conceptual photography such as that of Thomas Struth, Thomas Ruff,
and Bernd and Hilla Becher), but the concept can also be extended to her film work.
The concept echoes the dual nature of witnessing that I discussed earlier: counterpresence involves both seeing and what we cannot see. Just as Lockhart's *Exit* depicts a specific visual reality, it also refers to much a larger experience of labor that is not depicted,
gesturing toward that which lies beyond the visible domain. Not all of the films in this
new observational mode mobilize this rigorous strategy, or if they do, they differ from
Lockhart's signature style. Nonetheless, this concept of "counterpresence"—and the
kind of spectator attention it produces—provides a useful way of understanding the
conceptual dimension of these recent films about labor and industry.

FOREIGN PARTS

The feature-length film *Foreign Parts* is, in many ways, a more traditional observational documentary, using as it does a methodology inspired by ethnographic field
research, along with a more familiar nonfiction film style resembling *cinéma vérité*
(handheld camerawork, first-person interviews, interactions between filmmakers and
local subjects). Yet this film, too, is deeply concerned to witness the state of contemporary industry, or rather industrial waste, and it too updates the *vérité* tradition for

the digital age. This time, labor and industry are depicted in a landscape of junkyards and auto body shops that has been largely forgotten by—or rendered "foreign" to—the city that surrounds it. Likewise, this film utilizes the long take and, in many places, stationary framing; in the case of handheld shots, the long duration is determined by the interaction being recorded. Unlike the two films just discussed, which embody a dispassionate observational style, *Foreign Parts* reveals an intimate rapport between the filmmakers and their subjects. A different kind of portrait film than *Workers Leaving the Factory (Dubai)* or *Exit*, the filmmakers' relationship to their subject matter is here represented rather than elided, providing the spectator a way into the film via empathy and identification.

The Queens, New York neighborhood of Willets Point that the film documents is known for its auto repair shops and junkyards, and decaying machines are an important focus of the film. (The neighborhood was also featured in Ramin Bahrani's 2007 film *Chop Shop*, which is similarly concerned with questions of economics and labor, although, as a fiction film, it approaches the subject very differently.) But, more specifically, *Foreign Parts* explores the relationship between humans and machines, finding parallels between the treatment of junked cars and forgotten people in the larger economy of New York City (Figure 35.3). Although Willets Point is unhealthy (roads are unpaved and sewage pipes were never installed, and the dirt roads are perpetually filled with mud puddles), and in many ways dystopian (officially populated by only

FIGURE 35.3 *Foreign Parts* (Véréna Paravel and J. P. Sniadecki, 2008). Image courtesy of Véréna Paravel and J. P. Sniadecki.

one legal resident, along with others who sleep in their cars), the film finds much of value there.

Named after one of the many signs that compete for attention on neighborhood store-fronts, *Foreign Parts* depicts a multicultural community of 250 small businesses and the 2,000 people who work there. Willets Point is currently slated for a $3 billion redevelopment project, but the viewer is not informed of this fact until the end of the film, when a textual postscript explains the situation (and gives the numbers that I just cited). The harbinger of this urban redevelopment is the recently completed corporate-branded stadium for the New York Mets, Citi Field, visible in the background even in the film's first shot. At one point, one of the locals remarks, "This has become such a ghost town since they put that stadium up."

The industry of Willetts Point revolves around cars, and the film documents people working on them—painting, riveting, organizing parts—and also living in them—two of the film's main subjects, Sara and Luis Zapiain, have been living in a van for years. *Foreign Parts*, like the other titles I analyze here, avoids the commodity fetishism of the industrial film genre, following instead a different strategy of investing machines with uncanny soulfulness, framing junkyard cars so that they resemble dead animals. The film opens with a segment in which an old car is dismembered in such a way that it resembles a slaughterhouse beast. An engine is yanked apart, tubes are cut, brownish-yellow fluids pour forth, and the engine heaves, reminding the viewer of Georges Franju's 1949 documentary *Blood of the Beasts*. The film presents a landscape of decaying industrial production (a building marked "Feinstein Iron Works" is prominently visible in many shots), showing people who eke a living out of the end of the industrial supply chain, working in unhealthy conditions and trying to survive in a bleak economic climate. A young man says at one point, "This is a junkyard. Nobody ever wants to ever work here. I don't want to work here anymore."

Although the film does not treat the neighborhood's impending demolition and redevelopment as a major dramatic pivot point, as a more conventional "issues-oriented" documentary would, several of the people in the film discuss the proposed changes. In particular, the neighborhood's only official resident, 76-year-old Joe Ardizzone, is shown ceaselessly questing to challenge the city's redevelopment plans, although his struggle seems doomed to fail. At one point, while discussing the importance of "communication" with another man, he explains that he has missed a community meeting because the date was changed: everyone was informed by e-mail, but he didn't hear about the date change, because he doesn't have a computer. Joe explains, "Everybody's got computers. So they contact each other by computers…nobody called…so now I've got to get a, I got a rotary phone." "You've got to get a computer," the other man chuckles. "Because everybody's with a computer now." Joe responds, "Well it's like a nice thing, it's a great gadget, it's good, but I'm not into it, and I haven't got the time for computers. Why have I got to get all this equipment?" In the face of accelerating technological change and the planned obsolescence of consumer electronics, Joe and Willetts Point don't appear to stand a chance, for all their tenacious vitality.

The filmmakers, Véréna Paravel and J. P. Sniadecki, are both anthropologists affiliated with the Sensory Ethnography Lab at Harvard University (Paravel lectures in anthropology at Harvard, and Sniadecki recently completed his doctorate in anthropology there). For this film, they employed a methodology inspired by traditional field study techniques, filming and getting to know their subjects over the course of two years. The viewer does not necessarily know this, since it is not stated in the film, although at one point one young man, in the flush of a conversational monologue, says to the filmmaker (who is off-screen), "I hope you pass your test or your project, whatever you're doing. I hope you pass it, I hope you get a good grade out of this." The filmmakers' rapport with their subjects is made clear by the intimate moments to which they gain access.[24] Establishing a rapport with one's subjects is a cornerstone of the ethnographic method, a process that is today made easier by the unobtrusively small size of digital video cameras. The film's observational style utilizes classic *cinéma vérité* technique, pioneered by Jean Rouch (and exemplified in the 1960 film Rouch made in collaboration with sociologist Edgar Morin, *Chronique d'un été*): not just documenting the world but intervening in reality. The filmmakers can be heard and are briefly visible at a few points in *Foreign Parts,* along with pieces of the camera apparatus (tripod). Even though the filmmakers never become fleshed-out characters, this self-reflexivity gives the film an embodied point of view. In this way, the film is able to witness vitality in this dying industrial neighborhood and make a plea against gentrification and urban renewal without pretending to journalistic "objectivity." Indeed, journalism, too, becomes an object of study in the film, as a Spanish-speaking newscaster is shown setting up her camera and filming a story in the neighborhood.

Foreign Parts witnesses the both the hardships of Willets Point and the vibrancy of this community, in which small trades and independent businesses have managed to survive on scraps for generations. The film presents numerous scenes of wordless, small joys, such as a couple dancing in their shop, or two men having a snowball fight. A woman named Julia (who may be homeless, although that is never explicitly stated) dances happily in a bar as she drinks from a mini J&B bottle, and later celebrates her birthday with cake and her local friends. Alongside these fragmentary moments of happiness, the film details many of the obvious depravations of life in the neighborhood. In one scene, Luis talks about how difficult it is to sleep in their van when it's freezing outside while Sara cries quietly in the background. At another point, when Luis is in jail, Sara reveals the knife and tire iron she sleeps with for protection. The film shifts between such intimate sequences, in which local people divulge private experiences to the camera/filmmakers, and external sequences focusing on landscapes and cars. The external sequences tend to be carefully framed with a stationary camera, but the intimate sequences in which the camera/filmmakers interact with their subjects tend to be handheld long takes. Similarly, location sound is used throughout the film, which is sometimes muddy or inaudible, mirroring the handheld intimacy of certain shots.

Foreign Parts is important to this analysis because it provides a contrasting view of industry to the other films discussed here. What I am calling a "conceptual" observational style does not necessarily imply a "structural" interrogation of film form;

acknowledging the filmmaker as a presence in the world of the film is also a way of challenging outmoded notions of documentary objectivity. Rather than production, this
film explores decay; rather than formal austerity, this film echoes the messy contingency
of experience in its loose stylistics. Shot on HD video with sync-sound, even the film's
digital shadows and color evoke an ephemeral quality. Instead of a negative space that
gestures toward a larger world off screen, this film evokes the specificity of place in the
fullness of the present, which appears to be already outmoded. Mechanical industry
here appears as a dying marvel from the past; the future seems to offer no place for this
formerly vibrant habitat.

THE UNSTABLE OBJECT

Daniel Eisenberg's *The Unstable Object* is a precise and subtle meditation on three different instantiations of labor: state-of-the-art auto manufacturing in Dresden, Germany;
the relatively old-fashioned production methods at a factory that makes wall clocks
in Chicago; and the traditional handmade manufacturing of cymbals in Turkey. This
rigorously observational film resists overt social commentary, and yet, in its three-part
depiction of contemporary labor, the film portrays a kind of geography of early
twenty-first century capitalism, functioning as a witness to the phenomenon of uneven
development. Eisenberg's film illustrates the classic Marxist notion of uneven development visually and sonically, but for the purposes of explication, a textual definition will
be helpful. The social theorist David Harvey describes today's "capitalist spatiotemporal
logic" in terms of geographically uneven development:

> The general diminution in transport costs [for goods and material] in no way disrupts
> the significance of territorial divisions and specializations of labor. Indeed, it makes
> for more fine-grained territorial divisions since small differences in production costs
> (due to raw materials, labor conditions, intermediate inputs, consumer markets,
> infrastructural or taxation arrangements) are more exploitable due to highly mobile
> capital. Reducing the friction of distance, in short, makes capital more rather than
> less sensitive to geographical variations. The combined effect of freer trade and
> reduced transportation costs is not greater equality of power through the evolving
> territorial division of labor, but growing geographical inequalities.[25]

Eisenberg's film is not concerned so much with documenting inequalities as with
exploring the process of labor and comparing different experiences of labor. Resolutely
dispassionate (in places where one can imagine a different kind of documentary would
be fairly screaming to explain and argue), *The Unstable Object,* like the other films I have
been discussing, demands an attentive viewer. Here, though, the theme is not only labor
and its landscapes, but the way the landscapes of labor vary in time and space.

Stylistically, Eisenberg's film is nothing like the Lumière *Workers* film or a traditional
industrial, and yet it appears to have taken the classical industrial film as its inspiration

and model. Shot in HD color video, with a sparse and carefully considered soundtrack, *The Unstable Object* is a triptych of sorts, each third running about 20 minutes to comprise a feature-length running time of 69 minutes. Moving across three different industries—cars, clocks, and cymbals, whose production processes we might dub the postmodern, the modern, and the traditional—Eisenberg's film asks us to witness the specificities of these various forms of labor but also to make connections across these disparate practices. Each different national context, too, remains understated yet ever present, never spelled out but rather left to emerge from out of the larger context.

As has been noted by other scholars, Eisenberg's films defy categorization.[26] Although his work certainly falls into the category of avant-garde cinema, his films also engage with the traditions of nonfiction film, and *The Unstable Object* makes clear references to the old industrial film genre. The film documents the different stages of production in each factory, just as classic industrial films break industrial production down into discrete parts. Eisenberg's film also presents laborers without naming them, just as in a classic industrial film. Yet the film is deeply attentive to the workers it depicts, unlike traditional industrial films that focus on commodities rather than workers. And, more than anything, it is the film's careful three-part structure that transcends the industrial film formula to become a much more complicated and less celebratory depiction of labor. The film is carefully attuned to sound, for example, moving from a subdued audio presence in the first part to an increase in volume in the second part, until the sound becomes a loud din at the end of the third part as workers pound cymbals into shape. The sync-sound was recorded entirely on location, with the exception of three moments in which spare piano tones announce the start of each new section. This kind of meticulous detail is certainly absent from the classical industrial film tradition, which was more concerned with use-value than aesthetic form. Although *The Unstable Object* bears traces of that tradition of "useful cinema"—alongside its contemplative style, it does in fact document how things are made—this is no ordinary industrial film, but a magisterial statement about the contemporary experience of labor.

The first part of the film takes place at a high-tech Volkswagen plant in Dresden, Germany. The first several shots show the factory's ultra-modern exterior, which is unnamed in the film, although it is identified in the screening notes as the famous "transparent factory" ("Gläserne Manufaktur"), which manufactures Volkswagen's luxury Phaeton model.[27] Inside this glass-walled factory, laborers in clean white jumpsuits and white gloves concentrate on executing the final steps of manufacturing luxury cars while affluent consumers and factory tourists look on (Figure 35.4). Workers for the most part engage individually with each car, presenting the illusion that these luxury sedans are not made on an assembly line but produced like artisanal crafts. Although the film does not tell us this, it is apparent that the heavy assembly of the cars is done elsewhere, and this "factory" exists to put on a show for consumers. Indeed, an article in *Car and Driver* published the year after the factory opened in 2002 verifies that "all the smelly, noisy operations such as stamping and welding...take place elsewhere," but opines that "if the process convinces customers they're getting something special, maybe it's worth the added expense."[28] Designed not so much for manufacturing but for

FIGURE 35.4 *The Unstable Object* (Daniel Eisenberg, 2011). Image courtesy of Daniel Eisenberg.

spectacle, this factory evokes not the grease and exhaust of an auto repair shop but the cleanliness and efficiency of a bakery, as though the cars are not being made to drive on a gritty road, but to be eaten. As this section of the film illustrates, postmodern industry has masterfully transformed the act of production into a spectacle for consumption.

This work takes place in reverential silence; we hear many ambient sounds, but the workers do not speak to each other, nor are their tasks particularly loud. We see customers quietly speaking to white-coated factory technicians, but we cannot hear what they say. In fact, this wordlessness carries forward into the other two parts of the film; although words are spoken, they are often muffled and are never translated (parts one and three are in German and Turkish), so that the overall effect is an avoidance of the dialogue-driven nature of most cinema, including documentary film. When words are spoken, they tend to be registered visually (we see mouths moving) rather than aurally (the people speaking are often too far away to be heard), letting the images and the other sounds signify rather than language. Perhaps because of this downplaying of words, other ambient sounds rise to the foreground in part one: drilling and hammering, the clanking of metal parts, the squeaking of workers' shoes on the factory's polished hardwood floor.

One segment in this part of the film shows strange machines that seem to move independently of any human direction. These machines exit and enter elevators seemingly of their own volition, gliding effortlessly across the floor and changing direction with no visible intervention from people. This illusion of machine subjectivity is enhanced by Eisenberg's framing and editing, which eliminate any trace of human-machine interaction. The machines and the people in this factory seem to have equal function (and equal vitality), all of them uniformly mute before the onlooking consumer. The first part of *The Unstable Object* concludes, appropriately enough, with footage of workers leaving the factory, shot from inside the factory rather than from outside. Unlike the Lumière film, which elided labor by focusing on the world outside the factory gates, this film begins inside the factory and never leaves it.

The second part of the film takes place at a clock manufacturing plant staffed by visually impaired workers. Again, we are not given any information about the location beyond what we can see, but the film's screening notes explain that this segment was shot at the Chicago Lighthouse Industries manufacturing facility in Chicago, Illinois, which makes wall clocks for federal, state, and local government offices. The film does not tell us anything about the history of this facility, but instead simply shows us this reality, beginning with the visually impaired workers as they enter the factory and work throughout the day. Compared to the silent workers in part one, however, this part of the film is relatively vocal as the workers sing quietly to themselves, chat, and communicate throughout their day. Throughout this segment, we also hear the persistent, intermittent sound of air being sprayed to clean the clock faces. This more lively sound presence contributes to our understanding of these workers as blind or visually impaired: this factory is a sonic experience for its workers rather than a visual one (Figure 35.5).

In contrast to the work performed in the previous segment, this is a more traditional form of labor, in which a single kind of product is manufactured by a group of workers, each performing a different task. The equipment for this production is emblematic of the analog era: the clocks move down a slow conveyor belt and are assembled by hand. Each worker performs a single task repeatedly: one person places clock faces into a cutting machine, another attaches clock arms, another folds the cardboard boxes in which the clocks will be shipped, and so forth. Eisenberg emphasizes the repetitive nature of

FIGURE 35.5 *The Unstable Object* (Daniel Eisenberg, 2011). Image courtesy of Daniel Eisenberg.

these tasks by showing certain actions over and over, editing to create a sense of the repetitive rhythm of the day. We see that progress is made: the cardboard boxes eventually stack so high that they surround the man folding them, clocks accumulate on pegboards for testing until there is no room left. These white pegboards, too, show their age by the presence of shadowy black clock outlines on the empty walls stained by years of use. The irony here, of course, is that many of these workers, whose hands we see feeling for tools, cannot see the very clocks they are assembling. Yet this segment presents a vision of self-sufficiency in which these workers are empowered by their employment in the kind of jobs that are increasingly scarce in the United States.

Part three begins without an establishing shot, inside a room in which molten metal is being cast, we do not yet know where or for what. This is the only segment in which the workers are all men, and other than the modern clothes (jeans, flannel shirts, sneakers), there is little to indicate that this is the contemporary world. This turns out to be the Bosporus cymbal factory in Turkey, where traditional production methods are used to handcraft high-quality and much-prized cymbals. Here there is no factory division of labor—several men sit together in a room hammering cymbals by hand. The sound of all this hammering is extremely loud, and although words are spoken, an English-speaking audience cannot understand them. A great deal of time and care are devoted to the creation of these cymbals, but still the film avoids fetishizing the final product, instead focusing on the process of production and the experience of labor (this is how it looks, this is how it sounds; Figure 35.6).

By now, because the viewer has watched two other examples of contemporary labor, the comparisons and contrasts begin to pile up. All three kinds of labor involve production, but only the clock-making and the cymbal-making are divided into discrete

FIGURE 35.6 *The Unstable Object* (Daniel Eisenberg, 2011). Image courtesy of Daniel Eisenberg.

repetitive tasks. None of the workers appear to be in exploitative labor situations, but our knowledge about them is limited to what we can see. Cymbal-making appears to be the most hazardous process, due to the hot metal that is poured into molds. Everyone in each factory has been trained, and, for the most part, they go about their work silently. In taking such a contemplative tone, the film forces the viewer to fall back on his or her own thoughts, just as Sharon Lockhart's *Exit* does. Ending in a traditional factory that uses production processes that have been unchanged for hundreds of years, *The Unstable Object* concludes on a note of departure. If labor used to look like this, and still does now in some places, might the future of labor look different, less bleak than one imagines it now?

These recent works of experimental nonfiction witness the state of labor today by using various open-ended observational styles and techniques. These films demand attentive viewers who are ready to meet the contemplative challenge they present. In particular, these films utilize the classical technique of the long take, not to create a more believable representation of reality but to gesture toward the larger realities that reside off-screen. Long takes in these films are not more "real" but more partial and contingent. Perhaps the long take in the digital era can be understood as a particular kind of counterpresence, a new kind of negative space whose representation evokes everything surrounding it that remains unseen. In the spirit of witnessing, these films make labor visible, but not necessarily knowable.

ACKNOWLEDGMENTS

I would like to thank Jeanne Liotta and David Gatten for film suggestions that helped shape this article. Thanks also to Daniel Eisenberg for making the complete version of *The Unstable Object* available to me, and to all of the filmmakers for generously providing images of their work. This essay is for L. P., who happily retired his lunchbox four years ago.

NOTES

1. See Fredric Jameson's account of this historical shift in "Culture and Finance Capital," *Critical Inquiry* 24 (Autumn 1997): 246–265.
2. Although the films I analyze closely in this article do not fictionalize, it should be said that some of the other titles I cite do utilize scripted elements. Staging has become an important strategy of contemporary documentary, which often self-consciously blurs boundaries between fiction and nonfiction. Indeed, the tradition of staging in nonfiction goes back to Robert Flaherty's 1922 film *Nanook of the North,* and even before. There is a great deal of scholarship on staging and the construction of truth in documentary film; a good place to begin reading is Alexandra Juhasz and Jesse Lerner, eds., *F Is for Phony: Fake Documentary and Truth's Undoing* (Minneapolis: University of Minnesota Press, 2006).

3. There are numerous other examples of recent experimental nonfiction films about labor, including additional titles by a number of the filmmakers I have already cited. See for example the list of films tagged "labor" distributed by Video Data Bank at www.vdb.org/category/tags/labor.

4. Kelly Oliver, *Witnessing: Beyond Recognition* (Minneapolis: University of Minnesota Press, 2001), 16.

5. Jane Blocker, *Seeing Witness: Visuality and the Ethics of Testimony* (Minneapolis: University of Minnesota Press, 2009), 32.

6. The 47-second version with horse-and-carriage can be viewed here: www.youtube.com/watch?v=HI63PUXnVMw. The 40-second "no-horse" version can be viewed here: www.youtube.com/watch?v=LnVwgLORy2Y. For what it's worth, this is not actually "the first film," as is often claimed. Although I believe it is important to avoid the rhetoric of "firsts," we might still note that at least two other projected film shows occurred before the Lumière *cinématographe* debuted in December 1895 (the Phantoscope in Atlanta in September and the Bioskop in Berlin in November); moreover, it is worth emphasizing that early cinema historians today refer to a gradual "emergence" of cinema through a series of overlapping practices (fast motion photography, peephole viewers, magic lantern lectures, vaudeville) rather than a single invention that sprang forth full-born.

7. Sean Cubitt, *The Cinema Effect* (Cambridge, MA: MIT Press, 2004), 20.

8. On early travelogues and other nonfiction genres, see Jennifer Lynn Peterson, *Education in the School of Dreams: Travelogues and Early Nonfiction Film* (Durham, NC: Duke University Press, 2013).

9. For a fuller description of the industrial film genre in early cinema, see Jennifer Peterson, "industrial films," in *The Encyclopedia of Early Cinema*, ed. Richard Abel (New York: Routledge, 2005), 320–323.

10. On the Ford Motor Company films, see Lee Greiveson, "The Work of Film in the Age of Fordist Mechanization," *Cinema Journal* 51, no. 3 (Spring 2012): 25–51.

11. On the Westinghouse Works films, see Oliver Gaycken, "The Cinema of the Future: Visions of the Medium as a Modern Educator, 1895–1910," in Devin Orgeron, Marsha Orgeron, and Dan Streible, eds., *Learning with the Lights Off: Educational Film in the United States* (New York: Oxford University Press, 2012), 67–89. A link to the 1904 Westinghouse Works Films can be found here: http://memory.loc.gov/ammem/papr/west/westhome.html. A synopsis of the film *A Visit to Peek Frean and Co.'s Biscuit Works* (1906) can be found here, along with a link for viewing if one is in the United Kingdom at a registered library, college, or university: www.screenonline.org.uk/film/id/711535/index.html. A shorter version of this film is available in the United States on volume 3 of the DVD box set, *The Movies Begin: A Treasury of Early Cinema, 1894–1913*. The *Fish Processing Factory at Astrakhan* (1908) can be viewed here: www.europafilmtreasures.eu/PY/291/see-the-film-the_fish_processing_factory_at_astrakhan.

12. Jennifer Peterson, "Efficiency and Abundance: Industrial Films and Early Educational Cinema" (paper delivered at the Society for Cinema and Media Studies conference, New Orleans, March 12, 2011).

13. See Vinzenz Hediger and Patrick Vonderau, eds., *Films that Work: Industrial Film and the Productivity of Media* (Amsterdam: Amsterdam University Press, 2009); and Rick Prelinger, *The Field Guide to Sponsored Films* (San Francisco: National Film Preservation Foundation, 2006). On nontheatrical films more generally, see Charles R. Acland and Haidee Wasson, eds., *Useful Cinema* (Durham, NC: Duke University Press, 2011); and

Orgeron, et al,, *Learning with the Lights Off.* Many historical industrial films have lately been made available online; for a virtuosic example, see *Master Hands,* made by the Jam Handy Organization for the Chevrolet Motor Company in 1936, available at www.archive. org/details/MasterHa1936.

14. These remakes are not to be confused with the *hommages* produced by various acclaimed directors for the 1995 film *Lumière and Company.*

15. Harun Farocki, "Workers Leaving the Factory," trans. Laurent Faasch-Ibrahim, in Thomas Elsaesser, ed., *Harun Farocki: Working on the Sightlines* (Amsterdam: Amsterdam University Press, 2004), 238; originally published as "Arbeiter verlassen die Fabrik," in *Meteor* (Vienna) no. 1 (December 1995): 49–55.

16. Nancy Davenport's DVD installation *WORKERS (Leaving the Factory)* (2005–08) is another important example, but unfortunately I have not been able to see this work in person; for a well-illustrated analysis, see Ingrid Hölzl, "Blast-Off Photography: Nancy Davenport and Expanded Photography," *History of Photography* 35:1 (February 2011), pp. 33–43. Other *Workers* "remakes" are embedded into longer works, such as Daniel Eisenberg's *Something More Than Night* (2003) and Peter Hutton's *At Sea* (2007). Another (less meticulous) example of a *Workers* remake is *Workers Leaving the Googleplex* (Andrew Norman Wilson, 2011), which can be viewed at http://vimeo.com/15852288. Finally, I can't resist mentioning Martin Scorsese's *Workers* homage in his 1985 black comedy *After Hours,* which occurs at the beginning of the film when the main character, played by Griffin Dunne, leaves his job as a word processor, exiting the building in a shot that directly quotes the Lumière film.

17. *Workers Leaving the Factory (Dubai)* can be viewed at http://vimeo.com/7528954.

18. Bazin's theory—that spatial and temporal continuity (particularly when rendered by a long take and in real time) produce realism in the cinema—has been subject to much reassessment lately. See, for example, Phil Rosen, *Change Mummified: Cinema, Historicity, Theory* (Minneapolis: University of Minnesota Press, 2001), esp. 3–41; Daniel Morgan, "Rethinking Bazin: Ontology and Realist Aesthetics," *Critical Inquiry* 32, no. 3 (Spring 2006): 443–481; Tom Gunning, "Moving Away from the Index: Cinema and the Impression of Reality," *differences* 18, no. 1 (2007): 29–52; Dudley Andrew, *What Cinema Is! Bazin's Quest and Its Charge* (Chichester, West Sussex: Wiley-Blackwell, 2010); Dudley Andrew, ed., *Opening Bazin: Postwar Film Theory and Its Afterlife* (New York: Oxford University Press, 2011).

19. Lev Manovich, *The Language of New Media* (Cambridge, MA: MIT Press, 2001).

20. San Francisco Museum of Modern Art, "SFMOMA Presents Lunch Break by Sharon Lockhart." August 30, 2011, www.sfmoma.org/about/press/press_exhibitions/releases/891.

21. *Lunch Break,* an exhibition of twenty-seven photographs and two films, debuted in the United States in November 2009 at Blum & Poe gallery in Los Angeles, and has since shown at numerous other museums and art spaces, including the San Francisco Museum of Modern Art. The films have also been shown separately from the photographs at theaters such as the Harvard Film Archive and the REDCAT Theater in Los Angeles. Needless to say, the experience of *Exit* is entirely different if one views it in an art gallery (where the viewer can walk in and out of the viewing space) or a movie theater (where one sits immobile for the duration)…or online. *Exit* can be viewed in its entirety at UbuWeb: www.ubu.com/film/lockhart_exit.html.

22. Norman Bryson, "Sharon Lockhart: From Form to Flux," *Parachute* no. 103 (July 1, 2001), 88.

23. Bryson, "Sharon Lockhart," 89.

24. In an online interview about the film, Paravel says that her nickname in the neighborhood was "la mamacita con la película," (the hottie with the movie). This interview can be viewed at www.youtube.com/watch?v=pOk6sUVvzO4.

25. David Harvey, *Spaces of Global Capitalism: Towards a Theory of Uneven Geographical Development* (London: Verso, 2006), 77.

26. For analysis of Eisenberg's earlier body of work, see the essays in Jeffrey Skoller, ed., *Postwar: The Films of Daniel Eisenberg* (London: Black Dog Publishing, 2010).

27. See screening notes at www.filmlinc.com/pages/the-unstable-object.

28. Frank Markus, "VW's Transparent Factory," *Car and Driver*, September 2003, www.caranddriver.com/features/vws-transparent-factory.

SELECT BIBLIOGRAPHY

Blocker, Jane. *Seeing Witness: Visuality and the Ethics of Testimony*. Minneapolis: University of Minnesota Press, 2009.

Bryson, Norman. "Sharon Lockhart: From Form to Flux." *Parachute* 103 (July 1, 2001): 86–107.

Cubitt, Sean. *The Cinema Effect*. Cambridge, MA: MIT Press, 2004.

Farocki, Harun. "Workers Leaving the Factory." Translated by Laurent Faasch-Ibrahim. In *Harun Farocki: Working on the Sightlines*. Edited by Thomas Elsaesser, 49–55. Amsterdam: Amsterdam University Press, 2004. Original work published as "Arbeiter verlassen die Fabrik." *Meteor* no. 1 (December 1995).

Harvey, David. *Spaces of Global Capitalism: Towards a Theory of Uneven Geographical Development*. London: Verso, 2006.

Hediger, Vinzenz, and Patrick Vonderau, eds. *Films that Work: Industrial Film and the Productivity of Media*. Amsterdam: Amsterdam University Press, 2009.

Manovich, Lev. *The Language of New Media*. Cambridge, MA: MIT Press, 2001.

Oliver, Kelly. *Witnessing: Beyond Recognition*. Minneapolis: University of Minnesota Press, 2001.

Peterson, Jennifer. "Industrial films." In *The Encyclopedia of Early Cinema*, edited by Richard Abel, 320–323. New York: Routledge, 2005.

Skoller, Jeffrey, ed. *Postwar: The Films of Daniel Eisenberg*. London: Black Dog Publishing, 2010.

PART XI

MODES OF COMPOSITION: DIGITAL CONVERGENCE AND SOUND PRODUCTION

CHAPTER 36

THE ABSENT IMAGE IN ELECTRONIC MUSIC

ERIC LYON

IN 1877, Thomas Edison's phonograph introduced a new kind of audio media consumption in which a geographically distributed audience could listen to sounds and music without any visual indicators of how they were produced. The phonograph's severing of sound from image inspired sustained artistic research throughout much of the twentieth century and continues to inform artistic practices. Today's mediated world is largely audiovisual. However, in this essay, we lean toward the sonic side, treating electronic and digital music as a launch pad for new and emerging relationships between sound and image. In the post-World War II period, studio-based composers of electronic music exploited the separation of aural and visual media to investigate the phenomenology of sound, which we refer to here as *aurality*. The advent of the digital since the late 1950s facilitated unprecedented fluidity between sound and image, which can now be treated as pure information; the perceptual modalities differ, but, from the computer's perspective, it's all just ones and zeros. Our story begins with the loss of traditional sound–image relationships, continuing with the radical reconfiguration of music as electronic sound art, and finally exploring recent art forms in which image and sound pose new questions for each other.

LOSS OF THE IMAGE IN CLASSICAL MUSIC

In the common practice of European classical music, composition and performance are tightly bound to a visual object—the score—which arranges visual symbols that encode musical structure. Because this notation predates the invention of sound recording, the symbols primarily capture perceptual abstractions of sound events and their ordering in time: pitch, loudness, relative onset time, and duration. The emphasis on abstraction in this notational system has shaped the kinds of music that composers write with it, generally favoring quantized structures based on pitch and time grids. Once internalized by composers, the common practice notation system makes the creation of classical music a visual-sonic process.

In the performance of classical music, the audience receives a different, but equally important set of visual cues: the spectacle of musicians creating sounds with their bodily movements as they interact with their instruments and with each other. The abstractions of the musical score are "made flesh" as sounds are visually bound to specific physical gestures performed by the musicians. The performer is the key actor at the center of this visual transduction, taking in the visual stimuli of the score and producing a new set of visual stimuli with the physical actions of a musical performance.

"Tape music," an important subgenre of electronic music, eliminates the performer, thereby obviating the need for a score and removing all visual cues of performance. The anachronistic term "tape music" refers to electronic music that is stored, then later played back from a fixed medium. This was originally magnetic tape, but, more recently, "tape music" is stored on compact disk, DVD, or hard drive. The absence of traditional visual elements in tape music has produced both anxiety and enthusiasm. When tape music is performed in a traditional concert hall setting, the audience has nothing to look at except for loudspeakers, and there is no way to guess from watching a loudspeaker what sounds will emerge from it next.

The common practice of playing back tape music into a darkened room implicitly acknowledges that there's not much to see at tape music concerts. For commentators such as Pierre Boulez, this is a serious problem. "I, personally, have never been much of a believer in taped music played in a concert all. I have always been painfully embarrassed by the resemblance to a crematorium ceremony, and found the absence of *action* a redhibitory vice. Playing a tape where people are walking about, or for a small group of professionals, is a quite different matter. But for a larger audience—let alone huge crowds—it is a very lame, one-sided affair with nothing visual to correspond to what is heard."[1] Boulez's critique focuses on what is missing, rather than considering any new experiential possibilities inherent in the concert presentation of tape music. By contrast, Karlheinz Stockhausen focuses on these new possibilities. "I will always tell the audience...I have had a little spotlight installed, like a moon, for those who are afraid of the dark. But I still request that you close your eyes and remember that your very own, wonderful inner world opens up. And identifying with your eyes is not that important in music. Music is the opening of an inner world. And we are spirits, it is not necessary for us to lay our hands on it or open our eyes to check on it. The year 1953 brought such radical renewal, that we have no language to describe the sounds that have been made possible since then."[2] Stockhausen's mention of the year 1953 doubtless refers to the composition of his *Studie I*, a pioneering tape piece in which all sounds were painstakingly constructed from sine waves. A sine wave is the simplest possible sound, and Stockhausen's compositional system, in which more complex timbres were designed "from the ground up" by summing sine waves in various proportions, constitutes a genuinely new way of thinking about music that would have been impossible in the absence of tape recording technology.

ELECTRONIC MUSIC ABSENT THE IMAGE

The absence of visual imagery in early tape music invited a greater concentration on the phenomenological experience of raw sound. Much of the groundwork for this approach was developed by Pierre Schaeffer, working at Radiodiffusion-Télévision Française (RTF), both with the establishment of *musique concrète* and through the theoretical writings in his "Traité des Objets Musicaux."[3] Schaeffer developed three concepts that have remained central to European tape music: the sound object (*l'objet sonore*), reduced listening, and acousmatic music. Visual imagery is notably absent from each of these concepts. A sound object is a recorded sound that may be repeatedly experienced without change to its internal structure. The repeatability of the sound object offers up microdetails that could never be repeated in live acoustic performance. When a chord is played repeatedly on the piano, the complex acoustical systems involved assure that each successive chord will sound subtly different from the last one. Recording technology is therefore a prerequisite for the sound object. Schaeffer's notion of the sound object depends on the practice of "reduced listening," in which a sound is considered exclusively in terms of its intrinsic acoustic properties and with a deliberate disregard for its origin and the circumstances of its production. The concept of reduced listening may seem impractical—it is very difficult to divorce the sound of a car crash from a visual mental image of the crash. But the degree to which reduced listening can be put into effect is much less important than the intent of the practice. The twofold goal of reduced listening is to focus the listener on the aurality of the sound and to finally divorce the sound from its associated image. And, although reduced listening may be difficult, it is not impossible. A group of words spoken aloud repeatedly can become a nonreferential sound in the listener's mind, divorced from the semantic meaning of the phrase, in a psychological effect known as "semantic satiation." This effect manifests itself in Steve Reich's 1966 tape piece *Come Out*[4] in which the semantic meaning of the spoken phrase "come out to show them" gradually erodes in favor of musical effects, notably the composing out of a minor third and the increasingly complex phase relations among multiple overdubbed layers of the speech. And a car crash in the right context might come to seem as musically logical as a Mozartian V-I cadence. Indeed, Gordon Mumma's 1980 tape piece *Cirqualz*[5] accomplishes precisely that result with a combination of local and formal contextualization and canny mixing technique. The work is packed full of samples produced by a prodigious amount of tape splicing of sounds taken from vinyl recordings. *Cirqualz* begins with a spoken word sample from Leonard Bernstein's 1966 lecture on Beethoven's *Eroica Symphony*, "we begin at the beginning with those two whiplashes of sound that shattered the elegant formality of the 18th century."[6] Mumma allows Bernstein's lecture to continue at length to just the moment when he would have played the two opening E-flat chords on piano, at which point Mumma swaps in a pair of E-flat "stingers" sampled from a recording of circus music screamers. The musical irony is that a stinger is a cadence, a musical ending; Mumma shows here how endings and beginnings can be made interchangeable. At the same time, by taking the stinger out of context, Mumma turns it into a sound object. A cadence is a syntactically charged moment in tonal music that derives its meaning from what precedes it. Taken out of context, a cadence becomes literally meaningless. Mumma, a classically trained composer, fully understands and exploits this situation to create new contexts and meanings for the many deracinated stingers that populate the remainder of *Cirqualz*. A combination of tonal musical samples and noise-like sounds throughout the piece prepares us for Mumma's final trick. The final passage of a screamer leads to a V-I cadence in E-flat, but superimposed on the V chord is a slow-motion car crash that continues beyond the tonal cadence to bring the piece to its final resting place. Pitch elements in the car crash sample harmonize closely enough with the cadence to make the mixture of the two improbably linked sounds completely convincing. The rude use of stingers throughout *Cirqualz* suggests that an abrupt cadence might function metaphorically as a musical car crash. The final ending demonstrates that a tonal cadence and car crash can literally serve the same musical purpose, simultaneously. The semantic overloading of that final car crash gives the listener so much to think about from a purely aural standpoint that a literal-minded visualization of a car crash becomes completely unnecessary to the aesthetic enjoyment of the moment. Of course, the extent to which reduced listening is actually achieved depends on the individual listener, but Mumma's witty cadence makes a very strong case for the viability of reduced listening in electronic music.

Hearing Without Seeing

The third Schaefferian concept is the acousmatic, the sound that one hears without seeing the causes behind it. Schaeffer borrowed the term from Pythagoras's practice of lecturing from behind a screen, so that students would focus on the meaning of his words without being distracted by his physical presence. The acousmatic concept has been embraced in a genre of electronic music referred to as "acousmatic music," in which the source of sounds is deliberately kept from the listener.[7] Although acousmatic composers are often interested in a break from real-world sonic causality, they are also interested in the construction of internal causality based on perceptual attributes of the acousmatic sound. Denis Smalley, extrapolating from Schaeffer's acousmatic proposition, developed the idea of musical structuring through spectromorphology. Spectromorphology is an approach to sound that focuses on the evolution of its spectrum in time. It is intended to intensify aurality in both listening and composition. In setting out the axioms of his theory, Smalley states, "Listeners can only apprehend music if they discover a perceptual affinity with its materials and structure. Such an affinity depends on the partnership between composer and listener mediated by aural perception. Today we continually need to assert the primacy of aural experience in music."[8] Smalley's theory of spectromorphology remains influential for several subgenres of electroacoustic music. It is notable that the theory so adamantly asserts the primacy of aurality. For Smalley, aurality is counterpoised, not to the visual, but to what he considers an overly conceptual approach to composition in which the sounds are manipulated without concern for their perceptual attributes. However, once aurality is asserted, any reference to visual attributes or perception is studiously avoided. Music composed according to spectromorphological principles is understood to be fully apprehensible through the agency of the ears. As a fitting successor to Schaeffer's theories, spectromorphology keeps the visual at a distance in order to situate investigation of sonic experience at the center of electronic music composition.

MUSIQUE CONCRÈTE: THE ABSTRACT BECOMES CONCRETE

Pierre Schaeffer aptly named the genre of his early electronic compositions *musique concrète*. In classical music, musical structure comes into focus through the relations among sonic abstractions organized within the complex hierarchies of tonal music; in *musique concrète*, the sound object in all its perceptual richness and complexity emerges as the central musical fact. Of course, the two approaches are not completely opposed. Classical instrumental music has its sonically sensuous aspect, explored in depth through the art of orchestration. And *musique concrète* employs a grammar of sorts regarding the combination of sound objects, particularly in the subgenre of acousmatic music. But, despite these overlapped concerns, the turn toward *musique concrète* involves a fundamental shift of emphasis from sonic abstraction to phenomenological perception of the sound object. Through this shift of emphasis, the potential palette of musical sound expands considerably. Early *musique concrète* compositions of Schaeffer incorporate familiar sounds from daily life, such as train sounds and speech, sounds that would not have previously been considered inherently musical. By contrast, the sounds of classical music—violins, flutes, timpani, and the like—are almost always culturally encoded as music-related. On hearing a violin outside the concert hall (say, in a subway station), most people are still inclined to think of the violin's sound as music. The same could not be said of environmental sounds such as speech, train whistles, or bird song.

The incorporation of recognizable recorded sounds in *musique concrète* reverses a general tendency toward abstraction in twentieth-century modernist art forms. With the advent of photography, painting moved toward increasing abstraction, culminating in the 1940s work of abstract expressionists such as Mark Rothko and Jackson Pollock. Writing became increasingly concerned with word play, stream of consciousness, and other formal experiments in the work of authors such as James Joyce and Virginia Woolf and in the noise poetry of the futurists. Film moved toward the abstract and away from conventional narrative in the work of artists such as Oskar Fischinger and Stan Brakhage, as well as that of earlier surrealists filmmakers such as Luis Buñuel in his famed 1929 film *Un Chien Andalou*,[9] produced in collaboration with Salvador Dali. Instrumental music also moved toward the abstract as Arnold Schoenberg's 12-tone method melted down fully formed melodies into an abstract pitch-class series, a kind of musical stem cell, which could then be formed into any number of derived musical objects. The relations among musical objects derived from a 12-tone series are often quite difficult for nonspecialist listeners to comprehend, when compared to motivic transformations in the music of Beethoven and Brahms.

THE SCORE REVISITED

Despite the absence of the performer in tape music, the score returned rather quickly. In some cases, the score was a sketch of the intended timeline of events, as in Edgard Varèse's work score to *Poème Électronique* (see Figure 36.1). Such scores, however, were intended primarily for the composer and any technical assistants and were not for use in the performance of the work. (Later, spatial diffusion performers would sometimes prepare diffusion scores for themselves, informing performances that are essentially interpretations of the composer's work.) Karlheinz Stockhausen's score for his *Studie II* is an important early example of a score that specifies both musical structure and production techniques with sufficient detail to be re-created (see Figure 36.2). In addition to

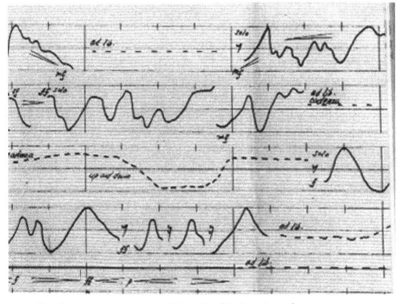

FIGURE 36.1 Sketch score excerpt from Edgard Varèse's *Poème Électronique*.

Studie II   Stockhausen

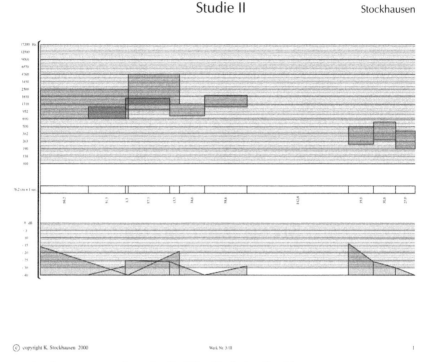

FIGURE 36.2 Score excerpt from *Studie II* by Karlheinz Stockhausen.

providing precise details on frequency content, timing, and duration of each tone mixture, the score provides precise guidelines on how to produce the desired stochastic timbral properties with tape splicing and reverberation. It is notable that the score to *Studie
II* provides exclusively detailed information for recreating the sound objects in the piece.
Interpretive performance guidance is completely absent, despite Stockhausen's observation that the piece was "performed" in the studio by Stockhausen and his engineering
assistants.[10]

   It is appropriate that the most detailed early electronic music score was produced by a
member of the *elektronische musik* school and not that of *musique concrète*. *Elektronische
musik* practice derives in large part from serialism, an instrumental conception at its
core. Serialism is a combinatorial calculus of musically abstract properties. At its outset,
in Arnold Schoenberg's 12-tone method, serial transformations were applied exclusively
in the pitch class domain. In the post-World War II era, the practice of integral serialism
organized dynamics, rhythm, timbre, and other elements as well. The serial principle is
extended in Stockhausen's electronic *Studien* to affect elements such as envelope shape
and reverberation patterns. Major post-World War II serialists such as Stockhausen,
Boulez, and Berio were all actively engaged in creating both electroacoustic music and
scored instrumental music. By contrast, Pierre Schaeffer and his collaborator Pierre
Henry were focused primarily on producing electroacoustic music.

RETURN OF THE IMAGE IN ELECTRONIC MUSIC

The previous examples have considered the heightened emphasis on aurality in elec-troacoustic music, explored with particular intensity in the "tape music" medium and extensively theorized by Pierre Schaeffer and the *musique concrète* group since the late 1940s. We now turn to examples of mixed-media work in which the image returns to occupy new relationships with sonic elements of the work.

NONCAUSAL AGGREGATIONS OF ELECTRONIC MUSIC AND IMAGE

A particular strain of multimedia work followed John Cage's ideas on indeterminacy.[11] John Cage's partner, choreographer Merce Cunningham, very often employed inde-terminacy in the creation of his dance pieces. In most cases, the accompanying elec-tronic music was improvised live, and often the dance incorporated a significant degree of improvisation as well. With no predetermined structure for either dance or music, the sound–visual mixture that evolved in performance would often be significantly uncorrelated.

A superposition of work in different media was characteristic of multimedia per-formances given at the ONCE Festival in Ann Arbor, Michigan, during the 1960s.[12] A similar intersection of media was pursued by FLUXUS, also in the 1960s, dubbed "intermedia" by Dick Higgins.[13] Sal Martirano's provocative 1968 intermedia work *L's GA*[14] incorporated taped music, films, and a live performer speaking through a gas mask.

FUSED AUDIO-VISUAL COMPOSITIONS

A nearly opposite situation obtains in the process called *sonification*, which is a special kind of articulation of visual (or visualized) data in sound. Sonification was originally intended for scientific purposes, to enable researchers to detect patterns aurally with much greater ease than they could by scanning the data. The Geiger counter, invented in 1908, is considered one of the earliest forms of sonification, converting ionizing radiation into audible clicks. More recently, data analysis was replaced with purely aesthetic applications of the technique, in which data is rendered as both digital video and audio. When combined, each modality represents the same underlying dataset, and thus audio and video can be maximally correlated (although how well this works in practice depends on the skill of the sound designer). In the case of seismic events, such as earthquakes, the waveform of the event can be sped up into the audio range, in a literal-minded but highly effective sonification. A sonification of the Tohoku earthquake is currently available online.[15] Sonification of live nonaudio performance events occurs in two of Alvin Lucier's compositions, *Music for a Solo Performer*,[16] composed in 1965, in which the strength of alpha waves in the performer's electroencephalogram (EEG) corresponds to increasing amounts of mechanical energy sent to speakers, which then excite percussive instruments. As the performer becomes more relaxed, more acoustic sound is released into the space. In Lucier's *Vespers*,[17] from 1968, blindfolded performers navigate their space using echolocation devices (similar to the way a bat hears) that emit audible clicks that occur closer together as the wearer comes closer to another object.

Visually Prominent Live Manipulation of Electronic Sound

A shopworn criticism of laptop performance of computer music asserts that the performer's actions are almost entirely unseen, leaving the audience unable to determine if the performer is actively creating the music or rather playing back a digital audio file while checking e-mail to keep busy. This paucity of visual information creates a different problem for live electronic music than for tape music, with its complete absence of observable performers. The laptop musician, by contrast, invites visual observation of a performance that could present a frustratingly parsimonious set of visual cues for the audience.

It might appear that a similar situation obtains for audience members watching a concert pianist while seated opposite the performer, such that they are not able to observe the pianist's hands. For such listeners, the only visual performance cues are projected from the upper arms, shoulder, and head. However, despite this visual limitation, listeners bring with them a culturally acquired model of the relation between physical actions by the pianist and the sounds thereby produced. Faster, larger arm gestures produce loud sounds, compared to delicate motions mainly coming from the wrist. Keys struck toward the upper end of the piano keyboard produce high-pitched sounds, and toward the lower end, low-pitched sounds. This internal model allows the audience to empathize with the performer and to understand when the performer is playing a difficult passage, even when they do not have a full view of the performer's hands. John Cage's invention of the prepared piano sharply undercuts this model. On a prepared piano, objects placed on or between the piano strings radically alter the resulting sound, such that there is often scant correlation between the physical location of a piano key and the perceived pitch of its struck tone. But even for the prepared piano, there is still a directly observable cause and effect between striking a key and reliably producing *some* sound in response to the performer's actions.

For laptop music, by contrast, there is no inherent relationship between the manipulation of the computer keyboard interface and the production of the resulting sound, which is entirely dependent on the audio software configuration employed. The obvious remedy to this situation is to develop physical controllers for the computer that can result in audience-observable performance gestures. Since 2001, the New Interfaces for Musical Expression (NIME) conference has brought together researchers who have addressed this problem by developing an astounding variety of interfaces to control digital sound synthesis on computers. Given the focus on expression, it is important that the control aspect of NIME interfaces designed for human performance should be readily apparent to the audience. Often, the novelty of the interface contributes strongly to any performance that utilizes it. A good example of this is Eric Singer's Sonic Banana,[18] a rubber tube which is flexed to control musical textures synthesized in the digital media language Max/MSP. Although NIME interfaces often solve the problem of the disconnect between the audio and visual aspects of laptop performance, in many cases, they also restore the *status quo ante* by developing new musical instruments that aspire to many of the same performance criteria as established acoustic instruments. Simply put, these instruments are then used to perform compositions in a traditional concert setting. We now venture beyond that setting.

Sound Without Hearing

Performance artist Christine Sun Kim returns the image to electronic sound in a manner that, in a certain sense, mirrors the practice of tape music. As a deaf artist concerned with sonic phenomena, Kim reclaims sound in the sensory domains available to her, primarily the visual and the tactile. Kim's performances involve the production of sound, in which the sound is an artifact of her physical gestures. String, pigment powder, paint, microphones, speakers, and other objects are used to render sound vibrations visible, sometimes as transient observable motions, and sometimes as a mechanism for leaving a permanent visual trace, as in her seismic calligraphy. Whereas many electronic musicians, particularly acousmatic composers, feel the need to make a case for aurality in the face of the apparent cultural domination of the image, Kim is ideally situated to investigate sound from the opposite perspective. She states, "I'm seeking a way to rearrange the hierarchy of information, remove language constraints, and place value on non-linearity and spatiality. It's also about the ownership of sound; I'm reclaiming sound as my property and challenging its orthodoxy."[19] As she points out, "There are social norms surrounding sound that form our speech development and our way of handling sound with care. They're so deeply ingrained that, in a sense, our identities cannot be complete without sound."[20] For Kim, it is the perception of sound itself that is absent from sound; aural sound is of necessity replaced by tactile sound and visual sound. Just as tape music calls attention to the aurality of sound by separating sound from its image, Kim's artistic practice encourages non-deaf listeners to separate the phenomenon of sound vibration from their perception of it.

NONCAUSAL MUSICAL GESTURES

Mark Applebaum's 2010 composition *Aphasia*[21] develops the deliberately absurd premise of reinstating a sonically superfluous performer to a tape piece. The composition is assembled from a large sound library of vocalizations recorded by Nicholas Isherwood under the direction of the composer. The tape piece comprises predominantly isolated sonic gestures that would lend themselves quite well to the acousmatic performance practice of diffusion. However, rather than adopt a diffusion strategy to spatially enhance the gestural content, the work is played back in stereo and is augmented with the visual presence of a "mute singer" who performs physical gestures precisely correlated to the sounds on the tape.

The piece is, in the first instance, very funny. Many of the gestures, although apparently causal, also appear to mock their corresponding sounds, such as an *en garde* gesture to accompany a barely plausible sound effect for a sword thrust, or a swiping motion to accompany a sensitive reverb tail. While enacting the gestures, the performer's face is completely devoid of emotion. Given the manifest absurdity of the musical framework, this lack of affect easily reads as the deadpan delivery of standup comedy. More darkly, the lack of affect suggests the presence of anhedonia—the inability of the performer to enjoy the absurdity of the musical gestures that he enacts. The lack of facial involvement underscores a more literal separation: with all vocal activity relegated to the recording, the performer is stripped of his natural voice.

The performer's gestures inhabit a world of fictional causality, in which each gesture appears as a hypothetical instigator or enactor of its corresponding sound on tape. The gestures are detailed in a musical score with obsessive precision (see Figure 36.3). The performer "sings" with the utmost seriousness, as if responsible for the precise temporal placement of each sound. The performer appears utterly convinced that he controls the sound, although it is equally clear to the audience that the performer controls nothing. Instead, the performer exercises the virtuosity of his ability to enact the illusion of control, and this is the pathos of the piece.

The performer is a forlorn figure who is physically present, yet absent of agency. He must enact a strenuous, technically difficult part while completely unable to affect the predetermined sonic outcome in any way. The ending of the piece is particularly poignant, as the expressive vocabulary of the performer is reduced to a single hand gesture (the American Sign Language sign for "finished") gradually diminishing in intensity and only responding to the spoken word on tape "one." An increasingly dense montage of number-based vocal sounds on the tape remains unanswered by the performer, who finally abandons all physical motion and sits impassively through the remaining seconds of the composition. The performer reminds us that even doing nothing is a gesture of sorts. The tape part tapers to a gradually slowing spoken count—97…98…99…and then, silence. As in an earlier Applebaum work, *Pre-Composition*, the final goal of the piece is clearly telegraphed, only to be thwarted at the last minute, thereby revealing the genial sense of tragedy that underlies the surface comedy of the project.

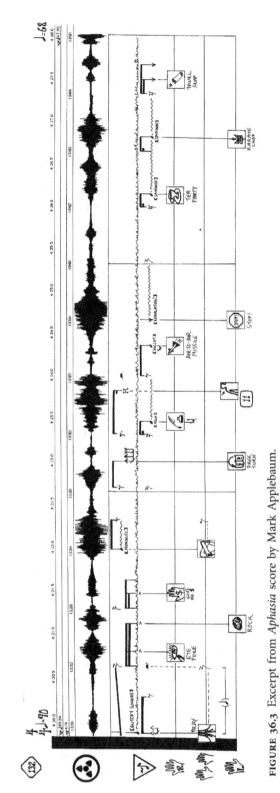

FIGURE 36.3 Excerpt from *Aphasia* score by Mark Applebaum.

Music Guided by the Unseen Image

Having considered new performance relationships between the aural and the visual that have emerged since the advent of sound recording, we now turn to cases in which image functions as an audio generator, one that is not intended to be seen.

Visual Music

The term "visual music," coined by Roger Fry in 1912, originally referred to visual artwork that imported concepts of musical structure, with Wassily Kandinsky an early proponent of applying musical concepts to painting.[22] Visual music later was adopted by early abstract filmmakers, such as Oskar Fischinger, whose *Allegretto*[23] of 1936 imports musical notions to the structuring of abstract video imagery. In Fischinger's *Allegretto*, the film closely follows a big band jazz instrumental score by Ralph Rainger. In addition to following the score with rhythmic precision, matching a recurring repeated three-note motif with an analogous visual articulation, the tonal characteristics of solo instruments such as piano, clarinet, and muted trumpet are matched to expressive geometrical shapes on the film. A recurrent background image of intersecting circular waves suggests the acoustic counterpoint of sound waves.

Drawn Sound

A more mechanical application of the concept of visual music reverses the flow of information, creating sound by means of drawn images. The earliest applications were in film, in which patterns were drawn directly onto the optical sound track of a film by such artists as Arseny Avraamov and Norman McLaren. Although the graphical layout of the optical track allowed for rather precise rhythmic and even pitch specification, in a painstaking process (see for example, McLaren's film *Neighbors*), the ability to affect timbre is extremely limited, since the optical sound track is a time-domain representation of the sound. A much more flexible use of the visual for the creation of electronic music, the UPIC system, was developed by Iannis Xenakis in the 1970s.[24] Composers work in UPIC by describing basic waveforms either through their harmonic weights or by drawing the waveform directly, and then sketching the form of the piece with a light pen. Thus, UPIC is a mechanism for directly creating a graphical score that is then realized by the computer in sound. Its layout is similar in graphical mapping to a spectrogram, a visual representation of sound, which corresponds somewhat to human hearing cognition, or at least more so than a graph of a sound pressure wave. The palette of waveforms (static timbres) makes explicit the connection to a painting program. Through the ability to zoom in to the details of a waveform or out to display the entire form of a composition, UPIC captures the basic principles of a traditional score.

Digital Image to Sound

In the early 1990s, Christopher Penrose developed Hyperupic,[25] a software application that powerfully updates UPIC. Hyperupic transduces a TIFF image to sound by
mapping pixel color and intensity to the weighting of particular grains. The algorithmic nature of the synthesis allows for multiple sonic realizations of the same image.
Since any TIFF image may be used as input to Hyperupic, line drawings may be transformed, but, unlike the original UPIC system, scanned photos and paintings can be
transduced as well. Penrose details this in his notes to the 1992 version of the program: "*Hyperupic* is an image to sound transducer implemented on a NeXT workstation. That's right, with *Hyperupic* you might be able to *hear Whistler's mother.*
I think that he did all the whistling, actually. Meanwhile, you need to know that this
implementation of *Hyperupic* only accepts 24-bit RGB TIFF images as transduction
sources. Now don't turn blue. You can still scribble with Icon, save the masterwork as
a 24-bit alpha-free image (even with JPEG compression if you like!) and *Hyperupic*
will transform the image into a soaring melody. It's just information." Penrose cryptically adds, "You are a glue gun." Penrose's whimsical documentation confirms the
porous nature of digital information across visual and audio domains and suggests
that the composer, traditionally defined as someone who puts things together, could
have a powerful new role in the digital age. Penrose's 1994 composition *I Can't Believe
It Isn't Music!* opens with a short motif reminiscent of the sound of a modem, an
analog relay device for digital information. A spectrogram of this motive reveals an
ironic, post-McLuhan text message inscribed into the spectrum of the sound—"the
medium is not always the only message" (see Figure 36.4.) This is a truly absent image,
existing as an artifact of audio steganography that is recoverable only through digital
forensics. Penrose blurred the text before transducing it to sound, thereby rendering
the source image more difficult to read as text, but broadening the bandwidth of the
post-transduction spectrum to produce a richer sound. This cross-modal application
of digital signal processing is a dramatic demonstration of Penrose's assertion that "it's
just information."

MetaSynth, a commercial program based on the same principles as Hyperupic,
extends Penrosian audio steganography capabilities to sound artists who are not versed

FIGURE 36.4 Spectrogram of the opening to *I Can't Believe It Isn't Music* by Christopher
Penrose.

in audiovisual digital signal processing using a general-purpose programming language like Objective-C. Aphex Twin used MetaSynth extensively on his album *Windowlicker* (Leander Kahney reported on spectrographic analyses of Windowlicker in a Wired article[26]). Venetian Snares produced some striking spectral images for his album *Songs About My Cats*. (See Figure 36.5) There is a characteristic, hazy broadband sound to this kind of image-to-sound transduction. (The earlier Penrose example is a sonically distinctive application of the digital image to sound transduction technique.) A specialized digital sound synthesis technique will often impress its particular sonic stamp on the resulting work, and this is certainly the case with MetaSynth.

Image to Sound-Space

Creative spatial aspects of computer music have received increasing attention in recent years.[27] Although the spatial projection of sound was present in some of the earliest electronic music, notably Edgard Varèse's *Poème Électronique* and Karlheinz Stockhausen's *Gesang der Jünglinge*, electronic music has predominantly been composed and distributed

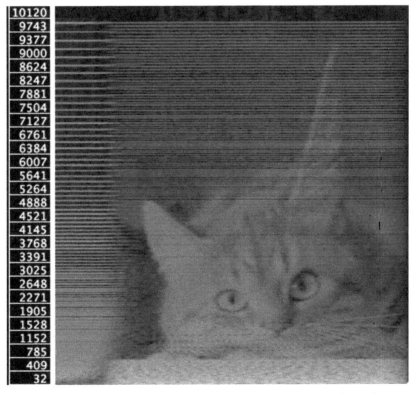

FIGURE 36.5 Spectral view from "Look" by Venetian Snares from the album "Songs About My Cats."

in stereo format. However 5.1 and 8-channel surround systems have become commonly available in university electronic music studios and festivals for electronic music, such as SEAMUS and The International Computer Music Conference. The next step up from these two-dimensional (2D) surround arrays is three-dimensional (3D) multichannel performance spaces such as Audium,[28] the Klangdom at ZKM,[29] and the Sonic Lab[30] at Queen's University Belfast. Such spaces are still relatively rare, but it seems likely that they will become increasingly common, following a similar trajectory to that of electronic music studios (extremely rare in the 1950s; nearly ubiquitous by the 1980s). Both 2D and 3D surround sound systems considerably enhance the possibilities for crafting spatial experiences for an audience compared to stereo sound projection. 3D systems in particular offer the possibility for the sensation of envelopment and for constructing electronic compositions much like sculptures, which reveal different aspects of a composition when viewed from different vantage points. Such artistic opportunities are tempting to electronic music composers in much the same way that the symphony orchestra offers a tantalizing richness and largeness of sonic possibilities that cannot be achieved by smaller ensembles.

Since 2004, I have composed computer music that treats spatial structure with equal status to that of pitch, rhythmic, and timbral structure. One promising technique I have developed to achieve this result involves transforming digital images to sound, such that the visual structure of the image translates to spatial properties for the sound. In my composition *Spaced Images with Noise and Lines* (2011),[31] each horizontal line of an image is mapped to thirty-two virtual sound locations on the perimeter of an 8-channel speaker array. Digital image-to-space-sound transduction affords the opportunity to apply image filters to spatial trajectories, smoothly transitioning from stark linear panning to blurred spatial diffusion (see Figure 36.6.) The mapping of image to space-sound is a relatively straightforward technical process, one that is easily grasped when the two media are viewed/listened to together. In performance, however, only the 8-channel audio composition is presented, not the generating images. Sound becomes the mediator between image and space. The fundamental difference between listening to music and viewing an image must first be bridged: performed music is sound fixed in time by the musician, but an image may be studied for any amount of time, with any sequence of visual focus, by the viewer. In image-based spatialization, the image is fixed in time by the spatial mapping process. Any sound can then be used to mediate between image and space, thus a wide variety of aesthetic results can be achieved. In *Spaced Images with Noise and Lines*, image-based spatial movement activates melodies, harmonies, timbres, and resonances. The spatial vocabulary includes trajectories, spins, blurs, diffusions, and maelstroms, all inseparable from the activating sonic elements. The transduction of image to space-sound offers a direct link between the spatiality inherent in an image and the spatiality of sonic motion through a hall. The absent generating image is then heard as pure movement.

FIGURE 36.6 A space-generating image used in *Spaced Images with Noise and Lines* by Eric Lyon.

CONCLUSION

The invention of recorded sound on media in the late nineteenth century introduced a profound schism between auditory and visual stimuli in the arts. The artistic implications of this break were extensively explored throughout the twentieth century. The development in the later twentieth century of digital storage of audio and video, along with digital signal processing techniques to alter this data, has led to a more fluid approach to artistic digital information in general. The works considered here have shown numerous ways that these epochal changes in media have manifest themselves in individual artistic projects. Taken in aggregate, these works invite us to consider how profoundly our perception of music may have changed since the mid-nineteenth century.

NOTES

1. Pierre Boulez, *Orientations: Collected Writings* (Cambridge, MA: Harvard University Press, 1986), 201.

2. Karlheinz Stockhausen, "We In Music Are Like Physicists," *Karlheinz Stockhausen Official Website*, last modified September 17, 2001 and accessed June 13, 2012, http://www.stockhausen.org/Physicists.pdf.

3. Pierre Schaeffer, *Traité des objets musicaux* (Paris: Editions du Seuil, 1966).

4. Steve Reich, "Come Out, for Tape," on *Steve Reich: Early Works*, Nonesuch 7559791692, 1992, compact disc.

5. Gordon Mumma, "Cirqualz," on *Electronic Music of Theatre and Public Activity*, New World Records 80632, 2005, compact disc.

6. Leonard Bernstein, "How a Great Symphony Was Written—Leonard Bernstein Discusses the First Movement of Beethoven's Eroica with Musical Illustrations" (lecture), on *Beethoven: Symphony No. 3 "Eroica"; Bernstein: How a Great Symphony was Written*, Sony Classical, 1999, compact disc.

7. Brian Kane, "*L'Objet Sonore Maintenant*: Pierre Schaeffer, Sound Objects and the Phenomenological Reduction," *Organised Sound* 12, no. 1 (2007): 15–24.

8. Denis Smalley, "Spectro-Morphology," in *The Language of Electroacoustic Music*, ed. Simon Emmerson (London: Macmillan Press, 1986), 62.

9. Luis Buñuel, *Un Chien Andalou* (Transflux Films, 2004), DVD.

10. Mya Tannenbaum, *Conversations with Stockhausen*, trans. David Butchart (Oxford: Clarendon Press, 1987), 21–22.

11. John Cage, "Composition as Process: Indeterminacy," in *Audio Culture*, ed. Christoph Cox and Daniel Warner (New York: Continuum, 2004), 177–186.

12. Gordon Mumma, "The Once Festival and How it Happened," *Arts in Society* 4, no. 2 (1967): 394.

13. Chris Salter, *Entangled* (Cambridge, MA: MIT Press, 2010), 199.

14. Salvatore Martirano, *L's GA—Ballad—Octet*, Polydor 24-5001, 1968, 33⅓ rpm.

15. Oliver Brodwolf and Florian Dombois, "Sonification of Tohoku Earthquake/Sendai Coast, Japan, 2011/03/11," YouTube video, 2:34, posted by "Sonifyerorg," March 20, 2011 and accessed June 13, 2012, http://youtu.be/3PJxUPvz9Oo.

16. Alvin Lucier, *Music for Solo Performer*, Lovely Music LP1014, 1982, 33⅓ rpm.

17. Alvin Lucier, *Vespers and Other Early Works*, New World Records 80604, 2002, compact disc.

18. Eric Singer, "Sonic Banana 2," YouTube video, 1:08, posted by "esinger3141" July 2, 2006 and accessed June 15, 2012, http://youtu.be/F7ojvS3PgVY.

19. Christine Sun Kim, "Performance Artist Christine Sun Kim Shares More with NOWNESS," Facebook note, posted by "NOWNESS" November 8, 2011 and accessed June 15, 2012, https://www.facebook.com/note.php?note_id=10150343313240095.

20. Ibid.

21. Mark Applebaum, "Aphasia," Vimeo video, posted January 2012 and accessed June 15, 2012, http://vimeo.com/34303981.

22. Kerry Brougher, et. al., *Visual Music* (London: Thames and Hudson, 2005), 25.

23. Oskar Fischinger, *Ten Films* (Los Angeles: Center for Visual Music, 2006), DVD.

24. Iannis Xenakis, *Formalized Music* (Hillside: Pendragon Press, 1992), 329–334.

25. Christopher Penrose, "HyperUpic for OS X," *MacMusic*, posted by "clouvel" February 13, 2004 and accessed June 15, 2012, http://www.macmusic.org/news/view.php/lang/en/id/1491/.

26. Leander Kahney, "Hey, Who's That Face in My Song?" *Wired Magazine*, May 10, 2002. Accessed June 24, 2012, http://www.wired.com/culture/lifestyle/news/2002/05/52426.

27. Felipe Otondo, "Recent Spatialisation Trends in Electroacoustic Music," in *Electroacoustic Music Studies Network, EMS07—The "languages"of electroacoustic music—Leicester*, 2007, accessed June 15, 2012, http://www.ems-network.org/IMG/pdf_OtondoEMS07.pdf.

28. Audium: Sound-Sculpture Space, accessed June 15, 2012, http://www.audium.org/.

29. "Klangdom/Zirkonium," *Zentrum für Kunst und Medientechnologie*, accessed June 15, 2012, http://www.zkm.de/zirkonium.

30. "The Sonic Lab," *The Sonic Arts Research Centre*, accessed June 15, 2012, http://www.sarc.qub.ac.uk/sites/sarc/AboutUs/TheSARCBuildingandFacilities/TheSonicLab/.

31. Eric Lyon, "Image-Based Spatialization," *Proceedings of the 2012 International Computer Music Conference* (San Francisco: ICMA, 2012): 200–203.

Select Bibliography

Boulez, Pierre. *Orientations: Collected Writings*. Cambridge, MA: Harvard University Press, 1986.

Brougher, Kerry, Jeremy Strick, Ari Wiseman, and Judish Zilczer. *Visual Music: Synaesthesia in Art and Music Since 1900*. London: Thames and Hudson, 2005.

Cox, Christoph, and Daniel Warner. *Audio Culture*. New York: Continuum, 2004.

Emmerson, Simon. *The Language of Electroacoustic Music*. London: Macmillan Press, 1986.

Manning, Peter. *Electronic and Computer Music*. New York: Oxford Press, 2004.

Miranda, Eduardo, and Marcelo Wanderley. *New Digital Musical Instruments: Control and Interaction Beyond the Keyboard*. Middleton: A-R Editions, 2006.

Moritz, William. *Optical Poetry: The Life and Work of Oskar Fischinger*. Eastleigh: John Libbey Publishing, 2004.

Salter, Chris. *Entangled: Technology and the Transformation of Performance*. Cambridge, MA: MIT Press, 2010.

Schaeffer, Pierre. *Traité des objets musicaux*. Paris: Editions du Seuil, 1966.

Xenakis, Iannis. *Formalized Music*. Hillside, NY: Pendragon Press, 1992.

....

CHAPTER 37

HUGUES DUFOURT'S CINEMATIC DYNAMISM

Space, Timbre, and Time in L'Afrique d'après Tiepolo

....

JANN PASLER

MANY major works by the French spectral composer Hugues Dufourt (b. 1943) have been inspired by paintings—from Rembrandt's *Le Philosophe* and Goya's *La Maison du sourd* to Jackson Pollock's *Lucifer*.[1] Since 2005, he has been attracted to Tiepolo's huge frescos on the vaulted ceiling of the Würzburg Palace (1752–53) for the bold dynamism of their imagery, freed of the constraints of gravity, and for the will they express to surpass human physiology. Dufourt finds in them both a "premonition of cinematographic writing" and an "*Ars poetica* of the music of the future."[2]

Tiepolo, as Dufourt observed, introduced into fresco technique "an assemblage of isolated moments and overflow framing that challenged the limits of scenic representation." This evoked for him the American cinema he had grown up with, cinema "whose scenic realism reached its highest point with the fatal convolutions of aerial battles shot during the Pacific war." As he explains in the program notes for the recording of the first two works in his Tiepolo cycle, "flux, swirling, lateral tensions, swelling, projections, and various degrees of distance are the new categories of these poetics."[3] Translating almost unconsciously into musical terms his visual perceptions of the fresco images and their three-dimensionality, reinforced by the architecture and the large sculpted characters bordering their frame, Dufourt observes "an entire range of tempi, a spectrum of speeds, of turbulences, teetering spaces, overhanging structures, interwoven axes and loops." These aspects of Tiepolo's art also point to two further characteristics shared with cinema: "the effects of dramatic acceleration and the simultaneous coexistence of fragments from disparate realities." In each case, he continues,

It's a question of overcoming obstacles. What's at stake is not only producing illusions of movement and speed, but also finding visual configurations endowed with a dynamic nature. Thus there are images cut off and twisting, inverted curves, and deformed perspectives. The baroque style had already explored various kinds of dynamic expression, but Tiepolo's abstract way of thinking most likely allowed him to proceed in radical ways. Technological invention constantly contributes to his stylistic innovations.[4]

In Tiepolo's frescos, Dufourt thus found not only "the characteristics of modernity...organic vitality disproportionate to man, a sense of the possible, and technical ambition," but also a dynamism—"organisms deformed by tensions and thrown into the anonymous movements of the universe"—which he called "explosive, unstable, and evolutionary, the expression of which called for a new musical 'grammar.'"[5] Grammar suggests rules and processes based on an organizational principle, and thus narrativity. But what does this mean when the work's purpose is to generate and maintain constant flux? For Dufourt, it was less important that his music refer to some external reality, than it produce a world of its own.[6] To understand this, we must look at how the elements of music and the new technologies of sound point to one another rather than to plot, thought, or character; that is, how motivic gestures, rhythms, instrumental textures, and harmonies create the interplay of stasis and turbulence, transparency (or pure sound) and distortion, "the identical and the ambiguous."[7] Such a sound world is characterized by instability and a dialectic of continuity and discontinuity, especially important to the French spectralists of which Dufourt was a co-founder.[8]

   In his Tiepolo cycle—compositions based on each of the four continents featured on the Würzburg frescos (Africa, Asia, Europe, and the Americas)—Dufourt explores sound at its liminal edges, playing with the boundaries between the commensurable and the incommensurable. In doing so, he deconstructs sound as Tiepolo deconstructs color.[9] As in any microanalysis of sound phenomena, timbre and acoustics are fundamental, dynamic parameters. But on the macrolevel, for both Tiepolo and Dufourt, form, too, is the "becoming [*devenir*] of the texture."[10] *L'Afrique d'après Tiepolo* (2005), the first of four works, "marks a return to the intuition of time and to the concrete perception of change." Change here is no longer linked to the idea of "trajectory"; rather, it results from "imperceptible transitions, indeterminate passages" and can be "multidirectional."[11] For Dufourt, "To write is to transform, that is, to establish correspondences and introduce relationships of equivalence or substitution as well as logical rules deriving from implications."[12] Transformation in *L'Afrique* operates both in the moment-to-moment succession of musical ideas, sometimes as "contrary predicates,"[13] a technique he expands on later in the cycle, and through an exchange of materials or their function from one section to the next.[14] Responding in part to what Alpers and Baxandall refer to as "the mobile play of perception"[15] that results from such dynamism, Dufourt further describes his compositional process as constructing "internal equilibriums and exchanges, separations and fusions, transitions and mutations."

Moreover, like Tiepolo, he is drawn to "combining diametrically opposed scales of grandeur: the infinite smallness of microstructures alongside the immensity of distant horizons."[16] This means not only unleashing musical tensions, but also taming them and, in doing so, shaping the chaos of sound into perceptible form. Such musical ideas, which first appear in *L'Afrique*, find fuller development in the Tiepolo-inspired works that follow.

The Tiepolo frescos also intrigued Dufourt for their social dimension as the incarnation of "the ideology of a world gone astray." Venetian society was "seeking to ward off the darkest omens by drowning its sorrows in the exuberance of decorative painting.... At first woven through with light and erected for the glory of God, the pictorial world of Tiepolo eventually gave way to the pallor of faded pearls. The celestial hierarchy [at the center of these frescos] freezes in cold detachment, meaning either happy passivity or a moment of bitterness." At the same time, he points out,

> Tiepolo attains a kind of grandeur that can be called the dynamic sublime, a dimension we also admire in Tintoretto, Rubens, or Goya, one characterized by centralized force-fields, the tumult of fluid masses, and the violent confrontation of volumes. Deprived of a stable base and with its abrupt character, Tiepolo's world nonetheless has a paradoxical assurance. Vertical forces dominate, preventing fatal dissipation of the cosmos.[17]

For Dufourt, Tiepolo thus shares many affinities with our own times: not only a "common dynamic concept of art" but also "the rhetoric of propaganda, spectacular splendor, a style of intoxication and surfeit, the ultimate bravado of the insane who, in spite of everything, count on surviving the shipwreck."[18]

Taking inspiration from these attitudes and processes, although without using the fresco as an "anecdotal model," in *L'Afrique* Dufourt meditates on the continent not only as depicted by Tiepolo, but also as understood today. Full of pottery and tents, Tiepolo's *Africa* has no permanent structures, in contrast to the architectural references in the fresco depicting Europe; its allegorical female lies sensually draped on a seated camel while turbaned merchants engage in the commerce of people, animals, and commodities. This ambiguous world, full of enigmas, forms a "strange counterpoint to the ceremonial splendor" of the apotheoses at the work's center. For Dufourt, *Africa* can be summed up as "crushed [*écrasé*]," its time not yet the time of Hegelian or Marxian self-consciousness.[19] The composer understands its cultures, at least during Tiepolo's time, as turning in place, not yet part of history. Working with such concepts at the core of *L'Afrique* allowed him to explore an ontology of being, time as space, that resists objectification and remains dynamic, albeit without teleological progress. As such, the work offers a kind of implicit critique of history in the West and of Western imperialism, with its power to conquer and shape as well as obliterate time.

Tiepolo: Space and an Art of Oppositions

The Residenz in Würzburg was one of the largest construction projects of the period. As Dufourt points out, the architect Balthasar Neumann used this as the occasion to enact a "geometric mode of thinking" in the way he "conceived and combined volumes as well as orchestrated surfaces and depth effects." Art historians have referred to his "innovative

FIGURE 37.1 Tiepolo's *Olympus and the Four Continents* at Würzburg.

handling of structures" and his "resolution of spatial problems" as "syncopated interpenetration." Resonating with his own aesthetic, Dufourt notes, Neumann "liked
ampleur [large, enveloping spaces], not *la pompe pittoresque* [picturesque pomp]."[20] To
support Neumann's vision of a "grandiose structure of universal significance," Giovanni
Battista Tiepolo was commissioned to create a "monumental" ceiling fresco over the
central staircase depicting Olympus and the Four Continents.[21] With long, narrow representations of Africa, Asia, the Americas, and Europe over the moulding on the four
walls, Apollo at the center, the "god of light" evokes "an impression of irresistible and
dizzying emergence from the depths." Dufourt calls this a "mythological portrayal of the
sunrise."[22] See Figure 37.1.

In his first work written in response to Tiepolo's frescos, *L'Afrique*, Dufourt is not so
much drawn to the triumphant figure of Apollo and his heavenly entourage, nor to the
opposition of heaven and earth so prominently on display, although arguably at times
his music seems to aspire to the sublime, the "dynamic sublime" he admired in Tiepolo's
fresco. Instead, he focuses on the continents—the parade of humanity, the animal kingdom, and various modes of human interaction, emblems of knowledge, and cultural
mores (Figure 37.2). In *Africa*, Dufourt sees "groups of traders and smokers, a camel,
pearl merchants, and an immense blue-and-white striped tent, then the allegorical figure, *Afrique*, along with the god of the Nile." What he doesn't mention is the opposition
of female and male, black and white, young and old that both structure and complicate this scenario. In addition to the young black slave on the far left and the old white
God of the Nile on the far right—these framing the tableau—a fully clothed, bearded,
light-skinned older male dominates the left half of the fresco and a bare-breasted,
younger black woman the right half. Moreover, this gender opposition is reinforced by
the similarly dressed black man, perhaps a tribal chief, who is standing beside the large

FIGURE 37.2 *Africa.*

merchant, while behind *Afrique* is a veiled white girl, possibly a slave. The surrounding context suggests the nature of their power. For the male, brute strength, with its capacity for abduction and domination, is here suggested by the leg of a prisoner in shackles and a large animal with huge muscular hind legs, his upper body here covered with a large rug, perhaps to suggest his domestication. For *Afrique*, straddling a comfortably seated camel, her physical beauty is such that an elegantly attired black man kneels before her, with incense in one hand and umbrella in another, as if courting her. What are we to make of all this, with the tableau's central characters facing away from one another? The space, divided almost equally into two parts, emphasizes their irreconcilable differences. Are we expected to encounter them one after the other, or experience their simultaneity? There is no action, but there is movement, with bodies twisting, arms raised, and the winds ever blowing.

Dufourt recognized the complexity of this scene, but it was not the picturesque elements that appealed. And neither was he interested in forging musical emblems of Africanness, be it with the sounds of a marimba or tam-tam, or with tunes borrowed from this part of the world. Nothing about the music signifies Africa or acts as a indexical sign to it. Tiepolo, too, eschewed any reference to musical instruments in his African tableau, unlike elsewhere in the fresco, where Native Americans have their drums and Europeans play string instruments. Indeed, Dufourt is not an Orientalist, a hypercharged position no longer tenable in the twenty-first century, nor a voyeur like Pierre Loti or Victor Segalen anxious to dream, to escape the constraints of Western culture, nor a rational modernist like Félix Regamey, intent on portraying aspects of modernity on these continents. Yet, like Saint-Saëns in his own *Africa* (1892), a fantasy also featuring the piano in dialogue with other instruments, Dufourt takes care to express the diversity and coexistence represented in this fresco and a certain kind of dynamism associated with African life. As he points out, "a work that does not encounter the Other,

FIGURE 37.2 *Continued*

encounter Otherness, develops only according to immanent and peaceful parameters."[23] Otherness, at its essentialist core, challenges us to come to grips with difference and potential conflict without the collapse of heterogeneity.

Difference as duality, audible in Dufourt's *L'Afrique d'après Tiepolo*, is fundamental. Whether intended to mirror the various binary oppositions in the fresco or not, duality—unassailable and yet irreconcilable, as in the frescos—characterizes the entire work at several levels. Most important, registral oppositions of extremely low and extremely high pitches, as well as temporal oppositions between extremely fast and extremely slow notes dominate throughout, both in simultaneous as well as successive articulations. Whether consciously or not, these echo the omnipresence in the fresco of both the earthly beings on the four sides, depicted as close to the viewer, and the heavenly ones, increasingly distant as one looks to the center. The perception of difference in how they occupy the space creates the remarkable experience of depth and height.

In the initial measures, the piano's very low bass thirty-second note, E flat⁻³, played *sffffz*—its gong-like sound maintained by a depressed pedal—serves as an upbeat to the chordal cluster of E⁻² / F#³G#³ / F⁴G⁴A⁴, spanning six octaves, also played *sffffz*, and lasting the measure in 3/4. With its registral and temporal oppositions, this musical idea—a short low bass appoggiatura on an upbeat to a much longer chord cluster on a downbeat—is the central one in the composition, serving as the basis of the musical phrases that follow and ensuring continuity and coherence (Figure 37.3). We immediately hear it repeated five times in the relatively slow tempo of quarter note = 63. This ritual-like stasis allows the listener to focus on its timbre, consisting of registral extremes. With them, Dufourt shows that even the sounds of a single instrument can seem irreconcilably different, refusing to fuse, and how the piano, the quintessential Western instrument, can play with the boundaries of sound and noise. While the dissonance and extreme dynamic levels produce tension, this insistent registral juxtaposition also leaves the center almost empty—the middle register, also spanning six octaves—as in Tiepolo's depiction of Africa, where little bridges the gulf between *Afrique* and the merchants. Occasional short arpeggios that rapidly traverse this terrain attempt to negotiate this space, but ultimately serve to reinforce its barrenness. These registral and temporal juxtapositions thus open a sound-space of potentiality, like the space created by the arched

FIGURE 37.3 *L'Afrique*, mm. 1–7 the central idea. *L'Afrique d'après Tiepolo* by Hugues Dufourt © 2005, Editions Henry Lemoine, Paris.

ceiling over the staircase, or in the tableau framed by the black slave on one side and the white god of the Nile on the other.

For Dufourt, the most important duality in the fresco comes from the juxtaposition of light and dark, the result of not only Tiepolo's design, but also of constantly shifting light in the hall itself. The fresco for "*Africa*, located on the vault's side, receives the most direct and complex light through the immediately opposite west window and the north window to the left."[24] Perhaps this is why, ironically, in one of Tiepolo's earlier sketches, the image of *Afrique* appears in full sunlight, with the ominous gray clouds instead over the allegorical female representing *Europe*. In his final version, however, Tiepolo shrouded this side of his fresco in clouds, thereby changing the meaning of the tableau. Neither Dufourt nor Alpers and Baxandall have remarked on the opposition of light and dark in the fresco as echoing or emblematic of the racial oppositions underlined in the visual structure. Yet, in his liner note, Dufourt brings a certain political consciousness and historical awareness to his interpretation that suggests that he may have intuited this connection. Responding to this melancholic, even ominous tone, Dufourt notes:

> *Afrique*, who is already in the clutches of the European thieves, is illuminated by a dull light. In the midst of these pale clouds, one no longer recognizes the sunny, shimmering paradises of rural culture. The sky seems oppressive. My music evokes the pale sun of Tiepolo's *Africa* and its thick, sulphurous clouds. The musical work is defined by the use of color.[25]

Color, Narrative, and Musical Form in *L'Afrique d'après Tiepolo*

Inspired by the Tiepolo fresco, color is the composer's mode (what is being "imitated," in the Aristotelian sense) as well as his means and manner of "imitation." It is the "evocation" of Tiepolo's colors, a technique for producing the evocation, and the manner in which the evocation is produced. The variability of cloud colors in Tiepolo's fresco inspired the constant variability of this work's musical colors. Other than the highly resonant individual bass note appoggiaturas in the piano, most notes are never heard alone, in their pure state, but rather "colored" by pitches or pitch classes a semitone or tone away, producing dissonances that rub against one another without bristling like "cactuses."

As it arises from both light and interaction with other colors, color poses not just the question of difference, but also that of coexistence. This coexistence can result from the simultaneous juxtaposition of sounds that perceptually remain distinct or from new sounds resulting from their fusion, often the product of sophisticated methods of writing. For example, flutter-tongued flutes sometimes double the vibraphone oscillations in the same registral space, adding complexity to the sound, while later the clarinets and English horn add depth to it. Moving beyond Tiepolo's clouds to his human figures, such hybrid sounds seem to argue for the benefits of coexistence among likes, even if they point to the impossibility of fusion among unlikes—a notion with significant racial implications historically, especially in Africa.[26]

But clouds are not just about color. And clouds are never static—they move—and often at different rates. Like the unstable nature of light itself, ever changing from morning to evening, Tiepolo's clouds assure an inherent vitality. What impressed Dufourt in the frescos was how "space alternately swells up and narrows, expanding or breaking apart."[27] Moreover, on the concave surface of the arched ceiling, the figures, too, seem to change, as Alpers and Baxandall point out, leaning in one direction or another depending on the viewer's position in the hall.[28] Similar processes characterize the treatment of timbre in *L'Afrique d'après Tiepolo*. Dufourt likewise understands color and its perception as dynamic. Building on the timbre-chords of Varèse and Messiaen and the recent theoretical work of psychoacousticians, he views instability and irregularity as essential to musical timbre.[29] And, as with the principal figure in each fresco, his principal musical idea in *L'Afrique d'après Tiepolo* also appears somewhat different from one moment to the next. Commenting on this, the composer explains,

> The sound's substance has its own dynamism that polarizes and rhythmizes the space even before it becomes the object of the composition. Composing consists in suggesting dynamic impressions with movements without actually shifting them. The new dimensions are depth, transparency, fluidity, and luminosity.[30]

The music challenges the listener to follow these subtle timbral variations, consubstantial with the musical process that gives rise to the work's form. As Dufourt points out, "Space is no longer the idea of immobility. It is form in all its power.... Musical form is a mold made of masses and empty spaces, forces and qualities in flux."[31]

The first section of *L'Afrique d'après Tiepolo* (mm. 1–74), for piano solo, is a good example of the importance of color, this kind of composing, and the nature of narrative in the work. Both the piano and its central idea are like narrative agents in that they begin pregnant with possibility and then undergo transformation. With each iteration, the chords, shifting between p and mp, begin to move melodically, articulate textural and rhythmic variants, and suggest the occasional cadence, even if, harmonically, the pitch classes and pitch clusters (around E and E flat) change minimally. Moreover, as the composer points out, "one and the same chord can seem homogenous on the surface and heterogeneous deeper down: at first lively and lucid, and then raw and dark in its convolutions, reflecting a tension that is just beginning to arise."[32] The rhythmic regularity of the central idea is also made dynamic by slight temporal variations—a delay and shortening of the chords by an eighth triplet, by three sixteenth triplets, by one quarter note, and by their collapse at one point to single notes (at mm. 40 and 42), as well as by their expansion by various temporal intervals in the measures that follow.

Transformation helps to define the end of part one. A peripety, in the Aristotelian sense of "a change by which the action veers round to its opposite,"[33] gives the section its shape. The appoggiatura itself evolves from the short low gong-like notes or quick rising arpeggios into longer chords, now, significantly, in the middle register. From mm. 45 to 53, they remain around the same pitches (F⁻¹ E flat¹ G¹) but extend in length to more or less a quarter beat, then to more than a half-note. These middle-to-upper register chord progressions, once established, then alternate with the central idea. Chord clusters (now as F⁻¹ Fflat⁻¹ C¹ G#¹) end the section by breaking into their arpeggiated form, ffff. This gives melodic, harmonic, rhythmic, and dynamic substance to this heretofore barren sound-space. Part one not only begins a process that the rest of the work will continue, it also suggests that tension produced by color, texture, and rhythm can be followed by resolution, if you will, in those same terms, even if partial and momentary. Such transformation, as in many narratives,[34] depends on mutually entailing implications within these elements themselves, or what Dufourt calls "logical rules deriving from implications," here a kind of timbral gap-fill.

In part two (mm. 75–124), the composer returns to the central idea and his exploration of registral extremes in the piano, but this time in dialogue with the vibraphone. The opening arpeggiated upbeat appoggiatura in the piano flows almost imperceptively into the grace-note appoggiatura of the vibraphone on the downbeat of the next measure. Then the vibraphone's chords, sounding as tremolos wavering between its own registral extremes, underpin and in part double the piano's chordal clusters, supporting a sound now able to last longer than one measure. As such, the composer treats the two instruments as if one. They continue to move together even when the appoggiatura-to-chord idea changes into two dotted half-notes or four measures of variations on the appoggiatura followed by four measures of chord clusters. And yet the electronic sound of the vibraphone cannot fuse with the pure, acoustic sound of the piano. This contradiction constitutes a third form of binary opposition in the work. It results not from the registral or temporal differences in the notes, but from within the sound itself, as produced by two incompatible technologies. Through their shared function as part of the same melodic gestures, Dufourt nonetheless shows a way to bridge their differences.

In this section, transformation again comes in the form of a peripety, an exchange of roles between the instruments. At m. 109, the vibraphone, solo, takes over the piano's opening gestures, as if it can stand in for the piano. Ironically, given its technology and previous function in the piece, this instrument turns the short–long rhythm and spaced-out intervals of the central idea into a kind of lilting melody of two-measure groups (in each of them, two eighth-note chords followed by a half-note chord). The piano loses its earlier preeminence and, when it returns, is reduced to an accompaniment of long single notes in the low bass that end on E⁻³ in the section's final measure. After a kind of cadential descent a fifth lower on A⁻⁴, the next part begins again with the piano.

Part three (mm. 125–189) features three timbral groups: a duo of piano and vibraphone, a trio of strings, and a trio of winds, treated as distinct groups, but also capable of exchanging material and roles. This section begins like the other two, but with the central idea of appoggiatura-to-chord cluster proceeding much more slowly, the former extending to an entire measure and the latter to three measures. Moreover, from mm.

125 to 142, the piano holds the gong-like opening note in the low bass under the chord clusters for two, four, and then five measures, while the wind and string trios answer each appoggiatura with a phrase made of three to four chord clusters per phrase. This new pattern is subtly different from what we've heard before: under the last measure of the chord clusters, the piano moves down a semitone for a measure and then, in the last measure of the second phrase, up an octave. These shifts are supported by a change in the pedaling. In the winds and strings, the notes of the individual parts interact as counterpoint. Here, close associations within three pairs of instruments result in new timbral colors. For example, each phrase by the flute and violin begins a semitone apart, and when the flute plays F#^{2} C^3 F#^{2} G^2, simultaneously the violin plays E^2 B flat^2 A^1 G flat^2. Simultaneously, each phrase in the English horn begins a tone or semitone away from that of the viola, but then reverses direction, leaping down a fourteenth and then back up a thirteenth, this echoed in the viola's leap down of a thirteenth. The clarinet and cello in this passage begin in parallel motion, a tone away, but then also divert, with the cello rising an eleventh to counterbalance within the strings the viola's descent. When the vibraphone enters, it joins the chordal clusters in the winds and strings, leaving the role of appoggiatura to the piano alone.

Beginning in m. 143 comes a rapid alternation between two meters associated with the two parts of the central idea: 2/4 for the low bass piano appoggiatura (with the bass slowing and dropping from E flat^{-3} to B^{-4}), and 3/4 for the chords in the instrumental ensemble (each lasting one measure). After their rapid alternation comes an extraordinary duet between a series of dynamically shaped tremoli chords in the vibraphone (in 2/4) and chordal harmonics in the strings, also subtly shaped dynamically into phrases (in 3/4). Eventually, the winds and piano add to the chordal and timbral texture, although almost inaudibly, ppp. Adding the metric alternation draws attention to the duality within the central idea and the various ways the composer uses musical color to shape our perception.

At the midpoint of part three (m. 155), the metrical alternation continues, albeit gradually elongating each metrical grouping and adding measures in 4/4. But perception of the central idea is inhibited as the ensembles break away from one another and establish distinctive independent gestures, rhythms, and timbres. The piano becomes the only instrument in the very low register, returning to the low A^{-4} where part three began and proceeding slowly to the lowest note in the piece, C^{-4}. But its first low bass appoggiatura, rather than being sounded, is implied: that is, held over from the last note in its previous iteration. The strings, all playing extremely high notes, beyond their normal registers, articulate only long chord clusters, lasting five or six measures, each of them animated by subtly shaped dynamics (from pp to p or mf to pp). This special string timbre remains constant until the end of the section. The winds punctuate the long string clusters with their own much shorter ones, but with staggered entries and a counterpoint of dynamics. For example, the clarinet reaches mf at its middle point while the flute plays forte. The vibraphone, with each of its tremoli shaped dynamically, is the only instrument that moves through a quicker succession of chords, helping to articulate the meter (Figure 37.4).

FIGURE 37.4 *L'Afrique*, mm. 176–184, *tuilage*. *L'Afrique d'après Tiepolo* by Hugues Dufourt
© 2005, Editions Henry Lemoine, Paris.

With these four timbres, Dufourt builds form through a process he calls "tilings
(*tuilage*)."[35] "Tilings" address the problem of form made of different densities and volumes, sound oppositions and sound fusions of various sizes, shapes, and colors, suggesting a response to the way architecture and painting relate in the hall. Like Neumann's
"syncopated interpenetration," it describes not only the way the four instrumental timbres here build on one another and interpenetrate, but also the succession of phrases

that layer one on the next, similar to the effect of various superimposed tiles ("*tuiles*") that make up roofs. That the same musical idea recurs throughout helps to make the "tiling" audible, just as the use of the same tile on a roof would render visible any pattern made with it. Through time, however, these distinctions collapse into the flux of form. The different rates of motion among these four timbres, the very quiet dynamic level with especially long notes in the piano and strings sounding at the very edges of the possible, and the subtle dynamic shadings of each instrumental ensemble, sometimes in contradiction with one another, result in such distention of the central idea as to make it virtually inaudible. The effect of tilings, like the shifting clouds in the fresco, thus points to a tension in the piece between the non-narrative structures that organize its flow and the stronger sense of narrativity imposed on the piece by sectional contrasts.[36]

In the rest of the piece, the timbral and temporal aspects of the central idea continue to be explored in myriad ways, including through momentary or structurally significant transformation. There are exchanges of earlier functions, such as at m. 189, between the piano and instrumental ensemble, when the strings take on the appoggiatura and the piano/vibraphone the chord-clusters, and in m. 212, with the cello now moving in its low register and the piano exclusively in its middle register, after which, at m. 225, the piano returns to its low register to accompany the winds and strings in increasingly complex counterpoint. Occasionally, the timbral groups reinforce one another, blurring their functional differences, especially with the return to long notes being held for many measures beginning in m. 199 and creating tension by virtue of their length. In m. 283, the string ensemble breaks up, and the texture is transformed with its pizzicato violin and viola quarter notes, heard with whole-note chord-clusters in the cello, piano, vibraphone, and winds. At other times, instrumental areas sound independently of one another and do not progress at the same rate, such as accompanying the return of the central idea in mm. 314–372. Despite the local-level transformations that characterize the end of each major section, the main musical idea never develops into something else. In other words, although duality may be inherent in the central idea and there is change, there is no development, no progress. Without a second idea, a counterpart with which to engage in dialectical conflict, there can be no internal struggle and thus no genuine growth.

But there are interludes, moments when the central idea retreats momentarily. Mm. 321–325 is one such interlude, with the shift to 4/4 and *sul ponticello* writing in the strings under rapid vibrato tremoli in the vibraphone, dynamically shaped from pp to mf to pp, and then with trills in the flute, English horn, and violin. Mm. 340–347 is another, with the sudden shift to forte, 3/4, and its remarkable superimposition of flutter-tongue trills in the woodwinds, doubled by tremoli in the vibraphone, over trills in the somewhat lower strings and a trill on D^3 in the piano, increasing from p to f. Like the clouds in the fresco that in some places move from the background into the foreground, these interludes provide space for timbral exploration for its own sake and prepare the listener for the explosion of timbral innovation at the end of the work.

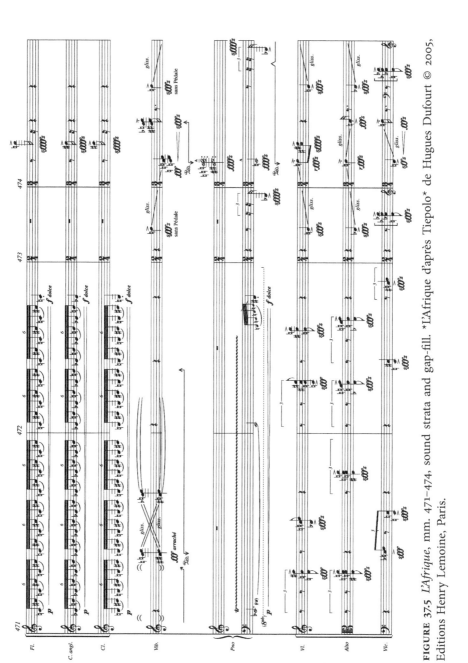

FIGURE 37.5 *L'Afrique*, mm. 471–474, sound strata and gap-fill. *L'Afrique d'après Tiepolo* de Hugues Dufourt © 2005, Editions Henry Lemoine, Paris.

After a long, relatively static, and quiet chordal section (mm. 373– 442), the last major section of *L'Afrique d'après Tiepolo* (mm. 443–493) unfurls a frenzy of musical activity, beginning with music marked in the composer's hand, "*extra dure.*" It is as if, in the last fifth of his piece, the composer's focus shifts—like the perspective of the viewer while climbing the stairs of the hall—from the magnificent procession of the clouds to the figures themselves. Highly original timbres abound, with writing that makes it difficult to know which instruments are performing and the incommensurability of the sound challenging rational expectations. As in the fresco, such writing plays with the limits of order and chaos. Shrieking glissandos in the strings, scraping up and down the vibraphone, all of this colonizing the entire sound universe, suggests the conflict of life on earth, driven by desire, frustration, anger, and other strong emotions. For example, beginning in m. 443, the central idea returns in the alternation of the piano appoggiatura and the instrumental chord clusters, but everything is fff. Moreover, the technologies producing them range from super-high trills in the woodwinds, playing fff, to double glissandi in contrary motion in the vibraphone, ff to sfff, to extreme registral oppositions in the piano at fff, to six parallel glissandi in the strings, rising and then falling, sff to fff or fffz. The string glissandi destabilize the sound, as do its very high notes, extremely difficult to perform. These timbres, superimposed over one another, continue until m. 466, when the trills shift to the low bass of the piano under oscillating seconds in the clarinet, thirds in the English horn, and fourths in the flute. Here, the strings turn to chord clusters, alternating from one string to the next and articulated at erratic intervals. At m. 474, glissandi return in the strings, but as if to fill the space between these chord clusters; in other words, another gap–fill process, while the winds and piano dialogue with their short and long chord clusters (Figure 37.5).

In the work's climax (mm. 481–491), the central idea alternates with measures in which all previous distinctions between instrumental groups dissolve in a shared texture of continuous motions, with a succession of rapid, parallel, arching arpeggios in one-measure phrases, each of which expands from rfz to sfff. This shift in the work from slow, subtle transformations of color to sudden, dramatic explosions and extremely animated rhythms leads to the critical moment, so important in all narratives, after which everything is different. While the sound-space is completely saturated in mm. 489–491, churning with oscillating octaves or arpeggios in all parts, in m. 492, the piano returns abruptly to A^{-4}, ffff, then the other instruments stop on a long tremolo chord; finally, the piano, now alone, returns to the opening idea, but in the middle register.

With the frenzy at an end, a kind of catharsis follows, a slow, lyrical duet between piano and clarinet (mm. 494–511), functioning as a coda. Here, instead of articulating the work's characteristic registral oppositions, the two instruments come together in dialogue. After its middle-register appoggiatura, the piano moves in chord clusters, mostly in the two outer registers, a reversal of how these appeared in the work's opening. This leaves to the clarinet the middle register, where it almost suggests the human voice—although a voice, as the composer points out, "without consequence," a voice in the desert that "speaks to no one." In bringing closure to the work, this moment of quiet lyricism can be understood as cynical, an empty gesture associated with narrative dénouement, or as comforting, a release from the work's relentless tension. I hear this as similar to *Afrique*'s gesture of openness, her eyes raised and looking hopeful, her left arm lifted and gesturing outward as if addressing the heavens. Or is it Europe, the fresco to the right, or the viewer? Or what comes next? Possibly the future? In any case, the final measures ready the listener for the next adventure, Dufourt's musical meditations on the other three continents.

As we have seen, color in *L'Afrique* results from harmonic, melodic, and rhythmic interactions not only within each timbral group, but also between them. New sound colors emerge from the juxtaposition and interpenetration of contrasting instrumental families, each with distinct technologies for their sound production, and from the effect of distortion caused by variations in the nature of the central idea from one moment to the next. If the individual gestures in continual flux and the *tuilage* create the effect of nontelelogical heterogeneity, what renders its complexity comprehensible are its narrative elements: one basic idea—its two parts treated as narrative agents undergoing constant change—and structural transformations, often involving peripeties and, after its climax, signaling the end of the work.

TIME PRESENT

Although one discovers the fresco only gradually when mounting the huge staircase, in many ways, Tiepolo's work foreshadowed today's concern with collapsing time to the present. In the frescos, as Dufourt points out, this results from "the overlapping and intersection of simultaneous developments, the superimposition and alternation of various episodes [in the overall narrative], retrospective development, and mobility as expressed by effects of transparency."[37] In *L'Afrique d'après Tiepolo,* too, there are "very different speeds of unfolding [*déroulement*], types of development, and writing," albeit with no development, ideas expanded upon in the works which follow. The distinction of timbres and timbre-masses facilitates perception of their contrasting rates of movement, what Dufourt calls "paradoxical temporalities," a technique he first explored in *Saturne* (1979). Given the rate and dynamic level at which the musical ideas succeed one another, the complexity of the micro- and macrophenomena are almost impossible to grasp in all their rich detail. Instead, they serve to focus the listener on the present, whether quiet and barely audible or screechingly frenetic.

What holds all this together is a "common meter and metronomic pulse," often articulated by the piano. Because Dufourt composes at the piano, one might think of it as the voice of the composer, its pulse as his breathing. And, yet, despite having the "main role from the beginning to the end" and "exhibiting acoustic vehemence … [it] never manages to arrive at an authentically personal formulation."[38] There is no self-glorification of the subject. Flux and form in *L'Afrique d'après Tiepolo* depend on the relentlessness of its slow, deliberate pulse, to which the appoggiaturas draw attention throughout the work. The composer calls it "obsessive." If the chord clusters point to the influence of Schoenberg's "Farben," from his *Five Orchestral Pieces* (1909), it is because of their similar unfolding in time.

This is the paradox of space becoming time and time becoming space, "creating a new type of network of interconnection," and thereby paving the way for digital art. But with color as both the subject and the medium of the music, there is no Bergsonian melody. Sonority, which takes attention away from the dialectic of consequence, does not push forward to something else. It invites immersion. The pulse, too, draws us in, taking us along with it, in part because it is slow enough here to regulate the listener's breathing. Dufourt, citing Edgar Allen Poe, refers to this as "the clock of eternity," its repetitiveness taking the place of any directionality and thus of history. Its regularity, never rigid— arguably responsible for a continuity, as Dufourt puts it, "more profound than the apparent discontinuity of its phenomena"[39]—suggests the "ontological time" of the universe, to cite Pierre Souvtchinsky, as opposed to the "psychological time," or time of becoming or desire, associated with the human psyche. Ontological time, the essence of time itself or "pure time,"[40] underlies and makes possible the experience of all other kinds of time. Music of ontological time absorbs human subjectivity because it requires submission to the music. Gisèle Brelet once saw social implications in this kind of music, an expression of the living reality of social experience as opposed to individual duration. The pulse in *L'Afrique d'après Tiepolo* thus contributes to the experience to which Dufourt refers in thinking of Africa as "crushed," in the sense of forced into submission. Although this, the first of his works on Tiepolo's continents, proceeds with a "temporality that is disproportionately distended," in those that follow, *L'Asie* and *L'Europe*, time becomes more condensed, leading to a "cataclysmic acceleration."[41]

Digital Versus Acoustic

For the past fifty years, French spectral composers have been exploring the "sound-space as a space of transitions."[42] Most of the research and compositions have taken place with the aid of computers. Dufourt, whose research lab was next to IRCAM for fifteen years, explains that digital sound led to new kinds of sensations, "renewing, expanding, and organizing our sensory inheritance":

> Science, so to speak, has allowed us to realize artificial syntheses of sensory impressions—a cultural phenomenon without precedent.... Digital techniques have given the human ear access to hearing on the microscopic level.... Microanalysis of sound phenomena has revealed that musical sounds are spectrums that behave dynamically...that instability and irregularity are essential to the musical phenomenon.... The perceptual experiences created by computer music have produced unclassifiable anomalies—sounds that rise and descend, glissandi without end, diffractions of timbre into harmony, liquidations of metallic and brass sounds— that have thrown into question the traditional division between musical theory and practice. [43]

But it is not the computer that Dufourt used in writing his music inspired by Tiepolo's frescos. Instead, he preferred to work as an "artisan," writing by hand on large architectural tracing pages on which he draws musical staves and, every centimeter, vertical lines that disappear when the music is engraved. Using ink permitted him to work much more quickly than with a computer, to "open as many windows" as he wished on the page, and, with tracing paper, to superimpose structures, a technique he finds stimulating while composing.[44] In this way, he composed for the symphonic orchestra, bringing his understanding of psychoacoustics and computer music to acoustic music all the while calling on our "cognitive and creative capacities" to navigate the "frontiers of fusion."[45] For Dufourt, the symphonic orchestra doesn't necessarily represent "the old academic tradition, just barely good enough to create monumental works," but rather is fully capable of "constructing phenomena without precedent, such as certain depth effects." The orchestra is ideal for creating synthesis that escapes analysis. In effect, what has interested Dufourt increasingly in his Tiepolo cycle is creating "multi-phonic sounds," especially with the flute, oboe, and clarinet, sounds that create a sound world "diffracted and hypertensive," resembling what can otherwise be produced by electroacoustics, and one that, especially in the works that follow L'Afrique, "with their violent accelerations, create asymmetries of perception." In the Tiepolo cycle as a whole, moving beyond even cinema, he thus aims to integrate "noise, tension, and distortion" into what he calls "consonant inharmonicity."[46]

Like Jacques Attali, Dufourt believes that music can be a "social symptomotology heralding real change."[47] Music "signals the world of tomorrow, of which it is the mirror and the prophecy.... Not only does it integrate the most advanced forms of rationality, but its aptitude for research and formalization provides it with the means to probe the depths of the human soul and to hold onto the shocks of history."[48]

NOTES

1. Dufourt's works based on paintings are *Saturne* (1979), referring to Panofsky's analysis of Durer's etching; *La Tempesta* (1977) to Giorgione; *Le Philosophe* (1991) to Rembrandt; *La Maison du sourd* (1996–99) to Goya; *Les Hivers* (1992–2001) to four paintings by Poussin, Rembrandt, Breughel, and Guardi; and *Lucifer* (1992–2000) to Pollock.

    The analysis of *L'Afrique d'après Tiepolo* in this essay, especially the sections "Tiepolo: Space and an Art of Oppositions," and "Color, Narrative, and Musical Form in *L'Afrique d'après Tiepolo*," draws on my "Hugues Dufourt's 'Manifesto of the Music of Our Times': Narratives Without History in *L'Afrique* and *L'Asie d'après Tiepolo*," *Perspectives of New Music* 49, no. 1–2 (summer 2011): 198–231.

2. The quotations from Dufourt, when not specifically indicated, come from three of my interviews with the composer, 2010–2012, the most recent one involving his written response to questions posed by the editors of this volume, John Richardson and Carol Vernallis, and myself, which I have translated. The first of these citations comes from the 2012 unpublished interview; the second from Hugues Dufourt, Liner notes for *D'Après Tiepolo: L'Afrique & L'Asie d'après Tiepolo,* Ensemble Recherche, Kairos 0013142 KAI, 2010, 14.

3. Dufourt, Liner Notes, 14. Throughout these, I have retranslated parts of the English version and reintegrated aspects of the original French left out of this translation.

4. Dufourt, unpublished interview (2012).

5. Ibid. and Dufourt, "Notice on *Surgir*," cited in Martin Kaltenecker, "Parcours de l'oeuvre," on the website for the composer at IRCAM: http://brahms.ircam.fr/composers/composer/1167/workcourse/#parcours

6. When questioned, Dufourt admitted that these works have narrative in the sense of Cassirer's symbolic forms. See Ernst Cassirer, *Language and Myth*, trans. Suzanne Langer (New York: Harper, 1946; repr., New York: Dover, 1953), 8.

7. In his "De la dimension productive de l'intensité et du timbre et leur intégration au système des 'éléments porteurs de forme,'" in *Composer au XXIème siècle, pratiques, philosophies, langages et analyses,* ed. Sophie Stévance (Paris: Vrin, 2010), Dufourt writes of the "play of colors" as permitting "the development of a dialectic of the identical and the ambiguous" (116).

8. The concept of spectral music first arose in a manifesto that Dufourt wrote in 1979 for Radio-France and the Société Internationale de Musique Contemporaine. It expressed the concerns about timbre and time associated with the group, L'Itinéraire, which included Michaël Lévinas, Tristan Murail, Gérard Grisey, Roger Tessier, and Dufourt.

9. Svetlana Alpers and Michael Baxandall, *Tiepolo and the Pictorial Intelligence* (New Haven, CT: Yale University Press, 1994), 46. The composer read this book as he wrote his music.

10. Dufourt, "*Eléments porteurs de forme*," 118.

11. Ibid., 118, and Dufourt, Liner notes, 21.

12. Hugues Dufourt, "Mathesis et subjectivité," Lecture taken from his *Essai sur les principes de la musique*, vol. 1, *Mathesis et subjectivité* (Paris: Editions MF, 2008), 18.

13. This concept comes from Kant's *Critique of Pure Reason* and Hegel's *Science of Logic*. In his article, "Gérard Grisey: La fonction constituante du temps," *Musicae Scientiae* 3 (2004), Dufourt explains, "Le principe de la synthèse instrumentale consiste précisément à réaliser une synthèse contradictoire, une synthèse qui ne peut pas s'achever car elle met en présence des prédicats contraires" (61).

14. For Tzvetan Todorov, in *Poétique de la prose* (Paris: Éditions du Seuil, 1978), transformation is the essence of narrative, representing a synthesis of difference and similarity; for Eero Tarasti, in "Music as a Narrative Art," in *Narrative across Media: The Languages of Storytelling*, ed. Marie-Laure Ryan (Lincoln: University of Nebraska Press, 2004), 283–304, it is the minimal condition of narrative. Paul Ricoeur, in *Time and Narrative*, translated by Kathleen McLaughlin and David Pellauer, 2 vols. (Chicago: University of Chicago Press, 1984; 1985), sees transformation as responsible for configuration, turning a series of events into a coherent whole. See also my "Narrative and Narrativity in Music," *Writing Through Music: Essays on Music, Culture, and Politics* (New York: Oxford University Press, 2008).

15. Alpers and Baxandall, *Tiepolo,* 44.

16. Dufourt, unpublished interview (2012).

17. Ibid.

18. Ibid.

19. Dufourt, unpublished interview (2010).

20. Dufourt, Liner notes, 12.

21. As Alpers and Baxandall point out in *Tiepolo*, the Treppenhaus *Four Continents and Apollo* at Würzburg was not unique, but a theme also used on a similar ceiling at the Schloss Weissenstein in Pommersfelden by Johann Byss in 1717–18. The idea of Apollo at its center came from Versailles (110).

22. Dufourt, Liner notes, 12.

23. Dufourt, cited in Martin Kaltenecker, "Resounding Conflicts" in the liner notes to Kairos 0013142KAI (2010), 16.

24. Dufourt, Liner notes, 13.

25. Ibid.

26. With increasing contact with the rest of the world has come preoccupation with racial "mixing." The French anthropologist Paul Broca once argued that when racial hybridity results from "proximate species," "unions between allied races are fertile" and can have advantages. Stronger races necessarily absorb weaker ones. The French exemplify "eugenesic hybridity," a people "formed by the intermixture [*croisement*] of two or more races" that is "indefinitely prolific." Such discourse was important to colonialists who sought to extend their impact on the world. When the French first arrived in Senegal, they promoted racial intermarriage as a way of assuring not only assimilation, but also stable and long-term influence on the culture. However, both Broca and Gobineau believed that, among distantly related races, mixing or "fusion" can threaten to erase the distinctions of difference. Hybridity eventually became a lightning rod for what was wrong with French assimilationist colonial policy from Africa to Indochina. See Paul Broca, *On the Phenomena of Hybridity in the Genus Homo*, ed. C. Carter Blake (London: Longman, Green, Longman, and Roberts, 1864), 8–9, 12,16–18, 25–28 and my "Theorizing Race in 19th-Century France: Music as Emblem of Identity," *Musical Quarterly* 89, 4 (Winter 2006): 459–504.

27. Dufourt, Liner notes, 13.

28. Alpers and Baxandall, *Tiepolo*, 128. Compare *Africa* from three perspectives on p. 128 and *Asia* as seen from the left and the right on p. 131.

29. Dufourt, *"Eléments porteurs de forme,"* 116.

30. Dufourt, Liner notes, 13. See also ibid.

31. Ibid., 21.

32. Ibid., 13.

33. Aristotle, *Poetics*, trans. Ingram Bywater (New York: Modern Library College Editions, 1984)

34. Pasler, *Writing Through Music*, 35–36.

35. *"Tuilage"* has traditionally referred to a singing practice in Brittany whereby one singer picks up on a former one's last syllables, thereby avoiding any interruption. *Wikipedia*, s.v. "Tuilage," accessed April 21, 2011, http://fr.wikipedia.org/wiki/Tuilage. In contemporary music, it refers to a kind of heterophony. See also the articles on tiling in *Perspectives of New Music* 49, no. 1–2 (summer 2011) and examples of patterns in Conway's Game of Life. *Wikipedia*, s.v. "Conway's Game of Life," accessed July 16, 2012, http://en.wikipedia.org/wiki/Conway%27s_Game_of_Life

36. I'm grateful to Nick Reyland for this last point.

37. Dufourt, unpublished interview (2012).

38. Ibid.

39. Dufourt, Liner notes, 13. I have written on a similar phenomena in "Debussy, *Jeux*: Playing with Time and Form," *19th Century Music* 6, no. 1 (June 1982): 60–72, and "Resituating the Spectral Revolution: French Antecedents and the Dialectic of Discontinuity and

Continuity in Debussy's *Jeux*" in *Aspects of Time in the Creation of Music*, ed. Irene Deliège and Max Paddison, special issue, *Musicae Scientiae* 3 (2004): 125–140; Reprinted in my *Writing Through Music*, 82–98.

40. Gisèle Brelet, *Le Temps musical* (Paris: Presses universitaires de France, 1949), 451. For more on these notions of time, see also my "Experiencing Time in the Quartet for the End of Time," in *La la la Maistre Henry. Mélanges de musicologie en hommage à Henri Vanhulst*, ed. Valerie Dufour (Turnhout: Brepols, Collection musical, 2009), 477–485.

41. Dufourt, e-mail to the author (15 July 2012).

42. Dufourt, "*Eléments porteurs de forme*," 116.

43. Dufourt, unpublished interview (2012).

44. Ibid. See "Hugues Dufourt," *Pandore*, accessed September 28, 2012, www.pandore.tv/index.php/joomla-license/papier-a-musique/166-hugues-dufourt

45. Dufourt, "*Eléments porteurs de forme*," 114, 116.

46. Dufourt, unpublished interview (2012).

47. Ibid.

48. Ibid.

Select Bibliography

Alpers, Svetlana, and Michael Baxandall. *Tiepolo and the Pictorial Intelligence*. New Haven, CT: Yale University Press, 1994.

Dufourt, Hugues. "Gérard Grisey: La fonction constituante du temps," *Musicae Scientiae* 3 (2004): 47–69.

——. "Mathesis et subjectivité." Lecture taken from his *Essai sur les principes de la musique*, vol. 1, *Mathesis et subjectivité*. Paris: Editions MF, 2008.

——. Liner notes to Hugues Dufourt, *D'Après Tiepolo: L'Afrique & L'Asie d'après Tiepolo*, KAIROS, 0013142 KAI, 2010.

——. "De la dimension productive de l'intensité et du timbre et leur intégration au système des 'éléments porteurs de forme,'" in *Composer au XXIème siècle, pratiques, philosophies, langages et analyses*. Edited by Sophie Stévance. Paris: Vrin, 2010.

——. "Notice pour *Surgir*." Cited in Martin Kaltenecker. "Parcours de l'oeuvre." On the IRCAM website for Hugues Dufourt, 2008. Accessed September 28, 2012, http://brahms.ircam.fr/composers/composer/1167/workcourse/#parcours.

Pasler, Jann. "Debussy, *Jeux*: Playing with Time and Form." *19th-Century Music* 6, no. 1 (1982): 60–72.

——. "Resituating the Spectral Revolution: French Antecedents and the Dialectic of Discontinuity and Continuity in Debussy's *Jeux*." In *Writing Through Music: Essays on Music, Culture, and Politics*. New York: Oxford University Press, 2008.

——. "Experiencing Time in the *Quartet for the End of Time*." In *La la la Maistre Henry. Mélanges de musicologie en homage à Henri Vanhulst*. Edited by Christine Ballman and Valerie Dufour, 477–485. Turnhout: Brepols, 2009.

——. "Hugues Dufourt's 'Manifesto of the Music of Our Times': Narratives Without History in *L'Afrique* and *L'Asie d'après Tiepolo*." *Perspectives of New Music* 49, no. 1–2 (summer 2011): 198–231.

CHAPTER 38

SCORING FOR FILM AND VIDEO GAMES

Collaborative Practices and Digital Post-Production

RONALD H. SADOFF

THE music for Hollywood feature films and "Triple A" video games has undergone an extraordinary transformation over the past decade. The proliferation of digital technologies has spawned innovative ways of creating film music, as well as redefined the post-production landscape. Using excerpts from interviews with prominent practitioners,[1] I analyze the soundtrack through in-depth and enlightening accounts of compositional and post-production processes. What becomes clear is that the collaborative efforts of composers and post-production professionals are now indispensible for the channeling of an expanding array of technologies that are being used toward creative ends.

Although modeled on its filmic counterpart, video game music diverges notably in its creative practices, which answer to the demands of a dynamic, nonlinear medium. Here, I portray the production of music that is adapted for games within a modular workflow that divides the tasks of the composer from those of the audio director and programmers.

These relatively new innovative ways of creating film scores and video game music have begun to cross-pollinate, with both drawing from their respective technologies, proprietary production techniques, and eclectic compositional styles. In demonstrating this cross-pollination, I present examples drawn from real-world contexts. I will also raise the alarm about what this cross-pollination and the repeated reuse of digital sound libraries may mean to the eventual suppression of individual voices.

THE POST-PRODUCTION LANDSCAPE OF
DIGITAL FILM: A STATE OF CONVERGENCE

Current post-production sound practices reflect a thirty-year evolution in digital technologies, but, in the past decade, there has been an accelerated convergence. The creative practices now employed by composers for commercial media were initially shaped by the digital technologies that emulated analog models used in the production of popular music. Among the core technologies were the MIDI Protocol in 1982,[2] the virtual multitrack recorder (sequencer), and digital synthesis and sampling technologies.[3] With the appearance of Digidesign's ProTools[4] "digital audio workstation" (DAW) in the early 1990s, the record industry initiated its conversion to digital audio production.

Filmmaking underwent an analogous shift to the digital domain through its rapid adoption of Avid System's Digital Nonlinear Editing Systems (NLE). As computers increasingly began to be used in video editing, venerable tape-based traditions were abandoned. Walter Murch's 1997 Oscar for his editing of *The English Patient* heralded the adoption of nonlinear editing by the entertainment and media industries. Simultaneously, film-music editors adopted ProTools for creating their temp tracks[5] and for effecting audio conformations. The term *conformations*, or *conforms*, refers to the process (and the product) used by music editors to resynchronize, realign, and reconstruct the music track to accommodate picture changes made by the new edit of a scene. These changes are routine and occur frequently, both during the composing and after the recording sessions of the score. Very compatible with Avid NLE systems, ProTools became the de facto software for sound editors, score recordists, and recording engineers. As a result, the workflows of all aspects of post-production have adapted around the hyperspeed conditions kindled by increasingly homogenized digital systems. This shift has, in turn, impacted the creative perspectives of those forging interactions among music, sound, and moving images. Mike Barry, re-recording mixer[6] for *Amelia* (2009) and *Men in Black* (1997) portrays a fundamental reshaping:

> What's changed most is that they [directors] have much more time to pay attention to detail, with the digital world. They don't necessarily have to make decisions about anything due to the technology, it seems to me. They can shoot something and then change it in the DI[7] later. They can change the color of whatever that thing is, or erase the telephone lines, all in post-production. With sound, they can post and fix almost everything all the time—in a constant way, from the beginning to the end—as a continuous process, rather than [as] before, [when] you had to commit to physically recording it. You couldn't have everything be "live" all the time. With computers, we more or less can do that now.[8]

A benchmark for efficient, high-speed workflow was set by Studio Area Networks[9] (SAN) in establishing an innovative post-production environment for recording Howard Shore's score for *Lord of the Rings: The Return of the King* (2003). The approach used was revolutionary at the time: no other major film project had yet engaged with the technology to this extent. Music editor Tim Starnes describes the process:

> For the recording and editing of Howard Shore's score for *Lord of the Rings: The Return of the King* at Abbey Road Studios, all of the hard drives were kept in Studio 1, the main recording room. They were then linked to computers throughout Abbey Road, allowing the interactive dynamic of three music editors to work simultaneously off of different drives: one dedicated for mixing and another set of drives used for the recording of live music. Previously, hard drives were accessed discretely, i.e. physically passed from editor to editor, and thus reducing workflow to an inefficient linear mode, dictated as per the prioritized needs for individual access.[10]

A decade later, the digital post-production landscape now enables instantaneous access and simultaneous manipulation of all filmic elements. Tim Starnes opines, "The result of the ever-evolving technology for film post-production is that the lines between offline editing,[11] online editing, and the finished product have become thoroughly blurred."[12] The industrial workflow has been transformed by the wholesale rendering of high-quality filmic elements from offline mixes. This production includes superb quality soundtrack mixes produced offline and routinely inserted into the mix (DI) far earlier than analog, tape-based systems permitted. Pristine "temp mixes" now appear in audience preview screenings. Mike Barry notes a pronounced effect in practice:

> For us [re-recording mixers], in a practical sense, it's very, very complicated to keep track of all that information all the time, on an ongoing basis. So they [directors] come in for their first temp mix—which should not even be called a temp mix anymore, because it's so large. There [are] just as many tracks as you have in a final mix, often—maybe not the music being quite as robust because it hasn't been recorded yet—it's all demoed stuff. The effects are hundreds and hundreds of tracks, and the dialogue is many, many tracks, and there's ADR[13] already and there's Foley[14] already. That's where they really invent the sound of the movie, is in the first temp. And they don't want to then go back and then start over again, which historically is what we did [with analog tape]. We couldn't keep it. Now it doesn't have to be changed every single time you come in to do the next change because it's just digitally remembered, and you can just build upon that—and that's what they expect now.[15]

Facilitating the complex interworking of collaborative post-production personnel, the internet has become an indispensible messenger, invoking a state of hyperconvergence born from its sheer speed and immediacy via hyperlinks. Composer Sean Callery, who has created the music for television shows such as *24*, *Bones*, and *Homeland*, notes:

> [Over the past 10 years,] the thing that has probably changed the most for me personally and professionally is the Internet and the communication that is established through the Internet. As that gets faster and more immediate, I am finding the environment with producers and with editors, and so forth, is changing dramatically.... Whenever they had to edit a relocked picture, they had to coordinate

a whole other delivery. Eventually it went to VHS and eventually to DVD. And now, ten years later, most of the episodes that I receive are posted online and you pull them down. What that does is it seriously truncates the turnaround schedule because editors will work on until the last minute because they are not getting notes fast enough. The technological advances with the speed of the Internet have completely changed the workflow.

DIRECTORIAL VISION, UNDERSCORE, AND MUSIC CONFORMS: *THE DEPARTED* (2006)

A director's concept for the soundtrack may be fully realized prior to the score's recording and editing in the post-production phase. The flexibility with which a director may now audition source music and develop underscoring relies on software that facilitates transparency between composer and music editor. The process by which Martin Scorsese incorporated Howard Shore's tango into *The Departed* is a perfect example of how these digital technologies expedite the composer's task of achieving the director's vision. Scorsese's inventive and idiosyncratic approach to applying music to his films is reflected in his remarkably varied soundtracks: the 1960s songs throughout *Goodfellas* (1990), Elmer Bernstein's period score for *The Age of Innocence* (1993), and a hybrid blend of original and preexisting music for *Gangs of New York* (2002). For *The Departed* (2006), Scorsese combined provocative preexisting songs with an underscore that revolved around a kind of leitmotif in the form of a tango. Atypically, while the movie was still in production, Scorsese asked Shore to compose thematic material for the film that resulted in a tango composed for guitars. The director envisioned intrigue stemming from the sensual form of a tango combined with the complexities woven from the melodic and rhythmic counterpoint invoked by the guitars. Strategically placing the tango in scenes throughout the film, Scorsese intensified the narrative entanglements that defined its morally bereft characters, characterizing them through a lethal dance.

Based on the script and discussions with the director, Shore initially created variations of his tango through a series of recording sessions, each featuring a guitarist[16] whose genre specialization was in some way germane to the characters' interactions within the film. This approach resulted in a diverse pool of cues, embodying a variety of styles, sonic designs, and rhythmic structures. As Scorsese progressively placed and contextualized Shore's tango within the specific narrative demands for each scene, the variations were utilized in much the same way as the other preexisting music chosen for the film. Like the Rolling Stones' "Gimme Shelter" and Dropkick Murphy's "I'm Shipping Up to Boston," a tango has a distinctive style and is culturally resonant. By way of example, Scorsese relied on the underlying musical conventions and lyrics for "Shipping Up to Boston" to intensify a scene in which Billy (Leonardo DiCaprio) is being released from prison (19:10). Its triplet rhythms conjure a boisterous Irish feel, and a violent tenor emanates from its underling rock beat, aggressive vocal strains, and macabre lyrics. A confluence of cultures is invoked by the song's accordion, its traditional Irish sound virtually synonymous with the uilleann pipes that signaled decorum in Colin's (Matt Damon) graduation from the police academy (6:45).

Shore's "*Departed* Tango" variations appear in nearly a dozen scenes throughout *The Departed*. However, Scorsese initially dispersed them throughout the film as though they were *temp tracks*, that is, a preexisting underscore, skillfully composed and proportioned but intended for a scene from a different film of related dramatic import. In addition, Scorsese edited the film *after* Shore had composed and recorded his tangos, thus requiring conforms to accommodate the director's fine editing of each scene. As a preemptive measure to ensure quality, compositional integrity, and a workflow capable of adapting to extensive editorial changes, Shore devised a system by which potential changes to the music's tone, texture, rhythms, and timings could be more fluidly affected.

To begin, an enormous production library of tango gestures and phrases had accrued from his initial recording sessions with the four guitarists. Variations of the tango melody had been performed, varied rhythmic accompaniments were recorded in the same tempo for synchronization purposes, performances were recorded in combinations of steel strings and nylon strings, and electric guitars using rock-style distortion effects were intermixed. Then, using ProTools, music editor Tim Starnes assembled the hundreds of discrete melodic and rhythmic variations into a loop-based digital editing system. As a result, virtually any of the musical elements could be mixed and matched to suit the director's dramatic needs for a scene and could then be swiftly implemented by Shore. A vast array of combinations was possible, such as a rhythmic loop performed by Larry Salzman mixed with a solo riff by G. E. Smith. Over a period of months, a library of permutations evolved, although some scenes still required Shore to return to the recording studio to overdub a string section or augment a cue that reached beyond the library's dramatic capacity for a particular scene. Shore's flexible, modular solution for attaining dramatic consonance in the wake of the directorial freedom accorded by a digital post-production environment is a representative scenario that depicts a revamping of the creative process while retaining compositional control and integrity.

VIDEO GAMES: POST-LESS PRODUCTION

RON SADOFF: Film re-recording mixers Mike Barry and Dominick Tavella[17] have noted that with the robust inclusion of technology, the post-production phase has essentially evolved into a continuation of production.

JEAN-LUC COHEN: And similarly, in the gaming industry, there has never really ever been post-production, but has simply only been "production." The technology has always facilitated change throughout the production of a game.[18]

Video games have largely inhabited the digital realm since the 1972 release of Atari's *Pong*, whose modest soundscape consisted of a few noise-generated tones that were synchronized with gameplay.[19] As with the development of film sound—from the live, off-screen sound of silent films,[20] through the inception of synchronized sound for *The Jazz Singer* (1927), and now Dolby Digital Surround Sound—the development of game sound has flourished through technical advancements. Modeled on their Hollywood counterparts, "Triple A" games now embody a cinematic breadth replete with complex audio mixes in surround sound. However, the implementation of game sound and its myriad of functional synergies within gameplay diverges significantly from live-action film's post-production practices. The unique set of conditions necessary to create non-linear adaptive music[21] does not incorporate a post-production phase, but rather a protracted timeframe spent in production. The development of music for video games is more closely akin to that of the underscore for an animated narrative film; music is incorporated quite early in production and develops continually forward as an "evolving temp track."[22]

THE AUDIO DIRECTOR: ENVISIONING GAME SOUND, MASHUPS, AND MANAGEMENT

Audio directors Clint Bajakian and Paul Gorman develop the soundtrack for a game by first formulating a musical style guide. Facilitated by the ease of editing within digital multitracking and looping programs, their process may be initiated by merging disparate styles through audio "mashups." For *Dante's Inferno* (2010), Gorman's initial conception of the music[23] was discovered through his "mashing up" of elements of Penderecki's *St. Luke Passion* (1966), the remake of the film *War of the Worlds* (2005), and percussion hits.[24] Similar to a film-music editor's process for creating a temp track, source material is teased from existing sources, and a demo "hybrid" composed of inventive combinations materializes. The broad range of game types tends to encourage experimentation with more original approaches than those generally utilized for film. This trend suits veteran game composers like Garry Schyman and Tom Salta, who are accustomed to the idiosyncratic techniques necessary for scoring games. However, for derivative works, whether in video games or film, this creative mode is trumped by producers who purposefully seek out expected iconic styles and the associated and visible Hollywood composers. The musical profiles for film franchises like *Harry Potter* feature signature musical themes, massive orchestral and choral forces, and well-trod stylistic and syntactical conventions, such as a proliferation of mediant chord progressions. John Williams' scores for the *Star Wars* films are so culturally resonant that LucasArts,[25] publisher of the *Star Wars* games, can virtually cut in portions of Williams' cues ported directly from the original film score. His varied orchestrations and constant shifts of mood and intensity provide audio editors with a dynamic organic flow and strong potential for spontaneous synchronizations ("happy accidents") to occur with events in the course of gameplay.

"Triple A" games typically require between 70 and 120 minutes of composed music to provide enough source material to subsequently create the additional music needed to cover between 10 and 100 hours of potential gameplay.[26] By comparison, an original score for a dramatic film generally requires between 30 and 40 minutes of music. In facilitating this creation, a game composer works under the guidance of a multitasking audio director who oversees the development, administration, and implementation of the entire soundtrack. Hence, the combination of musical and technical skills needed renders the production of game music a segmented and intrinsically collaborative process. GarrySchyman, composer for *Bioshock* (2007) comments:

> Very often they [the Audio Director] choose the composer, as well…. They tell you what kind of music they need, and they give you input so that you do your job and make music that works and fits. In some instances, they're the final word on music…. They are very much responsible for generating the theme and the creative ideas. In essence, the closest parallel in film would be the director. When you work with the director, they are talking with you on a daily or whenever they need to basis, and telling you what kind of music and approving cues, and telling you if they don't like something or if they do, or if you're right on, etc.[27]

Veteran game composer Tom Salta:

> I deal with an audio director who is unusual in the sense that he is a musician himself, and thinks outside of the box more than most people, and he comes up with suggestions that I would never have thought of. He'll suggest combining elements like taking a drum feel from this, an orchestral feel from this, a bass line from this— and I'll make them work. Sometimes they come out so great that I wonder if he knew that it was going to sound like it does.[28]

Audio directors, who possess an amalgamation of technical skills, managerial acumen, and strong musical instincts, play the most active and influential role in producing the adaptive score for a video game. Their oversight takes direct lineage from video game production practices of the early 1980s, when programmers also served as the composers of sparse, quirky, and infectious soundtracks. The music was largely governed by the limitations of sound technology, the programmers' deficient compositional backgrounds, and pop music sensibilities. As a result, catchy sonic signatures emerged from such wildly popular games as *PacMan* (1980) and *Super Mario Brothers* (1985). In the cacophonous, carnival atmosphere of game arcades, their rudimentary soundscapes became iconic and enhanced the gaming experience. An array of varied game types ensued, authored for gaming platforms that were designed for both home use and use on handheld devices.

Buoyed by the iPhone, iPad, and Android devices, a growing segment of "boutique games" continues to proliferate, although they are far more technically evolved. At the high end of today's spectrum, sophisticated motion detectors and haptic controllers powered by hardware platforms like Microsoft's Xbox and the Sony Playstation 3 now afford immersive, hyperreal cinematic experiences. Tom Salta highlights the creative breadth of video games and the malleability afforded to composers:

> [Today], the variety of types of games is staggering. I venture to say that there is so much more variety in the video-game world—in terms of the mechanics, under the hood—than film. If a film is about a little girl in a balloon or some huge futuristic apocalyptic thing, the mechanics are still the same. In games, there are mechanics that enable them to do certain things you just cannot do with regular playback of music to picture. *Super Mario* games still do the music with MIDI or a hybrid of MIDI and prerecorded stuff. And they can do so much more. And they don't do it because they don't have the technology. You can dynamically change certain components in the music in real time. You break it down into micro-bits of music— there was a game called *Flower*[29] where someone did this, and it was like playing a poem and you literally are the wind and you're flying around bringing all of these fields from these dull black and white colors to life. The music was devised from these repeating motifs. As you bring more flowers up to life another motif would appear in counterpoint, which would develop the music as you moved ahead in the gameplay. You can't compare that to a film. It's a whole different thing.[30]

Given the market share that video games now command, the genre has become a viable venue for composers from film and other media. In the process of selecting a composer for a "Triple A" game, an audio director will audition hundreds of music library tracks and peruse composer demo reels, as well as seeking opinions from key personnel in his production unit. Although initially culling from a broad stylistic musical swatch, the audio director ultimately seeks a composer with an individual voice, whose music can provide added value to the dynamic of the game.

J. P. Walton, audio director for Double Helix Games:

> When I hire a composer, I'm hiring that composer because I want their style. There's going to be direction given to them, and they might have to do certain things to fit a scene.... but I'm not going to ask the composer to do a Hans Zimmer imitation.[31]

Scoring "Adaptive Music": The Compositional Process for Video Games

In providing a cinematic experience, "Triple A" games incorporate sophisticated motion capture graphics and rousing orchestral/electronic "hybrid" scores, some penned by distinguished Hollywood film and television composers. Hired primarily for their visibility and musical personas, these composers rarely possess the technical backgrounds or compositional skills applicable to video game production. Therefore, audio directors have amended their production workflow to accommodate film composers' linear approach that was originally intended for scoring to "locked" visual sequences. Television composer Sean Callery has been hired to score video games based on the stylistic traits present in his widely known scores for the television series *24* (2001–2010) and *Medium* (2005–2011).

> RON SADOFF: Judging from the "mockup reel" that you showed me for a current game you're scoring, it seems very similar to a rough-cut that you might be handed when scoring a film. It appears that you are not expected to deal with the host of technical matters like compression schemes or even middleware like FMOD or Wwise.[32] It sounds as though you are writing primarily toward dramatic ends.
>
> SEAN CALLERY: Yes, what's happening is, like a movie, they send me a script. And the script has about nine chapters in it—nine little areas—and within those areas there's probably two or three missions per…chapter. And the chapters to me are sort of like reels of the picture—a reel of a movie. It's very relevant, so I kind of treat the scoring of a game like I would if I were scoring a movie or other "long-form" medium.[33]

Yet, with the exception of "cutscenes"—that is, transitional "in-game movies"—the compositional approach must continually gauge music in terms of its capacity to adapt dynamically to variations within gameplay. This requirement bears a close resemblance to the film-music editor's task of creating temp tracks, in which he or she must take into account specific genres, moods, and musical/cultural encodings. For adaptive music, however, it is the audio director who embeds the composer's score throughout the game, invariably drawing on the myriad variations that he has assembled from the composer's preexisting score. Garry Schyman, composer for *Dante's Inferno*, describes his approach, which consciously refrains from synchronizing music and moving image:

> While I locked the picture [to a game mockup reel], I was constantly changing the reference of the start point so that I was constantly aware that I am not scoring this particular scene. All I am doing is creating mood music for this particular portion of the game.[34]

In this respect, just as a film composer relies on a film-music editor to perform conformations, a game composer depends on an audio director to synchronize his music to gameplay. Another key compositional approach is to ensure that the music is flexible enough to be readily broken down and then reassembled into a series of interlocking and coherent musical segments. Paul Gorman, audio director for Electronic Arts, offers his perspective:

> [My] approach with a composer is to first approach music as a linear piece, and giving him [Schyman] scenes from gameplay. Once we arrive at music that we like, we decide…how we'll slice this up…. Many compositions are divided into orchestration "food groups." [For a scene from *Dante's* Inferno] we typically use three layers: skirmish cue—back-and-forth with fighting—and [without]. The solution is

to fade layers up and down as opposed to flipping [i.e., making sudden shifts from one layer to another].

Regarding another scene from *Dante's Inferno,* Gorman notes that Schyman composed a static underlying loop, intended as an atmospheric and supportive undercurrent. Schyman also provided Gorman with numerous individual musical "layers," each matched to the underlying loop by key, tempo, duration, and so on. Each layer embodied a specific function, like "tension" or "angelic choirs," designed to empower Gorman with the freedom to mix and superimpose the layers that would reflect a succession of events likely to occur in the course of gameplay. Thus, a variety of adaptive mixtures may be triggered by a player's progression within a scene. Callery describes this challenge of creating the range of musical illustrations necessary for a war game and its host of potential "game states":

> I was also in a mindset where, during the mission, you kind of understand…the permutations—…the possibilities—that the character that you're controlling will go through. There were times where the character would get wounded, but not killed, or get wounded even further. So I was designing musical colors that would depict if he was off his game. If he was getting wounded, the music would tackle that a bit there. Or if he got some bonus or he was doing great, he would be in a "plus" category. So I designed the music so that I would have that option. If they [game programmers or designers] wanted to go where he gets wounded, the music could jump to that area.[35]
>
> One might theorize that it's a bit modular in the way things are getting done, and nowhere is that more prevalent than in the video-game world.[36]

MODULAR WORKFLOW: FILM SCORING AND CONFORMS FOR *THE LORD OF THE RINGS*

Sparked by the creative freedom afforded directors via nonlinear editing, the processes by which films are scored have become increasingly similar to those utilized in producing soundtracks for video games. For instance, the conformations performed by film-music editors in answering to a steady stream of new picture cuts parallel the tasks of game audio directors who continually synchronize linear musical elements with the fluctuations generated throughout gameplay. In the production practices for both film and video games, a bifurcation of creative and technical skill sets continually emerges, spawning new specialists who develop novel approaches to workflow. Howard Shore's inventive solution for shaping dramatically concise variations of his "*Departed* Tango" is a perfect example. But far more complex and extensive music editing was required to support his composition of the monumental scores for

The Lord of the Rings: The Two Towers (2002) and *The Lord of the Rings: The Return of the King* (2003).

For these movies, director Peter Jackson's recurring picture edits occurred primarily prior to the orchestral recording sessions, necessitating a measured and efficient workflow to maintain the timetable necessary for composing a massive score. To avoid any time-consuming and debilitating rewrites that would arise with new picture edits, Shore devised a system by which music conforms would systematically alleviate many of the problems. In brief, the music that Shore initially composed and synchronized for a scene would be harvested and rendered largely intact, for inclusion within Peter Jackson's re-edited versions. Traditionally a film-music editor conforms music that has already been recorded, but in this framework, music editor Tim Starnes executed conforms prior to the orchestral recording sessions. This approach involved a complex series of conforms incorporating Shore's audio versions of his MIDI mockups, Digital Performer files of his MIDI sequences, and Finale notation files, as well as the reconciliation of new picture edits via Final Cut Pro. This rigorous operational mode continued throughout Shore's scoring of the films, entailing elaborate conforms for each and every re-edited scene. Starnes, however, notes the benefits achieved through this method for the finished score: "It doesn't sound like an audio edit...it actually sounds like an intentional performance." Judicious conformations faithfully resynchronized major portions of the original score with the new picture edits, retaining the integrity of Shore's music. Shore then had to "recompose" music only for selected portions of edited scenes, such as transitions and the expected gaps that Starnes' conforms could not cover. In sum, the composer's intended relationships between his score and the film's narrative and visual structures were sustained. Furthermore, the process allowed Shore to move forward consistently with scoring new cues.

Executing conforms in the course of scoring a film is now a common practice. However, as described earlier, it demands an eclectic skill set that combines a compositional background with the working knowledge of an integrated suite of audiovisual software tools. In general, the breadth of tasks assumed by a film-music editor has expanded, leading these individuals to exert more influence on the creative process and thus making the job more comparable to those endeavors engaged in by game audio directors.

BRIDGING FILM AND VIDEO GAMES: THE HOLLYWOOD SOUND

From the inception of synchronized scores, from Alfred Newman to Randy Newman and Thomas Newman, film music has always been a product and a reflection of undergirding cultural codes articulated via orchestral traditions and popular music sensibilities. Although the music for video games evolved along a far different path, the robust orchestral-electronic hybrid soundtracks of today's "Triple A" games now emulate the cinematic breadth of film scores. Insofar as commercial film, video games, and popular songs are produced within collaborative environments, they are shaped by a modular editorial apparatus and mediated by decisions made by corporate committees. Among the most influential forces that bridge innovative music production processes to high-profile films and video games is the composer "collective" within Hans Zimmer's Remote Control Productions. Zimmer has developed a system, cast in a highly efficient industrial mold, that exploits the varied talents in Remote Control's eclectic mix of composers. Infusing conventional musical practices with pop-based forms and soundscapes, their soundtracks are hewn from both live and sample-based instruments and then maneuvered through a bevy of leading-edge post-production processes. Costly techniques such as recording the orchestra's four choirs individually are often employed to provide stems[37] that permit an extraordinary level of flexibility and control for a final film mix.[38] Divested of a sound aesthetic modeled on the concert hall, a "hyperorchestral cinematic sound" has emerged. This phenomenon is exemplified by the "Hollywood sound" present in both Hans Zimmer's score for *Deception* (2010) and Harry Gregson-Williams' soundtrack for the video game *Metal Gear Solid 4: Guns of the Patriots* (2008).

MIDI-Mockups and the DNA of Sound Materials

The efficacy of a score is initially tested through a composer's MIDI mockup, a picture-locked electronic version of the finished score. Mockups have become an indispensible tool for communication between director and composer, providing the director with a full-scale preview and granting considerable editorial 'flexibility' by virtue of their modular and thus malleable design. At the sonic-DNA level, composers draw from a common pool of virtual instrument libraries. Orchestral libraries are professionally mastered and provide composers with "the Hollywood sound in a box." Multitrack sequencing software, in tandem with sophisticated virtual instruments and studio effects, can result in orchestral mockups that are nearly indistinguishable from their acoustic counterparts. Virtual synthesizers produce a tantalizing range of preprogrammed soundscapes and programmable instruments that reflect popular trends or the iconic retro-sound of a Minimoog synthesizer. A cornucopia of virtual ethnic instruments proliferates, and experimental libraries born from the recordings of natural objects, like kitchen utensils, are digitally processed into useful and playable instruments.

Sequencers (virtual multitrack recorders) shed the confines of linear-based composition, providing alternative creative tools more germane to producing loop-based music for popular and ethnic genres. Composers now create tracks assembled from vast palettes of "virtual" instruments, from the conventional to the rarified. Their fluid access to diverse sound libraries encourages experimentation and the cross-pollination of genres and cultures. The most extreme ideas may be readily implemented: for instance, *Klangfarben*, where each melodic and harmonic pitch sounds from a discrete virtual instrument. Furthermore, popular musical instruments and gestures may be interlaced with orchestral sounds, and diverse genres may be readily mixed together to form the recombinant "mashups" associated with urban music and the production of video game soundtracks.

As a result, composers function much like producers, exercising command over sample libraries and the evolving mechanisms within their sequencers. Additionally, they must assemble teams to assist them in managing the ongoing communications among editorial personnel, complex recording session protocols, synchronization, and mixing issues. Ultimately, all elements of composition and collaboration must coalesce for the score to sound like a coherent musical entity.

Reappropriating Genres and Codes

Virtual instrument libraries constitute a broad, yet selective sonic ethnography spanning popular, traditional, and world cultures. They provide an expansive pool of sounds that all commercial media composers draw from. Their file names reflect the practical, prejudiced, and esoteric: "viola solo legato mp," "tundra travel," "Singapore squeak," and "Jihad" (an evolving soundscape combining dark "Middle Eastern" timbres, a driving rhythmic loop, and a male chorus chanting "Arabic" phonemes). Extensive performance articulations enable faithful emulations of acoustic instruments, and modulation provides expressive control of synthesizers and digital signal processors. Acoustic libraries are packaged by related instruments: "Galaxy Pianos," "Ministry of Rock," and "Symphonic Orchestra." In the case of non-Western instruments, they are often assembled as an aggregate of culturally related sounds, such as "Silk" and "Desert Winds," which contain ethnic "eastern" instruments that may encompass the music of entire continents. They contain familiar and identifiable instruments like the *shakuhachi* and *tabla*, as well as the *ney* flute and *rag-dung*, for which only selective timbres may be provided. In effect, a rich cultural heritage may be reduced to disembodied sounds and restricted nomenclature. Similarly, the aptly named "Hollywood Strings" library reflects the current Hollywood orchestra studio sound of *Gladiator* (2000) and *Avatar* (2009), which no longer reflects the live sound aesthetics of the concert hall or the Hollywood sound of earlier generations. The aesthetic choices utilized in creating virtual instruments invoke the Western-centric perspective of its producers and composers, who must operate within the boundaries of Hollywood's musical and cultural conventions, as well as their audience's expectations.

For example, collating the virtual instrumental forces necessary for producing an orchestral mockup is straightforward, guided by venerable underlying musical conventions established in Europe and transformed by Hollywood. Conversely, the potential for assembling and homogenizing thoroughly diverse and disparate elements is equally viable. In essence, non-Western instruments may be easily appropriated, but they are not often utilized specifically by virtue of their core values as cultural artifacts. Rather, they may be "discovered" through sheer proximity and subsequently chosen for use by virtue of their color and visceral impact. Their cultural currency is assessed primarily within the scope of Western sensibilities and the needs of the project at hand. Concomitantly, the intrinsic performance practices of an ethnic instrument may be eschewed or reappropriated only partially, in order to provide a specific texture that might embellish or color a cue. A *kantele*[39] might be selected entirely for its distinctive, ethnic "zitherish" sound, yet, in the process, become divorced from its ontological rooting and performance practices. Although the *kantele* maintains cultural currency in parts of the world, to the extent that producers and their audiences remain oblivious to this fact, a composer may essentially recontextualize and recodify the instrument within the purview of Western audiences. By way of example, the *duduk* is now a common, recognizable, accepted, and representative "ethnic flavor." Whether its presence in *Gladiator* (2000) is culturally accurate is of no consequence because the instrument had been well established through its recurrent use in related films like Scorsese's *The Last Temptation of Christ* (1988). This kind of compositional shorthand represents a venerable practice exemplified by Miklos Rozsa's use of "invented" instruments for the music of antiquity in *Quo Vadis* (1951) and for the simulated Arabic music composed by Ira Newborn for the opening of *Naked Gun: From the Files of Police Files!* (1988).

Over the course of nearly two decades of digital filmmaking, scoring practices have diverged vastly from those heard in the classical Hollywood era. The early Hollywood sound was firmly entrenched in cultural and musical codes born from late Romanticism. Embedded in the scores of Max Steiner, "film music is the only music that began in its 'Golden Era.'"[40] The orchestral film score has evolved and is no longer a scion of late Romanticism. Virtual orchestral instruments have infused the symphony orchestra with pristine re-recorded versions, digitally processed as today's film sound. The musical gestures and instrumental palettes are modeled squarely on the zeitgeist of twenty-first-century sensibilities, as Danny Elfman, composer for *Spiderman* (2002) and *Dark Shadows* (2012) observes:

> I never pretend to excel at my ability to pull from so many different sources. People with much more classical training have a much wider palette to pull from. I'm actually pulling [musical references] from film music rather than from classical music…. After I did *Batman* (1989), someone said there was this passage that was obviously very Wagnerian. Well, I've never actually listened to a Wagner opera, but I have listened to a lot of Korngold, and I know Korngold often quoted Wagner, so I probably got a second-hand Wagner. But my sources come from those [film] composers.[41]

Although the budgets for Hollywood feature films and "Triple A" video games afford their composers extensive technical support and recording sessions with live orchestras, for much of the ubiquitous music heard in television, advertising, music production libraries, and low-budget projects, the MIDI mockup often serves as the final product. Therefore, the proliferation and rehashing of deeply similar sounds, gestures, and codes are spread across all media. As such, they are permeating and can breed staid uniformity while constricting creative breadth. Nevertheless, composers like James Newton-Howard utilize these sound technologies for creating exquisite mockups and unique "hybrid" soundscapes that integrate with live musicians. Ironically, sample libraries often feature distinctive soundscapes that emulate those inventive musical sculptures. But, with overexposure, the impact of an original voice is eventually reduced to a convention or even devalued as a cliché. For example, most virtual piano libraries provide an emulation of Thomas Newman's austere and intimate piano timbre from his score for *The Shawshank Redemption* (1994). Newman evokes an ethereal yet expressive atmosphere through a combination of acoustic instruments, processed timbres, and richly coded harmonies. Moreover, music editors utilized Newman's cue "Brooks Was Here" extensively in temp tracks throughout the 1990s and early 2000s. As a result, it was defined as the contemporary expression of Americana and, ultimately, the alternative to Aaron Copland's America.

* * *

The collaborative practices present in the digital post-production realm have evolved as its practitioners have adapted their creative workflows to modular systems. Robust hardware and software frameworks have generated the means for unprecedented speed and accessibility. This development has facilitated innovative recasting of the interactive pathways by which technical and creative tasks are accomplished. Tasks requiring new specialists have arisen with the bifurcation of technical and creative responsibilities. However, the technology has also enabled concurrent and collaborative efforts. For the first time in history, thanks to the digital domain of zeros and ones, all content is interchangeable. As is true of the internet, nonlinearity enables the dissemination of information and permits the homogenization of varied data. Moreover, a chronological perspective has yielded to juxtaposition and to the assimilation of heterogeneous elements, as though plucked from within our "field of vision." Similarly, those who construct temp tracks, music loops, and mashups, as well as effect conformations, appropriate music and repurpose it within new contexts. Audio editors and film-music editors have thus been emboldened and their scope of influence expanded.

A sea change is still in progress. The stylistic scope and compositional backgrounds of composers for Hollywood feature films and "Triple A" video games have diversified in the wake of an evolving digital production environment. The musical and political gulf that once applied between writers of popular forms and conservatory-trained composers has diminished, shrunk by the intersections of technology and eclectic compositional approaches. The increased visibility of video game music and the proliferation of songs in soundtracks over the past two decades have brought about a more malleable interplay between preexisting music and underscore. Although the symphony orchestra remains the primary scoring vehicle for blockbuster films and "Triple A" games, the frequent inclusion of synthesized timbres and popular music syntax suggests an essential shift in aesthetic perspective. The panoply of platforms that comprise *Broadcast Music*—from traditional outlets in television to evolving mobile devices—are now fortified by digital fingerprinting and the promise of lucrative royalty streams for composers of all stripes. Eminently accessible, commercial media has become a bastion for the cross-pollination of heterogeneous sounds and styles, but with tendencies toward the repeated reuse of conventions and clichés. Regardless, creative opportunities abound in the digital realm, where audio "mashups" and hybrid scores may inspire innovation as they blur stylistic lines.

NOTES

1. This essay draws directly from personal interviews, as well as from the panels noted below. My perspective is contextualized through experience that straddles the academy and the industry—that is, as the architect of the NYU Steinhardt program in "Scoring for Film and Multimedia" and as a member of the East Coast Steering Committee for The Society of Composers and Lyricists (SCL); as co-founder/co-editor of the UIP journal *Music and the Moving Image* and as a professional composer for commercial media.

   Personal Interviews:

   Michael Barry, re-recording mixer (*Men in Black*; *Fargo*), June 10, 2011.
   Scan Callery, composer (*24*; *Bones*; *James Bond: Everything or Nothing* (video game), June 2 and 13, 2011.
   Tom Salta, video game composer (*H.A.W.X.*; *Prince of Persia*), June 13, 2011.
   Jean-Luc Cohen, game sound editor (*Doom*), July 25, 2011.
   Tim Starnes, music editor (*Lord of the Rings*; *Hugo*; *The Departed*), July 7, 2011.
   Dominick Tavella, re-recording mixer (*Requiem for a Dream*; *Black Swan*), June 7, 2011.

   Conference Panels:

   "Video Games Scoring: Working with Audio Directors." Panel presentation hosted by the SCL. Panelists: Clint Bajakian, Paul Gorman, Dave Rovin, J. P. Walton, Garry Schyman. The American Film Institute, Los Angeles, October 6, 2009.
   "The Game Music Business: Relationships Between Composers and Large Corporations." Panel presentation hosted by the SCL. Panelists: Chuck Doud, Adam Levinson, and Victor Rodriguez. The American Film Institute, Los Angeles, January 13, 2009.
   "Following the Score: Film Music from Composition to Recording to Postproduction." Panel workshop at the 127th Audio Engineering (AES) Convention, Jacob Javitz Center, New York City. Ron Sadoff, chair; Lawrence Manchester, recordist/mixer (*The Good Shepherd*); Ira Newborn, composer (*The Naked Gun*); Tim Starnes; Dominick Tavella. October 9, 2009.
2. As a collective initiative of musical instrument manufacturers in 1982, the Musical Instrument Digital Interface (MIDI) Protocol established industry standards for communication and synchronization between electronic musical instruments, keyboard controllers, drum machines, and computers. The MIDI Protocol broke new ground by offering composers and performers direct access to the spectrum of electronic instruments

through traditional means like keyboards and virtual multitrack recorders. Today, "MIDI" is a generic term referring to music that is produced synthetically.

3. The digital hybrid sample/synthesis of the Fairlight Computer Music Instrument (CMI) and New England Digital's Synclavier 9600 formed an underlying element of the 1980s sonic signature. Priced at $125,000–500,000, only the most visible and iconic recording and performing artists, such as Sting, Frank Zappa, Laurie Anderson, and Michael Jackson, owned these instruments. Composer Jan Hammer relied on the signature sound of the Fairlight CMI for his soundtracks to the original *Miami Vice* series. Other early adopters included television composer Mark Snow, who continued to apply the Synclavier's distinctive range of electronic sounds to his atmospheric scores for the *X-Files* television series, which debuted in 1993.

In 1983, the Kurzweil 250 ($11,000) was created for Stevie Wonder; it was the first digital, sample-based musical instrument, featuring realistic acoustic sounds burned into its ROM. From the late 1980s through 2000, hardware samplers from Akai and Roland proliferated, offering increasingly affordable options for all composers and performers. Yet only over the past decade have computer processing speeds and inexpensive hard drives permitted robust "virtual instruments" and integrated software suites.

4. Avid Systems acquired Digidesign in 1995.

5. Ronald Sadoff, "The Role of the Music Editor and the 'Temp Track' as a Blueprint for the Score, Source Music, and Scource Music of Films," *Popular Music* 25, no. 2 (2006): 165–183.

Temp tracks serve as the primary conceptual blueprint for a film score: a robust musical topography of score, songs, culture, and codes in which a balance must obtain among the director's vision, the music's function, the underlying requirements of genre, and the spectator's perception.

6. A re-recording mixer, once referred to as a "dubbing mixer," is part of a postproduction sound team that combines all previously recorded dialogue, music, and sound effects tracks to create the final (re-recorded) soundtrack.

7. The digital intermediate (DI) provides a repository for all production elements in a digitally converted form; thus, they are available for editing and mixing throughout a project's postproduction phase.

8. Mike Barry, interview by author, June 10, 2011.

9. Studio Network Solutions produces and configures Studio Area Networks (SAN) by incorporating fiberoptic drive networks [www.studionetworksolutions.com/].

10. Tim Starnes, interview by author, July 7, 2011.

11. "Offline editing" is a postproduction process by which filmic elements, like music, are copied from the original footage for editing and then prepared for the "online editing" stage. There, all filmic elements are reassembled for the final edit. Over the past decade, the quality of offline editing has been buoyed by technologies that render them indistinguishable from those utilized for online edits.

12. Tim Starnes, interview by author, July 7, 2011.

13. Automated Dialogue Replacement or Additional Dialogue Recording (ADR) refers to the process of an actor re-recording lines spoken during filming in order to improve the audio quality, intelligibility, or any dialogue changes.

14. Foley, named after Jack Foley, whose pioneering efforts established the craft in the silent era, refers to the postproduction process of reproducing everyday sounds that bring realism to a film. These sounds may include footsteps, squeaky faucets, or doors opening. Like ADR, they are re-recorded to improve sound quality, intelligibility, or to enhance the overall realism.

15. Mike Barry, interview by author, June 10, 2011.
16. The guitarists Sharon Isbin, G. E. Smith, Larry Saltzman, and Marc Ribot, were recorded by Howard Shore in his upstate New York Studio. The recording procedures were noted by Tim Starnes in an interview on July 7, 2012.
17. Dominick Tavella is a distinguished re-recording mixer working from the *Sound One* postproduction facility in New York City. His extensive credits include Aronovsky's *Black Swan* (2010) and Ken Burns' *Baseball* (1994–2010).
18. Jean-Luc Cohen, interview by author, July 25, 2011.
19. Karen Collins, *Game Sound: An Introduction to the History, Theory, and Practice of Video Game Music and Sound Design* (Cambridge, MA: MIT Press, 2008).
20. Gillian B. Anderson, *Music for Silent Film (1892–1922): A Guide* (Washington, DC: Library of Congress, 1988).
21. *Adaptive music* refers to video game music conceived and designed to react in response to the events that occur during gameplay.
22. Jack Curtis Dubowsky, "The Evolving Temp Score in Animation," *Music, Sound and the Moving Image* 5, no. 1 (2011): 1–24.
23. Clint Bajakian, Paul Gorman, Dave Rovin, J. P. Walton, and Garry Schyman, "Video Games Scoring: Working with Audio Directors" (panel presentation hosted by the SCL, the American Film Institute, Los Angeles, October 6, 2009). Noted by Paul Gorman, Audio Director for Electronic Arts (EA).
24. *Percussion hits* are individual percussion sounds generally obtained from sample libraries. Composers and sound designers tend to draw such sounds, which are digitally processed and often feature the sounds of gargantuan impacts, from highly regarded libraries such as *Storm Drums* (East-West Libraries).
25. LucasArts, founded by director-producer George Lucas in 1982, is a leading publisher and designer of video games in tandem with its sister company Industrial Light and Magic (ILM).
26. Chuck Doud, Adam Levinson, and Victor Rodriguez, "The Game Music Business: Relationships Between Composers and Large Corporations." Panel presentation hosted by the SCL, the American Film Institute, Los Angeles, January 13, 2009. Noted by Adam Levinson, Director of Audio Management for Activison. By comparison, a 70- to 120-minute score for a feature film is generally only required for such genres as science fiction, fantasy, narrative animation, and space or deep-sea epics.
27. Garry Schyman, "Video Games Scoring" (panel presentation). Schyman was the composer for *BioShock* (2007), *Biochock 2* (2010), and *Dante's Inferno* (2010).
28. Tom Salta, interview by author, June 13, 2011. Salta composed for *Red Steel* (2006) and Tom Clancy's *H.A.W.X.* (2009).
29. *Flower* is a Sony Playstation 3 game released in 2007 and developed by Thatgamecompany. The score was composed by Vincent Diamante.
30. Tom Salta, interview by author, June 13, 2011.
31. Noted by J. P. Walton on a panel presentation hosted by the SCL at the American Film Institute in Los Angeles, October 6, 2009. Walton is an audio director for Double Helix Games.
32. Wwise, manufactured by AudioKinetic, is referred to as "middleware"—that is, software that provides a dynamic link between sound designers/composers and the game engine. It serves as a "staging" platform for the purpose of programming, demonstrating, and testing the functionality of sound and music within simulated gameplay.

33. Sean Callery, interview by author, June 2, 2011.
34. Garry Schyman, "Video Games Scoring" (panel presentation).
35. Sean Callery, interview by author, October 13, 2011.
36. Ibid.
37. *Stems*, created from the multitracks of a complete audio recording, are separate groups and subgroups of instruments that are delivered to the re-recording mixer for the "final mix." These individual tracks (i.e., percussion instruments only, guitar solo, harp, and so on) allow the re-recording engineer greater latitude by which he or she can accommodate the sonic space, clarity, and dynamics necessary for mixing music with dialogue and effects.
38. Dominick Tavella, interview by author, June 7, 2011. "Music stems are routinely provided by composers." As Tavella describes it, "Usually, we'll get a 5.1 mix, which is how the composer wants it to sound mixed totally together. And they'll submit a breakdown: a 5.1 of the drums, a 5.1 of the horns, a 5.1. of the strings; and so on, so you can make small corrections. It's a lot of material to ferret through sometimes, but it lets you really tone music exactly right for the scene."
39. The *kantele*, of Finnish decent, is an instrument from the zither family. Although it is a plucked instrument, virtual instruments often program in nonstandard performance techniques that are not possible with the actual instrument.
40. Paul Chihara, conversation with author, September 24, 2010. Chihara is a composer and a professor at the University of California–Los Angeles (UCLA).
41. Danny Elfman, panel presentation hosted by the SCL and the Directors Guild of America, Hollywood, California, February 17, 1999. Although Korngold never actually quoted Wagner, film composers in Hollywood's Golden Age drew liberally from Wagner's core compositional techniques, such as the use of *leitmotivs* and common-tone harmonic progressions.

SELECT BIBLIOGRAPHY

Collins, Karen. *From Pac-Man to Pop Music: Interactive Audio in Games and New Music.* Burlington, VT: Ashgate, 2008.

Collins, Karen. *Game Sound: An Introduction to the History, Theory, and Practice of Video Game Music and Sound Design.* Cambridge, MA: MIT Press, 2008.

Dubowsky, Jack Curtis. "The Evolving Temp Score in Animation." *Music, Sound and the Moving Image* 5, no. 1 (2011): 1–24.

Gilreath, Paul. *The Guide to MIDI Orchestration.* 4th ed. Oxford: Focal Press, 2010.

Marks, Aaron. *The Complete Guide to Game Audio: For Composers, Musicians, Sound Designers, Game Developers.* 2nd ed. Oxford: Focal Press, 2008.

Pejrolo, Andrea, and Richard DeRosa. *Acoustic and MIDI Orchestration for the Contemporary Composer.* Oxford: Focal Press, 2007.

CHAPTER 39

···

VISUALIZING THE APP ALBUM WITH BJÖRK'S *BIOPHILIA*

···

NICOLA DIBBEN

On its launch in July 2011, Björk's *Biophilia*[1] was received as the birth of a new music format—the "app album"—a music album designed for mobile digital devices. It was greeted as the way forward for musicians and developers and likened to the birth of cinema.[2] Although I'll consider such grand claims, I'll focus in this essay on the emergence and characteristics of this new format, focusing on the implications of the app for audio-visual aesthetics.

Biophilia is a multimedia project conceived and created by the musician Björk, comprising an audio album, a suite of apps for mobile devices (tablet and smartphone), live shows, residencies with "pop up" music schools, and a variety of other activities and artifacts. My analysis, focusing on the app suite, draws on participant observation, informal discussion, and formal interviews carried out during my time as a collaborator on the project from September 2010 to July 2011. This is supplemented by material drawn from published interviews, critical reception, music industry statistics, analysis of the music and apps, and an interview study with members of the general public.[3]

I start by putting the app into its historical context and then consider the consequences and opportunities of the app album format for audiovisual aesthetics as realized in *Biophilia*.

THE MUSIC APP AS A NEW DIGITAL MEDIUM

···

Although software applications have existed for decades, the idea of "apps"[4] —applications for mobile devices that are low cost, function specific, and downloadable—reached

the mass market in the first decade of the twenty-first century via the widespread availability of smartphones and digital distribution platforms. Since their initial launch, such
products and services have increased exponentially,[5] and mobile devices and services
are now an important part of how lives are lived.[6] Consequently, the app medium fits
into a projected future for digital media as mobile rather than fixed personal computer
services.

Music apps are usually a type of "immersive app," characterized by a focus on the content and a user experience that can be customized,[7] and are fairly popular compared to
other app categories.[8] Apps associated with established musicians emerged from 2009.
However, these tended to be promotional items for albums. For example, the French
band Nouvelle Vague released a promotional app for their album *3* in 2009, which
included material that might normally be found on an artist website, such as news, videos, and the option to purchase the album. Custom-made apps are expensive; therefore,
many artist apps are based instead on a toolkit comprising a selection from different
modules including free streaming services for an artists' audiovisual content, photographs, news, chat rooms, and the option to buy music, tickets, and other merchandise.
The Madonna app by Mobile Roadie is one such toolkit app.[9]

In addition to these music and social content apps, which arguably serve a gateway
function similar to a website, a range of other artist apps offer interactive functions more
akin to computer games. Remix apps allow the user to create new versions of an artist's song from the original instrumental and vocal tracks (*Remix David Bowie,*[10] *iDaft
2,*[11] *David Bowie Golden Years App*[12]), in some cases while playing a game (*Goldfrapp
Pinball*[13]). Musical instrument and sequencer apps allow the user to generate sound
and create music from samples (Kraftwerk—*Kling Klang Machine*—*No1*[14]). Sing-
and play-along apps enable the user to perform along with the artists' tracks (*Piano
Complete: Elton John's Greatest Hits Vol. 1,*[15] *David Archuleta Open Mic*[16]). In music action
game apps, the user performs missions within an artist-themed virtual world (*Linkin
Park 8-Bit Rebellion,*[17] *Gorillaz Escape to Plastic Beach for iPad*[18]). In a few cases, the app
can be thought of as a new audiovisual music "album" release. For example, 2manyDJs'
RadioSoulwax[19] is a series of twenty-four 1-hour mixes of classic tracks with animated
album cover art synchronized with the music sampled, and Bluebrain's *The National
Mall* is a site-specific app whose music changes according to the listener's proximity to
particular locations.[20]

Björk's *Biophilia* was unique in being a suite of apps structured as an album and
released in synchrony with the physical and digital album.[21] The app suite consists of
a "mother app" (referred to by the developers as the "box"), which has its own song
("Cosmogony") that serves as the interface from which users can access a suite of apps
corresponding to nine additional songs. These ten songs form the basis of the physical release of the album, although the mix in each version is unique. Nested within the
Biophilia app, each song has its own "box" within which is a suite of items: "play" is the
song presented as an interactive audiovisual semieducational game; "animation" is
a scrolling graphic score with playback; "score" is a scrolling notated score with MIDI
playback; plus lyrics, credits, and essays (see Figure 39.1).[22] Each app is an interactive

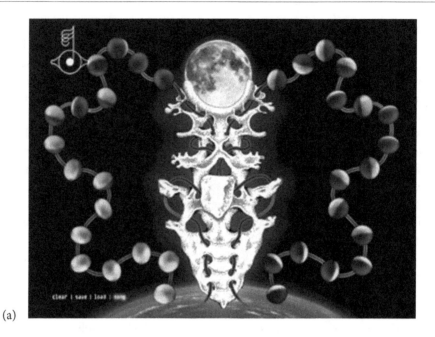

(a)

(b)

FIGURE 39.1 Illustrative images from Björk *Biophilia* app (One Little Indian/Wellhart, 2011). (a) "Moon," musical instrument song app; (b) "Crystalline" essay; (c) "Virus" animation; (d) "Virus" score. Screen shots by the author.

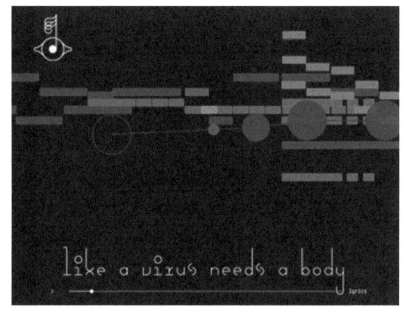

(c)

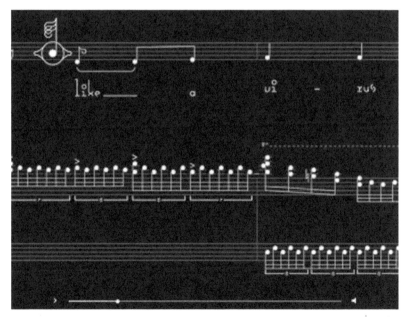

(d)

FIGURE 39.1 *Continued*

exploration of each song's concept and musical structure, taking a variety of forms, from new musical instruments through to linear music video. In some respects the apps can be thought of as digital music videos, and, therefore, as one example of the extension and diversification of traditional music video.[23] For the purposes of this essay, I consider the *Biophilia* app in the context of the music album, noting that it brought the term "app album" into widespread use.[24]

WHY MAKE *BIOPHILIA* AN APP ALBUM?

Biophilia is a concept album that presents an artistic vision of the relationships among nature, technology, and music. The hundreds of interviews, press releases, and other information released about the project since just before its press launch in June 2011 are a way of "storying" *Biophilia*, in which the genesis of *Biophilia* is made and remade in the telling. For example, it would be easy to see *Biophilia* as the natural extension of Björk's creative vision, whereas the stories told about *Biophilia* might more properly be thought of as the creative vision reimagined in the light of the eventual product. Nonetheless, it is possible to identify a range of factors that contributed to the making of the *Biophilia* app album.

Most notably, *Biophilia* was shaped by precursor tools, rather than by the app as a preexisting thing best suited to realizing her ideas. Björk recounted using touchscreens and other interactive electronic physical devices, including Lemur touchscreens and Reactable, to perform and compose since 2007:

> [T]he initial idea, in a way, was because of the arrival of the touch screen. I was already on my last tour from 2006 to 2008, the "Volta" tour. I had a touch screen instrument called the Lemur and another one called Reactable. And I was performing or people who were playing with me in the band were on those. Once the tour was finished in 2008, I was excited not just to perform with touch screens, but to write with them or kind of use it as much as you could.[25]

Björk believed that touchscreens offered a more intuitive and easily accessible form of instrumental accompaniment, which allowed her to change her usual compositional habits of composing vocally:

> Because I don't play the piano or guitar, and usually I've always written my music when I am just walking outside, I've finally found something that's appealing to me as an accompaniment.... I can just scrabble with my fingers—it's a breakthrough for me.[26]

When the iPad came out it offered a way of realizing her project as an interactive app. *Biophilia* was originally intended as a three-dimensional (3D) film to be directed by Michel Gondry, and then as a "music house" (like a museum) in which each room would represent one of the songs and contain interactive exhibits corresponding to its natural science subject matter.[27]

> We were trying to make the film behave like an app, but it wasn't.... I also kept thinking about the music house—that's how I wrote these songs. But the house is, like, rooms—like the apps.[28]

The key point about the project conception for the purposes of this essay is the relationship between the visuals and sound, which, in each case, is intended to relate directly to musical structures and processes. Björk's idea was to use touchscreens as an intuitive tool for music making and as a means for interactive, educational experiences that would allow the user to learn about some aspect of musical structure through natural-world phenomena. According to the lead app developer on the project, interactive artist Scott Snibbe, the song apps are "not merely a music video, and also not just some kind of pure musicological analysis, but they're actually a new creative experience that uses music, nature, technology and interactivity."[29] Hence, at a meeting in September 2010, Björk illustrated her ideas for how *Biophilia* might be manifested as an interactive semieducational project by showing me two types of app: high-quality educational apps (including *The Elements*,[30] *Solarwalk*[31]) and sound-art apps, some of which combined nature and music (*Soundrop*,[32] *Bubble Harp*,[33] *Bloom*[34]).

Biophilia addresses themes found in Björk's previous work, which reconfigures the relationship between nature and technology and emphasizes the "instinctive."[35] But events simultaneous with the making of *Biophilia* also point to a very practical engagement with questions of the relationship between nature and technology: Björk's involvement in the *Náttúra* campaign for environmental protection in Iceland, her involvement in a venture fund for start-up companies that emphasized the role of renewable energies and sustainable industry, and the Icelandic economic crash in 2008. A distinctive feature of the way that *Biophilia* addresses the relationship between nature and technology is the positive perspective in which new technologies can be used to go "forward to nature," in Björk's words.[36] The interactive music-educational aspect of the project is part of this positive proactive approach in two ways: by celebrating the natural world through a thematic focus on natural phenomena ("nature") and by using touchscreen technologies to enable intuitive, spontaneous, and embodied forms of music-making and learning ("the natural").

As this illustrates, the digital and multimodal character of the project can be seen as an integral component of its concept and aesthetic. However, for an artist like Björk, whose music is part of a larger concept realized through a range of media, a digital format that encompasses the multimedia is important strategically as well as aesthetically. From a personal perspective, Björk was influenced by the shift from physical to digital formats and distribution platforms:

> I have a lot of musician friends and they're all like it's the end of music and it's all going downhill, and music's going to die, and there's no more CD shops...and I'm

including myself, you know? It was so sort of a reaction to that: "Let's just clear the slate. And what do we got?" We got people that want to hear music, and people that make music, and they're exchanging it online.[37]

Prior to *Biophilia*, Björk's fans tended to buy her physical releases in preference to digital downloads,[38] so by releasing a digital artifact that retained and expanded the multimedia component of her work, fans would be encouraged to engage with downloads as a format for her music. Perhaps, too, she would be able to reach new audiences who wouldn't normally have bought her music. It is no coincidence that the emergence of music apps occurred simultaneous with a decline in global music sales, a reduction in physical sales, and growth in digital sales.[39] In 2011, 32 percent of global record industry revenue came from digital sources, and, in the United States, revenues from digital sources surpassed those from physical sources.[40] Thus, creation of music apps is a response to the broader shift toward digital as opposed to physical sales.

The end to Björk's record contracts in 2007 made this unusual venture feasible. Two difficulties from the perspective of a record label were the absence of agreed-on publishing rates for music in apps and the risk that the apps would undermine music sales. Rather than sign to a major record label for the project, it was funded through a profit share with the app developers[41] and released independently, and the audio album was signed to Nonesuch records as a one-off deal.

This account of the history of the *Biophilia* app album highlights factors that contributed to the development of its concept and aesthetic. In the remainder of this essay, I analyze the audiovisual character of the app suite and its implications for music making and consumption and briefly consider its position in relation to music video and album formats.

IMPLICATIONS OF THE APP ALBUM FOR AUDIOVISUAL EXPERIENCE

The app format, as realized in *Biophilia,* has three main consequences for musical and audiovisual experience, which I deal with in turn: first, music is visualized in a way that seems to encourage attentive listening to and playing with musical structures and processes; second, it offers a multimodal experience by virtue of touchscreen interactivity; and third, it presents a curated experience of a coherent artistic vision that is the product of collaborative work.

Visualizing Music

The *Biophilia* app emphasizes the visual dimension of music that in some respects was greatly diminished by the advent of recorded sound.[42] Adopting Korsgaard's summation of audiovisual relationships in music video, the app can be said to "visualize music" (by recasting preexisting songs in visual form) and, drawing on Vernallis,[43] to "musicalize vision" (by allowing the images to "respond" to musical structures).[44] What's distinctive about the particular audiovisual relationship in *Biophilia* is that a specific (and different) musical parameter of each of the ten songs is recast in relation to different natural phenomena.[45]

The audiovisual relationships in the song apps serve a pedagogical purpose in drawing attention to particular musical features of individual songs that function as sonic analogues of natural phenomena; conversely, too, natural phenomena are used as metaphors for musical processes. In the case of "Solstice," for instance, the user can learn how complex looping procedures work in music by seeing melodic sequences visualized as planets circling a sun on the screen. In "Thunderbolt," the user can learn that arpeggios are a kind of musical structure that retains the same basic interval arrangement even when range and tempo change by altering the length and height of lightning arcs on the app screen. As one informant stated: "The stuff you can do is really cool and I like how it relates to the actual song that it's talking about as well, they're not like completely random" (student, aged twenty). One criticism of the pedagogical approach is that it fragments the musical experience by treating different aspects of musical structure as completely separate: musical materials are isolated so that they become separable parameters of form, scales, chords, meter, and tempo. It could be argued that this even reinforces a rather traditional idea of what music is and how it should be taught—one that reflects Björk's own rather negative experience of music education perhaps.

The choice of natural phenomena and musical structures (Table 39.1) was driven by a variety of factors. For example, Björk focused on some natural phenomena because she thought of them as examples of nature at its grandest, such as electricity (performed by a Tesla coil in "Thunderbolt"). Others were chosen for personal reasons, such as the virus, which was an example of a symbiotic relationship inspired by her own battle with a throat infection. In each case, there is a connection to the apparently personal lyrical content of the songs, as in "Hollow," whose subject matter is genetic descent and

Table 39.1 Categorization of songs for press launch (Derek Birkett, e-mail message to author, June 12, 2011). This categorization also appears in naturalist and broadcaster David Attenborough's recorded narration to the *Biophilia* live show.

Technology	Nature	Music
Dark matter	Dark matter	Scales
Mutual core	Tectonic plates	Chords
Crystalline	Crystal structure	Structure and spatial musical environments
Moon	Moon phases	Musical sequencer and liquid forms in music
Solstice	Earth's tilt/seasons	Gravity as counterpoint in music
Virus	Viruses	Generative music
Cosmogony	Music of the spheres	Equilibrium
Sacrifice	Interaction of the sexes	Musical notation and fonts
Thunderbolt	Thunder and lightning	Arpeggios
Hollow	DNA	Rhythm and speed

DNA. The choice of which musical structure to visualize in which track was, in some instances, guided by rather than determined by the songs. Comparing the early briefs given by Björk to developers of the apps with the final realizations of the apps reveals this malleability. For example, Björk's initial brief for "Pneuma" (subsequently titled "Dark Matter") suggested the app should feature a human face, the mouth and throat of which would be manipulated to control the flow of breath and resulting vowel sounds.[46] However, Björk subsequently used this app to explore musical scales instead.

The audiovisual relationships between the natural phenomena and musical structures are idiosyncratic and reflect the way Björk conceives of and hears music. For example, Björk likened the way she hears verse-chorus form in pop music to the experience of traveling through intersections, and the idea of crystal structures as analogous to that:

> I've sat a lot of my life in buses and taxis from 20 years of touring and somehow all these different types of intersections have gone on file in my brain. Like some have 3 streets meeting with very tall buildings on all sides while others are complex with like 5 streets meeting but all buildings are low and so on...seems like each one of them has a different mood, different spatial tension or release. Part of my obsessive nature wants to map out each intersection in the world and match it with a song...to me crystal structures seem to grow in a similar way.[47]

The app realization of "Crystalline" combines these ideas by representing song sections as tunnels which the user travels down (by virtue of the camera's gaze flying through the tunnels), and representing the boundaries between song sections as tunnel intersections at which the listener selects a route by tilting the device. The aim of the game is to collect crystals from the sides of the tunnels, which accumulate to form larger crystals corresponding to a particular route through the song form. Interestingly, the visual aesthetic of "Crystalline," the first single and app released, is a retro video arcade game, highlighting the continuity between new and old gaming technologies and aesthetics.

One distinguishing feature from the traditional narrative pop video in each case is the (almost total) absence of the star persona. In other words, what is being visualized is the music, rather than the image of the artist herself. Björk's central idea was that the audiovisual relationship should always visualize musical structures and that the visual scale of any natural phenomena should be either very big or very small, but never human scale. This presented some difficulties for the app developers who, to some extent, wanted to use the human scale to provide an emotional connection and also because the subject matter of songs are as much about human experience as they are about natural phenomena (arguably the songs present natural phenomena as analogies for human emotional experiences).[48]

The absence of the author image was a problem in the case of "Hollow," which is also arguably the most traditional because it is the only linear music video that tracks the song. The animated video uses increasing levels of magnification to take the viewer from the level of human blood tissue to that of DNA akin to the visual technique used in the science documentary *Powers of Ten*[49] that was an inspiration for the video. The "falling effect" created by this increasing magnification is also a metaphor for musical processes (changes of tempo and meter) and the lyrical content (in particular, the narrative idea of falling through time and through genetic ancestry). An early version of the video featured Björk's face as the human-scale starting point for the animated journey but, under Björk's direction, her face was removed on the basis that although such a literal representation might be suitable for MTV or YouTube, it was less appropriate for the app, which should focus instead on the idea of the "ghost in the machine." Hence, in the final version Björk's visual image features twice: a brief glimpse as the camera exits the body at the end of the video and a mask-like representation made from protein strands midway.

In addition to the song apps, music is visualized in the scrolling music notation and animated graphic scores. These were created by the composer, inventor, and educator Stephen Malinowski, whose work Björk had seen online. Malinowski's "Music Animation Machine," from which these animations derived, was influenced by the work of twentieth-century abstract animator Oskar Fischinger, and, as Korsgaard notes, they can be regarded as a return to the prehistory of music video.[50] Significantly for *Biophilia*'s educational agenda, the animations have a pedagogical function:

> One of the things about a musical score is that if there's something in there that you're not perceiving, because it requires more attention than you're giving it, it gives you another way in to hear something. I've had people say, about pieces of music they've loved and known all their life, that after watching one of my videos they see something in it that they'd never heard before and now they hear it every time they listen to that piece of music. It's part of the education, people don't realize that when you're listening to a piece of music you're learning how to hear it, how to make sense of it.[51]

A review of *Biophilia* by a deaf person even notes how the animations provided a musical experience of Björk's music otherwise absent.[52]

The variety of music representation in the *Biophilia* app also has a deliberate purpose. Traditional sheet notation, graphic scores, MIDI, and mp3 each have different educational and musicological histories that Björk characterizes as old, "elitist," and new "street" representations.[53] The juxtaposition of music scores and graphic scores, MIDI and mp3, academic analyses and educational games highlights the equivalence between old and new, elitist and street. According to Björk, "It's sort of trying to blur these lines … that it's actually sort of the same thing."[54]

Beyond the characteristics of the individual apps, the app suite is united by a particular design aesthetic: a virtual environment that aims to create an immersive interactive experience. The designers M/M Paris created the star field "mother" app ("Cosmogony"), which visualizes the musical work as a 3D virtual environment that contains the songs (Figure 39.2), and exploited the possibilities of the newly emerging HTML5 for Björk's website. Everything within the environment moves making it feel live and organic, a model for this being *The Elements* periodic table app in which the contents are interactive and 3D. In the star field interface, stars corresponding to the song apps glow and pulse; each song increases and decreases in volume as the user

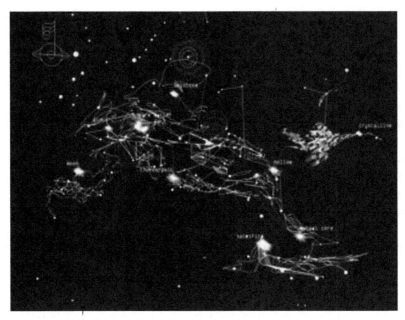

FIGURE 39.2 "Cosmogony" navigational interface from Björk *Biophilia* app (One Little Indian/Wellhart, 2011). Screenshot by the author.

approaches them in the 3D space by pinching the screen and zooming nearer and farther away; even song names in the track listing screen move and bob as if suspended in space.

The app suite also uses a particular color palette distinctive to each song and two custom-made fonts developed by M/M Paris while working on production of Björk's sheet music as part of another project: Bjotope for text and Allegretto for music notation. These are used in the app (and other associated products) and combined in a new font, Bjotope-staff, within the "Sacrifice" app, which introduces those without musical training to music notation through text and in which the iPad becomes a musical instrument. It is not just the type of visual material but also the high definition of the iPad screen that makes the visual experience of the apps so compelling.

One consequence of these audiovisual relationships is that the app encourages immersion in the audiovisual experience and attention to sound—in effect, a (re) new(ed) listening mode. The games, scrolling musical notation, and graphic scores draw attention to musical details of the song materials and structures by virtue of the musical parameters they choose to represent; the metaphorical relationship between natural phenomena, musical processes, and lyrical content; and the hands-on interactive medium. These relationships work against accusations that (interactive) images distract from the music, turning music into something akin to "unheard" film music[55]—an accusation also leveled against interactive video and early music video.[56] Furthermore, amid claims that the ubiquity of music on mobile devices is shortening attention spans and structuring musical experience as something "background" to other activities, it could be argued that the *Biophilia* app counters this by encouraging users to make music listening a central activity.

As evidence of this, informants in my interview study remarked on the high degree of attention demanded by the apps and viewed this positively or negatively depending on their primary mode of musical engagement and particular situation of listening (whether music was habitually background or foreground to some other task). Many said they would be most likely to use interactive music apps while traveling by train, indicating that the app experience benefits from focused attention.

Interactivity

A key to the immersive experience just described is the interactivity offered by touch-screen technology. The audiovisual aesthetic of touchscreen technology is cinematic and interactive. As Scott Snibbe notes, the first commercially available mass computers were interactive: you turned the computer on to be greeted by a flashing cursor and "you had to do something."[57] Subsequent operating system design and language conceptualized the computer interface in terms of "desktops" and "windows," which are both non-interactive flat spaces. Snibbe remarks that touchscreen technologies like the iPad restructured the interface using a cinematic language of swipes, cuts, and dissolves and achieved a more immersive experience.

The interactive aspect of *Biophilia* can be seen as continuous with related developments in interactive video, its precursors in video games and other forms of participatory consumption involving user-generated content and open-ended forms,[58] and, from a musical perspective, can be seen as a reflection of experimental musical practice post-Cage. Each song app allows a traditional, linear listening and viewing experience, but most also allow users to create their own versions of the songs. Indeed, with the exception of the "Cosmogony" and "Hollow" apps, songs do not exist in fixed versions: the apps allow users to improvise a bassline ("Thunderbolt"), create a route through the song structure ("Crystalline"), delay song progression ("Virus"), compose musical sequences ("Moon," "Solstice," "Hollow," "Dark Matter"), and write music notation ("Sacrifice"). This means that the listener personalizes the experience in so far as the album can be heard in different ways on revisits.[59]

Within this context, the song becomes process rather than a fixed, single object that is remade in different performances according to available resources: not only are the versions of songs on the app suite and music album different, the versions on the song app, score, and animation also differ. Other features also allow interactivity and user-generated content. The sheet music and graphic scores can be used to aid listening or performance: Björk and the choir used the graphic notation as a teleprompt in live performance. In addition, the music score feature allows MIDI playback, enabling users to reorchestrate the music or sing and play along. Björk had noted that whereas people can grab a guitar and sing rock songs together, they couldn't do that as easily with electronic music.[60]

This interactive experience is contrary to the receptive mode of consumption privileged by the advent of recorded music. However, the degree and type of interactivity
differs throughout the suite, reflecting the different approaches to interactivity of the
different developers. Some of the apps are instrument-like in their capabilities, and,
although, as with computer console music games, they may lack the flexibility of real
musical instruments, they entertain and may teach some elements of music and encourage users to explore further beyond the app. Scott Snibbe's work on *Biophilia* and elsewhere is concerned with open-ended interaction within simulated environments, hence
the apps he designed reflect this:

> I'm not as into the kind of push button kind of interactivity, but more that you are
> interacting with a simulated model of reality. So, the two apps that we did, "Virus,"
> where you're interacting with the simulated microscopic world and, "Thunderbolt,"
> where you're manipulating simulated electricity and lightning, both of those are
> completely open ended. They are different every time. You can explore them as if you
> can do that thing in reality. That is probably our specific angle on interactivity and
> you can see other peoples' personalities and approaches to interactivity came out in
> the apps.[61]

The digital interactive format of the touchscreen device is also central to the project
through the way that it makes electronic music making and learning a more embodied
process. As Korsgaard notes,

> *Biophilia*'s use of touchpad-based devices activates the sense of touch in a way normal
> music video do not. Both the images and sounds of the "music video" apps can be
> "touched" and thereby altered. This allows for a more tactile way of experiencing
> music *and* images.[62]

He contextualizes this "mediated embodiment" as "a response to the coldness and dema-
terialization of digitality." The introduction of touch and movement to the audiovisual
experience is crucial for understanding the *Biophilia* project. Björk saw touchscreens as
the tool by which she could facilitate "the natural" and "spontaneous" in her own and
others' music making, teaching, and learning.

As regards her own music making, Björk characterized touchscreens as offering a
more spontaneous and embodied mode of engagement. The standard tool for electronic
music composition is the Digital Audio Workstation, yet tangible musical interfaces
such as touchscreens can allow a more embodied form of composition and performance,
both for performers and audiences of electronic music.[63] As regards music teaching and
learning, Björk saw touchscreens as a way to make music education a more embodied
experience, countering what she saw as its unnecessarily dry and abstract theorization
of musical structures and processes:

> [T]he core or idea of this project is taking something that has usually been quite
> academic or bookish and making it impulsive and tactile. So actually explaining it

or doing an interview about it or writing or reading a press release about it, makes it sound like 500 times more complicated that it actually is. It's like trying to explain how to dance in an e-mail. If you would just turn it on and do it together, it'd be way easier. I am hoping that it would sort of dissolve this VIP status that musicology has—that it's only for the chosen few, if you are super clever, and you've studied for billions of years, you understand about scales.[64]

Curation

One notable feature of the *Biophilia* app suite as an audiovisual entity is the way it offers a curated vision. This is particularly pertinent given the increase of digital downloads and streaming services within which the unit of exchange is the song rather than the album. Streaming and download platforms fragment albums and, even if a listener chooses to listen to a whole album instead of a mix of singles from different albums, intervening adverts interrupt the continuity of the listening experience. The *Biophilia* app suite both communicates a project concept and adds creative value to the album at a time when the creative value of music alone seems to be proving insufficient to sustain industry sales and income. Indeed, in many ways, *Biophilia* potentially reinvigorates the idea of the album. Scott Snibbe remarks that the multimedia character of the app recalls the traditional physical album experience:

> In some reviews of *Biophilia*, people said, "Wow, I haven't had this experience in 20 years. Before CDs came out, I'd buy an album and hold the 12-inch cover in my hand, sitting cross-legged on the floor while I listened to the music, read the liner notes, and looked at the pictures." People used to have this very tactile, multimedia experience when they bought an album. But with the digitization of music, we've lost that special moment. You can think of the app as, finally, that chance to unwrap the box and have a personal, intimate experience again with music.[65]

The app suite deliberately recalls the album format in its architecture. Indeed, many of the difficulties encountered during the process were in trying to mimic the physical and chronological structure of the physical album release. For example, the app box design mimics the architecture of the physical album: the individual song apps are housed within a song box app alongside the other elements of the release, and these song boxes are housed within the mother app, "Cosmogony." Scott Snibbe noted that it was technically difficult to nest apps within each other[66] and to mirror the standard staggered release of three audio singles followed by the full album in the App store because it was the first time either had been attempted.[67]

This staggered release is standard industry practice designed to maximize media exposure and consumer desire, yet this album cycle is potentially undermined by the opportunities that digital formats offer for more continuous releases. For example, the constellation design of the *Biophilia* interface, and contractual agreements, meant she could add new song apps in the future should she wish. Other artists have increasingly used a variety of release formulae. For example, Ash released one single every two weeks for a year because, according to them, it suited their creative flow and meant there was no need to tie everything together.[68] A similar point has been made by other artists. For example, David Hockney remarked that "I draw flowers everyday on my iPhone and send them to my friends, so they get fresh flowers every morning," recalling the spontaneity so attractive to Björk. He also went on to remark: "[The iPad is] like an endless piece of paper that perfectly fitted the feeling I had that painting should be big."[69] Hockney's idea of a canvas with no boundary is similar to the open-ended music of some of the music apps and, less directly, the idea of a continuously expanding constellation of songs as described by Björk. However, whether Björk will use the star field in this way remains to be seen since the relationship between record labels and media is still currently structured by marketing that relies on the temporal build up to a release.

For the app user, the star field interface provides a less hierarchical and arguably less dictatorial means of music selection than is frequently the case, as noted by one informant:

> [M]ost of the music apps or software that I've seen is mainly just lists and it's like a grid format, it's quite, what's the word . . . it kind of takes out the artistry of the music, cos its like this is what you're going to listen to next and there's a queue of music and you don't get the "play about with it" kind of thing [reference to 3D navigation within the star field] . . . I think the whole spread-out idea's quite good, rather than "this is the top one you've got to listen to," you can pick and choose what you're going to do. (female student, aged twenty)

What's particularly interesting about the way this is realized is that, even though navigation and choice is not dictated by the *Biophilia* interface, a curatorial vision is retained through the consistency of the interface's design with the album's concept—interactivity and the natural world.

Although there is insufficient space here to discuss the creative process in detail, it is difficult to consider the artistic vision in a project such as *Biophilia* without also mentioning the collaborative character of the work that went into its creation.[70] Scott Snibbe describes his experience of collaboration, noting that:

> [S]he acts like a director. She has a very strong, high level vision for the project that she articulated in a long manifesto and in many meetings, playing the songs, explaining what they meant. But quite often she let us go off and interpret what she said in our own way, as long as we were sticking to the big message, the narrative, and the broad strokes she was painting. There was room for us to improvise within that.
>
> So it was a lot like working on a movie—there was a clear area where each person could make their own contribution, but there is an over-arching ultra-powerful vision from Björk at the top. And of course like any project, she makes corrections along the way.[71]

In practical terms, Björk presented a manifesto and design brief to collaborators, including detailed references to visual sources for the look and concept of each song app. These were then realized as storyboards and prototype apps with limited functionality, which were refined through developments and testing. In parallel with this, collaboration went on to develop the music scores, animations, and, in my case, the written text, and the designers and developers worked to create an architecture that would house this material. This work entailed a combination of face-to-face meetings, e-mails, and shared documents and artifacts in virtual storage spaces.

As an example of the strong creative vision exerted by Björk over the project, many of the final apps are very close to Björk's original conception: Björk's brief for "Solstice," for instance, is almost identical to its final realization:

> [T]he app could be a "circular" harp, which moves in planetary orbits . . . in brief: there is a central "sun" from which you draw the strings of the harp out. you then throw a planet in orbit and each time it passes a "string" it plucks it. you can fiddle with the size of the orbit, the speed of the planet, the length and spacing of the strings until you like it . . . and then you tap the central sun, change the colour, and pull out a new set of strings, plucked by a new planet. you can keep doing this, assigning different sounds to different planets, until you have a solar system of sound.[72]

Other apps changed during the course of realization as one or another element of the concept gained greater weight according to aesthetics and the practicalities of usability. For example, the original image for the "Moon" app depicted Björk's idea of fluid pulled up through a spine with the fullness of the moon and with notes of the song arrayed in horizontal lines like ribs.[73] However, this wasn't particularly easy to manipulate and didn't fully convey the idea of music as fluid and was subsequently changed to the ribbon design seen in the final "Moon" app. Like other collaborative music products, the presence of the author-image for the work is still an important part of how it is valued and understood,[74] both for audiences and other collaborators: as Max Weisel commented: "Collaboration is definitely a huge aspect of a project like this. If we were to release an app without any feedback along the way, you wouldn't get this sense that it's actually something from Björk."[75]

VIZUALIZING THE FUTURE

Considering *Biophilia* in the broader contexts of music albums, music videos, and computer games highlights the distinctive features of the app suite as a new format. In the context of music albums, the growth in digital album sales to 2011 shows there is still a demand for a body of work by an artist,[76] and, in this case, the app format is well-suited to produce the curated album experience central to the conceptual character of the project. More generally, it offers a way of retaining and reinvigorating the album format in a context of music dissemination that tends to fragment the whole. From the perspective of video, the app suite extends the form: it is similar in presenting close relationships between music and image and differs as regards their interactivity and in not fixing song length and structure.[77] In the context of gaming, the apps extend the notion of music games in that they also allows users to create and perform music, but focus on musical structures and processes through metaphors of natural phenomena; as one informant noted, comparing the *Biophilia* app to the status of music within computer games: "you're coming from music and you're sort of bringing in, you're 'game-ifying' the album" (male computer technician, aged thirty).

As regards the relationship between the app album as a format on the one hand and downloadable MP3s and the physical album on the other, there are perhaps two key features of the *Biophilia* app suite: the perceived materiality of apps in comparison to MP3s and the creative value that apps add to music.

Whereas some see the app as disposable (something to load, play with, and then delete if it doesn't sustain interest), others see it as having greater materiality than the MP3 file format and therefore as being more desirable. The just quoted informant went on to note:

> I suppose the attraction then is you've got an application that's on the iPad, so you're getting that extra bit, you know, it's putting value back to the music by going back to buying that physical object, which is not the case now really. I still like buying CDs, if I really like an album I like to physically have the CD. There's something about ... I'm just a hoarder, maybe, but yeh there's something about physically owning a physical object and you don't get that now with files but that ... I don't know, is that [the app] a physical object? It feels more physical, it feels more real. (male computer technician, aged thirty)

Another informant notes the added value that the multimedia content of the app brings to the music:

> I think it's really interesting how much stuff you get and how involved it is and how much more interesting it is than just having the song, cos like for music piracy there's a lot of stuff I will obtain in less than legal means because you think, well it's the soundtrack to *The Avengers*, they're gonna make a gazillion pounds, they don't need me to pay for it. But then all you pretty much get is the bare bones of the music, but if you've got something like this, there's more meaning to it, it seems to have weight to it, it's more interesting than you just having all the MP3s. (female student, aged twenty-two)

In some regards, this idea of added creative value is also evidenced in the stratified market for physical music formats. The physical release of *Biophilia* comprised three types of low-end physical release, including the standard CD in jewel case and two high-end releases: a limited edition (retailing at £35) and an ultimate edition of 200 copies available for preorder at £500 each. The Ultimate Edition includes a set of tuning forks in an oak box: one fork for each of the ten songs in the album, each tuned to the pitch center of the track (Figure 39.3). This unique packaging, produced by print and packaging consultant Daniel Mason, embodies some of the same ideas found in the app realization of the album: they are tactile, interactive, have educational potential, and can be used to make music.

The existence of this high-end physical release indicates a desire on the part of consumers for a covetable, tactile experience, previously noted in relation to the switch from CD to MP3 formats.[78] One consequence of a move to digital, then, is that digital media frees print from the communication process and opens an opportunity for the music industry to exploit the market for an enhanced physical product.

At its crux, *Biophilia* (re)introduced multimodality into digital audiovisual formats and used this to realize a creative vision of intuitive and embodied forms of music making and learning in which the natural world provides productive metaphors for emotional experiences and musical processes. Although there is a contradiction implicit in producing an artifact to make music theory less elitist for a device that currently restricts its use to the moderately wealthy, *Biophilia* explores the possibilities of a new technology that will soon become cheap and available to most people. As an innovative use of a new format, this is a tantalizing glimpse of things to come, one in which digitalization changes not just the way we buy or store music, but the very modality of music listening.

FIGURE 39.3 Björk, *The Ultimate Art Edition*, 2011. Photograph by the author.

NOTES

1. Björk, *Biophilia*, One Little Indian/Well Hart, 2011.
2. Jason Lipshutz, "Björk's App Designer Scott Snibbe Talks In-Depth About 'Biophilia,'" *Billboard.biz*, last accessed July 26, 2011, http://www.billboard.biz/bbbiz/industry/digital-and-mobile/bjork-s-app-designer-scott-snibbe-talks-1005293722.story.
3. The interview study conducted in June and July 2012 was designed by the author and conducted by Research Assistant James Rhodes. A convenience sample comprising fifteen informants was recruited through personal contacts and e-mail announcement to the University of Sheffield volunteers list. Respondents varied in age (age range 9–52) and experience with music apps (including no prior experience). Informants were asked about their experience of apps, music listening habits, and preferences before being given 15 minutes to play with the *Biophilia* app. They were then interviewed about their experience of the app. Interviews were recorded and transcribed for subsequent analysis using Interpretational Phenomenological Analysis.
4. The term "app" is an abbreviation of "application program" and distinguishes software programs, generally encountered by users, from "systems programs," which are those used by the computer itself. The term "app" was popularized by Apple's trademarked advertising slogan for the App Store ("There's an app for that"), although it had been in circulation prior to that.
5. From Apple's initial 2008 launch of the iPhone 3G and digital store application to March 2012, available apps have increased from 500 to 585,000. ("Android Overtakes Apple with 44% Worldwide Share of Mobile App Downloads," ABI Research, last accessed October 24, 2011, http://www.abiresearch.com/press/3799-Android+Overtakes+Apple+with+44%25+Worldwide+Share+of+Mobile+App+Downloads.) The iPhone has total sales of 116 million to date ("Android Expected to Reach Its Peak This Year as Mobile Phone Shipments Slow, According to IDC," IDC.com, last accessed June 6, 2012, http://www.idc.com/getdoc.jsp?containerId=prUS23523812), and the iPad tablet computer, 55 million. ("Apple Total Sales for the iPad Reaches 55 million," *Talking New Media*, last accessed January 25, 2012, http://talkingnewmedia.blogspot.co.uk/2012/01/apple-total-sales-for-ipad-reaches-55.html.)
6. Anthony Elliott and John Urry, *Mobile Lives* (Abingdon, Oxon: Routledge, 2010).
7. Suzanne Ginsburg, *Designing the IPhone User Experience: A User-Centered Approach to Sketching and Prototyping iPhone Apps* (Upper Saddle River: Addison-Wesley, 2010).
8. "Play Before Work: Games Most Popular Mobile App Category in US," *NielsenWire*, last accessed July 6, 2011, http://blog.nielsen.com/nielsenwire/online_mobile/games-most-popular-mobile-app-category.
9. *Madonna*, Madonna, 2012.
10. *Remix David Bowie*, EMI, 2009.
11. *iDaft 2*, dothedaft.com, 2010.
12. *David Bowie Golden Years App*, EMI, 2011.
13. *Goldfrapp Pinball*, Mute Records, 2010.
14. *Kling Klang Machine – No1*, Kraftwerk, 2011.
15. *Piano Complete: Elton John's Greatest Hits Vol. 1*, Better Day Wireless, 2011.
16. *David Archuleta Open Mic*, Sony, 2011.
17. *Linkin Park 8-Bit Rebellion*, Artifical Life, 2010.
18. *Gorillaz Escape to Plastic Beach for iPad*, Matmi New Media, 2010.

19. *RadioSoulwax*, Our Patience is Limited, 2011.

20. *The National Mall by Bluebrain*, Bluebrain, 2011.

21. *Biophilia* received huge international coverage in press and broadcast media on its release. Sales figures are not publically available, but rankings indicate it has performed fairly well. *Biophilia* for iPhone was ranked in the top ten of downloaded music apps in eight countries, and top 100 in thirty-two countries; *Biophilia* for iPad was ranked in the top ten in one country and top 100 in sixty-two countries; it was in the top ten for top grossing music apps in one country, and top 100 for eight others. ("App Database, Björk: Biophilia.")

22. For a video tour of the app see Björk, *Björk: Biophilia: Cosmogony App Tutorial*, online video, 1:44, posted by "bjorkdotcom," January 17, 2012, http://www.youtube.com/watch?v=3dlRg6lM4mQ.

23. See Mathias Bonde Korsgaard, "Music Video Transformed," in *The Oxford Handbook of New Audiovisual Aesthetics*, ed. Claudia Gorbman, John Richardson and Carol Vernallis (Oxford: Oxford University Press, 2013), 501–524.

24. Google Trends analysis shows that the volume of news containing the term "app album" on Google (all regions) first registers on the scale in mid-2011, which coincides with the release of *Biophilia* ("Google Trends – app album").

25. Jonathan Binder, "Bjork's 'Biophilia' Takes Music to the App World," *CNN*, last accessed October 10, 2011, http://articles.cnn.com/2011-10-10/tech/tech_innovation_bjork-app-album-biophilia_1_apple-app-store-app-world-bjork?_s=PM:TECH.

26. Liam Allen, "Björk on Biophilia and Her Debt to UK Dance Music," *BBC News*, last accessed July 28, 2011, http://www.bbc.co.uk/news/entertainment-arts-14318593.

27. Björk, in discussion with the author, September 2010.

28. Björk, in Charlie Burton, "In Depth: How Björk's 'Biophilia' Album Fuses Music with iPad Apps," *Wired*, July 26, 2011, http://www.wired.co.uk/magazine/archive/2011/08/features/music-nature-science?page=all.

29. Scott Snibbe, in Lipshutz, "Bjork's App Designer Scott Snibbe Talks In-Depth About 'Biophilia.'"

30. *The Elements*, Theodore Gray, 2010.

31. *Solarwalk*, Vito Technology, 2009–2012.

32. *Soundrop*, Develoe, 2009.

33. *Bubble Harp*, Scott Snibbe, 1997–2011.

34. *Bloom*, Opal, 2008.

35. For further discussions of the relationship between Björk's work and constructions of nature and technology, and how that relates to a more widespread Nordic ecological agenda, see Nicola Dibben, *Björk* (London: Equinox Press, 2009), and "Nature and Nation: National Identity and Environmentalism in Icelandic Popular Music Video and Music Documentary," *Ethnomusicology Forum* 18, no. 1 (2009); Charity Marsh and Melissa West, "The Nature/Technology Binary Opposition Dismantled in the Music of Madonna and Björk," in *Music and Technoculture*, ed. René T. A. Lysloff and Leslie C. Gay, Jr. (Middletown, CT: Wesleyan University Press, 2003) Mathias Bonde Korsgaard, "Emotional Landscapes: The Construction of Place in Björk's Music and Music Videos," in *Globalizing Art: Negotiating Place, Identity and Nation in Contemporary Nordic Art*, ed. Bodil Marie Stavning Thomsen and Kristin Ørjasæter (Aarhus: Aarhus University Press, 2012).

36. James Merry, e-mail message to author, June 8, 2011.

37. Björk, in Brandon Stosuy, "Stereogum Q&A: Björk Talks *Biophilia*," *Stereogum*, last accessed June 29, 2011, http://stereogum.com/744502/stereogum-qa-bjork-talks-biophilia/top-stories/lead-story/.

38. Björk, in discussion with the author, September 2010.

39. IFPI, *Recording Industry in Numbers 2012* (IFPI, 2012).

40. IFPI, *Digital Music Report 2012* (IFPI, 2012).

41. Scott Snibbe, in Lipshutz, "Bjork's App Designer Scott Snibbe Talks In-Depth About 'Biophilia.'"

42. Mark Katz, *Capturing Sound: How Technology Changed Music* (Berkeley: University of California Press, 2004), 18–24.

43. Korsgaard, "Music Video Transformed."

44. Carol Vernallis, *Experiencing Music Video:Aesthetics and Cultural Context* (New York: Columbia University Press, 2004), 44.

45. One exception to this is "Sacrifice," whose visual representation is a music text writer—particularly significant, given that it was developed by designers who created the fonts used in the app.

46. A brief from Björk to the app developers, e-mail from Derek Birkett to Scott Snibbe, June 30, 2010.

47. Björk, interview with the author, November 2010.

48. Scott Snibbe, in Julia Kaganskiy, "Interactive Artist Scott Snibbe Gives Us the Scoop on Björk's Biophilia Apps," *The Creators Project*, last accessed February 21, 2012, http://thecreatorsproject.com/blog/interactive-artist-scott-snibbe-gives-us-the-scoop-on-björks-ibiophiliai-apps.

49. *Powers of Ten*, documentary film, directed by Charles Eames and Ray Eames (IBM, 1977).

50. Korsgaard, "Music Video Transformed."

51. Kevin Holmes, "Animating Björk's Biophilia: Q&A with Stephen Malinowski," *The Creators Project*, last accessed February 14, 2012, http://thecreatorsproject.com/blog/animating-björks-ibiophiliai-qa-with-stephen-malinowski.

52. William Mager, "Björk's Biophilia Brings the Music Back," *Holy Moly!*, last accessed July 29, 2011, http://www.holymoly.com/music/reviews/bjorks-biophilia-brings-music-back58397.

53. Björk, in Stosuy, "Stereogum Q&A: Björk Talks *Biophilia*."

54. Ibid.

55. Claudia Gorbman, *Unheard Melodies: Narrative Film Music* (London: BFI, 1988).

56. Stan Hawkins and John Richardson, "Remodeling Britney Spears: Matters of Intoxication and Mediation," *Popular Music and Society* 30, no. 5 (2007).

57. "Scott Snibbe," mini-documentary, *The Creators Project*, last accessed July 11, 2012, http://thecreatorsproject.com/blog/björk-expands-her-ibiophiliai-educational-programs-in-nyc.

58. Korsgaard contextualizes *Biophilia* within a history of music video and video games in Korsgaard, "Music Video Transformed."

59. The equivalent in music video is that the user can edit images, control the camera, or mix the sound, thereby empowering the viewer, as noted by Korsgaard, "Music Video Transformed," and Carol Vernallis, "Music Video's Second Aesthetic?," in *The Oxford Handbook of New Audiovisual Aesthetics*, ed. Claudia Gorbman, John Richardson, and Carol Vernallis (Oxford: Oxford University Press, 2013).

60. Björk, in discussion with the author, November 2010.

61. Scott Snibbe, in Kaganskiy, "Interactive Artist Scott Snibbe Gives Us The Scoop On Björk's Biophilia Apps."
62. Korsgaard, "Music Video Transformed."
63. Jordà, Sergi, Günter Geiger, Marcos Alonso, and Martin Kaltenbrunner, "The Reactable: Exploring the Synergy Between Live Music Performance and Tabletop Tangible Unterfaces," *Conference on Tangible and Embedded Interaction*, 2007, http://mtg.upf.edu/node/510.
64. Binder, "Bjork's 'Biophilia' Takes Music to the App World."
65. Scott Snibbe, in Eliot Van Buskirk, "Björk's Lead App Developer Riffs on Music, Nature and How Apps Are Like Talkies," *Wired News*, last accessed July 26, 2011, http://www.wired.com/underwire/2011/07/bjork-app-part-1/all/1.
66. Ibid.
67. The mother app and first single were available in the App store in July 2011, subsequent single releases were in August and September, and the complete app suite was released in October 2011.
68. Eamonn Forde, "What Now My Love?," *The Word*, November 2011, 54.
69. David Hockney, in Nicholas Wroe, "David Hockney: A Life in Art," *The Guardian*, last accessed January 13, 2012, http://www.guardian.co.uk/culture/2012/jan/13/david-hockney-life-in-art.
70. For discussions of Björk and collaboration see Laura Ahonen, *Constructing Authorship in Popular Music: Artists, Media and Stardom* (Saarbrucken: VDM, 2008) and Dibben, *Björk*.
71. Scott Snibbe, in Kaganskiy, "Interactive Artist Scott Snibbe Gives Us The Scoop On Björk's Biophilia Apps."
72. E-mail from Björk to Scott Snibbe, June 30, 2010.
73. "Moon" storyboard, April 14, 2011.
74. Ahonen, *Constructing Authorship in Popular Music: Artists, Media and Stardom*.
75. Max Wiesel, in Eliot Van Buskirk, "Meet the 19-year-Old Building 3 Bjork Song Apps - and Some of the First iPhone Apps Ever," *Evolver.fm*, last accessed August 25, 2011, http://evolver.fm/2011/08/25/meet-the-19-year-old-who-built-bjorks-virus-app-and-some-of-the-first-iphone-apps-ever/.
76. IFPI, *Digital Music Report 2012* (IFPI, 2012), 10.
77. Korsgaard, "Music Video Transformed."
78. Katz, *Capturing Sound: How Technology Changed Music*, 171. One example of the covetability of the *Biophilia Ultimate Art Edition* is evident in one online gallery site that shows the edition in 210 extreme close-ups showing partial shots of the product in various states of opening—an example of a wider phenomena of "packaging porn." See "Biophilia Ultimate Edition," accessed June 20, 2012, http://gallery.me.com/shffl#100060&view=grid&bgcolor=black&sel=214.

SELECT BIBLIOGRAPHY

Ahonen, Laura. *Constructing Authorship in Popular Music: Artists, Media and Stardom*. Saarbrucken: VDM, 2008.
Dibben, Nicola. *Björk*. London: Equinox Press, 2009.
———. "Nature and Nation: National Identity and Environmentalism in Icelandic Popular Music Video and Music Documentary." *Ethnomusicology Forum* 18, no. 1 (2009): 131–151.

Jordà, Sergi, Günter Geiger, Marcos Alonso, and Martin Kaltenbrunner. "The Reactable: Exploring the Synergy between Live Music Performance and Tabletop Tangible Interfaces." Proceedings of the First International Conference on Tangible and Embedded Interaction, 2007. New York, ACM. Available at http://mtg.upf.edu/node/510.

Kaganskiy, Julia. "Interactive Artist Scott Snibbe Gives Us the Scoop on Björk's Biophilia Apps," The Creators Project. Last modified February 21, 2012. http://thecreatorsproject.com/blog/interactive-artist-scott-snibbe-gives-us-the-scoop-on-björks-ibiophiliai-apps.

Korsgaard, Mathias Bonde. "Music Video Transformed." In *The Oxford Handbook of New Audiovisual Aesthetics*, edited by Claudia Gorbman, John Richardson, and Carol Vernallis, 501–524. Oxford: Oxford University Press, 2013.

Stosuy, Brandon. "Stereogum Q&A: Björk Talks Biophilia," Stereogum. Last modified June 29, 2011. http://stereogum.com/744502/stereogum-qa-bjork-talks-biophilia/top-stories/lead-story/.

Vernallis, Carol. *Experiencing Music Video: Aesthetics and Cultural Context*. New York: Columbia University Press, 2004.

Vernallis, Carol. "Music Video's Second Aesthetic?" In *The Oxford Handbook of New Audiovisual Aesthetics*, edited by Claudia Gorbman, John Richardson, and Carol Vernallis, 437–465. Oxford: Oxford University Press, 2013.

PART XII

DIGITAL AESTHETICS ACROSS PLATFORM AND GENRE

CHAPTER 40

ACCELERATED AESTHETICS

A New Lexicon of Time, Space, and Rhythm

CAROL VERNALLIS

IT can feel delirious trying to be open to everything—YouTube, cinema, music video, television, video games—wishing to know and take it all in. It's an absurd desire, of course, as media content proliferates exponentially. Across the globe populations are participating as producers, and vast quantities of historical content are being rediscovered and uploaded, every moment. The mediascape starts to resemble a world, and to see it all might be a kind of overwhelming sublime. Such a stance has rewards—it means nothing less than the dream of being interested in almost everything.

But for this essay we might resist the lure of ubiquity and adopt a more restricted perspective: for the first time we have seemingly unlimited access to an array of digitally enhanced media that present new configurations of time and space. With our smart devices we can conjure up these media instantly, anywhere, often jarringly, with one clip up against another. We also access these heightened segments through home and work computers, or as brief moments embedded in feature films, video games, television shows, and trailers: we may become facile and fleet as we shift attention from one experiential mode to another. Now, I can't say there's an exact homology, or determine cause-and-effect relations, but I'd like to note that at the same time as we have digitally enhanced, aesthetically accelerated media, our work and leisure has become infiltrated by global financial and work flows that themselves are digitally enabled.

In other words, contemporary digital media present forms of space, time, and rhythm we haven't seen before, and these new forms bear some similarities to contemporary experiences like work speedup, multitasking, and just-in-time labor. While a Frankfurt School perspective might note that forms of entertainment replicate labor so we can better toil under our oppressive conditions, Marshall McLuhan might claim that the digital has infiltrated entertainment, finance, and labor, and hence there's a homology between them.[1] My intuition is that both perspectives grasp something. I wonder if becoming more aware of the patterns of space, time, and rhythm in media and work speedup might help us to adapt to social change. We might even work to train our forms of attention so that we can handle the shocks of contemporary society with more grace, care, and awareness.

I don't have time to fully show that we are experiencing accelerating cultural configurations, but let me offer one quick, banal example drawn from my personal experience. My adolescence lacked cell phones and computers. I occupied myself with books, played instruments, or, much worse, engaged in the low-stimulus activity of hanging out at the nearby suburban shopping mall with other teens. For entertainment we'd stand on the corner of a suburban cul-de-sac, and when a lone car passed, we'd yell, "Floor it." I doubt the driver knew what we meant. Our sense of time and horizons differed. Today, however, young people, through smart devices and multimedia forms, often take flight through the imaginarily held worlds of Facebook, texting, and video games. Theirs is a denser, more richly articulated world. YouTube clips viewed on a smart phone may provide one of the quickest, and truest, exits, and here's why. When we see moving media with some semblance of the human, our brain's mirror cells light up, replicating the patterns and shapes we see before us. With mirror cells, you see someone perform a gesture onscreen and somewhere in your brain, your cells model it. It's as if you've gone through the thought-motion without performing the external gesture.[2] With much media moving faster than can be biologically processed, we're leaping to catch up. Both work and leisure have become faster and more pressured.

First, what are the rhythms of today's multitasking and work speedup? If you're an IT worker laboring at the computer, your attention may be drawn along consistent paths. Sometime in your session, you might experience a hunter's drive, an attention that reaches beyond the monitor into the future. This form of attention resembles moments in recent action films and video games. At some point, you'll feel a pull back to the work at hand, and in the interim, you might experience a moment of task switching or even a stutter—the brain misfiring. Then there might be a short period of hyperfocus when you're riveted by details and your consciousness contracts to the microsecond. Soon the brain may seek to take a break and you might daydream. Or you might go into a zone of very productive work. Either way you're engaged in a different, slower form of time. Suddenly, outside pressures impinge. You have to shift tasks and it's "all at once": everything tumbles in at an instant. Though you may feel flooded you also must close this work session, so you can start again and cycle through these same modes of labor. And in the future, I suspect, our ability to control our workflow by bracketing these work sessions may diminish, and we'll become more disoriented as the borders among aesthetics, work, and leisure activities merge.

I have a dystopian picture of how multimedia and work will be coupled in the future. Then, I'll sit at the computer doing my tasks. A device will read my biological outputs and the computer will measure my workflow. An algorithm will inform me to stop and participate in a multimedia clip (for example, calisthenics in an Xbox "Kinect-like" environment). These forms of monitoring and behavioral regimes, shaped to my attention, will help me break, refocus, and return to the task at hand. We'll all feel pressured to participate in these practices because we'll desire to become more employable.

In the near future, however, I think methods of working with multimedia and labor will be less uniform. I can imagine a smartphone having not just audio but also audiovisual playlists containing byte-sized clips configured for the person. These would work to call up where one wants to go or where one wants to turn back to. People may not always be aware of what they're doing, but that would be the underlying purpose of these clips. Such compendia would be as finely tuned and articulated as the enormous music and sound libraries for today's films, which allow you to choose between "graceful with a lilt," "ominous but still urbane," and so on. One might catch a clip to intervene in a cycle of rising panic or to enable a leap into a project.

Amplifying and refashioning the self has become an increasingly prevalent theme in today's digital culture; it's called the "totally quantified life."[3] Health-conscious people wear plastic wristbands to count their steps or measure their heart rates. Others chart sleep-wake cycles or moments of insight and downtime. Positive aphorisms come chiming into cell phones throughout the day. *Wired* magazine has become one locus for sharing these forms of self-management. (One article asks whether documenting one's daily diet supports higher cognition.)[4] These protocols may become increasingly common, and the following description of how we can trace paths of attention through audiovisually intensified media provides one possible example. I place this description in the context of broader shifts, perhaps across media, away from traditional narratives to more open forms. States induced by audiovisually intensified clips might serve as a guide for creating new forms and modes of art-making. Below is one possible routine a viewer might practice and one possible way of reconfiguring a new media work.

Protocols for Practicing New Patterns of Attention

(1) Core
(2) Convoluted and Extended Space
(3) Stutter and Focus
(4) Slo-mo and Bullet Time
(5) All-at-once
(6) Blurred Sectional Demarcations
(7) Line

Core

Before we consider digitally accelerated clips that reproduce features from multitasking and just-in-time labor (items 2 through 6 from the list above), let's look at a few that can establish a sense of ground, balance, and center. The first audiovisual clip I consider here

FIGURE 40.1 Oren Lavie's "Her Morning Elegance": a sense of grounded everydayness.

is Oren Lavie's "Her Morning Elegance." The clip is characterized by a gently circling 3/4 fast waltz against a rolling hypermeter; a smoothly-flowing chord progression of vi, IV, I, V, vi; softly articulated timbres; and breathy singing seeks to please rather than demand exegesis. It seems peacefully active. The plunking bass, mumbled blasé singing, and little bells assert that the bourgeois lead a charmed life; and one little bell encourages the viewer onward. "Her Morning Elegance" has a subtly dark undertow, however. Our protagonist never emerges from sleepwalking nor makes it past her bed's confines. Also, the digital has invaded her domestic space. The quasi-two-dimensional environment resembles several computer-program screen interfaces, like the gridded windows and timelines of Avid and Pro Tools (Figure 40.1).

Here is a second clip to establish a sense of ground. Anusara Yogi Bridget Woods Kramer contains timbres with no attacks; a long, flat pedal tone articulating G major and rare appoggiatura passing tones of A and C; and a breathy voice stretched and smoothed out that suggests no change. Peaceful and passive, it feels inward but expansive (Figure 40.2).[5]

A third clip features a chakra-balancing meditation. My hunch is that many global workers including Americans will feel pressured to take designer drugs for the brain to maintain a competitive edge. An example is Adderal, which improves focus and endurance under boring labor conditions. Maybe we'll end up wired to miniature MRI biofeedback machines. And their outputs might look like the depiction in Figure 40.3.

FIGURE 40.2 Anusara Yogi Bridget Woods Kramer's meditation clip.

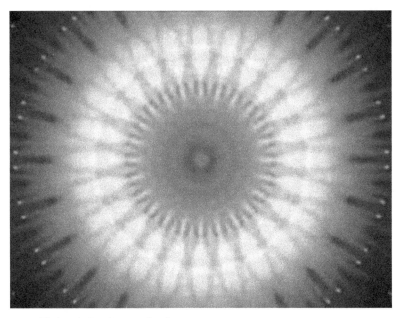

FIGURE 40.3 Chakra-balancing meditation.

Convoluted and Extended Space

Okay. Let's be workers. Ready to rock. Let's spread out. *Gamer* is one of my favorites for convoluted and extended space. I understand little about the body I'm supposed to identify with, where I am in space, or whether the space is 2-D or 3-D. One moment I'm in a music-video-like slide show of global cities. Next, an explosion fills the screen and I'm dropped in with some figure that is silhouetted and then stilled, fuzzed out, sped up, and slowed down, with breathing that's out of sync with the body. The camera pans much more quickly and abrasively than my muscles can respond to, and in the lag or disconnect I feel a roughness or jerkiness. Our protagonist seems to run toward a corner that's constantly expanding backward as if toward a vanishing octagonal point. The soundtrack, made up of breath, gunfire, metal, whooshes, and pitched tones, encourages us to pay attention, because we never ascertain the status of the sounds—some may have been chosen as punctuation, to create a musical line, others to define the environment (Figure 40.4).

Speed racer has a utopian, ever-expansive space, with the broad arcs and expanses that we dream by. There's no horizon. The color strips run to infinity, and I too, fingers and feet, flow out without boundary. I feel as if I cross effortlessly from hand-drawn line animation, to live action, to motion control, through an explosion, to 2-D and 3-D checkered squares. Or do I? At the clip's end, I feel uneasy. Some part of me can't assimilate the pen-and-ink mandala of red-and-white checkered squares that morphs into a tin checkerboard, becoming hard as a shiny concrete or marble showcase floor. So fast, broad, and dense I can't take it all in, but I still love it for all of its capitalistic excess (Figure 40.5).

FIGURE 40.4 Gamer: thrown, fragmented and dispersed audiovisual relations.

FIGURE 40.5 *Speed Racer:* utopian, ever-expansive space.

Stutter and Focus

Okay, let's contract. This Lady Gaga clip thematizes the problem of task-switching: right in the midst of an all-out girls-in-prison, hair-to-fist fight, you get a phone call and you don't want to take it because you're focused on getting your booty onto the dance floor (Figure 40.6). The clip has many layers of stutter, including slow and fast, audio and visual. Is it that nothing is more piercing than a stutter? Does a stutter suggests mechanical failure? A brain misfiring? Recent media are so taken up by the stutter it seems like it's the central meme.[6]

This Rihanna clip, so digitally manipulated, is hyperembodied (Figure 40.7). The slick viscosity of the lips; their lurid shine; the sharp points of the spiky headdress and the eyelashes with their smeared brushstroke-like traces; followed by an "rrrr" sound, which seems to smear the visual stroke into an aural blur; the smoke and digital pixels so sharply demarcated, cloaking the body. All these features meticulously placed against each other, give the sense of overwhelming tactility—ultra physical. Incessantly, points

FIGURE 40.6 Lady Gaga's "Telephone": stutter and focus.

of focus rapidly direct our attention: lips, spikes, eyelashes, gun, so that only too late do we notice a trauma. Rihanna's singing, "I told you baby, I told you, uh oh," has been mutilated, the sonic envelope for "baby" abbreviated into an absence as the word "baby" smashes into the cry of "oh." This opening contains an impossible kernel, a moment suggestive of a violent act, which, in our hyperfocused, constantly moving, distracted attention we've failed to witness.[7]

We can flip media and find this hyperfocus in the soundtrack. Ke$ha may be the queen of accelerated sonic pop aesthetics (Figure 40.8). In " TiK ToK" her voice is meshed with the electronic arrangement. When she sings "tipsy" the lyrics are slowed down, and autotune is applied in special isolation to "on—the—clock." The "Oh, oh" echo's a signature trope of Gwen Stefani's. The arrangement's squeaky sounds are so tactile I can't help but activate the sensation of rubber boots on flesh. My attention can't drift from "here, here, here."

Slo-mo and Bullet Time

I'd claim that bullet time is a technology grounded in narcissism and crisis (Figure 40.9). Think of Neo dodging a bullet in *The Matrix*. We're only willing to grant bullet time to a person, not an animal or a natural event like a volcano, and the moment most often is riven with threat.[8] We can see this effect in the CSI (Crime Scene Investigation TV series) clip (which uses a similar technique known as "stop time").

Bullet time's sensations may be similar to the experiential temporal elongation of a car crash; a near-death epiphany; or a long-distance plummeting to the ground. But the temporality of bullet time is uncertain. Linda Williams notes three genre-based forms

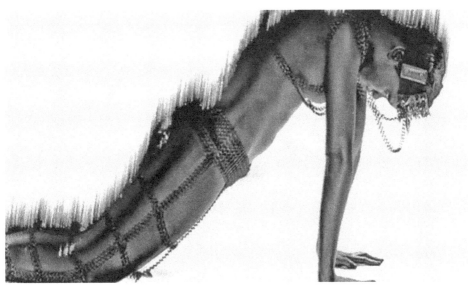

FIGURE 40.7 Rihanna's "Rock Star": hyperfocus in the soundtrack and image.

of time we might attend to: (1) Melodrama, where the villain demands the maiden's rent or threatens the wife and baby, and an illicit affair produces an out-of-wedlock pregnancy—here you're too late. (2) Horror, when you've come too early, you pull the door and a knife is waiting for you. (3) Porn, which is just in time.[9] But what is the time of bullet time? Perhaps it's past tense, already remembered. Yet, paradoxically it's still unfolding in present time, so when music is added, the soundtrack is called upon to serve as a witness and provide all temporal materials, like pulse and duration. Bullet time's time may surpass our biological capabilities. Nevertheless, drawing from bullet time,

FIGURE 40.7 *Continued*

FIGURE 40.8 Ke$ha's "TiK ToK": synaesthetic, close audiovisual relations.

I wouldn't mind having a few more moments like that in my life. I see a face, for instance, that means something to me. A taste that sweeps over me like a shock. As I pour my coffee, I would like bullet time. I would give so much to extend my life with these potholes of moments.

Nuit Blanche's slow-mo time is unusual because of its genre hybridity: it blends the human under threat with romance. It's haunted by the question of whether true love exists, or our attachments are arbitrary, simply moments of cathexis linked to some previous lost relationship. Or are we only DNA receptacles struggling for our chromosomal matter's continuance?[10] Formally *Nuit Blanche* reflects this dichotomy. It's warm and authentic, but it's artificial; almost all of it was composed from still photographs,

FIGURE 40.8 *Continued*

matte-painted in Photoshop, and then stretched over texture maps. The glass never broke—it was animated. No street, building, or car existed in this space; the actors, shot in green screen, might never have met, and the music was recorded in a cathedral. Like much recent media, *Nuit Blanche* is vertiginous. Objects and people roll over and turn: the building lurches forward like the *Titanic*, and the male protagonist, buckling gently, drifts as he's hit by a car. The kiss, nestled among glass shards, starts to turn, like in Hitchcock's *Vertigo*, with both a rotation and a swerve. These large turns create a sense of disequilibrium and sleep. All this sleep, I want to argue, saturates much of contemporary media. *Nuit Blanche* literalizes McLuhan's conundrum. If we are to work with new media forms as prostheses, they must become natural for us. To do this, we must, at least for a while, fail to see them, undergo narcissus narcosis. But if we're building a new form of embodiment and so much of it involves sleeping or sleepwalking, we have put ourselves at risk (Figure 40.10).[11]

FIGURE 40.9 *CSI:* "stop time"

FIGURE 40.9 *Continued*

All at Once

Does this "all at once" replicate our current experiences of work and play—our trying to keep up with email, instant messaging, chat windows, cell-phone calls, projects due? I can tell you that, as a professor, I'll find myself in the rush of backlogged email, preparing for a lecture, trying to submit a grant, adding a last bit of copyediting for a journal, and making a department meeting, and I'm trying to do these simultaneously. Or is "all at once" simply a response to the excitement of all the newly available media? A replica in miniature of the sublime surplus? Or is it simply what the brain delights in? "All at once" may be everywhere now because we never had as good a technology to produce this. Or is it that we like "all at once" because we feel more sharply the trajectories of other people's lives and the ones that our own lives might take? Perhaps we've made a wrong turn?

Never before *Inception* has a film asked us to hold so many separate worlds, all simultaneously, within our conscious attention for such a long duration (Figure 40.11). Director Chris Nolan felt the Edith Piaf song was so central to the film's design he couldn't decide whether to first give it to the composer or the sound designer. Each of *Inception*'s seven layers has a different set of sound effects—the way water sounds, or wind, or clocks are all particular. The Wagnerian V to flat-VI runs through the film, always hovering, never resolving. The low foghorn belongs to everything, the crashing city, the crumbling

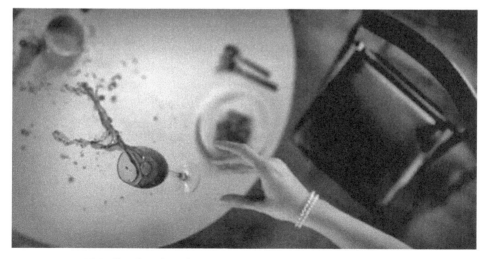

FIGURE 40.10 *Nuit Blanche*: ultra slow-mo.

FIGURE 40.10 *Continued*

buildings, the avalanche, the car going over the bridge and nose-diving into the water. That horn suggests slumber, but it is part of the ping, the Piaf trigger, so it should be constantly waking us up. On each level, the characters are subtly different as well. Films now are not so much about story as about pathway. All I want to do is to learn the lilt, the turn of each of the characters, the ways objects work in each layer, and hold these against the other layers and against the music. I'd like to learn this map or build.[12]

One more example of "all at once." Studies show that in reality people can't multitask. What we're really doing is one task at a time, with a short lag, as the brain switches focus. But multimedia say, "screw the science." Our brains are pliant. We can refigure the brain so we can follow along with this Lynyrd Skynyrd/Beyoncé clip, hearing both lines of music simultaneously, with equal attention, as two ongoing channels or streams. (The two songs are different keys separated by a whole step.) (Figure 40.12).

Blurred Sectional Demarcations

I've mentioned it's important to bracket work experiences into sections as a means to control the amount and flow of stimulus. In the future, however, I believe borders between leisure and work will become less clear. Santigold's "L.E.S. Artistes" points to such a future. The music video quivers between an arty, fashion-plate tableau and a narrative with current, pressing global issues, like militant activism in the face of violent repressive regimes.

Santigold's video exploits our cultural understandings about color through the fine modulations made possible by Digital Intermediary.[13] A shift from pure primaries and

FIGURE 40.11 Inception: seven layers "all at once."

FIGURE 40.12 Lynyrd Skynyrd/Beyoncé mashup: clashing media "all at once."

soft pastels to a muted burnt-sienna orange two-thirds in suddenly takes us away from a playful imaginary into a suggestively real world with tragic consequences. We have to ask: Do new technologies make it possible for our politics and aesthetics to mingle this way? What does it mean for our lives when we have many streams coming in and we're not sure what's authentic and what's stylized? Santigold's clips show there are stakes

FIGURE 40.13 Santigold's "L.E.S. Artistes": blurring the lines between leisure, work, and politics.

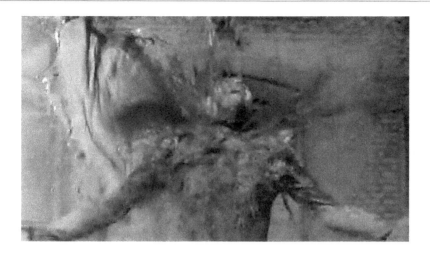

FIGURE 40.13 *Continued*

here—we may be experiencing not only a shift in aesthetics and attention but also in politics and community (Figure 40.13).[14]

Line

I've started with "Core" as a technique for negotiating shifting modes of attention. Let me close with another adaptive mode, which I'll call "Line." To make it in today's increasingly globalized society, we need to be "just in time," able to work within a large organization, to retool and reconfigure our personalities and roles. Those who succeed will be "fleet"; as they move quickly through contexts, they'll no more than momentarily touch on incidents as they continue onward. An audiovisual corollary to the experience of Line is in Bekmambetov's *Day Watch,* To's *Full-Time Killer,* or the trailer for *The Town* (Figure 40.14). One could argue that "the Line" is amoral, or even immoral. It's not for those who take the time to consider all perspectives, to brood over the ramifications of an event. If everyone embodies this sense of Line, it'll be another form of sleepwalking. But for someone trapped by the past or too reactive, this kind of Line might be liberatory. To travel lightly and to keep going. To not overjudge and to let go.

Justin Bieber's music video "Somebody to Love" uses the concept of Line with perhaps a positive moral valence (Figure 40.15). I've interviewed Dave Meyers, the video's director, about making it. The gig came through in two days. Meyers didn't know he'd have Usher until the night before. The backdrop was simply green screen. Meyers threw up the stalactites. He liked the choreographer and dance group, and they quickly came on

FIGURE 40.14 *Full Time Killer*: Johnnie To's sense of line.

FIGURE 40.14 *Continued*

FIGURE 40.15 "Somebody To Love": ways to make it through.

FIGURE 40.15 *Continued*

board. Everyone brought unique, finely honed skills to the table, and somehow helped create a sense of community. Watch and listen to the way the video creates a finely articulated, constantly moving, yet always transitioning Line (we follow from a hand gesture by Usher, to the unfolding of Japanese women's fans, to the rising and falling of dancers dressed in black moving-like pistons). The video suggests that even if the context that brings people together is dissembled, a new one—also involving active, attentive, and engaged participants—might emerge. It suggests if we can find a way to go forward like this, we just might make it through.

NOTES

1. Max Horkheimer and Theodor Adorno, *Dialectic of Enlightenment (Cultural Memory in the Present)*, trans. Edmund Jephcott (Stanford, CA: Stanford University Press, 2002), 7. See also Marshall McLuhan, "The Playboy Interview: Marshall McLuhan," *Playboy Magazine*, March 1969, repr. 1994, 11.
2. R. C. Miall, "Connecting Mirror Neurons and Forward Models," *Neuroreport* 14, no. 17 (2003): 2135–2137.
   "Entrainment occurs when two oscillators come to oscillate together...entrainment is the coordinating of the timing of our behaviors and the synchronizing of our attentional resources." Satinder P. Gill, "Entrainment and Musicality in the Human System Interface," *AI & Society* 25 (2007): 567–605.
3. See "QS: Quantified Self, Self Knowledge Through Numbers," http://quantifiedself.com/.
4. Gary Wolf, "The Data-Driven Life," in *The New York Times* (April 28, 2010), http://www.nytimes.com/2010/05/02/magazine/02self-measurement-t.html?pagewanted=all&_r=0.
5. Many people experience weird YouTube vortices, where they're not only moving laterally, clicking from link to link, but also trying to pursue some sort of connoisseurly obscure topic like abrasive, gauche regional carpet cleaning commercials from the seventies. I've

started collecting meditation clips, in part for their oxymoronic qualities. There's little Benjaminian aura here. The ads blare, and the low-res images compete with the snarky commentary. Some person may be reaching out, but just as well she might be trying to peddle a DVD, and, in the middle of the viewer's vulnerably hypnotic meditative state, an intrusive loud blaring sound might appear. (I've kept one eye open for such complaints in the commentary.) People before me have come and gone leaving little trace, so the "sacred" of meditation is tainted with that of a peep-show. But some of it actually works. Perhaps yoga is so popular today because it's effective at combating social and economic demands.

6. Audiovisual stutter has historical precedents, and what's exciting about new media is that my intertextual precursors for this effect most likely differs from yours. Mine features the 1970s Purina Cat Chow commercials in which (with primitive video editing) the cat goes, "Chow chow chow." Today, perhaps nearly everyone enters a clip from a different vantage point. Perhaps we're less in sync than we thought. For new research on the glitch and the stutter, see Laura Marks, "A Noisy Brush with the Infinite: Noise in Enfolding-Unfolding Aesthetics" (chapter 7) and Caetlin Benson-Allott, "Going Gaga for Glitch: Digital Failure @nd Feminist Spectacle in Twenty-First Century Music Video" (chapter 9) in *The Oxford Handbook of Sound and Image in Digital Media*, ed. Carol Vernallis, et al. (New York & Oxford: Oxford University Press, forthcoming).

7. Film theorists have recently become obsessed with the digital versus analog. Digital and analog can sometimes be understood as a state of mind or experience—something can seem digitalish or analogish based on context. (In a scene in a very digitally embodied film, *Inception*, the femme fatale Mal sits in her mission house and the sun glints on a knife and on cut, glowing, golden tomatoes. The digital should feel cold, abstracted, nonearthly, but this is one of the most quotidian and holy of scenes—notably warm.) With accelerated aesthetics, categorical attributes attributed to the digital and analogue can confound us. See D. N. Rodowick, *The Virtual Life of Film* (Cambridge, MA: Harvard University Press 2007).

8. Technologically, for bullet time, still cameras are placed around the circumference of the profilmic event and then recombined into a moving image.

9. Linda Williams, "Film Bodies: Gender, Genre, and Excess," in *Film Theory and Criticism*, ed. Leo Braudy and Marshall Cohen, 5th ed. (New York: Oxford University Press, 1999), 711.

10. Several recent films, such as *Fifty First Dates* (2004), *Eternal Sunshine of the Spotless Mind* (2004), and *500 Days of Summer* (2009) reflect the same themes.

11. Is a possible subspecies or genre-blending of "slow-mo" and "all at once" the scroll? If we're watching a television newscaster in a dazed state, the scroll can seem to pull our distracted attention in a flow terminating nowhere. This two-state, split configuration is inassimilable.

12. In contemporary film, we often follow an avatar-like character against a shifting landscape; sometimes, this character itself changes. In these archipelago-like forms, we cleave to sound image relations. We simply want the feel and pattern, a kinesthetic response we can match with the film's own routines comprised of varied forms of time, space, and rhythm. Consider, for example, *Moulin Rouge* (2001), *Bourne Ultimatum* (2007), and *Life Aquatic* (2004).

13. In the case of "L.E.S. Artistes," I'll argue that the driver's simply digital intermediary, or in industry parlance, DI. DI functions like Photoshop's processes for altering images, but it works with real-time moving media. You can tweak an individual pixel's color, isolate it, and modulate it thereby fracturing the moving image, pulling it away from its referent in

the world. Even if the Santigold video had not been designed with DI, I'd say it relies on DI's safety net: that a piece can be "made in post."

14. Epochs in the throes of change may produce their own antidotes and remedies. The *New York Times* published a study recently suggesting that IT workers who multitasked were deskilling. They were over-responding to a surfeit of stimulus and failing to identify important elements within a field of information. I took the test and was pleased at how well I'd done. I've spent years studying music video, however, and have learned to hunt and track one item at a time as it threads through the material. I've also taught and done production. The benefits of participating in media (through criticism, teaching, or production) may be also why so many of my students, regardless of their discipline, now turn to video production. Production practice provides a way to make manageable and find patterns within an onslaught of stimuli, and to begin to articulate one's own dreams rather than more simply reenvisioning the dreams of others. Part of me is hopeful about new media. We will become more shotgun, staccato-like readers, but also listeners and viewers who might, through new configurations of the senses, take part in a public conversation.

SELECTED BIBLIOGRAPHY

Gill, Satinder P. "Entrainment and Musicality in the Human System Interface." *AI & Society* 25 (June 2007): 567–605.

Horkheimer, Max, and Theodor Adorno. *Dialectic of Enlightenment (Cultural Memory in the Present)*. Translated by Edmund Jephcott. Stanford, CA: Stanford University Press, 2002.

McLuhan, Marshall. "The Playboy Interview: Marshall McLuhan." *Playboy Magazine* March 1969, repr. 1994.

Miall, R. C. "Connecting mirror neurons and forward models." *Neuroreport* 14 no. 17 (December 2, 2003): 2135–2137.

Rodowick, D. N. *The Virtual Life of Film*. Cambridge, MA: Harvard University Press, 2007.

Williams, Linda. "Film Bodies: Gender, Genre, and Excess." In *Film Theory and Criticism*, 5th ed., edited by Leo Braudy and Marshall Cohen, 701–715. New York: Oxford University Press, 1999.

CHAPTER 41

ACOUSTIC AUTEURS AND TRANSNATIONAL CINEMA

JAY BECK

THIS essay considers two fields of inquiry within cinema studies today: the circulation and reception of global cinema and the growing discipline of sound studies. Over the past twenty years, scholars have noted that digital convergence has transformed the ways audiences experience cinematic sounds and images. With the consolidation of transnational media corporations, films from commercial studios now reach into almost every corner of the globe and, with them, come a set of audiovisual codes that have become a worldwide lingua franca. Yet, within these flows of mainstream global cinema, it is possible to trace patterns of resistance, especially in the soundtrack. One trend emerging in the past decade is the new "acoustic auteur" who constructs personal sound aesthetics that rework the rules of commercially driven audiovisual relations. This essay considers how global audiences listen to and make sense of these emerging aesthetics. What follows are critical observations and postulates about a new contemporary global sound praxis that reveals evolving patterns of cinematic and cultural forms.[1]

TRANSNATIONAL CINEMAS AND CONTINGENT COMMUNITIES

In this essay, I use the term "transnational cinema" to describe a cinematic practice and style that both consciously acknowledges its site of origin and is in dialogue with other filmmakers and cinematic forms. Throughout the twentieth century, Hollywood cinema had extended its reach into other national cinematic practices, shaping both their representational and stylistic codes. But, starting in the 1990s, circulation of cinema via digital technologies like DVDs/Blu-rays and the internet created a new dynamic. Film and other media began to move freely across borders, between oppositional nations, and, most importantly, among contingent communities of diverse cinematic viewers who came together around shared affinities rather than national allegiances.[2] For me and other scholars, twenty-first century transnational cinema is no longer dependent on the old centers of cinematic power—the American media industries, the commercial cinemas of Western Europe and India, and the large national cinemas of Eastern Asia—that once dominated the flow of cinema around the globe. As Lúcia Nagib observes cinema circulating in the digital era escapes the discursive binary of US–Europe/rest-of-the world and decenters the unidirectional flow of cinematic influences. Multiple centers influenced by regional interactions cultivate cinematic diversity.[3]

Traditional mainstream American cinema had specific characteristics—subordination of time and space to cause–effect logic, editing patterns designed to reinforce continuity, mise-en-scène and cinematography that emphasize diegetic verisimilitude—and these worked together to ensure the stability of the narrative system.[4] Regarding sound practices, primary emphasis was placed on dialogue intelligibility, character development supported by an empathetic musical score (generally based on repeated themes or leitmotifs), rigid boundaries between diegetic and nondiegetic sounds (such as a clear distinction between off-screen voices and voice-over), and the use of clearly sourced and narratively justified sound effects (including the occasional use of source music).

But transnational cinemas have countered with a variety of oppositional techniques based around the alteration of film form for local audiences. Exemplars of this approach were Danish directors Lars von Trier and Thomas Vinterberg, as part of the Dogme 95 movement, who sought to return cinema to its basic properties. Instead of relying on studios, genres, special effects, and postproduction sound techniques, their films embraced digital cinema's ability to capture profilmic events. Dogme 95 was an attempt to open up narrative structure and cinematic style, and it demonstrated that smaller European cinemas could stand up to the popularity of American cinema through what Dudley Andrew calls "indigenous local narrations,"[5] local variations that differently inflect the codes of mainstream narrative cinema to cater to local audiences.

Most of the filmmakers examined in this essay fall into what is referred to generally as "transnational art cinema," owing to a combination of their national origins, funding structures, and cinematic styles. Their films, funded transnationally and distributed internationally, seek both regional and multinational audiences. The circulation of these films has inaugurated an international dialogue among makers and audiences on a level impossible in the predigital era. It is my contention that the primary way transnational filmmakers construct stylistic linkages, made possible only in an era of digital convergence, is through a reconfiguration of the rules governing sound and image relations. This is by no means a systematic or unified resistance to the codified structure of mainstream narrative cinemas; rather, it represents an emergent set of stylistic practices that cut across national boundaries and connect filmmakers via shared acoustic techniques. This essay presents a theoretical distillation of several emergent sound tropes and how they are changing the construction and meaning of cinema around the world.

THE ESCHEWAL OF THE SCORE

As part of this strategy of cultivating indigenous local narrations, filmmakers from around the world find themselves exploring new representational strategies to connect with local as well as transnational audiences. A prominent practice that reconfigures the rules of cinematic representation is the eschewal of empathetic score music. There is a strong tendency among directors outside the commercial mainstream to dispense with nondiegetic orchestral scores in favor of constructing carefully detailed sound-scapes. Again, this trend can be heard in the films produced by the Dogme 95 filmmakers, whose Vow of Chastity states "the sound must never be produced apart from the image or vice-versa."[6] This practice has its origins in the 1970s—starting in France with filmmakers Eric Rohmer, Chantal Akerman, Jean-Marie Straub and Danièle Huillet—and a preference for the use of direct sound recording in many European cinemas.[7] Concomitant with the use of direct sound was a refusal to use nondiegetic score music so as not to undercut the acoustic verisimilitude of the films. This idea, reinvigorated by the Dogme movement, is found in a growing number of global filmmakers who refuse to use music for affective purposes. As Argentine filmmaker Lucrecia Martel explains:

> What's interesting about sound is that it lacks a harmonic organization, which allows the viewer to predict feelings and anticipate events.... Music, like the plot and like language, always allows the viewer to anticipate and even prejudge what's next. Conversely, sound only allows the simultaneity of the experience. That's very important when you're trying to share emotions. It only allows you to face what you are seeing at that moment. [8]

Along with Martel, there are a growing number of directors who do not use nondiegetic scores in many or all of their films, including Lisandro Alonso, Andrea Arnold, Pedro Costa, Jean-Pierre and Luc Dardenne, José Luis Guerín, Michael Haneke, Hong Sang-Soo, Jia Zhang-ke, Abbas Kiarostami, Yorgos Lanthimos, Lee Chang-Dong, Carlos Reygadas, Jaime Rosales, Alicia Scherson, Athina Rachel Tsangari, Apichatpong Weerasethakul, Keren Yadaya, and even American independent filmmakers such as Kelly Reichardt and Gus Van Sant. Within their films, it is possible to hear how the absence of a score changes the way that audiences perceive film sound. As an example, sound theorist Michel Chion notes of Michael Haneke's *Caché*, "one could argue that this absence has no precise meaning. In the majority of films, characters don't go to the bathroom either, nor do they usually wait for change when paying, and this does not mean that the omission of such scenes is meaningful for the film. But music, diegetic or not, is such an important element in the majority of films, as well as in the sonorous tissue of today's private moments, that films that do not offer such sounds 'sound' different to us."[9] Instead of relying on the empathetic quality of the score to define character emotions and prompt audience reaction, the films resist passive interpretation; according to director Andrea Arnold, "You have to tune in on a different level."[10]

Parallel to this trend are filmmakers who choose to use music in their films as source sounds coming from the diegesis only. A cluster of films using this approach appears in Argentine cinema, where filmmakers like Marcelo Piñeyro, Adrián Caetano, and Martín Rejtman use diegetically sourced local music and performers in lieu of a score. Film scholar Gustavo Costantini observes this tendency in his taxonomy of Argentine cinema music, "La banda sonora en el nuevo cine argentino," yet he misses a larger trend by not realizing that this phenomenon extends well beyond the boundaries of Argentina or South America.[11] In fact, from the minimal use of music in the films of Hou Hsiao-Hsien or Edward Yang to the diegetically sourced popular music in Alfonso Cuarón's *Y tu mamá también* and Lynne Ramsay's *Morvern Callar*, the move away from the directly affective nondiegetic score is a global trend in film sound aesthetics.

In addition, many of these directors use diegetic music as a sound effect, giving it the same weight and substance as other effects in their acoustic landscape. Although audiences may still react to the music affectively, these filmmakers do not rely on the signifying properties of nondiegetic music to prompt emotional responses. For example, rather than instructing an audience how they are supposed to react to the narrative, music in Lynne Ramsay's *Morvern Callar* takes on a different function. The film's titular character is deliberately opaque, and the audience is placed in a position to gauge their own moral response to her actions without being prompted by either the musical selections or the character's internal thoughts as voice-over (a feature Ramsay dispensed with when she adapted Alan Warner's novel). In interviews, Ramsay has expressed a disdain for traditional film scores, saying, "Look at the music. You know, . . . 'Feel happy, feel sad, feel good.' Personally, I go to see films a lot and feel completely manipulated, like someone telling me I'm dumb. I like to give the audience quite a lot of room, and some audiences like that and some don't."[12] What is important in the film is not necessarily the music that is heard—a mix tape given to Morvern as a Christmas gift from her boyfriend before he committed suicide—but how it is heard (Figure 41.1). According to Linda Ruth Williams, "Ramsay's approach is to make almost everything we hear emerge from her protagonist's Walkman. Morvern's Christmas tape is the film's primary music source, diegetic or otherwise. The aural landscape sweeps across and between the direct sound which is Morvern's earphones-in experience and that irritating, tinny buzz you get from someone else's Walkman at a distance."[13] By refusing voice-over as well as a score, Ramsay makes her audience work to interpret the actions of the central character (see AV example 41.1◐).

Innovative patterns of sound and music usage are replacing the established narrative cinematic conventions of theme songs and leitmotifs in numerous transnational films. We can hear these changes in the rigorously structural repetition of popular songs in Wong Kar-Wai's films, drawn from his memories as a youth growing up in Shanghai and Hong Kong, interwoven with a highly contemplative use of voice-over. Other formulations include the incongruous heavy metal music over the titles of Lisandro Alonso's

FIGURE 41.1 As Morvern listens to her mix tape, the audience hears the music from her point of audition (*Morvern Callar*, Lynne Ramsay, 2002).

profoundly affectless films, the titular character Wendy humming her own theme song in Kelly Reichardt's *Wendy and Lucy*, or the eruption of Grace Chang musical numbers into the hyperrealistic diegetic spaces of Tsai Ming-Liang's films. Indeed Tsai, along with Jean-Luc Godard, is identified by Claudia Gorbman as an "auteur *mélomane*," or a music-loving director who utilizes prerecorded music in his films as "a key thematic element and a marker of authorial style."[14] In addition to Tsai and Godard, it is possible to include Apichatpong Weeresethakul's canny use of Thai and Japanese pop songs in *Tropical Malady* and *Syndromes and a Century*, the counterpoint between British new wave music and Türkü folk songs as commentary on the cultural conflict of Turkish *Gastarbeiter* working in Germany in Fatih Akin's *Head-On*, or the improbable references to British post-punk groups Wire and Young Marble Giants amid the slums of Lisbon in Pedro Costa's films. In dispensing with the score, in both its affective and commercial functions, new models of sound techniques and their relationship to storytelling are unfolding.

EMERGING SOUND TROPES IN GLOBAL CINEMAS

The larger strategy of eliminating nondiegetic score music has opened up the potential for the soundtrack to be remobilized as an expressive space, and it is possible to identify resistant patterns of vernacular sound usage to reinvent the local narrations. To better understand these connections, this chapter examines seven emerging sound tropes in contemporary transnational cinemas.

Subjectivity

Subjective sound never has taken hold in American cinema because it generally replicates or contradicts the effect of visual point of view and conflicts with the long-established rules of narrative continuity. The rare incidents of aural subjectivity are linked almost exclusively to traumatic events or aural hallucinations based around moments of character delirium. Yet a few engaged transnational filmmakers explore the expressive potential of aural subjectivity through the shift between third- and first-person hearing.

Instances of subjective hearing serve to overturn classical models of sound–image relations that posit the structural subordination of sound to the dominance of the image and the valorization of dialogue intelligibility over scale matching between sound and image.[15] The use of music heard through headphones in *Morvern Callar* allows the audience to experience Morvern's point of audition directly, without the need to reinforce subjectivity through a point-of-view shot. Other filmmakers, like Carlos Reygadas, tug at the fabric of acoustic verisimilitude by shifting between third-person and first-person perspectives, both visually and acoustically. At several points in Reygadas's films, the soundscape expands or contracts to represent the point of audition of the main character, and this is often married to a tracking camera movement that shifts from an objective over-the-shoulder shot to a subjective point-of-view shot.

First used to represent the existential crisis of the unnamed central character in *Japón* as he wanders through a remote mountainous region of Mexico, the shifts between subjective and objective sound mimic his internal ethical vacillations during the journey. In *Battle in Heaven*, Reygadas uses this technique to grant audiences an interior glimpse of the otherwise inscrutable central character, Marcos. At several points in the film, the soundscape collapses to express Marcos's shifting attention and how he perceives the world around him. In what seems like a comic interlude at the beginning of the film, Marcos is seen with his wife selling cheap alarm clocks in a passageway leading to the Mexico City Metro. As the camera tracks in closer, the cacophony of the beeping alarms fades away, leaving just the sound of commuters passing through the tunnel once the film cuts to Marcos's point of view. After several minutes of his perceptual activity— scanning the cross-section of city's demographic while listening to the changes in reverberation as they pass—the film cuts to a long shot of Marcos and his wife with the alarm sounds restored (see AV example 41.2 ◑).

Reygadas continues this shifting sound aesthetic throughout the film, until the point at which Marcos sleeps with his employer's daughter, Ana. The tryst is initially seen and heard through Marcos, his point of audition reinforced by a shallow focus image to represent his vision without his glasses. Yet, as the couple continues, the camera cuts to a medium-long shot and drifts away through a window, looping through a courtyard in a 360-degree pan. As the camera reveals views of the neighboring buildings, the soundscape shifts from the noises of lovemaking to objective audio missives of the city on a summer afternoon: the clank of workers removing television antennas, the flutter and chirrups of unseen birds in the trees, the steady-state murmur of distant traffic, the laughter of children playing on a rooftop, the rattle of utensils as the evening meal is prepared in a nearby apartment, and the intermittent dripping from a leaky water spigot. Reygadas experiments with this technique in all of his films and explains his rationale: "I sometimes believe that sound design is almost half of cinema, especially in terms of expression. Sound can be objective or subjective. I would say that Tarkovsky is a master of subjective sound and Kiarostami is a master of objective sound. I try to use both."[16] In doing so, his films construct a valuable slippage between listening regimes and ask spectators to experience the diegetic world the same way his characters experience it.

Rendering

Nearly all films rely on the realistic reproduction of sound, whether through the recording of synchronous dialogue during production or the postproduction practice of adding sounds to fill the diegetic world. In most Hollywood narrative films, this occurs on a one-to-one basis designed to reinforce a perceived ontological link between image and sound: we see an old wooden door opening, and we hear the creaking noise of a door with rusty hinges. Of course, because film and sound recordings can be manipulated, it is entirely possible and very often probable that the sounds we hear are not those that were produced when the image was photographed. Michel Chion notes that through *synchresis*—a process of linking a sound to an image that it does not match by way of synchronization—an audience can be made to believe that sounds and images fit together.[17] The logic behind this is that when we see an object and hear a sound simultaneously, our empirical experience tells us that they are connected. The theory of synchresis opens up a broad range of expressive possibilities for filmmakers beyond the basic correspondence between sound and image. Yet it is remarkable just how few filmmakers have sought to explore these possibilities and how many still rely on a putative ontological link between sound and object.

The synchresis effect grants film an affective power and becomes a unique expressive tool for creating emotional resonances in audiences. Chion defines this practice as "rendering" and elaborates its function as follows:

> In considering the realist and narrative function of diegetic sounds (voices, music, noise), we must distinguish between the notions of rendering and reproduction. The film spectator recognizes sounds to be truthful, effective, and fitting, not so much if they reproduce what would be heard in the same situation in reality, but if they *render* (convey, express) the feelings associated with the situation.[18]

This notion of rendering allows for the objective perception of a sound—even if that sound is a construction—to merge with an affective function. In this way, sounds can take on more meaning than just signification and lead to what sound editor Walter Murch calls a "conceptual resonance" between the sounds of the film and the emotions of the story being told.[19]

Rendering sounds to exploit their affective power is a broad-ranging trope among contemporary transnational filmmakers. This is in strong contrast to the classical Hollywood norm and the majority of international commercial cinema, in which sound effects are added to create a passive verisimilitude rather than an active sense of engagement with the diegesis. The standard model for effects usage is to include sounds for objects that correspond to a visualized presence in the frame and to provide only those off-screen sounds that are relevant to the narrative.[20] As a point of contrast, many global filmmakers take differing approaches to using sound effects to render experiences. Claire Denis emphasizes diurnal sounds of routine in her films, such as the percolations of a coffee maker in *Nenette et Boni*, the washing and ironing of clothes in *Beau Travail*, and the inevitable Parisian traffic of *Vendredi Soir*. Takeshi Kitano lets his sound editors build up a realistic soundscape by adding in effects that correspond to the sound sources present in the diegesis, yet, during the film's mix, he removes sounds, paring down the soundtrack to just a few signal effects to persuade the audience emotionally.

Another important aspect of rendering is its ability to extend the diegetic world beyond the space of the frame. The way that most narrative films achieve this is through the visualization of active sound sources and the inclusion of a general ambience to hint at the presence of a passive off-screen world. Yet in the films of Lucrecia Martel, just the opposite occurs. In Martel's films, "the relationship between cause and effect is inverted; only after hearing a sound do we see the source that produces it."[21] From the beginning of her first feature, *La ciénaga*, Martel shows only short bits of action in tightly framed close-ups and fills the off-screen space with numerous sound effects: distant thunder, muffled gunfire, bird cries, cicadas, ice clinking in glasses, and, most disturbingly, the abrasive scrape of metal chairs being dragged across concrete. As she explains, "Off-screen space becomes far more important when you don't show the entire scene, but rather show fragments of the scene."[22] (See AV example 41.3.◉) As a result, the sounds take on a centrifugal force, constantly pulling at the edge of the frame and reminding the audience of the larger world that exists beyond. Moreover, Martel exploits the effects of rendering to a point at which the sounds become haptic, engaging other senses through a synthesis of sight and sound that borders on synesthesia. There is a physicality and weight to the sounds in Martel's films, and the sonic miasma of *La ciénaga* perfectly matches the lassitude of its characters. Martel describes her working process, saying:

> I think out the sound track well ahead of shooting—even before writing the script—and it gives me the grounding for the visuals. I first try to define the sonic atmosphere. I find the sound in most films disturbingly loud and disruptive. I hope the sound [in my films] works in a different way. Sound is what connects the film, the spectator, and the director.[23]

Tsai Ming-Liang provides a different approach to rendering through his technique of long take location filming in the spaces of globalization around Taipei. Chris Wood expresses the distinction between ontological realism and Tsai's rendered realism as follows: "Where Bazinian realism purports to capture the actual, Tsai's realism performs a conception of the real."[24] In his films, Tsai expunges the characteristic sounds of the local to leave a generic palette of electrical hums, light flickers, and air handling noises. These sounds are mated to conversationless restaurants, anonymous theaters, and liminal zones of airports, public walkways, and basements. This method, although relying on many of the same sound effects, is precisely the opposite of Martel's centrifugal sound-scapes: in Tsai's films, sound works centripetally, pushing in on the frame and fixing the characters in their claustrophobic environments. Although the sonic spaces in Tsai's films adhere to a realism born from their locations, the increased levels of ambience and off-screen sound effects contain and demarcate the diegesis.

Perhaps the most ubiquitous spaces in Tsai's films are Taipei's high-rise apartment complexes that provide the main sites of interaction. Central to the construction of this world are the reverberations of shoes in hallways, the whoosh of air from elevator shafts, the whine and groan of defective plumbing, and the ubiquitous buzz of fluorescent light-ing (Figure 41.2). This preference for signature sounds over dialogue shifts the audience away from semantic listening to become absorbed in the same acoustic framework as the characters. Thus, without the common set of contextual cues coming from dialogue or score music, the viewer's perceptual activity is engaged in a search for meaningful patterns and aural motifs, such as the beeping of alarm clocks in *What Time Is It There* and *The Skywalk Is Gone* or the never-ending rain in *The Hole*.

Architectural Acoustics

Another trope, related to the concept of rendering, is an increased attentiveness to the sound of spaces and urban environments. This is evident in the films of Tsai Ming-Liang,

FIGURE 41.2 The offscreen space in Tsai Ming-Liang's films is filled with the quotidian elec-trical and mechanical sounds of urban Taipei (*The Wayward Cloud*, Tsai Ming-Liang, 2005).

and it also is put to strong narrative effect in Pedro Costa's trilogy of films set in the Lisbon slum of Fontainhas. Starting with *Ossos*, through *In Vanda's Room* and *Colossal Youth*, the distinct acoustic ambience of Fontainhas evolves as the community undergoes radical change. In each film, the spectator is kept within a restricted visual perspective, forced to experience the labyrinthine space of the slum in the same way that the characters live their lives. We are never given an establishing shot of the world outside, yet we hear the city's renovation workers digging their way into the decaying district. In counterpoint with the drug addicts and low-wage denizens of this community, the ubiquitous sound of gentrification reminds viewers of how the neighborhood is literally being erased before their eyes. This sound of urban transformation cuts across the three films and the shallow visual depth of field is superseded by the films' deep focus sound (see AV example 41.4 ◐). The exterior sounds of the city penetrate Fontainhas as a form of "*audio vérité*," a direct sound approach that emulates the *cinéma vérité* documentaries of the 1960s. Although this approach posits sound as providing a documentary parallel to Costa's fixed camera and digital video images, the relative directness of the soundtrack hides the intricate layering of sounds made possible in postproduction. Despite the observational quality of his images, Costa is a true architect of sound space. Through his richly constructed soundscapes, the director reproduces his version of Fontainhas even after the real community itself has crumbled to dust.

Similarly, in *Goodbye, Dragon Inn*, Tsai Ming-Liang uses the space of Taipei's decaying Fu Ho movie theater to highlight the interplay between regional acoustic practices. His film interpolates a screening of the 1967 King Hu film *Dragon Gate Inn*—the last film screened before the theater is shuttered—and makes the viewer aware of Hong Kong cinema's sound aesthetics by reauditioning them in the space of the auditorium. In King Hu's film, the spatial codes of sound are routinely subordinated to the demands of a re-recording process in which all of the sounds of the film were added in postproduction. In part, this was due to the difficulty of recording live on location in the remote settings of rural Taiwan, but primarily it allowed for the dubbing of Mandarin dialogue into other languages, principally Cantonese, for international distribution. The plenitude of dialogue and stylized martial arts sound effects in *Dragon Gate Inn* is contrasted by the dearth of communication and interaction among the spectators watching the film in the auditorium. The long takes and reverberant sound space of *Goodbye, Dragon Inn* are a radical counterpoint to the fast cutting and shallow soundscape in King Hu's epic. Through this acoustic juxtaposition of the films' sound aesthetics Tsai draws an allegory between the economic vibrancy of Hong Kong cinema within the region since the 1960s and the concurrent decline of Taiwanese film.

Sound and Epistemology

One trademark of sound usage in mainstream commercial cinema is that sounds are regularly defined by and tied to the sources that produce them. Christian Metz comments on the epistemological nature of this relationship by noting that sounds function as adjectives used to modify or describe visualized objects, and it is through their visualized presence that these objects are concretized as nouns. For example, we don't consider a "whistling" sound to be an object unto itself but rather a characteristic of the kettle that produces it. Yet Metz opens up for debate whether sounds in cinema are simply secondary qualities of the visualized objects that produce them and whether we perceive all sounds the same way because, as Metz observes, "the perceptual object is a constructed unity, *socially constructed,* and also (to some extent) a linguistic unity."[25] Therefore it is possible that certain sounds can function as acoustic objects and carry with them more than just the signification of their source.

Indeed, a new generation of filmmakers is experimenting with the indeterminacy of sound and image relations through the evocation of off-screen space. Lisandro Alonso, Martín Rejtman, and Julio Bressane each construct complex sound puzzles in their films that force the viewer into a new epistemological relationship with the characters and their world by playing with audience perception of sounds and sources. The expressive effect of unseen and unrevealed "aural objects" in their films activates a different relationship between spectator and character. As Edward Branigan explains:

> [O]ne possible outcome of juxtaposing sound and image is that the sound may allow the inference that the space represented by the image contains motion and volume which is both nearby and contemporaneous; or, to state it differently, the space of the theater sound may come to stand for the space implied by the image.[26]

This effect can be heard in Lisandro Alonso's *Fantasma,* in which the meanderings of its characters in the unfamiliar environment of Buenos Aires' Teatro San Martín extend the soundtrack's acoustic maze into the space of the audience. The two central characters—the respective stars of Alonso's previous films *La libertad* and *Los muertos*—wander around the urban theater while the audience, hearing primally, discovers the space at the same time that the characters do. In the process of moving from one room to another, the sources of certain sounds are revealed whereas others remain cloaked in their status as pure aural objects (see AV example 41.5 ◐).

In a similar fashion, Julio Bressane's films provide a shallow visual perspective complemented by numerous off-screen sounds that never enter the frame. Aural motifs—such as the noises from an unseen train station, the rattle and rhythmic footsteps of an off-screen horse carriage, and the regular chiming of clock towers—are dispersed across his film *Nietzsche em Turin,* in which the sounds flesh out a world that Bressane's images do not reveal. This technique can be traced back to his roots in the *udigrudi* or underground movement of Brazilian cinema in the late 1960s. In contrast to the rigidly imposed realism of the early Cinema Novo movement, underground filmmakers like Bressane, Rogerio Sganzerla, and Joachim Pedro de Andrade experimented with expressive sound usage and a strong counterpoint between sound and image. Since this early period, Bressane has refined his visual cinematic technique, yet he still prefers to construct the dieqeses of his films through evocative soundscapes. *Filme de amor* and *Cleopatra* each use flat, stage-bound framing techniques and expansive soundtracks that hint at larger, unseen worlds. Through the interplay between the limited views of the scenes on screen and complex off-screen sounds, Bressane's films offer the viewer an imagined evocation of space that is accepted as real via its acoustic plenitude.

In contrast, Iranian filmmaker Abbas Kiarostami regularly builds highly complex soundtracks by balancing two differing codes of realism. On the one hand, his films adhere to the international standard that foregrounds dialogue intelligibility. During his numerous long-shot/long-take driving sequences, conversations inside a vehicle are heard directly despite the camera's varying distances. On the other hand, the sounds of the vehicle moving through the landscape are rigorously tied to a scale that matches the position of the camera. In this way, Kiarostami constructs a sense of objective hearing through what is actually a complexly layered and structured sound track. According to Kiarostami:

> Basically anything seen through a camera limits the view of a spectator to what's visible through the lens, which is always much less than what we can see with our own eyes. No matter how wide we make the screen, it still doesn't compare with what our eyes can see in life. And the only way out of this dilemma is sound.... The viewer always has this curiosity to imagine what's outside the field of vision; it's used all the time in everyday life. But when people come to a theater they've been trained to stop being curious and imaginative and simply take what's given to them. That's what I'm trying to change.[27]

Whereas his earlier films showed a fascination with the textural quality of sounds—one thinks of the timbre of the rolling can of spray paint as it rattles down a street in *Close-Up*—his later films show a willingness to let sounds take on their own autonomy. He achieves this by letting many sounds function as pure aural objects.

Perhaps the prime example of this is Kiarostami's well-tuned ornithological ear. Despite never showing most of the birds heard in his films, a great deal of attention is paid to the signifying power of bird sounds. As the character of Mr. Badii drives his Range Rover through the hills surrounding Tehran in *Taste of Cherry*, the audience hears a broad range of different birdcalls and animal noises. And when he makes a return journey, these sounds are heard in reverse order, each taking on an indicative function to mark the specific locations that Mr. Badii passes. What seem like minor details at first take on weighted significance when he returns to the hills at night to the spot where he plans to commit suicide. Despite the darkness, the cawing of crows and the unmistakable trilling of a pheasant indicate that he is at the chosen location, which previously was signified visually by the lone tree that stands above the shallow grave. In addition to their locative role, the birdcalls also carry an affective function, reminding Mr. Badii, as well as the audience, of the living creatures that surround him every day. By relying on unseen sounds to advance the narrative, Kiarostami trains audiences how to listen to his films.

The Voice and Culture

Taking Argentina as a case study, we find that the function of the spoken voice reveals much more about Argentine culture than just narrative information. Gonzalo Aguilar has written that Argentina, like much of South America, was inundated with empty political rhetoric on television and radio, as well in US films in theaters, during the *guerra sucia* from 1976 to 1983.[28] A resulting distrust of language manifested itself after the restoration of democracy in a variety of cinematic portrayals, from the overtly verbal swindlers and use of slang in *Nine Queens* and *Pizza, Birra, Faso* to the laconic characters and paucity of dialogue in *Los guantes mágicos* and all of Lisandro Alonso's films.

In direct opposition to dialogue intelligibility, many recent Argentine films confront the audience with deliberate unintelligibility. Instead of clearly enunciated lines, dialogue is often whispered, mumbled, overlapped, distorted, misinterpreted, or accidentally overheard. The multilayered speaking voices in Lucrecia Martel's films resist translation since much of the emphasis is not on the semantic value of the words, but on their phatic qualities and spatial characteristics. Martel explains:

> [T]he narrative structure that I use as a point of departure to tell a story stems from conversations—conversations I heard growing up as a child. There was not a lot of communication, but there was a lot of conversation.... But the total sense of a conversation has little to do with the words exchanged. It has much more to do with the sound, dramatic structure, and rhythm of the exchange.[29]

In Martel's films, this unintelligibility is often the essence of the story being told as she replicates the circuitous speech characteristic of the northern Argentine middle class. According to the director, "the meaning isn't very direct when people talk. People go round and round in circles, stories appear, and in the end you realize what it's all about. To understand or to have a clear idea about events you have to be patient as with the sound."[30] This strong emphasis on orality in all of her films utilizes the characteristics of the spoken voice to distinguish between class, race, location (especially the *porteños* of Buenos Aires versus the criollos and mestizos of inland and northern Argentina), and nationality. Luciano Monteagudo summarizes this effect, noting: "One might say words in Martel's film are as polished as the magnificent sound design, a composition in itself where silence also has its own dimension. Observations, criticism, and banal comments weave a dense plurality of meaning. Even though nothing is spelled-out, the never-ending friction—family, social, racial—becomes evident through the use of language."[31]

Another example of the relationship between language and culture comes in Yorgos Lanthimos's 2009 film, *Dogtooth*. The premise, which takes the viewer some time to discern, is that the industrialist patriarch of an upper-middle-class Greek family has kept his three children, along with his presumably willing wife, completely isolated from society to indoctrinate them with his own teachings. Unexposed to external media, the children have grown up with their own twisted logic about the world: airplanes are actually only four inches long and can be knocked out of the sky with stones, and the area outside of the family's compound is unimaginably dangerous and policed by fearsome carnivorous predators known as "cats." The father exerts tyrannical rule over his children, using the preferred method of control: language. Philip Brophy points out that "key to this film's chilling aura is its reliance on the oral, the vocal, and the acoustic.... The father dictates outlandish missives, truisms, and explications into a cheap recorder like a series of Homeric verses, which the children spend each day learning and memorizing."[32] Through this memorization and recitation process, the children become verbal automatons, and their main form of entertainment is repeating the dialogue that they have learned from home videos after innumerable viewing. "The parents also lie about language," notes Jonathan Romney. "*Dogtooth* begins with the children learning new words on a cassette recorded by their mother: '"Sea" is a leather armchair… "Motorway" is a very strong wind….' Later, the parents use distortions of language to protect their children from adult realities: when one child queries the word 'pussy,' glimpsed on one of the parents' porn tapes, the Mother explains that it means a 'big light.'"[33]

Cracks in the linguistic system appear when Christina—a security guard at the father's plant and the only character named in the film—is blindfolded and brought in to service the oldest sibling sexually. Although she interacts with his younger sisters only briefly, Christina surreptitiously lends them two of her own videotapes: *Jaws* and *Rocky*. The eldest daughter watches the films and, as she has done before, dutifully learns the dialogue by heart. It is only when she spouts lines from *Rocky* verbatim and insists that her siblings call her "Bruce" that her parents discover what has happened. In perhaps one of the film's strangest scenes, the parents discuss the children's behavior in the kitchen; to avoid being overheard, they mouth the dialogue to each other, producing only guttural sounds. Although this is unsettling for a foreign audience, the lack of verbal information is mitigated by the inclusion of subtitles. Yet it forces a Greek audience into a very different relationship with the film because they must work to read the characters' lips to discern their intentions (see AV example 41.6 and Figure 41.3 ◐). Not only

FIGURE 41.3 To avoid being heard by their children, the parents hold a discussion in their kitchen by mouthing the words to each other (*Dogtooth*, Yorgos Lanthimos, 2009).

does the film draw attention to the ontology of the spoken voice, it also foregrounds the cultural construction of language and its malleability as the children take their parents' proclamations literally. Having been told that they are able to leave the compound only after their cuspid, or "dogtooth," falls out, the eldest daughter forcibly extracts her own tooth and hides in the trunk of the father's car to escape into the world outside. "When the father teases the children with the rule that they may venture beyond the wall once their 'canine' teeth have grown and fallen out, he sets the scene for demonstrating how the children take their Zeus 'at his word,' symbolically returning myth to its oral poetic tradition in the most uncompromising of ways."[34]

Sound and Ethics

The rules of sound and image construction in cinema carry with them ideological and ethical implications. Just the simple idea of closure in most films reinforces the motivated protagonist's pursuit of clearly defined goals and their achievement by the end of the film. The result is what Thomas Elsaesser refers to as an ideology of progress, projecting an "a priori optimism" rooted in individual triumph that has been a mainstay of classical Hollywood cinema and American culture.[35] In relation to sound practices, emphasis on dialogue intelligibility ensures that audiences hear every line that is narratively significant, and musical scores encourage audiences to empathize with characters at the proper moments. Yet lurking behind these representational forms are ethical questions regarding how filmmakers treat their audiences. In the case of most blockbusters and spectacle-laden films, the reality is that all of the films' effects are chosen to unify and intensify audience reactions. In this way, the autocratic formal address of most mainstream narrative films contrasts sharply with the populist ideologies they promulgate.

As a challenge to the ideological conflicts of mainstream cinema, many global filmmakers actively deconstruct cinematic form. In addition to her eschewal of score music, Lucrecia Martel uses source music anempathetically. The distorted *cumbias* playing out of car radios in *La ciénaga* and the theremin music in *The Holy Girl* are not used to direct audience emotional responses; rather, they construct a sense of locational and spatial verisimilitude in the films. An excellent example of how Martel uses music anempathetically is when Middle of the Road's 1971 pop hit "Soley Soley" plays on a car radio in *The Headless Woman*. While listening to the music, the film's central character Vero is distracted by a cellular phone call and hits an unseen object on a country road. Despite the horrific lurch and bump of the car, the music continues to play after she stops and contemplates what to do. Not only is this the opposite reaction to what we would expect—in most commercial films, the cheery pop music would stop abruptly and be replaced by portentous score music—but the effect is made even more chilling when she puts her sunglasses back on and drives away. In addition, the very presence of the music opens up a strong ethical question in relation to Vero's actions and our response to it: just as the music denies an emotional response to the event, so, too, do Vero's actions. Amy Taubin made an astute observation that Vero's callous act can be read allegorically as a comment about her generation and their complicity with the *guerra sucia*. She observes that, "[t]he use of anachronistic detail such as the song 'Soleil Soleil' suggests a parallel between the privileged classes in the Seventies that partied while the dictatorship tortured and murdered thousands, and the contemporary middle and upper classes that ignore the deadly effects of poverty on a huge segment of the population."[36]

Another moral question examined in films from around the globe is the ethics of hearing. Although this question has been addressed in American cinema, most eloquently in Francis Ford Coppola's *The Conversation*, in most Hollywood films there is a clear bias toward vision; the visual elements tend to carry the weight of veracity whereas the presence of a sound is confirmed only by the visualization of its source. If sounds or voices are heard off-screen and not revealed—what Michel Chion refers to as "acousmatic sounds"—they generally don't carry much narrative significance in American cinema.[37] Yet, in many transnational films, the acousmatic retains a power, as well as a mandate, to examine what it means to overhear something without seeing its source. Because sound has an ability to penetrate boundaries that vision cannot, what are the ethical implications of hearing?

In *La ciénaga*, Martel leaves several of the sound sources off-screen and never reveals them visually. This grants them an evocative power and ties them to the perceptual activity of the listeners. Although we hear the sound of a large dog barking just beyond the wall of Tali's courtyard, she never acknowledges its presence. Only her son Luchi reacts to the sound, and, ultimately, his curiosity leads to his accidental death. The floors and walls in Tsai Ming-Liang's films are especially permeable, and the characters regularly are exposed to the bodily sounds of their neighbors. In *Code Unknown*, Michael Haneke constructs a pivotal scene around overhearing a fight in a neighbor's apartment. The character of Anne pauses while ironing to listen to the row between a father and his young daughter, but instead of intervening she turns up the volume of her television to drown out the altercation. As the narrative continues, Haneke makes it clear that Anne's inaction contributes to the death of the girl and triggers a series of events that ultimately destroy her relationship (see AV example 41.7 ◑).

Revealing the Everyday Sublime

A unique acoustic trope in contemporary cinema is the valorization of the expressive power of the soundscape to grasp the spectator on a purely pleasurable level. Jean-François Augoyard and Henry Torgue, two sound theorists from the Centre for Research on Sonic Space and the Urban Environment (CRESSON) in Paris, rediscovered a useful term for describing the sheer pleasure that comes from hearing an unexpectedly rich sonic field. They call this the *sharawadji effect*, a word introduced to Europeans from China by way of seventeenth-century travelers to describe "beauty that occurs with no discernible order or arrangement."[38] Augoyard and Torgue apply it to the realm of acoustics to refer to the feeling of plenitude generated by a sound motif or complex soundscape of inexplicable beauty. Such moments in American cinema are extremely rare and generally limited to sound-sensitive directors like David Lynch and Terrence Malick. Both experiment with the affective power of sound, and their films feature moments when the plenitude and beauty (or ugliness) of the soundscape overwhelms the narrative drive. Perhaps the best example comes from the nearly wordless second reel of Malick's *The Tree of Life*, in which the audience is treated to the sounds and visions of his version of the origin of the universe. Despite the dearth of examples from American cinema, it is possible to discover regular *sharawadji* moments in transnational cinema, most notably in the films of Apichatpong Weerasethakul.

Having received his cinematic training at the School of the Art Institute of Chicago, Weerasethakul developed a strong background in experimental film and video art. These elements can be seen in the experimental form of his films, as well as heard in their highly expressive soundtracks. Each of his films features a surface sense of realism derived from location filming, nonprofessional actors, and the use of production dialogue tracks recorded with wireless microphones. Yet behind this surface realism is a carefully constructed ambience "of all-enveloping sound forms, such as the crickets and cicada noises (in *Uncle Boonmee* [*Who Can Recall His Past Lives*]) or electronic hums (in *Syndromes and a Century*)" that surround his audience and draw them into the world of the film.[39] As Lucrecia Martel reminds us, "Lynch and Apichatpong oblige you to lose your mind."[40]

For example, *Tropical Malady* is a bifurcated story in which the semidocumentary depiction of a small-town romance between two young men in the first half is contrasted by the immersive environment of Thailand's northeastern jungle in the second half. The diegesis is rendered through location cinematography, as well as through a finely crafted soundscape constructed from atmospheric field recordings. As Dennis Lin observes, "[t]he jungle is infinitely vast and dark, home to restless spirits and elaborately gnarled trees that emit ominous burbling noises; the rustling, chirping, buzzing cacophony suggests a demented white-noise machine."[41] In the film's penultimate sequence, the soundscape transforms itself by redeploying a motif of radio static that had punctuated a soldier's voyage through the jungle as the sound of the spirit world. The effect is a moment of the sublime, lifting the character as well as the viewers out of the physical world and granting them access to the spiritual (see AV example 41.8 ◐).

Weerasethakul's films all display an interest in differentiating the sounds of spaces and establishing a connection between the human voice and the spirit. To achieve this, he sets up relays between on-screen characters and off-screen sounds that diverge from the codes of cinematic realism. Philip Brophy notes that this trend breaks down the ontological distinction between on- and off-screen space, and that:

> [I]t is remarkable how much sound in non-Western cinema is not empirically matched to a visible source. The ease with which non-Western cinema generally incorporates this supposed breach links up with Weerasethakul's core concerns: the incorporation of spiritual post-embodiment in everyday life. The anxiety with

which traditional sound design in English-speaking cinema mandates on-screen audio-visuality and is averse to off-screen aurality uncannily recalls the same disconnect experienced by those naïve listeners of bygone times who assumed the recorded voice was a spirit from beyond. That voice was simply off-screen.[42]

In his soundtracks, Weerasethakul sets up a fantasmatic relationship between sound and image that mirrors the characters' transitions between the human and spiritual worlds. In doing so, the spectator is regularly struck by the uncanny beauty of the films' soundscapes and the *sharawadji* effect.

In summary, the creative sound work being done by these contemporary transnational filmmakers points to acoustic expressions of cultural identities that need further investigation. For, even as mainstream commercial cinema seems to have achieved a stylistic equilibrium in the postclassical era, we need to consider that rules of cinematic construction are being rewritten across national boundaries in the postclassical art film. The strong economic effects that place much of the world's cinematic output in continuity with the narrative standards of American cinema are being challenged, and filmmakers from around the globe are changing cinema at a rapid rate. New models of sound techniques and their relationship to local storytelling are more than just expressive devices for directors—they are political imperatives and methods for retaining local cultures. As new contingent communities form via the internet and digital distribution, cinema will continue to evolve to accommodate new voices and perspectives. The shift to the transnational study of cinema sound reminds us that the standards by which we listen to film also dictate how we study them; therefore, it is imperative to learn to listen to films differently and to be attentive to how sound usage is changing cinema.

Notes

1. My thanks to Cecilia Cornejo Sotelo, Peter Franco, Dennis Hanlon, Aaron Han Joon Magnan-Park, and the editors for their help in revising this essay.
2. Andrew Higson, "The Limiting Imagination of National Cinema," in *Cinema & Nation*, eds. Mette Hjort and Scott MacKenzie (New York: Routledge, 2000): 63–74.
3. Lúcia Nagib, "Toward a Positive Definition of World Cinema," in *Remapping World Cinema: Identity, Culture and Politics in Film*, eds. Stephanie Dennison and Song Hwee Lim (London: Wallflower, 2006): 30–37.
4. See David Bordwell, "The Art Cinema as a Mode of Film Practice." *Film Criticism* 4, no.1 (1979): 56–64.
5. Dudley Andrew, "An Atlas of World Cinema," in *Remapping World Cinema*, 22.
6. Lars Von Trier and Thomas Vinterberg, "The Vow of Chastity: Dogme Manifesto," presented at "Le cinéma vers son deuxième siècle" conference in Paris, March 22, 1995.
7. See Claudine Nougaret and Sophie Chiabaut, *Le son direct au cinéma* (Paris: Institut de Formation et d'Enseignement pour les Métiers de l'Image et du Son, 1997).
8. Jason Wood, *Talking Movies: Contemporary World Filmmakers in Interview* (London: Wallflower Press, 2006), 171.

9. Michel Chion, "Without Music: On *Caché*," in *A Companion to Michael Haneke*, ed. Roy Grundmann (Chichester: Wiley-Blackwell, 2010), 161.

10. Fiona Cook, "Andrea Arnold's *Wuthering Heights*," *Dazed Digital*, June 6, 2012, http://www.dazeddigital.com/artsandculture/article/11997/1/andrea-arnolds-wuthering-heights.

11. Gustavo Costantini, "La banda sonora en el nuevo cine argentino," *Cuadernos Hispanoamericanos* no. 679 (2007): 7–17.

12. Ray Pride, "Sound and Vision: Lynne Ramsay on *Morvern Callar*," *Cinema Scope* no. 13 (2002): 8.

13. Linda Ruth Williams, "Escape Artist," *Sight & Sound* 12, no. 10 (2002): 24.

14. Claudia Gorbman, "Auteur Music," in *Beyond the Soundtrack: Representing Music in Cinema*, eds. Daniel Goldmark, Lawrence Kramer, and Richard Leppert (Berkeley: University of California Press, 2007), 149.

15. See Rick Altman, "Sound Space," in *Sound Theory/Sound Practice*, ed. Rick Altman (New York: Routledge, 1992), 46–64.

16. Jason Wood, *Talking Movies*, 195.

17. Michel Chion, *Audio-Vision: Sound on Screen*, ed. and trans. Claudia Gorbman (New York: Columbia University Press, 1994), 63–65.

18. Ibid., 109. Emphasis in original.

19. Walter Murch, "Foreword" to Michel Chion, *Audio-Vision*, xxii.

20. See *Dolby Surround Mixing Manual*, San Francisco: Dolby Laboratories, Inc. (1998): Ch. 5.

21. Gonzalo Aguilar, *Other Worlds: New Argentine Film* (New York: Palgrave MacMillan, 2008), 90.

22. Natalija Vekic, "Soundscape Artist: Lucrecia Martel Wants You to Listen," *Release Print* (2005): 29.

23. Amy Taubin, "Vocational Education: An Interview with Lucrecia Martel," *Artforum* 43, no. 8 (2005): 175.

24. Chris Wood, "Realism, Intertextuality & Humour in Tsai Ming-liang's *Goodbye, Dragon Inn*," *Journal of Chinese Cinemas* 1, no. 2 (2007): 108.

25. Christian Metz, "Aural Objects," trans. Georgia Gurrieri, *Yale French Studies* no. 60 (1980): 31. Emphasis in original.

26. Edward Branigan, "Sound and Epistemology in Film," *The Journal of Aesthetics and Art Criticism* 47, no. 4 (1989): 312.

27. Mehrnaz Saeed-Vafa and Jonathan Rosenbaum, *Abbas Kiarostami* (Urbana: University of Illinois Press, 2003), 114.

28. See Gonzalo Aguilar, *Other Worlds*.

29. Natalija Vekic, "Soundscape Artist," 28.

30. Luciano Monteagudo, "Lucrecia Martel: Whispers at *Siesta* Time," in *New Argentine Cinema: Themes, Auteurs and Trends of Innovation*, eds. Horacio Bernades, Diego Lerer, and Sergio Wolf (Buenos Aires: Ediciones Tatanka, 2002), 74.

31. Ibid., 71.

32. Philip Brophy, "The Prisonhouse of Language: Yorgos Lanthimos's *Dogtooth* Makes Greek Mythology Modern," *Film Comment* 47, no. 2 (2011): 16.

33. Jonathan Romney, "Bad Education," *Sight & Sound* 20, no. 5 (2010): 42.

34. Philip Brophy, "The Prisonhouse of Language," 16.

35. Thomas Elsaesser, "The Pathos of Failure: American Films in the 1970s: Notes on the Unmotivated Hero," *Monogram* no. 6 (1975): 14.

36. Amy Taubin, "Identification of a Woman," *Film Comment* 45, no. 4 (2009): 23.
37. Michel Chion, *Audio-Vision*, 71–73.
38. Jean-François Augoyard and Henry Torgue, *Sonic Experience: A Guide to Everyday Sounds* (Montreal: McGill-Queen's University Press, 2009), 117.
39. Michael Sicinski, "Dreaming in Cinema: Capturing the Imagination of Apichatpong Weerasethakul," *Cineaste* 36, no. 2 (2011): 27.
40. Chris Wisniewski, "When Worlds Collide: An Interview with Lucrecia Martel, Director of *The Headless Woman*," *Reverse Shot* no. 23 (2008), accessed June 26, 2011, http://www.reverseshot.com/article/interview_lucrecia_martel.
41. Dennis Lim, "To Halve and to Hold," *The Village Voice* (June 21, 2005), accessed June 26, 2011, http://www.villagevoice.com/2005-06-21/film/to-halve-and-to-hold/.
42. Philip Brophy, "Gone Native: Speaking in Tongues with Apichatpong Weerasethakul," *Film Comment* 45, no. 5 (2009): 20.

Select Bibliography

Altman, Rick, ed. *Sound Theory/Sound Practice*. New York: Routledge, 1992.
Augoyard, Jean-François, and Henry Torgue. *Sonic Experience: A Guide to Everyday Sounds*. Montreal: McGill-Queen's University Press, 2009.
Beck, Jay, and Tony Grajeda, eds. *Lowering the Boom: Critical Studies in Film Sound*. Urbana: University of Illinois Press, 2008.
Branigan, Edward. "Sound and Epistemology in Film." *The Journal of Aesthetics and Art Criticism* 47, no. 4 (1989): 311–324.
Chion, Michel. *Audio-Vision: Sound on Screen*, ed. and trans. Claudia Gorbman. New York: Columbia University Press, 1994.
Gorbman, Claudia. "Auteur Music." In *Beyond the Soundtrack: Representing Music in Cinema*, eds. Daniel Goldmark, Lawrence Kramer, and Richard Leppert, 149–162. Berkeley: University of California Press, 2007.
Metz, Christian. "Aural Objects," trans. Georgia Gurrieri. *Yale French Studies* no. 60 (1980): 24–32.
Pride, Ray. "Sound and Vision: Lynne Ramsay on *Morvern Callar*." *Cinema Scope* no. 13 (2002): 5–8.
Vekic, Natalija. "Soundscape Artist: Lucrecia Martel Wants You To Listen." *Release Print* (2005): 28–29, 46.
Weis, Elisabeth, and John Belton, eds. *Film Sound: Theory and Practice*. New York: Columbia University Press, 1985.

CHAPTER 42

INSTRUMENTAL VISIONS

Electronica, Music Video, and the Environmental Interface

ALLAN CAMERON

MUSIC is almost always a matter of technology. In the case of electronic music, how-ever, technology occupies a special position. For one, technology is often central to the semiotic connotations and affective charge of such music, from the robotic aesthetics of Kraftwerk to the metronomic beats and synthetic tones of Detroit techno and its descen-dants. Furthermore, rapid changes in hardware and software over the past four decades (from analog synthesizers to digital samplers to computer-based generative programs) have conspicuously shaped the contours of electronic music's generic field. Just as the characteristic "squelch" of the Roland TB-303 synthesizer helped to define the sound of acid house in the 1980s, contemporary genres such as dubstep have relied increas-ingly on software-based sequencers and effects. Electronic music is thus informed by technological shifts, as well as inflected by technological themes. In addressing this diverse field of cultural production, I use the term "electronica" to encompass an array of subgenres. Writing in 2000, Kim Cascone describes electronica as "an umbrella term for alternative, largely dance-based electronic music (including *house, techno, electro, drum'n'bass, ambient*)," and notes that the genre has experienced a marked increase in influence and popularity from the mid-1990s onward.[1] Although Cascone's description elides the aesthetic and contextual features of different subgenres, it nonetheless serves as a useful way of highlighting a significant network of thematic connections.[2] Linking together these electronic subgenres, I propose to connect them in turn to the format of the music video, exploring how such videos elucidate and extend electronica's ongoing engagement with technological themes.

Electronic music, however, cannot be defined simply by its dependence on electronic technologies. As music journalist Simon Reynolds points out, there is generally more "space-age technology" put to work in the production of MOR pop than in the genera-tion of cutting-edge techno music.[3] Rather, in defining electronica, we need to look for a certain disposition toward the technological. Because electronica tends to eschew or de-emphasize vocal performance, attention is directed more emphatically toward the material features of the soundscape. Qualities such as timbre, resonance, and rhythm are frequently given precedence over melody and lyrics (the voice, when it does appear, is often heavily processed or treated like another instrument in the mix). As a result, the technological basis of the music comes to the forefront, manifested not only in the juxtaposition of analog and digital sound sources but also in the digital sequencing that typically provides the music's structural "scaffolding."

Importantly, electronica's technological orientation is not merely a product of technology itself, but can be understood within the broader context of what Charlie Gere calls "digital culture." According to Gere, digital culture is derived not simply from binary digital computing, but from an array of elements that presaged its arrival, including "Cold War defence technology; avant-garde art practice; counter-cultural techno-utopianism; postmodernist critical theory; [and] new wave subcultural style."[4] Spanning an array of social contexts, digital culture is characterized by "ways of thinking and doing" that include "abstraction, codification, self-regulation, virtualization and programming."[5] Electronica, I suggest, not only draws on all of these "ways of thinking and doing," but also makes them a prominent aesthetic feature by foregrounding the selection and/or juxtaposition of synthetic or organic tones, smooth or granular textures, and regular or random patterns. This emphasis on the technical underpinnings of the music, together with the high-tech discourse that often accompanies it, suggests two ways of regarding electronica as instrumental: first, electronica tends to privilege instrumentation over the human voice; and second, it carries associations with instrumental technologies in other spheres, including science, industry, and combat.

Significantly, Gere's description of digital culture's development explicitly places cultural factors alongside instrumental factors: his list of "ways of thinking and doing" consists of processes that span science, industry, philosophy, avant-garde aesthetics, and popular culture. Therefore, to consider electronica as a component of digital culture is to acknowledge its affinity to those industrial and bureaucratic techniques of automation and regulation that also incorporate "abstraction, codification, self-regulation, virtualization and programming."[6] For some critics, this is cause for concern. Julian Stallabrass, for example, criticizes contemporary "computer culture" for what he sees as a continuation of modernist tropes, evident in "its technophilism, its fetishization of functionality, and its steadfast ideology of progress."[7] Digital culture, by this account, is thoroughly shot through with an instrumentalist mindset: it submits the world to human agency via the medium of technology. I would argue, however, that digital culture's engagement with instrumentality is more multifaceted than Stallabrass's account allows. Central to my argument here is the notion that much electronic music is engaged, explicitly or implicitly, with the question of how to regard this alignment of the aesthetic and the instrumental. Juan Atkins, one of the pioneers of Detroit techno, invokes this issue directly, linking music technologies with popular notions of instrumental power: "with technology, there's a lot of good things, but by the same token, it enables the powers that be to have more control."[8] In what follows, I hope to show how videos for electronic music provide a window on the genre's exploration of this question. Before discussing these multimedia texts, however, I want to explore further the relationship between music and instrumentality.

DIGITAL MUSIC AND INSTRUMENTALITY

What might it mean to say that digital music is instrumental? Aden Evens offers an extraordinarily detailed account of the processes behind digitally mediated sound, before concluding that digital composition separates musicians from a direct engagement with music itself. The notion of instrumentality is central to his critique. For Evens, all musical instruments are, by their nature, instrumental. Yet acoustic instruments overcome the negative connotations of instrumentality by exceeding their instrumental function: "Like any instrument, a *musical instrument* is a means.... But a musical instrument is no mere means: it does not disappear in its use."[9] This quality of material resistance and unpredictability is what is lacking in computer-based composition tools, according to Evens: "the digital implements an immaculate ordering that isolates desired properties and gives verifiable, repeatable, and measurable definitions."[10] Evens's concern is therefore that digital instruments, in their very controllability and knowability, are "*merely* instrumental, nothing but means to ends."[11] Evens's critique, like Stallabrass's, strongly recalls Martin Heidegger's argument that modern technology has been defined by an instrumental orientation, leading mankind to an estrangement from the world.[12]

Yet digital culture in general and electronic music in particular are more sophisticated and fluid than Evens's and Stallabrass's accounts might suggest. First, these accounts overlook the fact that digital audio production technologies are commonly actualized in ways that have not been determined in advance by engineers, programmers, or even producers (since it is usually possible to generate unforeseen results, whether by intention or by accident). Second, digitally created music and other media are delivered via a host of channels and mediated by countless social contexts, so that such work is almost never, from the perspective of reception, *merely* instrumental.

At the same time, however, instrumentality does form an important discursive thread within digital culture and electronic music. Indeed, electronica is often productively engaged with the theme of instrumentality, via an approach that runs the gamut from benign endorsement to critical resistance, but is commonly defined by a more ambivalent and exploratory attitude. This type of engagement follows on from experimental music's repurposing of functional technologies for aesthetic ends, an approach that extends from the *musique concrète* of Pierre Schaeffer and Pierre Henry to the "industrial" noise of Throbbing Gristle and Einstürzende Neubaten. In electronica, sampling and digital synthesis are often used to evoke incidental or functional sounds including sirens, beeps, clicks, and chimes, calling up soundscapes associated with work and practical instrumentality. Moreover, the names of prominent electronic acts (Cybotron,

Mantronix, Autechre) and music festivals (Sonar, Mutek) suggest engagements with cutting edge technology, much of it associated with the spheres of science, industry, or combat.[13] The creative repurposing of such technologies is thus a recurrent trope in electronic music generally.

The development of more powerful software-based production tools over recent years has introduced a further level of abstraction to electronica, giving producers the ability to single out and independently modify discrete parameters of sound and to generate "new" sounds through granular synthesis and sample processing. Digital software is now capable of complex audio processing tasks that would have been beyond the reach of bulky hardware units only a few years earlier. Meanwhile, the instrumental "noises" associated with electronica are as likely to resemble the clicks, whirrs, and beeps of digitally mediated work and leisure as they are to evoke the industrial context of the modern factory. This movement toward software-based tools and aesthetics imbues electronic music with a sense of light instrumentality that is consonant with Zygmunt Bauman's description of our contemporary sociohistorical situation as one of "liquid modernity." Under liquid modernity, the instrumental tools of "heavy" modernity (factories and bulky industrial equipment) are superseded by techniques and technologies involving speed, mobility, and instantaneous communication.[14] These techniques and technologies have reshaped both industrial and cultural production.

This sense of light instrumentality is also found in discursive currents that circulate in and around electronica. For example, members of the listening community engage in extensive online discussions regarding the software being used by producers and often speculate on the extent to which producers are actively "playing" the music as opposed to triggering preprogrammed sequences.[15] This has led to the recurrent complaint that performers who make use of laptop computers on-stage often look as if they are "checking e-mail." Here, the production of music becomes indistinguishable from digitally mediated office routine. Similarly, the Daft Punk track "Technologic" (2005) sends up the parallels between aesthetic production and mundane office work by featuring a high-pitched robotic vocalist who recites a list of computer-based tasks: "Write it, cut it, paste it, save it/ Load it, check it, quick-rewrite it/ Plug it, play it, burn it, rip it/ Drag and drop it, zip-unzip it." In this case, the digital instrumentalism with which Aden Evens is so concerned is not simply a technological byproduct but also a key thematic component of the music.[16]

Yet, whereas Daft Punk's music tends to emphasize patterns of regularity and repetition, some producers use new software tools to disrupt such patterns and, by extension, instrumentalism itself. As Steve Goodman points out, programs such as Supercollider, MaxMSP, and PureData "deploy mathematical algorithms to simulate the conditions and dynamics of growth, complexity, emergence, and mutation of evolutionary algorithms and transcode them to musical parameters."[17] This approach, based around the notion of "artificial life," aims to introduce elements of "creative contingency" into the composition process.[18] Similarly, the emergence in the late 1990s of "glitch" music, which draws on static, clicks, pops, and the sounds of digital errors, signaled a desire to overcome the predictability of much conventional electronica.[19]

Electronica has not, however, been purged of its instrumental connotations by these new developments. Algorithmic composition has arguably allowed for increased control over a host of additional sonic parameters. At the same time, a great deal of glitch electronica has retained the regularity and structural logic of existing genres (house music in particular). More importantly, electronica's most extreme experiments with randomness in composition have more often than not foregrounded instrumentality. The German group Oval gained notoriety during the 1990s for sampling damaged compact discs and using the resulting sounds as the basis for their stuttering, skittering compositions. Yet it is repetition itself that allows these compositions to read as music, while their constitutive clicks, drones, and bursts of noise serve to highlight rather than conceal their basis in digital data.

In the case of electronica, the "problem" of instrumentality has a further dimension, since it is often very difficult to identify what counts as an instrument. Although it is commonly claimed that the Beatles' stereo experiments in the late 1960s refigured the recording studio itself as a kind of instrument, electronica's increasing reliance on digital production tools takes this tendency a step further. As Ken Jordan and Paul D. Miller argue, software can work "to dematerialise the musical instrument. It does this by distributing the qualities of an instrument across the various peripherals that control the sounds that the software generates."[20] Programs like Max/MSP even allow for the creation of "virtual instruments" by allowing users "to make an aggregate of whatever sounds you run through its parameters."[21] Furthermore, these tools (and studio production generally) frequently blur the boundaries between instruments and the spaces in which they resonate. Even the application of relatively simple effects such as delay and reverb can create a sense of cavernous "space" that bears no direct relation to any "real-world" location. Electronic "instruments" are thus distributed across the field of audition in complex and unpredictable ways. Because it is often impossible to identify the "original" source of a given sound within the mix, listeners are reminded once again of the music's technological provenance.

GRAPHING DIGITAL SPACE-TIME

The visualization of electronica through music videos illuminates the technological imaginary of digital culture, as well as related questions regarding agency and control. As a popular genre, however, electronica is conspicuous for the relative scarcity of music videos, despite the fact that live performances are often accompanied by projected visuals. Indeed, visual media have a paradoxical role in relation to electronic music, appearing to be at once superfluous and crucial to it. The scarcity of videos may be due to the fact that electronic acts, unlike pop and rock performers, tend not to feature a prominent (and hence visible) public persona. Moreover, the creation of self-sufficient sonic "spaces" in electronica seems to suggest that visual accompaniment is unnecessary.[22] For example, under the influence of 1970s dub reggae producers like King Tubby and Lee

"Scratch" Perry, electronica often deploys reverb and delay effects to create a sense of spatial depth. Similarly, the use of the "filter sweep" in trance, techno, and other electronic genres can evoke the sensation of moving from one space into another by temporarily occluding, and then reintroducing, high frequencies in the music. As Andrew Goodwin argues, real or virtual sonic environments inscribe "a synaesthetic process" into musical recordings "by aurally representing the physical space within which sounds appear to be recorded."[23] It therefore seems no accident that the sonic representation of such spaces is known as the "*stereo image.*"[24] Electronica's foregrounding of technique and texture intensifies this "synesthetic" process.

Despite the fact that electronica often appears not to "need" visual accompaniment, mediated visuality is central to the production process. Particularly given the accelerating uptake of software-based tools for composition and live performance, electronica increasingly *depends* on the visual, in the form of graphical user interfaces and analytic representations of audio waveforms. This ability to visualize and spatialize the music may contribute further to the sense of instrumental control that attends the genre. Sean Booth of electronica duo Autechre expresses a sense of ambivalence regarding the visual aspect of digital audio production: "There's nothing better than turning the screen off and just going analogue...The worst things are the timeline sequencers where you can see on the screen what's coming up."[25] As I go on to argue, music videos for electronic music often capture this sense of ambivalence through an aesthetic of instrumentality. The spatialized control associated with audio interfaces is frequently evoked in these videos, which emphasize analytic perspectives, machinic movements, and striated spaces. By choosing to draw out or conceal digital textures and patterns in the music, such videos articulate affective and conceptual perspectives on the instrumental.

One approach to visualizing electronic music is extreme abstraction, through the creation of what I will call "synesthetic datascapes." Nicholas Cook, drawing on a narrower definition than Andrew Goodwin, uses the concept of synesthesia to analyze the confluence of sound and moving images. Observing that it is a clinical term frequently applied as a metaphorical model for describing multimedia experiences, Cook defines synesthesia as the "tendency for an input in one sensory mode to excite an involuntary response in another."[26] He points out, however, that it is, generally speaking, a poor model for understanding multimedia, since "multimedia is predicated on difference."[27] Relations of extreme similarity between sound and image (a phenomenon that Cook dubs "conformance") are in fact very rare.[28] For Cook, instances of multimedia are more likely to demonstrate contest (relations of contradiction) or complementation (relations of "undifferentiated difference") than conformance (relations of similarity).[29] Nonetheless, the usage of the synesthetic metaphor is justified by certain electronica videos, in which sound and image are tied together by an aesthetic of abstract conformance. Multimedia artist Ryoichi Kurokawa's video for Aoki Takamasa's track "Mirabeau" (2006) is an excellent example of such conformance. The clean tones and glitchy rhythms of Aoki's piece are mirrored precisely by Kurokawa's abstract black and red shapes, which pulse and contort in time to the music. Constituting these shapes are an array of fine lines resembling musical waveforms. The video thus resembles a more sophisticated version of automated audio visualization programs (such as the iTunes "Visualizer") that use waveforms as the basis for abstract shapes.

The abstract character of these "synesthetic" effects can invite reflection on their material basis. For the abstract painter Wassily Kandinsky, synesthesia possessed a spiritual dimension, notes Nicholas Cook. Kandinsky saw his own works as synesthetic and was also impressed by the composer Alexander Skriabin's attempt to synchronize his music with colored light displays. As Cook puts it, Kandinsky was drawn to the idea that "sound and colour do not relate directly to one another, but relate indirectly through a common relationship with the spiritual."[30] In the case of "Mirabeau," there is a similar sense that tone and color, line and timbre, meet in some abstract space beyond the senses. Here, however, sound and image converge not as spiritual truth but as data. This video thus explores, in oblique fashion, the mutual digital provenance of the music and the visuals. It evokes instrumentality not simply by gesturing toward this world of data, however, but also by deploying abstract visuals that resemble the spidery contours of statistical graphs. The video thus constitutes a graphing of musical and visual space that references the quantification and probabilistic logic of information science.

Similarly, musician and multimedia artist Ryoji Ikeda has created a number of installations in which abstract or quasi-abstract datascapes are accompanied by his detached, schematic soundscapes. Works like *Formula* (2000–05) and *Datamatics* (2006–) feature grids of numbers, geometrical shapes containing rapid montages of images, digital lines that "scan" down or across the screen, and representations of three-dimensional (3D) digital "space" in which axial lines are tagged with numerical coordinates. Ikeda's explicit project is to make perceptible "the invisible multi-substance of data that permeates our world."[31] In doing so, he uncovers a space where the sphere of information management and geospatial datamapping is coextensive with the aesthetics of digital culture.

The video for Autechre's "Gantz Graf" (Alex Rutterford, 2002) moves further away from abstraction, but maintains a strong degree of conformance. In time with the track's clattering, unpredictable rhythms, a 3D shape shifts and changes, abruptly shedding and accreting digital lines and layers. As the music is striated by digital noise and the sounds pulled apart, the shape itself, which resembles an engine or a piece of industrial machinery existing in virtual space, undergoes an analogous process of warping and stretching (Figure 42.1). The machinic qualities of this shape again point to the confluence of data and audiovisual affect, emphasizing what is digital about the music and tying it to connotations of utilitarian form. However, this machine's aggressive performance of digitality seems to communicate a type of self-determination, its mutability and dynamic unpredictability suggesting that it is ultimately beyond human control. Like "Mirabeau," *Formula*, and *Datamatics*, "Gantz Graf" presents a synesthetic datascape in which abstract digital shapes oscillate between two-dimensional (2D) and 3D form, an effect that is underlined by virtual camera movements, including tracking and pivoting. Yet this invocation of extraterritorial power and spatial mastery is short-circuited in each case by the presentation of audiovisual spaces and codes that resist deciphering. In this way, these videos simultaneously invoke and exceed instrumentality.

FIGURE 42.1 "Gantz Graf" (Alex Rutterford, 2002).

ANALYTIC AUDIOVISION

The tracking and pivoting movements that organize these videos can also be found in other, less abstract, works. In such clips, cities, buildings, or bodies are subjected to a type of analytic vision that is represented by lateral and longitudinal camera movements, bands of light and color that pass across subjects, or the visual penetration of material surfaces. The modern city is the object of this analytic vision in the video for Kid 606's ambient track "Sometimes" (Pleix, 2006). As the gentle, beatless music plays, CGI skyscrapers fall apart into digital fragments. Although this scenario instantly recalls the destruction of New York's World Trade Center, there is a quality of calmness, flow, and even order to the clip as the shiny, black, quasi-abstract pieces tumble through space in slow motion. Rather than scattering chaotically, the pieces seem increasingly to be moving in parallel clusters. This impression is confirmed by the final shot, which shows a collection of shards falling into place to complete the final corner of a "new" intact skyscraper (or, alternatively, to represent the initial "explosion" of the skyscraper played in reverse). Here, the video creates an ambiguous perspective, suspended between the desire for wholeness and the desire for freedom (an effect that is heightened by the flowing yet structureless and almost reversible quality of the music). Ultimately, order emerges from chaos, but it is an order that seems inextricably attached to the abstract, overtly digital "structure" of the building.

A similar approach to urban space is evident in the video for dubstep producer Scuba's track "Before" (Sam Geer, 2010). Video footage of a drive through city streets is mirrored symmetrically across four quadrants of the screen, creating a kaleidoscopic effect that is synchronized with the heavily reverbed female vocals. The scanning movement of the camera (tracking along and through urban streets) is thus multiplied fourfold and folded together, turning the space of the city inside out. The Prefuse 73 video "Half of What?" (Ed Holdsworth, 2003) creates a similar effect by layering urban tracking shots, CGI skyscrapers, and shifting patterns of lines and dots over glitchy hip-hop beats and noirish tones. Each of these videos features a dispassionate visual style, evoking the presence of an analytic gaze that is capable of looking at, but also through, the spaces of the city. The cityscapes in these clips thus parallel, or even overlap with, the datascapes foregrounded more emphatically in the "abstract" videos discussed earlier.

Bodies in electronica videos also tend to become the objects of analytic vision. In Oval's "Ah!" (Darko Dragicevic, 2010), the camera takes a clinical view of a female dancer who performs mechanically and without expression, contorting her body into uncomfortable poses. Scanning across her body and those of the male figures who periodically accompany her, this clip strips the human body of its expressive intentionality, making it into an instrument for the track's melodic yet machinic progression. Bodies in Matmos's "Exciter Lamp and the Variable Band" (M. C. Schmidt, 2008) and Darkstar's "Gold" (Evan Boehm, 2010) are also submitted to a machinic scanning operation. In the former video, the jerky bleeps and bloops of the track itself are accompanied by vertical lines of red and green light that move laterally across the bodies of the band members, decomposing them into shifting chromatic strips. In "Gold," the faces of the three band members appear in a series of close-ups, scanned by lines of illumination, overwritten by lines of resolution, and finally broken into digital fragments. Interpolated between these shots are images of brain scans and 3D renderings of the performers' heads, embellished with networks of digital lines that appear to represent synaptic connections (Figure 42.2). "Gold" (Evan Boehm, 2010) In this case, the emotional weight of the delicate vocal performance is offset not only against the synthetic tones and fidgety, dubstep-influenced rhythms of the track itself, but also the clinical visual movement of the scan, which renders the group itself as projections of digital data. Despite their

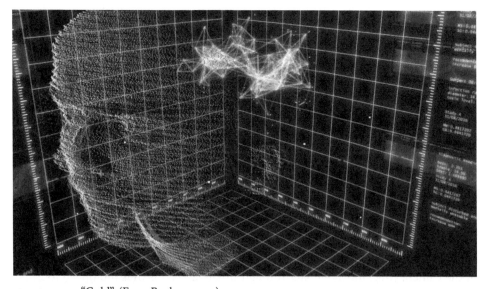

FIGURE 42.2 "Gold" (Evan Boehm, 2010).

analytic aesthetic, however, these videos function neither as celebrations of rationalism nor as dystopian visions of technology run amok. Rather, they chart the uncertain space between these two extremes, cautiously exploring instrumentalism's limitations, boundaries, and gaps.

The technological orientation of many of these works recalls Brooks Landon's observation that music videos have borrowed science fiction's "themes and icons,"[32] as well as its tendency to showcase "up-to-the-moment filmic and video technology that is itself futuristic."[33] Yet, whereas Landon argues that science fiction films almost always express a sense of ambivalence, typically "directed toward science, the military, and public authority in some combination,"[34] music videos are less direct in their questioning of instrumentalism. Although science fiction films often end with the rejection of the spectacular technologies that motivate their narratives (including doomsday weapons, sentient machines, and virtual reality), music videos generally do not seek to discover a space outside technology. The "ambivalence" that Landon sees in science fiction is therefore much less pronounced in music videos, although this has not stopped directors from presenting technology in a more menacing light. For example, in the video for Amon Tobin's track "Esther's" (Charles de Meyer, 2010), the relentless mechanical creep of the music is paralleled by a customized multipurpose machine (visualized through CGI) that is deployed by a young man to infiltrate a woman's apartment. The sinister, constantly transforming machine sneaks inside, hides under a table, and surveils the woman before menacing her, finally, with a large spike that turns out, in the last instance, to be the vehicle for delivering her a beautiful flower. The sinister connotations of the machinic are (partially) overturned by this comedic "victory" of the aesthetic. Unlike most of the science fiction films Landon discusses, this clip therefore moves toward a reconciliation with technology rather than a rejection of it.

The video for "9Samurai," by Kode9 and the Spaceape (Mo Stoebe and Jasmin Jodry, 2006), retains a dystopian flavor but aligns technology with pleasure rather than making it the motivation for escape. Here, the invocation of rationalism is very explicit. In stark black-and-white, the video depicts a scientist studying the effect of bass-driven music on lab rats. Wearing ear protection and goggles, he plays a vinyl record while reading about the spread of an illness known as the "hyperdub virus."[35] At the end of the video, we see human figures dancing in silhouette to the music before their heads are radically deformed. In this 2D monochromatic presentation, it is possible to read the deformations as splattered blood, abstract shapes, or a representation of pleasure (in a literal sense, these individuals have had their "minds blown"). Kode9's bass-heavy and skittery music is the scientist's object of analysis, and the effects it produces are both disturbing (representing a violent extension of the technoscientific into the realm of cultural reception) and benign (producing a heightened aesthetic charge by means of advanced technology). The "ambivalence" here is qualitatively different from that articulated by most of the science fiction films Landon discusses, since there is no sense that technology is something to be overcome by "human" values and morality. Science fiction may offer thematic and stylistic templates for both electronica and music videos, but these templates do not fully determine the ways in which such cultural forms grapple with the question of instrumentality.[36]

THE ENVIRONMENTAL INTERFACE

In her book *Digital Encounters*, Aylish Wood describes how the creation, layering, and compositing of images in cinema and other media offer spectators different types of "encounters" with technological processes. Wood argues that analog and digital production processes are embedded in images in ways that are both "seamless" and "non-seamless,"[37] so that "screens are not only places where images appear, but also interfaces on which technologies are inscribed."[38] Although Wood focuses principally on cinematic examples, music videos spanning all musical genres are notable for their sheer density of technological inscription and for the tendency of this inscription to be "non-seamless." Juxtaposing abstraction and representation, live action and animation, and digital and analog, these videos seem to invite us to actively navigate our way across their contrasting spaces and temporalities. The screen thus becomes not simply a window but also an interface. Although this feature is endemic to contemporary music videos, it is particularly prominent in the case of electronica clips because of their tendency to privilege spaces and textures over vocal and kinetic performance.

Electronica clips are often reflexively engaged with this notion of the screen as interface. In "Game Over" by Ken Ishii (Tanaka Noriyuki, 1999), and "Derezzed" by Daft Punk (Warren Fu, 2010), this is communicated in fairly straightforward fashion through the referencing of video game aesthetics. In these videos, virtual human figures enter and interact with digital environments. These clips are reminiscent, in turn, of video games like *Rez* (Sega, 2001), *Guitar Hero* (RedOctane, 2005), and *Rock Band* (MTV Games/ Electronic Arts, 2007), in which players generate musical compositions by moving "forward" through gridded virtual spaces. Moreover, these interactive screenscapes function as representational (and instrumental) extensions of the abstract datascapes I discussed earlier. In what follows, however, I wish to explore the way that certain videos project this instrumental view outward onto existing landscapes. Such videos, I suggest, explore both the potentialities and the limits of the environmental interface.

Loscil's "Motoc" (Scott Morgan, 2006), and Oval's "Kastell" (Darko Dragicevic/ Austin Stack, 2010) blend images of plants (trees in the former and long blades of grass in the latter) with abstract, vertically oriented patterns. In "Motoc," areas of the frame decompose into shifting strips; in "Kastell" a simple shot of grass waving in the breeze is augmented by thin white lines that appear and disappear almost imperceptibly. Although these shifting vertical lines recall the aesthetic of scanning described earlier, the analytic perspective is here imbricated with a "natural" setting. These simple yet suggestive clips explore a zone of ambiguity in which the analytic view and the organic environment are neither opposed nor conflated. This ambiguity is framed more directly in the video for the dubstep track "Night," by Benga & Coki (Jess Gorick, 2008). In this clip, the hollow, booming synth line is accompanied by a CGI squid, which pulsates in time to the music as its body lights up with vivid colored patterns. The squid also sports a spinning mechanical apparatus under its semitransparent hood, and two dangling audio leads. At the end of the clip, the underlying metaphor of the control interface is made explicit when we briefly see two audio control knobs attached to the outside of the squid's body. The technological provenance of the music is thus foregrounded via the trope of the environmental interface, which overlays nature and technology without collapsing them together or suggesting a one-way relationship of instrumentality.

Although these examples are overtly digital, the environmental interface has also been imagined via analog media. Analog technology is central to the music and visuals in the clip for "Dayvan Cowboy" by Boards of Canada (Melissa Olson, 2006). Like Boards of Canada's other work, which typically deploys analog synths and production processes to create fuzzy, deformed sonic textures, this track foregrounds the "warmth" of the analog. Here, a processed guitar sample is used to create an ambient bed of sound that gradually builds until a down-tempo hip-hop beat kicks in at the track's midpoint, followed by sweeping strings, washes of white noise, cymbal splashes, and a chiming melody. Although Boards of Canada commonly combine digital and analog techniques to make their music, the video heavily emphasizes the analog, since it consists entirely of recut archival film material. As Steve Marchese describes it, the clip begins with "grainy NASA footage documenting Joseph Kittinger's astonishing Project Excelsior high-altitude parachute jumps during the late '50s and early '60s," before introducing "stunning footage of another impossible-to-believe feat—Laird Hamilton's perfect ride of a giant wave" at Teahupoo, Tahiti.[39] The transition between these two halves of the clip is so seamless that the entire movement from stratosphere to surf appears as a continuous progression. Here, a high-tech instrumental project (involving the testing of military technology and human endurance) is smoothly diverted into an activity in which instrumentality appears subsumed by natural forces (surfing). The vertical orientation of the clip's spatial progression and the seamless transition between different instrumentalities together transform the very matter of sea and sky into a virtual interface. Via this interface, a space of military control is imaginatively reconfigured as a space of sensory exploration and free play.

At the structural level, this music video is based on a logic of sampling. That is, like the guitar sample that provides the basis for the track, the Kittinger and Hamilton footage provides the raw material for the video's experiential narrative. Moreover, just as the datascapes of "Mirabeau" and "Gantz Graf" invite us to consider the common digital materiality of audio and video, the action of sampling sounds and images places both on the same ontological plane. Focusing in particular on the Coldcut video "Timber" (Stuart Warren Hill, 1997), Timothy Warner argues that the logic of sampling has migrated from musical to visual production.[40] Although he seems to overlook the fact that techniques of looping and media manipulation have long been present in experimental film, it is nonetheless important to acknowledge the way that audio and video production interfaces have become increasingly similar within the digital context. More importantly, Warner's analysis of "Timber" shows that sampling can be deployed to show a more critical perspective on instrumentality than is offered by the airy fantasy of "Dayvan Cowboy." In "Timber," footage of lumberjacks cutting down trees is looped and staggered to match precisely the sampled chainsaws and other tree-felling noises that are significant components of the audio track. These sounds and images of tree-felling are counterposed against the plaintive vocals of a native woman, who provides a chorus of sorts. Significantly, the cutting of the trees and the cutting of audiovisual media are tied together by an instrumental logic. As Warner puts it, "'Timber' is about machines—machines that are destroying an important natural resource—but is also made by machines (samplers, signal processors, sequencers), and requires machines for its realization: CD players and computers equipped with a CD-ROM drive."[41] Thus, whereas "Dayvan Cowboy" offers a utopian repurposing of the instrumental, "Timber" foregrounds the negative material consequences of instrumentality while highlighting the instrumental operations of sampling and cutting that produce the track. The environmental interface here is therefore no innocent object of play but bears within it the potential for producing political and ecological harm. Very few music videos display this degree of political engagement, although, as I have already argued, it would be wrong to assume that they provide an uncritical perspective on instrumentality.

TRACKING SOUNDSCAPES

In certain music videos, the environmental interface displays a distinctly horizontal orientation. This is evoked by lateral movements through cityscapes and landscapes, movements that again recall the "scanning" aesthetic common to many electronica videos. Examples include Prefuse 73's "Half of What?," in which urban and abstract imagery move across the frame; Amon Tobin's "Verbal" (Alex Rutterford, 2002), in which computer-generated cars race through the streets of a virtual city; and Four Tet's "She Moves She" (Ed Holdsworth, 2003), in which shuffling drum samples accompany the view from a train window moving through an urban landscape. In the latter video, the image has been split and mirrored along the horizontal axis, so that the passing cityscape oscillates between abstraction and concrete presence. Such examples function as quasi-reflexive treatments of the relationship between music and movement. As Carol Vernallis argues, tracking shots are of central importance to music videos in general: "instead of experiencing the music from a stationary position, as it rushes past, the viewer can get the sense of running along the soundstream."[42] Furthermore, such shots refer not only to the horizontal inscription of musical notation (which is key to Western society's sense of musical spatiality and temporality), but also to the production interface of the digital timeline. As Steve Goodman observes, the timeline is "a common feature of all time-based media" that "typically stratifies the on-screen workspace into a metric grid, adjustable in terms of temporal scale."[43] In the videos for "Verbal" and "She Moves She," images of cityscapes provide a concrete manifestation of this virtual grid. Significantly, Vernallis suggests that such patterns may be embedded within the form itself: the "forces of music, editing, and framing" in music video "can be imagined as casting a grid across the video's frame."[44] The clips discussed here can therefore be seen as reflexive engagements with music video's characteristic structures of production and textual arrangement.

The video for "Star Guitar" by the Chemical Brothers (Michel Gondry, 2002) brings together the timeline and the grid to provide one of the genre's most sophisticated soundscape visualizations. In this clip, physical features of the environment are looped and multiplied to match the insistent beat of the music. Depicting a continuous rail journey through a contemporary European setting as seen from the perspective of an anonymous passenger, "Star Guitar" draws attention to all of its constitutive tracks, from the tracks that make up the audio mix to the tracks along which our visual perspective travels. Although the repetitive nature of the visuals lends them a synthetic quality, they are in fact made up of video footage taken on the French railway system. Segments of this footage were painstakingly composited together to create seamlessly articulated loops that are then repeated and varied over time. Like Coldcut's "Timber," the video is built on a sampling and looping operation that echoes the production methods of much popular electronica.

Furthermore, as in the examples mentioned earlier, the visuals in "Star Guitar" are subject to the "gridding" operation common to both musical notation and to the electronic production software that has been used to create the music.[45] The frame itself is made up of a number of distinct strata. Via a process of *synchresis*, certain percussive sounds are linked with visual objects appearing on each stratum.[46] For example, in the opening section, the kick drum corresponds to a storage silo that appears repeatedly on a middle layer and the "snare" is matched by a strut that moves across the top of the frame. This spatial arrangement parallels the design of ProTools and other music production programs, which present music as a series of horizontal tracks that run in parallel across the screen. The visual tracking of the train across the landscape is thus paralleled by a metaphorical audio tracking. In "Star Guitar," audio processing effects are also represented visually: filter sweeps, for example, are accompanied by rising banks that obscure the sonic "objects" providing the track's percussive scaffolding.

"Star Guitar" thus invokes instrumentalism in two ways: first, by visualizing the digital tools that have been used to arrange the music and, second, by projecting its environmental interface into a space of mechanized transport and industry. In the process, Gondry's video obliquely reviews the historical connection between cinema and the railroad. In her book *Parallel Tracks*, Lynne Kirby argues that the railroad was "a precursor to, and a paradigm for early cinema," as both institutions compressed space and time, combined physical stasis with the experience of speed, and encouraged a state of distraction, constituting modern subjects both as tourists and consumers.[47] The train, she argues, was an extension of imperialist power, imposing order and rationality on "what modern Western culture sees as irrational: nature and tradition."[48] Like the modern railroad, "Star Guitar" seems to treat its landscape as instrumental: as an extension of modern technology's control over the environment, and also, more directly, as a *musical* instrument. The video appears to position the viewer as precisely the sort of subject that Kirby describes, as the stasis of the train's projected "passenger" is emphasized by the way the train's window frames the unrolling view. At the same time, the video actually seems to literalize Kirby's argument about the railroad's transformation of the landscape. Here, the environment is looped and composited to fit the standardized, metronomic beat of the music. We are invited to be distracted tourists, gazing out on a vista that transforms itself for us alone. I will argue, however, that this clip's treatment of instrumentality goes beyond blind affirmation.

REFRAMING INSTRUMENTALITY

The vista framed by the train window in "Star Guitar" oscillates between landscape and technoscape. A wavering synth tone that opens the clip is paired with wide green fields, while the introduction of the track's structural components (percussive sounds, an arpeggiated bass, and guitar samples) signals a move into industrial settings (represented by buildings, poles, wires, smokestacks, and bridges; see Figure 42.3). "Star Guitar" (Michel Gondry, 2002) Two-thirds of the way through the track, the introduction of a gentle rising and falling melody motivates the train's emergence into a more pastoral environment. Despite the prominence of industrial infrastructure in this clip, its panoramic framing of depopulated physical spaces recalls the tradition of landscape art.[49] Tracing the history of Western landscape painting from its emergence during the late Renaissance, Martin Lefebvre observes that landscapes are always distinct from the idea of "nature" because they are framed from a human perspective, informed by cultural codes of representation.[50] "The form of landscape is thus first of all the form of a view, of a particular gaze that requires a frame. With that frame nature turns into culture, land into landscape."[51] In a chapter that echoes Kirby's emphasis on instrumentality,

FIGURE 42.3 "Star Guitar" (Michel Gondry, 2002).

Lefebvre comments that aesthetics and tactical judgement are often united through the concept of landscape. He notes geographer Yves Lacoste's argument that landscapes identified as "beautiful" are often "the most advantageous for tactical and military purposes."[52] From this perspective, instrumentality is already embedded in the idea of the landscape.

In "Star Guitar," the framing of landscape is foregrounded by the implied presence of the window frame around the view. Furthermore, the codedness of the landscape is made literal in the way that the video "writes" the rhythm across it. By synchronizing elements of the represented world with the beat of the music, "Star Guitar" deliberately intertwines nature and culture. Yet, as I have already noted, the landscape presented in the video is not nature in the raw. In fact, the video tracks across an everyday extraurban environment, in which fields and lakes alternate with industrial buildings and shunting yards. This imagery calls to mind not only the opening shot of Walter Ruttman's *Berlin: Symphony of a Great City* (1927),[53] in which a train carries the film's viewers into the outskirts of Berlin, and the railroad imagery of Kraftwerk's video for "Trans-Europe Express" (Günther Fröhling, 1977), but also the works of Canadian structuralist filmmaker David Rimmer. As Catherine Russell argues, many of Rimmer's films make use of the "metaphoric inscription" of a window frame[54] and work to overcome the division between nature and technology by deconstructing perspectival vision, so that the "instrumentalized gaze" is destabilized.[55] Here, I suggest that "Star Guitar" achieves something similar, although the visual challenge presented by the fragmentation of its landscape is domesticated by the invisible stitching (in the form of digital compositing) that holds it together as a cohesive image. Nonetheless, by providing tacit evidence of this compositing operation, the video gestures toward the mutual infiltration of nature and culture. The digital edits that articulate the video's looping footage are invisible yet conspicuous, underlining the representational and technological apparatus that constitutes any field of vision as a "landscape."

If the physical environment in "Star Guitar" can be regarded as the object of an instrumental gaze, it is nonetheless equally possible to view it as a subject, which itself "plays" the music. As Russell says of the landscape in David Rimmer's films: "It looks back, it is in constant movement, it has presence."[56] Moreover, Gondry's exploration of sound-image relations suggests a model of understanding digital multimedia that goes well beyond "mere instrumentality." The uncanny nature of this landscape/technoscape, which seems itself to be autonomously "performing" the musical score, suggests the presence of other temporalities, at once parallel and divergent. Although the clip rigidly synchronizes certain elements (linking percussive noises with industrial hardware, for example), other elements produce their own, partially autonomous rhythms. Despite the overarching gridlike structure, the video consists of segments of indexical time, fleeting byproducts of the initial footage that are not precisely matched to features of the music.[57] There is, moreover, a tension between the 2D "grid" that overlays the track and the spatial "excess" produced by the images themselves, which occupy a 3D perspectival space. Thus, the precisely timed "tracking" of objects across the foreground of the shot is counterposed against the "slower" movement of background features, which, at certain moments, transcend the logic of the grid. The instrumental associations of the tracking shot are also softened by the way that the camera is directed slightly backward, so that the landscape is constantly receding from us, connoting nostalgia rather than an instrumentalized push into the future.[58]

In "Star Guitar," heavy modernity (represented by the technoscape of transportation and industrial infrastructure) meets light modernity (represented by digital technology's command over space and time). At the confluence of the two, we are offered a space of play and performance, where the environmental interface takes on a life of its own. Without articulating anything resembling a fully fledged political vision, "Star Guitar" nonetheless sets up a three-way dialogue among the human, technological, and "green" worlds. Central to this dialogue are the mediating functions offered by music, by visual technologies, and by the framing traditions of landscape art and cinema. In "Star Guitar," the reverie of the spectator inside the train is both extended and confronted by the uncanny performance offered by the worlds of nature and technology. This video invites us to enjoy its seamless technical accomplishment (the orchestration and synchronization of multiple audiovisual elements) while simultaneously making us aware of the disjuncture and fragmentation that must underlie its smooth trajectory. The multiple temporalities of the music and the visual strata that accompany it produce a mesmerizing display that, without organizing itself as narrative or critical discourse, nonetheless invites reflection on past and present relations among technologies, environments, and aesthetic practices.

CONCLUSION

Collectively, the videos I have discussed here work to remind us that, as Sean Cubitt puts it, "not all technologies are instrumental."[59] Paralleling Catherine Russell's analysis of David Rimmer's films, Cubitt sees nature, the technological/technical, and the human/social as interrelated rather than distinct spheres.[60] He is, furthermore, critical of those works, including many science fiction films, that plot a path back to nature by rejecting technology.[61] By this account, cultural engagements with technology should be measured not by their repudiation of it, but by their creative exploration of its possibilities and limits. I have argued that many music videos for electronica tracks do precisely this, by probing and in some cases challenging the instrumental connotations of digital media technologies and, by extension, the role of technical instrumentality in shaping contemporary experience. These videos are not uniform in their approach, but can be characterized by a loosely articulated aesthetic of instrumentality, with recurrent features that include abstraction, architectural and machinic forms, scanning and tracking imagery, and the projection of environmental interfaces. Many of these features are commonly found in videos outside of the generic field covered by the term "electronica." Yet no other musical genre seems quite as determined to engage with the technological materiality of media or to grapple with the "techno-logic" of contemporary experience.

In a world where work and leisure activities are increasingly shaped and defined by interactions with digital technology, it may be that these multimedia works provide ways of grappling with digital culture's instrumental dimension.

NOTES

1. Kim Cascone, "The Aesthetics of Failure: 'Post-Digital' Tendencies in Contemporary Computer Music," *Computer Music Journal* 24, no. 4 (2000): 15.
2. Nick Collins observes that the word "electronica" has been "charged by some as a deliberate marketing term for popular electronic music," and that its relationship with the master category of "electronic dance music" (or EDM) has varied widely: "in the United States it might simply denote EDM and in Europe electronic music outside the core EDM territory." Collins also suggests, however, that this term's technological connotations reveal parallels with digital art and other spheres of media production. See Nick Collins, "Electronica," in *The Oxford Handbook of Computer Music*, ed. Roger T. Dean (New York: Oxford University Press, 2009), 335.
3. Simon Reynolds, *Generation Ecstasy: Into the World of Techno and Rave Culture* (New York: Routledge, 1999), 49.
4. Charlie Gere, *Digital Culture* (London: Reaktion Books, 2002), 201. The "countercultural techno-utopianism" mentioned here has resurfaced across a number of electronic genres and is particularly evident in the Detroit techno scene that developed during the 1980s and 1990s. For more on this, see Dan Sicko, *Techno Rebels: The Renegades of Electronic Funk*, 2nd ed. (Detroit: Wayne State University Press, 2010) According to Sicko, techno's "underlying philosophy" emphasizes "the power of individual and personal visions of Utopia" (12).
5. Gere, *Digital Culture*, 13.
6. Ibid.
7. Julian Stallabrass, "The Ideal City and the Virtual Hive: Modernism and Emergent Order in Computer Culture," in *Technocities*, ed. John Downey and Jim McGuigan (London: Sage, 1999), 116
8. Quoted in Reynolds, *Generation Ecstasy*, 19.
9. Aden Evens, *Sound Ideas: Music, Machines, and Experience* (Minneapolis: University of Minnesota Press, 2005), 83.
10. Ibid., 63. According to this view, whereas acoustic instruments' outputs are contingent on variations in temperature, tension, space, and performance, digital technologies always produce the same results in response to a given input.
11. Ibid., 83.
12. See Martin Heidegger, *The Question Concerning Technology, and Other Essays*, trans. William Lovitt (New York: Harper and Row, 1977) For Heidegger, technology can serve, like poetic creation, as a "way of revealing" essential truths (10–12). This special capacity has been undermined, however, by the modern tendency to view natural energies as regulated, measurable resources (14–15).
13. The techno group (and record label) Underground Resistance has displayed a particularly strong engagement with military instrumentalism. Emerging in the late 1980s, Underground Resistance made extensive use of military imagery and track titles to complement the aggressive high-tech aesthetic of their music and underline their political

activism, which was grounded in the context of Detroit's urban decay, racism, and social inequality.

14. Zygmunt Bauman, *Liquid Modernity* (Cambridge: Polity Press, 2000) Whereas progress under "heavy modernity" was judged in terms of "growing size and spatial expansion" (115), "velocity of movement and access to faster means of mobility" now constitute "the principal tool of power and domination" (9). Bauman associates this shift in spatial dynamics with "the near-instantaneity of software time" (119).

15. For examples of such discussions, see the discussion boards at http://www.gearslutz.com and http://www.futureproducers.com, as well as the website for popular audio production software package Ableton Live: http://forum.ableton.com/.

16. For Kodwo Eshun, this digital instrumentalism is something to be embraced because it points the way toward a radical posthumanism. See Kodwo Eshun, *More Brilliant than the Sun: Adventures in Sonic Fiction* (London: Quartet Books, 1998). As Eshun remarks approvingly, the emergence of Kraftwerk in the 1970s ushered in an era in which "[t]he musician becomes an electronic programmer, a push-button percussionist who taps ENTER with the fingertips" (105). The posthuman flipside of this push-button instrumentality is the notion that humans themselves have become instruments: "[t]he producer is now the modular input, willingly absorbed into McLuhan's 'medium which processes its users, who are its content'" (106). Although Eshun is right to suggest that these developments have helped to carry contemporary culture beyond naïve humanism, he underemphasizes the way that anxieties about instrumental control have continued to shape discourses of and about electronic music.

17. Steve Goodman, "Sonic Algorithm," in *Software Studies: A Lexicon*, ed. Matthew Fuller (Cambridge, MA: MIT Press, 2008), 230.

18. Ibid., 233.

19. See Cascone, "The Aesthetics of Failure."

20. Ken Jordan and Paul D. Miller aka DJ Spooky that Subliminal Kid, "Freeze Frame: Audio, Aesthetics, Sampling, and Contemporary Multimedia," in *Sound Unbound: Sampling Digital Music and Culture*, ed. Paul D. Miller aka DJ Spooky that Subliminal Kid (Cambridge, MA: MIT Press. 2008), 103.

21. Ibid.

22. For Kodwo Eshun, techno music rejects popular music's emphasis on visuality and "grasps the chance to recede from the visible. To listen to Underground Resistance is to have your vision deleted, plunging you into midnight sunshine. Nothing to see, so much to feel." See Eshun, *More Brilliant than the Sun*, 120.

23. Andrew Goodwin, *Dancing in the Distraction Factory: Music Television and Popular Culture* (Minneapolis: University of Minnesota Press, 1992), 57 See also Michel Chion, *Audio-Vision: Sound on Screen*, ed. and trans. Claudia Gorbman (New York: Columbia University Press, 1994) According to Chion, artworks that transmit kinetic sensations "through a single sensory channel" are able to "convey all the other senses at once" (137).

24. Goodwin, *Dancing in the Distraction Factory*, 57.

25. Quoted in Paul Tingen, "Autechre: Recording Electronica," *Sound on Sound*, April 2004, http://www.soundonsound.com/sos/apr04/articles/autechre.htm, accessed February 3, 2012.

26. Nicholas Cook, *Analysing Musical Multimedia* (Oxford: Clarendon Press, 1998), 25.

27. Ibid., 56.

28. Ibid., 106.

29. Ibid., 102–103.

30. Ibid., 46.

31. Ryoji Ikeda, "Datamatics," *Ryoji Ikeda* website (2010), http://www.ryojiikeda.com/project/datamatics/, accessed February 3, 2012.

32. Brooks Landon, *The Aesthetics of Ambivalence: Rethinking Science Fiction Film in the Age of Electronic (Re)production* (Westport, CT: Greenwood Press, 1992), 101.

33. Ibid., 103.

34. Ibid., 20.

35. The "hyperdub virus" is something of an in-joke, since it takes its name from the record label managed by Steve Goodman (Kode9).

36. See Kodwo Eshun, *More Brilliant than the Sun.* Eshun observes that music's orientation toward technology appears to set it apart from other cultural discourses: "in mainstream society, science is *still* the science that drains the blood of life and leaves everything vivisected. But in music it's never been like that; as soon as you hear the word science, you know you're in for an *intensification* of sensation" (175).

37. Aylish Wood, *Digital Encounters* (Oxford: Routledge, 2007), 6.

38. Ibid., 93.

39. Steve Marchese, "Sky's the Limit," *Res* 9, no. 4 (2006): 27.

40. Timothy Warner, "Narrating Sound: The Pop Video in the Age of the Sampler," in *Changing Tunes: The Use of Pre-existing Music in Film*, ed. Phil Powrie and Robynn Stilwell (Aldershot: Ashgate, 2006), 174.

41. Ibid., 178.

42. Carol Vernallis, *Experiencing Music Video: Aesthetics and Cultural Context* (New York: Columbia University Press, 2004), 35.

43. Steve Goodman, "Timeline (Sonic)," in *Software Studies: A Lexicon*, ed. Matthew Fuller (Cambridge, MA: MIT Press, 2008), 256.

44. Vernallis, *Experiencing Music Video*, 132.

45. Indeed, Gondry planned the video for "Star Guitar" by writing a visual "score" mapping the location of sync points across different strata within the frame.

46. Michel Chion uses the term "synchresis" to describe "the spontaneous and irresistible weld produced between a particular auditory phenomenon and visual phenomenon when they occur at the same time." See Chion, *Audio-Vision*, 63.

47. Lynne Kirby, *Parallel Tracks: The Railroad and Silent Cinema* (Exeter: University of Exeter Press, 1997), 250.

48. Ibid., 27.

49. In its layering of sounds and images, "Star Guitar" seems to affirm Sergei Eisenstein's declaration that, when it comes to communicating emotion through art, "*landscape lies closest to music.*" See Sergei Eisenstein, *Nonindifferent Nature*, trans. Herbert Marshall (Cambridge: Cambridge University Press, 1987), 218.

50. Martin Lefebvre, "Introduction," in *Landscape and Film*, ed. Martin Lefebvre (New York: Routledge, 2006), xiii.

51. Ibid., xv.

52. Martin Lefebvre, "Between Setting and Landscape in the Cinema," in *Landscape and Film*, ed. Martin Lefebvre (New York: Routledge, 2006), 53.

53. Significantly, *Berlin* has been criticized extensively for its framing of instrumentalism. See, for example, Carsten Strathausen, "Uncanny Spaces: The City in Ruttmann and Vertov," in *Screening the City*, ed. Mark Shiel and Tony Fitzmaurice (London: Verso, 2003), 15–40.

"Ruttmann's 'symphony,'" argues Strathausen, "depicts the instrumentalization of people as part of the city's interior machinery" and attempts "to reconcile the conflict between nature and culture by merging cyclical and linear movement, static and moving imagery" (32).

54. Catherine Russell, "The Inhabited View: Landscape in the Films of David Rimmer," in *Landscape and Film*, ed. Martin Lefebvre (New York: Routledge. 2006), 153.

55. Ibid., 160.

56. Ibid., 161.

57. To use Nicholas Cook's terminology, this video displays multimedia relations characterized not by straightforward "conformance" but by "complementation," in which the identification of cross-media similarities provides a frame for the acknowledgment of differences. See Cook, *Analysing Musical Multimedia,* 102–103.

58. As Vernallis observes, "Videos utilizing tracking and slo-mo often seem imbued with nostalgia, as they make us aware that, even if our perceptions reside in the present, past events are irretrievably slipping away." See Vernallis, *Experiencing Music Video,* 178.

59. Sean Cubitt, *EcoMedia* (Amsterdam: Rodopi, 2005), 4.

60. Ibid.

61. Ibid., 16.

Select Bibliography

Cook, Nicholas. *Analysing Musical Multimedia.*Oxford: Clarendon Press, 1998.

Evens, Aden. *Sound Ideas: Music, Machines, and Experience.* Minneapolis: University of Minnesota Press, 2005.

Gere, Charlie. *Digital Culture.* London: Reaktion Books, 2002.

Goodman, Steve. "Timeline (Sonic)." In *Software Studies: A Lexicon,* edited by Matthew Fuller, 256–259. Cambridge, MA: MIT Press, 2008.

Jordan, Ken, and Paul D. Miller. "Freeze Frame: Audio, Aesthetics, Sampling, and Contemporary Multimedia." In *Sound Unbound: Sampling Digital Music and Culture,* edited by Paul D. Miller (aka DJ Spooky that Subliminal Kid), 97–108. Cambridge, MA: MIT Press. 2008.

Kirby, Lynne. *Parallel Tracks: The Railroad and Silent Cinema.* Exeter, UK: University of Exeter Press, 1997.

Russell, Catherine. "The Inhabited View: Landscape in the Films of David Rimmer." In *Landscape and Film,* edited by Martin Lefebvre, 149–166. New York: Routledge. 2006.

Vernallis, Carol. *Experiencing Music Video: Aesthetics and Cultural Context.* New York: Columbia University Press, 2004.

Warner, Timothy. "Narrating Sound: The Pop Video in the Age of the Sampler." In *Changing Tunes: The Use of Pre-existing Music in Film,* edited by Phil Powrie and Robynn Stilwell, 167–179. Aldershot, UK: Ashgate, 2006.

Wood, Aylish. *Digital Encounters.* Oxford: Routledge, 2007.

INDEX

....

Page numbers followed by *t* or *f* indicate tables or figures, respectively. Numbers followed by "n" indicate notes.

3|1|14